A Review of the Events of 1976

The 1977 World Book Year Book

The Annual Supplement to The World Book Encyclopedia

Field Enterprises Educational Corporation
Chicago Frankfurt London Paris Rome Sydney Tokyo Toronto
A subsidiary of
Field Enterprises, Inc.

Staff

Editorial Director
William H. Nault

Editorial Staff
Executive Editor
Wayne Wille

Managing Editor
Paul C. Tullier

Chief Copy Editor
Joseph P. Spohn

Senior Editors
Robert K. Johnson
Edward G. Nash
Kathryn Sederberg
Darlene R. Stille
Foster P. Stockwell

Assistant Copy Editor
Irene B. Keller

Index Editors
Marilyn Boerding
Judith L. Deraedt

Editorial Assistant
Madelyn Krzak

Executive Editor
The World Book Encyclopedia
A. Richard Harmet

Art Staff
Executive Art Director
William Dobias

Art Director
Alfred de Simone

Senior Artists
Joe W. Gound
Marge Kathan

Artist
Richard B. Zinn

Photography Director
Fred C. Eckhardt, Jr.

Photo Editing Director
Ann Eriksen

Senior Photographs Editors
Blanche Cohen
Marilyn Gartman
John S. Marshall

Assistant Photographs Editor
Jo Anne M. Ticzkus

Research and Services
Head, Editorial Research
Jo Ann McDonald

Senior Researcher
Robert Hamm

Head, Research Library
Vera Busselle

Head, Cartographic Services
H. George Stoll

Pre-Press Services
Director
Richard A. Atwood

Manager, Manufacturing Liaison
John Babrick

Supervisor, Keyboarding Section
Lynn Iverson

Manager, Film Separations
Alfred J. Mozdzen

Assistant Manager, Film Separations
Barbara J. McDonald

Manager, Production Control
J. J. Stack

Supervisor, Distribution
Marguerite DuMais

Supervisor, Scheduling
Barbara Podczerwinski

Manufacturing Staff
Executive Director
Philip B. Hall

Production Manager
Jerry R. Higdon

Manager, Research and Development
Henry Koval

Year Book Board of Editors
Harrison Brown, Alistair Cooke, Lawrence A. Cremin, John Holmes, Sylvia Porter, James Reston, Walter (Red) Smith

World Book Advisory Board
Phillip Bacon, Professor and Chairman, Department of Geography, University of Houston; George B. Brain, Dean, College of Education, Washington State University; Alonzo A. Crim, Superintendent, Atlanta Public Schools; William E. McManus, Chairman, Committee on Education, United States Catholic Conference; A. Harry Passow, Jacob H. Schiff Professor of Education and Director, Division of Educational Institutions and Programs, and Chairman, Department of Curriculum and Teaching, Teachers College, Columbia University; John Rowell, Director, School Libraries Programs, School of Library Science, Case Western Reserve University; William M. Smith, Professor of Psychology and Director, Office of Instructional Services and Educational Research, Dartmouth College.

Printed in the United States of America
ISBN 0-7166-0477-9
Library of Congress Catalog Card Number: 62-4818

Preface

"I opened my eyes upon a strange and weird landscape. I knew that I was on Mars." The words are those of a character in *A Princess of Mars,* a novel by Edgar Rice Burroughs published in 1917. The fictional landscape the narrator went on to describe was wildly different from the one pictured at the bottom of this page. The photograph, taken on Mars in 1976, is of Mars as it actually is. Hardly a strange and weird landscape. More like Arizona. Still, now we know what Mars really looks like. And now we will learn more about the planet. Is there life beyond that rock-strewn horizon? Perhaps we will find out.

Similarly, we saw other new horizons in 1976, here on earth. And eventually we will learn what lies beyond them, too. The deaths of Mao Tse-tung and Chou En-lai in China may bring major changes. The whole of southern Africa was seething, foretelling—what? For the first time, scientists created in a test tube a gene that worked in a living cell. What might that lead to? A presidential election in the United States marked the changing of the guard. Did it also mark a new approach to solving problems?

The major events of 1976—its horizons—are reported on in this edition of THE YEAR BOOK. Future editions will tell what lies beyond the horizons. And for those who find meaning, or merely pleasure, in coincidence: Burroughs' narrator looking out over a "strange and weird landscape" was named Carter. He was a Southerner.   WAYNE WILLE

A field of reddish rocks and sandlike material stretches to the horizon 2 miles (3.2 kilometers) from the *Viking 2* lander on Mars's Utopian Plain.

Contents

A chronology of some of the most important events of 1976 appears on
pages 8 through 16. A preview of 1977 is given on pages 607 and 608.

Contributors

Abrams, Edward, Ph.D.; Director of Technical Development, Chemetron Corporation. [CHEMICAL INDUSTRY]

Alexiou, Arthur G., M.S., E.E.; Associate Director, Office of Sea Grant Programs, National Science Foundation. [OCEAN]

Anderson, Alfred T., Jr., Ph.D.; Associate Professor of Geology, University of Chicago. [GEOLOGY]

Anderson, Joseph P., M.S., LL.D.; Editor, *Washington Bulletin.* [COMMUNITY ORGANIZATIONS; SOCIAL SECURITY; SOCIAL WELFARE; YOUTH ORGANIZATIONS]

Anderson, Leo S., B.A.; Editor, *Telephony Magazine.* [COMMUNICATIONS]

Araujo, Paul E., Ph.D.; Assistant Professor, Human Nutrition, University of Florida. [NUTRITION]

Banovetz, James M., Ph.D.; Chairman, Department of Political Science, Northern Illinois University. [CITY; City Articles; HOUSING]

Barber, Peggy, B.A., M.L.S.; Director, Public Information Office, American Library Association. [AMERICAN LIBRARY ASSOCIATION]

Beaumont, Lynn; Travel and Public Relations Consultant. [BICENTENNIAL, UNITED STATES; FAIRS AND EXPOSITIONS; TRAVEL]

Beckwith, David C., J.D.; Correspondent, *Time* Magazine. [COURTS AND LAWS; CRIME; PRISON; SUPREME COURT]

Benedict, Burton, A.B., Ph.D.; Professor of Anthropology, University of California at Berkeley. [WORLD BOOK SUPPLEMENT: SEYCHELLES; VICTORIA]

Benson, Barbara N., A.B., M.S., Ph.D.; Assistant Professor, Biology, Cedar Crest College. [BOTANY; ZOOLOGY]

Berkwitt, George J., B.S.J.; Chief Editor, *Industrial Distribution Magazine.* [MANUFACTURING]

Bornstein, Leon, B.A., M.A.; Labor Economist, U.S. Dept. of Labor. [LABOR]

Boyum, Joy Gould, Ph.D.; Professor of English, New York University. [MOTION PICTURES]

Bradsher, Henry S., A.B., B.J.; Reporter, *Washington Star.* [Asian Country Articles]

Brana-Shute, Gary, Ph.D.; Assistant Professor of Social Sciences, University of Florida, Gainesville. [WORLD BOOK SUPPLEMENT: PARAMARIBO; SURINAM]

Brown, Kenneth, Editor, *United Kingdom Press Gazette.* [EUROPE and European Country Articles; EUROPE (Close-Up)]

Brown, Lester R., B.S., M.A.; President, Worldwatch Institute. [WORLD BOOK SUPPLEMENT: FOOD SUPPLY]

Cain, Charles C., III, B.A.; Automotive Editor, Associated Press. [AUTOMOBILE]

Carlson, Eric D., Ph.D.; Senior Astronomer and Education Supervisor, Adler Planetarium. [ASTRONOMY]

Carr, Archie, Ph.D.; Graduate Research Professor, Department of Zoology, University of Florida. [Special Report: LAST CHANCE FOR THE SEA TURTLE]

Clark, Phil, B.A.; Free-Lance Garden and Botanical Writer. [GARDENING]

Cook, Robert C., former President, Population Reference Bureau. [POPULATION, WORLD]

Cromie, William J., B.S.; Executive Director, Council for the Advancement of Science Writing. [SPACE EXPLORATION]

Csida, June Bundy, former Radio-TV Editor, *Billboard* Magazine. [RADIO; TELEVISION; TELEVISION (Close-Up)]

Curry, Wesley, B.S., B.S.E.E.; Manager, Periodicals, American Hospital Association. [HOSPITAL]

Cuscaden, Rob, Editor, *Building Design & Construction* Magazine; Architecture critic, *Chicago Sun-Times.* [ARCHITECTURE]

Cviic, Chris, B.A., B.Sc.; Editorial Staff, *The Economist.* [Eastern European Country Articles]

Dale, Edwin L., Jr., B.A.; Reporter, *The New York Times*, Washington Bureau. [INTERNATIONAL TRADE AND FINANCE]

DeFrank, Thomas M., B.A., M.A.; Correspondent, *Newsweek.* [ARMED FORCES]

Delaune, Lynn de Grummond, M.A.; Assistant Professor, College of William and Mary; Author. [LITERATURE FOR CHILDREN]

Derickson, Ralph Wayne, Public Information Associate, Council of State Governments. [STATE GOVERNMENT]

DeSimone, Daniel V., LL.B., J.D.; Deputy Director, Office of Technology Assessment, U.S. Congress. [METRIC SYSTEM]

Dewald, William G., Ph.D.; Professor of Economics, Ohio State University. [Finance Articles]

Dixon, Gloria Ricks, B.A.; Director of Public Relations, Magazine Publishers Association. [MAGAZINE]

Douglas, John H., M.S., M.J.; Associate Editor, *Science News Magazine.* [SCIENCE AND RESEARCH]

Eaton, William J., B.S.J., M.S.J.; Washington Correspondent, *Chicago Daily News.* [U.S. Political Articles]

Esseks, John D., Ph.D.; Associate Professor of Political Science, Northern Illinois University. [AFRICA and African Country Articles]

Evans, Earl A., Jr., Ph.D.; Professor of Biochemistry, University of Chicago. [BIOCHEMISTRY; BIOLOGY]

Farr, David M. L., D. Phil.; Professor of History, Carleton University, Ottawa. [CANADA and Canadian Province Articles; LÉGER, JULES; TRUDEAU, PIERRE ELLIOTT]

Feather, Leonard, Professor of Jazz History, University of California, Riverside; Author, *The Encyclopedia of Jazz in the Sixties.* [MUSIC, POPULAR; RECORDINGS]

Fernandez, James W., B.A., Ph.D.; Professor of Anthropology, Princeton University. [WORLD BOOK SUPPLEMENT: SÃO TOMÉ; SÃO TOMÉ AND PRÍNCIPE]

Ferrell, Ann H., B.A.; Laboratory Assistant, Biochemistry Department, Stanford University. [WORLD BOOK SUPPLEMENT: GENETIC ENGINEERING]

French, Charles E., Ph.D.; Head, Agricultural Economics Department, Purdue University. [AGRICULTURE]

Gann, Lewis Henry, M.A., B.Litt., D.Phil.; Senior Fellow, Hoover Institution, Stanford University. [WORLD BOOK SUPPLEMENT: ANGOLA; COMOROS; LUANDA; MAPUTO; MORONI; MOZAMBIQUE]

Gayn, Mark, B.S.; Foreign Affairs Columnist, *The Toronto Star*; Author. [ASIA and Asian Country Articles]

Goldner, Nancy, B.A.; Critic, *Dance News, The Nation,* and *Christian Science Monitor.* [DANCING]

Goldstein, Jane, B.A.; Publicity Director, Santa Anita Park. [HORSE RACING]

Goy, Robert W., Ph.D.; Director, Wisconsin Regional Primate Research Center; Professor of Psychology, University of Wisconsin. [PSYCHOLOGY]

Graubart, Judah L., B.A.; former Columnist, *Jewish Post and Opinion* (Chicago). [JEWS AND JUDAISM]

Griffin, Alice, Ph.D.; Professor of English, Lehman College, City University of New York. [THEATER]

Gwynne, Peter, M.A.; Science Editor, *Newsweek.* [Special Report: WHO DISCOVERED AMERICA SECOND?]

Hagan, Robert L., Acting Director, U.S. Bureau of the Census. [CENSUS]

Hartmann, Ernest L., M.D.; Professor of Psychiatry, Boston State Hospital. [Special Report: THE WAY WE SLEEP]

Havighurst, Robert J., Ph.D.; Professor of Human Development and Education, University of Chicago. [OLD AGE]

Healey, Gerald B., Midwest Editor, *Editor & Publisher* Magazine. [NEWSPAPERS; PUBLISHING]

Hechinger, Fred M., B.A.; member, Editorial Board, *The New York Times.* [Special Report: THE LOSING WAR AGAINST ILLITERACY; EDUCATION]

Henry, Kristin W., B.A., M.A.; former Lecturer in English, American University, Cairo. [WORLD BOOK SUPPLEMENT: CAPE VERDE; PRAIA]

Hershey, Robert D., Jr., B.A.; Reporter, Washington Bureau, *The New York Times.* [INTERNATIONAL TRADE AND FINANCE (Close-Up)]

Jacobi, Peter P., B.S.J., M.S.J.; Professor, Medill School of Journalism, Northwestern University. [MUSIC, CLASSICAL]

Jessup, Mary E., B.A.; former News Editor, *Civil Engineering* Magazine. [DRUGS; Engineering Articles; PETROLEUM AND GAS]

Joseph, Lou, B.A.; Manager, Media Relations, Bureau of Public Information, American Dental Association. [DENTISTRY]

Karr, Albert R., M.S.; Reporter, *The Wall Street Journal.* [TRANSPORTATION and Transportation Articles]

Kind, Joshua B., Ph.D.; Associate Professor of Art History, Northern Illinois University; Author, *Rouault;* Contributing Editor, *New Art Examiner.* [VISUAL ARTS]

King, Micki, B.S.; Gold Medal Winner, Diving, 1972 Olympics. [WORLD BOOK SUPPLEMENT: DIVING]

Kingman, Merle, B.A.; Senior Editor, *Advertising Age.* [ADVERTISING]

Kisor, Henry, B.A., M.S.J.; Book Editor, *Chicago Daily News.* [LITERATURE]

Klis, John B., M.S.; Director of Publications, Institute of Food Technologists. [FOOD]

Knechtges, David R., B.A., A.M., Ph.D.; Associate Professor of Asian Languages and Literature, University of Washington. [WORLD BOOK SUPPLEMENT: CHINESE LITERATURE]

Koenig, Louis W., Ph.D., L.H.D.; Professor of Government, New York University; Author, *Bryan; A Political Biography of William Jennings Bryan.* [CIVIL RIGHTS]

Langdon, Robert, Executive Officer, Pacific Manuscripts Bureau, Australian National University. [PACIFIC ISLANDS]

Lea, David A. M., B.A., Ph.D.; Professor of Geography, University of New England, Australia. [WORLD BOOK SUPPLEMENT: PAPUA NEW GUINEA; PORT MORESBY]

Levy, Emanuel, B.A.; Editor, *Insurance Advocate.* [INSURANCE]

Lewis, Ralph H., M.A.; Collaborator, Division of Museum Services, Museum Operations, National Park Service. [MUSEUMS]

Litsky, Frank, B.S.; Assistant Sports Editor, *The New York Times.* [Sports Articles]

Livingston, Kathryn, B.A.; Senior Editor, Special Projects, *Town and Country.* [FASHION]

Maki, John M., Ph.D.; Professor of Political Science, University of Massachusetts. [JAPAN]

Martin, Everett G., A.B.; South American Correspondent, *The Wall Street Journal.* [LATIN AMERICA and Latin American Country Articles]

Marty, Martin E., Ph.D.; Professor, University of Chicago. [PROTESTANTISM; RELIGION]

Mattson, Howard W., B.S.; Director of Public Information, Institute of Food Technologists. [FOOD]

Mauldin, Bill; Cartoonist, *Chicago Sun-Times.* [Special Report: CARTOONS WITH A CONSCIENCE]

Mayer, Jean, Ph.D., D.Sc.; President, Tufts University. [WORLD BOOK SUPPLEMENT: FAMINE]

Miller, J. D. B., M.Ec.; Professor of International Relations, Research School of Pacific Studies, Australian National University. [AUSTRALIA; NEW ZEALAND]

Moore, Clement Henry, A.B., Ph.D.; Associate Professor of Political Science, University of Michigan. [WORLD BOOK SUPPLEMENT: CAPE VERDE; PRAIA]

Morton, Elizabeth H., LL.D.; former Editor in Chief, Canadian Library Association. [CANADIAN LIBRARY ASSOCIATION; CANADIAN LITERATURE]

Mullen, Frances A., Ph.D.; Secretary-General, International Council of Psychologists, Inc. [CHILD WELFARE]

Murray, G. E., M.A.; Poetry Critic, *Chicago Daily News.* [POETRY]

Neil, Andrew F., M.A.; Political/Economic Correspondent, *The Economist.* [GREAT BRITAIN; IRELAND; NORTHERN IRELAND]

Nelson, Larry L., Ph.D.; Executive Vice-President, Snyder Associates, Inc. [AGRICULTURE]

Newman, Andrew L., M.A.; Information Officer, U.S. Department of the Interior. [CONSERVATION; ENVIRONMENT; FISHING; FISHING INDUSTRY; FOREST AND FOREST PRODUCTS; HUNTING; INDIAN, AMERICAN]

Oatis, William N.; United Nations Correspondent, The Associated Press. [UNITED NATIONS]

O'Connor, James J., E.E.; Editor in Chief, *Power* Magazine. [ENERGY]

Offenheiser, Marilyn J., B.S.; Free-Lance Writer. [ELECTRONICS]

O'Leary, Theodore M., B.A.; Special Correspondent, *Sports Illustrated* Magazine. [BRIDGE, CONTRACT; CHESS; COIN COLLECTING; GAMES, MODELS, AND TOYS; HOBBIES; PET; STAMP COLLECTING]

Pearl, Edward W., Supervisory Meteorologist, University of Chicago. [WEATHER]

Plog, Fred, Ph.D.; Associate Professor of Anthropology, Arizona State University. [ANTHROPOLOGY; ARCHAEOLOGY]

Poli, Kenneth, Editor, *Popular Photography.* [PHOTOGRAPHY]

Pye, Lucian W., Ph.D.; Ford Professor of Political Science, Massachusetts Institute of Technology. [CHINA, PEOPLE'S REPUBLIC OF (Close-Up)]

Rabb, George B., Ph.D.; Director, Chicago Zoological Park. [ZOOS AND AQUARIUMS]

Rafalik, Dianne, B.A., M.S.; Editor, *The New Physician.* [HEALTH AND DISEASE; MEDICINE; MENTAL HEALTH; PUBLIC HEALTH; PUBLIC HEALTH (Close-Up)]

Rowen, Joseph R., A.B.; Vice-President, National Retail Merchants Association. [RETAILING]

Rowse, Arthur E., I.A., M.B.A.; President, Consumer News, Inc. [CONSUMER AFFAIRS]

Schmemann, Alexander, S.T.D., D.D., LL.D., Th.D.; Dean, St. Vladimir's Orthodox Theological Seminary, New York. [EASTERN ORTHODOX CHURCHES]

Schubert, Helen C., B.S.; Home Furnishings Writer. [INTERIOR DESIGN]

Selye, Hans, M.D., D.Sc., Ph.D.; Professor and Director, Institute of Experimental Medicine and Surgery, University of Montreal. [WORLD BOOK SUPPLEMENT: STRESS]

Shaw, Robert J., B.S., B.A.; former Editor, *Library Technology Reports,* American Library Association. [LIBRARY]

Shearer, Warren W., Ph.D.; former Chairman, Department of Economics, Wabash College. [ECONOMICS]

Sheerin, John B., C.S.P., A.B., M.A., L.L.D., J.D.; General Consultor, American Bishops' Secretariat for Catholic-Jewish Relations. [ROMAN CATHOLIC CHURCH]

Spalding, Jack J., A.B.; Editor, *Atlanta Journal.* [WORLD BOOK SUPPLEMENT: CARTER, JAMES EARL, JR.]

Spencer, William, Ph.D.; Professor of Middle East History, Florida State University; Author, *Land and People of Algeria.* [MIDDLE EAST and Middle Eastern Country Articles; North Africa Country Articles]

Thompson, Carol L., M.A.; Editor, *Current History* Magazine. [U.S. Government Articles]

Thompson, Ida, Ph.D.; Assistant Professor, Department of Geological and Geophysical Sciences, Princeton University. [PALEONTOLOGY]

Tofany, Vincent L., B.L.; President, National Safety Council. [SAFETY]

Van Rossen, Don, Ph.D.; Aquatics Director and Head Swim Coach, University of Oregon. [WORLD BOOK SUPPLEMENT: SWIMMING]

von Smolinski, Alfred W., Ph.D.; Associate Professor of Chemistry, University of Illinois at the Medical Center. [CHEMISTRY]

White, Thomas O., Ph.D.; Lecturer in Physics, Cambridge University, Cambridge, England. [PHYSICS]

Contributors not listed on these pages are members of the WORLD BOOK YEAR BOOK editorial staff.

Chronology 1976

January

S	M	T	W	T	F	S
				1	2	3
4	5	6	7	8	9	10
11	12	13	14	15	16	17
18	19	20	21	22	23	24
25	26	27	28	29	30	31

1   **Venezuela,** chief supplier of foreign oil to the United States, officially nationalizes its oil industry.

7   **Italian Prime Minister Aldo Moro** and his Cabinet resign after Socialists withdraw support for his coalition government.

U.S. Appeals Court rules that former President Richard M. Nixon's presidential papers and tapes are public property.

8   **Chou En-lai,** 78, premier of the People's Republic of China since the Communists took power in 1949, dies of cancer in Peking.

11   **Ecuador's president is deposed.** A three-man military junta replaces General Guillermo Rodriguez Lara, whose Cabinet quit earlier.

12   **United Nations (UN) Security Council** debate on the Middle East begins. Council votes 11 to 1 to allow the Palestine Liberation Organization (PLO) to participate as though it were a UN member. Israel boycotts the session.

Prime Minister Odvar Nordli appoints his Cabinet and assumes power in Norway following the resignation of Trygve Bratteli.

13   **Organization of African Unity (OAU)** ends talks without solving the Angola conflict.

14   **Spain drafts thousands of postal workers** into the army to end a two-day stoppage and stem a growing tide of labor unrest.

John T. Dunlop quits as U.S. secretary of labor, effective February 1.

26   **The United States vetoes** a UN Security Council resolution calling for total Israeli withdrawal from all Arab territories occupied in the 1967 Arab-Israeli war and affirming an independent state in Palestine.

27   **George H. W. Bush is confirmed** by the U.S. Senate as director of the Central Intelligence Agency (CIA).

Anne Armstrong is confirmed as the U.S. ambassador to Great Britain.

U.S. Congress votes to ban aid to all factions in Angola during fiscal 1976.

28   **Spanish Prime Minister Carlos Arias Navarro** announces plans to reform parliament, modify the antiterrorism law, and legalize some political groups.

Congress overrides President Ford's veto of a bill appropriating $45 billion for the Department of Labor and the Department of Health, Education, and Welfare.

31   **The International Energy Agency (IEA)** adopts a long-term policy to reduce members' dependence on imported energy.

Jan. 1

Jan. 11

Jan. 26

February

S	M	T	W	T	F	S
1	2	3	4	5	6	7
8	9	10	11	12	13	14
15	16	17	18	19	20	21
22	23	24	25	26	27	28
29						

2   **Elliot L. Richardson is sworn in** as U.S. secretary of commerce.

Canadian Prime Minister Pierre Elliott Trudeau ends a state trade tour of Mexico, Cuba, and Venezuela.

3   **Daniel P. Moynihan resigns** as chief U.S. representative to the United Nations.

4   **Major earthquake in Guatemala** causes massive destruction and leaves an estimated 22,000 persons dead.

U.S. Secretary of Transportation William T. Coleman, Jr., approves limited service for 16 months by the British-French Concorde supersonic transport to Washington, D.C., and New York City.

4-15   **The 12th Winter Olympic Games** are held at Innsbruck, Austria, with more than 1,000 athletes from 37 nations competing.

March

S	M	T	W	T	F	S
	1	2	3	4	5	6
7	8	9	10	11	12	13
14	15	16	17	18	19	20
21	22	23	24	25	26	27
28	29	30	31			

Feb. 4

Feb. 4-15

March 5

March 20

April 5

April 12

16 **Great Britain's Prime Minister Harold Wilson** announces he will quit as soon as a successor is selected.

20 **Kidnaped newspaper heiress Patricia Hearst** is convicted of bank robbery and using a firearm in the commission of a felony.

21 **U.S. closes its last military base** in Thailand following demonstrations in Bangkok.

24 **Argentine President** María Estela (Isabel) Martínez de Perón is overthrown in a bloodless coup d'état.

26 **U.S.-Turkish pact** gives the U.S. military bases in Turkey for four years in return for $1 billion in military aid.

28 **Federal Bureau of Investigation (FBI)** papers show the FBI burgled the New York City office of the Socialist Workers Party more than 90 times between 1960 and 1966.

29 **Argentina's army commander,** Lieutenant General Jorge Videla, is sworn in as president. Cabinet includes six military officers and two civilians.
One Flew Over the Cuckoo's Nest wins best picture, best director, best actor, and best actress Oscars at the 48th annual awards of the Academy of Motion Picture Arts and Sciences.

31 **Vice-President Nelson A. Rockefeller,** visiting in Australia, pledges that the United States will match any Russian fleet build-up in the Indian Ocean.

April

S	M	T	W	T	F	S
				1	2	3
4	5	6	7	8	9	10
11	12	13	14	15	16	17
18	19	20	21	22	23	24
25	26	27	28	29	30	

5 **Foreign Secretary James Callaghan** succeeds retiring British Prime Minister Harold Wilson.
Cambodia's Prince Norodom Sihanouk and his Cabinet resign. Khieu Samphan replaces Sihanouk as chief of state.

7 **Hua Kuo-feng is named premier** of China and first deputy chairman of the Communist Party; Deputy Premier Teng Hsiao-ping is ousted.

9 **Syrian troops enter Lebanon** in an attempt to force a political solution to the civil war.

12 **Thousands of Greek Cypriots** storm the U.S. Embassy in Nicosia to protest U.S.-Turkish defense agreement.

13 **More than 90,000 Canadian teachers strike** for one day in Quebec province over antistrike legislation.

14 **Mauritania and Morocco** agree to divide the disputed Western Sahara at a meeting in Rabat, Morocco.
Australia announces a three-year, $108-million aid program for Indonesia.

15 **Greek-U.S. pact** approves four U.S. military bases in Greece in return for $700 million in military aid over four years.
India and China resume relations for the first time since their 1962 border war.
President Ford signs $135-million mass immunization bill to guard against swine flu.

15-18	**Spain allows** the General Worker's Union, once Spain's largest socialist union, to meet in Madrid, the first such meeting in Spain since 1932.
17	**Prime Minister Constantine Caramanlis** of Greece proposes a peace pact with Turkey.
23	**Thousands of persons march** in Boston to protest antibusing violence earlier in the year.
25	**Portugal's Socialist Party wins** 107 of 265 seats in the first free parliamentary elections in 50 years.
26	**Vietnamese elect** a joint National Assembly, that nation's first unified government in 30 years.
27	**U.S. Secretary of State Kissinger** delivers a major policy address in Lusaka, Zambia, opposing white minority rule in Rhodesia and apartheid in South Africa.
28	**The U.S. Senate Select Committee** on Intelligence offers 96 recommendations to stem "illegal or improper" spying on U.S. citizens by the FBI and other agencies.
30	**Italian Prime Minister Aldo Moro** and his Cabinet resign. Moro agrees to remain as caretaker until new elections are held.

May

S	M	T	W	T	F	S
						1
2	3	4	5	6	7	8
9	10	11	12	13	14	15
16	17	18	19	20	21	22
23	24	25	26	27	28	29
30	31					

5	**The UN Conference on Trade** and Development opens in Nairobi, Kenya, and hears U.S. Secretary of State Kissinger call for better economic relations between rich and poor nations.
7	**The UN Law of the Sea Conference** adjourns its fourth session in New York City without reaching agreement between industrialized and developing nations on how to share the ocean's mineral wealth.
8	**Lebanese parliament elects Elias Sarkis** to replace President Sleiman Frangie. **FBI Director Clarence M. Kelley** apologizes to the American public for agency activities that he termed "clearly wrong and quite indefensible."
10	**Jeremy Thorpe resigns** as head of Britain's Liberal Party.
10-11	**France and 19 African nations meet** in Paris to discuss economic cooperation.
11	**President Ford signs** legislation to re-create Office of Science and Technology Policy.
17-22	**French President Valéry Giscard d'Estaing** visits the United States.
18	**Allan Joseph MacEachen,** secretary of state for external affairs, announces an end to Canada's nuclear cooperation pact with India. **Inter-American Development Bank** members, meeting in Cancún, Mexico, call for more U.S. aid for the bank's lending programs.
19	**The U.S. Senate creates** a permanent Select Committee on Intelligence having exclusive jurisdiction over the CIA. It will share jurisdiction over other U.S. intelligence organizations with other committees. **South Africa establishes** a 1,000-mile

(1,600-kilometer) buffer zone against guerrilla attacks allegedly launched from Namibia (South West Africa).

20-21	**North Atlantic Treaty Organization** (NATO) foreign ministers, meeting in Oslo, Norway, charge that Russia's military build-up might jeopardize détente and call for continued efforts to relax tensions. **The International Energy Agency** agrees to conduct joint experiments in nuclear energy and to share oil reserves in the event of another Arab oil embargo.
21	**Prime Minister Fidel Castro** agrees to withdraw Cuban troops from Angola.
23-25	**Latin American and European** social democratic party leaders meet in Caracas, Venezuela, to discuss "transatlantic cooperation" on economic, political, and social issues.
24	**The British-French Concorde** supersonic jetliner begins trial service to Dulles International Airport near Washington, D.C.
26	**The UN Security Council adopts** a statement deploring Israel's policy of establishing settlements in occupied Arab land.
28	**The UN Security Council** extends for six months the Golan Heights observer force. **U.S. and Russia sign a treaty** that limits the size of underground nuclear explosions for peaceful purposes and provides for on-site U.S. inspections of Soviet tests.

April 23

May 11

May 17-22

May 24

June

S	M	T	W	T	F	S
		1	2	3	4	5
6	7	8	9	10	11	12
13	14	15	16	17	18	19
20	21	22	23	24	25	26
27	28	29	30			

1   **Great Britain and Iceland** sign an interim pact to end the "cod war," a dispute over fishing rights.
Australian Prime Minister Malcolm Fraser criticizes Russia's attempts to "expand its influence throughout the world."

5   **The Teton River Dam bursts** in Idaho, flooding 300 square miles (777 square kilometers) and causing an estimated $1-billion damage.

7   **International $5.3-billion loan** is approved to bolster the sinking British pound.

10   **The Arab League agrees** to send a peacekeeping force to Lebanon to enforce a new truce for the war-torn country.

10-11   **NATO defense ministers** meet in Brussels, Belgium.

12   **Uruguay's military ousts** President Juan M. Bordaberry Arocena.

16   **Rioting erupts in Soweto,** a black township near Johannesburg, South Africa. More than 170 persons, mostly black students, die.
Kidnapers slay U.S. Ambassador Francis E. Meloy, Jr., his aid, and his chauffeur in Beirut, Lebanon.

19   **Jamaica's government declares** a state of emergency following months of political unrest on the island.

20   **The U.S. Navy evacuates** more than 100 Americans from Beirut, Lebanon.
Turkish Cypriots elect Rauf Denktash as president of the self-proclaimed Turkish Federated State of Cyprus.

20-21   **Italy's Communist Party gains** in national elections, winning 116 of 315 elected seats in the Senate and 228 of 630 seats in the Chamber of Deputies.

23   **The United States vetoes** Angola's bid for UN membership in a Security Council vote.

23-24   **South Africa's Prime Minister** Balthazar Johannes Vorster and U.S. Secretary of State Kissinger discuss the evolution to majority rule in southern Africa during talks in West Germany.

25   **Polish workers riot** over government plans to raise food prices.

27   **Portugal's first free presidential election** in 50 years goes to army Chief of Staff Antonio Ramalho Eanes.

29-30   **European Communist Party leaders** meet in East Berlin. Some challenge Russia's sole leadership role and support autonomy for each country's party.

June 16

June 20-21

June 20

July

S	M	T	W	T	F	S
				1	2	3
4	5	6	7	8	9	10
11	12	13	14	15	16	17
18	19	20	21	22	23	24
25	26	27	28	29	30	31

1-5   **At least 75 Argentines die** in political violence as the toll passes 600 since January 1.

2   **The U.S. Supreme Court upholds** the death penalty for murder convictions, saying it is not "cruel and unusual punishment."
North and South Vietnam officially reunite as the Socialist Republic of Vietnam.

3   **Israeli commandos rescue** 103 hostages in a raid on Uganda's Entebbe Airport. Seven pro-Palestinian guerrillas who hijacked an Air France plane on June 27 die in the fighting.
Spain's King Juan Carlos I names Adolfo Suarez Gonzalez as prime minister to replace Carlos Arias Navarro, whom he fired July 1.

4   **The United States celebrates** its 200th birthday with festivities throughout the land. An estimated 6 million people watch Operation Sail — an international flotilla of sailing ships — sail from New York Harbor up the Hudson River.
Mexico elects Jose Lopez Portillo as president.

6   **French President Giscard d'Estaing** and West German Chancellor Helmut Schmidt meet in Hamburg, West Germany, to discuss common problems.

Queen Elizabeth II of Great Britain arrives in Philadelphia for a six-day tour of the United States.

12 **Over 2 million Australian workers strike** for 24 hours to protest proposed changes in Medibank, the country's health plan.

The European Council of the Common Market agrees on a distribution plan for the 410 elected seats in a new European parliament.

13 **Giulio Andreotti succeeds Aldo Moro** as Italy's prime minister.

14 **James Earl (Jimmy) Carter, Jr., wins** presidential nomination on the first ballot at the Democratic National Convention in New York City. Carter selects Senator Walter F. Mondale (Minn.) as his vice-presidential running mate.

Aparicio Mendez is named Uruguay's president.

17 **Spain's Cabinet announces** that legislative elections will be held by June 30, 1977.

The Summer Olympic Games open in Montreal, Canada, amid political controversy.

West German Chancellor Schmidt ends a three-day visit to the United States.

19 **Drought-stricken European farmers** seek Common Market economic aid.

20 *Viking I* **lands on Mars** and relays crisp surface photos.

21 **The British ambassador to Ireland dies** when a land mine is set off beneath his car.

21-24 **A mystery ailment strikes** 179 persons attending conventions in Philadelphia, killing 29.

22 **Congress overrides President Ford's veto** of a $3.95-billion public-works jobs bill.

26 **Italy's Communist Party** gains the chairmanships of four key legislative committees.

26-30 **Australian Prime Minister** Malcolm Fraser visits the United States.

27 **Former Japanese Prime Minister** Kakuei Tanaka is arrested in connection with an alleged bribery scandal involving the U.S.-based Lockheed Aircraft Corporation.

28 **Earthquakes rock northern China,** killing an estimated 655,000 persons.

August

S	M	T	W	T	F	S
1	2	3	4	5	6	7
8	9	10	11	12	13	14
15	16	17	18	19	20	21
22	23	24	25	26	27	28
29	30	31				

1-8 **The 41st International Eucharistic Congress** of the Roman Catholic Church meets in Philadelphia and discusses the theme "Hungers of the Human Family."

3-4 **Congress overrides President Ford's veto** on new regulations for leasing federal lands with coal reserves.

7 **Iran announces plans** to buy $50 billion worth of U.S. goods by 1980.

14 **President Ford signs an energy bill** that raises the price of U.S. oil and encourages conservation.

16-20 **Representatives of 85 nonaligned nations** meet in Colombo, Sri Lanka, and urge richer nations to share their wealth.

July 4

July 14

July 20

Aug. 19

Sept. 4-6

Sept. 6

19   **President Ford narrowly defeats** Ronald Reagan for the presidential nomination at the Republican National Convention in Kansas City, Mo. He selects Senator Robert J. Dole (Kans.) as his running mate.

19-23   **Danish workers strike** over passage of an economic plan that would limit wage hikes.

24   **British Prime Minister** James Callaghan appoints Denis Howell to oversee water conservation as Europe's worst drought in more than 200 years continues.

25   **French Prime Minister Jacques Chirac resigns** and is replaced by Raymond Barre, former minister of foreign trade.
The U.S. Interior Department accepts $1.13-billion in bids by oil companies to drill for oil in the Atlantic Ocean.

26   **Prince Bernhard of the Netherlands resigns** nearly all his military and business posts because of questionable relations with the Lockheed Aircraft Corporation.

28   **Striking U.S. rubber workers end** a walkout that began on April 21.

31   **Mexico floats the peso,** which plummets 40 per cent in value. Action ends 22 years of fixed parity to U.S. dollar.

September

S	M	T	W	T	F	S
			1	2	3	4
5	6	7	8	9	10	11
12	13	14	15	16	17	18
19	20	21	22	23	24	25
26	27	28	29	30		

1   **Congressman Wayne L. Hays** (D., Ohio) resigns in the wake of a sex scandal.
Aparicio Mendez assumes power as president of Uruguay and suspends the political rights of the leaders of all political parties in the country for 15 years.

2   **The European Commission** on Human Rights reports that some British officials tortured suspected terrorists in Northern Ireland in 1971.

3   *Viking 2* **spacecraft** lands on Mars.

4-6   **U.S. Secretary of State Kissinger** and South African Prime Minister Vorster meet in Zurich, Switzerland, to discuss majority rule for southern Africa.

6   **Russian pilot lands MIG-25 jet** in Japan and asks for U.S. asylum.
U.S. and North Korea accord partitions Panmunjom joint security area in the Demilitarized Zone to prevent clashes such as that in which North Koreans killed two U.S. officers on August 18.

8   **Prime Minister Malcolm Fraser** announces plans to aid drought victims in southwestern Australia.

9   **Chairman Mao Tse-tung dies** at 82. He had been the principal leader of the People's Republic of China since its birth in 1949.

10   **British Prime Minister Callaghan** reshuffles his Cabinet after Home Secretary Roy Jenkins resigns to become president of the European Commission.

| 13 | **The U.S. National Academy of Sciences** recommends that fluorocarbons be regulated by 1978 to prevent destruction of the earth's protective ozone shell. |

13 **The U.S. National Academy of Sciences** recommends that fluorocarbons be regulated by 1978 to prevent destruction of the earth's protective ozone shell.

14 **U.S. Secretary of State Kissinger** arrives in Dar es Salaam, Tanzania, to begin talks with black African leaders to resolve political conflicts.

Prime Minister Pierre Elliott Trudeau shuffles his Cabinet as Canadian Liberal Party's popular support sinks to its lowest level in 20 years. He reassigns eight ministers.

15 **Japan's Prime Minister Takeo Miki** dismisses 13 ministers and appoints 13 new members to his Cabinet.

17 **The UN Law of the Sea Conference** ends its fifth session in New York City without reaching agreement on mining minerals from the sea floor.

20 **Sweden's Social Democrats lose** parliamentary elections for the first time in 44 years.

21 **Orlando Letelier,** a former Chilean Cabinet minister, dies in a terrorist bomb explosion in Washington, D.C.

22 **Prime Minister Barre** announces wage-and-price controls and tax reforms to curb inflation in France.

The Council of Europe formally accepts Portugal as its 19th member.

23 **President Ford** and former Governor Jimmy Carter debate economic issues in Philadelphia in the first of three televised campaign confrontations.

19 **A UN Security Council resolution** to ban arms to South Africa is vetoed by Great Britain, France, and the United States.

20 **First U.S. copyright revision since 1909** is signed into law. It extends protection to 50 years after a copyright holder's death.

21 **The Cincinnati Reds** defeat the New York Yankees, 7-2, to win the World Series and become the first National League team to win two consecutive series since 1922.

23 **Vietnam and U.S. agree** to talks on improving relations.

22-24 **Millions of Chinese demonstrate** in major cities in support of Chairman Hua Kuo-feng and the purge of "radical" leaders including Chiang Ching, the widow of Mao Tse-tung.

25 **Russian leader Leonid I. Brezhnev** announces a possible record grain harvest following 1975's disastrous harvest. He also says the pace of détente has slowed.

26 **Transkei** becomes the first of South Africa's *bantustans* (black homelands) to gain independence. The UN votes 134 to 0 on a resolution calling Transkei independence a sham — a way for the South African government to continue white minority rule.

27 **The U.S. Department of Defense** announces plans to boost the number of fighter planes in NATO by 20 per cent.

28 **The British pound drops** to a new low of $1.56.

October

S	M	T	W	T	F	S
					1	2
3	4	5	6	7	8	9
10	11	12	13	14	15	16
17	18	19	20	21	22	23
24	25	26	27	28	29	30
31						

3 **West German Chancellor Schmidt's** coalition government majority is sharply reduced in parliamentary elections.

4 **U.S. Secretary of Agriculture Earl L. Butz** resigns for "gross indiscretion" amid rising protest over racist remarks.

The U.S. Supreme Court convenes for its 1976-1977 term and refuses to reconsider its July decision upholding the death penalty for murder.

6 **Thai military leaders seize power** after students and police clash in Bangkok.

President Ford and Jimmy Carter discuss foreign policy and national defense in their second debate, in San Francisco.

7 **Thorbjorn Falldin,** a farmer, takes office as prime minister of Sweden.

12 **Hua Kuo-feng succeeds Mao Tse-tung** as chairman of the Chinese Communist Party.

13 **Syrian troops in Lebanon** attack Palestinian forces near Beirut in an attempt to force a settlement in the civil war.

18 **Six Arab leaders sign a peace pact** for Lebanon in Riyadh, Saudi Arabia, calling for a 30,000-man peacekeeping force to supervise the withdrawal of troops to positions they held before April 1975.

Sept. 9

Oct. 3

Oct. 6

November

S	M	T	W	T	F	S
	1	2	3	4	5	6
7	8	9	10	11	12	13
14	15	16	17	18	19	20
21	22	23	24	25	26	27
28	29	30				

2   **James Earl (Jimmy) Carter, Jr.,** is elected President of the United States with 50.08 per cent of the popular vote. Senator Walter F. Mondale (Minn.) is elected Vice-President.

8   **The U.S. Conference of Mayors,** meeting in Chicago, urges President-elect Carter to "set a national tone of concern for urban America."
The U.S. Supreme Court refuses to block federal funds for abortion by choice.

9   **The UN General Assembly** passes 10 resolutions against South Africa's policy of racial separation.
Patrick J. Hillery is declared president-elect of Ireland to succeed Cearbhall O Dalaigh, who resigned in October.

11   **Russia, the United States,** and 13 other countries begin top-secret talks in London to curb the spread of nuclear weapons.

Nov. 15

Dec. 17

Dec. 1

15   **Quebec's separatist party,** the Partí Québécois, wins control of the province's National Assembly.
The United States vetoes Vietnam's application for membership in the United Nations.
Syria's peacekeeping troops complete the occupation of Beirut, Lebanon, effectively ending the civil war that claimed more than 35,000 lives in 19 months.
China rejects friendlier ties with Russia.

18   **Spain's *Cortes* (parliament)** approves a plan changing it to an elected body.

28   **Australia devalues its dollar** 17.5 per cent.

December

S	M	T	W	T	F	S
			1	2	3	4
5	6	7	8	9	10	11
12	13	14	15	16	17	18
19	20	21	22	23	24	25
26	27	28	29	30	31	

1   **Jose Lopez Portillo** is sworn in as president of Mexico. He calls for national unity and tells Mexicans to look forward to "austerity as a way of life."

Italian parliamentary commission implicates former Prime Minister Mariano Rumor in connection with the Lockheed Aircraft Corporation bribery scandal.

Angola gains UN membership.

5   **Japan's ruling Liberal Democratic Party** is set back in general elections, but keeps power with help from independents in the *Diet* (parliament).

9   **Secretary of State Kissinger** warns NATO foreign ministers to reject a Russian proposal that NATO and the Warsaw Pact members pledge never to be the first to use nuclear weapons.

Lebanon's Prime Minister Salim Ahmad al-Huss names a Cabinet composed mainly of non-politicians to lead the war-torn country's reconstruction.

14   **Britain adjourns the conference on Rhodesia** in Geneva, Switzerland, until Jan. 17, 1977.

15   **Spanish voters** overwhelmingly approve parliamentary reform.

16   **U.S. health officials halt** the swine-flu immunization program because of a possible link to at least 50 cases of paralysis and four deaths.

17   **Organization of Petroleum Exporting Countries** announces a bi-level price hike; Saudi Arabia and the United Arab Emirates will boost prices 5 per cent, and the 11 other members, 10 per cent.

20   **Chicago Mayor Richard J. Daley dies** of a heart attack at age 74.

Prime Minister Yitzhak Rabin of Israel resigns after losing his majority in Parliament the day before when he ousted members of the National Religious Party from his coalition.

24   **Japan's parliament narrowly elects** Takeo Fukuda, 71-year-old leader of the conservative Liberal Democrats, as prime minister.

Section One

The Year In Focus

THE YEAR BOOK Board of Editors analyzes some significant developments of 1976 and considers their impact on contemporary affairs. The Related Articles list following each report directs the reader to THE YEAR BOOK's additional coverage of related subjects.

Focus on The World

John Holmes

The year 1976 was clearly a climactic one, as memorable, perhaps, as 1776—but at the same time, it was mostly a year of postponement

The year 1976 was clearly a climactic one, as memorable perhaps as 1776. Events in China and Africa alone made this likely, not to mention the Middle East, Europe, and the United States. But at the same time, not much actually changed. It was mostly a year of postponement, of waiting to see who would rule in Peking and Washington, D.C., and how Moscow would move, and how negotiations in progress would turn out. Things did happen, of course, that were bound to affect the world's course, but the consequences were only dimly predictable.

The long-awaited transfer of power in China may prove to have been the most important event of 1976. Chou En-lai died, and then Mao Tse-tung. The new regime of Hua Kuo-feng established swift authority over Mao's widow and the other "radicals," but what this triumph of the so-called "moderates" would mean was uncertain. A more pragmatic approach in internal policies could mean better relations with the West, but also with Russia. The unsettling doctrine of incessant revolution was disposed of and a greater disposition of welcome trade and technology from the West was indicated, but China was not renouncing its own way to Communism and its isolation. Western leaders watched nervously and discreetly. They feared the consequences of Russian-Chinese discord going out of control, but they were aware that the Chinese breach with Moscow had become an important factor in calculating the prospects for détente and the Russian military threat. The Russians, with their enemy Mao out of the way, invited reconciliation, but Peking continued its vitriolic attacks. Mao was mourned in the West, not as a friend but as a leader of consequence who had kept China a stable element in the balance. His passing could loose incalculable forces. Hua's stance was reassuring, but, overall, it was a year of uncertainty in China.

For Communism in general, it was a year of disintegration. Where could Communists now look for leadership? Mao was dead, and with him the glowing idealism of pure revolution. Hanoi, now the capital of a united Vietnam, showed signs of going its own way. President Josip Broz Tito was nearing the end in Yugoslavia. The Western European and Japanese Communists were not only rejecting Russian hegemony, but also trying to disengage from the crude Russian tradition of Communism. They publicly criticized Soviet suppression of human rights. Europe's Communist parties met in East Berlin in June and stressed the principle of equality and sovereign independence of each party. A generation gap emerged at the meeting between the elderly leaders of the Russian and East European parties and the Italian, French, and Spanish spokesmen seeking "Communism with a human face." The Western European leaders formally rejected the

John Holmes

19

"dictatorship of the proletariat" and "proletarian internationalism," the code word for party discipline under Russian leadership. Tito attended such a meeting for the first time in 19 years to reassert the doctrine of independence. The more disciplined party chiefs from Czechoslovakia and Poland rejected the new doctrines, but at home their restless people clearly wanted a more European version of the doctrine according to which they must live.

The trends were viewed with optimism and skepticism in Western capitals. The electoral triumph in the spring of Social Democrats over the Communists in Portugal had been followed by gains for the Italian Communists. The Italian Communists, however, were dedicated to the Western European tradition of achieving and holding power by democratic means and working with other parties. Their leader, Enrico Berlinguer, said he favored keeping Italy in the North Atlantic Treaty Organization (NATO) until there could be a dismantling of both military blocs in Europe. Some Europeans thought that a government with Communist participation could not stay in NATO, but others were wary of seeming to interfere in Italian politics. In Cold War terms, there was no clear gain for Russia, though on broad world issues the Italian and French Communists held orthodox views about the struggle with "imperialism" and took a harsh view of the United States.

Further events of profound but still incalculable consequences were the outbreak of black militancy in South Africa and the recognition by Prime Minister Ian Smith of Rhodesia that white-minority rule must be abandoned. Although it was American pressure that forced his hand, Secretary of State Henry A. Kissinger's tardy attention to Africa looked to many Africans like an effort to counter what Russia had gained by backing the winning faction in Angola's civil war. The black leaders of Zimbabwe (their name for Rhodesia) met with Smith in Geneva, Switzerland, to arrange for majority black rule in two years. As was to be expected, there were strong confrontations and the disunity of the black leaders made agreement more difficult. But with encouragement from leaders of other African states and the British chairman of the Geneva meeting, a serious effort was at last underway to make the transition peaceful, if at all possible.

The British and Americans could expect little credit from Africans, whatever happened, but their intervention was recognized as an opportunity. Some African leaders, at least, would like to avoid unbalanced dependence on Soviet support. African alignments, however, were likely to be determined by the passions roused over the imminent struggle for power in southern Africa to which Rhodesia is only the preliminary. The showdown in South Africa might come sooner than expected, and it would involve much more powerful forces.

While they gained friends in Black Africa, the Russians were losing them in the Middle East—and bases as well. The "Ugly Russian," given time, could become as obnoxious as any other imperialist. Egypt renounced its Treaty of Friendship and Cooperation with the Soviet Union and canceled Russia's rights of access to its Mediterranean

A showdown in South Africa might come sooner than most expect

Kissinger in Africa

20

ports. President Anwar al-Sadat then turned toward Peking as well as Washington. Syria defied Moscow by intervening in the Lebanese Civil War to counter the pretensions of radical Palestinians. The fragile truce and disengagement in the Sinai that Kissinger had maneuvered between Egypt and Israel in 1975 was holding under strain, and United States influence was still crucial. What might prove a turning point in the Middle East was the shifting alignment resulting from the war in Lebanon. The complexity of these shifts defied simplistic analysis. So far, conservative Arabs had prevailed over radicals, and the bloody strife was a sobering experience that made explicit or tacit understandings with Israel at least conceivable. The United States, as the Arabs could see, was pressing the Israelis in that direction. The fear of an oil embargo by the Arab states may have affected the thinking of some Americans, but an evenhanded policy was understandable on its own merits. The Middle East was still the tinderbox, however.

The complexity of the shifts in the Middle East defied easy analysis

Another enigma was the United States election. It looked as if the new Administration would change the style more than the substance of United States policy, but the world watched nervously. Kissinger may not have been praised abroad, but he would be missed. He had sought to make the United States a stabilizing rather than a crusading nation, and it seemed more reliable than it had been as the frantic power of the 1960s. Nevertheless, a Democratic Administration was expected to be more liberal on economic matters and perhaps better able to check the quarrelsome role of Congress in foreign policy, a trend popular with neither friends nor adversaries abroad.

Détente was a continuing fact of international life. Russian Communist Party General Secretary Leonid I. Brezhnev reaffirmed it at the 25th Party Congress in Moscow. So did the East European leaders who met in Bucharest, Romania. It was hailed even by the dissident European Communists, though it was denounced by Peking as a Russian fraud. Many Westerners questioned whether Soviet and Cuban intervention in Angola was compatible with détente, and they were alarmed by the rapid expansion of Soviet armed might. Others pointed out that Russia had never pretended it would suspend the ideological conflict or cease to support "wars of liberation." They saw the armed thrust as the predictable fulfillment of the Soviet determination some years back to "close the gap" and establish Russia's position as a world military and naval power equal in status to the United States. Russian arms were coming off the production line at a pace not likely to cool tensions or the arms race. Still, the Strategic Arms Limitation Talks and the efforts by NATO and the Warsaw Pact to achieve mutual and balanced force reductions, though stalled, were not renounced as goals by either side.

Middle East tinderbox

Skepticism about détente was encouraged by what were seen as the meager results of the Helsinki agreements of 1975, which had promised more freedom of movement, commerce, and ideas. Neither the Russians nor the East Germans showed much will to let people out or ideas in. The West Germans, however, made a deal by which trade

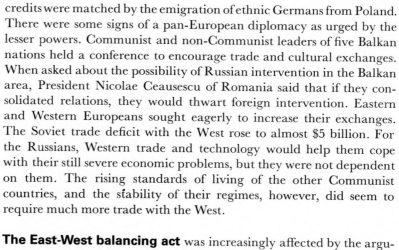

credits were matched by the emigration of ethnic Germans from Poland. There were some signs of a pan-European diplomacy as urged by the lesser powers. Communist and non-Communist leaders of five Balkan nations held a conference to encourage trade and cultural exchanges. When asked about the possibility of Russian intervention in the Balkan area, President Nicolae Ceausescu of Romania said that if they consolidated relations, they would thwart foreign intervention. Eastern and Western Europeans sought eagerly to increase their exchanges. The Soviet trade deficit with the West rose to almost $5 billion. For the Russians, Western trade and technology would help them cope with their still severe economic problems, but they were not dependent on them. The rising standards of living of the other Communist countries, and the stability of their regimes, however, did seem to require much more trade with the West.

North-South arguments affected the East-West balancing act

The East-West balancing act was increasingly affected by the argument between North and South—the developing countries versus the industrial countries. The "capitalist" powers, and especially the United States, took most of the abuse at the United Nations (UN); at the Non-Aligned Conference in Colombo, Sri Lanka; and at the UN Conference on Trade and Development sessions in Nairobi, Kenya. At those meetings, however, the Communists did not get away with the argument that this was a simple struggle with capitalist exploiters. At Nairobi, a resolution was passed calling for more aid from the Communist countries and more equitable trade arrangements than the barter systems they had hitherto imposed on the poorer countries. Prime Minister Lee Kuan Yew of Singapore told the "nonaligned" that they could make progress only in cooperation with the West.

It was obvious that the plight of the third world depended on the will of the Western powers to agree to better terms in the "New Economic Order." The Communist states took only 5 per cent of third world trade, and the aid they gave to the developing countries was negligible. The West might be the third world's problem, but it was also their only answer. So they continued the discussions at the UN and in the Commission for International Economic Cooperation (CIEC) in Paris. The pragmatic note struck at the Special Assembly of the UN in September 1975 continued, though the rhetoric was still vehement. The CIEC was not making much progress, and it was a question how long this stage of negotiations could last. The Western powers were far from united, with the United States and West Germany sometimes isolated in opposition to third world demands.

On key political issues, there was more restraint. The third world did not press its case against Israel to extremes, either in the UN General Assembly or in the United Nations Educational, Scientific, and Cultural Organization, where it had dangerously alienated the major contributors. The oil-producing states, though they raised the price of oil again in December, were still in the hands of men who appreciated the importance for the third world of a solvent West.

Western leaders were trying to come up with workable schemes for

United Nations meeting

more equitable cooperation with the third world, but conditions at home were hardly propitious. The economies of the most responsible industrialized powers, especially Britain, were in desperate straits. Almost nowhere could there be found a strong government, not even in West Germany, where the government was narrowly returned to power in an October election. From Australia to Mexico and Sweden, there was a swing toward a more conservative mood. It was not a time of confident and easy rule in the Communist countries, either.

In a world intermeshed, government had become awesomely complex. Was an interdependent world governable? Were even countries any longer governable? Could governments that had to tell their people to restrain their appetites stay in power? Could the world's peoples—increasingly aware that their resources were finite, that population must be checked, that the arms race could destroy them—find the ways or the will to discipline themselves? There were grounds for despair, but the effort to regulate was still going on—most notably in the UN Law of the Sea Conference. This greatest effort in history to place the whole world under a rule of law held two more sessions in which the areas of difference were at least narrowed.

If the future looked bleak to many, it was perhaps because people had worked their way through the alternatives that had sustained earlier generations and found them wanting: world government, collective security, liberalism, Socialism, and Communism in various forms. Disillusion, however, meant the shedding of illusions, and the inclination to move from the abstractions of ideology to cope with the inescapable facts of 1976 was a hopeful sign.

Not only friends, but also antagonists were hoping that the United States might now offer an exception to the rule of uncertain government, because their hopes for better living or for détente depended on a stable America. On its 200th birthday, America was not beloved abroad as the Founding Fathers had hoped, but it was respected—by some for its moral values, its recuperative powers, and its constructive energy, and by others for its productivity, its efficiency, and its economic, military, and diplomatic power. The revelations of irregular activities by the Central Intelligence Agency and of bribery by industrial concerns didn't help; but there was still no serious rival in strength across-the-board. Russia and East Germany did better at the Olympic Games, but the United States gained all the Nobel Prizes. Leadership by the new Administration of James Earl (Jimmy) Carter, Jr., would certainly be welcomed, even though the day of the *Pax Americana* had passed.

Despite cause for despair, the effort to regulate was still going on

Nobel Prize ceremony

Related Articles

For further information on international relations in 1976, see the articles on the various nations in Section Four, and also the following:

Focus on The Nation

James Reston

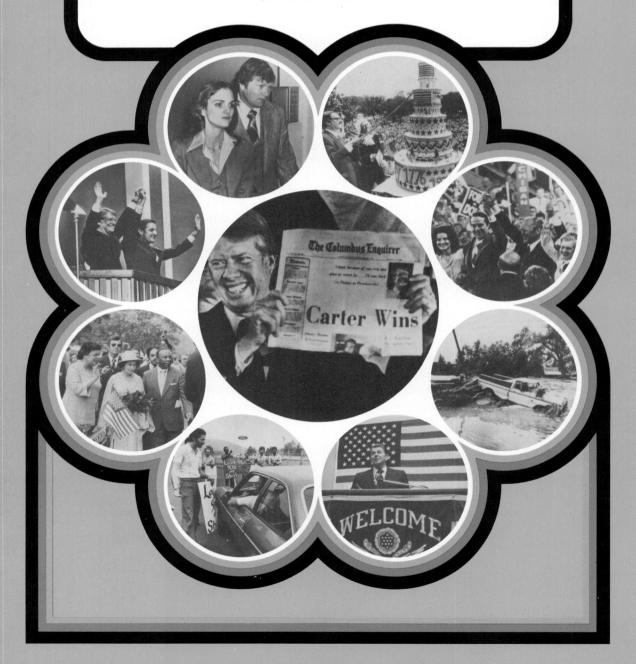

**Like most years, 1976 had its disappointments
and its anxieties, but it brought forth a new
generation to grapple with the new challenges**

Most years in the long story of the United States slip away from
memory, but some have unforgettable names: 1776, the Year of Independence; 1789, the Year of the Constitution; 1861, the Year of
Sorrows; 1932, the Year of the Great Depression; 1945, the Beginning
of the Atomic Age; 1969, the Year of Man on the Moon. These, among
others, are the milestones of our history, and while 1976 did not quite
rank with such memorable years, it stands apart as a special time at
the beginning of the last quarter of the 20th century.

It marked the 200th anniversary of the Declaration of Independence. It provided a new beginning for a nation that had ended the
most calamitous international war in its history. And, in a way, it
finally unified the nation politically by electing as President of the
United States a true son of the Old South–James Earl (Jimmy) Carter,
Jr., of Georgia–for the first time since before the Civil War.

Like most years, 1976 had its disappointments and anxieties. It was
a time of excessive unemployment, with almost 8 million of its people
out of work, with high prices and rates of inflation, and with unresolved conflicts over taxation, education, and the distribution of
wealth and social services, particularly in the growing and financially
depressed urban centers of the North.

Nevertheless, America's Bicentennial year was a period of comparative economic and psychological recovery at home, and of peace abroad
for the first time in almost a generation. After the constitutional crises
of the Vietnam War and the White House Watergate scandals, the
nation somehow survived its first major defeat in war, the resignation
of a President, and the turmoil of a hard and close presidential election campaign–all in good order and reasonable calm.

Americans were asked in 1976 to remember the men and women
who founded the nation and wrote the most enduring constitution in
the history of free peoples, but they didn't have to go back to their
history books to understand the thought and achievements of Thomas
Jefferson, James Madison, and Alexander Hamilton. The warnings of
the Founding Fathers against human pride, power, and corruption
had been in the newspaper headlines for years. And the safeguards of
the Constitution had ended a war and caused the departure of a
President who violated the principles of 1776 and 1789.

More than that, 1976 saw the end of one of the strangest chapters in
American political history, during which both a President, Gerald R.
Ford of Michigan, and a Vice-President, Nelson A. Rockefeller of New
York, had occupied the two highest offices of the nation without having
been elected by the people to do so.

Maybe "moderation" was the name for 1976 on the national scene.
It was a time of change, as usual, but of corrective change, of pulling

James Reston

back or edging away from some of the extremes of the immediate years before. The mood of the country seemed more cautious, reflective, and skeptical of elaborate plans to cure all the historic ills of the human family.

Alarmed by the rise of prices, unemployment, welfare payments, and excessive deficits, the opposition to inflationary spending policies increased. Politically, the appeal of partisan arguments declined, and the fiscal crisis of New York City, threatening bankruptcy, produced strong support for presidential vetoes of previously popular programs. Even in the field of foreign policy, there was rising opposition to what was regarded as one-sided cooperation with Russia and to interventionist policies elsewhere in the world.

And yet, though the sentiment of the voters seemed more conservative, they rejected in the 1976 presidential primary elections the two most conservative candidates, Governor George C. Wallace of Alabama on the Democratic side, and former Governor Ronald Reagan of California on the Republican.

Also, despite over 40 per cent unemployment among black teenagers, the racial demonstrations abated in the cities, and the university campuses, once the center of radical turmoil, were comparatively calm. In short, almost all the economic, social, and security problems of the first half of the 1970s remained, but during the election and the Bicentennial year, militancy was at least temporarily out of favor among student activists and in the controversies between the races, the regions, and labor and management.

Perhaps the paradox of 1976 was that, when confronted by a choice between a cautious, familiar, and predictable President and a comparatively unfamiliar and unpredictable challenger, the American people voted for the risk of the unknown rather than for the risk of going on about as before. They made factual history out of one of the oldest fictional tales of America—the story of the small-town man (in this case a peanut farmer from Plains, Ga.) who dreams of becoming President, and then by hard work and against incredible odds achieves his ambition. Jimmy Carter changed the balance of political power in America in 1976, but by the narrowest of margins:

■ In the years since the end of World War II, the two major political parties had each held the presidency for 16 years. But Carter not only ended eight years of Republican control of the executive branch, he also defeated an incumbent President for the first time since Franklin D. Roosevelt overwhelmed President Herbert Hoover in 1932.

■ His victory was based on sweeping all of the states of the Civil War Confederacy except Virginia and all of the border states except Oklahoma, but even so his electoral margin of 57 votes—297 to 240 (Ford carried Washington, but 1 elector cast his vote on December 13 for Ronald Reagan)—was the closest since Woodrow Wilson defeated Charles Evans Hughes by 23 electoral votes in 1916.

■ Nevertheless, the Democrats not only recaptured the White House, but also increased their majorities in the House and the Senate and

Ford campaigning

The American people voted for the risk of the unknown

even added to their dominant control of the state governorships and legislatures. In sum, the Republican Party, which won the presidency in 1972 with 60.7 per cent of the popular vote and 520 electoral votes to 17, was reduced to a minority party with a deficit of 38 seats to 61 in the Senate, with 1 Independent; 143 to 292 seats in the House; 12 out of the 50 governorships; and control over both houses in only 5 of the 50 states.

Even after President Carter was sworn into office in January 1977, political observers were still debating what all these changes meant for the political future of the nation. On the positive side, there was general agreement that, after a period of unusual stress, the American political system was working fairly well, with more flexibility and stability than most. It had produced the 25th Amendment to the Constitution, which enabled the nation to survive the resignations of both President Richard M. Nixon and Vice-President Spiro T. Agnew much more tranquilly than most observers had thought possible.

It introduced a new government-supported campaign finance system that limited the corrupt private financing of the past. It endured an excessively long primary election season and demonstrated once more that the highest position in the nation is open to any citizen who can win the confidence of the people—regardless of the preference of the party leaders.

Also on the positive side, it ended the North's century-old prejudice against a President from the old Confederacy, and it gave that half of the nation that is under 30 years of age a sense that the system is open and capable of producing new Presidents and new beginnings.

Finally, American blacks demonstrated that they could use the franchise to gain an important and maybe even a decisive voice in the election of an American President. They voted 4 to 1 for Carter in the North and by even larger margins in the South, and helped Carter prevail, though he ran behind Ford in the overall vote of white Americans, 48 per cent to 51 per cent.

On the negative side of the 1976 election was the fact that the trend toward nonvoting continued for the fourth straight presidential election. Though more voters went to the polls than ever before—about 80 million—only some 53 per cent of the eligible voters actually cast their ballots, compared with 55 per cent in 1972. In fact, of all Americans over 18 years of age, 27 per cent voted for Carter, 26 per cent voted for Ford, and 47 per cent stayed home.

Accordingly, while vast changes occurred on the political landscape during the Bicentennial year, the margin of Carter's victory was so small and the percentage of nonvoters was so large, that observers were hesitant to conclude that the results of 1976 necessarily marked an enduring course for the 1980s.

A careful analysis of the results by Michael Barone of the Peter D. Hart polling organization reached the following conclusion: "We are unlikely to see an enduring Democratic or Republican majority at a time when people's party ties are weakening, as they undoubtedly are.

After a period of stress, the system was working well

TV tallies the votes

In the last four [presidential] elections, every state except Massachusetts, Arizona, and the District of Columbia has voted for both Republican and Democratic candidates. So don't look for the partisan patterns of 1976 to be repeated. The primary lesson of the 1976 campaign is that many things can occur, but that it takes a lot of mistakes for a candidate to lose when the basic currents of public opinion are working in his favor."

No political party was sure it had all the answers to a changing world

Coming into the last quarter of the century, however, "the basic currents of public opinion" in America were obviously changing. Despite Southern pride that helped elect President Carter, regional patterns of thought were breaking down under the relentless barrage of national television. Even the remotest villages on the continent were getting the same news every day from the same national networks. The mobility of the American people over national highways and national airlines was increasing. Vast crisscrossing migrations were taking place, out of the South and into the urban North and, simultaneously, out of New England and the Middle West into the South. Meanwhile, the West and the Southwest, the so-called Sunny Crescent, was booming with larger populations, new industries, and new commercial and financial centers.

The Middle West, once the most isolationist part of the country, was exporting its grain in ever larger quantities overseas, and backing the freetraders it used to oppose. The old assumption of a self-sufficient America was breaking down in the face of oil shortages and the imperative need to export other raw materials. And even the assumption of American military, scientific, and technological supremacy was being challenged by the progress of other advanced industrial nations.

As a result, no section of the nation dominated the others as clearly as it had in the past, no nation had a monopoly or even a domination of power, and no political party in America was sure that it had the answers to a rapidly changing world or could count on winning a majority of the states in a national election.

By 1977, however, American opinion was adjusting to these hard facts and regaining the confidence that had waned during the military, social, moral, and political crises of the 1960s and early 1970s. After more than a generation of preoccupation with international affairs, there seemed to be a new concern with the internal stability of the nation and a realization that security abroad depended in large measure on the unity of the regions, the races, and the classes at home.

For example, Potomac Associates, a social-research organization based in Washington, D.C., found a marked shift in the concerns of Americans during 1976. In 1964, Potomac's studies showed that the five major concerns of the American people were all in the field of international affairs, whereas in 1976, the 10 leading problems on the American mind had to do with domestic problems.

In order of importance, these concerns were: (1) crime in America; (2) the amount of violence in American life; corruption or law-breaking on the part of government officials; and the rise in prices and the cost

The President-elect

of living—a three-way tie; (5) the problem of drug addicts and narcotic drugs; (6) ensuring that Americans in general, including the poor and elderly, get adequate medical and health care; (7) improving the educational system; (8) unemployment in the country; (9) cleaning up our waterways and reducing water pollution, and protecting consumers against misleading advertising, dangerous products, and unsafe food and drugs—a two-way tie.

It was only after these primary concerns that the respondents said they were concerned with keeping our military and defense forces strong and with the growing dependence of the United States on foreign nations for supplies of oil and other natural resources.

So the agenda of problems remained a long one as President Carter started his Administration, but the focus of the nation had turned more inward, though not isolationist. Reflection on the Bicentennial had heightened the mood of self-appraisal and produced a new emphasis on the inner unity and coherence of American society.

In this sense, 1976 was a landmark year, dramatizing the departure of old leaders and minimizing the concerns of former years, but also bringing to the fore new concerns and a new generation calling for a more equal society of men and women of all races to grapple with the new challenges at the end of the 1970s.

The focus of the nation was more inward, but it was not isolationist

Related Articles

For further information on United States affairs in 1976, see also Section One, Focus on The Economy and Focus on Education; Section Five, Carter, James Earl, Jr.; and the following articles in Section Four:

<table>
<tr><td>Cabinet</td><td>Economics</td><td>Republican Party</td></tr>
<tr><td>Carter, James Earl, Jr.</td><td>Elections</td><td>Rockefeller, Nelson A.</td></tr>
<tr><td>City</td><td>Ford, Gerald R.</td><td>State Government</td></tr>
<tr><td>Congress of the United States</td><td>Labor</td><td>Supreme Court of the United States</td></tr>
<tr><td>Courts and Laws</td><td>Mondale, Walter F.</td><td></td></tr>
<tr><td>Democratic Party</td><td>Nixon, Richard M.</td><td>Taxation</td></tr>
<tr><td>Dole, Robert J.</td><td>President of the U.S.</td><td>United States, Government of the</td></tr>
<tr><td></td><td>Reagan, Ronald</td><td></td></tr>
</table>

Focus on The Economy

Sylvia Porter

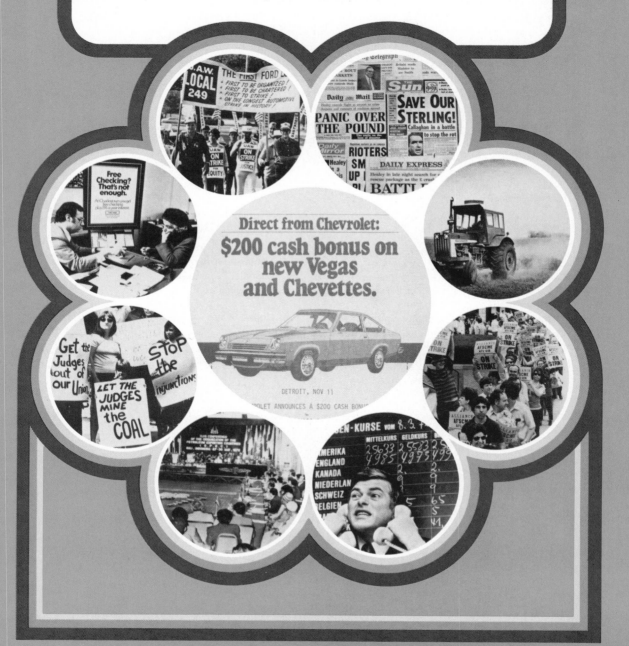

The United States economy continued its recovery, but there were many challenges—shrugged off so far—that should not be pushed aside much longer

The United States economy in 1976 continued to recover from the worst business slump of the entire post-World War II era, and by year's end, its total dollar output of goods and services had reached an annual rate of almost $2 *trillion*, the highest peak ever. But while the direction was upward throughout, the pace of the expansion turned disturbingly erratic as the year wore on. While the rate of inflation was slashed in half from its 1974 double-digit level, the annual inflation rate remained in an intolerably high 5 to 6 per cent range. While total employment climbed to a new record, the rate of unemployment also remained stuck in an unacceptable range of more than 8 per cent. And while some of the great economic challenges of the closing decades of the 20th century were being vaguely acknowledged by the politicians in power in Washington, D.C., most of them weren't even perceived—much less met.

That 1976 was a year of expansion, though, was beyond dispute. "Real" gross national product (GNP)—total output with the impact of price increases on the dollar figures eliminated—rose 6 to 6.25 per cent. Total employment leveled off at about 88 million in the second half of the year, almost 4 million higher than at the low in 1975. Corporate profits ended up a healthy 15 to 25 per cent over 1975. Workers' paychecks increased, so for those persons with jobs, the pay hikes plus the slower rate of rise in prices meant some relief from the prolonged cost-of-living squeeze. Industrial production expanded during most of the year. Consumers were reported by Conference Board economist Fabian Linden to be "in the middle of an awesome yawn," but consumer spending kept climbing even in the most sluggish months later in the year, and the consumer was generally acknowledged to be the prime force behind the overall expansion of the United States economy.

But the total growth in GNP hid the fact that the pace of expansion slid from 9.2 per cent in the first quarter of 1976 to 4.5 per cent in the second to 3.9 per cent in the third and then sputtered along to average out at 6 to 6.25 per cent. The pace of rise at year's end was not sufficient to cut into our high rate of unemployment or to assure business of sufficient profits to expand or to maintain the United States as an economic leader of the Free World. When James Earl (Jimmy) Carter, Jr., won the White House on November 2, the economy had slowed to a "pause," and the gnawing fear was that the nation was heading into another recession. A sluggish economy may help to curb price rises, but putting the unemployed on the first line of defense is a cruelly expensive, barbaric way to fight a price spiral.

As for the cut in the inflation rate from the 12.2 per cent reached in December 1974 to the 5 to 6 per cent range of 1976, it was akin to

Sylvia Porter

the sense of release you feel when the acute misery of a toothache is replaced by a throbbing pain. The pain is still there, but it is not as intense, so you feel "better."

But the "better" 5 to 6 per cent rate of inflation in 1976 was merely an improvement, *not* a great achievement. It is *not* tolerable, and it is *not* acceptable for the long run. We actually invite the ruin of our free economy if we indulge in complimenting ourselves for only this improvement.

For even an annual rate of 5 per cent inflation compounded—meaning each year's 5 per cent would be piled on top of the previous year's, which would have been piled on top of the rate the year before that, and so on—would mean that the dollar that bought you 100 cents worth of goods and services in the market place in 1974 would buy you only a bit more than 50 cents worth in 1988. It would purchase only about 34 cents worth in 1996, and only about 28 cents worth at the end of this century. It would mean that a market basket of goods and services priced at $100 in 1974 would cost you almost $180 in 1986, more than $265 in 1994, and more than $356 in the year 2000. You couldn't plan ahead for anything with a double-digit rate of inflation. And you couldn't make confident plans for the future with a 5 to 6 per cent rate, either—not for your own security or the education of your children or care for your elderly or for anything else.

Equally significant, side by side with high inflation rates go stiflingly high interest rates—placing a stranglehold on housing, penalizing all borrowers (particularly smaller businessmen and middle- to low-income individuals), and slamming a lid on essential financing for business expansion. Investors will not save and lend their money unless they believe that the interest rates they earn on savings and on loans will at least offset the loss in purchasing power they suffer from relentless inflation.

The unemployment problem was among the most visible of all the challenges during the entire year—and small wonder, with a rate of over 8 per cent translating into more than 7.8 million real people and even that total probably wildly understated.

The year marked the 30th anniversary of the historic Employment Act of 1946. This law, pledging the federal government to the pursuit of "maximum" employment, reflected the deep concern at the end of World War II that without this commitment, the U.S. economy would plunge back into an era of great depression and joblessness.

It was an eerie anniversary, because we were fighting the battle of full employment all over again in 1976. The words of the act were still on the statute books, but the commitment was not. And in its birthplace, the United States, the spirit of that world-heralded law had been rejected. What has happened in the three decades since the Employment Act to bulge the jobless rolls and raise the nation's tolerance threshold for a high unemployment rate?

A key change has been the explosive expansion in our labor supply and a fundamental change in its composition. From 1947 to 1976, the

Unemployment problem

The "better" inflation rate of 6 per cent is unacceptable

number of women in the labor force soared 123 per cent, more than double the rise in the female population and centering around the 25-to-34-year-old bracket. Along with women, teen-agers joined the labor force in record numbers. Many left school because they didn't see any job opportunities for which to train, while others remained in school unwillingly and searched for part-time jobs. Meanwhile, earlier retirement—out of choice or because of age discrimination—eliminated males from the market. In 1947, 89 per cent of the men between 55 and 64 years of age held or were seeking jobs. Some 30 years later, 12 per cent fewer were doing so.

Because of this tremendously significant and still only dimly understood change in the composition of our labor force and because of the inflation push inherent in periods of labor shortages, it well may be that the "maximum" unemployment rate will now be accepted as 5.5 to 6 per cent instead of the previous 4 to 4.5 per cent.

Translated into human terms and based on 1976 labor force totals, that would mean roughly 5 million men and women without jobs in the "best of times." And translated into social terms, that would mean the everpresent danger of an explosion of resentment among the jobless against the economic system that forced them into their inferior position.

And the economy in 1977? This trend already is assured. It will be upward, though predictions were widespread as the year began that the pace would remain inadequate.

The first key point is that an upswing, not a new recession, is probable into 1978. The second key point is that the pace of expansion can (almost surely will) be accelerated by higher federal spending, selective programs to create jobs, and tax reductions for both consumers and business. Even before he took office, President-elect Carter pledged specific targets for 1977: a real growth in GNP of 6 per cent and a decline in the total unemployment rate of 1 to 1.5 per cent. While possibly unrealistically optimistic, for these goals, Carter had the full support of the powerful chairman of the Federal Reserve Board, Arthur F. Burns.

Merely by yardsticks of the recent past, the current recovery is still young. It was only 22 months old when 1977 began. If it does no more than match the average of the five previous expansions of the post-World War II period, its duration will be 50 months. Even if the extraordinarily prolonged boom of the decade of the 1960s is eliminated, the average of the past expansions has been a full three years. Thus, a conservative average would support this expansion through 1977 and into 1978.

In contrast to the nightmare credit squeeze and double-digit interest rate peaks of 1974-1975, credit policy was geared to supporting a solid economic expansion as 1977 began, loans were comparatively easy to get, and interest rates had slid way down from their highs. The housing industry seemed poised at last for a recovery in 1977, with new housing starts at year's end at the highest level in three years.

The economy should climb upward during 1977, into 1978

Women at work

This fundamental industry—usually in the lead of U.S. expansions—had lagged throughout the recovery of 1975 and 1976. If it resumes its customary role as a leader in 1977, the bullish impact of housing activity alone would be enormous. Signs accumulated, too, that with promised tax incentives, business also would soon be ready to add modestly to its spending on new plants and equipment.

Consumer, business, and government spending—the three types of spending that determine our economy's health—will bolster our economy in 1977, but as of January 1, there were only 36 months left to go in what we initially hailed as the decade of the "Sizzling Seventies." Instead of sizzling, this has turned out to be a decade of the "Sad," "Stagnating," often "Sliding" Seventies. Instead of moving comfortably into history as a 10-year span of steady economic expansion, the period has been characterized by utterly unanticipated economic turbulence.

Instead of "sizzling," the Seventies are "stagnant"

Moreover, the economic-financial challenges emerging clearly in earlier years of the decade have mostly been swept under the rug at every level of government—federal, state, and local. Even when New York City's fiscal crisis exploded across the nation's front pages in 1975 —flashing similar catastrophes to come in other cities and sending borrowing costs of the strongest municipalities soaring in sympathy with New York's—the response of the Gerald R. Ford Administration to New York was, as immortalized in the New York *Daily News* headline, "DROP DEAD." Even when America's voters emphasized in poll after poll that a prime concern was the skyrocketing cost of health care, no action was taken either by the Ford White House or by lawmakers in Congress.

Now, though, time is growing short. It is a statistical conceit to measure fundamental economic movements in terms of specific dates on the calendar, but there is a symbolism about the start of a new decade. And it is most improbable that many of the challenges shrugged off in the 1970s—to the jeopardy of millions of us—can be pushed aside much longer. To suggest merely a few of those challenges:
- National health insurance: For far too many years, Americans have been yearning for a health system that would protect us from financial catastrophe in the event of a costly, prolonged illness or accident and yet would not be so expensive that it would threaten to tumble our nation into bankruptcy.
- Our cities: This challenge goes far beyond the survival of New York City, of course. The most powerful and youngest of our cities also are struggling under the mounting burden of welfare, in addition to ever more expensive public services, debt interest, and so on. If New York goes, so eventually will other great cities from coast to coast. The solutions range from short-term stopgap federal loans to limited federal guarantees of state and city bonds to removal of some of the welfare burden from local governments to many others. This is essentially a national, not a local, problem. How much longer can it be brushed aside?

Challenge of health care

■ Inflation: The inflation rate in the United States actually averaged out to zero from the Civil War in the mid-1800s to World War II in the mid-1900s, with declines offsetting the increases. Until the era of President Richard M. Nixon, our annual inflation rate averaged under 2.5 per cent (except during the two full years of the Korean War). We cannot settle, we need not settle, for the inflation rates of the 1970s. There are solutions consistent with our private enterprise system. What's needed is the courage to seek the solutions and to try them.

■ Unemployment: Once the changing structure of our labor force is recognized and accepted, the appropriate policies to reduce our jobless rolls to acceptable levels will follow.

■ Our tax structure: Our tortuously complicated tax code must be simplified, and infuriatingly unfair loopholes must be closed.

■ A trustworthy, relevant international monetary system: The patchwork structure of 1976 must be reformed to help promote stabilization in currency rates and to stimulate expansion in world trade.

On top of these, we need an energy policy that will lessen our vulnerability to oil import controls, a realistic approach to pollution control, a strengthened social security system, a reformed welfare system. And this is just a sampling of the challenges that leap to mind. There are others, and still more will emerge. We have drifted without true leadership in the economic sphere through almost an entire decade.

In the economic sphere, we have been drifting for a decade

Related Articles

For further information on economics in 1976, see Section Four, AGRICULTURE; BANKS AND BANKING; ECONOMICS; INTERNATIONAL TRADE AND FINANCE; LABOR; MANUFACTURING; STOCKS AND BONDS.

Focus on Science

Harrison Brown

The year saw the most momentous of all our efforts in space so far in terms of scientific achievement, but it still left many questions about life on Mars

On Aug. 20, 1975, an unmanned *Viking* spacecraft was launched from the John F. Kennedy Space Center in Florida and placed in a trajectory that would take it to the planet Mars. Three weeks later, a backup spacecraft was launched, also destined for Mars. *Viking 1* went into orbit around Mars on June 19, 1976, followed by *Viking 2* some seven weeks later.

As it orbited the planet, *Viking 1* took almost 1,000 photographs of the Martian surface and transmitted them back to Earth, where scientists studied them carefully, searching for a safe landing site. Nearly four weeks went by before a decision was finally made. Then, on July 20, the three-legged landing craft separated from the orbiter and descended into the Martian atmosphere. Some 3 hours and 22 minutes later, with the help of a retrorocket and a parachute, the instrument-laden craft landed safely. Immediately, the lander's cameras took two pictures of the Martian landscape, and they were received on Earth less than an hour later. Thus began what has turned out to be the most momentous of all our efforts in space so far in terms of scientific achievement.

Both *Viking 1* and *Viking 2* were filled with complicated instrumentation designed to investigate a number of characteristics of the planet's atmosphere and surface. Incredibly, almost all of the experiments were successful. The results of the measurements, together with the surprisingly clear photographs, give us a picture of the planet that is detailed, beautiful, awesome, and mysterious. Scientists will study the new information for many years in attempts to unravel the geologic history of Mars and what it tells us about the origin and evolution of our planetary system.

When we view the surface of Mars from the *Viking* orbiter, we see numerous meteorite impact craters, though they are not nearly as frequent as they are on the Moon. We also see what appear to be volcanoes. Most startling of all, however, are the huge systems of canyons that were discovered several years ago by *Mariner 9.* They look as though they were formed by the violent action of rapidly flowing water. Indeed, photographs taken by the *Viking* orbiter provide abundant new evidence that running water played a major role in shaping the surface of the planet. But there is no liquid water of any consequence on Mars today, in part because the planet is so cold, though there is some water vapor in the atmosphere. There is ice, some of which forms clouds but most of which is trapped in the polar icecap.

The thin Martian atmosphere is composed primarily of carbon dioxide, but small quantities of nitrogen and oxygen are also present. These substances play major roles in life processes on Earth, so their presence, together with that of water, suggests that Mars, like Earth,

Harrison Brown

Photographs showed pink sky, barren rocks, and red sand

might be an abode of life. And, in fact, Mars has long been thought to be the planet, next to Earth, most likely to support the evolution of life.

Our current knowledge concerning biological processes and the chemical and physical evolution of the Earth tempts scientists to conclude that given certain special conditions, life will inevitably emerge as the end product of a complicated sequence of chemical events. First, there must be enough carbon, nitrogen, and oxygen to permit these elements to combine in endless varieties of complex chemical compounds. Second, the environment should not be very hot or very cold. Complex chemical compounds are destroyed by heat, and chemical reactions take place too slowly in the cold to permit the formation of the extremely large and complex molecules that are the building blocks of living organisms. Third, there must be a medium, such as an ocean or an atmosphere or both, in which chemical reactions can take place. Given all these conditions, scientists reason, chemical evolution will lead eventually to the formation of molecules capable of making duplicates of themselves from the materials of their environment and thus give birth to life. Once that happens, chemical evolution will be replaced by biological evolution.

All of these conditions are met on Earth, but have they been met elsewhere in our solar system? Certainly they are not met on the Moon, which is too small to hold an atmosphere, or on Mercury, which is both too small and too hot. Venus comes closer, but its very high surface temperature and the virtual absence of water would seem to rule it out. Mars comes still closer, though the conditions there are very rugged. Nevertheless, at the time the *Viking* mission was being planned, the Martian environment appeared favorable enough to warrant the concentration of a large proportion of *Viking*'s scientific capability on the search for life.

The numerous photographs sent to Earth by the two landing craft, however, showed no evidence of life. Nothing was seen to move. Nothing was seen resembling plants. All that could be seen were barren rocks, red sand, and pink sky.

But might there not be microorganisms buried in the Martian soil? On Earth, such organisms abound even in regions that otherwise appear to be sterile—certain areas of the Antarctic possibly being the only exception. Because of this possibility, *Viking* included equipment for three basic biology experiments on samples of Martian soil. A mechanical arm that received its directions from Earth scooped up soil samples, then poured them into *Viking*'s automated laboratory.

In one experiment, a soil sample was mixed with a nutrient solution of organic substances. Before the actual mixing, water vapor from the solution was permitted to humidify the soil, and—much to the surprise of scientists reading the data sent back to Earth—there was an immediate, large, and puzzling increase of oxygen pressure. When the soil was actually wet by the nutrient solution several days later, there was no further release of oxygen, but there was a slow increase in the pressure of carbon dioxide. From the point of view of indicating the pres-

Launching *Viking 1*

ence or absence of life, these results were ambiguous. Biological processes could not be ruled out, but neither could they easily explain the initial rapid production of oxygen.

In another experiment, the soil sample was introduced to a solution of water and amino acids "labeled" with radioactive carbon. These acids are compounds that organisms on Earth decompose rapidly to carbon dioxide. In the *Viking* experiment, large quantities of radioactive carbon dioxide were released, but the explosive nature of the release was not like that brought about by organisms on Earth. Further, the later addition of radioactive nutrient solution did not give rise to the liberation of more carbon dioxide.

In the next experiment, a mixture of carbon monoxide and carbon dioxide labeled with radioactive carbon was introduced to the soil sample. The material was then irradiated by a xenon lamp, simulating Martian sunlight, in the presence of simulated Martian atmosphere. If photosynthesis took place, radioactive carbon would become incorporated in any organic material that was photosynthesized. The material could then be heated, any organisms present would be decomposed, and the resultant gases could then be analyzed for radioactive carbon. The results obtained by both *Viking 1* and *2* were weakly positive.

Finally, two soil samples were heated to high temperatures, and the gases that evolved were analyzed. The results showed that organic compounds have not accumulated in the Martian soil to an extent greater than about a few parts per billion – if at all.

The results of these experiments could be seen as evidence that there is some sort of biological material very sparsely distributed in the Martian soil. Unfortunately, that explanation fails to account adequately for some of the observations. On the other hand, it seems quite possible that virtually all of the observations can be accounted for on a nonbiological chemical basis.

The evidence indicates that the surface of Mars is highly oxidized. Ozone has been detected, and hydrogen peroxide might exist in the atmosphere. It has even been suggested that significant concentrations of metallic peroxides might be present on the surfaces of rocks and grains of sand. Some scientists believe the results of the three biological experiments could be explained satisfactorily if it could be proved that the Martian surface is in such a superoxidized state. But many more experiments must be done, both in laboratories on Earth and on *Vikings 1* and *2*, before this hypothesis can be proved conclusively.

Some scientists think life might exist farther to the north on Mars. The first *Viking* lander is in an extremely dry desert, and the second is not far enough north to encounter water precipitated in the form of frost. In far northern regions, slopes that face south might receive sufficient heat to melt ice and provide liquid nourishment for living organisms. One day this hypothesis may be tested. In the meantime, the best guess is that Mars is sterile.

If in truth Mars is devoid of life, we can probably blame it on the

A series of experiments tested Mars's "soil" for signs of life

Martian landscape

fact that the planet apparently never has had an ocean of any great size. There was sufficient liquid water in past eons to produce the vast canyon system, but there never was enough to cover large areas of the planet for any appreciable length of time. By contrast, Earth was endowed from the beginning with huge quantities of water and almost from birth had oceans that remain to this day. Those oceans provided the medium in which chemical reactions took place that led eventually to the emergence of the first terrestrial replicating molecules. The same oceans then nurtured biological evolution until organisms reached sufficient complexity to survive on land.

Earth may be the only planet in our solar system that supports life

Earth appears to be the only planet in our solar system that has oceans. As a result, it might be the only planet in our solar system that has life. The philosophical consequences of such a finding would be profound. Would this mean that life in the universe is truly a miracle, that Earth is unique in being an abode of life? Or can we continue with the widely accepted scientific view that life is probably abundant in the universe as a whole? Are there steps that can be taken to help answer such questions?

Here, scientists stress that the most urgent next steps are to learn much more about Mars. More landers are needed equipped to undertake varieties of experiments, to take more pictures, and to roam about the surface of the planet searching for new and interesting details. Perhaps in such quests life will be found. But if it isn't found, it is important that we understand why. It is important that we learn what the environmental constraints to the emergence of life really are.

If life is not found on Mars, will it mean that we humans, who are a part of the scheme of life on Earth, are alone? With respect to our solar system, this would almost certainly be true. But with respect to our galaxy and the universe as a whole, such a conclusion would be unwarranted, at least at present.

The evidence we now have concerning the process of star formation suggests strongly that planetary systems probably are very abundant in the universe. It is conceivable that most stars have planets of various sizes in orbit about them. The question then becomes, how many of those planets have environments conducive to the emergence of life? Most will be too small or too large, too far away from their suns or too close. How many will be just the right size and the right distance from their suns? How many will have oceans? Almost certainly, only a small proportion of them. In our own system, one planet out of nine meets the specifications. But even if the proportion were as small as 1 out of 100, the absolute numbers of planets that could support life would be huge.

Is there any possibility of our detecting life that might exist on planets attached to other stars in our galaxy? Unfortunately, most stars are so far from Earth that there is no known way of detecting ordinary life forms using Earth-based instruments. And it will be a very long time, if ever, before our space vehicles can reach even the nearest of the stars, make observations, and send back their findings.

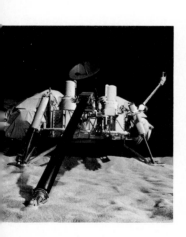

Viking lander model

However, one possibility remains that many scientists believe should be explored intensively. On Earth, biological evolution led to the emergence of a creature possessing the power of conceptual thought—the ability to ask questions, to solve problems, and to communicate its knowledge to others. Once that creature—the human being—emerged, it became the dominant life form, and biological evolution was replaced by cultural evolution. Is it possible that this process has occurred elsewhere, perhaps numerous times? Many scientists believe that it has.

Intelligence enabled human beings to create civilizations, to destroy them, and to build new ones based upon ever-expanding technologies. Human technology has now reached a level of development that makes it possible, in principle, to communicate with civilizations associated with other stars, using electromagnetic radiation, provided that they also possess the requisite technology and have the desire to communicate. Recognizing this possibility, a number of scientists have seriously proposed that we attempt to make contact.

A group of scientists and engineers, with Massachusetts Institute of Technology physicist Philip Morrison as chairman, met periodically in 1975 and 1976. Under the auspices of the National Aeronautics and Space Administration's Ames Research Center in California, they discussed the problems of communicating with intelligent beings elsewhere in our universe. The group agreed that there might well be other civilizations in our galaxy that possess the level of technology necessary to communicate. The group proposed a systematic program—the Search for Extraterrestrial Intelligence (SETI)—that would search for other planetary systems and try to detect signals that might have their origin in other civilizations.

It is possible, of course, that we on Earth are the first creatures in our galaxy to reach this "communicative state." But when we consider that our galaxy contains billions of stars and possibly tens of billions of planets, and that biological evolution on those planets conducive to life might have gone on for billions of years, the likelihood that we are the first civilization able to communicate seems remote. Indeed, some scientists have suggested that civilizations elsewhere may already be linked together in a communications network, and that they might have established "beacons" that transmit signals automatically, century after century, designed to attract the attention of newcomers such as ourselves.

At first glance, this might seem far-fetched. But the serious scientists who proposed SETI do not believe it is.

Are "beacons" transmitting signals in space, century after century?

Related Articles

For further information on science and technology in 1976, see the articles on the various sciences in Section Four.

Philip Morrison

Focus on Education

Lawrence A. Cremin

A gap between expectation and reality was troubling Americans in 1976, and they were asking about what results to expect from a universal school system

Almost a million young Americans took the Scholastic Aptitude Test (SAT) in 1976, which in itself was scarcely newsworthy. Growing numbers of high school juniors and seniors had been taking the SAT for half a century, as one measure of their ability to do college-level work. And their performance on the SAT and on other tests like it had become a fairly standard element in decisions as to who would be admitted to the nation's more selective colleges.

What was indeed news in 1976 was the concern with which the American public observed their performance. For more than a decade, scores on the SAT had been declining, and in 1975 and 1976 that decline suddenly moved to the forefront of public concern. The College Entrance Examination Board, which supervises and administers the SAT, appointed a blue-ribbon panel of experts to investigate the causes of the decline, and newspapers across the country carried articles on what it portended for the future of the nation.

The SAT itself was first devised in 1926 for the explicit purpose of obtaining a more "objective" predictor of academic success in college. At that time, most of the tests administered by the College Entrance Examination Board were essay-type examinations that sought to measure achievement, or how much a student had learned, in such school subjects as English, history, mathematics, foreign languages, and the natural sciences. The SAT was designed as a multiple-choice examination that would supplement the results of the various achievement tests with a more general measure of the student's ability to deal with such intellectual problems as definition, classification, reading comprehension, logical inference, arithmetic calculation, and number series.

From the beginning, arrangements were made to conduct research on the effectiveness of the SAT as a predictor of academic success in college. The assumption of the test makers was that an effective test would have to be valid; that is, it would have to be accurate in its predictions of subsequent academic achievement. It would have to be reliable; that is, it would have to be consistent in the way it made its predictions for the same individual at different times. And it would have to be relatively unbiased; that is, it would have to be as insensitive as possible to the effects of such irrelevant factors as the particular region of the country in which a person had attended school, or his or her ethnic or religious background, or whether he or she had been coached for the test. The research was initially done by educators and psychologists at the College Entrance Examination Board. After 1947, when the Educational Testing Service (ETS) was founded to carry forward the technical work of the Board and a number of other testing organizations, it was done by educators and behavioral scientists at ETS.

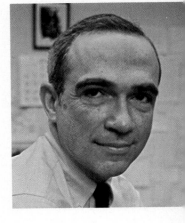

Lawrence A. Cremin

43

**What did the
decline in the
Scholastic
Aptitude Test
scores mean?**

It was on the basis of that continuing research—probably more research, incidentally, than had previously been done on any single test—that the present-day version of the SAT had evolved. As given in 1976 it was a three-hour test of six 30-minute sections dealing with such indicators of verbal aptitude as reading comprehension, analogizing ("*Hot* is to *cold* as *near* is to   "), and the ability to complete and correct sentences, and such indicators of mathematical aptitude as the ability to compute, to reason geometrically, and to derive information from graphs and charts. Three scores were given on the test: a score representing verbal aptitude, on a scale running from 200 to 800; a score representing mathematical aptitude, also on a scale running from 200 to 800; and a score representing aptitude in written English, on a scale running from 20 to 60.

With respect to the scales for the verbal and mathematical scores, the assumption over the years had been that the mean or average score for each of the two measures would be 500. And it was the steady decline of the average verbal and mathematical scores on the SAT since 1963 that had become a matter of public concern. The average verbal score for all students taking the SAT in 1962-1963 had been 478; in 1975-1976 it was 429. The average mathematical score for all students taking the SAT in 1962-1963 had been 502; in 1975-1976 it was 470.

What did the decline in the average scores mean? The simple explanation that projected the SAT into the headlines in 1976 was that young Americans were learning less because the schools were teaching less, and that the fault was therefore with the schools. Actually, whatever truth there might have been in that particular explanation would have had to be stated quite differently in order to be accurate. The American school curriculum had undergone profound changes during the 1960s and 1970s, particularly in the direction of allowing more options to students, with the result that teachers had indeed shifted the allocation of their time and effort. It was not that the schools were teaching fewer things, however, but rather that they were teaching different things. Of course, one could lament the curricular changes of the 1960s and 1970s and the newer emphases that had flowed from them, but to do so was to transform the question from whether the schools were teaching enough to whether they were teaching what any particular critic thought they ought to be teaching.

Yet, to settle hastily on the schools as the prime source of the decline in test scores was to ignore a number of alternative explanations. One possibility, for example, was that either the SAT itself or the overall group of students taking it had changed significantly, thereby altering the averages. Was the test slowly becoming more difficult? Was a more diverse group of students taking the test—more disadvantaged students or more black or Hispanic or American Indian students, who would not have taken the test 20 years earlier because they would not have contemplated going to college in the first place? Were more students taking the test in their junior year rather than their senior year? Were more students taking the test twice, once in their junior year and again

Working a math problem

in their senior year? Changes of this sort might well have affected the averages, and one of the things the panel of experts was doing was gathering data to make the determination. For this reason, at least, their report, due in 1977, was eagerly awaited.

Another possibility was that the principal sources of the decline lay not inside the school but outside, in the education young people received in the family and via television. More and more children were growing up in single-parent households during the 1960s and 1970s, and more and more mothers of children under 18 were taking full-time jobs, with the result that children generally were receiving less direct instruction from parents, and teachers generally were able to count on less direct assistance from parents. Furthermore, even in two-parent households where one parent remained home full time to look after the children, youngsters were spending more and more time watching television, with the result, once again, that they were probably receiving less direct parental instruction. They doubtless learned a good deal from television, some of it beneficial, some of it harmful; but whatever they did learn was likely to be different from what their parents might have taught them 20 years earlier.

An explanation of the decline would be both complex and controversial

In sum, then, the possible explanations for the decline in average SAT scores were various: They could lie within the school, or within the family and television, or within the testing situation itself. And beyond these possibilities, there were all the continuing questions as to whether the SAT actually measured aptitude in the first place, with some psychologists arguing that it was essentially a test of innate intelligence largely dependent on genetic factors and others arguing that it was essentially a test of what had been learned at school and elsewhere and largely dependent on the quality of previous education. Even in advance of the report of the College Entrance Examination Board's panel of experts, it seemed probable that any ultimate explanation of the decline in test scores would be complex and itself the subject of additional controversy.

Yet, granted that likelihood, one fascinating question remained. The decline, after all, had been occurring over more than a decade. Why had it burst into the forefront of public concern in 1975 and 1976? To put the question that way was to go considerably beyond the SAT, or any other test for that matter, to the question of what Americans actually expected of their schools. And on that issue there were significant shifts of opinion in 1976.

Some clues to those shifts came in a Gallup Poll on popular attitudes toward education conducted during the spring of 1976. On the question of the probable reason for the decline in national test scores, 65 per cent of the respondents mentioned decreasing parental supervision and concern, 49 per cent mentioned too much television viewing, 49 per cent thought society had become too permissive, 39 per cent remarked that teachers were giving less attention to students, and 10 per cent suggested that the curriculum had expanded too broadly. In other words, most respondents were not ready to place the burden of

A testing situation

blame exclusively on the schools (and the parents of schoolchildren, interestingly enough, were even less ready than others). Yet, on the specific question of whether the decline in national test scores actually meant that the quality of education had been deteriorating, 59 per cent of the respondents answered yes, 31 per cent answered no, and 10 per cent voiced no opinion. Finally, on the question of whether high school students should be expected to pass a nationwide examination in order to receive a high school diploma, 65 per cent of the respondents answered yes, 31 per cent answered no, and 4 per cent voiced no opinion.

As is often the case with surveys, the findings were not all of a piece. The respondents who supported a national examination for a high school diploma also voted overwhelmingly in favor of greater emphasis on career preparation in the high schools, while the respondents who indicated their belief that declining test scores meant a deterioration in the quality of education also chose "high moral standards" as the single most neglected area of schooling. Taken as a whole, however, the Gallup findings indicated a pervasive concern with the intellectual outcomes of schooling.

The reasons were not difficult to determine. The quarter century since 1950 had witnessed a considerable expansion of American schooling at all levels. The holding power of the elementary and secondary schools had increased steadily, to the point where 90 per cent of 16- and 17-year-olds were enrolled. And, although the actual number of young people in the schools had been decreasing during the 1970s, owing to the decline in the American birth rate, the holding power of the schools remained the highest in the world, and by a considerable margin. In addition, both the absolute numbers of students enrolled in preschool programs and in college and university programs and the percentages of their respective age groups in the population they represented had risen substantially since 1950. As a result, the average number of years of schooling completed by Americans over the age of 25 had climbed from 9.3 in 1950 to 12.3 in 1974, with the averages of younger adults being substantially higher than the averages of older adults and with the gap between white and black adults steadily narrowing. In order to pay for the expansion, Americans had increased their expenditures for education from 3.4 per cent of the gross national product in 1949-1950 to 7.8 per cent of the gross national product in 1974-1975. The accomplishment was prodigious and unprecedented, and it ought to have been a source of considerable national pride.

Yet, when the 1976 Gallup Poll asked respondents to rate the public schools on a scale from A to F, 13 per cent assigned the grade of A, 29 per cent B, 28 per cent C, 10 per cent D, and 6 per cent F, with 14 per cent venturing no answer. Moreover, when one turned to the actual performance of children and adults on a number of nationwide achievement tests designed to assess the efficacy of the schools, the results were mixed at best. Youngsters generally were reading better at all levels. Yet 11 per cent of the 17-year-olds questioned on a 1974 test of func-

The holding power of U.S. schools was the highest in the world

Looking at test results

tional literacy proved unable to read a newspaper, fill out a driver's license application, or understand the labels on packaged foods or household medicines. Similarly, 99 per cent of the 17-year-olds and 84 per cent of the young adults questioned on a 1972-1973 test of mathematical ability proved unable to balance a checkbook, owing primarily to carelessness in addition, subtraction, multiplication, and division. In the realm of writing, the results were even more distressing: National samples of 13-year-olds and 17-year-olds tested in 1969 and 1974 revealed a significant decline in the quality of student essays —there were more ungrammatical phrases, more run-on sentences, and more incoherent paragraphs. And, indeed, in colleges across the country, including some of the most selective and prestigious institutions, entering freshmen were being assigned in unprecedented numbers to remedial writing courses so that they could pursue undergraduate studies effectively. One could add the horror stories about 13-year-olds who thought that the Supreme Court was part of the United States Congress and 17-year-olds who could not calculate 70 per cent of 4,200. But perhaps the point has been made. The results of American schooling seemed at best imperfect and at worst alarming.

In colleges, some entering students were taking remedial reading courses

It was this gap between expectation and reality that was troubling Americans in 1976. Educators and the public had long recognized that the popularization of schooling would inevitably involve a broadening of the school curriculum and a concomitant provision of alternative modes of satisfying academic requirements. And there had long been talk of equivalent but differing standards of academic success. Yet granted this, Americans were asking about what results they might legitimately come to expect from a universal school system. And their concern was manifesting itself in a growing number of state-mandated examinations for high school graduation, in sharpening demands for more detailed blueprints of what might constitute a "thorough and efficient education," and in a more general "back to basics" movement that was seeking to attract the attention of educators, parents, and school board members across the country. It was this larger concern that had projected the SAT into the headlines in 1976, and that was the real educational news of the year.

Related Articles

For further information on education in 1976, see Section Two, THE LOSING WAR AGAINST ILLITERACY; Section Four, EDUCATION.

Using a basic skill

Focus on The Arts

Alistair Cooke

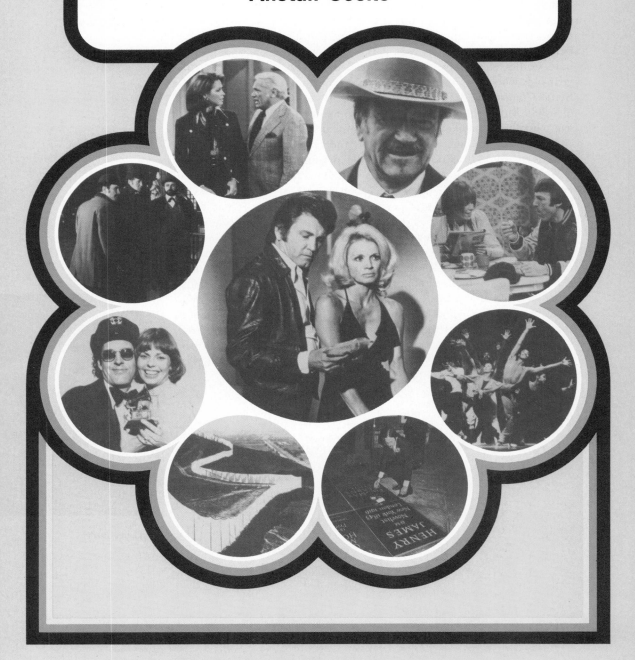

Even tentative judgments on what is good, better, and best in the arts are really hunches, so reports such as this one look instead at *trends* in the arts

When I began these Focus chronicles 15 years ago, I remarked that there is a problem, peculiar to the United States, in doing an annual survey of the arts. "The well-established categories that we should look for elsewhere," I wrote, "are not necessarily the ones in which Americans are excelling.... In fact, we all know that the United States is often truest to its best traditions when it is upsetting tradition and, incidentally, breaking the European mold. The first genuine American invention in public architecture was the sky-scraper, and one of the last in domestic architecture was the bath-room." (H. L. Mencken, no philistine, once wrote–after a tour of Europe harassed by Neanderthal plumbing–that he would gladly swap the Parthenon for an American bathroom.)

So though it is easy, it is also dangerous, to take a rapid look at what's being done in the usual arts: painting, music, sculpture, novels, ballet, opera, theater, even the motion picture, which, of all art forms, can be said to have been an American original. Quite apart from the fact that there is no American alive who has the omniscience to speak with equal authority on all the arts, the danger of looking for original achievement in the usual arts is the danger of blinding oneself to originality that is flourishing in *un*usual places, and in some places where the regular critics never expect art to flourish at all. It is now a commonplace to say that Mark Twain is a great, perhaps the first great, American writer or that Jackson Pollock is a giant of modern American painting. But for much of their own time, their critics in-dignantly denied that they were artists at all. Twain was thought of, by intelligentsia of the Eastern seaboard, as a buffoon who wrote stories not much more respectable than comic strips (another indig-enous American art form, elevated in the past decade into the solem-nity of pop art capable of fetching astronomical prices in auction rooms). Pollock was for long dismissed as a hysterical dauber.

And outside America, too, the expert critic is, more than he or she is ever prepared to admit, a victim like the rest of us of the waves of fashion. The Nobel Prize committees can boast an impressive record in choosing scientists whose contributions can now be seen to be his-toric. But in the arts, it is a very different story. Look over the list of the Nobel Prizewinners for Literature in the 75 years the awards have been made, and you will come on such names as Sienkiewicz, Heyse, Pontoppidan, Spitteler, Reymont, Deledda, Andrić–which in America might be guessed at as a baseball team and which in Europe not one bookworm in a thousand would ever have heard of. As often as the Nobel committee has picked a writer whose reputation is likely to be lasting (Shaw, Mann, O'Neill, Eliot, Asturias), just as often its cer-tificate of award has been a passport to oblivion.

Alistair Cooke

All this is by way of saying, to young readers especially, that when somebody sets himself up as a critic, there is no reason to assume that he has been endowed with the gift of prophecy or even with the gift of distinguishing the first-rate from the nearly first-rate, or a masterpiece from a fraud. Sixty years ago, an American expatriate, the Baroness von Hutten zum Stolzenberg, wrote a novel called *Pam*. It was a furious best seller. I picked it up for 75 cents in London last summer. It is a jaunty, hilariously sentimental bit of hackwork. Yet at the time, Thomas Hardy thought it was a work of great profundity, and he compared it favorably with his own *Tess of the d'Urbervilles*. Lately, we have had the fascinating case of the playwright Harold Pinter, who should be due any year now for the Nobel Prize for Literature, judging from the almost reverential acclaim that critics in London, New York City, and Hamburg, West Germany, have given his most recent plays—*Landscape, Silence,* and *No Man's Land*. Compare the judgments of two of America's acknowledged critical masters. Harold Clurman calls Pinter "a superb craftsman [who evokes] baffling and nightmarish circumstances and states of mind" and is thus "a representative voice of contemporary society." John Simon, just as dogmatically, declares him to be "a clever ex-actor turned playwright full of surface theatricality under which resides a big, bulging zero."

What I am saying is that professional critics, even as you and I, are playing hunches and hoping that their passing impressions will endure as true insights. Fifteen years ago, I quoted old Longinus, and I will quote him again: "The judgment of contemporary work is the last and ripest fruit of much experience." And, often as not, even vast experience does not save a veteran critic—whether in ancient Greece or present-day America—from seeing a mountain as a molehill, and vice versa. So what is to be expected from such reports as this Focus is not even a tentative judgment on what is good, better, and best; but a running report on *trends* in the arts, what is being pursued and what is being rejected.

In that first Focus piece, I remarked on the sudden national urge to build "cultural centers" in the cities. It was an impulse universally praised at the time. Many a colossal building, in New York City, Los Angeles, Dallas, was seen as a symbol of our final emergence from a frontier society in which virile men plowed the plains and "culture" was left to women. But it has turned out that buildings are not enough. You must have something to put in them. And although they have increased the number of concert halls for serious music, they have strikingly failed to breed or foster new playwrights. All except Minneapolis, which has splendidly maintained the momentum given by its founder, the late Sir Tyrone Guthrie, and which could justifiably claim the title of American National Theater—certainly much more than that memorial mausoleum, the John F. Kennedy Center for the Performing Arts in Washington, D.C. Most of the pioneer work among new playwrights, and all the encouragement to a remarkable crop of young black talent, has best been demonstrated in the small, scruffy basements, churches,

Harold Pinter

converted garages, and the like that, a decade or more ago, were restricted to what we called "off-Broadway" and that now bloom, like flowers in the desert, in such cities as San Francisco, Chicago, and Los Angeles.

The American Revolution Bicentennial might have been expected to produce some such rousing work as Benjamin Britten's *Gloriana*, composed for the coronation year of Elizabeth II of Great Britain. But if we have had anything comparable, I haven't heard of it. There were "retrospective" concerts of such hardy old music men as Richard Rodgers and George Gershwin, a boisterous review of American music in San Francisco misnamed "The Evolution of the Blues," and a disastrously inept—and short-lived—attempt to make a musical out of the lives of six Presidents, called *1600 Pennsylvania Avenue*.

Museums in many cities paid a passing tribute to the founding of the republic (or, rather, to the outbreak of the American Revolutionary War) with displays of colonial and federal artifacts, the most highly praised of which was the "Jefferson and Franklin" exhibit put on by New York City's Metropolitan Museum of Art. It was a handsomely mounted tribute to the elegance of late 18th-century America. It showed a handful of unknown and interesting paintings, and in one room it housed a small and exquisite collection of American furniture. But it gave scarcely a hint of the rich and excited turmoil of life in America in 1776. That was left, I'm sorry to have to say, to a magnificent exhibition called simply "1776," researched, collected, and put on by two British scholars outside London in the shadow of the noble Royal Naval College. A series of tents followed the progress of the war, each one devoted to a national participant—Britain, the Continental Army, France—or such groups of concerned onlookers as the Indians and the Loyalists. (I shall not soon forget the pathos and terror invoked by the tent devoted exclusively to the plight of the Loyalists—precious paintings of their flight and of the choking of the seaports, relics of their possessions, maps of the routes of their exodus, congressional proclamations of their fate—the entrance dominated by a huge and horrifying figure of a tarred and feathered Loyalist.) The exhibit ended with a display of the tart and final exchange of letters between "your most obedient servant, Cornwallis" and "your most obedient servant, Geo. Washington" and a recording of the famous exchange of greetings between King George III (spoken by Prince Charles) and John Adams, the first United States minister to Great Britain (spoken by former Ambassador Elliot L. Richardson). The great pity of this incomparable exhibition is that it is not likely to be shown in the United States. The researchers did their ransacking too well: They unearthed so many precious artifacts and original paintings not seen or known before that the insurance premiums for an overseas journey were calculated at several million dollars.

The television networks were agog with Bicentennial "tributes," but most of them were either blaringly chauvinistic, or patriotic outbursts amplified to the requirements of show biz. On the Fourth of

Museums in many cities paid passing tribute to the Bicentennial

Sir Tyrone Guthrie

51

July, two networks spent fortunes whisking their cameras around a score or more cities and small towns of the United States, picking up "live" a series of various high jinks—a festival of a sort that many Americans believe gave a palpable lift to the nation's morale. Speaking coldly as a reporter on the arts, I can only say that the Public Broadcasting System's "Adams Chronicles"—though too often indulging the national fondness for making all famous men recognizable as such from the cradle on—was practically alone in redeeming television's Bicentennial tribute.

Which brings us, sadly, to a dominant trend in the two liveliest arts, the ones, at any rate, that most continuously affect the lives of most Americans: the movies and television. There was a time, only 30 years ago, when literary critics used to fret for the fate of what they called "minority culture" (books, painting, music) before the onslaught of "mass entertainment" (represented most incessantly by the movies). In those days, it was figured that about half the American population —80 million persons—went to the movies once or twice a week. Going to the movies entailed at the least a short excursion out of the home. But television is there at your elbow, and the temptation to use it as an accompaniment to daily living, a sort of audible wallpaper, is apparently irresistible. The most reliable surveys report that the average American spends between four and five hours a day in front of the tube. I mentioned in last year's Focus that while fewer Americans now go to many movies, more Americans than ever go to, say, three or four movies a year. Thirty years ago that would have guaranteed the bankruptcy of the industry. And it has meant the end of the half a dozen or more big Hollywood corporations that had been financing and producing hundreds of films a year with huge resident staffs and a stable of stars under contract. It has also produced undreamed-of fortunes for independent (sometimes one-shot) companies that have had the luck or cunning to exploit the seemingly insatiable public hunger for violence and brutality.

In 1975, the few movies that half the population saw were *The Godfather* (I and II), *The Exorcist*, *Earthquake*, *The Towering Inferno*, and *Jaws*. In 1976, the itch for making films with a visceral shock spread to otherwise intelligent and gifted directors. We had the appalling end sequence of *Taxi Driver*, in which the hero, who is presented for half the film as a sensitive young man disturbed by his experiences in the Vietnam War, suddenly is revealed as a psychopath who goes berserk with a handgun in a brothel. He sprays every human in sight at point-blank range, and the screen is glutted with broken bone and rivers of blood as the large metropolitan audience (when I saw it) whoops and cheers. The juicy moments in *Grizzly* are the ripping of a man's arm by a bear and the decapitation of a horse. *The Omen* begins as an apparently respectable film about the private ordeal of an American ambassador with a disturbed son. Very soon, the son is made out to be the Devil reincarnated, capable of transfixing a meddlesome priest with a bolt of lightning made actual as a sword, of throwing his

Taxi Driver

mother out the window to her death, and of causing the very visible decapitation of an inquisitive reporter. Like *Taxi Driver, The Omen* tricked its family audience into thinking it was going to see a serious psychological study of ill health, till both films turned into festivals of blood and guts. At last report, *The Omen* was said to be vying with *The Godfather, Gone with the Wind,* and *The Sound of Music* (the valentines of an innocent era) as one of the all-time box-office successes. Toward the end of the year, we began to see themes, sights, and sounds formerly relegated to slummy hard-core pornographic theaters burgeoning in full-length feature films in downtown theaters.

Television has not yet dared to go so far. Because, so goes the standard argument, it is a home theater available to youngsters helpless to know what they might see. But there are very disturbing signs indeed that the networks are committing themselves more and more to the two genres that pay off most lucratively: situation comedies and violent police dramas. The television critic of *The New York Times,* not normally an alarmist of the faintest hue, wrote a bitter piece in September 1976 accusing the networks of so obsessive a concern with their advertising revenues that they are turning down such proposals as a series of "family classics," to be underwritten by American Telephone and Telegraph Company, and are packing the airwaves with dramas in which "there isn't a single problem that isn't settled by violence, a single characterization that isn't rampantly sexist."

Later in the year, a federal judge ruled that the networks' own tradition of restraint, whereby sex and violence is barred from television during the so-called "family viewing hours" of early evening, is a violation of the First Amendment to the Constitution. The judicial argument is now at hand for any parent who wishes to assert the "right" of an 8-year-old to watch rape on the home screen. It is one more example of what, to this critic, is the almost lunatic stretching to which the doctrine of freedom of speech has recently been subjected.

A judge said television's family hour violated the Constitution

Related Articles

For further information on the arts in 1976, see the following articles in Section Four:

The family hour

Focus on Sports

Red Smith

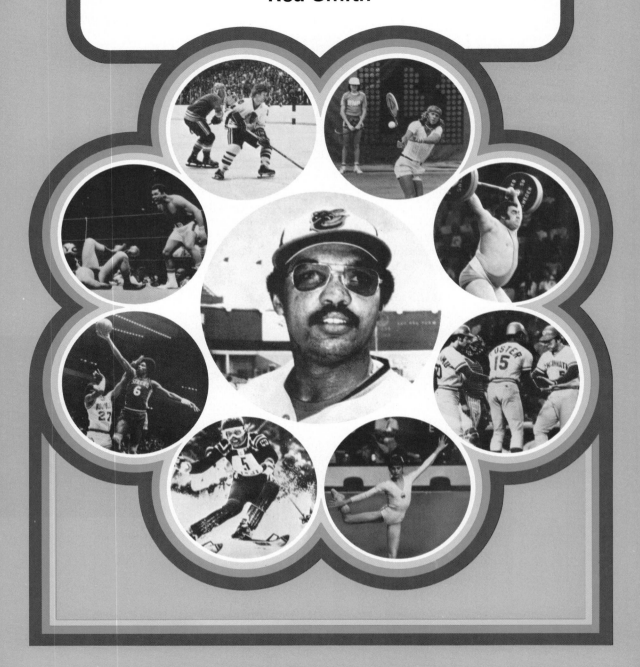

**Events of 1976 — the Year of Jock Lib — meant
that professional athletes would have for
the first time a voice in their own future**

A little before noon on Dec. 23, 1975, a small drama was acted out in the Lincoln Building at 60 East 42nd Street, New York City. Three men sat checking through a 65-page document that concluded: "The grievances of Messersmith and McNally are sustained." Having read it, the men signed the paper—Peter Seitz as impartial chairman of baseball's arbitration panel; Marvin Miller, executive director of the Players Association, concurring; John J. Gaherin, labor relations representative of the major-league club owners, dissenting.

Then, in painful embarrassment, Gaherin handed Seitz a paper containing a single paragraph. It advised the arbitrator that the owners no longer desired his services.

The performance was over in minutes, but it signaled a revolution whose effect will be felt as long as professional team sports are played. It meant that starting in 1976, players would have for the first time some voice in their own future. In the past, an athlete signing his first contract as a professional became the property of his employer until the employer released him or disposed of his contract in a trade or sale. This was called the reserve system, and Peter Seitz's decision in the Messersmith-McNally case blew a big hole in it.

Pro football, basketball, and hockey all have operated under reserve systems similar to baseball's, and all were under attack in 1976. Up to now, however, the revolt has had its most dramatic effect in baseball, where 1976 was truly the Year of Jock Lib.

Before 1976, baseball had several rules that combined to give a club what amounted to outright ownership of its players. One established the standard contract, which bound the player for one year and gave his employer an option on his services for the next year. Another was the "no tampering" rule that forbade making offers to any player deemed to be the property of another club. A third provided that if a player declined to sign a new contract—with the standard one-year option—the employer could renew the old contract and all its terms for a period of one year.

Andy Messersmith, a pitcher with the Los Angeles Dodgers, and Dave McNally, a pitcher for the Montreal Expos, refused to sign 1975 contracts. The clubs renewed their old ones. Messersmith played out the season, but McNally retired in June. At the season's end, both men filed grievances contending that their "option year" was over and that they should be free agents.

In collective bargaining over the years, the Players Association had won the right to arbitration of grievances by the panel of Miller, representing the players, Gaherin for the owners, and Seitz, who had the deciding vote. This time, however, the owners went to court to keep the grievance out of arbitration. United States District Judge John W.

Red Smith

Oliver told them to go to arbitration and come back if they didn't like the decision.

During arbitration hearings, Seitz urged the other two parties to take the case out of his hands and settle it through collective bargaining. The owners declined. They argued that when an old contract was renewed with all its terms, those terms included another one-year option that could be exercised a year later with still another option and so on throughout the player's career.

Suddenly, the owners were seeing free agents under their beds

Seitz, with Miller concurring, decided that "a period of one year" meant 12 months, not eternity. He ruled that Messersmith and McNally had fulfilled their contractual obligations and were free to sell their services on the open market. The owners fired Seitz and went back to Judge Oliver, who upheld the arbitrator. The owners went on to the United States Circuit Court of Appeals, which upheld the judge.

Suddenly the owners were seeing free agents under the bed. Now any player who didn't sign a 1976 contract could play out his option and be free at the end of the World Series. The baseball hierarchy foresaw chaos—gypsy caravans of players shuttling from team to team, all the best talent monopolized by the richest clubs, players deserting Milwaukee and Atlanta for the "glamour" cities of New York and Los Angeles. Constant movement of players from town to town would destroy "fan identification" with the home team, said men accustomed to moving hundreds of players arbitrarily in trades and sales. The new freedom would upset competitive balance, they said, meaning the balance that had concentrated five straight divisional championships in Oakland, five out of six in Baltimore, five of seven in Cincinnati, five of six in Pittsburgh.

"So let's try collective bargaining," the owners said.

The players conceded that when an owner invested heavily in the new talent, he should have a chance to get his money's worth out of that talent before losing it. On the other hand, they could not, acting as a union, bargain away the freedom individual players had won. So they compromised: For 1976 and 1977, anyone could play out his option and be free; after that, players would need six years of major-league service before applying for free agency.

Most teams opened the 1976 season with some players unsigned, but most managed to satisfy the holdouts and get their names on contracts as the summer wore on. The least successful owner in this respect was Oakland's uninhibited Charles O. Finley. Facing the prospect of losing his stars with nothing in return, he set out to get something for them. First he traded Reggie Jackson, a flamboyant outfielder, and Ken Holtzman, a pitcher, to Baltimore. Then he sold another outfielder and another pitcher, Joe Rudi and Rollie Fingers, to Boston for $1 million each and still another pitcher, Vida Blue, to the Yankees for $1.5 million.

Scandalized by the prices, Bowie Kuhn, the baseball commissioner, vetoed the sales and ordered the trio back to Oakland. Finley filed a $10-million damage suit against the commissioner.

Charles O. Finley

Instead of the rush for freedom that had been prophesied, only 24 of the 600 players in the big leagues became free agents. Eight of these, including Rudi and Fingers, were Finley's employees, and he got nothing for them.

Of those who went over the hill, half were good enough to inspire spirited—not to say frenzied—bidding. Kuhn, who was aghast when Finley stood to collect $3.5 million for three players, sat by helplessly while one free agent after another sold himself for a million or more.

Choicest item in the flesh market was Reggie Jackson, who had refused to sign with the Orioles after they landed him in the trade with Oakland. The Yankees, who had already signed Cincinnati pitcher Don Gullett for an estimated $2 million over six years, committed themselves to about $3 million for a five-year lien on Reggie's muscles.

That wasn't even the highest offer Jackson received. Montreal offered more, and Ray Kroc, the McDonald's hamburger potentate who owns the San Diego Padres, was prepared to go to $4 million. Contrary to predictions, money was not the decisive factor with Jackson and several others. Contrary to predictions, New York City attracted only two migrants and Los Angeles none. Contrary to predictions, the strongest teams did not get stronger, except for the Yankees. Because teams that most needed help bid most aggressively, most players went to weaker teams than the ones they had left. It looked as though competitive balance had been improved.

While this was going on in baseball, the natives were growing more and more restless in other sports. As early as 1974, Federal Judge William T. Sweigert in San Francisco had declared football's draft of college players and the so-called Rozelle Rule—also known as the Ransom Rule—both unreasonable. The no-tampering rule he called "patently unreasonable," and he used the same words for the rule that made Pete Rozelle, commissioner of the National Football League (NFL), the court of last resort in grievance cases.

In 1975, Federal Judge Robert L. Carter in New York had this to say in regard to pro basketball: "It is difficult for me to conceive of any theory or set of circumstances pursuant to which the college draft, blacklisting, boycotts, and refusals to deal could be saved from Sherman [antitrust] Act condemnation....The life of these restrictions, therefore, appears to be all but over."

In 1976, other federal judges spoke up—Warren J. Ferguson in San Francisco; Earl R. Larson in Minneapolis; William B. Bryant in Washington, D.C.; the Eighth Circuit Court of Appeals in St. Louis. All agreed that professional teams illegally deprived athletes of their right to play for an employer of their choice. Consider football's college draft:

A boy grows up in the Louisiana bayous, goes to high school and college there, and excels in football. Never in his life has he heard the name of Dominic Olejniczak, president of the Green Bay Packers. Olejniczak didn't help the boy through school, never bought him a meal, never met him. The Packers have no financial, legal, or moral

It looked as though the competitive balance had been improved

Bowie Kuhn

57

claim to the boy's services. But because a club official stood up at a draft meeting in New York City and said, "We select running back Armand Thibidoux of McNeece State," Armand must go up to frozen Wisconsin and play for Dominic Olejniczak or be barred from making a living in the United States at the one thing he does best. And even if the Packers never sign him, they own him as a pro football player as long as he lives.

This is, of course, immoral.

Before Messersmith punctured baseball's reserve system, the standard football contract had a built-in escape hatch, but the Rozelle Rule kept the hatch closed. The football people did not claim perpetual control of a player. Their contract permitted him to play out his option and become a free agent, but the Rozelle Rule provided that when another NFL team hired a free agent, the team that lost him must be compensated, and if the teams could not agree, Commissioner Rozelle would fix the amount.

Since nobody knew what exorbitant price Rozelle might set in players or draft choices, teams were wary of hiring free agents. The Rozelle Rule effectually restricted the player's freedom to change jobs.

Obviously, if existing practices are illegal, it is imperative that owners and players get together and agree on compromises that the courts will not disapprove. However, the contract between the NFL and the NFL Players Association expired in January 1974. The 1976 season was the third without a collective bargaining agreement.

As the season closed, negotiations were proceeding like wet cement. Nobody knew when or whether a 1977 draft could be held.

Pro basketball now operates without a reserve system. Under agreement reached when the National Basketball Association merged with the American Basketball Association, a player may be hired for one, three, or five years. On a one-year contract, he must get the league's minimum salary ($30,000) or more. After that he is free. If he signs for three years, his pay over that period must average $90,000 a year. If it's five years, the average is $100,000.

Through the season of 1979-1980, a Rozelle Rule applies in basketball. That is, a team hiring a free agent must compensate his old team. After 1980, there will be no compensation, but the player's old team can keep him by matching his best offer.

In hockey, there is competitive bidding for talent between the National Hockey League and the World Hockey Association. While that remains the case, players do not worry about the reserve system. They have reserved the right to reconsider the situation anytime the leagues merge.

It all comes down to a simple fact. From now on, pro sports must operate within the law, like people.

Andy Messersmith

From now on, pro sports must operate within the law, like people

Related Articles

For further information on sports in 1976, see OLYMPIC GAMES; SPORTS; and the articles on individual sports in Section Four.

Section Two

Special Reports

Six articles give special treatment to subjects
of current importance and lasting interest.

Cartoons with A Conscience

By Bill Mauldin

One of America's leading political cartoonists talks about the role of the artistic gadfly, where he gets ideas, and how he executes them

One night back in 1960, when the civil rights movement was a burning national issue, with sit-ins, demonstrations, and explosive reactions, I was watching the evening news on television, wondering what I would do for the next day's cartoon. The camera moved to an Alabama city. I watched a group of burly white men, armed with toy baseball bats from a nearby department store, beating up peaceful demonstrators—men, women, and children, both blacks and whites.

Violence is not new to me. I have witnessed it often as a soldier and as a newspaperman, but I have never been able to get used to it. But unlike most viewers who watched the Alabama scene and other horrors of our turbulent times with a sense of angry, gnawing helplessness, I had one consolation. I could express my feelings immediately and effectively, simply by drawing an editorial cartoon that I knew would be printed the following day in some 250 newspapers around the country—including Alabama. One of the fringe benefits of being a political cartoonist is freedom from ulcers.

This kind of cartooning, devoted to criticism and satirization of individuals and institutions, got its start in the 1700s. A typical cartoonist of that time, such as James Gillray or George Cruikshank of Great Britain, would think up a drawing about a prominent person or situation that irritated him, etch the drawing on a stone, print a number of copies, and peddle them on the street until he ran out of stock, starved, or was put away. These early cartoons, or caricatures, no doubt had some nuisance value, but not much social force. Political cartooning did not really hit its stride until the advent of mass-circulation printing in the early 1800s. Honoré Daumier, a Frenchman who was perhaps the greatest cartoonist in history, used the new medium to such effect that King Louis Philippe jailed him for six months in 1832 for his caustic caricature of the king.

The execution of a political cartoon is quite unlike producing comic strips or humorous "gag panels." The latter have to be done seven days a week, including a large Sunday page. They involve a great deal of work, but they also command more money. This enables the creator to hire helpers, including idea men if he needs them. Also, strips and gags can be done weeks or even months in advance. The political cartoonist usually produces only five drawings a week, but he has to think up and turn out all the work himself, and he must deal strictly with the news of today, not tomorrow or yesterday.

First, the cartoonist must think up an idea. Even though on the night of the Alabama incident I was sure what the subject of the next day's drawing would be, I went to bed as usual with three or four pencils, a notebook, and a small collection of news magazines, opinion journals, and newspapers. This habit goes back to my art school days in Chicago before World War II. I decided then, at the age of 17, that ideas are the most important ingredient in editorial cartooning. Drawing ability and training are important, of course—nothing adds more authority to a good thought than a well-done illustration—but good drawing can't save a poor idea.

Every night, before going to sleep in my YMCA room, I forced myself to think up 10 cartoon ideas and make quick sketches of them. These are called *roughs*. Some nights stretched into the dawn, and my other work at art school often suffered. Still, I was young and ambitious, I stuck with my regimen, and it paid off. Even now, after all these years, I still knock out six or eight roughs almost every night.

Normally, while skimming through my bedside reading matter, I find three or four topics to play around with. This time, even though I knew my subject, the going was not easy. How would I approach the civil rights incident? Humorously? The thought of people being bloodied in the streets does not exactly inspire chuckles—but then, not all humor is laughter. Humor is the classic complement to tragedy, and is often the best way to cope with grim situations. I had learned that

SCHOLAR

MORALIST

DIRECTOR

ARTIST

The author:
Bill Mauldin, twice a winner of the Pulitzer Prize, finds himself playing many roles as editorial cartoonist. He is on the staff of the *Chicago Sun-Times*.

One of Mauldin's favorite cartoons takes aim at Southern racism of the 1960s. TV news programs and bedtime reading spark many of his ideas.

"LET THAT ONE GO. HE SAYS HE DON'T WANNA BE MAH EQUAL."

The daily mail provides a cartoon idea, *below.* Mauldin quickly sketches an overloaded mailman, *bottom left,* and then traces the final drawing carefully, *bottom right.*

much in the Army, where the ability to smile internally could actually mean salvation in some situations.

I remember thinking that night of Thomas Nast, the leading United States cartoonist in the 1800s, who popularized the Democratic donkey and Republican elephant along with many other symbols that have become cartoon standards. Nast, who was somewhat short of humor but long on righteous wrath, would have had his own way of dealing with the subject. His style was perfectly suited to a day when printed journals were the public's only source of news. The average New York City reader was an immigrant, still struggling with printed English, and political cartoons had immense impact because they were easy to read and instantly understandable.

William Marcy (Boss) Tweed, the corrupt founder of New York City's Tammany Hall and one of the most ruthless politicians in the sorry history of American big-city political machines, was systematically and single-handedly destroyed by Nast through a series of brilliant, angry drawings. At one point, before he was stripped of power and jailed as a result of public attention generated by the cartoons, Tweed even tried vainly to buy the artist off with an offer of half a million dollars in gold.

"My people couldn't read much," the old tyrant was heard lamenting in his cell, "but they sure understood them damn pictures."

No, Nast wouldn't have bothered with humorous subtleties in the case I was pondering. Just as he showed Tweed with a vulture's body, feeding on the remains of a taxpayer, and as a bloody-jawed tiger crouching over a mangled maiden representing civic virtue, he would probably have drawn the Alabama scene as a Roman circus, with loutish gladiators pounding on early Christians. Or perhaps he would

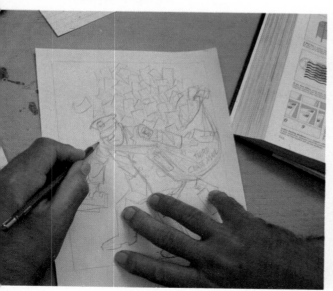

have shown a pack of ravening wolves amid a piteous flock of black and white sheep.

The Nast approach, with the cartoonist as an avenging angel, is a tempting solution tonight, I thought, as I lurched out of bed to make some coffee. Something simple and heavy-handed would not only get me to sleep earlier, but it would also relieve my outrage. Every editorial cartoonist is a moralizer at heart—a sort of ink-stained, self-ordained preacher with a drawing board for a pulpit. That's what keeps him from getting rich drawing comic strips.

Besides, I reasoned, there are plenty of distinguished, modern examples of an angry pen wielded by a righteous hand. Look at Herbert Block (Herblock) of the *Washington* (D.C.) *Post,* and recall his memorable cartoon campaign against the controversial Senator Joseph McCarthy, the Republican from Wisconsin who, with his shotgun charges of Communist infiltration of the government, attacked the reputations of so many Americans in the 1950s. And there was the great British caricaturist, David Low, who did such devastating drawings of Adolf Hitler in his heyday that the German dictator once even put a price on the artist's head.

Herblock didn't actually destroy McCarthy, as Nast clobbered Tweed, nor did Low stop Hitler. A crusading cartoon today does not pack the punch it did a century ago. Readers are more sophisticated now, and less easy to inflame. But there is no doubt that Herblock and Low scored effective hits and hurried their respective targets along the way to oblivion by constantly attacking them—with wrath one day and contempt the next—and repeatedly raising questions in the minds of readers who might otherwise have ignored the rascals.

Two factors finally made me decide against a heavy approach to the civil rights matter. First, there was no single person for me to attack. The bat-men were a mob. Second, why take them seriously and build them into satanic figures, when they were merely scruffy, evil-tempered little bullies? They would have liked to know their behavior created a lot of angry reaction. Why not figure out a way to laugh at them? No bully can stand to be laughed at. Satire would triumph over belligerence, I decided.

Exhausted by all this pondering and secure in the knowledge that I had a topic and an approach to it,

After completing the cartoon in ink, *top*, Mauldin is ready to send it to his office at the *Chicago Sun-Times* by telecopier, *above*.

Cartoon styles vary widely. Honoré Daumier portrayed peace after the Napoleonic wars as a skeleton brooding over Europe. Thomas Nast cast Boss Tweed as a vulture, and David Low treated Adolf Hitler with contempt.

A GROUP OF VULTURES WAITING FOR THE STORM TO "BLOW OVER."—"LET US *PREY*."

"YOU MAY HAVE BEGUN MAN — BUT *I*, ADOLF HITLER, WILL FINISH HIM."

I ignored the freshly made coffee and went to sleep after struggling through a few listless roughs, none of which were very good or very humorous. At this point, it's probably time to confess that I seldom use any of those thousands of midnight inspirations—even those bought at considerable cost in sleep and comfort. Ideas thought up late at night often cannot stand the scrutiny of morning. The main function of the roughs in my life has been disciplinary, to keep my mind on my work. If one goes to bed thinking of cartoons, he is not likely to wake up thinking of something else. At least, that's true for me.

My real working trick in the morning (every cartoonist has his own) is to get into a tub of extremely hot water, Japanese style, and let my brains boil. Sometimes it takes a while, but it never fails. Although I have never been able to figure out, let alone explain, the mental processes involved in converting current events into cartoons, I think it is a sort of filter system, like an automatic coffeemaker, combined with what psychoanalysts might call free association. One morning, I might sit in the steam thinking about Congress, which would lead me to the Senate, which might point to the White House (several senators have become President lately), thereby bringing to mind the secretary of state, then the Defense Department, raising the specter of nuclear warfare, which causes fallout, creating air pollution, which takes me back again to congressional debate. Somewhere along the line, one of these subjects will mate with a news topic, giving birth to an idea—an interesting feat for an automatic coffeemaker.

Incidentally, any old bathtub will do for this exercise. I have sampled plenty of them in 30-odd years of this work. I travel a lot because I start drawing elephants and donkeys too much when I stay in an office. Once I justified my restlessness by saying I needed to look at my victims in order to caricature them properly. Photos are too one-dimensional. Now that I can see politicians constantly on TV and can tell which are tall and which are not without having to go near them, I still travel a lot. I've come to realize that I simply need to see new people and new places.

For the past few years, I have carried with me a telecopier machine about the size of a portable typewriter, which transmits and receives written copy and drawings over the telephone. Usually, I prefer to mail drawings to my office at the *Chicago Sun-Times* because they lose some quality when transmitted by machine. But the telecopier saves my day when events are moving too fast or the mail is too slow. Also, through this device, the office can send me details of news stories when I need them and, in an emergency, can even transmit photographs of individuals whose faces I can't remember. So if the water is hot enough (showers are only for rinsing) and there is a telephone line, I can think and work almost anywhere. I have left eraser crumbs in some of the world's worst hotels.

Anyway, I was simmering in my own tub at home the morning after seeing the baseball bats when I suddenly realized how I should handle

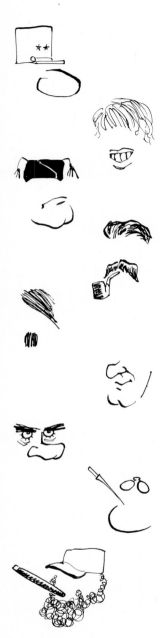

the fellows who had swung them. There would be no drawing of carnage and pathos. In fact, there would be no victims in the scene. This sort of staging can be very effective, as I learned while doing war cartoons. Go look at some of the cartoons I did for *Stars and Stripes* during World War II—Willie and Joe and the others—and you will see that I never once drew dead soldiers, yet I always tried to leave the impression that there were plenty of them in the wings, just out of sight. Restraint of this sort is usually more dramatic, in my opinion, than explicit gruesomeness.

All right, I would show only the attackers and their weapons. In my case, this would save a lot of work. These were anonymous thugs, so I wouldn't have to draw any well-known faces. Caricature comes easier to some cartoonists than to others. I have always had to work hard at it, and it often takes me weeks to master the shape of a new politician's head, the way he holds it, and the location of its features in relation to each other. (I say "he"—the proliferation of statespersons of the female persuasion creates new problems. How do you caricature a woman without becoming ungallant? We're going to need more lady cartoonists to handle that.)

Some faces, notably those of Dwight D. Eisenhower and John F. Kennedy, always gave me trouble. When drawing either of them, I often had to fall back upon what I call "nightclub caricature." This refers to the technique of those quick-sketch artists who hang around night spots and draw patrons in a few seconds for half a dollar or so, grossly exaggerating facial defects to achieve a likeness. Thus, Eisenhower's wide mouth and bald head and Kennedy's moplike hair became mainstays of the art.

Not that there is anything wrong with displaying Charles de Gaulle's huge nose or, more recently, Gerald Ford's prominent chin or Jimmy Carter's Chiclet teeth, but a conscientious cartoonist should not depend upon these things. Low, who in my opinion was one of the two best caricaturists in recent times (the other is New York City's David Levine), used to follow his subjects everywhere. He would trail them into restaurants, down streets, even into their offices and homes if possible, to see how they walked, sat, and gestured, and whether they scratched with their left or right hands. As a result, his drawings showed the whole personality, not isolated details, and were immensely effective. To a politician of his day, only one thing was worse than being "done" by Low, and that was being ignored by him.

So, casting would be simple in the cartoon about Alabama civil rights. Now, what sort of person clubs unarmed women and children? A man so full of meanness, insecurity, bitterness, and self-pity that he has to feel there are subhumans even lower than himself, creatures he can abuse without consequence. All of us have learned in recent years that this sort of brute is just as likely to be wearing a pinstriped suit in a northern city as rougher garb in Dixieland, but this incident occurred in the rural South, so I would dress my cast accordingly. A cer-

A Siamese cat naps placidly in Mauldin's lap as the cartoonist toys with a sketch.

tain amount of license is allowed cartoonists in cases such as this: Although none of the bat wielders I had seen on TV were barefooted, I couldn't resist taking the boots off one of my characters.

In center stage, I placed two of the sorriest rowdies I could concoct —unshaven, beady-eyed, with tobacco juice dribbling down the chin of one and a pre-owned cigar butt in the snaggled teeth of the other. In the background were two more of the same type, viciously swinging their bats at the offstage victims.

Theatrical terms are not inappropriate when describing the creation of a political cartoon. You are staging a drama and planning its impact. First, the cartoonist is a playwright. Having worked out his theme and its message, he writes his script, or caption. Next, he becomes a casting director, deciding what characters he needs to act out his daily dreams. Then, as stage manager, he positions stars and supporting cast in the most effective composition. Finally, he is a director, putting expressions into their faces and actions.

Like playwrights, cartoonists differ widely in style, yet they occasionally run in packs. Some artists favor highly decorated sets. A current fad among many younger artists is to imitate the well-known British satirical illustrator Ronald Searle, who fills his drawings with delightful embroidery. This, coupled with the fact that there is much unintentional duplication and near-duplication of ideas (everyone gets the same news at the same time and we all work within the same limited frames of reference), means that today you often have to decipher signatures to know who drew what.

I have always preferred a severe, somewhat stark style in which every line and word must justify itself by being vital to the message. Political cartoons used to be packed with words. Take a look at a 19th-century Currier and Ives print. Not only is it full of quotes from various characters, but the figures and objects in the drawing are

Who's who on opposite page, *top to bottom:* Charles de Gaulle, Jimmy Carter, Benito Mussolini, Joseph Stalin, Adolf Hitler, Lyndon B. Johnson, Richard M. Nixon, Franklin D. Roosevelt, and Fidel Castro.

Mauldin's cartoons over the years have ranged over a wide variety of subjects in war and peacetime.

labeled in detail. A globe covered with continents and crisscrossed with lines and meridians is labeled "The Earth." None of this appears in today's cartoons, and nobody misses it. In my cartoons, I try to edit wordage down as close as possible to nothing. If I can manage to do two cartoons in a week that can be understood without any captions, I'm proud of myself.

This cartoon, however, would need a caption. As usual, the words had come into my head with the picture. One of the cretinous clubbers points offstage to his right and speaks to his partner, the barefooted one with the cigar:

"Let that one go. He says he doesn't want to be my equal."

Not bad. The drawing needed nothing more—no labels, no explanations. I've always felt that an editorial cartoonist is not an entertainer, out to capture and please the largest possible audience. He is addressing himself to people who are sufficiently informed and interested enough in current events to be browsing through the opinion section of the paper. Gone are the innocent, gullible readers of Nast's day, and a cartoonist who tries to draw for this kind of audience will lose credibility fast. I decided as a very young man in this profession that I

SOLE SUPPORT

"BACK UP FIRST AND WE'LL NEGOTIATE LATER."

"SOMEHOW, WE'VE GOT TO BREAK THAT UP."

"DON'T FORGET, NOW....WOMEN AND CHILDREN FIRST."

"I PREFER MOVING SECRETLY."

"IT'S GETTING SO BAD THAT EVEN PEOPLE ARE COMPLAINING."

Editorial cartoonists took these varying approaches to the 1976 U.S. presidential election. They are by Pat Oliphant, *top right*; Jeff MacNelly, *right*; Herblock, *bottom right*; and Paul Conrad, *below*.

FORD ALREADY HAS A RUNNING MATE

"— BUT IF I WERE PRESIDENT —"

would always rather risk puzzling a customer than insulting his intelligence and sense of humor.

Being near my office—I was working for the *St. Louis Post-Dispatch* at this time—I made a rough sketch of my idea and bounced it off a few reporters and editorial writers, a secretary, and a copy boy. I only parade my work around like that when I think I have done something great—and I never bounce anything off editors if I can help it. I have sometimes gone for years without so much as speaking to one. (Unfortunately, however, I don't know any way that beginners in this work can avoid editors. The only way to get started is to bombard them with your work—and if you are allergic to rejection slips, forget the whole thing. I own one of the world's most comprehensive collections of these slips, mostly from sending stuff to magazines during my art school days.)

In this case, to my chagrin, several people thought the cartoon itself effective, but the caption deficient.

"I've got it," an editorial writer finally told me. "That man should be talking redneck."

I explained that I had given up regional and ethnic dialect in captions years before, on the grounds that it is often needlessly insulting.

"You draw a weird bunch of hillbillies like that and then worry about insulting them with an *accent*?" he asked.

The caption became: "Let that one go. He says he don't wanna be mah equal."

When searching for an idea, Mauldin sometimes seeks inspiration by turning to his airplane control panel simulator. He exercises his fingers by playing the guitar.

I retired to my office, dusted off the drawing board—which I hadn't seen for weeks because I had been hiding out and sending in my work from my home in Santa Fe, N. Mex.—and started drawing the picture. When I was an art student, black India ink was sturdy stuff, and red sable brushes, with which I once did all my line drawing, could hold a point indefinitely. This meant I could carry all the supplies I needed, other than paper, in my shirt pocket—brush, ink bottle, pencils, eraser, and a package of single-edge razor blades for sharpening and scraping. But not today. While other people complain about the lack of quality control in the manufacture of automobiles and similar goods, I bemoan the fact that even if I could manage to ink in a complete cartoon with a brush before it limply spread its bristles, the ink is so poor that the work would be rubbed off when I tried to clean it up with an eraser.

Most people learn to do their chores faster over the years. My stuff takes twice as long as it once did because I must trace over the lines twice as often as I used to. First, I pencil in the drawing, often referring to the best of half a dozen or so tiny thumbnail sketches I have made for composition and placement of characters. Then I ink lightly and loosely over the pencil work with a fine-pointed pen because, with today's rotten ink, only a pen line will stand up when I vigorously erase the underlying pencil line. Next I do whatever shading I want with a lithographic pencil and spray fixative over everything. Finally,

Mauldin gets his best ideas while simmering in a hot morning bath. He uses a mirror in his studio and photos of himself to help him get gestures and poses right.

I go over the drawing one more time with a brush to strengthen the lines where they need it. After processing by engravers and printers, my work is ready for the newsstands.

And what about the complaints that follow publication? My cartoons are syndicated for publication in a couple of hundred papers, reaching people in all parts of the country. The reaction to the bat-men cartoon was quite substantial. For one thing, as soon as it appeared, an Alabama paper announced it would no longer run my work. Several cranks I hadn't heard from in years began sending me obscene mail again. It is amazing what some people will put into an envelope. I even got feedback from a few of my relatives, most of whom are Deep Southerners.

The cancellation by the Alabama paper surprised me mildly. Most of the papers I lost by doing strong cartoons about civil rights when it was a hotly controversial topic were in the North where, as we have learned, bigotry takes more forms and in many ways is more deep-seated than in the South. After all, cancellation is the only weapon an editor has to punish a syndicated cartoonist. My cartoons have appeared in as many as 280 papers and as few as 79, depending upon whose shins I've kicked. Many of the papers sign up again once tempers have cooled.

The problem is that many people fail to realize that political cartooning is not an objective form of journalism. Also, because of the nature of his work and the present state of libel law, which encourages fair comment and open debate on matters of public interest, the cartoonist is seldom, if ever, held le-

Using the photos of himself, plus some others, for reference, Mauldin sketches the cartoon in pencil, *above left.* He uses a litho pencil for shading, *above,* then inks the lines, *left.*

gally accountable for what he does. The potential for irresponsible mischief in this line of work is considerable. The only real checks on a cartoonist are his own conscience and the fact that if he makes reck-lessness a habit, he will soon have no audience. Although this is not an objective art, it behooves the artist to be scrupulously fair in searching out facts to determine the direction of his nonobjectivity. For all the seeming simplicity of his pictures, a political cartoonist must have, or acquire, a thorough education in history, economics, sociology, and anything else that touches upon his work. I once even went so far as to run for Congress—unsuccessfully—in order to understand better the mentality of candidates.

Based on all this input, the cartoonist is ready to speak his piece. I'm assuming, of course, that he wants to be an independent thinker, not a hack at the service of his publisher or editor. The difference between a cartoonist and an editorial writer is that the cartoonist is not anony-

"Interesting lining on your flag here, Mister."

Mauldin sorts through cartoons to be published in a collection of his work. One cartoon he did for a National Park Service book depicts the common soldier in the American Revolution.

mous. The editorial writer is presenting the viewpoint of the paper and its management. The cartoonist is producing signed work, and it should be his own.

This brings up a touchy matter. How truly independent can the cartoonist be? It varies, of course, from paper to paper. Some publishers think it is necessary for an employee to reflect the boss's thinking. I have never been able to work for such people. On the other hand, if you constantly produce work that is in opposition to your newspaper's editorial policy, you make both yourself and the paper look foolish. Some conflict makes for credibility; too much is too much. The trick, therefore, is to find an editor and a publisher with whom you are in general agreement, and wish them both a long life.

Political cartoonists proliferate in times of upheaval, suffering, and tyranny. Good cartoonists tend to be mavericks, flying in the face of the Establishment, holding to the maxim that power tends to corrupt. Thus, most independent-minded American cartoonists found themselves siding with unions when labor was waging an uphill struggle for its rights. Now that many unions have become at least as large, powerful, and arrogant as their old adversaries, they have themselves become legitimate targets for the satirist. A good rule of thumb for the political cartoonist is: If it's big, you probably should hit it. Obviously, this art does not flourish in totalitarian societies, except in a few underground publications that usually find themselves with very limited and short-lived circulations.

"Why can't you guys do something constructive for a change?" readers sometimes ask. Try to imagine a "constructive" cartoon. Do you de-emphasize the wart on your subject's nose? Do you put a halo over the head of the candidate you favor? You would only make him look silly. A cartoon without a point of view is one of the world's most worthless objects, and political satire is by nature somewhat destructive. The trick is for the artist to be destructive in a constructive way. If you discover that you approve of a politician, the way to help him is to go after his opponent.

Victims of editorial cartoons generally react more mildly than do their loyal supporters. No political person with enough savvy to be successful is going to admit that a cartoonist got his goat. While his friends search for a rope and a tree to hang you from, the victim himself is much more likely to ask for the original drawing. Sometimes this show of sportsmanship is genuine. Senator Barry Goldwater (R., Ariz.), for example, is an avid collector of cartoons about himself. I have never done anything about him that wasn't critical, yet he has asked for nearly all of them, and I have reason to believe that he has a genuine sense of humor. Jimmy Hoffa, long-time head of the Teamsters Union, used to ask for everything drawn about him, too.

"Have you ever done a cartoon you've regretted?" I've been asked. Of course I have. You can't deal constantly with controversy without tripping over your own conclusions sometimes. For example, I started drawing cartoons as early as 1962 against our increasing involvement in Vietnam. Then I went to South Vietnam in early 1965, following my belief that cartoonists need exposure to real life as much as do other journalists, and became somewhat involved myself, possibly in part because one of my sons was there. I drew a number of hawkish cartoons supporting the war during the next several months before I gradually came back to my senses. There have been other, lesser occasions when I have wished I could eat my own drawings, but Vietnam was my biggest and longest goof.

There is no way of knowing how much or how little I contributed to a tragic situation in that case. As for drawings about individuals, it's probably a good thing that when we cartoonists decide to play Saint George we can't really kill our dragons anymore, as Nast did. You can't revive a dead dragon if you learn that you got the wrong one. Generally, however, the political scene is not crowded with Saint Georges and dragons. Gray predominates, not black and white.

I think the function of the modern political cartoonist in most situations is not so much that of a destroyer as of a gadfly, using whatever wit and talent he possesses to amuse, irritate, or infuriate his audience into paying attention to his subject. I have never really cared much about converting readers. I'm satisfied to get their emotions focused, because I cling hopefully to the belief that if enough people look at any problem or situation they will usually arrive at the proper conclusion—even when it doesn't agree with my own.

The Losing War Against Illiteracy

By Fred M. Hechinger

The number of illiterates in the developing nations is increasing, and many persons in wealthier societies cannot read and write well enough to cope with everyday life

It was a glum year for those who believe in the universal right to read. In February 1976, the United Nations Educational, Scientific, and Cultural Organization (UNESCO) formally issued a report acknowledging that its crusade against illiteracy, which began in 1966, was a dismal failure. Not only did the UNESCO effort fail to bring the benefits of literacy to great masses of people in developing nations, but the worldwide total of illiterates over 15 years of age actually increased to 800-million from 735 million in 1965.

Although the UNESCO program targeted 11 countries–Algeria, Ecuador, Ethiopia, Guinea, India, Iran, Madagascar (Malagasy Republic), Mali, Sudan, Syria, and Tanzania–it reached only about a million adults. And not all of them succeeded in learning how to read and write.

An illiterate person can function in a simple culture, but you must know how to read to cope with a complex society.

But the curse of ignorance is not confined to the poorer nations of Africa, Asia, and Latin America. Americans, for example, consider themselves a well-educated, literate people, spending $100 billion a year for education at all levels. Nearly half of all U.S. high school graduates go on to college, creating a higher-education enrollment of more than 9 million students—the largest number in the world.

Yet, in October 1975, the U.S. Office of Education reported that 23 million Americans between ages 18 and 65 could not read or write well enough to function adequately in U.S. society. This was revealed during a four-year study by the University of Texas at Austin. "It is surprising, perhaps even shocking," the report said, "to suggest that approximately 1 of 5 Americans is incompetent or functions with difficulty, and that about half of the adult population is merely functional and not at all proficient in necessary skills and knowledge."

It is easier to understand how a great many people can be illiterate in the poorer nations. Few children in developing countries have an opportunity to attend school, but every child in America must go to school. To people who believe that learning to read is a natural result of going to school, the news about American incompetency came as quite a jolt. Surely American schools cannot be producing illiterates?

Without some further explanation, comparing the U.S. and world-wide situations would be like comparing apples and oranges. There are two kinds of illiteracy involved—absolute illiteracy and functional illiteracy. Absolute illiterates cannot write even their names or read in any language. Functional illiterates can read and write, but not well enough to function in their own societies.

In a remote village in India, those who can write their names and read a few simple sentences are looked upon by fellow villagers as educated persons. But in a modern industrialized nation, citizens who have only these limited skills are considered ignorant. They are constantly frustrated and confused by the complexities of the world around them and most likely doomed to a life of poverty. For example, 85 per cent of American adults with three years of schooling or less have incomes at the poverty level. By contrast, only 11 per cent of those who graduated from high school are listed as poor.

To test the complexity of life in modern America, Ted R. Kilty, an educational researcher at Western Michigan University in Kalamazoo, analyzed some of the materials an ordinary person might have to read, and reported the results in early 1976. He found that the modern version of Psalm 23 is written at the fifth-grade reading level. The manual a person must study to get a driver's license and the instructions on how to make coffee are written at the sixth-grade level. Directions for making gelatin are at the seventh-grade level, and those to prepare a frozen TV dinner are at the eighth-grade level. Instructions for taking aspirin require 10th-grade reading ability, and it takes 12th-grade ability to understand life insurance policies. An apartment lease is comprehensible only to college-level readers.

Understanding the instructions in a driver's manual, *above left,* or
on a package of frozen food, *above right,* requires reading skills
that many Americans do not have, according to recent literacy studies.

America's Report Card	Percentage of U.S. adults		
	Have Difficulty	Fair	Proficient
Reading	21.7	32.2	46.1
Problem solving	28.0	23.4	48.5
Arithmetic	32.9	26.3	40.8
Writing	16.4	25.5	58.1
Learns and uses job skills	19.1	31.9	49.0
Can shop economically	29.4	33.0	37.6
Understands laws and how government works	25.8	26.2	48.0
Knows fundamentals of health care	21.3	30.3	48.3
Can find community help and resources	22.6	26.0	51.4
Overall ability to function in society	**19.7**	**33.9**	**46.3**

Source: University of Texas study

But according to the U.S. Office of Education, 22 per cent of U.S. adults between ages 18 and 65 read at the fifth-grade level; another 32 per cent read at the sixth- or seventh-grade levels. "This is tragic," says Kilty. "This means that 54 per cent of the [adult] population either can't read materials they come in contact with or do it with great difficulty."

Functionally illiterate persons in the United States cannot read help-wanted ads or fill out employment applications. They are unable to understand the labels or instructions on cans or boxes in the supermarket or to compute prices.

On the other hand, a peasant in Africa or India does not need reading or writing skills to deal with the reality of daily life. The peasant struggles just to find enough food to live from day to day and to have adequate shelter to sleep through the night.

Considering the two kinds of societies, it is clear that there must be different causes for the two types of illiteracy in today's world. But both societies share one common problem—poverty. In the United States, as in the developing countries, poverty still remains a serious hindrance to learning. Even though the United States is almost unbelievably affluent when compared with many other nations, pockets of poverty remain in city slums and in rural areas. Cramped living space, poor nutrition, and a lack of books and stimulating conversation are the enemies of learning.

Educators have long known the value of good nutrition in learning. As early as 1931, experimenters in Oslo, Norway, began serving a nutritious breakfast daily to all schoolchildren. They found that the pupils produced far better schoolwork than they had previously. Yet, millions of U.S. children go to school each morning without a nutritious meal, perhaps after spending a restless night in a tenement that is hot during summer and cold during winter. Under these conditions, learning obviously suffers.

Also, many American children are struggling to overcome backgrounds of social disadvantage. Black children in particular suffer as descendants from the days of slavery, when their ancestors were forbidden by law to learn reading and writing. Even after slavery was abolished, black children were restricted to inferior schools. Many of today's black adult functional illiterates are undoubtedly the unwilling heirs of this discrimination against their parents and grandparents.

In addition, the United States continues to be a haven for immigrants. These newcomers find it difficult to cope with the sophisticated problems of U.S. civilization, and their difficulties are often heightened by the language barrier. They may be functionally literate in their native tongue, but find it difficult to learn English.

However, functional illiteracy is not confined to immigrants and racial minorities. Too often, public schools have simply not lived up to the demands of a complex society. Every year, many elementary, high school, and even college students graduate with inadequate reading

Functional illiteracy in the United States has many causes. Newcomers to America, *left,* often have difficulty surmounting the language barrier, and television, *below,* has made many children less concerned with learning to read. Poverty and the legacy of social disadvantage, *bottom,* also seriously hinder learning.

and writing skills. For example, open admission to the City University of New York was introduced in the late 1960s, allowing anyone with a high school diploma to enroll. University officials soon discovered that great numbers of students had not reached the eighth-grade level in reading ability. The problem has grown steadily worse. Today, colleges and universities throughout the United States are burdened with the necessity of teaching remedial English and arithmetic skills to an increasing number of freshmen.

Many experts believe that a major reason why these students read poorly is that elementary-school teachers are not properly trained to teach reading. They claim many teacher-training colleges offer theories about teaching children to read, but do not give the future teachers enough practical experience. One elementary-school teacher recalled her own first day in the classroom. "It's as if you trained doctors only in the theory of diseases," she said, "then, after they get their license, let them get at live patients for the first time."

Writing also takes a back seat in many schools. Some experts believe this is another result of poor teacher training. It is possible for an English teacher to complete college without having taken a single composition course – let alone a course on how to teach composition. In addition, written exercises tend to feature creative self-expression to the exclusion of grammar. But many students are not required to write very much at all. Illustrating this, a student who attended his first five years of school in England complained that he was bored because his American teachers rarely gave written assignments. The boy's mother passed this criticism along to the principal. "You must understand," the principal answered, "we can't ask our children to do much writing, because they write so badly."

Finally, television has made Americans far less reading oriented. Many children watch TV more hours a day than they spend in school. Consequently, they no longer consider the printed and written word important. If they can get news and entertainment by simply turning on the TV set, why learn to read and write well?

Whatever the reasons, the fact is that literacy has declined in the United States. The National Assessment of Educational Progress, a panel of U.S. educators, has been conducting nationwide evaluations since 1969. They have found that 9-year-olds have virtually no understanding of spelling and grammar. In late 1975, this panel of educators reported that many young adults over 18 years of age are reluctant to write at all. These two discoveries may be closely connected. Deprived of effective early training in the basics, adults may become progressively more functionally illiterate.

The reasons for massive illiteracy in the poorer, developing nations differ substantially from those in the industrial world. Although the UNESCO project failed dismally, in fairness we must note that the percentage of illiterates throughout the world actually declined. But the total number of illiterates increased because the population continued to increase. On the basis of the UNESCO experience, it seems clear that educational efforts are not able to keep pace with rapidly expanding populations.

In many countries, the UNESCO literacy program reached only a tiny fraction of the population, and the dropout rate was usually more than 50 per cent. In Algeria, for instance, the project enrolled fewer than 1 per cent of the estimated 6 million illiterates. A program sponsored by the Algerian government enrolled another 5 per cent. But only half of those who took part in the programs attained fifth-grade reading ability.

Since 80 to 90 per cent of the people in developing countries live in rural areas, transportation was another obstacle. In Madagascar, public transportation was frequently nonexistent, and some people had to travel for several days to reach classes. Getting supplies was also a big problem. In one instance, a year elapsed between the date books were purchased and the time they were delivered. In another case, it took suppliers 23 months to deliver a bookmobile.

Often the teaching materials were not geared to adults. Some of the books used to teach illiterate adults were simply reprints of children's texts in which the word *child* was replaced by *adult*. In many places, no books were available for those who had learned to read. Unless a country can set up printing facilities, libraries, or bookmobiles, a newly literate person quickly sinks back into illiteracy.

Furthermore, going to school seems demeaning to illiterate adults. UNESCO experts observed that "there is often something of a stigma attached to adults who take part in education, which is normally thought to be reserved for children." To make matters worse, classes were often conducted in the village school, which many adult illiterates perceived as a strange and foreign place. According to UNESCO experts, this had the effect of "cutting learners off, psychologically and physically, from the reality around them."

Some of the most successful literacy classes were conducted outdoors or in factories, churches, or private houses. In Ethiopia, students sometimes built their own classrooms. Tanzania provided funds for literacy training only if the students contributed materials and labor for simple school buildings.

Literacy program administrators in Algeria, Ethiopia, Iran, and Mali organized classes in factories to combine literacy training with vocational training. In Ecuador, India, Iran, and Tanzania, much of the teaching was done on agricultural demonstration plots. However, professional teachers recruited from elementary schools were unfamiliar with the factory or farming occupations of their adult pupils. In addition, many of the teachers had the authoritarian attitudes typical of educated persons toward illiterates in countries where only a few people enjoy a formal education.

Language posed other hurdles. In India, functional literacy programs were organized in nine languages. In one case, Russian teach-

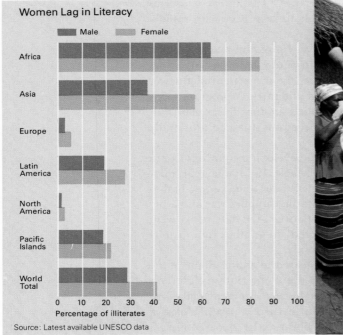

Women Lag in Literacy

■ Male ▨ Female

Africa

Asia

Europe

Latin America

North America

Pacific Islands

World Total

0 10 20 30 40 50 60 70 80 90 100
Percentage of illiterates

Source: Latest available UNESCO data

ing materials were translated into English for discussion by the international staff, then retranslated into the various national languages. This is reminiscent of the children's game in which players sit in a circle and pass on a whispered sentence. Under such circumstances, a great deal tends to get lost in translation.

Communications between leaders of the UNESCO literacy drive and people in the developing countries were not easy. A study in Mali showed that many Western symbols for getting simple messages across —an arrow to indicate direction or a skull and crossbones to indicate poison—were incomprehensible to African and Asian peasants.

In addition to these obstacles, substantial ideological and political disagreement hampered progress. Education experts disagree about the actual purpose of literacy. Those holding a pragmatic view believe reading and writing should help people in their jobs, such as farming, construction, and simple businesses. They contend that the teaching of reading and writing should be linked with those jobs.

Other experts, such as Majid Rahnema, Iran's special adviser to the prime minister and former minister of higher education, insist that "the goal of literacy is not to teach a person to decode a few symbols, but to provide him with all the tools needed for decoding the world...." Rahnema agrees with UNESCO experts who maintain, "Literacy is not the simple reading of a word, of a set of associated symbols and sounds, but an act of critical understanding of man's situation in the world."

These more idealistic educators believe that those who learn to read and write will also become more powerful as citizens. A literate people can take part in decision making in community, governmental, and economic affairs.

But many less-than-democratic governments were lukewarm toward such a goal. These governments had little interest in creating a mass of literate citizens and therefore did not give wholehearted support to the UNESCO efforts. Educated citizens want to improve their lives and may begin to question the established order. Undoubtedly, an absolute ruler feels safer with subjects who have not learned that there may be more to life than eking out a miserable living.

As long as great masses of a society's people do not need to read complex instructions for survival or even for minimal success, then few feel left out because they cannot read. And as long as the ruling powers do not need many literate people, they naturally assign a relatively low priority to literacy training.

This leads to a kind of rationing of literacy in many developing countries. Because of the difficulty of educating illiterates, the UNESCO efforts, hampered by limited resources, were often aimed at those among the uneducated who showed the greatest ability, motivation, and potential. With this approach, a limited number of people learned to read and write, but the majority remained illiterate.

As might be expected, the rationing of limited educational resources also tends to discriminate against women. Before universal education was part of the American scene, only boys were given access to advanced education. And the general social and cultural atmosphere encouraged discriminatory attitudes. As late as the mid-1800s, respected medical experts warned that excessive education would leave females with "monstrous brains and puny bodies; abnormally active cerebration and abnormally weak digestion; flowing thought and constipated bowels...." So too, today, cultural considerations and limited educational facilities work against women in underdeveloped societies. These societies tend to shunt women aside. Consequently, UNESCO reports that nearly two-thirds of the world's 800 million illiterates are women.

Given the two types of illiteracy that plague industrial and developing societies, what are some possible solutions?

One successful—but largely forgotten—approach was pioneered in 1929 by U.S. educator and missionary Frank C. Laubach, who died in 1970 at the age of 85. The essence of Laubach's approach lay in his favorite slogan, "Each one teach one." He used simple, basic teaching materials and encouraged each newly literate person to teach someone else to read and write.

Laubach traveled to more than 100 countries, developing simple literacy textbooks in more than 165 languages. He was directly or indirectly responsible for teaching an estimated 100 million persons to read. But he had no illusions about the long-term effects of his work.

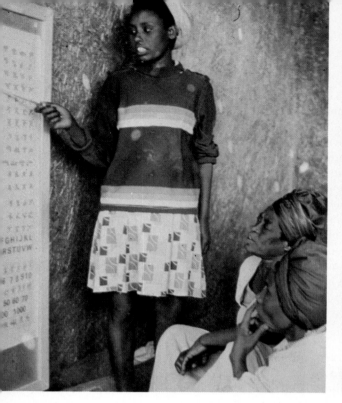

Developing nations have set up reading classes, *above left,* even having
children teach adults, *above right.* But many, fearful that literacy may
lead to protests, *below,* have not fully supported reading programs.

"I haven't even kept up with the birth rate," he once said. "And besides, about 20 million or more who've learned to read have lapsed back into illiteracy for lack of reading materials."

More recent programs have also stressed the simplicity that Laubach valued so highly. The first stage of a literacy program in Algeria covers only 304 basic Arabic words. In Tanzania, where few books are available, a major national daily newspaper sets aside one page for stories written in a simple, easily understood style. An entire newspaper has been developed for new readers in Mali.

Some countries have tried drastic steps to wipe out illiteracy. Cuba, which claims to have virtually eliminated illiteracy, shut down all its high schools in 1961 and sent the students into the countryside to teach adults how to read and write. During that year, Cuba claimed to have cut its illiteracy rate from 23 per cent to 4 per cent.

In 1974, Somalia followed Cuba's example by closing its high schools and sending 30,000 students to teach proper health care as well as reading and writing to rural citizens, 95 per cent of whom were illiterate. However, the campaign was complicated by the fact that the first written alphabet for Somalia's Cushitic language was not introduced until 1972.

Algeria has undertaken an ambitious illiteracy campaign. Like other developing nations, Algeria must fight illiteracy on two fronts—in the traditional school system for children and in adult education programs. The adult programs are divided into two approaches. One offers instruction to anyone who asks for it, the other combines literacy training with the illiterate's job. In both instances, classroom work is augmented with radio, television, and correspondence courses.

The Algerian government enlisted thousands of young volunteers to teach older people. To combat the stigma of adults in school, the government sponsored posters and skits that ridiculed illiterate adults. Nevertheless, a scarcity of funds and teachers, combined with inefficient administration, made the effort less than a total success.

Brazil also has a rural illiteracy program and claims to have decreased the illiteracy rate from 33 per cent in 1970 to 26 per cent of the country's 110 million inhabitants 2½ years later. "The biggest problem now," said one of the program's organizers, "is to persuade students to stay in rural areas once they've learned to read and write." One local teacher taught his students to write only their first names; he was afraid they would instantly move to the cities if they learned to write their full names.

One of the most successful efforts to provide developing countries with books has been carried out since 1952 by the Franklin Book Programs, Incorporated, a nonprofit organization. It has begun programs to stimulate book publishing in Africa, Asia, Latin America, and the Middle East. Through Franklin, more than 3,000 books have been translated and produced in such languages as Arabic, Bengali, Persian, and a number of African languages.

Controversy continues between back-to-basics educators, who favor formal class settings, *above left,* and those who prefer the freedom of less structured open classrooms, *above right.*

A large part of the illiteracy problem is tied to social and economic issues. Without substantial improvement in a nation's economy and the creation of skilled jobs, there is little incentive for citizens to learn to read and write. This raises a "what comes first, the chicken or the egg?" question. Without economic improvement, people have no reason to learn; but without learning, it is difficult for people to raise their economic expectations.

In the United States and other industrial nations, many educators believe the problem of functional illiteracy can be solved only by a return to the basic skills of reading, writing, and arithmetic. Heated debate is going on between what are loosely called educational progressives and educational conservatives. But after years of experimenting with informal, or open, classrooms—in which children worked largely on their own and the teacher assumed the limited role of an adviser—the new conservative trend is toward a more formal structure. In the 1960s, so-called alternative schools sprang up offering informal education. New alternative schools are now coming on the scene—but they feature the basics.

The back-to-the-basics movement will undoubtedly get further support from a report issued in April 1976 by a research team at Lancaster University in England. The report showed that children learn the basic skills faster and better when taught in the old-fashioned, formal way. The fact that these findings came from a study in Great Britain is particularly significant, because British educators pioneered the open-classroom movement. Their system served as a model for many progressive American schools.

From Arizona to Oregon to Florida, an increasing number of states have instituted or are considering basic competency tests that students must pass to receive a high school diploma. In March, representatives from 32 states met in Denver—which has had such a testing program since 1962—to discuss minimum standards for these tests.

Public elementary schools are also beginning to examine the progress of their students. For example, the Chicago Board of Education in April resolved that the city's public school students be tested after completing the third, sixth, and eighth grades. Those failing the tests would be given special help in learning the basics.

The growing popularity of competency testing may one day even extend to prospective teachers. In 1975, the Stamford, Conn., Board of Education passed a rule that all of its teachers must pass an oral and written English examination.

We have looked at some specific causes of and proposed cures for illiteracy. But given the enormousness of the problem, we might ask: What is the purpose of educating great masses of people?

One obvious answer lies in the realm of economics. In the United States particularly, education during the 1950s and 1960s came to mean earning power—the more education a person has, the better the job he or she can get. It would seem to follow that through education, people in developing nations could automatically raise their standard of living. However, in the United States of the 1970s, this connection between education and earning power appears to have broken down. College graduates are driving taxis and clerking in stores. The so-called overeducated find themselves in the same unemployment lines as the undereducated.

If the education-equals-jobs equation no longer holds true, why expend effort and money on literacy programs when peasants in Africa and Asia can get by without knowing how to read and write?

One of America's Founding Fathers, Thomas Jefferson, advocated basic schooling for children at government expense. But his reason was not primarily economic. The larger goal of literacy in Jefferson's view was to educate citizens as to their rights and responsibilities in a free society. The voters who elect the leaders must be informed, and to be informed, they must be educated.

Jefferson's views are shared today by idealistic educators in developing nations and UNESCO experts who link literacy with the entire issue of enlightened citizenship and self-government. "If a nation expects to be both ignorant and free in a state of civilization," said Jefferson, "it expects what never was and never will be."

America's Big Birthday Party

By Edward G. Nash

On July 4, 1976, the United States held its Bicentennial party by being itself — joyful, troubled, commonplace, and extraordinary

When 218 million Americans decide to celebrate a birthday, their efforts are wonderfully diverse, yet always flavored by the American character, which is common to all parts of the country but adapted to each. On the following pages is a scrapbook, a family album, showing some of what happened on one birthday – July 4, 1976.

On that day, the people of the United States feasted, marched, danced, played, and worshiped to commemorate the 200th anniversary of the signing of the Declaration of Independence. That document launched the American Experiment, and gave voice to the American Promise – life, liberty, the pursuit of happiness, equality, and justice. It was, and is, a noble statement, perhaps even more inspiring after 200 years.

While a platoon of youthful firecrackers marches in Milwaukee, Wis., covered wagons roll in Pine Plains, N.Y. Meanwhile, a woman in Redmond, Wash., and a man in Washington, D.C., dress for the occasion.

The author:
Edward G. Nash is a Senior Editor of THE WORLD BOOK YEAR BOOK and SCIENCE YEAR.

Many parade floats, such as this one in Millerton, N.Y., show scenes from early American life for spectators who, like these in Los Angeles, line the nation's main streets from coast to coast.

Sixteen of the Tall Ships, the world's last great sailing vessels, are among hundreds of sailing ships from other countries gathered in New York Harbor to observe the Fourth with Operation Sail.

Ethnic groups add their distinctive styles to the celebration, reminding us that much of America's strength comes from the unique diversity of its people—such as Italians in New York City, *left,* and Philadelphia's Chinese and Middle Easterners.

No birthday party is complete without a cake, and America has dozens. A young Redmond, Wash., cyclist parades one, and a five-story concoction, the largest ever baked, rests in Memorial Hall in Philadelphia. President Gerald R. Ford cuts another on the U.S.S. *Nashville* in New York Harbor.

Many Americans fashion unique birthday cards to show how they feel about their country. Among them are a yard sign in Lawrenceville, N.J., and a sidewalk greeting in New York City.

Americans gather in all settings—a Philadelphia front porch, *right,* a St. Louis high-rise, *below right,* and a family home in Nashville, *below*—to mark a special Fourth.

Fourth of July picnics of communities, social clubs, church groups, and families feature the most American of foods — sweet corn in Oriental, N.C.; hamburgers in West Barnstable, Mass.; and juicy watermelon in Independence, Va.

The Fourth is more than just feasting and fun. Americans in Denver, *right;* Dickinson, W. Va., *below;* and elsewhere remember to give thanks for the nation's blessings.

In a land born of protest, some people mark the Fourth by protesting. One group gathers at the nation's Capitol, while Indians, blacks, and others marching in Philadelphia call for equal rights.

The Stars and Stripes is everywhere — in an Ohio wheat field, on a rubber raft in North Carolina, and in a Virginia re-enactment of the flag-raising on Iwo Jima in World War II.

Traditional games and contests on the Fourth range from a marathon race in Atlanta, Ga., to a pie race held in West Barnstable, Mass., and a horse-pull near Cleveland.

At the end of a long day, a bone-weary young colonial in Independence, Va., is ready for bed, and Uncle Sam pauses for a refreshing drink in Philadelphia. But there is still work for the cleanup crews in Redmond, Wash., and elsewhere.

Heading for home in Virginia, two paraders who represented the 1800s in America move along a modern highway.

Now the party is over. The picnic areas and the parade grounds, the streets and the beaches, have been swept and cleared. The celebrants have gone home, happy and weary. But a birthday is more than a time for celebration. It is also a time for reflection, for taking stock of where we are and where we are going. Millions of thoughtful Americans considered these questions on July 4, 1976.

If the Declaration of Independence was a Promise from the people of the Thirteen Colonies to the people of the future in the United States, how much of that Promise has been fulfilled? How far do we have to go? The answers are many, because we Americans are many. But the Promise remains unchanged, ringing in these words from the declaration: "We hold these truths to be self-evident, that all men are created equal, that they are endowed by their Creator with certain unalienable Rights, that among these are Life, Liberty and the pursuit of Happiness."

The Way We Sleep

By Ernest L. Hartmann

**Researchers who chart our nighttime journeys
have found two complex states of slumber**

A 30-year-old Frenchman spent more than two years at a sleep-research laboratory where investigators verified that he seldom slept more than 15 minutes a night. At the Boston State Hospital Sleep and Dream Laboratory, we recently studied a 22-year-old graduate student who slept about 16 hours each day for weeks at a time.

Neither person was psychologically normal. The Frenchman suffered nightly from hallucinations and died after two years of his unusual sleep pattern. Although the cause of death was not certain, slight brain abnormalities might have been related to both his unusual sleep pattern and his death. The student was quite depressed and disturbed about her life. After she recovered from her depression, she regularly slept about 7½ hours each night.

Nevertheless, these people and their unusual sleep patterns raise questions that are important to all of us. We spend one-third of our lives in sleep, yet we know relatively little about it. What is sleep? Do all humans and all animals sleep? Do all people need the same amount of sleep? Is dreaming an important part of sleep? These queries lead to the big questions: Do we need to sleep, and if we do, why?

At my sleep laboratory in Boston and at dozens like it throughout the world, researchers study sleepers and search for answers to these questions. Several thousand persons have slept in the bedrooms of these laboratories while polygraphs in special equipment rooms recorded certain body activities on moving paper. If you were to spend a night in a sleep lab, you would don a nightcap made of several electrodes that the experimenter would paste to your face and head. The electrodes detect faint electrical signals caused by brain waves, eye movements, or muscle activity. Electronic equipment in the polygraph processes the signals, and the polygraph traces them as squiggly lines along with patterns of pulse and respiratory rates. A typical night's sleep patterns fill about 1,000 feet (300 meters) of paper.

Some people are unable to sleep normally for the first night or two in a sleep laboratory, but by the third or fourth night recorded sleep patterns usually stabilize. The patterns are surprisingly similar from person to person and from night to night. For example, follow the activities of a typical sleeper, Helen, through a night's sleep. As Helen falls asleep, her muscles gradually relax. Her eyes roll slowly and then stop moving. Her pulse rate and respiratory rate slow down. Helen's brain waves gradually change in a definite four-step sequence. First, the alpha rhythm, the normal pattern of electrical oscillations in the awake brain, drops out. Next, sleep spindles—short bursts of high-frequency brain waves—appear. In the third stage, large-amplitude slow waves begin. After 15 or 20 minutes, these slow waves take over and Helen is in the fourth and deepest stage of sleep.

Deep, slow-wave sleep does not continue throughout the night, however. After about an hour, sleep appears to lighten. Slow waves stop and Helen's brain waves become irregular like those in the first stage. Her eyes begin to move as though she is watching an object move. Pulse rate and breathing become somewhat faster and less regular, and her blood pressure changes from minute to minute.

In many ways, Helen appears to be lightly asleep, yet she is very soundly asleep. Almost as loud a noise is needed to awaken her from this stage as from deep slow-wave sleep. If Helen is awakened, she will likely report that she was dreaming. If left to sleep, however, her eye movements stop after about 5 to 10 minutes, and she progressively returns to the deep slow-wave sleep for another 60 to 90 minutes. Then she has another dream period. This cycle of events repeats itself four or five times during the night. Late in the night, sleep time between

The author:
Ernest L. Hartmann is a professor of psychiatry at the Tufts University School of Medicine and director of the Sleep and Dream Laboratory at Boston State Hospital.

Illustrations by John Faulkner

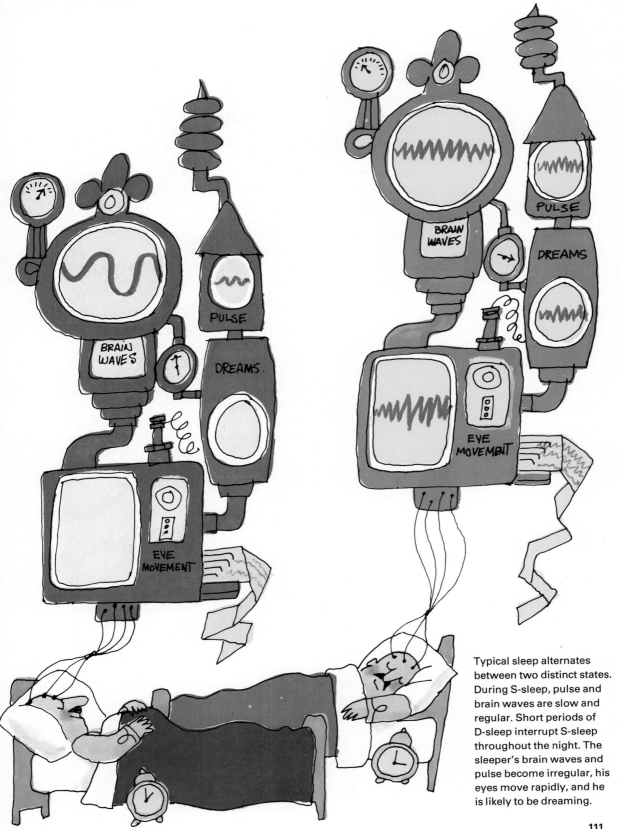

Typical sleep alternates between two distinct states. During S-sleep, pulse and brain waves are slow and regular. Short periods of D-sleep interrupt S-sleep throughout the night. The sleeper's brain waves and pulse become irregular, his eyes move rapidly, and he is likely to be dreaming.

dreams is spent in the second or third stages. Her later dreams last somewhat longer than her first dream, perhaps 20 to 30 minutes. Overall, she dreams for about 100 minutes, or one-fourth of her sleep.

The two distinct states of sleep that we all experience differ in so many ways that they are usually given two separate names. The state characterized by eye movements, dreams, and irregular, desynchronized brain waves is called D-sleep for dreaming or desynchronized sleep. Such sleep is also called rapid eye movement (REM) sleep, or paradoxical sleep, because it is very light in some ways and very deep in others. The other state of sleep—which accounts for three-fourths of sleep time—is called S-sleep for synchronized sleep. It is also referred to as nonrapid eye movement (NREM) sleep or orthodox sleep. S-sleep is characterized by slow brain waves, regular pulse and breathing, and the absence of rapid eye movements. Only rarely do people awakened during S-sleep report that they have been dreaming.

Although we can describe in detail changes in brain waves and body physiology during sleep, these changes are not themselves sleep. Sleep is basically a behavioral state that occurs regularly and is easily reversed; the body is quiet and the person or animal responds less readily to a loud noise or some other prominent external event than when awake. According to this basic behavioral definition, all *vertebrates* (animals with backbones) experience some form of sleep during which their activity stops or almost stops one or more times every 24 hours and they have difficulty responding to their surroundings. Of the five major classes of vertebrates, fish and amphibia show no changes in brain wave patterns along with behavioral sleep, while reptiles show definite changes in brain activity. Clear-cut brain changes relating to sleep have been recorded in birds and mammals. In fact, both D-sleep and S-sleep occur in all mammals that have been studied except in the echidna, a close relative of the platypus.

If mammals experience D-sleep, do they actually dream? We do not yet know how to ask them, but I believe they do dream. You may have watched sleeping dogs and cats move their eyes as if they were running or hunting. The parts of their brains involved with sensation, especially vision, are very active in D-sleep. In one study, monkeys were trained to press a bar whenever they saw pictures projected on a large screen. After these monkeys had been asleep for an hour or two, their paws moved and they seemed to be pressing bars.

We can ask people about their dreams, but only about 2 of every 3 persons normally remember them. Almost every subject recalls dreaming vividly when awakened during D-sleep in the laboratory, however. Light sleepers who awaken several times during the night are likely to remember dreams. People who are very imaginative, introspective, or fascinated by strange or ambiguous things are likely to remember dreams. A conscious interest in dreams also makes a difference in dream recall. You are more likely than usual to remember a dream tonight, simply because you read this article.

The mental events that we call dreams involve pictures, and research shows that most dreams are in color. Unless you recall a dream immediately, however, the color is forgotten quickly. A dream often begins with a bizarre or illogical event followed by a story sequence for a few seconds or minutes until the scene suddenly shifts. Each story unfolds in about the same amount of time that would be required for the same sequence of events in waking life.

The exact meaning of a story sequence cannot be determined by any simple code or key. Sometimes a dream presents an obvious wish or thought that hardly needs interpretation. For example, a child who fell asleep still hungry for some strawberries dreamed, "I ate all the strawberries." Sigmund Freud considered this to be the simplest case of wish fulfillment. He suggested that dreams, when properly understood, are fulfillments of a wish. Not everyone agrees with his view. Some dreams present fears or simply restate in visual terms a problem in the dreamer's mind. There is little question, however, about Freud's major discovery that dreams are meaningful revelations of mental activity, not random events.

In fact, sleep as we now know it in people and animals is definitely an active, not a passive, state. Brain cells are active during sleep. Their

Adults and mature animals spend less time asleep — and experience much less D-sleep — than do infants or young animals.

Adults who regularly sleep at most only six hours a night tend to be ambitious and energetic people who are satisfied with their lives, *above*. Those who sleep at least nine hours each night, however, tend to worry about world problems and change their daily routines often due to dissatisfaction, *opposite*.

activity changes as we slip from waking to S-sleep, and then into D-sleep, but they never turn off. Sleep is also an active state in terms of brain chemistry. Although the details are still uncertain, we know that a substance called serotonin plays an important role in inducing sleep. Because it cannot pass from the blood to the brain, serotonin must be made in the brain from tryptophan, a building block of proteins found in meat and milk. Drinking a glass of milk before bed has a calming psychological effect on many people, and milk may provide a vital chemical factor in sleep.

Sleep is also related to the life of the sleeper. One of the best-known relationships is between sleep and age, and laboratory studies have confirmed that young children sleep more than adults. A newborn child sleeps from 16 to 18 hours a day. Sleep time falls rapidly to about 12 hours daily for 1-year-olds, then gradually drops to 7 or 8 hours in the young adult.

The percentage of time spent in D-sleep falls off even more dramatically than total sleep time. A newborn child spends over half of its 16 hours of sleep in D-sleep, but a young adult spends one-fourth of his sleep in D-sleep and slightly less as he or she grows older. It is hard to imagine what a young infant might be dreaming about for eight hours

—perhaps the joys of nursing at his mother's breast. However, infants are probably incapable of having well-defined dreams before they have well-formed thoughts or images while awake, and this process does not occur until at least 6 to 12 months of age. Whether or not they dream, infants obtain a great deal of D-sleep.

Kittens, puppies, young mice, and most other young mammals always spend more time asleep—and much more time in D-sleep—than do adult mammals. This relationship may be important in eventually answering the big question: Why do we sleep? Whatever it is that sleep does for us, we seem to need more of it when we are very young, a time of rapid body and brain growth and dramatic increases in learning, memory, and other functions of the human mind. Sleep and dreaming may play a crucial role in growth, learning, and memory.

Another way to look at the question of what sleep does for people and animals is to examine the effects of sleep deprivation. If we want to know what vitamin C does for an animal, we can remove vitamin C from its diet and record what happens. In the same way, we can try to find out if animals need sleep and what happens when they do not get it. Such studies indicate that all animals seem to require some sleep in order to survive, especially young animals.

There are two well-known cases of people who went without sleep for extremely long periods of time. Disk jockey Peter Tripp stayed awake continuously for 200 hours in 1959 during a fund-raising marathon. While crowds watched, he broadcast daily from a windowed booth in New York City's Times Square. Tripp appeared unaffected until the final days when he began imagining he heard sounds at night. He also believed that unknown enemies were trying to sabotage his marathon by slipping sleeping pills into his food. Psychiatrists who were observing Tripp's behavior diagnosed this abnormal mental state as "nocturnal psychosis." While in this state of irrational distrust of others, Tripp refused to take tests that sleep researchers had designed to measure changes in his performance.

Tripp's "trip" convinced many people that psychosis was the inevitable outcome of going too long without sleep. But in 1964, 17-year-old San Diego high school student Randy Gardner and two classmates began a science fair project to break the world record for continuous wakefulness. Every six hours, Randy's classmates tested and recorded his performance on such tasks as identifying familiar smells and remembering numbers. On the fourth day, a U.S. Navy physician volunteered to supervise the project. On the seventh day, William C. Dement, a psychiatrist at Stanford University, began monitoring Randy's brain waves. The youth stayed awake easily during the day, but he had to stay active in order to avoid sleep at night. Throughout the test he showed no signs of mental imbalance other than a few brief hallucinations toward the end. By the end of his 11-day vigil, Randy was the center of national attention. He conducted a press conference, then slept for nearly 15 hours. He resumed his normal sleep pattern after only one night of long sleep.

Randy was in top physical condition, and the attention of newsmen boosted his strong motivation. Sleep researchers believe that high motivation and good physical condition are necessary for prolonged sleeplessness. They also tend to discount the notion that sleeplessness necessarily causes the kind of mental state that Peter Tripp experienced. They view sleeplessness as just one possible stressful situation that can trigger a mental breakdown.

In fact, our studies of subjects who were deprived of sleep show few dramatic effects. When a person goes without sleep for just one day or a few days there are few measurable body changes. Your pulse rate may be high and your brain waves slightly slower, but neither of these changes is very striking. Although you may feel miserable, you can still spell, do arithmetic tests, and perform similar brief tasks surprisingly well. However, you are likely to perform badly on really long and boring tests. You may even fall asleep for brief periods while trying to do such tests. In addition to a generally tired look and physical dragging, people who are deprived of sleep have trouble dealing with others. When very sleepy, both children and adults tend to be irritable, grouchy, easily upset, and generally unpleasant.

By monitoring a sleeper's brain waves and waking him at the right time, we have deprived people of only D-sleep or only deep S-sleep. One study showed that depriving a person of D-sleep could cause personality changes, even a mental breakdown. Recent carefully controlled studies have not shown anything so dramatic. We now believe that lack of D-sleep may produce some difficulty in normal attention and learning functions and in social interaction, while a lack of deep S-sleep produces a sort of physical tiredness. These findings suggest that D-sleep is necessary for mental restoration and S-sleep is needed to prevent physical fatigue.

Although all humans and mammals require some sleep, we do not all need the same amount. Our sleep laboratory in Boston recently completed several studies of long and short sleepers in collaboration with physician Frederick Baekeland of the State University of New York at Brooklyn. We wanted to find out if people with different sleep needs act and think differently. We were interested in those who always slept unusually long or short periods. We were not interested in students who sometimes slept for four or five hours and then caught up after exams, nor in insomniacs, those who have difficulty in sleeping. We advertised in newspapers for individuals who always slept more than nine hours per day (long sleepers) or less than six hours (short sleepers) and functioned normally on that amount. We selected 30 and studied each of them for eight nights in the sleep laboratory.

We found interesting differences in life style and personality. The short sleepers as a group were efficient, energetic, generally ambitious people who tended to work hard and to keep busy. They seemed to be satisfied with themselves and their lives and had few complaints about the laboratory, their lives, or the state of the world. Most of them were extroverts and they seldom stopped to think about problems. In marked contrast, many of the long sleepers were mildly anxious or depressed and complained of minor aches and pains and concerns. They also expressed far more worry and concern about serious world problems than did the short sleepers. In computer terms, we found ourselves thinking of the short sleepers as "preprogrammed"—they had a way of doing things that worked well and they did not vary their routine much from day to day. On the other hand, the long sleepers tended to be dissatisfied with their programs and often changed them.

Some famous men and geniuses reputedly were either very long or very short sleepers. Thomas A. Edison and Napoleon Bonaparte got along on from four to six hours of sleep per day, while Albert Einstein was a very long sleeper at times. Their sleep patterns tend to agree with our findings. Edison and Napoleon were efficient, hard-working men who achieved in an active, worldly sense. Einstein was a deep thinker who also worried a great deal about general world problems.

Our laboratory tests show clearly that long sleepers and short sleepers, despite the difference in total sleep, had identical amounts of the third and fourth stages of S-sleep. The major difference between the two groups was in D-sleep—the long sleepers had twice as much D-sleep as the short sleepers. Using the number of rapid eye movements during D-sleep as a rough measure of the intensity of a dreaming period, we found that the long sleepers had three times as many eye movements as the short sleepers. The long sleepers also remembered their dreams much more often. Perhaps we all need about the same amount of deep S-sleep, while our needs for D-sleep, and dreaming, differ depending on our personalities and our life styles.

To learn if an individual's sleep needs can change, we studied several hundred persons whom we classed as variable sleepers. All of them had stable enough sleep patterns so that they could note changes. On questionnaires and in interviews, they reported periods of weeks or months when they slept either much longer or shorter times than usual. We then tried to find out as much as possible about what was going on in their lives during those periods. The only common characteristic during periods when some subjects needed less sleep was that they said "everything was going well." We found some physical situations associated with the need for more sleep. For example, those who greatly increased their exercise slept more, especially if they were unused to heavy exercise. Women slept more when they were preg-

Most dreams are in color, and some express thorny problems in vivid pictures in the dreamer's mind.

nant. Certain psychological situations were almost always associated with the need for more sleep–greater mental activity, periods of stress, such as a new job, and depression or worry.

One man was a striking case of a changing need for sleep. He had spent his twenties as a physical laborer. He did reasonably heavy work, but not much thinking or worrying, and slept about seven hours per night. At age 30 he enrolled in a university, and his life changed a great deal as a student. He had to study and learn a tremendous amount and was under stress because of his goals, the way he spent his time, and the competition with bright, younger students. He reported that he then required about nine hours of sleep–almost two hours more than previously. At times, people sleep more or less when it is convenient for them to do so, but this young man needed more sleep at a stressful time when it would have been convenient for him to sleep less in order to study more.

These studies of variable sleepers led us to the same conclusions as did the studies of long and short sleepers. People seem to need more sleep during times of worry, change, or new learning; they require less sleep when they are not worrying and when everything is going well. A number of experiments in which conditions of worry, stress, or new learning are artificially created tend to support this view. For example, subjects fitted with inverting prisms–eyeglasses that make the world appear upside down–seemed to need more D-sleep while they adjusted to the unusual situation.

Sleep researchers are also studying a state that we all find ourselves in frequently–tiredness. They have found at least two distinct patterns of tiredness. There is a tiredness that comes after a day of purely physical activity–usually a relaxed or even pleasant feeling in the muscles, without accompanying mental change. The second kind comes after a tough mental or emotional day. Our muscles are somewhat tense, we may have a headache, and we are often uncomfortable, irritable, and unable to concentrate. When this second kind of tiredness appears in children, we often say they are "just too tired to get to sleep." It seems logical to associate the two kinds of tiredness with the two states of sleep. The first state, physical tiredness, may indicate a need for S-sleep, the second a need for D-sleep.

From all of these studies, my conclusion is that sleep serves a definite role in keeping with a common-sense notion–sleep restores. William Shakespeare said it best, "Sleep that knits up the ravel'd sleave of care." In fact, it may serve two related restorative functions. S-sleep appears to be a time of physical restoration, while D-sleep appears to be a time of mental restoration that is especially necessary during times of worry, stress, and new learning. S-sleep, which always precedes D-sleep in healthy people, may play a preparatory role in the functions of D-sleep. In chemical terms, the body makes large molecules during S-sleep that the brain may need for mental restoration during D-sleep.

Insomnia, the inability to sleep, may be caused by worry or by more serious psychological or medical problems. But sleeping pills, unless wisely used, can turn a temporary case of sleeplessness into a drug habit that actually causes insomnia.

Many sleep researchers do not agree with the idea that sleep restores. One alternative view is that sleep kept our ancestors out of harm's way in the distant past but has no definite restorative function now. In other words, it was once advantageous for a human or small mammal to curl up in a place safe from enemies and to save energy. Those who hold this view claim that sleep has persisted since then as a sort of habit, and that we might not need to sleep at all if we could figure out how to break the habit. This theory, however, does not explain why so few people who try can sleep less than five or six hours, nor does it explain the complexity and richness of the two distinctly different states of sleep.

In any case, if sleep does have a restorative function, it performs the function well. Most of us spend our waking time reasonably well rested, and this may be why we pay little attention to the one-third of our lives spent sleeping. However, many people often think about their sleep because they have serious sleep problems. For instance, a person who has narcolepsy falls asleep in the daytime and occasionally suffers cataplectic attacks, a sudden loss of muscle control. The patient may collapse unconscious, even during an exciting activity. Sleep recordings show that narcolepsy appears to be related to too much D-sleep at the wrong time. D-sleep occurs early during the night and also during daytime sleeps.

Treatments are now available for narcolepsy and another recently discovered illness, sleep apnea. The apnea patient complains either of feeling sleepy all day, of his sleep not doing much good, or of difficulty in remaining asleep. All-night sleep recordings show that his breathing often stops for periods of 15 seconds or more during sleep. The patient awakens, takes a few breaths, goes back to sleep, and then the pattern repeats itself. Some people have hundreds of apnea attacks during a single night. When the apnea is caused by a physical condition in the throat or surrounding areas, a small operation can sometimes prevent further attacks. When the brain is responsible, treatment is more difficult, but stimulant medication can help.

These somewhat special sleep disorders occur far less often than insomnia, which represents a great public-health problem because millions of people who get insufficient sleep do not work efficiently, and they spend more than $1 billion annually on various sleep remedies. These sleep potions range from weak, sometimes ineffective pills that you can buy without a prescription to potent prescribed medications. Used as remedies for insomnia, drugs can be worse than the disease. For example, a person may begin taking a drug to get more sleep. However, he may soon be sleeping less again and then must raise the dosage or face the sleepless discomfort of withdrawal. Eventually, what may have started as a minor case of insomnia caused by worry ends up in chronic insomnia and drug dependency.

We all experience temporary insomnia when faced with an impending important task or extra worries that we cannot quickly resolve. The important point is that insomnia is a symptom—the result of one or more causes. Hypnotics in carefully controlled dosages can relieve the symptom, but it is essential to discover the cause of the insomnia—whether it be medical, psychological, or simply something in the environment—and then correct or treat the cause.

Sleep research holds promise of discovering cures for specified sleep disorders, but its greatest use may be in helping us to better understand the mind and the body and thus eventually help society with many ills not specifically connected with sleep. For instance, many psychologists and psychiatrists active in sleep research are interested in the similarity between the way we all function in our dreams and the way certain psychotic persons function while awake. Now that we know when someone is dreaming, we can better examine the biology of the dreaming state. Understanding the biology of dreaming may help us to understand the biology of mental illness and to develop more effective treatments. But beyond these intriguing medical payoffs lies the fundamental question: Why sleep? Until we know, sleep researchers will continue their sleepless vigils while machines chart their subjects' journeys through the night, and they will look for clues in the squiggly lines left behind.

Who Discovered America Second?

By Peter Gwynne

The Indians were first, but adventurers from many countries may have braved the oceans to reach the New World before Columbus

Brendan, Ericson, Hanno, Herjulfsson, Hoei-shin, Hoel, Madoc, Maol, Pining, Scolvus, Zeno—these names might be found in the telephone directory of any large city in the United States or Canada. But the list is really an exclusive one with significance in American history. Each name belongs to an explorer reputed to have discovered the New World before Christopher Columbus landed on Oct. 12, 1492.

Every few years, an expert or amateur in archaeology, ancient history, lost languages, or boat navigation produces new and apparently compelling evidence for the primacy of some previously unheralded discoverer who landed on American shores before Columbus. These

Some say that Egyptians actually reached the New World in ancient times. Norwegian explorer Thor Heyerdahl sailed the papyrus-reed boat *Ra 2* across the Atlantic Ocean in 1970 to prove that they could have done it.

claims often cause distress and indignation among Italian Americans, archaeologists, and others. But every new claim delights those who share a national heritage with the newly reputed explorer. And because the list of early explorers is a long one, most American ethnic groups can point to one of their own as the real finder of the Western Hemisphere. As the title of one book succinctly puts it, "They All Discovered America."

The evidence for these pre-Columbian explorers is limited. Many of the claims are based merely on nationalistic myths and legends that have been embellished by reports of strange finds in remote parts of the New World—tales of pale Indian tribes, peculiar markings on rocks, and unusual religious practices. Some of the claims are based on all but unprovable resemblances between the pottery of ancient Asian and Mediterranean peoples and that of certain American Indian tribes. And some partisans have gone so far as to sail across the ocean in primitive vessels to demonstrate that the explorers they champion also could have made such a trip to America.

Among anthropologists, the arguments for and against the various claims of pre-Columbian discovery are held by those known as *diffusionists* and *antidiffusionists*. The diffusionists argue that objects of similar design found in two different parts of the world must be evidence of some contact between the people who used the objects. They say that the same invention cannot be made independently by several different people. The antidiffusionists, on the other hand, argue that such independent invention must have occurred many times in history, and that it is the only way to account for the multitude of similarities between the crafts and customs of the Old and New Worlds.

Of course, the term *discovery* is actually a misnomer. *Rediscovery* would be more correct, because no one doubts that the people who became the American Indians were the first to find the continents of the New World. Most archaeologists think the Indians first came to North America between 20,000 and 40,000 years ago by walking from Asia over a land bridge that once linked Siberia with Alaska. A few experts place the long march much further back in time. What is indisputable is that Indians peopled the entire hemisphere by 9000 B.C. from Alaska above the Arctic Circle to Cape Horn, close to the Antarctic. If the legends are to be believed, the descendants of those settlers greeted a succession of adventurers from Europe, Asia, and Africa before Columbus' ships arrived.

The earliest claim—so far—for pre-Columbian discovery comes from Turkey. Scholars in Turkey reported in the mid-1960s that the languages of the Mayans and Aztecs, the Indians who lived in Central America and the northern part of South America before Columbus arrived, contained words of Turkish origin. They also argued that Mayan and Aztec stone architecture resembled Turkish designs of 7,000 years ago. They concluded that Turks must have followed the Indians over the land bridge between Siberia and Alaska about 5000

The author:
Peter Gwynne is science editor of *Newsweek* magazine.

B.C. Like many of the other claims, this one is basically circumstantial; there is no direct evidence.

The same applies to a claim that Japanese preceded Columbus. The 1964 discovery in Ecuador of pottery decorated in a fashion similar to pottery made in ancient Japan about 2500 B.C. led archaeologists Betty Meggers and Clifford Evans of the Smithsonian Institution to theorize that people from that nation somehow managed to sail across the Pacific Ocean in prehistoric times.

There is also circumstantial evidence that adventurers came from the other side of the world, crossing the Atlantic Ocean about 1100 B.C. According to Italian archaeologist Mario Gattoni Celli of the Institute of Etruscan Studies in Florence, the traditional customs of the Akawayo Indians of Guyana and Surinam on the north coast of South America are so similar to those of the ancient Etruscans that a link between the two peoples is almost certain. The Etruscans lived in northern Italy more than 3,000 years ago, controlled trade in the Mediterranean Sea, and were among the first people to use the metallurgical technology of the Iron Age. But it was their religion that convinced Celli of their link with the New World. Both the Akawayo Indians and the Etruscans used religious symbols that show men with wings. Furthermore, some words in the two languages are similar. However, most other archaeologists disagree with Celli's conclusions and point out that many people in widely separated parts of the world have independently developed similar cultural practices.

There are also those who claim that Egyptian ships, sailing under orders from the pharaohs, crossed the Mediterranean and then the Atlantic Ocean to reach the New World. They point to a map drawn

The pyramid at Chiapas in Mexico, *below left,* is strikingly similar to stepped Zoser pyramid at Saqqarah, Egypt, and provides proof to some people of ancient contact between the builders of the Old and New Worlds.

How They Reached America

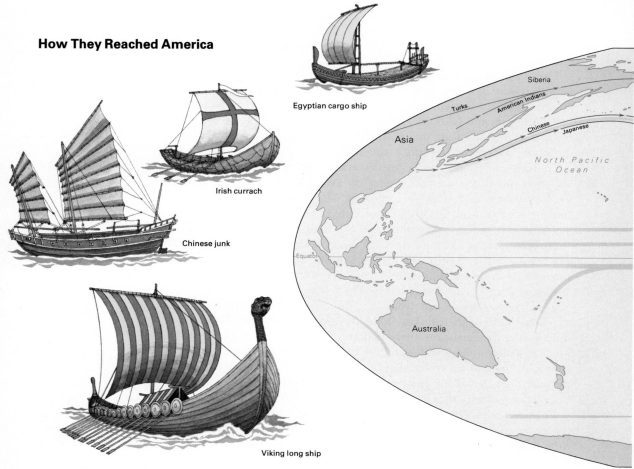

Egyptian cargo ship

Irish currach

Chinese junk

Viking long ship

Siberia

Turks

American Indians

Chinese

Japanese

Asia

North Pacific Ocean

Equator

Australia

The evidence of arrival is often hazy, but ocean and wind currents suggest that ancient explorers could have reached the Americas.

for the Turkish Admiral Piri Reis in A.D. 1513, which outlines the eastern coastline of South America in surprisingly accurate detail and also gives the correct distance from Africa. The post-Columbian date of this map is remarkable only in that the map was based on maps from the great library of Alexandria, Egypt, a structure that was totally destroyed sometime before A.D. 640.

In less concrete terms, scholars have suggested that Egyptians influenced the development by the pre-Columbian civilizations of South and Central America of their sophisticated calendars, hieroglyphics, and pyramids between 3,000 and 4,000 years ago. At that time, the Egyptians sailed the Mediterranean in rafts made of thin papyrus reeds. In A.D. 1969, Norwegian explorer Thor Heyerdahl, who had sailed a balsa-wood raft, the *Kon-Tiki*, across the South Pacific from Peru to the Polynesian islands in 1947, decided to prove that a papyrus raft could actually make it across the Atlantic Ocean.

Heyerdahl copied his papyrus boat, *Ra*, after the ancient Egyptian craft, with a curved prow and stern, a broad beam, and a square, brown-cotton sail. He then set out to pilot it across the Atlantic, but

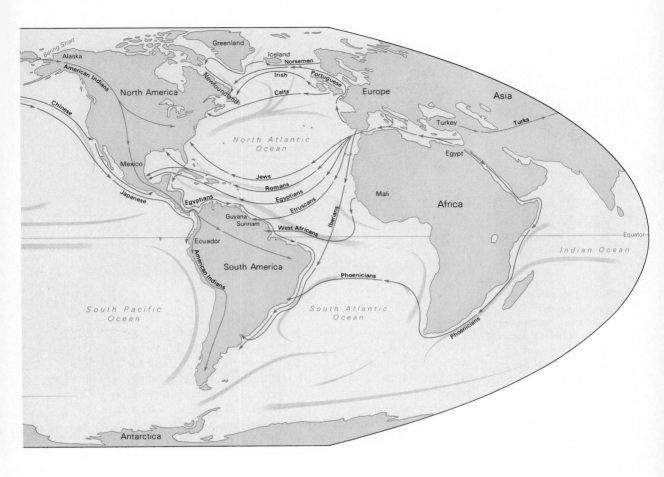

failed. However, on the second try, in 1970, Heyerdahl managed to sail *Ra-2* from Morocco to Barbados in the West Indies in 57 days. "I think we have proved what we set out to do," he stated.

According to pre-Columbian buffs, there was a surge of discovery and settlement on American shores starting in about 800 B.C. Investigations and interpretations by Barry Fell suggest that North America hosted at least two major groups of settlers and one major voyage of discovery during the period from 800 to 200 B.C. Fell, a Harvard University marine biologist, became interested in ancient voyages as a result of his research into ocean currents.

He believes that Basques, from the region that is now northern Portugal and Spain, lived in the Susquehanna Valley, about 100 miles (160 kilometers) from what is now Philadelphia, from 800 to 600 B.C. Fell cites a series of inscriptions on about 400 stones collected in the area in the 1940s. These writings had earlier been dismissed as the scrawls of illiterate Vikings. However, Fell believes that they are related to Bronze Age writings found in the ancient province of Trás-os-Montes, in present-day northern Portugal.

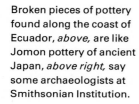

Broken pieces of pottery found along the coast of Ecuador, *above,* are like Jomon pottery of ancient Japan, *above right,* say some archaeologists at Smithsonian Institution.

Fell worked out the language, which he called Lusitanian, and dated it by its relation to the Punic dialect the Phoenicians used. According to Fell's translations, the inscriptions include such words and phrases as "alas" and "I remain in tears," suggesting that the stones were gravestones. And references to women and children, such as "Anez, a little girl of three summers," indicate to him that the stones were put there by settlers rather than explorers.

According to other stone inscriptions examined by Fell in New Hampshire and Vermont, another group of Europeans, a company of Celts, was making itself comfortable in the New World between 800 and 200 B.C. Fell and his colleagues in the Epigraphic Society, which studies ancient languages, have identified writings on stones found at Mystery Hill, near North Salem, N.H., and in the foothills of Vermont's Green Mountains as ogam, the language of the ancient Celts who once lived from southwestern Germany to Spain and the British Isles. According to the translations, these settlers boasted such names as Hoel, Maol, and Da. Fell suggests they died out as a distinct race because of intermarriage with Indian tribes.

The most controversial claim asserted by Fell centers on a voyage by a group of sailors he describes as Iberians, who apparently sailed from the southern tip of Spain and disembarked at various points along the shores of North and South America about 480 B.C. Fell is convinced that stone inscriptions located as far afield as Sherbrooke, Canada; Tihosuco, Mexico; and Paraguay were written in a combination of Iberian Punic, a language spoken in the Spanish port of Cádiz 2,500 years ago, and Libyan, which was spoken in ancient Carthage on the North African coast at about the same time. Fell's translations indicate that a sea captain named Hanno, who is also identified in ancient Greek accounts as a circumnavigator of Africa, marked various parts of the American coast with proclamations that have the flavor of the World War II catch phrase "Kilroy was here." One typical example is "Hanno, out of Tamu, reached this place."

Experts in ancient languages question Fell's academic qualifications to identify and translate what they regard as nothing more than meaningless scratches on stones. They question the type of sentiments expressed in his translations, saying they sound like statements by such modern adventurers as Arctic explorer Richard E. Byrd. "A Punic inscription that sounds as if it came straight from Admiral Byrd is obviously a hoax. They just didn't write that way," asserts Yale University history professor Robert S. Lopez. The wide variety of languages and locations that Fell reports also concerns pre-Columbian scholars. "He is doing too much cross-country running," says Frank M. Cross, a Harvard professor of Semitic languages.

But Fell has his defenders. "In general, Fell strikes me as very original, very much a genius," says Swiss linguistics professor Linus Brunner of the University of Neuchatel. And language professor Thomas Lee of Laval University in Quebec says that Fell's contentions can be proved or disproved only after long and painstaking study by experts in linguistics and pre-Columbian archaeology. "Until that is done," Lee says, "I don't see how criticism can be valid."

Another man who arouses anger among members of the archaeological establishment is Cyrus H. Gordon, who recently retired as professor of Mediterranean Studies at Brandeis University in Waltham, Mass. Gordon's interpretations hint that Phoenicians and Jews traveled from the eastern edges of the Mediterranean to the Western Hemisphere several times between 600 B.C. and A.D. 200.

Gordon's evidence for the Phoenicians, who were itinerant merchants in ancient times, is a copy of a stone inscription, since lost, that was found by plantation slaves in Paraíba, Brazil, in 1872. Until a decade ago, Gordon and other scholars thought the copy was a sophisticated forgery. Then the Brandeis professor re-examined the text and decided that some of the grammar and vocabulary paralleled that in authentic Phoenician texts. The Paraíba inscription starts: "We are Sidonian Canaanites from the city of the merchant king. We were cast up on this distant island, a land of mountains. . . ." Idiosyncrasies of the script and references in it put the date of the inscription at 531 B.C., according to Gordon.

But his critics strongly disagree. "It says just what someone who wants to believe that the Phoenicians crossed the Atlantic would want it to say," complains archaeologist Gordon F. Eckholm of the American Museum of Natural History in New York City. And Harvard's Frank Cross declares the inscription is a hodgepodge of Phoenician writing from different periods.

Gordon's case for Jewish exploration results from his interpretation of markings on another stone, discovered when Smithsonian archaeologists excavated an ancient grave at Bat Creek in Monroe County,

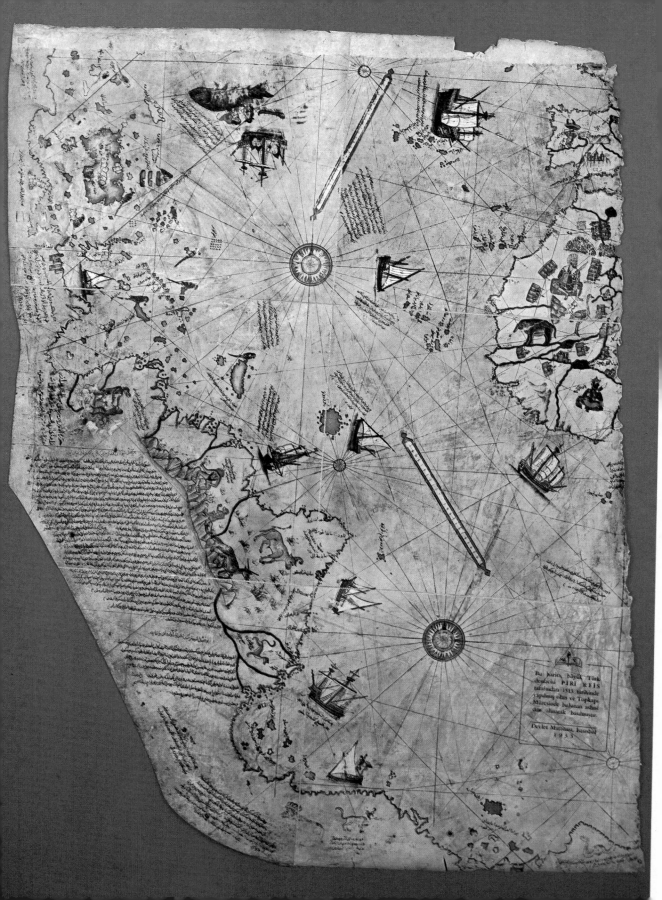

Tennessee, in the 1880s. They believed the markings to be written in Cherokee, but Gordon decided that the writing is ancient Hebrew from the first or second century A.D. He argues that the lettering is clearly old-script Hebrew and that, though the inscription is short, it includes the word *Judea*. He speculates that it was inscribed by Jews who had fled their homeland in A.D. 78 or between 132 and 135 after an unsuccessful revolt against the Romans.

It was about this time in history, if circumstance is a reliable guide, that the Romans began to extend their declining empire to the New World. In 1961, West German archaeologist Robert Heine-Geldern dug up a sculptured head in Calixtlahuaca, Mexico, that he ascribed to Roman origin from about A.D. 200. Several years earlier, Joseph Bray of Louisville, Ky., discovered buried Roman coins from the 100s in his backyard. Are these coincidences, hoaxes, or real evidence of Roman voyages? Nobody knows. Most archaeologists discount them. In the case of the Roman coins, Israel T. Naamani, an expert on the Middle East at the University of Louisville, says that he suspects the coins were minted recently rather than in ancient times.

Copy of a map drawn for Turkish Admiral Piri Reis in 1513 has African and South American coasts in surprisingly accurate detail. The map is said to be based on maps from a library in Alexandria, Egypt, that was ruined by fire about A.D. 640.

An ancient Chinese narrative provides the claim of an Asian-American pioneer. In 1962, Chinese linguists translated Buddhist monk Hoei-shin's account of a voyage with four companions in 459 from China to a land far to the east. The monk's diary accurately describes the customs of tribes that lived in Mexico and Central America at the time, particularly those of a Mayan tribe known as the Itzas.

Researchers at the University of California's Institute of Archaeology in Los Angeles added a small but intriguing piece of evidence to the Chinese puzzle in 1975. Their study of mysterious boulders discovered by scuba divers Wayne Baldwin and Bob Meistrell in 15 to 30 feet (4.5 to 9 meters) of water off California's Palos Verdes Peninsula indicated that these might be ancient Asian anchors. Such anchors were used by the Chinese. The stones weighed from 150 to 700 pounds (70 to 320 kilograms), and each had a hole, obviously man-made, in its center. The archaeologists said that the stones, which are perhaps 1,000 years old, could not have been produced by Indians that lived in the region. However, James Muche, an archaeologist working for the Fathom 8 diving organization, says that he doubts that the stones are more than 100 years old, because they were not covered with enough marine growth when found to have been underwater longer.

One of the most compelling claims to the rediscovery of America is that of the Irish. A mixture of legend, saga, and observation suggests that the Irish landed on the shores of the New World sometime before 1000. The most famous legend concerns Saint Brendan, who set forth on an island-hopping journey with a crew of monks from his Clefort monastery in Galway about the year 650 to convert the people of the North Atlantic islands to Christianity. During the seven-year missionary voyage, according to an odyssey written in the 1000s, Brendan and his companions encountered a miraculous array of creatures and places, including sea birds that sang psalms, Judas Iscariot, numerous Irish monasteries, and a whale on whose back they prepared a fire. Some people believe that these well-traveled monks must have beached on an American shore sometime during their wanderings.

Brendan himself may or may not have made it, but there is strong evidence that others of Irish descent did between 600 and 1000. According to the Icelandic sagas, which recount the exploits of the Norsemen in the North Atlantic, the pagan Vikings drove the Christian Irish from settlements in Iceland late in the 800s. The sagas report that most of the Irishmen sailed back to their homeland, but at least one band drifted west over the ocean.

No Irish artifacts have been located in North America. But the late geographer Carl O. Sauer of the University of California, Berkeley, argued in *Northern Mists* (1968) that there is plenty of indirect evidence of Irish occupation in Newfoundland, Canada. This evidence includes the remains of an iron-smelting industry similar to that of craftsmen in Ireland, as well as reports by early French missionaries in Canada of an Algonquin Indian ceremony similar to the Irish Roman Catholic observance of Passion Week.

In 1976, English author Timothy Severin decided to do for the Irish what Thor Heyerdahl did for the Egyptians. He built a *currach,* a boat with leather stretched over a wooden frame that has been used in Ireland at least since Saint Brendan's time. Severin's boat was large enough to carry a crew of 14, the number said to have accompanied Saint Brendan some 1,300 years ago. Severin and a four-man crew—to prove that someone of Brendan's time could have made it to the New

Joseph Bray of Louisville, Ky., holds Roman coin he found buried in his backyard. The two sides of the coin were stamped with Hebrew inscriptions, a common practice in ancient times when the money of one nation was used by another.

Remains of an ancient house that was found at L'Anse aux Meadows in Newfoundland mark the site of an early Viking settlement in America.

World—sailed the little vessel from Crosshaven, Ireland, to Iceland, a voyage that took two months. They went no farther, leaving the boat there in the hope of completing the journey in the summer of 1977.

Even if the Vikings didn't drive the Irish as far as the New World, there is unassailable evidence that the Norsemen themselves reached North America and had a small settlement there for many decades. The Vikings conquered much of Ireland in the early Middle Ages, reached Iceland in 870, and sailed to Greenland 115 years later. The leader of the Greenland expedition was Eric the Red, who had been banished as an outlaw from the Iceland colony. After he found Greenland, Eric went back to Iceland and persuaded 15 shiploads of emigrants to return with him and start a settlement in Greenland.

About 1000, according to the Norse sagas, Eric's son Leif met a Norwegian named Bjarni Herjulfsson, who had touched on two well-forested lands to the west of Greenland after missing his course. Herjulfsson subsequently disappeared into the mists of history. But Leif Ericson sailed to this land of salmon streams and meadows full of wild berries that could be pressed into wine. He named it Vinland.

When the Icelandic sagas that told of Vinland were published in 1837, they set off a flurry of activity aimed at locating the site of the Vinland colony. But the search produced no concrete evidence for 125 years. Supposedly Viking inscriptions found in Minnesota in 1898 and in Oklahoma in the early 1900s were largely discredited. Even the famous Vinland map owned by the British Museum, reportedly drawn about 1440, was eventually proved to be a forgery.

By then, however, the Norsemen's claim had been established by Norwegian archaeologists Anne and Helge Ingstad, who found a site at L'Anse aux Meadows in northern Newfoundland, Canada, in 1961 that contained the traces of two large homes similar in design to that of the indisputably Norse dwellings in Greenland. Subsequent excavations have confirmed that this settlement lasted for scores of years—but that the Vikings did not live there when Columbus made his voyage.

This colony probably died out because of dwindling communication between Scandinavia and its far-western Viking settlements. After the bubonic plague scourged Europe in the 1300s, the visits of supply ships to Iceland, Greenland, and Vinland must have diminished. No ships from Europe visited Greenland after 1412. The little settlement founded at Vinland by Leif Ericson slowly starved and died out by the mid-1400s. Some persons have also suggested that it might have been destroyed by hostile Indians.

The Vikings did not, apparently, make the last voyages to America before Columbus. Harvard botany professor Li Hui-lin announced in 1961 that his perusal of Chinese documents relating to early diplomatic contacts between the Chinese and the Arabs indicated an Arab presence in South America. The records discussed journeys in which Arab sailors traveled "due west for full a hundred days ... in ships with sails as wide as clouds." As evidence that America was the final destination of the voyagers about 1100, Li cited descriptions of plants and

One of the first pictures of Columbus' discovery of America shows three ships, the king of Spain, and some welcoming Indians. It illustrated a letter from Columbus that was printed in Florence, Italy, in 1493.

animals otherwise unknown to the Old World before Columbus. They included "a gigantic gourd big enough to feed 20 to 30 people"–presumably a pumpkin–and "a tall sheep with a tail as broad as a fan"–probably a guanaco, a South American animal related to the llama.

West Africa has also found support as a starting point for pre-Columbian explorers. The early Arab historian Ibn Fadi Allah al-Omari reported two expeditions into the Atlantic by sailors from the Mali Empire during the early 1300s. The historian's text is not clear on whether the sailors reached the New World, but American anthropologists have found skeletons in the Virgin Islands predating Columbus that resemble those found in Africa. In February 1975, for example, Smithsonian Institution scientists reported that the teeth of an individual buried in the Virgin Islands in 1250 had been broken in a ritual manner peculiar to the people of some early African cultures.

One purported journey has been commemorated by the Daughters of the American Revolution. In 1953, the group erected a bronze marker at Fort Morgan, overlooking Alabama's Mobile Bay. There, according to the marker inscription, Prince Madoc ap Owain Gwynedd of Wales, who made two trips to the New World, landed after his second voyage in 1170. According to legend, the prince recruited settlers to take back with him on his second trip, after finding the American shoreline a year earlier. He was never heard of again in Wales. But there were occasional reports in the 1700s and 1800s of fair-skinned, blue-eyed Indians whose languages bore an uncanny resemblance to Welsh. The Comanche, Conestoga, Delaware, Shawnee, and other tribes both real and imaginary, have all been designated by one person or another as the pale-skinned, blue-eyed, Welsh-speaking Indians.

And the list continues. A story printed in Venice, Italy, in 1558 credits the Venetian Zeno brothers with discovery of huge islands in the western Atlantic in 1380. The Danes have a legend that two Danish pirates named Pining and Pothorst were piloted to North America in 1476 by a Pole, Johannes Scolvus. The Portuguese argue that their extraordinarily skilled sailors must have reached the New World by accident or design in the early 1400s. The French and Hindus also make such claims. Some English sources claim that Bristol merchants financed sailors who discovered America in 1480.

Who really was the first to reach America after the Indians? No one knows. Even if one of the many claims was conclusively proved, this would not reduce the importance of Columbus' voyage. His voyage, in contrast to the others, will always hold a high place in history because it was followed by a series of successes by other European explorers.

But we can be sure that as long as the American continents remain the nationalistic melting pots they are today, the debate will continue. It is a great and fascinating mystery, comparable to that of whether or not beings from other planets ever visited the earth, but it is a mystery with many more clues and intriguing details.

Last Chance For the Sea Turtle

By Archie Carr

Scientists are working to plug the gaps in our knowledge of the life of the sea turtle — and to save it from extinction

Never in the memory of the Torres Strait islanders had the big sea turtles failed to arrive for their yearly nesting on the beaches of Bramble Cay, 75 miles (120 kilometers) north of Cape York, Australia. Every year, hundreds of female green turtles, some of them weighing as much as 400 pounds (180 kilograms), dragged themselves onto the sandy beaches. They would make their way onto the shore and each one would dig a shallow hole in the sand with her flippers and lay her spherical eggs in it, usually as many as 100 or more. This done, she would carefully fill the hole, pushing in sand with her hind flippers to cover the eggs and throwing sand about with her front flippers to conceal the site. Then she would crawl ponderously back to the water. Each female might repeat this process several times, then disappear until the next nesting season, leaving the many turtle eggs to hatch in the warm, moist sand.

But in 1975 only a few sea turtles came back to Bramble Cay, and the turtle hunters who live on the neighboring islands of Torres Strait –which lies between Australia and New Guinea–are worried. Their lives have long been interlocked with the annual cycle of the green turtle. It provides them with meat and eggs to eat. The mysterious failure of the turtles to appear for the annual nesting poses a serious threat to these islanders' food supply.

With the help of the Australian government, the Torres Strait islanders had been trying for several years to develop small turtle farms to provide a constant supply of these animals, whose meat would go into international trade. On some of the islands, the farms were stocked with eggs taken from the huge Bramble Cay nesting ground. But in 1975, for the first time, Bramble Cay could not provide nearly enough eggs for the turtle farms.

Nobody has the vaguest idea why the turtles failed to appear. Something must have happened to them either in their home feeding grounds or along their migratory routes to Bramble Cay. Since nobody knows where the turtles go when they leave the beach, there is nothing the islanders or anybody else can do but hope that the failure of the nesting is only temporary, that it does not signal the disappearance of the green sea turtle as a breeding visitor to their islands.

One colony of another kind of green turtle, one known as the East Pacific black turtle, will probably disappear forever if fishermen using scuba-diving equipment continue to kill its members in great numbers. Scientists only recently learned that these turtles hibernate in the Gulf of California, between Sonora state and Baja California in Mexico, lying half-buried in the bottom mud during winter months. This was the first evidence that any kind of sea turtle hibernates.

However, the Seri Indians, a primitive hunting and fishing tribe in Sonora, have known for a long time that these turtles hibernate, and they have adapted accordingly, spearing the sleeping reptiles with long harpoons from boats. But in 1972, Mexican fishermen with scuba equipment and motorized boats also found the hibernating grounds. Now they are rapidly wiping out the unique turtle colony–and with it, the meat supply of the Seri Indians.

Human destruction cannot be blamed for the crisis facing another species of sea turtle, the huge leatherback. These turtles nested for many years on the Organabo beach along the French Guiana coast, 90 miles (145 kilometers) northwest of Devils Island. That leatherback nesting site, which may have been the largest in the world, was found only in 1968 by zoologist Peter Pritchard of the Florida Audubon Society. In 1975, ocean storms devastated the shore at Organabo, leaving no suitable sand for the leatherbacks to nest in. Turtles frustrated in their nesting sometimes shift to another shore. Sometimes they drop their eggs in the water, where no young can hatch. What most of the Organabo colony of leatherbacks will do when their next egg-laying season comes remains to be seen. Some apparently found

The author:
Archie Carr, professor of zoology at the University of Florida, is a leading expert on green turtles.

**The Five Kinds of Sea Turtles:
What They Weigh and How Big They Are**

Green turtle
Chelonia mydas
36 to 48 inches (91 to 122 centimeters)
250 to 450 pounds (113 to 204 kilograms)

Leatherback turtle
Dermochelys coriacea
54 to 70 inches (137 to 178 centimeters)
650 to 1,200 pounds (295 to 544 kilograms)

Loggerhead turtle
Caretta caretta
31 to 45 inches (79 to 114 centimeters)
170 to 350 pounds (77 to 159 kilograms)

Hawksbill turtle
Eretmochelys imbricata
30 to 35 inches (76 to 89 centimeters)
95 to 165 pounds (43 to 75 kilograms)

Ridley turtle
Lepidochelys olivacea
23 to 28 inches (58 to 71 centimeters)
80 to 100 pounds (36 to 45 kilograms)

Where Sea Turtles Live and Breed

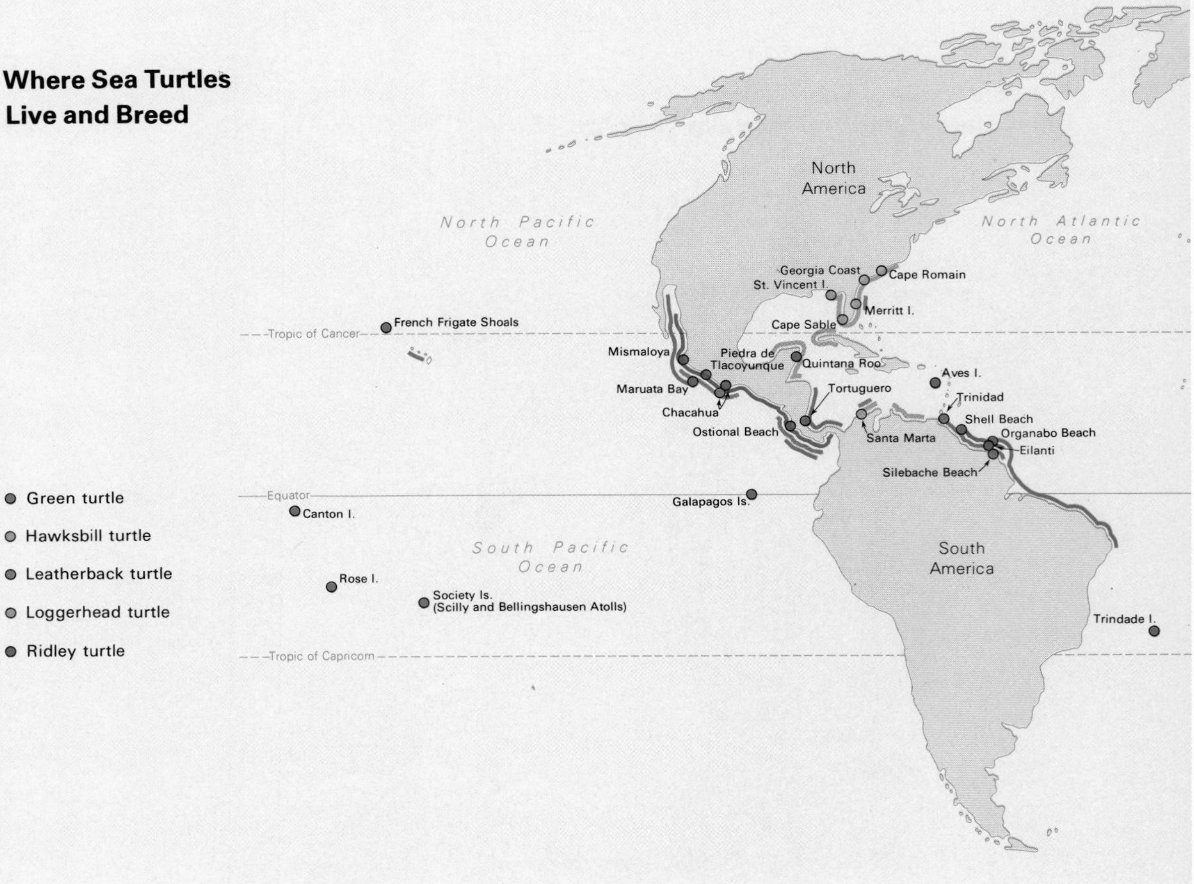

North America

North Pacific Ocean

North Atlantic Ocean

Georgia Coast
Cape Romain
St. Vincent I.
Merritt I.
Cape Sable

Tropic of Cancer — French Frigate Shoals

Mismaloya
Piedra de Tlacoyunque
Quintana Roo
Aves I.
Maruata Bay
Trinidad
Tortuguero
Chacahua
Shell Beach
Ostional Beach
Organabo Beach
Santa Marta
Eilanti
Silebache Beach

Equator
Canton I.
Galapagos Is.

South America

South Pacific Ocean

Rose I.

Society Is.
(Scilly and Bellingshausen Atolls)

Trindade I.

Tropic of Capricorn

- Green turtle
- Hawksbill turtle
- Leatherback turtle
- Loggerhead turtle
- Ridley turtle

Sea turtle feeding areas (shown by lines on map) and breeding sites (dots) are diminishing as turtle hunters find and exploit them. Scientists know little about the routes turtles take between the living and breeding areas, and there may be many areas that are not known.

their way to other beaches along the coast of Surinam, west of French Guiana, to nest during the 1976 season, but it is still too early to determine how disastrous the beach washout has been to the total leatherback population.

For centuries, men have marauded the sea turtle's nesting grounds without eradicating the species, though the harvest of meat, eggs, skin, and shells destroyed many turtle colonies completely. But today the turtles are being killed in much greater numbers. René Márquez, a sea turtle biologist in Mexico, estimates that the Gulf ridley species has dwindled to fewer than 5,000 females from 40,000 in 1947.

It is now clear that the very existence of the sea turtles is being threatened by people seeking profit from the harvest. Turtle steaks—especially those of the green turtle—grace the menus of growing numbers of gourmet restaurants. Soup made from the shell cartilage, or calipee, has long been a prestige dish. Some turtle hunters have even been known to remove only the cartilage from their killed turtles, throwing the rest of the animal away. Turtle skins are tanned and used for expensive shoes and handbags. Turtle oil is promoted as an ingredient of cosmetic lotions. And turtle shells are made into jewelry and are used for inlaid furniture.

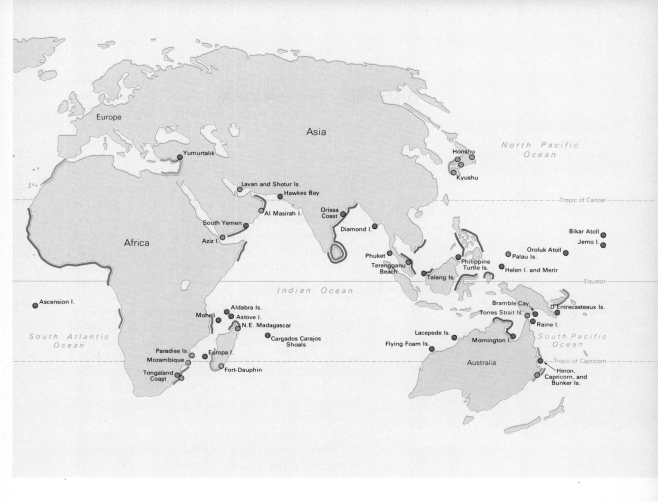

A fundamental factor in the present predicament of sea turtles is that they nest in large groups on limited sections of shoreline, where they are particularly vulnerable to human and animal predators who kill them and steal their eggs. There was a time when they were relatively safe when they were out in the ocean, away from shore. But today even the open sea is unsafe. Shrimp trawlers, a fast-growing menace to all the species, inadvertently kill sea turtles that become trapped in their nets. Most modern trawlers drag much larger nets along the ocean floor today than they did 20 years ago, and they leave them in the water longer. Sea turtles that are accidentally caught in these nets often suffocate because they cannot escape and swim to the surface to get air.

Sea turtle populations are declining so rapidly that the United States Department of the Interior placed all species on the threatened and endangered species list in 1976. The International Union for the Conservation of Nature and Natural Resources also lists all of them as either threatened, endangered, or rare.

There are five distinct kinds, or genera, of sea turtles—leatherback, green, ridley, hawksbill, and loggerhead—and some of them have more than one species. The leatherback is the largest sea turtle, weigh-

Polynesian fishermen drag big sea turtles onto the beach, *below.* Then they remove the meat to prepare a feast, *bottom.*

ing from 650 to 1,200 pounds (295 to 544 kilograms) when fully grown. It can be distinguished from the other sea turtles by its body covering—which, instead of a hard shell composed of separate plates, is a leathery surface with seven bony ridges running the length of its back and five along its belly. Until it was washed out, the Organabo beach was the largest known leatherback nesting area. The largest known nesting site now is one on the South China Sea coast of the Malay Peninsula. Leatherback eggs are collected there by Malaysians and auctioned off as a gourmet item.

There are three recognizable forms of green turtles—the worldwide, the black turtle of the eastern Pacific, and the Australian flatback. The largest nesting ground for the worldwide type is probably one recently discovered by zoologists in northern Queensland, Australia. That colony is well protected. Green turtles are not as well protected in the Caribbean, where commercial interests have built large turtle-freezing plants. The demand for turtle meat, which is frozen for sale in Europe, North America, and Japan, is increasing, and the turtles are netted and harpooned in growing numbers on the important feeding ground in Nicaragua and even off the big nesting beach in Costa Rica.

There are two species of ridleys. The olive ridley, sometimes called the Pacific ridley, lives mainly in the Indian and Pacific oceans. H. Robert Bustard, a British zoologist who works in India, has recently located an enormous nesting site of the olive ridley near Wheelers Island in the Bay of Bengal on the Orissa coast of India. These turtles also nest on the coast of West Africa, on the Pacific coast of Costa Rica, and on the Atlantic coast of Guyana. The Gulf ridley, sometimes called the Atlantic ridley, nests only on the Tamaulipas coast of Mexico, north of Tampico.

The two largest hawksbill nesting areas are on a little island off Yemen (Aden) in the Gulf of Aden and in Torres Strait. The most important loggerhead nesting is on United States, Australian, and South African shores, though some leave their eggs on beaches in Colombia, Cuba, and a few Pacific sites. The loggerhead is the most frequently seen sea turtle in Florida, where some of its nesting beaches are being disrupted by land development.

Sea turtles could probably live to be 100 years old if human beings would let them. Once they grow to adult size, few natural predators attack them. Each female is capable of laying several hundred eggs, usually every two or three years—though in some cases, at one- or five-year intervals. Sea turtles lay their eggs at night. As a female nears the shore to make her nest, she pauses in the shallow surf wash before moving up onto the sand. She is nervous, and any unnatural sound or sight will send her out to sea again. When she is finally satisfied that the beach is safe, she lumbers across the beach to the edge of dunes or beach vegetation. Laboriously, she thrashes out a depression to rest in while she lays her eggs, then delicately scoops out an urn-shaped nest hole with her hind flippers and drops her eggs into it. She may come up onto the beach to nest several times during one laying season, which may last more than two months.

The eggs hatch about two months later. The little hatchlings scramble out of their sandy nest and instinctively head for the water, even though it may be hidden from their view by dunes, debris, or beach vegetation. They are in great danger at this time, easy prey for raccoons, crabs, vultures, frigate birds, and other beach predators. And the hatchlings that finally get to the water run the risk of being eaten by sharks and other fish that cruise close to the shore. Those few baby turtles that survive and manage to reach the safety of the deeper water disappear for almost a year. Nobody knows where they go. That is one of several mysteries of sea turtle life yet to be solved.

Most of what scientists know about the behavior and ecology of sea turtles has been learned by observing and marking the mature females when they come ashore to nest. They are marked with small metal tags that bear an address and sometimes an offer of a reward for the tags' return. The tags are clipped through the skin of one of their front flippers. Tagging does not harm them, and the tags can be identified on later encounters. The travels of turtles tagged on a single beach can be slowly pieced together when the tags are returned by fishermen and turtle hunters, and when the turtles return to the nesting beach.

We have been tagging members of a green turtle colony at Tortuguero beach in Costa Rica for 21 years, and each year we learn more about the turtle's life cycle. For example, we have found that when the Tortuguero turtles return to the beach, it

Poachers who rob their nests, *below,* and shrimp nets that trap and drown them, *bottom,* are two threats to the survival of the world's sea turtles.

Hundreds of olive ridley
turtles crawl onto a
Pacific beach to lay eggs,
above. Predators are
not the only hazard that
nesting turtles face. A
leatherback is trapped
by driftwood, *right,* as
it heads back to the sea.

is usually surprisingly close to previous sites—rarely more than a few hundred yards or meters from the spot where they nested before. The precision of this site fixity varies somewhat with the changing condition of the beach, however.

Tagging also provides data on remigrations—returns to the same beach in later seasons. We learned years ago that most of the Tortuguero turtles, like those then being studied on the islands in the South China Sea off Sarawak, Borneo, return to lay eggs every three years. However, we also found that a smaller group comes back every two years. And later on we learned that individual turtles can change their nesting interval from two to three years, or vice versa. A growing number of four-year absences suggests that there may be a minor cycle that long or even longer. However, no Tortuguero turtles have ever been found that nest each year.

Our tagging at Ascension Island has revealed similar cycles for the turtles that nest there. But other zoologists report that green turtle colonies they studied include some females that nest every year. This variability undoubtedly has an important bearing on the ecology and survival of a turtle colony, but we cannot explain its causes.

Nevertheless, our knowledge of sea turtle breeding habits has grown faster than our understanding of any other aspect of their life. There is only one way we can learn where green turtles that show up at the breeding ground have come from and where they go, and that is by collecting the tags sent in by the fishermen who harpoon or net them. By then, the turtle has been eaten or sent to market—so that is the end of its record. As a result, we must work back to the breeding place from the locations of returned tags to determine whether females from various places behave and nest differently, and we are only now beginning to have enough returned tags to let us make any helpful guesses.

Perhaps the most puzzling gap in our knowledge is where the young sea turtles live during the first year after they enter the sea. They might be expected to stay in shallow coastal waters. However, exhaustive searching and innumerable interviews with fishermen have failed to produce any evidence of that. The most plausible assumption now appears to be that they swim out to sea and live in the mats of brown sargassum weed that drift with ocean currents. This theory presupposes that the hatchlings that get through the surf can swim far enough on a proper course to reach the currents that carry these mats of weeds. Hatchlings do not need to eat for the first few days of life; they live off the stored yolk in their bodies. The sargassum mats would provide them with both food and refuge from predators. No systematic search for little turtles has yet been made in sargassum mats, but each year a few loggerhead hatchlings are found in or around the mats that drift in the Gulf Stream off the nesting beaches on the lower east coast of Florida. Baby turtles of all species are involved in this lost-year mystery, so huge numbers of them must be hiding somewhere.

One way to get clues to solve this mystery is to trace the paths taken

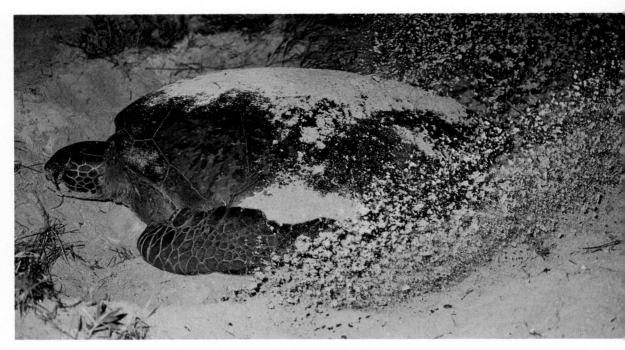

A green turtle digs a pit in the sand, *above,* then lays her eggs there, *right.* After the babies hatch and dig their way out of the sand, *far right,* they head for the sea, *below.*

by hatchlings as they swim out to sea. Jane Frick, a young zoologist working at Nonesuch Island in Bermuda, has followed them for long distances by swimming after them. Day after day she swam behind them for hours at a time, tracking some of them as far as 6 miles (10 kilometers) from shore. She has found that the hatchlings can swim for hours, and probably days, on courses that take them directly away from shore. What guides them is unknown, but the paths they take obviously remain oriented long after they move out of sight of fixed landmarks. Because this ability to swim straight away from the shore would eventually take the hatchlings into a mat-bearing current, the studies seem to lend weight to the sargassum-mat theory. Although these studies were made only with green turtles, I think it is reasonable to conclude that hatchlings of other species also live in the current-borne mats.

Hungry crabs waiting on the beach and birds that swoop down from the sky take their toll before the newly hatched baby turtles can reach the sea.

Another baffling gap in our understanding of the natural history of sea turtles is what guides mature turtles across great expanses of open ocean to gather, on schedule, at specific places to breed. Turtles that nest on a mainland shore are no doubt helped in their search for their nesting ground by landmarks along the coast, underwater bottom conditions, and the different kinds of water that flow into the sea from coastal streams. However, circumstantial evidence indicates that there is much more to the guidance process than that. Scientists know that olive ridley turtles mass in enormous groups, or schools, far out at sea and then move along the shore, sometimes for great distances, to the point on the shore where they nest. Nobody knows how these sea bands form, or even where the turtles come from.

The green turtle's breeding journey is different. Its nesting aggregations are less concentrated than those of the olive ridley, and individuals seem to arrive at the nesting area separately or in small groups. But we do not understand how green turtles locate the breeding shore, and their precisely scheduled arrival at tiny islands after they have traveled hundreds or thousands of miles or kilometers in the open ocean is a classic puzzle.

So far, about all we have been able to do is identify some conceivable explanations. These include *celestial navigation* (taking direction from the stars and sun); *Coriolis force* (sensing differential rotation of the earth with changing latitude); some kind of internal inertial-guidance system that might resemble a ship's gyroscope; random searching; effortless drift with the ocean currents; *chemoreception* (the smell-taste kind of perception)—or perhaps a combination of two or more of these. My own unenthusiastic choice of a mechanism that may guide one group of turtles that cross the vast stretches of ocean between Brazil and their nesting ground at Ascension Island is a combination of chemoreception and celestial navigation. This is not really a good theory; it merely seems less preposterous than any of the other theories that have so far been proposed.

One weakness in it is that birds also nest on most of the islands used by turtles. The green turtle, for example, shares Ascension Island with the sooty tern as well as other birds that make long migrations to get to the island. When two kinds of animals show up on schedule at the same speck of rock in a trackless spread of ocean, we are tempted to look for a common guidance system. Obviously, however, birds cannot be guided over water by their sense of smell, however keen it might be. Aroma-carrying air currents are too erratic. Predictable water currents are the only possible smell-taste carriers for such tremendous distances, and these are available to the turtles but not to the birds.

Continued theorizing is not likely to solve this engrossing mystery. Some progress could probably be made by laboratory experiments. It would be interesting to know, for example, whether green turtles can detect changes in magnetic fields or can maintain a constant heading from a simulated moving sun. The most needed experiments, however, are tracking tests to trace the exact paths taken by turtles migrating across open sea. The green turtle is particularly suitable for open-

Scientists staple a metal identification tag on a flipper, *below,* and weigh the turtle, *below right,* in charting a record of its size and travels. Some turtles get numbers on their shells, *bottom.*

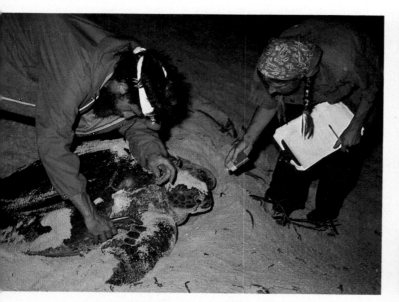

ocean tracking experiments, because it travels slowly, stays at or near the surface, and breathes air. It also is big enough to tow tracking buoys or to carry substantial packages of instruments without any seeming inconvenience.

The instruments may be attached to floating buoys that are tied to the turtles by long lines. The turtles pull the buoys through the water with no apparent discomfort. Instrument packages can also be attached directly to a turtle's back, and if these operate properly, a tracking airplane or satellite can pick up the signals when the animal surfaces every few minutes for air.

We learned long ago that when you move a female green turtle away from her nesting ground before she has finished nesting, she will stubbornly return. We have also shown that the turtles are not hindered by a towline and buoy fastened to their shells. So radio tracking should be the ideal way to test the chemoreception-celestial navigation theory of island-finding navigation. One group of instrumented turtles at Ascension Island could be moved downstream in the current that flows past the island toward the Brazilian coast, and another group could be placed away from and across the flow of the current from the island. If the downstream group showed clear superiority in getting back to Ascension, we could conclude that they were responding to chemoreception from the island. But if the turtles placed across the current were the most successful at getting back, the chemoreception theory could be ruled out. If, in other tests, the ability of the turtles to find their nesting area should decrease during darkness or when skies are overcast, celestial navigation would likely be a major guidance component. Special sensors in the instrument package could transmit data on depth, temperature, speed, and other factors. All of this would give us a firm basis for evaluating the various navigation theories, if only a record could be kept over long periods of time and for many turtles. So far, however, a dismal series of instrument failures has held up progress in this promising research.

While radio tracking may help us explain the mechanisms involved in turtle migration, it will not solve the mystery of how natural selection was able to produce a green turtle that lives and feeds most of the time directly off the northeast coast of Brazil and then makes a 1,200-mile (2,000-kilometer) trip eastward to tiny Ascension Island to lay its eggs. The green turtle does this even though there are beaches suitable for egg laying on the mainland not far from the feeding grounds. No matter what sensory mechanisms guide such a journey, it is puzzling how evolution could have given rise to a strain of animals that travel so far to breed when there are equally good nesting grounds nearby.

The solution to this mystery may lie in the geologic process of sea-floor spreading. About 100 million years ago, when the turtles' urge to nest was probably established, the islands they used may have been within hailing distance of the Brazilian coast. But as sea-floor spreading widened the South Atlantic and the distance between South

Attendants bury olive
ridley eggs at a hatchery
on a Surinam beach, and
later release the babies
hatched from the eggs.

America and Africa increased, the islands moved farther out to sea.
Consequently, as time passed and the spreading sea floor grew to its
present dimensions, the turtles would have had to swim a bit farther
each breeding season. As a result of this slow, gradual change, evolution produced a strain of green turtles with both the urge and the
ability to migrate to the distant islet.

Of all the problems that sea turtles present, their poor survival
outlook is the most urgent. Anxiety over their decline is growing, and
people are clamoring for ways to save them. The fact that they are
now on official endangered species lists has slowed, but by no means
stopped, international trade in turtle products. The most important
immediate need is for more breeding sanctuaries and better enforcement of turtle laws everywhere. Everything possible should be done to
free every nesting colony from exploitation and interference. It is the
human turtle-egg robbers and the human turtle hunters that are causing the most destruction to these ancient animals. Along shores where
people are settling, or in remote places such as Aves Island in the
Caribbean Sea off Guadeloupe or the Lacepede Islands in the Indian
Ocean off northern Western Australia, it is difficult for government
authorities to prevent illegal poaching. Nevertheless, effectively protected breeding sanctuaries appear to be the single best hope for the
survival of the sea turtle.

Other than protecting sea turtles against human exploitation, the
only management techniques that seem to hold any promise are either
incubating eggs in hatcheries where they will be safe from predators,
or trying to establish new turtle-nesting sites, or rearing young turtles

until they are so big that predators of hatchlings are no longer a menace to them when they are released.

In places where predators are numerous, moving eggs to protected hatching sites seems reasonable, if great care is used in handling them. Such egg hatcheries have been established on the coasts of Florida, Georgia, and South Carolina, and in various other parts of the world. Transplanting eggs or young turtles in order to establish new colonies or rehabilitate old ones is a possibility based on the assumption that the hatchlings will return to the new hatching site—not the one where the eggs or baby turtles came from—when they have reached sexual maturity. A long-term experiment to determine whether this is feasible is now in progress on beaches in Bermuda.

Rearing young turtles for a year or so until they are so big that the host of hatchling predators are no longer a menace is known as head-starting. The only way to test the effectiveness of such a project is to tag the young turtles when they are released, and see how many are recovered—and under what circumstances. Preliminary findings from such studies suggest that much depends on the kind of place in which the yearlings are released. None of the several hundred yearlings released off Costa Rican beaches have been heard from. Those that are released in lagoons, bays, or reef-protected water have a better chance of survival. Recoveries of tagged yearlings released in Bermuda, Surinam, and elsewhere are more encouraging. On the other hand, there have been some interesting returns from a project at Stuart, Fla., where yearlings are released on open sea beach. So much remains to be learned before head-starting should be recommended for widespread use as a conservation technique for sea turtles.

It once seemed that turtle farming, using natural turtle grass to feed stock kept in pens or pastures along the shore, might satisfy the commercial demand for green turtles and thus save them from extinction. The belief was based on the assumption that the first farms would be nonprofit, experimental projects that would not attempt commercial production until pilot studies showed that such

Her nesting finished, a female green turtle lumbers slowly across the beach to the sea.

farming would be feasible. Meanwhile, pen-reared breeding stock could be developed to furnish all the eggs needed to maintain production and eventually even to provide a domesticated strain of sea turtle distinct from all wild stock. While this was going on, a realistic marketing analysis would be made to determine if such an enterprise would be profitable without having to create new demands and outlets for turtle meat and other turtle products.

Although these rearing, pasturing, and marketing conditions have not been met, turtle farmers claim that their efforts will help save the green turtle from extinction. They say that mass production will saturate markets for turtle products, prices will drop, and the hunting of wild turtles will decline.

Most of the eggs for hatcheries and head-starting pens are now taken from natural turtle sanctuaries. Proponents say that the eggs are taken only from badly placed nests that would otherwise be washed out by high waves or raided by predators. But it seems unlikely that such doomed nests could supply enough eggs for a growing industry. The turtle farmers also say that eggs for commercial turtle farming will soon be produced on man-made beaches by turtles that have been reared in breeding pens. Although no farm has yet reached that stage, advances have been made. A few pen-reared turtles have reached maturity and are nesting on artificial beaches. However, there remains serious doubt that the volume of eggs required for a profitable large-scale commercial operation can be produced.

As an effort to justify taking eggs from natural sanctuaries, turtle farmers release a certain number of pen-reared, head-started yearlings at the original nesting ground. They say that each returned yearling, which has a better chance of escaping predators, is the equivalent of hundreds of eggs removed. It is possible that this is true. But there is no statistical evidence to show that it is, and so we must await the accumulation of tag recoveries in numbers sufficient to show that head-started turtles survive, breed, and return to the nesting beaches from which the eggs were taken. Without such proof it seems unwise to raise false hopes by recommending either head-starting or turtle farming as conservation practices.

The most effective way to save sea turtles would be to stop all commercial exploitation of such animals. Market hunting—legal and illegal—results in huge amounts of turtle meat, shell, and leather being shipped or smuggled from one country to another each year. Setting up more breeding and feeding sanctuaries and giving those that exist better protection than they are now getting would also help. But to do this is not simple. It is much easier to comfort ourselves by protecting a few hundred nests from predators, or by releasing a few thousand head-started yearling turtles from time to time. If they could get better protection of their natural breeding and foraging habitats, there might still be time to cure the other ills that make it so hard for sea turtles to live in the same world with human beings.

A Year In Perspective

THE YEAR BOOK casts a backward glance at the furors, fancies, and follies of yesteryear. The coincidences of history so revealed offer substantial proof that, though the physical world continually changes, human nature—in all its inventiveness, amiability, and even perversity—remains fairly constant, for better or worse, throughout the years.

Little Acorns, Giant Oaks

By Paul C. Tullier

It is one of history's quirks that the minutiae of one era frequently play significant roles in another era

It is in the seeming trivia of one era that history sows the seeds of another time's sturdiest oaks. Or so it might have seemed to Charlie Smith—had he given it some thought—as he led the American Revolution Bicentennial parade down the main street of Bartow, Fla., on July 4, 1976. Smith, physically fragile but mentally alert and well aware of the day's significance, was enjoying not only his prestige as grand marshal of the local pageant, but also his singular status in the United States. According to the Social Security Administration's records, Smith was the oldest beneficiary on their rolls. He was 134 years old. It was generally supposed that he was the nation's oldest citizen.

In every sense of the word, Smith was unique. During his lifetime, he had seen the number of states in the Union grow from 26 to 50. The U.S. population had soared nearly tenfold—from 23 million to 217.5-million. Smith had lived under 28 of the country's 38 presidents; eight generations had either been born, matured, or died in his lifetime.

Leading events of 1876 included, *clockwise from upper right,* Rutherford B. Hayes running for President; Custer's last stand; casting of the Statue of Liberty; and the opening of the U.S. Centennial Year in Philadelphia.

Smith could easily have qualified as a judge of two premises that many historians hold to be self-evident truths. The first of these–that history repeats itself–had some obvious proof in the analogies that could be drawn between international events during the Centennial year, 1876, and those during the Bicentennial celebration in 1976. In 1876, Spain had replaced a dictatorship with a king, but the transition, including the adoption of a new Constitution, was not an easy one. It was the same in 1976. Black uprisings against the white government in South Africa made world headlines in 1876 as blood flowed in the streets of Cape Town. The scene was the same in 1976.

In Latin America, unstable governments and border wrangles disrupted internal and external relations among most of the nations in 1876. In Ireland, anti-British sentiment and religious strife fed the fires of discontent. There was political unrest in China and in India. Marauding guerrillas made life difficult in some sections of Mexico. In Lebanon, the predominant Maronite Christian sect competed bloodily with the Muslim minority for control of the government. Corruption and bribery surfaced in Italy with the discovery of a "black book" recording the misdeeds of government officials. Even papal authority was under worldwide challenge. And in the United States, a presidential election contest between Republican Rutherford B. Hayes and Democrat Samuel J. Tilden established new highs in vilification. Hayes was accused of having "a permissive attitude toward business and industrial bribes." Tilden was charged with being "a man of unknown capacity." A splinter group, called "Half-Breeds" attacked both parties for "me-tooism." "Significant differences," they said, "no longer separate the parties." Even the nation's international reputation was impugned. "It is painfully apparent," wrote a former senator, "...that [we] stand before the world in an attitude of...humiliation and shame." (Hayes won, but the electoral vote was challenged; not until March 2, 1877, was he declared the winner.)

But it was the second premise–that history has an almost wayward way of planting its future oaks in the minutiae of yesteryear–that held the most merit. Who, even with the aid of a cosmic crystal ball, could have foreseen that the birth in 1876 of an infant named Willis H. Carrier presaged the age of air conditioning? Or that other newborns of that year–Constantin Brancusi, the sculptor; Manuel de Falla, the composer; and novelists Jack London and Willa Cather–would leave their mark on future generations? Or that two German nestlings–Erich Raeder and Karl von Rundstedt–would be key cogs in the Nazi war machine of World War II while Konrad Adenauer, born the same year, would help repair the damage they had wrought? Who could have foretold, in 1876, that Elisha Graves Otis' new improved "passenger elevator" on display in Philadelphia would contribute to the development of today's skyscraper by facilitating vertical transit? Or that an instrument patented in that year by Alexander Graham Bell as "an improvement in telegraphy" would eventually intercon-

The author:
Paul C. Tullier is Managing Editor of THE WORLD BOOK YEAR BOOK.

nect not merely individuals and their homes but cities and even continents under the name "telephone"?

Foresight is not one of mankind's strongest suits, and the average citizen considered these inventions to be either amusing diversions or curiosities—but nothing more. Yet if people shortsightedly failed to see any long-range dividends in these minutiae, they were quick to perceive the instant value inherent in others. Thus, they took enthusiastically to the first U.S.-manufactured hair clipper when it was produced in 1876. It had a practical application. Perfected by Henry Coates of Worcester, Mass., it was so superior in workmanship and performance to those imported from Europe that Coates's initial order for 5,000 clippers had to be greatly increased to meet the demand. A portent of today's great canning industry was the first successful sardine cannery, which began operating in Eastport, Me. The proprietor, Julius Wolff, of Wolff and Reesing, New York City, had cleverly produced a container consisting of three pieces—top, bottom, and side —that, when soldered together, made the container airtight. Both Coates and Wolff may have expressed their joy at the financial returns by joining their homefolks in singing some of the popular songs of the day, which included "Grandfather's Clock," "I'll Take You Home Again Kathleen," and "Rose of Killarney." A religious song—"What a Friend We Have in Jesus"—was also enjoying huge sheet-music sales.

Polo, a British import, promised a new kind of diversion for America's well-to-do class when it was introduced at Jerome Park in New York City in 1876. Equipment, including the mallets and balls, was imported.

Black resentment over white minority rule flared into bloody war in South Africa in 1876. Here, British troops attack a black village near Cape Town.

The homefolks, at least those in New York City, could also appreciate the values of fine cooking, thanks to the first school devoted entirely to the culinary arts—the New York Cooking School—which was opened in November 1876 by Juliet Corson at her residence in St. Mark's Place. She had previously given cooking instruction in the Ladies Cooking Class of the free Training School for Women in New York City. (Coincidentally, a boon to future cooks with plumbing problems at the kitchen sink was the patenting, in 1876, of the first practical pipe, or screw, wrench by Daniel C. Stillson. Stillson's original model was whittled out of wood.)

The first cooking school enrollees were considered "daring" because they were accused of competing with professional cooks, but no more so than the first woman to wear trousers especially designed as an article of feminine apparel—the irrepressible French actress Sarah Bernhardt, who was photographed in 1876 costumed in a jacketed trouser-suit of extraordinarily modern appearance. Sarah's "suit" created quite a stir among the menfolk, whose "male sensibilities," wrote a reporter, "suffered grave consequences."

Even greater offense was taken by parents on both sides of the Atlantic Ocean with the appearance in 1876 of the first sex-education manual for children. Entitled *Counsel to Parents on the Moral Education of their Children*, and published by Elizabeth Blackwell, Great Britain's first female physician, it aroused a storm of controversy. Parental concern was also growing over a tendency to commercialize Christmas. The prototype American Santa Claus, with his rotund figure, jolly appearance, and white beard, had been created in 1862 by Thomas Nast in a series of Christmas cartoons for *Harper's Weekly*. By 1876, Santa's helpers at the R. H. Macy Company of New York City had created the first promotional window displays with an exclusively Christmas motif. One window, featuring Macy's doll collection, sold out within a week.

Christmas, however, was only a seasonal affair. Manufacturers vied with one another to provide new products to keep the consumer spending on a year-round basis. One such product was the first practical carpet sweeper. Its inventor was Melville Reuben Bissell of Grand Rapids, Mich. The Singer Sewing Machine Company kept pace, introducing in 1876 a new "lamp bracket for sewing" that "quite obviated the difficulty experienced by operators when sewing at night." The lamp, claimed the Singer company, would not "jar off the table or upset" and it could "be moved without soiling the fingers." To this domestic "must" was added another: the first one-day, backwind alarm clock in a metal case, manufactured by the Seth Thomas Clock Company of Thomaston, Conn.

Luxuries being made available included the first electric organ, which was built by Hilborne Lewis Roosevelt and eventually installed in Chickering Hall at Fifth Avenue and 18th Street in New York City. A competitor, William F. and H. Schmoele of Philadelphia, produced a mechanical Orchestrion or Electro-Magnetic Orchestra that reproduced music by means of paper rolls similar to those used later on the player piano.

Thomas A. Edison of Menlo Park, N.J., probably the world's greatest inventor, obtained on Aug. 8, 1876, a patent on a new device that would provide "a method of preparing autographic stencils for printing." It eventually became known as a mimeograph machine. Earlier in the year, John Celinergos Zachos of New York City obtained a patent on a "typewriter and phonotypic notation device for printing legible text in the English alphabet at a high reporting speed." It was the forerunner of the stenotype machine. Both devices had commercial potentials. The same could be said of the cigarette-manufacturing machine that Albert H. Hook introduced on Nov. 7, 1876. Although about 50 million cigarettes were already being produced in the United States every year, mostly by hand-operated machines, the Hook machine made it possible to increase output enormously—to the despair of antismoking crusaders.

Ministers hoped, in print and from the pulpit—in vain, it turned out—that the "noxious weed" would be banned from the Coast Guard Officers' Training School that was established July 31, 1876, in New Bedford, Mass. It was also to be hoped, according to an editorial in *Leslie's Illustrated Weekly Newspaper*, that the school's student body

Following two pages: An enthusiastic crowd surges into the vast Grand Plaza for the Centennial Exposition's opening in Philadelphia's Fairmont Park. The speaker's platform is crowded with notables. Spectators overflow the stands, left, and some perch on the plaza's colossal statues to get a better view.

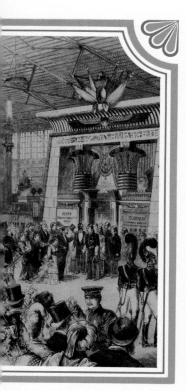

During an opening-day tour of exhibits in the Centennial Exposition's Main Hall, President Ulysses S. Grant greets foreign commissioners at the display erected by Egypt and the Sudan.

would not follow in the footsteps of the cadets at West Point, six of whom had been dismissed for cheating.

A quicker way of reaching a wider audience of newspaper readers was being explored by the *Philadelphia* (Pa.) *Times*, which, in 1876, installed the first high-speed newspaper printing press and folding machine. Using a gathering cylinder with a rotary folding cylinder, the new press printed and folded a four-page sheet at the rate of 400 a minute. It was a boon to the growing publishing industry, which in 1876 saw the birth of the *Chicago Daily News* and *McCall's Magazine*.

Harvard University began publishing the *Lampoon*, the first undergraduate humor magazine in America. Not to be outdone, Princeton brought out *The Princetonian;* the day it made its bow—June 14, 1876—a Princeton student named Woodrow Wilson confided to his diary that he would "patronize it because it promises to be a very lively, interesting journal."

Meanwhile, a Chicago-based firm—Donnelly, Lloyd and Company—introduced a series of phenomenally cheap "paperback" books under the Lakeside Library imprint. They cost 10 cents apiece, a price made possible by the fact that they were reprints of works no longer under copyright. They were instant best sellers. So, too, was a modest book that had been rejected by all publishers, printed at the author's expense, and finally sold to the public through a Chicago book firm. It was Henry M. Robert's *Pocket Manual of Rules of Order for Deliberative Assemblies.* The first edition of 4,000 copies, priced at 75 cents each, was sold out in six weeks. Robert's *Rules of Order*—since revised—is still the standard guide for parliamentary procedure.

Also high on the best-seller list was Mark Twain's new book, *The Adventures of Tom Sawyer*. It was also somewhat notorious, following its exclusion from the Children's Room of the Brooklyn Public Library and its being banned altogether by the Denver Public Library. The language was considered too "coarse" for young readers. No such opprobrium attached itself to John Habberton's book *Helen's Babies*, which, according to the subtitle, gave *"Some account of their ways, Innocent, Crafty, Angelic, Impish, Witching, and Repulsive."* The book, the subtitle went on, was *"Also a Partial Record of Their Actions During Ten Days of Their Existence, by their Latest Victim."* The book was an immediate success—as were Horatio Alger, Jr.'s books *Sam's Choice* and *Shifting for Himself*. For the mature readers, there was *Roderick Hudson*, a novel by Henry James (who had finally settled in London), and *The Spagnoletto*, a verse tragedy by Emma Lazarus whose sonnet "The New Colossus" would eventually be inscribed on the base of the Statue of Liberty, then being cast in sections in France.

The growth of the publishing industry coincided with similar advances in education. Of great interest in 1876 was the opening of Johns Hopkins University (for men) in Baltimore; the University of Oregon at Eugene and Portland (for men and women); and, at Yale, the granting of the first Doctor of Philosophy degree to a black. The recipient was Edward Alexander Bouchet, who was also the first black to be elected to Phi Beta Kappa, the national scholastic fraternity. Another first was the free kindergarten opened by Samuel Lapham Hill in Florence, Mass., on Jan. 3, 1876. It was followed in October by the founding of the American Library Association (ALA) at a meeting in Philadelphia. One of the ALA founders was Melvil Dewey, whose decimal system of book classification would vastly simplify the classifying and shelving of books. Dewey also was instrumental in founding the association's *Library Journal* the same year. There was great need for both: Altogether, there were 3,647 libraries with 300 or more books in the United States in 1876; Harvard had the largest collection.

A book certain to be included in many libraries was the first translation of the Bible made by a woman—Julia Evelina Smith of Glastonbury, Conn., whose knowledge of Latin, Greek, and Hebrew enabled her to make the translation. A number of church officials considered the "style" a drawback—Smith had translated the verbs in the future tense—but all welcomed it as one more weapon in the offensive being waged in 1876 against Charles Darwin's theory of evolution. The chief spokesman for the "evolutionists" was an Englishman named Thomas H. Huxley, who toured the United States in 1876 lecturing on "Evidence as to Man's Place in Nature"—a direct assault on the six-day theory of creation. The editors of *Scientific America* considered his lectures "a waste of time and an insult to American intelligence." A derogatory song in great vogue was entitled "Too Thin, or Darwin's Little Joke. A Humorous Song with words by Grace Carlton and music by 'O'Rangoutang.'"

Huxley, undisturbed by the tumult, was intrigued by the concept behind the Ethical Culture Society, which was founded in New York City in 1876 by Felix Adler, a German-born educator and reformer who was an ardent advocate of nonsectarian religion and a moral life independent of formal creeds. Men of many faiths were alarmed by the development of cremation, which threatened the old established rituals. Its advocates strongly urged its worldwide adoption as a way to eliminate the "disease-carrying gases and offensive odors emanating from the graves." One champion of the cause, Francis Julius LeMoyne, built the first U.S. crematory in Washington, Pa., in 1876.

Disease, however carried, was a concern of many Americans in 1876. Among the major topics discussed at the annual American Medical Association (AMA) meeting that year were ways to control tick fever, contagious pleuropneumonia in cattle, hog cholera, and the horse plague. Yellow fever was also high on the list because of a serious outbreak of the disease in the South, particularly around Savannah, Ga., where 1,500 persons died between July and November.

Prominent among those at the AMA meeting was S. Weir Mitchell, the best-known medical man of his time, who would eventually be credited with inventing the rest cure and with foreshadowing psychosomatic medicine. Another was Edward Robinson Squibb, who was

Examples of American ingenuity displayed at the exposition ranged from Alexander Graham Bell's new telephone to the Minnehaha, an elaborately decorated soda water dispenser.

campaigning to revise the U.S. Pharmacopoeia, the official list of drugs and medicines, which he described as "little more than a catalogue." His plea to update and improve the pharmacopoeia, however, fell on deaf ears at the meeting; his motion was tabled. Squibb would eventually succeed, however, and along the way establish the pharmaceutical house that bears his name. Not present at the AMA meeting but destined to be Squibb's rival was Colonel Eli Lilly of Indiana, a Civil War veteran who had just started his own drug business. By year's end, Lilly's firm had grossed $4,470 from the sale of pills, fluid extracts, elixirs, and cordials.

Such "prescriptions" were the mainstays of medicine in the United States in 1876; there were 456 identified bottles of bitters alone, as well as untold numbers of balms, balsams, compounds, and cordials. Medicine cabinets bulged with drops, elixirs, emulsions, liniments, and mixtures. There were also oils, sarsaparillas, specifics, and syrup and water concoctions—most of which contained alcohol. Almost all were bottled in distinctive blue glass, including a new product named Lydia E. Pinkham's Vegetable Compound, which, in 1876, became the first nationally distributed home remedy. The original formula contained 18 per cent alcohol.

The year 1876 also saw the publication of a pioneering medical textbook, *The Atlas of Skin Diseases,* by Louis Adolphus Duhring, a professor at the University of Pennsylvania medical school. The mathematical physicist Josiah Willard Gibbs published the first half of *On The Equilibrium of Heterogeneous Substances* in the *Transactions of the Connecticut Academy of Arts and Sciences.* Gibbs's work, which is among the great achievements of science, would eventually make possible many new manufacturing methods in industry as well as help advance biological and medical science. The American Chemical Society was formally organized on April 20 "to encourage the broadest and most liberal advancement of all the branches of chemistry." John William Draper, a physicist and astronomer at New York University, was named the society's first president. (Draper scored some other "firsts": He was credited by several European authorities with being the first to photograph the solar spectrum, and the first to take a photograph of the moon.)

In 1876, a new concept was introduced into a different kind of science—criminology—by Cesare Lombroso, a professor of anthropology at the University of Turin in Italy. Lombroso, after painstakingly investigating and examining dozens of imprisoned criminals, published his conclusions in a book entitled *L'Uomo delinquente (Criminal Man).* Criminals, wrote Lombroso, are "born" and are easily identified by such distinguishing marks as receding foreheads, massive jaws,

President Ulysses S. Grant activates the gigantic Corliss engine in Machinery Hall on the Centennial Exposition's opening day, May 10, 1876. The engine's unprecedented power was a harbinger of the expanded role that technology and energy was destined to play in the development of the United States.

projecting ears, feline eyes, and left-handedness. Lombroso's premise, which in one way or another touched everyone, stimulated both dissent and further research by his colleagues. Many of their subsequent conclusions, diametrically opposed to Lombroso's, are accepted today.

The Lombroso furor nearly obscured the news that the first reformatory for juvenile offenders was founded in Elmira, N.Y.; that the Pinkerton detective agency adopted the "Private Eye" symbol as its official trademark; and that the Legal Aid Society was founded in New York City. None of these, unfortunately, could do anything about crime in New York City streets, because of which visitors were warned, in booklet form, that the city was a dangerous place at night and that they would be well advised to stay off the streets after dark. "If possible, reach the city in the daytime," the traveler was admonished. "Avoid being too free with strangers and avoid all crowds, particularly at night."

It was fortunate, at least for New York City's entertainment centers, that such strictures were invoked only for outdoor activities. Indoors, crowds in the hundreds gathered nightly in Gilmore's Gardens (beginning in May) to hear the famous Parisian composer Jacques Offenbach lead his orchestra of 100 players in popular music of the day (John Philip Sousa was among the instrumentalists). For Offenbach's visit, Gilmore's Gardens had been redecorated with lush tropical plants and cascading "waterfalls" to replace the austere décor left by evangelist Dwight L. Moody and his assistant, Ira D. Sankey, who had used the hall for a series of meetings.

Other crowds were flocking to New York City's new German-language Stadt Theatre, which had opened under the management of Oscar Hammerstein, an erstwhile cigar-maker from Germany who had decided to enter show business. Hammerstein's instinct for making entertainment pay found an echo in Buffalo Bill (William Frederick) Cody, whose career included successful appearances in such melodramas as *Scouts of the Prairies,* which won cheers from the reviewers and paying customers alike. Applause was loud, too, at the Union Square Theater for Victorien Sardou's French drama *Ferréol,* one of the hits of the season. One of the play's stars was Kate Claxton, the popular "Miss Kate," who later in the year was playing a lead role in the melodrama *The Two Orphans* at the Brooklyn Theatre when it was destroyed by fire. Of 1,200 in the audience, 295 died (197 victims were identified, 98 remained unidentified). The tragedy was headlined in newspapers throughout the country and affected attendance at theatrical performances nearly everywhere for almost a year.

In vaudeville, the sensation of the year was Etta Morgan, who toured the country as a member of the Berger Family's Ladies Orchestra. Her chief claim to fame was her saxophone. In the opera houses, a warm welcome was extended to the great German soprano Therese Tietjens, who, on January 24, made her American debut in *Norma* at the Academy of Music in New York City. In a startling reversal of roles, Teresa Carreño, the famous pianist, essayed a brief operatic career as a soprano, making her debut at the academy on February 15 as Zerlina in Mozart's *Don Giovanni*. In addition to these sterling artists, Americans heard first performances in the United States of Johannes Brahms's *Symphony No. 1 in C minor*, Peter Ilich Tchaikovsky's *Romeo and Juliet*, Richard Wagner's *Siegfried*, and Léo Delibes' ballet composition *Sylvia*.

The big music event of 1876, however, was unquestionably the opening of the Bayreuth Festspielhaus (Festival Play House) in Germany, featuring the first complete performance of Richard Wagner's *The Ring of the Nibelung*. The opening performance, on August 13, featured *Das Rheingold*. The audience included Emperor Wilhelm I of Germany, King Ludwig II of Bavaria, Friedrich Nietzsche, and an impressive gathering of Wagner's fellow composers—Franz Liszt, Edvard Grieg, Anton Bruckner, Gustav Mahler, Camille Saint-Saëns, and Tchaikovsky. But the audience was more intrigued by the innovations in the 1,800-seat theater. It was darkened; no applause was permitted while the curtain was up; and singers were forbidden to acknowledge applause except between acts. Further, Wagner had covered the orchestra pit and reverted to the ancient Greek-style amphitheater for his seating plan. Despite all this, the first season was a flop. Artistically, it fell below expectations—"Wagner," sneered Nietzsche, "presumes a false omnipotence." Financially, it lost $125,000.

Classical music, as in all eras, left large segments of the population unmoved. They preferred action, be it as participant or spectator. And in 1876, there was plenty of action for both. On February 2, the National League of Professional Baseball Clubs was organized to replace the discredited National Association of Professional Baseball Players. It included teams in Boston; Chicago; Cincinnati, Ohio; Hartford, Conn.; Louisville, Ky.; New York City; Philadelphia; and St. Louis. In the first National League game, on April 2, Boston beat Philadelphia 6 to 5 in Philadelphia before 3,000 spectators. On May 23, Joe Borden pitched the league's first no-hitter. Chicago won the league's first pennant with a season record of 52 wins and 14 losses.

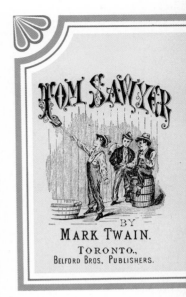

Mark Twain's classic, *Tom Sawyer*, became a best seller in 1876. Its popularity was somewhat diminished when a few librarians banned it from their bookshelves because they deemed some language "too coarse" for young readers.

Another "first" was scored by Frederick Winthrop Thayer of Waverley, Mass., who was captain of the Harvard University Baseball Club. Thayer, working with a Cambridge, Mass., tinsmith, invented a catcher's mask that, after first being tried out in the university's gymnasium, proved an excellent safeguard on the baseball diamond.

On November 23, at the invitation of Princeton, delegates from Columbia, Harvard, Princeton, Rutgers, and Yale universities met at Massasoit House, in Springfield, Mass., to discuss football rules. Princeton had recently adopted Harvard's rules, which in turn were based chiefly on rules of the British Rugby Union, and these were adopted by all colleges represented at the meeting. The American Intercollegiate Football Association, the first such organization, grew out of this weeklong meeting.

The Intercollegiate Association of Amateur Athletes of America (AAA) was founded in Saratoga Springs, N.Y., by delegates from 14 U.S. colleges participating in the crew and track events held there on July 20 and 21. The organization was the earliest significant intercollegiate sports organization in the United States; its original members included Amherst, Bowdoin, Brown, City College of New York, Columbia, Cornell, Dartmouth, Harvard, Princeton, Trinity, Union, Wesleyan, Williams, and Yale. Princeton won the first track meet with four firsts and four seconds.

In horse racing, Shirley won the Preakness purse ($1,950); Vagrant won the Kentucky Derby ($2,950); and Algerine took the $3,700 Belmont Stakes purse. The first greyhound race using an artificial hare was run on October 7 in Hendon, England. In boxing, Joe Goss of England became the world bare-knuckle champion when Tom Allen was disqualified in the 27th round for fouling during their bout in Covington, Ky.

Newspaper publisher James Gordon Bennett, just back from England—where polo, the ancient Persian sport, was enjoying a revival—arranged an indoor match at Dickel's Riding Academy in New York City. It was the first time polo was played in the United States. Bennett imported white-painted willow balls, rattan mallets, knee guards, spurs, and other accessories for the players. The horses were brought from Texas by Harry Blasson, a New York riding master. On May 11, a team captained by Bennett played Lord Mandeville's British team at Jerome Park in Westchester County, N.Y. (The park had been built by and named for Leonard Jerome, the father of Jennie Jerome, a Brooklyn belle who was destined to become Winston Churchill's mother.) Polo was never to become a widely popular sport; the expense of maintaining a stable of thoroughbred polo ponies was too great for the average citizen.

But despite all these varied activities, there was one overriding interest in the United States in 1876: the Centennial celebration of American independence. It permeated the nation's thinking, stirred its imagination, and aroused its pride. America's literati were lavishing their talents on the subject. In commemoration of the occasion, William Cullen Bryant composed two of his most memorable poems, "A Lifetime" and "The Flood of Years." Sidney Lanier wrote an official Centennial Ode entitled "Psalm of the West." James Russell Lowell composed "An Ode for the Fourth of July 1876." Walt Whitman, keeping abreast of the times, brought out a two-volume Author's, or Centennial, Edition of his *Leaves of Grass*, the sixth edition of the collection.

The Centennial celebration was not, however, the exclusive domain of the poets. It was a major preoccupation of most Americans in 1876, and the 236-acre (95-hectare) Philadelphia Exposition with its 50 buildings and 60,000 items on display was its focal point. The exposition opened on May 10 with a spectacular parade, a specially commissioned but less-than-inspiring march composed by Richard Wagner, the singing of a Centennial hymn with words by John Greenleaf Whittier, and a platitudinous speech by President Ulysses S. Grant. Emperor Pedro II of Brazil was an honored guest. By November 10, the day the exposition closed, 9,789,392 persons had passed through its newly invented turnstiles.

It was a show of shows, a mammoth potpourri with something for everyone. Statuary was tastefully scattered throughout the grounds. There was a much-admired bronze of Robert R. Livingston, the man who had sworn in George Washington as the first President of the United States, and, from the skilled hands of architect Larkin G. Mead, a huge figure of Revolutionary War hero Ethan Allen, who was depicted demanding the surrender of Fort Ticonderoga. There were many more, but the center of attraction was Thomas Hall's gigantic statue of Daniel Webster, which stood 14 feet (4.3 meters) high. Later in the year, it would be given a place of honor in New York City's Central Park, a masterpiece of urban planning by Frederick Law Olmsted and Calvert Vaux that had just been completed.

There were numerous fountains on the grounds. Some, like that of the Woman's Christian Temperance Union, spurted jets of pure clean water to slake one's thirst; others splashed cascades of perfumed water with which to bathe one's hands and face. There were elaborately decorated restaurants featuring German, French, Japanese, Hungarian, Brazilian, Austrian, or Tunisian food. One of the most popular oases was operated by a man named Charles E. Hires, who prepared before the eyes of his customers a concoction called root beer. There

The Prince of Wales invests an Indian rajah with the Grand Cross of the Star of India in Calcutta during a good-will tour in 1876 designed to soothe ruffled feelings over Queen Victoria's new title: empress of India.

was even a narrow-gauge railroad circling the exposition grounds to transport footsore sightseers.

But only inside the buildings could one get the kind of kaleidoscopic view that gave a truly composite picture of America's first 100 years. Multiform and multipurpose, the objects on display ranged from "guaranteed impregnable" Yale locks to a novelty called linoleum, from Pullman berths to inks for all purposes. There were candy, chewing tobacco, and popcorn machines, as well as hydraulic rams and automatic railroad switches. Toys, pottery, and porcelain competed for attention with watches, roofing slate, steamship models, and fire engines. There was even a machine, run by a little girl, that could stick 180,000 pins into paper in a day. The mind reeled at the seemingly unending parade of objects: horseshoes, baking powder, and rotary lamps for lighthouses; laundry soap, grindstones, and totem poles; a piece of California redwood and a model of a Pennsylvania oil well; guns, books, and aquariums filled with saltwater fish; John Paul Jones's original flag, Benjamin Franklin's printing press, and George Washington's camping equipment. (After June 25, however, there was one exhibit–of famous American Indians modeled in papier-mâché– that drew hostile glances from fairgoers; on that date in 1876, Lieutenant Colonel George A. Custer and his troops were massacred by Indians at the Battle of the Little Bighorn–"Custer's Last Stand"–in the Montana Territory. The sole survivor on the battlefield was a horse named Comanche, which was retired with honors at Fort Riley and never ridden again.)

The major attraction of the exposition was an engine–a gleaming black behemoth–that stood in the Great Hall of the Main Building. Built by Cornell University engineers, the Corliss engine–it was called a "beneficent Titan"–was a double-acting, duplex vertical engine, capable of generating, through 20 tubular boilers outside the building, a then-unbelievable 1,400 horsepower of energy.

The Corliss engine's significance lay in its ability to generate, within one giant unit, enough energy to supply the needs of the 8,000 other, multipurpose machines operating simultaneously in the hall. It was a stunning concept of power usage. Yet those who failed to foresee the implications that the engine held for future technological development could not be faulted for lack of foresight. Who in 1976, for example, would have dared predict unequivocally where genetic engineering or the landing of *Viking 1* on Mars would lead? Similarly, what present-day seer could have foretold unerringly which infants being held along the thousands of Bicentennial parade routes on July 4, 1976, might one day add new dimensions to the world of knowledge?

There were none. Yet as surely as the seeds of Centennial 1876 had grown into the oaks of Bicentennial 1976, so those of Tricentennial 2076 were taking root amid the minutiae of today. The seedlings–the future Bells, Otises, Carriers, and even the long-lived Charlie Smiths– may not have been discernible. But they were indisputably there.

The Year On File, 1976

Contributors to THE WORLD BOOK YEAR BOOK report on
the major developments of 1976 in their respective fields. The
names of these contributors appear at the end of the articles
they have written. A complete roster of contributors,
giving their professional affiliations and listing the articles
they have prepared, appears on pages 6 and 7.

Articles in this section are alphabetically arranged by subject
matter. In most cases, their titles refer directly to articles in
THE WORLD BOOK ENCYCLOPEDIA. Numerous cross-references
(in bold type) are a part of this alphabetical listing. Their function
is to guide the reader to a subject or to information that
may be a part of some other article, or that may appear under
an alternative title. *See* and *See also* cross-references appear
within and at the end of articles and similarly direct the reader
to related information contained elsewhere in THE YEAR BOOK.

ADVERTISING

ADVERTISING. The worldwide advertising picture brightened in 1976. Among advertising agencies, J. Walter Thompson Company led the pack, entering 1976 with worldwide billings reported at $900.1 million. Young & Rubicam International led in U.S. billings with $476.6 million.

By far the largest proportion of advertising dollars continued to be spent in the United States. A $4-billion increase raised the 1976 U.S. ad total to a record $32.4 billion. The figures are conservative estimates based on the annual compilation by McCann-Erickson, New York City.

Bicentennial promotion activities contributed to the advertising surge, as did the presidential election campaign, the Olympic Games, and a gradually recovering economy. The results showed in retail sales, which rose 11.3 per cent in the 12 months ending in April 1976, compared with a 9.6 per cent boost in the eight-month period extending from the recession low point in May 1975 to year-end. The Marketing Economics Institute reported that top sales increases in the first half of 1976 were in durable goods, led by automobile dealers, whose sales rose 29.3 per cent.

Top Advertisers. Biggest contributor to the U.S. advertising total was Sears, Roebuck and Company, the nation's largest advertiser, whose annual ad expenditure is now estimated at $510 million. This total includes $285 million in retail advertising for stores and $225 million in national advertising. More than half of the total is for its famous catalogs. Most of the remainder is in television and magazines. Biggest national advertiser, excluding retail ads, was the Procter & Gamble Company, with an annual total estimated at $360 million.

Brightening the picture for incorporated agencies, net profit after taxes rose to an average of 3.91 per cent of gross income. The American Association of Advertising Agencies said this was the highest level since net profit hit 4.03 per cent in 1969. Bolstering the increase was a notable achievement—more advertising from fewer people. At last count, 414 member shops of the association had 36,000 employees, compared with 365 members with 42,-000 employees in 1968. During that period, billings rose 38 per cent, while the ratio of employees per $1-million of billings dropped from 7.1 to 4.5.

Supreme Court Ruling. One of the most significant developments of 1976 was a May 24 decision by the Supreme Court of the United States broadening the protection of freedom of commercial speech (advertising) under the First Amendment. The decision strengthened the hand of advertisers against critics who would ban some ads and against Federal Trade Commission (FTC) efforts to impose standardized rules.

Although lower courts and the FTC have agreed that ads dealing with public issues have First Amendment protection, the new decision went much further. It held that advertising that tells what is available and at what price is also in the public interest for varied reasons, including its indispensable role in the operation of a free-enterprise market place. The court stressed that ads still can be regulated on such grounds as deception.

Ironically, the case originated with consumer groups that defended advertising's First Amendment status in contention with businessmen—Virginia pharmacists—who opposed the idea. The court ruling upset a Virginia law prohibiting pharmacists from advertising prices for prescription drugs. The question raised, the court said, was whether commercial speech involves sufficient public interest to qualify for First Amendment standing. A 7-to-1 majority said yes.

Another Legal Development with potentially big repercussions was the start of hearings in May in an FTC antitrust case against the Big Four cereal makers—Kellogg, General Mills, General Foods, and Quaker Oats. The FTC alleged that the companies maintained profits and market control without necessarily engaging in a conspiracy. By marketing ever more cereal brands, using heavy advertising to differentiate these brands in the consumer's mind, and controlling market shelf space, the companies kept out competitors and "shared a monopoly," the FTC maintained.

An advertising campaign—"Roll up your sleeves, America"—urged the public to get vaccinated for protection against the threat of swine flu.

Advertising men and women from throughout the world watch a slide film
of the industry's history during an Advertising Week observance in Chicago.

If the FTC wins the case, which might drag on for years, it could mean a court-ordered breakup of cereal operations of the companies. "Every industry has a few leaders and a lot of small marketers," General Mills attorney and former FTC Chairman Edward Howrey said in defense of the companies.

The Cost Squeeze. Advertisers sought relief in "alternative media" from the rising advertising cost crunch, particularly in television, where time was scarce and prices the highest in history. TV production houses suggested that advertisers set up their own quasi-networks to furnish groups of stations with quality programs — supplied by the production houses, of course. Nearing the start of the fourth quarter, Archa Knowles, director of media services for General Foods, a major TV advertiser, urged creation of a fourth commercial television network to relieve cost pressure and improve the quality of programs.

With magazine ad rates more stable than television's rates, the Magazine Publishers Association launched the biggest ad campaign in eight years in the fall. Jack Kauffman, president of the Newspaper Advertising Bureau, told a meeting of newspaper executives in July that 1976 would end up as a boom year, with $9.7 billion in newspaper ad revenues, partly because of advertisers avoiding the soaring television rates. Merle Kingman

AFARS AND ISSAS. See AFRICA.

AFGHANISTAN improved relations with neighboring Pakistan and Iran in 1976 and started a seven-year economic development plan to mark the third anniversary of the Republic of Afghanistan. President Mohammad Daoud exchanged state visits with Pakistan's Zulfikar Ali Bhutto in June. Although no definite steps were taken to resolve their differences, which stem mainly from Afghan support of autonomy for the Baluchi tribesmen and their ethnic cousins the Pathans in Pakistan, each agreed not to intervene in the other's affairs.

Feasibility studies began on various projects to be carried out with the help of $700 million pledged by Iran in October 1975. The proposals included a trans-Afghan railway, textile and sugar mills, and development of a livestock industry.

The Afghan National Oil Company's oil strike in August at Qashqari in northern Afghanistan increased oil reserves to an estimated 7.7 million short tons (7 million metric tons), with two refineries in the area producing 55,000 short tons (50,000 metric tons) annually.

The seven-year plan, issued in March, set $310-million for development, with 63 per cent of this amount to come from outside sources. Russia agreed to postpone collection of $75 million in loans until 1986 to relieve Afghanistan's balance of payments problem. William Spencer

See also ASIA (Facts in Brief Table).

AFRICA

Southern Africa became a major world trouble spot during 1976. A violent civil war in Angola that drew in foreign powers ended early in the year, but Rhodesia faced the threat of all-out civil war between blacks and whites if a negotiated settlement could not be worked out. Meanwhile, negotiations and guerrilla warfare went on simultaneously in Namibia (South West Africa), and the white minority government of South Africa was shaken by many months of violent black protests in urban areas.

Self-government came peacefully to the Seychelles in 1976, and the last French colony in Africa, the Territory of Afars and Issas, made progress toward gaining independence. But Burundi's government was overthrown by a military coup d'état, and there were coup attempts in several other African nations.

Angola's Civil War between black nationalist factions ended in February. However, scattered guerrilla fighting continued throughout the year. The winning side, the Popular Movement for the Liberation of Angola (MPLA) under Agostinho Neto, received military aid from Cuba and Russia. Cuba provided from 10,000 to 12,000 soldiers to fight alongside MPLA forces. The Russians supplied weapons that gave the MPLA-Cuban offensives superior firepower. President Gerald R. Ford's efforts to supply MPLA rivals were thwarted by the U.S. Congress, which prohibited arms shipments to Angola. Many congressmen feared that the United States would have another Vietnam on its hands if arms were sent.

The MPLA's rivals lost control of all major towns by the end of February. But they were still able to mount guerrilla attacks, especially in the southern part of Angola. See ANGOLA.

Rhodesian Tensions. An increased number of black guerrillas infiltrated Rhodesia from Mozambique. The guerrilla activity began in 1972, and the present situation stemmed from Nov. 11, 1965, when a white government under Prime Minister Ian D. Smith unilaterally declared independence from Great Britain. Britain, which insisted upon a transition to black-majority rule, responded with diplomatic and economic sanctions against the Smith regime. Blacks outnumber whites in Rhodesia by about 25 to 1.

In 1966, the United Nations (UN) Security Council acted, prohibiting UN members from purchasing Rhodesia's major exports.

These sanctions had limited success, because both South Africa and Mozambique, which was then ruled by Portugal, refused to comply. However, newly independent Mozambique joined in the UN economic sanctions on March 3, 1976, and closed its border with Rhodesia (see MOZAMBIQUE). Rhodesia, left surrounded by black African nations, was dependent solely on white-ruled South Africa for its trade with the outside world.

South Africa's government, however, appeared not to want the economic and military burden of supporting Rhodesia's whites through a prolonged civil war. In August, South Africa withdrew pilots and technicians who had been aiding Rhodesia in

Black protesters back away in fear as a white policeman brings in an attack dog to break up a demonstration near Cape Town, South Africa.

military operations against black guerrillas. On September 19, South Africa's Prime Minister Balthazar Johannes Vorster reportedly told Smith not to expect continued military aid.

Faced with these economic and military pressures, Smith's government agreed on September 24 to a U.S.-British plan allowing black-majority rule within two years. A conference between black nationalists and Smith's government opened in Geneva, Switzerland, on October 28, but it soon deadlocked over the timetable for independence and the nature of the interim government. See RHODESIA.

Namibian Talks. On the surface, negotiations between Namibia's blacks and whites made considerable progress in pushing Namibia toward inde-

pendence from South African colonial rule. A constitutional conference representing the territory's 11 ethnic groups on August 18 agreed on independence by the end of 1978 and on a multiracial interim government. However, the most influential black nationalist party, the South-West Africa People's Organization (SWAPO), was excluded from the conference. SWAPO rejected the conference's plan for transition to independence. But SWAPO's cooperation, or at least compliance, seemed necessary, because it had developed a significant guerrilla-warfare capability with the help of Russian arms and bases in neighboring Angola. The UN also rejected the plan, calling it "ambiguous and equivocal." See NAMIBIA.

Facts in Brief on African Political Units

Country	Population	Government	Monetary Unit*	Foreign Trade (million U.S. $) Exports	Imports
Algeria	17,890,000	President Houari Boumediene	dinar (4.2 = $1)	4,442	5,861
Angola	6,340,000	President Agostinho Neto; Prime Minister Lopo Do Nascimento	escudo (31 = $1)	1,202	614
Botswana	747,000	President Sir Seretse M. Khama	pula (1 = $1.15)	77	125
Burundi	3,981,000	President Jean-Baptiste Bagaza; Prime Minister Edouard Nzabimana	franc (90 = $1)	27	62
Cameroon	6,649,000	President Ahmadou Ahidjo; Prime Minister Paul Biya	CFA franc (249.5 = $1)	448	599
Cape Verde	305,000	President Aristides Pereira; Prime Minister Pedro Pires	escudo (31 = $1)	2	34
Central African Empire	1,880,000	Emperor Bokassa I; Prime Minister Ange Patasse	CFA franc (249.5 = $1)	47	54
Chad	4,187,000	Supreme Military Council President F. Malloum Ngakoutou Bey-Ndi	CFA franc (249.5 = $1)	37	87
Comoros	320,000	Chief of State Ali Soilih; Prime Minister Abdellah Mohamed	CFA franc (249.5 = $1)	5	15
Congo	1,104,000	President Marien N'Gouabi; Prime Minister Louis Sylvain Goma	CFA franc (249.5 = $1)	243	254
Dahomey (Benin)	3,239,000	President & Chief of Government Mathieu Kerekou	CFA franc (249.5 = $1)	53	113
Egypt	38,859,000	President Anwar al-Sadat; Prime Minister Mamduh Muhammad Salim	pound (1 = $2.56)	1,402	3,751
Equatorial Guinea	316,000	President Macias Nguema Biyogo Negue Ndong	ekpwele (66.6 = $1)	32	36
Ethiopia	28,115,000	Provisional Military Government Chairman Teferi Bante	birr (2.1 = $1)	239	310
Gabon	1,026,000	President Omar Bongo; Prime Minister Leon Mebiame	CFA franc (249.5 = $1)	942	469
Gambia	543,000	President Sir Dawda Kairaba Jawara	dalasi (2.4 = $1)	44	60
Ghana	10,407,000	Supreme Military Council Chairman Ignatius Kutu Acheampong	new cedi (1.15 = $1)	820	805
Guinea	4,627,000	President Ahmed Sekou Toure; Prime Minister Lansana Beavogui	syli (20.7 = $1)	70	100
Guinea-Bissau	540,000	President Luis de Almeida Cabral	escudo (31 = $1)	3	44
Ivory Coast	5,123,000	President Felix Houphouet-Boigny	CFA franc (249.5 = $1)	1,181	1,127
Kenya	14,379,000	President Jomo Kenyatta	shilling (8.4 = $1)	601	938
Lesotho	1,084,000	King Motlotlehi Moshoeshoe II; Prime Minister Leabua Jonathan	rand (1 = $1.15)	10	70
Liberia	1,860,000	President William R. Tolbert, Jr.	dollar (1 = $1)	394	331
Libya	2,661,000	Revolutionary Command Council President Muammar Muhammad al-Qadhaafi; Prime Minister Abd as-Salam Jallud	dinar (1 = $3.38)	6,121	4,400
Malagasy (Madagascar)	7,810,000	Supreme Revolutionary Council President Didier Ratsiraka; Prime Minister Justin Rakotoniaina	franc (249.5 = $1)	244	281
Malawi	5,309,000	President H. Kamuzu Banda	kwacha (1 = $1.07)	137	250

Violent Protests by urban blacks challenged South Africa's white-minority rule. Beginning on June 16, there were unprecedented disorders, sometimes involving arson and looting. The protests were confined mostly to segregated black townships outside cities. About 400 persons were killed during these disorders from June to December. The protests brought minor concessions from the white government, including limited desegregation of competitive sports and improved property rights for blacks living in townships. See SOUTH AFRICA.

The Transkei on October 26 became the first tribal homeland to formally gain independence. South Africa's official policy of "separate development" provides that blacks have political rights only in the tribal "homelands" established by the white government. The 10 homelands comprise 13 per cent of South Africa's land. Each is supposed to become a sovereign state. See TRANSKEI.

Russian-U.S. Rivalries. Russian influence in southern Africa grew because of the region's instability. Angola's President Neto signed a 20-year treaty of friendship and cooperation with Russia on October 8. The treaty also provided for military aid, needed in part to help combat Angola's internal guerrillas. SWAPO forces operating from Angola were armed with Russian weapons, as were Rhodesian guerrillas based in Mozambique. President Samora Moises Machel of Mozambique visited Moscow in May.

Country	Population	Government	Monetary Unit*	Foreign Trade (million U.S. $) Exports	Imports
Mali	5,840,000	President & Prime Minister Moussa Traore	franc (498 = $1)	64	179
Mauritania	1,398,000	President Moktar Ould Daddah	ouguiya (45 = $1)	181	121
Mauritius	899,000	Governor General Sir Abdul Raman Osman; Prime Minister Sir Seewoosagur Ramgoolam	rupee (6.7 = $1)	298	332
Morocco	18,360,000	King Hassan II; Prime Minister Ahmed Osman	dirham (4.5 = $1)	1,543	2,567
Mozambique	9,810,000	President Samora Moises Machel	escudo (31 = $1)	298	467
Namibia (South West Africa)	956,000	Administrator B. J. van der Walt	rand (1 = $1.15)	no statistics available	
Niger	4,714,000	Supreme Military Council President Seyni Kountche	CFA franc (249.5 = $1)	53	97
Nigeria	66,310,000	Head of State Olusegun Obasanjo	naira (1 = $1.60)	8,096	6,035
Rhodesia	6,797,000	President John Wrathall; Prime Minister Ian D. Smith	dollar (1 = $1.60)	652	541
Rwanda	4,432,000	President Juvenal Habyarimana	franc (92.8 = $1)	42	96
São Tomé and Príncipe	84,000	President Manuel Pinto da Costa; Prime Minister Miguel Trovoada	escudo (31 = $1)	13	10
Senegal	4,666,000	President Leopold Sedar Senghor; Prime Minister Abdou Diouf	CFA franc (249.5 = $1)	450	561
Seychelles	62,000	President James Richard Mancham; Prime Minister France Albert Rene	rupee (6.7 = $1)	3	27
Sierra Leone	2,834,000	President Siaka Stevens; Prime Minister Christian A. Kamara-Taylor	leone (1 = $1.13)	131	185
Somalia	3,315,000	President Mohamed Siad Barre	shilling (6.3 = $1)	62	129
South Africa	24,995,000	President Nicolaas J. Diederichs; Prime Minister Balthazar Johannes Vorster	rand (1 = $1.15)	5,383	8,293
Sudan	18,655,000	President Gaafar Muhammed Nimeiri; Prime Minister El Rashid El Tahir	pound (1 = $2.87)	438	887
Swaziland	548,000	King Sobhuza II; Prime Minister Maphevu Dlamini	lilangeni (1 = $1.15)	139	92
Tanzania	15,980,000	President Julius K. Nyerere; Prime Minister Rashidi Kawawa	shilling (8.4 = $1)	370	772
Togo	2,328,000	President Gnassingbe Eyadema	CFA franc (249.5 = $1)	189	120
Transkei	1,500,000	President Botha Sigcau; Prime Minister Kaiser Matanzima	rand (1 = $1.15)	no statistics available	
Tunisia	6,057,000	President Habib Bourguiba; Prime Minister Hedi Nouira	dinar (1 = $2.37)	856	1,424
Uganda	12,309,000	President Idi Amin Dada	shilling (8.4 = $1)	258	200
Upper Volta	6,234,000	President Aboubakar Sangoule Lamizana	CFA franc (249.5 = $1)	44	151
Zaire	26,315,000	President Mobutu Sese Seko	zaire (1 = $1.15)	1,374	990
Zambia	5,319,000	President Kenneth D. Kaunda; Prime Minister Elijah Mudenda	kwacha (1 = $1.25)	763	1,075

*Exchange rates as of Dec. 1, 1976.

U.S. Secretary of State Henry A. Kissinger tried to offset the growing Russian military influence by promoting negotiated settlements in Rhodesia and Namibia. He made two trips to Africa during 1976 – from April 24 to May 6 and from September 14 to 24. He also met with South Africa's Prime Minister Vorster in West Germany on June 23 and 24 and again in Switzerland from September 4 to 6. He needed Vorster's aid to promote independence under black rule for Namibia and to pressure Rhodesia to accept a black-majority government.

Kissinger also met with the leaders of Tanzania and Zambia, hoping that they would persuade the black nationalists to negotiate. Kissinger's African "shuttle diplomacy" reached its peak with a Sep-tember 19 meeting in Pretoria, South Africa, during which he and Vorster persuaded Smith to accept a transition to black rule within two years.

In the campaign to counter Russian influence in Africa, the United States provided military aid to two friendly governments. In June, Donald H. Rumsfeld made the first official visit to Africa by a U.S. secretary of defense. He agreed to supply Kenya with 12 F-5 jet fighters, and he promised increased U.S. military assistance to Zaire.

Ending Colonial Rule. Great Britain on June 28 ended its rule over the Seychelles, a group of 92 islands off the east coast of Africa with a population of about 62,000 people. It became independent under a coalition government with James Richard

Carrying their belongings and children, Angolans flee the fighting between rival nationalist groups vying for control of the country.

Mancham, leader of the Democratic Party, as president and France Albert Rene of the United Party as prime minister. See SEYCHELLES.

The French government announced on August 4 that a referendum on the independence of France's last colony on the African continent, the Territory of Afars and Issas, would take place in early 1977. The territory's future was clouded by conflict between its two major ethnic groups, the Issas and the Afars. Because the Issas are a Somali people, the Afars fear that neighboring Somalia will try to annex the colony after its independence. During the year, there were clashes between French and Somali troops and also between Afars and Issas tribesmen.

In the Indian Ocean nation of Comoros, the people of one island, Mayotte, voted on February 9 by a large margin to stay linked with France. Comoros' Chief of State Ali Soilih had unilaterally declared the islands independent of France in July 1975. The French National Assembly recognized the independence of only three of the four islands and called for the referendum on Mayotte.

Fighting Future Droughts. In May, the U.S. government announced its support for a $7.5-billion international program to develop the drought-prone Sahel region of west and central Africa south of the Sahara. The Sahel covers seven countries—Mauritania, Senegal, Gambia, Mali,

Upper Volta, Niger, and Chad. The development program will be financed by these countries, plus any interested foreign powers.

The program will help the region to recover from the severe effects of the 1968 to 1973 drought. It will also help to develop the capacity for surviving future droughts with less destruction of crops, livestock, and human life. The 1976 harvests were expected to be satisfactory in most of the Sahel. But Chad again suffered from inadequate rainfall.

Organization of African Unity (OAU) grew to 48 members by adding Angola and the Seychelles in 1976. The OAU's 13th annual summit meeting, in Port Louis, Mauritius, in July, endorsed increased guerrilla warfare against the white Rhodesian government and voted new financial aid for guerrillas based in Mozambique. It also required all member governments not to recognize the "fraudulent pseudo-independence" of Transkei.

The OAU recommended boycotting the 1976 Olympic Games if New Zealand participated, because New Zealand's government permitted sports ties with South Africa. The International Olympic Committee refused to oust New Zealand, and most African countries withdrew their teams. Only two nations, the Ivory Coast and Senegal, remained in the games (see OLYMPIC GAMES). Sir Seewoosagur Ramgoolam, prime minister of Mauritius, became the new OAU chairman.

Regional Economic Relations. The new Economic Community of West African States, established in 1975, held its first ministerial council meeting in Accra, Ghana, in July. The meeting ended with an agreement for cooperation in trade policy and funding for economic development.

The economic cooperation programs of the East African Community (EAC) continued to suffer from political conflict among member states. Kenyans employed in EAC agencies in Uganda reportedly fled the country, fearing reprisals after Kenya aided an Israeli commando raid on July 3 and 4 to rescue Jewish hostages held in Uganda by airplane hijackers. See ISRAEL; UGANDA.

Kenya subsequently prohibited Ugandan pilots flying EAC planes from entering Kenyan airspace. Kenya also expelled Tanzanians and Ugandans working for EAC corporations in Kenya. In July, Tanzania's government took over the administration of railways and harbors in its territory from an EAC corporation.

The Afro-Malagasy Common Organization (OCAM), a cooperative grouping of French-speaking states, was weakened by the withdrawal of one of its richest members, Gabon, on September 8. Gabon was the seventh nation to leave OCAM. This reduced OCAM's membership to nine African countries.

A dancer entertains Kenya's President Kenyatta and Henry Kissinger during the U.S. secretary of state's first visit to black Africa, in April.

Turbulent Southern Africa

Cameroon
Equatorial Guinea
Gabon
Congo
Uganda
Kenya
Equator
Rwanda
Burundi
Lake Victoria
Zaire
Lake Tanganyika
Tanzania
Cabinda (Angola)
Angola
Lake Nyasa
Zambia
Malawi
Salisbury
Rhodesia
Mozambique
South West Africa (Namibia)
Botswana
Walvis Bay (South Africa)
Indian Ocean
Johannesburg
South Atlantic Ocean
Swaziland
South Africa
Lesotho
Transkei
Cape Town

0   500 Miles
0   500 Kilometers

Coups and Plots. In November, Burundi's armed forces overthrew the government of President Michel Micombero in a coup d'état. Micombero had come to power by a military coup in 1966, replacing a monarchy with a one-party government. Coup leader Lieutenant Colonel Jean-Baptiste Bagaza dissolved the party and suspended the Constitution.

On February 3, plotters attempted to kill President Jean-Bedel Bokassa of the Central African Republic. In December, Bokassa changed the country's name to Central African Empire and made himself emperor.

The military crushed a coup attempt on February 13 in Nigeria. However, the insurgents succeeded in killing the head of Nigeria's military government, General Murtala Ramat Muhammed. See NIGERIA; OBASANJO, OLUSEGUN.

Niger's military government was also the target of a miscarried coup in March. The attempt, the third in three years, was reportedly headed by two army officers and a labor union leader. On April 13, three persons were killed during a grenade attack on Chad's President F. Malloum Ngakoutou Bey-Ndi, who escaped unharmed.   John D. Esseks

See also Section Five, ANGOLA; CAPE VERDE; COMOROS; LUANDA; MAPUTO; MOZAMBIQUE; SÃO TOMÉ; SÃO TOMÉ AND PRÍNCIPE; SEYCHELLES; VICTORIA.

AGRICULTURE

AGRICULTURE. The world food supply improved in 1976. But a United Nations Food and Agriculture Organization report in November cautioned that world supplies, though increasing, were still lagging behind the needs of the world's hungry. A National Academy of Sciences report to the United States government warned that important scientific breakthroughs in food production must be made by the end of this century if drastic international upheavals over food supplies are to be avoided.

World grain and rice production hit a record 1.4 billion short tons (1.3 billion metric tons) in 1976. Rice production was down slightly from 1975's record output, but bumper crops of other grains, especially wheat, brought world production to a level that exceeded consumption by 28.6 million short tons (26 million metric tons). This is the first time since 1971 that production has significantly exceeded consumption. In the span from 1971 to 1976, world consumption topped production by an average of 13.2 million short tons (12 million metric tons).

These record crops are attributable primarily to generally good weather and a continuing increase in the area harvested. The area harvested throughout the world has increased almost 9 per cent from 1.67 billion acres (676 million hectares) to 1.82 billion acres (735 million hectares) since 1970.

A cow poisoned by polybrominated biphenyls (PBBs) in its feed is buried in Michigan. More than 32,000 have been destroyed in two years.

Russian grain production rebounded from the disastrous 1975 crop. The 1976 grain crop of 246.7-million short tons (224 million metric tons) exceeded the previous record of 245 million short tons (222 million metric tons) harvested by Russian farmers in 1973.

Drought Conditions that began in Western Europe in the spring and extended into Eastern Europe during the summer reduced production in that area. France was especially hard hit by drought, and grain production there was 25 per cent below normal and 15 per cent below the country's poor crop of 1975.

The world cotton crop was larger than in 1975, but it did not equal the record 1974 crop. A significantly bigger U.S. crop provided most of the increase in world production. Coffee production fell 15 per cent, the smallest crop since 1970. Reduced production was due primarily to a severe frost in Brazil in July 1975.

Soybean production dropped almost 10 per cent from the record 1975 crop, but it was still the second largest crop on record. Most of the decline resulted from a major U.S. reduction. American farmers switched acreage from soybeans to corn and cotton in 1976.

World output of meat—beef, veal, pork, and poultry—was up in 1976. A decline in production by European Community (Common Market) countries was more than offset by increased U.S. production. However, the number of cattle in the world on Jan. 1, 1976, showed an increase of less than 1 per cent, compared with an average 3 per cent annual increase since 1972. Hog numbers fell over 5 per cent from January 1975 to January 1976. This sharp drop resulted primarily from a 20 per cent reduction in both the United States and Russia.

American Agriculture had a good year, with two large harvests back-to-back and record livestock production. Many farmers earned the largest income of their careers, with large supplies and a good demand both in the United States and other countries.

But by year's end, farmers were restless and concerned. They recalled the 1972-to-1974 pressure from dire world food needs and the volatile prices, high costs, and erratic weather in many areas. The number of livestock was up and stocks of grain were mounting, but world export competition was also increasing. Finally, nearly all major farm legislation was due to expire in 1977.

The U.S. crop harvest, though down from the 1975 record, was still the third highest in history, exceeded only by 1975 and 1973. The all-crops production index was at 118 (1967=100), compared with 122 in 1975 and 110 in 1974.

A record corn crop and substantially higher cotton production led the way. Corn production was 5 per cent above the 1974 record, mainly because of a 6 per cent increase of land planted in corn. Increased acreage was also the major factor in the 19 per cent increase in cotton output.

Farmers' shift of production acreage to corn and cotton resulted in an 8 per cent drop in soybean acreage. The reduced acreage, combined with a lower yield per acre, caused total U.S. soybean production to fall 18 per cent from the 1975 record.

The good overall crop harvest was achieved in spite of severe drought conditions throughout the spring and summer in the North Central States, especially in Minnesota and the Dakotas.

Livestock Production rebounded from 1975's low levels but was still below 1974's. The overall livestock production index was 103 in 1976 (1967=100), compared with 100 in 1975 and 110 in 1974. Chicken and turkey production registered the largest gains, up 12 per cent and 13 per cent, respectively. Beef, pork, milk, and eggs registered smaller gains.

Farm Prices rose early in the year, but fell off somewhat by year's end. The index of prices received by farmers climbed to 195 (1967=100) in June and July, but had receded to 173 by November, 6 per cent below November 1975.

The year-end price decline covered many major commodities. Wheat was $2.46 per bushel in November, down 31 per cent from 1975; corn was $2.02 per bushel, down 13 per cent; sorghum grain was $3.30 per hundredweight (cwt.), down 19 per cent; beef cattle averaged $31.10 per cwt., down 4 per cent; and hogs were $31.10 per cwt., down 37 per cent. Soybean and cotton prices were up 37 per cent and 28 per cent, respectively.

While prices received by farmers rose and fell during the year, the index of prices farmers paid for supplies and equipment held relatively constant at an index of 194 to 195 (1967=100). Nevertheless, the November index was 5 per cent higher than a year earlier.

American Farm Finances again set records. Total farm assets rose 8.3 per cent to a record $634-billion. However, farm debt also rose 11 per cent to a record $101.5 billion. Thus, the debt-to-asset ratio, which measures how much farmers owe against the value of their assets, rose from 15.7 per cent to 16 per cent during 1976. Despite the rise in debt and the slight rise in the debt-to-asset ratio, farmers' liquidity improved. Their commercial bank deposits and currency rose to $16.1 billion from $15.6-billion in 1975.

A major portion of the increase in farm assets was attributable to the continued upward movement in land prices. Between March 1, 1975, and Feb. 1, 1976, the average value of an acre (0.404 hectare) of farmland climbed almost $50 to $403.

The Farm Work Force dropped 4 per cent in numbers from October 1975 to October 1976.

Agricultural Statistics, 1976
World Crop Production
(million units)

Crop	Units	1975	1976	%U.S.
Corn	Metric tons	318.9	327.6	47.0
Wheat	Metric tons	349.3	407.2	14.3
Rice	Metric tons	355.1	346.8	1.5
Barley	Metric tons	144.8	172.1	4.8
Oats	Metric tons	47.0	49.1	16.7
Rye	Metric tons	23.7	29.6	4.8
Soybeans	Metric tons	67.5	61.9	55.1
Cotton	Bales**	55.1	58.8	17.5
Coffee	Bags‡	73.5	62.8	0.3
Sugar (centrifugal)	Metric tons	81.9	87.0	7.2

**480 lbs. (217.7 kilograms) net
‡ 132.276 lbs. (60 kilograms)

Output of Major U.S. Crops
(millions of bushels)

Crop	1962–66†	1975	1976*
Corn	3,876	5,767	6,063
Sorghums	595	758	731
Oats	912	657	564
Wheat	1,229	2,134	2,127
Soybeans	769	1,521	1,252
Rice (a)	742	1,276	1,124
Potatoes (b)	275	319	349
Cotton (c)	140	83	99
Tobacco (d)	2,126	2,182	2,071

†Average; *preliminary
(a) 100,000 cwt. (4.54 million kilograms)
(b) 1 million cwt. (45.4 million kilograms)
(c) 100,000 bales (50 million lbs.) (22.7 million kilograms)
(d) 1 million lbs. (454,000 kilograms)

U.S. Production of Animal Products
(millions of pounds)

	1957–59†	1975	1976*
Beef	13,704	23,976	25,775
Veal	1,240	873	785
Lamb & Mutton	711	410	375
Pork	10,957	11,503	12,050
Eggs (a)	5,475	5,362	5,433
Chicken	5,292	11,034	12,350
Turkey	1,382	2,278	2,575
Total Milk (b)	123	115.5	118.6

†Average; *preliminary
(a) 1 million dozens
(b) billions of lbs. (454 million kilograms)

Wage rates continued to climb, up to $2.80 per hour from $2.63 in 1975. A U.S. Department of Agriculture (USDA) study showed that the average age of American farmers dropped for the first time in more than 50 years. The average age of farmers was 43.5 years in 1910. It climbed steadily to more than 53 years by 1970, but by 1975 had dropped to 50.4. Moreover, the number of farmers under 35 years of age rose 35 per cent, while the number over 60 fell 23 per cent.

U.S. Agricultural Exports reached $22.1 billion in fiscal 1976, a gain of $500 million. Expanded volume more than offset lower prices. Record export volumes were recorded for corn, soybeans, pork, cattle hides, burley tobacco, and fruits.

A Kansas farmer prepares his dusty field for spring planting. A dry winter and summer drought hit parts of the Great Plains and reduced crop yields.

The substantial increase in grain shipments to the Soviet Union was the most important boost to exports. The United States exported 15.4 million short tons (14 million metric tons) of grain to Russia in fiscal 1976, and total shipments of agricultural products to Russia were valued at approximately $2 billion.

Japan, which expanded its imports of U.S. agricultural products eightfold from fiscal 1956 to fiscal 1976, is still the largest single-country market for U.S. agricultural exports. It is also the largest net importer in the world, relying on imports for more than half its food.

Increases in world grain production suggest that 1977 U.S. agricultural exports may not equal those in 1976. But the drought in Europe has caused continued heavy demand for U.S. grain. Increased hog and poultry numbers in the Common Market and in Japan also helped to sustain the heavy demand for grain.

U.S. Agricultural Imports broke the $10-billion mark in fiscal 1976 as imports of most commodities except sugar rose. Raw sugar imports fell 6 per cent in volume and 44 per cent in value, to $1.4 billion.

The greatest dollar value increases in order of magnitude were for coffee, beef, dutiable cattle, pork, cacao beans, hides and skins, bananas, and dry form rubber. Green coffee imports reached a record value of $2 billion. Largest suppliers of imports were Brazil, Mexico, Australia, and Canada.

Federal Farm Policy changes provided some tax breaks for farmers. These included breaks on estate gifts; exemption for one year for most farmers from regulation by the Department of Labor's Occupational Safety and Health Administration; tighter grain-inspection laws; a packer-bonding law to protect livestock producers; and a Bureau of Land Management Organic Act freezing for a year the grazing fees ranchers pay to run their herds on public land. USDA's program of guaranteed loans to help stockmen survive periods of economic stress was extended for 21 months.

The Rice Production Act of 1975, passed in February 1976, suspended marketing quotas and penalties for 1976 and 1977 crops and removed restrictions on rice production. On January 30, President Gerald R. Ford vetoed a bill to increase price supports for dairy products. The 1976 national marketing quotas on burley tobacco were set at 630 million pounds (286 million kilograms). A national marketing quota of just over 2.2 million short tons (2 million metric tons) was announced on December 1 for the 1977 peanut crop.

The Environmental Protection Agency issued final regulations in March for the operation of livestock feedlots and estimated that 3,240 of the nation's 718,800 beef-, dairy-, and swine-feeding operations would require permits. The USDA asked the Department of Labor in November to establish an Agriculture Labor Relations Board.

Domestic food aid programs cost $7.8 billion, about two-thirds of the USDA's budget, in fiscal 1976. More than 45 million persons received food assistance of some type — 17.5 million received food stamps and 25.9 million received school-lunch program aid.

The first World Conference on Agriculture Education convened in Kansas City in early November as an international version of the Future Farmers of America (FFA) convention. It emphasized two changing aspects of agriculture — young people from 22 countries attended, and five of the U.S. state-chapter presidents attending were women.

Key Year? Farm policy has pivotal years in which major changes occur. Such years were 1933, 1949, and 1962. But the affluence and anxiety of agriculture in 1976 set the stage for such a year in 1977. Acting Secretary of Agriculture John A. Knebel said on November 23, "The new farm bill which must be written next year will be the most important piece of legislation to come before the 95th Congress in 1977."

But at the same time, the ability of the agricultural community to influence such legislation has diminished. "Consumers, labor, and a number of other groups have more clout than agriculture," Knebel said on November 15. "Fifty years ago, there were 251 congressional districts in which farm population contributed 20 per cent or more of the total. Today there are only 49 congressional districts with 20 per cent or more farm population."

New Technology. Direct control of pressure irrigation to use the least amount of water necessary was applied in many areas and increased the efficiency of water use. Scientists at the Snake River Conservation Research Center in Idaho used small irrigation furrows within the rows to reduce the amount of water used by 30 to 50 per cent. Irrigation systems have traditionally been aboveground, but USDA scientists have designed a system of buried irrigation pipes that allows other fieldwork to be done without disturbing the irrigation system.

University of California scientists at Riverside have developed an alfalfa variety that is smog-resistant. When exposed to smog, yields of other alfalfa varieties have been reduced as much as 60 per cent.

One of the most dramatic changes in culturing crops is minimum tillage. USDA scientists reported plowless farming was practiced on 6 million acres (2.4 million hectares) in 1976 and predicted that conventional tillage methods will be practiced on only 5 per cent of the cropland by the year 2010.

Iowa State University scientists have developed a workable way to spray fertilizers directly into soybean plants, and they report that the new spray may increase yields as much as 50 per cent. Soybean plants have been remarkably resistant to increases in yields by traditional scientific breeding and cultural techniques. USDA scientists in Texas and Hawaii have had promising success in controlling the blowfly, one of the most destructive pests to the livestock industry. They administer methoprene, a growth and reproduction inhibitor, in the cattle's drinking water. The methoprene infects the flies that bite the cattle. Scientists think that this method could open a new dimension in insect control, even for the common housefly.

Earl L. Butz Resigned as secretary of agriculture on October 4 after a storm of public protest over a racist remark. Undersecretary John A. Knebel became acting secretary on November 4. On December 20, President-elect James Earl (Jimmy) Carter, Jr., said he would nominate Representative Bob Bergland (D., Minn.) to be secretary of agriculture in his Administration. Charles E. French and Larry L. Nelson

AIR FORCE. See ARMED FORCES.
AIR POLLUTION. See ENVIRONMENT.
AIRPORT. See AVIATION.
ALABAMA. See STATE GOVERNMENT.
ALASKA. See STATE GOVERNMENT.

ALBANIA continued its harsh anti-Russian stance in 1976 but improved relations with its Balkan neighbors, especially Greece and Yugoslavia. First Secretary Enver Hoxha declared at the Communist Party Congress in Tiranë on November 1 that Albania would help Yugoslavia in case of a Russian attack. But Albania did not send delegates to the first conference on Balkan cooperation, held in Athens from January 26 to February 5.

World recession hurt Albania's economy. The proposed five-year plan published in November showed a slower pace of industrialization. But agricultural production was to increase 55 per cent by 1980. Hoxha announced that Albania was self-sufficient in grain for the first time in 1976.

Albania remained ideologically, politically, and economically close to China. A new steel mill at Elbasan, built with Chinese aid, was officially opened on October 15, while a cement works began production on October 26. Albanian officials ceremoniously mourned Mao Tse-tung's death and congratulated his successor, Hua Kuo-feng.

A government decree in February gave municipal authorities the right to change, by force if necessary, any citizen's first or family name in order to make the individual conform to the country's "political, ideological, and moral standards." Chris Cviic

See also EUROPE (Facts in Brief Table).

Albanian Communist Party First Secretary Enver Hoxha visits with factory workers during one of his rare public appearances.

ALBERTA. Canada's westernmost Prairie Province gained large revenues from its oil resources in 1976. It set aside some of these funds for future generations by establishing the Alberta Heritage Savings Trust Fund, a $1.5-billion public endowment. The act authorizing the fund provided that 30 per cent of oil royalties would be paid into it annually.

The Progressive Conservatives dominated the 75-seat Legislative Assembly, holding 69 seats. There were also 4 Social Credit members, 1 New Democratic Party representative, and 1 Independent. The Assembly passed 58 bills during its 51-day session, including a measure creating a home-mortgage corporation and a plan to reorganize provincial courts. A $2.9-billion budget presented on March 19 called for a 7.7 per cent increase in expenditures, modest when compared to the 25 per cent growth each year over the previous five years. There were no tax increases, retaining Alberta's distinction of having the lowest provincial taxes in Canada.

A new policy for exploiting Alberta's billions of tons of coal — half Canada's reserves — was announced in June. A complicated formula will net the province much larger revenues from future coal royalties. The $2-billion Syncrude Canada, Limited, plant on the Athabaska tar sands passed the halfway point in construction. David M. L. Farr

See also CANADA.

ALGERIA. The government of President Houari Boumediene announced a new national charter on April 26, 1976, that is designed to lay the base for a representative socialist system. Officials and party leaders of the National Liberation Front (FLN) then explained the charter's provisions at public meetings where attendance averaged about 200,000 persons. Boumediene's leadership and Algeria's commitment to socialism were not arguable, but all other facets of the charter were subject to popular criticism and change.

Algerian voters approved the charter in a June 26 referendum by a 98.5 per cent margin, and it went into effect on July 5. The charter declared Algeria "irrevocably committed to socialism," with the FLN as the only legal political organization. Islam is the state religion, and the weekly holiday was changed from Sunday to Friday to conform to Muslim practice.

Boumediene issued the charter in response to mounting criticism of his failure to introduce parliamentary reforms. On March 11, members of the original nationalist movement, including its founder, Ferhat Abbas, and Assembly Speaker Benyoussef ben Khedda, distributed an "Appeal to the Algerian People" calling for free elections, an end to one-man rule, and unity for North Africa. A Constitution, based on the new charter, and providing the machinery for the election of a new national assembly in January 1977, was overwhelmingly approved by the voters on November 19.

Saharan Fighting. Algeria's opposition to Moroccan control of the former Spanish Sahara brought the two neighbors close to war. In March, after a series of border clashes, Algeria recognized the anti-Morocco Saharan Arab Democratic Republic formed in the territory. The republic's military arm, the Popular Front for the Liberation of Sakiet el Hamra and Rio de Oro (Polisario), was armed and equipped by the Algerians and operated from the oasis of Tindouf. See MOROCCO.

Economic Development slowed because of skilled manpower shortages, port congestion, and inadequate transport facilities. Other problems were aggravated by Algeria's population growth. At an estimated 3.4 per cent a year, Algeria has one of the highest rates in the world. Major projects in the current $27.5-billion four-year plan were postponed. There were some bright spots. A record harvest provided grain to meet domestic needs.

In September, a nine-year, three-cycle program of basic education in primary, middle, and secondary schools began for the new class of 332,000 primary pupils. It replaced the two-cycle (primary and secondary) system. William Spencer

See also AFRICA (Facts in Brief Table).

AMERICAN LEGION. See COMMUNITY ORGANIZATIONS.

AMERICAN LIBRARY ASSOCIATION (ALA). About 9,000 librarians and others celebrated the ALA's 100th anniversary during the group's annual conference in Chicago in July 1976 (see Close-Up). Clara Stanton Jones, director of the Detroit Public Library, took office as ALA president. Eric Moon, president of Scarecrow Press, Metuchen, N.J., is president-elect. William Chait, director of the Dayton and Montgomery County Public Library in Ohio, was elected to a five-year term as treasurer.

Funds Problem. The ALA was faced with finding additional funds for libraries struggling under the double burden of rising costs and dwindling revenues. During the annual conference, Librarian of Congress Daniel J. Boorstin helped to launch Project Survival, an ALA campaign aimed at increasing public awareness of the financial plight of libraries. The ALA and Urban Library Council also cooperated in urging Congress to amend the Library Services and Construction Act to authorize federal grants to states for large urban libraries.

Other Actions. President Gerald R. Ford on July 19 announced that the first White House Conference on Library and Information Services would be held in accordance with a law passed in 1974. The conference, expected to be held in 1978, will provide a national forum for librarians, library users, and government officials to discuss the condition and future of libraries in the United States.

The ALA Council passed a resolution outlining specific steps to eliminate racism and sexism in library services and within the library profession. The ALA also established a permanent committee on the status of women in the profession.

The ALA also presented the views of librarians and library users to congressmen working on a revision of the U.S. copyright law. The new law, signed by the President on October 20, affects the ability of librarians to photocopy materials for patrons. The ALA also continued to distribute a manual to guide libraries in establishing literacy classes. Through this national campaign, the ALA hopes to reduce the number of functional illiterates, now estimated at 1 out of every 5 adults (see Section Two, THE LOSING WAR AGAINST ILLITERACY).

The Year's Awards. The ALA's official journal, *American Libraries,* and one of its divisions, the Association of College and Research Libraries, shared the 1976 J. Morris Jones-World Book Encyclopedia-ALA Goals Award and the Bailey K. Howard-World Book Encyclopedia-ALA Goals Award. The annual awards are intended to improve library service by supporting programs that further the goals of the ALA. Peggy Barber

See also CANADIAN LIBRARY ASSOCIATION (CLA); LIBRARY; LITERATURE FOR CHILDREN.

ANDORRA. See EUROPE.

The American Library Association stages a fair as part of its centennial year celebration at its annual conference, held in Chicago in July.

Guiding America's Libraries

Some 9,000 members of the American Library Association (ALA) met in Chicago in July 1976 to celebrate the 100th anniversary of the organization. They also made plans for the future of the more than 85,000 libraries in the United States. They discussed federal support for local libraries and focused on expanding the role of the library by providing a service to answer questions about other community resources — from art and music to food stamps.

The sheer size of the gathering was in sharp contrast to the ALA's founding meeting 100 years earlier. Only 103 librarians attended that first conference in Philadelphia in 1876.

Richard R. Bowker, the publisher of *Publisher's Weekly,* and Melvil Dewey, who had just invented a decimal system for classifying books, invited U.S. librarians to meet and discuss common goals and problems in 1876. At that time, there were about 3,600 private, public, and school libraries in the United States, but only about 200 full-time librarians. Most private and public libraries then used part-time workers. Young teachers were assigned to tend most school libraries. Librarians had little professional standing, and this was one of the first problems the ALA tackled.

For example, ALA founders had difficulty persuading the Librarian of Congress, who considered such conferences "wordy outlets for impracticables and pretenders," to attend the first meeting. However, ALA prestige grew so rapidly that by 1899 it could persuade President William McKinley to appoint ALA President Herbert Putnam as Librarian of Congress.

Another step in establishing librarians as professionals came in 1887 when Dewey founded the first library school at Columbia University in New York City. The ALA has since been active in setting standards for educating and training librarians.

The ALA's principal goals have always centered around providing schools and communities with high-quality library service. In its early years, it tackled the problem of efficiently keeping track of books. It compiled and published bibliogra-

100 years of service

phies, catalogs, and indexes and also drew up book-selection lists for libraries and reading lists for children and such special groups as immigrants, who were then flocking to America.

The ALA's growth inspired the formation of state and local library associations. Meanwhile, such specialists as children's, catalog, and reference librarians formed their own interest groups within the ALA.

Library use grew rapidly during the ALA's first 100 years, as did the role of libraries. New features were added, such as collections of photographs, paintings, and phonograph records. The ALA's concerns also expanded, ranging from adult education and the development of rural libraries to adequate pay and benefits for librarians. In the early 1900s, the ALA went to the Carnegie Corporation of New York to get philanthropic grants for libraries and library schools. In the 1950s, it began lobbying for federal funds for libraries.

In addition, the ALA began to involve itself in social issues as they apply to libraries and librarians. It has been a leader in the quest for equal opportunity for women and minorities in the library field. It has also opposed those who want to censor books. Among the books the ALA has defended from censorship is John Steinbeck's *The Grapes of Wrath.*

The association has always stood for the freedom to read, believing that Americans are entitled to find books and publications in their libraries that present a variety of viewpoints. Consequently, the association formed its Intellectual Freedom Committee in 1940 to watch over this basic right.

Today, the ALA, supported by more than 33,000 members, offers a variety of programs and publications from its headquarters in Chicago. It encourages excellence on the part of those serving the reading public by sponsoring such awards as the prestigious Caldecott and Newbery medals for children's books. And, now entering its second century, the ALA continues to promote the library as "an institution of education for democratic living."   Darlene R. Stille

ANDREOTTI, GIULIO (1919-   ), was sworn in as prime minister of Italy on July 30, 1976. He succeeded Aldo Moro and was serving as Moro's budget minister at the time of his appointment. Andreotti had previously served as Italy's prime minister in 1972. See ITALY.

Andreotti, in forming his Cabinet, deliberately excluded members of the Communist Party by choosing only members of the ruling Christian Democrat Party. Because the Communist Party was the country's second-largest political movement, however, it was feared that Andreotti's new government could not survive a vote of confidence in the Chamber of Deputies and the Senate. Both parliamentary bodies gave Andreotti an affirmative vote, however, primarily because the Communist members absented themselves or abstained from voting.

The new prime minister was born in Rome on Jan. 14, 1919, and earned a law degree from the University of Rome. He became a deputy to Parliament in 1947 and subsequently served in Christian Democratic governments from 1947 to 1953.

From 1954 to 1970, he held several important posts, heading the ministries of the interior, finance, treasury, defense, and industry and commerce.

Andreotti is married and has four children. He likes to write and is a Latin scholar. He heads a center for research on the famous Roman orator and politician, Cicero.   Paul C. Tullier

ANGOLA. The civil war ended in February 1976 as the Popular Movement for the Liberation of Angola (MPLA) captured the last important towns held by its rivals, the National Front for the Liberation of Angola (FNLA) and the National Union for the Total Independence of Angola (UNITA). MPLA leader Agostinho Neto became Angola's head of government. See NETO, AGOSTINHO.

The tide of battle had favored the FNLA-UNITA coalition in late 1975. South African troops were fighting alongside coalition forces, and military supplies were coming in from France, the United States, and other countries. However, in November, the MPLA began receiving greater support from Communist countries. By the end of January 1976, about 10,000 to 12,000 Cuban troops were in Angola aiding the MPLA. Russia sent arms that gave the MPLA superior military equipment.

With Cuban Forces, the MPLA launched an offensive in January that routed FNLA troops from strongholds in the north of Angola and UNITA soldiers from positions in central and southern regions. On February 12, UNITA announced it was preparing to wage guerrilla warfare.

The Administration of U.S. President Gerald R. Ford hoped to bolster the FNLA-UNITA forces by increasing U.S. military aid. However, many U.S. congressmen feared that such aid would lead to a Vietnam-like involvement. The House of Representatives voted 323 to 99 on Jan. 27, 1976, to prohibit further military assistance to the FNLA-UNITA coalition. The Senate had voted 54 to 22 against further aid on Dec. 19, 1975.

Diplomatic Recognition. Following its military successes, the MPLA won important diplomatic victories. On January 13, a special Organization of African Unity (OAU) session on Angola deadlocked—22 nations against 22 others—on the question of recognizing the MPLA. But on February 11, the OAU recognized the MPLA regime as the legitimate government of Angola. Great Britain, Canada, and several West European nations recognized the People's Republic of Angola in February. France, Zaire, and Zambia, which had aided the MPLA's rivals, also reversed their earlier position against granting diplomatic recognition. The United States, however, withheld recognition and on June 23 vetoed Angola's application to join the United Nations (UN), insisting that Cuban troops must first leave Angola. However, the United States withdrew its objection to Angola's UN membership in November, and Angola was admitted on December 1.

Neto's government on July 10 executed an American and three British mercenaries for committing war crimes during the civil war.   John D. Esseks

See also AFRICA (Facts in Brief Table).

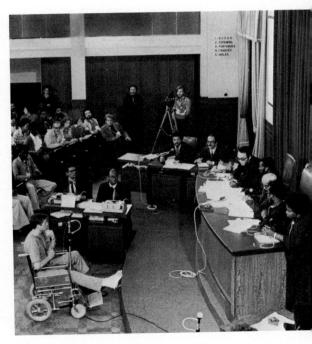

Mercenary Gary Acker of Sacramento, Calif., was sentenced to 16 years in prison in Angola in June for war crimes there.

ANGUILLA, a tiny island in the Caribbean, became a self-governing territory on Feb. 10, 1976, when its new Constitution was ratified by Great Britain. The former British colony had been part of the West Indies Associated States of St. Kitts-Nevis-Anguilla formed in 1967.

Under the new Constitution's provisions, Britain retained ultimate responsibility for Anguilla's defense, judiciary, external affairs, internal security, public service, and finance branches of government. British commissioner David F. B. Le Breton was confirmed as the official representative of Queen Elizabeth II.

In elections held on March 15, the People's Progressive Party led by Ronald Webster captured six of the seven elective seats in the 12-member House of Assembly. The other five members are appointed by the British commissioner. About 78 per cent of the eligible voters cast ballots in the election.

Britain retained responsibility for continued financial aid to develop Anguilla's main exports, lobsters, which earned about $200,000 in foreign funds in 1976, and salt from evaporated seawater, which brought in about $130,000. There was also some hope that Anguilla might be able to stimulate its tourist industry by building new facilities at its resort complex on Rendezvous Bay.   Paul C. Tullier

ANIMAL. See CONSERVATION; PET; ZOOLOGY; ZOOS AND AQUARIUMS.

ANTHROPOLOGY. C. Donald Johanson and Richard Leakey jointly described in March 1976 how their recent discoveries of human fossils have added to the growing understanding of the earliest stages of human evolution. Johanson, a curator of the Cleveland Museum of Natural History and associate professor of anthropology at Case Western Reserve University in Cleveland, made his finds in Ethiopia. Leakey, director of the National Museums of Kenya, made his in Kenya.

As recently as 1970, most anthropologists would probably have said that the earliest ancestors of human beings lived no more than 2 million years ago. But the new fossils recovered by Leakey and Johanson, combined with evidence reported by Leakey's mother, Mary N. Leakey, in October 1975, lead to a conclusion that our direct ancestors lived no less than 3.5 to 3.75 million years ago.

The evidence Johanson discussed includes 150 bones from at least two children who died when they were 4 or 5 years old and at least three adults, all found in the same location. He believes these individuals may have been a family unit that was trapped and killed in a flash flood.

Leakey described his fossil finds of *Homo erectus,* another ancestor of man that lived more recently than Johanson's group. Leakey's data indicates that *Homo erectus* existed as early as 1.5 million years ago, a million years earlier than anthropologists

had previously assumed. Thus, there was probably a period about 1.5 million years ago when the australopithecines, one of our early ancestors, and the slightly more advanced *Homo erectus* were contemporaries in East Africa. The somewhat more efficient *Homo erectus* hunting techniques may have caused the extinction of the australopithecines.

Salem Witchcraft. Linnda R. Caporael of the University of California, Santa Barbara, suggested in April that the Salem witch trials in 1692 may have been associated with an outbreak of ergotism, a disease caused by the growth of the fungus ergot on stored grains. Ergot poisoning results in hallucinations of the type associated with the witchcraft fear. The hot and damp weather in the Salem area in 1692 was ideal for the growth of the fungus, according to Caporael, and there is some evidence that the girls involved in the early stages of the incident may have eaten grain from the same source. Caporael also cited evidence of an association between ergotism and accusations of witchcraft in Europe.

Diet and Disease. Mahmoud El-Najjar and Betty Lozoff of Case Western Reserve University and Christy Turner and Dennis Ryan of Arizona State University reported on a study of diet deficiencies in 539 prehistoric skulls from archaeological sites in the Southwestern United States. All of

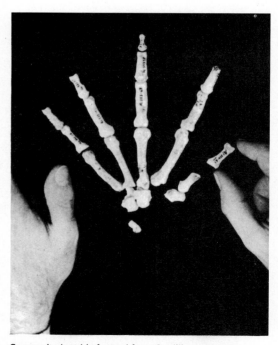

Composite hand is formed from 3-million-year-old bones found in central Ethiopia by C. Donald Johanson of Case Western Reserve University.

the skulls came from sites where the population depended on corn for food. Thirty-four per cent of these skulls had a spongy bone growth that indicated the individuals probably suffered from severe iron deficiency anemia. When the skulls were separated into two groups — those that lived in canyon-bottom sites and those that lived on the plains — anemia predominated among the children who lived in the canyon-bottom sites. Anemia was found to be three to four times more common among those who lived in the canyon bottoms. The scientists suggested that while corn agriculture made living in the canyon bottoms possible, there were too few natural foodstuffs available to provide the iron that corn lacks. The resulting anemia may have reached epidemic proportions and forced these people to abandon some parts of the Southwest.

Male Supremacy. William Devale of the City University of New York and Marvin Harris of Columbia University used data gathered from 112 societies to draw some interesting conclusions about why male supremacy is so prevalent today. Their studies indicate that the males who survived the wars fought in pre-industrial societies emerged as the dominant force. In later societies, the males assumed control of the wealth, power, and decision-making. Along with this, the associated pattern of female subordination in political, economic, and social life grew.   Fred Plog

ARCHAEOLOGY

Recent excavations by Paolo Matthiae and Giovanni Pettineto of the University of Rome 30 miles (48 kilometers) from Aleppo, Syria, have revealed the discovery of the previously unknown state of Ebla, which existed between 2400 and 2250 B.C. At its peak, the state had more than 250,000 persons living in the area between Sinai and the mountains of Iran. Prior to the Italians' discoveries, the area was thought to have been inhabited only by nomads. Over 15,000 cuneiform tablets recovered from the site indicate that previously known nearby cities traded with and paid tribute to Ebla. Only a small percentage of the tablets have yet been studied, but they have already provided rich details on life in Ebla. Some individuals mentioned in the texts are apparently the same people mentioned in the first books of the Bible.

The Pharaoh Akhenaton. The reign of the pharaoh Akhenaton, who ruled Egypt between 1367 B.C. and 1352 B.C., has been difficult to document by archaeological discoveries. Because Akhenaton advocated *monotheism* (the worship of one god), his temples were destroyed by later pharaohs who advocated polytheism. Donald B. Redford of the University of Pennsylvania found what he believes to be one of Akhenaton's temples in the Gem-Pa-Aton area of Karnak while investigating the *talatats* (engraved building blocks) that were made during Akhenaton's reign. When his temples were destroyed, they were used as rubble fill in the temples of later pharaohs. Computer and other techniques were used in matching more than 40,000 broken pieces of talatats. Information recovered during this process led to the discovery of the temple.

Early New World Civilizations. Two archaeological projects produced evidence in 1976 that may cause important changes in our view of the earliest civilizations in the New World. Robert F. Heizer and John A. Graham of the University of California, Berkeley, in April described their findings near Retalhuleu, in western Guatemala. They found monuments at the site of Abaj Takalik, including a series of sculptured stone altars and *stelae* (stone pillars). One of the stelae had the date June 3, A.D. 126, inscribed on it in the Mayan calendric system. This date is 166 years earlier than the oldest previously known date for Mayan sites.

The other stelae at Abaj Takalik, which in local legend is known as "where the world was created," may prove even older. This evidence suggests that the Maya, until now believed to have developed from ancestral groups living in the lowlands of Mesoamerica (middle America), may have evolved from groups that lived in the highlands and moved to the lowlands.

Donald W. Lathrop of the University of Illinois in Urbana, working at Real Alto, found evidence of a village near Guayaquil, Ecuador, that was occupied by as many as 1,000 individuals about 2800 B.C. The village was adjacent to mangrove swamps, which would have provided some of the food the people needed. But Lathrop also found evidence that the villagers practiced agriculture. While sites in Mexico and Peru were previously believed to be the earliest such agricultural villages, this Ecuador site was occupied from 1,000 to 1,500 years earlier than those in Mexico and Peru. Thus, the apparent similarities between Mesoamerican and Andean civilizations may reflect their common origin in Ecuador or some other intermediate area.

Archaeologists in Bolivia uncovered the ruins of trapezoid-shaped buildings of a previously unknown people whose culture disappeared some 500 years ago. The find included a citadel, discovered in the mountainous jungle about 190 miles (300 kilometers) north of La Paz. The citadel has been named Iskanwaya.

Asian Metallurgy. Chester Gorman of the University of Pennsylvania and Pifit Charoenwongsa of the National Museum of Bangkok, Thailand, detailed evidence in May that was recovered in recent excavations near Ban Chiang, Thailand. The evidence shows that the people of the area were apparently manufacturing a variety of bronze artifacts about 3600 B.C., some 600 years before similar artifacts were produced in the Middle East and 2,500 years before any that have been found in India or China. The Thai artifacts are so sophisticated that

University of California archaeologists uncover a sacrificial altar
used by the ancient Maya near present-day Retalhuleu, Guatemala.

the archaeologists believe much earlier artifacts will yet be discovered. The bronze items were made by villagers who were part-time farmers and hunters.

Bamboo Laws. Chinese archaeologists reported in March that they had found a series of early laws inscribed on about 1,000 bamboo slips in an excavated tomb in Yunmeng county in central China. The writings dated back 2,200 years. The tomb was discovered by workers digging a drainage canal.

The finds date from the late years of the Warring States period of China's history, 475 B.C. to 221 B.C., just before the Ch'in dynasty was established. They "provide important historical evidence of how the Ch'in dynasty followed the legalist line and imposed the dictatorship of the landlord class over the slaveowning class," according to the Chinese archaeologists.

"The records of laws and acts of the Ch'in dynasty and of earlier periods had been lost for centuries," the Chinese archaeologists said.

Preliminary studies show that the bamboo slips include a document from a governor in 227 B.C., laws, acts, judicial cases, a book on the "ways of officials," and a chronicle of major events from 306 B.C. Also included are specific cases showing how court trials were conducted. The finds also include acts on farmland, currency, official appointments of self-exiled Ch'in subjects, and the dismissal of government officials. Fred Plog

ARCHITECTURE. Given the nation's mood against elaborate civic projects, few United States cities announced grandiose building schemes in 1976. And few of those proposed were actually constructed. Instead, the design profession concentrated its Bicentennial year efforts on preserving and restoring historic and architecturally important buildings. Philadelphia nicely managed to combine the old and the new in architecture in a number of projects.

Some Bicentennial Buildings. Because the cramped quarters in Philadelphia's Independence Hall could never accommodate the Bicentennial crowds desiring to view the Liberty Bell, the National Park Service decided to move the historic relic to a separate facility. Philadelphia architects Mitchell/Giurgola designed the Liberty Bell Pavilion, located immediately north of the hall on Independence Mall. The small, one-story, glass and white-granite structure was likened to both a jewel box and a drive-in branch bank. Nevertheless, it accomplished its purpose, becoming the official new home of the bell on January 1.

The same architects designed another permanent structure in Philadelphia, the Living History Center, which opened in stages during the summer. This seven-story, stepped-down, concrete building faces the mall. It provides an 875-seat film theater and about 20,000 square feet (1,860 square meters)

of exhibition space, which was designed by R. Loewy International.

Architects Venturi & Rauch (V&R), also of Philadelphia, designed a "ghost" structure where Benjamin Franklin's house and printing shop once stood, just off Market Street. No plans or drawings of these structures exist, and V&R decided not to fake any design details. Instead, they simply used steel tubing to indicate the general outline of what these buildings probably looked like. The site also contains an underground Franklin Museum designed by V&R.

The AIA Convention. Philadelphia hosted the annual meeting of the American Institute of Architects (AIA) in May. The convention theme was "An American City: The Architecture of Information." But the primary information the architects wanted was how to stay in business. The AIA's ranks continued to be decimated by the lack of design and construction work. Consequently, convention attendance was down for the second year in a row. Only 1,185 members attended in 1976, compared to 1,500 in 1975.

Many members believed the key to survival would be a radical change in AIA's code of ethics. They debated such ethical taboos as advertising, giving out free sketches, paying agents, and allowing architects to become building contractors. Final action on these matters was deferred until 1977.

Architectural historian, critic, and Yale University professor Vincent J. Scully, Jr., was to accept two AIA honors at the convention. But when Scully learned that the AIA's College of Fellows had denied membership to renowned Philadelphia architect Robert Venturi, Scully refused the honors. Scully protested, "I cannot in good conscience accept an award, however welcome, in the same year that the most important architect of my generation is denied a fellowship." The affair revived charges of cronyism in the fellowship program.

The 1976 Olympic Games in Montreal, Canada, generated exotic architectural structures. Parisian architect Roger Taillibert sculptured in concrete the velodrome, for cycling events, and the main stadium, which sported 17 pairs of columns of different sizes. Montreal architects D'Astous & Durand's designed the Olympic Village — four 19-story, half-pyramid-shaped structures.

The total bill for the Olympic buildings came to more than $1 billion, with $40 million reportedly going to Taillibert. Labor troubles and strikes contributed to enormous cost overruns.

Noteworthy Trends. A movement away from academic architecture may have been heralded when philosophically similar new heads were appointed to two of the United States most prestigious architectural schools. James I. Freed became dean of architecture, planning, and design at Chicago's Illinois Institute of Technology; and Cesar Pelli,

dean of the Yale University School of Architecture. Both men are practicing architects and each said that he would stay with his architectural firm. "Mies van der Rohe was at his most influential as a teacher during the time he was most actively building," said Freed.

Three major architectural exhibitions, devoted to earlier, more ornamental styles, drew large crowds and provoked much discussion during the year. New York City's Museum of Modern Art (MOMA) displayed "The Architecture of the École des Beaux-Arts" and the Metropolitan Museum of Art offered "Architectural and Ornamental Drawings." At the Art Institute of Chicago, "Art Nouveau in France and Belgium: 1880–1920" focused on the architecture designed in this short-lived style.

The interest in these shows seemed to represent a broad-based hunger for something more than today's skin-and-bones, steel-and-glass, box architecture. No one believes that a beaux-arts revival is in the works, or even desirable. But as Arthur Drexler, director of MOMA's Department of Architecture and Design, commented, "A more detached view of architecture as it was understood in the 19th century might provide a more rigorous critique of philosophical assumptions underlying the architecture of our own time."

Rob Cuscaden

AIA-award-winning Waterside apartment building in New York City, designed by Davis, Brody & Associates, was cited for its sculptured look.

ARGENTINA. In the early hours of March 24, 1976, the armed forces overthrew the faltering government of President María Estela (Isabel) Martínez de Perón in a bloodless, meticulously planned coup d'état. The army commander in chief, Lieutenant General Jorge Rafael Videla, was named president of the new ruling junta, which included the commanders of the navy and air force.

General Videla immediately announced that the "fundamental objective will be to restore the essential values which guide the state." This meant that he intended to end the chaotic state of affairs in the country. Labor strife, inflation threatening to exceed 400 per cent, and a clandestine war between left wing guerrillas and right wing "death squads" were wracking the country.

Ouster Expected. The coup had been predicted for more than a year. The day before it took place, a military spokesman openly told journalists, "What you are all expecting will take place anytime." Perón was seized as she left her office in the Casa Rosada and flown to a remote government-owned retreat in the Andean lake region of Neuquén province, while the junta investigated charges of corruption against her. On September 18, Telam, the official news agency, quoted court sources as saying Perón had transferred more than $8 million from a Peronist Party charity to her own bank account. An unknown number of union leaders, who had formed the backbone of the Peronist movement, were also arrested and facing charges.

Perón's downfall was inevitable. During about two years in power, she paid political debts by swelling national, provincial, and municipal government payrolls and expanding the payrolls of state-owned industries by 24 per cent.

To meet public salaries, the Peronists printed money to cover 80 per cent of the national budget. The resulting currency glut all but destroyed the peso's value and caused a 335 per cent increase in prices in 1975. Even with the austerity program, imposed by the junta after the coup, inflation reached about 500 per cent in 1976.

Meanwhile, foreign trade suffered not only from the effects of the worldwide recession, but also from an embargo placed on Argentine beef exports to the European Community (Common Market), which the market had imposed to protect their own beef farmers. As a result, Argentina's foreign income was not large enough to import the raw materials needed to keep factories running or to pay on an estimated $10-billion international debt.

Proposed Recovery Program. The junta named José Martínez de Hoz, a 51-year-old businessman, as economics minister. His proposed recovery program emphasized a free-market economy, a cutback in the government role in industry, and encouragement of foreign investments. He also advocated a sharp curtailment in wage increases.

Continued Violence in the country caught world attention. More than 1,000 persons died during the year; and though there was no way to keep a tally, most were probably left wing victims of the death squads. Human-rights groups abroad criticized Videla for not eliminating these death squads for their extralegal acts. The most important government victory over left wing terrorists came on July 19, when police and soldiers killed Mario Roberto Santucho, founder and leader of the People's Revolutionary Army, in a gun battle in Buenos Aires.

International Concern was expressed over the safety of some 10,000 leftist refugees who had fled to Argentina from Bolivia, Chile, Peru, and Uruguay while Perón was in power. The bodies of former Uruguayan legislators Zelmar Michelini and Héctor Gutierrez Ruíz were found on May 20, two days after they were taken forcibly from their homes. Former leftist Bolivian President Juan José Torres was also found dead on June 2. Twenty-five refugees — most of them Chilean — were taken on June 11 from a Buenos Aires hotel administered by the United Nations. They were beaten, tortured, then released with instructions to leave Argentina within 48 hours.   Everett G. Martin

See also LATIN AMERICA (Facts in Brief Table).

ARIZONA. See STATE GOVERNMENT.

ARKANSAS. See STATE GOVERNMENT.

Supporters of Argentina's deposed President Isabel Perón wave farewell as she leaves Casa Rosada palace aboard an army helicopter.

ARMED FORCES. The United States and Russia worked to extend their agreement on strategic arms limitations in 1976, but they made little progress. As a result, both sides proceeded with the development of a variety of new strategic programs.

Meanwhile, annual world spending on arms approached the $300-billion mark, according to a privately sponsored study published in February. The analysis, prepared for private U.S. arms control groups, said that arms spending had increased 45 per cent since 1960. Although the United States and Russia accounted for 60 per cent of the total, the highest relative increases were recorded in the developing countries of Africa, Asia, and Latin America. As in previous years, the United States ranked as the world's largest arms dealer.

New Hardware. The keel was laid for the U.S. Navy's first *Trident* ballistic missile submarine in April, while development continued on air- and submarine-launched cruise missiles, a new warhead for the Minuteman III missile, and a new strategic missile, the M-X. At a Pentagon briefing in September, Secretary of Defense Donald H. Rumsfeld noted, "The Soviets continue to press ahead with aggressive development programs for both land-based and submarine-launched systems . . . [and] reinforce one's concern about the purposes behind their energetic activities."

B-1 Bomber. One of the Pentagon's priority strategic weapons systems, the controversial B-1 supersonic bomber, became enmeshed in politics, and its future was thrown into question by the outcome of the 1976 presidential election. Congressional opponents of the multibillion-dollar project successfully allocated only $87 million per month in B-1 procurement funds until Feb. 1, 1977, in the fiscal 1977 defense appropriations bill, not enough for full production. The action was a defeat for President Gerald R. Ford's Administration, which had hoped to authorize nearly $1 billion for its production in late 1976. On December 2, the Air Force awarded contracts that extended the monthly commitment through June 1977. The contracts, totaling more than $700 million, provided for the first three production models of the warplane.

B-1 opponents argued that the costly bomber is unnecessary in view of existing land-based and sea-based strategic-missile systems. Democratic presidential candidate James Earl (Jimmy) Carter, Jr., frequently criticized the program during the campaign, leading to speculation that he might cancel or curtail it.

Korean Dispute. Two U.S. Army officers were killed by ax-wielding North Korean soldiers during a clash on August 18 in the Panmunjom demilitarized zone (DMZ) separating North and South

A female plebe, one of 77 who entered the U.S. Naval Academy in 1976, gets help from a drill instructor while learning how to present arms.

Korea. A U.S.-South Korean work party was trimming a large tree when the attack occurred. President Ford promptly labeled the killings "vicious and unprovoked murder" and ordered a build-up of U.S. forces in South Korea. Several squadrons of jet fighters flew in from Okinawa, 20 F-111 fighter-bombers were dispatched from the United States, and B-52 bombers began practice bombing runs near the DMZ. After several days of negotiations, the United Nations Command and North Korean representatives signed an agreement on September 6 designed to prevent further incidents, and U.S. forces in South Korea returned to normal duty status.

Pilot Defects. In what was described by Western analysts as the greatest intelligence coup in years, a defecting Russian pilot flew his MIG-25 Foxbat swing-wing jet fighter to the Japanese island of Hokkaido on September 6. Lieutenant Viktor Belenko received political asylum in the United States, while the Japanese, reportedly with "unofficial" help from U.S. aviation specialists, began dismantling the plane to decipher the secrets of what was thought to be the world's most sophisticated jet fighter. Russia accused Japan and the United States of conspiring to prevent Belenko from returning to his base, claiming he had landed in Hokkaido merely because of a fuel shortage.

West Point Scandal. Secretary of the Army Martin R. Hoffmann in August appointed a special panel to review the U.S. Military Academy's honor code in the aftermath of a cheating scandal in which more than one-fourth of the academy's junior class was officially implicated. The panel, headed by former astronaut Frank Borman, president of Eastern Airlines and West Point graduate, was to assess the code and recommend appropriate changes. The scandal was triggered when some third-class students convicted of cheating on a take-home engineering examination alleged that several hundred classmates were equally guilty and charged the Army with narrowing the scope of the inquiry to avoid unfavorable publicity. Reporting in mid-December, the Borman panel urged the speedy readmission of the cadets and called for revisions in the academy's honor code.

Military Strength. The United States continued to trim its military forces in 1976. On October 31, troop strength stood at 2,085,866, the lowest level in 25 years and 11,000 fewer than in 1975. Nearly 465,000 troops were stationed overseas, including 208,500 in West Germany, 45,300 in Japan, and 40,000 in South Korea. At the insistence of the Thai government, the U.S. closed its remaining installations in Thailand on July 20, leaving only about 250 military advisers.

Japanese technicians examine a Russian MIG-25 fighter plane after a defecting pilot landed the top-secret craft in Japan in September.

In his annual report, General George S. Brown, chairman of the Joint Chiefs of Staff, warned that U.S. power was continuing to decline with respect to Russia. "If this trend continues," he said, "the U.S. will draw closer and closer to that indefinable point where our deterrent power will no longer lend forceful credibility to our foreign policy."

Defense Budget. The U.S. Department of Defense submitted a budget request for fiscal 1977 (Oct. 1, 1976, to Sept. 30, 1977) of $100.1 billion, an increase of $9.9 billion. The budget would support 16 Army and 3 Marine divisions, 26 Air Force tactical wings, 16 Navy and Marine air wings, and a Navy fleet of 491 vessels. An estimated $9.4 billion was recommended for strategic forces, $40.1 billion for conventional forces, and $10.9 billion for research and development. The Navy was scheduled to receive the largest share of the budget, $32.2 billion; the Air Force, $27.7 billion; and the Army, $24.5 billion.

The Navy asked for $2.9 billion for the *Trident* submarine and its ballistic missile, $1.3 billion for nuclear attack submarines, $1.3 billion for guided missile frigates, $708.2 million for F-14 Tomcat jet fighters, $346.9 million for the first F-18 carrier-based fighter plane, and $182.5 million for the submarine-launched cruise missile.

The Air Force requested $1.5 billion for the F-15 Eagle jet fighter, $1.5 billion for the B-1 bomber, $619.7 million for the first F-16 lightweight jet fighter, $584.3 million for the AWACS radar plane, $471.6 million for Minuteman III missiles, and $617.8 million for the A-10 close-support fighter.

The Army asked for $503.6 million for M-60 tanks, $141 million for the XM-1 main battle tank, $213 million for a new utility helicopter, $180 million for the SAM-D (Patriot) missile, $147.2 million for Lance and Stinger missiles, and $112.1 million for an advanced attack helicopter.

Congress passed a $32.5-billion military procurement bill for fiscal 1977 on July 1, and President Ford signed it on July 14. The bill provided only $1.7 billion less than the Ford Administration had sought. The major loss was a supplemental Pentagon request to increase from eight to 12 the number of authorized guided missile frigates.

Command Changes. John L. McLucas was appointed head of the Federal Aviation Administration and replaced as secretary of the Air Force by Thomas C. Reed on January 2. General Bernard W. Rogers became Army chief of staff on October 1, replacing retiring General Frederick C. Weyand. Samuel L. Gravely became the Navy's first black three-star admiral on August 4 when he was nominated for promotion to vice-admiral and named commander of the U.S. Third Fleet. Admiral Maurice F. Weisner became commander in chief of U.S. forces in the Pacific on September 1, succeeding Admiral Noel A. Gayler.   Thomas M. DeFrank

ARMSTRONG, ANNE LEGENDRE (1927-   ), was confirmed as United States ambassador to Great Britain on Jan. 27, 1976. She is the first woman to hold the post.

Anne Legendre was born in New Orleans on Dec. 27, 1927. She attended the Foxcroft School in Middleburg, Va., and graduated from Vassar College in 1949. Her first political activity came as a volunteer worker for President Harry S. Truman in the 1948 campaign while she was in college.

After marrying Texas rancher Tobin Armstrong in 1950, she plunged into politics as a Republican. She was vice-chairman of the Texas Republican Party and a national committeewoman. She was a delegate to the 1964 and 1968 Republican National Conventions and served on the Republican National Committee's executive committee in 1969. In 1971, she was the first woman elected co-chairman of the party, and in 1972, she became the first woman to deliver a convention keynote address.

She became a counselor to President Richard M. Nixon in 1973 with Cabinet rank. She acted as liaison between the Administration and Spanish Americans, women, and young people. She also advised on matters relating to the American Revolution Bicentennial.   Kathryn Sederberg

ARMY. See ARMED FORCES.

ART. See ARCHITECTURE; DANCING; LITERATURE; MUSIC, CLASSICAL; POETRY; VISUAL ARTS.

ASAD, HAFIZ AL- (1928?-   ), president of Syria, sent Syrian troops into war-torn Lebanon on April 9, 1976, in a move to settle the conflict between Lebanese Christians and the Lebanese Muslims and Palestine Liberation Organization (PLO). By fall, more than 20,000 Syrians controlled almost all of Lebanon as the core of an Arab peacekeeping force, which in November finally imposed a working cease-fire on the battling Christians and Muslims. It was a bold—but apparently successful—gamble for the prudent, pragmatic Syrian leader to take. It was also a move that underscored and enhanced Asad's popularity at home and his influence in Middle Eastern affairs. See LEBANON; MIDDLE EAST; SYRIA.

Hafiz al-Asad was born in Qardahah, the oldest son of farmers. His family belonged to the Alawis sect, a Muslim group that is strongly represented in the Syrian Army and the ruling Baath Party. After a military education, Asad rose quickly in both the air force and the party. He was a key figure in the 1963 coup that brought the Baathists to power and was minister of defense during the six-day Arab-Israeli war in 1967.

Asad seized power in 1970 and has been president since 1971. He is considered more moderate on Israel than are many other Arab statesmen. During his regime, Syria has had economic progress and improved relations with the West.   Edward G. Nash

ASIA

By and large, 1976 was a year of peace for this vast continent. The war in Indochina was over, and Hanoi began negotiating with the United States for aid it claimed America had promised to provide Vietnam. After a war in 1971, India and Pakistan resumed normal relations in 1976. The ominous clouds on the Chinese-Russian frontier seemed to have lifted, though Peking charged Russia with provoking more than 150 border incidents in the first eight months of 1976. Portugal's territory of Macao on the south coast of China received broad executive and legislative autonomy after negotiations between China and Portugal over Macao's future reached an impasse.

Here and there, of course, blood still flowed. Indonesia annexed East Timor and crushed the groups that wanted independence. Communist guerrillas continued their hit-and-run raids on the Thai-Malaysian border and in Thailand's barren northwest. With China's help, the Communists and the hill tribesmen in Burma continued to battle government forces. And Bangladesh accused India of helping Bangalee "miscreants" to attack its border villages.

As elsewhere in the world, dreams in Asia were often built on oil—and harsh words were exchanged when claims to rich oil deposits became the focus of international disputes. Not the least of these confrontations saw two Communist allies, China and Vietnam, decorously but firmly press their rival claims to Spratly Island, an offshore island thought to be rich in oil.

But still, peace prevailed. And the continent's leaders were again able to focus on Asia's basic problems—too many infants, the struggle to produce enough food, the rising debt, and the hunger for development funds. China had gone through another political convulsion. Indochina had settled under increasingly harsh Communist rule. India, once the greatest democracy in Asia, had become a one-party dictatorship. But all of these countries, leftist or rightist, shared these crushing problems.

Too Many Babies. The high birth rate was regarded as one of the most urgent problems. But most Asians were reluctant to accept the idea of family planning. For the Asian farmer, a large family remained a form of social insurance—a son meant one more pair of hands for work in the fields and support in old age. In some areas, religion or tradition stood in the way of birth control. By 1976, nearly all the Asian states had some form of family-planning program, but far too many were ineffective—more a concession to pressure from the World Bank than any real national effort.

A block-long banner announces Prime Minister Indira Gandhi's 20-point economic-development plan for India to the people of New Delhi.

In Bangladesh, the late President Mujibur Rahman used to answer questions about birth control with, "We Bangalees love our children." He had a family-planning program that satisfied no one but its own bureaucracy. Mujibur's successor, Major General Ziaur Rahman, established a new birth-control scheme, complete with a huge new staff.

The birth rate in Bangladesh in 1976 was an awesome 46 per 1,000 persons, compared with 36 in India and 14 in the United States. In Indonesia,

which boasts of a family-planning program, the island of Java expected its population, estimated at 80 million, to rise to 130 million by the year 2000. And even in China, which uses powerful social pressures to keep the marriage age at about 26 for women and 29 or 30 for men, the birth rate rose. And the rate was appreciably higher in inland farming areas than in the coastal cities.

"Stop at Two." India has long had a family-planning organization that is heavily financed by the West, but the population has grown from 350-million in 1950 to 624 million. The program's effectiveness was limited until 1976, when Prime Minister Indira Gandhi's son, Sanjay, took charge of it. His platform for progress included the slogan,

"Stop at Two." Punitive steps were taken against civil servants who had more than three children. Maharashtra state had a law requiring male sterilization after the birth of the third child. The coercion produced violent reaction in various places. In Mrs. Gandhi's home state of Uttar Pradesh, police fired on people rioting in October against the forced sterilization of some young men, and about 50 persons were killed.

Oddly, in India, as in many other countries, the problem was made worse by progress. The population was growing not only because so many babies were born, but also because, with better health care, fewer people died. Since India's emergence as an independent state in 1947, the death rate has

A sign of peace in Asia, a poster in Hanoi
shows the constituency for the newly elected
National Assembly for a reunited Vietnam.

been halved to 14 per 1,000, and the life expectancy
has risen by 20 years.

Feeding the Multitudes. Feeding these multi-
plying millions has been the main preoccupation of
most Asian states. Those in South Asia, from Vietnam to Pakistan, depend on the whims of the monsoons to bring them rain, and the people go hungry
when the monsoons fail. Apart from the monsoons,
most of Asia relies on primitive farming methods.
The 1976 harvest was excellent in India and Bangladesh and good in China. But the cities in Burma
went short of rice, mainly because of inefficiency.
Quite properly, most governments gave their top
priority to the development of agriculture. The
World Bank spent an estimated $1.8 billion in 1976
on farm projects around the world, most of it in
Asia. Still, Pakistan did not expect self-sufficiency
in food until perhaps 1978, and Indonesia set its
dreams for self-sufficiency at a later date.

The World Food Council, set up by the United
Nations in June, named 11 "food priority" countries in Asia – those it expected to have a grain deficit by 1985 unless major changes were made in
agriculture. These countries included India, Indonesia, Pakistan, Sri Lanka, and the Philippines.
Only in the Philippines did the gross national product per capita exceed $300 a year.

The World Food Council said the Green Revolution has achieved only modest progress. Not enough
new seed varieties have been developed, the testing
and distribution of the seed has been faulty, and
mechanization has been inadequate. But, even
more important, the council said, was the pattern of
land ownership. In the priority countries, tiny holdings are worked by millions of sharecroppers. Un-
sure of their tenure, the tenants have little incentive
to improve the land they rent. In spite of all the
claims emanating from New Delhi in 1976, this
problem was most acute in India.

Fertilizer and Electronics. Although desperately
short of funds, many Asian countries continued
their industrial and technological progress. China,
India, Pakistan, and South Korea rushed to complete dozens of fertilizer plants. Steel and petrochemical capacity was being expanded from South
Korea to Pakistan. There was also a growing sophistication. Only China and India had the capacity in 1976 to produce nuclear weapons and missiles,
but half a dozen other nations stood on the edge of
the atomic age.

But industry did not grow rapidly enough to absorb the millions of people pouring into the cities
from the impoverished countryside. China solved
this problem by sending 12 million educated youths
for whom there were no urban jobs into the country, purportedly to be "re-educated." Vietnam,
with a million jobless people in the cities, simply
shipped them out to villages. But in India, Indonesia, and Sri Lanka, the problem of urban unemployment was acute – and politically explosive.

All these nations suffered from a shortage of investment funds – a need only marginally met by
Western donors. The difficulties increased greatly
in 1973 when the oil producers quadrupled their
prices. This action not only wiped out funds the
underdeveloped countries had earmarked for capital investment, but it also forced these countries to
cut their imports of oil, which slowed their economy. The Organization of Petroleum Exporting
Countries decision to raise oil prices 5 per cent to 10
per cent on Jan. 1, 1977, could only create more
problems.

The oil producers made no price concessions to
their have-not clients. Only Pakistan received large
credits from the Arabs, but these merely met the
increase in the oil price. For the other countries, it
meant a growing debt burden. Many nations
passed the "danger mark" in 1976 – that is, they
had to spend more than one-fifth of their export
earnings merely to service their foreign debt.

Nonaligned? When the so-called nonaligned nations met in Colombo, Sri Lanka, in August 1976,
these burdens were uppermost in the minds of most
of the delegates. They wanted a new economic
order – which meant higher prices for the raw materials they produce, huge Western credits, and a
moratorium on, or even forgiveness of, existing
debts. The West was expected to set up a fund,

Facts in Brief on the Asian Countries

Country	Population	Government	Monetary Unit*	Foreign Trade (million U.S. $) Exports	Imports
Afghanistan	20,036,000	President & Prime Minister Mohammad Daoud	afghani (45 = $1)	210	276
Australia	13,548,000	Governor General Sir John R. Kerr; Prime Minister Malcolm Fraser	dollar (1 = $1.02)	11,872	11,115
Bangladesh	75,437,000	Martial Law Administrator Ziaur Rahman; President Abu Sadat Mohammed Sayem	taka (16.1 = $1)	326	1,269
Bhutan	1,241,000	King Jigme Singye Wangchuck	Indian rupee	no statistics available	
Burma	32,375,000	President U Ne Win; Prime Minister U Sein Win	kyat (6.8 = $1)	167	118
Cambodia (Khmer)	8,470,000	President Khieu Samphan; Prime Minister Pol Pot	riel (1,650 = $1)	7	80
China	854,306,000	Communist Party Chairman & Premier Hua Kuo-feng	yuan (2 = $1)	6,300	7,400
India	624,212,000	President Fakhruddin Ali Ahmed; Prime Minister Indira Gandhi	rupee (8.7 = $1)	4,299	6,135
Indonesia	140,200,000	President Suharto	rupiah (415 = $1)	7,103	4,709
Iran	35,226,000	Shah Mohammad Reza Pahlavi; Prime Minister Amir Abbas Hoveyda	rial (71.4 = $1)	19,977	10,343
Japan	114,091,000	Emperor Hirohito; Prime Minister Takeo Fukuda	yen (297 = $1)	55,817	57,853
Korea, North	16,849,000	President Kim Il-song; Premier Pak Song-chol	won (1.1 = $1)	482	779
Korea, South	35,200,000	President Chung Hee Park; Prime Minister Choe Kyu-ha	won (484 = $1)	5,081	7,274
Laos	3,498,000	President Souphanouvong; Prime Minister Kayson Phomvihan	kip (60 = $1)	10	52
Malaysia	12,550,000	Paramount Ruler Yahya Petra ibni Sultan Ibrahim; Prime Minister Datuk Hussein Onn	ringgit (2.5 = $1)	3,825	3,590
Maldives	125,000	President Amir Ibrahim Nasir	rupee (8.7 = $1)	2	3
Mongolia	1,524,000	People's Revolutionary Party First Secretary & Presidium Chairman Yumjaagiin Tsedenbal; Council of Ministers Chairman Jambyn Batmonh	tugrik (5 = $1)	113	156
Nepal	13,011,000	King Birendra Bir Bikram Shah Dev; Prime Minister Tulsi Giri	rupee (12.5 = $1)	99	171
New Zealand	3,130,000	Governor General Sir Denis Blundell; Prime Minister Robert D. Muldoon	dollar (1.1 = $1)	2,160	3,152
Pakistan	76,892,000	President Fazal Elahi Chaudry; Prime Minister Zulfikar Ali Bhutto	rupee (9.6 = $1)	1,049	2,151
Papua New Guinea	2,667,000	Governor General Sir John Guise; Prime Minister Michael Somare	kina (1 = $1.15)	480	588
Philippines	45,267,000	President Ferdinand E. Marcos	peso (7.4 = $1)	2,275	3,883
Russia	259,151,000	Communist Party General Secretary Leonid I. Brezhnev; Supreme Soviet Presidium Chairman Nikolay Viktorovich Podgorny; Council of Ministers Chairman Aleksey Nikolayevich Kosygin	ruble (1 = $1.40)	33,310	36,969
Singapore	2,337,000	President Benjamin Henry Sheares; Prime Minister Lee Kuan Yew	dollar (2.4 = $1)	5,376	8,133
Sri Lanka	14,285,000	President William Gopallawa; Prime Minister Sirimavo Bandaranaike	rupee (8.7 = $1)	559	709
Taiwan	16,769,000	President Yen Chia-kan; Premier Chiang Ching-kuo	new Taiwan dollar (37 = $1)	5,302	5,959
Thailand	45,130,000	King Bhumibol Adulyadej; Prime Minister Thanin Kraiwichian	baht (20 = $1)	2,373	3,075
Vietnam	45,134,000	President Ton Duc Thang; Prime Minister Pham Van Dong	dong (2.5 = $1)	no statistics available	

*Exchange rates as of Dec. 1, 1976

perhaps about $6 billion, to help maintain prices of key raw materials. But the conference also demonstrated to many observers the weaknesses of the nonaligned bloc. Fear of having their oil supplies cut off kept them silent on the failure of the Arab states and Iran to consider their plight. And with so many Communist members in their nonaligned ranks, the majority found themselves pushed into ideological detours of little value.

Similar concerns and problems plagued the meeting of five Asian nations held in February to establish the formal mechanism for the Association of Southeast Asian Nations (ASEAN). These nations—Thailand, Malaysia, Singapore, Indonesia, and the Philippines—agreed on the broad outlines of a treaty of friendship and cooperation, but on little else.

Unlike some of the world's other regional organizations, the ASEAN countries have little in common ancestrally on which to build their cooperation. In the five nations of 230 million people there are three major religions (Christianity, Buddhism, and Islam) and three distinct racial groups (Chinese, Thai, and Malay-Polynesian). In addition, four of the five countries have different colonial backgrounds, while Thailand was never a colony. As a result, they have different administrative systems, and establishing an administrative body for ASEAN may be particularly difficult.

SEATO Ends. With a military band playing "Auld Lang Syne," the Southeast Asia Treaty Organization (SEATO) completed its last international exercise in the Philippines in February. The closing ceremonies for what was probably the last regional project involving Western and Asian troops were witnessed by diplomats and officials of the countries that originally formed SEATO. The proceedings were muted and simple, in stark contrast with those at the 1954 Manila Conference, when the alliance was born. The decision to abolish SEATO was made in September 1975, and the last international exercise was civic rather than military in nature. In this exercise, the SEATO troops were building roads and other facilities for Philippine communities.

Arms for the Have-Nots. One of the more ominous developments in Asia in 1976 was the growing sophistication in weaponry. With at least four nuclear tests during the year, China continued to improve and expand its nuclear arsenal. Having conducted one test in 1974, India was working on both nuclear devices and missiles. India's example was infectious, and Pakistan made strenuous efforts to acquire a French reprocessing plant that would give it weapons-grade plutonium. There were rumors that Iran, Taiwan, and South Korea were planning to develop nuclear weapons.   Mark Gayn

See also the various Asian country articles; Section One, Focus on The World.

ASTRONOMY. The successful landings of two *Viking* spacecraft on the surface of Mars in 1976 marked a major turning point in the history of space exploration. The landers carried with them the first experiments designed to test for the presence of life on another planet. While the landers photographed their surroundings and dug samples of Martian soil to place inside their biology testing chambers, their sister spacecraft in orbit around Mars relayed the results to Earth and took dramatically clear photographs of the Martian surface.

Viking 1 landed on Mars on July 20 in the northwest part of a broad, flat basin known as Chryse Planitia. The *Viking*'s cameras revealed a flat expanse of red soil dotted with rocks. Scientists believe the red color may be caused by the action of solar ultraviolet rays on iron-rich minerals.

East of the spacecraft are rolling sand dunes, dark rocks, and distant hills. To the south are rocks as large as 6 to 10 feet (2 to 3 meters) across, and on the horizon are low hills that resemble the rim of a crater. In the west are patches of sand or dust, a dune field, and a large rock with sand or dust piled against it on the side away from the wind. No rocks known on Earth exactly match the chemical analysis of the soil at Chryse.

Sky and Atmosphere. The brightness of the Martian sky and its pink-orange color were a surprise, because the ultrathin air of Mars was expected to produce a dark, deep-blue sky. Apparently, many fine dust particles remain suspended in the thin air for long periods. They reflect sunlight, thus producing the unusual brightness and color.

Wind speeds are fairly steady at 15 miles (24 kilometers) per hour. During the daytime, the winds are out of the northeast, but they reverse direction between midnight and dawn. Temperatures climb to about $-5°F.$ $(-20°C)$ in the afternoon, but drop to a frigid $-122°F.$ $(-85°C)$ each night. The air pressure decreased slightly after the landing as carbon dioxide gas froze out of the atmosphere at the southern polar cap during the southern winter. About 95 per cent of the Martian atmosphere is carbon dioxide.

One of *Viking*'s major discoveries was that nitrogen makes up 2 to 3 per cent of Mars's atmosphere. Nitrogen is an essential element for life chemistry on Earth. The inert gas argon was also detected, as well as traces of two other inert gases, krypton and xenon.

Viking 2 entered orbit around Mars on August 7. After its cameras showed that its intended landing site on Cydonia was too rough, the *Viking 2* lander finally settled to the surface on an immense plain, Utopia Planitia, on September 3. The site is at the edge of Mars's northern winter polar icecap, and scientists hope that the *Viking 2* cameras can photograph the coming of the winter frosts about one Earth year after the landing date.

The flat terrain at the Utopia site is surprisingly similar to that at the Chryse site. The soil is the same red color, there are even more rocks, and the sky is the same pink-orange color. Winds are a little weaker, and daytime high temperatures are a little colder. Night temperatures are somewhat warmer, however, because the summer nights are shorter at Utopia's high northern latitude.

Tests for Life. The prime mission of the *Viking* landers was to test for the possible presence of living organisms on Mars. Soil samples at both sites were deposited successfully into the biology experiment packages. They produced provocative, but inconclusive, results. Some experiments suggested that a biological process might be involved, while others indicated the opposite. The organic chemistry experiment at both sites failed to detect any·breakdown products of living or dead organisms.

Other experiments were designed to test for the absorption by living organisms of carbon dioxide or the processing of a nutrient fluid, nicknamed "chicken soup." Again, results were inconclusive.

Water Evidence. Meanwhile, the two *Viking* orbiter spacecraft were producing the finest photography of Mars ever obtained on a planetary scale. The first photographs in the Chryse basin revealed enormous areas carved dramatically by fluid erosion — meandering channels, teardrop-shaped islands, partially eroded craters, and vast regions apparently hit by flash floods at some time in the past.

Other orbiter instruments found that the ice fields remaining at the northern polar cap are frozen water, not frozen carbon dioxide. They appear to be from 300 to 3,000 feet (90 to 900 meters) thick. Vast areas on Mars seem to be permafrost regions that melted and collapsed. The main unanswered question, now that large quantities of water ice have been identified on Mars, is: What caused the water ice to melt at times in the past?

Other Developments. The largest optical telescope in the world, the 237-inch (6-meter) telescope on top of Mount Pastukhov in Russia, began making regular observations on February 7 after 16 years of construction.

A new method involving the decay of rhenium 187 into osmium 187 has increased the estimated age of the universe to 20 billion years. Because the half-life of the rhenium decay process is 44 billion years, the new method is less subject to error than the previous dating method using the decay of uranium to thorium, which has a shorter half-life.

The first precise measurement of a pulsar's mass gave a value of 1.3 times the mass of the Sun. This falls comfortably within the predicted range of masses for neutron stars, supporting the idea that pulsars are neutron stars. The pulsar measured was Hercules X-1.

Powerful Earth-based radar produced new pictures of Venus showing a long rift valley nearly

The *Viking 2* orbiter obtained this picture of Mars's inner satellite Phobos in September, the most detailed photograph to date.

1,000 miles (1,600 kilometers) long and 100 miles (160 kilometers) wide, somewhat like the immense Valles Marineris found on Mars. A region of 15 to 20 mountain peaks, possibly a cluster of volcanoes, was also found on Venus.

Final results from the Russian *Venera 9* and *10,* which landed on Venus in October 1975, showed that Venus' clouds are surprisingly thin, more like haze than heavy clouds. The surface is therefore much brighter than expected, comparable to the Earth on an overcast day. Planetary astronomers believe the clouds are composed of tiny droplets of sulfuric acid.

Three astronomers at Kitt Peak National Observatory near Tucson, Ariz., reported in April that Pluto may have substantial amounts of frozen methane. Methane had not previously been found in its frozen state anywhere in the solar system. Methane ice on Pluto means that the planet may be much more reflective, and hence smaller, than previously thought, because a small, bright surface reflects the same amount of light as a larger, darker surface. The estimated smaller size also casts doubt upon previous estimates of the planet's mass and density. Scientists have decided that no reliable estimates are possible until a spacecraft flies past the planet. Eric D. Carlson

See also SPACE EXPLORATION; Section One, FOCUS ON SCIENCE.

ATLANTA. The Georgia World Congress Center, one of the world's largest exhibition and convention facilities, opened in Atlanta on Sept. 14, 1976. In dedicating the $35-million state-owned center, Georgia Governor George D. Busbee said it made Atlanta a "city of international significance" and announced that he would create an Institute of World Commerce to further the city's international posture.

Discrimination Charges. Twenty-seven demonstrators were arrested on September 15 for protesting what they termed "blatant racism" by center officials. Joseph E. Boone, leader of the demonstration, charged that center construction companies had hired too few blacks and that too few construction contracts had been given to black contractors.

There were also charges of reverse discrimination during the year. A Fulton County Superior Court judge recommended on September 7 that a grand jury investigate possible reverse discrimination against whites by the county and the city governments. An Atlanta police planning and research officer testified in federal court on September 22 that he had found what he believed to be evidence of discrimination against white police personnel.

Mayor Maynard H. Jackson disputed the allegations, pointing out that less than 1 per cent of the local government's contracts went to firms owned by nonwhites and that only 47 per cent of the city's

administration were black. About 60 per cent of the city's population were black.

Reorganization and Planning. Mayor Jackson proposed a major city-government reorganization on September 20. His plan called for eliminating three city departments and creating several new agencies that would report directly to the mayor.

The Metropolitan Area Regional Transportation Authority marketed its first bond issue in October for a planned 53-mile (85.3-kilometer), $2.1-billion rapid transit system. The U.S. Urban Mass Transportation Administration committed $560 million to build the first 13.7 miles (22 kilometers).

Healthy Economy. The average annual income of factory workers in the Atlanta area rose 15.7 per cent to $10,874 between August 1975 and August 1976. Living and food costs rose 4.7 per cent and 2.8 per cent, respectively, during approximately the same period. Unemployment stood at 7.1 per cent at midyear, with total employment up 1.1 per cent from 1975. The U.S. Department of Labor estimated that a family of four would need an annual income of at least $9,400 to live in the area.

Federal Bureau of Investigation figures showed that serious crime in Atlanta rose 21.9 per cent between 1970 and 1975. But there were sharp declines in five of the seven major crime categories through June 1976. Local figures showed that city crime declined between 1974 and 1976. James M. Banovetz

AUSTRALIA. The tone of politics in 1976 was tame compared with the high drama of 1975. Although Liberal Prime Minister Malcolm Fraser could have governed without Country Party assistance after the December 1975 elections – the Liberal Party gained 68 seats in the House of Representatives to 23 for the Country Party and 36 for the Labor Party – he included several Country Party members in his 24-man Cabinet. The coalition government set the reduction of inflation and the increase of business confidence as its main task.

The Labor Party, weakened by the electoral defeat, received another blow in March when its national executive censured leader Gough Whitlam and the party's national secretary for seeking money from Arab sources for the 1975 election. No money was received, but the revelation that it had been secretly sought was bad for the party's image. However, on May 1, Labor overthrew a Liberal-Country Party government in New South Wales, winning a close election by two seats. But Labor lost heavily in the Victoria state elections on March 20, when the Liberals increased their majority.

The Fraser Government was pledged to establish a system giving the states more control over their revenues. Despite some progress, the states complained about inadequate federal grants. A constitutional convention in Hobart in October recommended constitutional amendments to provide a

Prime Minister Fraser of Australia and his wife admire a stone lion in the Imperial Palace in Peking's Forbidden City on a June visit to China.

retiring age for federal judges and to conduct simultaneous elections for the Senate and House of Representatives. Fraser also planned to set up an advisory council on intergovernmental relations.

The federal government received much advice on administrative change during the year. This included the report of the Royal Commission on Government Administration under H. C. Coombs, and a special series of reports from Sir Henry Bland, who was asked to advise on reduction or transfer of departmental responsibilities.

The Economy was the government's main concern. In some respects, its performance was good—early in the year, overseas reserves grew, and the rate of increase of inflation slowed. Both wages and prices dropped from an annual growth rate of 13 or 14 per cent to about 10 per cent. Nonetheless, business remained sluggish, with sales, exports, capacity utilization, and manufacturing employment below normal. Private investment continued to be low, except in housing, which increased somewhat. Following increased movement of capital out of the country, the Australian dollar was devalued by 17½ per cent on November 28. Ten days later, it was revalued upward 2 per cent.

The main problem was unemployment. About 4.3 per cent of the work force was unemployed in August, about the same as in 1975. The government tried to reduce public spending in order to stimulate private investment. Although it provided increased assistance to unemployed young people, it stiffened penalties against people on relief who would not accept work when it was offered.

Foreign Trade. Exports continued to grow, especially minerals. With the government providing new incentives for foreign investors, mining prospects were good. It was hoped that oil production would increase following an Industries Assistance Commission recommendation that oil prices should go up. Australia produced just over 70 per cent of its crude oil needs in 1975. Further development of natural gas deposits on the northwest shelf also seemed likely. Wool exports were good, but beef continued to meet import restrictions in Northern Hemisphere markets.

Debates over tariff protection sharpened, with manufacturers complaining of the Industries Assistance Commission's hostile attitude. Textiles, clothing, footwear, and shipbuilding were all hit by inexpensive imports, in spite of high tariffs and other barriers. Nobody disagreed with Deputy Prime Minister Douglas Anthony when he said on June 17 that Australia had the highest wages in the world; but there was plenty of argument about whether these wages inhibited further development through their effect on costs.

The government amended the existing Medibank health insurance system to provide a general levy on the incomes of those receiving Medibank benefits, and also to open opportunities for private insurance plans. The new system began October 1.

Affairs Abroad. In some respects, the Fraser government's foreign policy differed sharply from that of its predecessor. Foreign Minister Andrew S. Peacock said on January 8 that Australia would support United States plans for a base at Diego Garcia in the Indian Ocean, and the government continually emphasized the threat from Russian naval activity in that area. United States nuclear-powered warships were welcomed in Australian ports, in spite of left wing objections. The government on March 23 approved the establishment of a United States Omega navigational aid station near the Tasman Sea. The new government was determined to stand well with the United States, and Fraser visited President Gerald R. Ford in Washington, D.C., in July.

In other respects, there was not much change. Fraser and Peacock, like former Prime Minister Whitlam, were sharply criticized for acquiescing in Indonesia's absorption of Timor. Visiting Tokyo in June, Fraser signed a treaty of friendship and cooperation with Japan, which had been initiated by Whitlam, and maintained the same note of admiration for Chinese achievement on a visit to China.

Australia signed a new financial agreement on March 4 with Papua New Guinea to provide a minimum of $1.15 billion in aid over five years. Papua New Guinea thus continued to be the principal beneficiary of Australian aid. The importance of Pacific Ocean areas to Australia was further emphasized by Peacock's announcement at the South Pacific Forum meeting in Suva, Fiji, on October 12 of $74 million aid to other South Pacific countries during the next three years.

Australia officially commemorated the American Revolution Bicentennial by founding a chair of Australian studies at Harvard University, publishing a special history of Australian-American relations, and dispatching an Australian historical exhibition to tour the United States in 1976 and 1977.

Domestic Developments. The population continued to increase slowly. Preliminary figures from the June 30 census put the total at 13,548,472, an increase of 6.4 per cent in five years. More people left the country than arrived. The new government showed more interest in immigration than did its predecessor, but was cautious about stimulating the flow of immigrants because of unemployment. Immigration was confined largely to people joining families already in Australia, and to those qualified for jobs that could not be filled locally. In addition, a growing number of refugees came in from Cyprus, Lebanon, Indochina, and Timor. The government decided to expand certain services to immigrants, including ethnic radio programs, and offered amnesty to illegal immigrants.

Fraser announced on January 21 that "God Save the Queen" would be the national anthem on vice-regal occasions, while any of four songs—"God Save the Queen," "Advance Australia Fair," "Waltzing Matilda," and "Song of Australia"—could be used on other occasions.

Aborigines continued to receive considerable attention, including increased funds for welfare, health, and education, but there was much argument about the best policies to pursue. An Aborigine, Sir Douglas Nicholls, a former sports star in Victoria, took over as governor of South Australia.

Arts and Sports. The Archibald Prize for a portrait was taken away from the initial winner because he painted his picture from a photograph, rather than from life. The Australian Ballet performed in Washington, D.C., New York City, London, and Manila, the Philippines. Australian movies advanced with such films as *Caddie, The Devil's Playground,* and *Mad Dog Morgan.*

Australia's 5-1 defeat of the West Indies in the cricket test match series was some consolation for the country's poor performance at the Olympic Games in Montreal. The Sheffield Shield was won by South Australia and the Melbourne Cup by Van der Hum. Hawthorn was the top team in Australian Rules football in Melbourne, and Manly-Warringah in Rugby league in Sydney. J. D. B. Miller

See also ASIA (Facts in Brief Table).

AUSTRIA. Chancellor Bruno Kreisky emphasized a policy of "active neutrality" through Austrian participation in United Nations (UN) peacekeeping operations throughout the world when he visited Paris in June 1976. Kreisky proposed a summit meeting of Western European countries and the United States after the American elections to counter similar consultations in Eastern Europe. "To reduce Europe to the Community [Common Market] is an erroneous concept," he declared.

Kreisky showed interest in Middle East affairs by persuading President Anwar al-Sadat of Egypt to extend his April visit to Vienna for longer discussions of bilateral issues. Kreisky hoped the Geneva Middle East peace conference would be reconvened because he believed that continuing conflict in the Middle East posed the only immediate danger of war for Europe.

Austria continued construction of UN City, an office complex in Vienna for 4,500 United Nations officials to be leased at a nominal yearly rent. Switzerland objected to the development because it threatened UN rentals there.

Minority Rights. The Austrian Parliament adopted a minority-rights bill on July 7 despite strong opposition from Slavic groups. The bill allows minority groups to use their own languages in government, businesses, and schools and on signposts if they constitute at least 25 per cent of the

Vienna's 790-foot (240-meter) Empire Bridge, built in 1937, collapsed into the Danube River on Aug. 1, 1976, when a faulty pier gave way.

local population. Slovene groups in the southern province of Carinthia boycotted a nationwide language census held on November 14 to establish the size of minority populations.

Cabinet Changes. On August 16, Kreisky nominated Willibald Pahr, head of the federal chancellery's constitution department, as foreign minister to succeed Erich Bielka-Karltreu, who retired. Kreisky also elevated Finance Minister Hannes Androsch to vice-chancellor.

Growing Deficit. The government continued its expansionary economic policy despite an increasing deficit, estimated in late 1976 at $2.8 billion. A new economic program in June increased spending by $605 million, aided industrial investment, suspended tax on new investments, accelerated depreciation allowances, and increased provision for export-guarantee finance. The government also allowed the National Bank of Austria's interest rate to drop to 4 per cent by the end of June.

The Austrian Institute of Economic Research expected the gross national product to rise by 4 per cent in 1976. Greater exports to new markets in the Middle East and Communist countries and a slower inflation rate of about 7 per cent were factors in the economic recovery from the 1975 recession. Austria's commitment to full employment kept unemployment down to 1.6 per cent.   Kenneth Brown

See also EUROPE (Facts in Brief Table).

AUTOMOBILE. The United States automobile industry enjoyed a year of recovery in 1976 after a lackluster 1975. Labor problems, including a 28-day strike in September and October against the Ford Motor Company and a 12-hour ministrike against General Motors (GM) Corporation in November, highlighted the year. United States auto production for the year was estimated at 8.5 million cars, 29 per cent above the 6.7 million built in 1975. Sales in the United States were expected to finish up at about 10.1 million cars, including 1.5 million imports. That was 16 per cent ahead of 1975 and its 8.6 million total sales. Sales forecasts for 1977 were optimistic; Thomas A. Murphy, board chairman of GM, predicted car sales, including imports, would be close to 11.25 million.

The profit picture was bright at GM and Chrysler Corporation, but Ford was hit in its cash register by the strike, and American Motors Corporation (AMC) was hurt by declining sales. GM reported a third-quarter net of $397 million, up 63 per cent from last year; Chrysler posted an operating profit of $76.2 million, as against a third-quarter loss of $79 million in the same period in 1975. Ford earnings for the quarter dropped to $42.5 million, down from $56.3 million a year earlier. AMC lost $51-million in the quarter, against a profit of $15 million in the third quarter a year earlier.

Strong sales reports were not confined to the U.S. auto front. Henry Ford II forecast in December that Free World car and truck sales would total 33.8-million vehicles in 1976, a solid gain over the 30.8-million sold in 1975. He predicted the figure would jump to 35 million units in 1977.

The Price Tags on 1977 models increased substantially, though it was difficult to figure them exactly as automakers shuffled standard and optional equipment on various models. GM said the "average equipped car" went up $338 or 5.9 per cent, Ford boosted its prices $310 or 5.1 per cent; Chrysler, $326 or 5.9 per cent; and American Motors, $167 or 4.8 per cent.

Foreign cars joined the price-boost parade. Toyota and Volkswagen (VW) raised their base prices an average of $112, which figured out to 2.8 per cent for Toyota and 2.5 per cent for VW. Other foreign makes also upped their price tags.

When small-car sales slowed, AMC in November cut the price of its Gremlin by $253 to $2,995, making it then the least expensive U.S.-built car, $4 under the Chevrolet Scooter.

AMC later offered a $253 rebate on its Pacer, and GM got into the rebate act in November, offering $200 rebates on its Chevette, Vega, and Astre models in efforts to shore up sagging sales in the low end of the market.

Market Mix. American firms trimmed the number of 1977 models to 252, a reduction of 42. The trend has been downward since the 375 offered in

The last American-built convertible, a Cadillac
Eldorado, rolls off an assembly line in Detroit
in April, ending an era in automobile styling.

1970. The average 1977 car is smaller in both
weight and wheelbase for the second consecutive
year.

Labor Gains. The 28-day strike at Ford plants in
the United States and a 12-hour strike at selected
GM plants helped the United Auto Workers
(UAW) to get substantial gains in their new three-
year contracts. Using Ford as an example – it was
the primary strike target – the new agreement will
cost the company more than $3 billion additionally
over the life of the contract, or about $300 for every
car, truck, or tractor the company builds in the
United States during that time.

An assembler in a Ford plant will get a 3 per cent
hourly increase in each of the three years and an
additional 20 cents an hour in the first year. His
present hourly wage of $5.43, plus a $1.09 cost-of-
living allowance, gives him $6.52 per hour. The old
base rate of $5.43 will go up to $8.35 an hour,
including cost-of-living adjustments, in the third
year of the contract. One of the key victories from a
UAW standpoint was a provision that over the life
of the three-year pact, workers will get an additional 13 paid days off annually.

Import Cars. The Japanese-built Toyota held
onto the import-car sales lead in the U.S. market
for the second consecutive year. During the first 11
months of 1976, a total of 1.4 million foreign cars
and trucks were sold, about 6 per cent below the 1.5-

million sold in the opening 11 months of 1975. Imports picked up about 14.9 per cent of the U.S.
market in the opening 11 months of 1976, off from
the 18.7 per cent in that period a year earlier. Indications were that the imports would wind up with
about 15 per cent of the U.S. market. That would
put foreign-car sales for the year at about the usual
1.5 million vehicles. Toyota sold 321,293 cars between January and November. VW reported a total
of 252,744 sold; and Datsun, 244,230.

Auto Safety. In December, Secretary of Transportation William T. Coleman, Jr., took a major
step in the field of auto safety. He ruled against
making airbags mandatory on all new cars for the
time being. Instead, he suggested that at least two
auto manufacturers agree to make and market a
combined total of 500,000 1979 and 1980 model
cars in various sizes equipped with passive restraints, either airbags or passive belt systems such
as are found on the Volkswagen Rabbit. He said
the cost should not exceed $100 for the entire
front-seat installation or $50 for the driver's side
only. Company spokesmen indicated they believed
the cost of such a system would be closer to $300.

Consumer advocate Ralph Nader criticized the
Coleman decision. Nader called it "horrendous and
irresponsible." Some safety experts had said installation of airbags in all U.S. cars would probably
save 12,000 lives a year and would reduce injuries
in hundreds of thousands of crashes. Nader agreed
with this assessment and expressed hope that Coleman's decision would be reversed by Representative
Brock Adams (D., Wash.), who was slated to be
transportation secretary in the Administration of
President James Earl (Jimmy) Carter, Jr.

Experimental Engines. GM deferred future payments for licensing rights to the rotary-powered
Wankel engine, but insisted that the project was not
dead, just destined for more testing. The other
three United States automakers have done research
on the engine.

Seeking to counteract the high cost of gasoline,
auto companies showed renewed interest in diesel
engines for passenger cars and experimented with
alcohol-powered cars. Ford said it will have a six-
cylinder engine within two years that can be
switched to a three-cylinder operation to save on
fuel when desired.

Emissions. The auto companies said they would
have problems trying to meet the level of auto emissions set by the Environmental Protection Agency
(EPA) for 1978 models. UAW President Leonard
Woodcock said that Carter had agreed to meet with
Woodcock and heads of the four U.S. auto companies to work out compromises on EPA emissions
standards to avoid a possible shut-down of car
plants in the summer of 1977, when the auto industry is scheduled to begin manufacturing the 1978
models.   Charles C. Cain III

AUTOMOBILE RACING. James Hunt of England won the world driving championship by one point in the last race of 1976. He won despite a series of incidents that led him to call the series a "farce" and say, "They have spoiled it for everybody." He won because Niki Lauda of Austria, the 1975 champion, quit in the rain after one lap in the decisive race, Japan's Formula One Grand Prix in October.

"It's too misty," Lauda said. "Sometimes I couldn't tell which direction the car was going. For me, it was the limit. For me, there is something more important than the world championship." Hunt finished third in that race and picked up three points, enough to edge Lauda, 69 to 68, for the title.

Lauda drove an Italian Ferrari, as he did in 1975. Hunt switched sponsors. His 1975 car was an English Hesketh, but the 25-year-old Lord Hesketh quit racing after investing $1 million in his car. At the same time, Emerson Fittipaldi of Brazil, the 1972 and 1974 world champion, left the English McLaren team to drive a new car built by his brother. So Hunt replaced Fittipaldi on the McLaren team and watched Lauda win most of the early races. Then Hunt started winning races, and Lauda was critically injured in a crash.

Hunt's Obstacles. Hours after he won the Spanish Grand Prix on May 2 at Madrid, Hunt was disqualified because an aerofoil was $1/2$ inch (13 millimeters) too wide. An international appeals board later reinstated his victory. He won the British Grand Prix on July 18 at Brands Hatch, England, but was disqualified two months later because crewmen had pushed his car to the pits after a first-lap accident. He failed to place in the Italian Grand Prix on September 12 at Monza because he was accused of using illegal fuel in the trials and thus had to start at the rear of the field.

Hunt won seven of the 16 races, including two of the last three—Canada at Mosport, Ont., and United States at Watkins Glen, N.Y. Lauda won five races, all before his near-fatal accident on August 1 in the German Grand Prix at Neurburgring. He raced again six weeks later, having missed only three races.

The Indianapolis 500 on May 30 highlighted the United States Auto Club's championship circuit. Johnny Rutherford of Fort Worth, Tex., driving a four-cylinder McLaren-Offenhauser, won for the second time in three years.

When rain interrupted the race after 102 of the 200 laps, A. J. Foyt of Houston, a three-time winner at Indianapolis, replaced a damaged front sway bar that had caused serious handling problems. He seemed likely to challenge Rutherford, but the race was never resumed.

The Stock Cars on the Grand National circuit of the National Association for Stock Car Auto Racing (NASCAR) provided yearlong excitement. Cale Yarborough of Timmonsville, S.C., won the

Apartment dwellers in Long Beach, Calif., watch as Clay Regazzoni of Switzerland, the winner, makes a turn in the first U.S. Grand Prix West.

series title in a Chevrolet. Richard Petty of Randleman, N.C., driving a Dodge, led in earnings with $308,074. David Pearson of Spartanburg, S.C., in a Mercury, led in victories, winning 10 of 30 races.

The 41-year-old Pearson won NASCAR's richest race, the $343,300 Daytona 500 on February 15 at Daytona Beach, Fla., in a fictionlike finish. He took the lead by passing Petty on the final backstretch. Petty regained the lead coming out of the last turn, and the cars bumped. Both spun out, hit the wall, and stopped on the infield grass. Pearson's car, 50 yards (15 meters) from the finish and its front flattened, seemed dead, but he got it across the finish line at 15 miles (24 kilometers) per hour and won.

Other Races. Brian Redman of England won the Formula 5000 10-race series in a Lola for the third straight year. Jacky Ickx of Belgium and Gijs van Lennep of the Netherlands won the 24 Hours of Le Mans in a turbocharged Porsche 936.

Janet Guthrie of New York City and Shirley Muldowney of Mount Clemens, Mich., made racing history. Guthrie, a 38-year-old physicist, became the first woman to pass the driver test for the Indianapolis 500, and she might have qualified for the 33-car field if her car had been more powerful. She later drove in stock car races. The 35-year-old Muldowney became the first woman to win a major top fuel championship in the National Hot Rod Association's Springnationals.   Frank Litsky

AVIATION perked up in 1976 as economic revival and fare increases stimulated airline finances. Knut Hammarskjöld, director-general of the International Air Transport Association (IATA), predicted at the group's meeting in Singapore in November that the world aviation industry would grow 8 per cent per year from 1977 on. IATA estimated that scheduled airlines carried 13 per cent more paying passengers on heavily traveled North Atlantic routes through September, and cargo was up 11 per cent. United States carriers' international passenger traffic rose 8.7 per cent through November.

United States scheduled-airlines earnings rebounded from an $84-million loss in 1975. George W. James, the industry's chief economist, estimated in December that the carriers would show profits of about $350 million for 1976. A series of fare increases, a solid gain in passenger traffic, and industry restraint in adding flight capacity were behind the glowing prediction. Improvement was marred by some strikes, however. Domestic-airline passenger traffic through November was 10.3 per cent ahead of 1975. Total air freight rose 4.7 per cent through October; domestic air freight was up 5.5 per cent, and international air freight hauled by U.S. carriers rose 5.8 per cent.

The Civil Aeronautics Board (CAB) ruled on November 19 that the major route swap between Pan American World Airways (PanAm) and Trans World Airlines (TWA) that took place early in 1975 should be continued through March 2, 1978. A federal appeals court reopened the case in July 1976 and ruled that the CAB originally approved without a full investigation the exchange of transpacific and transatlantic routes, aimed at reducing overlapping service and improving the two lines' financial condition. The regulatory agency on October 4 granted PanAm its first domestic route, between Detroit and Boston. But the CAB turned down petitions by TWA, PanAm, and Eastern Airlines for government subsidy.

The CAB voted on July 21 to expand transatlantic service, approving new direct United States-to-Europe service for 11 U.S. cities. It also granted Delta Air Lines and Northwest Airlines their first routes in that market. President Gerald R. Ford returned the case to the CAB on December 27, for foreign-policy and other reconsideration.

Two countries expressed dissatisfaction with their share of service to and from the United States. The British government said in August that it would pull out of the "Bermuda" agreement governing aviation relations between Great Britain and the United States; it sought a bigger share of transatlantic passenger traffic for British Airways. The two governments began negotiations on a new pact. In September, Japan pressed for a larger portion of U.S.-Japan air traffic for Japan Air Lines.

Amid these disputes, the Ford Administration issued an international-aviation policy statement on September 8. It contained provisions aimed at protecting the economic interests of airlines based in the United States.

Domestic Policy. The CAB was liberal in granting fare increases and new routes. After a 1 per cent domestic air-fare hike on February 1, the agency approved 2 per cent boosts in March, May, and September. It rejected proposals in June and July for fare increases, however, as being excessive. The CAB approved, on May 12, fare increases on the North Atlantic averaging about 4 per cent. IATA members could not agree on a winter North Atlantic fare package, so individual airlines filed plans to raise fares up to 20 per cent on November 1.

Carrying out a new policy to encourage route expansion, the CAB approved new domestic and international routes in nine major cases. The CAB also moved to ease air-charter travel rules with a new Advance Booking Charter plan that became effective on October 7. See TRAVEL.

The Ford Administration's 1975 proposal to ease some regulations on the airline industry gained new support. The CAB on April 8 proposed its own plan to sharply cut back board control over airline fares and routes. The CAB plan helped persuade chairmen of the House and Senate aviation subcommittees to introduce their own airline regulatory reform bills. The Administration proposed new leg-

A British Airways Concorde supersonic transport takes off from Heathrow Airport, London, on January 21, launching commercial passenger service.

islation on March 29 to subsidize service to small towns by commuter airlines if larger carriers end such service after deregulation.

Supersonic Transport. The British-French Concorde began U.S. flights to Washington, D.C.'s Dulles International Airport from London and Paris on May 24. The flights were cleared by Secretary of Transportation William T. Coleman, Jr., who ruled on February 4 that the Concorde should be allowed a 16-month U.S. trial to judge its noise and other factors. Coleman's decision was backed by federal courts that heard lawsuits by environmental groups and counties affected by Concorde operations. The Port Authority of New York and New Jersey kept Concorde flights out of John F. Kennedy International Airport.

Federal Aviation Administration (FAA) monitoring of Concorde take-offs at Dulles showed them to be considerably noisier than subsonic planes, as was predicted. Britain and France said on November 2 that they might not build more Concordes after completing the original 16 aircraft. British Airways said on November 17 that it was negotiating with Braniff International to extend the London to Washington, D.C., Concorde flight subsonically to Dallas-Fort Worth, Texas.

Aircraft Noise. The Department of Transportation announced a timetable on November 18 that requires airlines to reduce noise by 1985 on their older aircraft, which comprise about 75 per cent of jetliner fleets, to the quieter level of new, wide-bodied jets. Coleman held a hearing on December 1 to explore his idea for using part of the airline-passenger ticket tax, in effect, to help pay for aircraft noise reductions.

Air Safety. Airline fatalities rose throughout the world, but fell sharply in the United States. The Flight Safety Foundation, a private U.S. group, estimated about 1,400 deaths worldwide in airline crashes through late December, ahead of 824 fatalities in 1975. In the United States, 45 airline-accident deaths occurred, according to the National Transportation Safety Board, against a 1975 total of 124. See DISASTERS.

John L. McLucas, FAA administrator, overruled a deputy's decision to allow airlines an extra year, until Dec. 31, 1978, to modify wide-bodied jets to protect against sudden fuselage punctures that could cause crashes. In November, McLucas gave the airlines until June 30, 1978, to modify the Boeing 747 and until March 31, 1978, to change the Lockheed L-1011.

Strikes. More than 1,000 pilots struck Continental Airlines for the first time on October 23 after 15 months of negotiations. The strike ended on November 17. Canadian pilots struck for a week in June (see CANADA). Albert R. Karr

See also TRANSPORTATION.

AWARDS AND PRIZES presented in 1976 included the following:

Arts Awards

Academy of Motion Picture Arts and Sciences. *"Oscar" Awards: Best Picture, One Flew Over the Cuckoo's Nest. Best Actor,* Jack Nicholson, *One Flew Over the Cuckoo's Nest. Best Actress,* Louise Fletcher, *One Flew Over the Cuckoo's Nest. Best Supporting Actor,* George Burns, *The Sunshine Boys. Best Supporting Actress,* Lee Grant, *Shampoo. Best Director,* Milos Forman, *One Flew Over the Cuckoo's Nest. Best Screenplay, One Flew Over the Cuckoo's Nest,* Lawrence Hauben and Bo Goldman. *Best Documentary Feature, The Man Who Skied Down Everest,* F. R. Crawly, James Hager, and Dale Hartleben, producers. *Best Song,* "I'm Easy," from *Nashville,* music and lyrics by Keith Carradine. *Jean Hersholt Humanitarian Award,* Jules Stein. *Irving G. Thalberg Award,* for achievement in directing, Mervyn Leroy. *Honorary Award,* for service to the motion-picture industry, Mary Pickford.

Antoinette Perry (Tony) Awards. *Drama: Best Play, Travesties,* by Tom Stoppard. *Best Actor,* John Wood, in *Travesties. Best Actress,* Irene Worth, in *Sweet Bird of Youth. Best Director,* Ellis Rabb, for *The Royal Family. Musical: Best Musical, A Chorus Line. Best Actor,* George Rose, *My Fair Lady. Best Actress,* Donna McKechnie, *A Chorus Line. Best Choreography,* Bob Avian and Michael Bennett, *A Chorus Line. Best Music and Lyrics,* Marvin Hamlisch and Edward Kleban, *A Chorus Line. Best Director,* Michael Bennett, *A Chorus Line.*

Avery Fisher Prize, for excellence among young instrumentalists, Ursula Oppens and Paul Shenly, pianists; Ani Kavafian, violinist; and Heidi Lehwalder, harpist.

Cannes International Film Festival. *Golden Palm Grand Prize, Taxi Driver,* United States. *Best Actor,* Jose Louis Gomez in *The Family of Pascal Duarte. Best Actress,* Dominique Sanda in *The Ferramonti Heritage* and Mari Torocsik in *Where Are You, Madame Dery? Best Director,* Ettore Scola for *Affreux Sales et Mechants.*

Capezio Dance Award, Jerome Robbins, choreographer and stage manager, New York City Ballet, "for bringing a new classicism and daring innovation, profundity, and hilarity to the world of ballet. . . ."

Dance Magazine Award, for contributions to the dance, Michael Bennett, Suzanne Farrell, and E. Virginia Williams.

National Academy of Recording Arts and Sciences. *Grammy Awards: Record of the Year,* "Love Will Keep Us Together," The Captain and Tennille. *Song of the Year,* "Send in the Clowns," by Stephen Sondheim. *Album of the Year, Pop,* "Still Crazy After All These Years," by Paul Simon. *Best Pop Vocal Performance of the Year, Female,* "At Seventeen," Janis Ian; *Male,* "Still Crazy After All These Years," Paul Simon; *Duo, Group, or Chorus,* "Lyin' Eyes," The Eagles. *Classical,* Beethoven's complete symphonies, the Chicago Symphony conducted by Sir Georg Solti. *Best Classical Performance, Orchestra,* the New York Philharmonic conducted by Pierre Boulez, Ravel's *Daphnis and Chloe. Best Solo Classical Performance with Orchestra,* pianist Alicia de Larrocha, *Concerto for Left Hand* and *Concerto in G major* by Ravel. *Best Chamber Music Performance,* Schubert Trios, Arthur Rubinstein, Henryk Szeryng, Pierre Fournier. *Best Opera Recording,* Mozart's *Così Fan Tutte,* Royal Opera House, Covent Garden, conducted by Colin Davis. *Best Classical Performance, Instrumental Soloist or Soloists,* Bach's *Sonatas and Partitas for Violin Unaccompanied,* Nathan Milstein. *Best Classical Vocal Soloist Performance,* Mahler's *Kindertotenlieder,* Janet Baker. *Best Classical Choral Performance,* Carl Orff's *Carmina Burana,* Cleveland Orchestra

Chorus and Boys' Choir, conducted by Michael Tilson Thomas. *Best Jazz Performance, Big Band,* "Images," by Phil Woods with Michel Legrand and his Orchestra; *Group,* "No Mystery," by Return To Forever featuring Chick Corea; *Solo,* "Oscar Peterson and Dizzy Gillespie," by Dizzy Gillespie. *Best Country Vocal Performance, Female,* "I Can't Help It If I'm Still in Love with You," by Linda Ronstadt; *Male,* "Blue Eyes Crying in the Rain," by Willie Nelson; *Duo or Group,* "Lover Please," by Kris Kristofferson and Rita Coolidge. *Best Country Song,* "(Hey Won't You Play) Another Somebody Done Somebody Wrong Song," by Chips Moman and Larry Butler.

National Academy of Television Arts and Sciences. *Emmy Awards: Best Actor and Actress in a Comedy or Drama Special,* Anthony Hopkins in *Lindbergh Kidnaping Case,* Susan Clark in *Babe. Best Single Appearance in a Comedy or Drama Series,* Edward Asner in "Rich Man, Poor Man" and Kathryn Walker in "The Adams Chronicles." *Best Actor and Actress in a Drama Series,* Peter Falk in "Columbo" and Michael Learned in "The Waltons." *Best Actor and Actress in a Comedy Series,* Jack Albertson in "Chico and the Man" and Mary Tyler Moore in "The Mary Tyler Moore Show." *Best Actor and Actress in a Limited Series,* Hal Holbrook in "Sandburg's Lincoln" and Rosemary Harris in "Notorious Woman." *Best Special, Drama or Comedy, Eleanor and Franklin. Best Drama Series,* "Police Story." *Best Comedy Series,* "The Mary Tyler Moore Show." *Best Limited Series,* "Upstairs, Downstairs." *Best Comedy, Variety, or Music Series,* "NBC's Saturday Night." *Special Citations,* "Bicentennial Minutes," "Tonight Show," and "Mary Hartman, Mary Hartman."

New York Drama Critics Circle Awards. *Best play, Travesties,* by Tom Stoppard. *Best American Play, Streamers,* by David Rabe. *Best Musical, Pacific Overtures,* music and lyrics by Stephen Sondheim, book by John Weidman.

New York Film Critics Circle Awards. *Best Film, Nashville,* directed by Robert Altman. *Best Actor,* Jack Nicholson, *One Flew Over the Cuckoo's Nest. Best Actress,* Isabelle Adjani, *The Story of Adele H. Best Director,* Robert Altman, *Nashville. Best Screenplay, The Story of Adele H.,* by François Truffaut, Jean Gruault, and Suzanne Schiffman.

Journalism Awards

American Association for the Advancement of Science (AAAS). *AAAS-Westinghouse Science Writing Award,* to David Perlman, *San Francisco Chronicle;* Elizabeth J. Maggio, *Arizona Daily Star,* Tucson; and Paul Brodeur, *The New Yorker.*

The Newspaper Guild. *Heywood Broun Award,* Kent Pollock, *The Philadelphia Inquirer,* for a three-part series that described and documented increased police brutality in Philadelphia.

The Scripps-Howard Foundation. *Roy W. Howard Public Service Award,* to *The Courier-Journal,* Louisville, Ky., and KGW-TV, Portland, Ore. *Edward J. Meeman Conservation Award,* to Kenneth L. Robison, *The Idaho Statesman,* Boise.

The Society of Professional Journalists, Sigma Delta Chi. *Newspaper Awards: General Reporting,* to seven reporters for *The Detroit Free Press* who spent a year investigating Michigan's mental health code. *Editorial Writing,* William Duncliffe, *The Boston Herald-American,* for a front-page editorial on school busing. *Washington Correspondence,* James Risser, *The Des Moines Register,* for uncovering corruption in grain exporting. *Foreign Correspondence,* Sydney H. Schanberg, *The New York Times,* for coverage of the fall of Cambodia. *News Photography,* Stanley J. Forman, *The Boston Herald-American,* for photographs of a woman and child falling from a collapsing fire escape. *Editorial Cartooning,* Tony

Auth, *The Philadelphia Inquirer,* for a cartoon on civil strife in Lebanon. **Public Service in Newspaper Journalism,** *The Louisville Courier-Journal,* for coverage on school busing. **Magazine Awards: Reporting,** Mike Mallowe, *Philadelphia* magazine, for an investigation of Philadelphia's Bicentennial program. **Public Service in Magazine Journalism,** *Philadelphia,* for its examination of the condition of children under foster care. **Radio Awards: Reporting,** WHBF AM-FM, Rock Island, Ill., for coverage of an explosion. **Public Service,** WRVA, Richmond, Va., for exposing the dangers of the chemical Kepone. **Editorializing,** Charles B. Cleveland, WIND, Chicago, for a series on delays in unemployment payments. **Television Awards: Reporting,** WHAS-TV News, Louisville, Ky., for coverage of school busing. **Public Service,** WCKT-TV, Miami, Fla., on abortion. **Editorializing,** Don McGaffin and Charles Royer, KING-TV, Seattle, for exposing the improper use of special-interest money in the state legislature. **Research in Journalism,** Marvin Barrett, Columbia University, for his book *Moment of Truth?*

Literature Awards

Academy of American Poets. Lamont Poetry Selection Award, to Larry Levis, for his second book of poems, *The Afterlife.*

Academy of American Poets and Copernicus Society of America. Copernicus Award, to Robert Penn Warren, for his life's work. **Edgar Allan Poe Award,** to Charles Wright for his book *Bloodlines.* **Walt Whitman Award,** for unpublished poets, to Laura Gilpin.

American Academy of Arts and Letters – National Institute of Arts and Letters. Awards, to Robert Coover, novelist and playwright; to Robert Craft, critic and biographer; to E. L. Doctorow, novelist; to Eugene D. Genovese, historian; to Kenneth Koch, playwright, poet, and novelist; to Charles Simic, poet; to John Simon, critic; to Louis Simpson, poet and critic; to Susan Sontag, novelist, critic, film writer, and director; to Louis Zukofsky, poet. **Rome Prize,** to Miller Williams, poet and critic. **E. M. Forster Award,** to Jon Stallworthy, biographer, poet, and critic. **Loines Award for Poetry,** to Mona Van Duyn. **Richard and Hilda Rosenthal Award,** Richard Yates, for his novel *Disturbing the Peace.* **Marjorie Peabody Waite Award,** to Rene Wellek, critic. **Morton Dauwen Zabel Award,** to Harold Rosenberg, critic.

American Library Association. Caldecott Medal, to Leo and Diana Dillon, for illustrating *Why Mosquitoes Buzz in People's Ears; A West African Tale.* **Newbery Medal,** to Susan Cooper for her book *The Grey King.*

Columbia University. Bancroft Prizes, for "books of exceptional merit and distinction in American history . . . diplomacy and international relations. . . ." David Brion Davis, for *The Problem of Slavery in the Age of Revolution, 1770-1823* and Richard W. B. Lewis for *Edith Wharton: A Biography.*

Ernest Hemingway Foundation. Award, for the "best first novel by an American" to Lloyd Little for *Parthian Shot.*

The Hudson Review. Bennett Award, to "a writer of achievement whose work has not yet received the full recognition it deserves," to Jorge Guillen.

National Institute of Arts and Letters. National Book Awards: Arts and Letters, Paul Fussell for *The Great War and Modern Memory.* **History and Biography,** David Brion Davis for *The Problem of Slavery in the Age of Revolution, 1770-1823.* **Children's Literature,** to Walter D. Edmonds for *Bert Breen's Barn.* **Contemporary Affairs,** Michael J. Arlen, for *Passage to Ararat.* **Fiction,** William Gaddis for *J.R.* **Poetry,** John Ashbery for *Self-Portrait in a Convex Mirror.*

Nobel Prizes. See NOBEL PRIZES.

Public Service Awards

Brandeis University. Louis Dembitz Brandeis Award, for distinguished legal service, to Elliot L. Richardson, secretary of commerce.

National Association for the Advancement of Colored People, Spingarn Medal, to Alvin Ailey, founder and artistic director, Alvin Ailey Dance Theater.

National Civil Service League. Career Service Awards, to Alfred L. Atherton, Jr., Velma N. Baldwin, Robert J. Blackwell, Talcott W. Edminster, Arnold W. Frutkin, Vernon C. Johnson, Porter M. Kier, John E. Thornton, Rufus H. Wilson, and John D. Young. **Special Achievement,** Edgar E. Hartwig.

Neils Bohr Gold Medal, for outstanding contributions to the peaceful use of atomic energy, to Hans A. Bethe, Cornell University.

New York Urban League. Whitney M. Young, Jr., Award, to the National Council of Negro Women, accepted by Dorothy Height, president.

Rockefeller Awards, established by John D. Rockefeller III to honor outstanding public service, to Ira DeMent, U.S. attorney in Montgomery, Ala., for work in court cases affecting the welfare of imprisoned persons; to Herbert Sturz, director, Vera Institute of Justice, New York City, for the development of new criminal justice programs; to Dale Bertsch, executive director, Miami Valley Regional Planning Commission, Dayton, Ohio, for leadership in a plan providing low- and moderate-income housing; to Ernest Green, executive director, Recruitment and Training Program, Incorporated, New York City, for development of the Outreach program to recruit, train, and place minorities in construction industry apprenticeship programs; to Bernice Sandler, project director, Association of American Colleges Project on Women in Washington, D.C., for her campaign to increase job opportunities for women; to Donald S. Brown and David Shear, U.S. Department of State, for creating a long-range U.S. development and investment program to assist drought-plagued areas in Africa.

Templeton Foundation. Templeton Award, for contributions to ecumenicity, to Leon-Joseph Cardinal Suenens, Roman Catholic primate of Belgium.

United States Government. Freedom Medal, the nation's highest civilian award, to pianist Arthur Rubinstein and dance pioneer Martha Graham.

Pulitzer Prizes

Journalism. Public Service, a gold medal to *The Anchorage* (Alaska) *Daily News,* for a series investigating a local Teamsters Union. **General Local Reporting,** to Gene Miller, *The Miami Herald,* for stories leading to the exoneration of two men sentenced to death in Florida. **Special Local Reporting,** to the staff of *The Chicago Tribune* for exposing abuses in federal housing programs. **National Reporting,** to James Risser, *The Des Moines Register,* for exposing corruption in grain exporting. **International Reporting,** Sydney H. Schanberg, *The New York Times,* for his coverage of the Communist take-over of Cambodia. **Editorial Writing,** Philip P. Kerby, *The Los Angeles Times,* for editorials attacking government secrecy and attempts at judicial censorship of trial proceedings. **Spot News Photography,** Stanley J. Forman, *The Boston Herald-American,* for photographs of a Boston fire, showing the five-story fall of a woman and child. **Feature Photography,** the photo staff of *The Louisville Courier-Journal,* for its coverage of court-ordered busing in Louisville. **Editorial Cartooning,** Tony Auth, *The Philadelphia Inquirer.* **Distinguished Commentary,** Walter W. (Red) Smith, *The New York Times,* for the "literary quality" of his sports column. **Distinguished Criticism,** Alan M. Kriegsman, *The Washington Post,* for his writing on the dance. **Special Citation,** John Hohenberg, Columbia University, for his contributions to journalism.

AWARDS AND PRIZES

Letters. *Biography,* to Richard W. B. Lewis for *Edith Wharton: A Biography.* *Drama,* *A Chorus Line* by Michael Bennett, James Kirkwood, Nicholas Dante, Marvin Hamlisch, and Edward Kleban. *Fiction,* Saul Bellow for *Humboldt's Gift.* *General Nonfiction,* Robert N. Butler for *Why Survive? Being Old in America.* *History,* Paul Horgan for *Lamy of Santa Fe.* *Music,* Ned Rorem for *Air Music, 10 études for orchestra.*

Science and Technology Awards

American Association for the Advancement of Science (AAAS). *AAAS Rosensteil Award in Oceanographic Science,* Kenneth O. Emery, Henry Bryant Bigelow Oceanographer, Woods Hole Oceanographic Institution. *AAAS Socio-Psychological Prize,* R. B. Zajonc, professor of psychology, University of Michigan, and Gregory B. Markus, assistant research scientist, University of Michigan Center for Political Studies.

American Chemical Society. *Priestley Medal,* Henry Gilman, professor emeritus of chemistry, Iowa State University of Science and Technology.

American Section, Society of Chemical Industry. *Perkin Medal,* Lewis H. Sarett, president, Merck Sharp & Dohme Research Laboratories in Rahway, N.J.

American Geophysical Union. *Maurice Ewing Medal,* Walter H. Munk, Institute of Geophysical and Planetary Physics, University of California, San Diego. *Robert E. Horton Medal,* Walter B. Langbein, U.S. Geological Survey, Reston, Va. *William Bowie Medal,* Jule G. Charney, Massachusetts Institute of Technology.

American Institute of Aeronautics and Astronautics. *Goddard Award,* Edward Price, visiting professor, Georgia Institute of Technology. *Louis W. Hill Space Transportation Award,* Glynn Lunney, National Aeronautics and Space Administration.

American Institute of Physics. *Dannie Heineman Prize for Mathematical Physics,* S. W. Hawking, Department of Applied Mathematics and Theoretical Physics, Cambridge University, England.

American Physical Society. *Bonner Prize in Nuclear Physics,* John Schiffer, Argonne National Laboratory. *Davisson-Germer Prize,* Ugo Fano, of the University of Chicago.

Columbia University. *Louisa Gross Horwitz Prize,* geneticists Seymour Benzer, California Institute of Technology, and Charles Yanofsky, Stanford University, for their studies of gene structure and functions, which, according to the awards, explain how genes code instructions for life, molecule by molecule.

Geological Society of America. *Penrose Medal,* Preston E. Cloud, Jr., Department of Geology, University of California, Santa Barbara. *Arthur L. Day Medal,* Hans Ramberg, Division of Mineralogy and Petrology, University of Uppsala, Sweden.

Kittay Scientific Foundation. *Kittay International Award,* James Olds, professor of behavioral biology, California Institute of Technology, and Hans Selye, director, Institute of Experimental Medicine and Surgery, University of Montreal, Canada, for their contributions to the field of mental health.

Albert and Mary Lasker Foundation Awards. *Albert Lasker Basic Medical Research Award,* Rosalyn S. Yalow, a nuclear physicist at the Bronx (N.Y.) Veterans Administration Hospital, for her role in developing a technique to measure the concentrations of hormones, viruses, vitamins, enzymes, and drugs in body tissues. *Albert Lasker Clinical Medical Research Award,* to Raymond P. Ahlquist, Medical College of Georgia, Augusta, and James W. Black, University College of London, England, for their independent research leading to the development of a class of drugs called beta blockers, which are used to lower blood pressure and prevent irregular heartbeat. *Albert Lasker Public Health Service Award,* to the

World Health Organization (WHO) for its "imminent eradication of smallpox — the first and only disease ever to be eradicated from the Earth." The award was accepted by Halfdan I. Mahler, director-general of WHO, and Donald Henderson, director of WHO's smallpox eradication program.

National Academy of Engineering. *Founders Medal,* Manson Benedict, professor emeritus, Massachusetts Institute of Technology. *Zworykin Award,* C. Kumar N. Patel, director, Electronics Research Laboratory, Bell Laboratories.

National Academy of Sciences. *Agassiz Medal,* for contributions to oceanography, to Walter H. Munk, Institute of Geophysics and Planetary Physics, University of California, San Diego. *U.S. Steel Foundation Award in Molecular Biology,* to Daniel Nathans, director, Department of Microbiology, Johns Hopkins University, Baltimore. *Selman A. Waksman Award in Microbiology,* to Wallace P. Rowe, chief, Laboratory of Viral Diseases, National Institute of Allergy and Infectious Diseases, Washington, D.C. *National Medal of Science,* for distinguished scientific achievement, to John W. Backus, International Business Machines Corporation's San Jose (Calif.) Research Laboratory, for contributions to computer programming; to Manson Benedict, professor emeritus, Massachusetts Institute of Technology, for his role in creating the discipline of nuclear engineering; to Hans A. Bethe, Cornell University professor emeritus of physics, for his explanation of the origin of the sun's heat, and for his work on atomic energy; to Shiing-Shen Chern, professor of mathematics, University of California, Berkeley, for work in geometry and topology; to George B. Dantzig, Stanford University professor of operations research and computer science, for inventing linear programming and methods for more efficient use of mathematical theory in computers; to Hallowell Davis, emeritus professor of physiology, Washington University of St. Louis, for research in neurology, acoustics, and pediatrics; to Paul György, late professor emeritus of pediatrics, University of Pennsylvania School of Medicine, for the discovery of three vitamins and related research in human nutrition (awarded posthumously); to Sterling Brown Hendricks, former chief chemist, U.S. Department of Agriculture, for basic research in the physical and chemical properties of soils and proteins; to Joseph O. Hirschfelder, University of Wisconsin professor of theoretical chemistry, for contributions to atomic and molecular quantum mechanics; to William H. Pickering, director emeritus, California Institute of Technology Jet Propulsion Laboratory in Pasedena, for leadership in exploring planets and the solar system; to Lewis H. Sarett, president of Merck Sharp & Dohme Research Laboratories in Rahway, N.J., for contributions to the chemical synthesis of cortisone and other chemotherapeutic agents; to Frederick E. Terman, vice-president and provost emeritus, Stanford University, for his role in creating modern electronics; to Orville Alvin Vogel, U.S. Department of Agriculture, for contributions to agronomic research; to E. Bright Wilson, Jr., Harvard University professor of chemistry, for theoretical and experimental contributions to the understanding of molecules; to Chien-Shiung Wu, Columbia University professor of physics, for experiments that led to the understanding of the decay of radioactive nuclei.

National Science Foundation. *Alan T. Waterman Award,* for outstanding accomplishment and promise as a young researcher, to mathematician Charles L. Fefferman, Princeton University.

Pepperdine University. *John and Alice Tyler Ecology Award,* Charles Elton, Oxford University, England; Rene J. Dubos, professor emeritus, Rockefeller University, New York City; and Abel Wolman, professor emeritus, Johns Hopkins University.   Edward G. Nash

BAHAMAS. See WEST INDIES.

BAHRAIN. Parliamentary government remained suspended in Bahrain in 1976. Amir Isa bin Salman Al Khalifa on August 25 ruled out reopening the National Assembly, which was suspended in 1975, in the near future.

Nevertheless, the government moved ahead with economic and social development plans. An important element in the program involved protection for Bahraini citizens from foreign labor and exploitation. On August 15, visas became mandatory for foreign workers; profiteering was banned; and workers were prohibited from joining trade unions until they had completed five years employment with a firm. Bahrain's first social insurance law also went into effect for all firms with more than 1,000 workers. Curbs were placed on the use of middlemen in contracts between foreign companies and Bahraini interests.

A record $487-million budget, up 46 per cent, was approved in February. Partly because of the collapse of Beirut in Lebanon's civil war, Bahrain became a major Middle East financial center in 1976. Some 32 international banks received licenses to conduct international banking operations at $25,000 per license. Twenty-four were in operation by the end of November. William Spencer

See also MIDDLE EAST (Facts in Brief Table).
BALLET. See DANCING.

French President Valéry Giscard d'Estaing greets Amir Isa bin Salman Al Khalifa of Bahrain, who visited France in January.

BALTIMORE. A federal judge, on March 8, 1976, ordered the U.S. Department of Health, Education, and Welfare (HEW) not to proceed with its administrative hearings regarding school desegregation plans. This ended a government threat to cut off $23 million in aid to Baltimore's public schools and at least $36 million in aid to Maryland's state colleges and universities. HEW officials had charged in 1975 that Maryland failed to carry out desegregation plans, and announced it would start hearings that could result in the fund cutoff. Maryland filed suit against HEW in January 1976, claiming that specific violations were not cited. In issuing his order to halt the hearings, the judge said that HEW had been "duplicitous and uncooperative" in its negotiations.

City Hall Shoot-Out. A man identified as Charles Hopkins entered Mayor William D. Schaefer's office on April 13 and wounded the mayor's appointments secretary. He then shot and killed a city councilman and took another councilman hostage. Hopkins was captured after a gun battle in which he, the hostage, and a policeman were wounded.

The day before the shootings, Hopkins had disrupted a meeting of the city's Board of Estimates. On March 12, he had ripped the U.S. flag from the courthouse and set it afire to show his displeasure over a dispute involving his restaurant lease.

Government Ratings. Baltimore's city government received the highest rating for responsiveness to citizen complaints in a study of 22 cities released by the Council on Municipal Performance in April. The Maryland General Assembly's Constitutional and Public Law Committee made a less flattering assessment, accusing the Baltimore Police Department of "a clear abuse of police powers" in a report released on January 14. The report charged that police routinely spied on private citizens.

A federal study released on March 2 showed that violent crime continued to increase in Baltimore despite $140 million that the Law Enforcement Assistance Administration gave to the city for 233 anticrime projects.

Living Costs in the Baltimore area rose 5.5 per cent between June 1975 and June 1976. Food costs rose 4.6 per cent during the same period. Baltimore continued to rank as one of the more expensive U.S. cities in which to live. The U.S. Department of Labor reported that an average family of four would need an income of $15,398 a year to live in moderate comfort.

Johns Hopkins University researchers in a study for the Environmental Protection Agency reported on February 16 that the lung cancer death rate among men living within a 0.5-mile (0.8-kilometer) radius of Baltimore's Allied Chemical Company plant was four times greater than that among men in nonindustrial parts of the city. James M. Banovetz

BANGLADESH went through a year of economic woe in 1976. It also had grave disputes with India, the country that helped to create this nation in 1971. Still, Bangladesh survived without the kind of calamities that marked the previous four years.

For the second successive year, the rice harvest was plentiful. But Bangladesh was still a long way from adequately feeding its 75 million people, and it needed imports of 2.2 million short tons (2 million metric tons) of grain. The country again received foreign credits of about $750 million.

Industry worked below capacity because of poor management and distribution and unchecked corruption. Imported grain rotted on the docks because of improper storage. Relief supplies were diverted into the black market, despite arrests, trials, and severe sentences. In an effort to revise the economy, the government offered to return to their Pakistani owners some of the factories confiscated in 1971 if the owners would bring in fresh investments. Quadrupled oil prices also posed a problem.

Strongman. Major General Ziaur Rahman, who came to power following a series of military mutinies in November 1975, retained his post as senior military administrator, though several groups of officers were arrested and charged with plotting to remove him. A member of the ruling group, Air Vice-Marshal Muhammad Ghulam Tawab, began to seriously disagree with Ziaur's policies and was ousted on May 1. The officers who murdered President Mujibur Rahman, the "father of Bangladesh," in 1975 sought to return from exile, but were turned away. On November 30, General Ziaur Rahman assumed full powers under martial law and had a number of prominent politicians, including former President Khandakar Mushtaque Ahmed, arrested.

Relations with India continued to deteriorate. After Mujibur's assassination, many of his followers fled across the border, and the Indian Border Security Force took them under its wing. Early in 1976, these India-based people began to raid villages in Bangladesh.

Bangladesh also accused India of using the enormous Farakka Dam, which was built in 1971, to divert water from the Ganges River that passes through Bangladesh to India's Hooghly River. India insisted it needed the water to flush silt from the port of Calcutta.

Bangladesh officials said that the low level of the Ganges caused salinity to spread up from the sea, ruining drinking water for the Bangladesh people, hindering industry, and damaging crops. Sporadic talks between the governments yielded no result. A march on the dam in May, led by 94-year-old Maulaua Bhashani, a popular Muslim leader, was called off at the border. Bhashani died in November. Mark Gayn

See also ASIA (Facts in Brief Table).

BANKS AND BANKING. Modest real economic growth was accompanied by little, if any, increase in interest rates around the world in 1976. Interest rates were well below the all-time peaks of 1974. Bank loans to businesses in the United States and Canada remained sluggish as companies financed most of their inventory and other investment needs internally, in contrast to earlier recoveries when the proportion of external financing generally increased. Individuals and businesses, as well as banks, were anxious to rebuild their financial soundness after being severely buffeted by inflation and recession in 1974 and 1975.

The Debt Market. In 1975, a number of money-market analysts had anticipated sharp interest rate increases in the United States because of the enormous amounts of debt sold to finance a huge $66-billion federal deficit for the year ending June 30, 1976. However, the deficit fell by more than half in the first six months of 1976, and a further drop was expected during the rest of the year. This contributed to substantially easier money markets. In addition, private borrowing grew comparatively little because of the sluggish economy.

As of June 30, private investors held $620.4 billion in public debt. Some $392.6 billion of that amount was marketable, most of it in short-term treasury bills and notes that would come due within one year. The federal government borrowed an additional $83 billion in fiscal 1976. Although part of this was held by the government itself, mainly by the Federal Reserve System and Social Security Administration, about $75 billion was purchased by private investors.

New issues of state and local government securities totaled $32 billion in the comparable fiscal year, and corporate stock and bond issues came to $61-billion. Although the average maturity of the federal debt remained quite short, the U.S. Department of the Treasury attempted to lengthen it by issuing a substantial number of bonds that would come due in more than 20 years. Private investors increased their holdings of these long-term securities by more than $1 billion in 1975 and 1976, and the Federal Reserve System increased its holdings by more than $2 billion. Nevertheless, most new issues of federal securities continued to be very short term.

Savings Deposits. Individuals as well as businesses used 1976 to rebuild their financial strength. Personal savings totaled 7 per cent of disposable personal income in the first half of the year, well above the 6.4 per cent that was saved in 1972, which was also the second year of an economic expansion. As real economic growth slowed to 4 per cent in the third quarter, consumers maintained their spending ratio by cutting savings to 6.4 per cent.

Thrift institutions gained a substantial flow of deposits through most of 1976. Savings and loan

Banks in six New England states were among the first in the United States to offer NOW accounts, interest-bearing checking accounts.

associations, whose financial soundness had been threatened in 1974 and 1975, rebounded with record capital inflows in 1976. Federal Reserve Regulation Q, which sets maximum interest rates on savings accounts, had held down deposit interest rates during the tight credit situation in 1974 and 1975. This led to withdrawals as depositors sought higher yields in money-market securities, such as short-term treasury bills. But with easier money-market conditions in 1976, interest rates on savings accounts became competitive again.

The growth in deposits permitted savings and loan associations not only to increase mortgage lending, but also to repay loans from Federal Home Loan Banks. Savings and loan associations make more mortgage loans than all other financial institutions combined. Despite a slower increase in new housing starts than the industry might have hoped for, mortgage loans increased more than 50 per cent in the first half of the year, pointing to substantial mortgage extension in the rest of the year. The increase in new housing starts reflected both lower mortgage interest rates and greater availability of mortgage money. See HOUSING.

Monetary Growth. Total private liquid assets increased nearly 10 per cent in the year ending Aug. 31, 1976. The most rapid growth occurred in time deposits at commercial banks and other savings institutions.

Overall monetary growth in currency and demand deposits largely hovered within the Federal Reserve's targets, which ranged between 4.5 to 7.5 per cent for the year. Federal Reserve Chairman Arthur F. Burns stuck to this goal in his quarterly appearances before congressional committees.

Nobel Prize Winner. Milton Friedman of the University of Chicago was awarded the 1976 Nobel Prize in Economics. Like Adam Smith, who founded modern economics with his *Wealth of Nations* in 1776, Friedman favors the quantity theory of money, which holds that changes in money supply importantly affect total spending and prices. Friedman's 1963 classic *A Monetary History of the United States 1867–1960,* written with Anna Schwartz, found that there had been a consistent cyclical relationship between changes in monetary growth and later changes in spending and prices.

Such observations persuaded the Congressional Joint Economic Committee to recommend in 1968 that the Federal Reserve Board limit variation in monetary growth to between 2 and 6 per cent annually. In 1975, Congress further required the Federal Reserve to announce each quarter its proposed growth targets for the following 12 months.

Friedman spent a lifetime criticizing the Federal Reserve and, most recently, Arthur Burns, his one-time colleague at the National Bureau of Economic Research. Despite this, Friedman was to retire from the University of Chicago in 1977 to become scholar in residence at, of all places, the Federal Reserve Bank of San Francisco.

New Banking Legislation was considered in both the United States and Canada. Canada is preparing new legislation affecting a wide range of banking activities. Its current banking law expires on June 30, 1977.

In the United States, Democrats in Congress initiated a major review of the banking system in a study called Financial Institutions and the Nation's Economy (FINE). The main FINE proposals, however, suffered the same fate that had befallen earlier bills proposed by the Richard M. Nixon Republican Administration's Commission on Financial Structure and Regulation – they all failed to make it into law.

The Administration bill and the FINE bill had several common elements, as well as some major differences. Both sought to increase competition among financial institutions. Both proposed the eventual elimination of Federal Reserve Regulation Q, setting maximum interest rates on term and savings deposits. Both bills anticipated that, after five years, financial institutions would be strong enough to stand alone without being protected from interest rate competition by Regulation Q. Both bills also proposed special programs to encourage home-mortgage loans, though they suggested different ways to achieve the goal.

Martha Clarke of Columbus, Ohio, holds a
fistful of $2 bills, which were reissued
in 1976 for the first time in a decade.

The FINE bill also proposed that bank regulation be centered in fewer agencies. The Office of the Comptroller of the Currency, which charters and regulates national banks, would be merged into a federal banking commission that would also incorporate the regulating authority of the Federal Reserve Board. The Federal Deposit Insurance Corporation would retain its present duty of examining and insuring commercial banks.

Foreign Currencies Fall. Comparatively high inflation rates in Great Britain, Italy, and Mexico in recent years culminated in substantial depreciation in the value of their currencies against other currencies. The Mexican peso, which had previously been held at 8 cents, dropped to 5 cents at the end of August and to 3.8 cents in October. The Italian lira hovered around 0.115 cents at year's end, compared to 0.146 cents in December 1975. The British pound steadied after touching an all-time low of $1.56 in October. In November, Great Britain began negotiating with the International Monetary Fund (IMF) for a $3.9-billion loan to shore up its sagging currency. The loan was approved on Jan. 3, 1977. With strong support from the United States, the IMF in October endorsed the existing floating exchange-rate system that allows major rate changes to occur without precipitating an international financial crisis. William G. Dewald

BARBADOS. See WEST INDIES.

BARRE, RAYMOND (1924-   ), succeeded Jacques Chirac as prime minister of France on Aug. 25, 1976 (see FRANCE). President Valéry Giscard d'Estaing called Barre "the best economist in the country" and urged him to fight inflation, meet French defense needs, and study possible political reforms. A political independent, Barre favors a united Europe through such steps as monetary union among members of the European Community (Common Market).

Barre was born on April 12, 1924, on the Indian Ocean island of Reunion, attended high school there, and studied law and political science in Paris. He taught economics at Caen, in Normandy, from 1954 to 1963 and at the Institute for Political Science in Paris, and also occupied the chair for economics at the Sorbonne. His textbooks became required reading for most French economics students.

From 1959 to 1962, Barre was chief aid to President Charles de Gaulle's minister for industry. France's chief representative to the Common Market from 1967 to 1973, Barre was also vice-president of the market's executive commission and a commissioner for economic and financial affairs. In January 1976, he became minister of foreign trade.

Friends describe the rotund Barre as jovial and relaxed. He enjoys eating gourmet food and going to the opera. He and his wife, Eve Hegedus, have two sons. Robert K. Johnson

BASEBALL. The Cincinnati Reds won the World Series for the second straight year in 1976, defeating the New York Yankees in four straight games. The World Series, and the April-to-October season that preceded it, served as an interlude in a baseball year dominated by labor strife and the historic freeing of many veteran players to sign with new teams.

The owners of the 24 major-league clubs refused to open spring-training camps on March 1. Their overall contract with the Major League Baseball Players Association had expired, and they had been unable to reach agreement on the reserve clause. That clause was part of the standard player contract that bound the player to his team permanently unless it sold, traded, or released him.

On March 17, after the players had softened their stand, Commissioner Bowie Kuhn ordered training camps opened immediately. On July 12, on the eve of the All-Star Game and after 13 months of negotiations, the owners and players agreed on a four-year contract.

The players won new freedom. After five years in the major leagues, a player could demand to be traded, and he could veto six clubs. If he was not traded, he would become a free agent. After six years in the major leagues, a player could become a free agent, subject to a draft of 12 clubs plus his own.

Although the owners signed the agreement,

many said it would ruin baseball, that most players would become free agents, and that the rich clubs would buy up the outstanding free agents. It did not turn out that way.

When the special free-agent draft was held on November 4 in New York City, it offered only 24 players from 13 clubs. Among them were eight members of the Oakland A's, including Reggie Jackson, Bert Campaneris, Joe Rudi, and Gene Tenace, plus such other stars as Bobby Grich, Gary Matthews, Dave Cash, and Don Gullett.

Thirteen of the 24 players were drafted by the maximum number of 12 clubs. Three players — first basemen Willie McCovey, Nate Colbert, and Dick Allen — were passed up by every club.

Most of the players signed multiyear contracts for far more money than they had been earning. Most signed with clubs that had not played as well as their own in 1976, and only a few signed with the so-called rich clubs. Jackson made the richest deal, with the Yankees for $2.9 million for five years.

The fear that they would lose good players in the future led clubs to sign their present players to multiyear contracts at higher salaries. For example, Don Sutton, who received $155,000 to pitch for the Los Angeles Dodgers in 1976, could have become a free agent after the 1977 season. The Dodgers gave him a four-year contract worth $1 million.

Oakland A's owner Charles O. Finley was angry that so many of his players were playing out the option year of their contracts. On June 15, he stunned baseball by selling three of his best players — pitcher Vida Blue to the Yankees for $1.5-million and relief pitcher Rollie Fingers and outfielder Joe Rudi to the Boston Red Sox for $1 million each, the highest price in history.

Finley, like the other club owners, was upset by a 1975 arbitrator's decision, upheld in 1976 by two federal courts, that any player who completed a season without having signed a contract would become a free agent at the end of that season, free to sign with any club. This ruling was modified by the July agreement between the club owners and players, but it governed baseball when Finley traded Jackson and Ken Holtzman, both unsigned, to the Baltimore Orioles on April 2 and then sold Blue, Fingers, and Rudi, all unsigned.

On June 16, the day after the sales, Kuhn ordered a hearing. On June 17, Finley said, "I only regret that I didn't sell more of them. I hope to wake the stupid owners to the facts of reality."

On June 18, Kuhn surprisingly voided the sales of the three, calling them "inconsistent with the best interests of baseball."

Finley sued Kuhn for $3.5 million, charging antitrust violations. He asked the court to allow the

Reds' catcher Johnny Bench, left, won the World Series Most Valuable Player award. Catcher Thurman Munson, right, was the Yankees' star.

sales, and he refused to let the three play for the A's until the dispute was settled. The other A's players threatened to strike unless their three teammates could play. Finley finally let them play.

Pennant Races. The Reds won the National League's Western Division race for the fifth time in seven years and the pennant for the fourth time in seven years. Their team batting average of .280 was the highest in the major leagues, and five of their eight regulars – including second baseman Joe Morgan, third baseman Pete Rose, and outfielder George Foster – batted over .300. The Reds swept by the Philadelphia Phillies in three games in the pennant play-offs.

Billy Martin, in his first full season as manager of the Yankees, created an aggressive team, and the Yankees won the American League's Eastern Division easily. Their best players were catcher Thurman Munson, the league's Most Valuable Player; outfielder Mickey Rivers; and first baseman Chris Chambliss. The Kansas City Royals held off the fast-closing A's to win the Western Division. The Yankees won the pennant on a ninth-inning home run by Chambliss in the fifth and final game of the play-offs against the Royals.

The World Series was a four-game sweep for the Reds. Johnny Bench, the Cincinnati catcher, was voted the Most Valuable Player in the series.

The major commotion came when the second game, on a Sunday, was played at night – in temperatures that dipped below 40°F. (4°C) – instead of in the afternoon. Although World Series weekday games were played at night, weekend games had always been day games. The change to night, which Kuhn called an experiment, was influenced by an extra payment of $700,000 by NBC, which preferred to televise the game at night.

Regular-season attendance reached 31.3 million, the highest ever and 1.2 million more than the record established in 1973. A further increase was anticipated in 1977, when the American League would add teams in Seattle and Toronto, Canada.

Hall of Fame. Pitchers Robin Roberts and Bob Lemon were voted into the Baseball Hall of Fame by baseball writers. The veterans' committee added Fred Lindstrom, Roger Connor, and umpire Cal Hubbard, and the Negro Leagues committee chose Oscar Charleston.

Henry Aaron played his 23rd major-league season, then retired at 42 and became vice-president in charge of player development for the Atlanta Braves, the team for which he played most of his career. Aaron finished his career with 755 home runs (more than anyone else in history) and 3,771 hits (second only to Ty Cobb). Frank Litsky

See also Section One, Focus on Sports.

Final Standings in Major League Baseball

American League

Eastern Division	W.	L.	Pct.	GB.
New York	97	62	.610	
Baltimore	88	74	.543	10½
Boston	83	79	.512	15½
Cleveland	81	78	.509	16
Detroit	74	87	.460	24
Milwaukee	66	95	.410	32

Western Division	W.	L.	Pct.	GB.
Kansas City	90	72	.556	
Oakland	87	74	.540	2½
Minnesota	85	77	.525	5
California	76	86	.469	14
Texas	76	86	.469	14
Chicago	64	97	.398	25½

Leading Batters

Batting Average—George Brett, Kansas City	.333
Home Runs—Graig Nettles, New York	32
Runs Batted In—Lee May, Baltimore	109
Hits—George Brett, Kansas City	215

Leading Pitchers

Games Won—Jim Palmer, Baltimore	22
Win Average—Bill Campbell, Minnesota (17-5) (162 or more innings)	.780
Earned-Run Average—Mark Fidrych, Detroit	2.34
Strikeouts—Nolan Ryan, California	327

Awards

Most Valuable Player—Thurman Munson, New York
Cy Young—Jim Palmer, Baltimore
Rookie of the Year—Harold (Butch) Wynegar, Minnesota
Manager of the Year—Dorrel (Whitey) Herzog, Kansas City

National League

Eastern Division	W.	L.	Pct.	GB.
Philadelphia	101	61	.623	
Pittsburgh	92	70	.568	9
New York	86	76	.531	15
Chicago	75	87	.463	26
St. Louis	72	90	.444	29
Montreal	55	107	.340	46

Western Division	W.	L.	Pct.	GB.
Cincinnati	102	60	.630	
Los Angeles	92	70	.568	10
Houston	80	82	.494	22
San Francisco	74	88	.457	28
San Diego	73	89	.451	29
Atlanta	70	92	.432	32

Leading Batters

Batting Average—Bill Madlock, Chicago	.339
Home Runs—Mike Schmidt, Philadelphia	38
Runs Batted In—George Foster, Cincinnati	121
Hits—Pete Rose, Cincinnati	215

Leading Pitchers

Games Won—Randy Jones, San Diego	22
Win Average—John Candelaria, Pittsburgh (16-7) (162 or more innings)	.700
Earned-Run Average—John Denny, St. Louis (162 or more innings)	2.52
Strikeouts—Tom Seaver, New York	235

Awards

Most Valuable Player—Joe Morgan, Cincinnati
Cy Young—Randy Jones, San Diego
Rookie of the Year—Larry Herndon, San Francisco
Manager of the Year—Danny Ozark, Philadelphia

BASKETBALL. Merger and labor peace came to professional basketball in 1976. On June 17, the 30-year-old National Basketball Association (NBA) and the nine-year-old American Basketball Association (ABA) agreed to merge the 18 NBA teams and 4 ABA teams into a 22-team NBA. On the court, the 1975-1976 champions were the Boston Celtics in the NBA, the New York Nets in the ABA, and Indiana University among the colleges.

In the nine years of NBA-ABA rivalry, competition for player talent became fierce. Untested players just out of college signed contracts worth more than $1 million. Veteran stars earned as much as $500,000 a year, and the average salary in the NBA reportedly exceeded $100,000 a year.

The ABA said it had lost $40 million since it began play in the 1967-1968 season. It always seemed on the brink of collapse, and it filed multimillion-dollar antitrust suits against the NBA. Merger seemed logical, but the players had opposed it because their salaries would suffer.

The Merger. Each ABA team in the merger — the New York Nets, Indiana Pacers, Denver Nuggets, and San Antonio Spurs — paid a $3.2-million franchise fee to the NBA. In addition, the Nets agreed to pay a $4-million indemnity to the New York Knickerbockers for invasion of the Knicks' NBA territory. The four ABA teams will not share in television revenue of $11 million a year through the 1977-1978 season and $11.5 million a year for the following two years. Nor will they share in a $5-million bonus CBS-TV promised to pay the NBA because it added four teams.

The ABA had hoped to have its six surviving teams in the merger. Instead, it had to pay about $3-million each to the Kentucky Colonels and the Utah Rockies (formerly the Spirits of St. Louis), the two teams excluded from the merger.

It recovered almost $3 million of the money in a dispersal draft by the existing NBA teams of Kentucky and St. Louis players. The cost of the players was set in advance. The highest was the $1.1 million the Chicago Bulls paid for Artis Gilmore of Kentucky. The 7-foot 2-inch (218-centimeter) Gilmore had been the only dominant center in the ABA and its rebounding leader in four of his five seasons, including 1975-1976.

The Robertson Case. Before the merger, the NBA achieved labor peace in February by reaching an out-of-court settlement with its players association in the Oscar Robertson case. Robertson, one of the great NBA players before he retired in 1974, filed a class action suit in 1970 contending that the college draft, option clause, and other NBA practices violated antitrust laws.

The players won all of their points. The option clause was dropped from new contracts after the 1975-1976 season. Starting in 1980, a player whose contract has expired can deal with any other team,

Final Standings in Major League Basketball

National Basketball Association

Eastern Conference

Atlantic Division	W.	L.	Pct.
Boston	54	28	.659
Buffalo	46	36	.561
Philadelphia	46	36	.561
New York	38	44	.463

Central Division	W.	L.	Pct.
Cleveland	49	33	.598
Washington	48	34	.585
Houston	40	42	.488
New Orleans	38	44	.463
Atlanta	29	53	.354

Western Conference

Midwest Division	W.	L.	Pct.
Milwaukee	38	44	.463
Detroit	36	46	.439
Kansas City	31	51	.378
Chicago	24	58	.293

Pacific Division	W.	L.	Pct.
Golden State	59	23	.720
Seattle	43	39	.524
Phoenix	42	40	.512
Los Angeles	40	42	.488
Portland	37	45	.451

Leading Scorers	G.	FG.	FT.	Pts.	Avg.
McAdoo, Buffalo	78	934	559	2,427	31.1
Abdul-Jabbar, Los Angeles	82	914	447	2,275	27.7
Maravich, New Orleans	62	604	396	1,604	25.9
Archibald, Kansas City	78	717	501	1,935	24.8
F. Brown, Seattle	76	742	273	1,757	23.1
McGinnis, Philadelphia	77	647	475	1,769	23.0
R. Smith, Buffalo	82	702	383	1,787	21.8

American Basketball Association

	W.	L.	Pct.
Denver	60	24	.714
New York	55	29	.655
San Antonio	50	34	.595
Kentucky	46	38	.548
Indiana	39	45	.464
St. Louis	35	49	.417
Virginia	15	68	.181

Leading Scorers	G.	FG.	FT.	Pts.	Avg.
Erving, New York	84	915	530	2,462	29.3
Knight, Indiana	70	768	415	1,969	28.1
Thompson, Denver	83	804	541	2,158	26.0
Gilmore, Kentucky	84	773	521	2,067	24.6
Barnes, St. Louis	67	678	251	1,616	24.1
Silas, San Antonio	84	718	564	2,000	23.8
Issel, Denver	84	751	425	1,930	22.9

College Champions

Conference	School
Atlantic Coast	North Carolina (regular season)
	Virginia (ACC tourney)
Big Eight	Missouri
Big Ten	Indiana
Ivy League	Princeton
Mid-American	Western Michigan
Missouri Valley	Wichita State
Ohio Valley	Western Kentucky
Pacific-8	UCLA
Southern	Virginia Military Institute
Southeastern	Alabama
Southwest	Texas A & M (regular season)
	Texas Tech (SWC tourney)
West Coast Athletic	Pepperdine
Western Athletic	Arizona
Yankee	Massachusetts

Highflying Julius Erving, the famed "Dr. J.," plays for the Philadelphia 76ers after a pay dispute forced his trade by the New York Nets.

but his old club can keep him by matching the best offer. See Section One, FOCUS ON SPORTS.

The NBA Season. Division winners were the Celtics, Cleveland Cavaliers, Milwaukee Bucks, and the defending champion Golden State Warriors. The Phoenix Suns finished 17 games behind Golden State, but they qualified for one of the wild-card play-off berths, reserved for the third-place team with the best record in each conference. The Suns surprisingly eliminated the Warriors, 4 games to 2, in the Western Division finals.

The Celtics defeated the Suns, 4 games to 2, in the play-off finals, and Celtic guard Jo Jo White was voted Most Valuable Player in the play-offs. The Most Valuable Player during the regular season was Kareem Abdul-Jabbar, the 7-foot 2-inch (218-centimeter) center traded before the season from the Bucks to the Los Angeles Lakers. The all-star team consisted of Abdul-Jabbar at center, Rick Barry of Golden State and George McGinnis of the Philadelphia 76ers at forward, and Nate Archibald of the Kansas City Kings and Pete Maravich of the New Orleans Jazz at guard.

In the ABA play-offs, the Nets defeated San Antonio, 4 games to 3, in the semifinals and Denver, 4 games to 2, in the final to win their second ABA championship in Kevin Loughery's three years as coach. The Nets' 6-foot 6-inch (198-centimeter) forward, Julius Erving, was voted the ABA's Most Valuable Player for the third consecutive season. He led the league in scoring (29.3 points per game) for the third time in four years.

The College Season. Many people felt that an Indiana era started in March, when the University of California, Los Angeles (UCLA), era ended. UCLA had won 10 National Collegiate Athletic Association (NCAA) championships in 12 years under coach John Wooden, who retired, and it reached the national semifinals under its new coach, Gene Bartow, before losing to Indiana, 65-51.

Indiana (27-0) and Rutgers (28-0) were the only major teams undefeated in the regular season. Michigan beat Rutgers, 86-70, in the national semifinals, and Indiana won decisively from Michigan, 86-68, in the final.

In his fifth year as head coach, the volatile Bobby Knight blended a strong team at Indiana. It had two all-Americans in 6-foot 7-inch (201-centimeter) Scott May at forward and 6-foot 11-inch (211-centimeter) Kent Benson at center.

The wire services chose May as College Player of the Year, and he helped the United States team win the Olympic gold medal in July in Montreal, Canada. So did Adrian Dantley of Notre Dame, the high scorer of the Olympic team (see OLYMPIC GAMES). May, Benson, and Dantley were chosen on most all-America teams with John Lucas of Maryland, Phil Sellers of Rutgers, and Rich Washington of UCLA.

Frank Litsky

BELGIUM climbed slowly out of its worst postwar recession during 1976, but recovery lagged behind its neighboring economic competitors: France, West Germany, and the Netherlands. Parliament passed a package of antirecession measures in March, including reduced social security contributions by businesses with large labor forces, lower taxes on company stocks, and tax relief on certain investments. But unions forced the government to abandon plans for a freeze on real wages.

Belgium suffered through its worst drought in a century, and on August 21, the government announced stiff measures to conserve water supplies. People caught watering lawns, washing automobiles, filling swimming pools, or hosing sidewalks faced jail terms and fines of from $100 to $1 million.

New Price Index. Prime Minister Leo Tindemans scored a major breakthrough when unions agreed on a new retail price index after July 1. The old index covered only 149 items and was considered inflationary because it was tied to wage scales. The index's inadequacy was highlighted in January when potatoes, which are served as chips with almost every main dish in Belgium, were in short supply and rocketed in price. Because the potato was the only vegetable listed, the price index also soared. The government clamped a price freeze on potatoes and invoked a wartime law to jail potato hoarders for up to five years.

Unemployment Peak. The inflation rate fell from a 1975 peak of 20 per cent to 10 per cent by the end of the summer of 1976, but unemployment reached a record 229,000 in mid-February – 8.7 per cent of the labor force. The government introduced retraining programs to try to find work for recent university and high school graduates.

King's Anniversary. King Baudouin I celebrated his silver anniversary on March 31. He told a session of both houses of parliament: "I commit myself fully to the service of the nation. I invite Belgium to go forward with dignity, courage, and confidence." Baudouin assumed the throne at the age of 20 in 1951 after his father, Leopold III, abdicated. Baudouin and Queen Fabiola criticized property developers at a civic lunch on March 31, saying that they had "spoiled the face" of Brussels.

Jet Contract. Belgium manufacturer Fabrique Nationale signed a $700-million deal in August with the U.S.-based Pratt and Whitney Company to coproduce jet engines in Belgium for the U.S. F-16 fighter aircraft. Belgium had ordered 102 F-16's in 1975, and many viewed the engine contract as compensation for ordering F-16's rather than French Mirages.

In March, and again in July, the National Bank raised the interest rate to bolster the Belgian franc against speculation.   Kenneth Brown

See also EUROPE (Facts in Brief Table).
BELIZE. See LATIN AMERICA.

BERLINGUER, ENRICO (1922-   ), as the secretary-general of Italy's Communist Party, led his party to important political gains in June 1976 elections for the Senate and Chamber of Deputies. The Communists won 228 seats in the Chamber of Deputies, a gain of 49. They took 116 seats in the Senate, a gain of 23. After the election, the hardworking, realistic Berlinguer relaxed his call for "historic compromise" – direct Cabinet participation with the Christian Democrats who have dominated Italian politics for 25 years – choosing to exercise power through cooperation and by gaining such key posts as the presidency of the legislature and four legislative chairmanships. See ITALY.

Berlinguer symbolizes European Communist independence from Moscow. At a meeting of European Communist Party leaders in East Berlin in June, he called for "free debate of ideas."

Berlinguer was born in Sassari, Sardinia, on May 25, 1922. His father was a Socialist Cabinet minister. He joined the Communist Party in 1944 and was active in its youth movement in Sassari, Milan, and Rome. He won election to the Chamber of Deputies in 1968 and became party leader in March 1972.

Slight of build and soft-spoken, Berlinguer shuns publicity. He lives with his wife, Letizia, in a Rome apartment.   Robert K. Johnson
BHUTAN. See ASIA.

BICENTENNIAL, UNITED STATES. In a patriotic salute that had ringing bells, exploding fireworks, blaring bands, and thousands of parades, the United States celebrated its 200th birthday on July 4, 1976. The highlight of the day's commemorative festivities occurred in Philadelphia at precisely 2 P.M., E.D.S.T., when the Liberty Bell, symbol of American independence, was struck 13 times – once for each of the original colonies that renounced allegiance to the British Crown in 1776. In a clamorous two-minute response, bells pealed in thousands of communities – in churches, fire departments, and schools across the United States. Thanks to television and radio, it was a sound heard around the world. See Section Two, AMERICA'S BIG BIRTHDAY PARTY.

The July 4 celebration was only a part of the yearlong festivities. The American Revolution Bicentennial Administration (ARBA) distributed $51-million appropriated by the U.S. Congress to finance projects and programs throughout the year. States and territories were given $20 million in matching grants, and revenue from other sources, such as the sale of Bicentennial medals, license fees, and royalties, totaled nearly $18.5 million. ARBA prepared a master calendar of events of local, state, national, and international significance. Altogether, it listed 27,146 active projects and events in 11,739 cities and towns.

Great Britain's Queen Elizabeth II becomes an honorary citizen of New York City in July during Bicentennial visit to the United States.

By year's end, 97 nations had joined in celebrating the nation's 200th birthday. Sixteen heads of state and others of high rank paid their respects on personal tours beginning with Israel's Prime Minister Yitzhak Rabin on January 26 and ending with Prime Minister Juan M. G. Evertsz of the Netherlands Antilles on November 16. The visitors included Prime Minister Liam Cosgrave of Ireland, King Hussein I of Jordan, King Carl XVI Gustaf of Sweden, Queen Margrethe II of Denmark, President Valéry Giscard d'Estaing of France, King Juan Carlos I of Spain, King Baudouin of Belgium, Prime Minister Pierre Elliott Trudeau of Canada, Prime Minister Takeo Miki of Japan, Crown Prince Harald of Norway, Queen Elizabeth II of Great Britain, Chancellor Helmut Schmidt of West Germany, and President Urho Kekkonen of Finland.

Bicentennial Gifts to the United States were as varied as the countries they came from. Notable was Japan's gift of a rare and priceless collection of 50 bonsai plants, some dating back more than 400 years. The National Arboretum in Washington, D.C., accepted them on behalf of the American people. Queen Elizabeth personally presented a replica of the original Liberty Bell in Philadelphia on July 6 and loaned one of the four original copies of the Magna Carta. West Germany gave a $1-million endowment to the New School for Social Research in New York City for a Theodor Heuss chair in the school's graduate faculty of political and social science and also presented a $1-million planetarium projector system to the Smithsonian Institution's National Air and Space Museum. France created a special sound and light show for Mount Vernon, re-enacting the life and times of George Washington. It also sent the Paris Opéra on its first American visit. Belgium launched a four-city tour of its Twentieth Century Ballet and loaned U.S. museums a valuable collection of 16th-century Flemish tapestries. Australia sent its ballet, its symphony, and its boys' choir, endowed a chair in Australian Studies at Harvard University, and presented six koala bears to the San Diego Zoo.

The people of Jordan, land of the ancient city of Philadelphia, presented a 2,000-year-old column to its American namesake, Philadelphia, Pa. Milan's famed La Scala opera made a historic debut at the John F. Kennedy Center for the Performing Arts in Washington, D.C., on September 8. Italy also gave the United States a rare 18th-century miniature portrait of Thomas Jefferson that had been in an Italian convent for more than 150 years. Egypt sent 55 artifacts from the tomb of Tutankhamon, never before displayed in another country; a nationwide tour of the artifacts began at the National Gallery of Art in Washington, D.C., on November 16.

Foreign Celebrations. The British laid out six Bicentennial trails, associated with American history, across the United Kingdom and staged a

"1776" exhibition at the National Maritime Museum in London. It opened on April 14 and included 570 paintings, uniforms, and contemporary 18th-century articles. At a cost of about $5 million, West Germany launched close to 4,000 separate Bicentennial events ranging from village parties to nationwide television programs. The Netherlands staged a Frontier America festival in The Hague and offered special tours to Leiden, where the Pilgrim Fathers had stayed for 11 years.

U.S. Projects. The most meaningful and enduring expressions of America's Bicentennial were manifested in the many restorations, beautification programs, arts and crafts projects, and compilations of pictorial and oral histories. Restorations included the St. Louis Cathedral in New Orleans; the downtown section of Indianapolis; the Alamo in San Antonio, Tex.; and the early fortifications at West Point in New York. Historic cemeteries were restored and preserved, trees planted, and parks built throughout the country. Ethnic groups in such cities as Boston, Cleveland, Detroit, Pittsburgh, San Francisco, and Tulsa, Okla., assembled oral histories dating from their immigration to the area.

About 5,000 locally sponsored one-day town meetings were held, using a specially designed format and materials from which community residents could identify and analyze the issues facing them and develop practical solutions. Nearly 13,000 Bicentennial Youth Debates on American history and values were held in high schools and colleges across the country, culminating in a national conference sponsored by ARBA in Washington, D.C., in June.

Special Bicentennial Salute. Participants from 36 nations joined more than 90 American communities in the annual Smithsonian Festival of American Folklife. The event was held from June 16 to September 6 on the Mall between the Washington Monument and the Lincoln Memorial.

Third Century America, the only exposition officially sponsored by the U.S. government, attracted more than 400,000 visitors to Florida's John F. Kennedy Space Center during its summer-long run that continued through Labor Day. The exposition was designed to provide a glimpse of America's life style in the century ahead.

The 10-car Freedom Train ended its tour of 140 cities in the 48 contiguous states in Miami, Fla., on December 31. Its exhibit of more than 700 objects portraying 200 years of American achievement in the arts, technology, culture, crisis, and innovation was seen by an estimated 8 million persons. The 222-Wagon Train pilgrimage carrying some 3,000 participants pulled into Valley Forge, Pa., on July 3, ending its historic trek through 47 states. The American Wind Symphony Orchestra's floating barge made a six-month tour of 76 cities that began in Biloxi, Miss., on April 30.

More than 500 events, ranging from one-day activities to year-round programs, took place in the nation's national parks. An unprecedented array of national organizations, newspapers, magazines, radio and television stations, and state and local community groups and organizations participated in the American Issues Forum, funded by a $7-million grant from the National Endowment for the Humanities and private contributions. The forum's nine-month calendar of topics focused on nationwide discussions of the country's political, economic, and social principles. More than 1,000 forum projects were documented by the endowment.

The July 4 Party. The Bicentennial reached its climax over the Independence Day period. The party began in the continental U.S.A. with a sunrise service on Maine's Mars Hill. Throughout the nation, millions of Americans turned out, from the smallest of communities to the largest of metropolitan centers. All 50 states, the territories, the District of Columbia, and the Commonwealth of Puerto Rico sealed documents and memorabilia in time capsules so that the citizens of 2076 might know how the nation's 200th birthday was celebrated.

In New York Harbor, ships from other countries and U.S. Navy units formed part of an armada of more than 50 vessels that included 16 square-rigged tall ships. Six million persons on the shore and countless others in 30,000 spectator craft watched

On the U.S.S. *Forrestal* in New York Harbor on the Fourth of July, President Ford strikes the ship's bell once for each original colony.

for three hours as they sailed up the Hudson River from the Verrazano-Narrows Bridge to George Washington Bridge in Operation Sail. Millions of others saw the parade on television.

In Washington, D.C., there were parades, speeches, music, a spectacular fireworks display, and the dedication of the largest building of the Smithsonian Institution's complex, the National Air and Space Museum. A 76-hour weekend vigil was held at the National Archives beginning at 9 P.M. on July 2 to honor the Declaration of Independence, the Constitution, and the Bill of Rights.

Boston's daylong festivities were climaxed with Arthur Fiedler conducting the Boston Summer Symphony in a program of patriotic music concluding with Peter Ilich Tchaikovsky's "1812" overture, complete with the ringing of church bells, the firing of howitzers, and a mammoth fireworks display on the Charles River Esplanade.

State and City Activities. A 111-day observance began on May 21 at Mount Rushmore National Memorial in South Dakota, with two days set aside for each state and territory. Some 7,000 Puerto Rican Boy Scouts held a massive demonstration of the "Spirit of '76" in San Juan. It was aimed at achieving a greater understanding of the problems to be faced in the future of the commonwealth and the nation. Saint Louis and New Orleans launched

a showboat to dramatize the Mississippi River's role in the nation's development. Fourteen states issued Bicentennial automobile license plates.

The renowned statue of the Venus de'Medici became the focal point for the most complex exhibition ever mounted by Washington's National Gallery of Art. This major Bicentennial exhibition, "The Eye of Thomas Jefferson," was based on the life of the third President and the visual arts of his day. It featured more than 550 fine examples of art, architecture, and design that Jefferson saw and that, through him, have influenced the nation. It opened on June 1 and ran through September 6.

"Remember the Ladies . . . Women in America 1750-1815," an exhibition at the Pilgrim Society and Plymouth Antiquarian Society in Plymouth, Mass., opened on June 30, then toured five American cities. The exhibit provided a detailed view of the nation's "founding women" and their wide-ranging participation in American society during that period.

Private Contributions to the Bicentennial were not fully recorded, but ARBA records indicated that about 345 companies contributed more than $38 million to programs and events, most of them nationally recognized. For example, the Sun Oil Company underwrote an examination of the Constitution's past, present, and future, prepared by

Flag-bedecked covered wagons, part of the U.S. Bicentennial Wagon Train, arrive at Valley Forge, Pa., after their yearlong trek from Blaine, Wash.

Chilean ship *Esmeralda* sails past the Statue of Liberty as part of a fleet assembled in New York Harbor for Operation Sail, a Bicentennial event.

four distinguished American law scholars and presented at a conference in Philadelphia's Carpenters' Hall on April 5. The Travelers Insurance Company, owners of the world's largest collection of Currier and Ives original lithographs, presented "The Story of the Revolution as Seen by Currier and Ives," which toured major cities in the 13 original states. Exxon Corporation activities ranged from support of the American Issues Forum to the sponsorship of television vignettes—"Bicentennial Minutes"—emphasizing the importance of individual effort in the development of the nation.

A Mobil Oil Corporation grant made possible a major exhibit of 200 significant American posters in Chicago's Museum of Science and Industry covering events and concerns of the nation between 1945 and 1975. The Continental Bank of Philadelphia refurbished the Tomb of the Unknown Soldier of the American Revolution.

There had been reports that dissident groups would try to disrupt Fourth of July activities in such cities as Chicago, Los Angeles, New York, Philadelphia, and Washington, D.C., but the threats failed to materialize. There were, however, marches and demonstrations by a number of groups that felt the United States had fallen short of its 200-year-old commitment to freedom and justice for all. The People's Bicentennial Commission, throughout the celebration, stressed that belief.   Lynn Beaumont

BIOCHEMISTRY

BIOCHEMISTRY. More than 100 years ago, French poet Charles Baudelaire wrote *"Chaque homme porte en lui sa dose d'opium naturel"* ("every man carries within himself his own opium") without realizing scientists would substantiate his idea in 1976—though probably not in the way he imagined. Biochemists found natural painkilling substances called *endorphins* in brain tissue. This brought them closer to understanding and perhaps to treating pain and narcotic addiction.

Scientists have known since about 1971 that nerve receptors in the brain interact with opiate molecules like morphine only if such molecules have both the correct chemical makeup and the right molecular shape. Molecular shape requirements must also be met by opiate *antagonists*, drugs that combine with the same receptors to block the opiate.

In 1974 and 1975, Lars Terenius and Agneta Wahlstrom of the University of Uppsala in Sweden and John Hughes of the University of Aberdeen in Scotland reported independently that small *peptides* (chains of amino acids) in pig and beef brain tissues have properties that closely resemble those of morphine. Avram S. Goldstein and his colleagues at Stanford University in California discovered similar activity in extracts from the pituitary gland.

Hughes and His Co-Workers at Aberdeen and elsewhere reported in December 1975 that the substance Hughes discovered, now called enkephalin, consists of two peptides, each containing five amino acids. Methionine enkephalin, the most potent and most abundant peptide, contains the amino acids tyrosine, glycine, glycine, phenylalanine, and methionine, in that order. The other peptide, called leucine enkephalin, contains tyrosine, glycine, glycine, phenylalanine, and leucine, in that order. James D. Beluzzi and his collaborators at Wyeth Laboratories in Philadelphia reported in April 1976 that injection of the two enkephalins into the brains of living rats produced morphinelike activity that could be completely reversed by the morphine antagonist naloxone. Meanwhile, scientists at the British National Institute for Medical Research at Mill Hill in London constructed a model of methionine enkephalin and showed that its shape is similar to that of one of the morphine molecules.

British scientists at the University of Birmingham produced morphinelike behavior in cats by injecting both types of enkephalin, but naloxone did not block the effects. Swiss researchers manufactured the two peptides and two slightly different chains of amino acids. The synthetic enkephalins induced *analgesia* (deadening of pain) in mice, but the different chains did not.

Pituitary Painkillers. Other scientists studied a variety of opiatelike peptides in the pituitary gland. Hughes noted that the amino acid sequence in methionine enkephalin was identical to that in a portion of "β-lipotropin," a hormone found in the pituitary glands of sheep, pig, and man. Choh Li and his colleagues at the University of California, Berkeley, isolated the hormone in 1964 and subsequently determined the amino acid sequences for the sheep and pig hormone. Li and David Chung, now at the San Francisco campus, reported in April 1976 the complete sequence for the human β-lipotropin hormone. In all three cases, the sequence of amino acids in positions 61 to 65 is identical to that of methionine enkephalin.

In collaboration with Li, Goldstein investigated the painkilling activity of the β-lipotropin hormone. The complete hormone, which contains 91 amino acids, has almost no opiate effect, while the sequence 61 to 91 has about the same potency as methionine enkephalin, he reported in June. Goldstein noted that β-lipotropin also contains a subsequence that is exactly identical to melanocyte-stimulating hormone, which acts on melanocyte cells in frog skin. He speculated that the whole sequence of the β-lipotropin contains a number of smaller hormonal molecules, a situation comparable to the large precursor molecule, proinsulin, which forms the pancreatic hormone insulin.

Roger Guillemin and his colleagues at the Salk Institute for Biological Studies in La Jolla, Calif., supported this idea in August at the 10th International Congress of Biochemistry in Hamburg, West Germany. Guillemin described three peptides that his group had isolated from hypothalami from about 250,000 sheep. All three peptides are duplicated in particular sections of the β-lipotropin molecule: α-endorphin is identical to the amino acid sequence from positions 61 to 76; β-endorphin to positions 61 to 91; and γ-endorphin to positions 61 to 77. Guillemin's group found that each peptide produced characteristically different actions in laboratory rats. Injections of α-endorphin produced a mild analgesia and tranquilizing effect, whereas rats injected with γ-endorphin behaved violently.

Guillemin reported that β-endorphin is "by far the most active of all the compounds we have studied." It produced a catatonic, or rigid, state in the experimental animals that lasted more than three hours. However, if the catatonic rats were given naloxone, they were "awake and running around" within a few seconds. Guillemin suggested that these results may lead to a biochemical explanation for certain types of mental illness.

On the other hand, Goldstein wanted scientists to explore the possibility that endorphin deficiency may play a key role in narcotic addiction. In the addict, morphine may inhibit the normal formation of endorphins. Then, a deficiency of endorphin may be responsible for the immediate and protracted symptoms during morphine withdrawal. Extensive and lively research is expected to yield valuable information concerning the central nervous system and these natural painkillers.   Earl A. Evans, Jr.

BIOLOGY. An international committee was formed in October 1976 to encourage countries to set up uniform policies to regulate potentially harmful genetic research. The International Council of Scientific Unions – which represents national academies of sciences, research councils, and international scientific unions – set up the Committee on Genetic Experimentation to promote safe genetic research and to inform the public about it.

In the United States, the National Institutes of Health published guidelines in June that prohibit the riskiest experiments and prescribe safety standards for others. The experiments in question use substances called restriction enzymes to selectively break the double-stranded genetic deoxyribonucleic acid (DNA) into small fragments that can be combined with other DNA fragments to form new genetic material. Such genetic-transfer procedures may make possible the cheap manufacture of drugs or other useful chemicals. But some biochemists fear that risks are too great, especially because *Escherichia coli* bacteria, commonly found in human beings, are widely used in the experiments.

Experimental proof that genes transferred from a higher organism into a lower organism actually function came from two California laboratories during the year. The scientists transferred a segment of DNA from baker's yeast – a *eucaryote* because it has a separate nucleus – into the genetic material of *E. coli,* a *procaryote* without a separate nucleus.

Ronald Davis, Kevin Struhl, and John Cameron of Stanford University in Palo Alto, Calif., inserted a segment of yeast DNA into the genetic material of a mutant of *E. coli* that cannot make the essential amino acid histidine. They found that some of the bacterial cells grew without added histidine, presumably as a result of the yeast genetic material.

John Carbon, Louise Clarke, Cristine Ilgen, and Barry Rathkais of the University of California, Santa Barbara, confirmed these results with the histidine-deficient *E. coli* mutant. However, instead of using a restriction enzyme to form DNA fragments from the yeast DNA, they used mechanical force. In addition, the Santa Barbara group demonstrated similar results with *E. coli* mutants that are unable to make the amino acid leucine.

Artificial Gene Works. Har Gobind Khorana and his research team at the Massachusetts Institute of Technology (M.I.T.) in Cambridge reported in August that they had made a gene that worked in a living cell. The gene is a copy of one found in *E. coli* called the tyrosine transfer ribonucleic acid (RNA) gene. It contains 126 subunits called nucleotides plus 56 more nucleotides at one end that act as a start signal and 25 nucleotides at the other end that act as a stop signal when the gene assembles a transfer RNA molecule.

The researchers worked nine years to complete

Har Gobind Khorana of Massachusetts Institute of Technology explains how his research team made an artificial gene that worked in a living cell.

their artificial gene, and many biologists hailed the feat as proof that DNA molecules are indeed the basis of life. Because the techniques used are so slow, the M.I.T. team does not plan to mass-produce artificial genes. They plan to build genes with known defects and see how they affect *E. coli*.

Plantimals? Two research groups fused human cells with plant cells for the first time. A group led by Harold H. Smith at the Brookhaven National Laboratory in Upton, N.Y., reported in July that they had fused protoplasts of tobacco cells and human tumor (HeLa) cells. Protoplasts are cells in which the cell walls have been removed. A group at the Hungarian Biological Research Center in Szeged fused HeLa protoplasts with carrot protoplasts. In related experiments, a British team fused animal red blood cells with yeast cells, and a group at Florida Atlantic University in Boca Raton fused rooster red blood cells with tobacco cells. They plan to use such hybrid cells to study genetic material.

Life on Mars? Two U.S. *Viking* spacecraft landed on Mars in July and September. The landers dug samples of Martian soil and placed them in biology testing chambers. Scientists who analyzed the test results found no proof of present or past life on Mars. See ASTRONOMY; Section One, FOCUS ON SCIENCE.   Earl A. Evans, Jr.

BIRTHS. See CENSUS, U.S.; POPULATION, WORLD.

BLINDNESS. See HANDICAPPED.

BOATING. A transatlantic single-handed sailing race was the major boating event in 1976. On June 5, 125 craft from 17 nations, with one man per boat, left Plymouth, England, for Newport, R.I. At least five craft sank, some in a severe gale in the North Atlantic. Michael Flanagan of Essex, Conn., was apparently drowned.

Eric Tabarly of France finished on June 29 in the 73-foot (22-meter) ketch *Pen Duick VI,* and won the trophy for big boats. Eighteen hours later, Michael Birch of England finished in the 32-foot (10-meter) trimaran *The Third Turtle,* the small-boat winner.

The yachts ranged from a 25-foot (8-meter) catamaran to the *Club Méditeranée,* a 250-gross-ton, four-masted schooner, 236 feet (72 meters) long, that cost more than $1 million.

Pen Duick VI had a busy year. Tabarly and a 14-man crew almost won the 3,600-mile (5,800-kilometer) race from Cape Town, South Africa, to Rio de Janeiro, Brazil, in January. Then he won the race from Rio de Janeiro to Portsmouth, England, in March.

America's Cup. The United States prepared to defend the America's Cup, yachting's most prestigious trophy, in 1977 against challenges from Australia, England, France, and Sweden. There were three candidates for the role of American defender—*Courageous,* which won the last defense in 1974, and the new yachts *Enterprise* and *Independence.*

The craft were sloops, more than 60 feet (18 meters) long, in the 12-meter class. They will compete off Newport in the summer of 1977 to pick an American defender. The winner and the winning foreign challenger will then meet off Newport in September.

Powerboats. Bill Muncey of La Mesa, Calif., the most successful driver in the history of unlimited hydroplane racing, became a successful owner-driver in 1976. He bought *Pride of Pay 'N' Pak,* which had won the national championship series the three previous years. He renamed it *Atlas Van Lines,* won five races, and became champion driver for the fifth time.

Joel Halpern, 37, of Bronxville, N.Y., won the national outboard series. He spent $150,000 on a 38-foot (12-meter) Cobra hull with twin 482-cubic-inch (7,900-cubic-centimeter) MerCruiser engines, and he owned the company that built the hull. Halpern decided in midseason to try for the world title, but he finished second to Tom Gentry of Honolulu, Hawaii, who drove a 36-foot (11-meter) Cigarette hull with twin 468-cubic-inch (7,670-cubic-centimeter) Kiekhaefer Aeromarine engines. Halpern's quest required five round trips to Europe in five weeks to race in England, France, Italy, and Sweden.   Frank Litsky

BOLIVIA. President Hugo Banzer Suarez in 1976 became one of the few Bolivian presidents in the 20th century to remain in office more than four years. Throughout most of the year, however, university students and union workers staged outbursts, allegedly attempts to break Banzer's military rule.

A strike that began January 24 at the Manaco Shoe Company near Cochabamba over the firing of 800 workers provided the excuse for nearly two months of on-and-off sympathy strikes by students and workers. Hundreds of people were subjected to overnight arrests. On February 19, the government declared it was dealing with a plot to overthrow Banzer. It further maintained the plot was engineered by former President Juan José Torres, who was in exile in Argentina. Nine alleged conspirators were exiled to Chile on February 22.

The government negotiated settlements on many of the strikers' grievances, and all seemed calm until Torres was found slain near Buenos Aires on June 2. Banzer condemned the slaying and tried to link it with the slaying of Bolivia's ambassador to France, General Joaquin Zenteno Anaya, who was shot on a Paris street on May 11 by terrorists calling themselves the International Ché Guevara Brigade. Zenteno had commanded the forces who killed Argentine revolutionary Ernesto (Ché) Guevara in 1967 when he was trying to organize a revolt against the Bolivian government. Torres was also a member of the force that tracked down Guevara, but no one came forward to claim credit for Torres' killing.

Banzer offered to give Torres a state funeral, but his widow demanded that the services be held in the miners' union headquarters. More unrest was touched off, and Banzer withdrew his offer. Torres' body was flown to Mexico for burial on June 7.

Despite These Problems, the year was mainly characterized by political stability and economic growth. The gross national product grew 7 per cent, and inflation was held to 12 per cent, a low figure by Latin American standards. A five-year development plan extending through 1980 aims at continued growth at this pace and calls for an investment of more than $3.4 billion. About 60 per cent of this must be borrowed abroad. The Banzer government has already increased Bolivia's foreign debt to $1.6 billion from $500 million in 1971, but economists say the payments are carefully spread out so they will not exceed 20 per cent of exports in any one year.

Government planners have some 300 projects in the works, ranging from new roads to oil and mineral exploration and agricultural and industrial development.   Everett G. Martin

See also LATIN AMERICA (Facts in Brief Table).

BOOKS. See CANADIAN LITERATURE; LITERATURE; LITERATURE FOR CHILDREN; POETRY; PUBLISHING.

BOSTON. A winter and spring of violence over busing to achieve school integration was followed by relative peace when Boston schools reopened in September 1976 for the third year of court-ordered desegregation. In early 1976, there were continual acts of violence. For example, police used tear gas to repulse antibusing protestors who were attacking them with clubs and stones on February 15.

Major Court Decisions contributed to the changed atmosphere in the autumn. U.S. District Court Judge W. Arthur Garrity announced on May 3 that he was leaving East Boston High School out of the autumn busing program, and the Supreme Court of the United States on June 14 let stand lower court rulings on which the busing program was based. In addition, an Appeals Court on August 17 upheld the court-ordered federal take-over in 1975 of South Boston High School, a center of much of the earlier violence. Some observers also believed the U.S. attorney general's decision on May 29 not to use Boston as a school-busing test case helped calm the situation.

After the court decisions, a massive antiviolence march through Boston in April, and a special $1.9-million federal grant to provide summer jobs for youths, the schools reopened in the fall with attendance up and violence limited to relatively minor evening clashes between antibusing demonstrators and police.

A puppet show entertains children at Boston's renovated Quincy Market, a wholesale market place dating from 1826 that reopened on August 26.

There were several bombing incidents in the Boston area during the year. A bomb exploded in the Suffolk County Superior Court Building on April 22, injuring more than 20 persons. Another bomb damaged the Middlesex County Superior Courthouse on June 21, injuring a custodian. Three bombs exploded early on July 2, one of which damaged a historic courthouse in Newburyport.

Expensive City. Boston continued to be the third most expensive U.S. city in which to live. It was exceeded only by Honolulu, Hawaii, and Anchorage, Alaska. The average factory worker in the Boston area earned $10,724 — less than the U.S. Department of Labor estimated an average family of four would need to sustain a minimum standard of living. Living costs rose 7.6 per cent between July 1975 and July 1976. Food costs rose 3.8 per cent, but earnings were up only 7 per cent by mid-1976. Unemployment in the city stood at 8.2 per cent. Department store sales showed no increase, and construction activity was down 15.8 per cent.

In the wake of New York City's brush with bankruptcy, the interest rate paid by Boston on its bond issues rose from 6 to 9 per cent early in the year. Budget deficits nearly forced Boston to close its schools early and forced the city to increase property taxes an estimated 28 per cent.

Mayor Kevin H. White was inaugurated for his third term as mayor on January 5. James M. Banovetz

BOTANY. British scientists in 1976 developed a surprising method of dealing with compacted soil. When soil is compacted, or nonporous and hard, plant roots become thick and twisted. But botanists Sheena M. Wilkins, Henry Wilkins, and Roy L. Wain of Wye College in Ashford, England, found that a chemical called 3,5-diiodo-4-hydroxybenzoic acid (DIHB) causes pea seedlings growing in compacted soil to produce longer and heavier roots.

They believe that the chemical action inhibits natural ethylene production in the soil and plants. Ethylene stunts root growth and is produced by microbes when there are low concentrations of oxygen, as would be present in nonporous soils, and by roots that have to grow against strong resistance. If DIHB is found to work in the same way with other kinds of plants, it may become highly valuable for farming in highly compacted soils.

D. C. Clarkson and his colleagues at Letcombe Laboratory in England found that nutrients move through the roots of barley and rye plants more quickly when the temperature of the soil falls. Both barley and rye grow in relatively cold climates. The botanists' studies show that when the speed of *ion transport* (the process by which nutrients move from plant cell to plant cell) is affected by the soil temperature, the nutrients most recently absorbed by a plant's roots are moving, rather than the nutrients already stored in root vacuoles.

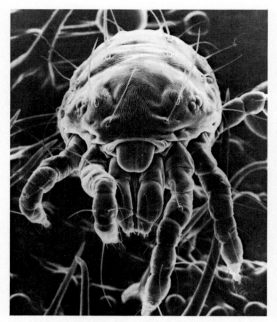

Tiny leaf mite, photographed by electron microscope at the University of Michigan, spends its entire life on a single leaf.

The scientists demonstrated the action in the plant roots by using radioactive tracers. The mechanism that causes the speed-up in ion transport is still unknown, but the researchers suspect that the temperature causes the cells to expend more energy to move ions across their membranes. If they can eventually understand this increase in root transport, they believe they will be able to better select and breed crop plants for farming in cold climates.

Photosynthesis. The rate of photosynthesis in an evening primrose, a desert plant that grows in Death Valley, California, was found to be exceedingly high by Stanford University researchers. Photosynthesis is the process by which green plants absorb the energy of the sun and use it to produce carbohydrates and oxygen from carbon dioxide and water. The evening primrose converts 8.5 per cent of all the photosynthetically active energy available into carbohydrates. This efficiency is 80 per cent of the maximum potential value of conversion.

Sugar beet, a plant previously used in describing the photosynthetic efficiency of leaves, shows an efficiency of only 30 per cent. The Stanford botanists think environmental selection in the desert has produced a species with a greater ability to capture light and fix carbon dioxide. In Death Valley, some plants must complete their growth and development in six to 10 weeks.   Barbara N. Benson

BOTSWANA. See AFRICA.

BOWLING. Earl Anthony of Tacoma, Wash., became bowler of the year for the third straight year in 1976 and broke the sport's most significant record. His victory in the Buzz Fazio Open on October 26 in Battle Creek, Mich., was the 26th of his career, the most by anyone in the 18-year history of the Professional Bowlers Association (PBA) tour.

The 38-year-old Anthony, a left-hander, bowled well week after week. In January and February, he lost one tournament by 1 pin, one by 4 pins, and one by 6 pins. Then, from February to December, he won seven tournaments. In 1975, he became the first bowler to top $100,000 in one year, winning $107,585, and in 1976 he led again with $110,833.

Anthony was a grocery clerk in 1969, and he did all his winning in the next seven years. Dick Weber of St. Louis and Don Johnson of Las Vegas, Nev., shared the previous record for career victories. Each won once during 1976 for his 25th triumph.

The PBA Tour started in 1959 with three tournaments worth $47,000. In 1976, there were 36 tournaments worth a record $2.7 million. Purses ranged from $60,000 to $125,000, and nine tournaments offered at least $100,000 in prizes.

Paul Colwell of Tucson, Ariz., did little on the winter tour because he was 20 pounds (9 kilograms) overweight. In the $85,000 PBA championship in June in Seattle, he rolled a *channel* (gutter) ball in the last frame of the title game against Dave Davis of Atlanta, Ga., and they tied at 191. Colwell covered his face in embarrassment. Then he defeated Davis, 49-48, in a two-frame play-off for the title.

Paul Moser of Medford, Ore., won the $100,000 United States Open in March in Grand Prairie, Tex., for his first tour title.

Marshall Holman, also of Medford, captured the tour's richest tournament, the $125,000 Firestone Tournament of Champions in April in Akron, Ohio. He beat Billy Hardwick of Louisville, Ky., 203-198, in the final.

Jim Schroeder of Buffalo, N.Y., won the classic singles division of the American Bowling Congress tournament. Nelson Burton, Jr., of Olivette, Mo., became the Masters champion. Mark Roth of Staten Island, N.Y., won three times on the tour and ranked second to Anthony in earnings. John Pezzin of Perrysburg, Ohio, playing in a sanctioned league, rolled 33 straight strikes on March 4 in Toledo, Ohio, and finished with 259-300-300.

Patty Costello, a left-hander from Scranton, Pa., won seven tournaments, including the women's U.S. Open and the Professional Women Bowlers Association national championship. Betty Morris of Stockton, Calif., won the Brunswick World Invitation and the Women's International Bowling Congress all-events title and barely lost to Costello, 235-233, in the U.S. Open final. Costello earned nearly $40,000 and Morris $35,000, far more than Morris' 1974 record of $26,547.   Frank Litsky

BOXING. Never since the heyday of Joe Louis had a world heavyweight champion defended his title as often as the tumultuous Muhammad Ali of Chicago. Ali regained the title in 1974 and defended four times in 1975 and four in 1976. Then he said he was retiring, something he had often said and retracted. In December, he talked of fighting again.

Before Ali's day, promoters dreamed of million-dollar gates. Ali made them pay million-dollar purses. In 1975 and 1976, his purses ranged from $1-million to fight Ron Lyle in 1975 and Jean-Pierre Coopman in 1976 to the $6 million he earned for barely outpointing Ken Norton in September 1976. His title-fight purses totaled $8.6 million in 1975 and $10.3 million in 1976, and he earned an additional $1.8 million in June 1976 for a martial-arts contest in Tokyo with Antonio Inoki, a Japanese wrestler.

Ali's First 1976 Opponents were not impressive fighters. They started with Coopman, an earnest but amateurish Belgian. Ali knocked him out in five rounds on February 20 in San Juan, Puerto Rico.

Ali did not take his next opponent, Jimmy Young of Philadelphia, seriously. Their April 30 fight in Landover, Md., was so close that many at ringside thought Ali had to win the 15th and final round to win the fight and keep the title. Ali won a unanimous decision, but not all the spectators agreed.

Ali hardly had time to rest for his May 25 fight in Munich, West Germany, against Richard Dunn, a courageous left-hander from England. Ali knocked him down five times before the fight was stopped in the fifth round.

The Inoki Affair. The title fights were interrupted by the June 26 draw with wrestler Inoki. Only two punches, both by Ali, were landed in 15 rounds. Inoki stayed on the floor like a crab, kicking Ali's legs. Ali's legs were so bruised that he was hospitalized with minor blood clots around the knees.

He recovered in time for his September 28 meeting with Norton in New York City. Ali won a unanimous decision, but many thought Norton had won.

Ali and Carlos Monzon of Argentina were the only champions recognized by both the World Boxing Association (WBA) and the World Boxing Council (WBC). Monzon was recognized as middleweight champion by both after he outpointed Rodrigo Valdes of Colombia on June 26 in Monte Carlo, Monaco.

Monzon had been a champion for six years, but not every champ had that much experience. Alfonso Lopez of Panama won the WBA flyweight title in his 23rd professional fight, then later lost it. Carlos Palomino of Los Angeles won the WBC welterweight crown in his 24th fight. Frank Litsky

BOY SCOUTS. See YOUTH ORGANIZATIONS.
BOYS' CLUBS. See YOUTH ORGANIZATIONS.

BRAZIL. A huge trade deficit, soaring inflation, and a greatly diminished growth rate created serious problems for the regime of President Ernesto Geisel in 1976. There were indications that their overall impact might affect Geisel's efforts to ease the military dictatorship's repressive controls.

Clearly, Brazil's economic miracle was over. Since 1968, Brazilian economic growth had been one of the most spectacular in the world with increases averaging about 9 per cent a year. Although critics had charged that the benefits fell disproportionately to the wealthy and upper middle class, it was also clear that more poor Brazilians were finding jobs and moving into the middle class.

Growing Debt. The boom was based largely on huge investments and loans from abroad, which, however, gave Brazil a constantly mounting international debt. By the end of 1976, these debts had reached nearly $29 billion.

Although the repayment program had been safely distributed over many years, Brazil would have to increase its exports every year in order to meet those obligations. Throughout the boom years, exports averaged a 25 per cent increase yearly. But trouble began when the Arab oil-exporting countries quadrupled the price of crude oil in 1973. Brazil, which imports 80 per cent of its oil, was hurt badly. In addition, a worldwide business slump cut demand for Brazilian products abroad.

World Champion Boxers

Division	Champion	Country	Year Won
Heavyweight	Muhammad Ali	U.S.A.	1974
Light-heavyweight	†John Conteh	England	1974
	*Victor Galindez	Argentina	1974
Middleweight	Carlos Monzon	Argentina	1970
Junior-middleweight	†Eckhard Dagge	West Germany	1976
	*Miguel Castellini	Argentina	1976
Welterweight	†Carlos Palomino	U.S.A.	1976
	*Jose Cuevas	Mexico	1976
Junior-welterweight	Declared vacant by WBA		
	†Saensak Muangsurin	Thailand	1976
Lightweight	*Roberto Duran	Panama	1972
	†Esteban de Jesus	Puerto Rico	1976
Junior-lightweight	†Alfredo Escalera	Puerto Rico	1975
	*Samuel Serrano	Puerto Rico	1976
Featherweight	Declared vacant by WBA		
	†Danny Lopez	U.S.A.	1976
Bantamweight	*Alfonso Zamora	Mexico	1975
	†Carlos Zarate	Mexico	1976
Flyweight	†Miguel Canto	Mexico	1975
	*Guty Espadas	Panama	1976
Junior-flyweight	†Luis Estaba	Venezuela	1975
	*Yoko Gushiken	Japan	1976

*Recognized by World Boxing Association
†Recognized by World Boxing Council

For a time, high world prices for Brazilian commodities such as coffee, sugar, and soybeans held off the effects. But by 1975, the balance-of-trade deficit totaled $3.5 billion.

Zero Net Gain. In 1976, the picture grew worse. Stringent import controls cut the trade deficit back to $2.5 billion, but the deficit was still higher than hoped for. Controls, however, meant that Brazil could import fewer machine tools and less of the technology vital to its continued growth. As a result, the gross national product increase of 3 per cent merely offset the population growth.

Among the unpopular measures the government took to cut its deficit was one forcing all Brazilians traveling abroad to deposit $1,200 for a year, without interest or adjustment for inflation. Importers also had to deposit under similar terms the full purchase price of anything they bought.

The government announced it would commit $23 billion to make Brazil self-sufficient in steel, paper, fertilizers, and petrochemicals by 1980 and to cut imports significantly in nonferrous metals and insecticides. Petrobras, the state oil monopoly, was ordered to open up new areas for exploration as part of an all-out effort to find new oil resources.

Unanswered Was the Question of how the economic slowdown would affect Geisel's efforts to ease the military dictatorship's repressive controls. If the state of the economy creates widespread criticism and labor unrest, it was feared, Geisel would be forced to yield to right wing forces within the military who oppose any easing of the dictatorship.

Geisel has been forced to walk a political tightrope between his own announced intentions to allow more political freedom and the objections of his military colleagues. When five opposition senators criticized the government on human-rights violations too freely, he expelled them from the Senate. Geisel, however, also lifted censorship on all major newspapers.

When Manoel Fiel Filho, a São Paulo metalworker, allegedly committed suicide in an army prison on January 17, Geisel fired the army chief, General Ednardo D'Avila. D'Avila, a hard-line officer, was one of the sharpest critics of Geisel's relaxation policy.

In the November 15 municipal elections – a test of the dictatorship's popularity – the pro-government Alliance for National Renewal Party took 55 per cent of the votes to give it control over 2,400 municipalities, compared with fewer than 500 for the opposition Brazilian Democratic Movement (MDB). The MDB, however, won in Brazil's largest cities.   Everett G. Martin

See also LATIN AMERICA (Facts in Brief Table).
BRIDGE. See BUILDING AND CONSTRUCTION.

U.S. tacitly recognizes Brazil as Latin America's major power as diplomats of both nations sign a pact in February creating a consultative committee.

BRIDGE, CONTRACT.

BRIDGE, CONTRACT. Italy's domination of team contract bridge ended in Monte Carlo, Monaco, on May 8, 1976, when the United States won the Bermuda Bowl, symbol of the world team championship. Brazil also bested Italy to win the Fifth World Bridge Team Olympiad in Monte Carlo on May 22. Usually the bridge Olympiad replaces the Bermuda Bowl in years the Olympic Games are held, but both were played in 1976.

The United States team consisted of Bill Eisenberg, Fred Hamilton, Paul Soloway, and Erik Paulsen, all of Los Angeles; Ira Rubin of Paramus, N.J.; and Hugh Ross of Oakland, Calif. They defeated the famed Italian Blue Team 232 to 198.

Brazil was the first country outside of Europe or North America to win a world championship team title. Gabriel Chagas, Pedro-Paul Assumpçao, Babino Cintra, Christian Fonseca, Marcelo Branco, and Sergio Barbosa represented Brazil.

In the American Contract Bridge League's (A.C.B.L.) spring tournament in Kansas City, Mo., the Harold A. Vanderbilt knockout team championship was won on March 19 by the defending team of George Rosenkranz of Mexico City, Mexico; Richard Katz, Larry Cohen, and John Mohan, all of Los Angeles; and Roger Bates of Las Vegas, Nev. The same team won the Spingold knockout team title at the A.C.B.L. summer tourney in Salt Lake City, Utah.   Theodore M. O'Leary

BRITISH COLUMBIA.

BRITISH COLUMBIA. The Social Credit administration of Premier William R. Bennett imposed policies of retrenchment and consolidation in 1976. The tone was set in the March 26 budget, which claimed that the previous New Democratic Party (NDP) government had engaged in such wasteful spending during the preceding $3^{1}/_{2}$ years that the province was faced with a $541-million deficit. The Bennett government's "recovery budget," totaling $3.6 billion, represented a 5.4 per cent spending increase over 1975. Personal and corporate income tax rates were raised, and the sales tax was boosted from 5 to 7 per cent.

The British Columbia Insurance Corporation, formed by the previous government to provide low-cost motor-vehicle insurance, faced a $181-million deficit by February. The new government, determined to make automobile insurance self-supporting, increased rates 40 per cent, making them more comparable with private company charges in other parts of Canada.

The government went ahead with the previous government's plan of a guaranteed monthly income for needy persons, extending benefits to those between 55 and 60. Former Premier David Barrett won election to the Assembly in June. The Social Credit Party then held 35 seats; NDP, 18; Liberals, 1; and Progressive Conservatives, 1.   David M. L. Farr
See also CANADA.

BUILDING AND CONSTRUCTION.

BUILDING AND CONSTRUCTION. Spending for construction in the United States in 1976 was estimated at $142.3 billion, an increase of 8 per cent from the $124 billion spent in 1975. Spending for housing units, not including mobile homes, was estimated at $57.5 billion, up from $46.8 billion.

The *Engineering News-Record*'s annual survey of the cost of construction materials in 20 key U.S. cities showed that inflation remained moderate, despite a sharp rise in lumber prices and a series of price increases by metal producers. The average price for Douglas fir rose 12 per cent during the year, while pine soared almost 19 per cent.

Under construction labor agreements negotiated during the year, the median first-year increase in wages and benefits was 75 cents an hour or 7 per cent, according to the Contractors Mutual Association (CMA). The median is based on 893 nonresidential wage settlements reported to the CMA.

Codes and Specifications. The American Institute of Architects produced a new edition of the standard agreement between owners and general contractors. The agreement gives the general contractor general management control, lessens the architect's involvement in actual construction work, and expands the owner's role in the project.

An unusual number of devastating earthquakes throughout the world led engineers and scientists to place new emphasis on the early prediction of quakes. To study land movements, the National Aeronautics and Space Administration (NASA) in May launched the Laser Geodynamic Satellite (LAGEOS), which will use laser beams to measure land shifts. NASA plans to have nine permanent and seven mobile stations transmitting beams by 1978. Scientists will concentrate on measurements along critical faults, such as the San Andreas Fault in California.

New Building Techniques. The General Services Administration opened its redesigned environmental demonstration office building in Saginaw, Mich., in October. The $5-million structure features a solar collector that will heat water and provide much of the building's heating and cooling requirements. Earth *berms* (dikes) are used as insulation to reduce heat loss through the walls of the building, and double-glazed windows and overhangs reduce cooling needs in the summer.

Many innovations in prestressed concrete were produced for the Olympic Games, held in Montreal, Canada, in July. Among them was a complex seashell-shaped stadium that seats 60,000 persons and cost between $685 million and $800 million, about 600 per cent above the original estimate. The stadium and a nearby track for bicycle and motorcycle racing introduced a construction technique never before used in North America – gluing precast concrete pieces together during erection, then applying tension after they had set.

BUILDING AND CONSTRUCTION

A barrel-arch roof using laminated wood won the American Society of Civil Engineers' Outstanding Structural Engineering Achievement Award for 1976. The roof, the world's longest-span structure, covers the University of Idaho stadium in Moscow, Ida. The arch spans 400 feet (122 meters) and rises 150 feet (46 meters) above the playing field. Although barrel-arch roofs of wood, steel, or concrete have been used before, the University of Idaho stadium is the first to combine both wood and steel. Because of the area's long, cold winters, university officials decided to replace a burned-out wooden football stadium with a multipurpose structure that would enclose both the playing field and the spectator area with a roof and walls.

Bridge Building. After decades of study and dispute, the Danish legislature cleared the way in June for construction of a bridge that will link the capital city of Copenhagen to the rest of the country. The bridge will cross the Great Belt, a channel of water 11 miles (18 kilometers) wide between two of Denmark's largest islands – Sjaelland, where Copenhagen is located, and Fyn, which is already connected to the mainland. Plans call for a low structure over the western section of the Great Belt, and a higher one over the eastern half, where there is considerable shipping. The bridge will carry six traffic lanes and a double-track railroad.

Construction of a new Hudson River bridge parallel to an existing bridge between Newburgh and Beacon, N.Y., started in June. The federal government will pay some 90 per cent of the $107-million cost because the bridge will be part of the interstate highway system. Scheduled for completion on Oct. 1, 1980, the new three-lane bridge will be similar to the existing structure, which is 7,860 feet (2,396 meters) long and has 14 spans.

The Florida Department of Transportation announced in January that it had abandoned plans to convert bridges connecting the Florida Keys into causeways. Instead, it will replace the crumbling spans with new bridges. All but seven of the 44 bridges need to be replaced. Replacing the deteriorated bridges will cost an estimated $155 million, with the federal government paying 70 per cent.

Dam Construction. The June 5 collapse of the Teton Dam in southeastern Idaho led officials to take a new look at the safety of other dams under construction (see DISASTERS). While the cause of the Teton Dam disaster was still unclear, preliminary reports by engineers and government officials pointed to failure of the structure's unusual triple-grout curtain, a kind of concrete wall finishing off the earth-fill dam. Congressional leaders asked the U.S. Army Corps of Engineers to respond to charges that four of its dams under construction and one

Aerial view looking upstream shows the huge breach in the Teton Dam through which a wall of water surged into southeast Idaho on June 5.

Montreal's Olympic Village has four 19-story half-pyramid structures that housed some 10,500 athletes and officials during the Summer Games.

proposed project may also be unsafe. Although Congress passed a Dam Safety Act in 1972, the Corps of Engineers had checked not one of the thousands of dams that Congress expected to be inspected.

By 1983, the world's largest thin-arch dam will span the American River near Auburn, Calif., after extensive fault treatment to lock the structure in place. The dam will be a double-curvature, elliptical-arch structure 4,150 feet (1,265 meters) long and 685 feet (209 meters) high. It will be 40 feet (12 meters) thick at the top and 196 feet (60 meters) thick at the base. Foundation work is well ahead of schedule. Because of the failure of two thin-arch dams in Europe, foundation studies at the site have been the most extensive ever undertaken for a Bureau of Reclamation dam.

Tunnel Bores. The city of Baltimore announced in February that it will build a steel tubular tunnel across Baltimore Harbor. The tunnel will carry an eight-lane highway extension under the harbor between Fort McHenry and Canton, Md. Completion is scheduled for 1982.

In April, Alpine tunnelers finished a safety bore paralleling what will be the world's longest vehicular tunnel, through the St. Gotthard pass in the Swiss Alps, southeast of Zurich. Work on the main tunnel, which will be 10.2 miles (16.4 kilometers) long, is two years behind schedule.   Mary E. Jessup

BULGARIA combined pro-Russian loyalty with greater flexibility toward its Balkan neighbors, Communist and non-Communist alike, in 1976. Bulgarian officials attended the Greek-sponsored Balkan conference on regional cooperation in Athens from January 26 to February 5 along with delegates from Romania, Turkey, and Yugoslavia. Communist Party First Secretary and State Council Chairman Todor Zhivkov visited Greece again in April. The two countries issued a communiqué after the visit saying that they had no outstanding territorial disputes.

Zhivkov visited Turkey in June and held a summit meeting in Varna on the Black Sea with President Nicolae Ceausescu of Romania. In September, the Macedonian question was discussed with a Yugoslav delegation in Sofia. At issue was whether the Macedonians in Yugoslavia were a "minority" group or, as Bulgaria insisted, ethnically Bulgarian.

The Communist Party Congress, held in Sofia from March 29 to April 2, re-elected Zhivkov as party leader and reaffirmed close economic and political ties with Russia. Three former senior leaders—Deputy Prime Minister Zhivko Zhivkov, philosopher Todor Pavlov, and Ivan Popov—were dropped from the party Politburo, reducing its size to nine members.

Leadership Shakeups. The National Assembly re-elected Zhivkov as state council chairman and

Stanko Todorov as prime minister on June 15. The leader and deputy leader of *Komsomol,* the Communist youth organization, were dismissed on April 23 for not doing enough to foster a Marxist-Leninist outlook among Bulgaria's youth. Georgi Bokov, president of the journalists' union, was dismissed on May 3 and four days later was replaced as editor of the party's main newspaper, *Rabotnichesko Delo.*

A special Central Committee meeting on July 1 and 2 discussed problems in industry, particularly low labor productivity. But the government claimed that industrial production was 8.2 per cent higher in the first nine months of 1976 than in the same period in 1975. Labor productivity growth of 6.9 per cent reportedly accounted for 85 per cent of the production increase. The government announced on August 5 that a large new unit of planning and management – the national agro-industrial complex – had been set up.

General Motors (GM) Corporation and the Bulgarian Balkancar enterprise signed a trade agreement in September. GM's Bedford Trucks Division in Great Britain will supply heavy-duty trucks to Bulgaria in exchange for fork-lift trucks produced by Balkancar. GM will use the fork-lift trucks in its plants throughout the world.   Chris Cviic

See also EUROPE (Facts in Brief Table).

BURMA. The rickety St. James Market in the heart of Burma's capital, Rangoon, gave way in 1976 to a new shopping center. Its name was simply the "Black Market." Instead of going to the stores of the 22 official government corporations, where shelves were usually bare, the people increasingly came to rely on the Black Market. Here, at highly inflated prices, one could buy car parts, coffee, cotton cloth, and drugs. In Rangoon, as elsewhere in Burma, the black market had more than ever become a way of life.

Economic Stagnation. A World Bank mission put the bleak picture in figures in March 1976, reporting that the gross domestic product had risen at an annual rate of 2.3 per cent during the previous 10 years. The population, meantime, grew by 2.2 per cent annually to about 32 million persons. Agriculture, forestry, mining, and transport had been neglected. The production of rice, the main export item, remained stagnant. The inflation rate was 40 per cent a year. And the gross national product per person was estimated at $80 a year, making Burma one of the world's poorest nations.

Other experts blamed the crisis on the haphazardness of "the Burmese way to Socialism," preached by President U Ne Win and the ineptness of the army officers running the economy. In March, Ne Win finally retreated from the rigid

Cuban Prime Minister Fidel Castro is greeted warmly by Bulgarians in Sofia in March as Communist Party First Secretary Todor Zhivkov watches.

Restoration work progresses slowly on ancient temples at Pagan, Burma. They were badly damaged by an earthquake that shook the area in July 1975.

neutrality he had pursued for 14 years to ask the World Bank for credits.

Work continued slowly on the repair and reconstruction of 2,500 ancient monuments and temples at Pagan that were heavily damaged in a 1975 earthquake. The government refused all foreign aid for this project, and many art experts feared that most of the treasures would never be recovered.

Plots and Wars. The sick economy nourished unrest. In July, 14 officers were arrested on charges of plotting to assassinate Ne Win and his defense minister, San Yu. The plotters' trial dragged on through the year's final months. For the third time in 16 months, there were student demonstrations and riots, and for the third time the government closed the universities.

Meanwhile, the army continued to wage war against two dangerous foes. One was a group of hill tribes, which have been fighting for independence for 26 years. In midsummer, nine of these tribes, including the well-armed Karens, formed the National Democratic Front, and called on China and the United States for support. The other foe was the Burmese Communists, reportedly armed by China. Ne Win visited China, seeking Peking's help. When he failed, the war was renewed.   Mark Gayn

See also ASIA (Facts in Brief Table).

BURUNDI. See AFRICA.

BUS. See TRANSIT; TRANSPORTATION.

BUSH, GEORGE H. W. (1924-   ), businessman, diplomat, and politician, was confirmed as director of the U.S. Central Intelligence Agency (CIA) on Jan. 27, 1976. When Bush assumed the CIA post, the agency was under heavy criticism for unlawful spying on U.S. citizens. In April 1976, the Senate Select Committee on Intelligence recommended that the CIA be barred from using such surveillance techniques as wire-tapping or opening mail inside the United States. See UNITED STATES, GOVERNMENT OF THE.

Bush was born on June 12, 1924, in Milton, Mass. He served as a Navy pilot in the Pacific theater during World War II. After his discharge in 1945, he attended Yale University and graduated in 1948 with a bachelor's degree in economics. He then moved to Texas and entered the oil industry.

He became involved in Republican politics in the Houston area and was elected to the U.S. House of Representatives in 1966, where he served two terms. He was U.S. representative to the United Nations from 1971 to 1973, when he became chairman of the Republican National Committee. From 1974 until his appointment as CIA director, he served as U.S. envoy to the People's Republic of China.

Bush married Barbara Pierce in 1945. They have four sons and a daughter.   Darlene R. Stille

BUSINESS. See ECONOMICS; LABOR; MANUFACTURING; Section One, FOCUS ON THE ECONOMY.

CABINET, UNITED STATES.

There were only three changes in President Gerald R. Ford's Cabinet during 1976. But as the year ended, attention focused on the Cabinet choices made by President-elect James Earl (Jimmy) Carter, Jr., for his Administration when it assumed power.

The Ford Cabinet. Secretary of Labor John T. Dunlop resigned on January 14, after Ford vetoed an on-site picketing bill that would have expanded the picketing rights of striking construction workers. Dunlop said he resigned because he believed that staying in the Ford Administration would damage his credibility with labor union leaders.

The most embarrassing incident involving a Cabinet member led to the October 4 resignation of Secretary of Agriculture Earl L. Butz. Butz made a racial slur against black Americans after the Republican National Convention in Kansas City, Mo. John W. Dean III, who was special counsel to President Richard M. Nixon, reported the incident in *Rolling Stone* magazine, and a great outcry ensued.

Ford reprimanded Butz on October 1 but was reluctant to fire him because the agriculture secretary was popular with farmers. However, public pressure was so great that Butz was forced to resign.

The only other Ford Cabinet change occurred on February 2, when Elliot L. Richardson was sworn in as secretary of commerce. Richardson replaced

President-elect James E. (Jimmy) Carter, Jr., in December presents his first Cabinet nominee, Cyrus R. Vance, designated secretary of state.

President Ford's secretary of agriculture, Earl L. Butz, was forced to resign in October after making a slur against black Americans.

Rogers C. B. Morton, who resigned to become a Ford counselor. See PRESIDENT OF THE UNITED STATES.

The Carter Cabinet. During his presidential campaign, Carter pledged to seek women and minority-group members for Cabinet posts. However, during the selection process, Carter revealed that several minority-group members and one woman turned down Cabinet appointments.

Carter completed all major appointments by December 23. On December 3, he made his first Cabinet appointment—Cyrus R. Vance, who served in earlier Democratic administrations, as secretary of state. He named two women—Juanita M. Kreps as secretary of commerce and Patricia Roberts Harris as secretary of housing and urban development. Kreps was a vice-president at Duke University and Harris, a prominent black attorney.

Carter chose two congressmen for Cabinet posts. Bob Bergland (D., Minn.) was named secretary of agriculture and Brock Adams (D., Wash.), secretary of transportation.

Carter's choice of Atlanta attorney Griffin B. Bell as attorney general drew fire from civil rights activists. Bell, a former appeals court judge, was criticized for his record on civil rights issues and for belonging to segregated private clubs. However, Carter bowed to pressure from women and minorities in his selection of a secretary of labor. Carter had seriously considered recalling Dunlop to the post. But instead, he chose F. Ray Marshall, an economics professor at the University of Texas who specialized in minority job programs. Environmentalists were pleased with the appointment of Idaho Governor Cecil D. Andrus as interior secretary.

In addition to Vance, Carter chose two other persons who held high-level posts in the Administration of former President Lyndon B. Johnson. He named Harold Brown, former secretary of the Air Force, as secretary of defense, and Johnson's chief domestic adviser, Joseph A. Califano, Jr., as secretary of health, education, and welfare.

Carter chose W. Michael Blumenthal, chairman of Bendix Corporation, to be treasury secretary.

Other High-Level Posts. Carter appointed Georgia banker Thomas Bertram Lance as director of the Office of Management and Budget; Representative Andrew Young (D., Ga.), chief U.S. delegate to the United Nations; Columbia University professor Zbigniew Brzezinski, special assistant for national security; Brookings Institution fellow Charles L. Schultze, chairman of the Council of Economic Advisers; and Theodore C. Sorensen, director of the Central Intelligence Agency. Former Secretary of Defense James R. Schlesinger was slated to be the new energy czar.   Darlene R. Stille

CALIFORNIA. See LOS ANGELES-LONG BEACH; SAN FRANCISCO-OAKLAND; STATE GOVERNMENT.

CALLAGHAN, JAMES (1912-   ), was named prime minister of Great Britain on April 5, 1976, after Labour Prime Minister Harold Wilson unexpectedly resigned the post (see GREAT BRITAIN). The genial Callaghan, nicknamed "Sunny Jim," has broad popularity within the Labour Party. He is regarded as a middle-of-the-road politician with a flexible approach to policy and a shrewd understanding of grass-roots opinion.

Leonard James Callaghan was born on March 27, 1912, in Portsmouth, England. He left school at 16 to help support his mother, widowed six years earlier. After passing a government examination in 1929, he became an income tax officer. Seven years later, at 24, he became a full-time trade union official with the Inland Revenue Staff Federation in London. There he developed skill as a labor negotiator and began rising within the ranks of the Trades Union Congress.

After serving with the Royal Navy during World War II, Callaghan entered Parliament in 1945. When the Labour Party took power in 1964, he became chancellor of the exchequer. He was home secretary from 1967 to 1970 and foreign secretary from 1974 until he was chosen as prime minister.

Callaghan married Audrey Elizabeth Moulton in 1938, an event he credits with adding middle-class stability to his working-class background. They have one son and two daughters.   Kathryn Sederberg

CAMBODIA. A new Constitution that changed the country's name from the Khmer Republic to Democratic Cambodia went into effect on Jan. 5, 1976. Following the traditional Communist practice, the Constitution said that "the important general means of production are the collective property of the people's state" and that Cambodia "practices the system of collective transport and labor."

A People's Representative Assembly will be elected every five years with 150 seats to represent farmers, 50 for "other workers and laborers," and 50 for the army. The Assembly will pass laws and elect "the administration," whose composition and powers were not defined.

The New Government. A reported 98 per cent of the voters chose the first Assembly in elections on March 20 from among 515 candidates. The Assembly met in Phnom Penh from April 11 to 13 and announced a new government on April 14.

Prince Norodom Sihanouk resigned his post as chief of state. He was replaced by President Khieu Samphan. The main leader of the new regime was Premier Pol Pot. Ieng Sary became deputy premier for foreign affairs, and Son Sen became deputy premier for defense.

Pol Pot was virtually unknown outside Cambodia. He was identified in a message from Laos as secretary-general of the Cambodian Communist Party, a job long reported held by Saloth Sar. Observers agreed that Pol Pot and Saloth Sar might be the same person.

Limited Achievements. In an interview on July 20, Pol Pot said the new regime "had not made any noteworthy achievements, except the revolutionary movement of the masses." He said the new government had established security and resettled people. "Since the war," Ieng Sary told the United Nations on October 5, "we have gradually solved many economic problems," including the food problem. He implied that internal resistance was continuing in the country by accusing the United States of creating "discord from the inside, interfering in our country's internal affairs."

The government charged that two U.S. warplanes bombed the city of Siem Reap on February 25, killing 15 persons and wounding 30. The United States denied the charge. Observers in Thailand suggested that resistance groups had set off bombs in the market place.

Refugee reports indicated that the large-scale killing and uprooting of people that followed the Communist victory in April 1975 might have ended by late 1976. Sihanouk was not heard of after he resigned. He failed to answer any of his mail. Some reports said that he was living somewhere near Phnom Penh.   Henry S. Bradsher

See also ASIA (Facts in Brief Table).

CAMEROON. See AFRICA.

CAMP FIRE GIRLS. See YOUTH ORGANIZATIONS.

CANADA

Economic conditions improved in Canada in 1976, but disputes over the policy of bilingualism threatened national unity. Prime Minister Pierre Elliott Trudeau's Liberal government served its eighth year in office, but its popularity declined significantly. There were several resignations from the federal Cabinet, Liberal standing in Parliament was reduced, and the separatist Parti Québécois came to power in Quebec in an election on November 15. See QUEBEC.

The forces of division appeared strong in Canada. René Lévesque, the new separatist premier of Quebec, spoke of an irreversible trend toward independence in that province and promised to hold a referendum on the issue in two years (see LÉVESQUE, RENÉ). Trudeau firmly rejected the idea of Quebec independence.

The Economy. Canada made some improvement in overcoming the worrying economic problems of the previous year. The gross national product in

An aerial view of Montreal shows the new sports stadium and other facilities that were built for the 1976 Olympic Games.

real terms grew modestly and was expected to reach $182.9 billion, a 5 per cent gain in real value. Unemployment remained at about the same level, even though there was a large increase in the labor force. The cost of living came down significantly, leading to lower wage settlements.

Exports picked up with the quickening pace of the world economy, and a small surplus in merchandise trade was expected for the year. But payments abroad for services and for interest and dividend charges meant that Canada's balance-of-payments deficit would be only slightly below the record $5 billion recorded in 1975.

Economic Controls. The Trudeau government's imposition of wage and price controls in October 1975 set the tone for 1976. Controls were intended to achieve successive reductions in the inflation rate, from 8 per cent in 1976 to 6 per cent in 1977 and 4 per cent in 1978, the last year of the controls. The cost of living rose about 6.5 per cent in 1976, attaining the first objective.

More significantly, controls broke the inflationary expectations that had appeared in recent years. Business, labor, and government seemed to have a more realistic appreciation of the demands that could be placed upon the economy. This was important; Canada's position as one of the world's leading trading nations depended upon its ability to compete internationally.

Controls were administered by an Anti-Inflation Board in Ottawa that laid down regulations for allowable wage and salary increases as well as business profits. Decisions could be appealed to a federally appointed administrator. Eight provinces agreed to apply the anti-inflation guidelines to workers and companies within their jurisdictions. Saskatchewan and Quebec appointed their own boards but agreed to follow the guidelines.

Labor Opposition. Although business leaders and bankers complained about government regulation, the Canadian Labour Congress (CLC) was the most vigorous critic of controls. The CLC raised a legal challenge to the anti-inflation legislation, arguing that it was beyond the federal government's power to enact. The Supreme Court of Canada rejected this claim in July.

The CLC showed its displeasure by withdrawing its representatives from government advisory bodies. It then decided to take its case to the people by sponsoring a national day of protest, coinciding with the first anniversary of controls on October 14. The day of protest was a mixed success. More than 1 million workers stayed off their jobs, but production was not seriously disrupted.

CLC President Joseph Morris led the labor movement in denouncing controls. In the general election of July 1974, the Liberals had gained labor support by opposing controls. They won the election decisively, but little more than a year later,

Trudeau saw the need for controls. In the CLC view, the labor movement's trust had been betrayed. The government dismissed these objections, saying that controls were necessary and effective, and that they would definitely be removed at the end of the statutory period. But the restraints were unpopular and worked to the political disadvantage of the Trudeau government.

The Language Issue was potentially more serious because it touched the fundamentals of the relationship between English- and French-speaking Canadians. Parliament had strongly backed the 1969 Official Languages Act, which provided for federal services in both languages, but implementing the policy in English-Canada had always been criticized. Many English-speaking Canadians believed that language measures were being introduced too quickly and where they were not required, and that public money was being wasted.

The federal case for bilingualism was not helped when the Quebec Assembly in 1974 passed Bill 22, a law declaring French the official language of the province and giving it a preferred position. Enactment of the bill convinced many English-speaking Canadians that French-speaking Quebecers were happy to see bilingualism adopted across Canada, but were not prepared to allow it in Quebec. One feature of the bill was especially objectionable – a clause that required the children of immigrants who were neither French- nor English-speaking to attend French schools unless they could demonstrate proficiency in English. In the past, such immigrants who came to Quebec had usually placed their children in the English educational stream.

Airline Objections. The concept of bilingualism was sorely tested by a dispute over the use of French in ground-air communications at major airports in Quebec and at Ottawa. English-speaking air controllers and pilots objected, claiming that two languages from the control tower would imperil safety in the air. In May, attorney John Keenan was appointed commissioner to study the question, but he resigned on June 7 when it became apparent he did not have the confidence of French-speaking air-transport groups. Keenan had formerly served as counsel to the Canadian Airline Pilots Association, which opposed bilingualism in the air. The 2,200 members of the Canadian Air Traffic Controllers Association, most of whom were English-speaking, then scheduled a strike for June 20. Although a court injunction stalled the controllers' walkout, English-speaking pilots struck and were joined a few days later by controllers. International airlines and pilots supported the strike by refusing to use Canadian airports.

The strike ended June 28 when Minister of Transport Otto Emil Lang negotiated a settlement. The controllers and pilots agreed to the appoint-

The Ministry of Canada
In order of precedence

Pierre Elliott Trudeau, prime minister

Allan Joseph MacEachen, president of the queen's privy council

Jean Chrétien, minister of industry, trade, and commerce

Donald Stovel Macdonald, minister of finance

John Carr Munro, minister of labor

Stanley Ronald Basford, minister of justice and attorney general of Canada

Donald Campbell Jamieson, secretary of state for external affairs

Robert Knight Andras, president of the treasury board

Otto Emil Lang, minister of transport

Jean-Pierre Goyer, minister of supply and services

Alastair William Gillespie, minister of energy, mines, and resources

Eugene Francis Whelan, minister of agriculture

W. Warren Allmand, minister of Indian affairs and northern development

James Hugh Faulkner, minister of state for science and technology

Daniel Joseph MacDonald, minister of veterans affairs

Marc Lalonde, minister of national health and welfare

Jeanne Sauvé, minister of communications

Raymond Joseph Perrault, leader of the government in the Senate

Barnett Jerome Danson, minister of national defense

J. Judd Buchanan, minister of public works

Roméo LeBlanc, minister of fisheries and the environment

Marcel Lessard, minister of regional economic expansion

Jack Sydney George Cullen, minister of manpower and immigration

Leonard Stephen Marchand, minister of state for small businesses

John Roberts, secretary of state of Canada

Monique Bégin, minister of national revenue

Jean-Jacques Blais, postmaster general

Francis Fox, solicitor general of Canada

Anthony Chisholm Abbott, minister of consumer and corporate affairs

Iona Campagnolo, minister of state for fitness and amateur sport

André Ouellet, minister of state for urban affairs

Joseph-Philippe Guay, minister without portfolio

Premiers of Canadian Provinces

Province	Premier
Alberta	Peter Lougheed
British Columbia	William R. Bennett
Manitoba	Edward R. Schreyer
New Brunswick	Richard B. Hatfield
Newfoundland	Frank Moores
Nova Scotia	Gerald A. Regan
Ontario	William G. Davis
Prince Edward Island	Alexander B. Campbell
Quebec	Réne Lévesque
Saskatchewan	Allan Blakeney

Commissioners of Territories

Northwest Territories	Stuart M. Hodgson
Yukon Territory	Arthur Pearson

ment of three judges to appraise the safety of bilingual air communications. If the judges' report were unanimous on the question of safety, it would be submitted to Parliament for debate.

The Lang settlement aroused a storm of criticism in Quebec. French-speaking controllers and pilots were convinced it was biased against them in requiring unanimity from the judges. To deny the use of French at Quebec airports, they said, would be to abolish the legal equality of French in federal government operations. *L'Association des Gens de l'Air* – a group of French-speaking pilots and controllers formed the year before – became their spokesman against the position of the two national controllers' and pilots' groups.

English-speaking controllers and pilots at the same time rigidly defended using one language in air communications, asserting that English was the language of international air traffic.

Ministers Resign. The Trudeau Cabinet itself was divided on the issue. This became apparent on June 30 when Jean Marchand, one of Trudeau's closest friends, resigned from the government. Marchand said he could not continue in a Cabinet that had undermined the principle of bilingualism through the Lang settlement. Marchand later resigned from Parliament, and was defeated by a separatist when he tried for a seat in the Quebec Assembly. Trudeau appointed him to the federal Senate on December 9.

Another minister left the Cabinet over bilingualism as Parliament assembled for its autumn session on October 13. James A. Richardson, minister of national defense and a strong spokesman for the western provinces, said he disagreed with Trudeau's apparent wish to entrench the principle of bilingualism in a revised Canadian constitution by giving Quebec a veto over changes. His concern sprang from Trudeau's long-standing desire to work out an amending formula for the constitution and then transfer the amending power from the British Parliament to the Parliament of Canada. Trudeau's plan would give Ontario and Quebec a veto over constitutional changes. This arrangement was not acceptable to the western provinces.

A third minister, Bryce Mackasey, a popular figure from Montreal, resigned as postmaster general in September after an undisclosed difference with Trudeau. On October 26, he resigned from Parliament after 14 years in Ottawa, to run as a Liberal in the Quebec election. While Mackasey won a Quebec seat, another Liberal member of Parliament who had also resigned lost in his election try.

The resignations and a death reduced the Liberal Party's strength to 135 seats in the House of Commons, down from 140 in January.

A Restructured Cabinet. Other Cabinet resignations were not connected with the language issue. André Ouellet, active in the organization of the

Liberal Party in Quebec, resigned as minister of consumer and corporate affairs on March 16. He was found guilty of contempt of court for publicly criticizing the decision of a Quebec judge in a price-fixing case launched by his department. Dissatisfaction in Parliament over Ouellet's behavior and Trudeau's handling of the matter led to Ouellet's resignation.

The conduct of another minister, Charles M. Drury, accused of interfering in the judicial process on behalf of Ouellet, was called "improper" by a judicial inquiry. Drury, minister of science and technology and public works, apologized to the House, but Trudeau refused to accept his resignation. Drury was allowed to resign in September, when there was a general shuffle of Cabinet posts.

The reconstructed Cabinet had seven new faces on September 15. Two were women, joining Communications Minister Jeanne Sauvé to give Canada its first Cabinet containing three women. Another first occurred when Leonard S. Marchand, an Indian from British Columbia, was named minister of state for small business. In addition to Mackasey and Drury, Mitchell Sharp, president of the privy council, also resigned from the Cabinet. Eight ministers were transferred to new portfolios and one received an additional post.

The most important shift was the move of Allan J. MacEachen, secretary of state for external affairs, to his old post as president of the privy council and government leader in the Commons. MacEachen's key role became apparent when he was also named deputy prime minister.

Ouellet returned to the Cabinet on November 3 after his appeal of the contempt decision had been rejected. Trudeau claimed he had been sufficiently punished for his misdemeanor. At the same time, Barnett J. Danson was named to succeed Richardson as defense minister.

Other Political Parties. The Progressive Conservative Party picked up two seats in by-elections on October 18. The victories gave them 96 seats in the House.

The Conservatives selected a new national leader, Joseph C. Clark, at an Ottawa convention on February 22. The 36-year-old former journalist and party organizer had represented the Rocky Mountain constituency in Alberta since 1972. Clark is bilingual, with middle-of-the-road positions on many issues. An able parliamentarian, he possesses a pragmatic approach and a cool style. See CLARK, JOSEPH C.

The Social Credit Party, with 10 seats in the House, chose André Fortin, 32, of Quebec as its new leader on November 7. He succeeded the ailing party founder, Réal Caouette, who died on December 16.

The New Democratic Party, with 16 seats, continued under the leadership of Edward Broad-

bent. There was 1 Independent member and 6 vacancies — one formerly held by the Conservatives, one by Social Credit, the others by the Liberals.

The Legislative Record was not impressive. Only about half the legislation promised when the session opened in 1974 was implemented. In a close vote on July 14, Parliament abolished the death penalty for civilian crimes. No executions have occurred in Canada since 1962.

Another controversial measure removed the 100 per cent tax deductions allowed for advertisers using Canadian editions of foreign magazines. To qualify for tax deductions for advertisers, a publication must have 75 per cent Canadian ownership, and at least 80 per cent of its content must be differ-

Federal Spending in Canada
Estimated Budget for Fiscal 1977*

	Millions of Dollars
Health and welfare	13,517
Economic development and support	5,317
Public debt	4,650
Defense	4,147
Fiscal transfer payments to provinces	2,851
Transportation and communications	2,617
General government services	1,703
Internal overhead expenses	1,334
Culture and recreation	789
Foreign affairs	753
Education assistance	740
Total	38,417

*April 1, 1976, to March 31, 1977

Spending Since 1971

Billions of dollars

| Fiscal Year | 1971-'72 | '72-'73 | '73-'74 | '74-'75 | '75-'76 | '76-'77 Est. |

Source: Treasury Board of Canada

Canadian Census Report

With partial tables of the preliminary population count

Canada's population grew an estimated 5 per cent in the five years from 1971 to 1976, according to preliminary 1976 census statistics. The preliminary figures, which do not include people living away from their usual homes, set the total population at 22,598,016, compared with 21,568,311 in 1971. All of Canada's 10 largest census metropolitan areas grew, but most of the growth took place outside the central cities.

Montreal, Que., remains Canada's largest city, with a population slightly over 1 million. This is far ahead of Toronto, Ont., the second largest city with just over 600,000 persons. Winnipeg, Man., with more than 550,000 persons, moved into third place.

Below is a listing of Canadian cities, towns, and villages with populations of more than 5,000 based on the preliminary figures. Final statistics will be issued in 1978.

Kathryn Sederberg

Alberta . . 1,799,771
Brooks 6,269
Calgary
  City 457,828
  Metro Area . . 457,828
Camrose. 9,947
Drumheller. 6,032
Edmonton
  City 452,095
  Metro Area . . 542,845
Fort
  McMurray 15,139
Fort
  Saskatchewan . . 8,142
Grande Prairie . . 17,471
Hinton 6,597
Leduc 8,498
Lethbridge 46,048
Lloydminster
  (Alta. and Sask.)
  10,147
Medicine Hat . . 32,263
Red Deer 31,723
St. Albert 23,960
Spruce Grove. . . . 6,827
Taber 5,243
Wetaskiwin. 6,695

British Columbia
  2,406,212
Castlegar 6,159
Chilliwack. 8,472
Comox 5,226
Courtenay 7,566
Cranbrook 13,310
Dawson Creek . . 10,316
Fort St. John . . . 8,872
Kamloops. 57,241
Kelowna 50,111
Kimberley 7,015
Langley 9,814
Merritt 5,581
Nanaimo 39,655
Nelson 8,919
New
  Westminster . . 37,171
North
  Vancouver. . . . 31,207
Penticton 21,017
Port Alberni . . . 19,304
Port
  Coquitlam . . . 23,686
Port Moody 11,515
Prince George . . 58,292
Prince Rupert . . 14,247
Quesnel 7,539
Sidney 6,464
Trail 9,872
Vancouver
  City 396,563
  Metro Area . . 1,135,774
Vernon 17,162
Victoria
  City 60,407
  Metro Area . . 212,466

White Rock 12,297
Williams Lake 6,132

Manitoba 1,005,953
Brandon 34,481
Dauphin 9,081
Flin Flon
  (Man. and Sask.)
  8,431
Portage la
  Prairie 11,719
Selkirk 9,741
Steinbach 5,905
The Pas 6,531
Thompson 17,083
Winnipeg
  City 553,148
  Metro Area . . 570,725

New Brunswick
  664,525
Bathurst 16,062
Campbellton. . . . 9,157
Chatham 7,517
Dalhousie 5,593
Dieppe 7,424
Edmundston . . . 12,530
Fredericton 44,572
Grand Falls 6,164
Moncton 53,418
Newcastle 6,296
Oromocto 9,915
Riverview 14,069
Sackville 5,695
Saint John
  City 82,976
  Metro Area . . 109,700
St. Stephen 5,211

Newfound-land 548,789
Channel-Port
  aux Basques . . . 6,080
Conception
  Bay South 9,559
Corner Brook . . . 24,798
Gander 9,117
Grand Falls 8,786
Happy Valley-
  Goose Bay . . . 8,114
Marystown 5,823
Mount Pearl 10,058
St. John's
  City . . . . . : . 84,994
  Metro Area . . 140,883
Stephenville . . . 10,120
Windsor 6,283

Northwest Territories
  42,237
Yellowknife 8,195

Nova Scotia . . . 812,127
Amherst 10,150
Bridgewater 5,931
Dartmouth 64,452
Glace Bay 21,484
Halifax
  City 113,036
  Metro Area . . 261,366
New Glasgow . . . 10,529
New Waterford. . . 9,106
North Sydney. . . . 8,192
Springhill 5,138
Stellarton 5,281
Sydney 30,087
Sydney Mines . . . 8,863
Truro 12,625
Yarmouth 7,644

Ontario . . 8,131,618
Ajax 20,669
Amherstburg 5,523
Ancaster 14,151
Arnprior 5,953
Aurora 13,853
Aylmer 5,030
Barrie 33,524
Belleville. 34,702
Bracebridge 8,186
Brampton 102,743
Bradford 5,031
Brantford 66,385
Brockville 19,566
Burlington 104,133
Caledon 22,210
Cambridge 71,798
Carleton Place . . 5,204
Chatham. 38,437
Cobourg 11,279
Collingwood 11,147
Cornwall 45,491
Deep River 5,527
Dryden 6,682
Dundas 19,115
Dunnville 11,556
Elliot Lake 8,730
Espanola 5,845
Essex 5,549
Fergus 5,980
Fort Erie 23,687
Fort Frances . . . 9,198
Gananoque 5,056
Goderich 7,243
Gravenhurst 7,908
Grimsby 15,510
Guelph 66,431
Haldimand 16,201
Halton Hills 34,232
Hamilton
  City 308,845
  Metro Area . . 525,222
Hanover 5,478
Hawkesbury 9,647
Hearst 5,161
Huntsville 11,092

Ingersoll 8,034
Iroquois Falls . . . 6,807
Kapuskasing 12,542
Kenora 10,361
Kingston. 59,804
Kirkland Lake . . . 13,486
Kitchener
  City 130,866
  Metro Area . . 269,828
Leamington 11,036
Lincoln 14,235
Lindsay. 12,872
Listowel 5,099
London
  City 234,968
  Metro Area . . 264,639
Markham 55,585
Midland 11,444
Milton. 20,581
Mississauga . . . 246,766
Nanticoke 19,136
New Liskeard . . . 5,554
Newcastle. 31,582
Newmarket 24,677
Niagara Falls . . . 69,450
Niagara-on-
  the-Lake 12,272
Nickel Centre . . . 12,993
North Bay 50,819
Oakville 68,444
Onaping Falls . . . 6,660
Orangeville 11,859
Orillia 24,090
Oshawa
  City 106,002
  Metro Area . . 133,959
Ottawa
  City 291,088
  Metro Area . . 668,853
Owen Sound . . . 19,223
Paris 6,487
Parry Sound 5,423
Pelham 9,879
Pembroke 14,722
Penetanguishene . 5,449
Perth 5,639
Petawawa 5,704
Peterborough . . . 59,077
Pickering 27,762
Port Colborne . . . 20,269
Port Hope 9,687
Rayside-Balfour . . 16,001
Renfrew 8,530
Richmond Hill. . . 34,504
St. Catharines
  City 121,657
  Metro Area . . 298,129
St. Thomas 26,721
Sarnia. 54,859
Sault Ste. Marie . 79,090
Simcoe 14,100
Smiths Falls 9,149
Stoney Creek . . . 29,944
Stratford 25,398
Strathroy 7,546
Sturgeon Falls . . 6,352

Sudbury
  City 96,038
  Metro Area . . . 155,013
Tecumseh 5,222
Thorold 14,599
Thunder Bay
  City 110,288
  Metro Area . . 117,988
Tillsonburg. 9,325
Timmins 44,010
Toronto
  City 611,171
  Metro Area . . 2,753,112
Trenton 15,211
Valley East 19,427
Vanier 18,327
Vaughan. 17,367
Walden 10,366
Wallaceburg . . . 11,066
Waterloo 46,057
Welland 43,930
Whitby 27,957
Whitchurch-
  Stouffville . . . 12,616
Windsor
  City 192,683
  Metro Area . . 243,289
Woodstock 26,396

Prince Edward Island 116,251
Charlottetown. . . 16,508
Sherwood 5,542
Summerside 8,404

Quebec . 6,141,491
Alma 25,294
Amos 8,985
Ancienne-Lorette 11,640
Anjou 36,071
Arthabaska 5,855
Asbestos 8,878
Aylmer 25,145
Baie-Comeau . . . 11,800
Beaconsfield . . . 20,275
Beauharnois 7,614
Beauport 54,990
Bécancour 8,947
Beloeil 15,805
Blainville 12,367
Boisbriand 9,986
Boucherville . . . 25,236
Brossard 37,088
Buckingham . . . 14,173
Candiac 7,153
Cap-de-la-
  Madeleine . . . 31,788
Chambly. 11,755
Charlesbourg . . . 62,366
Charny 6,426
Châteauguay . . . 36,242
Chibougamau. . . 10,443
Chicoutimi
  City 56,702
  Metro Area . . 127,181

Coaticook 6,334	Roxboro 7,048
Côte-St-Luc 24,979	St.-Antoine 6,792
Cowansville 11,843	St.-Basile-le-
Deux-	Grand 5,591
Montagnes 8,797	St.-Bruno-de-
Dolbeau 8,261	Montarville 20,842
Dollard-des-	St.-Constant 7,595
Ormeaux 36,315	St.-Eustache 21,018
Donnacona 5,730	St.-Georges 8,424
Dorion 5,804	St.-Georges-
Dorval 18,891	Ouest 6,349
Drummond-	St.-Hubert 48,385
ville 28,894	St.-Hyacinthe . . .36,832
Drummondville-	St.-Jean 34,048
Sud 9,354	St.-Jérôme 24,808
Farnham 6,434	St.-Lambert 20,129
Gaspé 16,694	St.-Laurent 62,826
Gatineau 71,474	St.-Léonard 78,619
Granby 36,674	St.-Luc 6,320
Grand' Mère 15,733	St.-Paul-
Greenfield	l'Ermite 6,083
Park 18,215	St.-Pierre 5,899
Hampstead 7,456	St.-Romauld-
Hauterive 14,283	d'Etchemin 8,924
Hull 58,160	Ste.-Agathe-
Iberville 8,769	des-Monts 5,393
Île-Perrot 5,202	Ste.-Anne-
Joliette 17,863	des-Monts 5,889
Jonquière 60,373	Ste.-Catherine . . .5,927
Kirkland 7,278	Ste.-Foy 70,356
La Baie 19,801	Ste.-Julie 8,519
Lac-Mégantic 6,388	Ste.-Thérèse 17,365
Lachenaie 7,121	Sept-Îles 30,185
Lachine 40,948	Shawinigan 24,388
Lachute 11,753	Shawinigan-Sud . .10,920
La Prairie 8,989	Sherbrooke 75,137
LaSalle 75,361	Sillery 13,203
La Tuque 11,956	Sorel 19,516
Lauzon 12,641	Terrebonne 10,838
Laval 241,297	Thetford Mines . .20,435
Le Moyne 7,137	Tracy 12,212
Lévis 17,507	Trois-Rivières . . .51,772
Longueuil 119,994	Trois-Rivières-
Loretteville 14,570	Ouest 10,463
Lorraine 5,289	Val-Bèlair 10,560
Magog 13,110	Val-d'Or 20,479
Malartic 5,029	Valleyfield
Maniwaki 5,924	(Salaberry-De-). 29,385
Mascouche 14,145	Vanier 10,515
Matane 12,598	Varennes 6,416
Mirabel 12,495	Vaudreuil 5,585
Mistassini 5,453	Verdun 67,458
Mont-Joli 6,464	Victoriaville 21,595
Mont-Laurier 8,493	Westmount 21,769
Mont-Royal 19,411	Windsor 5,608
Mont-St.-Hilaire . . .7,611	
Montmagny 12,178	
Montreal	**Saskatchewan**
City 1,060,033	. . . . **.907,650**
Metro Area	Estevan 8,754
. 2,758,780	Flin Flon
Montréal-Nord . .94,980	(Sask. and Man.)
Montréal-Ouest . .5,854	8,431
Noranda 9,574	Lloydminster
Outremont 26,556	(Sask. and Alta.)
Percé 5,171	10,147
Pierrefonds 34,647	Melville 5,101
Pincourt 7,835	Moose Jaw 31,884
Plessisville 7,181	North Battleford . .12,987
Pointe-aux-	Prince Albert 28,240
Trembles 37,463	Regina
Pointe-Claire 25,355	City 147,529
Port-Cartier 8,010	Metro Area . . .148,965
Québec	Saskatoon
City 173,959	City 132,291
Metro Area . . .534,193	Metro Area . . .132,291
Repentigny 26,470	Swift Current 14,523
Rimouski 27,550	Weyburn 8,805
Rivière-du-	Yorkton 14,965
Loup 13,012	
Roberval 8,514	
Rosemère 6,997	**Yukon** . . . . . **.21,392**
Rouyn 17,479	Whitehorse 13,045

ent from material appearing in other editions. *Reader's Digest* met these requirements when it was decided that material edited and condensed in Canada could be defined as "Canadian content." The magazine also agreed to set up a foundation to hold three-fourths of its Canadian subsidiary's shares. *Time* found it impossible to meet the conditions and ceased publishing its Canadian edition.

Parliament also imposed limits on health-care spending over the next two years by setting limits on increases in federal grants to the provinces for health-care purposes. A national lottery, Loto-Canada, was established to continue the Olympic lottery and raise funds for the 1978 Commonwealth Games in Edmonton, Alta.

Oil Prices. Canada moved toward applying the world price of oil in its domestic market. Ottawa agreed with Alberta, the chief oil-producing province, that the two-price system should be phased out. On July 1, the domestic wellhead price of Canadian oil was raised to $9.05 per barrel; it was to rise to $9.75 on Jan. 1, 1977. Natural gas prices increased proportionally.

Oil from western Canada began flowing into the Montreal market in June as a pipeline from Sarnia, Ont., went into operation. This diversion meant less oil was exported to the United States, though the average daily flow of 460,000 barrels was higher than predicted.

Foreign Affairs. Trudeau visited Mexico, Cuba, and Venezuela in January. Trudeau told Cuban Prime Minister Fidel Castro that Canada disapproved of Cuban volunteers intervening in the civil war in Angola. However, he affirmed that Canada would continue to trade with Cuba.

Visiting Japan in October, Trudeau signed an economic cooperation agreement with Prime Minister Takeo Miki and gained assurances that Japan would consider buying more manufactured goods from Canada. A similar agreement was signed with the European Community (Common Market) on July 6.

Canada staked out its claim to fishing zones extending 200 nautical miles off the Atlantic and Pacific coasts, to take effect on Jan. 1, 1977. A similar extension of fishing limits in the Arctic Ocean was to take effect on March 1, 1977.

In July, Canada hosted the summer Olympic Games in Montreal, which attracted visitors from all parts of Canada and other countries. See OLYMPIC GAMES.

Facts in Brief: Population: 22,598,016. Government: Governor General Jules Léger; Prime Minister Pierre Elliott Trudeau. Monetary unit: Canadian dollar. Foreign Trade: exports, $34,734,000,000; imports, $34,360,000,000.   David M. L. Farr

See also Canadian province articles; CANADIAN LIBRARY ASSOCIATION (CLA); CANADIAN LITERATURE; LÉGER, JULES; TRUDEAU, PIERRE ELLIOTT.

CANADIAN LIBRARY ASSOCIATION (CLA)

CANADIAN LIBRARY ASSOCIATION (CLA) explored ways and means for libraries to meet the needs of the Canadian multicultural society at its 31st annual conference, held in Halifax, N.S., from June 10 to 16, 1976. About 1,000 persons attended, and even the social events and refreshments were multicultural.

Medals and Awards. The Book of the Year for Children Medal was awarded to Mordecai Richler for *Jacob Two-Two Meets the Hooded Fang.* The Amelia Frances Howard-Gibbon Medal for the best illustrated English-language children's book went to William Kurelek for *A Prairie Boy's Summer.* The Merit Award of the Canadian Library Trustees Association went to Fred Pile of the North York Public Library Board, Willowdale, Ont., and the Margaret B. Scott Award of the Canadian School Library Association to John Wright of the University of Alberta Faculty of Library Science. The eighth Howard V. Phalin-World Book Graduate Scholarship in Library Science, sponsored by World Book – Childcraft of Canada, Limited, was awarded by a CLA standing committee to David H. Jenkinson, assistant professor at the University of Manitoba.

The CLA published *Canadian Business and Economics,* edited by Barbara E. Brown, and *Canadian Juvenile Fiction and the Library Market* by John P.

Wilkinson. The Canada Council awarded a grant of $88,000 to expand and automate the CLA's *Canadian Periodical Index.*

Libraries. The Library of Parliament, which dates back to 1791, celebrated the centenary of the opening of its building with festivities, a historical display, and the minting of a commemorative silver dollar. The National Library of Canada and the U.S. Library of Congress signed a nonexclusive exchange agreement. The National Library exhibit – "Canadian Children's Books: A Treasury of Pictures" – at the International Book Fair in Montreal from May 19 to 23 featured 83 books.

The Ontario Provincial Library Council released its survey report, *The Ontario Public Library: Review and Reorganization,* prepared by Albert W. Bowron, for discussion and recommendations by workshops meeting throughout the province. The Toronto Public Library issued *The Catalogue of the Osborne Collection of Early Children's Books, 1566-1910,* Volume 2. The Council of Federal Libraries held its first meeting on April 9. The Alta Vista regional branch of the Ottawa Public Library opened its spacious new building in July. The School of Librarianship of the University of British Columbia sponsored the Pacific Rim Conference on Children's Literature in Vancouver from May 10 to 15. Authors, illustrators, publishers, and critics from 11 countries took part.   Elizabeth Homer Morton

The Royal Canadian Mint in 1976 commemorated the 100th anniversary of the opening of the Library of Parliament building by issuing this silver dollar.

CANADIAN LITERATURE during 1976 continued the geographic historical trend begun a year earlier. For example, Pierre Berton wrote an instant history, *My Country; the Remarkable Past.* Meanwhile, several new small firms published poetry, fiction, and works with a local background. The book of the year was Canada's gift to the United States to celebrate the American Revolution Bicentennial – *Between Friends/Entre Amis,* prepared by Lorraine Monk and members of Canada's National Film Board. It is a magnificent folio of scenes along the undefended U.S.-Canadian border. The pictures were taken by 26 photographers and are enlivened by apt quotations.

The Canada Council established Children's Literature prizes for the two best books (one in English, one in French) for young people written by Canadians. The first awards went to Bill Freeman for *Shantymen of Cache Lake* (English) and to Louise Aylwin for *Raminagradu* (French), Aylwin's hand-lettered and illustrated collection of fantasy stories.

Birds and Birdmen books were plentiful. The interplay of camera and airplane was detailed in *Skyview Canada: a Study of Aerial Photography in Canada* by Don W. Thomson, historian, journalist, and poet. The book marked the 50th anniversary of the Canadian National Air Photo Library. Thomson covered technological progress and included interesting wildlife photographs, especially of birds in flight. *Prairie Birds in Color* by Doug Gilroy described 92 varieties of birds, their habits, habitats, and colorful details. *Birds of the West Coast,* Volume 1, by J. Fenwick Lansdowne contains color paintings, pencil drawings, and the author's notes about the birds.

Political Biography. Well-written and interesting accounts of Conservative prime ministers included: *MacDonald, His Life and World* by P. B. Waite, a well-rounded account of the father of Canadian confederation; *Robert Laird Borden,* Volume 1, by Robert Craig Brown, hailed as a significant work on Canada's prime minister during World War I; and *One Canada, The Crusading Years, 1895-1956, Memoirs of the Right Honorable John G. Diefenbaker,* which began the reminiscences of the first prime minister from western Canada. Biographies of Liberal prime ministers included *William Lyon Mackenzie King, Volume III, 1932-39; the Prism of Unity* by Blair Neatby, on the Great Depression and King's political leadership; and *My Years with Louis St. Laurent* by John W. Pickersgill, about King's successor.

Indian Art. A unique collection was featured in *"Bo'jou, Neejee!" Profiles of Canadian Indian Art,* with text by Ted J. Brasser and photographs from the Speyer Collection of Indian artifacts.

Fiction. Gabrielle Roy wrote *The Enchanted Summer,* "an adult fairy tale where fantasy and reality meet." *The Swing in the Garden* by Hugh Hood is the first of a series of interwoven novels planned to portray a century of Canadian life.

Poetry. Margaret Atwood published her *Selected Poems.* Works by other established poets included *The Price of Gold* by Miriam Waddington; *Wood Mountain Poems* by Andrew Suknaski; and *The Darkening Fire: Selected Poems, 1945-1968* by Irving Layton.

Governor-General's Literary Awards for books published in 1975 went to Milton Acorn for *The Island Means Minago* (English poetry); Marion MacRae and Anthony Adamson for *Hallowed Walls* (English nonfiction); Brian Moore for *The Great Victorian Collection* (English fiction); Pierre Perreault for *Chouennes* (French poetry); Louis-Edmond Hamelin for *Nordicité canadienne* (French nonfiction); and Anne Hébert for *Les enfants du Sabbat* (French fiction).

The Canada Council Translation Prizes. John Glassco won for his English translation of the *Complete Poems of Saint-Denys Garneau* and Jean Simard for *Mon père, ce héros,* a French translation of Mordecai Richler's *Son of a Smaller Hero.*

Stephen Leacock Memorial Award for humor went to Harry J. Boyle for *The Luck of the Irish; A Canadian Fable.* Elizabeth Homer Morton

CAPE VERDE. See AFRICA; Section Five, CAPE VERDE and PRAIA.

CARTER, JAMES EARL, JR. (1924-   ), former governor of Georgia, capped his two-year campaign for the U.S. presidency by winning the presidential election on Nov. 2, 1976. He defeated incumbent Republican President Gerald R. Ford, getting 50.08 per cent of the popular vote and 297 electoral votes. See ELECTIONS.

In Democratic primaries early in the year, the relatively unknown Carter – who prefers to use "Jimmy" instead of "James" – won substantial victories over his rivals. Although he lost several late primary elections, his momentum carried him to the presidential nomination on the first ballot at the Democratic National Convention in New York City on July 14. See DEMOCRATIC PARTY.

After his election victory, Carter, his family, and aides relaxed on St. Simons Island, Georgia, where Carter studied voluminous reports to help prepare for the transition from a Ford Administration to a Carter Administration.

In the weeks of transition that followed, the President-elect conferred with President Ford, Federal Reserve Board Chairman Arthur F. Burns, congressional leaders, CIA Director George H. W. Bush, and Secretary of State Henry A. Kissinger. On November 15, Carter announced that Jody Powell would be his White House press secretary. In December, he announced choices for his Cabinet. See CABINET. Carol L. Thompson

See also Section Five, CARTER, JAMES EARL, JR.

CELEBRATIONS and anniversaries observed in 1976 included the following:

Konrad Adenauer Centenary, honoring the birth of the former chancellor of West Germany (1949-1963) was observed on Jan. 4, 1976, in Rhöndorf, where he is buried. Events included a Mass said by his son Paul, a Roman Catholic priest.

American Chemical Society Centenary. A new commemorative stamp, honoring the founding of the society in April 1876 in New York City, was issued by the U.S. Postal Service. The stamp depicts experimental procedures in a chemical laboratory.

American Revolution Bicentennial. See BICENTENNIAL, UNITED STATES; Section Two, AMERICA'S BIG BIRTHDAY PARTY.

Bayreuth Festival Centenary. Performances of German composer Richard Wagner's *Ring of the Nibelung* were given in Bayreuth's Festspielhaus (Festival Play House) in July. Other opera companies, notably New York City's Metropolitan Opera, included commemorative performances of the Ring cycle in their 1976-1977 repertories.

Alexander Graham Bell Centennial, marking Bell's first telephone call, to Thomas A. Watson, was commemorated in a series of postage stamps issued by the United States and other countries.

Boys' Club of New York Centennial celebration was held in the club's seven-story building in New

A restored 1926 Swallow biplane soars over Chicago during its tour
of the United States to mark commercial aviation's 50th anniversary.

York City in October. A dinner attended by the board of trustees was followed by a performance of Frank Loesser's musical play *The Most Happy Fella.*

Pablo Casals Centenary honored the 100th birthday of cellist Pablo Casals, who left his native Spain in 1939 in protest of the Francisco Franco regime. In June, festivals were held in Puerto Rico; Mexico; Switzerland; Prades, France, where Casals organized his first festival in 1950; and Vendrell, Spain, his birthplace.

Caxton Quinquecentennial commemorated the founding in 1476 of England's first printing shop by William Caxton. A four-day Caxton International Congress attracted European scholars to London in September to discuss Caxton's work.

"Count Dracula" Quinquecentennial marked the 500th anniversary of the death of Prince Vlad Tepes of Walachia, who was known to his contemporaries as "The Impaler." The prince, who was born near the Transylvanian city of Braşov, Romania, was the subject of a vampire novel by Bram Stoker and a number of Hollywood motion pictures in which he was known as "Count Dracula."

Edward Gibbon Bicentennial marked the 200th anniversary of the publication of the first volume of Gibbon's *History of the Decline and Fall of the Roman Empire.* A highlight of the international observance was a conclave of British, U.S., Swiss, French, and Italian prelates in Rome, sponsored by the American Academy of Arts and Sciences and the Institute of the Italian Encyclopedia.

Little Bighorn Centenary marked the anniversary of the June 25, 1876, battle in which Lieutenant Colonel George Armstrong Custer made his famous "last stand" against hostile Indians. Memorial services were held at Custer Battlefield National Monument, which is located at the Montana battlefield.

Legal Aid Society Centenary honored the first group in the United States to provide legal assistance to the poor. At a ceremony in March at the New York State Theater in New York City's Lincoln Center for the Performing Arts, Justice Harry A. Blackmun was main speaker.

Phi Beta Kappa Bicentennial marking the 200th anniversary of the founding of the national scholastic society was celebrated in Williamsburg, Va., on Dec. 5, 1976, by scholars and delegates representing state chapters and universities.

Adam Smith Bicentennial, commemorating the birth of the Scottish economist, philosopher, and author of *The Wealth of Nations,* was held in Great Britain.

Winnie-the-Pooh. The 50th anniversary of A. A. Milne's classic for children was celebrated in England. The central event was a publisher's luncheon held in October at Cotchford Farm, Milne's former country home in Sussex.   Paul C. Tullier

CENSUS, UNITED STATES. President Gerald R. Ford signed a bill on Oct. 8, 1976, providing for mid-decade censuses beginning in 1985. These will help the Bureau of the Census maintain more accurate data on an increasingly mobile and changing society. Between 1970 and 1975, for instance, the South gained 2.6 million persons through migration and is presently attracting almost twice as many migrants as the West, long the United States growth leader in population. The South's gains contrast with the early 1950s, when the region lost 1.6 million persons through migration.

The U.S. population has been growing older, too, as the median age in 1975 rose to 28.6 years and the death rate dropped to a new low — 8.9 deaths per 1,000 persons. The 1975 death toll, 1,911,000, was lower than at any time since 1967, despite a larger and older population. The previous upward trend was reversed primarily by a continuing decline in deaths from heart diseases, cerebrovascular diseases, and accidents, particularly traffic accidents. This last reduction is attributed to the nationwide adoption of the speed limit of 55 miles (89 kilometers) per hour.

American Family Size also continued to diminish in 1975 as the birth rate declined to the lowest point in the nation's history and divorces reached a record high — 1 million in one year. A rate of 14.7 births per 1,000 persons (compared with 18.2 per 1,000 in 1970), plus the rapid increase of families headed by women (11 per cent of all white families and 35 per cent of all black families), resulted in the average family size dropping from 3.58 persons in 1970 to 3.42 in 1975.

In addition, almost 1 in every 5 U.S. households in 1975 consisted of a person living alone. Nearly 1 in 3 households had only 2 persons.

Other Census Findings:
- Two out of three adults 25 years of age or older were high school graduates in 1975 — compared with 1 out of 3 in 1950.
- Community colleges accounted for half of the increase in undergraduate enrollment during the past five years. From 1970 to 1975, two-year-college enrollments increased about 50 per cent; enrollment in other colleges increased 31 per cent.
- The recession and inflation caused the median U.S. family income to decline 3 per cent between 1974 and 1975. During that time, the total number of people below the low-income or poverty level increased 2.5 million, or 10.7 per cent.
- The Bureau of the Census estimated that more than 150 million Americans were eligible to vote in the November elections, nearly 10 million more than in 1972. The U.S. began 1976 with an estimated population of 214,435,000.   Robert L. Hagan

CENTRAL AFRICAN REPUBLIC. See AFRICA.

CEYLON. See SRI LANKA.

CHAD. See AFRICA.

CHEMICAL INDUSTRY. Concern over chemicals that are potentially dangerous to health and safety was widespread during 1976. Experts in Geneva, Switzerland, began assembling an International Register of Potentially Toxic Chemicals as part of the United Nations (UN) Environment Program. Data on the environmental hazards of a wide range of substances will be collected, stored in a computer, and made available to UN member countries. In the United States, President Gerald R. Ford signed the Toxic Substances Control Act on October 12. The new law requires companies to test before selling those substances that the Environmental Protection Agency (EPA) says pose potential hazards to the public.

Two Tragic Occurrences resulting from chemical industry operations underscored the need for concern. On July 10, an accident at the Icmesa chemical plant of Hoffman-La Roche and Company of Switzerland in Seveso, Italy, a suburb of Milan, released toxic fumes of 2,3,7,8 tetrachlorodibenzo-p-dioxin (TCDD) over Seveso. Because TCDD can cause kidney, liver, and lung damage, the townspeople were evacuated.

In the United States, District Court Judge Robert R. Merhige, Jr., of Richmond, Va., fined the Allied Chemical Corporation $13.3 million on October 5 for the discharge of Kepone, a highly toxic insecticide, into the James River from a Life Sciences Products Company plant in Hopewell, Va. Civil damages claims of nearly $200 million have been filed against Allied Chemical by commercial fishermen and by Life Sciences workers allegedly disabled by exposure to the chemical. Life Sciences stopped producing Kepone in 1975, but traces continued to show up in the James River and Chesapeake Bay. As a result, commercial fishing was banned in a portion of the river.

Commercial fishing was also banned in certain rivers in Alabama, Georgia, and South Carolina because of contamination by polychlorinated biphenyls (PCB's). Alabama and Georgia residents sued the General Electric Company in September, charging that plant operations in Rome, Ga., "either willfully, wantonly, negligently, or recklessly" discharged waste containing PCB's into streams. Monsanto Industrial Chemicals — named in the suit as the supplier of PCB's — began phasing out PCB production in January. On September 23, scientists at Colorado State University in Fort Collins presented findings that nursing American mothers had traces of PCB in their milk. Animal studies have shown that very low levels of PCB are dangerous to nursing offspring, but the scientists drew no conclusions about their findings.

Food Additives Banned. The U.S. Food and Drug Administration (FDA) on February 12 banned Red Dye No. 2 for use in foods, drugs, or cosmetics because it caused cancer in female rats.

A worker wearing a gas mask and protective clothing washes down tank
that accidentally released poisonous gases near Milan, Italy, in July.

However, both Canada and the European Community (Common Market) reaffirmed approval of Red Dye No. 2. The FDA also banned chloroform as used in medicines and toothpaste, trichloroethylene, Red Dye No. 4, and carbon black. The FDA retained its ban on cyclamate, an artificial sweetener, on May 11 despite a generally favorable report from the National Cancer Institute on March 8. See FOOD.

Aerosol Curb Urged. The U.S. National Academy of Sciences (NAS), after a 16-month study of fluorocarbons used as the propellant in aerosol spray cans, reported on September 15 that fluorocarbons pose a threat to the earth's protective stratospheric ozone layer and could lead to more cases of skin cancer. On October 15, the FDA proposed the phasing out of all nonessential uses of fluorocarbons as spray propellants. Meanwhile, manufacturers are switching to alternate spray-can propellants and devices.

Economic Recovery in the U.S. chemical industry slowed down in the second quarter. Nevertheless, output for the second quarter rose 10 per cent to $93.5 billion. Net chemical exports increased 8 per cent to $5.4 billion. Recovery overseas lagged behind that in the United States but was well underway by midyear. Drought hurt industry operations in France and Great Britain. Fertilizer and pesticide sales were hardest hit.   Edward Abrams

CHEMISTRY. Representatives of more than 100 scientific societies joined several thousand chemists in New York City in April 1976 to observe the 100th anniversary of the founding of the American Chemical Society (ACS). They saw the introduction and first-day sales of a new United States Postal Service stamp honoring chemistry, a time-capsule ceremony, and an ACS ceremonial session.

Anticancer Drugs. Two independent groups of scientists reported at the ACS meeting that they had synthesized the antitumor antibiotic adriamycin and some closely related substances. The National Cancer Institute considers adriamycin to be among the most effective anticancer drugs approved by the Food and Drug Administration for use in clinical research. Adriamycin is currently produced from a soil fungus by fermentation. But it is expensive and can cause heart failure.

Chemist Andrew S. Kende of the University of Rochester in New York used a new approach to synthesize the antitumor antibiotics daunomycin and carminomycin, two compounds related to adriamycin. David W. Henry and his co-workers at Stanford Research Institute in California synthesized adriamycin from adriamycinone and the amino sugar daunosamine. The researchers hope that the synthetic route may provide more effective, less costly, and less toxic variants of anticancer drugs than those produced from natural sources.

Laser Chemistry. Ernest M. Grunwald and his co-workers at Brandeis University in Waltham, Mass., disclosed results in the summer that buttress the view that molecules can absorb laser energy in a more efficient and selective way than thermal energy. The investigators reported that some molecules under certain conditions absorbed infrared energy from a carbon dioxide laser, and that energy remained localized in one of the molecular bonds during the time of the laser flash. Their finding was highly unexpected. Most chemists would have predicted that the vibrationally excited molecules quickly collide hundreds of times with other molecules and thus dissipate the absorbed laser energy as heat.

Grunwald, Kenneth J. Olszyna, and David F. Dever studied the laser-induced decomposition of a chlorofluorocarbon gas at high pressure. They plotted their data and calculated that if the absorbed energy were being used in a random, thermal manner, the plot would have been quite different. They could account for the experimental plot if they assumed all the absorbed energy remained in one excited bond. Theorists were hard-pressed to explain the unexpected result, which raises the possibility of using lasers to perform selective chemistry, in which specified molecular bonds can be broken at will.

Element 107? A team of Russian researchers led by Georgii N. Flerov at the Joint Institutes for Nuclear Research in Dubna, near Moscow, claimed to have made element 107, an element with 107 protons and 154 neutrons in its nucleus. The scientists bombarded a target of bismuth with a beam of energetic chromium nuclei. They first found evidence for a new nucleus that spontaneously broke apart into smaller nuclei in about five seconds. However, theoretical calculations predicted that element 107 would have a much shorter lifetime, about one millisecond.

Flerov's group adjusted their detectors and found a second nucleus that broke up spontaneously in about two milliseconds. They claimed that the short-lived nucleus is element 107, while the long-lived nucleus is element 105, which is made when element 107 breaks up. United States scientists who specialize in making heavy elements believe that detection of spontaneous break-up alone is insufficient proof for a new element.

Priestley Medal. Organic chemist Henry Gilman, 83, a research professor at Iowa State University at Ames, was named the 1977 recipient of the ACS's Priestley Medal "for distinguished services to chemistry." Gilman won the gold medal — considered the highest honor in U.S. chemistry — for his work in organometallic chemistry. William N. Lipscomb, Jr., of Harvard University in Cambridge, Mass., won the 1976 Nobel Prize in Chemistry (see NOBEL PRIZES).   Alfred W. von Smolinski

CHESS. The top six finishers from two 1976 interzonal chess tournaments qualified to compete for the right to challenge reigning world champion Anatoly Karpov of Russia in 1978. Karpov became world champion on April 3, 1975, by default over Bobby Fischer of the United States.

Henrique Mecking of Brazil won the interzonal tournament that ended on July 12, 1976, in Manila, the Philippines, with 13 points. Two other qualifiers, Vlastimil Hort of Czechoslovakia and Lev Polucaevsky of Russia, tied for second with 12½ points each.

Bent Larsen of Denmark, with 12½ points, won the interzonal tournament that ended on August 2 in Biel, Switzerland. Tigran Petrosian and Mikhail Tal, both of the Soviet Union, and Lajos Portisch of Hungary tied for second with 12 points. Petrosian and Portisch won a play-off to qualify for the candidates' contest. In addition, Fischer and Viktor Korchnoi, a Russian grandmaster, were automatically eligible. But Fischer failed to submit his entry by the Jan. 1, 1977, deadline.

Korchnoi Defects. Korchnoi, world's number two ranked player, defected from Russia on July 27. After playing in a tournament in Amsterdam, the Netherlands, he asked for political asylum there. Korchnoi has been a leader in Russian chess for about 25 years, winning three national champion-

Russian grandmaster Viktor Korchnoi plays in a chess tournament in the Netherlands before asking for political asylum in July.

ships. The Dutch Ministry of Justice announced on September 28 that Korchnoi could settle in the Netherlands for an indefinite period, but that he did not qualify for political asylum.

Korchnoi told a Dutch newspaper he had planned to seek asylum since 1974. He said he had many reasons, "the most important being the situation in the Soviet chess organization." The Soviet Chess Federation censured Korchnoi in 1974 for making derogatory remarks about Karpov.

The Russian government officially requested in September that Korchnoi be barred from the next world championship series. However, Max Euwe, president of the International Chess Federation, said Korchnoi could not be prevented from playing, because he was a candidate in his own right.

Other Champions. Anatoly Lein and Leonid Shamkovich of Russia tied for first place in the U.S. Open Chess Championship in August in Fairfax, Va. Diane Savereide of Culver City, Calif., retained her United States Women's Chess Championship in Teton Village, Wyo., in July.

For the third straight year, the International Association of Chess Writers in January awarded their World Chess Oscar to Karpov. On August 8, Euwe revealed that Karpov had pledged to renounce his title if he lost to Fischer in a proposed $5-million exhibition match.　　　Theodore M. O'Leary

CHICAGO. Mayor Richard J. Daley, 74, often called the last of the big-city bosses, died on Dec. 20, 1976, after 21 years in office. He suffered a heart attack in his doctor's office. Alderman Michael Bilandic was named acting mayor by the City Council, to serve until a special election in 1977.

A federal judge issued an injunction on Jan. 5, 1976, withholding revenue-sharing funds until the city ended racial and sexual bias in police-department hiring and promotion practices. In 1974, U.S. District Court Judge Prentice H. Marshall had issued a temporary injunction in the case, which involved procedures used in testing police applicants.

Mayor Daley yielded on June 25 and agreed to hire police officers under a system that set goals for employing 42 per cent white males, 42 per cent minority-group males, and 16 per cent females. Marshall then allowed the city to collect $19 million in revenue-sharing funds due on July 1 and October 1, but he continued to withhold $114 million to ensure compliance with his orders.

On September 7, the judge accepted a police plan to hire applicants from a roster of 1,091 persons who had previously taken the department test. However, in December he again threatened to cut off funds because the city did not pick enough minorities from the roster.

In his last public appearance, hours before his death on December 20, Mayor Daley, right, attends the dedication of a park district gymnasium.

City Employees. Mayor Daley, on May 4, ordered all city employees living in the suburbs to establish residency in the city by August 1 or face the loss of their jobs. Hundreds of employees reportedly moved back to the city.

The Supreme Court of the United States ruled on June 28 that public employees not occupying policymaking or confidential advisory jobs could not be fired because of their political beliefs. Employees of the Cook County sheriff's office brought the suit after being fired for refusing to pledge loyalty to the county's Democratic Party organization.

Public Housing. The U.S. Supreme Court ruled on April 20 that federal courts can order the construction of low-income housing in Chicago's suburbs to make up for past segregated housing practices within the city. See HOUSING.

The U.S. Department of Housing and Urban Development on June 7 announced a one-year trial program to place 400 minority-group families in need of public housing in rent-subsidized apartments throughout the metropolitan area. Most of these apartments must be located in white suburbs.

The Chicago Housing Authority announced on February 24 that it would start a federally funded rent-subsidy program for low- and moderate-income people. At least 60 per cent of the apartments in the program would be located in predominantly white neighborhoods.   James M. Banovetz

CHILD WELFARE. A Children's Act enacted in Great Britain in 1976 gave any adopted person over 18 years of age a right to find out who his natural parents are. A movement for similar legislation is growing in the United States.

In the United States, a report from the Children's Bureau of the Department of Health, Education, and Welfare (HEW) encouraged subsidies for adoptions. The report estimated that 100,000 handicapped, minority, and older children remain in institutions because of a lack of adoptive homes.

Bleak New York Picture. A study of child welfare in New York City suggested that even though the deplorable conditions in the city were increased by the city's financial crisis, they also have far deeper roots. The study presented a bleak picture of the education, health services, child welfare services, and judicial remedies offered to New York City children. It reported that 460,000 children in the city lived in poverty. Of these, 60 per cent lived in families headed by women, nearly half were black, and one-third were Puerto Rican. Black children were twice as likely as white children to be living in poverty. The number of children under foster care had increased 55 per cent since 1960, compared with decreases in other communities.

Foster Care. A New York study of children under foster care published in March reported that 36 per cent of the 624 children studied remained in foster care for at least five years. Because foster care is considered a temporary measure until a child can be returned to his own home or given in permanent adoption, this is a disturbing figure.

"There is growing public concern about children who seem fated to spend all their childhood in . . . foster care," the report concludes. "The failure of agencies to move vigorously toward termination of parental rights . . . is being viewed as unacceptable."

The U.S. District Court in New York City ruled in March that children in foster care for a year or more must have a court hearing before being transferred to another foster home, returned to their natural parents, or put up for adoption. The court said children have a constitutional right to have their views heard before they are moved.

Child Abuse. Public concern over child abuse was fueled in 1976. An article in the March-April issue of *Children Today* gave an international perspective by reporting on home violence in Canada and Great Britain. A National Conference on Child Abuse and Neglect in January tied the problem to a society that condones violence. Senator Walter F. Mondale (D., Minn.), chairman of the Senate Subcommittee on Children and Youth, asserted that the fundamental solution lay in developing and maintaining healthy families. Other speakers outlined specific protective, preventive, and remedial measures and new programs.

In February, the federal government proposed new regulations to make it easier to combat child abuse and neglect by pinpointing responsibility for child care. The HEW proposal would require the states to investigate reports of suspected child abuse and neglect under programs for child welfare and aid to families with dependent children.

Day Care. Preliminary reports on the federal government's three-year study of the effectiveness of day-care programs began appearing. Previous studies reported disappointing results from day-care programs. The first volume of the new study, which was descriptive, not evaluative, concentrated on the effect of such factors as staff-child ratio, staff education and training, and group size on children's progress. It also reported the cost per child for various programs.

President Gerald R. Ford on April 6 vetoed a day-care bill that would have provided funds for federally supported centers to meet new federal staffing requirements and state health and safety codes. Without the funds, many centers might have been forced to close. But the President reversed himself on September 7 when he signed a similar day-care bill that provided funds but delayed enforcement of the federal staffing standards until Oct. 1, 1977.   Frances A. Mullen

CHILDREN'S BOOKS. See LITERATURE FOR CHILDREN.

CHILE. Charges of human-rights violations by the Chilean secret police, the National Intelligence Directorate (DINA), continued to be leveled against Chile's military government in 1976. The United Nations Commission on Human Rights on February 19 condemned "institutionalized torture," and the Organization of American States urged, during its General Assembly meeting in Santiago, Chile, in June, that reforms be carried out. On June 25, the United States Congress limited economic assistance aid to Chile to $27.5 million for fiscal 1977.

To soothe critics, President Augusto Pinochet Ugarte – head of the military government – allowed a number of political prisoners to go into exile, and on January 28, he signed a decree guaranteeing certain rights to arrested persons. These included the right to be charged within 48 hours of arrest and an examination by a doctor for evidence of maltreatment.

Criticism against the government from abroad, which had begun to abate somewhat, flared anew on September 21, when Orlando Letelier, a former Chilean ambassador to the United States and a left wing critic of the junta, was killed in his car by a bomb explosion in Washington, D.C. United States congressional opponents of the junta as well as Chilean emigré organizations blamed DINA for the murder.

During the year, Pinochet appeared to consolidate his power within Chile by firing almost all the armed forces officers who had been active in the fight against the Marxist government of deposed President Salvador Allende Gossens. The most prominent man replaced was General Sergio Arellano Stark, chief of the armed forces general staff, who was sent into retirement. The lack of reaction within the army to the removal of one of its most popular leaders was seen as an indication that Pinochet had no opponents to his one-man rule. Military sources said DINA agents throughout the armed forces are a key to his control.

The Economy. Leftists abroad and former Christian Democrat President Eduardo Frei Montalva at home criticized the harsh austerity measures taken to try to end Chile's economic crisis. Mismanagement by Allende started the problems, and a drop in copper prices in 1974 made them worse. However, there were hopeful signs that the strict measures were beginning to pay off as copper prices revived in 1976. The government projected a balance-of-payments surplus even after paying off some $800-million on Chile's $4-billion foreign debt. Unemployment eased slightly, though it was still around 16 per cent in Santiago, and industrial production picked up slowly. More than $300 million in foreign investments have been committed to Chile, a sign that the business community approves of the economic discipline.   Everett G. Martin

See also LATIN AMERICA (Facts in Brief Table).

Raul Cardinal Silva Henriquez, left, meets with President Pinochet in an effort to reduce tensions between the Catholic Church and Chile's government.

CHINA, PEOPLE'S REPUBLIC OF. A meteorite fell in northeast China in March 1976. Northern China was later hit by a drought. In the south, there were earthquakes. By late May, Communist Party journals in Peking were anxiously exhorting the public not to believe, as people did in ancient days, that natural disasters meant the rulers were losing "the mandate of Heaven" and that "the land will be divided."

But Peking's pleas fell on unhearing ears; public uneasiness grew as the disasters multiplied. The worst of the calamities was an earthquake that devastated the industrial city of Tangshan, between Peking and the sea. The first tremor, at 3:45 A.M. on July 28, was measured at 8.2 on the Richter scale, making it the strongest in the world in a dozen years. The industrial city of Tientsin and Peking were also badly shaken by the quake.

The death toll in Tangshan reportedly was estimated by Chinese officials to be more than 655,000. The famous Kailan coal mines were heavily damaged, but Peking said most of the underground workers escaped. Heavy damage was also done to Tangshan's cement and power plants. China declined foreign aid, and sent in tens of thousands of medical aides, troops, and builders, as well as hundreds of trainloads of food, drugs, tents, and reconstruction supplies. On government orders, millions of Peking residents camped outdoors for weeks.

The Disasters heightened the anxiety produced by the deaths of some of the old revolutionaries who had ruled the land since the Communist take-over in 1949. One of these was Chu Teh, the general who commanded the Communist armies in the civil war. But no loss was as heavy as that of Premier Chou En-lai, who died on January 8, and Communist Party Chairman Mao Tse-tung, who died on September 9. See Close-Up.

Their deaths brought to a climax the struggle for succession that had been an underlying feature of Chinese politics for 10 years. Chou learned in 1972 that he had cancer. He then began to arrange for the transfer of his powers to a man who would share his belief in the need for a tranquil and orderly society and for economic development unhindered by politics. He chose Teng Hsiao-ping, another old revolutionary, a tough little man purged in 1967 as a leading "capitalist roader" but rehabilitated after the Cultural Revolution. By 1975, when Chou had to undergo yet more surgery, Teng had taken over the running of the nation.

The "Radicals." But, from the outset, Chou and Teng ran into fierce opposition from the so-called "radical" faction of four led by Mao's wife, Chiang Ching. Her allies, all leaders of the Shanghai Communist Party machine, were Wang Hung-wen, a textile worker who soared to eminence during the Cultural Revolution and was then chosen Mao's heir-designate; Chang Chun-chiao, a former journalist expected to succeed Chou as premier; and Chang's former aide in the Shanghai propaganda mill, Yao Wen-yuan. Yao's rise to the top began in 1965 when an attack he made on a Peking playwright — at Mao's urging — turned out to be the opening shot of the Cultural Revolution.

This band of four saw a threat to their own prospects in Teng Hsiao-ping's re-emergence. They were well placed for the struggle, forming a solid bloc in the top party leadership of eight or nine. They controlled the news media. Above all, they increasingly controlled access to the ailing Mao Tse-tung. The years from 1973 to 1976 saw a succession of propaganda campaigns that were often obscure but invariably aimed at the Chou-Teng leadership. These were apparently staged by the four radicals.

Teng was allowed to read the eulogy at a service for Chou on January 15. After that he vanished and in February, an obscure Hunanese politician, Hua Kuo-feng, was named acting premier. Peking sources said that he had been a compromise candidate picked when the two main factions became deadlocked. See HUA KUO-FENG.

Riot in Peking. On April 5, a festival day for honoring the dead, thousands of people assembled

Government and Communist Party leaders of China gather in Peking to pay their last respects to Chairman Mao Tse-tung, who died on September 9.

China's Mao-Chou Legacy

Mao Tse-tung and Chou En-lai, the two men who radically changed the face of modern China, died in 1976 – Chou in January and Mao in September. They had long worked closely together and, though their personalities and backgrounds were quite different, they complemented each other in their styles of leadership. In fact, Western observers had assumed that should Mao die first, Chou would naturally take his place as leader.

Chairman Mao Tse-tung was hailed in his lifetime as the greatest Chinese who ever lived, and his followers called him the Great Helmsman, the man whose Thoughts could solve all problems. Mao more modestly asked that he be remembered mainly as a teacher. As a teacher, he had sought to change the nation's values, which stemmed from the 2,000-year-old tradition of Confucius. Mao attacked the most revered Confucian values and insisted that the Chinese people should cast aside their search for harmony and welcome struggle, contradiction, and disorder.

Mao sought above all to restore China to a position of greatness in the world, and he believed that this could be accomplished only if revolutionary commitment replaced traditional practices. He recognized that China was poor and lacked machinery and technology, but he believed in the superiority of the human spirit. He was convinced that China could be modernized by transforming the Chinese people into "new men" who would possess a spirit of selfless dedication to the nation.

Mao was particularly concerned with the need to inspire the youth of China with his vision of revolutionary struggle and sacrifice. He distrusted government bureaucracy and worried that those who held high office would become self-satisfied and interested only in their personal well-being. Mao wanted more equality, and he was not sure that superior merit or ability should be rewarded. He valued peasant life and was against many aspects of academic training. At his direction, millions of Chinese students went to live and work in the country, and China's universities focused on political indoctrination rather than educational excellence.

Mao gave China a new ideology. In a sense, it is a new religious faith that negates some Confucian values but also preserves some core Confucian concepts, such as the need for correct thoughts, self-improvement, and group loyalty rather than any kind of individualism.

Only time will tell how deeply the Chinese have accepted Maoism as the purest expression of their highest ideals. In practical matters, compromises have already been made, and the new leaders, in rejecting extreme forms of Maoism, have stressed many of the qualities that made Chou En-lai great.

Throughout much of his public life, Chou En-lai provided a pragmatic, realistic balance to Mao's visionary spirit. Chou accepted Mao's ambitions to modernize China and make it a revolutionary influence in the world, but he focused his energies on practical issues such as economic development, rather than ideology. Chou recognized China's need for more science and technology, and therefore he worked to improve relations with industrialized countries in order to expand trade.

Mao Tse-tung and Chou En-lai unified China and mobilized the great masses of the Chinese people to modernize their country. Their accomplishments already rank among the extraordinary political achievements of recent times.

Mao will be remembered as the symbol of China's re-emergence as a world power. His greatest contributions were in spreading his version of Communism. His successors will undoubtedly continue to pay lip service to the Thoughts of Mao Tse-tung, but in time his influence is likely to decline in the practical, day-to-day management of affairs in China. Chou En-lai is less likely to be publicly revered by succeeding generations. But, if China is to realize its potential for world influence and to solve its most acute economic problems, it will have to adhere closely to the policies he initiated.

Mao Tse-tung (1893–1976)

Chou En-lai (1898–1976)

As a great charismatic leader, Mao Tse-tung's appeal reached far beyond the borders of China; he was both revered and hated throughout the world. To some, he was only a ruthless leader who had conducted a revolution that killed an estimated 2-million people. To others, he was a humanitarian and one of the most skillful political organizers in history. In recent years, many world leaders sought the honor of visiting Chairman Mao. They were impressed that a man born during the last Chinese imperial dynasty, who came from a rural village in central China, could have risen to command peasant armies and eventually gain control of all of China.

Mao never traveled abroad until after he came to rule China, and then he visited only Russia. Yet he was interested in world history and in current developments everywhere. He never lost his roots in the peasant culture of China, but at the same time he was a lonely man who did not have many close friends. Mao was rather introspective and he once characterized himself as being part "tiger" and part "monkey," that is, partly a firm, fierce, aggressive person and partly an impish, mercurial person.

Born at a time when China was torn by civil strife, overcome with terrible poverty, and used by more advanced foreign powers, he lived to fulfill his boyhood dream of restoring China to its traditional place as a great nation. In later years, he liked to compare himself with Shih Huang Ti, China's first emperor, who unified the nation in 221 B.C.

Despite the awesome power and prestige that Mao had in the later years of his life — from about 1960 onward — he was obsessed by an anxiety that the Chinese revolution he led might be in danger of slipping backward and into the kind of elitism and bureaucratic methods that were notorious in the days of imperial China. He rated this danger all the greater because it seemed to him that this process was taking place in modern Russia under what he termed "revisionism." In Mao's view, Nikita S. Khrushchev's emphasis on materi-al incentives to increase consumer-oriented production and the clear emergence in Russia of a privileged Communist Party were anathema.

To ensure that the revolution survived him and to cleanse the party and revitalize China, Mao launched the Great Proletarian Cultural Revolution in 1966. He conceded later that this Cultural Revolution had consequences he did not foresee.

Hundreds of thousands of Chinese youth were mobilized as Red Guards during this period. They were often unruly, were given to fighting among themselves, and roamed the country humiliating and chastising Mao's opponents in the party, after his call to "bombard the headquarters." At the end of two years of turmoil, economic disruption, and sometimes even bloodshed, order was restored by the army and some of the surviving party leaders, such as Premier Chou En-lai.

Chou, in contrast to Mao, came from a rich family, had a better education, and had lived abroad in Japan and France for nearly 10 years. Chou was a more modest man who was sensitive to the opinions of others. He had the qualities admired in Chinese mandarins — dignity, wisdom, and good judgment.

Like most of the other government leaders, Chou came under attack by the Red Guards during the Cultural Revolution, but he survived as premier mainly, it is said, because of the protection of Mao. After the turmoil ended and China began to expand its contacts with the rest of the world, Chou held a series of historic meetings with U.S. President Richard M. Nixon. They signed the joint Shanghai Communiqué in 1972 that re-established diplomatic contact between the two countries.

China will miss both Mao and Chou. Because they did not succeed in arranging a smooth transition to the rule of their successors, it is likely that China will experience considerable tension and uncertainty until the new leadership becomes established. During this time of uncertainty, many Chinese will appreciate more than ever what Mao Tse-tung and Chou En-lai did for China.   Lucian W. Pye

CHINA, PEOPLE'S REPUBLIC OF

The people of Peking turned to drain pipes and other makeshift shelters after disastrous earthquakes that rocked China in July.

in Peking's Tien An Men square to pay tribute to Chou's memory. Many bore flowers that they piled high at the Monument to the People's Heroes. But soon student speakers were reciting poems hailing Chou and Teng Hsiao-ping and ridiculing Chiang Ching. Some speakers cried that "the reign of the first emperor" — to whom Mao liked to be compared — had come to an end. Bloody skirmishes began as the crowd beat militiamen, tried to storm the Great Hall of the People, China's capitol, and set fire to an army barracks nearby. By midday, 100,000 persons milled about the vast square, and many hundreds were injured in clashes. (The government later charged that "a few of the bad elements sported crew cuts.") Thousands of troops and militia finally marched into the square at 9:30 P.M. and began a mass roundup.

The explosion of public fury sent shock waves through the party leadership. At a session that night, Teng Hsiao-ping was blamed for the riot and shorn of all party and state posts. On April 7, Hua Kuo-feng was named premier and, more important, was also named first deputy chairman of the Communist Party.

The Showdown. Government documents indicate that the struggle continued until October 4. Official evidence later suggested the "radicals" used a doctored quotation by Mao to strengthen their claim to power.

The two factions had their final clash on October 6 on the question of who was to succeed Mao Tse-tung as chairman of the Communist Party. It was resolved forcefully; the army unit that served as Mao's bodyguard arrested the four "radicals." At about the same time, Hua was chosen chairman of the party in Mao's stead. The victors met on October 7 and 8 and decided to set up a committee, under Hua, to edit the fifth volume of Mao's works and to build at once a mausoleum in Peking's Tien An Men square to hold Mao's embalmed remains.

The move to arrest Mao's widow was politically risky. But a greater danger to the new regime was presented by her three allies, who headed Shanghai's powerful party organization and its militia of 1 million members. Posters published later suggested that the followers of the Shanghai bosses plotted an insurrection there. But the Shanghai leaders were quickly displaced, with the army playing a decisive role. Within three weeks, after mammoth demonstrations, the workers, students, and militia vowed their undying loyalty to Hua.

At the same time, a campaign of denunciation against "the gang of four" was launched across the land. The quartet was accused of running a parallel government in the provinces, subverting agreed-upon decisions, sabotaging production with calls for more revolution, and converting the Cultural Revolution into a "bloody civil war."

258

Back to Normality. Mao's successor, Hua Kuo-feng, and his allies displayed political skill both in crushing the opposition and in shedding some of Mao's main revolutionary precepts. At mass rallies from mid-November on, the workers were told that China would now acquire foreign technology, expand foreign aid, restore managerial controls, and enforce labor discipline. The "gang of four" was accused of having sabotaged efforts to modernize industry.

The new rulers did not seek accommodation with Russia, as Moscow hoped they would; instead, they intensified the attacks on Soviet "social imperialism." Typical was Chiao Kuan-hua's description of Russia at the United Nations Assembly meeting on October 5 as "the biggest peace swindler and the most dangerous source of war today." By contrast, Peking's attitude toward the United States was almost temperate. The Chinese still denounced American imperialism and its "collusion" with Russia. But in September, they gave red-carpet treatment to former Defense Secretary James R. Schlesinger, whom they regard as a hard-liner in relations with Russia.

Economic Slowdown. As a result of the Tangshan earthquake and the acute political feuding that spread through the provinces, economic growth in 1976 dropped below 7 per cent, down 4 per cent. After their fall, Chiang Ching and her allies were blamed for many prolonged industrial work stoppages—some lasting as long as eight months—and for holding down purchases of Western technology. Vital coal production rose by less than 5 per cent, compared with an 11 per cent growth rate in 1975. This in turn served to curtail steel output.

The year also saw a drop in China's oil sales to Japan, down 8 million barrels to 48 million barrels. And trade with the United States declined from a high of $934 million in 1974 to about $420 million in 1976. But this drop was overshadowed by Washington's decision in October to sell two Cyber-172 computers to China. The computers could be put to military use, but the U.S. National Security Council felt it could overlook that possibility for the sake of political gains.

The political turmoil—and the debate on priorities—led to postponement of the Sixth Five-Year Plan that was to start on Jan. 1, 1976. The new rulers were expected to reintroduce the plan, originated by Premier Chou En-lai as part of his modernization program. The brightest spot in the economic picture was what Peking claimed was a record rice and wheat crop.   Mark Gayn

See also ASIA (Facts in Brief Table).
CHRONOLOGY. See pages 8 through 16.
CHURCHES. See EASTERN ORTHODOX CHURCHES; JEWS AND JUDAISM; PROTESTANTISM; RELIGION; ROMAN CATHOLIC CHURCH.

CITY. A Gallup Poll survey released on Nov. 21, 1976, indicated that most people living in the developing nations of the world would prefer to live in cities, while most citizens of industrialized nations would rather live in rural areas. According to the 70-nation study, 75 per cent of Nigeria's residents would prefer city living, but only 5 per cent are residents of urban areas. On the other hand, 80 per cent of Great Britain's population is in cities, but only 20 per cent live there by choice.

Tokyo was named the world's most expensive city in two separate surveys issued during the year. A study released by Business International on July 27 said that, after Tokyo, the world's most expensive cities were Osaka, Japan; Stockholm, Sweden; Zurich and Geneva, Switzerland; Oslo, Norway; Copenhagen, Denmark; Lagos, Nigeria; Paris; Vienna, Austria; Toronto, Canada; Jakarta, Indonesia; Düsseldorf, West Germany; and New York City. A study of 41 cities released by the Union Bank of Switzerland on October 27 indicated that Tokyo was the most expensive and Bogotá, Colombia, the cheapest city in which to live.

To and from Cities. Rural dwellers in developing countries continued to migrate to cities in 1976. A reverse migration seemed to be starting in industrialized countries. In the United States, for example, the Bureau of the Census reported in February that small towns were growing faster than urban and suburban areas. Nonmetropolitan areas had grown 5.5 per cent since 1970, while cities and suburbs increased only 3.4 per cent.

Researchers from the Brookings Institution told the U.S. Congress on October 1 that only about 20 per cent of U.S. cities provide residents with better education, jobs, housing, and employment opportunities than do their suburbs. The researchers saw the urban crisis as a regional problem afflicting the older cities in the Northeast and Middle West, rather than solely a big-city problem.

Revenue Sharing. A delegation of U.S. mayors went to Washington, D.C., in March to seek an extension of the federal revenue-sharing program, scheduled to terminate on December 31. Meeting under the joint auspices of the National League of Cities and the U.S. Conference of Mayors, they argued that city governments were being held hostage in election-year politics by Congress and President Gerald R. Ford. Ford aligned himself with the mayors, calling for early passage of legislation to extend the revenue-sharing program.

However, Congress delayed passage of the extension until September 30; Ford signed the measure into law on October 13. It authorized $25.6 billion in aid to state and local governments between Jan. 1, 1977, and Sept. 30, 1980.

The U.S. Conference of Mayors presented an economic report on U.S. cities during its annual conference in Milwaukee in June. The study

Kenneth Gibson, right, of Newark, N.J., is first
black president of the U.S. Conference of Mayors,
succeeding Moon Landrieu of New Orleans, left.

warned that 84 per cent of the nation's cities are in
serious financial straits. Without federal aid, they
face "massive personnel layoffs and/or cuts in essential municipal services."

The mayors met again in a two-day session in
Chicago following the November 2 election of
Democrat James Earl (Jimmy) Carter, Jr., as President. They called for a new national urban policy
and immediate help for the cities. Mayor Kenneth
A. Gibson of Newark, president of the U.S. Conference of Mayors, asked Carter to push for immediate
legislation to create jobs, consolidate the nearly
1,800 federal-assistance programs for cities, and
give the mayors a larger role in formulating federal
urban policies.

The 1976 Democratic Party platform had
claimed to offer "America's first national urban
policy." It called for continued general revenue
sharing, a massive financial effort to help older cities, antirecession grants for cities where unemployment is greatest, and more aid for rehabilitating
housing. President-elect Carter said he favored
removing states from the revenue-sharing program
and slating all the money for cities and counties.

Other Federal Aid. Congress finally passed a
public-works jobs bill over the veto of President
Ford on July 22. The $3.95-billion measure allotted
$2 billion for public-works projects that could be
started within 90 days; $1.25 billion to help states

and cities with high unemployment maintain essential community services; and $700 million for
water-pollution control. Ford had opposed the bill
on the grounds that it was inflationary and had
successfully vetoed a $6-billion version in February.

President Ford also vetoed on September 29 the
appropriation bill for the departments of Labor and
Health, Education, and Welfare. Congress overrode his veto on September 30, thereby providing
$56.6 billion in fiscal 1977 for school aid, community health centers, job training, and other social programs.

Urban Transit. The U.S. Department of Transportation announced on June 10 that it was giving
Buffalo, N.Y., a $269-million grant to build the first
light-rail transportation system in the United
States. Light rail is a modern version of the old
trolley-car system. The new Buffalo line will have a
roadway separate from car and truck traffic lanes.
See TRANSIT.

A crime wave struck the Metro, Paris' subway
system, highlighted by the first subway hijacking in
Paris history on July 2. The Paris police chief detailed four-man teams to begin patrolling subway
stations in October. On March 18, Scotland Yard
ordered armed protection for London's subway riders after a bomb was discovered on a subway train
in February. It was the first time in the 113-year
history of London's subway system that armed police rode as guards aboard trains.

Moscow's subway system moved a record 250-million passengers during the first six weeks of 1976.
The city's newly expanded system increased daily
passenger capacity to 5.5 million persons.

The first segment of Washington, D.C.'s planned
100-mile (161-kilometer) rapid-transit system
opened in March. See WASHINGTON, D.C.

City Workers. The Supreme Court of the United
States declared on June 24 that the 1974 amendment applying the federal minimum wage and
maximum hours regulations to employees of state
and local governments was unconstitutional. The
decision was hailed by city officials as a landmark
restriction on the authority of Congress to regulate
the policies and programs of state and local governments. However, Jerry Wurf, president of the
American Federation of State, County, and Municipal Employees, claimed that the decision meant
that "public workers are inferior, undeserving, and
to be discriminated against."

In other actions affecting city employees, the Supreme Court ruled that public employees could not
seek redress through the federal courts for personnel
decisions; that they could be forced to retire upon
reaching a set age; that school boards could fire
striking teachers; and that tests used to screen applicants for police positions could not be considered
discriminatory simply because black applicants experienced a higher failure rate.

A Rome sports arena is packed with 5,000 persons taking a test for 300 city jobs. They were among 30,000 who applied for the $220-per-month positions.

The U.S. Bureau of the Census reported on August 8 that U.S. city governments grew less rapidly in 1975 than in any of the previous 13 years. Nevertheless, city payrolls increased by 15,000 employees, bringing the total to 2.5 million.

The Census Bureau reported on March 9 that a record 51 per cent, or 4.7 million, of the nation's state and municipal public employees belonged to labor unions in 1975. Firemen were the most organized public workers, with 74 per cent belonging to unions. They were followed by teachers, with 72 per cent organized.

Strikes and slowdowns by public employees affected public services in many major U.S. cities during the year. See LOS ANGELES-LONG BEACH; NEW YORK CITY; NEWARK; PITTSBURGH; SAN FRANCISCO-OAKLAND.

Racial Issues. New school-busing programs were instituted in Dallas; Dayton, Ohio; and Detroit for the 1976 fall term. Louisville, Ky., began its second year of busing. No antibusing violence was reported in any of these cities. Boston schools also opened in an atmosphere of relative calm. See BOSTON; DALLAS; DETROIT.

Federal courts during the year ordered school officials in Cleveland, Denver, Milwaukee, and Omaha, Nebr., to prepare plans for busing of pupils to achieve racial balance. See CLEVELAND.

The number of black elected officials in the United States continued to increase. A survey by the Joint Center for Political Studies reported that there were 3,979 blacks in elective office as of June 30, 14 per cent more than in 1975. The largest increase was in Washington, D.C., where 184 blacks were elected to membership on neighborhood advisory commissions.

Local Laws and Regulations. The Russian Black Sea resort city of Sochi proclaimed itself the world's first "no-smoking city." It banned cigarettes from beaches, restaurants, schools, hospitals, and government offices and also from all public and private transportation.

The U.S. Supreme Court on June 24 upheld a Detroit ordinance regulating the location of so-called adult movie theaters. The ordinance was designed to forestall the development of inner-city skid rows. The decision spurred other localities, such as Indianapolis and Fairfax County, Virginia, to enact similar ordinances.

The Supreme Court also ruled on June 21 that voters can limit rapid growth in their communities by vetoing, through a referendum, zoning-law changes already approved by elected officials. The case arose in Eastlake, Ohio, where voters rejected a proposed zoning change that would have allowed construction of an apartment house. The local planning board and city council had approved the measure earlier. James M. Banovetz

CIVIL RIGHTS. In 1976, as in other years, the status of civil rights throughout the world presented a mixed picture. Spain, during the first full year of the restored monarchy, was racked by street demonstrations and disorders through much of 1976. The professed aim of King Juan Carlos I was to restore democratic liberties, and liberty made some gains. Spaniards voted overwhelmingly on December 15 to adopt a democratic form of government.

In neighboring Portugal, where a Russian-sponsored Communist Party appeared to be taking over in 1975, democratic liberties remained miraculously alive. Portugal elected a National Assembly on April 25 in the first free parliamentary election in 50 years and then elected a president on June 27 and held municipal elections on December 12.

In Africa, attention centered on Rhodesia and South Africa, where tensions between ruling white minorities and the black majorities they dominated evoked fears of civil war. United States Secretary of State Henry A. Kissinger negotiated fervently for the establishment of black-majority rule with safeguards for whites and other conditions, as an alternative to bloodshed.

Elsewhere in Africa, Malawi inflicted pogrom-style persecutions on thousands of its citizens who are members of the Jehovah's Witnesses religious sect. Despite tight government secrecy, reports leaked out about widespread torture and murder of Jehovah's Witnesses, whose beliefs bar them from saluting a flag and taking oaths of allegiance.

Democracy dwindled further in India. The Indian Supreme Court ruled in May that the right of habeas corpus, which guarantees a prompt hearing to anyone who is arrested, was suspended when Prime Minister Indira Gandhi imposed her one-woman rule in 1975.

U.S. School Desegregation. Thousands of adults and children, both white and black, marched in Boston on April 23 in a "Procession Against Violence," seeking to calm the city's racial tensions. Mayor Kevin H. White initiated the march after two of the worst weeks of violence since court-imposed school busing began in 1974.

Tensions and violence diminished after the march, though they did not disappear. When Boston's schools opened in September, the atmosphere was sufficiently relaxed to avoid the massive presence of police, helicopters, and rooftop riflemen that marked the city's 1975 school opening. Similar calm prevailed in other cities where large numbers of students were bused, including Louisville, Ky.; Omaha, Nebr.; and Dayton, Ohio.

President Gerald R. Ford remained critical of court-imposed school busing. He proposed legislation to restrict the power of courts to order busing as a means of desegregating schools. In May, the President asked Attorney General Edward H. Levi to "look for an appropriate and proper case" by

which to request the Supreme Court of the United States to "re-examine" the use of busing to integrate schools. But Levi counseled against this step. Levi was impressed by the contention of civil rights leaders and Assistant Attorney General J. Stanley Pottinger of the Civil Rights Division that intervention would encourage those who used violence against busing to believe that resistance could be rewarding.

In June, the Supreme Court let stand a lower court's decision declining to order further desegregation of Chattanooga, Tenn., high schools that were nearly all black. The high court also determined that lower courts cannot require school officials to adjust attendance zones each year to reflect population shifts. In a major ruling favorable to school desegregation, it held on June 25 that private nonsectarian schools may not exclude black children because of their race. The court thus extended the doctrine of the historic 1954 *Brown v. Board of Education of Topeka* ruling, which prohibited segregation in public schools.

In Other Rulings, the Supreme Court determined in April that federal agencies found guilty of contributing to housing discrimination within a city can be ordered to provide integrated housing in surrounding suburban areas. In June, the court held that portions of the 1964 Civil Rights Act and

Atlanta Mayor Maynard Jackson passes the hat to collect money for an appeal bond after a $1.25-million judgment against the NAACP.

other laws protect whites as well as blacks against racial discrimination.

The presidential election year found black political leaders uncertain and frustrated concerning the importance of their race as a political force. Some blacks felt that the Republicans more or less ignored them. There were fewer black delegates to both national conventions than in 1972, and civil rights and other issues of concern to blacks were soft-pedaled in both national campaigns. Despite the economy's improvement, black unemployment stayed at the same high level as it had in 1975, almost 13 per cent.

Judgment Straps NAACP. One of the most prestigious civil rights organizations, the National Association for the Advancement of Colored People (NAACP), was beset by financial troubles in 1976. It was forced to launch a major fund-raising drive after a Mississippi court on August 9 awarded 12 white merchants in Port Gibson, Miss., $1.25 million because of an NAACP boycott in 1966. In addition to the $1.25-million judgment, the NAACP needed to post a $1.6-million bond in order to appeal the court verdict.

Illegal Surveillance. Revelations of widespread violations of civil liberties by federal agencies persisted in 1976. The U.S. Department of Justice conducted a nationwide investigation of illegal burglaries by Federal Bureau of Investigation (FBI) agents since 1971 against leftist organizations and individuals, an inquiry that could ultimately involve hundreds of FBI agents and officials. A report released on May 9 by the Senate Select Committee on Intelligence disclosed that the FBI used wiretaps and bugging devices to gather information concerning contacts between members of Congress and foreign officials for Presidents Lyndon B. Johnson and Richard M. Nixon.

According to the Senate Intelligence Committee, the Central Intelligence Agency (CIA) was pressed by Presidents Johnson and Nixon to maintain surveillance over the mail, telegrams, and telephone calls of thousands of Americans to determine the extent of hostile foreign influence on domestic unrest. The surveillance continued from 1967 to 1974, despite the CIA's repeated negative findings.

The press benefited from a landmark Supreme Court ruling of June 30 that judges generally may not impose orders on the press that bar publication of information about criminal cases, even though a trial judge believes that such an order would help to ensure the defendant a fair trial by preventing prejudicial publicity. In the Nebraska case, a judge forbade news reporting of a murder trial. The ruling concerned members of the press because it culminated a period of judicially imposed gag orders upon reporters. Louis W. Koenig

See also articles on individual countries; COURTS AND LAWS.

CLARK, JOSEPH CHARLES (1939-   ), member of Parliament for Rocky Mountain, Alberta, became the youngest political party leader in Canadian history when he was elected to head the Progressive Conservative Party on Feb. 22, 1976. Clark won a narrow victory on the party's fourth ballot. He succeeded Robert L. Stanfield, 61, who resigned after failing three times to defeat the Liberals in the nine years he led the party.

Clark was born in High River, Alta., where he worked as a youth on his father's newspaper. He also worked for newspapers in Calgary and Edmonton. After receiving a master's degree from the University of Alberta in Edmonton, he taught political science there from 1965 to 1967. He entered politics in 1957, when he went door-to-door soliciting votes for Progressive Conservative candidates. He served as private secretary to a provincial party leader, as national president of the Progressive Conservative Student Federation, and as founding chairman of the Canadian Political Youth Council.

He was first elected to the House of Commons in 1972. There he won respect as a lucid speaker and a practical politician. His task as leader of the Conservatives is to weld a fractured party into a unified force for elections expected in 1978. Clark married Maureen McTeer, then president of the Young Progressive Conservatives, in 1973. Kathryn Sederberg

See also CANADA.

CLEVELAND. A United States District Court judge on Aug. 31, 1976, found the Cleveland Board of Education guilty of creating and maintaining a racially segregated public school system. The court also found that the Ohio Board of Education allowed the segregation to exist. This raised the possibility that Cleveland might become the first major U.S. metropolitan area in which court-ordered busing would shift students between city and suburban school districts.

Desegregation Ordered. Judge Frank J. Battisti ordered the Cleveland Board of Education to submit a school desegregation plan by Jan. 17, 1977. However, he did not indicate what kind of plan might go into effect nor did he respond to a plea by the National Association for the Advancement of Colored People (NAACP) for a metropolitan desegregation plan. An earlier NAACP suit to halt further school construction was turned down by Battisti on Jan. 6, 1976. School board president Arnold R. Pinkney announced that the board would appeal the desegregation decision. Of the city's 175 schools, 151 had almost all-black or all-white enrollments. But the school board contended it did not order busing within the city because it feared this would cause white flight to the suburbs.

High Wages. The average earnings of factory workers in the Cleveland area rose 17.6 per cent between August 1975 and August 1976, far above

CLOTHING

the 4.6 per cent increase in the area's cost of living recorded in May. The unemployment rate of 6.1 per cent in June was well below the 7.8 per cent national average. The $13,906 average annual earnings of factory workers was above the $10,000 that the U.S. Department of Labor estimated a family of four would need to sustain a minimum standard of living, but below the $16,000 needed to maintain a moderate standard of living in the area.

The Council on Municipal Performance on April 18 ranked Cleveland's responsiveness to citizens' complaints 12th among 22 U.S. cities studied.

Increased Crime. A government study released on March 2 reported that the violent crime rate in Cleveland had increased between 1972 and 1974, despite a major effort to reduce street crimes and burglary. Cleveland was one of eight cities given $140 million in federal funds for anticrime programs. The study blamed the programs' failure on political pressures to get them underway too quickly and lack of cooperation among law enforcement agencies.

However, Federal Bureau of Investigation figures in March showed that serious crimes in the Cleveland area rose only 1.6 per cent between 1970 and 1975, compared with a 38 per cent national rate of increase.   James M. Banovetz

CLOTHING. See FASHION.

COAL. The United Nations Economic Commission for Europe reported on Feb. 8, 1976, that coal would be used to meet 21 per cent of Western Europe's energy needs by 1985. The new estimate was almost double an earlier one and took into account Europe's reaction to the Arab oil embargo of 1973 and 1974 and growing concern about the growth and safety of nuclear power.

U.S. Coal. In the United States, Congress on August 4 overrode President Gerald R. Ford's veto of a bill to reform rules on the leasing of federal lands with coal reserves. Backed by the governors of the nine Western states that contain most of the coal, the new law increases the federal government royalty to 12.5 per cent of the coal's value, increases the state's share of royalties from 37.5 per cent to 50 per cent, and limits the amount of land any one company can lease to 100,000 acres (40,400 hectares). Commercial mining must start within 10 years or the lease expires.

The Department of the Interior issued rules on May 11 requiring coal companies to restore strip-mined federal land to approximately its original contour and degree of vegetation. The Supreme Court of the United States ruled on June 28 against the Sierra Club's attempt to block coal strip mining in Montana, North Dakota, South Dakota, and Wyoming until the Interior Department could prepare an environmental impact statement for the

Coal miners and their families demonstrate in West Virginia during a month-long strike by members of the United Mine Workers union.

entire region. The Supreme Court ruled on July 1 that coal-mine operators must pay benefits to miners who suffer from black lung disease, in accordance with all provisions of a 1972 amendment to the Coal Mine Health and Safety Act.

Eastern Coal. Thousands of coal miners went on strike in West Virginia on July 19, angered by what they called unfair federal court intervention in union labor disputes. More than 90,000 miners were idle at the height of the wildcat strike, which lasted until August 16 and involved mines in nine states. The United Mine Workers (UMW) leaders said the strike cost at least $12 million in uncollected royalties that mine owners pay the UMW for pensions and widows' benefits. See LABOR.

Two explosions in a mine near Whitesburg, Ky., spurred congressional action on mine safety. A methane gas explosion on March 9 killed 15 miners. Two days later, 11 members of a volunteer rescue team died in a second blast in the same tunnel. The disaster was described as the worst in the history of Letcher County.

Congress responded with a bill, strongly backed for several years by the UMW, that would transfer the enforcement of coal-mine safety standards to the Department of Labor from the Department of the Interior, which has long been criticized for lax enforcement.   Mary E. Jessup

See also MINES AND MINING.

COIN COLLECTING. Numerous coin and medal collectors protested in 1976 that the official gold United States Bicentennial medal was priced higher than many collectors could afford. The medal was offered in several sizes and metals, including three made of gold that ranged in price from $100 to $4,000. Many collectors also complained that the medals were overpriced in relation to their gold content. Herbert C. Bardes, coin editor of *The New York Times,* estimated that the gold-bullion value of the $4,000 medal was about $1,900.

In the first six months of the year, 269 of the $4,000 Bicentennial medals were sold. During the same period, sales of a 1½-inch (3.8-centimeter), $5 bronze medal, the least expensive of the set, reached about 373,800.

Canada's special Olympic coin issue, in honor of the 1976 Olympics in Montreal, also drew criticism. The series of 28 coins, which sold for $469.50, contained only about $117 worth of silver.

New $2 Bills. For the first time since 1966, the U.S. Bureau of Engraving and Printing produced $2 bills. They were issued on April 13, birthday of Thomas Jefferson, whose picture appears on one side of the bill. The U.S. Postal Service offered to postmark stamped $2 bills on the first day of issue. But some authorities claimed that postmarking encouraged collectors to hoard the notes.

This one-of-a-kind 1907 $20 Double Eagle gold piece sold for about $1 million in mid-1976 to the A-Mark Coin Company of California.

Even though 400 million $2 bills were scheduled to be printed every year, few were in circulation during 1976. "We figure a lot of the bills are being hoarded," a Department of the Treasury official said. The fact that many clerks and merchants feared confusing the $2 bills with $1 bills may have contributed to the bills' failure to circulate. To discourage people from collecting $2 bills, the Bureau of Engraving and Printing set up no special outlets for the bills. Consequently, "fast-buck" dealers offered them in first-day-of-issue packages for as much as $12.13.

Coin Shows. A coin auction at the American Numismatic Association convention in August in New York City grossed more than $4 million. Gold coins brought the highest prices despite a general decline in gold-coin values. Four gold stellas – 1879 and 1880 trial strikings for a $4 U.S. coin that was never issued – sold for $225,000. An uncirculated 1815 U.S. Half Eagle, a $5 gold piece, brought $75,000.

The average number of visitors to the U.S. Mint in Philadelphia jumped from 1,000 persons a day to about 5,000 after the coin collection of the late Louis Eliasberg, a Baltimore banker, went on display in April. It is the only collection that has a specimen of every coin struck for circulation by all U.S. coinage facilities since the mint was founded in 1792.   Theodore M. O'Leary

COLOMBIA. After nearly four months of chaos, elections for departmental (state) assemblies and municipal councils were held on April 18, 1976. During that period, at least 14 persons were killed, many injured, and hundreds arrested as teachers, bank and government employees, and other workers struck for higher pay. Simultaneously, there were antigovernment student riots and a wave of terrorism by leftist guerrillas.

President Alfonso Lopez Michelsen of the Liberal Party had promised on January 16 that he would lift the state of siege under which he had governed since June 1975. But the pre-election developments forced him to reverse himself on January 29 and keep the siege in effect. Worker protests were directed against Lopez Michelsen's refusal to negotiate wage increases beyond 15 per cent, one of the measures he had used to reduce the inflation rate from 30 per cent to less than 20 per cent in two years. Rioting students protested government repression; the guerrillas, representing various Marxist factions, were trying to challenge Colombia's entire democratic system.

The Election. Each group, for its own reasons, wanted a strong election showing by three small leftist parties against the dominant Liberals and Conservatives. In addition, the experts thought the election would show which of the three Liberal Party factions would prevail.

But the voters double-crossed everyone. Some 76 per cent of them stayed away from the polls. It was the worst turnout in Colombian history, and those who did vote strongly endorsed the status quo by giving the Liberals 52 per cent, the Conservatives 40 per cent, and the leftists only 8 per cent. The spread within the Liberal votes also contributed nothing to settling their dispute.

The Economy. The 1975 freeze that destroyed Brazil's coffee crop sent prices of Colombia's coffee soaring from 65 cents per pound (0.45 kilogram) to $1.50 in 1976. Coffee exports earned a record $1-billion and generated $700 million in hard currency reserves for the government.

The immediate effect was an avalanche of cash that threatened to bury Lopez Michelsen's inflation fight. Consequently, he set up special funds to keep some of the cash out of circulation. One fund would help coffee growers to withstand future crop failures; another provides low-interest loans to Colombians wanting to buy shares in foreign-owned corporations. Foreign companies have some $400-million invested in the country, and Lopez Michelsen wants to bring them under local control. Seven foreign-owned banks in Colombia were also ordered to start selling control of their operations to local interests.   Everett G. Martin

See also LATIN AMERICA (Facts in Brief Table).

COLORADO. See STATE GOVERNMENT.

COMANECI, NADIA (1961-   ), a 14-year-old Romanian gymnast, became the darling of the 1976 Summer Olympic Games in Montreal, Canada, in July with dazzling performances that won her three gold medals, a silver, and a bronze. She won the individual all-around, balance beam, and uneven bars competitions and completely overshadowed her chief rival, Russia's Olga Korbut. She received perfect scores of 10 in seven exercises, a feat previously unheard of in Olympic gymnastic competition.

Her tiny body—she is about 5 feet (153 centimeters) tall and weighs 86 pounds (39 kilograms)—appeared frail, but it was like a supple sliver of steel as she reeled off thrilling flips and twists with apparent ease.

Comaneci was born in Oneşti (now Gheorghe Gheorghiu-Dej), where her father is an automobile mechanic and her mother works in an office. She has a brother, Adrian, 10. She was discovered when she was 6 years old by her coach, Bela Karolyi. She finished 13th in her first competition, but has not lost since then.

Comaneci—pronounced *kawm uh NEECH*—practices about four hours a day after school. She likes to collect dolls and has about 200 on shelves in her bedroom.   Joseph P. Spohn

See also OLYMPIC GAMES.

COMMON MARKET. See EUROPE.

COMMUNICATIONS. The world celebrated the 100th birthday of the telephone in 1976 with numerous special programs. "We know that, even after 100 years, we have not finished inventing the telephone," said John D. deButts, chairman of American Telephone and Telegraph Company (A. T. & T.).

Events of the year bore him out. The United States got its first domestic satellite telephone system. Several new families of digital switching systems were introduced, promising faster, cheaper, and more trouble-free processing of phone calls. Optical transmission of telecommunications signals moved closer to practical use. And an all-electronic telephone was introduced.

Satellite Communications. The first of three *Comstar* "birds," providing telephone service to the 48 contiguous states and Hawaii, was launched on May 13 and went into service about a month later. A.T. & T. and General Telephone & Electronics Corporation (GTE), owner of the second-largest telephone system in the United States, lease the capacity of the satellite from Communications Satellite Corporation (COMSAT), the government-established corporation that runs the satellite program. A.T. & T. has four earth stations (in California, Illinois, Georgia, and Pennsylvania) and GTE has three (in California, Florida, and Hawaii) over which messages are transmitted.

Competition in satellite communication in the United States took a step forward during the year. COMSAT, International Business Machines Corporation, and Aetna Life and Casualty Company set up a new company, Satellite Business Systems, to establish an all-digital domestic satellite system to serve large communications users. Target date to begin operations is 1979.

MARISAT, a maritime satellite communications system, was also established to provide high-quality communications to the U.S. Navy and to commercial shipping and offshore industries. Satellites for the system were launched in February and March. MARISAT is owned by COMSAT and three international communications carriers based in the United States.

Internationally, satellite communications were provided to 94 countries by midyear. The countries are members of the International Telecommunications Satellite Consortium (INTELSAT). They range in size from the tiny sultanate of Oman to the United States, France, and Great Britain. Service began in February over the first of a new series of *Intelsat IV-A* satellites, each of which provides up to 6,250 circuits for voice transmission, plus two television channels.

Technical Developments. Digital switching was the big technical news. Currently, the world's telecommunications systems are predominantly *analog*—that is, the signals follow the wavy-line

Citizens Band Together

With ears, a handle, and a ticket from Uncle Charlie, you can take a quick trip around the horn. Which is to say – in the slang of citizens band (CB) radio – that with a CB transceiver, a nickname, and a license and official Federal Communications Commission (FCC) call letters, anyone over 18 can start a two-way radio conversation on one of 40 channels on the CB dial.

It does not take long for an answer. The FCC estimated that as many as 10 million CB sets were in use in homes, automobiles, and boats during 1976. More than half a million people applied for licenses in March, and some automakers offered CB transceivers as options on their 1977 models. By all accounts, CB radio was the communications craze of 1976.

The FCC provided 23 CB channels in 1958 for short-range personal communication. But the 1973 Arab oil embargo and the subsequent "double-nickel" nationwide speed limit of 55 miles (89 kilometers) per hour to conserve gasoline really started the craze. Truckers advised one another on *Smokey reports* – positions of police cars. Soon, average motorists tuned in to avoid speeding tickets, swap weather and travel advice, and just chat. The popular song "Convoy" by C. W. McCall spread the CB mystique over commercial radio, and clubs, magazines, and even a best-selling CB-slang dictionary were available to enthusiasts.

At first police resented the growing use of CB's to avoid speed traps, but they soon tuned in and turned the CB reports to their own advantage by moving to new spots while reports continued to give their previous positions. Moreover, CB-equipped motorists keep one another alert and aware of traffic hazards. And there is an official emergency channel (channel 9) over which to report mishaps or request assistance. The Chicago-based group REACT International Incorporated – REACT stands for Radio Emergency Associated Citizens' Teams – has more than 50,000 trained volunteers in more than 1,500 active teams that monitor channel 9. REACT also has teams in Canada, Mexico, Puerto Rico, Venezuela, and West Germany.

The CB boom has brought with it certain problems. A CBer transmitting illegally on a channel reserved for model-plane enthusiasts sent one plane crashing to the ground. Complaints of CB radio-transmission interference with television sets, stereos, automatic garage-door openers, and even hearing aids surged from about 40,000 in 1974 to well over 100,000 in 1976. Perhaps the biggest problem is overcrowding, which can turn "good buddies" into nasty rivals. CBers are supposed to limit calls to five minutes, and those who do not are called "ratchet jaws." But even without the ratchet jaws, some CBers on crowded highways or in urban and suburban areas never get a chance to talk.

To help alleviate the congestion, the FCC provided 17 new CB channels on Jan. 1, 1977. The FCC also required transceiver makers to comply with new technical standards aimed at reducing interference.

An effect beyond the control of Washington, D.C., may cause additional havoc for CBers. The Department of Commerce Institute for Telecommunication Sciences (ITS) in Boulder, Colo., warned that increased solar activity from about 1978 to 1980 may alter the earth's ionosphere in such a way that it will reflect CB waves across the continent. While some scientists believe there is no reason to worry, ITS scientists believe that unwanted long-distance conversations could further jam local CB communications.

Unlike pocket calculators and digital watches, the CB explosion did not result from a new electronic technology. It grew instead from a basic human need – the desire to talk back. Because we live in a world of mass communications, we are flooded with messages but rarely get a chance to respond. CB radio has already gone a long way toward ending the loneliness of the long-distance driver. If CB use continues to grow, it may well do what politicians so often promise in a world where people are often isolated and afraid – it may indeed bring us together. Robert K. Johnson

A CBer

COMMUNICATIONS

A new mushroom-shaped building for the French Ministry of Post and Telecommunications was to begin serving Parisian subscribers in 1977.

configuration of the human voice. In digital systems, signals are chopped into segments, each of which has a specific number value. The technique has been used for years to increase transmission capacity. Digital switching machines have been developed to route phone calls and computer communications without changing the mode of transmission from digital to analog and back again. The process promises to eliminate much expensive equipment and to provide a much more trouble-free, easily administered system.

Other major technological developments saw electronic systems, based on computer and semiconductor technology, swiftly replacing the old electromechanical systems. The Bell System put its 1,000th electronic central office into service in October in Chicago. Electronics also moved into the telephone itself, which has remained basically unchanged for years. L. M. Ericsson Company of Sweden introduced an all-electronic telephone that promises clearer transmission and the possibility of packing more functions into it.

Bell Laboratories demonstrated an experimental optical transmission system in which signals are transmitted by light impulses over glass fibers. Once fully developed, the systems will be less expensive than metal cable systems, take much less space, and eliminate electromagnetic interference in transmission.   Leo S. Anderson

COMMUNITY ORGANIZATIONS. In terms of disaster relief, 1976 was one of the costliest years in the history of the American Red Cross. The organization spent almost $33 million in aid after such events as the February 4 earthquake in Guatemala; the June 5 Teton Dam break in Idaho; and the July 31 flood through Big Thompson Canyon in Colorado. See DISASTERS.

The Red Cross published two important books during the year – *Blood: The River of Life* describes that life-sustaining substance, and *First Aid for Foreign Body Obstruction of the Airway* explains new techniques to aid choking victims.

The Salvation Army flew a team of Spanish-speaking officers into Guatemala less than 48 hours after the February earthquake. The Guatemalan government asked the army to aid in the reconstruction of Tecpan, a city leveled by the disaster.

The army, which has members in 82 countries, has been adapting its social services to meet changing needs. For example, women are now admitted to the army's alcoholic rehabilitation centers, and many youth crisis centers are now open on a 24-hour basis.

The Young Men's Christian Association (YMCA) had 9 million registered members in 1976, 34 per cent of them female. The YMCA gave increasing emphasis to its health, education, and physical fitness programs designed to reduce cardiovascular disease. YMCA officials hope to enroll 6 million persons in the program by 1981.

The Young Women's Christian Association (YWCA) held its 27th national convention at the University of Notre Dame in South Bend, Ind., in June. Elizabeth Steel Genné of Montclair, N.J., was re-elected president, and Sarah-Alyce P. Wright remained as national executive director. The organization emphasized training its professional and volunteer staff; as a result, 700 women received training in modern management techniques during the year. A grant from the National Endowment for the Humanities is financing research in the YWCA's early involvement in women's rights.

Service Organizations. Kiwanis International reported a 1976 membership of almost 300,000 in 6,000 clubs in 48 countries. Much of the increase in membership is due to Kiwanis emphasis on two new categories, youths and women.

The Lions Club began the Lioness Program, which seeks to unify Lions Ladies Auxiliaries throughout the world and provide new opportunities for service to the needy. In May, Lions International reported a membership of 1,165,000 in nearly 30,000 clubs in 146 countries.

Rotary International members elected W. Jack Davis of Hamilton, Bermuda, president at the national convention in New Orleans in June. Wolfgang Wick, an Austrian industrialist, withdrew as nominee in March in the face of charges that he was a Nazi Party member and a storm trooper during World War II. Rotary International reported that it had more than 16,000 clubs, with nearly 800,000 members.

Veterans Organizations. The Veterans Administration (VA) reported a record 2.8 million persons training under the GI Bill in 1976, a 4.8 per cent increase over 1975. The 1976 edition of "Federal Benefits for Veterans and Dependents" reflected the latest changes in VA benefits in such areas as pensions, medical care, disability compensation, and GI home loans. Nearly 1 million widows received pensions from nonmilitary-related deaths.

The American Legion, in several policy statements during the year, called for readjustments in compensation for disabled veterans, pension reform, adequate funding of VA medical care programs, and adjustments in monetary allowances for veterans training under the GI Bill.

The Veterans of Foreign Wars (VFW) vigorously opposed a proposal to cut the present 10-year time limit for completion of education under the GI Bill to eight years. At its convention in New York City in August, the VFW elected R. D. Smith of Toccoa, Ga., commander in chief. Joseph P. Anderson

COMOROS. See AFRICA; Section Five, COMOROS; MORONI.

CONGO (BRAZZAVILLE). See AFRICA.

CONGO (KINSHASA). See ZAIRE.

CONGRESS OF THE UNITED STATES. A stalemate between President Gerald R. Ford and the 94th Congress led to an unusually unproductive second session in 1976. President Ford characterized it as a Congress of "weak compromises and evasions." The Democratic congressional leadership retorted at the end of the session that the President had vetoed 22 bills in 1976, many of which dealt with such pressing problems as unemployment, health care, and needed social services.

The 94th Congress convened for its second session on Jan. 19, 1976, and adjourned on October 2. In the Senate, there were 61 Democrats, 37 Republicans, 1 Conservative, and 1 Independent. When the session began, there were 290 Democrats and 145 Republicans in the House of Representatives.

Several senior members of Congress were among the 53 who retired in 1976 — Senate Minority Leader Hugh Scott (R., Pa.), Senate Majority Leader Mike Mansfield (D., Mont.), and Speaker of the House Carl B. Albert (D., Okla.). House Democrats caucused in December to choose new leaders. On December 6, they elected Thomas P. O'Neill, Jr., of Massachusetts as speaker of the House. James C. Wright, Jr., of Texas replaced him as House majority leader.

Two members of the House of Representatives were chosen by President-elect James Earl (Jimmy) Carter, Jr., for Cabinet posts after his Administration took office in 1977. Bob Bergland (D., Minn.) was named secretary of agriculture; Brock Adams (D., Wash.), secretary of transportation. See CABINET, UNITED STATES.

Presidential Vetoes. Congress overrode five presidential vetoes in 1976 by the required two-thirds vote of both houses — a $45-billion appropriation for health, welfare, and manpower programs, passed in 1975, in January; a $3.95-billion public-works bill to provide employment, in July; a bill reforming coal-leasing arrangements on federal lands, in August; a $160-million program for developing an electric automobile motor, in September; and a $56.6-billion appropriation for the Department of Labor and the Department of Health, Education, and Welfare (HEW), in September.

However, Congress sustained most of the President's vetoes. Those sustained included an on-site picketing bill, in January; a bill raising milk price supports, in February; a $6-billion public-works employment bill, in February; a bill providing $125-million in federal aid for day-care centers, in May; a $4.4-billion foreign-aid bill, also in May; a bill establishing an automobile research program, in September; and a bill reorganizing the Bureau of Indian Affairs, in October.

Budget and Taxes. On January 21, President Ford presented a budget of $394.2 billion for fiscal 1977 (Oct. 1, 1976, to Sept. 30, 1977). The budget was characterized by increased defense spending and an attempt to save money by holding down spending on social programs.

The start of the fiscal year changed from July 1 to October 1 as of 1976. Therefore, funds were needed for the three-month transition period. In addition to the estimated $373.5-billion fiscal 1976 budget, $98 billion was slated for the transition.

On September 15, the Senate approved a binding 1977 budget ceiling of $413.1 billion, with a projected deficit of $50.6 billion. The House approved this budget the following day.

On June 30, the President signed legislation passed by Congress raising the temporary federal debt ceiling to $700 billion through Sept. 30, 1977. The permanent debt ceiling is $400 billion, but the federal debt is more than $200 billion above it.

The House and Senate approved tax-reform legislation on September 16, and President Ford signed it on October 4. Among other provisions, the act extended personal and corporate income tax cuts — estimated at $17.2 billion — through fiscal 1977. See TAXATION.

Social Welfare sparked most of the clashes between a welfare-minded Congress and the President, who regarded almost all new or increased federal spending programs as inflationary.

On April 6, President Ford vetoed a bill providing $125 million in federal aid to improve the safety

The Senate meets on June 16 in the historic Old Senate Chamber to dedicate the restored room where that body met from 1810 to 1859.

and health standards of day-care centers serving children of mothers on welfare. But on September 7, he signed a compromise bill providing $24 million for day-care centers serving low-income families and delaying implementation of the federal regulations to October 1977.

The Senate on September 22 completed congressional action on two employment bills, which the President signed. One extended a public-service jobs program for state and local governments through fiscal 1977; the other appropriated $3.7-billion for public-works construction projects, federal aid for state and local budgets, and federal funds for water-treatment plants.

On September 29, Congress completed action on a bill authorizing $4.9 billion over a three-year period for public-works construction in economically depressed areas. Ford signed it on October 12.

Congress overrode the President's veto of the appropriation for HEW and the Department of Labor on September 30. This bill included a provision forbidding the use of federal funds for Medicaid payments for abortions. But that provision was later declared unconstitutional in federal district court (see POPULATION, WORLD).

Among other social welfare acts passed by Congress and signed by the President were an extension through fiscal 1977 of Department of Housing and Urban Development programs, including loans to build housing for the elderly and rent subsidies for low-income families; an authorization of $20 billion for higher education and vocational training; and a $2.3-billion medical-education aid program, making many loans contingent on the doctors working in medically understaffed regions for two years, or repaying the loan threefold, plus interest. See HOUSING; SOCIAL SECURITY.

The Environment was the focus of several acts passed in 1976. The President on July 26 signed a bill providing $1.6 billion to aid coastal states in alleviating problems related to the development of offshore coal and gas reserves. On August 14, the President signed legislation eliminating price ceilings on some domestic oil, permitting 10 per cent annual price increases, and authorizing loans for energy-conservation investments.

The Toxic Substances Control Act was signed into law on October 12. It provides that the Environmental Protection Agency (EPA) must be notified 90 days before a new chemical is put on the market, or a process of "significant new use" begins, so that the EPA can test the product. The bill also calls for phasing out almost all of the production and sale of polychlorinated biphenyls.

Other environmental measures included increased federal funds for national parks and recreation areas; curbs on mining in national parks; and $366 million for solid-waste-disposal programs (see MINES AND MINING).

Members of the United States Senate

The Senate of the first session of the 95th Congress consists of 61 Democrats, 38 Republicans, and 1 Independent, compared with 61 Democrats, 37 Republicans, 1 Independent, and 1 Conservative for the second session of the 94th Congress. Senators shown starting their term in 1977 were elected for the first time in the Nov. 2, 1976, elections (with the exception of Wendell R. Anderson, who was appointed to fill the vacancy created in Minnesota when Walter F. Mondale was elected Vice-President). Those shown ending their current terms in 1983 were re-elected to the Senate in the same balloting. The second date in each listing shows when the term of a previously elected senator expires. For organizational purposes, the one Independent will line up with Democrats.

State	Term	State	Term	State	Term
Alabama		**Louisiana**		**Ohio**	
John J. Sparkman, D.	1946—1979	Russell B. Long, D.	1948—1981	John H. Glenn, D.	1975—1981
James B. Allen, D.	1969—1981	J. Bennett Johnston, Jr., D.	1972—1979	Howard M. Metzenbaum, D.	1977—1983
Alaska		**Maine**		**Oklahoma**	
Theodore F. Stevens, R.	1968—1979	Edmund S. Muskie, D.	1959—1983	Henry L. Bellmon, R.	1969—1981
Mike Gravel, D.	1969—1981	William D. Hathaway, D.	1973—1979	Dewey F. Bartlett, R.	1973—1979
Arizona		**Maryland**		**Oregon**	
Barry Goldwater, R.	1969—1981	Charles McC. Mathias, Jr., R.	1969—1981	Mark O. Hatfield, R.	1967—1979
Dennis DeConcini, D.	1977—1983	Paul S. Sarbanes, D.	1977—1983	Robert W. Packwood, R.	1969—1981
Arkansas		**Massachusetts**		**Pennsylvania**	
John L. McClellan, D.	1943—1979	Edward M. Kennedy, D.	1962—1983	Richard S. Schweiker, R.	1969—1981
Dale Bumpers, D.	1975—1981	Edward W. Brooke, R.	1967—1979	H. John Heinz III, R.	1977—1983
California		**Michigan**		**Rhode Island**	
Alan Cranston, D.	1969—1981	Robert P. Griffin, R.	1966—1979	Claiborne Pell, D.	1961—1979
S. I. Hayakawa, R.	1977—1983	Donald W. Riegle, Jr., D.	1977—1983	John H. Chafee, R.	1977—1983
Colorado		**Minnesota**		**South Carolina**	
Floyd K. Haskell, D.	1973—1979	Hubert H. Humphrey, D.	1971—1983	Strom Thurmond, R.	1956—1979
Gary Hart, D.	1975—1981	Wendell R. Anderson, D.	1977—1979	Ernest F. Hollings, D.	1966—1981
Connecticut		**Mississippi**		**South Dakota**	
Abraham A. Ribicoff, D.	1963—1981	James O. Eastland, D.	1943—1979	George S. McGovern, D.	1963—1981
Lowell P. Weicker, Jr., R.	1971—1983	John C. Stennis, D.	1947—1983	James G. Abourezk, D.	1973—1979
Delaware		**Missouri**		**Tennessee**	
William V. Roth, Jr., R.	1971—1983	Thomas F. Eagleton, D.	1968—1981	Howard H. Baker, Jr., R.	1967—1979
Joseph R. Biden, Jr., D.	1973—1979	John C. Danforth, R.	1977—1983	James R. Sasser, D.	1977—1983
Florida		**Montana**		**Texas**	
Lawton Chiles, D.	1971—1983	Lee Metcalf, D.	1961—1979	John G. Tower, R.	1961—1979
Richard B. Stone, D.	1975—1981	John Melcher, D.	1977—1983	Lloyd M. Bentsen, D.	1971—1983
Georgia		**Nebraska**		**Utah**	
Herman E. Talmadge, D.	1957—1981	Carl T. Curtis, R.	1955—1979	Edwin Jacob Garn, R.	1975—1981
Sam Nunn, D.	1972—1979	Edward Zorinsky, D.	1977—1983	Orrin G. Hatch, R.	1977—1983
Hawaii		**Nevada**		**Vermont**	
Daniel K. Inouye, D.	1963—1981	Howard W. Cannon, D.	1959—1983	Robert T. Stafford, R.	1971—1983
Spark M. Matsunaga, D.	1977—1983	Paul Laxalt, R.	1975—1981	Patrick J. Leahy, D.	1975—1981
Idaho		**New Hampshire**		**Virginia**	
Frank Church, D.	1957—1981	Thomas J. McIntyre, D.	1962—1979	Harry F. Byrd, Jr., Ind.	1965—1983
James A. McClure, R.	1973—1979	John A. Durkin, D.	1975—1981	William L. Scott, R.	1973—1979
Illinois		**New Jersey**		**Washington**	
Charles H. Percy, R.	1967—1979	Clifford P. Case, R.	1955—1979	Warren G. Magnuson, D.	1944—1981
Adlai E. Stevenson III, D.	1970—1981	Harrison A. Williams, Jr., D.	1959—1983	Henry M. Jackson, D.	1953—1983
Indiana		**New Mexico**		**West Virginia**	
Birch Bayh, D.	1963—1981	Pete V. Domenici, R.	1973—1979	Jennings Randolph, D	1958—1979
Richard G. Lugar, R.	1977—1983	Harrison H. Schmitt, R.	1977—1983	Robert C. Byrd, D.	1959—1983
Iowa		**New York**		**Wisconsin**	
Richard C. Clark, D.	1973—1979	Jacob K. Javits, R.	1957—1981	William Proxmire, D.	1957—1983
John C. Culver, D.	1975—1981	Daniel P. Moynihan, D.	1977—1983	Gaylord Nelson, D.	1963—1981
Kansas		**North Carolina**		**Wyoming**	
James B. Pearson, R.	1962—1979	Jesse A. Helms, R.	1973—1979	Clifford P. Hansen, R.	1967—1979
Robert J. Dole, R.	1969—1981	Robert Morgan, D.	1975—1981	Malcolm Wallop, R.	1977—1983
Kentucky		**North Dakota**			
Walter Huddleston, D.	1973—1979	Milton R. Young, R.	1945—1981		
Wendell H. Ford, D.	1975—1981	Quentin N. Burdick, D.	1960—1983		

Members of the United States House

The House of Representatives of the first session of the 95th Congress consists of 292 Democrats and 143 Republicans (not including representatives from the District of Columbia, Guam, Puerto Rico, and the Virgin Islands), compared with 286 Democrats and 145 Republicans with 4 seats vacant, for the second session of the 94th Congress. This table shows congressional districts, legislator, and party affiliation. Asterisk (*) denotes those who served in the 94th Congress; dagger (†) denotes "at large."

Alabama
1. Jack Edwards, R.*
2. William L. Dickinson, R.*
3. William Nichols, D.*
4. Tom Bevill, D.*
5. Ronnie G. Flippo, D.
6. John H. Buchanan, Jr., R.*
7. Walter Flowers, D.*

Alaska
† Don Young, R.*

Arizona
1. John J. Rhodes, R.*
2. Morris K. Udall, D.*
3. Bob Stump, D.
4. Eldon Rudd, R.

Arkansas
1. Bill Alexander, D.*
2. Jim Guy Tucker, D.
3. J. P. Hammerschmidt, R.*
4. Ray Thornton, D.*

California
1. Harold T. Johnson, D.*
2. Don H. Clausen, R.*
3. John E. Moss, D.*
4. Robert L. Leggett, D.*
5. John J. Burton, D.*
6. Phillip Burton, D.*
7. George Miller, D.*
8. Ronald V. Dellums, D.*
9. Fortney H. Stark, D.*
10. Don Edwards, D.*
11. Leo J. Ryan, D.*
12. Paul N. McCloskey, Jr., R.*
13. Norman Y. Mineta, D.*
14. John J. McFall, D.*
15. B. F. Sisk, D.*
16. Leon E. Panetta, D.
17. John H. Krebs, D.*
18. William M. Ketchum, R.*
19. Robert J. Lagomarsino, R.*
20. Barry M. Goldwater, Jr., R.*
21. James C. Corman, D.*
22. Carlos J. Moorhead, R.*
23. Anthony C. Beilenson, D.
24. Henry A. Waxman, D.*
25. Edward R. Roybal, D.*
26. John H. Rousselot, R.*
27. Robert K. Dornan, R.
28. Yvonne B. Burke, D.*
29. Augustus F. Hawkins, D.*
30. George E. Danielson, D.*
31. Charles H. Wilson, D.*
32. Glenn M. Anderson, D.*
33. Del M. Clawson, R.*
34. Mark W. Hannaford, D.*
35. Jim Lloyd, D.*
36. George E. Brown, Jr., D.*
37. Shirley N. Pettis, D.*
38. Jerry M. Patterson, D.*
39. Charles E. Wiggins, R.*
40. Robert E. Badham, R.
41. Bob Wilson, R.*
42. Lionel Van Deerlin, D.*
43. Clair W. Burgener, R.*

Colorado
1. Patricia Schroeder, D.*
2. Timothy E. Wirth, D.*
3. Frank E. Evans, D.*
4. James P. Johnson, R.*
5. William L. Armstrong, R.*

Connecticut
1. William R. Cotter, D.*
2. Christopher J. Dodd, D.*
3. Robert N. Giaimo, D.*
4. Stewart B. McKinney, R.*
5. Ronald A. Sarasin, R.*
6. Anthony J. Moffett, D.*

Delaware
† Thomas B. Evans, Jr., R.

Florida
1. Robert L. F. Sikes, D.*
2. Don Fuqua, D.*
3. Charles E. Bennett, D.*
4. William V. Chappell, Jr., D.*
5. Richard Kelly, R.*
6. C. W. Young, R.*
7. Sam M. Gibbons, D.*
8. Andy Ireland, D.
9. Louis Frey, Jr., R.*
10. L. A. Bafalis, R.*
11. Paul G. Rogers, D.*
12. J. Herbert Burke, R.*
13. William Lehman, D.*
14. Claude D. Pepper, D.*
15. Dante B. Fascell, D.*

Georgia
1. Ronald Ginn, D.*
2. Dawson Mathis, D.*
3. Jack T. Brinkley, D.*
4. Elliott H. Levitas, D.*
5. Andrew Young, D.*‡
6. John J. Flynt, Jr., D.*
7. Lawrence P. McDonald, D.*
8. Billy L. Evans, D.
9. Ed Jenkins, D.
10. Doug Barnard, D.

Hawaii
1. Cecil Heftel, D.
2. Daniel Akaka, D.

Idaho
1. Steven D. Symms, R.*
2. George Hansen, R.*

Illinois
1. Ralph H. Metcalfe, D.*
2. Morgan F. Murphy, D.*
3. Martin A. Russo, D.*
4. Edward J. Derwinski, R.*
5. John G. Fary, D.*
6. Henry J. Hyde, R.*
7. Cardiss Collins, D.*
8. Dan Rostenkowski, D.*
9. Sidney R. Yates, D.*
10. Abner J. Mikva, D.*

11. Frank Annunzio, D.*
12. Philip M. Crane, R.*
13. Robert McClory, R.*
14. John N. Erlenborn, R.*
15. Tom Corcoran, R.
16. John B. Anderson, R.*
17. George M. O'Brien, R.*
18. Robert H. Michel, R.*
19. Thomas F. Railsback, R.*
20. Paul Findley, R.*
21. Edward R. Madigan, R.*
22. George E. Shipley, D.*
23. Charles Melvin Price, D.*
24. Paul Simon, D.*

Indiana
1. Adam Benjamin, D.
2. Floyd J. Fithian, D.*
3. John Brademas, D.*
4. J. Danforth Quayle, R.
5. Elwood H. Hillis, R.*
6. David W. Evans, D.*
7. John T. Myers, R.*
8. David L. Cornwell, D.
9. Lee H. Hamilton, D.*
10. Philip R. Sharp, D.*
11. Andrew Jacobs, Jr., D.*

Iowa
1. James Leach, R.
2. Michael T. Blouin, D.*
3. Charles E. Grassley, R.*
4. Neal Smith, D.*
5. Tom Harkin, D.*
6. Berkley Bedell, D.*

Kansas
1. Keith G. Sebelius, R.*
2. Martha E. Keys, D.*
3. Larry Winn, Jr., R.*
4. Dan Glickman, D.
5. Joe Skubitz, R.*

Kentucky
1. Carroll Hubbard, Jr., D.*
2. William H. Natcher, D.*
3. Romano L. Mazzoli, D.*
4. Marion Gene Snyder, R.*
5. Tim Lee Carter, R.*
6. John B. Breckinridge, D.*
7. Carl D. Perkins, D.*

Louisiana
1. Richard A. Tonry, D.
2. Lindy Boggs, D.*
3. David C. Treen, R.*
4. Joe D. Waggoner, Jr., D.*
5. Jerry Huckaby, D.
6. W. Henson Moore, R.*
7. John B. Breaux, D.*
8. Gillis W. Long, D.*

Maine
1. David F. Emery, R.*
2. William S. Cohen, R.*

Maryland
1. Robert E. Bauman, R.*

2. Clarence D. Long, D.*
3. Barbara Mikulski, D.
4. Marjorie S. Holt, R.*
5. Gladys N. Spellman, D.*
6. Goodloe E. Byron, D.*
7. Parren J. Mitchell, D.*
8. Newton I. Steers, Jr., R.

Massachusetts
1. Silvio O. Conte, R.*
2. Edward P. Boland, D.*
3. Joseph D. Early, D.*
4. Robert F. Drinan, D.*
5. Paul E. Tsongas, D.*
6. Michael J. Harrington, D.*
7. Edward J. Markey, D.
8. Thomas P. O'Neill, Jr., D.*
9. John J. Moakley, D.*
10. Margaret M. Heckler, R.*
11. James A. Burke, D.*
12. Gerry E. Studds, D.*

Michigan
1. John Conyers, Jr., D.*
2. Carl D. Pursell, R.
3. Garry Brown, R.*
4. David Stockman, R.
5. Harold Sawyer, R.
6. Bob Carr, D.*
7. Dale E. Kildee, D.
8. Bob Traxler, D.*
9. Guy Vander Jagt, R.*
10. Elford A. Cederberg, R.*
11. Philip E. Ruppe, R.*
12. David E. Bonior, D.
13. Charles C. Diggs, Jr., D.*
14. Lucien N. Nedzi, D.*
15. William D. Ford, D.*
16. John D. Dingell, D.*
17. William M. Brodhead, D.*
18. James J. Blanchard, D.*
19. William S. Broomfield, R.*

Minnesota
1. Albert H. Quie, R.*
2. Thomas M. Hagedorn, R.*
3. Bill Frenzel, R.*
4. Bruce F. Vento, D.
5. Donald M. Fraser, D.*
6. Richard Nolan, D.*
7. Bob Bergland, D.*‡
8. James L. Oberstar, D.*

Mississippi
1. Jamie L. Whitten, D.*
2. David R. Bowen, D.*
3. G. V. Montgomery, D.*
4. Thad Cochran, R.*
5. Trent Lott, R.*

Missouri
1. William L. Clay, D.*
2. Robert A. Young, D.
3. Richard A. Gephardt, D.
4. Ike Skelton, D.
5. Richard Bolling, D.*
6. E. Thomas Coleman, R.
7. Gene Taylor, R.*

8. Richard H. Ichord, D.*
9. Harold L. Volkmer, D.
10. Bill D. Burlison, D.*

Montana
1. Max S. Baucus, D.*
2. Ron Marlenee, R.

Nebraska
1. Charles Thone, R.*
2. John J. Cavanaugh, D.
3. Virginia Smith, R.*

Nevada
† James Santini, D.*

New Hampshire
1. Norman E. D'Amours, D.*
2. James C. Cleveland, R.*

New Jersey
1. James J. Florio, D.*
2. William J. Hughes, D.*
3. James J. Howard, D.*
4. Frank Thompson, Jr., D.*
5. Millicent Fenwick, R.*
6. Edwin B. Forsythe, R.*
7. Andrew Maguire, D.*
8. Robert A. Roe, D.*
9. Harold Hollenbeck, R.
10. Peter W. Rodino, Jr., D.*
11. Joseph G. Minish, D.*
12. Matthew J. Rinaldo, R.*
13. Helen Meyner, D.*
14. Joseph A. LeFante, D.
15. Edward J. Patten, D.*

New Mexico
1. Manuel Lujan, Jr., R.*
2. Harold Runnels, D.*

New York
1. Otis G. Pike, D.*
2. Thomas J. Downey, D.*
3. Jerome A. Ambro, Jr., D.*
4. Norman F. Lent, R.*
5. John W. Wydler, R.*
6. Lester L. Wolff, D.*
7. Joseph P. Addabbo, D.*
8. Benjamin S. Rosenthal, D.*
9. James J. Delaney, D.*
10. Mario Biaggi, D.*
11. James H. Scheuer, D.*
12. Shirley Chisholm, D.*
13. Stephen J. Solarz, D.*
14. Frederick W. Richmond, D.*
15. Leo C. Zeferetti, D.*
16. Elizabeth Holtzman, D.*
17. John M. Murphy, D.*
18. Edward I. Koch, D.*
19. Charles B. Rangel, D.*
20. Theodore S. Weiss, D.
21. Herman Badillo, D.*
22. Jonathan B. Bingham, D.*
23. Bruce F. Caputo, R.
24. Richard L. Ottinger, D.*
25. Hamilton Fish, Jr., R.*

26. Benjamin A. Gilman, R.*
27. Matthew F. McHugh, D.*
28. Samuel S. Stratton, D.*
29. Edward W. Pattison, D.*
30. Robert C. McEwen, R.*
31. Donald J. Mitchell, R.*
32. James M. Hanley, D.*
33. William F. Walsh, R.*
34. Frank Horton, R.*
35. Barber B. Conable, Jr., R.*
36. John J. LaFalce, D.*
37. Henry J. Nowak, D.*
38. Jack F. Kemp, R.*
39. Stanley N. Lundine, D.*

North Carolina
1. Walter B. Jones, D.*
2. L. H. Fountain, D.*
3. Charles Whitley, D.
4. Ike F. Andrews, D.*
5. Stephen L. Neal, D.*
6. L. Richardson Preyer, D.*
7. Charles Rose, D.*
8. W. G. Hefner, D.*
9. James G. Martin, R.*
10. James T. Broyhill, R.*
11. Lamar Gudger, D.

North Dakota
† Mark Andrews, R.*

Ohio
1. Willis D. Gradison, Jr., R.*
2. Thomas A. Luken, D.
3. Charles W. Whalen, Jr., R.*
4. Tennyson Guyer, R.*
5. Delbert L. Latta, R.*
6. William H. Harsha, R.*
7. Clarence J. Brown, R.*
8. Thomas N. Kindness, R.*
9. Thomas L. Ashley, D.*
10. Clarence E. Miller, R.*
11. J. William Stanton, R.*
12. Samuel L. Devine, R.*
13. Donald J. Pease, D.
14. John F. Seiberling, D.*
15. Chalmers P. Wylie, R.*
16. Ralph S. Regula, R.*
17. John M. Ashbrook, R.*
18. Douglas Applegate, D.
19. Charles J. Carney, D.*
20. Mary Rose Oakar, D.
21. Louis Stokes, D.*
22. Charles A. Vanik, D.*
23. Ronald M. Mottl, D.*

Oklahoma
1. James R. Jones, D.*
2. Theodore M. Risenhoover, D.*
3. Wes Watkins, D.
4. Tom Steed, D.*
5. Mickey Edwards, R.
6. Glenn English, D.*

Oregon
1. Les AuCoin, D.*
2. Al Ullman, D.*
3. Robert B. Duncan, D.*
4. James Weaver, D.*

Pennsylvania
1. Michael Myers, D.
2. Robert N. C. Nix, D.*
3. Raymond F. Lederer, D.
4. Joshua Eilberg, D.*
5. Richard T. Schulze, R.*
6. Gus Yatron, D.*
7. Robert W. Edgar, D.*
8. Peter H. Kostmayer, D.
9. E. G. Shuster, R.*
10. Joseph M. McDade, R.*
11. Daniel J. Flood, D.*
12. John P. Murtha, D.*
13. Lawrence Coughlin, R.*
14. William S. Moorhead, D.*
15. Fred B. Rooney, D.*
16. Robert S. Walker, R.
17. Allen E. Ertel, D.
18. Doug Walgren, D.
19. William F. Goodling, R.*
20. Joseph M. Gaydos, D.*
21. John H. Dent, D.*
22. Austin J. Murphy, D.
23. Joseph S. Ammerman, D.
24. Marc L. Marks, R.
25. Gary A. Myers, R.*

Rhode Island
1. Fernand J. St. Germain, D.*
2. Edward P. Beard, D.*

South Carolina
1. Mendel J. Davis, D.*
2. Floyd D. Spence, R.*
3. Butler C. Derrick, Jr., D.*
4. James R. Mann, D.*
5. Kenneth L. Holland, D.*
6. John W. Jenrette, Jr., D.*

South Dakota
1. Larry Pressler, R.*
2. James Abdnor, R.*

Tennessee
1. James H. Quillen, R.*
2. John J. Duncan, R.*
3. Marilyn Lloyd, D.*
4. Albert Gore, Jr., D.
5. Clifford R. Allen, D.*
6. Robin L. Beard, Jr., R.*
7. Ed Jones, D.*
8. Harold E. Ford, D.*

Texas
1. Sam B. Hall, Jr., D.*
2. Charles Wilson, D.*
3. James M. Collins, R.*
4. Ray Roberts, D.*
5. James Mattox, D.
6. Olin E. Teague, D.*
7. Bill Archer, R.*
8. Bob Eckhardt, D.*
9. Jack Brooks, D.*
10. J. J. Pickle, D.*
11. W. R. Poage, D.*
12. James C. Wright, Jr., D.*
13. Jack Hightower, D.*
14. John Young, D.*
15. Eligio de la Garza, D.*
16. Richard C. White, D.*
17. Omar Burleson, D.*

18. Barbara C. Jordan, D.*
19. George H. Mahon, D.*
20. Henry B. Gonzalez, D.*
21. Robert Krueger, D.*
22. Bob Gammage, D.
23. Abraham Kazen, Jr., D.*
24. Dale Milford, D.*

Utah
1. K. Gunn McKay, D.*
2. Dan Marriott, R.

Vermont
† James M. Jeffords, R.*

Virginia
1. Paul S. Trible, Jr., R.
2. G. William Whitehurst, R.*
3. David E. Satterfield III, D.*
4. Robert W. Daniel, Jr., R.*
5. W. C. Daniel, D.*
6. M. Caldwell Butler, R.*
7. J. Kenneth Robinson, R.*
8. Herbert E. Harris, D.*
9. William C. Wampler, R.*
10. Joseph L. Fisher, D.*

Washington
1. Joel Pritchard, R.*
2. Lloyd Meeds, D.*
3. Don Bonker, D.*
4. Mike McCormack, D.*
5. Thomas S. Foley, D.*
6. Norm Dicks, D.
7. Brock Adams, D.*‡

West Virginia
1. Robert H. Mollohan, D.*
2. Harley O. Staggers, D.*
3. John M. Slack, D.*
4. Nick J. Rahall, D.

Wisconsin
1. Les Aspin, D.*
2. Robert W. Kastenmeier, D.*
3. Alvin J. Baldus, D.*
4. Clement J. Zablocki, D.*
5. Henry S. Reuss, D.*
6. William A. Steiger, R.*
7. David R. Obey, D.*
8. Robert J. Cornell, D.*
9. Robert W. Kasten, Jr., R.*

Wyoming
† Teno Roncalio, D.*

Nonvoting Representatives

District of Columbia
Walter E. Fauntroy, D.*

Guam
Antonio Won Pat, D.*

Puerto Rico
Baltasar Corrada, D.

Virgin Islands
Ron de Lugo, D.*

‡Was to be nominated in 1977 to serve in the Cabinet of President James Earl (Jimmy) Carter, Jr.

Democratic Senator Mike Mansfield of Montana, the Senate majority leader, retired after the second session of the 94th Congress ended.

Retiring senators, from top: Paul Fannin (R., Ariz.); Roman Hruska (R., Nebr.); Stuart Symington (D., Mo.); Hugh Scott (R., Pa.); and John Pastore (D., R.I.).

Consumer Interest. Congress passed and the President on May 11 signed a law expanding the authority of the Consumer Product Safety Commission. On October 19, President Ford signed a bill designed to protect consumers against corporate price fixing. The measure provides that state attorneys general can sue on behalf of a consumer for triple damages on charges of price fixing. It also gives the Antitrust Division of the Department of Justice subpoenalike powers to force corporations and individuals to release information in civil antitrust proceedings.

A so-called "government in sunshine act," signed on September 13, requires about 50 federal agencies to conduct most of their business in public. Regulatory agencies and commissions must schedule open public hearings, except on specifically exempted topics.

Government and Politics. Congress passed on September 30 a $25.6-billion appropriation extending revenue sharing through September 1980. The President signed it October 13. See CITY.

On January 30, the Supreme Court of the United States ruled that the Federal Election Commission performed executive duties, therefore its officers should be appointed by the executive branch of government, rather than Congress. The House approved the reconstituted commission, whose members would be appointed by the President, on May

3; the Senate approved it on May 4; and the President signed the measure on May 11. See SUPREME COURT OF THE UNITED STATES.

President Ford on September 14 signed legislation ending states of emergency that had been declared by Presidents Franklin D. Roosevelt, Harry S. Truman, and Richard M. Nixon. The bill also provided that Congress can end any new state of emergency declared by a President.

Foreign Policy. Congress acted early in the session to prevent U.S. involvement in the civil war in Angola. The House voted on January 27 to cut off $28 million in covert aid to pro-West factions in Angola, making the restriction an amendment to a $112.3-billion defense appropriation. The fund cutoff had earlier been approved by the Senate. The President disapproved of the amendment, but signed the defense appropriation bill on February 10. See AFRICA; ANGOLA.

The President signed a revised $6.9-billion foreign military aid bill on June 30. The act banned aid to Angola and Chile. A human rights provision warned that no nation may receive aid from the United States if it consistently violates internationally recognized human rights. On September 27, the House approved a foreign and military aid appropriation of $5.1 billion for fiscal 1977. The Senate approved the measure on September 28, and Ford signed it on October 1.

Scandals in Congress. Wayne L. Hays (D., Ohio) resigned his House seat on September 1 in the wake of a scandal surrounding his alleged use of public funds to retain Elizabeth Ray as a "secretary" for sexual favors. Because of the allegations, Hays had resigned as chairman of the Democratic National Congressional Committee and as chairman of the House Administration Committee in June.

Congressman Allan T. Howe (D., Utah) was convicted on a morals charge on July 23 and again in a second trial on August 24. He subsequently lost his bid for re-election. See ELECTIONS.

During the year, a South Korean lobbyist and several members and former members of Congress were reported to be the subjects of a grand jury investigation of influence peddling. Tongsun Park, a South Korean businessman, was at the center of the probe, because he allegedly gave money or gifts to members of Congress.

Intelligence Probes. Both the House and the Senate investigated the nation's intelligence-gathering agencies in 1976. The report of the House Select Committee on Intelligence, completed in January, was not made public, but newspaper summaries of the classified document said that the intelligence-gathering agencies had been operating secretly and without any congressional supervision. Almost one-third of the agencies' activities in recent years involved clandestine U.S. support of foreign political parties and heads of state. *The Village Voice,* a New York City newspaper, published part of the report on February 11. Newscaster Daniel Schorr admitted leaking the information and was suspended from his job with the Columbia Broadcasting System. Schorr refused to name his source, and the House began an investigation of the leak to Schorr in March. Six months later, it decided to drop the investigation.

The Senate Select Committee on Intelligence Activities published a summary of its report on April 28. The summary criticized some activities of the Federal Bureau of Investigation (FBI) and the Central Intelligence Agency (CIA) as illegal spying on U.S. citizens and called for reform through legislation to govern the agencies' activities. On May 19, the Senate voted to establish a Select Committee on Intelligence to oversee operations.

Assassination Probes. The Senate Select Committee on Intelligence charged on June 23 that the CIA and FBI investigations into the assassinations of President John F. Kennedy and civil rights leader Martin Luther King, Jr., were "lax." The House voted on September 17 to set up a special committee that will conduct a new inquiry into the two assassinations.   Carol L. Thompson

See also PRESIDENT OF THE UNITED STATES; UNITED STATES, GOVERNMENT OF THE.

CONNECTICUT. See STATE GOVERNMENT.

CONSERVATION groups saw renewed hope in 1976 for saving the whale from extinction, but they continued to demand a 10-year moratorium on whale hunting. The International Whaling Commission at its annual session in London in June reduced the number of whales that could be killed by about 40 per cent. On August 29, Russian officials said their country plans to stop hunting whales within two years. The Japanese, who along with the Soviet Union account for 90 per cent of the whale catch, accepted quota reductions after some United States conservation groups threatened to spread their boycott of Japanese products. See ENVIRONMENT.

United States conservation leaders viewed the election of James Earl (Jimmy) Carter, Jr., as President with hope for better support from the White House on environmental issues. They were pleased with the President-elect's choice of Idaho Governor Cecil D. Andrus, a staunch conservationist, as his nominee for secretary of the interior. Before the election, the League of Conservation Voters rated the former Georgia governor as "outstanding" and President Gerald R. Ford as "hopeless" on conservation issues. The league cited Carter's statement when he announced his candidacy that in the case of conflict between economic development and environmental quality he would support environmental quality. Ford's record was criticized as "chasing after energy at any price."

National Parks and Recreation. In a speech on August 29 in Yellowstone National Park, President Ford proposed a Bicentennial Land Heritage Act that would provide $1.5 billion over 10 years to expand and improve the national park and wildlife refuge systems. The program was aimed at halting the deterioration of many national parks because of insufficient funds for maintenance and staff.

The Ford proposal called for doubling the size of the park and refuge systems. Nearly all of the new acquisitions would be in Alaska, where about 63-million acres (25 million hectares) of federal land are scheduled to be set aside as park and wildlife preserves.

Environmentalists criticized the timing of the Ford proposal. For example, the Environmental Policy Center charged that the President had reached the "height of hypocrisy" in making the proposal so close to the end of the congressional session that it had no chance of passage.

In what he described as the first important step in carrying out the Land Heritage Act, President Ford signed legislation on September 28 that tripled the Land and Water Conservation Fund established in 1965 to create new outdoor recreation areas. The fund's authorized level of spending will reach a peak of $900 million annually in 1980.

Conservationists won a 14-year battle on September 11 when President Ford signed legislation to

Members of the Greenpeace Foundation, which wants whaling stopped, protest Russian ships searching for whales in the Pacific Ocean in June.

keep portions of the headwaters of the New River in North Carolina from being flooded by a private power project. The law made a 26.5-mile (42.6-kilometer) stretch of the New River part of the National Wild and Scenic River System and thus blocked an $845-million hydroelectric project that the American Electric Power Company had wanted to build since 1962. Conservationists fought the project vigorously because they feared dams would upset the area's ecology.

Congress imposed stiff controls on new strip mining in Death Valley National Monument and five other federal park areas in September (see MINES AND MINING).

But U.S. District Judge William T. Sweigert frustrated conservationists' efforts to protect the 62,000-acre (25,000-hectare) Redwood National Park, which was established in 1968 to preserve the world's tallest trees. Sweigert dismissed a Sierra Club suit on June 7 that sought to force the Department of the Interior to acquire additional land around the northern California park to offset logging operations just outside park boundaries.

Water Resources. The collapse of the Teton River Dam in southeastern Idaho on June 5 sent a torrent of water down the Teton River, killing 10 persons and causing damages estimated at more than $1 billion. Environmental organizations, which had charged in a 1973 court suit that the

dam was being built by the Bureau of Reclamation on a high-risk site, said the bureau had ignored their warnings. The dam collapse was the first in the bureau's 74-year history.

Severe droughts devastated some areas of the United States and Europe. Western Europe reported multibillion-dollar losses from a yearlong drought (see EUROPE). Great Britain appointed a water czar on August 24 to cope with its worst drought in more than 200 years. In the United States, lack of rainfall during the summer cut farm output in some areas and caused forest fires.

Preserving Wildlife. Conservationists won a number of legal battles in their crusade to save endangered species by protecting the places where they live. The desert pupfish, one of the rarest fish in the world, got a new lease on life on June 7 when the Supreme Court of the United States unanimously upheld the federal government's right to maintain the water level in the pupfish's only known habitat, Devil's Hole Cavern in Death Valley National Monument on the Nevada-California border. About 200 pupfish, stranded for 10,000 years in the deep pool when glaciers retreated, were threatened when pumping of ground water by nearby ranchers lowered the water level in Devil's Hole.

A federal judge ruled on May 25 that it would not be reasonable to halt construction of the $16-million Tellico Dam in Tennessee to save the rare snail darter fish's habitat. Environmental groups won an injunction on August 3, however, prohibiting the filling of the reservoir. The Tennessee Valley Authority, which is building the dam, maintained it is necessary to control floods. Conservationists contended the project would jeopardize the tiny fish's only habitat, a 16-mile (26-kilometer) stretch of the Tennessee River.

The Supreme Court upheld in November a lower-court ruling that blocked construction of a segment of a major interstate highway in southern Mississippi because it would run through a refuge being established for the 40 surviving Mississippi sandhill cranes. The court gave the Interior Department a virtual veto power over any highway plans that would endanger the habitat.

Clashes between environmentalists and government projects that threaten endangered species seem certain to multiply. In one of its most sweeping actions, the Interior Department added 159 animals to the list of endangered species on June 14, bringing the total to 585. The U.S. Fish and Wildlife Service said on June 18 that proposals to add 32 types of snails and 1,767 plants to endangered species listings could be "traumatic" because of the potential impact on many federal projects throughout the nation.   Andrew L. Newman

See also Section Two, LAST CHANCE FOR THE SEA TURTLE.

CONSTITUTION OF THE UNITED STATES.
The question of amending the U.S. Constitution to prohibit abortion on demand became a much-discussed issue in the 1976 presidential campaign.

President Gerald R. Ford, the Republican candidate, believed a constitutional amendment should give the states the power to decide whether abortion should be legal or illegal. Nevertheless, he endorsed the Republican Party platform, which supported efforts to enact a constitutional amendment protecting "the right to life for unborn children."

The Democratic Party took a different position. While acknowledging that many people have moral objections to abortion, the Democratic platform stated it would be undesirable to promote an anti-abortion amendment.

The Equal Rights Amendment (ERA), guaranteeing equal rights for women, again failed to win ratification by the necessary 38 states. As of December, 34 states had approved it. Ratification efforts were defeated in Arizona and Illinois, and the Kentucky House of Representatives voted to rescind its earlier ratification.

However, some observers believed that the pro-ERA forces might be regaining momentum after Massachusetts voters on November 2 approved a state ERA and Colorado voters defeated a move to rescind their state ERA. Darlene R. Stille

See also ELECTIONS.

CONSUMER AFFAIRS. The election of Democrat James Earl (Jimmy) Carter, Jr., as President in November 1976 and the return of a strongly Democratic Congress left consumer advocates both pleased and wary. The consumer advocates immediately began planning ways to collect on the promises made by Carter to push many goals previously blocked by the Administration of President Gerald R. Ford.

During his campaign, Carter endorsed the long-sought goal of an independent "watchdog" federal agency to ensure that the consumer point of view was adequately represented in regulatory activities. He also supported national health insurance, stronger environmental protection, stricter antitrust enforcement, more emphasis on energy conservation, and more citizen participation in government.

But Carter did not support all the goals of the consumer advocates. He said he was not ready to back the perennial effort to enact a national system of no-fault automobile insurance. Carter also opposed a ban on throwaway beverage containers, and he said he was against the use of government money to finance citizen participation in government proceedings.

Living Costs. During 1976, retail prices averaged nearly 6 per cent above the previous year. But in the fall, wholesale prices began rising faster than retail prices, even though those received by farmers – a large segment of the wholesale price index – lagged almost 6 per cent below 1975. At the same time, the gap between prices received by farmers and prices paid by consumers for the same products continued to increase, leaving retail prices of food 3 to 4 per cent higher in December than they were a year earlier.

When sales of 1977 automobiles began to fall below expectations in November, several manufacturers offered cash rebates to purchasers of small cars, the slowest sellers. General Motors Corporation offered $200 on its Vega, Pontiac Astre, and Chevette, while American Motors Corporation slashed the price of its subcompact Gremlin by $253, making it the lowest-priced domestic car at $2,995. American Motors also gave rebates of $25 to $225 on other models purchased by members of several senior-citizen groups. The rebates were a reaction to buyer resistance to the 6 per cent increase in auto prices for the 1977 models and the total boost of $1,000 in the price of smaller cars over a five-year period. See AUTOMOBILE.

Fuel prices, which had skyrocketed in recent years, generally held steady with one notable exception – natural gas. The Federal Power Commission (FPC), which controls interstate wholesale power rates, in July approved an increase from 52 cents to $1.42 per 1,000 cubic feet (28 cubic meters) of natural gas from "new" wells, those discovered or put in production since Jan. 1, 1975. Lesser rate increases were allowed for gas from older sources. Within some states, where the FPC had no authority, some gas prices went even higher. A coalition of consumer groups tried unsuccessfully to block the FPC rate increases in court. See ENERGY; PETROLEUM AND GAS.

Legislative Action. Consumer issues were not the dominant factors in many congressional elections, but the Consumer Federation of America claimed that 95 per cent of the candidates it endorsed won. These included 79 of the 82 endorsed House members running for re-election. It was the first time that the federation, the largest consumer lobbying group in the United States, had endorsed candidates for Congress.

Consumer-oriented measures that became federal law in October 1976 included the Toxic Substances Act, which authorizes the Environmental Protection Agency (EPA) to require safety tests on hazardous chemicals. The law requires producers to notify the EPA 90 days in advance of marketing a chemical. The EPA can add another 90-day delay and eventually ban the substance entirely if it is deemed too hazardous.

Also passed by Congress were measures requiring full disclosure of leasing arrangements for cars and other products and the banning of discrimination in granting credit. A law passed in 1975 banned credit discrimination on the basis of sex. The 1976 law

A former bill collector, masked to hide his identity, tells of some abusive debt-collection practices before a congressional committee.

were preparing more foods themselves in order to avoid the higher costs of factory-prepared items. Surveys conducted by grocery chains showed that shoppers were reading nutritional information on labels and watching unit prices more closely than in the past.

Several surveys showed householders were cutting down on their use of energy. More than half of those interviewed by the USDA said they had reduced heating fuel consumption and had cut home lighting, while 20 per cent used less air conditioning. Appliances also were being used less, but gasoline consumption increased.

At the same time, government regulations added some new consumer rights. A Federal Trade Commission rule that took effect in February requires mail-order merchants to ship orders within 30 days, unless a longer period was specified in advance. In case of failure to ship within 30 days or to notify the buyer of a delay beyond that time, the buyer must be given a refund if one is requested. A rule taking effect in May gave time-payment buyers the right to withhold payment for defective or undelivered goods without being sued for the total amount due. In effect, the rule canceled the "holder-in-due-course" doctrine, which allowed credit institutions that bought installment contracts to avoid responsibility for the products.

Voluntary Changes. Meanwhile, private businesses continued to make voluntary changes in their selling practices in anticipation of new laws and regulations. Many makers of aerosols, for example, eliminated fluorocarbon propellants shortly after scientific studies indicated fluorocarbons damage the earth's ozone shield. The National Association of Mutual Insurance Agents launched the first consumer action program in the insurance industry. Known as the Insurance Consumer Action Panel (ICAP), it was modeled after similar programs in the automobile, furniture, and appliance industries. The National Canners Association, whose members manufacture 90 per cent of the canned foods in the United States, announced a program of labeling the weight of "solid content," beginning with the 1977 harvest season. And the Monsanto Company said it would stop making cancer-causing polychlorinated biphenyls (PCB's) in October 1977, a year before the Toxic Substances Act officially bans them.

At the grassroots level, citizens' groups became more active in many areas. Committees were formed to press for the resolution of individual consumer complaints, even to the point of picketing stores. In such groups, each complainant was expected to work on another person's problem in return for group action on his own complaint. Such consumer action committees were especially active in San Francisco and Cleveland.   Arthur E. Rowse

COSTA RICA. See LATIN AMERICA.

extended the ban to cover age, race, color, religion, and national origin.

Several consumer measures approved earlier by Congress became effective in 1976. One, effective in July, strengthened penalties for tampering with automobile odometers. Another, effective in June, made it permissible for parents and students who are 18 or older to see most of their school records and challenge their accuracy. A revised law requiring disclosure of real estate settlement costs in advance also became effective in June.

Consumer legislation continued to flourish at the state level. And voter referendums decided an increasing number of consumer and environmental issues. Voters in Michigan and Maine voted in November to require deposits on most beverage containers, joining Vermont and Oregon. The aim was to reduce litter and cut the use of energy by the beverage-container industry.

Changing Customs. Living patterns shifted substantially, primarily because of continued inflation and high unemployment. Changes in consumer attitudes and practices were documented in a massive U.S. Department of Agriculture (USDA) survey. The study showed that food buyers, in particular, were becoming more fastidious. Thirty per cent of those interviewed said they checked newspaper ads for prices more often and saved more discount coupons than ever before. Twenty per cent said they

COURTS AND LAWS. A go-slow posture adopted in 1976 by the United Nations (UN) International Court of Justice at The Hague, the Netherlands, in a mineral-rights dispute led to agreement between Greece and Turkey on direct negotiations between the two countries. The International Court on September 12 refused a Greek request to order a temporary ban on Turkish oil-surveying in the Aegean Sea, but agreed to hear full arguments on the controversy if both parties agreed.

The court had initially urged the two countries to negotiate the matter themselves, as called for by a UN Security Council resolution approved on August 25. After Turkey offered to pull back its oil-search ship, Greece agreed on November 20 to take part in direct negotiations with Turkey. See GREECE; TURKEY.

The Hearst Case. Worldwide attention was focused on the California trial of Patricia Hearst, daughter of millionaire publisher William Randolph Hearst, Jr. On March 20, she was found guilty on federal charges of armed robbery and of using a firearm in the commission of a felony. On April 12, she was given an interim sentence of 25 years, and, on September 24, after psychiatric tests, she was sentenced to concurrent terms of seven years in prison on the first charge and two years on the second. The charges stemmed from the 1974 robbery of a San Francisco bank.

On November 19, Hearst was released in the custody of her parents on bail of $1.5 million, pending appeal of her federal conviction. She still faced 11 felony charges in a California state court.

The 1975 manslaughter conviction of Kenneth C. Edelin, a Boston physician, in the death of a fetus during a legal abortion was overturned by the Massachusetts Supreme Court on December 17. And, in New York, the two kidnapers of Samuel Bronfman, son of the chairman of the Seagram Company, were acquitted in December of charges of kidnaping. But they were convicted of grand larceny for extorting the $2.3-million ransom and sentenced to three and four years in prison.

Legal Ethics. The ethical responsibilities of attorneys continued to be hotly debated in the United States. A summary of the legal actions related to the Watergate scandal, released by an American Bar Association (ABA) committee in October, reported that seven lawyers, including former President Richard M. Nixon and former Attorney General John N. Mitchell, had been disbarred for their roles in Watergate. Eleven other lawyers were publicly disciplined — most of them by temporary suspension from practice — for their parts in the scandal.

Among the ethical reforms advocated for the legal establishment was a proposal to disqualify all associates and partners of former government attorneys from practicing in matters those public employees once handled. This proposal by the Legal

Patricia Hearst was sentenced to a prison term for bank robbery in April, then freed on bail in November, pending appeal of her conviction.

Ethics Committee of the District of Columbia Bar Association prompted a storm of protest among Washington lawyers, a large number of whom are former government employees. No action was taken on the Legal Ethics Committee recommendation during the year.

More Funds. In extending federal funding for the Law Enforcement Assistance Administration (LEAA) into 1979, Congress ordered a greatly expanded role for state courts in deciding how LEAA money should be spent. Judges and lawyers had complained that a disproportionate share of LEAA grants previously went to buy equipment for police departments, rather than to the courts. In a related development, the reorganized Legal Services Corporation, a group responsible for representing the nation's poor, received a large budget increase for 1977 – from $92.3 million to $125 million. This increase made possible the first improvement in legal services for the poor in five years.

The Supreme Court ruled in June that it is constitutional for states to allow judges who are not lawyers to preside over criminal trials, at least in cases in which the defendant can appeal for a second trial before a judge who is a lawyer. About three-fourths of the states have nonlawyer judges in some of their courts.   David C. Beckwith

See also CIVIL RIGHTS; CONSUMER AFFAIRS; SUPREME COURT OF THE UNITED STATES.

CRIME. Two forms of international wrongdoing dominated headlines in 1976. The first was the use of bribery by multinational corporations to obtain sales contracts with governments of other countries. The largest of the scandals involved the Lockheed Aircraft Corporation, the United States biggest defense contractor. As details of Lockheed payoffs of more than $25 million since 1967 became known, the governments of Japan and the Netherlands tottered, and officials in Italy, West Germany, and other countries were implicated. See INTERNATIONAL TRADE AND FINANCE (Close-Up).

A more violent form of international crime, airline hijacking for political motives, received a serious setback in July, when Israeli commandos rescued 103 hostages from Entebbe Airport in Uganda. See ISRAEL; MIDDLE EAST; UGANDA.

Nice Bank Job. History's biggest bank heist was completed on July 18, when a gang of thieves tunneled from a sewer into the basement of a Nice, France, bank and escaped with at least $8 million in money and jewelry. Police arrested seven suspects in October.

In the United States, the Federal Bureau of Investigation reported major crimes increased 3 per cent during the first half of 1976, well below increases in recent years. Six of the seven major crimes actually dropped – murder was down 12 per cent, robbery 10 per cent, burglary 5 per cent, and

auto theft 3 per cent, and both rape and aggravated assault dropped 1 per cent. But larceny-theft, the most frequently reported crime, rose 11 per cent, accounting for the overall rise. Figures released by the Law Enforcement Assistance Administration indicated that U.S. police solved 21 per cent of all reported crimes during 1975.

Most Spectacular Crime in the United States in 1976 was the abduction for $5 million ransom of 26 Chowchilla, Calif., schoolchildren and their bus driver on July 15. The victims were taken in vans about 100 miles (160 kilometers) from the kidnaping site and placed in a truck trailer that had been buried in a quarry near Livermore, Calif. They managed to dig their way out after 15 hours. Three young men were arrested and charged with kidnaping and theft on July 23 and 29.

An investigative reporter for *The Arizona Republic* newspaper, Don Bolles, 47, lost both legs and an arm when a bomb destroyed his car on June 2. Bolles, who was investigating land-fraud charges involving top state politicians, died of his injuries on June 13. Underworld figure John Adamson was tried for the murder, but the judge declared a mistrial in October. Police charged a nurse's aide with multiple counts of arson and murder after 18 elderly residents died in a Chicago nursing home fire on January 30.   David C. Beckwith

Workers pull a 30-foot (9-meter) truck van out of a hole in a California quarry where kidnapers imprisoned 26 schoolchildren and their bus driver.

CROSLAND, ANTHONY (1918-   ), became foreign secretary of Great Britain on April 8, 1976. He succeeded James Callaghan, who became prime minister on April 5 following the resignation of Harold Wilson. Crosland had been environment secretary in the Labour government.

Charles Anthony Raven Crosland was born on Aug. 29, 1918. He attended a private school in London, and Trinity College at Oxford University. During World War II, he served as a parachute officer in Italy, North Africa, and Austria. He returned to Oxford after the war and earned honors in politics, philosophy, and economics. From 1947 to 1950, he taught economics at Trinity College.

Crosland was elected to Parliament in 1950. He quickly emerged as a party theorist, publishing several books on socialist economics, including *The Future of Socialism* (1956), one of the most influential documents on the Labour Party.

When the Labour Party returned to power in 1964, Crosland was named minister of state for economic affairs. He was secretary of state for education and science from 1965 to 1967, president of the Board of Trade from 1967 to 1969, and secretary of state for local government and regional planning from 1969 to 1970.

He lives with his second wife, the former Susan Barnes, and her two daughters.   Kathryn Sederberg

See also CALLAGHAN, JAMES; GREAT BRITAIN.

CUBA. A warming trend in United States-Cuban relations cooled considerably in 1976. The presence of Cuban troops in Angola, where they helped turn the tide in the civil war in favor of the Marxist Popular Movement for the Liberation of Angola, caused the cooling. Estimates of the Cuban troops involved varied from a high of 16,000 to a low of 10,000. See AFRICA; ANGOLA.

U.S. Reaction. Senator Jacob K. Javits (R., N.Y.) told Panamanian government chief Omar Torrijos Herrera that Cuban intervention in Angola had "absolutely aborted" prospects for normal relations between Havana and Washington, D.C. President Gerald R. Ford in February called Prime Minister Fidel Castro an "international outlaw." Later in the year, Castro renounced a 1973 antihijacking agreement with the United States. He maintained that the United States was responsible for the sabotage of a Cuban airliner that crashed on October 7, killing 73 persons.

Cuba remained active in Latin America during the year. On February 23, the Venezuelan magazine *Resumen* reported that Cubans were giving paramilitary training to thousands of youths in Guyana. However, Guyana's Foreign Minister Frederick R. Wills denied this on March 3, charging that the allegation was part of a U.S. campaign "of destabilization against Guyana's socialist government." It was confirmed, however, that from 200 to 300 Cuban technicians were working on economic development projects in Jamaica and that some Jamaican police were training in Cuba.

At the Organization of American States (OAS) annual meeting in Santiago, Chile, in June, a secret 35-page OAS Human Rights Commission report accused the Cuban government of violating the human rights of political prisoners. The report was not debated publicly because, it was claimed, it had been completed too late.

On February 15, Cubans approved the first Constitution since the Castro revolution came to power. Under its provisos, a Communist system of democratic centralism was established in which a pyramid of lesser assemblies elect a National Assembly of People's Power. On September 10, Cuba's first elections under Castro were held for 169 municipal assemblies.

The Economy. Castro announced on September 28 that the Cuban people were in for a period of sacrifices because of a fall in world sugar prices and high import costs. After three years of drought, sugar production had fallen from 7.2 million short tons (6.5 million metric tons) in 1975 to 6.4 million short tons (5.8 million metric tons) in 1976. The world sugar price had dropped from a record 66 cents per pound (0.45 kilogram) in November 1974 to about 8 cents.   Everett G. Martin

See also LATIN AMERICA (Facts in Brief Table).

CYPRUS. The Greek Cypriot coalition of centrists, Socialists, and Communists won all 35 seats in parliamentary elections on Sept. 6, 1976. Their platform pledged full support for President Archbishop Makarios III and his policies of international nonalignment and long-term struggle against the continued Turkish occupation of the northern 40 per cent of the island. The anti-Makarios party of Glafcos Clerides, who favored a quick settlement with the Turks, won no seats.

Turkish Cypriots on June 20 elected Rauf Denktash president of the self-proclaimed Turkish Cypriot Federated State. Only Turkey recognizes the state, and Greek Cypriot leaders quickly called the election invalid. Turkish Cypriots held military parades on July 20 in the northern area they occupy to celebrate the second anniversary of the Turkish invasion of Cyprus.

Clerides resigned as chief Greek Cypriot negotiator at the intercommunal peace talks in Vienna, Austria, on April 9 after admitting that he made a secret agreement with Denktash about negotiating procedures. Tassos Papadopoulos, deputy president of the Cyprus House of Representatives, succeeded Clerides. Umit Suleiman Onan replaced Denktash as negotiator on April 15. Little progress was made in the negotiations.   Kenneth Brown

See also GREECE; MIDDLE EAST (Facts in Brief Table); TURKEY; UNITED NATIONS.

CZECHOSLOVAKIA

CZECHOSLOVAKIA pursued friendly diplomatic relations with the non-Communist world in 1976 but remained committed to repression at home. The Austrian chancellor, Bruno Kreisky, visited Czechoslovakia in February, the first such visit by a senior Austrian official since World War II. Archbishop Luigi Poggi, the Vatican's specialist in Communist countries, visited Prague in July, and Foreign Minister Bohuslav Chnoupek visited Great Britain in September.

Czechoslovakia's balance of trade with the Western world worsened during the first nine months of 1976. Exports dropped 3.3 per cent, while imports increased 7.1 per cent. About one-third of Czechoslovakia's foreign trade is with Western nations.

Economic Problems claimed the most attention at the Communist Party Congress in Prague in April. The more than 1,200 delegates re-elected Gustav Husak party leader. Right wing opportunism – the official name for 1968-style reforms – was declared still to be the main enemy, and only minor changes were proposed to deal with industrial obsolescence and lagging labor productivity. Husak hinted that some former party members expelled after the 1968 Russian invasion might be allowed to regain party membership. But on October 14, editor Jiri Hajek was replaced after pleading in a banned issue of the party magazine *Tvorba*

for a return to the party of those victims of the post-1968 purge who had "remained faithful to socialism."

Czechoslovakia had problems meeting the demand for fuel, electric power, and farm products. As a result, Husak dismissed two senior federal vice-premiers and Minister of Agriculture Bohuslav Vecera in September. But Husak and other senior officials assured Czechoslovaks that basic food prices, frozen since 1970, would not be raised soon.

Other Problems. A Politburo member, Josef Kempny, announced on September 5 that Russia would sell Czechoslovakia less oil in the 1976 to 1980 period than had been planned previously. Prague and other cities introduced energy-conservation measures on September 30.

On October 6, Prime Minister Lubomir Strougal conceded that the country faced a meat shortage and would have to import grain from the West. The grain harvest was 14 per cent below the 1975 harvest. Czechoslovakia's collective farms produced 3.1 per cent less meat and 2.3 per cent fewer eggs during the first half of 1976, compared with the same period in 1975. In contrast, industrial production gained 6 per cent.   Chris Cviic

See also EUROPE (Facts in Brief Table).

DAHOMEY (BENIN). See AFRICA.

DAIRYING. See AGRICULTURE.

President Gustav Husak signs autographs for some of the delegates to the 15th Communist Party Congress, held in Prague, Czechoslovakia, in April.

The new mayor of Dallas, Robert Folsom, and his wife celebrate his victory in an April runoff election.

DALLAS-FORT WORTH. School integration began in Dallas on Aug. 23, 1976. More than 17,000 black, white, and Mexican-American pupils were placed in a busing program to comply with a desegregation plan handed down by U.S. District Court Judge William M. Taylor, Jr., on March 10. No violence or other major problems were reported. The Fifth U.S. Circuit Court of Appeals continued an appeal from the National Association for the Advancement of Colored People to stop implementation of the plan because it did not go far enough in promoting integration.

The desegregation plan combined busing and voluntary integration for minority students with magnet schools. Magnet schools are those with superior facilities to attract pupils of all races. The plan divided the Dallas School District into six subdistricts, and it restricted busing within each of the subdistricts to those pupils in grades four through eight.

Twelve magnet schools were created to promote voluntary desegregation and attracted more than 17,000 pupils of all races. Also, under a voluntary transfer plan, a student could transfer from a school in which he or she was among the racial majority to a school in which he or she would be in the minority.

City Government. Robert Folsom, a millionaire land developer and former president of the Dallas School Board, was elected mayor of Dallas in a runoff election on April 24. He defeated Garry Weber, a millionaire stockbroker, who resigned from the city council to run for the office. The runoff election followed a five-way race on April 3 that failed to produce a clear winner.

The Dallas Police Department on June 13 abandoned a five-year, $300,000 program to hire black and Mexican-American police officers on a 1-to-1 basis with whites. Police officials indicated the program was discontinued because of a lack of interest on the part of minority-group members.

Culture and Costs. The Fort Worth Art Museum sponsored The Great American Rodeo in April as a Bicentennial tribute to the famous Fort Worth Fat Stock Show. The event was intended to give the museum a unique identity and attract visitors to the museum from the show and rodeo.

Living costs in the Dallas area rose 6.7 per cent from mid-1975 to mid-1976, but food costs rose only 3.6 per cent. The unemployment rate was 5.1 per cent in June. Earnings of factory workers increased 5.4 per cent to an annual average of $9,531 – about the amount the U.S. Department of Labor estimated an average family of four needed for a minimum standard of living. Department store sales increased 12.3 per cent, and construction was up 1.5 per cent at midyear.   James M. Banovetz

DAM. See BUILDING AND CONSTRUCTION.

DANCING

Choreographers and dance companies celebrated the American Revolution Bicentennial en masse in 1976. The most extravagant new dance in honor of the occasion was also the most offbeat—George Balanchine's *Union Jack.* This hourlong tribute to Great Britain's military and music-hall traditions was premièred by the New York City Ballet on May 13 during its two-month season at Lincoln Center's State Theater in New York City. *Union Jack,* which has a cast of 75, opens with a regal Scottish tattoo, then moves into a duet for the cockney Costermonger Pearly King and Queen, and concludes with the entire company semaphoring "God Save the Queen" in naval code. Presented by a company that usually favors austere productions over all-out bashes, *Union Jack* was a smash hit.

Other Bicentennial Offerings were in a more conventional mode. The Alvin Ailey Dance Company toured the nation with a Duke Ellington festival, in which they presented a number of works that were based on Ellington's music, such as Ailey's *Black, Brown and Beige* and *Three Black Kings,* Louis Falco's *Caravan,* and Lester Horton's *Liberian Suite.* For the spring season in New York City, Ailey devised *Pas de "Duke,"* which teamed the Ailey company's own star Judith Jamison with the dance superstar Mikhail Baryshnikov.

The Martha Graham Dance Company, celebrating its 50th birthday, drew on Graham's long-standing interest in American themes to present programs titled *In the American Grain.* These programs, which toured the United States and Europe, included *Frontier; Letter to the World,* based on poet Emily Dickinson's life; and *The Scarlet Letter,* a new work created for Rudolf Nureyev and first seen in New York City on Dec. 22, 1975. In recognition of Graham's position as the pioneer of an indigenous American art form, London's Royal Opera House in Covent Garden invited the company to dance there from July 19 to 31, 1976. This was the first time modern dancers had performed in that opera house.

The American Ballet Theater (ABT) also presented Americana evenings during its summer season at the State Theater in New York City from June 29 to August 7. The selections were highlighted by a revival of Agnes de Mille's *Rodeo* and a company première of her *Texas Fourth* on July 8.

The Joffrey Ballet, celebrating its own past, revived American-choreographed signature pieces that had not been given in several years. Ruthanna Boris' *Cakewalk* and Gerald Arpino's *Olympics* were seen from August 3 to 7 at Wolf Trap Farm in Virginia. For its four-week fall season at New York

City's City Center, beginning October 13, the Joffrey revived Arpino's *Sea Shadow* and Robert Joffrey's multimedia *Astarte.* A new production of De Mille's *Rodeo* was also added to the program.

Other major choreographers who jumped aboard the Bicentennial bandwagon included Erick Hawkins, who was preparing a dance about the Southwest to a commissioned score by Alan Hovhaness; Murray Louis, whose *Catalogue* was based on a turn-of-the-century Sears, Roebuck and

Margot Fonteyn basks in the midst of admirers in the ballet *The Merry Widow,* which was danced by the Australian Ballet in Washington, D.C.

Company catalog and set to music by Victor Herbert; and Twyla Tharp, who spoofed parades and parade mentality in *Give and Take.*

Other New Productions. Evaluating the year artistically, the U.S. birthday party receded in importance. For all the attention given Balanchine's *Union Jack,* the artistic sensation of the New York City Ballet was his *Chaconne,* premièred by the company on January 22. Set to music by Christoph Willibald Gluck, this suite of dances is a sublime example of Balanchine's classical style.

Other critically acclaimed new works included Tharp's *Push Comes to Shove* to music by Joseph Haydn, premièred by ABT on January 9 in a production starring Baryshnikov; Paul Taylor's *Cloven*

Kingdom, first danced by his company on June 9, and *Polaris,* premièred on August 26; and Merce Cunningham's *Torse,* unveiled January 13 in Princeton, N.J. The Joffrey Ballet's outstanding event was an entire program of Kurt Jooss dances, a rare chance to view four ballets created by the German expressionist in the 1930s and 1940s.

Internationalism was the keynote of ABT's year. Its most glamorous and important new productions were the Russian classic *Sleeping Beauty,* premièred on June 15 at the Metropolitan Opera House in New York City, and Baryshnikov's staging of *The Nutcracker,* which opened during the 1976 Christmas season at the John F. Kennedy Center for the Performing Arts in Washington, D.C. Much atten-

The Alvin Ailey Dance Company toured the United States with a program based on the late Duke Ellington's music, in a tribute to that jazz musician.

tion was drawn to ABT's international roster of guest artists—Rudolf Nureyev, Marcia Haydee, Lynn Seymour, Alicia Alonso, Erik Bruhn, Natalia Makarova, and Yoko Moroshita. These stars danced in a number of regular programs and gala performances throughout the year in Los Angeles, San Francisco, New York City, and Washington, D.C.

Television and Dance joined ranks as never before, perhaps in response to the dance boom, but definitely spurring a bigger boom. The most ambitious project was the "Dance in America" series, produced by WNET of New York City, which featured the Joffrey Ballet, the Pennsylvania Ballet, and the Graham and Tharp companies. The participation of both choreographers and television production crews in televising these programs accounted for their high quality. Other television efforts included the Bolshoi Ballet's production of *Romeo and Juliet.* Filmed in Moscow, it was aired nationally on June 27. A live performance of ABT's *Swan Lake* was broadcast from the New York City State Theater on June 30.

Visitors from Abroad. The Royal Danish Ballet received a mixed reception on its first visit to the United States in 11 years. It appeared at the Kennedy Center from May 11 to 16 and spent the next three weeks at the Metropolitan Opera House. The Danes specialize in 19th-century ballets by August Bournonville, which much of the public found old-fashioned and somewhat tame when compared to the virtuosity of the Russian tradition. Yet many critics were disappointed that the Danes did not bring more Bournonville. Some found Flemming Flindt's *The Triumph of Death*—a multimedia extravaganza featuring nudity and Danish rock music—dated and exploitative. Although the men's liveliness and charm were admired in the Bournonville works, the general level of dancing was considered to be below that of the Danes' last visit in 1965.

The exquisite professionalism of Britain's Royal Ballet, from ensemble to soloist, was universally cheered during its spring visit to New York City, Washington, D.C., and Philadelphia. Sir Frederick Ashton's *A Month in the Country,* his first ballet in several years, was the chief novelty. Most of the program was composed of tried-and-true full-length spectacles.

Igor Moiseyev's Russian Festival drew upon the diverse folk cultures of Russia, including the Eskimos of northeastern Siberia. It held forth at the Metropolitan Opera House for three weeks in July and then visited Boston, Washington, D.C., Chicago, Detroit, and St. Louis. Another visiting group was the Dutch National Ballet, which toured Canadian cities in October before coming to New York City's Uris Theater in November.   Nancy Goldner

DEATHS OF NOTABLE PERSONS in 1976 included those listed below. An asterisk (*) indicates the person is the subject of a biography in THE WORLD BOOK ENCYCLOPEDIA. Those listed were Americans unless otherwise indicated.

*Aalto, Alvar (1898-May 11), Finnish architect who pioneered in developing new forms of architecture and functional plywood furniture.

*Albers, Josef (1888-March 25), German-born painter and educator noted for his experiments with color relationships.

Arlen, Richard (1900-March 28), romantic actor who starred in the first Oscar-winning film, *Wings* (1927).

Auchincloss, James C. (1885-Oct. 2), Republican congressman from New Jersey from 1943 to 1964.

Baddeley, Angela (1904-Feb. 22), British actress who played the crusty but tender-hearted cook, Mrs. Bridges, in the "Upstairs, Downstairs" television series.

Ballard, Florence (1944-Feb. 22), original member of the Supremes singing trio.

Banting, Lady Henrietta (1912-July 26), Canadian physician and widow of Sir Frederick Banting, discoverer of insulin. She was director of the Cancer Detection Center at Women's College Hospital in Toronto from 1959 to 1971.

Barrett, William A. (1896-April 12), Democratic congressman from Pennsylvania since 1948.

Beecher, Henry K. (1904-July 25), anesthetist, chairman of Harvard Medical School's Committee to Examine the Definition of Brain Death.

Berkeley, Busby (1895-March 14), ingenious dance director of such Hollywood musical extravaganzas as *Gold Diggers of 1933*.

Bolles, Donald F. (1928-June 13), investigative reporter for *The Arizona Republic* whose car was bombed while he was working on an article about allegedly fraudulent land deals.

Boswell, Connee (1908-Oct. 11), popular singer whose recordings of such songs as "Stormy Weather" and "They Can't Take That Away from Me" sold more than 75 million copies.

*Britten, Benjamin (1913–Dec. 4), British composer and one of the 20th century's leading musical creators. He composed such works as the opera *Peter Grimes* (1945) and the acclaimed *A War Requiem* (1962), based on the Roman Catholic Mass for the dead blended with verses from the antiwar poems of Wilfred Owen.

Brown, Joe D. (1915-April 22), journalist and novelist whose book *Addie Pray* became the movie *Paper Moon*.

Browning, Gordon (1889-May 23), Democratic governor of Tennessee from 1937 to 1939 and 1949 to 1953 and congressman from 1923 to 1935.

Buchan, Alistair (1918-Feb. 3), British educator and an expert on international relations who founded the Institute for Strategic Studies in 1958. He served on the YEAR BOOK Board of Editors from 1970 to 1973.

*Calder, Alexander (1898-Nov. 11), sculptor whose witty and imaginative mobiles and stabiles enliven cities throughout the world.

Cambridge, Godfrey (1933-Nov. 29), black actor and comedian whose starring roles included *Purlie Victorious* (1964) on stage and *Cotton Comes to Harlem* on screen.

Carey, Max (1890-May 30), outfielder for the Pittsburgh Pirates and Brooklyn Dodgers, who stole 738 bases.

Cassin, René (1887-Feb. 20), French jurist who won the 1968 Nobel Prize for Peace for furthering the cause of human rights.

*Chou En-lai (1898-Jan. 8), prime minister of the People's Republic of China since 1949. See CHINA (Close-Up).

*Christie, Dame Agatha (1891-Jan. 12), prolific British author of detective fiction, noted for her ingenious plots. See LITERATURE (Close-Up).

Ted Mack presided over the "Original Amateur Hour."

Busby Berkeley, a Hollywood producer.

Lily Pons sang at the Met for more than 25 years.

Lin Yutang was a Chinese scholar.

Clapp, Anna (1893-Feb. 3), who turned her homemade vegetable soup into America's first commercially prepared baby food.

Clark, John (1886-Jan. 18), Conservative member of the Canadian Parliament from 1921 to 1929 and president of the Canadian Bar Association from 1950 to 1952.

Cobb, Lee J. (1911-Feb. 11), stage, screen, and TV actor who created the role of Willy Loman in Arthur Miller's *Death of a Salesman* in 1949.

Cogley, John (1916-March 28), proponent of reform in the Roman Catholic Church and an editor of *Commonweal* magazine.

Combs, Earle (1899-July 21), who batted ahead of Babe Ruth and Lou Gehrig in the New York Yankees' "Murderers' Row" batting order.

Cook, Piano Roll (J. Lawrence) (1900-April 2), composer of master rolls for player pianos.

*Costello, John A. (1891-Jan. 5), prime minister of Ireland from 1948 to 1951 and 1954 to 1957.

Cunningham, Imogen (1883-June 24), pioneer photographer noted for a fresh, witty approach.

*Daley, Richard J. (1902-Dec.20), Democratic mayor of Chicago since 1955, one of the most powerful political leaders in the United States.

Dam, Henrik (1895-April 17), Danish biochemist and co-winner of the 1943 Nobel Prize for Physiology or Medicine.

D'Arcy, Martin C. (1888-Nov. 20), British Jesuit philosopher who converted such famous people as Dame Edith Sitwell and Evelyn Waugh to Roman Catholicism.

Lord Thomson of
Fleet, publisher.

Angela Baddeley played
in "Upstairs, Downstairs."

Andrei Grechko,
Russian leader.

Lotte Lehmann was a
renowned opera star.

Dennis, Patrick (Edward E. Tanner III) (1921-Nov. 6), best-selling novelist whose wacky *Auntie Mame* (1955) was adapted into the hit musical *Mame.*

Dennison, David M. (1900-April 3), theoretical physicist who discovered the spin of the proton.

Deschler, Lewis (1905-July 12), parliamentarian, a powerful figure in Congress for over 46 years.

Deutsch, John J. (1911-March 18), Canadian educator, former chairman of the Economic Council of Canada.

Doering, Carl (1890-March 28), biostatistician who found the link between cancer and heavy smoking in 1928.

*Douglas, Paul H. (1892-Sept. 24), liberal Democratic senator from Illinois from 1949 to 1967, an early advocate of civil rights.

Dowling, Eddie (1894-Feb. 18), Broadway actor, playwright, and director who played in *The Glass Menagerie* (1945) and produced *The Time of Your Life* (1940) with William Saroyan.

Dwyer, Florence P. (1902-Feb. 29), Republican congresswoman from New Jersey from 1956 to 1971.

Dykes, Jimmy (1896-June 15), baseball player and manager whose major-league career spanned 50 years.

*Ernst, Max (1891-April 1), German artist and sculptor, a leader in the surrealism and Dada movements in art.

Erskine, Laurie York (1894-Nov. 30), English-born author of the *Renfrew of the Mounted* adventure series.

Evans, Dame Edith (1888-Oct.14), British actress known for her subtle performances in Shakespearean plays and Restoration comedies.

Faber, Red (1888-Sept. 25), baseball pitcher who was elected to membership in the National Baseball Hall of Fame in 1964.

Faith, Percy (1909-February 9), Canadian-born orchestra conductor whose easy-listening arrangements charmed a generation of radio listeners.

*Farley, James A. (1888-June 9), U.S. postmaster general from 1933 to 1940 and chairman of the Democratic Party from 1932 to 1940.

Fishbein, Morris (1889-Sept. 27), physician and editor of the *Journal of the American Medical Association* from 1924 to 1949.

Fisk, Sarah E. (1885-Jan. 9), a leader in the education of mentally retarded children.

Folsom, Marion B. (1893-Sept. 28), secretary of the Department of Health, Education, and Welfare from 1955 to 1958 and architect of the 1935 Social Security Act.

Friis, Harald T. (1893-June 15), Danish-born engineer whose work on microwaves included the design of the ubiquitous rabbit ear TV antenna.

Fuller, Lone Cat (Jesse) (1897-Jan.30?), folk-blues musician and one of the greatest one-man bands.

Gabin, Jean (1904-Nov. 15), French film actor since the 1930s who played the hero-victim in such roles as Jean Valjean in *Les Miserables.*

Gallico, Paul W. (1897-July 15), sportswriter and prolific novelist whose books include *The Snow Goose* (1941), *Mrs. 'arris Goes to Paris* (1958), and *The Poseidon Adventure* (1969).

*Getty, J. Paul (1892-June 6), oilman who was considered the world's wealthiest man. See Close-Up.

*Grechko, Andrei A. (1903-April 26), Russian military leader who became defense minister in 1967 and was named to the Politburo in 1973.

György, Paul (1893-March 1), Hungarian-born nutritionist and pediatrician who discovered three vitamins — riboflavin, pyridoxine (B6), and biotin.

Hackett, Bobby (1915-June 7), cornetist whose mellow tone and graceful style made him a favorite in both jazz and pop music.

Haddow, Sir Alexander (1907-Jan. 21), Scottish pathologist who pioneered in treating cancer with drugs and by stimulating the body's own defense system.

Haig-Brown, Roderick (1908-Oct. 9), Canadian writer and environmentalist, author of some 24 descriptive books on the outdoors.

Halop, Billy (1920-Nov. 9), actor who played Tommy, leader of the Dead End Kids in 1930s films.

Hart, Philip A. (1912-Dec. 26), liberal Democratic senator from Michigan since 1959, often called the "conscience of the Senate."

*Hastie, Judge William H. (1904-April 14), governor of the Virgin Islands from 1946 to 1949 and the first black on the U.S. Court of Appeals.

*Heidegger, Martin (1889-May 26), German philosopher who influenced fields ranging from physics to literary criticism. He said the most important question is, "Why is there something rather than nothing at all?"

Heinemann, Gustav (1899-July 7), president of West Germany from 1969 to 1974.

*Heisenberg, Werner (1901-Feb. 1), German nuclear physicist who won the 1932 Nobel Prize for Physics for founding quantum mechanics, which led to a more precise theory about atoms.

Hodgson, Peter C. L. (1912-Aug. 6), Canadian-born marketing executive who turned a seemingly useless silicone substance into an international rage called Silly Putty that sold for $1 a dab and made millions.

Howe, James Wong (1899-July 12), Chinese-born cinematographer who won Oscars for his work in *The Rose Tattoo* (1955) and *Hud* (1963).

Howlin' Wolf (Chester A. Burnett) (1910-Jan. 10), Mississippi blues singer and composer whose style influenced such rock groups as the Rolling Stones.

Of Men
And Money

When Howard Hughes died on April 5, 1976, he was 70 years old and worth perhaps $2.5 billion. When J. Paul Getty died at 83 on June 6, he was worth between $2 billion and $4-billion. But as he once ruefully pointed out, "A billion dollars isn't worth what it used to be."

That is true. The combined fortunes of these two remarkable men could scarcely have run the United States government in 1976 for five days. Still, such sums in the hands of individuals represent great power.

How Getty and Hughes made their money, and how it shaped their lives, is an interesting study of contrasts. Getty, patient, clever, and hard-working, seemed in later years to enjoy the notoriety of great wealth, as well as its other advantages. Hughes, flamboyant boy wonder of the 1920s and 1930s, ended life an eccentric prisoner of wealth.

Jean Paul Getty was born in Minneapolis in 1892. His father struck oil in Oklahoma in 1903 and was soon a millionaire. After college, Getty began buying oil leases in Oklahoma, and by the time he was 23, he was a millionaire. He accumulated oil companies during the Great Depression. In 1949, he obtained an oil concession in the neutral zone between Saudi Arabia and Kuwait. The oil that began to gush there in 1953 made him a billionaire.

Despite his wealth, Getty worked 10 to 14 hours a day until he died. Business was his first love – all five of his marriages failed. He was often suspicious of friendly overtures and worried that his money was more the attraction than he was. He hated being overcharged or being expected to pay for others. He installed a pay phone in his 72-room mansion near London for the use of his guests.

Getty's grandson was kidnaped in Italy in 1973, and the abductors demanded $16 million in ransom, sending Getty the boy's severed ear. But he refused to pay, saying that if he ransomed one grandchild, all 14 would be in danger. The youth was later freed for a much smaller sum.

Howard Robard Hughes was born in Houston in 1905. He inherited his father's firm, the Hughes Tool Com-

Howard Hughes (1905–1976)

J. Paul Getty (1892–1976)

pany, in 1924. With the profits from this company, the restless young man headed for Hollywood and an astonishing series of careers. He made movies, such as *Hell's Angels* (1930) starring Jean Harlow and *The Outlaw* (1943) starring Jane Russell. He set up the Hughes Aircraft Company in 1935 to build the planes he designed. He turned a small airline into the giant Trans World Airlines.

In the 1950s, Hughes began to withdraw from the world. Although he still ruled his empire with an iron hand, he was rarely seen. Suspicious of others, fearful of infections, he relied on his staff for contact with the outside world. He made his last public appearance in 1958.

Hughes lived in hotels, closing off entire floors and sealing and darkening the windows of his rooms. All the while, he prospered on defense contracts, gambling casinos, airlines, and other ventures. In the 1970s, he worked with the Central Intelligence Agency in trying to raise a Russian submarine from the Pacific floor.

In his final years, Hughes, clad in pajamas, often lived on fudge and cake. He weighed only about 90 pounds (40 kilograms) and suffered from malnutrition when he died.

The men and their money are now parted; only the money remains, still bearing the mark of its maker. Characteristically, Getty left a detailed will, with bequests to his family and friends. The bulk of the estate avoids the taxman and goes to charity. But the Hughes case is another story. No fewer than 30 wills, some obvious hoaxes, turned up after the death of the secretive billionaire. One man who claimed to be Hughes's son said he had been born in a flying saucer in 1946. It will take years to settle the Hughes estate. Battle lines were being drawn in 1976 between relatives in Houston, who had not seen him for 40 years, and the executives of his Summa Corporation.

Getty's body now lies at his Malibu, Calif., estate, and Hughes is buried beside his parents in Houston. At Hughes's burial service, the priest said, "We brought nothing into this world, and it is certain we can carry nothing out."   Edward G. Nash

Samuel E. Morison,
noted historian.

Lee J. Cobb, versatile
stage and screen actor.

Gregor Piatigorsky,
eminent cellist.

Mary Margaret McBride,
a radio personality.

Hubbard, De Hart (1903-June 23), first black American to win an Olympic gold medal when he won the long jump in Paris in 1924.

*Hughes, Howard R. (1905-April 5), eccentric industrialist, aviator, and film producer and one of the world's wealthiest men. See Close-Up.

Hunt, Herold C. (1902-Oct. 17), educator, undersecretary of the Department of Health, Education, and Welfare from 1955 to 1957, and a consultant for THE WORLD BOOK ENCYCLOPEDIA.

Johnson, Eyvind (1900-Aug. 25), Swedish novelist, co-winner of the 1974 Nobel Prize for Literature.

Jones, Mary Anissa (1958-Aug. 28), actress who portrayed Buffy, the little girl, in the television series "Family Affair."

Kampmann, Viggo (1910-June 3), Danish prime minister from 1960 to 1962.

Kerner, Otto (1908-May 9), Democratic governor of Illinois from 1961 to 1968. In 1973, as a federal judge, he was convicted in a race-track stock scandal.

Kirchwey, Freda (1893-Jan. 3), editor and publisher of *The Nation* from 1937 to 1955, a fearless crusader for liberal causes.

Kohler, Walter J., Jr. (1904-March 21), Republican governor of Wisconsin from 1951 to 1957.

Kubitschek, Juscelino (1902-Aug. 22), president of Brazil from 1956 to 1961 and builder of the futuristic capital Brasília.

Kuhlman, Kathryn (1916-Feb. 20), popular evangelist and faith healer.

Lang, Fritz (1890-Aug. 2), Austrian-born film director, best known for *M* (1932), a terrifying study of a psychopathic killer.

Lazarsfeld, Paul F. (1901-Aug. 30), Austrian-born sociologist and educator whose studies of U.S. voting patterns became classics.

*Lehmann, Lotte (1888-Aug. 26), German-born opera star, considered matchless in the role of the Marschallin in Richard Strauss's *Der Rosenkavalier.*

Leighton, Margaret (1922-Jan. 13), British actress of stage, screen, and television who won Tony Awards for her performances in *Separate Tables* (1956) and *The Night of the Iguana* (1962).

*Lin Yutang (1895-March 26), Chinese writer and philosopher whose books include *Moment in Peking* (1939). He invented a Chinese typewriter in 1946.

Lippisch, Alexander M. (1894-Feb. 11), German-born engineer who designed the first airplane to fly faster than the speed of sound.

Lisagor, Peter I. (1915-Dec. 10), chief of the *Chicago Daily News* Washington Bureau since 1959, a highly respected journalist whose reporting and commentary were laced with wit and wisdom.

Litton, Jerry L. (1937-Aug. 3), Democratic congressman from Missouri from 1972 to 1974. He ran successfully for the Democratic nomination for senator, but was killed in a plane crash hours after the primary election.

Livesey, Roger (1906-Feb. 5), British character actor for more than 50 years whose films include *The Entertainer* (1960) with Laurence Olivier.

Lowry, Judith (1890-Nov. 29), delightful actress who played the tart-tongued Mother Dexter on the TV series *Phyllis.*

Lyons, Leonard (1906-Oct. 7), journalist whose Broadway column "The Lyons Den" appeared in the *New York Post* for 40 years.

*Lysenko, Trofim D. (1898-Nov. 20), Russian biologist whose theories dominated Russian agriculture from the 1930s to the 1950s but were later proved faulty.

Macdonald, Torbert H. (1917-May 21), Democratic congressman from Massachusetts from 1955 who helped bring about the Federal Election Campaign Act of 1971.

Mack, Ted (William Edward Maguiness) (1904-July 12), host of Television's "Original Amateur Hour" for 22 years.

MacMillan, Harvey R. (1885-Feb. 9), Canadian lumberman and philanthropist, a major figure in British Columbia for more than 50 years.

Mainbocher (Main Rousseau Bocher) (1891-Dec.27), leading fashion designer since the 1930s.

*Malraux, André (1901-Nov. 23), eminent French writer, a hero of the French resistance during World War II and minister of culture from 1959 to 1969. His highly acclaimed works included *Man's Fate* (1933) and *The Voices of Silence* (1953).

*Mao Tse-tung (1893-Sept. 9), leader of the People's Republic of China. See CHINA (Close-Up).

McBride, Mary Margaret (1899-April 7), whose down-home radio talk shows entertained housewives and enriched sponsors five days a week for 20 years.

McDevitt, Ruth (1895-May 27), TV actress who portrayed delightfully daffy old ladies.

Mercer, Johnny (1909-June 25), composer of such Oscar-winning songs as "On the Atchison, Topeka, and the Santa Fe" (1946); "In the Cool, Cool, Cool of the Evening" (1951); "Moon River" (1961); and "Days of Wine and Roses" (1962).

Mineo, Sal (1939-Feb. 12), actor, best known for his roles in *Rebel Without a Cause* and *Exodus.*

Minkowsky, Rudolph L. (1895-Jan. 4), German-born astronomer who supervised the National Geographic Society-Palomar Observatory Sky Survey for many years.

Mitchell, Martha (1918-May 31), outspoken estranged wife of former Attorney General John N. Mitchell. She denounced the Nixon Administration during the Watergate scandal.

Monnington, Sir Walter (1902-Jan. 7), British mural painter, president of the Royal Academy since 1967.

*****Monod, Jacques** (1910-May 31), French biochemist who helped lay the framework for our understanding of gene action and protein synthesis. He shared the 1965 Nobel Prize for Physiology or Medicine with André Lwoff and François Jacob.

*****Montgomery, Field Marshal Bernard L.** (Viscount Montgomery of Alamein) (1887-March 24), British Army commander in World War II who directed the Allied victory over the Germans in North Africa in 1942 and led the British forces that landed in France on June 6, 1944.

Morgan, Joseph F. (1918-May 2), Canadian biochemist and cancer researcher who developed the medium in which the Salk antipolio vaccine was produced.

*****Morison, Samuel E.** (1887-May 15), historian who won a Pulitzer Prize in 1943 for *Admiral of the Ocean Sea: A Life of Christopher Columbus* and another in 1960 for *John Paul Jones.*

Moss, Robert V., Jr. (1922-Oct. 25), president of the United Church of Christ since 1969, a noted ecumenist.

Moulder, Morgan (1904-Nov. 12), Democratic congressman from Missouri from 1948 to 1962.

Nevers, Ernie (1903-May 3), one of the greatest fullbacks in football history, who played with the Duluth Eskimos and the Chicago Cardinals.

Ochs, Phil (1941-April 9), folk singer and lyricist whose 1963 song "I Ain't Marchin' Anymore" was one of the first protest songs of the Vietnam War.

O'Leary, Grattan (1889-April 7), Canadian senator from Ottawa since 1963 and former editor of *The Ottawa Journal.*

Onsager, Lars (1903-Oct. 5), Norwegian-born theoretical chemist who won the 1968 Nobel Prize for Chemistry for his work in thermodynamics.

Patman, Wright (1893-March 7), Texas congressman since 1929 who helped to pass the Employment Act of 1946 and create the Small Business Administration.

Pelletier, Denise (1928-May 24), Canadian actress who received the Canada Council's $20,000 Molson Prize in 1976.

Penfield, Wilder G. (1891-April 5), neurologist who founded the Montreal Neurological Institute in Canada and pioneered surgical techniques to treat epilepsy.

Petty, Mary (1899-March 6), cartoonist whose caustic commentaries on the upper crust appeared in *The New Yorker* magazine from 1927 to 1966.

Phillips, Nathan (1893-Jan. 7), mayor of Toronto, Canada, from 1955 to 1962.

*****Piatigorsky, Gregor** (1903-Aug. 6), Russian-born musician, one of the world's great cellists. Summing up his philosophy, he said, "Forget about modesty. Be a show-off. There has never been written a modest symphony or a humble rhapsody."

Pons, Lily (1904-Feb. 13), diminutive French-born coloratura soprano of the Metropolitan Opera in New York City for more than 25 years.

Porter, Charlie (1854-Jan. 13), born in slavery in Alabama, a witness to more than 121 years of tumultuous American history.

Ray, Man (1890-Nov. 18), American artist, a creator of the Dada movement in Paris 60 years ago and sometimes called the "Last of the Red-Hot Dadas."

Razak, Abdul bin Dato Hussein (1922-Jan. 14), prime minister of Malaysia since 1970.

Redfield, William (1927-Aug. 17), stage and screen actor who played Harding in the Oscar-winning film *One Flew over the Cuckoo's Nest.*

Reed, Sir Carol (1906-April 25), British director of such films as *Odd Man Out* (1947), *The Third Man* (1950), and the prize-winning musical *Oliver!* (1968), for which he won an Academy Award.

Max Ernst was a German artist and sculptor.

Field Marshal Bernard Montgomery.

Jacques Monod won a Nobel Prize for his work on cells.

Paul Robeson was a gifted performer.

Rethberg, Elisabeth (1894-June 6), German-born lyric soprano who sang with the Metropolitan Opera in New York City from 1922 to 1942 and was said to be the finest Aïda of her generation.

Reynolds, Milton (1892-Jan. 23), who marketed the ballpoint pen and wrote himself a fortune.

Rich, Daniel C. (1904-Oct. 15), a leading exponent of contemporary art and director of the Art Institute of Chicago from 1945 to 1960.

*****Robeson, Paul** (1898-Jan. 23), actor and bass-baritone, acclaimed for the sensitivity he brought to such productions as *The Emperor Jones* (1923) and *Othello* (1943). Dogged by racism, he thought he had found a better way in Communism, but he later said again and again, "I am an American." He won the Spingarn Medal in 1945.

Roche, Josephine A. (1886-July 29), first woman to be appointed assistant secretary of the treasury, in 1934.

Rosenbloom, Maxie (Slapsie Maxie) (1905-March 6), former world light-heavyweight boxing champion who went on to a movie career. He was elected to boxing's Hall of Fame in 1972.

Roy, Mike (1913-June 26), popular radio personality whose five-minute show "Mike Roy's Cooking Thing" was broadcast five days a week on CBS.

Russell, Rosalind (1911-Nov. 28), stage and screen actress best known for her performances as the zany *Auntie Mame* on stage (1956) and *Mame* on screen (1958).

Ryle, Gilbert (1900-Oct. 6), British philosopher who analyzed the language philosophy uses in speaking about

Alexander Calder, a
world-famous sculptor.

Ernie Nevers, a great
fullback in football.

Wright Patman,
Texas congressman.

Martin Heidegger, an
influential philosopher.

the world. His book *The Concept of Mind* (1949) became a classic in modern philosophy.

Schairer, Otto S. (1879-March 12), electrical engineer and former vice-president of RCA Corporation who directed programs during World War II that provided night-vision and radar devices.

*****Shepard, Ernest** (1879-March 24), British artist who illustrated Winnie-the-Pooh and his friends in the classic stories by A. A. Milne.

Sifton, Clifford (1893-April 8), Canadian lawyer and publisher of *The Leader-Post* of Regina, Sask., and *The Star-Phoenix* of Saskatoon.

Sim, Alastair (1900-Aug. 19), Scottish actor, known for his droll characterizations in such films as *The Lavender Hill Mob* with Alec Guinness and *The Belles of St. Trinian's,* in which he played the headmistress of a girls' school.

Sissman, L. E. (Louis Edward) (1928-March 10), advertising executive and gifted poet who celebrated his last years in such poems as "Dying: An Introduction."

Smith, Gerald L. K. (1898-April 15), self-ordained Arkansas preacher who was antiblack, anti-Semitic, anti-Catholic, and pro-Fascist and could never understand why so many people didn't like him.

Smith, H. Allen (1907-Feb. 24), newspaperman and humorist whose books include *Low Man on a Totem Pole* (1941) and the adventures of a cat who inherited a baseball team – *Rhubarb* (1946).

Snow, Raymond P. (1875-Nov. 24), one of Theodore Roosevelt's Rough Riders in the Spanish-American War.

Sparks, William J. (1904-Oct. 23), president of the American Chemical Society and winner of the 1965 Priestley Prize. With R. M. Thomas, Sparks invented synthetic butyl rubber, credited with a major role in the Allied victory in World War II.

Strand, Paul (1890-March 31), photographer and filmmaker who pioneered in social subject matter in his film *The Plow That Broke the Plains* (1936).

Streeter, Edward (1891-March 31), author of such best sellers as *The Father of the Bride* (1949).

Sullivan, Frank (1892-Feb. 19), humorist whose delightful annual Christmas verse appeared in *The New Yorker* magazine for more than 40 years.

Thomas, Sir James Tudor (1893-Jan. 23), British eye surgeon who demonstrated that healthy parts from the eyes of dead persons could be used to repair diseased or injured eyes.

Thomson of Fleet, Lord Roy (1894-Aug. 4), Canadian publisher who built a vast and influential publishing empire that included *The Times* of London.

Thorndike, Dame Sybil (1882-June 9), eminent British actress for whom George Bernard Shaw wrote *Saint Joan.*

Thornton, Dan (1911–Jan. 18), cattle rancher and governor of Colorado from 1951 to 1955.

*****Tobey, Mark** (1890-April 24), abstract artist known for his "white writing" – elaborate patterns of lines and small symbols.

Trumbo, Dalton (1905-Sept. 10), author of *Johnny Got His Gun* (1939), and screenwriter of such films as *Exodus* and *Hawaii.* Blacklisted by the film industry in the late 1940s because he had belonged to the Communist Party and had refused to cooperate with investigations of the House Committee on Un-American Activities, Trumbo won an Oscar under an assumed name in 1957 for writing *The Brave One.*

Visconti, Luchino (1906-March 17), Italian film director known for such sumptuously detailed melodramas as *The Leopard* and *Death in Venice.*

Wegner, Monsignor Nicholas H. (1898-March 18), director of Boys Town near Omaha, Nebr., from 1947 to 1973.

Weigle, Luther A. (1880-Aug. 2), dean emeritus of Yale Divinity School and director of the writing of the Revised Standard Version of the Bible.

Weil, Yellow Kid (Joseph) (1875-Feb. 26), king of the confidence men, who was so convincing that a detective taking him to prison in Illinois after a swindling conviction bought $30,000 worth of "stock" from him.

Wheeler, Sir R. E. Mortimer (1890-July 22), Scottish archaeologist who discovered relics in Somersetshire, England, believed to be from King Arthur's Camelot.

Whipple, George H. (1878-Feb. 1), pathologist, co-winner of the 1934 Nobel Prize for Medicine for demonstrating that a liver diet could control pernicious anemia.

White, Minor (1908-June 24), noted photographer and teacher at the Massachusetts Institute of Technology from 1965 to 1974.

Wiener, Alexander S. (1907-Nov. 6), physiologist who won the 1948 Lasker Award for co-discovery of the Rh blood factor.

Wilson, John A. (1899-Aug. 30), Orientalist, epigrapher, and authority on Egypt whose books include *The Burden of Egypt* (1951).

*****Yakubovsky, Ivan I.** (1912-Nov. 30), deputy defense minister of Russia from 1967 to 1976 and commander of the Warsaw Pact forces.

Zeckendorf, William (1905-Sept. 30), flamboyant real estate developer who arranged the purchase of land for United Nations Headquarters in New York City.

Zolar (Bruce King) (?-Jan. 15), popular astrologer whose books were translated into 10 languages.

Zukor, Adolph (1873-June 10), movie pioneer who built the Paramount Pictures Corporation.   Irene B. Keller

DELAWARE. See STATE GOVERNMENT.

DEMOCRATIC PARTY. The Democrats regained control of the White House in the November 1976 election with a stunning triumph by a Washington outsider, former Georgia Governor James Earl (Jimmy) Carter, Jr. Carter received 50.08 per cent of the popular vote to 48.02 per cent for Republican President Gerald R. Ford. Independent candidate Eugene J. McCarthy, a former liberal Democrat, got less than 1 per cent of the vote. In the Electoral College, Carter captured 297 electoral votes to 240 for Ford. A Washington state elector cast 1 vote for former California Governor Ronald Reagan when the Electoral College met on December 13.

The Democrats did remarkably well in congressional contests, preserving their 2 to 1 majority in the House and 3 to 2 advantage in the Senate.

In governors' races, the Democrats made a net gain of one governorship. The governors' line-up became 37 Democrats to 12 Republicans and 1 Independent. Democrat Dixy Lee Ray, former head of the Atomic Energy Commission, was elected governor of Washington. She became the second woman governor to be elected in her own right— rather than by succeeding a husband. Ella T. Grasso of Connecticut in 1974 was the first. See ELECTIONS.

The Biggest Surprise of the political year was Carter's emergence from a crowded field of better-known Democrats to win 20 of 30 primary elections and capture the party's presidential nomination.

Carter gained an early lead in the Iowa Democratic precinct caucuses on January 19. He then went on to win the first primary, which was held in New Hampshire on February 24. He decisively defeated another Southern contender, Alabama Governor George C. Wallace, in Florida on March 9. Carter came out on top in Illinois and North Carolina. He fell to fourth place in the New York state primary, barely won Wisconsin, but then scored a triumph on April 27 in a Pennsylvania showdown with Senator Henry M. Jackson of Washington.

As Carter scored early successes, Jackson and other Democrats withdrew from competition— former North Carolina Governor Terry Sanford, Senator Lloyd M. Bentsen of Texas, Senator Birch Bayh of Indiana, Pennsylvania Governor Milton J. Shapp, the 1972 Democratic vice-presidential nominee Sargent Shriver, and former Senator Fred R. Harris of Oklahoma. Carter carried Michigan on May 18, inflicting a mortal blow to Representative Morris K. Udall of Arizona, who was frequently a runner-up but never won a primary.

Meanwhile, union leaders and other supporters urged Senator Hubert H. Humphrey of Minnesota to enter the race. But Humphrey announced on April 29 that he would not enter any primary.

Jimmy Carter and running mate Walter Mondale rejoice with their wives after winning the Democratic Party's nomination in New York City in July.

Humphrey said he had no campaign organization and no funds. He also believed it was too late for him to begin his fourth bid for the presidency.

Late Entries. Two Westerners entered the primary battle relatively late – California Governor Edmund G. (Jerry) Brown, Jr., and Senator Frank Church of Idaho. Carter lost to Church in Nebraska on May 11 and in Idaho and Oregon on May 25. Brown defeated Carter in Maryland on May 18 and in Nevada a week later. On June 1, Church won Montana, and Carter took South Dakota, but Brown won a symbolic victory in Rhode Island with a slate of uncommitted delegates he supported.

On June 8, the final primary day, Brown carried his home state of California. But Carter won a decisive victory in Ohio, which virtually assured him the presidential nomination.

On June 9, Wallace and Chicago Mayor Richard J. Daley endorsed Carter and gave him more delegate strength, assuring him of enough votes at the Democratic National Convention to go beyond the 1,505 required to become the Democratic candidate. Jackson also promised to back Carter.

Secret of Success. For Carter, who began his campaign in 1974 as an obscure outsider, eclipsing his more prominent Democratic rivals was an incredible political feat. He had carefully constructed an organization of hard-working young volunteers, who helped him get a fast start.

Carter's theme was simple. The nation, he said, needed an efficient government as good and full of love as the American people. The Georgian promised that he would never lie, would reorganize the federal government, and would make U.S. citizens proud of their country once again. It proved to be a winning combination in a year when an anti-Washington mood seemed prevalent.

United Convention. A jubilant Democratic Party, with high hopes for a presidential victory, assembled in New York City on July 12. In an atmosphere more like that of a coronation than of a convention, the Democrats bestowed their nomination on the Georgian.

In addition to Carter, the names of Udall, Brown, and Ellen McCormack, an anti-abortion candidate, were placed before the delegates. Carter, however, won 2,238½ votes on the first ballot to become the Democratic nominee.

The dramatic highlight of the convention was Carter's selection of a running mate. Carter interviewed six senators – Church, Jackson, Edmund S. Muskie of Maine, John H. Glenn of Ohio, Walter F. Mondale of Minnesota, and Adlai E. Stevenson III of Illinois. Representative Peter W. Rodino, Jr., of New Jersey, who had also been on Carter's list of prospective running mates, withdrew because of a health problem.

In a break with tradition, Carter interviewed the six senators and Rodino at either his Plains, Ga.,

California Governor Edmund G. Brown, Jr., a late entrant in the Democratic race, addresses New Jersey voters before the presidential primary.

home or in New York City before announcing his choice. He settled on Mondale, which pleased organized labor and party liberals who had been cool toward Carter's candidacy. Carter said he had a "great compatibility" with Mondale.

In his convention acceptance speech, Carter said it was a "time for healing" in the nation. Certainly the convention helped to heal the wounds in the Democratic Party inflicted by the divisive candidacy of Senator George S. McGovern of South Dakota in 1972.

Representative Barbara C. Jordan of Texas became the first woman and the first black to give a Democratic National Convention keynote address. Martin Luther King, Sr., a Baptist minister and father of the slain civil rights leader, pronounced the final benediction.

The Democratic Platform, prepared a month in advance of the convention, drew wide support from all sections of the party. It reflected Carter's views but was endorsed by representatives of Wallace, Udall, and Jackson as well.

The platform favored national health insurance, tax reform, gun control, a guaranteed-income plan to replace the welfare system, and full pardons for Vietnam War draft resisters. It endorsed busing for school integration as a "judicial tool of last resort" and opposed a constitutional amendment to forbid abortions.

Presidential Campaign. Carter began his campaign by invoking memories of former Democratic Presidents Franklin D. Roosevelt and John F. Kennedy. After the Democratic convention he held a big lead in public opinion polls. However, his lead steadily slipped, particularly after the first televised debate with President Ford, who was regarded as the winner of that exchange on domestic affairs.

However, Ford made a major error in the second debate, devoted to foreign affairs, by saying that Eastern Europe was not under Russian domination. This appeared to halt his momentum. Nevertheless, Carter's lead was so thin by election eve that pollsters declared the race too close to call.

After his narrow victory, Carter acknowledged that he was not as good a campaigner as he might have been. Yet his strategy worked remarkably well. As planned, he carried the South from Texas through Florida, except for Virginia, and picked up all the Border States, except for Oklahoma. He then won New York, Pennsylvania, and Ohio, plus several smaller Northern states.

Democratic National Committee Chairman Robert S. Strauss announced on November 8 that he would resign as of Jan. 21, 1977, the day after Carter's inauguration.   William J. Eaton

See also CARTER, JAMES EARL, JR.; MONDALE, WALTER F.; Section Five, CARTER, JAMES EARL, JR.

DENMARK. The Social Democratic minority government called the *Folketing* (parliament) into an emergency session on Aug. 17, 1976, to rush through austerity economic measures. The legislation was designed to cut consumer and public spending and to correct a foreign-trade deficit that had soared to over $1 billion in the first half of 1976. The new laws limited wage increases in 1977 and 1978 to 6 per cent a year. They also froze dividends, continued price and profit controls, and sharply raised taxes on beer, coffee, gasoline, liquor, sugar, and wine.

Narrow Victory. Prime Minister Anker Henrik Jorgensen needed the support of the opposition Conservative Party to push through these tough economic measures on August 19 and to stay in office. Because Jorgensen promised that the tax increases would last for only two years, the 10 Conservatives supported him. The Liberals, largest of the opposition parties, voted against him, saying the measures would not save the economy. Trade unions denounced the wage clause, and 15,000 workers demonstrated in Copenhagen.

Strikes over Britons. About 800 construction workers struck in Copenhagen on March 5 to protest the use of British labor while nearly 200,000 Danes were unemployed. Eight Britons on a subcontract were receiving one-third the Danish pay rate. The contract with the British company was cut

short on April 7 when demonstrators ejected the workers from the construction site.

Greenland Move. Greenland, the world's largest island and a province of Denmark, considered greater independence in view of possible sudden revenue increases from substantial oil reserves off its west coast. Several international groups are prospecting there on a 10-year concession, on the promise of 80 per cent of net profits for the Danish government. Greenland's two representatives in the Folketing talked of leaving the European Community (Common Market) by 1982 and declared that Greenland should administer its own mineral resources. Greenland's complete independence from Denmark is unlikely, but the Greenland Provincial Council approved a plan in March that would give the island home rule by 1980.

Heavy Taxation. A Common Market study concluded that the Danes are the heaviest-taxed people in Europe and that their newspapers are preoccupied with the subject. More than half the gross national product is taken in taxes, and a middle-class wage earner typically pays about 60 per cent of his or her income in taxes.

The National Bank made large-scale purchases to support the krone on March 15 and raised the interest rate 1 point to 8.5 per cent.   Kenneth Brown

See also EUROPE (Facts in Brief Table).

Denmark's Queen Margrethe II lays a wreath honoring war dead at Chicago's Civic Center in May while Prince Henrik watches, center.

DENTISTRY. Researchers at the University of Washington in Seattle have found new evidence that orthodontic treatment can be beneficial to adults, according to a May 1976 report. Vincent G. Kokich and Benjamin C. Moffett discovered that the upper jaw does not completely unite with the frontal bone of the skull until people are more than 70 years old. As a result of this research, orthodontists can now use traditional orthodontic appliances in treating adults for protrusion of the upper jaw and other facial disfigurements.

The laser may replace the acid etching now used to prepare tooth surfaces for bonding with resin filling materials, a dental researcher at the State University of New York in Buffalo predicted in March. A. M. Patrignani explained that adherence of resin fillings, which are used for appearance, depends on the tooth surface being *pebbled* (roughed) by acid or a laser to allow a bond. No cement or additional material is used to hold the filling in place. "The dentist using a laser has more precise control over the area to be etched," Patrignani said, "whereas acid is applied less precisely and may trickle onto surrounding soft tissue." The laser etching requires only two milliseconds to create pebbling, compared with 60 to 90 seconds for acid etching.

Fluorides and Radiation. Cancer patients receiving head and neck radiation therapy need no longer lose all of their teeth to rampant decay, a University of Texas dental researcher reported in March. Samuel Dreizen of Houston found that topical fluoride treatment protects the teeth of oral-cancer patients from the rapid tooth decay that inevitably used to follow the radiation-induced dry-mouth condition called xerostomia.

Dreizen told the 54th General Session of the International Association for Dental Research in Miami Beach, Fla., that "patients given radiotherapy for cancer of the head and neck are inordinately susceptible to *caries* [tooth decay] when the major salivary glands are included in the radiation fields." The ravaging decay begins immediately after the loss of the salivary-gland function. But the daily application of a 1 per cent sodium fluoride gel to the teeth, plus strict oral hygiene, has greatly reduced decay.

Dental Costs. The cost of dental care in the United States has kept a closer relationship to the general rise in the cost of living than have other medical expenses, a study by the American Dental Association (ADA) revealed. The ADA comparison of medical costs with Consumer Price Index figures from 1967 to 1975 showed that dentists' fees had risen 61.9 per cent in those years, close to the general cost-of-living increase. The cost of all medical care rose 68.6 per cent and physicians' fees, 69.4 per cent. Hospital charges showed even greater increases, more than doubling.　　　　Lou Joseph

DETROIT. There were no disturbances on Jan. 26, 1976, when Detroit began busing to desegregate its public schools. Many observers attributed the absence of violence to the limited nature of the plan. Two-thirds of Detroit's black pupils remained in virtually all-black schools.

The National Association for the Advancement of Colored People challenged the plan in court, calling it too modest. The appeal was turned down on August 4 by an appellate court. However, the court ordered a reconsideration of the plan for three inner-city regions. But the Michigan attorney general asked for a delay pending a review by the Supreme Court of the United States.

Cutbacks and Crime. Detroit's Mayor Coleman A. Young said on February 25 that the city was in desperate financial condition and faced potential bankruptcy unless it received state or federal help. During the year, Young closed recreation centers, museums, libraries, and immunization clinics. He also laid off city employees, including about 1,000 police officers.

Meanwhile, crime by street gangs became a growing menace. The worst gang incident occurred August 15, when an estimated 150 gang members took control of Cobo Hall during a rock concert. The rampaging youths robbed, beat, and raped concertgoers before police arrived and arrested 47 persons.

The city then recalled 450 laid-off policemen, increased downtown patrols, and passed an emergency curfew ordering all persons under 18 years of age off the streets by 10 P.M. The Wayne County Board of Commissioners appropriated $243,000 to hire new judges, referees, prosecutors, and other staff for the juvenile courts. In an attempt to combat low police morale, Young appointed a new police chief, William L. Hart, on September 28.

To bolster the city's bank account, officials held a three-day auction in April of obsolete or unneeded city equipment. Billed as the world's largest garage sale, the event produced an estimated $170,000 in revenues. Additional aid came from the federal government, which announced on July 21 that the city would receive $10.1 million in grants for mass-transit programs. The city also hoped that Renaissance Center—with offices, shops, and a hotel scheduled to open in 1977—would improve conditions in downtown Detroit.

The Economy. Although employment rose 2.8 per cent between August 1975 and August 1976, a midyear unemployment rate of 11.2 per cent gave Detroit one of the worst employment problems in the nation. Still, factory workers' earnings rose an average of 18.2 per cent, the highest for any major U.S. city. Overall living costs rose 5.2 per cent between July 1975 and July 1976.　　James M. Banovetz

DICTIONARY. See Section Six, DICTIONARY SUPPLEMENT.

Sept. 10 – Southwest Japan. Two days of heavy rain caused floods that killed at least 12 persons.

Oct. 6 – Pereira, Colombia. A rain-swollen river burst a dike, drowning 58 persons.

Nov. 13-14 – East Java, Indonesia. Floods caused by torrential rains killed at least 136 persons.

Hurricanes, Tornadoes, and Other Storms

Jan. 3 – Great Britain and Western Europe. Hurricane-force winds killed more than 40 persons in Britain, the Netherlands, and West Germany.

Jan. 31-Feb. 1 – South Africa and Mozambique. A cyclone killed at least 20 persons.

April 22 – Bangladesh. The government reported that 81 persons were killed during two weeks of violent storms.

June 25 – Southwestern Japan. Torrential rains caused landslides that killed at least 24 persons.

Aug. 25 – Hong Kong. A tropical storm caused floods and landslides that killed at least 21 persons.

Oct. 1 – La Paz, Mexico. Hurricane Liza swept across Baja California Sur, killing at least 500 persons and injuring 14,000 others.

Mine Disasters

Mar. 9 – Near Whitesburg, Ky. A methane-gas explosion in the Scotia Coal Company mine killed 15 men. A second explosion in the same mine on March 11 killed 8 miners and 3 mine inspectors.

Sept. 7 – Watbrzych, Poland. An explosion ripped through a coal mine, killing at least 17 persons and injuring more than 30 others.

Sept. 17 – Near Tete, Mozambique. Three miners were known dead and 140 missing and feared dead after a gas explosion in a coal mine.

Dec. 30 – Near Ostrava, Czechoslovakia. An explosion in a coal mine trapped 45 miners. They were presumed dead.

Shipwrecks

Jan. 27 – Off Southern Bangladesh. A hundred fishing boats carrying a total of about 800 fishermen were reported missing.

Aug. 7 – Off Southern Thailand. At least 26 persons drowned and 50 others were missing after a ferryboat capsized.

Aug. 29 – Davao River, the Philippines. A boat capsized, leaving 19 persons missing and presumed dead.

Sept. 20 – Off the Netherlands. Two sailors were killed and 10 others were missing after two British warships collided in the North Sea.

Oct. 15 – Bermuda Triangle. A Panamanian freighter with 37 crew members disappeared in heavy seas.

Oct. 19 – Off Newfoundland. Fifteen crewmen abandoned a Dutch freighter after it began taking on water. Only two crewmen were found alive.

Oct. 20 – Near New Orleans. A Norwegian tanker rammed and sank a commuter ferry in the Mississippi River. Authorities recovered 76 bodies; two persons were still missing.

Nov. 11 – South Pacific Ocean. A cargo ship sank in heavy seas, leaving 18 crewmen missing and feared dead.

Dec. 24 – The Red Sea. An Egyptian passenger boat burned and sank, killing more than 100 persons.

Train Wrecks

Feb. 7 – Beckemeyer, Ill. A train struck a camper, killing 12 persons, 11 of them children.

May 4 – Rotterdam, the Netherlands. A commuter train and an express collided head-on, killing 23 persons.

May 23 – Seoul, South Korea. A passenger train struck a fuel truck, killing at least 19 persons.

June 14 – Near Sofia, Bulgaria. A passenger train collided with a freight train, killing 10 persons.

A resident surveys the destruction at his home in Big Thompson Canyon near Loveland, Colo., after a flood that killed at least 136 persons.

June 27 – Near Brussels, Belgium. At least 12 persons were killed and 59 injured when an express train derailed.

Sept. 9 – Southern Cameroon. Two passenger trains collided, killing about 100 persons and injuring 300 other passengers.

Oct. 11 – Sierra Madre, Mexico. A passenger train and a freight train collided, killing 24 persons and injuring 63 others.

Nov. 3 – Near Częstochowa, Poland. An express rammed a stopped passenger train in dense fog, killing 25 persons and injuring 60 others.

Nov. 29 – Near Nairobi, Kenya. A train derailed on a flood-damaged bridge and plunged into a river. At least 14 persons were killed.

Other Disasters

Feb. 12 – Near Esmeraldas, Ecuador. Officials reported that mud slides killed about 50 persons.

Feb. 12 – Bitlis, Turkey. Twenty-seven persons were killed by avalanches.

Feb. 14-15 – The Pyrenees, France. At least 11 skiers were killed by avalanches.

Mar. 9 – Near Trento, Italy. A cable car carrying skiers plunged to the ground when a steel cable snapped. Only one of the 43 passengers survived.

April 15 – Gulf of Mexico. An oil rig under tow sank during a storm, and the crew tried to escape in two disk-shaped survival capsules. However, one capsule capsized, killing 13 men.

May 2 – Near Fresno, Colombia. A landslide on a road through the Andes Mountains killed 13 persons and injured 16 others.

Sept. 13 – Karachi, Pakistan. A six-story apartment building collapsed, killing more than 90 persons who were sleeping.

Darlene R. Stille

DOLE, ROBERT J. (1923-   ), Republican senator from Kansas and former chairman of the Republican National Committee, was selected by President Gerald R. Ford as his vice-presidential running mate on Aug. 19, 1976. A fiercely partisan campaigner, Dole was regarded as acceptable to former California Governor Ronald Reagan, who had waged a close battle with Ford for the nomination. See REAGAN, RONALD; REPUBLICAN PARTY.

During the campaign, Dole was particularly active in the Midwest Farm Belt. On October 15, he faced Democratic vice-presidential candidate Walter F. Mondale in a televised debate in Houston.

Dole was born on July 22, 1923, in Russell, Kans. During World War II, he served with the Army in Italy, suffering a severe wound that left his right arm crippled. While a student at Washburn University of Topeka, where he received a law degree in 1952, Dole was elected to the Kansas legislature. He later served as Russell County prosecuting attorney. He won election to the U.S. House of Representatives in 1960, where he served until 1968, when he was elected to the Senate.

Dole married Mary Elizabeth Hanford, a federal trade commissioner, in 1975. He has one daughter by his first marriage.   Carol L. Thompson

See also ELECTIONS.

DOMINICAN REPUBLIC. See LATIN AMERICA.

DRUGS. Opium and heroin continued to arouse worldwide concern in 1976. Officials from 14 European and Asian countries at a July conference in Bangkok, Thailand, on ways to reduce the narcotics traffic were assured that Burma and Laos, Asia's two principal sources of opium, had agreed to reduce the traffic by cutting back supplies. Together, Burma and Laos supply more than 600 short tons (544 metric tons) of opium annually—nine times the amount grown in Thailand, the third major Asian supplier.

The United States and Mexico resumed their joint campaign to eradicate thousands of opium-poppy plantations in the hope of sharply reducing the flow of Mexican heroin into the United States. At the start of the poppy-growing season in September, more than 30 helicopters, donated to Mexico by the United States, started crisscrossing the Sierra Madre mountains to spray the plantations with a herbicide to kill the poppy plants. A number of U.S. technicians and four spotter aircraft were also sent to Mexico to work with 30 aides of the U.S. Drug Enforcement Administration stationed in Mexico. In March, Mexican police and troops seized trucks carrying 39 short tons (35 metric tons) of marijuana worth $12.5 million.

Drug Programs. A proposal to set up the first U.S. experiment in supplying heroin legally to

U.S. Coast Guard workers in Miami Beach remove some of the 160 short tons (145 metric tons) of marijuana seized on a Panamanian freighter in October.

hard-core addicts, either free or at low cost, was under serious study by San Diego County drug officials. The county grand jury recommended in a special report issued in September the decriminalization of the drug, particularly for those considered to be incurably addicted, as a means of coping with an epidemic of drug-related crimes by both users and peddlers. Theoretically, making heroin legally available would replace the county's controversial methadone detoxification program.

Two doctors who helped develop and promote the use of methadone, a synthetic drug used to treat heroin addiction, renewed their long-standing attack on federal and state regulatory agencies that have restricted methadone programs in the United States. Vincent P. Dole and Marie E. Nyswander said in the May 10 issue of the *Journal of the American Medical Association* that, while thousands of addicts have been rehabilitated by methadone, the great majority of heroin addicts remain on the streets and the methadone programs have lost their ability to attract these addicts to treatment.

The FDA. General Accounting Office (GAO) investigators issued a devastating indictment of the U.S. Food and Drug Administration (FDA) in July, charging it with exposing humans to needless risks in testing new drugs. The investigators also discovered that many doctors, drug manufacturers, and researchers failed to keep track of drugs with which they were experimenting, leaving hazardous drugs in the hands of unsuspecting patients.

Perhaps the most controversial FDA ban issued during 1976 was the February 12 prohibition on Red Dye No. 2, which had been the subject of controversy for more than 20 years. The most widely used food coloring in the country, Red Dye No. 2 was also used in pill coatings and cosmetics, particularly lipstick. The FDA decided to ban the dye when its toxicology department, after reviewing a study on laboratory rats, decided that the dye could be a cause of cancer. A number of European countries had already banned the dye after studies indicated that it caused both cancer and fetal deaths, and in 1972 the World Health Organization recommended strict limitations on its use.

The FDA moved in October to take a new and widely advertised arthritis painkiller off the market because the manufacturer allegedly had covered up damaging test results. The target of this crackdown was the prescription drug Naprosyn. After it went on the market in March, doctors reportedly wrote 100,000 prescriptions per month for the preparation. The FDA in September ordered stronger warnings on the labels of estrogen, a sex hormone taken by women to relieve the symptoms of menopause. Noting that the estrogens have medical value, the FDA stated it wanted to keep them on the market but to reduce harmful misuse. Mary E. Jessup

EARTHQUAKE. See DISASTERS.

EASTERN ORTHODOX CHURCHES. More than 100 theologians representing all Orthodox Church theological schools in Europe, the Middle East, and North America attended the Second Congress on Orthodox Theology in Athens, Greece, in August 1976. The first such congress was held in Athens in 1936. During the 1976 sessions, the theologians discussed the relationship between the church and the modern world but failed to agree on a final document.

Ethiopia's military rulers removed the patriarch of that country's Orthodox Church from office in February and accused him of a series of crimes against the people. Patriarch Abuna Theophiles was rumored to be under arrest. He was replaced by Abuna Onis, a priest from the province of Tigre.

In the United States, Orthodox churches actively participated in the celebration of the American Revolution Bicentennial. Special messages and encyclicals stressing the integration of Orthodoxy into American religious and cultural life were issued by Archbishop Iakovos, head of the Greek archdiocese and president of the Standing Conference of Orthodox Canonical Bishops in America; by Metropolitan Ireney, primate of the Orthodox Church in America; by Metropolitan Philaret, head of the Russian Church in Exile; and by the leaders of virtually every Orthodox body.

Greek President Constantine Tsatsos kisses the Holy Gospel held by Bishop Chrysostomos during the celebration of Epiphany in Athens in January.

The Antiochian Orthodox community in the United States mobilized itself to help the victims of the civil war in Lebanon. Metropolitan Philip, head of the Antiochian Orthodox Christian archdiocese, led a group of Arab religious leaders to the White House for an April 15 meeting with President Gerald R. Ford.

Reorganization Plans for the Greek archdiocese of North and South America continued to be discussed by the archdiocese and the patriarchate of Constantinople and within the archdiocese itself. It was also the primary item on the agenda at a clergy-laity congress held in Philadelphia in July. The proposed plans imply greater autonomy for the archdiocese in relation to the patriarchate of Constantinople, as well as a decentralization of the archdiocesan administration by giving more authority to regional diocesan centers.

Both the Orthodox hierarchy and Orthodox theologians reacted intensely to a decision by the Minneapolis Convention of the Protestant Episcopal Church in September to admit women to holy orders (see PROTESTANTISM). In October, the Holy Synod of the Orthodox Church in America, which was represented at the convention by Bishop Dmitri of Hartford and New England, adopted a resolution denouncing women's ordination as incompatible with the apostolic faith.   Alexander Schmemann

See also RELIGION.

ECONOMICS. For the United States economy, 1976 was clearly a year of recovery from a two-year recession. But as the year ended, economists were anxiously scanning the economic indicators to determine how long the recovery would last. Economic conditions in the rest of the world were less satisfactory than in the United States; high rates of inflation and unemployment continued to plague most countries.

U.S. Growth. In terms of current dollars, the U.S. gross national product (GNP) rose from $1.5-trillion in 1975 to about $1.7 trillion, almost a 15 per cent increase. Even better, the real GNP measured in constant 1972 dollars rose in 1976 to about $1.27 trillion after two years of decline. This was a new record, about 2.5 per cent above the previous high in 1973.

Nevertheless, certain aspects of this 1976 growth were disturbing. After rising at an annual rate of 9 per cent in the first quarter, the real rate of growth dropped to 4.6 per cent in the second quarter, and 4 per cent in the third. Most economic authorities estimated that the last quarter would show an even further decline to about 3.8 per cent.

At the same time, unemployment, which had averaged 8.5 per cent since 1975, still hovered around the 8 per cent mark in December, though it had averaged somewhat less than this for the entire year. Most economists define full employment as meaning an unemployment rate of 4 to 5 per cent. On this basis, 1976 levels were unsatisfactory.

On the brighter side, the rate of inflation declined markedly to about 5 per cent for all of 1976. Economists disagree whether unemployment can be significantly and rapidly reduced without touching off a new wave of inflation. Although nearly 88.5-million Americans were at work in December, 3-million more than in December 1975, the available labor force had grown by 2.5 million. Consequently, the number of unemployed was reduced only slightly.

Youthful Unemployment. If the unemployment rate were evenly distributed over the population, the problem might be less significant. Unfortunately, the unemployment rate for teen-agers was close to 19 per cent at year-end, about 2.5 times greater than the rate for the total population. Also, the unemployment rate among black workers was almost double that for the total population. The combination of these factors meant that unemployment rates among black teen-agers were running between 30 and 40 per cent in some large cities.

Economists are nearly unanimous in agreeing that a substantial portion of teen-age unemployment results from laws that set the minimum wage at a level that is above the capacity of unskilled and poorly trained young people to produce. It has been proposed that minimum wages be reduced for such workers, but the nearly unanimous opposition of trade unions has prevented serious consideration of such a proposal. Only a substantial expansion of the American economy offers much hope of absorbing marginal workers into productive labor.

In one sense, however, the unemployment figures overstate the problems for the American public. At least half of all American families have two wage earners, so that most families are not left without income, even if one member is unemployed. In addition, unemployment compensation and supplementary unemployment benefits provide a substantial cushion when a job is lost. The unemployment rate for heads of households was under 6 per cent, and more than one-third of the people unemployed in September had been out of work for less than five weeks. However, about 30 per cent had been out of work for more than 15 weeks, constituting the most serious problem.

Consumer Confidence. For those who were employed, conditions had never been better. Personal income was up 10 per cent, to almost $1.4 trillion. This worked out, after taxes, to almost $5,500 per capita. Real per capita disposable income, expressed in 1972 dollars, set a new record by exceeding $4,100.

A spurt in consumer spending, partly due to higher income levels, sparked the rise in the economy early in the year. Consumers apparently believed that prospects for continued price stability were good and that business was improving. As a result, they reduced their rate of saving from 7.8 per cent of disposable personal income in 1975 to about 6.8 per cent, a more normal ratio.

Business Optimism. Businessmen apparently were equally optimistic as they increased spending for new plant and equipment from $113 billion to approximately $121 billion. Although slightly below the levels forecast at the beginning of the year, this was still 7 per cent above the 1975 level.

The decline in interest rates made investment more attractive, and the drop in the sales-inventory ratio increased the incentive to expand capacity. Doubts began to creep in near the end of the year, however, and new orders for manufactured goods began to fall off, after rising sharply during the first six months. This, as well as other factors, led to caution about the future. See MANUFACTURING.

Leading Indicators. The index of leading economic indicators, those measures of the economy that presumably predict the state of business six to nine months in the future, rose slightly in October after small declines in August and September. Characteristically, a decline in this index for three successive months is the forerunner of a downturn in business activity. While most economists were cautiously optimistic that the expansion would continue at least into late 1977, the warning of a contrary situation was not unheeded.

Corporate profits during the first half were up sharply from 1975's depressed levels, but the rate of increase tapered off toward the end of the year. Economists anticipated that the final total, which will not be available until well into 1977, would show approximately a 25 per cent increase. This spurt in growth attracted considerable attention, but if profits were adjusted to reflect changing price levels over the past decade, they would be somewhat lower than in 1966 despite the tremendously increased amount of capital required to produce them. As a percentage of gross national product, profits were much lower than in 1966. By contrast, employee compensation as a percentage of national income has risen from 72 to 76 per cent.

Stock Prices. All of these uncertainties were reflected in the behavior of prices on the New York Stock Exchange. Industrial stock prices rose sharply during the first three months and then moved erratically for the balance of the year. They closed just above the peak achieved earlier in September. At the end of the year, stock prices were nearly 20 per cent above those at the close of 1975, whether measured by the broad New York Stock Exchange index or by the more popular, but less representative, Dow Jones industrial average. See STOCKS AND BONDS.

The housing industry was one of the brighter spots as the year closed. However, new private housing starts still fell far short of the record rate of

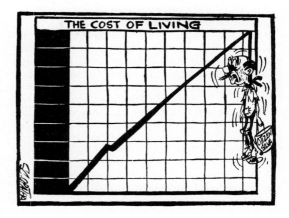

2.3 million units in 1972. About 1.5 million new units were started during the year, about 30 per cent above the level of 1975. See HOUSING.

Money Supply. While the economy moved forward, the Federal Reserve System (Fed), under the leadership of Arthur F. Burns, continued to emphasize restraint of the money supply. The Fed's primary fear was that easily available money would allow inflation to break out again and interrupt the economy's progress toward the goal of full employment without inflation. Thus, the primary money supply – currency in circulation plus demand deposits at commercial banks – was allowed to grow by something less than 5 per cent despite the unsatisfactory unemployment statistics. A broader measure of the money supply that includes the primary measure plus time deposits at commercial banks grew at a rate of about 10 per cent over the year. See BANKS AND BANKING.

The Federal Reserve Board believes that such rates are high enough to maintain a rate of economic growth that can be sustained over a long period of time without overheating the economy. The rates are deliberately set low to avoid the start-stop aspects of monetary economic policies that, in the past, have alternately generated inflationary pressures and then caused recession by tightening up on credit. The Fed's policy has succeeded in reducing the inflationary pressures of 1974 and 1975.

Success in reducing inflation, however, has been accompanied by an unsatisfactory level of unemployment, bringing the Fed under attack from those who place a higher priority on full employment than on stopping inflation. The Fed's policy has also been criticized by those who believe that, with industry operating well below capacity, a liberal increase in the money supply could be permitted without creating inflationary pressures.

The resolution of this controversy may well become one of the crucial decisions in the early days of President James Earl (Jimmy) Carter, Jr.'s Administration. During his campaign, Carter seemed to favor more rapid expansion of the economy as he strongly criticized both President Gerald R. Ford and Federal Reserve Chairman Burns. Some observers believe that this position on economic policy may have contributed to Carter's narrow victory. It came as somewhat of a surprise to these observers when, after the election, Carter began to sound more fiscally conservative. He and Burns indicated that they could work together, and Carter also indicated he had not made up his mind about what means to use to stimulate the economy.

Steel Prices. The major steel companies announced a price increase for flat rolled steel early in December, touching off protests from the Council on Wage and Price Stability, as well as from spokesmen for the incoming Carter Administration. Critics feared that the price increases would be reflected in higher prices for automobiles and home appliances, products in which steel is a major component. However, economists were by no means agreed that the effect of steel price increases would be nearly as serious as was alleged.

Some speculated that the increase was probably justified in terms of higher production costs, and that the announcement came when it did to beat a new round of price-wage controls feared under the Carter Administration. This led Carter to announce publicly that he had no intention of seeking such controls. When some steel users announced intentions of buying steel in other countries, doubts grew about whether the price increase would hold. See STEEL INDUSTRY.

Government Spending at all levels continued to play an important role in the economy. Total government purchases of goods and services amounted to slightly less than 22 per cent of the gross national product. Continuing the trend of recent years, state and local purchases grew more rapidly than those on the federal level, amounting to about 64 per cent of total government purchases.

Such purchases of goods and services should not be confused with total government spending. Only slightly more than one-third of the total federal outlays of about $390 billion went for the purchases of goods and services. The rest went for transfer payments, the largest items being social security payments, grants in aid to state and local governments, and net interest.

By function, the federal government spent the largest amount on health and income security — almost 70 per cent more than was spent on national defense. The total deficit was somewhat smaller than in 1975 and somewhat lower than had been anticipated — about $56 billion.

Trade Patterns. Total American merchandise exports were up nearly 10 per cent, or $11 billion, over 1975 levels. Imports rose even more rapidly, however, and converted the merchandise trade balance from a surplus of more than $3 billion in 1975 into a deficit of nearly $6 billion in 1976.

Income from private investments abroad and from providing services to foreign nations helped hold down the current transactions deficit. As a result of receipts of foreign capital, total United States official reserve assets continued to rise, reaching more than $18 billion by year's end.

The increased use of foreign crude oil was partially responsible for the rise in United States imports. But another important element was the increased U.S. prosperity. This brought an increase in imports as Americans found it possible and profitable to buy more goods from other countries.

As usual, heavy machinery and transportation equipment, along with meat and agricultural products, led the list of U.S. exports. Not unexpectedly,

Who Gets What

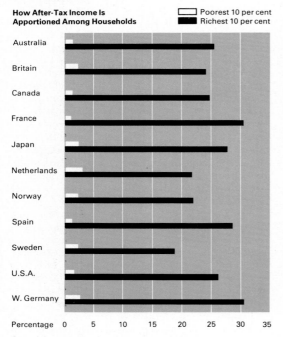

How After-Tax Income Is Apportioned Among Households

☐ Poorest 10 per cent
■ Richest 10 per cent

Australia

Britain

Canada

France

Japan

Netherlands

Norway

Spain

Sweden

U.S.A.

W. Germany

Percentage 0 5 10 15 20 25 30 35

Source: Organization for Economic Cooperation and Development

Selected Key U. S. Economic Indicators

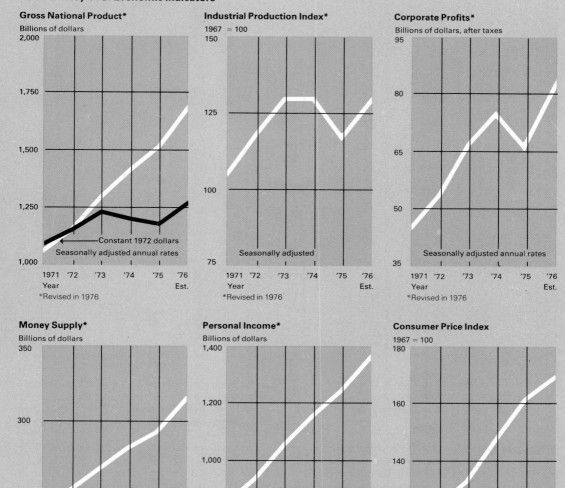

Gross National Product*
Billions of dollars

2,000

1,750

1,500

1,250

1,000

←— Constant 1972 dollars
Seasonally adjusted annual rates

1971 '72 '73 '74 '75 '76
Year   Est.
*Revised in 1976

Industrial Production Index*
1967 = 100

150

125

100

75

Seasonally adjusted

1971 '72 '73 '74 '75 '76
Year   Est.
*Revised in 1976

Corporate Profits*
Billions of dollars, after taxes

95

80

65

50

35

Seasonally adjusted annual rates

1971 '72 '73 '74 '75 '76
Year   Est.
*Revised in 1976

Money Supply*
Billions of dollars

350

300

250

200

Averages of daily figures,
seasonally adjusted

1971 '72 '73 '74 '75 '76
Year   Est.
*Revised in 1976

Personal Income*
Billions of dollars

1,400

1,200

1,000

800

600

Seasonally adjusted annual rates

1971 '72 '73 '74 '75 '76
Year   Est.
*Revised in 1976

Consumer Price Index
1967 = 100

180

160

140

120

100

All items

1971 '72 '73 '74 '75 '76
Year   Est.

The most comprehensive measure of the nation's total output of goods and services is the *Gross National Product* (GNP). The GNP represents the dollar value in current prices of all goods and services plus the estimated value of certain imputed outputs, such as the rental value of owner-occupied dwellings. *Industrial Production Index* is a monthly measure of the physical output of manufacturing, mining, and utility industries. *Corporate Profits* are quarterly profit samplings from major industries.

Money Supply measures the total amount of money in the economy in coin, currency, and demand deposits. *Personal Income* is current income received by persons (including nonprofit institutions and private trust funds) before personal taxes. *Consumer Price Index* (CPI) is a monthly measure of changes in the prices of goods and services consumed by urban families and individuals. CPI includes 300 goods and services. All 1976 figures are *Year Book* estimates.

United States President Gerald R. Ford, center,
talks with other world leaders during an economic
summit meeting at Dorado Beach, Puerto Rico.

petroleum headed the list of U.S. imports by a wide margin. Heavy machinery and transportation equipment were the next most important imports, followed by manufactured goods. These statistics indicate a continuation of the tendency for the immensely productive American agricultural sector to be the breadbasket of the world and of increasing U.S. dependence on foreign oil for energy needs. They also point up the significant exchange among industrialized nations of relatively sophisticated technological products, resulting in a two-way flow of manufactured goods and machinery. See INTERNATIONAL TRADE AND FINANCE.

There was little change in the geographic patterns of trade in 1976. The best customers of the United States, in order of importance, were Canada, Japan, West Germany, Mexico, and Great Britain. The primary U.S. suppliers were Canada, Japan, Saudi Arabia, West Germany, and Venezuela. Saudi Arabia and Venezuela made the list because of their heavy sales of crude oil.

World Economic Trends. Inflation continued to plague other countries much more than it did the United States. Switzerland, with only a 1.5 per cent

increase in consumer prices, and West Germany, with a rise of only 4 per cent, had the best records among industrialized nations. Next in line were the United States and Canada, both with increases of 5 to 6 per cent.

Most nations showed considerable declines in inflation from the prevailing rates in 1975. But Great Britain's drop from 25 to 14 per cent apparently was still not enough to ease the troubles of that country. Toward the end of the year, the British pound dropped precipitately on the foreign exchange markets. At year's end, it had risen from a low of $1.56 to $1.70, still 15 per cent below 1975's closing price. Unemployment also rose in Britain, giving support to the proposition that inflation is not a cure for unemployment, but probably serves to increase it in the long run.

Italy and France, with inflation rates of 15 and 9 per cent respectively, also suffered from increasing unemployment. Some experts worried that these countries might be hovering on the brink of a real recession, though industrial production in both countries continued to grow at a modest rate. If a recession were to materialize, it might well halt or slow the continuing recovery of such nations as West Germany and Japan, to say nothing of the United States.

Political Complications. Economic problems in the three troubled countries were complicated by

Prospects for 1977 appeared reasonably good for the United States, barring unforeseen events. Businessmen expected to increase spending for plant and equipment by 10 per cent. Modest stimulation of the economy by the Carter Administration's budget proposals was expected to produce further increases in the nation's output of goods and services. Increased retail sales during the Christmas buying season seemed to indicate that consumers had not lost their confidence. All these factors were expected to produce continued steady growth in the economy.

Although no startlingly rapid reduction is anticipated in the level of unemployment, some analysts believe that it could be well below 7 per cent by the end of 1977. If price increases can be held to a 5 to 6 per cent rate, 1977 should be a banner year for the United States.

Prospects abroad are not quite as glowing. If several of the major industrial countries were to experience recession at the same time, this could dampen prospects in the United States. Particularly troublesome would be any decline in the Canadian economy, which provides the largest single market for American goods. At year's end, some economists expressed fears that Canada might be headed into a significant slowdown in its rate of growth, if not an actual recession.   Warren W. Shearer

See also Section One, FOCUS ON THE ECONOMY.

---

political considerations. Britain ended the year locked in negotiations with the International Monetary Fund (IMF) for a loan of $3.9 billion to stabilize the pound. IMF authorities insisted on substantial cuts in British public spending before authorizing the loan on Jan. 3, 1977. The cuts roused widespread opposition from the left wing of Britain's governing Labour Party. See GREAT BRITAIN.

In both Italy and France, the problem revolved around the acceptance of the Communist Party as a part of a ruling government coalition. Although such a coalition was far from certain in either country, unsatisfactory economic conditions appeared likely to increase the chances of a Communist Party role in a coalition. At the same time, the prospect of such a coalition lessened the incentive for private economic growth.

Less-Developed Nations experienced even more severe inflation than the industrial countries. The annual rate of inflation in the troubled economies of Argentina and Chile was estimated at 800 per cent and 400 per cent, respectively. In Nigeria, economically the strongest of the African states, inflation ran at a rate of 34 per cent, a low figure for the equatorial African countries. Only in India, where increasingly stiff controls were being applied to the private economy, was there any apparent reduction in consumer prices, which were down 8 per cent.

ECUADOR. President Guillermo A. Rodriguez Lara was deposed in a bloodless coup d'état carried out by the armed forces on Jan. 11, 1976. The new military junta, which was headed by Vice-Admiral Alfredo Poveda Burbano, included army General Guillermo Duran Arcentales, and air force General Luis Leoro Franco. See POVEDA BURBANO, ALFREDO.

Rodriguez had been engaged in a political balancing act since September 1975, when he thwarted an attempt to oust him. He had been under attack by the Civic Junta, a conservative group, for delaying a return to civilian rule. Factions in the armed forces also opposed him for showing favoritism to other factions, and business and industry had censured him for the 1975 economic downturn into which he had led the country. It was, however, a series of student riots and a public-transportation strike in January – precipitated by a 20 per cent rise in urban transport fares – that provided the fatal spark.

Coup's Aftermath. The junta imposed a state of siege and declared martial law, but it also promised to follow a moderate political course and said it would keep Ecuador in the Organization of Petroleum Exporting Countries. The unmollified Civic Junta denounced the coup, however, and charged that the new leaders had been hand-picked by Rodriguez. The military responded by holding a series

Ecuador's President Guillermo A. Rodriguez
Lara leaves the presidential palace in Quito
after being deposed in a military coup d'état.

of meetings with civilian political leaders to discuss
Ecuador's return to constitutional rule in 1978.

The Economy rebounded from its 1975 slump
with an 8 per cent increase in the gross national
product. In response to strict import controls and a
more realistic government-set price for oil exports,
the balance of payments showed a surplus.

However, Ecuador's two leading exports, oil and
bananas, continued to be worrisome. The junta
formed a commission of banana producers to seek
new markets in Arab and Communist-bloc countries because competition from U.S.-owned fruit
companies was hurting Ecuador's sales in Western
Europe, Japan, and the United States.

While the junta improved somewhat on Rodriguez noncompetitive oil-pricing policy—which had
caused Ecuador crude oil to go begging abroad—it
continued a strong nationalistic policy that oil firms
termed little better than harassment. The junta demanded that the Texaco-Gulf consortium, which
developed most of the country's oil in the Amazon
region and built a $100-million pipeline over the
Andes Mountains to the Pacific Ocean, conduct
further exploration to increase average output from
175,000 to 210,000 barrels per day. Texaco and
Gulf said that Ecuador's heavy taxes, high royalty
claims, and hidden charges made such a venture
too costly.   Everett G. Martin

See also LATIN AMERICA (Facts in Brief Table).

EDUCATION in the United States faced acute economic pressures and problems associated with dras-
tically reduced growth in 1976. After years of struggling to keep up with the rising tide of pupils, local
communities across the nation had to begin closing
schools rather than building them.

Financial difficulties plagued schools at all levels.
An increasing number of big-city school systems
experienced severe budget crises. New York City
eliminated 5,000 teaching positions, enlarged its
classes, shortened the school day, and cut pupil
transportation and other services, such as guidance,
remedial studies, and library use. Chicago schools
ran out of money and had to close 16 days early in
June 1976. Chicago teachers accepted a contract
with no salary increases. Detroit abolished inter-
school sports, and New Orleans placed a moratorium on training courses for teachers.

A nationwide survey commissioned by *Change*, a
monthly magazine devoted to higher education,
showed that about half of the 2,163 colleges and
universities whose economic position was examined
were in poor financial condition, while some 300—
14 per cent of the total—were approaching insol-
vency and may not survive without outside aid. The
City University of New York had to shut down for
two weeks in May and June, when operating funds
ran out. The largest urban public institution of
higher learning in the world, it was forced to abandon its 129-year-old tradition of free tuition in September 1976.

In Higher Education, professional school enrollments dropped slightly, but the pressure to gain
admission to some, particularly in law, medicine,
and business administration, scarcely abated. However, after a 20-year trend toward ever more open
access to higher education, persistent questions
were raised about the wisdom of sending many
young people to college. Critics cited the declining
job market for college graduates and the fact that a
college degree no longer served as a guarantee of
high returns in earnings.

The public continued its demands for redoubled
emphasis on the teaching of basic skills at all school
levels. Generally conservative trends were also reflected in the accelerating competition among students for higher grades and the general abandonment of such noncompetitive devices as pass/fail
grades, which had been favored during the 1960s
by much of the student leadership.

Total Enrollment in American schools and colleges declined slightly for the fourth consecutive
year, after almost three decades of constant growth.
Although high school and college enrollments continued to increase, a drop of slightly more than
500,000 in the elementary schools—following an
average decline at that level of about 600,000 annually during the past three years—caused the downturn in the total curve. Total high school enroll-

ment in 1976 was expected to hit 15.8 million, an increase of less than 1 per cent over 1975. An anticipated increase of 4 per cent in higher education growth for the 1976-1977 school year appears to have been over optimistic. The latest estimate by the National Center for Education Statistics has scaled the increase down to 0.4 per cent. Only the two-year colleges showed a real gain, 2.1 per cent. But despite this slight overall increase, many colleges complained of insufficient students, largely because they had expanded their facilities on the basis of earlier, overly optimistic forecasts. Because of high tuition costs at a time of inflationary pressures and substantial unemployment, many students turned from expensive private colleges and universities to relatively low-cost public institutions.

The enrollment in public and private institutions dropped to 60.1 million in the fall of 1976 from 60.2 million the previous year. Elementary grades (kindergarten through grade 8) enrolled 34.1 million, with 30 million in public schools. High schools (grades 9 through 12) had a total enrollment of 15.8 million students, with 14.3 million of them in public high schools.

There were more than 3.1 million high school graduates in 1976. The graduating class of 1977 is expected to equal this record. For the 1976-1977 academic year, colleges and universities were expected to confer about 918,000 bachelor's degrees, 60,000 first professional degrees, 338,000 master's degrees, and 37,000 doctorates.

According to the U.S. Office of Education, education is the primary occupation, as learners or teachers, of some 63.6 million Americans. This means that 3 out of every 10 persons of a total population of 218 million participate directly in the educational process.

According to the latest available estimates, about 75 per cent of those 16 and 17 years old graduate from high school, and about 45 per cent of the graduates continue their education. About 25 per cent earn a bachelor's degree while 8 per cent and 1.5 per cent, respectively, gain master's or professional degrees and doctorates.

The Teachers. There were an estimated 3.2 million teachers at all levels of U.S education in 1976, including 687,000 in colleges and universities. About 400,000 of the total taught in private schools, half of them in higher education. The estimated 2.5-million elementary- and secondary-school teachers represented a very small increase over 1975. The substantial surplus of teachers continued, particularly in such fields as English, history, music, and the arts.

The average salary of teachers rose to $12,524 at all public school levels, and $12,130 for elementary-school teachers, a gain of about 7.5 per cent over the previous year. Averages ranged from Mississippi's $9,314 to Alaska's $19,880.

Thousands of Bostonians march on April 23 to protest violence against the city's controversial school-busing program.

EDUCATION

In higher education, the National Center for Education Statistics reported that faculty salaries rose an average of 6.6 per cent in 1975-1976. At the same time, salary inequalities between men and women increased, with salaries for men rising an average of 6.7 per cent, compared with only 6.1 per cent for women. The American Association of University Professors found the national average increase to be only 6 per cent.

Teachers' Unions. Fierce competition continued between the two largest U.S. teacher organizations, the National Education Association (NEA) with 1.8-million members and the American Federation of Teachers (AFT) with about 475,000 members. Earlier hopes for a merger of the two organizations were dampened when a trial merger in New York collapsed amid considerable acrimony in early 1976.

There were 210 teacher strikes in the United States during the 1975-1976 school year, 60 of them called by affiliates of the AFT. They ranged from a one-day stoppage in Waukegan, Ill., to an eight-week walkout in Pittsburgh.

The school year that started in September 1976 began with fewer teacher strikes. There were more than 2,000 unsettled teacher contracts, but the overwhelming majority either were settled or were in the process of being settled without strikes.

Education Expenditures at all levels for 1976-1977 were estimated by the Office of Education at $130 billion, an increase of some $11 billion. However, that increase was only slightly more than the rate of inflation, leaving the schools and colleges with a real gain of about $3 billion. Elementary and secondary schools were expected to spend $81.5-billion during the 1976-1977 academic year, compared with $75.3 billion the previous year. College and university spending was estimated at $48.8 billion, up from $44.5 billion. Public schools and colleges spent about $105.8 billion.

National educational expenditures were still about 8 per cent of the gross national product. State governments contributed a total of $45 billion, or 34.5 per cent; local governments, $38.2 billion, or 29.3 per cent; the federal government, $13.4 billion, or 10.3 per cent; and all other sources, $33.7-billion, or 25.9 per cent.

Student Achievements have been under increasingly critical scrutiny. Average scores on the Scholastic Aptitude Tests given to college-bound juniors and seniors by the College Entrance Examination Board have declined for at least 10 years — from 492 to 470 in mathematics and from 466 to 429 in verbal skills on a scale ranging from 200 to 800. In an effort to determine the cause, the board appointed a special panel in 1975 under the direc-

French police use tear gas and nightsticks to clear Paris streets of thousands of students striking to protest changes in university courses.

Classes go on for the cadets at West Point
as a special commission investigates the
academy honor code after a cheating scandal.

Bilingual Education. In April, the Department of Health, Education, and Welfare (HEW) issued a memorandum to clarify its policy on bilingual education for students whose first language is not English. HEW's position, one supported by a 1974 decision of the Supreme Court of the United States, is that bilingual education for such children is the best solution for language difficulties in schools, but is not required under Title VI of the 1964 Civil Rights Act. HEW said other remedies may be used instead, but it did not spell out what these remedies might be. HEW's ruling, and the court decision, affect about 1.1 million students in 333 school districts in 26 states whose primary language is not English.

Professional Schools reported a slowdown in enrollments. For years, schools of medicine, dentistry, nursing, and law had grown at a record pace. But September 1976 showed the first decrease in the growth rate of medical school applications in a decade, after more than doubling from 1966 to 1975. Applications to dental schools leveled off, and the number of nursing programs and students stopped increasing. The number of students taking the Law School Admission Test dropped for the first time in 10 years.   Fred M. Hechinger

See also Section One, FOCUS ON EDUCATION; Section Two, THE LOSING WAR AGAINST ILLITERACY.

tion of W. Willard Wirtz, former secretary of labor, to review factors that affect test performances.

At the same time, the National Assessment of Educational Progress, a federally funded project that periodically compares the achievements of different age groups, reported that children's reading ability has not deteriorated in the 1970s and that the skills of 9-year-olds in particular have improved markedly since 1971. The report also said that black children, though still trailing their white peers in reading skills, have shown a greater improvement rate than their white classmates.

President Gerald R. Ford signed the omnibus higher education and vocational education aid bill on October 12, but he criticized a provision that raises the maximum annual basic opportunity grant – which provides aid for college students from low-income families – from $1,400 to $1,800.

Integration. There was a growing acceptance of school desegregation in 1976. Peaceful school openings in communities with court-ordered integration, such as Louisville, Ky.; Dayton, Ohio; and Cleveland, indicated greater racial peace. Moreover, the United States Commission on Civil Rights issued a report on school desegregation in August that was generally positive, but it criticized the Ford Administration for supporting legislative proposals to limit the federal judiciary's authority to order busing for purposes of integration.

EGYPT. The second stage of the disengagement agreement with Israel proceeded smoothly in 1976. Egyptian forces reoccupied the Port Fuad-Kantara area east of the Suez Canal on January 26, following Israeli withdrawal, and Egypt re-established control on February 22 in an 89-square-mile (231-square-kilometer) area of the Sinai Peninsula up to the Mitla and Giddi passes.

Relations with Libya followed a rougher road. Former Libyan Planning Minister Omar Meheishi, who fled to Tunisia after an attempted coup d'état against President Muammar Muhammad al-Qadhaafi of Libya, was granted political asylum in Egypt in February. Meheishi's presence led to several attempts on his life by Libyan commandos. On July 11, three Libyans were given long prison terms for attempted assassination. Rivalry with Libya was also a factor in Egypt's support of Sudanese President Gaafar Muhammed Nimeiri, the target of a July coup attempt. Egypt and the Sudan signed a 25-year treaty of mutual defense on July 19. See LIBYA; SUDAN.

Free Elections. President Anwar al-Sadat was re-elected unopposed by a 99.93 per cent majority of the electorate on October 6. In a Sadat-encouraged liberalization of the Arab Socialist Union (ASU), Egypt's only legal political party, the first relatively free parliamentary elections since the 1952 revolution were held on October 28. The

Seeking aid for Egypt's sagging economy,
President Anwar al-Sadat, center, visited
Saudi Arabia and five other Arab states.

ASU presented candidates representing three groupings—the political left, center, and right. Egyptian voters gave the centrists a strong majority in the People's Assembly. Sadat said on November 11 that the groupings could be called political parties, thus reinstituting a multiple-party system.

Although hard-pressed economically, Egypt remained a vital source of skilled workers for other Arab states. On August 23, some 2,000 Egyptian teachers were recruited for Kuwaiti schools. Saudi Arabia agreed to provide $50,000 in aid to Egyptian universities for every Egyptian professor sent to a Saudi university.

Economic Gains. Sadat's forecast on March 29 of "five lean years" for Egypt did not seem to discourage foreign investment in the country. The compensation on May 2 of $10 million to American firms whose property had been expropriated under the Nasser regime was a further incentive. In July, the People's Assembly passed a foreign-currency law allowing banks to deal freely in foreign currency, a first step in relating the Egyptian pound to international money markets.

A major natural gas field was discovered in February south of Cairo. New oil fields in the Gulf of Suez and in the Western Desert will triple Egyptian oil production when they eventually go into full operation.   William Spencer

See also MIDDLE EAST (Facts in Brief Table).

ELECTIONS. Democratic challenger James Earl (Jimmy) Carter, Jr., defeated President Gerald R. Ford, his Republican opponent, on Nov. 2, 1976, in one of the closest elections of the 1900s. It was the first time in 44 years that an incumbent President seeking election was put out of office.

Carter, a former Georgia governor, received 50.08 per cent of the popular vote. Ford captured 48.02 per cent, and other candidates—including independent Eugene J. McCarthy—received less than 2 per cent. Carter's popular vote totaled 40,827,292; Ford's, 39,146,157. McCarthy received only 745,346, but he may have tipped the outcome against Carter in several states where the Ford-Carter race was extremely close.

The presidential candidates needed at least 270 electoral votes to win the election. Carter received 297 electoral votes. When the Electoral College met on December 13, one elector from Washington state cast his vote for Ronald Reagan, leaving Ford—who had carried the state—with 8, for a national total of 240. If Carter had won 10,000 fewer votes in Ohio and Hawaii, he would have lost the election even though he still would have led in the popular vote.

Although Ford lagged far behind in polls taken early in the campaign, he rallied to win most of the Western, Rocky Mountain, and Great Plains states. Carter captured the more populous states in the Northeast, South, and Midwest.

Only 53.5 per cent of the registered voters showed up at the polls on November 2. This was the lowest turnout since 1948 and below the 55 per cent who voted in the 1972 presidential election.

Campaign Strategies. Carter won by reassembling many parts of the New Deal coalition formed by President Franklin D. Roosevelt in the 1930s. Carter courted the South, minorities, organized labor, and liberals. He also ran better in the rural Midwest than most Democrats.

Ford's pardon of former President Richard M. Nixon was only a minor campaign issue. A sagging economy and persistent inflation probably contributed more to his defeat than the lingering memories of the Watergate scandal.

Carter, recalling the 1960 presidential campaign of John F. Kennedy, promised to "get the country moving again" if he were elected. He characterized Ford as a decent man but a do-nothing President.

Debates and Distractions. Ford and Carter engaged in three nationally televised debates. The first debate was held on September 23 in Philadelphia and covered the economy and domestic issues. The second, held in San Francisco on October 6, dealt with defense and foreign policy. The third debate, on October 22 in Williamsburg, Va., was open to all subjects.

Ford made a statement in the second debate that was widely viewed as a major blunder. He said that

Eastern Europe was not under Russian domination. Pollster George H. Gallup, Jr., claimed this was the "decisive event" in the campaign, halting Ford's momentum just as he was pulling even with Carter in the polls.

Carter, on the other hand, was plagued by an interview he gave to *Playboy* magazine. The magazine printed Carter's admissions about lustful thoughts, which caused a furor among some voters. Carter later said it was a mistake to grant the interview.

The November race was the first publicly financed presidential election in U.S. history. Both candidates accepted federal financing and limited their spending to $21.8 million.

Senate Races. The Democrats easily retained their 3-to-2 margin over the Republicans in the U.S. Senate. There was little change in party membership. The line-up remained almost the same, with 61 Democrats, 38 Republicans, and 1 Independent (see CONGRESS OF THE UNITED STATES). However, nine incumbent senators were defeated. With elected replacements for eight retiring senators and an appointed replacement for the seat left vacant by Vice-President-elect Walter F. Mondale, this made a total of 18 new senators.

Democrats ousted four incumbent Republican senators in November. Democrat Daniel Patrick Moynihan, former U.S. ambassador to the United Nations, unseated New York state's Conservative James L. Buckley. In Maryland, Democrat Paul S. Sarbanes replaced Republican J. Glenn Beall, Jr. Ohio Democrat Howard M. Metzenbaum defeated Robert Taft, Jr., and James R. Sasser upset Republican William E. Brock III of Tennessee.

Republicans toppled five Democrats in the Senate. In California, a 70-year-old semanticist from San Francisco State University, S. I. Hayakawa, beat Democrat John V. Tunney. Indianapolis Mayor Richard G. Lugar replaced Democrat Vance Hartke of Indiana. In New Mexico, Republican Harrison H. Schmitt, a former astronaut, defeated Joseph M. Montoya. Utah Democrat Frank E. Moss lost to a Republican novice, Orrin G. Hatch, and Republican Malcolm Wallop upset three-term Democratic Senator Gale W. McGee in Wyoming.

Five of the eight senators elected to replace retiring incumbents were Democrats. Dennis DeConcini defeated Sam Steiger in Arizona. Democrat Spark M. Matsunaga succeeded Republican Hiram L. Fong of Hawaii by defeating former Governor William F. Quinn. In Michigan, Democrat Donald W. Riegle, Jr., won over Marvin L. Esch. Montana Democrat John Melcher replaced retiring Senate Majority Leader Mike Mansfield by defeating Re-

The 1976 Electoral College Vote

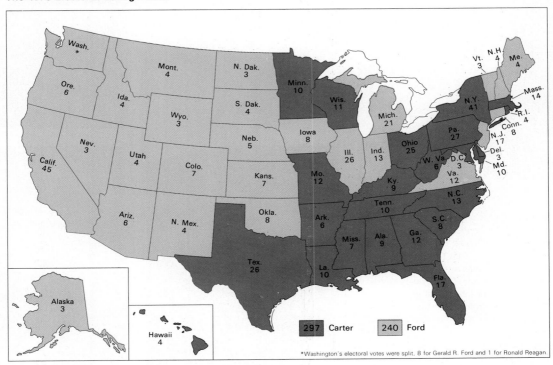

publican Stanley C. Burger. In Nebraska, Edward Zorinsky, a Republican-turned-Democrat and mayor of Omaha, beat Republican John Y. McCollister. Wendell R. Anderson resigned as governor of Minnesota to be appointed to fill the Senate seat vacated by Mondale.

In the Republican column, John C. Danforth, an Episcopal minister and Missouri state attorney general, won a Senate seat over former Governor Warren E. Hearnes. H. John Heinz III, heir to a processed foods fortune, won over Democrat William J. Green for the Pennsylvania Senate seat vacated by former Minority Leader Hugh Scott. In Rhode Island, liberal Republican and former governor John H. Chafee defeated Richard P. Lorber.

House Contests were a sharp disappointment to Republican officials. They had hoped to recapture many of the 43 seats the Democrats gained in 1974, when Watergate and high inflation took their political toll. However, the Democrats retained their 2-to-1 margin.

Most incumbent representatives retained their seats. Only 13 House members were ousted, including 2 of the 75 freshman Democrats elected in 1974—Allan T. Howe of Utah and Tim L. Hall of Illinois. Howe, doomed after being convicted of soliciting policewomen posing as prostitutes in Salt Lake City, was defeated by Republican Dan Marriott. Hall lost to Tom Corcoran, former lobbyist for the state of Illinois in Washington, D.C.

The Democratic and Republican parties both provided winners in the November 2 election who figure to be prominent on the national scene. They included, *clockwise from above:* three new senators, Daniel P. Moynihan, Democrat of New York, S. I. Hayakawa, a California Republican, and former astronaut Harrison H. Schmitt, now Republican senator from New Mexico; and new governors Dixy Lee Ray of Washington, a Democrat, and James R. Thompson of Illinois, a Republican.

Six other Democrats also lost seats. Two-term Representative Edward Mezvinsky lost to Republican James Leach in Iowa. Democrat Richard F. Vander Veen, who won President Ford's former Michigan district in 1974, was replaced by Republican Harold Sawyer.

Republican J. Danforth Quayle, a newspaper publisher, ousted eight-term Representative J. Edward Roush of Indiana. Six-term Democrat Joseph P. Vigorito lost to Marc L. Marks in northwestern Pennsylvania. In West Virginia, Democratic Representative Ken Hechler lost a write-in campaign against the Democratic Party's slated candidate, Nick J. Rahall. New Jersey Democrat Henry Helstoski, facing trial on bribery charges, was defeated by Harold Hollenbeck.

Four veteran Republican members of the House lost in November. Eight-term Representative Garner E. Shriver of Kansas lost to Democrat Dan Glickman. In Ohio, Democrat Thomas A. Luken ousted Donald D. Clancy. California's Burt L. Talcott was defeated by Democrat Leon E. Panetta. Albert W. Johnson of Pennsylvania lost to Democrat Joseph S. Ammerman.

The 16 black members of the House won reelection. The number of women in the House dropped from 19 to 18; three women left the House and only two new women were elected. The newcomers are Democrat Barbara Mikulski of Baltimore and Democrat Mary Rose Oakar of Cleveland.

In Gubernatorial Races, the Democrats picked up 1 governorship, giving them 37 governors to the Republicans' 12. There was also 1 Independent.

Nine new governors were chosen in 14 contests. A major Republican victory occurred in Illinois, where James R. Thompson, a former U.S. attorney in Chicago, easily defeated Democrat Michael J. Howlett. Another Republican candidate, Pierre S. du Pont IV, was elected governor of Delaware, ousting incumbent Democrat Sherman W. Tribbitt. In Vermont, Republican Richard A. Snelling defeated a conservative Democrat and a third-party candidate. In Missouri, Democrat Joseph P. Teasdale ousted Republican Governor Christopher S. Bond. Democrat John D. Rockefeller IV was elected governor of West Virginia over former Republican Governor Cecil H. Underwood.

Dixy Lee Ray, a marine biologist and former chairperson of the Atomic Energy Commission, won easily over Republican John Spellman for the governorship of Washington state. In Utah, Democrat Scott M. Matheson, a Salt Lake City lawyer, defeated Republican Vernon B. Romney.

Two lieutenant governors were elected to the top post in their states — North Carolina Democrat James B. Hunt, Jr., and Rhode Island Democrat J. Joseph Garrahy. Five incumbents kept their governor's chairs: Republicans Meldrim Thomson, Jr.,

of New Hampshire and Otis R. Bowen of Indiana and Democrats David Pryor of Arkansas, Thomas L. Judge of Montana, and Arthur A. Link of North Dakota.

Referendums. Several states used the November election to bring important issues before the voters. Proposed restrictions on the development of nuclear power were voted on in Arizona, Colorado, Montana, Ohio, Oregon, and Washington. All six states rejected the nuclear restrictions. California voters rejected a similar proposal in June.

Proponents of gun control suffered a setback when Massachusetts voters rejected a ban on the sale of handguns. Massachusetts also voted against mandatory deposits on beverage containers, as did Colorado. But Maine and Michigan voters adopted such regulation.

California voters defeated a proposition to ensure collective-bargaining rights and secret-ballot elections for farmworkers. They also rejected a proposal to introduce dog racing in the state. New Jersey voters approved a plan to allow legalized gambling in Atlantic City.   William J. Eaton

See also CARTER, JAMES EARL, JR.; DEMOCRATIC PARTY; FORD, GERALD R.; MONDALE, WALTER F.; REAGAN, RONALD; REPUBLICAN PARTY; ROCKEFELLER, NELSON A.; Section Five, CARTER, JAMES EARL, JR.

ELECTRIC POWER. See ENERGY.

ELECTRONICS. Some British television viewers read news, sports, weather, and even stock reports on their TV screens in early 1976 as tests began on sets equipped with special electronic adapters. Both the British Broadcasting Corporation and the Independent Broadcasting Authority transmitted "pages" of information piggyback on the regular television signal. Each page had 24 horizontal rows, and the viewer could select from about 800 pages by using a calculator-type keyboard.

In the United States, citizens band (CB) radio became the electronics craze. Millions of individuals bought CB transceivers for communications between automobiles, homes, and offices. With sales jumping from a steady $50 million annually to over $1.5 billion, such big names in electronics as RCA Corporation and Motorola joined more than 30 lesser-known manufacturers in making and selling CB sets. See COMMUNICATIONS (Close-Up).

Another industry highlight was the addition of new technology to an industry old-timer — television. New circuitry in the sets, a new kind of picture tube, and video games that hook up to TV sets reflected the changes. In the computer field, microprocessor technology grew rapidly, and semiconductor makers began selling two new types of computer memories.

Television Tuners. Although the typical TV buyer may never know it, TV tuners are better and

Blind students at the University of California,
Irvine, use a calculator that announces entries
and computation results in a male-sounding voice.

Video games, which are played on TV sets, were developed that generate games in color. In some cases, a single LSI chip contained all the circuitry for an entire game.

Computer Components. Microprocessor technology advanced in the areas of increased storage space and the development of powerful programming languages similar to those used with medium to large computer systems. A microprocessor is a complete computer core on a single LSI chip. Many manufacturers produced microcomputers — complete computers on single printed circuit boards — that were built around microprocessors.

Two new computer memories were introduced during the year. One, the 16,384-bit random access memory (16k RAM), is an extension of the 4k RAM, not a new technology. A bit is the basic unit of information in digital computers. The new memory offers more capacity in less space, thereby increasing computing power and decreasing costs.

The first practicable bubble memory for computers and terminals was also introduced. Aimed at replacing electromechanical disk- and drum-type storage memories, the bubbles are actually magnetized regions of a material that can store data in a relatively small area.   Marilyn J. Offenheiser.

EL SALVADOR. See LATIN AMERICA.

EMPLOYMENT. See ECONOMICS; EDUCATION; LABOR; SOCIAL SECURITY; SOCIAL WELFARE.

more reliable, thanks to new kinds of electronic circuits. Through large scale integration (LSI) — the manufacture of thousands of transistors and other interconnected components on one tiny "chip" of silicon — electronic tuners replaced electromechanical tuners in many sets. For example, Magnavox Corporation of Fort Wayne, Ind., introduced a relatively low-cost 20-channel electronic tuner that uses five LSI chips. The largest chip is about 0.2 inch (0.5 centimeter) square, yet it contains the equivalent of 1,750 separate components. The viewer selects channels by punching a keyboard, and the channel number appears on a light-emitting-diode display.

Electronic tuning made remote-tuning devices more practical. One RCA TV can be tuned only by a remote keyboard. The complete tuning system, which transmits ultrasonic energy from the hand-held unit to the set, uses 10 LSI chips.

Zenith Corporation of Chicago, in conjunction with the Corning Glass Works of Corning, N.Y., developed a new type of picture tube. The tube uses a 100° deflection angle, which makes it about 2.5 inches (6.4 centimeters) shorter than the 90° angle tube used by most U.S. TV makers. Japanese set makers use a 100° angle. Zenith said the new tube improves picture clarity and reduces production costs, but most other U.S. manufacturers continued to use the 90° angle tubes.

ENERGY. The United States and other oil-importing nations found out on Dec. 16, 1976, that their oil bills would be higher. The Organization of Petroleum Exporting Countries (OPEC) agreed then to a split-level increase in prices. Two members, Saudi Arabia and the United Arab Emirates, agreed to raise their prices 5 per cent effective Jan. 1, 1977. The other 11 OPEC nations agreed to raise their prices 10 per cent on the same date. See PETROLEUM AND GAS.

For much of 1976, the U.S. search for new energy sources and the inability to establish a well-defined energy policy that would be politically and socially acceptable continued.

A growing sector of American industry began looking for energy supplies on a do-it-yourself basis. The first natural gas produced by Republic Steel Corporation from 20 wells in Ohio began flowing through East Ohio Gas Company pipelines to Republic plants in northeastern Ohio. Some 20-million cubic feet (566,000 cubic meters) of new natural gas per day started flowing to Republic plants. The new gas also supplemented East Ohio's gas reserves for home heating use. Gas from the new wells could spell the difference between some of Republic's plants continuing to operate or being shut down during peak gas-demand periods.

Private Electric Generation by industrial plants received a boost from the Federal Energy Administration (FEA). The FEA's deputy administrator, John A. Hill, told a meeting of the Environmental Advisory Committee on October 8 of the gains that are possible if industrial firms can generate electricity on their own. Two federal studies—one coordinated by Dow Chemical Company for the National Science Foundation and the other produced by Thermo Electron Corporation for the FEA—have shown a rich potential for industrial firms generating electricity as a by-product of their steam requirements. Many companies could satisfy their own electrical needs and sell the surplus to the utilities. The Dow study stated that private industrial electric generation, or *co-generation*, could cut electric utility needs for capital spending by about $5-billion a year and could reduce residential electricity rates about 8 per cent by 1985.

Some industrial plants now operate on a co-generation basis with their utility. In February, the Hammermill Paper Company of Erie, Pa., started selling its surplus electric power to Pennsylvania Electric Company. Almost all the electric power in Hammermill's Erie plant is generated by passing high-pressure steam through turbogenerators, producing low-pressure steam for manufacturing needs and electric energy. During the winter season—when more steam is needed for manufacturing, drying, and heating—more electric power is made, and the surplus is sold to the utility. Conversely, lower steam demand during the summer results in lowered power production, so Hammermill must buy electricity from the utility.

Heat Recovery from a West German electric utility began in 1976 when the first 2-mile (3.2-kilometer) section of a pipeline through the Ruhr industrial area went into operation. The pipeline carries waste steam at 176° to 356°F. (80° to 180°C), depending on the season, from a 50-megawatt (Mw) generating station in Gelsenkirchen to homes and commercial buildings in the area. By the end of 1977, the double-pipe steam line is expected to stretch 19 miles (30.5 kilometers) and connect Gelsenkirchen with Essen and Bottrop. It will carry steam from coking plants and other industrial boilers, plus steam provided by regional utility generating stations.

Environmental Opposition to the Newport power plant in Australia prompted the Victoria State Electricity Commission to propose adding 7 per cent to the 10 per cent rate increase originally deemed necessary. The commission also planned to send officials abroad to buy gas turbines that would enable the stalled 1,000-Mw, gas-fired Newport station to generate the power it was expected to produce. Meanwhile, four old power stations are to be kept in service.

An engineer at the San Onofre, Calif., nuclear power plant reads about the June 8 defeat of Proposition 15, a proposal to curb nuclear power.

The completion of the Newport Station was delayed by the fear of increasing pollution. Environmental groups also threatened to block use of the three old oil-burning stations and one old briquette-burning station on the same grounds. Commission officials said that despite use of the old plants and the installation of the gas turbines, severe power shortages will occur in 1979 in Victoria, Australia's second most heavily populated and industrialized state.

Nuclear Power had another mixed year. Public opposition continued to be the toughest barrier to nuclear power growth. The nuclear industry recorded a gain in June, when California voters soundly defeated the antinuclear Proposition 15 in a referendum. Proposed restrictions on the development of nuclear power were also decisively rejected in the November elections in all six states where they appeared on the ballots — Arizona, Colorado, Montana, Ohio, Oregon, and Washington. The electric power industry hailed the results as evidence of a national consensus in favor of going ahead with nuclear energy.

The contribution of nuclear energy was underlined in May by an Atomic Industrial Forum report. With 61 operable reactors in the United States representing 42,699 Mw of capacity, nuclear plants produced 8.3 per cent of the electricity generated in the first six months of 1976. This saved 5 billion barrels of oil, or 27 million short tons (24.5 million metric tons) of coal.

U.S. Electric Utilities went through another disappointing year, the more so because 1976 was expected by many to be the best in recent years, with full economic recovery and a normally hot summer after three successive cool ones. The economy moved up steadily in the first half of the year, and kilowatt-hour sales responded eagerly. But a weak second half and only spotty summer heat damped the surge. Actual load growth in 1976 returned only to pre-energy-crisis levels. Utility management continued to hold back on capital spending and at year's end reported the following:

	1975	1976	% gain
	(in millions)		
Total capability (kw)	495	515	4
Utilities generation (kwh)	1,863,600	2,038,000	9
Utilities sales (kwh)	1,735,000	1,843,000	6
Utilities revenue*	$ 42,700	$ 47,200	11

*For investor-owned companies

The Heat Pump took on fresh promise. Sales of the energy-saving devices, which heat and cool with the same components, are booming. Sales reached 120,000 units in 1973 during the oil embargo and continued to climb through 1975, when sales totaled 167,000 units shipped. In the first seven months of 1976, manufacturers sold 170,000 units and approached 300,000 at year's end. Heat pumps — basically reversible central air conditioners — were being installed in nearly half the homes with electric heating built in the United States. In Cincinnati, Ohio, heat pumps are being used in 75 per cent of the new houses, and in Washington, D.C., even more — 80 per cent — of the new homes have them.

Their popularity stems mainly from the big energy price increases since 1973. Although heat pumps often cost more initially than other heating and cooling equipment, their efficiency can result in a saving for the homeowner.

Solar Energy made some advances during the year with financial backing from the federal Energy Research and Development Administration. United States engineers successfully tested a power-plant steam boiler designed to run on sunlight at the world's largest solar-energy test installation in Odeillo, France. During the test, mirrors focused sunlight to produce steam that could then power a conventional steam turbogenerator.

It was announced in September that construction will start in 1977 on a 160-unit housing project in North Easton, Mass., that will use solar energy for heating.   James J. O'Connor

See also COAL.

ENGINEERING. See BUILDING & CONSTRUCTION.

ENVIRONMENT. The Fifth United Nations (UN) Law of the Sea Conference ended on Sept. 17, 1976, without agreement on how to control deep seabed mining. Critics contended that representatives from the underdeveloped nations resisted compromise on the issue because they hoped for a change in U.S. policy after the November election. See MINES AND MINING; OCEAN.

A new law aimed at protecting domestic fisheries from overfishing by foreign trawlers was signed by President Gerald R. Ford on April 13. The law extended the United States fishing jurisdiction from 12 to 200 nautical miles. It was to take effect on March 1, 1977.

Clean Air. The Council on Environmental Quality, in its annual assessment of the ecological health of the United States, said on September 30 that the country is making "significant progress" in cleaning up air pollution, but that efforts to improve water quality are still lagging.

A last-minute filibuster on October 1, as Congress was rushing toward adjournment, killed amendments to the 1970 Clean Air Amendments Act over which Congress had fought most of the session. The bill would have delayed for one year the existing 1978 deadline for the automobile industry to further reduce emissions from exhausts on their new models. The industry had asked for an extension until 1982. See AUTOMOBILE.

A panel of the National Academy of Sciences on September 13 confirmed growing evidence that gases from aerosol spray cans may be damaging the ozone layer in the stratosphere that protects life on earth from the sun's most damaging rays. The panel recommended regulatory action within two years, after further study to determine the degree to which uses of the gases should be curtailed. See SCIENCE AND RESEARCH.

Energy Conflicts. The basic conflicts between environmentalists and energy developers heightened during the year and resulted generally in a stand-off unsatisfactory to both sides. The conservationists won unexpected support on August 24 when the General Accounting Office (GAO) recommended that the federal government stress energy conservation rather than developing more costly synthetic fuel. The GAO said conservation offers the greatest potential payoff.

A proposition that would have greatly restricted the development of nuclear power in California was overwhelmingly defeated by the voters on June 8. Consumer advocate Ralph Nader had strongly backed the proposal, which would have empowered the legislature to enforce strict safety standards in nuclear plants and to ban new nuclear plant construction. The vote was viewed as a major test of public attitudes on whether accident-prevention systems in reactors are adequate and whether nuclear wastes can be disposed of safely.

In Great Britain, a commission on environmental pollution recommended on September 22 that the national commitment to nuclear power be delayed as long as possible in the hope that it would become unnecessary through the development of other energy sources.

The U.S. Department of the Interior leased tracts for oil and gas development on the continental shelf off the coasts of Alaska and the Middle Atlantic states. Some environmental groups opposed the actions, but the department won court suits permitting it to proceed. Congress failed to enact legislation, bitterly opposed by the Ford Administration and the oil industry, increasing state participation in the leasing process.

Conservation groups charged on August 3 that the Interior Department had failed to vigorously enforce stipulations to ensure safety of the Alaska oil pipeline. Congressional investigators reported that construction problems made it doubtful that the line would go into operation on schedule. The pipeline was scheduled to begin moving 1.2 million barrels of oil daily from Alaska's North Slope by mid-1977.

Water Pollution. Russell E. Train, administrator of the U.S. Environmental Protection Agency

Scientists studying how to safely dispose of atomic waste products, such as these in Idaho, are considering burying them deep in the ocean floor.

Landslides after heavy rain on Japan's Izu Peninsula killed nine persons.
They were blamed on rapid land development that upset the balance of nature.

(EPA), said on August 17 that contamination by the toxic and long-lived pesticide Kepone might become a major environmental problem. Train cited tests that showed massive contamination by the pesticide in Virginia's James River, contamination that was now spreading through Chesapeake Bay, one of the nation's major seafood-producing regions. Part of the James River was closed to fishing in December 1975. A federal judge fined Allied Chemical Corporation $13.3 million on Oct. 5, 1976, for discharging Kepone into the river. See CHEMICAL INDUSTRY.

The EPA on July 23 ordered New York City and other communities to stop dumping sewage sludge into the Atlantic Ocean by the end of 1981. The order affected more than 100 communities and commercial firms in New York and New Jersey that have poured an estimated 5.8 million short tons (5.3 million metric tons) of sludge annually into the Atlantic. The action came after Long Island ocean beaches were contaminated early in July by garbage, and after a huge fish kill was reported on July 7 off New Jersey.

Land-Use Programs. Despite continued pressure from environmentalists, Congress adjourned without enacting legislation to control widespread strip mining. The House of Representatives, which had passed six strip-mining bills in recent years, was blocked from its final 1976 effort to enact the legis-lation when the House Rules Committee voted on September 15 to deny the bill floor consideration. The environmental groups had sought congression-al action because they feared that strip mining in the Rocky Mountain and Northern Plains states would greatly increase in 1977, following the Inte-rior Department announcement on January 26 ending a three-year moratorium on leasing the massive federally owned coal deposits in those areas. Congress also failed to resolve conflicting views about federal control of wetlands.

Toxic Substances. Legislation imposing the first controls on the manufacture and use of toxic sub-stances was approved by Congress on September 28, climaxing a bitter five-year battle conducted primarily by environmentalists. In signing the bill into law on October 12, President Ford called it "one of the most important pieces of environmental legislation." Under this law, the EPA may require testing of new chemical substances and may ban or limit their use if the agency concludes they are po-tentially hazardous. The legislation completely bans polychlorinated biphenyls (PCB's), chemical compounds widely used in electrical insulators, within two years. PCB's are known to be a cause of cancer and have been found in nursing mothers' milk. Andrew L. Newman

See also CONSERVATION.

EQUATORIAL GUINEA. See AFRICA.

ETHIOPIA. The secessionist war in the northern province of Eritrea continued during 1976 despite efforts by the central government to achieve a negotiated settlement. Eritrean nationalists began fighting for independence in the early 1960s.

On May 16, 1976, the head of Ethiopia's military government, Teferi Bante, announced a plan to end the war. The plan offered substantial autonomy for Eritrea and amnesty for most Eritrean political prisoners. But Eritrea would still remain part of Ethiopia.

Bante's government also dispatched diplomats to Yemen (Aden), Sudan, and other Arab countries that had supported the Eritrean nationalists, hoping to enlist the aid of those countries in persuading the Eritrean insurgents to negotiate. However, the Eritreans spurned the offer, apparently because the war was going well for them. By October, the central government controlled only the main towns and very little of the rural areas, where most of the Eritreans live.

In April, the central government mobilized thousands of peasants, armed with obsolete weapons, to aid about 25,000 soldiers and police officers stationed in Eritrea. There may have been as many as 100,000 of these peasant troops in June, when the government decided to send them home.

The central government publicly denied that the peasants ever fought in Eritrea. However, Eritrean guerrilla forces claimed they ambushed large columns of peasants in May.

Eritrean guerrillas released two U.S. servicemen in January, and two Americans and one British citizen taken hostage in 1975 were freed in May. The last U.S. hostage was released in June.

Internal Problems. The central government also faced opposition within its own ranks. The government in February arrested a number of right wing critics, including a prominent leader of the ruling military council, Lieutenant Colonel Atnafu Abate.

Another high-ranking council member, Major Sisay Habte, was implicated in an alleged coup d'état attempt in July. He and 17 others were subsequently executed. The council's first vice-chairman, Major Mengistu Haile Mariam, escaped an assassination attempt on September 23. There were reportedly many other political murder plots, including the killings of high-ranking civilian officials on October 1 and November 8.

The government linked the assassinations to a left wing opposition party, the People's Revolutionary Party (PRP). Although it shared the military government's Marxist orientation, the PRP advocated immediately handing over power to civilians. In November, the military government executed 50 dissidents, some of whom were accused of the assassination plots. Many of those executed were PRP members.   John D. Esseks

See also AFRICA (Facts in Brief Table).

EUROPE suffered one of the worst droughts in its history in 1976. Increasing pressure weakened most currencies, and the nine European Community (Common Market) countries failed to cut unemployment below 5 million persons. Industrial output mounted, and most countries continued to climb out of the 1975 recession, but inflation, which ran at an average annual rate of 12 per cent, continued to worry government leaders.

Belgian Prime Minister Leo Tindemans suggested a plan for "two-speed" European economic integration in January. It would allow such weaker market members as Great Britain and Italy to lag temporarily behind the more prosperous nations. But Tindemans had little success persuading other market members to implement his ideas for greater political, economic, and monetary integration. Britain and France totally opposed his plan.

Greece made progress in its bid for admission as the 10th member of the market. Spain, which moved slowly toward democracy during the year, and Portugal are also likely to join. See GREECE; PORTUGAL; SPAIN.

The North Atlantic Treaty Organization (NATO) was concerned about a possible conflict between Greece and Turkey over ownership of the oil-rich Aegean seabed. Political instability in Italy and the prospect of Communists playing an active role in government also worried NATO (see ITALY). But on June 1, the "cod war" between Britain and Iceland over Iceland's extended fishing limits ended, thus easing NATO concern for the future of its Icelandic base, which is at Keflavík (see Close-Up).

Two of Europe's major countries installed new prime ministers in 1976. Harold Wilson surprisingly resigned in Britain, and James Callaghan succeeded him on April 5 (see CALLAGHAN, JAMES; GREAT BRITAIN). In France, rising tension between President Valéry Giscard d'Estaing and Jacques Chirac led to Chirac's replacement by Raymond Barre (see BARRE, RAYMOND; FRANCE). Italy, Norway, Spain, and Sweden also gained new heads of government (see NORWAY; SWEDEN). West German Chancellor Helmut Schmidt's party won a narrow victory in parliamentary elections on October 3, and he was re-elected chancellor by a bare majority in parliament on December 15 (see GERMANY, WEST).

The Lockheed Aircraft Corporation bribery scandal had repercussions in Europe. Prince Bernhard of the Netherlands resigned many defense and business positions in August after a commission of inquiry found that he had shown himself "open to dishonorable requests and offers." See INTERNATIONAL TRADE AND FINANCE (Close-Up); NETHERLANDS.

Unemployment was a major worry in all Western European countries during 1976. In January, the Common Market's jobless total was a record 5.7-

Children walk along a dry section of the Thames riverbed in London as worst drought in modern history reduced the river to a trickle.

million. This figure fell only to 5.4 million in April, and European Commissioner for Social Affairs Patrick J. Hillery urged action to solve this problem by 1980. The European Commission – the market's principal executive body – decided that an annual growth rate of 4.5 to 5 per cent coupled to an annual inflation rate of no more than 5 per cent between 1976 and 1980 would reduce the group's unemployment dramatically.

Costly Drought. Europe's driest and hottest summer on record followed a 1975 grain harvest that was 10 per cent below that of 1974. Vegetables, particularly potatoes, were hardest hit by the drought. The market agreed on August 23 to increase vegetable imports and suspended import tariffs on cabbages, carrots, cauliflowers, celery, and fresh peas. Italian objections excluded beans and onions from these arrangements. European Commissioner for Agriculture Pierre Lardinois on August 30 forecast a 5 per cent reduction in the year's real production. But on September 16, he predicted normal supplies of basic foods during the winter at normal prices with ample reserves.

Tension and mistrust threaten the market's trading partnership with the United States, Lardinois said on August 24. "Our farmers are being unfairly treated by the U.S. phosphate cartel," he told soybean processors in Monterey, Calif. He accused Americans of "shutting Common Market farm ex-

ports out of one market after another." A commission proposal on July 7 to impose a tax on $500-million in exports of soybean oil and other vegetable oils angered the United States, which threatened to restrict market imports.

The market's annual farm-price review ended on March 6, after four days of hard bargaining, in a 7.5 per cent increase in guaranteed minimum prices paid to the market's 9 million farmers. Britain fought the increase because it feared a rise in British food prices at a time when inflation was slowing.

Monetary chaos threatened the Common Agricultural Policy (CAP). Lardinois warned that every 1 per cent decline in the value of the British pound added $17 million to the market's farm budget. But CAP costs soared as the value of the pound and the Italian lira fell further. The nine agriculture ministers met in emergency session on April 29 and cut $129 million from the farm budget. In July, representatives of 46 developing countries that trade with the market under the Lomé Convention sought better terms for their raw materials, particularly their sugar. But they made little progress toward agreement beyond 1977.

European Parliament. The Common Market was deadlocked for the greater part of the year over arrangements for an elected European Parliament. The number and distribution of seats for the assembly – seen as a first step toward a federalist

Europe – were at issue. The nominated European Parliament of 198 met in Strasbourg, France, on March 11 and called on European heads of government to schedule direct universal suffrage elections to the European Parliament in 1978. They envisaged a larger parliament of 355 members. France and Britain saw a directly elected European Parliament as a serious threat to the sovereignty of their national legislatures, and they deadlocked at the first summit meeting of 1976, held in Luxembourg on April 1 and 2.

The stalemate ended on July 12, when government heads agreed on a 410-member European Parliament to be elected in May or June of 1978. Britain, France, Italy, and West Germany will have 81 seats each; the Netherlands, 25; Belgium, 24; Denmark, 16; Ireland, 15; and Luxembourg, 6. After the decision, several hundred federalists demonstrated their support outside the Charlemagne building in Brussels, Belgium. Georges Spenale, French president (speaker) of the nominated parliament, said the decision was "a great victory for parliamentary democracy" and marked "the birth of the European citizen."

Currencies Falter. Most European currencies fell against the U.S. dollar, causing an added drain on European funds. Many countries dipped heavily into their reserves. In March, the British pound fell against the dollar to about $1.90, its steepest dip since June 1972. By October 1976, the pound had plummeted to a record low of about $1.57. An International Monetary Fund loan helped raise the rate to about $1.70 at year's end. The French franc also came under pressure, threatening a breakup of the *snake* of jointly floating European currencies. After spending $1.5 billion in January and February to support the franc, France withdrew it from the float on March 15. The Belgian franc and Danish krone, weaker links in the snake, had to be helped to keep them within agreed float margins.

Finance ministers of Common Market nations met in Brussels on July 26 and heard Dutch plans to put the market back on the road to economic and monetary union. But because pressure on the weaker currencies continued, a snake rearrangement was not formulated.

West Germany, in a surprise move on October 18, raised the Deutsche mark's value an average of 3 per cent against the other snake currencies. Central Bank President Karl F. Klasen called the small revaluation "a contribution to the building of Europe." The commission preferred the realignment to abandonment of the snake, but privately complained that West Germany had not consulted with other Common Market nations before it acted on the Deutsche mark.

European leaders pose for official photographs before a European Community (Common Market) summit meeting in Luxembourg in April.

Facts in Brief on the European Countries

Country	Population	Government	Monetary Unit*	Foreign Trade (million U.S.$) Exports	Imports
Albania	2,662,000	Communist Party First Secretary Enver Hoxha; People's Assembly Presidium Chairman Haxhi Lleshi; Prime Minister Mehmet Shehu	lek (9.75 = $1)	91	159
Andorra	27,000	The bishop of Urgel, Spain, and the president of France	French franc and Spanish peseta	no statistics available	
Austria	7,703,000	President Rudolf Kirchschlaeger; Chancellor Bruno Kreisky	schilling (17 = $1)	7,518	9,392
Belgium	9,914,000	King Baudouin I; Prime Minister Leo Tindemans	franc (36.9 = $1)	28,804 (includes Luxembourg)	30,685
Bulgaria	8,793,000	Communist Party First Secretary & State Council Chairman Todor Zhivkov; Prime Minister Stanko Todorov	lev (1.2 = $1)	4,691	5,408
Czechoslovakia	14,931,000	Communist Party General Secretary & President Gustav Husak; Prime Minister Lubomir Strougal	koruna (10.2 = $1)	8,358	9,081
Denmark	5,167,000	Queen Margrethe II; Prime Minister Anker Henrik Jorgensen	krone (5.9 = $1)	8,712	10,368
Finland	4,731,000	President Urho Kekkonen; Prime Minister Martti Miettunen	markka (3.8 = $1)	5,495	7,620
France	54,032,000	President Valéry Giscard d'Estaing; Prime Minister Raymond Barre	franc (5 = $1)	52,951	53,964
Germany, East	16,845,000	Communist Party Secretary General & State Council Chairman Erich Honecker; Prime Minister Willi Stoph	mark (2.5 = $1)	10,088	11,290
Germany, West	63,721,000	President Walter Scheel; Chancellor Helmut Schmidt	Deutsche mark (2.4 = $1)	90,166	74,924
Great Britain	56,555,000	Queen Elizabeth II; Prime Minister James Callaghan	pound (1 = $1.66)	44,124	53,576
Greece	9,224,000	President Constantine Tsatsos; Prime Minister Constantine Caramanlis	drachma (35.7 = $1)	2,278	5,321
Hungary	10,494,000	Communist Party First Secretary Janos Kadar; President Pal Losonczi; Prime Minister Gyorgy Lazar	forint (20.4 = $1)	6,091	7,176
Iceland	223,000	President Kristjan Eldjarn; Prime Minister Geir Hallgrimsson	króna (186.9 = $1)	306	462
Ireland	3,140,000	President Patrick J. Hillery; Prime Minister Liam Cosgrave	pound (1 = $1.68)	3,179	3,768
Italy	56,666,000	President Giovanni Leone; Prime Minister Giulio Andreotti	lira (865 = $1)	34,815	38,365
Liechtenstein	22,000	Prince Francis Joseph II	Swiss franc	no statistics available	
Luxembourg	366,000	Grand Duke Jean; Prime Minister Gaston Thorn	franc (36.9 = $1)	28,804 (includes Belgium)	30,685
Malta	313,000	President Sir Anthony J. Mamo; Prime Minister Dom Mintoff	pound (1 = $2.30)	164	375
Monaco	28,000	Prince Rainier III	French franc	no statistics available	
Netherlands	13,984,000	Queen Juliana; Prime Minister Johannes Martin den Uyl	guilder (2.5 = $1)	35,046	35,577
Norway	4,073,000	King Olav V; Prime Minister Odvar Nordli	krone (5.2 = $1)	7,206	9,717
Poland	34,578,000	Communist Party First Secretary Edward Gierek; President Henryk Jablonski; Council of Ministers Chairman Piotr Jaroszewicz	zloty (19.9 = $1)	10,283	12,536
Portugal	8,428,000	President Antonio Dos Santos Ramalho Eanes; Prime Minister Mario Alberto Nobre Lopez Soares	escudo (31 = $1)	1,939	3,841
Romania	21,588,000	Communist Party General Secretary & President Nicolae Ceausescu; Prime Minister Manea Manescu	leu (4.9 = $1)	4,872	5,553
Russia	259,151,000	Communist Party General Secretary Leonid I. Brezhnev; Supreme Soviet Presidium Chairman Nikolay Viktorovich Podgorny; Council of Ministers Chairman Aleksey Nikolayevich Kosygin	ruble (1 = $1.40)	33,310	36,969
San Marino	19,000	2 regents appointed by Grand Council every 6 months	Italian lira	no statistics available	
Spain	36,429,000	King Juan Carlos I; Prime Minister Adolfo Suarez Gonzalez	peseta (66.6 = $1)	7,691	16,264
Sweden	8,268,000	King Carl XVI Gustaf; Prime Minister Thorbjorn Falldin	krona (4.2 = $1)	17,433	18,065
Switzerland	6,776,000	President Kurt Furgler	franc (2.5 = $1)	12,953	13,303
Turkey	41,946,000	President Fahri S. Koruturk; Prime Minister Suleyman Demirel	lira (16.1 = $1)	1,401	4,739
Yugoslavia	21,807,000	President Josip Broz Tito; Prime Minister Dzemal Bijedic	dinar (18.1 = $1)	4,072	7,697

*Exchange rates as of Dec. 1, 1976

Fishy alarm

Defense. NATO viewed the growth of military power within the Warsaw Pact countries of East Europe as a disturbing trend. The 15 NATO foreign ministers were unimpressed when U.S. Secretary of State Henry A. Kissinger told them in Oslo, Norway, on May 20 that Russia's increasing military strength is an inevitable historical consequence of its growing economic and industrial power. Europe would have to learn to live with the strength of the Soviet Union, he said. NATO defense ministers met in Brussels on June 10 and 11 for their semi-annual conference, and agreed in principle to boost defense spending by up to 5 per cent between 1977 and 1982.

NATO published its force goals for the period from 1977 to 1982 in July. The goals emphasized the need for improved defense against submarine attacks, low-level air attack, and chemical warfare. On August 19, at the start of two months of NATO air, land, and sea exercises involving hundreds of thousands of troops, U.S. General Alexander Haig, commander of NATO forces in Europe, said the alliance must improve the efficiency of its conventional forces to avoid a "dangerous and undesirable overreliance" on nuclear weapons.

Communist Party leaders from 29 countries met on June 29 and 30 in East Berlin. They rejected Russia's sole leadership role and affirmed each party's right to adopt its own policies.

The Eastern European Council for Mutual Economic Assistance (COMECON) considered 10 investment projects costing $12 billion. Over a five-year period, the plans will exploit raw-material resources — asbestos, cellulose, copper, natural gas, nickel, phosphorus, steel, and timber — most of them in Russia, using Western equipment. Labor was the biggest problem in these enterprises. Czechoslovakia, East Germany, Hungary, and Poland had to supply workers they could ill spare from their own national efforts. Romania refused to send workers to the 1,700-mile (2,700-kilometer) Orenburg pipeline that will carry natural gas from the Ural Mountains to Russia's western border. Romania has large natural gas deposits of its own.

Gerhard Weiss, deputy chairman of East Germany's Council of Ministers, led a COMECON deputation to the Common Market meeting in Brussels on February 16. The two economic blocs discussed collective trade arrangements but made little progress, and the Common Market rejected a COMECON proposal in November.

Immigration Rules. Britain opposed a European Commission proposal on September 6 to tighten control on illegal immigration. Most members backed the plan to impose stiff fines on employers of illegal immigrants. Britain feared such action would hurt legal immigrants. It also resisted a plan to pay family allowances to a migrant worker from

Troubled Waters

The lowly cod became a highly volatile issue between Iceland and Great Britain before they reached a truce on June 1, 1976. Economics and national integrity were at the heart of the controversy, which ultimately led to naval clashes in the North Atlantic Ocean and severed diplomatic relations. The dispute even threatened the North Atlantic Treaty Organization (NATO). See ICELAND.

The "cod war," as it was known, was a three-part series of confrontations. It began on Sept. 1, 1958, when Iceland unilaterally extended its territorial waters from 4 to 12 nautical miles in order to save its only natural resource, its coastal fisheries. Almost 75 per cent of Iceland's exports are fish and fish products.

British trawlers, however, had been making increasingly heavy catches, particularly of cod, along Iceland's coastal shelf. The 12-nautical-mile limit would materially reduce the British catch, as well as that of other nations trawling in the waters.

But Britain's fishing industry depended on the Icelandic waters for about 15 per cent of its total annual catch, so Britain refused to stop fishing there. Instead, it deployed Royal Navy vessels to escort its trawlers. Ultimately, after a series of incidents involving cut fishing nets, the two nations reached a settlement in March 1961 that allowed Britain to fish for three years in certain parts of the outer 6 nautical miles of the zone.

But on Sept. 1, 1972, Iceland further extended its territorial waters, this time to 50 nautical miles, and the cod war intensified again. Iceland claimed that the cod supply had declined through overfishing.

Economic conditions in both nations were also important. Barring 100 British vessels from the waters would throw 20,000 fishermen out of work in a country where unemployment was near its highest point in 40 years. In Iceland, similar economic worries were coupled with resentment of "British bullying."

Britain, which had used the fishing grounds for centuries, demanded the right to an annual catch of 110,000 short tons (99,800 metric tons) of fish,

of which 90,000 short tons (81,600 metric tons) would be cod. Icelandic scientists, however, said the total catch — for Britain as well as Iceland — should not exceed 230,000 short tons (209,000 metric tons) and that Britain's share should not be more than 65,000 short tons (59,000 metric tons). Britain refused.

On Oct. 15, 1975, Iceland took control of fishing rights in all waters 200 nautical miles off its shores. The situation reached an impasse, with Britain refusing to withdraw the frigates protecting its trawlers and Iceland insisting it would not negotiate any adjustment in fishing rights until the frigates were removed.

Icelandic gunboats harassed British trawlers and cut their fishing-net towlines. Royal Navy frigates attempted to protect the trawlers; by Christmas 1975, the incidents were occurring almost daily and growing more belligerent.

On Jan. 12, 1976, Iceland played its ace in the hole by threatening to quit the NATO alliance. Tomas A. Tomasson, Iceland's ambassador to NATO, said bluntly there was a "definite link" between Iceland's alliance membership and continued use of the air base near Keflavík, which the United States uses for air surveillance of Russian submarines and aircraft in the area.

To cool the situation, Britain withdrew its frigates on January 19 and invited Iceland's Prime Minister Geir Hallgrimsson to London for talks. These failed, however, and on February 19, Iceland broke off diplomatic relations with Britain.

NATO Secretary-General Joseph Luns then tried to heal the breach. Informal talks were held in Oslo, Norway, and Britain and Iceland signed an agreement on June 1 in Oslo. The pact limits Britain's trawlers to a total of 24 a day within the 200-nautical-mile limit and bans them altogether within 30 nautical miles of the coast.

Both sides were pleased. Iceland's Foreign Secretary Einar Agustsson said: "We won at the conference table." Britain's Foreign Secretary Anthony Crosland called it "a victory for common sense." Kenneth Brown

Iceland's
Territorial
Waters

a country outside the market whose dependents still live in the country of origin.

A huge free-trade area spanning most of the Mediterranean area moved closer to reality in January when the market completed trade and aid deals with Algeria, Morocco, and Tunisia. Talks with the Arab League in Luxembourg in May ended inconclusively on Arab demands for political support in exchange for economic cooperation. In July, the market disbursed the equivalent of $86-million to African countries as compensation for export earnings lost under the Lomé Convention, the pact that linked African, Caribbean, and Pacific countries to the Common Market.

Antiterrorism. Common Market governments agreed on June 29 to intensify their fight against international terrorism by adopting a six-point program for the closer cooperation of security forces. The program includes moves to pool information on past acts of terrorism.

Women's Rights. The European Commission set up a women's bureau in the summer to promote equality in employment and in social security. A five-day conference on crimes against women brought more than 1,000 women from 30 countries to Brussels in March. They agreed to set up a permanent group to plan strategy on issues ranging from rape to wife-beating.   Kenneth Brown

EXPLOSION. See DISASTERS.

FAIRS AND EXHIBITIONS. More than 800 international trade fairs were held in 1976, according to the U.S. Department of Commerce. Of these, 604 were held in countries other than the United States. Sixty-three of them featured boats, camping, and sporting equipment. There were 29 international clothing and fashion fairs and 26 leather and footwear fairs. Among the 25 newly established fairs, there was a discothèque equipment exhibit in Denmark; "Animals and Us" in Switzerland; "Techniques for Environment" in Yugoslavia; and an international water-sports exhibition in Great Britain. Other fairs displayed a variety of products including hotel and restaurant equipment and food (17); office equipment and business machines (19); and machine tools (12).

The biggest air show of 1976 was staged in September in Farnborough, England. About 100 types of airplanes were exhibited, but new transport planes attracted the greatest interest among the industry representatives who attended. Mexico held its largest trade fair in San Antonio, Tex., a week-long show in September. More than 750 companies exhibited several thousand products.

The East-West Trade Fair in Leipzig, East Germany, in September reportedly had U.S. feed grains as the biggest seller. The People's Republic of China opened the largest trade fair it has ever presented in Southeast Asia on March 25 in Bangkok, Thailand. It had more than 1,000 exhibits, everything from farm tractors to lace doilies.

Other European Shows. The Venice Biennale was revived in August, following a four-year suspension, at a cost to the Italian government of $2.5 million. It offered a variety of art, dance, movies, music, seminars, and theater. The Frankfurt Book Fair, from September 16 to 21 in West Germany, was the biggest in its 28-year postwar history, and it attracted more than 200,000 visitors. It included displays from 68 countries with 278,000 titles, some 83,000 of them new. The United States was represented by 358 publishers. West Berlin's month-long 26th Fall Arts Festival included more than 100 performances of theater, dance, and classical music. An airlift carried artists and artworks from New York City in shifts from September 15 to October 17 at a cost to the West Berlin and West German governments of $400,000.

U.S. Exhibits. An estimated 160 million persons attended U.S. fairs in 1976. Agricultural state, district, and county fairs held in the United States totaled some 2,600. The State Fair of Dallas drew more than 3 million visitors, and the Ohio State Fair in Columbus over 2 million. The Minnesota State Fair in St. Paul and the Indiana State Fair in Indianapolis attracted more than 1 million each.

The country's oldest, the York (Pa.) Interstate

Fire flashes through the geodesic dome that was the U.S. pavilion at Montreal's Expo '67, leaving it a skeleton in minutes on May 20.

Fair was held September 10 to 18. It was first held in 1765 under a charter issued by the king of England and signed by Thomas Penn, the son of William Penn. A highlight of the Nevada State Fair, held in Reno from September 8 to 12, was the National Championship Air Races.

The Iowa State Fair, held annually in August, exhibited more than 12,000 head of the finest livestock in the United States. The fair is put on by some 5,000 Middle Western stock breeders. They claim that it is the world's greatest agricultural and livestock exhibition. The 10-day event grossed about $1.5 million and attracted 14,000 exhibitors with 35,000 entries.

An estimated 3,000 rodeos offered millions of dollars in prize money. Two of the largest were held in Arizona—La Fiesta de los Vaqueros in Tucson in February and the Phoenix Rodeo of Rodeos in March. The Phoenix show drew 50,000 spectators.

The 38th annual Premium Show in May at the New York Coliseum had 1,070 exhibitors showing 26,000 buyers everything from cameras to T-shirts. The New York-New Jersey Minority Purchasing Council held its first one-day trade show in New York City in May. It attracted 105 corporations from the Northeast, who offered both goods and service opportunities to 1,000 minority-owned firms.   Lynn Beaumont

See also BICENTENNIAL, U.S.

FALLDIN, THORBJORN (1926-   ), a farmer, became prime minister of Sweden on Oct. 7, 1976. His Center Party ended 44 years of rule by the Social Democrats in elections on September 20. Falldin made the hazards of nuclear power a central campaign issue. After he took office, Falldin allowed construction of one plant to continue. But he demanded that its owners provide plans by Oct. 1, 1977, for the safe reprocessing of spent fuel and the permanent storage of radioactive wastes.

Falldin was born on April 24, 1926, in Högsjö, a farming community in northern Sweden. His formal schooling ended at age 19. Active in agrarian politics since the late 1940s, Falldin was elected to the *Riksdag* (parliament) in 1958 and 1967. He lost his seat in 1964 by 11 votes. He became vice-chairman of the Center Party in 1969 and party leader in 1971. Falldin grew skeptical about nuclear power while serving on the National Nature Conservation Board.

Falldin lives with his wife and three children on a farm near Högsjö, but he has an apartment in Stockholm. He raises sheep, grows potatoes, and clears timber from his 590 acres (239 hectares) of forest. Falldin's opponents say he is inexperienced and unimaginative, but supporters describe him as honest and persistent.   Robert K. Johnson

See also SWEDEN.

FARM MACHINERY. See MANUFACTURING.

FASHION split in two distinct directions in 1976—fantasy costumes and clean-cut styles. The first was French in origin, and its excitement was generated mainly by the lushly romanticized peasant shapes of Yves Saint Laurent.

Halston, currently the number-one U.S. designer, was clearly on a different track. He was the foremost proponent of neat silhouettes, the free-wheeling ease and simplicity of modern American dressing that has its base in classic sportswear. While there was much controversy within the industry over the two divergent trends, customers were enthusiastic about the new fashions.

The Parisian Peasant first appeared in April when Saint Laurent introduced his Rive Gauche line that took an eclectic ethnic route. It mixed several sturdy rustic shapes—bright-hued blanket-wool jackets with Tyrolean closings, Slavic drawstring shirts, and longish dirndl skirts with cummerbunds. Finishing the urban nomad mood were Genghis Khan-type fur-framed knit caps, paisley babushkas, and crushy high-heeled boots.

However, the dazzling showmanship with which Saint Laurent presented the same fashion philosophy in his fall haute couture collection was hailed as raising the curtain on a whole new era.

Saint Laurent's small-waisted, puffy-sleeved, and bouffant-skirted silhouettes daringly offered a woman an image of herself as a heroine—Tosca, Violetta, Anna Karenina. For the first time in a long time, the rustle of taffeta was heard. Petticoats reappeared. Wildly romantic evening dresses, some costing as much as $10,000, came in extravagant fabrics and astonishing color combinations. Taffeta was shown in irresistible reds, parakeet greens, Byzantine blues, aquas, violets, and raspberry pinks. There were also emerald silk failles, ruby chiffons, printed gold lamés, passementeried wools, and velvets edged in sable.

Everything was braided, corded, tasseled, or ornamented with improbably lavish detail. Mediterranean, Alpine, Balkan, and Berber strains were echoed in velvet corselet bodices; ruched, ruffled, and plisséd hems; collarless jackets; burnoose coats; hooded capes; and plumed turbans.

Saint Laurent was not alone in glorifying folklore. Ungaro's avant-garde outfits were a bravado of unorthodox pattern on pattern; for example, ostrich leather with flower-sprigged challis and plaid voiles. Taffetas propped by petticoats were seen at such staid houses as Chanel and Ricci.

Clean-Cut All-American. For the legions who dismissed Saint Laurent's peasant styles as too costly, unrealistic, and pretentious, the uniform of the year was the man-tailored blazer, cowl-neck sweater, and slimmed-down skirt. Best-selling American designers Bill Blass, Calvin Klein, and Ralph Lauren reached back to the United States British heritage for the tweeds, plaids, corduroys, and mens-

Capes and turbans, rich fabrics and glowing colors, billowing skirts and puffy sleeves characterize Yves Saint Laurent's romantic peasant look.

wear flannels in beiges, grays, browns, heathery blues, and muted greens. Part of this inspiration were the kilts and tartans of Scotland, and the vests, knickers, Tattersall shirts, bridle belts, and riding pants of the Irish hunt country.

Mannish pinstriped trouser suits with bow-tied blouses were translated by night into women's tuxedos. Pants came in new shapes, oriented to varying boot lengths. They were cuffed to blouse at the ankles, mid-calf, or knees, or were flared in a gaucho style. Harem pants ballooned on the leisure circuit. Halston's unfettered tunic pajamas with asymmetrical necklines and one-shouldered or strapless evening dresses stepped out.

The duffel coat was rediscovered, and the hood became the starring feature of outerwear. Some of the freshest outdoor shapes were derived from the rugged U.S. pioneer past, paraphrasing the protective clothing of those ancestors who bundled up against the hazardous wilderness. Braving the 1976 elements were woolly lumberjack shirts, hunter's red jackets, trapper's down-filled coats, poplin anoraks, and earth-toned blanket ponchos that could have come from log-cabin beds. The whaler's slicker as well as the aviator's and astronaut's gear were sources for an outpouring of thin, foldable, parachute-nylon rainwear. North-woods boots and Western-stitched boots became status symbols. Completing this camping chic, especially popular with the young, were muffling scarves, cable-stitched gloves, knit legwarmers, cordovan belts, and pouchy canvas pathfinder carryalls.

Menswear enjoyed a never-before freedom as designers mixed styles, textures, and colors with new insouciance. The vest continued to grow in importance, even in summer, and played a vital role as color catalyst. Often two different tweeds were combined in a single suit, and it was not uncommon to see a man turned out in a plaid jacket, checked vest, and solid flannel pants during business hours. Adolfo's velvet jackets, cut like tuxedos with satin or grosgrain facings but worn over conventional pants, injected a note of elegant informality for more formal evenings. Irish country hats in Donegal tweed were headliners.

The Coty Awards. For the second consecutive year, the three nominees for the Winnie, the fashion industry's Oscar, were all women—Mary McFadden, Britta Bauer of Cinnamonwear, and Holly Harp of Los Angeles. The winner was McFadden, a socialite turned working woman. Sal Cesarani won the Coty menswear trophy. Kasper was elected to the Hall of Fame, while Return Awards went to John Anthony and Ralph Lauren. Lauren was also named to the menswear Hall of Fame along with Bill Kaiserman. Special award recipients were Barbara Dulien for women's work wear and Vicky Davis for men's ties.   Kathryn Livingston

FINLAND

FINLAND. Prime Minister Martti Miettunen resigned on Sept. 17, 1976, because the Communists would not agree with the other four parties in his ruling coalition on proposed 1977 budget measures to boost employment and build more homes. At the same time, the Social Democrats and Miettunen's Center Party were deadlocked on farm subsidies. Miettunen formed a minority government on September 29 with the Liberals and the Swedish People's Party.

Signs of a government collapse first appeared in May when the Communists rejected Miettunen's plan to raise the national sales tax. President Urho Kekkonen relaxed his rule that all major decisions had to be unanimous, thus allowing the Communists to vote against the tax measure and still remain in office.

Concern over a $2.2-billion trade deficit at the start of 1976 coupled with a 2 per cent drop in exports and a 9 per cent increase in imports led to the government's plans to boost the economy. Particularly worrying was a 30 per cent drop in Finland's main exports, forest products. Paper exports dropped 8 per cent in value, but production of paper and lumber was scheduled to rise by 5 per cent a year until 1985.   Kenneth Brown

See also EUROPE (Facts in Brief Table).
FIRE. See DISASTERS.

FISHING. United States District Judge John D. Larkins on March 3, 1976, upheld a National Park Service ruling that sportfishermen have exclusive use of Cape Point on North Carolina's outer banks on weekends from October 1 through April 30. Conflicts between surf and commercial fishermen on the point, said to be the best surf-fishing spot in the world, have grown since the Cape Hatteras National Seashore was established in 1953. The new rule was designed to give the weekend angler his sport and allow commercial fishermen the other five days to earn their living.

Warnings that fish were being contaminated by Kepone insecticide severely undermined both sport and commercial fishing in Chesapeake Bay in August. Operators of charter boats in the area between Maryland and Virginia reported their business was halved after Kepone contamination was found in the bay. The contamination spread from Hopewell, Va., where a plant had poured massive amounts of the highly toxic insecticide into the James River for several years. The river has been closed to most fishing since December 1975.

A record 27.5 million Americans spent about $141.6 million for state fishing licenses in 1975. California and Michigan sold the most licenses, while Wisconsin attracted the most out-of-state fishermen.   Andrew L. Newman

The Icelandic gunboat *Tyr*, right, passes close to two British trawlers during a February confrontation. A June fishing pact ended the "cod war."

FISHING INDUSTRY. United States District Judge Charles R. Richey on May 11, 1976, ordered a halt in commercial tuna-fishing practices that cause the killing of porpoises. The decision was hailed by environmentalists but attacked by industry spokesmen. The ban was upheld by the United States Court of Appeals on August 6, but implementation was delayed until Jan. 1, 1977.

Fourteen environmental organizations brought the suit, charging that the killing of porpoises by tuna fishermen was not being adequately controlled as required by the Marine Mammals Protection Act of 1972. Because porpoises and tuna swim together, fishermen use porpoises as pilots to locate tuna. An estimated 134,000 porpoises were killed in 1975 when the air-breathing mammals drowned after being caught in tuna nets.

On June 11, the National Marine Fisheries Service limited the number of porpoises that can be killed in tuna fishing to 78,000 for 1976. The appeals court said Judge Richey should determine if the new limit was properly reached and should set a limit for 1977.

The American Tuna Boat Association said on May 15 that a ban on using porpoises in tuna fishing could destroy the industry and that the price of choice white tuna could double.

American households consume more tuna than any other seafood. In 1974, each household used 9 pounds (4.1 kilograms) at an annual cost of $14. Total consumption was 657 million pounds (298-million kilograms).

Fish Catch. The commercial fish catch brought into U.S. ports in 1975 was valued at a record $970.8 million. United States exports of fishery products reached a record $304.7 million, and imports were valued at $1.6 billion. The Port of Los Angeles on San Pedro Bay ranked first in both the amount and value of fish landed.

The General Accounting Office (GAO) reported on Feb. 20, 1976, that ineffective state regulation of offshore fishing is resulting in the rapid depletion of some fish stocks, including lobster, shrimp, and clams. The GAO said the National Marine Fisheries Service needs greater authority over domestic fisheries to impose needed conservation measures.

Fishing Zones. A seven-month renewal of the "cod war" between Great Britain and Iceland over fishing rights ended on June 1, when the two countries signed an agreement. Britain agreed to limit for six months the number of trawlers allowed to fish in Iceland's fishing zone of 200 nautical miles and to respect special conservation areas. See EUROPE (Close-Up).

The United States enacted legislation in 1976 extending its fishing zone to 200 nautical miles, effective March 1, 1977. Several other countries, including Mexico, Canada, and France, declared similar fishing limits.   Andrew L. Newman

FLETCHER, LOUISE (1934-   ), on March 29, 1976, won the Academy of Motion Picture Arts and Sciences best actress award for her role as a head nurse in a mental institution in *One Flew Over the Cuckoo's Nest*. Jack Nicholson won the best actor award for his portrayal of a rebellious patient in the same film. The film also won best picture and best director awards. See AWARDS AND PRIZES; NICHOLSON, JACK.

In her televised acceptance speech, Fletcher thanked her parents for their inspiration in sign language, because they are deaf.

Louise Fletcher was born on July 22, 1934, in Birmingham, Ala. She attended a private girls' school in Vicksburg, Miss., and the University of North Carolina at Chapel Hill, where she received a B.A. degree in 1957.

She became a television actress in Hollywood, Calif., with roles in such shows as "Playhouse 90." In July 1959, she married producer Jerry Bick, and they had two children. Fletcher retired from acting in 1962 to attend to her family.

However, she resumed her career in 1973 with a small role in the film *Thieves Like Us*. Director Milos Forman was impressed with her talents and cast her in *Cuckoo's Nest*.   Darlene R. Stille

FLOOD. See DISASTERS.

FLORIDA. See STATE GOVERNMENT.

FLOWER. See GARDENING.

FOOD. In a year of continued, though slackened, inflation in the United States, 1976 retail food prices were a welcome exception. Overall, food prices were up only about 3 to 4 per cent for the year, the smallest annual increase since 1971. But a few weather-induced problems complicated the total picture. Coffee rose to well over $2 per pound (0.45 kilogram) because of poor growing conditions in Brazil. Meat and sugar, scarce in 1975, came back on the market in a glut, and their prices fell below what they were a year earlier. Good harvests throughout the world reduced the pressures on grain prices that existed in 1975.

A number of cured-meat products incorporating poultry, introduced in 1975, continued to receive considerable consumer acceptance. Included among these were hot dogs and bologna containing chicken and turkey meat alone or mixed with beef and pork. The use of soy extenders in ground meat, cured-meat products, and baked goods increased. A survey taken in October 1976 indicated that 14 per cent of all consumers had eaten foods containing soy protein frequently in the preceding 12 months, while another 40 per cent said they had eaten them at least a few times.

Another novel protein source did not fare as well. Mechanically deboned meat (MDM) — removed from the backbones and neck bones of beef, pork, and chicken as a fine paste — was banned from use in cured-meat products by the U.S. Department of Agriculture (USDA). Proponents of MDM claim that the process increases the yields of red meat by from 10 to 20 per cent, reduces the price of finished products, and reduces waste and pollution. Opponents warned of bone chips in the material and cited the relatively high calcium content of MDM in requesting the ban. They also contended that the finely ground meat was susceptible to microbial contamination and that the proposed labeling was inadequate or even fraudulent.

Food Additives other than protein extenders also came under pressure. For example, the U.S. Food and Drug Administration (FDA) revoked its provisional listing for Red Dye No. 2, the most widely used food coloring, in January and thereby prohibited its further use. Red Dye No. 4, used primarily in maraschino cherries, was banned on September 22. So was the carbon black used in licorice, jellybeans, and cosmetics. The main reason advanced for the bans was a lack of confidence on the part of the FDA in the safety of the dyes. These actions left the food industry with only one general-purpose red color, Red Dye No. 40, which has been banned in Canada; and, on December 16, the Center for Science in the Public Interest — a nonprofit consumer group — urged the FDA to ban its use in the United States.

"If you're not making any money, the packer isn't making any money, and the rancher isn't making any money, then the cows must have a bundle stashed away."

Another additive involved in controversy was cyclamate, a noncaloric sweetener. It was banned originally in 1969 as a suspected cancer-causing agent. Its manufacturer, Abbott Laboratories, filed a petition with the FDA in November 1973 asserting that new tests indicated "no cancer-producing or other adverse effects." However, the FDA rejected the petition on May 11, 1976, and once again refused to clear the product.

A new and sweeter version of corn syrup made large inroads into the sugar market during the year. Spurred originally by the high price of sugar, development work on the high-fructose syrup has been pushed heavily. Most major corn millers are now producing large quantities for use in soft drinks, ice cream, baked goods, and a wide variety of other food products.

Do It Yourself. More than half of all U.S. homeowners grew some of their own fruits and vegetables in 1976, and many also canned or froze some of the produce. Tomatoes and beans were the most popular crops for home gardeners, followed by cucumbers, peppers, and radishes. Canning-jar lids, in short supply in 1975, were plentiful in 1976. See GARDENING.

Manufacturers introduced a number of new products to make canning easier and more dependable. Among them were spice and acid tablets for preparing foods, and a variety of utensils. Some

Per Capita U.S. Food Consumption, 1975-1976

	1975	1976
	Pounds (Kilograms)	
Milk and cream	291.0 (132.0)	293.9 (133.3)
Potatoes	120.2 (54.5)	115.4 (52.3)
Fresh vegetables	92.8 (42.1)	96.5 (43.7)
Beef	88.9 (40.3)	94.2 (42.7)
Sugar	88.7 (40.2)	93.1 (42.2)
Fresh fruits	80.3 (36.4)	80.3 (36.4)
Canned vegetables	53.4 (24.2)	56.1 (25.4)
Pork	51.0 (23.1)	52.5 (23.8)
Chicken	40.3 (18.3)	43.9 (19.9)
Eggs	35.3 (16.0)	35.3 (16.0)
Canned fruits	18.9 (8.6)	20.0 (9.1)
Ice cream	18.6 (8.4)	18.4 (8.3)
Cheese	14.5 (6.6)	15.5 (7.0)
Frozen fruits and fruit juices	12.7 (5.6)	12.7 (5.6)
Fish	12.1 (5.5)	12.3 (5.5)
Margarine	11.2 (5.1)	11.5 (5.2)
Frozen vegetables	9.6 (4.4)	9.5 (4.4)
Turkey	8.6 (3.9)	9.1 (4.1)
Coffee	9.0 (4.1)	8.7 (3.9)
Butter	4.8 (2.2)	4.3 (2.0)
Veal	3.5 (1.6)	3.0 (1.4)
Lamb and mutton	1.8 (0.8)	1.7 (0.8)
Tea	0.8 (0.4)	0.8 (0.4)

consumers expressed concern during the year over the safety of canning new varieties of low-acid tomatoes, but the USDA assured them that normal water-bath canning procedures were completely satisfactory if the tomatoes were not overripe.

Other new products also applied the do-it-yourself concept. Dry powdered mixes for beverages, for example, were far and away the brightest stars among the new products introduced during the year. At least six major soft-drink and juice companies introduced fruit-flavored powders to be reconstituted at home. New-product introductions during the first 10 months were up 8.5 per cent from 1975. Building on the concern that Americans' low-bulk diet could contribute to stomach cancer and heart disease, several major bakers brought out high-fiber breads. These incorporate highly purified alpha-cellulose powder, which reduces the calories per slice because it has no food value, and adds bulk, as roughage, to the diet. This in turn is assumed to shorten the time that waste products remain in the body, reducing the probability of certain diseases.

Food Consumption in the United States was up about 2.5 per cent and was expected to exceed 1972's per capita record. This increase reflected larger supplies, increased demand, and improved economic conditions.   John B. Klis and Howard W. Mattson

FOOTBALL. On the field, professional and college football enjoyed wide success in 1976. Attendance increased slightly, television ratings climbed, and competition was exciting as the Oakland Raiders and the University of Pittsburgh won the major titles in the United States.

Off the field, there was uncertainty. Federal courts ruled that the National Football League (NFL) compensation clause, known as the Rozelle rule, and the draft of college players were illegal. The NFL's 28 teams played the season without a compensation rule, and there was little effect. The draft problem was more serious, and the NFL did not know whether it would hold a 1977 draft.

The major colleges faced a problem, too, because of the structure of the National Collegiate Athletic Association (NCAA), the most important governing body in college sports. The NCAA's four-year colleges were grouped in Divisions I, II, and III, according to size and strength. The 137 colleges classed as major made up Division I. Many of the traditional football powers in Division I wanted more control over their destiny, and there were veiled threats of secession unless they got their way.

NFL Season. The best regular-season records belonged to the Raiders (13-1) and Minnesota Vikings (11-2-1), and they proved best in the playoffs, too. The oddest records belonged to the Pitts-

Walter Iooss, Jr., *Sports Illustrated*, © Time Inc.

Tony Dorsett, shown running against Georgia in the Sugar Bowl, set a college career rushing record in 1976 and won the Heisman Trophy.

burgh Steelers and New England Patriots. The Steelers, winners of the two previous Super Bowls, started the season by losing four of five games. Then they won their last nine games, five by shut-outs, and allowed only 28 points in the four others. Their defense was inspired week after week.

The Patriots turned a 1975 record of 3-11 into a 1976 mark of 11-3. In successive games early in the season, they defeated the Miami Dolphins, the Steelers, and the Raiders, and they became the only new team of the eight in the play-offs.

The Raiders opened the American Football Conference (AFC) play-offs by beating the Patriots, 24-21, on a touchdown with 10 seconds left. The Steelers defeated the Baltimore Colts, 40-14; just

15 minutes later, a single-engine plane crashed into the empty stands in Baltimore. In the AFC final, the Raiders won 24-7 over the Steelers, who played without Franco Harris and Rocky Bleier, their injured running backs.

In the National Football Conference (NFC) play-offs, the Vikings beat the Washington Red-skins, 35-20, and the Los Angeles Rams subdued the Dallas Cowboys, 14-12. Then the Vikings scored after two blocked kicks and won from the Rams, 24-13.

The Super Bowl matched the Raiders against the Vikings on Jan. 9, 1977, in the Rose Bowl at Pasadena, Calif. The Raiders had won their fifth straight division title and the Vikings their fourth straight division title and their eighth in nine years, but in another sense both were losers. The Vikings had lost their three previous Super Bowl appearances, and the Raiders had lost their one previous Super Bowl and six previous conference play-off finals.

The Raiders finally won the big one. They whipped the Vikings, 32-14, in the most one-sided Super Bowl since the first. They set Super Bowl records of 429 yards total offense and 266 yards rushing. Fred Biletnikoff, a wide receiver with the Raiders for 12 years, caught four passes and was voted the game's Most Valuable Player.

Top Players. The season's outstanding players were quarterbacks Bert Jones of the Colts and Ken Stabler of the Raiders on offense and middle line-backer Jack Lambert of the Steelers on defense. The best rookies were wide receiver Sammie White of the Vikings and cornerback Mike Haynes of the Patriots.

The highest-paid player was O. J. Simpson, the exciting running back of the Buffalo Bills. Simpson insisted he would retire unless the Bills traded him to a California team so he could be near his family. The night before the season began, he signed with the Bills for $700,000 a year for three years.

After sluggish performances in his first five games, Simpson showed why he had become the premier runner in pro football. On November 25, he ran for 273 yards against the Detroit Lions, breaking his NFL record of 250 yards in one game. He won the league rushing title with 1,503 yards in 14 games. The next leading rusher was Walter Payton of the Chicago Bears with 1,390 yards.

Player Relations. For years, professional football had been governed by practices it said were needed to maintain competitive balance. One was the Ro-zelle rule, which said that when a player played out the option year of his contract and signed with an-other team, his new team had to compensate his old team. If the teams could not agree, compensation would be determined by NFL Commissioner Alvin (Pete) Rozelle. The rule had been invoked only five times in 176 cases in its 12 years, but the players

1976 College Conference Champions

Conference	School
Atlantic Coast	Maryland
Big Eight	Colorado-Oklahoma-Oklahoma State (tie)
Big Sky	Montana State
Big Ten	Michigan-Ohio State (tie)
Ivy League	Brown-Yale (tie)
Mid-American	Ball State
Missouri Valley	Tulsa-New Mexico State (tie)
Ohio Valley	Eastern Kentucky
Pacific Eight	Southern California
Southeastern	Georgia
Southern	East Carolina
Southwest	Houston-Texas Tech (tie)
Western Athletic	Brigham Young-Wyoming (tie)
Yankee	New Hampshire

The Bowl Games

Bowl	Winner	Loser
American	North 21	South 20
Astro-Bluebonnet	Nebraska 27	Texas Tech 24
Cotton	Houston 30	Maryland 21
Fiesta	Oklahoma 41	Wyoming 7
Gator	Notre Dame 20	Penn State 9
Liberty	Alabama 36	UCLA 6
Orange	Ohio State 27	Colorado 10
Peach	Kentucky 21	N. Carolina 0
Rose	USC 14	Michigan 6
Shrine	West 30	East 14
Sugar	Pittsburgh 27	Georgia 3
Sun	Texas A. & M. 37	Florida 14
Tangerine	Oklahoma State 49	Brigham Young 21

All-America Team (as picked by UPI)

Offense

Wide receiver—Larry Seivers, Tennessee.
Tight end—Ken McAfee, Notre Dame.
Tackles—Mike Vaughan, Oklahoma; Marvin Powell, Southern California.
Guards—Joel Parrish, Georgia; Mark Donahue, Michigan.
Center—Derrell Gofourth, Oklahoma State.
Quarterback—Tommy Kramer, Rice.
Running backs—Tony Dorsett, Pittsburgh; Rob Lytle, Michigan; Tony Franklin, Texas A. & M.

Defense

Ends—Ross Browner, Notre Dame; Duncan McColl, Stanford.
Tackles—Gerry Jeter, Southern California; Mike Fultz, Nebraska.
Middle guard—Al Romano, Pittsburgh.
Linebackers—Calvin O'Neal, Michigan; Robert Jackson, Texas A. & M.; Kurt Allerman, Penn State.
Defensive backs—Dave Butterfield, Nebraska; Oscar Edwards, UCLA; Bill Armstrong, Wake Forest.

insisted that it inhibited free movement because teams feared excessive compensation.

Another practice was the annual draft of college seniors, with the NFL teams with the poorest records in the previous season choosing first. The players said the draft prevented them from dealing with more than one bidder and was thus illegal.

During the year, federal courts ruled in separate cases that the Rozelle rule and the college draft violated federal antitrust laws. The NFL appealed. Meanwhile, 13 veteran players, including Larry Csonka, Paul Warfield, Calvin Hill, John Riggins, and Jean Fugett, signed with new teams for the 1976 season without their previous teams receiving any compensation.

The courts seemed willing to approve any compensation and draft agreement reached by the NFL and its players' association, but the players preferred to let the courts shape their future. They were in and out of court all year, and they played their third straight season without an overall labor contract. *Pro Football Weekly*, in an editorial, decried the situation, saying: "The game has become the property of lawyers who must be laughing all the way to the bank. It will take years before they finish dragging their writs through the courts of the land."

Canadian Football. With one month left in the regular season, the Canadian Football League (CFL) division races were so close that eight of the

Standings in National Football Conference

Eastern Division	W.	L.	T.	Pct.
Dallas	11	3	0	.786
St. Louis	10	4	0	.714
Washington	10	4	0	.714
Philadelphia	4	10	0	.286
New York Giants	3	11	0	.214
Central Division				
Minnesota	11	2	1	.821
Chicago	7	7	0	.500
Detroit	6	8	0	.429
Green Bay	5	9	0	.357
Western Division				
Los Angeles	10	3	1	.750
San Francisco	8	6	0	.571
Atlanta	4	10	0	.286
New Orleans	4	10	0	.286
Seattle	2	12	0	.143

National Conference Individual Statistics

Scoring	TDs.	E.P.	F.G.	Pts.
Moseley, Washington	0	31	22	97
Bakken, St. Louis	0	33	20	93
Cox, Minnesota	0	32	19	89
Herrera, Dallas	0	34	18	88

Passing	Att.	Comp.	Pct.	Yds.	TDs.
Harris, Los Angeles	158	91	57.6	1,460	8
Landry, Detroit	291	168	57.7	2,191	17
Tarkenton, Minnesota	412	255	61.9	2,961	17
Hart, St. Louis	388	218	56.2	2,946	18

Receiving	No. Caught	Total Yds.	Avg. Gain	TDs.
D. Pearson, Dallas	58	806	13.9	6
Foreman, Minnesota	55	567	10.3	1
Largent, Seattle	54	705	13.1	4
Galbreath, New Orleans	54	420	7.8	1

Rushing	Att.	Yds.	Avg. Gain	TDs.
Payton, Chicago	311	1,390	4.5	13
Williams, San Francisco	248	1,203	4.9	7
McCutcheon, Los Angeles	291	1,168	4.0	9
Foreman, Minnesota	278	1,155	4.2	13

Punting	No.	Yds.	Avg.	Longest
James, Atlanta	101	4,253	42.1	67
Jennings, New York	74	3,054	41.3	61
Wittum, San Francisco	89	3,634	40.8	68

Punt Returns	No.	Yds.	Avg.	TDs.
E. Brown, Washington	48	646	13.5	1
Bryant, Los Angeles	29	321	11.1	0
Metcalf, St. Louis	17	188	11.1	0

Standings in American Football Conference

Eastern Division	W.	L.	T.	Pct.
Baltimore	11	3	0	.786
New England	11	3	0	.786
Miami	6	8	0	.429
New York Jets	3	11	0	.214
Buffalo	2	12	0	.143
Central Division				
Pittsburgh	10	4	0	.714
Cincinnati	10	4	0	.714
Cleveland	9	5	0	.643
Houston	5	9	0	.357
Western Division				
Oakland	13	1	0	.929
Denver	9	5	0	.643
San Diego	6	8	0	.429
Kansas City	5	9	0	.357
Tampa Bay	0	14	0	.000

American Conference Individual Statistics

Scoring	TDs.	E.P.	F.G.	Pts.
Linhart, Baltimore	0	49	20	109
Stenerud, Kansas City	0	27	21	90
Smith, New England	0	42	15	87
Harris, Pittsburgh	14	0	0	84

Passing	Att.	Comp.	Pct.	Yds.	TDs.
Stabler, Oakland	291	194	66.7	2,737	27
Jones, Baltimore	343	207	60.3	3,104	24
Ferguson, Buffalo	151	74	49.0	1,086	9
Griese, Miami	272	162	59.6	2,097	11

Receiving	No. Caught	Total Yds.	Avg. Gain	TDs.
Lane, Kansas City	66	686	10.4	1
Chandler, Buffalo	61	824	13.5	10
Mitchell, Baltimore	60	555	9.3	3
Casper, Oakland	53	691	13.0	10

Rushing	Att.	Yds.	Avg. Gain	TDs.
Simpson, Buffalo	290	1,503	5.2	8
Mitchell, Baltimore	289	1,200	4.2	5
Harris, Pittsburgh	289	1,128	3.9	14
Bleier, Pittsburgh	220	1,036	4.7	5

Punting	No.	Yds.	Avg.	Longest
Bateman, Buffalo	86	3,678	42.8	78
Wilson, Kansas City	65	2,729	42.0	62
Guy, Oakland	67	2,785	41.6	66

Punt Returns	No.	Yds.	Avg.	TDs.
Upchurch, Denver	39	536	13.7	4
Haynes, New England	45	608	13.5	2
Fuller, San Diego	33	436	13.2	0

nine teams could have finished anywhere from first to last. The Ottawa Rough Riders and Saskatchewan Roughriders, two teams with confusing nicknames, won the division titles and survived the six-team play-offs. In the Grey Cup championship game on November 28 in Toronto, Ont., Ottawa beat Saskatchewan, 23-20, on a touchdown pass from quarterback Tom Clements to end Tony Gabriel with 20 seconds left.

Ron Lancaster, the 38-year-old Saskatchewan quarterback from Clairton, Pa., was voted the league's outstanding player. Gabriel was voted the leading Canadian native for the second time in three years.

Anthony Davis, the Toronto Argonauts' running back, and at $200,000 a year the highest-paid player in CFL history, quarreled with his coaches and walked off the practice field late in the season. Then he paid $150,000 to buy out his five-year contract and signed to play in 1977 for the Tampa Bay Buccaneers of the NFL. Johnny Rodgers, a $100,000-a-year wide receiver for the Montreal Alouettes, signed after the season ended with the San Diego Chargers of the NFL.

College Football. In 1972, after Pittsburgh had finished a disastrous season with a 1-10 record, it tried to reverse its fortunes by naming Johnny Majors as coach. Majors' first move was to recruit Tony Dorsett, a high school running back from Aliquippa, Pa.

In 1976, the fourth year for Majors and Dorsett at Pittsburgh, their team became unofficial national champions, undefeated in 12 games, and Dorsett won the Heisman Trophy as the outstanding college player. Then they left together. Dorsett went on to pro football. Majors, despite a year left on his contract, returned to his alma mater, Tennessee, as football coach and assistant athletic director.

As a 155-pound (70-kilogram) freshman, Dorsett ran for 101 yards in his first game. When he played the 43rd and last regular-season game of his four-year career in 1976, he was a 195-pound (88-kilogram) senior who had broken or tied 18 NCAA all-time records.

His most impressive record was 6,082 yards in career rushing. The previous record was 5,177 yards by Archie Griffin of Ohio State. Dorsett also set records of 1,948 yards rushing in one season (1976) and 356 points in a career, and he tied the career record of 59 touchdowns by Glenn Davis of Army teams three decades before.

Top Teams. Michigan was ranked number one nationally until it lost to Purdue, 16-14, on November 6 in the year's major upset. Then Pittsburgh became number one and remained there the rest of the season. It preserved its ranking by defeating Georgia, 27-3, in the Sugar Bowl. Dorsett rushed that day for 202 yards, a record for a bowl game.

Pittsburgh, Maryland, and Rutgers, each 11-0 in the regular season, were the only major teams undefeated and untied. Michigan, Georgia, Southern California, Texas Tech, and San Diego State all had 10-1 seasons.

Of the three unbeaten teams, only Pittsburgh won a bowl game. Maryland lost to Houston, 30-21, in the Cotton Bowl. When Rutgers failed to receive a bid to a major bowl, its players decided to reject all other bowl invitations.

Rutgers extended its winning streak to 18 games, longest of any major college. It became the first major team in 19 years to lead the nation in three defensive categories — total defense (179.2 yards per game); rushing defense (83.9 yards per game); and fewest points allowed (7.4 points per game, tying with Michigan).

Dorsett ranked first nationally in rushing (177.1 yards per game) and scoring (12.2 points per game). The best players, in addition to Dorsett, were running backs Ricky Bell of Southern California and Rob Lytle of Michigan, and defensive end Ross Browner of Notre Dame. Bell and Lytle finished behind Dorsett in the voting for the Heisman Trophy. Browner won the Outland Award as the Lineman of the Year.

College attendance increased for the 22nd time in 23 years, rising 2.2 percent to 32,012,008 for 637 colleges. The major colleges accounted for 74 per cent of the total.   Frank Litsky

FORD, GERALD RUDOLPH (1913-   ), the first non-elected Vice-President, who became President of the United States in 1974, lost his bid for election as President on Nov. 2, 1976. He won the Republican nomination over former California Governor Ronald Reagan but could not defeat Democratic challenger James Earl (Jimmy) Carter, Jr., for the presidency. Carter captured 50.08 per cent of the popular vote and 297 electoral votes to 48.02 per cent and 240 for Ford. One of Washington's votes went to Reagan. See ELECTIONS.

On the Campaign Trail. Before the Republican National Convention in August, President Ford met a challenge from the right wing conservative faction of the Republican Party by taking a more conservative stand himself. He made statements opposing court-ordered school busing for racial integration, abortion, and gun-control legislation. To counter Reagan's charge that he was selling U.S. interests short in negotiations with Russia, the President dropped the term *détente* from his vocabulary and downplayed his continuing efforts to maintain friendly relations with Russia. See REAGAN, RONALD; REPUBLICAN PARTY.

Ford's Campaigning gave the American people a clearer picture of the unpretentious man who inherited the presidency without being elected to that high office. But during his bid for election, Ford used all the authority of the presidency, signing

President Ford throws a discus while at the U.S. Olympic training camp; his wife, Betty, does a few steps with the Alvin Ailey Dancers.

legislation in public ceremonies in the Rose Garden of the White House or at carefully selected sites along the campaign trail.

He attempted to characterize Carter as ambivalent on important issues. He also underlined the record of his Administration – no U.S. soldiers fighting anywhere in the world; a lowered inflation rate; a declining rate of unemployment; and a check on inflationary congressional spending. Nevertheless, the economic recovery slowed before the election, and this may have hurt Ford's chances.

The President met Carter in three televised debates. Ford's unusual memory and interest in facts stood him in good stead. See TELEVISION.

Personal Finances. Public scrutiny of the President's finances was especially sharp during the 1976 election year. On February 12, Ford reported that his net worth was $323,489 at the end of 1975. From 1966 through 1974, he paid $256,615 in federal income tax on total earnings of $754,605.

On October 8, *The Wall Street Journal* printed an account of a 1973 Internal Revenue Service (IRS) audit of Ford's tax returns for 1967 through 1972. The IRS investigation revealed that the President had paid for clothing for the 1972 Republican National Convention out of a political account, which he later reimbursed from his personal funds. Travel expenses for a 1972 Colorado vacation were similarly financed.

The audit also revealed that Ford had reported spending about $5 a week in pocket money while he was minority leader of the House of Representatives. The White House pointed out that during that period he used an expense-paid car and enjoyed other fringe benefits that kept his out-of-pocket expenses low.

The office of the Watergate special prosecutor in September began investigating Republican campaign financing in the President's former Michigan congressional district. In response to the investigation, Ford on September 30 declared that he had never used campaign funds for personal expenses. On October 14, the special prosecutor announced he had found no evidence of any impropriety.

White House Intruder. On July 25, a Secret Service officer shot and killed an intruder who climbed the White House fence and refused to stop when challenged by guards. The man, Chester M. Plummer, Jr., was carrying a length of pipe. Investigators failed to discover any reason for the intrusion.

Sara Jane Moore, who tried to assassinate Ford in San Francisco in September 1975, was sentenced to life in prison on January 15.

After the election, the Fords rested in Palm Springs, Calif., for about a week.   Carol L. Thompson

See also CONGRESS OF THE UNITED STATES; PRESIDENT OF THE UNITED STATES; UNITED STATES, GOVERNMENT OF THE.

FOREST AND FOREST PRODUCTS. In an action strongly supported by the U.S. timber industry but opposed by environmentalists, Congress on Sept. 30, 1976, approved legislation that would permit resumption of clear-cutting in national forests under strict guidelines. Clear-cutting is the practice of cutting down all the trees in a wide area.

The legislation overturned a 1975 decision by a federal appeals court that an 1897 law prohibited clear-cutting in West Virginia's Monongahela National Forest. The timber industry contended that if the ban were extended to all national forests, the annual yield of softwood timber would be cut 50 per cent, resulting in prohibitive price increases. Environmentalists argued that the practice scars the landscape and heightens soil erosion. The legislation limits the size and location of clear-cuts and requires sustained-yield harvesting, under which timber sales from each forest would be limited to the number of new trees the forest could produce. About 40 per cent of the nation's lumber comes from its 155 national forests.

The federal "let burn" policy of permitting naturally caused forest fires to burn uncontrolled in selected areas came under renewed criticism in 1976 as a result of unusually dry conditions in many forest areas.   Andrew L. Newman

FOUR-H CLUBS. See YOUTH ORGANIZATIONS.

FRANCE. President Valéry Giscard d'Estaing accepted the resignation of Prime Minister Jacques Chirac on Aug. 25, 1976, and replaced him with economist Raymond Barre, a former minister of foreign trade (see BARRE, RAYMOND). Rumors of tension between Giscard d'Estaing and Chirac had persisted for some time.

"The Fifth Republic does not allow for two powers to exist within the state," the president said. He charged Chirac had "tried to enhance the position of his office . . . at the president's expense."

The resignation came during an economic crisis. The French franc, which had been withdrawn from the European *snake* of jointly floating currencies in March, was at a low level, and inflation continued at a 10 per cent rate.

New Cabinet. In forming his new government, Barre included right wing Gaullists, who had viewed his appointment with alarm because that party had lost the prime ministry for the first time since World War II. Barre named himself minister of economy and finance and immediately "declared war on inflation." On September 22, he announced a price freeze for the remainder of 1976, increases in personal and corporate income taxes, and higher taxes on automobiles, gasoline, and liquor. About 6-million workers struck in protest against the tax boost on October 7.

Barges block the Seine River at Argenteuil on the outskirts of Paris when hundreds of barge operators stage a strike on May 22.

these were new gardens. Increasing numbers of new gardeners planted in community or group gardens. The main gardening motive was economic, but there was also increasing interest in house plants and outdoor ornamentals. A novelty among new vegetables was a lush dandelion, "Stoke's Thick-Leaved," for salads and boiling greens.

The Herb Society of America (HSA) completed arrangements to establish an herb garden on the grounds of the U.S. National Arboretum in Washington, D.C. The $250,000 garden will "serve as a teaching garden, a historical garden, and a garden of the finest in design and planning," said Mrs. Andrew Jyurovat, HSA president.

New Plants won just one All-America Award for 1976: the midsummer-to-fall hollyhock "Majorette," which blooms in its first season. Just 24 inches (61 centimeters) tall, the plant produces spikes of single or double flowers in the rich gamut of hollyhock colors. "Majorette" was improved by a Dutch seed firm from a strain produced in Budapest, Hungary. A yellow petunia, "Summer Sun," was developed by Goldsmith Seeds.

All-America award-winning roses for 1977 were "Double Delight," a large-flowered, red-and-white hybrid tea; "First Edition," a coral floribunda; and "Prominent," a bright orange grandiflora. Phil Clark

GAS AND GASOLINE. See ENERGY; PETROLEUM AND GAS.

GEOLOGY. Major earthquakes wrought havoc on three continents in 1976, and destroyed loosely constructed masonry dwellings in China, Guatemala, Italy, Turkey, and the Philippines. They may have left more than 650,000 persons dead and thousands more injured. See DISASTERS.

Seismologists and geologists continued to improve their methods for predicting when and where major earthquakes might occur. Geophysicist James L. Whitcomb of the California Institute of Technology in Pasadena measured minute uplifting of the ground to predict earthquakes. He concluded in April that such uplifting in an area near Los Angeles indicated that a major earthquake will probably occur near that city sometime before mid-1978.

Predictions of this sort raise a number of social issues because there is no law or governmental policy to cover the problems raised by forecasts of disaster. Geophysicist Frank Press of the Massachusetts Institute of Technology in Cambridge has identified some of the legal questions: (1) Who should be authorized to make such predictions? (2) Who is liable for business losses related to disaster predictions? (3) Who has the authority or responsibility to act in the interest of life and property threatened by a predicted earthquake? (4) Can insurance companies cancel or refuse to renew policies in an area threatened with disaster? As long as these questions remain unanswered, the benefits of earthquake prediction may be minimal.

Volcano Eruption. La Soufrière volcano on the Caribbean island of Guadeloupe erupted on August 30, spewing lava and boiling mud in all directions. Three French scientists who were observing the volcano were injured and two others were rescued by helicopter. The eruption was minor and no deaths were reported. The 72,000 persons living at the base of the mountain had been evacuated.

***Viking* Mission to Mars.** Much geologic interest was focused on the landings on Mars by *Viking 1* on July 20 and *Viking 2* on September 3.

The season on Mars was midsummer, the most likely time for liquid water to occur beneath the surface, water that conceivably might foster life. However, no signs of life were found. Both landing sites are in flat valleys or plains, regions far from major volcanic structures. The pictures sent back by the spacecraft showed pitted rocks, probably of volcanic origin. Other features enabled scientists to infer that streams, lava flows, meteorite impacts, wind erosion, and chemical changes had affected the surface of Mars near the *Viking 1* landing site. The polar caps of Mars are now thought to consist mainly of water ice. Alfred T. Anderson, Jr.

See also ASTRONOMY; SPACE EXPLORATION; Section One, FOCUS ON SCIENCE.

GEORGIA. See ATLANTA; STATE GOVERNMENT.

Long-smoldering La Soufriere volcano pours out gaseous clouds and torrents of debris after erupting on island of Guadeloupe in August.

GERMANY, EAST. Relations with West Germany in 1976 reached their lowest point since the two countries acknowledged each other's existence by treaty in November 1972. In one of a series of shooting incidents along the 870-mile (1,400-kilometer) border, an Italian truckdriver was killed near the border post at Hirschberg, in the West German state of Bavaria, on August 5.

Neues Deutschland, the East German Communist Party newspaper, said on August 9 that treaty arrangements that have enabled millions of West Germans to visit relatives in East Germany were in jeopardy. West Germany protested on August 13, the 15th anniversary of the day East Germany started building the Berlin Wall, by reminding the East Germans that 171 people had been killed along the border since 1961, including 70 on the wall.

But opposition leaders in the West German *Bundestag* (one of the two houses of parliament) stressed West Germany's "helplessness" in the face of growing border tension in a debate on August 17. They demanded firmer government action and better marking of the West German side of the border.

Russia Intervenes. Russian Communist Party General Secretary Leonid I. Brezhnev held a surprise meeting at his Crimean holiday home on August 19 with Erich Honecker, head of the East German Communist Party. The Russian news agency Tass said that the two countries were resisting efforts by "certain circles"—meaning Western nations—to interfere in East Germany's internal affairs. West German diplomats interpreted the meeting as a Russian attempt to lower tensions. In negotiations in Berlin on September 9, East and West German representatives agreed on easing travel restrictions between the two countries.

Honecker's title was changed from first secretary to secretary general at the Ninth Congress of the East German Socialist Unity Party in East Berlin on May 22. The 2,500 delegates approved new party rules and an economic development plan for the period from 1976 to 1980. Solidarity and complete allegiance to Russia were recurring themes.

The Economy was stable and buoyant despite the recession that most Communist countries suffered. But energy and labor shortages made it difficult to meet 1976 targets for industrial output. In September, East Germany sought credits of more than $400 million to pay for grain and fodder imports to make up for its drought-stricken crops. East German cargo ships were allowed to call at United States ports for the first time under terms of a grain-purchase agreement reached in Washington, D.C., on November 11.   Kenneth Brown

See also EUROPE (Facts in Brief Table).

East Berlin's Palace of the Republic was completed in time to house the Ninth Congress of East Germany's Socialist Unity Party in May.

GERMANY, WEST. The ruling center-left coalition of Chancellor Helmut Schmidt won a narrow victory in parliamentary elections on Oct. 3, 1976. Social Democrats and Free Democrats held 253 seats in the 496-member *Bundestag* (lower house of parliament) after a recount of votes on October 20. The Christian Democrats, led by Helmut Kohl, won 190 seats, but with their Bavarian ally, the Christian Social Union, they held a total of 243 seats. That was only 10 behind Schmidt's coalition.

Kohl claimed the chancellorship on the basis of having the largest single group in the Bundestag. However, President Walter Scheel turned down his claim in favor of Schmidt after the Free Democrats announced that they would continue their alliance with Schmidt's Social Democrats. Schmidt won re-election as chancellor by two votes in the Bundestag on December 15.

The general election was largely a battle of personalities. Kohl, a newcomer to national politics, challenged Schmidt, who took over as chancellor when Willy Brandt resigned because of a spy scandal in 1974. Kohl announced on October 7 that he would resign as prime minister of the Rhineland-Palatinate state to lead the coalition of Christian Democrats and Christian Social Unionists in the Bundestag. After a brief split, the coalition reunited and elected Karl Carstens on December 14 as the first opposition Bundestag president.

Economic Upswing. After West Germany's gross national product (GNP) declined 3.6 per cent and industrial production fell 7.5 per cent in 1975, the long-promised upswing began in the spring of 1976. In March, an economic research institute reported increased production of consumer goods and a growing labor force.

Unemployment fell below the million mark in May for the first time in 16 months, but the high figure – 4.2 per cent of the work force – worried the government. The Organization for Economic Cooperation and Development (OECD) said in July that West Germany should increase its efforts to ease unemployment for hard-hit groups, especially the young. Unemployment was unlikely to fall below 900,000, however, because of low investments in recent prior years. The OECD forecast a GNP rise of 5.5 per cent by the end of 1976 and an annual increase in consumer prices of less than 5 per cent. Economics Minister Hans Friderichs said on August 4 that inflation was "a little more than 4 per cent," the lowest in 5½ years.

Wage Agreements. Talks with trade unions in the spring resulted in wage increases of 5.4 per cent for 1.1 million engineering workers and 5 per cent for 2 million public service employees. Both settlements fell short of union demands, but dispelled strike fears. Friderichs appealed to industry on April 28 to keep prices down and to improve profits by higher production and cost reductions. But the automobile manufacturers slapped on 5 per cent price increases.

The German Central Bank had to support the Deutsche mark to the extent of $25 million on March 18 to fend off pressure for revaluation. But the government bowed to pressure on October 18 and raised the value of the mark from 2 to 6 per cent with respect to the six other currencies in the *snake* system of closely tied European currencies.

Continuing Détente. Schmidt told the Bundestag in his annual "state of the nation" speech on January 29 that West Germany must press on with détente, notwithstanding disillusion, disappointment, and difficulties.

West Germany and Poland moved closer together on June 11 after an official three-day visit to Bonn by Polish Communist Party First Secretary Edward Gierek. Schmidt and Gierek signed a cultural cooperation agreement, a five-year economic development pact, and a joint declaration to hold regular ministerial meetings. Economic development covered 14 industrial agreements, including one for West German firms to build a coal-gasification plant in Poland. A package of treaties ratified in March covered a pensions settlement, financial credit to Poland, and exit permits for up to 125,000 ethnic Germans.   Kenneth Brown

See also EUROPE (Facts in Brief Table).

Chancellor Helmut Schmidt claims victory for the Social Democrats in close parliamentary elections on October 3 in West Germany.

GHANA. Relations with the United States were strained after Supreme Military Council Chairman Ignatius Kutu Acheampong abruptly canceled an official visit by U.S. Secretary of State Henry A. Kissinger on April 27, 1976, two days before his scheduled arrival. The Ghanaian government said that Acheampong was ill, but U.S. officials suspected a deliberate insult and recalled Ambassador Shirley Temple Black "for consultations."

On May 19, the military government announced that a retired brigadier general and several other army officers had been involved in a revolutionary plot foiled in December 1975.

The government's popularity was hurt by continuing high inflation. In June, the annual inflation rate was reportedly between 40 and 50 per cent. There were also shortages of consumer goods.

During the year, the government began a campaign to honor the late Kwame Nkrumah, Ghana's founding father, whose government was toppled in 1966. An expressway and a massive conference center were renamed for him.

For the first time since taking power in January 1972, the military government announced, on January 9, that it was making plans for a return to civilian rule. It gave no timetable.   John D. Esseks

See also AFRICA (Facts in Brief Table).

GIRL SCOUTS. See YOUTH ORGANIZATIONS.

GIRLS CLUBS. See YOUTH ORGANIZATIONS.

GOLF. Four professionals shared the four major men's golf titles in 1976. Ray Floyd won the Masters, Jerry Pate the United States Open, Johnny Miller the British Open, and Dave Stockton the Professional Golfers' Association (PGA) championship. Jack Nicklaus won two tournaments, both of them important.

In women's golf, Judy Rankin became the first to win $100,000 in prize money in one year on the Ladies Professional Golf Association (LPGA) tour. She won six tournaments, more than anyone else, and finished second four times.

The PGA tour listed 44 tournaments, 29 with at least $200,000 in prizes. Purses exceeded a record $9-million, $1 million more than in 1975. The 32 tournaments on the LPGA tour paid $2.8 million in purses, also a record.

Floyd started the major tournaments by winning the Masters in April at Augusta, Ga., with a 72-hole score of 271, eight strokes ahead of Ben Crenshaw. Floyd finished 17 under par. He played the four par-5 holes (16 holes in four rounds) in 14 under par.

Pate, a rookie on the tour, won the United States Open in June at Duluth, Ga., with 277, beating Tom Weiskopf and Al Geiberger by two strokes. Needing a par on the 18th hole to win, Pate put his tee shot in the right rough and seemed doomed to a bogey. But he hit a number-5 iron 190 yards (174 meters) to within 2½ feet (76 centimeters) of the pin, and he sank the putt for a birdie and victory. It was his first win on the tour.

The British Open was played in July at Southport, England. Miller, three strokes behind starting the final round, shot a 66 for 279. He defeated Nicklaus and 19-year-old Severiano Ballesteros of Spain by six strokes.

Stockton won the PGA championship in August at Bethesda, Md., with a 12-foot (4-meter) putt on the last hole. His 281 beat Don January and Floyd by a stroke.

Nicklaus won five tournaments in 1975, including two of the four majors. But in 1976, he tied for second in the British Open, tied for third in the Masters, tied for fourth in the PGA, and tied for 11th in the United States Open.

His victories came in $300,000 tournaments – the Tournament Players Championship from February 27 to March 1 at Lauderhill, Fla., and the expanded World Series of Golf from September 2 to 5 at Akron, Ohio. He won $60,000 for the first triumph, $100,000 for the second as he led the tour in earnings for the fifth time in six years and the eighth time in his 15-year career. He was named PGA Player of the Year for the fifth time.

Nicklaus earned $266,438 on the tour. Ben Crenshaw was second with $256,834, Hale Irwin third with $252,718, Hubert Green fourth with $211,406, and Al Geiberger fifth with $194,821. In all, 23 players exceeded $100,000.

In March, Green missed the 36-hole cut in the Florida Citrus Open in Orlando. He won the next three tournaments – the Doral-Eastern Open in Miami by six strokes, the Greater Jacksonville (Fla.) Open by two strokes, and the Heritage Golf Classic on Hilton Head Island, S.C., by five strokes. Then he skipped the next tournament, the Greater Greensboro (N.C.) Open, to spend a happy week with his wife, his 7-month-old son, and his tax accountant.

Ben Crenshaw and Miller also won three major tournaments each. Crenshaw also finished second three times.

The Women's Tour. On the LPGA circuit, Donna Caponi Young won the $205,000 Carlton, the richest women's tournament ever staged, in September at Calabasas, Calif. The victory brought her $35,000. JoAnne Carner won the United States Open, and Betty Burfeindt took the LPGA championship.

Rankin passed $100,000 in earnings by midyear, and she was the year's leading money earner with $150,734. Young was second in winnings with $106,553, Carner third with $103,275, Jane Blalock fourth with $93,616, and Sandra Palmer fifth with $88,417. Young and Carner won four tournaments each.   Frank Litsky

GOVERNORS, U.S. See STATE GOVERNMENT.

GREAT BRITAIN passed through a false dawn in 1976. Until early summer, hopes were high that the country was well on the way to the kind of economic recovery that would end its postwar decline. By autumn, however, Britain was in the midst of yet another financial crisis, and its long-sought economic miracle seemed as far away as ever.

The outlook had seemed so rosy in the spring. Thanks largely to the unions' agreement to limit wage raises to $12 per week, inflation had been halved in less than a year. The massive trade deficit had also been cut in half. Businessmen reported a high level of intended investment, and the outlook for profits and exports was favorable.

When the government published its spending plans in February, it announced cuts of more than $9.6 billion in planned spending for education, transport, social services, housing, and defense over the next four years. Chancellor of the Exchequer Denis Healey said that he was cutting back on public spending to switch resources to industry.

Next, Healey pulled off another 12-month wage restraint agreement with the unions. In his April 6 budget, he offered almost $2 billion in income tax concessions if the unions agreed to a 3 per cent limit on wage increases for the year after August 1976, when the $12 limit ran out. Some union leaders were shocked by the meager 3 per cent ceiling, and

Healey's scheme got a hostile reception at first. But after four weeks of talks, the government agreed to a 4.5 per cent limit on wage increases, with nobody allowed less than $5 per week or more than $8 per week. This was endorsed by a 17 to 1 majority at a special Trades Union Congress conference in London on June 16 – an amazing vote of confidence for the government.

Waning Confidence. Despite all this progress, the government still intended to spend far more than it received in tax revenue. The verdict of the financial world was that the government needed to cut public spending immediately rather than lop bits off its future plans. By March, the pound had fallen below $2. In April, the country's precious foreign reserves slumped by more than $1 billion in one month – the biggest fall ever. On April 23, the Bank of England raised interest rates by 1.5 per cent to steady the pound, but to little avail. On May 17, the pound fell below $1.80.

The government's huge budget deficit was not the only cause of this drop in confidence. Although Britain's inflation rate was falling quickly, it was still more than twice as high as the rate among most of its main competitors. Moreover, the improvement in the trade gap was short-lived. It was soon apparent that the balance-of-payments deficit for 1976 would still be close to $4 billion.

Not only Queen Elizabeth II, but also demonstrators greeted Brazil's President Ernesto Geisel when he arrived in London for a visit in May.

Healey's Efforts. Healey temporarily stemmed the flight from the pound with a $5.3-billion standby credit arrangement in June. On July 22, he introduced a second budget, cutting public spending by an additional $1.8 billion in fiscal 1978. But these cuts did not affect the 1976 budget deficit, and foreign confidence was not reassured.

Healey's July budget simply paved the way to a critical financial predicament in the autumn. By October, the bank interest rate reached 15 per cent, and the pound fell to $1.56 on October 28. Healey was forced to go to the International Monetary Fund (IMF) for a $3.9-billion loan to back the pound. The IMF agreed, but it wanted its pound of flesh in return — further cuts in public spending.

Healey introduced his third budget on December 15, cutting public spending again, for a total reduction of about $4.5 billion in 1977 and 1978. The budget, while sufficient to ensure the IMF loan, was a compromise between what the IMF wanted and what labor would stomach. The left wing of the Labour Party moaned and groaned, and so did the unions. But nobody wanted to rock the boat too much lest it bring into power a Conservative government committed to even bigger cutbacks.

Left Wing Assaults. Rumblings from the left had been growing louder all year. On January 29, more than 50 Labour Party members of Parliament abstained on a motion to protest mounting unemployment, then about 1.2 million. The government's spending-cuts plan was defeated on March 10 when 37 Labour rebels abstained. Next day, the government narrowly won a vote of confidence.

These left wing assaults made life difficult for a government that was already in trouble because of its wafer-thin parliamentary majority. A furious scene erupted in the House of Commons on May 27 after the government won a close procedural vote on its plans to nationalize the shipbuilding and aircraft industries. Labour members stood on their seats and sang "The Red Flag," an old Socialist song. One Conservative leader then grabbed the mace — a staff symbolizing authority — and charged the Labour members.

On June 9, the government survived a second vote of confidence. But by July, it had run into serious trouble with five controversial bills, including the nationalization bill. In the end, the government failed to get its nationalization bill through and re-introduced it in December in a new session.

New Prime Minister. The strength of the Labour Party left wing showed in the election of a leader to replace Prime Minister Harold Wilson, who unexpectedly announced his resignation on March 16. James Callaghan emerged as the candidate with the broadest support, but left winger Michael Foot was a close second. Callaghan won with 176 votes to Foot's 137 in the third and final ballot on April 5. See CALLAGHAN, JAMES.

His predecessor's portrait behind him, James Callaghan takes call from Buckingham Palace notifying him he is the new prime minister.

Labour Split. The gulf between the Labour government and its party activists was most visible at the annual party conference in Blackpool in September. While Callaghan waxed enthusiastic about profits and investment in an attempt to boost confidence, the conference supported the nationalization of banks and insurance companies.

Callaghan did not allow the swing to the left to influence his choice of Cabinet ministers. He made four changes when he became prime minister that kept the left-right balance roughly as before. On September 10, he brought Merlyn Rees back from Northern Ireland to become home secretary in place of Roy Jenkins, the leading Labour moderate. Jenkins had fared badly in the leadership contest and left to become president of the European Commission in Brussels, Belgium. Shirley Williams was made education minister.

In an unexpected move on December 21, Reginald Prentice, an outspoken member of Labour's right wing, resigned as minister of overseas development. The resignation came as a surprise to observers, who expected defections, if any, to come from the left wing. Prentice cited cuts in foreign aid and his opposition to governing assemblies in Scotland and Wales as reasons for leaving the Cabinet.

While the Labour Party tore itself apart, the unions stayed remarkably loyal to the government. They stuck rigidly to the pay policy. As long as Callaghan could count on the support of the union big guns, the left in Parliament could be ignored.

Home Rule. Callaghan's program for the new parliamentary session that began on November 24 was dominated by two important constitutional issues – creation of directly elected assemblies in Scotland and Wales and direct election of British members to a European parliament.

The proposal to give a measure of home rule to Scotland and Wales exposed the divisions within the Conservative Party. Conservative morale was bucked up by the government's problems, their own by-election successes – which left the Labour Party with a majority of only one – and the knife-edge parliamentary situation. But the rift between Tory leader Margaret Thatcher and Edward Heath, the former prime minister she defeated in 1975 to become party leader, was still wide.

The Conservatives outlined their policies to solve the economic crisis in October. The program marked a shift to the right from the Heath days, though not by as much as expected. But by late November, the rift was wider than ever. Thatcher, after appointing a much more right wing shadow Cabinet on November 19, decided to oppose the government's devolution plans – plans to set up separate legislatures in Scotland and Wales. Heath disagreed, and two leading Scottish Conservatives resigned from the Thatcher shadow Cabinet. At the second reading of the devolution bill, Heath and 27

With wealthy Arabs buying up expensive property in London, some for-sale signs appear in Arabic as well as in English.

other Conservatives defied Thatcher's instructions and abstained. The bill passed with a majority of 45, though 10 Labour members voted against it.

The Liberals were thrown into chaos by a leadership scandal early in the year. On January 29, Jeremy Thorpe, the leader of the Liberal Party, denied as "wild allegations" claims by a male model that he had a homosexual relationship with Thorpe in 1961. The Liberal Party backed Thorpe but the newspapers would not leave the matter alone.

Thorpe resigned on May 10 after nine years at the top, saying a three-month "sustained witch hunt and campaign of denigration" made it impossible for him to lead the Liberals. David Steel, a young Scottish member of Parliament, was elected Liberal leader on July 7, the first British party leader ever elected by rank-and-file party members.

Foreign Affairs. The "cod war" with Iceland ended on June 1 when both countries signed a six-month agreement allowing 24 British trawlers a day into a 200-nautical-mile zone over which Iceland claimed jurisdiction (see EUROPE [Close-Up]). The other major foreign initiative came when Britain agreed to convene a conference in Geneva, Switzerland, in November bringing together Rhodesia's Prime Minister Ian D. Smith and African nationalists to discuss steps toward majority rule in Rhodesia. See RHODESIA.   Andrew F. Neil

See also EUROPE (Facts in Brief Table).

GREECE. The dispute with Turkey over oil prospecting rights in the Aegean Sea flared up on July 29, 1976, after Turkey's new seismic research ship *MTA-Sismik I* arrived in the area. Tension mounted when Turkey brushed aside Greek protests on August 7 and kept the vessel between the Greek islands of Limnos and Lesvos. Greece invoked the Geneva Convention of 1958 to substantiate its claim of jurisdiction over the seabed, while Turkey claimed rights over the eastern half of the Aegean. Both countries placed their military forces on alert.

Greece called for an urgent meeting of the United Nations (UN) Security Council on August 9 and asked the International Court of Justice at The Hague, the Netherlands, to settle the dispute. The court on September 12 turned down Greece's request for an interim injunction ordering Turkey to stop explorations in the Aegean. The court urged both countries to pursue the Security Council's August 25 resolution calling on them to negotiate.

Common Market Entry. Prime Minister Constantine Caramanlis pursued his government's goal of full membership in the European Community (Common Market). But the European Commission, the market's chief executive body, ruled on January 29 that the action be delayed until the Greek economy could be altered to conform with those of other member nations. Caramanlis called this an offer of "second-class membership." The market's foreign ministers brushed aside the commission's plan on February 9 and urged early negotiations to grant full membership to Greece by 1980. Talks began in Brussels, Belgium, on July 27.

Greece and the United States on February 13 announced a new U.S. forces agreement that governs the 5,000 American military personnel in Greece. On April 15, U.S. and Greek representatives initialed a four-year defense cooperation pact that provides $700 million in arms assistance in return for continued American use of four military bases in Greece.

Balkan Nations Meet. Athens hosted a conference of delegations from five Balkan countries from January 26 to February 5. Officials from Bulgaria, Greece, Romania, Turkey, and Yugoslavia discussed such areas of cooperation as agriculture, energy, and transportation, but reached no agreements. Albania declined to attend.

The Greek economy continued its moderate expansion in 1976 as industrial output rose about 6 per cent.   Kenneth Brown

See also CYPRUS; EUROPE (Facts in Brief Table); TURKEY.

GRENADA. See LATIN AMERICA.

GUATEMALA. See LATIN AMERICA.

GUINEA. See AFRICA.

GUINEA-BISSAU. See AFRICA.

GUYANA. See LATIN AMERICA.

HAITI. See LATIN AMERICA.

HAMILL, DOROTHY (1956-   ), established herself as the best female figure skater in the world in 1976. She won the 1976 Winter Olympic Games gold medal in women's figure skating at Innsbruck, Austria, in February, then captured the women's world title in Göteborg, Sweden, in March. In April, she signed a contract to perform as a professional. See ICE SKATING; OLYMPIC GAMES.

Dorothy Hamill was born in Riverside, Conn., the daughter of a business executive. She received her first pair of ice skates for Christmas when she was about 8 years old, and started skating on a frozen pond near her home. Soon she asked her mother for skating lessons so she could learn to skate backwards. She dropped out of school at 14 to devote long hours to skating. She studied under a private tutor to earn her high school diploma.

Later, Hamill moved to Denver so she could train there. There she displayed her perseverance and discipline. She prepared for major competition by practicing seven hours a day, six days a week, for 11 months of the year.

Hamill became the leading amateur female skater in the United States when Janet Lynn became a professional in 1973. She won consecutive U.S. women's figure-skating titles in 1974, 1975, and 1976. She also finished second in the world championships in 1974 in Munich, West Germany, and in 1975 in Colorado Springs, Colo.   Joseph P. Spohn

HANDICAPPED. President Gerald R. Ford authorized a postponement of the White House Conference on Handicapped Individuals from December 1976 to May 25, 1977, to allow for a more thorough assessment of the problems facing mentally and physically handicapped Americans. The conference, which was established by a 1974 law, is to generate a national awareness of problems and potentials of handicapped individuals, and to recommend suitable legislation to improve living conditions for the handicapped.

The postponement gave national and state organizations for the handicapped additional time to organize state conferences to determine subject matter for the White House Conference. The conference planners said they were making every effort to ensure that handicapped individuals were taking part in the program. Eleven members of the National Planning and Advisory Council to the White House Conference are themselves handicapped.

On April 29, President Ford ordered the Department of Health, Education, and Welfare (HEW) to establish rules barring discrimination against handicapped workers in federally assisted programs. The executive order also instructed HEW to determine what constitutes such discrimination.

Print-to-Speech Devices. Significant progress was made in 1976 in developing machines to enable blind people to read at normal speed. This is done

Ray Kurzweil, the inventor, demonstrates his optical scanner that is computer-linked to change printed words into sounds for the blind.

by computerized machines that convert printed or typewritten texts into speech. Experts predicted that text-to-speech machines could become inexpensive enough within five years for at least some persons to own them. Prior to that, businesses and institutions are expected to provide them for their sightless workers.

As some of the new machines were being demonstrated in Cambridge, Mass., in January, a spokesman for the National Federation of the Blind cautioned against too much emphasis on them. He said that the new machine techniques for reading must be seen as "just one of the breakthroughs we need for equal opportunity." Experts have emphasized that the primary problem of blindness will not be solved by technology. They contend that the real problem is the misunderstanding of other people.

The most significant of the new text-to-speech systems is the *Optacon*. This device uses a handheld camera no bigger than a pocket flashlight to convert printed material into impulses that imprint letters or numbers onto the index fingertip via vibrating metal pins. The Optacon system, about the size of a book, was developed by James D. Bliss, president of Telesensory Systems of Palo Alto, Calif., and John G. Linvill, chairman of the Stanford University Electrical Engineering Department.

Another computerized text-to-speech device is being developed by the Kurzweil Computer Prod-

ucts Company of Cambridge, Mass. It has a tiny camera attached to a computer that turns print images into a singsong type of mechanical speech. The machines are to be tested at Perkins School for the Blind in Boston and in the Boston public school system.

Architectural Barriers. National Awareness for the Handicapped Week in May stressed the importance of eliminating physical barriers in public places. Leaders of various organizations for the handicapped urged that building codes require new buildings to have ramps, doorways wide enough to accommodate wheelchairs, grab bars in toilet facilities, and lower water fountains and elevator buttons. They also urged that the space between elevator cars and landings be decreased.

Educating the Handicapped is governed by state laws, and a number of states rewrote their laws in 1976 to reflect the trend toward *mainstreaming,* placing handicapped students with normal students. Even though most educators accepted this concept in principle, handicapped children were still in segregated classes in many school districts.

Parents of handicapped children were also indicating increasingly that their children have a right to a normal education. They pressed for special education within the school system. Joseph P. Anderson

HARNESS RACING. See HORSE RACING.

HAWAII. See STATE GOVERNMENT.

HEALTH AND DISEASE. Mysterious diseases in Africa and the United States baffled medical researchers in 1976. A fever that broke out in mid-September in northern Zaire in central Africa took more than 335 lives. A similar disease in southern Sudan, 500 miles (800 kilometers) from Zaire, claimed more than 100 victims. World Health Organization (WHO) scientists said the virus that causes the disease poses the gravest threat to human life in more than 25 years. The virus causes high fever, intense vomiting, and diarrhea.

Another mystery disease struck in Philadelphia in July 1976, killing 29 persons and hospitalizing more than 150 others. The victims, most of whom had attended an American Legion state convention in Philadelphia from July 21 to 24, suffered headaches, chest pains, high fevers, and lung congestion.

In an effort to identify the cause of the disease, scientists tested for metal poisoning, concentrating on nickel poisoning, which has similar symptoms. The first series of nickel tests was ruled invalid because of probable contamination of autopsy tissue, and on August 25 a second set was declared suggestive but inconclusive as a possible cause. On August 27, federal epidemiologists expressed confidence that the epidemic was over.

A New Form of Arthritis, or joint inflammation, was discovered in 1976 in Lyme, Conn. The disease, which afflicted residents of neighboring towns in southern Connecticut, caused swelling of the knee, wrist, or elbow, and headache and muscle pain. Unlike other known forms of arthritis in the United States, Lyme arthritis may be caused by an infection, perhaps by a virus, spread by insects. The Connecticut patients showed no signs of any of three distinct forms of arthritis linked to viruses carried by mosquitoes in Africa, Australia, and Asia. Researchers trying to isolate the new virus stressed that the disease is mild.

Drugs. Three brands of sequential oral contraceptives that contain high doses of estrogen, a female sex hormone, were taken off the market in 1976 after the Food and Drug Administration (FDA) concluded that they were less effective than birth-control pills that contain a combination of estrogen and progestin, another hormone. The FDA said that the drugs were associated with a higher incidence of uterine cancer and blood clotting.

The FDA in September also ordered manufacturers of estrogen drugs used by women to ease the unpleasant symptoms of menopause to issue stronger warnings about the higher risk of cancer among users. The risk of developing uterine cancer was reported to be 4.5 to 13.9 times greater for users of the drugs, and the risk increases the longer the drugs are used.

The FDA made sweeping changes in the way cough and cold remedies can be sold. In September, on the advice of a panel of experts, it made available for direct sale to the public seven drugs that had previously required a doctor's prescription for purchase. The advisory group also suggested in October that Americans, who spend $735 million on cold preparations each year, be offered fewer and more powerful ingredients in nonprescription cough, cold, asthma, and allergy medicines.

Health-Care Costs. According to a U.S. Department of Health, Education, and Welfare (HEW) report released in October, Americans are spending $1 out of every $9 they earn for health care – and the cost of such care appears likely to go higher. According to the HEW report, Americans spent $118 billion for health care in 1975, or about $540 for every man, woman, and child. This record-breaking amount accounted for 8.3 per cent of the gross national product. Health-care costs for the first quarter of 1976 were up an annually adjusted 14 per cent.

The HEW study showed that health-care costs would continue to soar, climbing almost 40 per cent to $224 billion a year by 1980, regardless of whether or not a national health insurance program is enacted. The various proposals for such a program remained stalemated in Congress.   Dianne Rafalik

See also DRUGS; MEDICINE; PUBLIC HEALTH.

HIGHWAY. See BUILDING AND CONSTRUCTION; TRANSPORTATION.

Using every precaution, a scientist at the Center for Disease Control in Atlanta, Ga., seeks clues to mysterious "legionnaires disease."

HOBBIES. Perhaps inspired by the United States Bicentennial celebration, which focused interest on the past, Americans in 1976 went on a collecting binge. Particularly favored objects included kewpie dolls, first made in 1913; so-called Depression glass; old fountain pens; and quilts.

Why Collect? Psychiatrists suggested that the desire to collect starts between the ages of 7 and 10, when children first try to master control of a small part of the outside world. This desire is partly satisfied by collecting small objects. As a person grows older, collecting fulfills different needs. For example, psychiatrists Aaron Koblentz and Josephine Peek of New York City suggested that many collectors of model railroad equipment are frustrated engineers. "There is everything good about being a collector," said the psychiatrists, "provided it doesn't interfere with other functions in life, and you don't impoverish yourself by spending all of your money."

American Memorabilia. Specimens of fountain pens, made virtually obsolete by ballpoints, were avidly sought. The Parker fountain pen familiarly known as Big Red—which sold for $7 in 1921—brought as much as $150. California fashion faddists even converted antique pens into jewelry.

Depression glass—brightly colored glass dishes, cups, and ashtrays mass-produced from the early 1920s until the start of World War II—was in demand. It sold originally for as little as $1.99 for a 20-piece dinner set. However, collectors were willing to pay hundreds of dollars for Depression glass pieces that have become rare because people simply threw much of the "worthless" glass away.

Record Prices. A New York City dealer, H. P. Kraus, paid a record $660,000 plus 10 per cent commission for an illuminated Flemish manuscript, "Hours of the Virgins," produced in the early 1500s. Kraus purchased the manuscript at a London auction on July 5.

In April, a Moravian bridal quilt fetched a record price of $5,100 at an auction in Reading, Pa. The same quilt had been purchased in 1973 for $75. At a New York City auction on September 16, a New York dealer paid $10,000 for a letter written by George Washington in 1789 discussing the responsibilities of child rearing. In San Francisco on June 16, Sam Gordon of Shingle Springs, Calif., paid $44,000 for a Wells, Fargo & Co. stagecoach.

On July 29 in New York City, a private collector paid $3,400 for a gem-studded Sword of Islam that was presented to Italian dictator Benito Mussolini in 1937. Two parade-car banners used by Adolf Hitler sold for $700 and $800. An unidentified corporation paid $160,000 in January for a bulletproof 1944 Mercedes-Benz touring car used by another Nazi, Hermann Goering.　　　　Theodore M. O'Leary

The armorplated 1944 Mercedes-Benz used by Nazi leader Hermann Goering was auctioned for $160,000 in Scottsdale, Ariz., in January.

HOCKEY. The Montreal Canadiens and Winnipeg Jets won the major-league hockey championships in 1976, then helped Team Canada beat the best Europeans in the first Canada Cup competition. But much of the attention then shifted from the ice to the courtroom.

Traditionally, hockey fights and occasional brutality during games were handled by referees or league officials. But in the 1975-1976 season, players were arrested and tried in court.

The Violence. The prime case involved a November 1975 National Hockey League (NHL) game between the Detroit Red Wings and Toronto Maple Leafs in Toronto, Canada. Dan Maloney of the Wings allegedly punched Brian Glennie of the Leafs to the ice, hit him again, and twice picked him up and dropped him to the ice. Glennie suffered a mild concussion. Maloney was arrested for assault, but a Toronto jury later acquitted him.

Another major incident happened in a World Hockey Association (WHA) play-off game between the Quebec Nordiques and Calgary Cowboys in April 1976. Rick Jodzio of Calgary, allegedly under orders from his coach, Joe Crozier, skated into Marc Tardif of Quebec, the WHA's leading scorer. Tardif suffered a severe concussion when Jodzio struck him with a hockey stick, jumped on him, and punched him. Jodzio and Crozier were suspended by the league. Crozier was reinstated after the Quebec play-off series. Jodzio was also arrested on an assault charge. He was reinstated by the league during the summer after posting a $25,000 surety bond guaranteeing payment of any league fines that may be assessed.

The NHL played its 59th season with 18 teams. The division champions were the Canadiens, Boston Bruins, Philadelphia Flyers, and Chicago Black Hawks.

The Canadiens had the league's best regular-season record — 58 victories, 11 defeats, and 11 ties. They won the Stanley Cup play-offs in 13 games, beating Chicago four straight, the New York Islanders by 4-1, and Philadelphia by 4-0. Philadelphia had won the Stanley Cup the two previous seasons, but Flyers coach Fred Shero said, "If we would have played better, maybe the Canadiens would have played even better."

Reggie Leach of Philadelphia led the regular-season goal scorers with 61 and set a Stanley Cup record with 19 goals during the play-offs.

Bobby Orr, the game's premier player, failed to make the all-star team for the first time in nine years. A knee injury allowed Orr to play only 10 games. He was still unsteady after the fifth operation on his left knee, and he sought financial security in a new contract with the Bruins.

After the season, as his contract was expiring, the Bruins offered him $2.4 million over five years or, as an alternative, 18.6 per cent ownership of the team.

Standings in National Hockey League

Clarence Campbell Conference

Lester Patrick Division	W.	L.	T.	Points
Philadelphia	51	13	16	118
New York Islanders	42	21	17	101
Atlanta	35	33	12	82
New York Rangers	29	42	9	67
Conn Smythe Division				
Chicago	32	30	18	82
Vancouver	33	32	15	81
St. Louis	29	37	14	72
Minnesota	20	53	7	47
Kansas City	12	56	12	36

Prince of Wales Conference

James Norris Division	W.	L.	T.	Points
Montreal	58	11	11	127
Los Angeles	38	33	9	85
Pittsburgh	35	33	12	82
Detroit	26	44	10	62
Washington	11	59	10	32
Charles F. Adams Division				
Boston	48	15	17	113
Buffalo	46	21	13	105
Toronto	34	31	15	83
California	27	42	11	65

Scoring Leaders	Games	Goals	Assists	Points
Guy Lafleur, Montreal	80	56	69	125
Bobby Clarke, Philadelphia	76	30	89	119
Gil Perreault, Buffalo	80	44	69	113
Bill Barber, Philadelphia	80	50	62	112
Pierre Larouche, Pittsburgh	76	53	58	111
Jean Ratelle, Boston	80	36	69	105

Leading Goalies	Games	Goals against	Avg.
Ken Dryden, Montreal	62	121	2.03
Michel Larocque, Montreal	22	50	2.46
Montreal Totals	80	174	2.18
Glenn Resch, N.Y. Islanders	44	88	2.07
Billy Smith, N.Y. Islanders	39	98	2.61
N.Y. Islanders Totals	80	190	2.38

Awards

Calder Trophy (best rookie)—Bryan Trottier, N.Y. Islanders
Hart Trophy (most valuable player)—Bobby Clarke, Philadelphia
Lady Byng Trophy (sportsmanship)—Jean Ratelle, Boston
Norris Trophy (best defenseman)—Denis Potvin, N.Y. Islanders
Art Ross Trophy (leading scorer)—Guy Lefleur, Montreal
Conn Smythe Trophy (most valuable player in Stanley Cup play)—
   Reggie Leach, Philadelphia
Vezina Trophy (leading goalie)—Ken Dryden, Montreal
Bill Masterton Trophy (perseverance, dedication to hockey)—
   Rod Gilbert, N.Y. Rangers

Standings in World Hockey Association

Canadian Division	W.	L.	T.	Points
Winnipeg	52	27	2	106
Quebec	50	27	4	104
Calgary	41	35	4	86
Edmonton	27	49	5	59
Toronto	24	52	5	53
East Division				
Indianapolis	35	39	6	76
Cleveland	35	40	5	75
New England	33	40	7	73
Cincinnati	35	44	1	71
West Division				
Houston	53	27	0	106
Phoenix	39	35	6	84
San Diego	36	38	6	78
Minnesota	30	25	4	64
*Ottawa	14	26	1	29

*Formerly the Denver Spurs; disbanded January 17

Scoring Leaders	Games	Goals	Assists	Points
Marc Tardif, Quebec	81	71	77	148
Bobby Hull, Winnipeg	80	53	70	123
Real Cloutier, Quebec	80	60	54	114
Ulf Nilsson, Winnipeg	78	38	76	114
Robbie Ftorek, Phoenix	80	41	72	113
Chris Bordeleau, Quebec	74	37	72	109

Leading Goalies	Games	Goals against	Avg.
Michel Dion, Indianapolis	31	85	2.74
Jim Park, Indianapolis	11	23	2.41
Leif Holmquist, Indianapolis	19	54	3.00
Andy Brown, Indianapolis	24	82	3.60
Indianapolis Totals	80	244	3.00
Joe Daley, Winnipeg	62	171	2.84
Curt Larsson, Winnipeg	23	83	3.87
Winnipeg Totals	81	254	3.11
Ron Grahame, Houston	57	182	3.27
Wayne Rutledge, Houston	25	77	3.17
Houston Totals	80	259	3.24

Awards

Gordie Howe Trophy (most valuable player)—Marc Tardif, Quebec
W. D. (Bill) Hunter Trophy (scoring champion)—
   Marc Tardif, Quebec
Dennis A. Murphy Trophy (best defenseman)—
   Paul Shmyr, Cleveland
Ben Hatskin Trophy (best goaltender)—Michel Dion, Indianapolis
Lou Kaplan Trophy (rookie of the year)—Mark Napier, Toronto
Paul Deneau Trophy (most gentlemanly player)—
   Vaclav Nedomansky, Toronto
Robert Schmertz Memorial Trophy (coach of the year)—
   Bobby Kromm, Winnipeg

Bobby Orr, center, signed a $3-million pact with the Chicago Black Hawks after his contract with the Boston Bruins expired.

Instead, Orr signed with Chicago for a reported $3-million for six years, the payments to be spread over 30 years to lessen the tax burden. The money was guaranteed even if injury prevented his playing.

WHA Season. In the 1974-1975 season, the second and newer major league lost its Baltimore and Chicago teams because of financial problems. It started the 1975-1976 season with 14 teams, but Minnesota withdrew in midseason and Denver moved to Ottawa, played two games there, and disbanded.

The Winnipeg Jets, Indianapolis Racers, and Houston Aeros became division champions. Winnipeg won the World Cup play-offs by defeating Edmonton in four straight games, Calgary by 4-1, and Houston in four straight games.

Canada Cup. The first Canada Cup tournament was played in September in Montreal, Toronto, Quebec City, Ottawa, and Philadelphia. National teams from Canada, Czechoslovakia, Finland, Russia, Sweden, and the United States participated. Team Canada, with almost every NHL star playing, won the round robin and then defeated Czechoslovakia in the 2-of-3-game finals. Russia won the Olympic Games gold medal and finished second to Czechoslovakia in the world amateur championships.   Frank Litsky

HOME FURNISHINGS. See INTERIOR DESIGN.

HONDURAS. See LATIN AMERICA.

HORSE RACING. Forego won horse of the year honor for the third consecutive year and dominated the handicap ranks of thoroughbred racing again in 1976. After winning the Brooklyn Handicap, the 6-year-old gelding electrified fans at New York's Belmont Park and television viewers by carrying 135 pounds (61 kilograms) to win the Woodward Handicap at 1 1/8 mile on September 18 and 137 pounds (62 kilograms) to beat Honest Pleasure by a head in the $250,000 Marlboro Cup Handicap at 1 1/4 mile on October 2.

The son of Forli, owned by Mrs. Edward H. Gerry's Lazy F Ranch, was sidelined by injury after the Marlboro but was to return to racing in 1977. The third leading thoroughbred earner in history, Forego is just $322,679 short of the record $1,977,896 set by Kelso. **Nelson Bunker Hunt** of Dallas made news around the world with his thoroughbred enterprises in 1976. His American-bred 3-year-olds Youth and Empery won the French and English derbies, respectively. Youth could be called "Horse of the World" after he finished third in Europe's championship event, the Prix de l'Arc de Triomphe, on October 3 in Paris; won the Canadian International Championship at Woodbine Race Course on October 23; and then took the Washington, D.C., International on November 6 by 10 lengths at the Laurel Race Course in Maryland.

Major Horse Races of 1976

Race	Winner	Value to Winner
Belmont Stakes	Bold Forbes	$117,000
Canadian Int. Championship	Youth	114,600
Champions	King Pellinore	240,000
Epsom Derby (England)	Empery	192,640
Grand National Steeplechase (England)	Rag Trade	71,098
Irish Sweeps Derby	Malacate	117,508
Kentucky Derby	Bold Forbes	165,200
King George VI & Queen Elizabeth Stakes	Pawneese	142,689
Marlboro Cup Handicap	Forego	170,220
Preakness	Elocutionist	129,700
Prix de l'Arc de Triomphe	Ivanjica	243,120
Prix du Jockey-Club (French Derby)	Youth	190,170
Queen's Plate (Canada)	Norcliffe	89,716
Santa Anita Handicap	Royal Glint	155,900
Washington, D.C., Int.	Youth	100,000

Major U.S. Harness Races of 1976

Race	Winner	Value to Winner
American Trotting Classic	Keystone Pioneer	$ 49,410
Cane Pace	Keystone Ore	100,000
Hambletonian	Steve Lobell	131,762
Kentucky Futurity	Quick Pay	43,600
Little Brown Jug	Keystone Ore	56,905
Messenger Pace	Windshield Wiper	80,645
Roosevelt Int.	Equileo	100,000

Hunt also raced Dahlia, who retired at the end of 1976 as the leading money-winning thoroughbred mare of all time and ranked behind third-place Forego on the list of all top earners. In her first season of competition in the United States, Dahlia won the $200,000 Hollywood Invitational Handicap on May 31.

A half-brother to Dahlia by champion Secretariat, bred and sold by Hunt, set a world record when he was purchased for $1.5 million by a six-man Canadian syndicate at the Keeneland, Ky., yearling sales on July 20.

Bold Forbes was the upset winner of the Kentucky Derby and Belmont Stakes. Both Bold Forbes and Preakness winner Elocutionist were forced into retirement to stud by injuries suffered before the end of the season.

Other distinct divisional leaders were the 3-year-old filly Revidere, who lost only twice in 10 races, and the 2-year-old colt Seattle Slew, unbeaten in three starts, including the $125,000 Champagne Stakes at Belmont Park on October 16.

Harness Racing. The 2-minute mile became commonplace at major harness race tracks with the introduction of a lighter aluminum sulky.

Quarter Horse Racing. Real Wind won the All-American Quarter Horse Futurity for 2-year-olds at Ruidoso Downs, N. Mex., on September 6 to earn $330,000. Jane Goldstein

HOSPITAL. Strikes by hospital workers in Chicago, New York City, and Seattle and a slowdown by Los Angeles doctors protesting higher malpractice insurance rates plagued hospital administrators in 1976. The 65-day Seattle strike by 1,800 nurses at 15 hospitals ended in September.

The 10-day New York strike against 33 private nonprofit hospitals, 14 nursing homes, and 10 municipal hospitals involved about 33,000 technicians and other nonmedical workers. It ended on July 17 with an agreement to submit issues to arbitration. The National Labor Relations Board in March delivered a crippling blow to a budding union movement among young doctors by ruling that hospital interns and resident physicians are students, not employees, and are not covered by federal bargaining laws. In Chicago, nurses struck public hospitals run by Cook County for 38 days.

A series of nationwide hearings by the Federal Council on Wage and Price Stability focused on the unusually sharp rise in health-care costs in recent years. The hospital service charge component of the Consumer Price Index rose 13 per cent in 1976, as against the overall index increase of 7 per cent.

The American Hospital Association registered 7,156 hospitals with a total of 1.5 million beds in 1975. Hospitals reported 36.2 million inpatient admissions and 254.8 million outpatient visits in 1975, and more than 3 million employees. Wesley Curry

HOUSING. United Nations (UN) estimates presented at a UN Conference on Human Settlement in Vancouver, Canada, in June 1976 revealed that 300 million persons live in squatter settlements — shacktowns — on the outskirts of major cities in the developing nations of Africa, Asia, and South America. The UN estimated that shacktowns harbor 50 per cent of the population of Ankara, Turkey; 40 per cent of Caracas, Venezuela; and 45 per cent of Lima, Peru.

The president of Bosporus University in Turkey told the International Association for Housing Science meeting in Atlanta, Ga., in May that such settlements should be turned into so-called village-towns. He suggested that the national governments should provide financing that would allow the squatters to buy their own land and build houses.

Industry Recovery. The U.S. housing industry recovered in 1976 after falling to a 30-year low in 1975. The upturn began in February 1976 when housing starts showed a record 25 per cent increase. Activity declined in March and April, but housing starts during the first four months of 1976 surpassed those of the same 1975 period by 45.4 per cent.

Apartment-house construction picked up in May, and overall housing starts continued a strong comeback throughout the summer and autumn, with increases of 10.9 per cent in August and 17.6 per cent in September. Although housing starts

Work resumed in 1976 on the Nevada, one of several New York City apartment buildings left incomplete because of the 1974-1975 recession.

ized $2.5 billion in loans for housing for the elderly and handicapped.

Rising Home Costs. The president of the National Association of Home Builders said on March 9 that taxes and inflation had increased home-maintenance costs 303 per cent since the mid-1950s and priced 80 per cent of potential home buyers out of the market. The Federal Home Loan Bank Board reported in October that the average price of a new home had risen to $50,500 as of September, a jump of more than $20,500 since 1966.

As of June 15, HUD and the Consumer Product Safety Commission required all new mobile homes to meet federal safety standards. The new standards covered all aspects of design, construction, and durability. Mobile homes, as of mid-1976, accounted for nearly half of all new homes produced.

Segregation Issues. The Supreme Court of the United States ruled on April 20 that federal courts could order HUD to construct public housing in suburban areas as a remedy for racial segregation in cities. See CHICAGO.

On Dec. 31, 1975, President Ford signed into law a measure that would hinder *redlining,* the practice by lending institutions of refusing to make loans to potential home buyers in certain neighborhoods. The new law, as of 1976, required all lending institutions to reveal what mortgage loans they made and where they made them.   James M. Banovetz

dropped 4 per cent in October, with construction proceeding at an annually adjusted rate of 1.8 million units, it was still at the second highest level since February 1974.

In Canada, housing starts rose in November to a seasonally adjusted annual rate of 304,500, compared with 223,600 in October. The increase was due to housing starts carried over from October because of a construction strike in Quebec.

Federal Aid. The U.S. Department of Housing and Urban Development (HUD) helped promote recovery in January 1976 by providing financial backing for $3 billion in loans at below-market interest rates for the construction of apartment houses. On March 30, HUD reduced the maximum interest rate allowed on mortgages backed by the Federal Housing Administration or the Veterans Administration from 9 per cent to 8.5 per cent. As a result, mortgage lending by savings and loan institutions rose to a record $8.2 billion by June. The federal government began accepting applications for a new form of home loan featuring reduced payments in the early years of the mortgage.

On August 4, President Gerald R. Ford signed an authorization act extending HUD programs through fiscal 1977. The new act provided $850-million for low-income rental subsidies; lowered the interest rate on HUD-subsidized, 50-year home loans from 9 per cent to 7.5 per cent; and author-

HOUSTON. The city's magnet school program, one of the largest voluntary integration experiments in the nation, failed in 1976 to meet all of the goals that school officials had set for it. Reports filed with the U.S. District Court in July showed that only 3,336 students, 514 fewer than anticipated, transferred into the program during its first year.

The court approved the magnet school program as an alternative to an unsuccessful attempt to achieve school integration. The $4.5-million program was designed to attract students to integrated magnet schools by offering special educational programs not available elsewhere. Under the court-imposed program, 5,000 minority and white students were to transfer into magnet schools by January 1977. The school board claimed to have met 70 per cent of its goal by mid-1976, and the school superintendent was confident that the program would meet its overall goals by the deadline.

Local Disasters. Up to 12 inches (30 centimeters) of rainfall on June 15 and 16 caused severe flooding, which drove more than 2,000 families from their homes and caused electric power failures that blacked out sections of the city. Texas Governor Dolph Briscoe declared the city a disaster area on June 17. Officials estimated millions of dollars in damage to property, including the Contemporary Arts Museum, where basement flooding caused heavy damage to artworks.

HUA KUO-FENG

An explosion on February 22 destroyed grain elevators along the Houston Ship Channel. The blast killed four persons and shattered windows over a large area.

A 290-foot (88-meter) barge broke apart in the channel on May 4, spilling nearly 200,000 gallons (757,000 liters) of heavy fuel oil into Galveston Bay. The resulting oil slick forced officials to temporarily close the channel.

Booming Business. The Texas Eastern Transportation Corporation announced plans to build a 46-story office tower in an urban-renewal project under development in downtown Houston. The urban-renewal effort is reportedly the largest ever financed privately, and Texas Eastern planned to spend more than $1 billion on the project.

Department store sales rose 15.4 per cent in the area, and construction activity increased 4.4 per cent between August 1975 and August 1976. Employment rose 3.3 per cent, leaving the unemployment rate at 5.9 per cent in June. Factory worker earnings registered an 8.5 per cent annual increase by mid-1976 to an annual average of $12,888.

The state attorney general in September accused Houston of being the state's worst polluter and joined a suit to stop the city from dumping raw sewage into its waterways. He threatened to stop the issuance of new building permits unless Houston moved to correct the situation. James M. Banovetz

Premier Hua Kuo-feng, virtually unknown to the West, succeeded the late Mao Tse-tung as chairman of the Chinese Communist Party.

HUA KUO-FENG (1922-   ), one of 12 vice-premiers, became prime minister of the People's Republic of China in February 1976. He replaced Chou En-lai, who died on January 8. Then, after the death of Communist Party Chairman Mao Tse-tung on September 9, Hua also became party chairman. The appointment of Hua as prime minister surprised analysts in the West. They had assumed that the post would go to Teng Hsiao-ping, who had undertaken much of Chou En-lai's work during the latter's long illness. However, in February, Teng was ousted as senior among the 12 vice-premiers and severely criticized for being a "capitalist roader" and an opponent of the teachings of Mao. See CHINA, PEOPLE'S REPUBLIC OF.

Hua is relatively unknown in the West. A native of Mao's home province, Hunan, Hua won Mao's favor by organizing irrigation projects there. Hua was promoted to vice-governor of Hunan Province in 1958 but was the target of left wing political attacks during the Cultural Revolution of 1966 to 1969. However, he later became chairman of the Hunan Revolutionary Committee, a post comparable to that of a state governor in the United States. He also became first secretary of the Hunan Provincial Party Committee. In 1971, he served as political commissar of the Hunan military district and second political commissar of the Canton military region. Foster Stockwell

HUME, GEORGE BASIL CARDINAL (1923-   ), the abbot of Ampleforth Abbey, in Yorkshire, England, was appointed the ninth archbishop of Westminster by Pope Paul VI on Feb. 17, 1976. He was made a cardinal on April 27. As archbishop, he is the spiritual leader of British Roman Catholics. The appointment came as a surprise to British Catholics because Hume, though he is a highly regarded teacher and theologian, was not a bishop at the time of the appointment. He was consecrated bishop on March 25.

George Basil Hume was born on March 2, 1923, in Newcastle upon Tyne in the north of England, the son of a noted heart surgeon. He was educated at Ampleforth College, a school connected with the abbey; Oxford University; and Fribourg University in Switzerland, where he studied theology. He took his vows as a Benedictine monk in 1945 and was ordained a priest in 1950.

Hume taught at Ampleforth College from 1952 to 1963, when he became abbot. After his appointment as abbot, he became deeply involved in ecumenical activities and is a personal friend of F. Donald Coggan, the archbishop of Canterbury and spiritual head of the Church of England.

Cardinal Hume is deeply interested in sports. He fishes and is a devoted fan of Newcastle United, a soccer team. He describes himself as "a very keen but very bad squash player." Edward G. Nash

HUNGARY pursued a moderate economic and political course at home in 1976, while it tried to improve relations with its neighbors Austria and Yugoslavia as well as with the Western powers. Communist Party First Secretary Janos Kadar paid his first visit to the West in December when he went to Austria at the personal invitation of Chancellor Bruno Kreisky. Prime Minister Gyorgy Lazar visited Austria in May, France in June, and Yugoslavia in October. Deputy Prime Minister Gyula Szeker paid a visit to the United States in August and held talks with Secretary of Commerce Elliot L. Richardson.

The Vatican moved to normalize relations with Hungary. On February 12, Pope Paul VI named Monsignor Laszlo Lekai archbishop of Esztergom to succeed Joseph Cardinal Mindszenty as the Roman Catholic primate of Hungary. Mindszenty was a staunch anti-Communist who died in exile in 1975. Lekai was made a cardinal on April 27.

Russia and Hungary concluded a new five-year trade agreement on March 27 under which Hungary will deliver beef, corn, and wheat to Russia, over and above earlier trade pacts. In return, Russia agreed to supply cellulose, cotton, crude oil, diesel oil, gasoline, timber, and other raw materials.

The Economy. Hungary's exports to the West rose 6 per cent and its imports fell 9 per cent in the first half of 1976, compared with the corresponding 1975 period. Total foreign trade dropped 2 per cent. Industrial output rose 4.4 per cent in the first eight months of 1976, but food production fell 1.2 per cent despite a 25 per cent larger wheat crop.

Hungary raised meat and poultry prices an average of about 30 per cent on July 5. Every wage earner and pensioner was given a $3 monthly compensation allowance.

The government issued a decree in November that gave artisans and small traders tax cuts in order to improve services to the public. Where their services are needed, artisans and retailers will get a tax-free three-year period instead of the present two years. In villages with fewer than 3,000 inhabitants, the three-year tax-free period will be followed by a 60 per cent tax reduction that is subject to an income limit.

The Ministry of Labor froze employment of all administrative personnel on January 1, except for cases given special permission by the minister. In July, the government tried to relieve the country's severe labor shortage by issuing a decree that covers procurement, recruitment, and redirection of labor. Arpad Pullai, who had been in charge of the party's personnel selection and cadre policy for 10 years, was dropped from the post of central committee secretary on October 27 and replaced by Sandor Borkely, head of the central committee department in charge of trade and industry.   Chris Cviic

See also EUROPE (Facts in Brief Table).

HUNTING. The total duck breeding population was down about 9 per cent in 1976, and U.S. waterfowl hunters found the fall flight did not match 1975's better-than-average flight. The major changes in the federal waterfowl-hunting regulations governed the use of steel shot in designated zones of the Atlantic Flyway.

The U.S. Fish and Wildlife Service had planned a complete ban on the use of lead shot but it was forced to modify its regulations hastily on September 13 when hunters protested that there was a shortage of steel shot. Under the modification, the use of lead shot was permitted in smaller gauge shotguns for the 1976 season.

The decision to require steel shot was based on the estimate that 2 million ducks die in the United States each year from lead poisoning after swallowing spent shotgun pellets. The use of nonlead shot will be required in other flyways in increasing quantities over the next three years in order to allow ammunition makers time to increase production.

Many hunters opposed the proposal to ban lead shot. They argued that steel pellets have less striking energy and would result in more unretrieved ducks than are now dying from lead poisoning. The Fish and Wildlife Service, however, cited field tests that showed little difference in the effectiveness of the two types of shot. A federal district court judge upheld the ban in December.   Andrew L. Newman

ICE SKATING. Sheila Young of Detroit, Dorothy Hamill of Riverside, Conn., and Sylvia Burka of Toronto, Canada, won major honors during 1976 in speed skating and figure skating, sports usually dominated by Europeans. Young was a 25-year-old speed skater and world champion in cycling; Hamill, a 19-year-old figure skater; and Burka, a speed skater.

Speed Skating. Young starred in the Olympic Games held from February 4 to 15 at Innsbruck, Austria; the world overall championships on February 21 and 22 at Gjøvik, Norway; and the world sprint championships in March in West Berlin.

She won three Olympic medals, finishing first at 500 meters, second at 1,500 meters, and third at 1,000 meters. Young led after three of the four races in the world overall championships, then finished third in the final standing behind Burka and Tatiana Averina of Russia. In the world sprint championships, Young swept the four races—a feat never before accomplished—and won the title for the second straight year and the third time in four years.

Her feats were remarkable because speed skating is a minor sport in the United States. West Allis, Wis., has the only Olympic-sized (400-meter) rink in the country, and many skaters spend hours commuting there daily. Peter Mueller of Mequon, Wis., and his fiancée, Leah Poulos of Northbrook, Ill., used family savings to train in West Berlin before

Sylvia Burka, center, of Toronto, Canada, beat Sheila Young of Detroit, left, and Tatiana Averina of Russia, right, for world speed-skating title.

the Olympics. Mueller won a gold medal and Poulos a silver, each at 1,000 meters.

Figure Skating. Hamill won Olympic, world, and United States championships, and her wedge haircut and liquid grace captivated an international television audience. She turned professional after the world championships in March in Göteborg, Sweden, signed with an ice show, and agreed to appear on television. See HAMILL, DOROTHY.

Hamill's coach was Carlo Fassi, a small, fiery, 48-year-old Italian and former European champion. Fassi also coached John Curry, the Olympic, world, and European men's champion.

Other Winners. Curry, a 26-year-old Englishman, lived in New York City and trained with Fassi in Denver. He skated artistically rather than athletically, with a grace unusual for a man. The style was not manly enough, said a West German judge.

"I threaten them, I guess," said Curry. "It's so ridiculous, as if someone has to skate in a little soldier way to win a gold medal. Skating should be beautiful. It's lost some of its elegance."

Dianne de Leeuw of Paramount, Calif., won the European championships, placed second in the Olympics, and third in the world championships. Although born in California, she competed for the Netherlands. She held dual citizenship because her parents were born there.   Frank Litsky

See also OLYMPIC GAMES.

ICELAND severed diplomatic ties with Great Britain on Feb. 19, 1976. The break came over a bitter dispute involving British trawlers fishing in Icelandic waters. See EUROPE (Close-Up).

The move, which followed a series of gunboat confrontations, marked the first diplomatic break between two members of the North Atlantic Treaty Organization. Ties were restored following the signing of a pact on June 1 that calls for the registering of British trawlers fishing the Icelandic banks, limits their number to an average of 24 per day within the 200-nautical-mile limit, and bans all British trawlers within 30 nautical miles of Iceland's coast.

Labor unrest continued to disrupt the economy. On February 17, about 40,000 union members struck for wage hikes of up to 25 per cent and greater fringe benefits. The strike forced shops and factories to close; rail and communication facilities as well as the fishing industry were also affected.

On January 13, Iceland was hit by one of its most powerful earthquakes in more than 40 years. It measured 6.3 on the Richter scale. All buildings in Kópasker in northern Iceland were destroyed, but no deaths were reported.   Paul C. Tullier

See also EUROPE (Facts in Brief Table).

IDAHO. See STATE GOVERNMENT.

ILLINOIS. See CHICAGO; STATE GOVERNMENT.

INCOME TAX. See TAXATION.

INDIA. Already armed with vast emergency powers, Prime Minister Indira Gandhi made certain in November 1976 that she would be beyond all future legal challenges. The lower house of parliament passed a set of constitutional amendments on November 2 that greatly expanded her authority. President Fakhruddin Ali Ahmed is now bound to follow the prime minister's instructions and for two years can amend the Constitution single-handedly. The amendments ended the courts' right to review such constitutional amendments except on procedural grounds. In addition, they empowered the government to disregard individual rights if it believed a person was engaged in vaguely defined "antinational activities." In January, the parliament also approved the permanent censorship of all of India's newspapers.

The lower house, which is controlled by Gandhi's Congress Party, voted 180 to 34 on November 5 to put off for another year an election that, under the old Constitution, would have had to be held no later than March 1977. The house thus added another year to its five-year term. In demanding that the election be delayed, Gandhi argued that "the gains of the emergency [proclaimed in June 1975] should not be dissipated." Outside the parliament, an opposition leader said, "Government without the verdict of the people is despotism."

Political Arrests. The number of those detained remained uncertain. The home minister in October put the total at about 12,000, some 30 per cent of whom were said to have been subsequently freed "once they had given up the path of violent agitation." Detached observers put the total at between 35,000 and 75,000. The most notable prisoners were 72-year-old Morarji Desai, once a close associate of the prime minister's father, Jawaharlal Nehru; and George Fernandes, a prominent labor leader who was captured in June after a year of underground resistance. His brothers are known to have been tortured in prison to make them reveal the labor leader's whereabouts. A presidential ordinance in mid-June doubled to two years the time that officials can detain people without citing the grounds for their arrest.

The Economy showed some improvement, with an excellent harvest and promising deep-sea oil strikes off the west coast. Production also went up in such industries as steel, where the government banned all strikes and restricted union activity. Although the government continued to speak of socialism, the budget offered exceptional incentives to private industry. Despite controls, prices began to soar in March.

Son as Adviser. Gandhi's closest adviser was her son Sanjay, 30. Although he held no official post, he

Sanjay Gandhi, son of India's Prime Minister Indira Gandhi, and a rising young political figure, reaches out to greet people on a street in Calcutta.

dominated the government and police, helped to shape policy, and was paid extravagant honors on tours of the Indian states. Foreign diplomats insisted Sanjay combined politics with lucrative business deals that increased his personal income. The belief in India was that the prime minister was grooming him as her political heir.

India's Foreign Relations improved in 1976. Diplomatic contacts were restored with Pakistan in mid-May after a five-year break, and ambassadors were exchanged with China in April. Relations with the United States were correct rather than warm, but U.S. aid was resumed on a modest scale. Russia, still India's principal ally, gave Gandhi a lavish welcome on her visit to Moscow in June. Russian aid included heavy water for the Indian nuclear establishment. However, Canada ended its nuclear-aid arrangement with India in May, charging that New Delhi had misused a reactor provided by Canada for India's "peaceful" 1974 nuclear test.

The government also announced that, after years of lagging efforts, it was making real progress in slowing the birth rate. Sterilization, the most common method of birth control in India, was running at more than three times the 1975 rate. In the first five months of 1976, 2 million persons were sterilized.   Mark Gayn

See also ASIA (Facts in Brief Table).

INDIAN, AMERICAN. Indian tribes struggled in 1976 for greater control of their resources of land, energy, and water. Great coal, oil, and uranium resources are located on Indian tribal lands in the Western United States. As these resources became more valuable because of the energy crisis, many tribes found themselves in a better bargaining position for development of their energy reserves, which are estimated to be worth billions of dollars.

Coal and Water Suits. The Crow, Northern Cheyenne, and Fort Berthold tribes in 1976 sued with some success to invalidate existing coal leases so that they could renegotiate contracts with better royalty payments. On July 12, the U.S. District Court in Billings, Mont., refused a motion by energy companies to dismiss the Crow suit. The Supreme Court of the United States ruled on May 19 that coal reserves on the Northern Cheyenne Reservation in Montana, worth an estimated $2-billion, belong to the tribe rather than to individual Indians. The unanimous decision opened the way for the tribe to negotiate development contracts for tribally owned and individually allotted portions of the reservation.

However, Indians seeking to protect their water rights in Western states received a sharp setback on March 24, when the Supreme Court held that Indian rights to water may be determined in state as well as federal courts. An Indian spokesman said

American Indians and sympathizers celebrate a not-guilty verdict in May for militant leader Dennis Banks, charged with possessing firearms.

that unless Congress passes legislation to deny state jurisdiction over water rights, the high court decision will mark the end of Indian reservations in the West.

Indian Claims of tribal sovereignty against state interference were strengthened on June 14 when the Supreme Court ruled unanimously that a 1953 law did not give the states power to tax reservation Indians. The federal law gave some states criminal and civil jurisdiction over most of the reservations in those states. The law is unpopular with many Indian activists, who see it as an erosion of tribal sovereignty.

The landmark tax case was brought by a Chippewa Indian living on the Leech Lake Reservation in Minnesota. He successfully challenged county efforts to collect a personal property tax on his mobile home, which was located on tribal land.

The Seminoles voted on January 22 to accept a federal government offer of $16 million in settlement of their claims to ownership of the Florida peninsula. The tribes had waged a 25-year legal battle for compensation for 32 million acres (13-million hectares) of Florida land. Chief Howard Tommie said the offer amounted to about 50 cents an acre (0.4 hectare).

An Indian claim to most of Maine in October halted the sale of $27 million in municipal bonds. The suit, filed by Indians in 1972, cast doubt on the ownership of 12 million acres (4.9 million hectares), including several towns. The suit claims the Indians gave up the land under an illegal treaty never approved by Congress. In December 1975, the U.S. government took over the case.

Sioux Election. In a hotly contested election for the presidency of the Oglala Sioux tribe, Albert Trimble, a former Bureau of Indian Affairs superintendent, defeated incumbent Richard Wilson on January 27. Trimble, who was backed by members of the American Indian Movement (AIM), pledged to bring improved law and order to the troubled Pine Ridge Sioux Reservation in South Dakota. Pine Ridge was the scene of the Wounded Knee take-over by AIM militants in 1973. One of their demands had been a U.S. Senate investigation of Wilson.

On July 16, a federal jury in Cedar Rapids, Iowa, found two AIM members innocent of shooting two Federal Bureau of Investigation agents on the Sioux reservation in June 1975. On August 6, AIM leader Russell C. Means was acquitted of a murder charge that stemmed from a tavern slaying. However, militant Menominee leader Michael Sturdevant was convicted on April 21 of nine felonies as a result of the 1975 occupation of a vacant Roman Catholic seminary located near Gresham, Wis.　　　　　　　　　Andrew L. Newman

See also NORTHWEST TERRITORIES.

INDIANA. See STATE GOVERNMENT.

INDONESIA was a rarity in 1976 among oil-producing countries—a nation in financial trouble. Jakarta issued rosy reports on the country's economy. But the reports could not conceal the depth of the crisis—the retrenchment and the foreign debt that had passed $17 billion.

The world recession accounted for some of Indonesia's difficulties. But the immediate cause was the 1975 collapse of the giant Pertamina company, which was established to handle the nation's rich oil resources. The company was financed on huge foreign loans and hampered by corruption and lack of proper accounting. Pertamina foundered in 1975 when it could not pay its $1.5 billion in short-term credits.

The stunned Jakarta government acted decisively in 1976. The national bank met the immediate debts and began to untangle the company's accounts. Foreign lenders continued their aid, but the World Bank predicted that Indonesia would be using one-fifth of its export earnings simply to pay its debts by 1979.

Not Enough Jobs. The government estimated that 2 million new workers were being added to the labor force each year, but only 600,000 new jobs were being created. Millions of jobseekers poured into the cities in search of work. The government bulldozed their shantytowns and trucked the people out, but this did not solve the problem. One reason for the crisis was the slow pace of industrialization. The other was Indonesia's high birth rate. Indonesia allotted $15.6 million for family planning in 1976 but still expected the population to double in the next 30 years.

And even though the country had become vastly richer in the past decade, the gap between rich and poor kept widening, thus fueling unrest. In December, the government freed 2,650 prisoners detained after a 1965 Communist uprising, but 29,000 were still in jail. The government said these would be freed within three years.

The economic disparity went in step with corruption. In 1976, President Suharto felt impelled to deny that he, his wife, or their families had been helped by the government "in launching enterprises aimed at easy and big profits." In mid-1976, the government began to prepare for the election of May 2, 1977, expected to be won hands down by the official Golkar Party.

East Timor became Indonesia's 27th province on July 17 when Suharto signed a bill incorporating it into Indonesia. Troops from the western part of Timor, which Indonesia administers, invaded the former Portuguese colony in December 1975 and completed the take-over despite a United Nations Security Council resolution in April 1976 calling on Indonesia to withdraw its forces from the island colony.　　　　　　　　　　　　　Mark Gayn

See also ASIA (Facts in Brief Table).

INSURANCE. Rate increases for many forms of insurance that were obtained late in 1975 finally outran inflation to bring about a drop in insurance underwriting losses of U.S. companies in the second quarter of 1976. Further rate hikes in 1976 and a tightening of the market for high risks were expected to bring the full year's underwriting loss to $2-billion, only half the $4 billion loss of 1975. The loss in the first quarter of 1976 was $1.3 billion and in the second quarter only $635 million.

Investment income improved appreciably and surplus funds increased substantially because of higher prices on the stock market. However, industry leaders and state regulatory officials remained apprehensive. They worried about the reduced availability of some kinds of insurance, the greater use of residual markets such as assigned risk plans and fire pools, the great cost of some types of coverage, and the possible need for even higher insurance rates if the inflationary cycle resumes.

Auto Insurance. The high cost of replacement parts for collision damage was blamed for the continued poor showing of automobile insurance. Some state officials called on the Federal Trade Commission to act against car manufacturers and dealers accused of restraining competition. The manufacturers vehemently denied the charge at a Washington, D.C., hearing.

Auto theft was another major loss producer. The Department of Justice reported that 1 million cars are stolen each year at a current cost of about $1.5-billion. The Justice Department said more effective locks are being sought, a better vehicle identification number system is under development, and stronger state title laws are needed.

A controversy over automobile insurance rates in Massachusetts brought about the end of the traditional system of rates being set by the state insurance commissioner. A competitive rating system was enacted, effective Jan. 1, 1977.

Fear for the solvency of one of the largest auto insurers in the United States, Government Employees Insurance Company, sent shock waves through the country during the first half of 1976. Worry subsided when steps were taken to bring the company back to financial stability.

No-Fault Insurance. The hectic efforts to enact no-fault automobile insurance laws that characterized 1973 and 1974 abated in 1976, with little legislative activity and no new laws. Massachusetts even repealed its no-fault property-damage law.

The Michigan Appeals Court ruled unconstitutional a provision in its no-fault law that subtracted from survivor benefits the amounts received from government sources, such as social security and workmen's compensation. The court ruled in August 1976 that the provision discriminated against poor people who could not afford private insurance. Differentiating between governmental benefits and private benefits is "patently unreasonable," the court held.

The Florida no-fault law was changed, effective October 1. A new provision requires proof of permanent injury or serious disabling temporary injury before a victim can bring suit for pain and suffering. It replaced a $1,000 claim threshold.

In New York, an insurance company in November challenged in federal court the provisions of the no-fault law mandating compulsory binding arbitration and guaranteed renewal of coverage by insurers for a stated period of years.

Medical Malpractice Insurance. During 1976, 16 states enacted some form of underwriting mechanism to provide liability insurance for doctors and hospitals when insurers declined to write the business. This brought the number of states with such arrangements to 41. Thirty-five of the 41 have pooling systems, mainly joint underwriting associations. Four states have reinsurance facilities, and four have state funds. Oklahoma authorized its existing state workmen's compensation fund to write malpractice insurance where necessary. Eleven states, including seven with pools, have laws permitting doctors or hospitals to form mutual or reciprocal insurance companies. In addition, states enacted a wide range of reforms relating to benefits and limitations in bringing legal suits, with additional laws expected in 1977.   Emanuel Levy

INTERIOR DESIGN. Contemporary design was the most popular style in 1976 in all types of furniture. With its clean, smooth lines and curves, contemporary — including decorative accessories — was available at all prices.

Many selections combined modern styling with natural-looking woods and fabrics. Wicker, rattan, and bamboo were frequently used. Contemporary design elements included flared arms, single-seat cushions on sofas and love seats, weltless tailoring, and an abundance of throw pillows. Wood was used for decorative detail on arms and legs.

The Nostalgia Look, a new style, reflected motifs and lines popular in the United States during the affluent Gay Nineties period. Nostalgia was popular because it brought back memories of the good old days to some and because, for the young, it represented warmth, security, and charm.

One manufacturer of wood furniture presented a 52-piece nostalgia group, the "Keepsake Collection," which was highly acclaimed. The collection included a washstand with cheval mirror (a mirror that swings between two supports), chifforobe (combination wardrobe and chest of drawers), icebox, mustache-shaving stand, gossip bench, sewing stand, and full-sized player piano with matching stool. Ornate carvings, scrolls, and antique brass hardware decorated the items.

Many large department and furniture stores

opened special American antique departments to serve the interest in American antiques. And the popularity of the nostalgia look expanded the already popular pastime of restoring discarded furniture, lamps, mirrors, and tables.

Fabrics and Colors. Velvet continued as the most popular covering for all types of furniture. Velvet coverings were found on traditional, contemporary, French, and English styles. Print fabrics in floral and leaf patterns were also favored, along with diamond prints, small stripes, and geometrics. Earth tones and nature colors were used with prints.

Gay Nineties colors such as rose, gray, and bottle-green gained growing acceptance. Furniture designers found these colors compatible with natural wood tones. Pewter-gray was a basic color in combination with copper, rust, white, and black. Rose and bottle-green were considered to be trendsetting colors.

Designs from Other Cultures. Manufacturers looked to other cultures for design inspirations, especially for fabrics. Ethnic influences, especially those from Mexico and South America, grew in importance. Bold, colorful Indian patterns were offered on linens, bedspreads, throw rugs, area rugs, and wallhangings. Manufacturers also revived the American Indian motifs popular in the early 1900s.

Oriental and Far East designs appeared in fabrics shown at the Southern Fall Furniture Market, which was held from October 14 to 22 at High Point, N.C. New fabrics included a flocked nylon velvet in Persian-carpet colors, batiks in stripes and patterns, and Oriental designs. Color combinations included blue and cinnamon, coral and brown, and gray and apricot.

Out of the Woodwork. Oak and woods with character were popular with all manufacturers. Statistics released in June by the Fine Hardwoods-American Walnut Association showed that about 17 per cent of all manufacturers used oak, including bold, flat, sliced red oak, white oak, and knotty oak. Knotty pine was second with 10.4 per cent. Following in popularity were pecan with 9.5 per cent, and walnut, 8 per cent.

Combinations of natural and man-made materials were used in all styles. Wood and glass appeared on tables, wood and leather on chairs, and chrome and leather on sofas. Chrome, plastic, and glass were also used together.

Industry Affairs. The U.S. home-furnishings industry responded to Federal Trade Commission requests to provide care instructions on furniture. The upholstered-furniture industry also continued hearings with the Consumer Product Safety Commission on ways to reduce the flammability of furniture.   Helen C. Schubert

An all-white bedroom, one of the model rooms at Bloomingdale's in New York City, is dedicated to the late composer Charles Ives.

INTERNATIONAL TRADE AND FINANCE

Japan's parliament, investigating the Lockheed payoff scandal, hears a millionaire friend of a former prime minister deny any involvement.

World trade resumed its growth in 1976 after a rare decline during recession-plagued 1975, but difficult problems emerged for the world economy. On the whole, the spirit of international cooperation remained good, particularly among the leading industrial countries. The main conflicts concerned relations between rich and poor nations. A number of governments were rocked by allegations that their officials had received bribes and other questionable payments from Lockheed Aircraft Corporation and dozens of other U.S. companies seeking to facilitate sales abroad. Among the countries that were most affected were Italy, Japan, and the Netherlands. See Close-Up.

Trade Policy. Although the pace faltered somewhat late in the year, an expansion in the economies of all the major countries boosted the volume of world trade by an estimated 8 to 10 per cent after adjusting for somewhat higher prices for exports and imports. This considerably benefited the less-developed nations, whose exports to the industrial countries showed a good gain.

The United States trade balance swung strongly into deficit after a big surplus in 1975, but this deficit was accepted calmly at home and was welcomed abroad. United States imports exceeded exports by about $4 billion for the first 10 months of the year. This trade deficit did not harm the value of the dollar in the floating system of currency exchange rates now in operation, but it helped improve the trade balances of other countries, particularly those of the less-developed nations.

However, U.S. trade policy was an issue during the year for a different reason. It was the first year of full operation for the sweeping 1974 U.S. trade law, which contains several provisions opening the way to import restraints. Early in the year, President Gerald R. Ford imposed a system of import quotas on stainless and other specialty steels after the International Trade Commission found that imports were hurting domestic producers. This led to fears in the United States and elsewhere that America was moving in a protectionist direction. But later cases involving shoes, automobiles, and other products brought decisions against import restraints, and the fears abated. As the year ended, a renewed appeal for restraints on shoe imports, as well as several other cases, was still undecided.

Tariff Talks. International negotiations for a further round of reductions in tariffs and other trade barriers plodded along in Geneva, Switzerland, with only limited progress. As in previous negotiations, the chief problem was agricultural trade barriers, with the United States and the European Community (Common Market) as the main adversaries. Negotiators also disagreed over a formula for reducing tariffs and over a new international code to limit various devices used to subsidize exports.

While the talks moved slowly, a general desire for their success emerged from economic summit meetings in Rambouillet, France, and Dorado Beach, Puerto Rico, among President Ford and his counterparts from Canada, France, Great Britain, Italy, Japan, and West Germany. They set a goal of completing the trade negotiations by the end of 1977. There was every evidence that President-elect James Earl (Jimmy) Carter, Jr., shared the desire to reduce trade barriers on a reciprocal basis.

Exchange Rates. The year's main troubles were monetary, not in trade. Three major countries – Britain, France, and Italy – saw the exchange rates of their currencies decline. By the end of the year, the British pound had plunged about 45 per cent from its value at the end of 1971 when measured against a cluster of other leading currencies. The drop of the Italian lira was comparable. The French franc did not decline nearly as much, but on March 15 France dropped out of the European currency *snake* – an arrangement by which the currencies of several countries, with West Germany at the center, float jointly against the U.S. dollar and keep their rates stable against one another.

While no leading country urged an early return to the old system of fixed exchange rates that broke down earlier in the decade, many experienced some painful problems associated with floating. The main difficulty mentioned by France, Italy, and others at the annual meeting of the International

Corporate Corruption Commotion

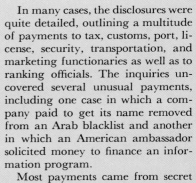

Broad investigations into corporate corruption in the United States produced startling results in 1976. By year's end, almost 300 U.S. companies had admitted making questionable or illegal payments, most of them overseas. The money went to obtain contracts by influencing the policy-making process in other countries and to speed up ordinary business procedures by paying lower-level officials to guarantee that they would do their jobs. Bribery was generally condemned when it was designed to win business that otherwise would have gone to a competitor. Smaller facilitating, or "grease," payments aroused less concern.

The Securities and Exchange Commission (SEC) flushed out disclosure of most of the payments. The SEC relied heavily on a voluntary program in which companies came forward, under the incentive of benign treatment, to admit their questionable or illegal payments. The SEC entered the matter because its job is to ensure that investors are told of all material corporate developments. Only a handful of cases—most prominently, the Lockheed Aircraft Corporation's bribes of at least $25 million to obtain orders for aircraft—involved amounts large enough to meet purely economic definitions of the SEC standard of corporate materiality. But the commission argued that a relatively small bribe could influence large business deals and also tended to reflect unfavorably on the integrity of a company's management.

Corporate filings with the SEC did not disclose the names of those bribed or their countries. But in the Lockheed case and a number of others, the foreign interests quickly became known. The resulting scandals jeopardized several governments. In Italy, a parliamentary committee accused former Prime Minister Mariano Rumor of fraud in his relations with Lockheed. Japan's former Prime Minister Kakuei Tanaka was arrested on charges of accepting a big Lockheed bribe. And Prince Bernhard of the Netherlands was forced out of some official posts for his dealings with Lockheed.

Japanese demonstrators protest Lockheed payoffs.

In many cases, the disclosures were quite detailed, outlining a multitude of payments to tax, customs, port, license, security, transportation, and marketing functionaries as well as to ranking officials. The inquiries uncovered several unusual payments, including one case in which a company paid to get its name removed from an Arab blacklist and another in which an American ambassador solicited money to finance an information program.

Most payments came from secret "slush" funds the companies created by such practices as overbilling customers or having them agree to pay kickbacks. Sometimes rebates were obtained from shipping companies.

As they disclosed their questionable practices, most companies adopted or strengthened policies forbidding bribes and other suspicious transactions. However, several said they would continue to make small "grease" payments when necessary.

It is not against United States law to bribe or make "grease" payments overseas; it is only illegal to fail to disclose significant corporate developments. Congress debated several measures to change this and prevent or discourage such payments. At least two bills sought to make it a crime to bribe foreign officials.

The SEC, however, pointed to enforcement and jurisdictional problems in trying to outlaw such payments, many of which were not considered improper or unusual in the country in which they were made. Instead of blanket prohibitions, the SEC fought to stiffen the penalties for falsifying corporate books so that slush funds could not be easily created or payments so easily made. The Ford Administration supported the SEC and submitted a bill that would require companies to report payments to the Department of Commerce, which might make them public only after a year. But in the end, Congress passed none of the proposed legislation, not even the relatively mild SEC bill. Nevertheless, the commission was convinced that the problem of questionable payments had been dramatically reduced.

Robert D. Hershey, Jr.

Monetary Fund (IMF) in Manila, the Philippines, in early October, was the "vicious circle" effect on countries with more rapid inflation than their trade partners. Their currencies soon decline in the markets, making imports more expensive. This intensifies the inflation problem. As the year ended, Britain had negotiated a $3.9-billion loan from the IMF to stabilize the pound, and Italy was also seeking massive financial aid.

The Debt Problem. Apart from the problems facing certain industrial countries was the separate matter of the rising debt of the less-developed countries. It had reached a total of $150 billion by the end of 1974, the latest date for which complete figures are available from the World Bank, and was estimated to have risen further in 1975 and 1976. Amid various expressions of concern, some spokesmen of the poorer countries urged a negotiated general debt relief of some kind. Most of the debt is owed to governments of the industrial countries and to the World Bank and other international lending agencies; about one-fifth is held by private banks.

The United States, most of the other industrial countries, and the World Bank took the position that the debt problem must be considered on a country-by-country basis and not as a general matter. Debts were rescheduled during the year for Zaire and Argentina, and there was no sign of massive defaults. Although negotiations on a general debt solution continued in the 27-nation Paris Conference on International Economic Cooperation, the industrial countries showed no sign of yielding in their firm insistence on dealing with debt on a case-by-case basis.

The Paris talks opened in February, after nine months of preparatory talks, and became deadlocked during the summer over procedural problems that had a bearing on the more substantive issues. In addition to the problem of the growing debt owed by the poorer nations to the industrial nations, a major issue before the conference was the prices paid for raw materials produced in developing countries. The developing countries were seeking language in the preliminary work program that would commit the industrial nations to decide whether or not to wipe out official debt. They also wanted a promise to discuss price-support formulas that would protect their raw material exports. The industrial nations, while differing somewhat among themselves on details, held out for more neutral language in the work schedules.

The insistence on a general debt moratorium was eased in October when finance ministers gathered in Manila for the annual meeting of the IMF and World Bank. There was no mention of wiping out the debt in preliminary meetings of the two key groups. A coalition of representatives from Latin American, Asian, and African countries urged only that aid on easy terms should be available to coun-

World Bank President Robert S. McNamara calls for an end to world poverty at a joint meeting with the International Monetary Fund in Manila.

tries that do not have access to private capital markets. Representatives also agreed that the industrial countries should give top priority to fighting inflation, rather than a quick return to full employment.

The basic problem for many less-developed countries, as well as for such nations as Britain and Italy, arose in part as the aftermath of the explosion of world oil prices in the winter of 1973-1974. The oil-producing countries as a group continued to run a large balance-of-payments surplus, more than $40 billion. This meant that the rest of the world had a counterpart collective deficit, much of which was financed by borrowing.

IMF Expands Role. The IMF played a growing role in financing deficits through several different lending facilities. The governing 20-nation Interim Committee agreed in January in Jamaica to expand IMF lending resources and revise its charter. The charter revision would include a formal endorsement of floating exchange rates as an option for member nations. The U.S. Congress ratified these changes in September, and approvals were expected from the necessary number of IMF members early in 1977. The changes will solve no immediate problems, but they will strengthen the role of the IMF in world finance.   Edwin L. Dale, Jr.

See also ECONOMICS; Section One, FOCUS ON THE ECONOMY.

IOWA. See STATE GOVERNMENT.

Expansion of Iran's Abadan oil refinery and other industrial development
was delayed because of lagging oil revenues and rising costs of imports.

IRAN. Shah Mohammad Reza Pahlavi in 1976 celebrated the 50th anniversary of his father's assumption of the throne, which began the Pahlavi dynasty, by continuing to strengthen Iran's prominent role in the Middle East. The agreement with Iraq negotiated in 1975 was formally ratified in June, ending border and navigational disputes that had festered for more than 50 years. Iran also closed the last of several refugee camps for Kurds who fled Iraq – another result of the agreement. See IRAQ.

Despite some criticism by the Arab states, the shah retained an Iranian military presence in the lower Persian Gulf in the form of an Iranian battalion detailed to assist the sultan of Oman in the war with Omani rebels in Dhofar province. See OMAN.

More Arms. Iranian political activity in the region was reinforced by continued arms purchases. On August 20, the shah ordered $114 million in military hardware from the United States plus a $200-million training and logistics-support program for the Iranian Air Force. The shah's absolute authority, enforced by security services and Savak, the Iranian secret police, generally met with only vocal opposition, though there were a few terrorist incidents. The most serious occurred on August 28, when three Rockwell International Corporation technicians working on a secret microwave monitoring system were ambushed and killed in Teheran while on their way to work.

October Elections for local, municipal, and regional councils, under the sponsorship of the Iran Resurgence Party established by the shah in 1975, produced surprising results. Candidates of such previously underrepresented groups as women, students, and workers defeated several Establishment politicians. Eleven new members were chosen for the 30-member Teheran City Council. In September, the party announced that its one-year membership drive had netted 5.2 million members, of whom 40 per cent were women and 3.7 million were from rural areas.

Oil revenues slumped a bit, and a national deficit was forecast for 1976, but the country's major problem was still how best to spend its money. A related problem was the lack of skilled manpower. A French-Iranian School of Management opened in October in Teheran to provide a four-year management training program for 200 Iranians each year. Agreements were also reached to train Iranians in Canada and in the Philippines to meet the critical shortage of medical personnel.

To lessen its dependence on oil revenues, Iran has been developing its mineral resources. More lead, iron, molybdenum, and zinc are being mined. The huge Sar Chesmeh copper mine, a $1-billion project in southern Iran, neared production capability in 1976. William Spencer

See also MIDDLE EAST (Facts in Brief Table).

IRAQ. The Revolutionary Command Council formally ratified the 1975 border agreement with Iran on June 13, 1976, ending an era of hostility between the two neighbors. Iran also closed the last Kurdish refugee camp, which was set up near Shiraz after the agreement ended Iranian support for Kurdish rebels fighting the Iraqi government.

Despite reports of occasional clashes, Kurdistan was relatively quiet as military rule and mass deportations of Kurds to remote southern areas of Iraq took effect. The deportations were halted on July 5, and, on August 26, a two-month amnesty was announced for Kurds still in opposition or in exile. Those who accepted would not be subject to military service or penalties. The government also designated Kurdish areas as primary beneficiaries of a new five-year plan initiated in April, with $100 million allocated for the immediate construction of schools and roads.

New Pipeline Route. Although disputes with its Arab neighbors were less severe than in previous years, Iraq essentially pursued a lone hand. President Ahmad Hasan al-Bakr's regime celebrated its eighth year in power with few domestic political changes. Failure to reach an agreement with Syria over transit fees and prices for Iraqi crude oil shipped through Syrian pipelines to Mediterranean refineries caused Iraq to halt all shipments on April 23. The government later completed a pipeline network through northern Iraq and Turkey to the Turkish port of Dörtyol on the Mediterranean Sea that by-passed both Syria and Lebanon.

The tension between Iraq and Syria, which have been feuding for years, was significantly reduced. A November 26 agreement, mediated by Egyptian diplomats, called for the withdrawal of most military forces along the Iraqi-Syrian border. The move greatly aided Syria, which had much of its army tied down in Lebanon, enforcing the pan-Arab cease-fire. See LEBANON; SYRIA.

The Economy continued strong, buoyed by the August discovery of a new 1-billion-barrel oil field near Basra by Brazil's state petroleum company Petrobras. Industrial projects costing $483 million were inaugurated in February. On August 23, the first phase of the Wadi Tharthar irrigation project, a Russian-built canal linking Wadi Tharthar with the Euphrates River 25 miles (40 kilometers) away, was completed. Poultry farms that will produce 70-million eggs a year and a paper mill near Basra employing 1,113 workers went into operation in October.

The first group of 350 Egyptian peasant families arrived in Iraq on April 1 to work on farms in the Baghdad region. If the program succeeds, it could boost agricultural production for land-rich, population-poor Iraq, and provide additional work for Egypt's huge population.   William Spencer

See also MIDDLE EAST (Facts in Brief Table).

IRELAND. The government lurched from economic to constitutional crises in 1976, and the strains within Prime Minister Liam Cosgrave's coalition of *Fine Gael* (Gaelic People) and Labour parties increased. An economic report prepared for the Bank of Ireland in November predicted that the republic was running "head-long for disaster." President Cearbhall O Dalaigh resigned on October 22 in a dispute over antiterrorist laws. The government's only consolation was that the opposition *Fianna Fáil* (Soldiers of Destiny) remained ineffective.

The Economy was a constant headache. Inflation stuck stubbornly at 16 per cent, unemployment leveled out at 12 per cent of the labor force, growth remained sluggish, the country dived even deeper into debt, and the government appeared helpless.

The crucial blow to the government's economic credibility came at the end of March when national pay talks between unions and employers failed to produce wage restraint. Government ministers had threatened statutory wage controls or extra taxes if restraint was not forthcoming. But the unions went on to press for inflationary wage hikes. The European Community (Common Market) was particularly annoyed. It had arranged a $300-million loan for Ireland on the promise of wage restraints.

Terrorism. As the economic gloom thickened—hardly helped by a two-month bank strike that

Police view the wrecked car in which Britain's ambassador to Ireland was killed when a land mine exploded under it in July near Dublin.

ended in August – public attention was diverted by the government's concentration on Irish Republican Army (IRA) terrorists. A law passed on March 3 was designed to stop IRA guerrillas from Northern Ireland from using the republic as a refuge. It authorized their trial in the republic, even if the terrorist offense had been committed elsewhere.

The IRA hit back on July 21 when Christopher T. E. Ewart-Biggs, Britain's ambassador to Ireland, was killed by a land mine as he drove down a quiet country lane. The Irish parliament was recalled on August 31 to debate far-reaching antiterrorist laws, while a state of emergency was declared. The proposed package increased the penalties for terrorism and gave the army powers of search, arrest, and detention. Despite criticism, the laws were passed largely intact.

President O Dalaigh referred the laws to the supreme court, which subsequently ruled them constitutional. But Defense Minister Patrick Donegan called the president a "thundering disgrace" on account of the delay. O Dalaigh demanded Donegan's resignation, but Cosgrave stuck by his defense minister, who did apologize, however. This did not satisfy the president, who resigned. In the constitutional uproar that followed, Patrick J. Hillery became president November 24.   Andrew F. Neil

See also EUROPE (Facts in Brief Table); GREAT BRITAIN; NORTHERN IRELAND.

ISRAEL. Prime Minister Yitzhak Rabin resigned on Dec. 20, 1976, after the collapse of a coalition that left him with a minority government. He remained as caretaker prime minister. An election to be held in May 1977 was seen as a showdown between politicians who demand a hard line toward the Arabs and moderates who would give up captured Arab land to get a peace treaty.

Until Rabin resigned, Israel had enjoyed relative tranquility in 1976. Its major problems were economic, though continued efforts by ultranationalists to convert the occupied West Bank and other former Arab territories into permanent parts of Israel produced tension with Israeli Arabs.

The question of the occupied territories sharpened in late February with Cabinet approval of the Galilee Development Plan. The plan would requisition 2,500 acres (1,000 hectares) – later increased to 6,000 acres (2,400 hectares) – of Arab-owned land in Galilee for Israeli projects.

Arabs Protest. Supported by Rakah, the Israeli Communist Party, which upholds the right to Palestinian self-determination, the Arab population held a "Day of the Land" general strike on March 30. Clashes between Arabs and police resulted in mass arrests, the deaths of five Israeli Arabs, and some 70 casualties. Rakah members and Arabs won 17 out of 65 seats in May 25 elections for town councils in Galilee, largely as a result of the land policy. Two

Arab *Knesset* (parliament) members quit the ruling Mapai Party to protest the expropriations.

The government also came under attack from other groups. On April 19, some 40,000 members of *Gush Emunim* (Band of the Faithful), an ultra-Orthodox group that believes that God's promise of Israel to Abraham and his heirs includes all Palestine, marched across the entire West Bank to underscore their demands of Jewish rights to the territory.

Entebbe Raid. Israel's national spirit, low since the 1973 war, received a much-needed boost on July 3 when Israeli commandos rescued 103 hostages, most of them Israelis, held at Entebbe Airport in Uganda by the pro-Palestinian hijackers of an Air France plane. The daring raid came after nearly seven days of negotiations with the hijackers, during which it appeared that Israel was backing down on its long-held refusal to deal with terrorists. The hijackers demanded the release of 53 terrorists held in Israeli and European prisons.

Three low-flying C-130 transport planes carried crack commando units, doctors, nurses, and a field hospital. With split-second timing, Israeli troops knocked out the control tower on the main air terminal and stormed an old terminal building where the hostages were held. A number of warplanes were destroyed on the ground to prevent pursuit by the Ugandans, who, under President Idi Amin

Arab women were allowed to vote for the first time in municipal elections held in April in Israeli-occupied West Bank.

Dada, had given considerable support to the terrorists. The action, which took scarcely an hour, cost the lives of three hostages and the American-born Israeli commando chief, Lieutenant Colonel Yehonathan Nethanyahu. Seven of the terrorists were killed, along with 20 or more Ugandan soldiers. See KENYA; UGANDA.

Economic Woes. A decline in gross national product for the first time in 22 years highlighted the Israeli economy's problems. The Israeli pound was devalued an average of 2 per cent per month, and when it reached a low of 8.1 to the U.S. dollar on July 29, it was allowed to float against other currencies. United States aid – originally targeted at $550-million for the June 1976 to October 1976 transitional U.S. fiscal period and $2 billion for the fiscal year from Oct. 1, 1976, to Sept. 30, 1977 – was reduced by the U.S. Senate to $275 million.

Faced with such pressures, the Israeli government announced an austerity program and higher taxes on April 25. A value-added tax on shops and businesses introduced on August 1 brought clashes between police and businessmen, who protested having to keep extra records in order to pay the tax. Government-imposed price increases hit the beleaguered Israeli consumer in November, as basic food prices went up 20 per cent, and fuel prices rose 11 per cent.   William Spencer

See also MIDDLE EAST (Facts in Brief Table).

Tina Anselmi stands next to President Giovanni Leone on July 30 after she became Italy's first woman Cabinet member, the minister of labor.

ITALY began 1976 in an economic crisis that persisted and generated serious new political tensions. The Communist Party, under the leadership of Enrico Berlinguer, increased its Chamber of Deputies strength by 49 to 228 seats and for the first time gained an official voice in the government (see BERLINGUER, ENRICO).

Prime Minister Aldo Moro's coalition government was toppled on January 7 by the economic crisis. Moro formed a new minority regime on February 11, but it lasted only until April 30. Its attempt to limit abortion to victims of rape or cases in which a woman's health was endangered was rejected by other parties, and 30,000 women marched in Rome on April 3, demanding an end to restrictions on abortion. Giulio Andreotti, a Christian Democrat, became prime minister on July 30, heading a one-party minority that could survive only if the Communists in Parliament abstained from voting (see ANDREOTTI, GIULIO).

The Communist Role in Italian politics worried Western diplomats, and the results of the general election on June 20 did nothing to ease their concern. Christian Democrats remained dominant, taking 38.9 per cent of the total vote. But the Communists maintained their post-World War II record of gains, advancing from 27.6 per cent of the vote in 1972 to 33.8 per cent. West German Chancellor Helmut Schmidt said in Washington, D.C., on July

16 that West Germany, Great Britain, France, and the United States would not provide loans for Italy's failing economy if Communists were included in the new Cabinet. United States officials warned that aid would be withdrawn if Italy should adopt a different policy toward the North Atlantic Treaty Organization.

Andreotti ruled out a coalition with the Communists, who, nevertheless, gained the key posts of president of the Chamber of Deputies and mayor of Rome. Andreotti's minority government won a vote of confidence on August 11 by 258 votes to 44 with 303 abstentions.

Economic Crisis. Italy closed its foreign exchange market on January 21 because of a run on the lira and foreign debts of $14 billion requiring annual interest payments of $1.3 billion. The market reopened on March 1 after the government adopted restrictive measures to protect the lira. An import-deposit scheme also helped to strengthen the lira. With inflation continuing at more than 16 per cent, the government began an austerity program in October that boosted telephone rates, gasoline prices, and electricity rates. The bank interest rate was raised to 15 per cent.   Kenneth Brown

See also CHEMICAL INDUSTRY; EUROPE (Facts in Brief Table).

IVORY COAST. See AFRICA.

JAMAICA. See WEST INDIES.

JAPAN

JAPAN. The Lockheed bribery scandal and its wide repercussions dominated politics in Japan in 1976. The U.S. Senate's Subcommittee on Multinational Corporations revealed in February that the Lockheed Aircraft Corporation had paid some $7 million to Yoshio Kodama, a right wing lobbyist who has been a shadowy figure in Japanese politics for many years. The payments were made to influence a Japanese airline company to purchase Lockheed passenger planes.

Subsequent revelations indicated that Lockheed had paid a total of about $12.6 million to Japanese individuals and companies. As a result, former Prime Minister Kakuei Tanaka was arrested and indicted on charges of bribery and violations of Japan's foreign exchange laws (for receiving money illegally brought into the country). He was later released on bail of $690,000. He was billed for $1.8-million in taxes and penalties relating to the $1.7-million he allegedly received. If he is convicted, the money will be confiscated and the taxes and penalties will be canceled.

Two members of the *Diet* (parliament) – the former minister and vice-minister of transportation – were arrested in August on charges of accepting bribes. About 15 others, most of them businessmen, were also arrested for their alleged roles in the Lockheed payoffs. There was no indication of when

trials might be held. Kodama's serious illness was impeding the investigation.

Cabinet Shaken. The scandal caused a crisis in Prime Minister Takeo Miki's Cabinet because he insisted on carrying out a full investigation, a move that won him popular support. Opponents within his Liberal Democratic Party resisted because they feared that additional Lockheed disclosures would be more harmful to the party. A key issue was the identification of *gray officials,* those alleged to have received payments but who were immune from charges because of the statute of limitations.

In September, strong pressure from his rivals nearly forced Miki to resign. But he stayed on and revised his Cabinet on September 15.

The political situation was further complicated when Miki's party suffered stunning reverses in the December 5 general election for the Japanese House of Representatives. Its working margin was cut to a slim majority. Miki resigned as prime minister in early December, and a party caucus began meeting to select a successor as head of the Liberal Democratic Party. On December 22, the party caucus elected Takeo Fukuda, the former deputy prime minister and head of economic planning. Two days later, a Diet vote made him the new prime minister.

The United States government cooperated with

Tokyo residents watch televised hearings in fascination as Japanese Diet investigates charges of Lockheed Aircraft Corporation payoffs.

the Japanese government by supplying information for the ongoing investigation. The Lockheed scandal apparently had no adverse effects on the general course of Japanese-American relations. See INTERNATIONAL TRADE AND FINANCE (Close-Up).

The Economy continued to improve from the 1974 recession low, when the rate of growth of the gross national product was 1.8 per cent under 1973. In the first quarter of 1976, the growth rate was 3.5 per cent, adjusted for inflation, and it was expected that the government's predicted rate of growth of 5.6 per cent for the year might possibly be reached. The government also predicted an 8 per cent increase in consumer prices and a 4.8 per cent increase in wholesale prices for the year. Exports were expected to total about $62 billion and imports about $68 billion.

The Organization for Economic Cooperation and Development announced that the annual increase in consumer prices in Japan was 9 per cent early in the year, compared with 30 per cent in 1974. Foreign currency reserves stood at $15.2 billion in August, an increase of about $3 billion over a 1975 low point.

Russian Pilot. On Sept. 6, 1976, a Russian Air Force lieutenant, seeking asylum in the United States, landed a MIG-25, probably the most advanced fighter plane in the Russian Air Force, at Hakodate Airport on the northern island of Hokkaido. The pilot was flown to the United States, and Japanese and U.S. Air Force personnel dismantled the plane. Analysis reportedly indicated that the plane's equipment was not as technologically advanced as had been thought and that the plane might be an older model MIG-25. Russia strongly criticized the Japanese government's handling of the case. The government returned the plane to Russia when its analysis was completed.

After some years of debate and controversy, the Diet ratified the Nuclear Nonproliferation Treaty on May 24. Japan thus became the 96th nation to sign the treaty, which was originally drafted in 1968. Opponents had argued that Japan should retain the right to develop its own nuclear weapons and that the treaty might inhibit research on nuclear energy.

Miscellany. A special ceremony on November 11 commemorated the 50th anniversary of Emperor Hirohito's accession to the throne on Dec. 25, 1926. His reign is the longest since the legendary Emperor Nintoku, who ruled in the 300s.

A new and architecturally controversial United States Embassy building was opened in Tokyo on September 24. Sadaharu Oh, first baseman of the Tokyo Yomiuri Giants, hit his 715th home run on October 11, surpassing Babe Ruth's total and placing him just 40 home runs behind Henry Aaron's current record.   John M. Maki

See also ASIA (Facts in Brief Table).

JEWS AND JUDAISM. Continuing incidents involving the actions of Arab terrorists against Israel plagued Jewish communities throughout the world in 1976. The most serious involved the June 27 hijacking of a French airliner carrying Israeli and other nationals. It landed at Entebbe, Uganda, where Israeli commandos rescued 103 passengers and crew in a daring raid on July 3. One passenger, Dora Bloch, who held British and Israeli citizenship, had to be left behind in a hospital. She was reportedly killed by Ugandan troops. See ISRAEL.

Relations between Jews and Christians improved. The first Protestant-Jewish and Roman Catholic-Jewish dialogues in history were held in Jerusalem under the joint sponsorship of the International Jewish Committee for Interreligious Affairs, the World Council of Churches, and the Vatican.

In Israel, there were a number of religious conflicts between Jews and Muslims. In January, a judge ruled that Jews could pray on Mount Moriah, a sacred hill where Muslim shrines stand over the ruins of King Solomon's Temple. Subsequent clashes between worshiping Jews and Muslims brought a police ban on Jewish prayers on the sacred hill, a ban that was upheld by the Supreme Court of Israel on March 21.

The West Bank of the River Jordan, a territory of 2,270 square miles (5,880 square kilometers) with roughly 600,000 Arab inhabitants that has been occupied by Israel since June 1967, was the scene of protests by the Gush Emunim, an Orthodox Jewish group. The group demanded the right to establish a settlement near Jericho.

In the United States, the Anti-Defamation League of B'nai B'rith charged in March that 200 U.S. corporations and 25 banks were cooperating with various chambers of commerce in the United States to evade laws that forbid cooperation by U.S. businesses with the Arab economic boycott of Israel. A similar charge was made in September by a U.S. House of Representatives subcommittee after an 18-month investigation. The subcommittee concluded that the Department of Commerce was encouraging American companies to avoid legislation forbidding compliance with the Arab boycott.

Rabbi Arthur Hertzberg, head of the American Jewish Congress, said in April that the American Jewish community, "no longer forced into a physical or psychological ghetto," had stopped regarding anti-Semitism as a problem. As a result, he said, "young American Jews have a weakening sense of Jewish identity and see their task as fighting for the rights of others — the disadvantaged at home and the beleaguered Jewish communities abroad."

At the same meeting, Simcha Dinitz, Israel's ambassador to the United States, warned that the Jewish people could survive "only if American Jews regarded Jews in Israel and in other foreign lands not as 'other' but as one with the Jewish people."

Dressed symbolically as prisoners, British Jews protest Russian limits on Jewish emigration during a Russian official's visit to London in March.

In February, Harvard University announced plans for a $15-million Center for Jewish Studies. The first nondenominational national Jewish women's magazine, *Lilith,* was founded in August.

Orthodox Leadership. Rabbi Walter S. Wurzburger of New York City was elected head of the Rabbinical Council of America in May. This is North America's largest and most influential Orthodox rabbinical body, representing more than 1,000 rabbis in the United States and Canada. Wurzburger heads a congregation in Queens, is a professor of philosophy at Yeshiva University in New York City, and is editor of *Tradition,* Orthodox Judaism's intellectual journal.

Russia. Stanley Lowell, chairman of the National Conference on Soviet Jewry, said in February that according to Russian officials, 750,000 Soviet Jews wanted to leave Russia. About 12,000 emigrated during the year. World Zionist Organization leader Yosef Almogi said in May that 60 per cent chose to emigrate to countries other than Israel once they were outside the Soviet Union.

World Population. The 1974 Jewish population, the most recent figure available, was 14,230,000, up from 14,150,000 in 1973. The *American Jewish Year Book,* which listed the figures in its 1976 edition, estimated the Jewish population in the United States at 5,732,000.　　　Judah Graubart

See also MIDDLE EAST.

JORDAN and Syria increased their cooperation in 1976 as part of their 1975 agreement establishing a joint military high command. The change came after years of estrangement. They agreed on May 1 to build a microwave telecommunications network linking the two countries. Jordan also supported Syrian intervention in the civil war in Lebanon. In July, a Syrian-Jordanian cement industry was set up to use Jordan's abundant limestone deposits to produce cement for Syria. On December 8, the two nations announced plans to unify some governmental systems after a two-day visit by Syrian president Hafiz al-Asad to Amman, the Jordanian capital.

Elections Postponed. Although Jordan was internally stable, continued instability outside its borders prevented an early return of parliamentary government. In a surprise move, King Hussein I reconvened the House of Representatives in February. But he did this in order to amend the Jordanian Constitution to postpone general elections "until the situation warranted them." Then the House was again dissolved. The Cabinet abolished the Arab National Union, successor to the 1971 Jordanian National Union and Jordan's only legal political body, on February 18.

Prime Minister Zayd Rifai resigned on July 13 because of poor health, after three years in office. He was succeeded by Mudhar Badran, former head of internal security. Badran said that control of inflation and improved relations with Syria were his major aims.

King Hussein traveled widely in his role as a moderate Arab spokesman. After much speculation, the United States on September 5 announced the sale – financed by Saudi Arabia – of 14 Hawk air-defense missile batteries to Jordan. Along with the anticipated increase in the Jordanian Army from 65,000 to 85,000 men, the missiles would add greatly to Jordan's military preparedness.

The government launched a new development plan on May 31 that envisaged an annual 12 per cent growth rate with annual expenditures of $2.2-billion. The foreign investment needed for this poured in. The United States Congress approved $223 million in economic aid, while other aid came from Iran, the Arab Fund for Economic and Social Development, the World Bank, and the European Community (Common Market). Jordan's liberal foreign investment law allowing tax and import duty exemptions had encouraged 89 foreign firms to establish branches there.   William Spencer

See also MIDDLE EAST (Facts in Brief Table).

JUDAISM. See JEWS AND JUDAISM.

JUNIOR ACHIEVEMENT (JA). See YOUTH ORGANIZATIONS.

KANSAS. See STATE GOVERNMENT.

KENTUCKY. See STATE GOVERNMENT.

KENYA. Concern over a successor to 85-year-old President Jomo Kenyatta dominated Kenya's politics during 1976. Three senior Cabinet ministers and 20 other members of Parliament supported a constitutional amendment to bar the vice-president from becoming Kenya's interim president. The Constitution called for the vice-president to assume the high office for 90 days following the death, retirement, or disability of the president.

The proposed amendment was directed against Vice-President Daniel Arap Moi, whose opponents did not want him in office for three months before the election of a new president. But on October 8, four Cabinet members and 98 members of Parliament issued a statement opposing the amendment.

United States Secretary of State Henry A. Kissinger visited Kenya in April and May as part of U.S. efforts to establish closer diplomatic ties with black Africa. United States Secretary of Defense Donald H. Rumsfeld visited Kenya in June and agreed to provide Kenya with 12 F-5 jet fighters.

Kenya's relations with neighboring Uganda were severely strained by disputes over trading ties and Kenya's role in an Israeli raid on Uganda's Entebbe Airport to rescue hijacked hostages in July. See UGANDA.   John D. Esseks

See also AFRICA (Facts in Brief Table).

KHMER. See CAMBODIA.

Kenyans living in Uganda flee in July, fearing harassment or death after Uganda accused Kenya of aiding the Israeli raid on Entebbe Airport.

KHULAYFAWI, ABDUL RAHMAN (1930-   ), became prime minister of Syria on Aug. 1, 1976, after Mahmud al-Ayyubi resigned. He had served as prime minister from April 1971 until he retired because of poor health in 1972. The new Syrian Cabinet line-up was announced shortly thereafter.

The retired army general's appointment was interpreted as an attempt to bolster President Hafiz al-Asad's standing with the military as Syria became more deeply involved in the Lebanese civil war. Khulayfawi, Asad's close personal friend and long-time associate, is widely respected in the Syrian Army. The change in government produced no major shifts in Syria's international policies.

Khulayfawi, a member of the Sunni Muslim sect, was born in 1930 and received a military and engineering education. He served in the army, rising to the rank of major general, and was Syria's representative on the Joint Arab Command in Cairo, Egypt, from 1964 to 1967. In 1967, he was named head of the Armored Forces Administration in Damascus. He became chief of the Officers' Board in Syria's Ministry of Defense in 1968. When Asad seized power in Syria in 1970, he appointed Khulayfawi interior minister.   Edward G. Nash

See also SYRIA.

KIWANIS INTERNATIONAL. See COMMUNITY ORGANIZATIONS.

KOREA, NORTH. North Korean troops killed two U.S. Army officers on Aug. 18, 1976, in the Panmunjom demilitarized zone on the 1953 Korean War cease-fire line. The murders occurred while American soldiers were trimming a tree that obstructed a United Nations (UN) observation post's view. UN forces went on alert, and military reinforcements were rushed from the United States.

On August 21, North Korean President Kim Il-song told the UN Command that the murders were "regretful." The U.S. government called this "a positive step," and American troops cut the tree down. An agreement was reached on September 6 to partition the security area.

Spurning U.S. proposals to make the cease-fire agreement more permanent, Kim called on July 22 for "a great national congress" of both Koreas to discuss the withdrawal of U.S. troops from South Korea and the overthrow of the government there.

Premier Kim Il resigned on April 30 and was succeeded by Pak Song-chol. President Kim's son, Kim Chong-il, reportedly was being groomed by his father to succeed him, but was seldom seen.

North Korea continued to default on its foreign debts. And in October, its diplomats were accused by Denmark and Norway of being active in black-market operations.   Henry S. Bradsher

See also ASIA (Facts in Brief Table).

North Korean troops attack a U.S.-South Korean crew of tree trimmers, in white helmets, in Panmunjom in August. Two U.S. officers were killed.

KOREA, SOUTH. Economic prospects improved during 1976. The country overcame severe balance-of-payments problems and increased its gross national product by an estimated 11 per cent. Exports, the key to prosperity because of a heavy dependence on imported raw materials, increased faster than expected. This made the large foreign debt more manageable. President Chung Hee Park announced on January 15 that oil, a major import item, had been discovered near Pohang.

The Opposition. In a Declaration on Democracy and National Salvation, 12 leading opponents of the government called on March 1 for the restoration of basic freedoms and parliamentary democracy and asked Park to resign. They said economic gains partly depended on exploited labor.

Eighteen persons were arrested and tried for this action. They included former President Yun Po-sun; Kim Dae-jung, who almost defeated Park in the 1971 presidential election and was kidnaped in Tokyo in 1973 by Korean agents; and various religious leaders. Yun, Kim, and two others were sentenced on August 28 to eight years in prison for violating an emergency decree that banned all criticism of the government. The other defendants, including former Foreign Minister Chung Il-hyung, were sentenced to prison for from two to five years. The prosecution charged that they "distorted the political situation by claiming there was no freedom in this country."

The leader of the opposition New Democratic Party, Kim Young-sam, was ousted in June because he failed to oppose Park sufficiently. He had been indicted in January on charges of violating Park's emergency decree, but he had not been arrested. Lee Chul-seung then became the opposition party leader.

U.S. Investigation. The United States government began an investigation in October of reports that South Korean agents had tried to buy influence in Washington, D.C., since the late 1960s. Tongsun Park, a South Korean businessman, admitted he made contributions to members of the U.S. Congress. Congressional protection of South Korean interests on food shipments, weapons supplies, and military protection were reportedly sought in a large-scale effort handled by the Korean Central Intelligence Agency. In December, President Park dismissed the head of the Korean Central Intelligence Agency over this matter.

United States Air Force and naval units were rushed to South Korea after the August 18 murder of two American Army officers by North Korean soldiers in the demilitarized zone at Panmunjom (see ARMED FORCES). Direct unification talks between North and South Korea, which began in 1972, remained in recess.   Henry S. Bradsher

See also ASIA (Facts in Brief Table); KOREA, NORTH.

KUWAIT. The one-year Kuwaiti experiment in representative government came to a screeching halt on Aug. 20, 1976. Prime Minister Jabir al-Ahmad al-Sabah resigned, blaming the elected National Assembly for obstruction of vital legislation. The ruler, Emir Sabah al-Salim Al-Sabah, then dissolved the assembly, suspended the Constitution, and clamped strict curbs on Kuwait's normally free press. On September 6, Jabir formed a new Cabinet, with key posts still held by the ruling family.

The parliamentary opposition, chiefly Palestinians and young radicals, criticized government support of Syria's intervention in the Lebanese civil war and denounced the Sinai interim agreement with Israel. The conflict between the government and the press and National Assembly was rooted in social tensions. The Kuwaitis, a minority of 47.5 per cent in their own country, feared loss of control in the face of increasing demands by non-Kuwaitis, notably the 250,000 Palestinians, for political rights. The fact that only male Kuwaiti property holders, who make up only 16 per cent of the population, could vote was another sore point.

Political instability did not affect the economic boom. In June, per capita income was estimated at $11,365, highest in the world. The budget set revenues at $7.1 billion, up 25 per cent, and expenditures at $3.2 billion.   William Spencer

See also MIDDLE EAST (Facts in Brief Table).

LABOR. Unemployment and inflation continued to afflict the United States work force in 1976. The unemployment rate stood at 8.1 per cent in November, compared with a rate of 8.3 per cent in December 1975. Unemployment averaged 8.5 per cent throughout 1975. The Bureau of Labor Statistics (BLS) Consumer Price Index (CPI) rose 5 per cent between November 1975 and November 1976.

The Jobless Rate hit a low of 7.3 per cent in May 1976, after having shown steady improvement since a recession high of 9.2 per cent in May 1975. However, unemployment began climbing again in June and remained close to the 8 per cent level for the remainder of the year. The number of jobless dipped to 7.3 million in May 1976, but rose to 7.8 million by November. The Ford Administration cited a "pause" in the recovery from the 1974 and 1975 recession, and the "extremely abnormal" number of people seeking jobs as factors in the high rate.

Total employment reached 88.1 million in November, 2.7 million more than the number employed in December 1975. This impressive improvement did not make much of a dent in the unemployment rate, because the civilian labor force increased by 2.8 million in the first 11 months of 1976. About half of these new labor force entrants were women, reflecting a 10-year-long trend of increasing female participation in the work force.

Nevertheless, there were signs as 1976 drew to a close that more than an increase in the labor force was keeping unemployment levels high. The layoff rate calculated by the BLS rose to 1.7 per cent per 100 manufacturing employees by October, a sharp upturn from the 1.1 per cent rate in July. In November, the key auto and steel industries announced layoffs. Providing another ominous sign, the November Wholesale Price Index rose 0.6 per cent and showed an 0.8 per cent increase in the industrial commodities index. This marked the sixth consecutive month of relatively large rises.

Preliminary BLS estimates given in the following table show major employment changes in 1976:

	1975	1976*
	(in thousands)	
Total labor force	**94,793**	**96,654**
Civilian labor force	92,613	94,511
Total employment	84,783	87,121
Unemployed	7,830	7,390
Unemployment rate	8.5%	7.8%
Change in real weekly earnings (Workers with 3 dependents— private nonfarm sector)	+0.1%	+0.8%†
Change in output per man-hour (Total private economy)	+2.1%	+3.3%‡

*January to September average, seasonally adjusted, except for armed forces data.
†For 12-month period ending Sept. 30, 1976.
‡Third quarter of 1976, compared with third quarter of 1975.

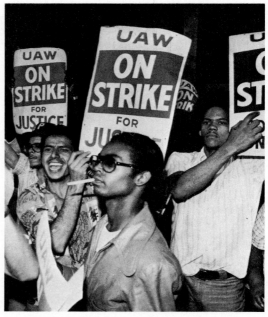

Automobile workers, on strike against the Ford Motor Company, won a new contract that provides a pay hike and 13 more paid days off.

Collective Bargaining. About 4.4 million workers were covered by major union contracts that expired or were reopened in 1976, compared with 2.5-million in 1975. Preliminary estimates showed that major collective-bargaining settlements in the first nine months of 1976 generally provided lower wage raises than agreements reached in 1975. Wage gains averaged 8.9 per cent in the first contract year, and 7 per cent a year over the life of the agreements, compared with 10.2 and 7.8 per cent, respectively, in 1975. With automatic cost-of-living escalator clauses covering an additional 156,000 workers, 6 million workers were covered. Union bargainers stood firm on having maximum payments on existing escalation clauses eliminated.

The United Automobile Workers (UAW) reached a three-year settlement with the Ford Motor Company that moved closer to the UAW goal of establishing a shorter workweek. The agreement was concluded on October 5. Local issues were resolved by November 1, ending the strike that began on September 14.

With the 1974-1975 wave of auto-industry layoffs in mind, the UAW negotiators emphasized cutting working time to create more jobs and preserve existing ones. UAW President Leonard Woodcock called the settlement a "step toward the four-day workweek." The UAW won 13 additional paid days off for Ford auto workers.

The 170,000 auto workers received a 3 per cent wage increase plus 20 cents an hour on Oct. 18, 1976, with additional 3 per cent raises due in September 1977 and September 1978. Skilled employees were to receive an additional 20 to 25 cents an hour over the term of the contract. The cost-of-living escalator clause was retained, and the contract provided for a possible one-time inflation bonus for Ford retirees.

The contract established more liberal medical benefits. The UAW also won tighter limits on Ford's right to contract out work that could be done by skilled tradesmen.

Ford, however, won some of its demands to cut health-care costs, including moving the effective date of health-care coverage for new employees from the second to the third month after hiring.

On November 5, the UAW reached a similar agreement with Chrysler Corporation for 118,000 workers. The same terms were extended to 390,000 auto workers at General Motors Corporation. The general pattern of the contracts was also extended to cover 100,000 UAW members employed by the major farm-implement manufacturers.

Rubber Strike. The major U.S. tire producers were hit by the United Rubber Workers (URW) 4½-month strike in 1976, beginning on April 21. The first settlement came about on August 24 at the Goodyear Tire & Rubber Company. The Firestone

Tire & Rubber Company settled on August 26, and settlements were then reached at Uniroyal, Incorporated, and B. F. Goodrich Company, ending the lengthy walkout by mid-September.

The agreements established unlimited cost-of-living adjustments. The workers received wage increases of $1.35 an hour over the life of the three-year contract, with additional increases given to Firestone, Goodrich, and Uniroyal workers to equalize pay differences resulting from different contract terms negotiated in 1973. Skilled tradesmen received an additional 40 cents an hour. The pacts also improved pension and layoff provisions, night-shift pay differentials, and insurance benefits.

Trucking Settlement. Serious harm to the economy was averted when the International Brotherhood of Teamsters reached three-year settlements with the trucking industry on April 2 and 3. An industrywide strike began April 1. The agreements gave 300,000 local truckdrivers a $1.65-an-hour wage hike over three years. Some 100,000 long-haul drivers received comparable increases.

A dispute centered around an 11-cent-per-hour annual ceiling on cost-of-living adjustments. In return for unlimited adjustments in 1977 and 1978, the union agreed to smaller increases in relation to rises in the cost of living. The employers also agreed to increase their contributions for pensions and health and welfare. The Teamsters won three days annual sick leave. Similar terms were extended to about 40,000 Chicago-area drivers, who did not participate in the nationwide bargaining.

Electrical Workers' Contracts. On June 27, the General Electric Company (GE) reached three-year agreements with the International Union of Electrical Workers (IUE) for 70,000 workers, and with the unaffiliated United Electrical Workers for 17,000. Another 27,000 GE workers represented by 10 unions won similar contracts. The contracts raised wages by $24 a week on June 28, 1976. The workers would receive either $10 a week or 4 per cent increases — whichever was larger — in 1977 and 1978. Some 21,000 skilled tradesmen received from $2 to $20 more a week. Other provisions included six weeks of paid vacation for workers with 30 or more years of service and improved pension, early retirement, and insurance provisions. Brief walkouts preceded similar settlements for 40,000 workers at Westinghouse Electric Corporation in July.

Other Agreements benefited 180,000 members of the International Ladies' Garment Workers' Union and 90,000 workers employed by menswear manufacturers; more than 30,000 members of the Amalgamated Meat Cutters and Butchers union; and 60,000 cannery workers in California represented by the Teamsters.

The Washington (D.C.) *Post* reached agreements with three craft unions in February, ending their role in a strike that began in October 1975. Howev-er, the pressmen were still picketing as 1976 ended. In April, the financially ailing *Washington Star* reached accords with 10 unions, eliminating 200 of 1,700 union jobs to save $6 million a year.

Federal White-Collar Employees received an average 4.83 per cent pay raise on October 1, prompting three of five union officials on the Federal Employee Pay Council to resign. The unions contended a flat 8.25 per cent raise was called for.

President Gerald R. Ford signed a bill on October 1 excluding members of Congress, federal judges, and high-level federal appointees from receiving the raise. The legislation eliminated the 1 per cent bonus from cost-of-living adjustments on pensions.

Strike Activity increased in 1976. The BLS reported 33.6 million days of idleness in the first nine months, 8.3 million more than a year earlier.

The Teamsters staged two strikes against the United Parcel Service (UPS). A walkout by 14,000 workers that ended on May 17 crippled UPS Midwest facilities for 17 days. About 18,000 Teamsters struck UPS in 15 Eastern states from September 15 to December 9.

About half of Canada's unionized workers staged a one-day strike in October to protest wage controls. See CANADA.

A month-long wildcat strike that eventually involved 90,000 United Mine Workers (UMW)

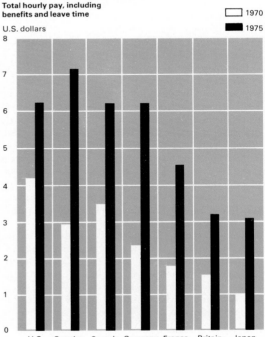

Closing the World Wage Gap

Total hourly pay, including benefits and leave time

☐ 1970 ■ 1975

U.S. dollars

Source: U.S. Bureau of Labor Statistics

Copies of a Paris newspaper litter the Champs Élysées on February 21 after striking newspaper workers intercepted and ended private deliveries of it.

members began on July 19 over a job-posting dispute by a UMW local in West Virginia. A federal judge fined the strikers $50,000. The strike then spread through the Appalachian region as miners became angered over what they felt was unfair federal intervention with their right to strike.

Farmworkers in California suffered a setback on November 2, when voters defeated Proposition 14, which would have solidified rights gained under the 1975 Agriculture Labor Relations Act. The act would have been written into the state constitution, and several pro-labor provisions would have been added, including the right of union organizers to campaign on growers' property for three hours a day. The United Farm Workers of America contended that such campaigning was necessary, because many farmworkers live on the farms and ranches. The growers, however, argued this provision would violate their property rights.

Union Affairs. The 350,000-member Amalgamated Clothing Workers of America and the 160,000-member Textile Workers Union of America approved their merger on June 1, to form the Amalgamated Clothing and Textile Workers Union. Clothing workers' chief Murray H. Finley became president of the new union, while Sol Stetin, who headed the textile workers, became its senior executive vice-president.

UMW President Arnold R. Miller saw his power eroded at the union's annual convention, which began on September 23 in Cincinnati, Ohio. The convention advanced the union's scheduled December 1977 presidential election to June 1977. The delegates also restored control of dues collections to UMW districts, out of Miller's direct control.

Edward Sadlowski, director of the United Steelworkers of America's Chicago area district 31, announced in September that he would seek the presidency of the 1.4-million steelworkers union in its February 1977 election. He stated that the current leadership had "grown soft" and said he would seek tougher contract provisions on job security and occupational health and safety issues. In response to Sadlowski's challenge, retiring Steelworkers President I. W. Abel accused unnamed "outsiders" of trying to take over the union.

IUE President Paul Jennings retired for health reasons on June 1. He was replaced by David J. Fitzmaurice, who had been secretary-treasurer.

Most of the 16 board members of the Teamsters' Central States Pension Fund resigned in October. Because of federal pressure, the board was then streamlined to five representatives of the union and five for the employers. The fund was under federal investigation because of its questionable lending practices.   Leon Bornstein

See also CABINET; ECONOMICS; NEW YORK CITY; NEWARK; SAN FRANCISCO.

LAOS. The Lao People's Revolutionary Party tightened its hold on the country in 1976, enforcing rigid discipline. Former officials and army officers, as well as ordinary citizens regarded as suspect, were shipped to camps for "re-education."

Paramilitary units began to patrol restless areas. Townspeople by the thousands were resettled in the countryside, and the first collective farms were set up. Private shops were tolerated, but only until the official People's Collective stores could be established. Shops suffered from a shortage of essentials.

Heavy-Handed Measures were, in part, a reaction to continued armed resistance. An estimated 150,000 Laotians fled to Thailand, and some of them formed guerrilla units. Frequently, however, the "enemy saboteurs" turned out to be peasants recrossing the Mekong River to reclaim a family water buffalo.

But economic stress, much more than armed opposition, lay at the root of the new regime's woes. The off-and-on sealing of the Thai border denied landlocked Laos most of its essentials, from soap to spare parts. One deputy premier argued that the border closing was a blessing because "we now have vegetables, chickens, and meat [of our own]." But the foodstuffs were so scarce that every government ministry and department in Vientiane, the capital, was required to grow its own vegetables and raise its own beef on the hoof.

Friends Help. In this crisis, help came from three sources. The principal one was Vietnam, where many of the new Laotian leaders, including Prime Minister Kayson Phomvihan, had been trained. Russia supplied oil, food, and transport equipment. Russians also replaced many of the United States technical advisers and provided air service. In June, Russia promised to build a town for 15,000 persons. China's main effort was the continued building of highways from China across Laos to the borders of Cambodia and Thailand.

The U.S. aid mission was forced out of the country in mid-1975. At that point, Washington halted all assistance to the fragile Laos economy but kept open the U.S. Embassy, which had a staff of 27. A Laotian deputy premier was quoted as saying of the U.S. ambassador: "If he wants to leave, we cannot prevent him. If he chooses to stay, he can remain here as a good friend." But Kayson told an interviewer that "many difficulties still lie ahead . . . because the United States has not yet given up its dark design against our country. It's seeking all means to check our advance."

In September, the government banned contraceptives and all other forms of birth control in order to build up the nation's population, which has been decimated by more than a decade of war. A government official explained that a larger population is needed to fill the empty land.   Mark Gayn

See also ASIA (Facts in Brief Table).

LASSER, LOUISE (1942-   ), an American actress, won popularity in 1976 playing the title role in a new television series, "Mary Hartman, Mary Hartman." Lasser portrays a member of a disaster-plagued family in a show that is described as a satire on soap operas.

Her hair in braids and clad in juvenile dresses, Mary Hartman views the unbelievable problems that confront her, her troubled husband, and others with a blank stare and such forgettable pronouncements as, "Language is half the problem of communicating."

Louise Lasser was born in New York City, the only child of S. Jay Lasser, a tax expert. She attended private progressive schools in New York City, then studied political theory at Brandeis University.

She studied philosophy and literature at the New School for Social Research in New York City, acting under Sanford Meisner, and improvisational acting as a member of Elaine May's revue *The Third Ear.*

Lasser married comedian Woody Allen in 1966, but they were divorced in 1970. Her television roles include parts in Ingmar Bergman's *The Lie* and the TV movie *Isn't It Shocking.* She has had film roles in *Slither* and three Allen movies — *Bananas, Take the Money and Run,* and *Everything You Always Wanted to Know About Sex.*   Joseph P. Spohn

See also TELEVISION (Close-Up).

LATIN AMERICA. Inflation, trade deficits, and recession continued to bedevil the governments of Latin America during 1976. Many countries began turning from the Marxist, socialist, or populist economic theories that they had hoped would solve their problems, to seek solutions in more orthodox approaches. Indeed, if the ideas of any one economist could be said to command the most respect in Latin America, they were those of Nobel Prize winner Milton Friedman of the University of Chicago, a conservative whose monetarist theories stress balanced budgets and minimal government interference in free enterprise.

In every case of government change during the year, the shift was apparently toward conservatism in varying degrees. As a result, foreign investors, who had been all but shut out by radical governments, found many new regimes offering them at least a qualified welcome once again.

Mexico, which has one official political party, changed presidents in an election held on July 4. The new president, Jose Lopez Portillo, took office on December 1 even as the once-stable peso was declining sharply in value. He was expected to follow a less radical economic and political course than his predecessor, Luis Echeverría Alvarez. See LOPEZ PORTILLO, JOSE.

Other Government Switches during the year came about through military intervention. The

The Organization of American States meets in Santiago, Chile, in June. Violations of human rights were an important topic of discussion.

most dramatic took place in Argentina when army Lieutenant General Jorge Rafael Videla overthrew President María Estela (Isabel) Martínez de Perón on March 24 in a bid to counter the threat of hyperinflation, widespread corruption, and mounting attacks from terrorists. In Ecuador, Vice-Admiral Alfredo Poveda Burbano headed an armed forces movement that unseated another military president, General Guillermo A. Rodriguez Lara, on January 11. In Uruguay, the military, openly exercising the control they were known to hold over the government, replaced President Juan M. Bordaberry Arocena on June 12 with another civilian, Aparicio Mendez Manfredini.

Even Peru's populist military regime, the most radical and innovative in Latin America, showed signs of becoming more conservative. President Francisco Morales Bermudez Cerruti, who took over in a bloodless coup d'état in 1975, moderated the course of the so-called Peruvian Revolution under pressure of a heavy foreign debt burden, a severe trade deficit, and obvious shortcomings in some of the most radical programs.

Human Rights. The Argentine coup left Colombia and Venezuela as the only major countries on the South American continent still under civilian rule. Efforts by military regimes to wipe out their enemies on the left brought international charges of torture and brutality against several governments.

Chile was again cited for violations of human rights in reports to the United Nations (UN) and in a study presented by the Inter-American Commission on Human Rights during the Sixth General Assembly of the Organization of American States (OAS) held in Santiago, Chile, in June. International human rights organizations also leveled charges against alleged excesses by the military and police in Uruguay, Argentina, and Paraguay.

A report detailing "cruel, inhuman, and degrading" treatment of political prisoners in Cuba was also presented to the OAS assembly; but officials said it arrived too late to be debated, and it received little publicity. Panamanian exiles charged the government of strongman Omar Torrijos Herrera with human rights violations; United States congressmen denounced Mexico for torture and brutal treatment of Americans held in Mexican jails, mostly on drug charges. United States and Mexican authorities "agreed to study" proposals to exchange prisoners so that nationals of each country could serve their sentences in their own countries.

The OAS meeting in Santiago was dominated by the alleged human rights violations committed by the host country. Mexico, which had already broken diplomatic relations with Chile over the 1973 ouster of the late Marxist President Salvador Allende Gossens by the military, refused to attend. On June 18, despite an adverse report concerning widespread torture and human rights violations in Chile, the assembly passed a mild resolution urging Chile "to continue to improve the treatment of political prisoners and to continue to cooperate with future OAS investigations of the situation."

Diplomatic Journey. United States Secretary of State Henry A. Kissinger attended the assembly from June 7 through June 10 as part of a Latin American tour that included stops in the Dominican Republic, Bolivia, and Mexico. His June 8 speech went further than any previous U.S. declaration on violations of human rights in the Western Hemisphere. Kissinger noted that Chile was making progress in curbing abuses, but said, "The condition of human rights as assessed by the OAS Human Rights Commission has impaired our relationship with Chile and will continue to do so."

The ruling Chilean junta allowed the full text of the condemnatory OAS report to be printed in *El Mercurio,* a Santiago newspaper. It was followed, however, by a long refutation of the charges by the Chilean junta, which claimed the report was based on "declarations of persons without scruples or badly informed." The junta also argued that it was necessary to "maintain legal and administrative measures that limit the freedoms and rights of man in order to protect precisely the most important right of all, the right to a secure life."

Trade Act Deplored. The OAS delegates also condemned the U.S. Trade Reform Act of 1974, which denied preferential benefits to Venezuela and Ecuador as members of the Organization of Petroleum Exporting Countries (OPEC) even though they did not take part in the 1973 oil embargo. The delegates, in addition, expressed hope that a new Panama Canal treaty would be concluded between the United States and Panama by the end of 1976. Kissinger promised that the United States would take a number of unilateral steps to improve trade relations with OAS countries. On June 10, he expressed Washington, D.C.'s displeasure with the structure and financing of the OAS. He said the OAS bureaucracy should be cut back and the U.S. share of its budget reduced.

Earlier in the year, Kissinger made his first official tour of Latin America. In February, he stopped in Venezuela, Peru, Brazil, Colombia, and Costa Rica. Most of the discussions centered around Latin American complaints against the trade act. Kissinger declared that President Gerald R. Ford's efforts to modify it were being blocked by Congress.

Mixed Reactions. Kissinger's reception by leaders in Venezuela, Peru, and Colombia was described as "cordial but cool." Peruvian President Francisco Morales reportedly made him wait outside his office for 10 minutes before their 55-minute interview. In Costa Rica, however, Foreign Minister Gonzalo Facio hailed him as "one of the greatest architects of world peace" and said that Costa Rica proudly counted itself a U.S. ally.

Kissinger's meetings in Brazil with President Ernesto Geisel and other top officials were the highlights of the trip. On February 21, he signed a pact in which the United States in effect recognized Brazil as the major power in Latin America. The pact stipulated that the United States and Brazil would hold consultations twice a year on any issues that either side wished to raise and that the U.S. secretary of state would travel to Brazil once a year to consult with the Brazilian foreign minister. Newspapers in Mexico, Colombia, and Venezuela immediately denounced the pact as an affront to their countries, and U.S. Senator Edward M. Kennedy (D., Mass.) chided Kissinger for favoring a country with a military government.

Central America. Kissinger had planned to hold a summit meeting with all the Central American presidents on February 24 in Costa Rica, but he had to content himself with conferring only with the foreign ministers of Honduras, El Salvador, Panama, Nicaragua, and Guatemala. The leaders of Guatemala, El Salvador, and Honduras said they would be unable to attend because of pressing domestic matters, but it was thought in diplomatic circles that they questioned the propriety of presidents traveling to meet with a secretary of state.

Troops of the U.S. 193rd Infantry Brigade carry out a training exercise in the Panama Canal Zone, a continuing source of U.S.-Panamanian friction.

On his way back to Washington, D.C., Kissinger's plane touched down briefly in Guatemala so that he could view Guatemala City, which had been devastated by an earthquake on February 4 that killed more than 22,000 persons and injured about 74,000. Officials estimated that as many as 5,000 more victims might be buried under rubble. The number of homeless was placed at 1 million persons — nearly one-sixth of Guatemala's population. The quake registered 7.5 on the Richter scale, and its epicenter was placed 30 miles (48 kilometers) southwest of Guatemala City, but it sent out shock waves that were felt as far away as Mexico City, Mexico.

In Honduras, the earthquake destroyed parts of three towns near the Guatemalan border and caused flooding and power failures. But it resulted in no deaths. Honduras was still recovering from the ravages of Hurricane Fifi, which killed about 10,000 persons in 1974.

The U.S. government provided an immediate $3.6 million in emergency aid, and nearly $15 million came in voluntary contributions from the United States within six days of the quake. The OAS contributed $500,000, and most other Latin American countries sent food, clothing, medical supplies, doctors, and relief experts.

United States Army helicopters ferried supplies to isolated villages, and U.S. military personnel from the Panama Canal Zone helped Guatemalan

Facts in Brief on Latin American Political Units

Country	Population	Government	Monetary Unit*	Foreign Trade (million U.S. $) Exports	Imports
Argentina	25,776,000	President Jorge Rafael Videla	peso (238 = $1)	2,962	3,947
Bahamas	228,000	Governor General Sir Milo B. Butler; Prime Minister Lynden O. Pindling	dollar (1 = $1)	2,216	2,482
Barbados	251,000	Governor General Sir Deighton Harcourt Lyle Ward; Prime Minister J. M. G. Adams	dollar (2 = $1)	107	217
Belize	150,000	Governor Richard Neil Posnett; Premier George Price	dollar (1.9 = $1)	45	45
Bolivia	5,907,000	President Hugo Banzer Suarez	peso (20 = $1)	443	558
Brazil	123,208,000	President Ernesto Geisel	cruzeiro (11.7 = $1)	8,659	13,558
Chile	10,942,000	President Augusto Pinochet Ugarte	peso (13.9 = $1)	1,661	1,811
Colombia	26,326,000	President Alfonso Lopez Michelsen	peso (33.3 = $1)	1,248	1,268
Costa Rica	2,115,000	President Daniel Oduber Quiros	colón (8.6 = $1)	489	699
Cuba	9,455,000	President Fidel Castro	peso (1 = $1.21)	2,669	2,652
Dominican Republic	4,988,000	President Joaquin Balaguer	peso (1 = $1)	894	889
Ecuador	7,688,000	Supreme Council President Alfredo Poveda Burbano	sucre (25 = $1)	912	943
El Salvador	4,349,000	President Arturo Armando Molina Barraza	colón (2.5 = $1)	515	601
Grenada	95,000	Governor General Sir Leo V. DeGale; Prime Minister Eric M. Gairy	dollar (2.4 = $1)	12	24
Guatemala	6,187,000	President Kjell Eugenio Laugerud Garcia	quetzal (1 = $1)	647	800
Guyana	814,000	President Raymond Arthur Chung; Prime Minister Forbes Burnham	dollar (2.6 = $1)	363	341
Haiti	4,710,000	President Jean-Claude Duvalier	gourde (5 = $1)	78	121
Honduras	3,070,000	Chief of State Juan Alberto Melgar Castro	lempira (2 = $1)	283	400
Jamaica	2,131,000	Governor General Florizel A. Glasspole; Prime Minister Michael Norman Manley	dollar (1 = $1.10)	784	1,124
Mexico	62,314,000	President Jose Lopez Portillo	peso (20 = $1)	2,909	6,581
Nicaragua	2,280,000	President Anastasio Somoza Debayle	cordoba (7.1 = $1)	375	517
Panama	1,774,000	President Demetrio B. Lakas; Chief of the Government Omar Torrijos Herrera	balboa (1 = $1)	283	870
Paraguay	2,650,000	President Alfredo Stroessner	guarani (126 = $1)	176	213
Peru	16,128,000	President Francisco Morales Bermudez Cerruti; Prime Minister Guillermo Arbulu Galliani	sol (65 = $1)	1,301	2,556
Puerto Rico	3,209,000	Governor Carlos Romero Barcelo	dollar (U.S.)	3,303	5,022
Surinam	490,000	President Johan H. E. Ferrier; Prime Minister Henck A. E. Arron	guilder (1.8 = $1)	277	262
Trinidad and Tobago	1,116,000	President Ellis Emmanuel Innocent Clarke; Prime Minister Eric E. Williams	dollar (2.4 = $1)	1,773	1,471
Uruguay	3,138,000	President Aparicio Mendez Manfredini	peso (3.6 = $1)	384	547
Venezuela	12,612,000	President Carlos Andres Perez	bolivar (4.3 = $1)	10,134	5,401

*Exchange rates as of Dec. 1, 1976

soldiers keep order. The efficiency of the Guatemalan military drew praise from observers who had witnessed the chaos and official corruption that hampered the distribution of relief supplies in Managua, Nicaragua, after the devastating earthquake there in December 1972.

Regional Groups. The Latin American Economic System (SELA), a regional grouping that excludes the United States, held its first ministerial meeting at its new headquarters in Caracas, Venezuela, in January. The delegates denounced the U.S. Trade Reform Act and voted to support efforts of developing nations at the UN to establish a "new international economic order." They also proclaimed the right of Latin American nations to "regulate the operations of transnational corporations" within their borders. A major goal of SELA is to establish Latin American multinational corporations, presumably state-owned enterprises, to compete with big foreign firms. Mexico and Venezuela presented specific plans for 60 such enterprises for the SELA secretariat to analyze.

Bank Policies Questioned. At the annual meeting of the Inter-American Development Bank (IADB) held in Cancún, Mexico, in May, the bank's lending policies came under heavy fire from Peru, Bolivia, and Ecuador. Peru charged that the IADB discriminated against Peru, Chile, and Colombia because they were countries of "intermediate" development and that (1) it had refused to aid the Andean Group's Andean Development Corporation, (2) had neglected to finance exports adequately, and (3) had ignored urban development needs. Bolivia claimed the IADB consistently favored Argentina, Brazil, Mexico, and Venezuela, the region's most developed countries, with its loans. Ecuador complained that it received fewer loans than the other countries and also got harsher payment terms.

The Andean Common Market (ANCOM), the most successful regional trade agreement in Latin America, suffered a setback in 1976 when Chile withdrew. The Chileans quarreled with the other members – Venezuela, Colombia, Ecuador, Peru, and Bolivia – over the strict rules that all members are required to apply to foreigners wishing to invest in an ANCOM country. Chile wanted to relax the rules in order to encourage foreign investment. The others agreed to liberalize the rules somewhat, but not as much as Chile wished. Chile also wanted to lower tariff barriers within ANCOM and to the outside world more rapidly, but the other countries wanted to go slow to protect their own infant industries. Everett G. Martin

See also articles on the various Latin American countries in this section and PARAMARIBO and SURINAM in Section Five.

LAW. See CIVIL RIGHTS; COURTS AND LAWS; CRIME; SUPREME COURT OF THE UNITED STATES.

LEBANON. Civil war continued to tear the country apart through most of 1976. More than 55 cease-fires were made and broken; the 30th, and shortest, lasted just 15 minutes on May 14. During fighting that pitted Muslims against Christians, Christians against the Palestine Liberation Organization (PLO), and elements of both against invading Syrian forces at times, Lebanese politicians struggled to find an acceptable formula for the reorganization of national life.

On January 28, when Lebanon's de facto partition into Christian and Muslim sectors was effectively completed, Prime Minister Rashid Karame's Cabinet proposed a 12-point political reform program. It included equal representation of Muslims and Christians in the Chamber of Deputies, civil service reforms, and election of a prime minister by majority vote in the Chamber. The program theoretically met most of the Muslim demands that had set off the original conflict, but distrust between the various factions prevented its adoption.

The Election. In addition, President Sleiman Frangie refused to resign so that a government of national unity could be formed. The Chamber met in Beirut on April 10 and voted to amend the Constitution to allow presidential elections to be held six months prior to the expiration of an incumbent's term of office. Frangie signed the amendment under protest on April 24. After several delays, the election was held on May 8, and a majority of 66 deputies elected Elias Sarkis, governor of the Central Bank, who had lost to Frangie by one vote in 1970. Muslim deputies boycotted the election. Sarkis took office on September 23 under Syrian Army protection. See SARKIS, ELIAS.

The New President faced monumental problems. What little stability existed resulted from the presence of Syrian military forces. As early as February, the cost of the civil war was estimated at $4-billion in 10 months, with 30 per cent of Lebanon's industry destroyed and 250,000 workers jobless. By year's end, the death toll approached 100,000 persons, with tens of thousands more wounded, and hundreds of thousands displaced or homeless.

The most promising development was a cease-fire negotiated in late October in Riyadh, Saudi Arabia, by Arab leaders and PLO leader Yasir Arafat. It set up a joint Arab peacekeeping force. On November 15, Syrian troops, the main element of the Arab force, occupied Beirut and imposed a cease-fire. Later in the month, the Syrians occupied other important Lebanese cities and Christian and Muslim strongholds. In December, Sarkis named a new prime minister, Salim Ahmad al-Huss, who then formed a largely apolitical interim Cabinet to begin the long and painful process of rebuilding national unity. William Spencer

See also MIDDLE EAST (Facts in Brief Table); SYRIA.

LÉGER, JULES (1913-   ), governor general of Canada, carried out a full round of public duties in 1976 after recovering from a stroke suffered six months after taking office in 1974. A speech difficulty made it necessary for his wife, Gabrielle, to share the reading of the formal speech from the throne at the opening of the second session of the 30th Parliament of Canada on October 12.

The governor general and Madame Léger took an active part in ceremonies at the Olympic Games in Montreal. They were present when Queen Elizabeth II, as the formal head of the Canadian state, opened the games on July 17. The governor general went to Vancouver, B.C., on May 31 to open Habitat, the United Nations Conference on Human Settlements, as well as a new Museum of Anthropology housing the University of British Columbia's collection of Pacific Northwest Indian material. The Légers' travels during 1976 took them to the Northwest Territories and the Yukon Territory in late May and to Washington, D.C., for a private visit in April.

The governor general made his customary summer visit to Quebec City despite a fire earlier in the year that damaged part of the Citadel, his official residence. He used the Canadian destroyer *Iroquois,* docked at Quebec, Que., as a base from which to work in September.   David M. L. Farr

LESOTHO. See AFRICA.

LÉVESQUE, RENÉ (1922-   ), an advocate of independence for the Canadian province of Quebec, and his Parti Québécois scored a stunning victory in an election held on Nov. 15, 1976. By defeating the governing Liberal Party in the largely French-speaking province, Lévesque greatly escalated the growing question of independent status for Quebec. See CANADA; QUEBEC.

Lévesque was born on Aug. 24, 1922, in New Carlisle on the Gaspé Peninsula. Under the tutelage of his father, a lawyer, Lévesque learned to read before starting school; he also acquired studious habits that made him an excellent scholar. In 1943, he dropped out of law school at Laval University to work for the French-language services of the U.S. Office of War Information.

He left a notable radio and television career in May 1960 to enter politics on the Liberal Party ticket. He was elected a deputy and subsequently served as provincial minister of public works, of hydraulic resources, of natural resources, and of family and social welfare.

In 1967, Lévesque broke with the Liberals and founded the Sovereignty Movement Association, which in 1968 developed into the Parti Québécois. In elections held in 1970, his party won 23 per cent of the vote; in 1973, it captured 30 per cent; and in 1976, it captured 41 per cent.   Paul C. Tullier

LIBERIA. See AFRICA.

LIBRARY. Drastic funding cutbacks and consequent reductions in library service continued to plague libraries in 1976 in the United States and Canada. Among the hardest hit were the San Francisco Public Library and New York City's Queens Borough Public Library. The latter was forced to discontinue its bookmobile program, cancel its building program, and cut hours at branch libraries. A cutback in city aid forced the Riverside (Calif.) City and County Public Library to reduce its staff, hours of service, and book buying. The National Library of Canada had to eliminate its reference services on weekends and holidays. There were numerous other cutbacks in the two countries.

The American Library Association (ALA) estimated that U.S. libraries spend $1.5 billion a year. It called for an expansion of about 20 per cent in library funds, to be provided by the federal government. At present, only about 5 per cent of the funds supporting U.S. libraries are federal.

The National Center for Educational Statistics reported in April that 52.9 per cent of the average library budget goes for salaries, while only 12.4 per cent is used to buy books. The rest goes for plant operation and improvement and audiovisual and microfilm acquisitions.

Library of Congress. Daniel J. Boorstin faced his first crisis as the new Librarian of Congress when the U.S. House of Representatives, led by Teno Roncalio (D., Wyo.), attempted to convert the nearly completed James A. Madison Memorial Building of the Library of Congress into a fourth House office building. Aroused librarians mustered enough public support to force House leaders to abandon the plan.

In a turnabout, the House on February 24 authorized $33 million to complete the building for library use. The additional money was required because bids on the final phase pushed the total cost beyond the $90 million originally appropriated for the marble building.

New Buildings. The Rensselaer Polytechnic Institute in Troy, N.Y., dedicated its new Richard Gilman Folsom Library in May. The $6.9-million library has a capacity of 500,000 volumes and can seat 800 students. The John F. Kennedy Library Corporation finished plans for the construction of a $12-million library complex on a 9.5-acre (3.8-hectare) site overlooking Boston Harbor. The eight-story building will have a museum and public visitor facilities on the lower two floors and archives and research facilities on the upper six levels. The site is on the Columbia Point commuter campus of the University of Massachusetts in Dorchester.

The annual ALA conference, held in Chicago in July, celebrated the 100th year of the ALA. About 9,000 persons attended.   Robert J. Shaw

See also AMERICAN LIBRARY ASSOCIATION; CANADIAN LIBRARY ASSOCIATION.

LIBYA. President Muammar Muhammad al-Qadhaafi held his post and most of his popularity in Libya during 1976, despite complaints by other Arab nations against his meddling in their internal affairs. His principal opponent was Egypt, where former Planning Minister Omar Meheishi took refuge after breaking with Qadhaafi in 1975. Efforts by Libyan agents to kidnap Meheishi led Egypt to arrest 27 persons accused of being Libyan spies. Libya reacted by expelling 3,000 Egyptians who lacked work permits.

Qadhaafi was also implicated in a July 2 attempt to oust Sudan's President Gaafar Muhammed Nimeiri. The rebel force, made up of Sudanese tribesmen and African mercenaries, was trained and launched from bases in Libya. See SUDAN.

Without public protest from the other countries involved, Libya issued new official maps in September that expanded its southern lands to include some 52,000 square miles (135,000 square kilometers) of possibly mineral-rich land in Algeria, Chad, and Niger.

Opposition to Qadhaafi involved mainly university students. There were demonstrations in January, and on April 7 a riot between pro- and anti-Qadhaafi students in Tripoli caused 250 casualties. In May, Qadhaafi issued an amnesty for all Libyans abroad. The action followed demands by a Paris-based Libyan exile organization, the Libyan National Grouping, and by Meheishi, for general presidential elections, trade unions, and the restoration of democratic rights.

Difficulties developed with Tunisia in March. Several Libyans were arrested in Tunis when a plot against President Habib Bourguiba was foiled. Tunisia charged that Libya was seeking to "avenge the collapse of the Libyan-Tunisian merger" in 1974. As relations worsened, Libya expelled some 6,800 Tunisian workers.

The Economy continued to emphasize industrial diversification to reduce Libya's dependence on oil. The budget issued on January 8 showed an increase of $84 million to a total of $1.7 billion. The five-year plan that went into effect on January 30 earmarked $395 million for power projects. Russia and France agreed to supply Libya with nuclear power stations for Libya's electric power network.

A glass factory that is expected to meet all domestic requirements began production on May 8 in Al Aziziyah. A prefabricated-housing plant opened in Tripoli on July 2, and Bengasi cement-plant production capacity was enlarged to 440,000 short tons (400,000 metric tons) annually.   William Spencer

See also AFRICA (Facts in Brief Table).

LIECHTENSTEIN. See EUROPE.

LIONS INTERNATIONAL. See COMMUNITY ORGANIZATIONS.

Libya's New Boundaries

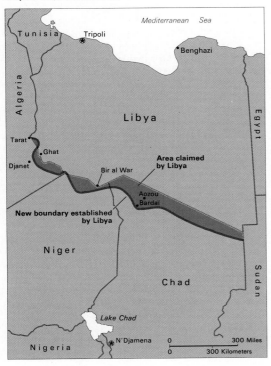

Mediterranean Sea

Tunisia — Tripoli

Benghazi

Algeria

Egypt

Libya

Tarat
•Ghat

Djanet

Area claimed by Libya

Bir al War

Aozou
•Bardaï

New boundary established by Libya

Niger

Sudan

Chad

Lake Chad

Nigeria   N'Djamena   0 — 300 Miles

0 — 300 Kilometers

LITERATURE. The year 1976 was mildly disappointing for American literature, especially in fiction. Although the publishing industry did well at the cash register, its efforts produced few home-grown landmarks. But the reader was not cheated. If there were few noteworthy American novels, for example, the influx of new fiction from abroad more than made up for that dearth. And the best of these foreign novels came from Latin America.

The most avidly awaited was Gabriel García Marquez' *The Autumn of the Patriarch,* a novel of a tyrant's death that was packed with the surreal thunder and lightning that characterizes this brilliant Colombian's work. While not equal to his 1967 novel *One Hundred Years of Solitude,* already an acknowledged masterpiece, *The Autumn of the Patriarch* satisfyingly displayed the vitality and passion once characteristic of U.S. fiction but now found mostly south of the border.

Other fine novels from Latin countries were *The Chronicles of Bustos Domecq,* by the Brazilian Adolfo Bioy-Casares; *The Buenos Aires Affair,* by the Argentine Manuel Puig; and the epic *Terra Nostra,* by the great Mexican writer Carlos Fuentes.

Canada was not to be outdone by her Southern Hemisphere competitors. From Robertson Davies, long a literary power north of the border, came *World of Wonders,* a magical novel built around a magician. The accomplished Margaret Atwood

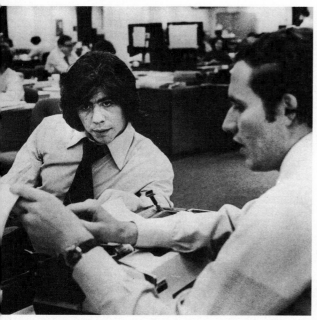

A 1976 best seller was *The Final Days,* an account of President Nixon's downfall by *Washington Post* writers Carl Bernstein, left, and Robert Woodward.

wrote *Lady Oracle,* a first-class entertainment, and Marian Engel offered the surreal *Bear.*

Great Britain also contributed important novels during the year. Anthony Powell completed his enormous *A Dance to the Music of Time* series with *Hearing Secret Harmonies,* the 12th volume (see POWELL, ANTHONY). Two British women, Beryl Bainbridge and Muriel Spark, offered *Sweet William* and *The Takeover,* respectively, both characterized by the graceful English wit that just seems arch when Americans attempt it.

From Australia came *Gossip from the Forest,* Thomas Keneally's inspired fictionalization of the behavior of the Allied and German signers of the 1918 armistice. Other English-speaking nations were represented by Irishmen Sean O'Faolain and Flann O'Brien, who gave us *Foreign Affairs and Other Stories* and *Stories and Plays,* respectively. The accomplished South African novelist Nadine Gordimer published her *Selected Stories.*

France sent Marguerite Yourcenar's bewitching historical novel *The Abyss,* and the exiled Russian Alexander Solzhenitsyn offered *Lenin in Zurich,* a fictionalization of the events that led to the Russian Revolution. Ruth Prawer Jhabvala, a Polish-Jewish novelist educated in England, married to an Indian, and long a resident of New Delhi, produced *Heat and Dust,* a fascinating tale of Anglo-Indian life. Germany contributed two important novels:

Heinrich Böll's *The Bread of Those Early Years,* a 1955 work published in America for the first time; and Siegfried Lenz's *An Exemplary Life,* a fine exercise in sustained tragicomic satire.

U.S. Authors gave their countrymen no comparable novels in 1976, but there were a few bright spots, especially among women writers. Young black novelist Alice Walker's *Meridian* was a powerful story of the civil rights movement in the South, and poet Marge Piercy's *Woman on the Edge of Time,* together with journalist Francine du Plessix Gray's *Lovers and Tyrants,* and Renata Adler's *Speedboat,* helped lift feminist fiction out of the morass of polemics. Lisa Alther's *Kinflicks,* the story of a young woman's coming of age in the South in the 1960s, was bouncy and breezy, the year's best American first novel. Another fine first novel was the tragicomic *Chilly Scenes of Winter,* by Ann Beattie, whose short-story collection, *Distortions,* also won fine notices.

Of veteran U.S. novelists' efforts, the best was John Gardner's *October Light,* a dazzling combination of mystic and pastoral themes in the tragicomic tale of a farmer's war against the corrupting influences of modernity.

There were craftsmanlike, if hardly groundbreaking, American novels in 1976 from such other established talents as Gore Vidal; John Hawkes; Clancy Sigal; Harry Mark Petrakis; Evan S. Connell, Jr.; Richard Condon; Wallace Stegner; Peter De Vries; Wright Morris; Joyce Carol Oates; Kurt Vonnegut; Ishmael Reed; Richard Yates; John Updike; Paul Theroux; and Vance Bourjaily.

Arts and Letters. This category of American books displayed a reasonably productive year. *The Letters of E. B. White* showed a pleasant new side of the distinguished essayist. Lillian Hellman's *Scoundrel Time* told of the playwright's experiences during the witch-hunt years of McCarthyism.

Critic Susan Sontag edited and offered valuable commentary in *Antonin Artaud: Selected Writings,* a collection from the works of the visionary French dramatist. Lawrence L. Langer's pioneering *The Holocaust and the Literary Imagination* explored how the atrocities of the Hitler years gave literature a new tradition of the phantasmagoric and horrific. Psychiatrist Bruno Bettelheim investigated the real literary and psychological values of fairy tales in *The Uses of Enchantment.*

Two posthumous volumes added considerably to the reputations of their authors. The late poet John Berryman displayed a talent for criticism as well as the essay form in *The Freedom of the Poet,* and John Steinbeck's *The Acts of King Arthur and His Noble Knights* was an uncompleted but provocative rendering of Sir Thomas Malory's classic.

Biography, ever the most satisfying genre in American publishing, offered a large number of good books, especially in political biographies. John

The Queen Of Murder Mysteries

Agatha Christie, who probably made more profit out of murder than any other woman since Lucrezia Borgia, died on Jan. 12, 1976, at the age of 85. The queen of crime fiction, she was the most widely translated writer in the English language.

In the course of her writing career, Dame Agatha wrote more than 100 works. Her books were translated into 103 languages and sold more than 400 million copies. Most of her books were mysteries, but she turned out a few romances under the pen name Mary Westmacott. She also wrote nine volumes of short stories and 17 plays. Her plays include the record-breaking *The Mousetrap*, which, when she died, was in its 23rd year in London, the longest-running play in theater history. In still another book, *Come, Tell Me How You Live* (1947), she described her field explorations with her second husband, a noted British archaeologist.

Agatha Christie wrote her first detective story on a dare from her sister. That novel, *The Mysterious Affair at Styles* (1920), introduced the short and dandified Belgian detective Hercule Poirot, who relied on "the little gray cells" in his head to solve crimes. She used this character in many of her books, and he became perhaps the most popular detective in the pages of crime fiction since Sherlock Holmes.

She was ingenious at unmasking the least likely character as the villain in each mystery's final chapter. She always laid her tantalizing plots so precisely and dropped false leads so cunningly that readers could seldom guess the villain's identity.

She used another detective, the elderly spinster Jane Marple, as a central figure in many books. Dame Agatha described Miss Marple as "fluffy, pink, innocent, tall," with "china-blue eyes and a wrinkled face." As an amateur detective, Miss Marple used her simple observations on human nature to help the professionals unravel the intricate details of complex crimes.

Agatha Christie once revealed in an interview that most of her story ideas were conceived "while doing some monotonous chore around the house. In fact," she said, "some of my best plots have come to me while working at the sink." Once she had the idea, she completed most of her books in from six weeks to three months. "I don't like messy deaths," she once said. "Give me a murder in quiet, family surroundings."

Agatha Mary Clarissa Miller was born in Torquay (now part of Torbay), in Devon, England, the daughter of an English mother and a rich American father. Her father died while she was still quite young, and she was educated at home, with her mother as tutor.

Although gifted with a good singing voice, she gave up a promising stage career because of her shyness. She married British air force Colonel Archibald Christie in 1914 but the marriage ended in divorce in 1928. The double trauma of her mother's death and discovery of her husband's infidelity produced what the doctors diagnosed as a classic case of amnesia. She disappeared for more than a week, and newspapers were filled with stories about the search for her. She was finally found in a Yorkshire resort hotel where she was registered under the name of her husband's paramour.

Four years later, she married the distinguished archaeologist Sir Max Edgar Lucien Mallowan, whom she met in Iraq, where he was excavating ruins. She developed a deep interest in her husband's work and accompanied him on most of his annual expeditions. She even used sites of ancient ruins as the settings for several of her stories.

"An archaeologist is the best husband any woman can have," she said at the time of their 25th wedding anniversary. "The older she gets, the more interested he is in her." In their 45 years of marriage, the Mallowans shared an interest in travel and properties. The couple owned eight houses at one time in their lives.

On the evening of her death, the houselights were dimmed in London's St. Martin Theatre, where *The Mousetrap* was in its 9,611th performance. Dame Agatha undoubtedly would have considered this a sufficient memorial.   Foster Stockwell

Agatha Christie
(1891-1976)

A commemorative plaque honoring American-born novelist Henry James is unveiled in Poets' Corner of London's Westminster Abbey in June 1976.

Bartlow Martin's *Adlai Stevenson of Illinois* took the life of the great Midwestern politician to the election of 1952 in this first of a two-volume biography. Doris Kearns turned out a surprisingly sympathetic life of the controversial President in *Lyndon Johnson and the American Dream.* In *Norman Thomas,* W. A. Swanberg renewed for the American Socialist leader the mantle of true radicalism, which had been frayed as other politicians adopted his ideas and made them respectable. Peter Collier and David Horowitz turned out a popular biography in *The Rockefellers: An American Dynasty.*

Literary biographies also were well served. Ring Lardner, Jr., chronicled his illustrious family in *The Lardners.* C. David Heymann helped restore to Ezra Pound his poetic reputation – nearly lost in the controversy over Pound's collaboration with the Italian Fascists in World War II – in *Ezra Pound: The Last Rower.* Geoffrey Wolff's *Black Sun: The Brief Transit and Violent Eclipse of Harry Crosby* resurrected the strange career of the forgotten, failed poet in a brilliant slice of the literary life of the 1920s. In *The Life of Raymond Chandler,* Frank MacShane ably explored the detective novelist's mysterious life.

Among the most popular memoirs were two rather artless but quite engaging books that shed some new light on Ernest Hemingway. A son, Gregory, told of Hemingway the father in *Papa,* and Hem-ingway's last wife, Mary, revealed the husband in *How It Was.*

Probably the year's most interesting literary phenomenon was *Roots,* a flawed but riveting biographical novel of Alex Haley's search for his black family's history from West Africa in the 1700s through the ante-bellum U.S. South to the present. Largely fictionalized but built upon 12 astonishing years of research, *Roots* was an epic journey to the heart of the hurts of the country – slavery.

There also were some strong biographies from other countries, especially Great Britain. That land exported Elizabeth Longford's elegant, witty *Byron,* Alun Chalfont's engrossing *Montgomery of Alamein,* Philippa Pullar's craftsmanlike *Frank Harris,* and John E. Mack's superb psychobiography *A Prince of Our Disorder,* the finest life of T. E. Lawrence yet published. Also from Britain came three biographical works on Bertrand Russell, all valuable: *My Father Bertrand Russell,* by Katherine Tait; *The Tamarisk Tree,* by Dora Russell, one of his wives; and the full-scale *The Life of Bertrand Russell,* by Ronald W. Clark.

Germany contributed *Spandau: The Secret Diaries,* by Albert Speer. This was a former Nazi's reflection on his crime and punishment, a valuable addition to the lore of World War II. The Frenchman Jean Lacouture's *André Malraux* separated the man from his self-made myth, yet found a great deal to praise in the life and works of the French novelist and essayist who died late in the year. *A Voice from the Chorus* was a collection of biographical meditations from a Russian prison by Andrei Sinyavsky, writing under the name of Abram Tertz – his exile *nom de plume.*

History and Politics. The heritage of American blacks continued to dominate American history, even in this Bicentennial year. One landmark study was Herbert G. Gutman's *The Black Family in Slavery and Freedom,* which attacked the idea that black families have been dominated by women in the absence of male leadership. Another was *Simple Justice: The History of Brown v. Board of Education* by Richard Kluger, a monumental study of the black struggle for legal rights in America.

The 200th birthday of the United States elicited a number of histories, most of which were transparently staged for the occasion. But there were some valuable books, among them *John Jay, the Making of a Revolutionary: Unpublished Papers 1745-1780,* edited by Richard B. Morris; *Tom Paine and Revolutionary America,* by Eric Foner; and the outstanding *Atlas of Early American History: The Revolutionary Era, 1760-1790,* edited by Lester J. Cappon, Barbara Bartz Petchenik, and John Hamilton Long, heading a large panel of distinguished historians. Its stunningly beautiful maps, created with the highest standards of historical scholarship, made it well worth the $125 price tag.

Other notable histories: Irving Howe's *World of Our Fathers,* exploring the life of Eastern European Jews in America; Terrence Des Pres's *The Survivors: An Anatomy of Life in the Death Camps,* challenging orthodox studies of the Hitlerian "Final Solution"; and George Dangerfield's *The Damnable Question,* probably the best study yet made on the vexatious relations of England and Ireland.

Watergate Books have become almost a cottage industry. While the definitive study of this national scandal has yet to be written, one book did approach this lofty status. This was *The New Yorker* magazine writer Jonathan Schell's brilliant *The Time of Illusion,* which explored the illusory nature of presidential power and the evils to which it so often has been put. *Nightmare: The Underside of the Nixon Years,* by former *New York Times* reporter J. Anthony Lukas, was another in the long line of ordinary journalistic studies of the case.

A number of actors on the Watergate stage produced books, none of which added much of import to our knowledge, but some of which clarified details and offered new points of view. These were *At That Point in Time,* by Fred Thompson, a somewhat self-serving memoir of the Ervin Committee's minority counsel; *Chief Counsel,* by Samuel Dash, who held that position on the committee; *The Right and the Power,* by Leon Jaworski, special U.S. prosecutor; *Born Again,* a peculiar memoir by Nixon aide Charles W. Colson; and *Blind Ambition,* by John W. Dean III, also a former White House counsel.

The most talked-about was *The Final Days,* by reporters Bob Woodward and Carl Bernstein, a popular reconstruction of President Richard M. Nixon's waning hours in power that was controversial but for the most part was considered accurate.

Miscellaneous. American novelist Saul Bellow's first nonfiction work, *To Jerusalem and Back* — an elegant argument for Israel — was published just as Bellow won the Nobel Prize for Literature (see NOBEL PRIZES). Other important books were Daniel Bell's *The Cultural Contradictions of Capitalism,* a bright star in the murk of literary sociology; Claude Levi-Strauss's *Structural Anthropology,* Volume II, a collection of essays that found a structure of rationality and order beneath the flux and disorder of the modern world; Ivan Illich's *Medical Nemesis,* a deeply muckraking if somewhat overstated indictment of modern medicine; and *The Wild Boy of Aveyron,* Harlan Lane's fascinating study of a feral child discovered in France in the 1700s whose case had great implications for the study of language. Henry Kisor

See also AWARDS AND PRIZES (Literature Awards); CANADIAN LITERATURE; LITERATURE FOR CHILDREN; POETRY.

LITERATURE, CANADIAN. See CANADIAN LIBRARY ASSOCIATION; CANADIAN LITERATURE.

LITERATURE FOR CHILDREN. Growing adult interest in children's literature was shown by the proliferation of conferences, lecture series, and institutes on the subject held at universities and colleges throughout the United States and Canada in 1976. At the same time, the predicted decrease in full-color illustrations in children's books became apparent. Publishers, pressed by rising costs, turned to two- or three-color illustrations and even cut back on the number of picture books published. Science fiction continued to be a popular subject, with survival of children in a desolate world a recurring and somber theme.

Some of the outstanding books of 1976 were:

Picture Books

Merrily Ever After, by Joe Lasker (Viking). Although truly a picture book, this is not just for very young children, but for everyone with an interest in the people of other times. This distinguished book has a short, interesting text and brilliantly colored paintings reminiscent of medieval times that show us how marriages in noble and peasant families might have been celebrated in the 1400s, near the end of the Middle Ages. Ages 9 and up.

Mr. and Mrs. Pig's Evening Out, by Mary Rayner (Atheneum). Engaging full-color illustrations of Mr. and Mrs. Pig dressed for their evening out and 10 little piglets happily engaged in a number of playful activities are the chief appeal of this story of a pig family that unsuspectingly hires a wolf as a baby sitter. Ages 4 to 8.

The Well-Mannered Balloon, by Nancy Willard, pictures by Regina and Haig Sherkerjian (Harcourt). James draws a pirate face on his balloon and soon finds it has a personality — and a ravenous appetite — of its own. The humor in this story should be appealing to children from 4 to 8.

My Nursery School, by Harlow Rockwell (Greenwillow). A little girl tells about activities in her nursery school, providing a simple, inviting introduction to what is sometimes a child's first venture into the unknown. Ages 4 to 8.

The Bed Book, by Sylvia Plath, pictures by Emily Arnold McCully (Harper). A series of unusual beds described in verse and shown in imaginative full-color illustrations should appeal to the child who enjoys the unusual. Ages 4 to 8.

Zoo City, by Stephen Lewis (Greenwillow). The top half of each page in this divided book shows a piece of equipment photographed so as to suggest an animal's head; the bottom half shows the head of the animal suggested. The child flips through the half pages matching up the pairs, sharpening his imagination as he goes along. Ages 4 to 8.

The Great Green Turkey Creek Monster, by James Flora (Atheneum/McElderry). A delightful account of the strange and humorous events that take place in Turkey Creek when a great green hooligan vine starts taking over the town. Ages 5 to 9.

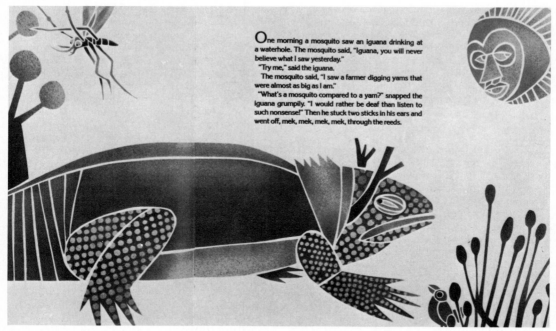

One morning a mosquito saw an iguana drinking at a waterhole. The mosquito said, "Iguana, you will never believe what I saw yesterday."

"Try me," said the iguana.

The mosquito said, "I saw a farmer digging yams that were almost as big as I am."

"What's a mosquito compared to a yam?" snapped the iguana grumpily. "I would rather be deaf than listen to such nonsense!" Then he stuck two sticks in his ears and went off, mek, mek, mek, mek, through the reeds.

A chatty mosquito and a grumpy iguana appear in the prizewinning *Why Mosquitoes Buzz in People's Ears: A West African Tale* by Verna Aardema.

The Easter Egg Artists, by Adrienne Adams (Scribners). Orson Abbott Rabbit likes decorating everything, and children will enjoy seeing beautiful full-color illustrations of a car, a trailer, a house, an airplane, and a bridge (not to mention eggs), all decorated for Easter. Ages 5 to 9.

Sweetly Sings the Donkey: Animal Rounds for Children to Sing or Play on Recorders, by John Langstaff, pictures by Nancy Winslow Parker (Atheneum/McElderry). Humorous illustrations with a medieval air add much to these rounds, which should be fun to sing or play; treble musical notation is included. Ages 8 and up.

Mooch the Messy, an I Can Read Book, by Marjorie Weinman Sharmat, pictures by Ben Shecter (Harper). Mooch is a rat who writes messages in the dust and hangs his socks on the bedpost, but he has to adjust somewhat when his neat father comes for a visit. For the beginning reader.

No More Work, by Anne Rockwell (Greenwillow Read-Alone Book). Three monkey sailors decide they are tired of working and slip away to an island. What they find there makes them decide to go back to their ship. For the beginning reader.

The Noah's Ark ABC and 8 Other Victorian Alphabet Books in Color, edited by Ruari McLean (Dover). Nine alphabets with interesting period illustrations should make this book a favorite. Preschool through age 7.

Just for Fun

The Improbable Book of Records, compiled by Quentin Blake and John Yeoman, illustrated by Quentin Blake (Atheneum). Ridiculous illustrations match the outlandish records that everyone—especially *Guinness Book of Records* fans—should find hilarious. Ages 8 and up.

Hurry, Hurry, Mary Dear and other Nonsense Poems, by N. M. Bodecker (Atheneum/McElderry). Deft and amusing line illustrations team up with humorous nonsense verses that sometimes twist surprisingly for a happy combination. Ages 9 and up.

Sports and People

Sports Star: Franco Harris, by S. H. Burchard (Harcourt). Easy enough for the early reader, this book shows the famous Pittsburgh Steeler fullback as a child and high school student, and tells of some of his professional games. Ages 6 to 10.

Olympic Games in Ancient Greece, by Shirley Glubok and Alfred Tamarin (Harper). A painless way to acquire some background in the life of ancient Greece, this account takes up the events of each day of the Olympic Games of 400 B.C., recounting known facts and the legendary achievements of some of the winners. It is illustrated with photographs of Greek art showing the athletes in action. Ages 10 to 14.

Getting Along in Your Family, by Phyllis Reynolds Naylor, drawings by Rick Cooley (Abingdon).

This book is helpful for adults as well as children. It deals with problems all families encounter in some degree — sharing duties, arguing, and understanding the other generation. It also tells the abused child where to seek help. Ages 9 to 12.

We All Come from Someplace: Children of Puerto Rico, by Julia Singer (Atheneum). This is a good survey of modern-day Puerto Rico. Excellent photographs show holiday celebrations, casual shopping expeditions, crop harvesting, and other aspects of life on the island. Ages 8 and up.

Born on the Circus, by Fred Powledge (Harcourt). Seeing things through the eyes of a talented young juggler and circus acrobat, this account pictures a young performer at work and at home, giving an inside look at life in the circus. Ages 10 to 14.

Amish People; Plain Living in a Complex World, by Carolyn Meyer (Atheneum/McElderry). The author gives an inside glimpse of life that an outsider seldom sees — an Amish family at home, at school, at work, and in church. Ages 12 and up.

The World of Horseback Riding, by Neal Shapiro with Steve Lehrman (Atheneum). The author, a famous equestrian, says this book is a basic introduction to the sport rather than a technical book. He gives information on the care and training of horses, basic techniques in English and Western riding, and showing. Ages 10 to 14.

Animals, Science, and Information

Camping Adventure; The Playful Dolphins; Animals That Build Their Homes; Wonders of the Desert World (National Geographic Society). These four additions to the excellent Books for Young Explorers Series continue the high standards set by the previous books. The text is clear and easy; color photographs are excellent, appealing, and informative; and there is real understanding of the things that appeal to children. Ages 4 to 12.

Small Habitats, by Lilo Hess (Scribners). Text and high-quality photographs provide detailed information on how to put together a terrarium that can serve as a habitat for a variety of small, unusual animals. Ages 8 to 14.

Frozen Snakes and Dinosaur Bones, by Marjorie Facklam (Harcourt). A fascinating introduction to many facets of natural history museums, this book asks the reader questions that arouse interest and lead into new areas of information about museums. It also tells how to dig for artifacts. Ages 9 to 14.

Is There Life in Outer Space? by Robert Kraske (Harcourt). This book provides a variety of scientific opinions on this fascinating question, including information on past searches for extraterrestrial life, the equipment used, and the possibilities that should be considered. Ages 10 and up.

How to Buy a Used Car, by Ross R. Olney, illustrated by Mary Ann Duganne (Dodd, Mead). This is a useful book with practical information on what to look for, where to look, and even when to look. It contains information many shoppers — experienced adults as well as the young driver out to buy his first car — would never think of. Ages 14 and up.

Things to Do

Fun with Weaving, by Alice Gilbreath, illustrated by Judith Hoffman (Morrow), has directions for 21 projects in various techniques. The book gives a clear introduction to a fascinating and popular craft and offers instructions on how to make some unusual and intriguing items. Ages 8 to 12.

Christmas Crafts for Everyone, by Evelyn Coskey (Abingdon). The author discusses simple Christmas tree decorations based on the traditional decorations of various countries. She also gives a calendar of Christmas observances and religious practices, and includes recipes for some well-known traditional holiday foods. Ages 10 and up.

Mythical Beasts Coloring Book, by Fridolf Johnson (Dover). Large outline drawings of such legendary things as the griffin and the hippocampus offer an opportunity for artistic coloring or copying. The book also includes a brief background of each creature. Ages 7 and up.

Miniature Needlepoint Rugs for Dollhouses, by Susan McBaine (Dover). This book offers the miniaturist and dollhouse or needlework enthusiast charts in authentic colors for making 41 miniature needlepoint rugs. Ages 10 and up.

Bicentennial Bookshelf for Children

The teachers, librarians, authors, and publishers who are members of the Children's Literature Association voted in 1976 to choose the 10 best children's books published in America in the past 200 years.

Their choices:

1. *Charlotte's Web* by E. B. White
2. *Where the Wild Things Are* by Maurice Sendak
3. *The Adventures of Tom Sawyer* by Mark Twain
4. *Little Women* by Louisa May Alcott
5. *The Adventures of Huckleberry Finn* by Mark Twain
6. *The Little House in the Big Woods* by Laura Ingalls Wilder
7. *Johnny Tremain* by Esther Forbes
8. *The Wonderful Wizard of Oz* by L. Frank Baum
9. *The Little House on the Prairie* by Laura Ingalls Wilder
10. (tie) *Island of the Blue Dolphins* by Scott O'Dell; *Julie of the Wolves* by Jean Craighead George

LITERATURE FOR CHILDREN

Fiction

The Trouble with Magic, by Ruth Chew (Dodd, Mead). When a plump little man with a magic umbrella comes out of the bottle Rick and Barbara bought at the store, the adventures begin. The magic is simple but interesting, and the fact that the magic umbrella works only when it rains adds to the fun. Ages 8 to 10.

The Magical Cupboard, by Jane Louise Curry, illustrated by Charles Robinson (Atheneum/McElderry). When a cold Felicity decides to crawl into the cupboard she was supposed to watch, she finds herself in a snug, warm room with a window that looks out into 1976 and a door opening onto the same scene in 1776. Ages 8 to 12.

Into the Painted Bear Lair, by Pamela Stearns, illustrated by Ann Strugnell (Houghton). Gregory goes into a painted lair in a toy store and finds himself in a new country, where he has a series of exciting adventures with a lady knight named Sir Rosemary and a large hungry bear named Bear. A nice sense of humor and several original touches enliven this fairy-tale adventure. Ages 8 to 12.

By Crumbs, It's Mine! by Patricia Beatty (Morrow). "A terror on two feet," 14-year-old Damaris Boyd inadvertently becomes the owner of a traveling hotel in this sprightly account of life in the Arizona Territory in the 1880s. Ages 10 to 14.

The Cats, by Joan Phipson (Atheneum/McElderry). When word gets out that their parents have won the lottery, Jim and Willy are kidnaped by two of the town's teen-aged toughs. Their journey into the Australian scrub beyond their village and what they encounter there gives this tale a strong sense of atmosphere and suspense. Ages 10 and up.

Mad Martin, by Patricia Windsor (Harper). Martin, called "Mad" because he never defends himself against bullies at school, has to go to live with the Crimp family when his grandfather goes to the hospital. Martin gradually discovers a new way of thinking about the world. Ages 10 and up.

A Messenger for Parliament, by Erik Christian Haugaard (Houghton). The narrator looks back at himself as an 11-year-old boy on his own during the English Civil War. A feeling of authenticity pervades this account of the boy's adventures in that troubled time. Ages 12 and up.

The Wraiths of Time, by Andre Norton (Atheneum/McElderry). A young black archaeologist finds herself thrown back into ancient time and another civilization when she opens a box containing an ankh, the ancient Egyptian symbol of life. Ages 12 and up.

Very Far Away from Anywhere Else, by Ursula K. LeGuin (Atheneum). A brief but memorable account of a teen-age boy who begins to feel he belongs in this world, though he feels different from all his high school acquaintances. Both he and the girl who helps him to appreciate his uniqueness are unusual people, but their experiences convey to the young reader some universal teen-age uncertainties. Ages 14 and up.

Pimm's Cup for Everybody, by Paige Dixon (Atheneum). Derek has just finished a spectacular year as a freshman basketball star when he starts out on a public relations tour with a visiting Englishman. The unexpected events of the tour enable Derek to see his own priorities in a clearer light. Ages 12 and up.

Awards in 1976 included:

American Library Association Children's Service Division Awards: The *Newbery Medal* for "the most distinguished contribution to American literature for children" was awarded to *The Grey King,* by Susan Cooper (Atheneum/McElderry). The *Caldecott Medal* for "the most distinguished American picture book for children" went to *Why Mosquitoes Buzz in People's Ears: A West African Tale,* retold by Verna Aardema, illustrated by Leo and Diane Dillon (Dial).

National Institute of Arts and Letters: National Book Awards. The *National Book Award for Children's Literature* was given to *Bert Breen's Barn,* by Walter D. Edmonds. Lynn de Grummond Delaune

LIVESTOCK. See Agriculture.

LONG BEACH, CALIF. See Los Angeles-Long Beach.

LOPEZ PORTILLO, JOSE (1920-   ), a lawyer and author, and finance minister under former President Luis Echeverría Alvarez, was elected president of Mexico on July 4, 1976, and took office on December 1. Lopez was the only candidate on the ballot, but he campaigned vigorously. He pledged economic reform to boost production and raise the standard of living. Lopez appealed for unity and selflessness in his inaugural speech. He asked Mexicans to accept austerity, and he promised a frugal government "not as a passing fad or fashion, but as a way of life." See Mexico.

Lopez Portillo was born on July 16, 1920, in Mexico City. He received his law degree in 1946 from the National University Law School and then joined the faculty.

Lopez joined the ruling Institutional Revolutionary Party in 1958 and served in a succession of administrative posts. He was director of legal affairs for President Gustavo Díaz Ordaz from 1965 to 1968, then became undersecretary of the presidency. Under Echeverría, Lopez was undersecretary of national resources from 1970 to 1972, then director of the Federal Electricity Commission. He became minister of finance in 1973.

Lopez has written books on law, politics, and even fiction. His *Don Q.,* a dialogue between a young lawyer and a philosopher, was published in English in 1976. Robert K. Johnson

LOS ANGELES-LONG BEACH. Doctors in the metropolitan area started a work slowdown on Jan. 1, 1976, to protest rapidly rising malpractice insurance costs. About 75 per cent of Los Angeles County's 4,400 doctors participated.

The problem arose when Travelers Insurance Company sought a 486 per cent increase in malpractice rates, effective January 15. The California state insurance commissioner reduced the increase to 327 per cent. But this satisfied neither the company, which challenged the reduction in court, nor the doctors, who began withholding their services. Efforts to develop a state-run insurance pool finally resolved the crisis on February 5.

Reading Test. The Los Angeles School Board adopted a rule on January 5 requiring students to pass a reading proficiency test before they could receive a high school diploma. The students must read well enough to follow such directions as those for filling out simple forms and must understand such items as labels, traffic signs, and news stories. The program will begin with the class of 1979.

Racial Balance. The Professional Educators of Los Angeles, an 11,000-member teachers' group, filed suit in May to block a faculty desegregation plan. The plan called for reassignment of public-school teachers to achieve racial quotas. The teachers' group objected, saying that assignments should be based upon merit.

The California Supreme Court ruled on June 28 that Los Angeles must take steps to desegregate its schools. The decision probably means that Los Angeles will have to devise a busing program.

The Los Angeles City Council in late January halted all purchases of cars, trucks, and parts totaling more than $5,000 from the Ford Motor Company because of a dispute over the firm's minority-hiring program. A city ordinance requires any firm doing business with the city to meet the city's affirmative action standards for hiring, training, and promoting minorities.

Local Economy. Average annual earnings of factory workers in the area rose 6.5 per cent to $10,936. However, the U.S. Department of Labor estimated that maintaining a minimum standard of living for a family of four required $10,236. Living costs rose 6.8 per cent between July 1975 and July 1976. The unemployment rate in the area stood at 9.2 per cent in mid-1976.

Voters on November 2 defeated a proposal to split Los Angeles County into two counties.

An estimated 750,000 commuters in four surrounding counties were stranded on August 23 when drivers and mechanics of the Southern California Rapid Transit District went on strike in a wage dispute. The work stoppage continued until September 27.   James M. Banovetz

LOUISIANA. See NEW ORLEANS; STATE GOV'T.

LUMBER. See FOREST AND FOREST PRODUCTS.

LUXEMBOURG. Socialist Labor Minister Bernard Berg was appointed to succeed Raymond Vouel as deputy prime minister on July 21, 1976. Vouel became the 13th member of the European Commission, the chief executive body of the European Community (Common Market).

The economy climbed slowly from the 1975 recession, strengthened by new short-term orders for steel. But Luxembourg's chemical and textile industries, which depend heavily on imports, were less buoyant. The Belgian-Luxembourg Economic Union (BLEU) surplus, which stood at $663 million in 1974, shrank to below $150 million in 1976. A steep fall in demand for, and prices of, intermediate goods, including steel, accounted for much of the shrinkage. Pressures on the Belgian franc added to the BLEU deficit.

The Organization for Economic Development and Cooperation estimated in July that BLEU exports would grow by 11 per cent in 1976. The key to growth was the economic upswing in West Germany and France, two of BLEU's main customers. Nevertheless, the balance of trade deteriorated with rising prices of imported materials.

The government took steps to keep employment high. It reduced immigration, cut the workweek to 40 hours, and spent $180 million to find public service jobs for unemployed steelworkers. Kenneth Brown

See also EUROPE (Facts in Brief Table).

MAGAZINE advertising revenues in the United States climbed to a record $1.6 billion in 1976, a 22 per cent increase over 1975, according to the Magazine Publishers Association (MPA). The number of ad pages rose about 17 per cent. Total circulation for the 330 U.S. consumer- and farm-magazine members of the Audit Bureau of Circulations was 253 million for the first six months of 1976, a 1.7 per cent increase compared with the same period in 1975. Newsstand sales increased 7.9 per cent, and subscriptions dropped 1.3 per cent.

As circulations continued to grow, magazine publishers passed on higher publishing costs to the readers. In fact, more than 75 per cent of the leading magazines increased their cover price during the years from 1972 through 1976. The average cover price went up 52 per cent, from 63 cents in 1971 to 96 cents in 1976. Subscription prices rose 45 per cent over the same five years.

New Magazines. An estimated 500 new consumer and business magazines started publication in 1976, compared with the 254 that were launched during 1975. Many of them were so-called special-interest publications, with editorial material aimed at readers with specified interests. For example, *CB Times,* a monthly published by Charlton Publications, Incorporated, premièred in June to report on citizens band radio. *New West* magazine, a Westernized version of publisher Clay Felker's successful

McCall's editor Robert Stein, *left,* marks the magazine's 100th anniversary. *New West, above,* began biweekly publication in April.

New York magazine, began publication in April as a biweekly aimed at Californians.

Sophisticated women interested in high fashion welcomed the September introduction of *L'Officiel/USA,* the American edition of the 55-year-old French fashion magazine *L'Officiel.* It is published in English in the United States by executives of Universal Publishers Representatives on a bimonthly basis. *Working Woman,* a new service magazine for single and married working women, began publication in November. It is published by WW Publications and covers both the private and business lives of women who work.

Also in November, *Joe Namath National Prep Sports Magazine* was introduced to provide coverage of high school sports. The bimonthly magazine features both boys and girls and covers major and minor sports.

Among the magazines that ceased publication during the year were *Archives of Environmental Health* and *Prism,* both American Medical Association publications, and *CITY of San Francisco,* published by film director Francis Ford Coppola.

Celebrating anniversaries were *McCall's,* 100 years; *Progressive Farmer,* 90; *House & Garden,* 75; *Parents',* 50; and *Skin Diver,* 25.

Canadian Developments. Time, Incorporated, halted publication of its Canadian edition with the March 15 issue because of a change in Canada's income tax law. Other foreign publications ceased because they could not meet the two new requirements that would allow their advertisers to deduct advertising expenses from taxable income — 75 per cent Canadian ownership and editorial content that is at least 80 per cent different from the non-Canadian edition. French and English editions of *Reader's Digest* continued under a new ownership agreement and editorial selection process.

Award Winners. The MPA named Richard J. Babcock, president and chairman of Farm Journal, Incorporated, and Emory O. Cunningham, president and publisher of The Progressive Farmer Company, as Publishers of the Year.

National Magazine Awards in 1976 went to *Audubon* for reporting excellence; *Business Week* for public service; *Essence* for fiction; *Horticulture* for visual excellence; *Modern Medicine* for service to the individual; and the *United Mine Workers Journal* for specialized journalism.

Time magazine won a special award — the first in the history of the awards — for its Bicentennial issue dated July 4, 1776. The awards are sponsored by the American Society of Magazine Editors and administered by the Columbia University Graduate School of Journalism.   Gloria Ricks Dixon

MAINE. See STATE GOVERNMENT.
MALAGASY REPUBLIC. See AFRICA.
MALAWI. See AFRICA.

MALAYSIA. Prime Minister Abdul Razak bin Dato Hussein died of leukemia in London on Jan. 14, 1976, after a month's illness. During his final illness, leaders of the ruling United Malays National Organization (UMNO) fought for succession. Victory finally went to Razak's brother-in-law, Deputy Prime Minister Datuk Hussein Onn, a 53-year-old lawyer (see ONN, DATUK HUSSEIN).

Onn may have won because he was regarded as weak and sick, but he did not prove to be weak. His first year in office was filled with plots, hatched in an atmosphere he described as "witch-hunting, innuendoes, and character assassination." UMNO split into two factions, in which the old guard, led by Malaysia's first prime minister, Tunku Abdul Rahman, overpowered the more modern Razak group, which included Onn.

Terrorist Activity. The political battles were fought against a background of government reports of increased activity by about 2,000 Communist guerrillas in the jungle along the Thai-Malaysian border. The government used this threat to justify tougher restrictions, surveillance of Chinese and intellectuals, and the indefinite detention of arrested persons without trial under the 1975 Internal Security Act. More important, the government's third five-year plan put less emphasis on the Malaysian peasant's welfare than on security. However, the official reports cast some doubt on the scale of the guerrilla threat. In the first seven months of 1976, the government reported only 10 "engagements," in which 11 guerrillas were killed and five captured and five weapons were recovered.

Repression of Chinese also increased. Key civil service posts were all but barred to the Chinese, who make up more than one-third of the population. School classes were conducted only in Malay, and Chinese could no longer buy land. Under a 1976 decree, all newly established private companies were required to have Malay partners. Malays form about half the population.

The Economy provided the one bright spot in the picture. Business recovery abroad led to a 30 per cent increase in the demand for such Malaysian products as rubber, tin, and lumber at higher prices. Malaysia also looked forward to increased exploration and production of its offshore oil, which in 1976 provided 14 per cent of the country's nearly $5 billion in exports. There were, however, fears that a new slump in Europe, the United States, and Japan would badly hurt Malaysia. Unemployment stood at about 7 per cent of the labor force. Mark Gayn

See also ASIA (Facts in Brief Table).

MALDIVES. See ASIA.

MALI. See AFRICA.

MALTA. See EUROPE.

Thousands of mourners in Kuala Lumpur, Malaysia, push their way in to view the body of Prime Minister Abdul Razak, who died in January.

MANITOBA. The provincial legislature passed 72 bills in a session that lasted from Feb. 12 to June 11, 1976. The most important established rent control and a home-warranty plan covering major structural defects in dwellings. The New Democratic Party formed the government with 31 seats in the 57-seat Legislative Assembly. The Progressive Conservatives' new leader, Sterling Lyon, entered the house in a by-election on November 2, bringing party strength to 23. The Liberals had 3 members.

Premier Edward R. Schreyer, who is also the finance minister, presented a budget on April 13 that estimated spending at $1.1 billion, 12 per cent over 1975, a growth rate corresponding to the increase in the province's gross economic output. Most of the spending increase was for health care and social development. The budget imposed a surtax on higher incomes for individuals and corporations, as well as new taxes on cigarettes and liquor.

Manitoba criticized the federal anti-inflation program when the Anti-Inflation Board cut back wage increases for some classes of provincial civil servants. Schreyer said the board did not show sufficient flexibility in dealing with workers who were completing contracts of several years duration. He threatened to withdraw Manitoba from the control program when its commitment to the program ends in April 1977.   David M. L. Farr

See also CANADA.

MANUFACTURING. The United States economy turned sluggish in the spring of 1976 and continued slow for the rest of the year. As new orders fell during the summer, manufacturers' inventories continued to rise, an involuntary build-up that was a direct result of the economic lull. These circumstances caused a decline in industrial production in September and October.

Some economists saw this as a sign that an inventory adjustment was developing and spreading at the manufacturing level. Others were optimistic because most excess stock was in finished goods, which would be more responsive to a pickup in demand than would materials and supplies inventories. However, all agreed that the lull in the economy would carry over into the first quarter of 1977.

Industrial Production in October stood at a seasonally adjusted 130.4 per cent of the 1967 average, down 0.6 percentage point from September. At this level, output was no higher in October 1976 than it had been in October 1974. Prior to September, production had risen for 17 consecutive months.

Factory inventories rose to an adjusted $156.1-billion in October, marking the 10th straight month of inventory build-up. Shipments declined, however, to an adjusted $93.6 billion. It was the third time in four months that shipments fell.

Factory orders rose to a seasonally adjusted $94.3 billion in October from $93.6 billion in Sep-

tember. Durable goods orders rose 2.1 per cent to $48 billion, but orders for nondurable goods fell 0.6 per cent. Unfilled orders rose 0.7 per cent to a seasonally adjusted $117 billion.

Plant Utilization. Factories operated at 80.9 per cent of capacity during the third quarter. Expansion of facilities could be a positive factor in 1977. Significantly, orders for nondefense capital goods rose 4 per cent in October, the ninth increase in 10 months.

Outlays for plant and equipment in 1976 were only barely up, reflecting business uncertainty about the economy. Plant and equipment spending was estimated at about $121.2 billion, up 7.4 per cent from $112.8 billion in 1975. However, this increase shrank to only 2.5 per cent after adjustment for inflation. The total was nearly 10 per cent below the prerecession high in 1974.

Manufacturing productivity in the third quarter rose at a 5.7 per cent adjusted annual rate, down from 8.7 per cent in the second quarter. Unit labor costs in manufacturing fell 1 per cent as the productivity increase more than offset the 4.7 per cent gain in hourly compensation.

Manufacturing Employment. The Brookings Institution blamed the slow growth of the economy for "inhibiting rehiring and work-force expansion." Manufacturing employment peaked at 20.6-

Red and white stripes are sewn together to make United States flags, which were in great demand during the Bicentennial year of 1976.

"I'm pleased to tell you, gentlemen, that in addition to serving the public, helping find the answers to some of the world's problems, improving the quality of life in America, and providing new and better products for the consumer, this quarter we made a *bundle!*"

million in the last quarter of 1973 and declined by 2.5 million during the recession, reaching a low of 18.1 million in July 1975. By the end of the third quarter of 1976, even after manufacturing output rose for six straight quarters to surpass its prerecession peak, employment was still only 19.4 million.

Total unemployment continued high throughout the year, edging up in November to 8.1 per cent from 7.9 per cent in October. Even more disturbing than the 185,000 increase in the number of unemployed was the drop of more than 200,000 in the number employed between August and October. Earlier in the year, the number of persons employed rose even though the unemployment rate was also increasing.

Time lost to strikes in October was the highest for any October since 1971. The Department of Labor estimated that 0.29 per cent of October's working time was lost to walkouts. Strike-related idleness for the first 10 months amounted to 0.23 per cent of work time, up from 0.16 per cent in 1975.

The major labor-management battle was the five-week strike by the United Automobile Workers against Ford Motor Company. The three-year agreement that ended the strike in October provided for a wage increase of about 3 per cent per year and automatic cost-of-living increases. The agreement also opened the door to a four-day week by giving the workers more paid days off. See LABOR.

New Technology. Computer technology took a major step forward when Sperry Rand Corporation and International Business Machines Corporation (IBM) introduced communications systems in which several computers and their input-output terminals can be linked together in the same data-processing network. Linking two or more System 370 computers, the IBM system allows customers to use any terminal to work with any computer in the network. The Sperry system also expands a customer's ability to deal with a variety of dispersed computers in the network. More unusual, Sperry's products can be used in the same network with IBM's System 370 computers.

International Computers Limited, U.S.A., introduced a small-scale computer that has many features of large-scale systems. It is intended for small businesses and first-time computer users. The system has six communications channels that can service data terminals, video terminals, and printers and can be linked to larger systems.

Concern about energy supplies sparked increased interest in alternate energy sources. One project was the General Electric Company's $7-million contract to build a 150-foot (46-meter) windmill capable of providing enough energy for a small commercial plant or a community of 500 houses. The federal government is now operating an experimental windmill in Sandusky, Ohio.

MANUFACTURING

Manufacturers of microwave ovens were busy in 1976 trying to keep supply up to meet a steadily growing demand for the appliances.

General Electric was also active in solar-energy projects. The company operates a solar-energy system at its Valley Forge, Pa., plant. At the end of the year, it was designing a system for Riegel Textile Corporation's mill in La France, S.C. Honeywell, Incorporated, was involved in a similar project for an Alabama textile mill.

Conoco Coal Development Company produced a sustained output of synthetic pipeline gas from lignite coal at its Rapid City, S. Dak., pilot plant, using an advanced carbon dioxide acceptor process. This was the nation's first continuous, integrated pilot-plant conversion of coal to synthetic gas that has the heat content of natural gas.

Machine Tool Orders picked up as the year progressed. Orders for these machines that shape and form most metal parts climbed to $239.8 million in October, a 5.7 per cent gain over September's $227 million and more than double the orders in October 1975. The National Machine Tool Builders' Association reported that it was the highest month since the $247.4 million recorded in July 1974.

Shipments wavered throughout the year, however, reflecting the poor order rates of 1975 and early 1976. October shipments were only $163.5-million, down 13 per cent from September's $187.4 million and 21 per cent below October 1975. Industry backlogs rose in the second half of 1976, totaling $1.4 billion at the end of October.

Innovative tools were the big gainers in the new-order surge. Flexible turning machines and machining centers that perform many operations without requiring the metal to be repositioned for each operation sold strongly. Warner & Swasey Company introduced a new family of turret lathes, vertical turning systems that can mount up to 18 different cutting bits. Kearney & Trecker Corporation recaptured some of its lost share of the market with a new line of sophisticated, numerically controlled turning and machining centers.

Electrical Products shipments totaled $69.9 billion, up 7.6 per cent over 1975. All categories registered advances, except power equipment, which still suffered the effects of deferments and cancellations by utilities. The largest gain was in the smallest product category – insulating materials – which increased 20 per cent to $1.1 billion. The largest product category – electronics and communications equipment – had a healthy 10 per cent gain, from $22.4 billion to $24.6 billion. Other major product categories showing increases were consumer products, up 5 per cent from $13.7 billion to $14.4 billion, and industrial equipment, up 10 per cent from $10.4 billion to $11.4 billion.

The Rubber Market. Natural rubber took a bigger share of the market in 1976, jumping to 27 per cent of total consumption after accounting for only 22 per cent two years earlier. Radial tires were the major reason for the increase. Natural rubber withstands heat better than synthetic rubber, and is considered better for radial tires for that reason. With tire makers turning out more radials, industry experts expect natural rubber to claim an even greater share of the market in years to come.

Total rubber consumption in 1976 was 3.1 million short tons (2.8 million metric tons). Automobile and truck tire shipments rose about 11 per cent to 211 million tires despite a four-month strike against manufacturers. Automobile tire sales totaled 191 million, with 138 million sold as replacements and 53 million to the automakers.

The Paper Industry. Based on production during the first nine months, paper and paperboard production was expected to reach 61 million short tons (55 million metric tons) for the year. Uncertainty about the economy acted to restrain capacity expansions that had been planned earlier. At the beginning of the year, industry sources estimated that 2.3 million short tons (2.1 million metric tons) would be added to capacity. Actual capacity increased by only 1.5 million short tons (1.4 million metric tons).   George J. Berkwitt

MEDICINE. Advances in the treatment of breast cancer raised new hopes for its victims in 1976. In February, Italian doctors reported a new postoperative drug treatment program that may increase survival rates as much as five times for breast cancer victims.

With a new combination of three anticancer drugs — cyclophosphamide, methotrexate, and 5-fluorouracil (CMF) — to treat women who had undergone surgery to remove cancerous cells in one or more lymph nodes, the doctors reported a success rate that was hailed as spectacular. After 27 months, only 5.3 per cent of the women on CMF showed signs of cancer, while 24 per cent of a control group that had received no drugs reported a reappearance of the disease. The researchers concluded that CMF destroyed the cancerous cells.

In the United States, 37 institutions in the National Surgical Adjuvant Breast Project reported encouraging results with L-phenylamine mustard (L-PAM). It is a relatively safe anticancer drug that has fewer side effects than CMF. L-PAM was found to reduce significantly or delay reappearance of cancer in the 1 of every 2 breast cancer patients whose risk of recurrence was high.

Prostate Cancer is the second most common form of cancer in men. These victims also were given new hope in 1976. Studies showed that treatment of prostate cancer victims with cyclophosphamide and CMF prolonged the patients' lives significantly.

In other cancer research, many patients were found to develop second and sometimes third distinctly different cancers. Scientists are now trying to determine if the multiple cancers are caused by hereditary predisposition, prolonged exposure to cancer-producing agents, or the therapy used to treat the initial cancer.

Multiple Sclerosis. Medical researchers at Children's Hospital in Philadelphia and at the Institute for Research on Mental Retardation produced evidence that multiple sclerosis is caused by a virus. The disease produces weakness, loss of muscle control, and speech disturbances. If the virus can be isolated and cultured, a vaccine may be developed to prevent the malady, which is a progressive disease of the brain and spinal cord that afflicts about 250,000 Americans.

Unnecessary Surgery. The controversy over unneeded surgery heated up in May when Eugene McCarthy, a Cornell University researcher, released a study indicating that at least 11 per cent of all elective surgery in this country is unnecessary. The study was based on negative second opinions given to patients to whom the doctors they contacted first had recommended surgery. It was attacked by the American Medical Association.

Concern over unnecessary operations prompted Blue Cross and Blue Shield, the largest private health insurance programs in the United States, to announce a pilot program in which they would pay the cost of second opinions for subscribers considering surgery.

Medical Ethics. The first right-to-die law in the United States was enacted in California on September 30. Under this law, healthy persons can sign "living wills" that order their physicians to disconnect life-support equipment that, in the doctor's opinion, serves only to postpone the inevitable moment of death. See STATE GOVERNMENT.

The most famous right-to-die case — that of Karen Ann Quinlan, a young New Jersey woman who was kept alive by life-support systems for a year after she lapsed into a drug-and-alcohol-induced coma on April 15, 1975 — was settled in the courts. The New Jersey Supreme Court on March 31 overturned a lower court's decision that had blocked the Quinlan family's efforts to have her removed from the respirator. Weaned from the respirator in May, Quinlan continued to live and breathe on her own. On June 9, she was transferred to a nursing home. Doctors expressed no hope that she would ever emerge from her comatose state.

Medical Education. A record 57,236 students entered the 116 U.S. medical schools in the fall of 1976. However, the rate of increase was not as great as in past years, and many medical educators saw

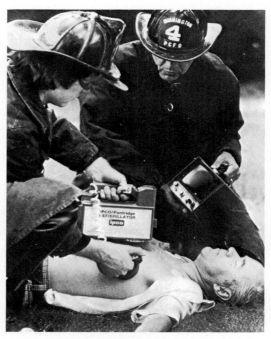

Dallas firemen demonstrate a new and smaller portable defibrillator, used to shock a coronary victim's failing heart back to a normal beat.

1976 as the end of an era of ever-increasing medical enrollments.

Medical school enrollments have increased steadily for the past 10 years, reflecting widespread recruitment because of fears of an impending doctor shortage. But the Carnegie Foundation's prestigious Council on Policy Studies in Higher Education, which had called for more medical schools and more students in a 1970 report, warned in 1976 that there may be too many rather than too few doctors in the future. It recommended cutbacks.

The medical profession manpower problem is not one of numbers, the Carnegie report said. Rather, it is one of getting the right kind of doctors into the areas that need them most — rural and poor urban communities. This concern with medically underserved areas was reflected in the health manpower legislation signed into law by President Gerald R. Ford on October 13. The law, which had been stalled in Congress for three years, ties almost all federal scholarship aid to medical students to commitments by them to serve after graduation in areas that need doctors. The law also requires medical schools with teaching hospitals to set aside an increasing proportion of their residency training programs for the primary-care specialties that need physicians most.   Dianne Rafalik

See also HEALTH AND DISEASE; PUBLIC HEALTH.

MENTAL HEALTH. Researchers in the United States and Denmark in 1976 developed new theories about the cause of schizophrenia, the most common form of psychosis. The studies, both made in cooperation with the U.S. National Institutes of Health (NIH) and reported at neuroscience conferences in May, may lead to more effective treatment and even to prevention of this disorder.

The American researchers formulated the "dopamine hypothesis" after observing people who took large doses of amphetamines. These drugs increase the amount of dopamine, a natural chemical involved in the transmission of nerve impulses, that is released in the brain. Amphetamine abusers exhibit all the hallmarks of schizophrenic behavior — hallucinations, loss of insight, and delusions. The researchers concluded that schizophrenia may be caused by a chemical abnormality in the brain involving either an excess of dopamine or increased sensitivity of nerve endings to dopamine.

The American researchers conducting the Denmark study concluded that nature, not nurture, is the crucial factor in the development of schizophrenic personalities. They studied the records of adopted children in Denmark because the records in that country are among the best in the world. They found that some children whose biological parents were schizophrenic also had the disorder.

"I don't suppose it's much compared with other inferiority complexes."

The scientists failed to discover any environmental component in schizophrenia. Previous studies of the children of schizophrenics had been confounded because the children studied were not adopted and the parents who supplied the genes also provided the environment.

Psychosurgery. After two years of study, the National Commission for the Protection of Human Subjects of Biomedical and Behavioral Research concluded in September that psychosurgery – which includes any brain surgery, such as lobotomy, performed to change or control the behavior or emotions of an individual – should not be categorically prohibited. Two teams of physicians and scientists evaluated four psychosurgical procedures in more than 60 mental patients and found that at least half seemed to benefit from the surgery. Their data also suggested that the risks of psychosurgery may be less than those of continuing chemotherapy or electroshock.

A California statute was amended in August to affirm the rights of mental patients to refuse psychosurgery or convulsive treatment. The law requires voluntary informed consent and unanimous agreement by a three-physican review committee before such procedures are done.

Right to Medical Treatment. The Massachusetts Supreme Judicial Court broke new legal ground in July by ruling that a profoundly retarded 67-year-old mental institution inmate should not be given chemotherapy for acute leukemia. Doctors favored nontreatment for the patient, a man with a mental age of 3 who has spent his last 53 years in state institutions for the retarded, because he could neither understand nor withstand chemotherapy. The ruling could become a landmark in the controversial field of withholding medical treatment if it is applied to other cases in which a person is not capable of choosing for himself.

Alcoholism. A report issued in June by the Rand Corporation set off controversy over whether reformed alcoholics can ever drink again. Challenging the traditional assumption that alcoholism is an incurable disease, the Rand report showed that a majority of the 600 alcoholics studied in detail for 18 months after initial treatment had resumed drinking (an average of one drink a day) with no ill effects.

The study drew fire from Alcoholics Anonymous, the National Council on Alcoholism, and other sources. However, studies by the Rutgers University Center on Alcohol also showed that some reformed alcoholics can drink in moderation.

Drug Abuse. The Drug Abuse Warning Network reported that alcohol, heroin, and diazepam, a tranquilizer better known by the brand name Valium, are the most frequently abused drugs in the United States.   Dianne Rafalik

See also DRUGS; PSYCHOLOGY.

METRIC SYSTEM. The United States delayed naming members to its Metric Conversion Board in 1976. However, many sectors increased their use of metric standards and measures.

The U.S. Office of Consumer Affairs began using primarily metric units in its *Consumer News* in January. An increasing variety of consumer goods were measured and identified in metric measures. For example, the two largest cola companies began marketing their products in liter bottles.

Citizens are receiving more weather data in metric units. Throughout Canada, which is leading the way for the United States, weather forecasts are given exclusively in degrees Celsius, kilometers per hour, and other metric measures.

A new translation of the Bible called the *Good News Bible* gives all weights and measures in metric units. Thus, Goliath stands nearly 3 meters tall, no longer 6 cubits and a span; God instructs Noah to make his ark 133 meters long, 22 meters wide, and 13 meters high; and Aaron's procedure for the daily lamb sacrifice calls for 1 kilogram of fine wheat flour mixed with 1 liter of pure olive oil, and a liter of wine to be poured out.

The U.S. Senate considered a resolution that would require the use of metric units in its bills and documents. Most governors have named representatives to an Interstate Metric Committee to coordinate the metric changeover.   Daniel V. De Simone

MEXICO. It was no surprise when Jose Lopez Portillo won a landslide victory in the presidential election on July 4, 1976. His party, the Institutional Revolutionary Party (PRI) had won every election since 1929, and he was running unopposed as the candidate of outgoing President Luis Echeverría Alvarez. See LOPEZ PORTILLO, JOSE.

Two of the three tiny, legally registered opposition parties also backed Lopez, but the third was so wracked with internal squabbles that it could not decide on a candidate. The unregistered Communist Party ran a write-in candidate who received few votes. Lopez received 17.5 million of the 18.5-million votes cast. Only 28.6 per cent of the voters failed to cast ballots, compared with 33 per cent when Echeverría won his six-year term in 1970.

Lopez, who was Echeverría's finance minister, had campaigned tirelessly despite his lack of opposition, traveling some 50,000 miles (80,000 kilometers), visiting 924 cities, and making 1,550 speeches. PRI officials said the extensive travel was prompted more by a need to acquaint Lopez with Mexico's problems than to win him votes.

Echeverría's Role. After Lopez took office on December 1, however, his most immediate problem was how to get Echeverría to fade quietly into the background. Mexico's ritualistic political system requires the outgoing president to begin his fade-out during the presidential campaign, but Echeverría

MICHIGAN

ruled determinedly until the end. Consequently, Lopez was forced to run a subdued campaign in which he carefully endorsed Echeverría's efforts to project Mexico as a key leader of the third world.

Several press commentaries abroad speculated that Echeverría might try to continue to upstage Lopez, at least in the field of foreign policy. Although his hopes of becoming secretary-general of the United Nations ended when Kurt Waldheim was re-elected on December 8 to a second 5-year term, Echeverría continued his espousal of such ideals as the new international economic order in his capacity as rector of the University of the Third World study center. Echeverría had set up the center near his Mexico City home.

The Economy remained in a shaky condition, with a worrisome trade deficit and a fiscal deficit that reached $2.2 billion, up 4.2 per cent. Government spending grew at an annual rate of 35 per cent, while tax revenues increased at a rate of only 30 per cent. On September 1, Echeverría ended 22 years of pegging the peso at 8 cents in U.S. money and cut it loose to float. By November 20, when the peso had fallen to 4 cents, Echeverría suspended foreign exchange dealings altogether. He also clamped strict curbs on spending and hiring and ordered 25 state companies and agencies disbanded.

Oil discoveries provided the brightest economic news. Stepped-up exploration resulted in the discovery of new petroleum deposits in the western state of Baja California Sur. By year's end, Mexico was producing 1 million barrels of crude oil a day and exporting 200,000 barrels. On May 4, the natural resources secretary, Francisco Javier Alejo, declared that Mexico had 7 billion barrels in proven crude reserves.

U.S.-Mexican Relations grew tense over the alleged mistreatment of about 600 American prisoners in Mexican jails, some 90 per cent of whom faced charges or were serving sentences for narcotics offenses. Many of the prisoners charged they were being beaten and tortured regularly. In November, both nations tentatively agreed to a prisoner exchange under which Americans sentenced in Mexico could serve out their terms in U.S. jails. The U.S. government would reciprocate by returning all Mexicans in U.S. jails to Mexico.

Land Distribution. On November 19, the federal government expropriated nearly 250,000 acres (101,000 hectares) of privately owned farmland in Sonora state for distribution to landless peasants. Lawyers representing the owners obtained a court injunction on November 30 declaring the take-over was illegal. The peasants, however, refused to vacate already occupied land and, on December 15, many of them began a mass march to Mexico City to protest the court's decree.   Everett G. Martin

See also LATIN AMERICA (Facts in Brief Table).

MICHIGAN. See DETROIT; STATE GOV'T.

MIDDLE EAST. Hopes that the Sinai disengagement agreement between Israel and Egypt, negotiated in 1975 by United States Secretary of State Henry A. Kissinger, would pave the way for an overall Arab-Israeli peace settlement were not fulfilled during 1976. Instead, the Arab states became deeply enmeshed in the civil war in Lebanon, though their success in halting that war by collective action in November was an encouraging sign.

The Arab preoccupation with Lebanon left Israel in the unusual position of a wary bystander. The United States, itself preoccupied with a presidential election, produced little in the way of new Middle Eastern policy initiatives. Both U.S. presidential candidates — and their party platforms — affirmed full support for Israel. But to balance this position, U.S. diplomacy stressed an evenhanded approach that officials hoped would bring about renewed face-to-face negotiations for a peace settlement.

The Struggle in Lebanon was the major Middle East problem in 1976. Cease-fires were negotiated there only to be broken — one of them lasted a scant 15 minutes — as Muslims, Christians, right wing Phalangists, the Palestine Liberation Organization (PLO), and many smaller factions battled in Beirut and throughout the country. A series of political reforms that would give Muslims a greater role in the government — social and political inequities were a cause of the civil war — was approved on February 14. But it quickly became a dead issue. Nor did the September accession of a new president, Elias Sarkis, who replaced the embattled Sleiman Frangie, have much effect on the fighting.

Syria's intervention in May triggered the developments that finally halted the conflict in November, after 19 months of bloody fighting. In a major policy speech on July 20, Syrian President Hafiz al-Asad said that his country had intervened to keep Lebanon from being split into Muslim and Christian enclaves and to ensure that no faction or group would be forced into an untenable position. The May 31 invasion aided beleaguered Christian forces who were in danger of being overrun by a combination of Palestinians and a Lebanese Army splinter group. The Syrian presence enabled Christian Phalangist militia to capture two Palestinian refugee camps, Jisr el-Pasha and Tel Zaatar, said to be bases for guerrilla activity. The latter was besieged for 51 days, and Palestinian losses reached 2,000.

The Death Toll at Tel Zaatar was a particularly deadly example of a conflict that respected neither age, sex, nor nationality. By the time of the "final" truce in October, deaths in the civil war totaled more than 35,000. Some death estimates reached 100,000. They included U.S. Ambassador Francis Meloy, shot down in June in the neutral zone of Beirut by unknown gunmen. About 1.7 million of Lebanon's 3.6 million residents were homeless.

On December 9, President Sarkis named Salim

Ahmad al-Huss, a 46-year-old Muslim banker, as prime minister. Huss promptly formed an interim Cabinet composed of four Muslims and four Christians. All were technical experts not closely associated with past political strife. See LEBANON.

PLO Losses. The Syrian offensive against Palestinian strongholds in September accelerated efforts to reach a more durable cease-fire. Syrian forces administered severe defeats to PLO units, forcing the PLO to reconsider its involvement in the war. By an unofficial PLO estimate, the Palestinians lost 20 per cent of their leaders and at least 3,000 fighting men in the Lebanese struggle, as well as thousands of civilians. Sarkis, Syria's Asad, and the leaders of Egypt, Kuwait, Syria, and the PLO met on October 18 in Riyadh with Saudi Arabian King Khalid ibn Abd al-Aziz Al-Saud and hammered out the details of the 55th cease-fire. This agreement was acceptable to all factions. Its key provisions were a commitment by the PLO to respect Lebanese sovereignty, and recognition by Lebanon of the PLO as the legitimate representative of Palestinian interests.

The cease-fire was enforced by the 20,000-man Syrian force that already occupied much of Lebanon. Syrian contingents entered Beirut on November 21 to complete their occupation as an "Arab deterrent force." Other Arab states were to boost the occupation force to 30,000. See SYRIA.

Israel remained officially aloof from the Lebanese debacle, but it set up entry points and mobile clinics to treat Lebanese villagers caught in the fighting along the border. Israeli authorities admitted on October 21 that Israel also supplied military equipment to Christian forces in southern Lebanon. A tacit agreement by Syria to respect the Israeli "red line" along the Litani River, near the Lebanese-Israeli border, as its limit of occupation eased Israeli fears. A similar understanding by Israel allowed Syria to transfer forces from the Golan Heights to Lebanon.

PLO Gains. Despite serious losses in Lebanon, the PLO continued to gain international recognition and to draw attention to the Palestinian cause. When the United Nations (UN) Security Council began full debate on the Palestine question on January 12, PLO observers took part in the proceedings. The Council proposed a resolution on January 26 that affirmed the right of Palestinians to establish a state of their own and called for Israel to withdraw from all territories occupied since June 1967. But the United States vetoed the resolution.

However, a subtle U.S. policy shift emerged as the Arabs moved toward successful collective action to resolve their problem in Lebanon. On November 11, the United States supported a UN Security Council resolution that criticized Israel for establishing Jewish settlements in the occupied territories and for "profanement" of Muslim holy places in

A joint force of Libyan and Syrian soldiers rolls through the ruins of Beirut during a June attempt to bring peace to Lebanon.

Jerusalem. The U.S. delegation voted with the Arabs again on November 23, calling on Israel to halt the resettlement of Arabs in the occupied territories by unilateral Israeli action. For its part, the PLO, pressured by its Arab backers to moderate its demands, began to talk publicly for the first time of a Palestinian state that would coexist with Israel.

Terrorism Declined almost as spectacularly on the international scene as it had arisen. Aside from the new-found respectability of the PLO and its affiliates, the chief reason for the decline was the effectiveness of security measures. The major hijacking of the year provided an important psychological deterrent. An Air France jet on a flight from Tel Aviv, Israel, to Paris was commandeered on June 27 by a guerrilla group and diverted first to Bengasi, Libya, and then to Entebbe Airport at Kampala, Uganda. The hijackers, a mixture of nationalities, tried to bargain the lives of the 258 passengers for the release of some 53 political prisoners in various countries, 40 of them in Israel. Later, all the hostages except those of Jewish descent, plus the Air France crew, were released.

Israeli commando units swept down on the airport on July 3, killed 7 of the 10 guerrillas plus about 20 Ugandan soldiers guarding Ugandan planes, and freed 103 hostages. Three hostages were killed in crossfire. Although technically a violation of Ugandan sovereignty, the Entebbe raid was widely supported abroad as an example of effective treatment of hijackers and the right of a nation to protect its citizens. See UGANDA.

Israel's Borders Quiet. Israel enjoyed the unaccustomed experience of entirely tranquil borders with its neighbors. The disengagement of Egyptian and Israeli forces under the terms of the Sinai agreement was completed in February (see EGYPT). The American-manned early-warning system between Israel and Egypt began operations on February 21. In November, the UN, Israel, and Syria approved a six-month extension of the UN force on the Golan Heights.

Although the outlook for an eventual Arab-Israeli settlement seemed more favorable than in many years, Israel's short-term internal prospects were less reassuring. The shaky coalition of Prime Minister Yitzhak Rabin's government, beset by staggering economic problems, faced divisions in its own ranks and political opposition on the issue recognizing the Palestinians. In December, Rabin broke up the coalition and called for new elections.

A growing number of "doves" favored negotiations, but an equal number of Jewish ultranationalists wanted to incorporate the West Bank into Israel in accordance with Biblical prescription. Jewish efforts to settle in the West Bank aroused the Arabs,

Ecstatic Israelis welcome one of the commandos who rescued hostages from Uganda's Entebbe Airport in July. His face is obscured for security reasons.

Facts in Brief on the Middle East Countries

Country	Population	Government	Monetary Unit*	Foreign Trade (million U.S.$) Exports	Imports
Bahrain	244,000	Amir Isa bin Salman Al Khalifa; Prime Minister Khalifa bin Salman Al Khalifa	dinar (1 = $2.53)	1,107	1,189
Cyprus	697,000	President Archbishop Makarios III	pound (1 = $2.42)	152	308
Egypt	38,859,000	President Anwar al-Sadat; Prime Minister Mamduh Muhammad Salim	pound (1 = $2.56)	1,402	3,751
Iran	35,226,000	Shah Mohammad Reza Pahlavi; Prime Minister Amir Abbas Hoveyda	rial (71.4 = $1)	19,977	10,343
Iraq	11,857,000	President Ahmad Hasan al-Bakr	dinar (1 = $3.41)	7,278	2,365
Israel	3,686,000	President Ephraim Katzir; Prime Minister Yitzhak Rabin	pound (8.3 = $1)	1,941	5,997
Jordan	2,921,000	King Hussein I; Prime Minister Mudhar Badran	dinar (1 = $3.01)	153	732
Kuwait	1,106,000	Emir Sabah al-Salim Al-Sabah; Prime Minister Jabir al-Ahmad al-Sabah	dinar (1 = $3.44)	8,644	2,392
Lebanon	3,639,000	President Elias Sarkis; Prime Minister Salim Ahmad al-Huss	pound (2.6 = $1)	613	1,283
Oman	819,000	Sultan Sayyid Qaboos bin Said Al Bu Said	rial (1 = $2.90)	1,344	668
Qatar	96,000	Amir & Prime Minister Khalifa bin Hamad Al-Thani	riyal (3.9 = $1)	1,788	413
Saudi Arabia	9,466,000	King & Prime Minister Khalid ibn Abd al-Aziz Al-Saud	riyal (3.4 = $1)	27,673	7,199
Sudan	18,655,000	President Gaafar Muhammed Nimeiri; Prime Minister El Rashid El Tahir	pound (1 = $2.87)	438	887
Syria	7,846,000	President Hafiz al-Asad; Prime Minister Abdul Rahman Khulayfawi	pound (3.9 = $1)	930	1,669
Turkey	41,946,000	President Fahri S. Koruturk; Prime Minister Suleyman Demirel	lira (16.1 = $1)	1,401	4,739
United Arab Emirates	231,000	President Zayid bin Sultan al-Nuhayan; Prime Minister Maktum ibn Rashid al-Maktum al-Falasa	dirham (3.9 = $1)	6,822	2,669
Yemen (Aden)	1,730,000	Presidential Council Chairman Salim Ali Rubayya; Prime Minister Ali Nasir Muhammad	dinar (1 = $2.90)	203	187
Yemen (Sana)	6,820,000	Command Council Chairman Ibrahim Mohamed al-Hamdi; Prime Minister Abdulaziz Abdul Ghani	rial (4.6 = $1)	11	294

*Exchange rates as of Dec. 1, 1976

and there were riots throughout the territory in March. The municipal elections in the West Bank on April 12 confirmed the extent of Palestinian nationalism. Most of the winning candidates were young professionals rather than long-established leaders or landowners. See ISRAEL.

In Other Areas. With Arab attention riveted on Lebanon, much of the rest of the Middle East enjoyed a relatively quiet year. Feuding over the former Spanish Sahara occupied Morocco and Algeria. Tunisia and Libya squabbled briefly, and Sudanese President Gaafar Muhammed Nimeiri survived another coup d'état attempt, which he blamed on Libya. See ALGERIA; LIBYA; MOROCCO; SUDAN; TUNISIA.

Iran, Saudi Arabia, and the other Persian Gulf states carried on a yearlong dialogue about the price of oil, as the rest of the world waited for the Organization of Petroleum Exporting Countries (OPEC) to raise its prices. On December 16, Saudi Arabia and the United Arab Emirates raised prices 5 per cent, effective Jan. 1, 1977. The other OPEC nations raised prices 10 per cent at the same time. See IRAN; PETROLEUM AND GAS; SAUDI ARABIA.

Turkey, ailing economically, suffered a stunning blow on November 24 when the worst earthquake in nearly 40 years struck the eastern part of the country, killing about 4,000 persons and destroying more than 100 villages. See TURKEY. William Spencer

MINES AND MINING. The United Nations Law of the Sea Conference closed a seven-week session on Sept. 17, 1976, deadlocked over how to exploit the mineral wealth of the deep seabed. Participants from 156 countries failed to resolve conflicts over a proposed international seabed authority with power to mine the copper, nickel, and other minerals lying in nodules on the ocean floor. Fearful that technologically advanced companies from the United States and other Western nations will rush to exploit the minerals, underdeveloped and landlocked countries insisted on a dominant role for the proposed seabed-mining authority.

U.S. Prices. The U.S. Council on Wage and Price Stability announced in May the start of a long-term comparative study of prices in several metal-producing industries, including aluminum, copper, lead, magnesium, steel, and zinc. The General Services Administration announced plans in October to rebuild stockpiles of 72 of the 93 raw materials that the federal government customarily keeps for military and other emergency needs. Experts predicted higher metals prices as a result, especially for copper. The plan calls for the purchase of about 400,000 short tons (360,000 metric tons) per year between early 1977 and 1980.

Brazil's Boom. What may be the richest iron-ore deposits ever discovered have created a mining boom in the Serra dos Carajás mountain range of

407

A rescue worker grabs a last tool before he descends into Kentucky's Scotia Mine, where two blasts killed 26 coal miners in March.

Mount McKinley National Park in Alaska; Crater Lake National Park in Oregon; and Coronado National Memorial and Organ Pipe Cactus National Monument in Arizona.

The U.S. Department of the Interior adopted rules on May 11 governing the restoration of strip-mined federal land. More than 90,000 members of the United Mine Workers (UMW) union went on strike in nine states in July and August. See COAL.

Yablonski's Killers Sentenced. Former UMW President W. A. Boyle began serving three consecutive life sentences in a state penitentiary in Pittsburgh in April for his part in the 1969 murders of Joseph A. Yablonski, his wife, and daughter. Yablonski was a reform critic of Boyle's UMW regime. Three other men, implicated in the slayings, were sentenced to life in prison on September 3.

About 1,800 UMW delegates held a stormy convention from September 23 to October 2 in Cincinnati, Ohio. Opponents of Arnold R. Miller, who succeeded Boyle as UMW president, returned dues collections to the district level, diluted the president's power to select convention committees, retained simple executive board veto of presidential appointments, and re-scheduled the union's presidential election to June 1977, six months before Miller's term expires. Miller barely retained control over union organizing, safety inspection, and political action.   Mary E. Jessup

MINNEAPOLIS-ST. PAUL. The Minnesota state legislature in 1976 gave the Twin Cities Metropolitan Council planning authority unequaled in scope in any other metropolitan area in the United States. A law set up an integrated system of planning for the entire metropolitan area and gave the council wide powers to govern growth within the seven-county urban region.

Long-Range Planning. By mid-1977, the Metropolitan Council must advise city and suburban governments of projected future populations and of future available facilities such as metropolitan sewer tie-ins, major highways, and mass transit. Each county and municipality must then submit a comprehensive land-use plan to the council by 1980, including a statement of how it plans to meet its share of the area's need for new moderate-income housing. School districts must also submit capital improvement plans. Differences between a local government's plans and those of the council will be settled by an independent hearing officer. A $1.1-million grant program was established to assist localities in putting together their plans.

Construction began in April on the first building of the Loring Park Development District in the downtown area of Minneapolis. The project calls for a four-block development at the south end of Nicollet Mall. It will include a new hotel and residential buildings.

northern Brazil. The ore averages 66 per cent iron content – among nature's highest known concentrations. It runs from the surface in bands about 250 feet (76 meters) deep that stretch for miles or kilometers – enough to supply the world's needs for several hundred years. More than 60 foreign mining companies have joined Brazilian concerns to survey and exploit not only the iron ore, but also deposits of bauxite, chrome, manganese, nickel, phosphate, and scores of other minerals.

Panama announced plans to develop its vast Cerro Colorado copper deposits with British and U.S. engineering companies. The project is expected to result in an annual copper production of 200,000 short tons (180,000 metric tons) by 1982.

Canadian Potash. Saskatchewan Premier Allan Blakeney pledged in September that the western Canadian province's vast potash industry would maintain adequate supplies and competitive prices to U.S. farmers. The pledge came after moves to partially nationalize the industry and a U.S. Department of Justice price-fixing suit against eight American companies with Canadian subsidiaries.

Strip Mining. President Gerald R. Ford signed legislation on September 28 to sharply curtail strip mining in the picturesque Death Valley National Monument in California. The law would also restrict mining in five other National Park System units – Glacier Bay National Monument and

New St. Paul Mayor. George Latimer, an attorney, was elected to a two-year term as mayor of St. Paul on April 27. Running as a candidate of the Democratic-Farmer-Labor Party, he defeated George Vavoulis, who ran as an Independent Republican. Vavoulis had served as a Republican mayor from 1960 to 1966.

Local Economy. Employment in the Twin Cities area rose 2 per cent between August 1975 and August 1976. Unemployment stood at 5.8 per cent in June. Living costs rose 7.6 per cent during the year ending in April, while food costs rose 5.9 per cent. The annual earnings of an average factory worker increased 6.2 per cent to $12,212.

Cultural institutions in the Twin Cities suffered economic setbacks during the year. The Minneapolis Institute of Arts, the Minnesota Orchestra, the Children's Theater Company, and the Walker Art Center all suffered from fund shortages. The State Theater in downtown Minneapolis, a major entertainment center for 54 years, closed on January 1.

Federal Bureau of Investigation figures showed that serious crime increased 6.5 per cent in Minneapolis and 15.1 per cent in St. Paul between 1970 and 1975.   James M. Banovetz

MINNESOTA. See MINNEAPOLIS-ST. PAUL; STATE GOVERNMENT.

MISSISSIPPI. See STATE GOVERNMENT.

MISSOURI. See SAINT LOUIS; STATE GOV'T.

MITTERMAIER, ROSI (1950-   ), a West German alpine skier, won two races and finished second in a third at the 1976 Winter Olympic Games at Innsbruck, Austria, in February. Mittermaier's outstanding performance included victories in the women's downhill and special slalom and second place behind Kathy Kreiner of Canada in the giant slalom. See OLYMPIC GAMES.

She also won the coveted crystal World Cup trophy in 1976, which is given annually to the world's leading woman skier in the World Cup series. She is the first German to win it. Later, she retired from competitive skiing to design sports clothing.

Rosi Mittermaier was born in Reit im Winkl, a village in southern Bavaria where her parents operate a mountain inn and ski school. She learned to ski when she was 7. At 16, she succeeded her sister Heidi in the world class of alpine skiers when Heidi retired. Another sister, Evi, placed eighth in the giant slalom at Innsbruck.

Mittermaier won her first German championship at the end of the 1966-1967 season and captured her first World Cup slalom race in 1970. She finished in 1976 with 10 World Cup victories.

Mittermaier has worked as a hotel business apprentice. She likes ceramics, gymnastics, and mountain climbing.   Joseph P. Spohn

See also SKIING.

MONACO. See EUROPE.

MONDALE, WALTER FREDERICK (1928-   ), a liberal Democratic senator from Minnesota, was elected Vice-President of the United States on Nov. 2, 1976. A protégé of Minnesota's Democratic Senator Hubert H. Humphrey, Mondale had been mentioned as a candidate for the Democratic presidential nomination. But he was overshadowed by President-elect James Earl (Jimmy) Carter, Jr.'s primary victories. The Democratic National Convention in New York City confirmed Mondale as Carter's running mate on July 15.

Mondale debated his opponent, Republican Senator Robert J. Dole of Kansas, on national television in Houston on October 15. Their 75-minute debate was the first ever held between vice-presidential candidates of major parties.

Mondale was born on Jan. 5, 1928, in Ceylon, Minn. He received a bachelor's degree from the University of Minnesota in 1951 and a law degree in 1956, after serving with the Army in Korea. He was Minnesota attorney general from 1960 to 1964, when he was appointed to fill the Senate seat left vacant when Humphrey became Vice-President. Mondale held the seat until his own election as Vice-President. He married Joan Adams in 1955. They have three children.   Carol L. Thompson

See also DEMOCRATIC PARTY; ELECTIONS.

MONGOLIA. See ASIA.

MONTANA. See STATE GOVERNMENT.

MOROCCO. The last Spanish personnel left Spain's former colony of Spanish Sahara on Feb. 26, 1976, completing the transfer of power to joint Moroccan-Mauritanian control. Moroccan forces moved rapidly to occupy the few scattered settlements in the territory, and a formal agreement on April 22 divided the phosphate-rich region between Morocco and Mauritania.

The boundary extends from El Aiun on the Atlantic Ocean eastward to the intersection of 23° north latitude and 13° west longitude. The agreement gave Morocco all the known phosphate deposits and iron mines. Because Mauritania lacks sufficient forces to police its territory, Morocco assumed the responsibility for security in both parts.

Following the agreement, Morocco formed three additional provinces, El Aiun, Semara, and Bojador (formerly Villa Cisneros), each named for its principal town.

Phosphate King. In addition to its territorial gains, Morocco became the world's largest phosphate producer with the purchase on February 9 of a 65 per cent interest in the Spanish-owned Bu Craa phosphate deposits. But guerrillas destroyed parts of the conveyor-belt system carrying phosphates from the mines to El Aiun, 44 miles (70 kilometers) away, in April.

Disagreement with Algeria over the latter's support of the right to self-determination of the Saha-

Driven from their villages by fighting on the Morocco-Algeria border,
Saharan women meet to discuss problems while their men wage war.

ran people, and intermittent guerrilla warfare by
the Algeria-backed Polisario Front against Moroccan forces, raised doubts about the value of King
Hassan II's new territory despite its economic potential. Nearly one-third of Hassan's 100,000-man
army was facing about 5,000 guerrillas based near
the Algerian oasis of Tindouf. See ALGERIA.

On July 9, his 47th birthday, Hassan repeated
previous promises to restore parliamentary government. He said elections would be held in time for a
new parliament to meet in April 1977. The statement came as trials resumed for 300 persons
charged with attempting to overthrow the king in
1973. Many who had been acquitted previously
were convicted of lesser offenses.

The Economy. Phosphate exports declined 3.3-
million short tons (3 million metric tons) to 19.6-
million short tons (17.8 million metric tons), and
poor grain harvests helped produce a budget deficit
of $899 million by mid-July; the gross national
product averaged a 5.3 per cent gain instead of the
7.5 per cent forecast.

New agro-industrial developments included a
tomato-processing plant built by the H. J. Heinz
Company at Kenitra that will net Morocco $4 mil-
lion a year in tomato-concentrate exports. The
World Bank provided $100 million for power and
irrigation development.   William Spencer

See also AFRICA (Facts in Brief Table).

MOTION PICTURES. The year 1976 was a disappointing one for the motion-picture industry
throughout the world. After two consecutive years
of significant increases in attendance, movie houses
were losing their audiences in an equally significant
downward trend. By late fall, the industry in the
United States was predicting that 1976 would show
a decline in gross box-office receipts of as much as
10 to 15 per cent from 1975's all-time high of well
over $2 billion gross. Because the worldwide decline
corresponded with a general improvement in the
economic climate, the old axiom that movies do
worse when the economy is strong and better when
the economy is depressed seemed to be holding true.

Perhaps the only encouraging development in
the industry was the increase in the number of films
exported and imported. For example, U.S. movies
accounted for as much as 50 per cent of the total
box-office gross in France, a country with a highly
developed motion-picture industry of its own. Aside
from France and such predictable overseas outlets
as the English-speaking countries of Australia,
Canada, Great Britain, and South Africa, the key
foreign markets for American films were Brazil,
Italy, Japan, Spain, and West Germany.

Film Imports. Similarly, in the United States,
there was a marked increase in the popularity of
foreign movies. As recently as 1971, not a single
import had earned $1 million at the box office, but

as many as six imports surpassed that mark in the first five months of 1976. Among these was a charming version of Mozart's opera *The Magic Flute,* directed by Ingmar Bergman. His brilliant and harrowing study of a divided personality, *Face to Face,* featuring a superb performance by Liv Ullmann and released later in the year, also made a considerable impact at the box office. Two films by Italian director Lina Wertmuller were even more successful, at least financially. They were *Swept Away by an Unusual Destiny in the Blue Sea of August,* a sharply intelligent comedy concerning an arrogant, upper-class woman and an embittered Marxist sailor who are shipwrecked and left alone together on a desert island; and *Seven Beauties,* a stunning and provocative, if ultimately unresolved, study of human survival set in a World War II concentration camp.

The fact that Lina Wertmuller's movies were markedly more popular in the United States than abroad pointed to a curious phenomenon – the tendency of certain films to achieve notable success once they were exported after only mild success where they were made. For example, *Barry Lyndon,* Stanley Kubrick's visually breathtaking but disconcertingly static adaptation of a minor novel by William Makepeace Thackeray, met with a mixed critical reception in the United States and even more unimpressive results at the box office on its release in December 1975. When distributed in Europe in late 1976, however, *Barry Lyndon* received ecstatic critical notices and an astounding response from the moviegoing public. It was one of the highest-grossing films in such countries as France, Sweden, and West Germany. Also relatively more popular abroad than at home was France's *Cousin, Cousine,* a light and charming comedy about a man and a woman finding true love outside marriage.

Co-Production. Just as the international market reflected growth in 1976, so too did international co-production. But most of these efforts turned out to be commercial and/or artistic failures. The American-Russian co-production of Maurice Maeterlinck's *The Bluebird* was distinguished only by its startling ineptitude, and the Russian-Japanese *Dersu Uzala,* though premièred at the prestigious New York Film Festival, was considered so unpromising commercially that it was never distributed. The French-Japanese *In the Realm of the Senses,* directed by Nagisa Oshima, met an even more disastrous fate. Immediately after being previewed for the New York City critics prior to its scheduled première, it was seized by the U.S. Customs Service as obscene. Although it was later released, it was never shown commercially, but it was seen at some museums and festivals.

Amid all this failure, there was one truly noteworthy achievement – Marcel Ophuls' *The Memory of Justice.* This 4½-hour documentary compiled

Taxi Driver, winner of the Cannes Film Festival's grand prize as the best picture, stars Robert De Niro as a lonely cabdriver.

from old newsreels and interviews is a profound and moving exploration of the Nuremberg trials and how the legal and moral principles established there have withstood the test of time.

Money-Makers. Significantly, the top-grossing new release in America's Bicentennial and election year was one that concerned recent events in American politics – *All the President's Men,* the story of the uncovering of the Watergate cover-up. Based on the book by *Washington Post* reporters Carl Bernstein and Bob Woodward, tautly directed by Alan J. Pakula, and with exemplary performances by Robert Redford, Dustin Hoffman, and Jason Robards, *All the President's Men* emerged not only the most profitable American film in 1976, but also the most aesthetically satisfying.

The same could hardly be said for the year's other big money-maker, *The Omen.* This preposterously plotted movie concerning an infant Antichrist obviously owed its success to its blatant exploitation of religious themes on the one hand and violence and terror on the other. Another of the year's top-grossing films, *Taxi Driver,* also dealt in horror, though of another kind and to distinctly different ends. The film was clearly a work of substance and a major achievement for both its director, Martin Scorsese, and its star, Robert De Niro. A deeply unsettling study of alienation, it was the official United States entry at the Cannes Film Festival, where it won the prize for best motion picture of the year.

But aside from these three movies and a handful of comedies — *Silent Movie,* a farcical parody of silent films starring and directed by Mel Brooks; *Murder by Death,* a Neil Simon take-off on detective movies; and *The Bad News Bears,* a satiric view of Little League baseball starring Walter Matthau and Tatum O'Neal — the keynote sounded in American movies was disappointment, both artistic and financial. *The Missouri Breaks,* directed by Arthur Penn of *Bonnie and Clyde* fame and starring America's two most powerful actors, Marlon Brando and Jack Nicholson, was a critical and financial disaster. *Buffalo Bill and the Indians,* directed by Robert Altman, though much more effective than *The Missouri Breaks,* was nowhere near as accomplished as some of Altman's previous films. *Family Plot,* directed by the usually reliable Alfred Hitchcock, turned out to be a distinctly inferior item, while the much-awaited movie about blacklisting, *The Front,* with Woody Allen in his first dramatic role, seemed both unequal to its important theme and unsatisfying as a film.

Big Productions. Even the presumably sure-fire money-maker, *Marathon Man* — produced by Robert Evans, directed by John Schlesinger, starring Dustin Hoffman, and with a script by William Goldman based on his best-selling novel — fell far short of expectations. Although this extremely violent thriller involving American double agents and crazed Nazi war criminals reached the top of *Variety*'s weekly chart of high-grossing movies shortly after its October release, its box-office performance was still considerably under par for such a heavily promoted commercial product.

It was only by default, then, that all hope at the end of the year for a major turnabout in the downward box-office trend seemed to rest in a single film, Dino de Laurentis' remake of *King Kong.* Produced at the staggering cost of $24 million, *King Kong* nevertheless managed to earn back its expenses even before it opened and was a prime example of the only truly new development in movies in recent years, the pre-sold blockbuster. Booked to open simultaneously in no less than 1,200 theaters, the owners of which had paid in advance for the privilege, *King Kong* was also the beneficiary of a huge, $15-million promotional campaign. Indeed, so much interest was generated about the movie prior to its Christmas opening that King Kong, rather than the presidential candidates, appeared on the cover of *Time* magazine during the week of the November 2 elections.   Joy Gould Boyum

See also AWARDS AND PRIZES (Arts Awards); FLETCHER, LOUISE; NICHOLSON, JACK.

Ingmar Bergman's film adaptation of Mozart's light-hearted fairy-tale opera *The Magic Flute* was one of the top motion pictures of the year.

MOZAMBIQUE. President Samora Moises Machel closed his country's borders on March 3, 1976, and severed all links with Rhodesia. He acted following a series of raids on villages in Mozambique by the Rhodesian Air Force. Rhodesia maintained that the villages were training areas for Rhodesian guerrillas. See RHODESIA.

The border closing had an immediate impact on Mozambique's economy, which was already faltering. Unemployment was rampant. Food production was down 75 per cent in some areas, and major cash crops such as sugar and cotton were off nearly 50 per cent. Machel announced a new austerity program under which all employed persons had to contribute one day's salary per month to a fund to be used at the government's discretion. To relieve a housing shortage, Machel nationalized all houses, freeing hundreds abandoned when white residents left Mozambique in 1975 after the country became independent.

Severing ties with Rhodesia added another economic burden. By refusing to permit landlocked Rhodesia's imports and exports to move by rail or road across Mozambique, the country was expected to lose annually about $165 million in transit fees. In addition, about 10,000 persons, including railroad workers, were left jobless.　　　Paul C. Tullier

See also AFRICA (Facts in Brief Table); Section Five, MOZAMBIQUE and MAPUTO.

MUSEUMS. In addition to visiting the United States in 1976, Queen Elizabeth II marked the American Revolution Bicentennial by opening the exhibition "1776" at the British National Maritime Museum in London and lending 25 drawings by Leonardo da Vinci from her personal collection to the National Museum of History and Technology in Washington, D.C. The British Library organized a display, "The American War of Independence 1775-1783," which later was loaned to the Museum of Our National Heritage in Lexington, Mass. The National Gallery of Art in Washington, D.C., showed a Bicentennial exhibition, "The Eye of Thomas Jefferson," containing many objects from European museums. To encourage such exchanges, the United States activated the Arts and Artifacts Indemnity Act, which spares museums high insurance costs on specimens borrowed from abroad.

The Field Museum of Natural History in Chicago prepared an exhibition of Ecuadorean ceramics, dating from 3000 B.C. to 300 B.C., for display in the United States and Ecuador. The Royal Ontario Museum in Toronto, Canada, and the Denver Art Museum showed collections of gold artifacts, one borrowed from Peru, the other from Colombia.

Museum Growth. President Gerald R. Ford dedicated the $40-million National Air and Space Museum in Washington, D.C., on July 1. In January, the Palm Springs (Calif.) Desert Museum moved into a new $5.5-million building, and the Virginia Museum of Fine Arts in Richmond opened its north wing.

Two Philadelphia museums celebrated their centennials and the U.S. Bicentennial by reopening after extensive renovations. Restoration of the Pennsylvania Academy of the Fine Arts' century-old building and installation of protective systems cost $5.1 million. Modernization at the Philadelphia Museum of Art totaled $9 million. The National Museum of Modern Art, part of the Georges Pompidou National Center for Art and Culture, opened in Paris, France.

Operations Crunch. Museums found it harder to raise money for daily operations than for development. The Council on Foundations projected a 12 per cent increase in U.S. museum deficits for 1976. The Detroit Historical Museum closed in April because the city could not pay essential employees. Appropriations by the Michigan state legislature allowed the museum to reopen and provided enough money for the Detroit Institute of Arts to continue statewide programs and remain open five days a week. The Hudson River Museum in Yonkers, N.Y., lost 60 per cent of its income when the city had to drop its support. On the hopeful side, both houses of Congress voted in September to give operational support to U.S. museums.　　Ralph H. Lewis

The National Air and Space Museum, the newest addition to the Smithsonian Institution, was opened in Washington, D.C., on July 1.

MUSIC, CLASSICAL. Families picnicking at the Hollywood Bowl in Los Angeles, Calif., on July 4, 1976, watched fireworks and listened to music. They heard baritone Sherrill Milnes sing Stephen Foster songs, a 300-voice interdenominational choir perform gospel and soul music, and the Los Angeles Philharmonic play the music of George Gershwin, Charles Ives, Aaron Copland, and John Philip Sousa. Similar scenes were common across the United States in 1976, the American Revolution Bicentennial.

In early January, the Cleveland Orchestra presented "The Sounds of America: 1776-1976," a concert that included a Revolutionary War hymn by William Billings (1746-1800) and works by other American composers such as Leonard Bernstein, Duke Ellington, Scott Joplin, and Gershwin.

Programs totally devoted to American composers were given in Dallas, Houston, New Orleans, New York City, and San Francisco by symphony orchestras that usually lean heavily on European works. Under the huge Gateway Arch in St. Louis, people listened to a string quartet by Founding Father Benjamin Franklin.

The Chamber Music Society of New York City's Lincoln Center for the Performing Arts traveled to Charleston, S.C., in June to commemorate the first public concerts given in the American Colonies in 1731. The New Yorkers gave three concerts at the historic Dock Theater and highlighted the programs with the première of a chamber work by U.S. composer Stanley Silverman patterned after colonial music in instrumentation and style.

Home-Grown Opera also enjoyed more than the usual number of revivals. The Houston Grand Opera and the Lake George (N.Y.) Opera Festival did Gershwin's *Porgy and Bess;* the Houston production went on tour and ended up with a highly successful run on Broadway. Virgil Thomson's evocative look at suffragist Susan B. Anthony, *The Mother of Us All,* was revived by the Chicago Opera Studio, the Boston Opera, and the Santa Fe Opera. Opera New England toured with Copland's *The Second Hurricane,* while the Baltimore Opera and New York City's Bronx Opera performed his *The Tender Land.* Douglas Moore's *The Ballad of Baby Doe* was produced at Chautauqua, N.Y., Kansas City, and Central City, Colo., where it premièred in 1956. The San Diego Opera performed Gian Carlo Menotti's *The Saint of Bleecker Street,* as did the New York City Opera. The Seattle Opera Association presented Carlisle Floyd's *Of Mice and Men,* and the New York Bel Canto Opera did Deems Taylor's *The King's Henchman.*

A performance of historical interest occurred in August at New Jersey's Washington Crossing state

Italy's La Scala Opera makes its U.S. debut in September in Washington, D.C., with Shirley Verrett and Piero Cappuccilli in Verdi's *Macbeth.*

Spanish conqueror Cortés, right, confronts Aztec ruler Montezuma, left, in Boston Opera Company's U.S. première of Roger Session's *Montezuma*.

park. It was the nation's first musical theater piece, a ballad opera originally published in 1767 but performed only once—and then in a censored version—in 1796. The work, called *The Disappointment, or The Force of Credulity,* was developed around popular tunes of that day.

The Nation's Heritage was celebrated in a number of new works that premièred during 1976. John La Montaine's opera *Be Glad Then America,* premièred at Pennsylvania State University in February, was pieced together from 18th-century letters and journals to show in words and music how the colonists looked upon the events that led to the signing of the Declaration of Independence.

Bilby's Doll, Carlisle Floyd's latest work, was introduced by the Houston Grand Opera in February and concerns a French orphan girl taken to New England at the time of the Salem witch trials who turns to witchcraft to combat the hostility around her. The story is based on the historical novel *A Mirror for Witches* by Esther Forbes, but Floyd considers the opera less about history than about "the protection of the poet, the rebel, the nonconformer in our society."

Menotti had a June première in Philadelphia. *The Hero* recounts the adventures of a Rip Van Winkle type who has been asleep for 10 years. He wakes up to discover that his wife and the leading citizens of the town have been exhibiting him dur-

ing his sleep as a tourist attraction. His awakening is a disaster to the town. Another day of sleep would have meant a record. His bed could then have become a monument, and replicas of it could have been sold to souvenir hunters. So should he fake sleep for another day? He decides to be honest. The opera suggests themes of love and conscience that have always interested the composer.

Richard Owen's *Mary Dyer* made its debut at an outdoor amphitheater in Suffern, N.Y., in June. Like *Bilby's Doll,* it concerns the injustices of colonial times, based on a historical incident. Mary Dyer, a Quaker in Puritan Massachusetts, commits an act of civil disobedience by returning to Boston despite a law that prohibits Quakers from re-entering the colony. She is tried and hanged, and—just as she expected—the act so repels people that the law is repealed.

Other operatic premières included Hugo Weisgall's *The Hundred Nights,* based on a Japanese No play, and William Schuman's *The Mighty Casey,* about the old baseball tale. Both were performed in New York. Thomas Pasatieri's *Ines de Castro,* a drama of intrigue in 13th-century Portugal, was done in Baltimore; his *Washington Square,* the Henry James story, was performed at Detroit's Michigan Opera Theatre; and Alva Henderson's version of James Fenimore Cooper's *The Last of the Mohicans* was introduced in Wilmington, Del.

Symphonic Premières approached flood stage. Baltimore heard Elie Siegmeister's *An Entertainment for violin, piano, and orchestra; Folk Song* for orchestra by Lukas Foss; and Jean Eichelberger Ivey's *Testament of Eve.* Boston presented *Renga with Apartment House 1776* by John Cage, and Chicago did Alan Stout's *Passion* and David Del Tredici's *The Final Alice.* Raymond Premru's *Concerto* for orchestra, Eugene Kurtz's *Three Songs from Medea,* and *Dialogus* by George Walker premièred in Cleveland; Del Tredici's *In Wonderland Part 2* was presented in Denver; and Benjamin Lees's *Concerto* for woodwind quintet and orchestra had its première in Detroit. In Milwaukee, there was Otto Luening's *A Wisconsin Symphony;* conductor Kenneth Schermerhorn's *Monodrama* for soprano and orchestra, written for his wife, soprano Carol Neblett; and Lester Trimble's *Panels VIII.*

Minnesotans heard *New People* by Michael Colgrass; and the National Symphony in Washington, D.C., performed 12 commissioned works, including pieces by Gene Gutche, Roy Harris, Lees, Gunther Schuller, and the orchestra's own conductor, Antal Dorati. The Philadelphia Orchestra played Norman Dello Joio's *Colonial Variants,* Leslie Bassett's *Echoes from an Invisible World,* and Menotti's *Symphony No. 1.* San Francisco heard *Street Music* by William Russo; and Seattle, William Bolcom's *Piano Concerto.*

The bigger orchestras were not the only groups involved in commissions. The Cuyahoga Valley Arts Ensemble in Akron, Ohio, introduced Ned Rorem's *Serenade on Five English Poems,* and the Tucson Symphony premièred Margaret Richter's *Landscapes of the Mind I,* inspired by the paintings of Georgia O'Keeffe.

The National Endowment for the Arts (NEA) furthered the commission flow. One set of grants supported six composers to write for six orchestras — Cage for the Boston Symphony; Del Tredici for the Chicago Symphony; Jacob Druckman for the Cleveland Orchestra; Morton Subotnick for the Los Angeles Philharmonic; Elliott Carter for the New York Philharmonic; and Leslie Bassett for the Philadelphia Orchestra — and committed each orchestra to perform all the compositions during the 1976-1977 season.

With NEA support, 20 orchestras in the Southeastern United States are collaborating in the commission of works by Ulysses Kay and Norman Dello Joio. Another grant went to Colgrass for *Best Wishes, USA,* a musical panorama that quotes a Mark Twain after-dinner speech, a Civil War song, and the conclusion of Thoreau's *Walden.* This work will be presented by the Springfield, Mass.; Albany, N.Y.; Hudson Valley, N.Y.; and Portland, Me., orchestras and the Rhode Island Philharmonic. The NEA committed itself to opera, with a $2.7-million grant split among 40 opera companies.

Dealing with Deficits. But such gifts and more to a cluster of orchestras only partially alleviated the financial problems that continued to plague not-for-profit musical organizations. New union contracts aided musicians in Chicago, Dallas, Houston, Indianapolis, and St. Louis and at the New York City Opera, and increased pressure on already strained budgets. The Cleveland Orchestra's deficit touched $1 million, and the Metropolitan Opera sought $12.7 million to balance its 1976-1977 budget. Chicago's Lyric Opera was looking for $3.1 million.

Such financial realities led to increasing use of crowd-drawing pop concerts with such personalities as Peter Nero and Skitch Henderson in special concerts, cameo opera performances in shopping centers, and radio marathons.

Carnegie Hall in New York City initiated a fund drive with a superstellar concert in May that brought $1.2 million in one night's cash and pledges after the guests heard pianist Vladimir Horowitz, violinists Yehudi Menuhin and Isaac Stern, cellist Mstislav Rostropovich, baritone Dietrich Fischer-Dieskau, and the New York Philharmonic.

Honors and Happenings. Pianist Arthur Rubinstein received the Medal of Freedom, America's highest civilian award, and Boston Pops conductor Arthur Fiedler was given the American Symphony Orchestra League's Golden Baton award.

Boston Opera conductor Sarah Caldwell became the first woman to conduct at the Metropolitan Opera. The renowned Russian pianist Lazar Berman finally made his first U.S. tour. Newscaster Walter Cronkite narrated Copland's *Lincoln Portrait* with the Indianapolis Symphony. Former British Prime Minister Sir Edward Heath conducted a pension concert for the Chicago Symphony. Filmmaker Robert Altman gave roles to three opera singers — Evelyn Lear, Bonnie Leaders, and Noelle Rogers — in his *Buffalo Bill and the Indians,* starring Paul Newman. Said Lear: "Joanne Woodward [Newman's wife] told me that using opera singers in the film even rubbed off on Paul. He now sings 'Caro mio ben' in the bathtub."

James Levine officially took over as music director of the Metropolitan Opera. William Steinberg retired as musical director of the Pittsburgh Symphony after 24 years, handing the baton to André Previn. In Seattle, Milton Katims bowed out after a 22-year directorship, and Rainer Miedel assumed the role.

Viktor Ullmann's and Peter Klein's *Emperor of Atlantis* was introduced in Amsterdam. It is based on experiences during World War II when they were prisoners at Terezin, a Nazi concentration camp in which both men were killed. Their score was discovered recently in London. The performance caused many in the audience, some with memories from the Nazi era, to weep.   Peter P. Jacobi

MUSIC, POPULAR. Rock and roll, disco music, rhythm and blues, and other long-established forms of popular music maintained their hold on the public in 1976. But a strong, new trend was the upsurge of so-called "crossover" jazz throughout the United States. This term referred to the work of jazz artists whose popularity overlapped into other musical areas, enabling them to enjoy unprecedented success with general audiences.

The performer most strongly associated with this development was guitarist George Benson. His album "Breezin'" became a platinum record, with sales of 1 million units. It was the first record by a jazz artist to reach the number-one position in popular, jazz, and soul markets alike. A single record from the album, "This Masquerade," also was a major hit. Composed by Leon Russell, the song featured Benson as both vocalist and guitarist.

Other jazz artists who achieved crossover popularity were the trumpeter Freddie Hubbard; composer-pianist Herbie Hancock; bassist Stanley Clarke; drummer Tony Williams; and saxophonists Ronnie Laws, David Sanborn, John Handy, and John Klemmer.

The Rock Scene. Heavy rock remained a vital force. One of the most broadly accepted groups was Aerosmith, whose lead singer, Steve Tyler, was compared with Mick Jagger of the Rolling Stones. During the year, this group had two million-dollar gold albums and a platinum album.

Boz Scaggs, the white rhythm-and-blues singer and guitarist, reached a new peak of success with his album "Silk Degrees." His stylish appearance and manner led one observer to describe him as "the Gatsby of rock and roll."

Former Beatle Paul McCartney opened his first American tour in 10 years in May with a triumphant appearance in Fort Worth, Tex. The tour of U.S. and Canadian cities was the final leg of a worldwide tour that began in Great Britain in late 1975 and took McCartney and his band, Wings, through Europe and Australia.

New Stars. Barry Manilow, who struck out on his own after serving as musical director for Bette Midler, emerged as a superstar in his own right. He sang and played the piano, and wrote most of the compositions for his records.

Eric Carmen, a singer, multi-instrumentalist, and composer with a classical background, was another popular new artist. Some critics compared his compositions to the works of John Lennon and Paul McCartney. A five-member vocal and instrumental group called the Bay City Rollers appealed to the teeny-bopper market; young girls screamed fanatically at the group's extrovert performances.

Peter Frampton, a 25-year-old British favorite, emerged in the United States early in the year. He has been a teen-age idol in Britain since he was 16. He made his impact on American audiences with a blend of soft and hard rock, a virtuoso guitar style, and an agreeable baritone voice. Sales of his album "Frampton Comes Alive!" passed albums by such established artists as Bob Dylan and Carole King during the spring to become the best-selling album in the United States. His single "Show Me the Way" enjoyed comparable success.

Black Soul Music. The nine-man group known as Earth, Wind, and Fire remained pre-eminent in black soul music. Four of their albums and three of their singles have each sold at least a million records. Their visually startling and rhythmically aggressive presentations combined heavy percussion and funky South Side Chicago soul-and-blues with jazz and rock elements.

The tendency among some white artists to emulate the sounds of black music was reflected in the work of Daryl Hall and John Oates, who extended their popularity from Philadelphia to a nationwide audience.

Other Developments. One of the year's most emphatic successes in the single-record world was scored by Wild Cherry, a quartet whose members described their music as "electrified funk." Their leader, producer, lead vocalist, and lead guitarist was Robert Parissi, and he composed the group's million-selling single, "Play That Funky Music."

The progressive country music sound continued

Jazz guitarist George Benson rose to the top of the popular music charts in 1976 with his album "Breezin'" and its hit single "This Masquerade."

Former Beatle Paul McCartney and his band, Wings, visited 20 U.S. and Canadian cities in 1976 during his first American tour in 10 years.

to dominate in some areas, typified in the work of such "outlaw" artists as Waylon Jennings, Kris Kristofferson, and the group Asleep at the Wheel.

The Captain and Tennille, an unusual husband-and-wife duo, debuted in a new TV show in the fall. The Captain is Daryl Dragon, the son of Carmen Dragon, conductor of the Burbank, Calif., symphony orchestra. His partner is Toni Tennille, whose bright personality contrasts with the more sedate manner of her husband. Among their hits were "Lonely Nights" and "Muskrat Love."

The Jazz Scene. Although the crossover trend was the most conspicuous aspect of jazz, some artists gained respect through pure jazz performances that reached a small but loyal audience. Notable among them were guitarist Kenny Burrell, long a familiar name but now enjoying greater acceptance; cornettist Nat Adderley, who formed his own quintet after the death in 1975 of his saxophonist brother Cannonball Adderley; and veteran vibraphonist Milt Jackson, who recorded with strings and in a variety of other settings.

Jazz festivals multiplied during the year, but the 11-day Newport Festival in New York City and the Monterey, Calif., Festival still were the best known. The second annual jazz festival in Nice, France, brought together more than 100 American and European musicians in July for almost two weeks of lively jam sessions.   Leonard Feather

NAMIBIA. After 10 years of conflict over the issue, South Africa in 1976 agreed to independence for Namibia (South West Africa). A constitutional conference convened in Windhoek, Namibia, by South Africa announced on August 18 that it had reached agreement on independence by the end of 1978. The constitutional conference was attended by representatives of Namibia's 11 ethnic groups — including whites, who make up about 10 per cent of the territory's 956,000 residents. The agreement calls for a multiracial transitional government to take over internal administration by June 1977, but South Africa would still have responsibility for Namibia's defense and foreign affairs.

However, South-West Africa People's Organization (SWAPO) President Sam Nujoma said on September 6 that the conference's black delegates were "puppets" in a South African plan to retain economic and political domination of Namibia. The United Nations and the United States also denounced the agreement, because SWAPO had no part in the conference. SWAPO was reportedly increasing its capacity to wage guerrilla war against white rule. This may eventually compel South Africa to negotiate with SWAPO.   John D. Esseks

See also AFRICA (Facts in Brief Table).

NATIONAL DEFENSE. See ARMED FORCES.

NAVY. See ARMED FORCES.

NEBRASKA. See STATE GOVERNMENT.

NEPAL. The tourist season in Nepal was good in 1976. An American promoter opened a casino—owned by the king's uncle—in Kathmandu, and tours of gamblers from India were flown there.

But the many tourists could not obscure Nepal's economic and political straits. The country, as an official put it, "is not landlocked but India-locked." Good relations with the government in New Delhi are essential to Nepal's survival, but in 1976, India showed signs of displeasure with Nepal. A five-year trade treaty between the two countries expired without renewal. Late in the year, travel restrictions barred Nepalese traders and peasants from some Indian border areas.

Under such circumstances, King Birendra Bir Bikram Shah Dev sought friends elsewhere. In June, he visited China's Tibet and was greeted by singing and dancing crowds. Chinese engineers were helping with Nepal's extensive roadbuilding program. In late November, he received an equally warm welcome—and pledges of aid—in Moscow. The Russians agreed to provide 120,000 short tons (109,000 metric tons) of oil products in 1976, goods previously supplied by India. Japan granted a $10-million loan, and the United States sought to help. But Nepal's deficit grew, and development projects made slow progress.   Mark Gayn

See also ASIA (Facts in Brief Table).

NETHERLANDS. Prince Bernhard, Queen Juliana's consort, resigned on Aug. 26, 1976, as inspector general of the Dutch armed forces and from all other business and defense positions he had held. His resignation came after a formal inquiry into allegations of bribery by the U.S.-based Lockheed Aircraft Corporation reported that he had "shown himself open to dishonorable requests and offers" and had created the impression that he was "susceptible to favors." When the inquiry was set up on February 8, the prince denied receiving any payment in return for his influence in arranging sales of Lockheed fighter planes.

The royal couple cut short an Italian vacation to return home on August 17, amid talk of abdication, as the commission's report on the alleged $1.1 million in bribes went to Prime Minister Johannes Martin den Uyl. But on August 26, Den Uyl said there would be no criminal investigation or judicial inquiry.

". . . My relations with Lockheed have developed along the wrong lines," Prince Bernhard said in a letter to parliament. "I have not been critical enough of initiatives presented to me. I have written letters which I should not have sent. I accept full responsibility for this and thus accept the disapproval expressed by the commission." Parliament endorsed the Cabinet's decision not to prosecute the

Queen Juliana opens the Netherlands parliament on September 21 while Prince Bernhard, censured because of Lockheed bribery scandal, listens.

prince on August 30 and thanked Queen Juliana for not abdicating.

Coalition Tested. The Socialist Party and its four coalition partners faced heavy pressures on issues as varied as increased worker participation in factory management, abortion-law reform, and the loss of a contract for supplying parts for South Africa's first nuclear power plant. But the center-left closed ranks and defeated opposition attempts at censure.

No Tax Changes. The government said on September 21 that there would be no tax changes. However, Queen Juliana told parliament that strict wage and price controls would continue through fiscal 1977. The government vowed to continue the fight against 5.8 per cent unemployment and inflation, which ran at 12 per cent annually. In March, the Organization for Economic Cooperation and Development predicted an economic growth rate of over 2 per cent following a 2 per cent fall in the gross national product in 1975.

About 1,000 women held a sit-in at an abortion clinic threatened with closure in Haarlem on May 25 to protest abortion laws. The Second Chamber approved in September a bill to legalize abortion, but the First Chamber voted 41 to 34 against the reform bill on December 14. Kenneth Brown

See also EUROPE (Facts in Brief Table); INTERNATIONAL TRADE AND FINANCE (Close-Up).

NETO, AGOSTINHO (1922-   ), became president of Angola in February 1976. Aided by Russian arms and Cuban troops, his Popular Movement for the Liberation of Angola (MPLA) defeated the National Front for the Liberation of Angola and the National Union for the Total Independence of Angola. This ended a civil war that began before Portugal granted Angola independence in November 1975. See AFRICA; ANGOLA.

After assuming power, Neto worked to set up a socialist state. His government received aid from East European countries, but Neto reportedly did not want to limit ties to Communist nations.

While studying medicine in Portugal during the early 1950s, Neto became involved in revolutionary politics. He returned to Angola to practice as a gynecologist, and he also wrote poems about the plight of black Angolans under Portuguese colonial rule. The Portuguese sent him to prison on several occasions.

In the mid-1950s, Neto and other intellectuals and labor leaders formed the MPLA. Neto was arrested again in 1961 and taken to Portugal. However, he escaped in 1962, went into exile in Zaire, and became head of the MPLA. Along with other black nationalists, the MPLA conducted guerrilla activities until Portugal agreed in 1974 to grant Angola independence. Darlene R. Stille

NEVADA. See STATE GOVERNMENT.

NEW BRUNSWICK. Restraint pervaded the New Brunswick budget presented on March 16, 1976. The budget offered no new programs and held spending increases for the 1976-1977 fiscal year to 15 per cent. It estimated expenditures at $1.1 billion, revenues at $1.06 billion. Borrowing requirements were expected to increase the province's total debt to $607 million, almost $900 for each person in the province.

Federal contributions through equalization payments and cost-sharing agreements accounted for about 45 per cent of New Brunswick's revenue. If federal ceilings on these grants were maintained, the budget warned, the poorer provinces would be unable to provide public services at national standards. The budget proposed no new taxes, but announced reductions in the number of hospital beds, in education, and in social services.

The Legislative Assembly passed more than 80 bills. The Progressive Conservative government headed by Richard B. Hatfield held 33 seats to the Liberals' 25. On July 29, a senior government member retired, leaving one vacancy in the 58-member Assembly. David M. L. Farr

See also CANADA.

NEW HAMPSHIRE. See STATE GOVERNMENT.

NEW JERSEY. See NEWARK; STATE GOVERNMENT.

NEW MEXICO. See STATE GOVERNMENT.

NEW ORLEANS. The Supreme Court of the United States approved a redistricting plan for the New Orleans City Council on March 3, 1976, despite objections from the Administration of President Gerald R. Ford that the scheme discriminated against black voters.

Before the redistricting, whites held a majority in all five wards. Under the approved redistricting scheme, New Orleans' black residents, who make up 45 per cent of the city's population, would hold a slight majority in one ward. Despite objections that the plan did not go far enough, the court justified its action on the grounds that the Voting Rights Act of 1965 required only that any redistricting plan not involve any setback to racial minorities in the election process.

One of the worst Mississippi River disasters in history occurred on October 20, when an ocean tanker rammed and capsized a Mississippi River ferry about 20 miles (33 kilometers) upstream from New Orleans. Only 18 of the estimated 96 passengers on the ferry survived the accident. The New Orleans coroner testified at a hearing on October 27 that the ferry captain was almost legally drunk when the accident occurred.

Violent Crime. According to Federal Bureau of Investigation statistics released on March 25, violent crime in New Orleans dropped during 1975. New Orleans' murder rate fell 22 per cent, and the overall rate of serious crime in the city was up only 2 per cent. Serious crime increased nationally by 9 per cent. The New Orleans district attorney's office attributed the improvement to mandatory prison terms, longer sentences, and less plea-bargaining.

New Orleans police called in sick for two days, on September 5 and 6, to protest holiday pay cuts. Community relations and police academy officers manned squad cars during that time.

Grain Scandals continued to plague the New Orleans port. Three giant grain export companies, the Garnac Grain Company, Archer-Daniels-Midland Company, and the St. Charles Grain Elevator Company, were each fined $10,000 on March 4 for falsifying the weight of grain loaded onto ships and substituting poor grades of grain for grain sold at good-grain prices. The companies made about $1.7 million annually from their illegal activities. The Continental Grain Company was fined $500,000 on May 4 for rigging weight scales.

Improved Economy. The average annual earnings of factory workers rose 10.4 per cent to about $11,000 a year between August 1975 and August 1976. Department store sales rose 11.7 per cent, and construction activity increased 1.9 per cent. Total nonfarm employment increased 1.6 per cent. However, 8.6 per cent of the labor force was still unemployed at midyear.   James M. Banovetz

NEW YORK. See NEW YORK CITY; STATE GOV'T.

NEW YORK CITY continued its efforts in 1976 to cope with the fiscal crisis that had threatened it with bankruptcy in 1975. The new year began badly. A report prepared for the U.S. Department of the Treasury in January noted that the city was lagging in its budget-balancing efforts. It had a $1-billion deficit for fiscal 1976, which ended on June 30.

Optimism v. Pessimism. Mayor Abraham D. Beame and U.S. Secretary of the Treasury William E. Simon reported to Congress in early April that the city was almost on schedule in paying back federal loans.

However, Comptroller General of the United States Elmer B. Staats testified that the city had no long-term solutions to its financial problems. Business leaders in the city also predicted that the city would eventually be forced to default. When the state court of appeals ruled in November that the city's moratorium on short-term debt payment was unconstitutional, city officials scrambled to find a new financial solution.

The City University of New York shut down for two weeks in June because it could not meet its payroll. It reopened on June 14 after the state granted $27 million in aid, but the school had to agree to begin charging tuition in September.

No Raises. The city averted a transit strike on April 1, when workers agreed to a new contract providing for no pay raises other than cost-of-living

adjustments. However, off-duty police staged demonstrations in October over a pay dispute.

A 10-day strike involving 37,000 nonmedical workers at 57 medical facilities ended on July 16 when both sides agreed to submit a dispute over cost-of-living raises to binding arbitration. A second strike, by 18,000 nonmedical workers at 16 municipal hospitals, lasted from August 4 to 7. The workers protested the layoff of 1,350 persons. They agreed to forego cost-of-living increases in exchange for the rehiring of 992 employees.

Economic Conditions remained poor. United States government figures showed that though New York City had the eighth highest per capita income among major U.S. cities, it was also one of the most expensive in which to live. Unemployment remained high – 10.3 per cent at midyear – and total employment dropped 2.5 per cent from 1975. At the same time, living costs rose 6.5 per cent.

The Environmental Protection Agency on July 23 ordered the city to stop dumping sewage sludge in the ocean by the end of 1981. The U.S. Department of Health, Education, and Welfare (HEW) on November 9 accused the school system of discriminating against women and minorities in hiring, promotion, and school assignments. HEW gave the system 90 days to develop a remedy or risk losing $200 million in federal aid.   James M. Banovetz

The Roosevelt Island Tramway, which opened in May, carries commuters from a new housing development over the East River to Manhattan.

NEW ZEALAND

NEW ZEALAND became a center of controversy in July 1976 when 32 African, Arab, and Caribbean countries withdrew from the Olympic Games in Montreal in protest against a tour of South Africa by the New Zealand Rugby Union team. Robert D. Muldoon's National Party government, elected on Nov. 29, 1975, had promised it would not ban sports tours of South Africa, as the previous Labour Party government had done, but would leave the decision to sports groups. New Zealand opposed *apartheid* (racial separation), but the Organization of African Unity was not appeased, and the walkout resulted. At the games, New Zealand's John Walker won the men's 1,500-meter race, and its field hockey team also won a gold medal.

The Economy was marked by a high inflation rate of 17 per cent and a balance-of-payments deficit caused by falling export prices and increased imports. Muldoon discouraged imports by raising taxes and imposing import deposits. He also restricted wage hikes; froze professional fees, prices, and rents; and imposed a tax on most foreign travel. New Zealand devalued its dollar by 6.2 per cent on November 29. The Labour government's national pension scheme, financed by employer and employee contributions, was replaced by a pay-as-you-go scheme funded by taxes.

Considerable industrial unrest resulted in legisla-tion in October to outlaw political strikes and those in essential industries, and to allow voluntary unionism. The government's overall aim was to increase production and reduce inflation, while at the same time recognizing that New Zealand's foreign exchange position made a temporary drop in living standards necessary. Abroad, there were encouraging rises in the price of wool, but meat exports continued to encounter difficulties.

Government Affairs. Muldoon's foreign policy differed sharply from his predecessor's in rejecting the idea of a nuclear-free zone in the Pacific Ocean and in welcoming U.S. nuclear-powered warships to New Zealand ports while proclaiming the threat of Russian expansionism. In spite of protests from port unions and others, the U.S.S. *Truxton* and *Long Beach* visited Auckland and Wellington.

The March 23 census set New Zealand's population at 3,130,083, an increase of 9.3 per cent since 1971. In spite of partial restoration of immigration from Great Britain and continued arrangements with Pacific Island countries, more people left New Zealand than entered it.

The country's reputation for social progressiveness was reinforced by the Anglican Synod decision to allow women to be ordained priests. The government also placed women on the same footing as men for jury service.   J. D. B. Miller

See also ASIA (Facts in Brief Table).

NEWARK. A judge ordered five members of Newark's city council to jail on June 4, 1976, for refusing to vote for court-ordered re-evaluation of property for tax purposes. They appealed the sentence on the grounds that it was unconstitutional to punish elected officials for following their conscience and their constituency. The Supreme Court of New Jersey ruled the question moot – at least until January 1977 – because the state legislature placed a 6-month moratorium on the tax issue after the council members were charged with contempt of court. A citizen task force was then set up to work out an acceptable tax plan. The incident stemmed from a civil suit brought against the entire nine-member city council by the state attorney general's office on behalf of the Essex County Board of Taxation.

Protests and Strikes. Councilman Anthony Carrino on March 23 led a crowd of 75 persons to Mayor Kenneth A. Gibson's office to protest the appointment of an out-of-towner as police precinct captain in the city's north ward. The protesters broke through the locked door of Gibson's city-hall office, and Gibson filed assault and battery charges against Carrino. An Essex County grand jury, however, refused to indict the councilman.

A snowstorm on February 2 followed by a teachers' strike closed the Newark public schools for a week. The strike continued despite a court restraining order issued on its third day. The teachers ap-

New Zealand's John Walker raises his arms in triumph as he crosses the finish line to win the 1,500-meter race at the Montreal Olympics.

proved a new contract on February 8, calling for 8.5 per cent pay increases over a 2½-year period.

Transit workers staged a two-week strike against Transport of New Jersey, the state's biggest commuter-bus line, in March. The strike ended on March 22.

Income and Taxes. A U.S. Department of Commerce study released on October 12 reported that the Newark metropolitan area's per capita personal income – $6,861 in 1974 – was the sixth highest in the nation. A Western Kentucky University study released in July showed that Newark residents bore one of the heaviest state and local tax burdens in the country. A family of four earning $10,000 per year paid 14.4 per cent of its income in taxes, compared with a national average of 8.9 per cent.

Factory workers' wages in the Newark area increased at the rate of 9.2 per cent between August 1975 and August 1976. The number of persons employed in Newark rose 1.3 per cent during the same period, but 8.4 per cent of the labor force was unemployed. Living costs rose 6.5 per cent and food prices increased 5 per cent over the one-year period ending in June. Department store sales, meanwhile, increased 16.4 per cent, while construction activity fell by 4.2 per cent.

A black priest, Joseph A. Francis, became an auxiliary bishop in the Roman Catholic diocese of Newark on May 4. James M. Banovetz

NEWFOUNDLAND suffered an economic blow on March 12, 1976, when the Come-by-Chance oil refinery on the south coast was forced to close. The provincial supreme court ruled that subsidiaries of the John M. Shaheen Company of New York City, which were operating the refinery, were bankrupt. The refinery, with a potential capacity of 100,000 barrels per day, lost $130 million in 2½ years of operation.

Newfoundland went to court to try to recover 800 megawatts of electric power pledged to Quebec from the massive Churchill Falls hydroelectric development in Labrador. Quebec Hydro planned to sell the power to the United States, but Newfoundland wanted it for its own economic growth.

Three by-elections were held on June 30 to correct invalid contests in the September 1975 provincial election. The ruling Progressive Conservatives, led by Premier Frank Moores, won 2 of the 3 seats, giving them 29 seats. The Liberals held 20 seats, having absorbed the splinter Liberal Reform Party; there was 1 Independent and 1 vacancy.

An austerity budget was presented on March 26. Totaling $1.2 billion, it included new gasoline and diesel oil taxes, a hike in the sales tax from 8 to 10 per cent, higher provincial income taxes, and a cutback in public services. David M. L. Farr

See also CANADA and articles on the other provinces.

NEWSPAPER. Economic problems and threats to press freedom bedeviled newspaper publishers throughout the world in 1976. Great Britain's newspapers found themselves caught in a morass of sagging readership, rising newsprint costs, and stagnant advertising revenues. A report in March from the Royal Commission on the Press stirred uneasy debate on Fleet Street when it recommended sharp manpower cuts and private loans of at least $100-million to the ailing industry.

The West German printers union went out on a 12-day strike against large newspapers in May, while allowing papers with under 50,000 circulation to continue publishing. In Paris, 11 major newspapers signed an agreement with a Communist-led printers union in July that allowed the financially pressed dailies to modernize plants and lay off and transfer printing-plant personnel.

In the United States, several newspapers also encountered labor difficulties. Picketing briefly shut down the *Philadelphia Inquirer* in March in a complicated dispute in which construction workers protested what they said was the newspaper's anti-union bias. The *Washington* (D.C.) *Post* continued its feud with striking pressmen who had temporarily shut down the paper in October 1975. Other craft unions signed a new contract with the paper in February 1976, but the dispute with the pressmen seemed unresolvable, and the paper began replacing them with nonunion workers. Meanwhile, the hard-pressed *Washington* (D.C.) *Star* reached an unprecedented agreement with 10 unions in April that would eliminate 200 jobs and save the paper about $6 million a year.

Declining circulations caused major problems for many U.S. papers. But the Newspaper Advertising Bureau reported ad linage was up 20 per cent.

Booth Newspapers, Incorporated, publisher of eight Michigan newspapers and the supplement *Parade,* in October approved a take-over by Samuel I. Newhouse in the largest newspaper transaction in U.S. history. Newhouse offered to buy Booth's outstanding stock at $47 a share, for a total of over $250 million. Robert O. Anderson, chairman of the Atlantic Richfield Company, agreed to buy *The London Observer* in late November. Also in November, Dorothy Schiff, publisher of *The New York Post,* said she had agreed to sell the paper to Australian publisher Rupert Murdoch.

Press Freedom was threatened by a proposal from a United Nations Educational, Scientific, and Cultural Organization meeting in Nairobi, Kenya, in October that would make national governments responsible for the international operations of all news organizations under their jurisdiction. The proposal was temporarily buried by sending it to committee for further study. Gerald B. Healey

See also SUPREME COURT OF THE UNITED STATES.
NICARAGUA. See LATIN AMERICA.

NICHOLSON, JACK (1937-   ), received the Academy of Motion Picture Arts and Sciences Award (Oscar) for best actor of 1975 on March 29, 1976, for his portrayal of a rebel in a mental institution in *One Flew Over the Cuckoo's Nest.* Considered one of Hollywood's best actors, Nicholson had been nominated three times previously as best actor: in 1970, for *Five Easy Pieces;* in 1973, for *The Last Detail;* and in 1974, for *Chinatown.*

Nicholson was born in Neptune, N.J., on April 22, 1937. His parents separated in his infancy, and his mother, Ethel May Nicholson, ran a beauty shop to support her son and two daughters. Nicholson began acting in high school. On a 1957 visit to his sister, a Los Angeles showgirl, he found a job as an office boy at Metro-Goldwyn-Mayer studios. Later, producer Joseph Pasternak encouraged him to join a theater group and study acting. In 1958, in the first of more than 20 B movies, he was the gunman in Roger Corman's *Cry Baby Killer.*

Since 1966, Nicholson has written and produced several films, including *Head,* an offbeat 1968 musical starring The Monkees. His big break came with his 1969 role as a boozy Southern lawyer in *Easy Rider,* for which he was nominated for the Oscar as best supporting actor. Nicholson married Sandra Knight in 1961, and they divorced in 1966. They have one daughter.   Edward G. Nash

NIGER. See AFRICA.

NIGERIA. A group of army officers on Feb. 13, 1976, staged an unsuccessful attempt to overthrow the Nigerian government. During the attempt, they killed Head of State Murtala Ramat Muhammed and held the Lagos radio station for several hours. By nightfall, the government had regained control.

The coup d' état was led by a junior officer, but the defense minister was also involved in the plot. He and 29 other accused participants were executed on March 11. Most of the plotters reportedly came from north-central Nigeria – as did former President Yakubu Gowon, deposed in July 1975. They apparently wanted to restore Gowon to power.

Lieutenant General Olusegun Obasanjo took over as head of state after the assassination. He had been the second-ranking member of the military government under Muhammed. See OBASANJO, OLUSEGUN.

Internal Reorganization. On February 3, the federal government announced the establishment of seven new states, carved out of five existing ones. This brought the number of states in Nigeria to 19.

The creation of the new states was intended to satisfy ethnic or regional interests as the military government went ahead with its plan to hand over power to a civilian government by 1979. The government published a draft of a proposed constitution on October 7 that provided for a federal system of government similar to that of the United States.

It called for universal suffrage, a two-house national legislature, and an elected president with strong executive powers. To prevent the election of someone representing just one group or region, a winning candidate would need to receive from 25 to 50 per cent of the votes in either a majority or two-thirds of the states – depending on the number of candidates competing. The merits of the draft constitution will be debated by a constituent assembly scheduled to convene in 1977.

Foreign Relations. Nigeria's relations with the United States deteriorated in early 1976. It objected strongly to alleged pressure by the United States aimed at getting Nigeria to withdraw its support of the Cuban- and Russian-backed faction in the Angolan civil war. On January 7, Nigeria publicly characterized the American pressure as insulting. Then, in April, it canceled a scheduled visit by U.S. Secretary of State Henry A. Kissinger.

The government told foreign investors on June 29 that they had to sell 40 to 100 per cent interests in their businesses to Nigerians. The percentage varied according to the type of enterprise. Foreign banks were required to give up a 60 per cent interest by September 30. Other businesses had until December 1978 to change to Nigerian control.

With the fall semester, Nigeria introduced free universal primary education.   John D. Esseks

See also AFRICA (Facts in Brief Table).

NIXON, RICHARD MILHOUS (1913-   ), the former President of the United States, who resigned in 1974, remained in seclusion for most of 1976. For the first time since 1948, Nixon did not attend the Republican National Convention. When the Republicans met in August in Kansas City, Mo., Nixon remained in San Clemente, Calif., watching the proceedings on television. Nixon spent most of his days working on his memoirs. In them, he reportedly blamed his enemies for the Watergate scandal that forced him to resign.

Trip to Peking. Nixon, his wife, Patricia, and a party of aides visited China for eight days in February as guests of the Chinese government. A reception was held in his honor in the Great Hall of the People in Peking on February 22.

On February 25, the Nixons hosted a dinner party in the Great Hall. The following day, they left Peking for a visit in southern China, and returned to the United States on February 29.

The publicity surrounding Nixon's China visit provoked criticism. Administration and congressional leaders were disturbed by remarks he made in China regarding U.S. foreign policy. The White House unceremoniously noted on March 22 that President Gerald R. Ford had found a written report from Nixon "very interesting and useful."

Aftermath of Scandal. The covert intelligence activities of the Nixon Administration were still

424

Flanked by daughters Tricia, left, and Julie, former President Nixon
wheels wife Patricia out of hospital where she recovered from a stroke.

being criticized and investigated in 1976. A deposition from Nixon made public on March 10 revealed that he ordered wiretaps in 1969 to locate news leaks, and that Secretary of State Henry A. Kissinger had given the Federal Bureau of Investigation a list of persons to be wiretapped. This conflicted with earlier sworn testimony by Kissinger. On December 16, a federal judge ruled Nixon liable for the tapping of an aide's telephone.

In a sworn statement published on March 11, Nixon revealed that he had ordered secret U.S. aid for the opponent of Salvador Allende Gossens in Chile's 1970 election to prevent a socialist victory.

The dispute over control of Nixon's presidential papers and tape recordings continued. In January, a three-judge federal panel upheld the 1974 law that awarded possession of his papers to the government. But on November 29, the Supreme Court of the United States agreed to hear Nixon's challenge to the law.

More Troubles. On July 8, Nixon was disbarred by the Appellate Division of the New York State Supreme Court on five charges stemming from the Watergate scandal. He can no longer practice law in New York.

Patricia Nixon suffered a stroke on July 7 and was hospitalized for 15 days. Daily therapy helped to restore strength in her arms and legs and to clarify her slightly slurred speech.　　　Carol L. Thompson

NOBEL PRIZES. Americans won all five prizes for literature, economics, and science that were presented in 1976. No peace prize was awarded. The Nobel committee last failed to award a peace prize in 1972.

Literature Prize was given to author Saul Bellow, 61, "for the human understanding and subtle analysis of contemporary culture that are combined in his work." Canadian-born, Bellow grew up in Chicago and is a professor of English at the University of Chicago. His novels are marked by a wry humor that touches on the theme of man trying to make sense of himself and the world. The Swedish Academy of Literature, which awards the Nobel for literature, said Bellow's first work, *Dangling Man* (1944), was a sign of change in American narrative art. They called *Seize the Day* (1956) "one of the classic works of our time," and *Henderson the Rain King* (1959) "the writer's most imaginative expedition." They went on to say that the book showed, as did most of Bellow's works, a fascination with a variety of settings — in the case of *Henderson*, the jungles of Africa — as well as a continuing, lively interest in his most identifiable subject, the "man with no foothold . . . who can never relinquish his faith that the value of life depends on its dignity, not its success."

Economics Prize was awarded to Milton Friedman, 64, who is a professor at the University of

"The child in me is delighted; the adult
is skeptical," novelist Saul Bellow said
upon learning he had won a Nobel Prize.

Chicago. He was cited for his work showing that economist John Maynard Keynes's theory of the consumption function—the relation of consumption to income—was wrong. Therefore, there were serious deficiencies in Keynesian and other earlier models for explaining economic behavior and developing policies to increase economic growth and stability. Friedman has long been a leader among conservative economists in advocating looser controls in monetary economics. He was an early supporter of floating exchange rates, instituted by the United States in 1971, and he was a leader in recognition of the importance of having a stable Federal Reserve System policy.

Chemistry Prize went to William N. Lipscomb, Jr., 57, of Harvard University, who was cited for studies of the structure of compounds called boranes that have illuminated problems of chemical bonding. This was the first award in many years for discoveries in pure inorganic chemistry. *Borane* is the currently accepted name for various unstable hydrides of boron, compounds first defined in 1912. Lipscomb was the first to explain the nature of their chemical bond, how such compounds are built, and why they exist.

Physics Prize was shared by Burton Richter, 45, of Stanford University and Samuel C. C. Ting, 40, of the Massachusetts Institute of Technology for the discovery of a new type of elementary particle:

the psi, or J, particle. They made the discovery independently in 1974. Many new elementary particles discovered in the preceding 15 years showed kinship to one another in groups or families. But the new particle, called J by Ting and psi by Richter, is separate and different and has formed the beginning of a new family of particles.

Physiology or Medicine Prize was shared by Baruch S. Blumberg, 51, of the University of Pennsylvania Medical School and D. Carleton Gajdusek, 53, of the National Institute of Neurological and Communicative Disorders and Stroke at Bethesda, Md., "for their discoveries concerning new mechanisms for the origin and dissemination of infectious diseases." Both men made their discoveries as a result of disease studies among primitive tribesmen. Blumberg's research resulted in the discovery of the so-called Australian antigen and the production of an experimental vaccine against the most severe form of hepatitis. Gajdusek's work led to the discovery that kuru, a disease found in a New Guinea tribe, is caused by a slow virus, the first identified among humans. As a result of this work, slow viruses have been tentatively identified as the cause of several neurological diseases.   Foster Stockwell

NORTH ATLANTIC TREATY ORGANIZATION (NATO). See EUROPE.
NORTH CAROLINA. See STATE GOVERNMENT.
NORTH DAKOTA. See STATE GOVERNMENT.

NORTHERN IRELAND spent 1976 in a political and military stalemate. Any chance that Roman Catholic and Protestant politicians would agree to form a power-sharing government finally vanished. Terrorism escalated as paramilitary groups on both sides of the religious divide rushed to fill the political vacuum with bombings and killings. The British government settled down to a prolonged period of direct rule of Northern Ireland from London. With no hope of political progress to isolate the terrorists or of military victory over them, there seemed to be no solution to Ulster's troubles.

No Political Progress. Merlyn Rees, Britain's secretary of state for Ulster, reconvened its constitutional convention on February 3. The government had already rejected a 1975 report from this Protestant loyalist-dominated body that advocated a return to old-style Protestant supremacy. But Rees hoped that more talks would bring Catholics and Protestants closer.

It was a forlorn hope. The convention broke up in disorder in March. Secret talks with the Catholic Social Democratic and Labour Party (SDLP) continued for a while, but they were in vain. The Protestants would offer the SDLP no more than seats on legislative committees. The SDLP would settle for nothing short of seats in the Cabinet.

So ended yet another attempt to find a lasting and acceptable form of government for Ulster. The

Protestant and Roman Catholic women stage a peace rally in Londonderry to protest the continued violence in Northern Ireland.

SDLP was further from power than ever, but the Protestant coalition had little to celebrate. Once the convention was dissolved, the Protestants split badly between relative moderates and extremists.

Terrorism Escalates. With the failure of the constitutional convention, the Irish Republican Army (IRA) mounted a new terrorist campaign, and Protestant murder gangs stalked the streets once more. By August, more than 200 people had been killed. Street rioting, barricades, and hijackings were organized by the IRA. Portrush, Ulster's premier holiday town, was destroyed by bombs. Rees was replaced on September 10 by Roy Mason, a former defense minister. Mason was greeted in Belfast with more violence. In one incident, troops killed an IRA gunman at the wheel of his car. The car swerved, killing three children. A peace movement, organized by women appalled at the slaughter of the children, gathered momentum. Peace marches united Catholics and Protestants all over Ulster, giving hope that if enough of the people shunned the terrorists, they would be forced out of business. But seasoned observers predicted the movement would soon peter out.

Meanwhile, the IRA agitated against the loss of political status for convicted terrorists. Maire Drumm, a spokesperson for the IRA political wing, was killed by gunmen on October 28.   Andrew F. Neil

See also EUROPE (Facts in Brief Table).

NORTHWEST TERRITORIES. Debate over the construction of a gas pipeline through the Mackenzie River Valley from the Arctic coast dominated the territory in 1976. The National Energy Board was charged with recommending a pipeline route to the federal Cabinet. By September, the board had three proposals to consider. One was a Canadian-American venture to transport gas from Prudhoe Bay in Alaska and from the Mackenzie Delta south through the Mackenzie Valley to markets in both countries. Another was a Canadian company's plan to bring only Canadian gas south along the same route. The third was to move Alaskan gas into Canada along the Alaska Highway to connect with existing distribution networks.

Indian and Eskimo land claims were another prominent issue. Some 7,000 Indians, most of them living in the Mackenzie Valley, on October 25 demanded an autonomous region to be the home of the Dene (pronounced *DEN-ay*) nation. The Indians claimed title to 450,000 square miles (1.2 million square kilometers) of territory.

On February 27, about 15,000 Inuit (Eskimos) presented a claim to 250,000 square miles (650,000 square kilometers) of Arctic land north and east of the tree line. They also claimed hunting rights and a 3 per cent share of mineral royalties in another large tract of land.   David M. L. Farr

See also CANADA.

NORWAY

NORWAY. Trygve Bratteli resigned as prime minister on Jan. 9, 1976, as he had promised to do in September 1975, when support fell for the ruling Labor Party. His successor was Odvar Nordli, former Labor Party parliamentary leader. In announcing his Cabinet on January 12, Nordli said there would be no change in foreign and domestic policies. He replaced six Bratteli ministers, and politicians saw the change as a handover of power from the World War II generation of leaders to a postwar generation.

Nordli's immediate task was to win back support from the left wing alliance of parties in readiness for general elections in 1977. A proposal by leftists in the *Storting* (parliament) to abolish the monarchy and establish a republic was rejected on March 16.

Incomes Program. The government, trade unions, and farmers' organizations agreed to a "combined income settlement" on April 5. The pact guaranteed an increase of 3 per cent in real incomes for wage earners and higher increases for farmers to bring them to the income level of industrial workers over five years. The settlement's goal was to reduce inflation from 12 per cent to 8 or 9 per cent by the end of 1976. Subsidies and tax cuts based on future oil revenues will foot the bill. Without this deal, a 20 per cent wage increase would have been needed to give a 3 per cent rise in real income.

Economic Zone. Nordli announced on October 5 that in 1977 Norway would begin to enforce an economic zone extending 200 nautical miles from its coastline in order to protect dwindling fish stocks. The move would exclude foreign fishermen from some of Europe's richest fishing grounds. Maritime Law Minister Jens Evensen said in September that the deterioration of cod-rich northern waters made quick solutions imperative. But Norway wanted to keep its right to catch certain types of fish in British coastal waters in exchange for giving British fishermen special rights within Norway's new zone. The failure of the European Community (Common Market) to reach a common fisheries policy presented a stumbling block to agreement. But Norway and Russia agreed on October 15 to recognize each other's right to a 200-nautical-mile economic zone in the Barents Sea.

Oil Exports. Norway became a net exporter of oil in 1976, and set a target of 88 million short tons (80-million metric tons) by 1980. Investment in the oil sector counteracted a weakening of foreign demand for other goods and services, and the economy suffered less from general recession than most other European countries. Vast public-works projects and job-training programs helped to keep unemployment below 25,000.   Kenneth Brown

See also EUROPE (Facts in Brief Table).

Oil drilling and production rigs in the North Sea helped make Norway a net exporter of oil in 1976, which offset reduced foreign demand for other goods.

NOVA SCOTIA. The high cost of energy dominated affairs in 1976. The price of gasoline, heating oil, and electricity rose steeply. In an effort to delay the impact of mounting energy costs, Premier Gerald A. Regan extended the freeze on oil prices for 30 days beyond the date fixed for the rest of Canada. The new Canadian national price for oil products, effective elsewhere in August, went into effect in Nova Scotia at the end of September.

Efforts to obtain federal subsidies for higher electrical costs failed. But a new hydroelectric generating station nearing completion at Wreck Cove on Cape Breton Island offered hope of some relief. It should provide 100 megawatts of power in 1977 and an equal amount a year later.

The Regan government presented the first billion-dollar budget in the province's history. Finance Minister Peter Nicholson managed to achieve a small surplus after increasing taxes on liquor and tobacco, raising the sales tax from 7 to 8 per cent, and boosting vehicle registration fees.

The governing Liberals retained a seat, Cape Breton West, in a by-election on September 7, the first electoral test for the government since it won re-election in 1974. That left the Liberals with 31 seats, the Progressive Conservatives with 11, the New Democrats, 3, and 1 vacancy.   David M. L. Farr

See also CANADA.

NUCLEAR ENERGY. See ENERGY.

NUTRITION. A December 1976 report issued by the Worldwatch Institute, a research organization, said that overnutrition—eating too much of the wrong kinds of foods—is as serious a world health problem as undernutrition. The authors, Erik Eckholm and Frank Record, believe that governments must develop policies that will fight both forms of malnutrition.

Scientists have increasingly linked the high-calorie, high-fat diet of the more affluent with the spread of such diseases as cancer, coronary heart disease, diabetes, hypertension, and obesity. Coronary heart disease accounts for one-third of all deaths in the United States, for example; its occurrence in Japan has tripled in the past 15 years. The disease is related to many factors, such as smoking and lack of exercise, but it also appears to be linked to a high-fat diet.

Diet and Cancer. The affluent diet, characterized by a high intake of meats, dairy products, and refined flour and sugar, may also be related to as many as half of all cancers in women and one-third in men, the two researchers said.

"Doctors and drugs alone can seldom cure the diseases of malnutrition," the report said. "Preventive measures are the sole effective means of control. With diet apparently a factor in more than half of all deaths in Western countries, the new stronghold of preventive medicine must be the pantry."

Reducing the number of calories in the diet inhibits the development of cancer in female mice, according to Gabriel Fernandes and Edmond J. Yunis of the University of Minnesota Medical School. They reported in October that a 10-calorie daily diet prevented the spontaneous development of breast cancer in a group of young female mice. Meanwhile, 71 per cent of the mice in another group that was fed the standard rodent diet of 16 calories per day developed breast cancer within 500 days. An equivalent caloric reduction for humans would be from 2,200 to 1,200 calories per day.

Australian Researchers Henry M. Whyte and Nathalie Havenstein of the John Curtin School of Medical Research in Canberra published in 1976 a complete review of the usefulness of a lower blood cholesterol diet in preventing heart attacks. They concluded that reducing saturated fat, cholesterol, and the total amount of fat and calories in the diet can be beneficial. Their report said that about 14 in a group of 100 nonsmoking 35-year-old men with normal blood pressure could expect to have heart attacks in the next 20 years. But if they adjusted their diet and lowered their blood cholesterol levels by as little as 16 per cent, about half of the 14 could avoid heart attacks.

New Milk. Lactose intolerance, a common condition among blacks and Orientals, prevents many people from drinking milk. Marvin L. Speck of the University of North Carolina's School of Dairy Sciences has developed a new milk that these persons can drink. Speck adds a culture of the bacteria *Lactobacillus acidophilus* to the milk. These bacteria break down lactose into lactic acid in the human intestinal tract, providing the nutritional value of milk to lactose-intolerant people.

Careful Shoppers? In September, the U.S. Food and Drug Administration published the results of a study of U.S. food-shopping habits. About 75 per cent of the shoppers surveyed checked "open dating" information, which indicates the shelf life of a food item. The list of ingredients on cans or packaged foods was considered by 46 per cent, but only 33 per cent consulted nutrition labels when buying food. More women than men considered nutritional values, and younger shoppers tended to be more nutrition-conscious than those over 35.

Starvation. While the rich, developed nations grapple with the problems of overnutrition, much of the rest of the world still faces serious undernutrition. Clifton R. Wharton, Jr., president of Michigan State University, warned at the 1976 World Food Conference in Ames, Iowa, in June that millions may starve in the next decade and millions more will suffer from undernutrition. Some authorities estimate, for example, that from 10 to 30 per cent of the children in Latin America are undernourished.   Paul E. Araujo

OAKLAND. See SAN FRANCISCO-OAKLAND.

OBASANJO, OLUSEGUN (1937-   ), a lieutenant general in the Nigerian Army, became the head of Nigeria's military government on Feb. 14, 1976. He replaced Murtala Ramat Muhammed, who was assassinated on February 13 during an attempted coup d'état. Obasanjo had served as chief of staff and second in command under Muhammed since July 1975. He directed the day-to-day administration of the government. See NIGERIA.

Obasanjo was born on March 5, 1937, in Abeokuta, Nigeria. He joined the army in 1958 and was commissioned in 1959, after attending officer training school in Great Britain. His military career flourished, and he rose rapidly through the ranks, becoming a brigadier general in 1972.

An engineer by training, Obasanjo served as chief of army engineers in the late 1960s. He then headed a marine commando division during the Nigerian civil war, when the state of Biafra tried to secede from the federal government. His troops broke through the Biafran lines in 1969, and the Biafran Army surrendered to him in 1970.

He also played a vital role in overthrowing the government of Yakubu Gowon in July 1975. Obasanjo, a member of the Yoruba people, was instrumental in winning support for the coup among Yoruba soldiers and officers.

Obasanjo is married, and he and his wife have four children.   Darlene R. Stille

OCEAN. France and Germany in 1976 joined Great Britain, Japan, and Russia in the International Phase of Ocean Drilling—a new stage of the Deep Sea Drilling Project (DSDP), which was started by the United States 10 years earlier. The new goal is to drill through sediments into the volcanic rocks that form the backbone of the ocean floor.

Ocean scientists completed the first voyage of the international phase on January 20. At a site about 1,500 nautical miles northeast of San Juan, Puerto Rico, the DSDP drilling ship *Glomar Challenger* penetrated 330 feet (100 meters) of sea-floor sediment and then drilled a remarkable 1,890 feet (576 meters) into subbasement rocks. Scientists had to remove the drill, replace worn drill bits, and guide it back into the same drill hole nine times, a record number of re-entries. Water depth at the drill site was 14,710 feet (4,484 meters), also a record for re-entry drilling.

The Deepest Hole. In a cruise that ended on May 12, scientists on the *Glomar Challenger* drilled a record 5,710 feet (1,740 meters) beneath the sea floor in water 12,760 feet (3,890 meters) deep west of Portugal in the North Atlantic. They found evidence of massive avalanching at the edge of the African continent.

On the summer cruise at the western edge of the European continent in the Bay of Biscay, new drilling revealed the remains of unknown swamplands fringed with coral reefs about 10,800 feet (3,300 meters) below sea level. Layers of carbon-rich shale 100 million years old indicated that the swamplands slowly sank to their present depth. A great mountain range that once extended between Greenland and Europe also sank to a depth of some 4,300 feet (1,300 meters) below sea level. Ocean scientists believe that both sinkings are related to the forces responsible for continental drift.

Practical Drilling. After a final legal test before U.S. Supreme Court Justice Thurgood Marshall, the U.S. government on August 17 opened bids for the first sale of offshore oil- and gas-drilling leases off the Atlantic Coast. The tracts, which lie in the Baltimore Canyon from 47 to 92 nautical miles off the coast of Delaware and New Jersey, may contain as much as 1.4 billion barrels of oil and 9.4 trillion cubic feet (0.27 trillion cubic meters) of natural gas. Earlier, a consortium of 31 oil companies conducted exploratory drilling on the edge of George's Bank, off Cape Cod.

Cod War. Iceland broke off diplomatic relations with Great Britain on February 19, but Britain agreed on June 1 to cut back its cod-fishing fleet for six months. The agreement ended a dispute over Britain's fishing rights within Iceland's declared 200-nautical-mile territorial seas. See EUROPE (Close-Up).

Goose barnacles are part of the New York Aquarium's display of rare deep-sea animals from the Gulf of Mexico—first time they have been exhibited alive.

Bigger Conservation Zone. On April 13, President Gerald R. Ford signed the Fisheries Conservation Act of 1976. Effective on March 1, 1977, the new law extends exclusive United States management rights over all fish and shellfish except tuna to a distance of 200 nautical miles from U.S. shores. See FISHING INDUSTRY.

The Fifth United Nations (UN) Law of the Sea Conference ended in deadlock on September 17 after seven weeks of sluggish negotiations over who should control the mineral wealth of the deep seabed. See MINES AND MINING.

The U.S. Navy, on November 11, recovered a highly secret F-14 Tomcat fighter aircraft that rolled off the deck of the U.S. aircraft carrier *John F. Kennedy* on September 14 and sank in about 1,890 feet (576 meters) of water 75 nautical miles northwest of Scapa Flow, Scotland.

The federal ocean program for fiscal 1977 totals $952.3 million, an increase of $79.1 million. The largest percentage increases went to the National Aeronautics and Space Administration's ocean satellite programs, to the Energy Research and Development Administration's renewable ocean energy programs, and to the outer continental-shelf oil-and-gas activities being carried out by the Department of the Interior.   Arthur G. Alexiou

OHIO. See CLEVELAND; STATE GOVERNMENT.

OKLAHOMA. See STATE GOVERNMENT.

OLD AGE. Elderly people in a 1976 national opinion poll named "fear of crime" as the most serious personal problem they faced. They selected the crime problem from a list that included "poor health" and "not enough money." A detailed local survey was made in Portland and surrounding Multnomah County, Oregon, and reported in September 1976 at the National Conference on Justice and Older Americans, held in Portland.

The Portland pollsters asked people over 60 years of age about their experience with crime. Half said that they had been a victim of crime within the previous 10 years, and one-third within the previous three years. The types of crime included: burglary, theft, or vandalism, 63 per cent; harassment or fraud, 23 per cent; and assault or robbery, 12 per cent. About 75 per cent of the crimes occurred in the victims' homes, and 11 per cent occurred on nearby streets. Slightly more men than women were victims. Fewer than half the victims reported the crimes to police.

Retirement Age. The Supreme Court of the United States on June 25 upheld the right of a state to set a mandatory retirement age for state employees. The case involved a challenge to a Massachusetts law requiring state police to retire at 50. The court ruled that such a limit does not discriminate against the elderly, but "marks a stage that each of us will reach if we live out our life span."

The National Council on the Aging (NCOA) met in Chicago in September and called on the U.S. Congress to amend the Age Discrimination in Employment Act. The council wants the law to cover people over 65 who want to keep working. The NCOA proposed that retirement plans should be based on a person's ability to work and not solely on chronological age. It cited a program at the Industrial Health Counseling Service in Portland, Me., as an example of such a flexible program.

The NCOA also focused attention on public financial support for education for the aged. Several states provide free tuition in public community colleges and state universities for people over 60 or 65. Directors of educational extensions in state universities devoted one day of their meeting in Dallas in September to discussions of programs for the elderly.

Housing was another concern of the NCOA, which called for renewed federal support for public housing for elderly people with low incomes, and low-interest loans. President Gerald R. Ford signed a housing bill on August 3 that raised the amount of funds available for housing loans to the elderly and handicapped to $1.48 billion in fiscal 1977, $2.39-billion in fiscal 1978, and $3.3 billion in fiscal 1979. See HOUSING.   Robert J. Havighurst

See also SOCIAL SECURITY.

Senators Percy of Illinois, left, and Moss of Utah look at backache drugs collected during investigation of Medicare and Medicaid fraud.

OLYMPIC GAMES

The world's greatest sports spectacle, the Olympic Summer Games, was held on schedule and without incident from July 17 through Aug. 1, 1976, at Montreal, Canada. That surprised those who feared that the facilities would not be ready, or that politics or terrorist activity would disrupt the games and perhaps end them.

The games went on, and they attracted huge crowds that paid up to $40 per ticket for the opening and closing ceremonies (scalpers got as much as $400 per ticket) and up to $24 for such sports as track and field, swimming, and gymnastics. The competition was good, and there were few surprises. Swimming and track and field, the showcase sports, were dominated by American men and East German women. The United States also regained the basketball gold medal it lost to Russia in 1972.

Nadia Comaneci. Olga Korbut of Russia, the darling of the 1972 Olympics as a 17-year-old gymnast, won a gold and a silver medal in Montreal and went almost unnoticed. She was upstaged by a new gymnastics prodigy, the 14-year-old Nadia Comaneci of Romania.

Comaneci was near perfection as she won three gold medals, one silver, and one bronze. Comaneci became the first gymnast in Olympic history to earn a perfect score of 10 from the judges. She earned seven 10's in the uneven parallel bars and the balance beam. The scoreboard designers were so sure no one would get a 10 that they built the board to show no score higher than 9.95. When Comaneci scored a 10, it showed as 1.00. See COMANECI, NADIA.

Construction Problems. For two years, it appeared there might be no Olympics. Excavation for the Olympic Stadium and the swimming pool did not start until 19 months before the games. Labor strife caused so many delays that the provincial government took charge of construction in November 1975. All facilities were ready, but work was suspended on the 552-foot (168-meter) tower adjoining the stadium until after the Olympics.

The original cost of the Montreal Olympics was projected as $310 million. The stadium alone cost between $685 million and $800 million, and the entire Olympics cost at least $1.4 billion. Much of that was in permanent facilities, such as a new subway line to downtown Montreal. But even with revenue from 3.3 million attendance, souvenir medals, a national lottery, and other sources, a deficit of $800 million remained.

Some of that money would be recovered in the sale of the Olympic Village, which housed more

Gold medalists in the 1976 Olympic Games include American figure skater Dorothy Hamill, *right,* and, *clockwise from bottom, opposite page,* American Sheila Young, 500-meter speed skating; East German Kornelia Ender, who won four in swimming; American John Naber, who also won four in swimming; American Bruce Jenner, decathlon champion; and Cuban sprinter Alberto Juantorena, winner of the 400- and 800-meter races in track and field competition.

than 10,000 athletes and officials in four 19-story buildings, shaped like half pyramids, half a mile (0.8 kilometer) from Olympic Stadium. The organizers hoped to sell the village to real estate developers for $50 million (it cost $85 million).

The Political Problems that always seem to plague the Olympics started after the facilities were completed. The first problem concerned Taiwan, which planned to compete as the Republic of China and was recognized by that name by the International Olympic Committee (IOC). But the People's Republic of China persuaded Canada, its trading ally, to make Taiwan compete as Taiwan. Taiwan was convinced that if it gave in this time, it would never again be known as the Republic of China.

The IOC was angry at what it called political interference by Canada. It threatened to call off the Olympics, and Canada almost certainly would have had to give in if the committee had maintained its threat. Instead, the IOC announced that the Olympics would be held regardless of the Taiwan solution. The U.S. Olympic Committee (USOC) helped arrange a compromise under which Taiwan would compete under another name. But Taiwan refused and called its athletes home.

The Taiwan problem was still simmering when a boycott of New Zealand unfolded. Many nations had sports relations with South Africa. The IOC had barred South Africa from competing because of its policy of *apartheid* (racial separation).

OLYMPIC GAMES

The New Zealand national rugby team, ironically known as the All Blacks after the color of the New Zealand national uniform, was touring South Africa. Black African nations demanded that New Zealand be barred from the Olympics because of this tour, and they said that if New Zealand did not leave, they would. New Zealand Olympic officials said they had no control over rugby, a non-Olympic sport. They decried South Africa's racial policies, but they would not withdraw.

Most black African nations, a few from Asia, and Guyana withdrew. In all, 32 nations quit. Some had potential Olympic champions and medalists, such as Filbert Bayi of Tanzania, whose 1,500-meter race against John Walker of New Zealand was a prospective highlight of the Olympics. With Bayi absent, Walker won easily.

Tight Security. During the 1972 Olympics in Munich, West Germany, Arab terrorists sneaked into the Olympic Village and eventually killed 11 Israeli athletes, coaches, and officials. Canada spent $140 million to prevent a repetition of that tragedy. Officials used 9,000 Canadian soldiers, 5,200 Montreal police officers, 1,500 Quebec provincial police officers, 1,400 members of the Royal Canadian Mounted Police, and 5,000 communications and support workers. In all, more than 22,000 security people guarded 24,000 athletes, and others.

Romanian gymnast Nadia Comaneci, 14, was the center of attention at the Summer Games as she made perfect scores of 10 seven times.

There were a few death threats — to American high jumper Dwight Stones and Russian sprinter Valeri Borzov among others — but there were no attempts on anyone's life. As Esther Rot, a hurdler who was the only member of the 1972 Israeli Olympic team to compete in Montreal, said dryly, "The security here is good, better than at Munich."

East Germany. Russia, which led in the 1972 Olympics with 50 gold medals and a total of 99, led again with 47 and 125. The United States, which won 33 gold and 94 total in 1972, took 34 and 94. East Germany advanced from 20 gold and 66 total in 1972 to 40 and 90, and its success was impressive and predictable.

Like the other Communist-bloc nations, East Germany uses sports as an instrument of state policy. It spends about $50 million per year on sports, much of it on 25 sports schools. Most of these institutions are boarding schools that take children as young as 6 years old who have been screened for their athletic ability. The children spend five or six hours per day, before and after classes, on sports. The program succeeded. East Germany sent 293

Alpine skier Rosi Mittermaier of West Germany won two gold medals and one silver in the Winter Olympic Games in Innsbruck, Austria, in February.

Official Results of the 1976 Olympic Games

Winners of the Winter Olympics in Innsbruck, Austria, in February

Event	Winner	Country	Mark
Men's Skiing			
Downhill	Franz Klammer	Austria	1:45.73
Giant Slalom	Heini Hemmi	Switzerland	3:26.97
Slalom	Piero Gros	Italy	2:03.29
15-kilometer cross-country	Nikolai Bajukov	Russia	43:58.47
30-kilometer cross-country	Sergei Saveliev	Russia	1 30:29.38
50-kilometer cross-country	Ivar Formo	Norway	2 37:30.05
40-kilometer cross-country relay	Matti Pitkaenen, Juha Mieto, Pertti Teaurajaervi, Arto Koivisto	Finland	2 07:59.72
Nordic combined	Ulrich Wehling	E. Germany	423.39 pts.
70-meter jump	Hans-Georg Aschenbach	E. Germany	252 pts.
90-meter jump	Karl Schnabl	Austria	234.8 pts.
Women's Skiing			
Downhill	Rosi Mittermaier	W. Germany	1:46.16
Giant Slalom	Kathy Kreiner	Canada	1:29.13
Special Slalom	Rosi Mittermaier	W. Germany	1:30.54
5-kilometer cross-country	Helena Takalo	Finland	15:48.69
10-kilometer cross-country	Raisa Smetanina	Russia	30:13.41
20-kilometer cross-country relay	Nina Baldicheva, Zinaida Amosova, Raisa Smetanina, Galina Kulakova	Russia	1:07:49.75
Men's Speed Skating			
500 meters	Evgeny Kulikov	Russia	39.17*
1,000 meters	Peter Mueller	U.S.A.	1:19.32*
1,500 meters	Jan Egil Storholt	Norway	1:59.38*
5,000 meters	Sten Stensen	Norway	7:24.48
10,000 meters	Piet Kleine	Netherlands	14:50.59*

Event	Winner	Country	Mark
Women's Speed Skating			
500 meters	Sheila Young	U.S.A.	42.76s*
1,000 meters	Tatiana Averina	Russia	1:28.43*
1,500 meters	Galina Stepanskaya	Russia	2:16.58*
3,000 meters	Tatiana Averina	Russia	4:45.19*
Figure Skating			
Men's Singles	John Curry	Great Britain	192.74 pts.
Women's Singles	Dorothy Hamill	U.S.A.	193.80 pts.
Pairs	Irina Rodnina, Alexandr Zaitsev	Russia	140.54 pts.
Ice Dancing	Ludmila Pakhomova, Alexandr Gorshkov	Russia	209.92 pts.
Biathlon			
Singles	Nikolai Kruglov	Russia	1:14:12.26
Relay	Alexandr Elizarov, Ivan Biakov, Nikolai Kruglov, Alexandr Tikhonov	Russia	1:57:55.64
Bobsledding			
Two-man	Meinhard Nehmer, Bernhard Germeshausen	E. Germany	3:44.42
Four-man	Meinhard Nehmer, Jochen Babok, Bernhard Germeshausen, Bernhard Lehmann	E. Germany	3:40.43
Ice Hockey		Russia	10 pts.
Men's Luge			
Singles	Detlef Guenther	E. Germany	3:27.688
Doubles	Hans Rinn, Norbert Hahn	E. Germany	1:25.604
Women's Luge			
Singles	Margit Schumann	E. Germany	2:50.621

Winners of the Summer Olympics in Montreal, Canada, in July

Event	Winner	Country	Mark
Archery			
Men	Darrell Pace	U.S.A.	2,571 pts.*
Women	Luann Ryon	U.S.A.	2,499 pts.*
Boxing			
Light-flyweight	Jorge Hernandez	Cuba	
Flyweight	Leo Randolph	U.S.A.	
Bantamweight	Yong Jo Gu	North Korea	
Featherweight	Angel Herrera	Cuba	
Lightweight	Howard Davis	U.S.A.	
Light-welterweight	Ray Leonard	U.S.A.	
Welterweight	Jochen Bachfeld	E. Germany	
Light-middleweight	Jerry Rybicki	Poland	
Middleweight	Mike Spinks	U.S.A.	
Light-heavyweight	Leon Spinks	U.S.A.	
Heavyweight	Teofilo Stevenson	Cuba	
Canoeing, Men			
500-meter kayak singles	Vasile Diba	Romania	1:46.41
500-meter kayak tandems	Mattern, Olbricht	E. Germany	1:35.87
500-meter Canadian singles	Alexandr Rogov	Russia	1:59.23

Event	Winner	Country	Mark
500-meter Canadian tandems	Sergei Petrenko, Alexandr Vinogradov	Russia	1:45.81
1,000-meter kayak singles	Rudiger Helm	E. Germany	3:48.20
1,000-meter kayak tandems	Sergei Nagorny, Vladimir Romanovsky	Russia	3:29.01
1,000-meter kayak fours	Chuhray, Degtiarev, Filatov, Morozov	Russia	3:08.69
1,000-meter Canadian singles	Matija Ljubek	Yugoslavia	4:09.51
1,000-meter Canadian tandems	Sergei Petrenko, Alexandr Vinogradov	Russia	3:52.76
Canoeing, Women			
500-meter kayak singles	Carola Zirzow	E. Germany	2:01.05
500-meter kayak tandems	Gopova, Kreft	Russia	1:51.15

(*) Indicates new Olympic record; (†) new world record; (≠) ties world record; (//) disqualified for using banned drugs

Event	Winner	Country	Mark
Cycling			
Individual road race	Bernt Johansson	Sweden	4:46.52
Sprint	Anton Tkac	Czecho-slovakia	10.78; 11.13
1,000-meter time trial	Klaus-Jurgen Grunke	E. Germany	1:05.927
4,000-meter individual pursuit	Gregor Braun	W. Germany	4:47.61
4,000-meter team pursuit	Braun, Lutz, Schumacher, Vonhof	W. Germany	4:21.06
100-kilometer team time trial	Chukanov, Chaplygin, Kaminsky, Pikkuus	Russia	2:08.53
Equestrian			
Three-day event, individual	Tad Coffin	U.S.A.	114.99 pts.
Three-day event, team	Tad Coffin, Mike Plumb, Mary A. Tauskey, Bruce Davidson	U.S.A.	441 pts.
Dressage, individual	Christina Stueckelberger	Switzerland	1,486 pts.
Dressage, team	Boldt, Klimke, Grillo	W. Germany	5,115 pts.
Prix des nation, individual	Alwin Schockemoehle	W. Germany	0.00 pts.
Prix des nation, team	Hubert Parot, Marcel Rozier, Michel Roche, Mare Rogust	France	40 pts.
Fencing, Men			
Individual foil	Fabio Dal Zotto	Italy	
Team foil		W. Germany	
Individual épée	Alexander Pusch	W. Germany	
Team épée		Sweden	
Individual saber	Viktor Krovopouskov	Russia	
Team saber		Russia	
Fencing, Women			
Individual foil	Ildiko Schwarczenberger	Hungary	
Team foil		Russia	
Gymnastics, Men			
All-around	Nikolai Andrianov	Russia	58.25 pts.
Long horse vault	Nikolai Andrianov	Russia	19.450 pts.
Side horse	Zoltan Magyar	Hungary	19.700 pts.
Horizontal bar	Mitsuo Tsukahara	Japan	19.675 pts.
Parallel bars	Sawao Kato	Japan	19.675 pts.
Rings	Nikolai Andrianov	Russia	19.650 pts.
Floor exercises	Nikolai Andrianov	Russia	19.450 pts.
Team		Japan	576.8 pts.
Gymnastics, Women			
All-around	Nadia Comaneci	Romania	79.275 pts.
Balance beam	Nadia Comaneci	Romania	19.950 pts.
Uneven parallel bars	Nadia Comaneci	Romania	20.000 pts.
Vault	Nelli Kim	Russia	19.800 pts.
Floor exercise	Nelli Kim	Russia	19.850 pts.
Team		Russia	390.35 pts.
Judo			
Lightweight	Hector Rodriguez	Cuba	
Light-middleweight	Vladimir Nevzorov	Russia	
Middleweight	Isamu Sonoda	Japan	
Light-heavyweight	Kazuhiro Ninomiya	Japan	
Heavyweight	Sergei Novikov	Russia	
Open	Haruki Uemura	Japan	
Modern Pentathlon			
Individual	Janusz Pyciak-Peciuk	Poland	
Team		Great Britain	

Event	Winner	Country	Mark
Rowing, Men			
Single sculls	Pectti Karppinen	Finland	7:29.03
Double sculls	Frank Hansen, Alf Hansen	Norway	7:13.20
Pairs without coxswain	Jorg Landvoigt, Bernd Landvoigt	E. Germany	7:23.31
Pairs with coxswain	Harald Jahrling, Friederich Ulrich, Georg Spohr	E. Germany	7:58.99
Four sculls	Guldenpfennig, Reiche Bussert, Wolfgramm	E. Germany	6:18.65
Fours without coxswain	Brietzke, Decker, Semmler, Mager	E. Germany	6:37.42
Fours with coxswain	Eshinov, Ivanov, Kuznetsov, Klepikov, Lukianov	Russia	6:40.22
Four sculls with coxswain	Borchmann, Lou, Poley, Zobelt, Weigelt	E. Germany	3:29.99
Eights with coxswain	Baumgart, Dohn, Klatt, Luck, Wendise, Kostulski, Karnatz, Prudahl, Danielowski	E. Germany	5:58.29
Rowing, Women			
Single sculls	Christine Scheiblich	E. Germany	4:05.56
Double sculls	Otzetova, Yardanova	Bulgaria	3:44.36
Pairs without coxswain	Kelbetcheva, Groutcheva	Bulgaria	4:01.22
Fours with coxswain	Metze, Schwede, Lohs, Kurth, Hess	E. Germany	3:45.03
Eights with coxswain	Goretzki, Knetsch, Richter, Ahrenholz, Kallies, Ebert, Lehmann, Muller, Wilke	E. Germany	3:29.99
Shooting			
Skeet	Josef Panacek	Czechoslovakia	198 pts.
Trapshooting	Don Haldeman	U.S.A.	190 pts.
Free pistol	Uwe Potteck	E. Germany	573 pts.
Rapid-fire pistol	Norbert Klaar	E. Germany	597 pts.*
Small bore rifle, prone	Karlheinz Smieszek	W. Germany	599 pts.
Small bore rifle, three positions	Lanny Bassham	U.S.A.	1,162 pts.
Rifle, running game target	Alexandr Gazov	Russia	579 pts.*
Swimming and Diving, Men			
100-meter free-style	Jim Montgomery	U.S.A.	49.99 †
200-meter free-style	Bruce Furniss	U.S.A.	1:50.29 †
400-meter free-style	Brian Goodell	U.S.A.	3:51.93 †
1,500-meter free-style	Brian Goodell	U.S.A.	15:02.40 †
100-meter backstroke	John Naber	U.S.A.	55.49 †
200-meter backstroke	John Naber	U.S.A.	1:59.19 †
100-meter breaststroke	John Hencken	U.S.A.	1:03.11 †
200-meter breaststroke	David Wilkie	Great Britain	2:15.11 †
100-meter butterfly	Matt Vogel	U.S.A.	54.35
200-meter butterfly	Mike Bruner	U.S.A.	1:59.23 †
400-meter medley	Rod Strachan	U.S.A.	4:23.68 †
400-meter medley relay	John Naber, John Hencken, Matt Vogel, Jim Montgomery	U.S.A.	3:42.22 †
800-meter free-style relay	Mike Bruner, Bruce Furniss, John Naber, Jim Montgomery	U.S.A.	7:23.22 †
Platform diving	Klaus Dibiasi	Italy	600.51 pts.
Springboard diving	Phil Boggs	U.S.A.	619.52 pts.

Event	Winner	Country	Mark
Swimming and Diving, Women			
100-meter free-style	Kornelia Ender	E. Germany	55.65†
200-meter free-style	Kornelia Ender	E. Germany	1:59.26†
400-meter free-style	Petra Thumer	E. Germany	4:09.89†
800-meter free-style	Petra Thumer	E. Germany	8:37.14†
100-meter backstroke	Ulrike Richter	E. Germany	1:01.83*
200-meter backstroke	Ulrike Richter	E. Germany	2:13.43*
100-meter breaststroke	Hannelore Anke	E. Germany	1:11.16†
200-meter breaststroke	Marina Koshevaia	Russia	2:33.35†
100-meter butterfly	Kornelia Ender	E. Germany	1:00.13*
200-meter butterfly	Andrea Pollack	E. Germany	2:11.41*
400-meter medley	Ulrike Tauber	E. Germany	4:42.77†
400-meter free-style relay	Kim Peyton, Wendy Boglioli, Jill Sterkel, Shirley Babashoff	U.S.A.	3:44.82†
400-meter medley relay	Ulrike Richter, Hannelore Anke, Andrea Pollack, Kornelia Ender	E. Germany	4:07.95†
Platform diving	Elena Vaytsekhovskaia	Russia	406.59 pts.
Springboard diving	Jennifer Chandler	U.S.A.	506.19 pts.

Event	Winner	Country	Mark
Track and Field, Men			
100 meters	Hasely Crawford	Trinidad-Tobago	10.06
200 meters	Donald Quarrie	Jamaica	20.23
400 meters	Alberto Juantorena	Cuba	44.26
800 meters	Alberto Juantorena	Cuba	1:43.50†
1,500 meters	John Walker	New Zealand	3:39.17
5,000 meters	Lasse Viren	Finland	13:24.76
10,000 meters	Lasse Viren	Finland	27:40.38
110-meter hurdles	Guy Drut	France	13.30
400-meter hurdles	Edwin Moses	U.S.A.	47.64†
3,000-meter steeplechase	Anders Garderud	Sweden	8:08.02†
Marathon	Waldemar Cierpinski	E. Germany	2h9:55.00
400-meter relay	Harvey Glance, Johnny Jones, Millard Hampton, Steve Riddick	U.S.A.	38.33
1,600-meter relay	Herman Frazier, Benjamin Brown, Fred Newhouse, Maxie Parks	U.S.A.	2:58.65
20-kilometer walk	Daniel Bautista	Mexico	1h24:40.60
High jump	Jacek Wszola	Poland	7 ft. 4.6 in. (2.25 m.)
Long jump	Arnie Robinson	U.S.A.	27 ft. 4.7 in. (8.35 m.)
Triple jump	Viktor Saneyev	Russia	56 ft. 8.7 in. (17.29 m.)
Pole vault	Tadeusz Slusarski	Poland	18 ft. 0.5 in. (5.50 m.)*
Discus	Mac Wilkins	U.S.A.	221 ft. 5.5 in. (67.50 m.)
Javelin	Miklos Nemeth	Hungary	310 ft. 3.6 in. (94.58 m.)
Shot-put	Udo Beyer	E. Germany	69 ft. 0.7 in. (21.05 m.)
Hammer	Yuriy Sedyh	Russia	254 ft. 4.0 in. (77.52 m.)
Decathlon	Bruce Jenner	U.S.A.	8,618 pts.†

Event	Winner	Country	Mark
Track and Field, Women			
100 meters	Annegret Richter	W. Germany	11.08
200 meters	Baerbel Eckert	E. Germany	22.37*
400 meters	Irena Szewinska	Poland	49.29†
800 meters	Tatiana Kazankina	Russia	1:54.94†
1,500 meters	Tatiana Kazankina	Russia	4:05.48
100-meter hurdles	Johanna Schaller	E. Germany	12.77
400-meter relay	Oelsner, Stecher, Bodendorf, Eckert	E. Germany	42.55*

Event	Winner	Country	Mark
1,600-meter relay	Doris Maletzki, Brigitte Rhode, Ellen Streidt, Christina Brehmer	E. Germany	3:19.23†
High jump	Rosemarie Ackermann	E. Germany	6 ft. 4 in. (1.93 m.)*
Long jump	Angela Voigt	E. Germany	22 ft. 0.6 in. (6.72 m.)
Discus	Evelin Schlaak	E. Germany	226 ft. 4.5 in. (69.00 m.)*
Javelin	Ruth Fuchs	E. Germany	216 ft. 4.1 in. (65.94 m.)*
Shot-put	Ivanka Christova	Bulgaria	69 ft. 5.1 in. (21.16 m.)*
Pentathlon	Siegrun Siegl	E. Germany	4,745 pts.

Event	Winner	Country	Mark
Weight Lifting			
Flyweight	Alexandr Voronin	Russia	535 lbs. (242.5 kg.)*
Bantamweight	Norair Nurikyan	Bulgaria	579 lbs. (262.5 kg.)*
Featherweight	Kinolai Kolesnikov	Russia	628 lbs. (285.0 kg.)*
Lightweight	Zbigniew Kaczmarek	Poland	678 lb. (307.5 kg.)*//
Middleweight	Yordan Mitkov	Bulgaria	739 lbs. (335.0 kg.)*
Light-heavyweight	Valeri Shary	Russia	805 lbs. (365.0 kg.)*
Middle-heavyweight	David Rigert	Russia	843 lbs. (382.5 kg.)*
Heavyweight	Valentin Khristov	Bulgaria	882 lbs. (400.0 kg.)*//
Super-heavyweight	Vassili Alexeev	Russia	970 lbs. (440.0 kg.)*

Event	Winner	Country
Wrestling (Free Style)		
Paperweight (105.6 lbs.)	Khassan Issaev	Bulgaria
Flyweight (114.4)	Yuji Takada	Japan
Bantamweight (125.4)	Vladimir Umin	Russia
Featherweight (136.4)	Jung-Mo Yang	S. Korea
Lightweight (149.6)	Pavel Pinigin	Russia
Welterweight (163)	Date Jiichiro	Japan
Middleweight (180.4)	John Peterson	U.S.A.
Light-heavyweight (198)	Levan Tediashvili	Russia
Heavyweight (220)	Ivan Yarygin	Russia
Super-heavyweight (over 220)	Soslan Andiev	Russia

Event	Winner	Country
Wrestling (Greco-Roman)		
Paperweight	Alexei Shumakov	Russia
Flyweight	Vitaly Konstantinov	Russia
Bantamweight	Pertti Ukkola	Finland
Featherweight	Kazimier Lipien	Poland
Lightweight	Suren Nalbandyan	Russia
Welterweight	Anatolyi Bykov	Russia
Middleweight	Momir Petkovic	Yugoslavia
Light-heavyweight	Valery Rezantsev	Russia
Heavyweight	Nikolai Bolboshin	Russia
Super-heavyweight	Alexandr Kolchinski	Russia

Event	Winner	Country
Yachting		
Finn monotype	Jochen Shumann	E. Germany
Tornado	White, Osborn	Great Britain
Class 470	Huebner, Bode	W. Germany
Soling	Jensen, Bandolowski, Hansen	Denmark
Flying Dutchman	Diesch, Diesch	W. Germany
Tempest	Albrechtson, Hansson	Sweden

Team Sports		
Basketball (men)		U.S.A.
Basketball (women)		Russia
Field hockey (men)		New Zealand
Handball (men)		Russia
Handball (women)		Russia
Soccer (men)		E. Germany
Volleyball (men)		Poland
Volleyball (women)		Japan
Water polo		Hungary

athletes to the games in Montreal, and 159 of them won medals.

Manfred Ewald, president of the East German Olympic Committee, said this performance "proves the success of our socialist system and our training methods." Swimmer John Naber of Menlo Park, Calif., who won four gold medals and one silver, expressed his disagreement.

"Politics has nothing to do with any of this," he said. "Gold medals don't mean the White House is better than the Kremlin. It means I swam faster than anybody else, that's all."

East German officials insisted that their athletes did everything for their nation. In a post-race interview, Roland Matthes, the East German 1968 and 1972 Olympic champion backstroker who lost to Naber in Montreal, was asked why he had returned to swimming at the advanced competitive age of 25 after a brief retirement.

"I did it for my teammates," Matthes answered in German. An East German translator, putting the words into English, said, "He said he did it for his country."

No matter why he or the other East Germans competed, they succeeded. The USOC had hoped for greater success than in the 1972 games by American athletes, especially in the so-called minor sports. It spent more than $11 million over a four-year period covering the Summer and Winter Olympics and the Pan American Games. The money came from corporations and individual contributors, but the United States remained the only nation in the Olympics without government financial support. The USOC said it needed $25 million per year, and it hoped for federal money without federal control. At year's end, the USOC said it would spend more than $10 million to develop athletes for the 1980 Olympics. Much of this money would be used for three year-round training centers.

Individual Stars. The United States, which won six gold and a total of 19 medals in men's track in the 1972 Olympics, equaled those totals in Montreal. East Germans captured nine of the 14 events for women. Lasse Viren of Finland, Alberto Juantorena of Cuba, and Tatiana Kazankina of Russia won two races each. Bruce Jenner of San Jose, Calif., won the decathlon with a record performance.

In swimming, American men won 12 of their 13 events, East German women 11 of their 13. Kornelia Ender of East Germany, like Naber, won four gold medals and one silver. The American women won only one gold medal.

Gymnastics commanded wide attention, and Comaneci's heroics rewarded the capacity crowds of 15,000 that turned out for every session. Russia's Nelli Kim, like Comaneci, received a perfect score of 10, in her case in the vault. Russians and Japanese dominated the men's competition.

For the second consecutive Olympics, the United

Flyweight Leo Randolph of the United States wins a decision over Ramon Duvalon of Cuba to garner an Olympic gold medal in boxing.

States won both gold medals in archery, and Americans took five of the 11 gold medals in boxing and two of the four in diving. Russian athletes won five of the 10 golds in free-style wrestling, seven of the 10 in Greco-Roman wrestling, six of the 11 in canoeing, three of the eight in fencing, five of the nine in weight lifting, and both men's and women's in team handball. East Germans took five of the eight golds in men's rowing and four of the six in women's rowing. Japanese won three of six in judo.

There were familiar gold medalists—Klaus Dibiasi of Italy for the third straight time in platform diving, Teofilo Stevenson of Cuba in heavyweight boxing for the second straight Olympics, and Vassili Alexeev of Russia in superheavyweight weight lifting for the second straight Olympics.

The 34-year-old Alexeev, weighing 344 pounds (156 kilograms), set a world record of 561 pounds (254 kilograms) in the clean and jerk.

Moments to Remember. Shun Fujimoto of Japan and Howard Davis of Glen Cove, N.Y., showed unusual courage in winning gold medals. Fujimoto broke a knee in the free-exercise portion of team gymnastics, but he insisted on performing on the rings and dismounted with a triple somersault. The pain when he landed on his feet was horrible, but he helped his team win. Davis, saying his mother would have wanted him to go on, boxed two days after she died.

There were moments of humor. When a ticket scalper was acquitted in court and his tickets returned, he was surrounded by lawyers who tried to buy the tickets at almost any price. When two Britons finished 14th among the 16 entries in Tempest Class yachting, they calmly burned their yacht and waded ashore.

The Winter Olympics involved 1,054 athletes from 37 nations, far fewer than at Montreal. They were held from February 4 to 15 at Innsbruck, Austria, and the "simple games" Innsbruck had promised cost $150 million. But they were extraordinary as an athletic spectacle.

The same nations that would win the most medals at Montreal won the most at Innsbruck. Russia captured 13 gold, 6 silver, and 8 bronze – a total of 27 medals. The East Germans were next with 7–5–7–19. The United States gained 10 medals, including 6 in speed skating, an impressive performance for a nation that gave little support to winter sports.

The outstanding competitors included Rosi Mittermaier of West Germany, who won two gold medals and one silver in Alpine skiing; Sheila Young of Detroit, who won a gold, a silver, and a bronze medal in speed skating; Dorothy Hamill of Riverside, Conn., winner of the women's figure skating; and Franz Klammer of Austria, winner of the men's downhill skiing. See HAMILL, DOROTHY; MITTERMAIER, ROSI.

Frank Litsky

OMAN. Fighting continued early in 1976 in Dhofar Province despite Sultan Sayyid Qaboos bin Said Al Bu Said's announcement that the rebellion had ended after a major offensive in late 1975 against the rebel Popular Front for the Liberation of Oman (PFLO). Omani-Yemeni border tension grew when the few remaining PFLO rebels took sanctuary in Yemen (Aden), but it eased with a cease-fire negotiated by Saudi Arabia on March 11. At the same time, Oman and the United Arab Emirates agreed on marking their common border.

A two-month amnesty was issued on March 10 for PFLO members, and about 332 rebels were said to have surrendered by April 30. The PFLO continued its radio broadcasts from Yemen (Aden), but the lack of outside support diminished its effectiveness. Great Britain agreed in July to remove its troops from Al Masirah Island and Salalah air bases in March 1977. This would leave Iranian forces as the only foreign troops in Oman.

Although Oman was the only Arab oil producer to increase production in 1976, revenues failed to keep pace with expenditures. The budget estimated income at $1.4 billion and expenditures at $1.8 billion, a 20 per cent increase. Qaboos approved a five-year plan on August 3 to increase agricultural production 164 per cent and make Oman self-sufficient in food by 1980.

William Spencer

See also MIDDLE EAST (Facts in Brief Table).

ONN, DATUK HUSSEIN (1922-　　), became prime minister of Malaysia in January 1976. He succeeded his brother-in-law, Abdul Razak bin Dato Hussein, who died in a London hospital. See MALAYSIA.

Malaysia's third prime minister was born on Feb. 22, 1922, in Johor Baharu, across the causeway from Singapore in what was then the sultanate of Johor. The son of a prominent national politician, Onn attended an English primary school in Johor and the Indian Military Academy at Dehra Dun, India. He studied law at Lincoln's Inn in London and later established a successful law practice in Kuala Lumpur, Malaysia.

Onn was active until 1953 in the United Malays National Organization, which his father had helped to establish. Then party dissension forced him and his father to resign. They both retired from political life.

Abdul Razak later persuaded him to rejoin the United Malays party, and Onn ran for his first elective office in May 1969. He was elected as a member of Parliament from Johor. He rose rapidly in government. As minister of finance he was instrumental in obtaining large foreign loans for Malaysia from commercial sources. He became deputy prime minister in 1973.

Onn is married to Datin Suhalia, the sister of Abdul Razak's wife.

Foster Stockwell

ONTARIO. Teachers, granted the right to strike in 1975, proved a militant force in Ontario politics in 1976. Nearly 9,000 teachers in metropolitan Toronto were ordered back to work by a special session of the legislature in January after a two-month strike. They were obliged to accept binding arbitration of their demand for a 43 per cent pay hike.

William G. Davis' minority Conservative government survived two votes of confidence in the 64-day session of the legislature. It increased its standing to 52 seats in a house of 125 members when a Liberal joined its ranks on August 3. The New Democratic Party served as the official Opposition with 38 members. The Liberals, down to 35 members, elected a new party leader at a convention on January 25. Stuart Smith, a Hamilton psychiatrist, succeeded Robert Nixon, who had made three unsuccessful attempts to oust the Conservative government.

The budget announced on April 6 made a determined effort to reduce the province's deficit. It raised taxes and health insurance charges to provide revenues of $11.3 billion, while spending increased less rapidly to $12.5 billion. Ten small hospitals were closed, and 36 others were ordered to eliminate 3,000 beds from service.

David M. L. Farr

See also CANADA.

OPERA. See MUSIC, CLASSICAL.

OREGON. See STATE GOVERNMENT.

PACIFIC ISLANDS. China and Russia moved to establish themselves in the South Pacific in 1976. The People's Republic of China opened an embassy in Fiji's capital, Suva, and the Russians offered technical and economic assistance to the governments of Tonga and Western Samoa. The sudden Communist interest in the South Pacific caused consternation in Australia, New Zealand, and the United States.

Prosperous Year. Papua New Guinea, by far the largest and most populous of the Pacific Islands countries, celebrated its first year of independence on September 16. Continued high prices for copper from the huge mining venture on the island of Bougainville kept export income rolling in despite a serious recession in the copra industry. Moreover, Australia promised to provide about $1 billion in aid over the next five years. Economic prospects looked so bright that the government revalued its currency upward by 5 per cent against the Australian dollar. The World Bank announced that the newly independent country need no longer rely on guarantees from Australia, its former colonial master, when raising loans. A happy omen for the future was a decision by secessionist leaders on Bougainville to accept the central government's authority. See Section Five, PAPUA NEW GUINEA; PORT MORESBY.

Fiji's Problems. The opening of the largely uninhabited interior of Fiji's main islands, Viti Levu and Vanua Levu, was one of the chief strategies of a five-year development plan launched during 1976. Meanwhile, tourist revenue fell considerably, and other problems beset the country. In six years of independence, Fiji's crime rate has risen alarmingly and there were charges of widespread government corruption. Many crimes were attributed to liquor and were apparently prompted by rapid changes in the traditional social structure and economy, and by an undermanned, underpaid, and ill-equipped police force.

Fiji also has a potentially dangerous land problem. About 80 per cent of the land is owned communally by 250,000 native Fijians who are reluctant to lease it for long periods to the country's more numerous Indians for fear they might not get it back.

The French Territories of New Caledonia and French Polynesia continued to agitate for more self-government. Boycotts, demonstrations, and other maneuvers in French Polynesia persuaded the French government to abandon a plan to make the territory a virtual department of France. On June 10, about 1,200 Tahitians, led by autonomist politicians, formed a human barrier to prevent the governor from entering the Territorial Assembly build-

Bougainville leaders, who wanted to secede from Papua New Guinea in 1975, reconsidered in 1976 and agreed to remain part of that new nation.

ing to try to reconvene the Assembly after a boycott of eight months.

Independence Moves. Two of Great Britain's remaining Pacific territories moved closer to independence. The Solomon Islands, whose leaders are opposed to early autonomy, gained internal self-government on January 2. The Gilbert Islands achieved self-government in November as a prelude to independence, probably in 1978. Meanwhile, Tuvalu, formerly the Ellice Islands, became a fully self-governing British colony on January 1.

In Micronesia, the Mariana Islands began steps to commonwealth status when President Gerald R. Ford signed a deed of covenant on March 24. Seven days later, the Marianas government was created. However, the Marianas can achieve complete commonwealth status only when the United Nations Trust Territory of the Pacific Islands, of which they are a part, is formally dissolved. To permit the dissolution, new arrangements must be made for governing the Caroline and Marshall Islands. On June 2, Micronesian representatives initialed a free association pact with the United States. To go into effect, the compact, which can be terminated by either side after 15 years, must be approved in a referendum by at least 55 per cent of the voters in four of the six administrative districts of the trust territory.   Robert Langdon

PAINTING. See VISUAL ARTS.

Prime Minister Zulfikar Ali Bhutto, left, is welcomed by Premier Hua Kuo-feng on his arrival for a visit to mainland China in May.

PAKISTAN. Prime Minister Zulfikar Ali Bhutto pronounced his people to be "in fairly good shape" in 1976. The judgment was reasonably accurate. The country had survived the loss of East Pakistan, now Bangladesh, in 1971. But the four provinces that now form Pakistan were in recurrent turmoil. The economy was sustained only by large amounts of foreign aid, and economic growth barely stayed ahead of the birth rate.

The economy was caught between the soaring prices of oil and machinery that Pakistan needed and the dropping prices of the rice, cotton, and textiles that it exported. Pakistan sold 855,394 short tons (776,000 metric tons) of rice in 1972 and 1973, but three years later the total had shrunk to one-third of that amount, at half the price.

Oil Money. Bhutto was able to balance the books with the help of credits from the oil-rich states of the Middle East. But this produced its own problems. The aid figure has been steadily declining, and neither the shah of Iran nor the Arab oil sheiks would lower the price of the oil they sold to Pakistan. Thus, in 1976, all of the $400 million in credits from the oil states was spent on the purchase of oil. The largely Western consortium aiding Pakistan provided roughly $700 million. But the nation's foreign debt by the end of 1976 exceeded $6 billion, and payments on loans amounted to more than 25 per cent of export earnings.

The confidence needed to promote private investments was shaken in 1972 when Bhutto nationalized many industries, from steel to fertilizer. Bhutto shook investors' confidence even further in July 1976 with a sweeping nationalization of agriculture-based industries, except sugar and textiles, with an annual turnover of $1.4 billion.

Plus Factors. But there were some positive developments in the economic picture. The building of fertilizer plants continued apace. By early 1977, the billion-dollar Tarbela Dam, the world's largest earth-filled barrier, should be completed after many mishaps. By 1978, a Russian-built steel mill is expected to begin operation. In a bold political step, Bhutto curbed the virtually unlimited powers of the Sardars, the feudal tribal leaders in Baluchistan.

The Bolan Dam, one of Pakistan's main instruments in irrigating the arid tracts of Baluchistan province, broke in September, inundating more than 5,000 square miles (12,950 square kilometers) of land.

Elections were clearly in store for 1977, but Bhutto was assured of victory. His key opponents were in jail, and some of them begged for admission to Bhutto's Pakistan People's Party. Bhutto's position was enhanced by renewed diplomatic ties with India in July, ties that had been severed in 1971 over the issue of Bangladesh.   Mark Gayn

See also ASIA (Facts in Brief Table).

PALEONTOLOGY. The date for the oldest known fossil vertebrates was pushed back to the beginnings of the Ordovician Period (480 million years ago) by the discovery of fossil fragments of heterostracan fish in Norway in 1976. Scientists from Oslo's Paleontology Museum and from the British Museum in London found the fossils on Spitsbergen Island in March. Until then, the oldest heterostracans came from Ordovician sandstones in Colorado. But these were dated 20 million years later.

Pre-Cambrian Fossils were found in shales in Russia in March by geologists B. V. Timofeev, T. N. Hermann, and N. S. Mikhaylova. They discovered microscopic spheroidal cells no more than 0.02 inch (0.5 millimeter) in diameter embedded in shale and dated them at about 1 billion years old. The Pre-Cambrian cells are the largest single cells from this time that have been found, and their size suggests that they are advanced cells, or eucaryotes.

Scientists also found what may be the oldest multicellular animal fossils from the United States and possibly from North America. Geologists Preston E. Cloud, Jr., and James Wright of the University of California, Santa Barbara, and Lynn Glover of Virginia Polytechnic Institute and State University in Blacksburg said in July they found more than a dozen fossils that are up to 4 inches (10 centimeters) long in rocks near Durham, N.C. Because the fossils were J- or U-shaped impressions in the rock, they may be the remains of soft-bodied worms or trails left by the worms. The rocks were dated to 620-million years ago, making them the oldest fossils of this type found in the continental United States.

Warm-Blooded Dinosaurs. Until Robert T. Bakker, a Johns Hopkins University vertebrate paleontologist, suggested in 1975 that dinosaurs were warm-blooded, most paleontologists assumed they were cold-blooded animals, much like living reptiles. But his studies have sparked new interest in dinosaur physiology. Bakker studied many dinosaur fossils and calculated the ratio of predators to prey among the fossils. He found that this ratio was closer to that found in present-day mammal communities than to reptile communities. Warm-blooded predators require 10 to 30 times more food to maintain their higher rate of metabolism than cold-blooded predators need.

Bakker found that dinosaur bone has a texture more like mammalian bone than reptilian bone. He noted that many of the bones were found in places where the weather was quite cold at the time these animals lived. Because dinosaurs were so large, they probably did not hibernate. Only warm-blooded animals would be expected to survive polar winters without hibernating. Ida Thompson

See also GEOLOGY.

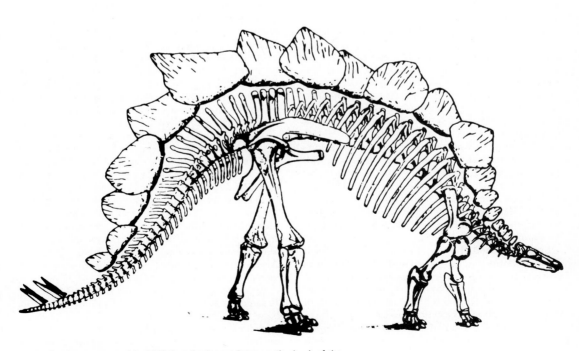

Yale scientists suggested in 1976 that the bony plates on the back of the Stegosaurus served as fins for dissipating the dinosaur's excess body heat.

PANAMA. The negotiation of a new Panama Canal treaty with the United States became a U.S. presidential election campaign issue in 1976. The candidates for the Republican nomination, Ronald Reagan and President Gerald R. Ford, held differing views concerning control of the canal, and their charges and countercharges concerning U.S. rights in the Canal Zone led Panama's Chief of the Government Omar Torrijos Herrera to accuse both of "irresponsibility" in dealing with the canal issue. Consequently, negotiations that began on February 7 reached an impasse and were not resumed until October 19. Torrijos Herrera indicated that if the talks failed, Panama "would have to resort to violence." He added, however, that he hoped a new treaty would be concluded in 1977.

The United Brands Company announced on January 8 that it would sell its 100,000 acres (40,000 hectares) of banana lands to the government for $151,500 and then lease 37,500 acres (15,000 hectares) for $2 million a year. United Brands promised to maintain production at 22 million boxes of bananas a year. Each box contains 42 pounds (19 kilograms) of bananas. The agreement settled a long dispute. *Everett G. Martin*

See also LATIN AMERICA (Facts in Brief Table).

PAPUA NEW GUINEA. See ASIA; PACIFIC ISLANDS; Section Five, PAPUA NEW GUINEA and PORT MORESBY.

PARAGUAY. The Roman Catholic Church in Paraguay clashed openly with the dictatorial regime of President Alfredo Stroessner in 1976. On July 12, the bishops' council of Paraguay denounced the government for repression of students and peasants; the torture and disappearance of political prisoners; and such measures against the church as raids on its educational institutions, imprisonment of priests, expulsion of eight priests from Paraguay, and a determined propaganda campaign to defame the church.

The document was a direct response to mass arrests of more than 1,000 persons following a gun battle on April 3 in Asunción between police and leftist guerrillas. Reportedly, the guerrillas belonged to the Politico-Military Organization (OPM). The government claimed the OPM had links to the Roman Catholic Church as well as to Argentine left wing terrorists.

School Closed. In March, Cristo Rey, a Jesuit school in Asunción, was closed and 28 of its teachers arrested on charges of teaching Marxism and encouraging guerrilla activities. Those arrested included one French and six Spanish Jesuits, four of whom were among those deported.

The Inter-American Commission on Human Rights of the Organization of American States estimated that there were 1,000 political prisoners in Paraguay.

Other Charges. The International League for the Rights of Man (ILRM) charged that the government had closed down a service project for Paraguayan Indians that was sponsored by Catholic University of Asunción and funded by the U.S.-based Inter-American Foundation. The foundation's director, Miguel Chase Sardi, and four staff members were arrested on charges of aiding Communist subversives. The ILRM accused the U.S. Department of State of covering up evidence of the arrests and condoning human-rights abuse.

A crisis developed with Argentina in February when a brigade of Paraguayan marines clashed with Argentine border guards, apparently over arms smuggling. There were reports that arms were being sold by Paraguayan smugglers to terrorists in Argentina—traffic that the Argentine border guards were determined to stop. Tensions were eased when Stroessner dismissed Admiral Hugo Gonzales, who was in charge of the Paraguayan marine brigade.

The National Assembly, on July 16, began paving the way for Stroessner to be re-elected president when his fifth term ends in 1978. It called for the convening of a constituent assembly in February 1977 to amend a constitutional restriction that would have prevented Stroessner from seeking a sixth 5-year term. *Everett G. Martin*

See also LATIN AMERICA (Facts in Brief Table).

PARENTS AND TEACHERS, NATIONAL CONGRESS OF (PTA), began a nationwide advertising campaign in the United States in 1976. The campaign was intended to stimulate awareness of PTA programs and to increase membership.

At the annual convention in Louisville, Ky., in May, the PTA passed a resolution urging the U.S. attorney general "to intervene in any court-ordered forced-busing case" that comes before the Supreme Court of the United States.

The PTA also obtained money for a national project to study the effects of television violence on children and youth. Hearings will be held in eight parts of the country. PTA members were encouraged to monitor TV programs and write letters protesting those with excessive violence. Another project sought to increase community support for more effective health-education programs. Also, for the fourth consecutive year, the PTA collaborated with the National Institute on Alcohol Abuse and Alcoholism in an effort to combat the misuse of alcohol among teens and preteens.

Continuing in two-year terms are Mrs. Walter G. Kimmel of Rock Island, Ill., president; Mrs. William C. Baisinger, Washington, D.C., first vice-president; and Wilson C. Riles, Sacramento, Calif., second vice-president. *Joseph P. Anderson*

PENNSYLVANIA. See PHILADELPHIA; STATE GOVERNMENT.

PERSONALITIES OF 1976 included the following newsmakers:

Alia, queen of Jordan, surprised two Chicagoans in April by inviting them to breakfast with her and King Hussein. The royal couple were in Chicago on an overnight visit. Jim Zavislak and Mary Frances Bubek had been students with the queen in 1969 at Loyola University's Rome Center in Italy. Said Zavislak later: "I thought she might just have time to say 'hello.' But, golly, we talked for nearly an hour. It was like Old Home Week."

Anderson, Andy, of Twin Falls, Ida., celebrated the American Revolution Bicentennial in a unique way in March when he received a set of red, white, and blue dentures. Learning that Anderson was getting a new set of teeth, his friends obtained the impressions and surprised him with the new dentures. He now sports shiny red canines inset with diamonds, which frame four white and blue incisors that proclaim 1976 in red and white enamel.

Andre, Valerie, became France's first woman general on April 21, her 54th birthday. A member of the armed forces medical corps since she received her medical degree in 1949, Andre flew on dozens of mercy missions to Communist-held zones in Indochina. She is credited with saving the lives of nearly 200 French soldiers before the French pulled out of Indochina in 1954. She is also an enthusiastic helicopter pilot. Her husband is an air force reserve colonel.

Berry, Fredd, state senator in Tennessee, had his proposal to name a state fossil nearly backfire on him in March. After his colleagues amended the bill to make him the official state fossil, Berry withdrew the measure.

Blanda, George, 48, hung up his football cleats for the last time on August 25 when the Oakland Raiders put him on waivers. Blanda, whose career spanned 26 years, started his professional career in 1949 as a rookie quarterback for the Chicago Bears. He holds National Football League records for the most seasons played (26); most games played (342); and most points scored (2,002). He had been a place-kicker for the Raiders since 1967.

Brooks, Gwendolyn, Chicago poet, became the first black woman elected to the National Institute of Arts and Letters in March. Brooks was born in Topeka, Kans., and published her first volume of poetry in 1945. She won a Pulitzer Prize for her work in 1950.

Brennan, Nancy, raised the eyebrows of British customs officers in May when she arrived in Great Britain with a 4-pound (1.8-kilogram) container filled with a white, granular substance labeled "grits." Official concern eased when she explained that she and her husband had come to London for a five-day cooking demonstration of specialties from their New Orleans restaurant. Among the dishes was one called grillades and grits.

George Burns signals his pleasure after winning an Oscar at 80 for his supporting role in the movie *The Sunshine Boys.*

Hartman, David, 26, became the first blind person to graduate from a United States medical school in May. Hartman, blinded by glaucoma at the age of 8, received his degree from Temple University in Philadelphia. He plans to specialize in psychiatry and rehabilitative medicine after completing his residency requirements.

Heath, Edward, former Conservative prime minister of Great Britain, went back to his first love when he conducted the Chicago Symphony Orchestra on September 28 in a benefit performance for the orchestra's pension fund. Originally destined for a career in music, Heath was sidetracked into politics while a student at Oxford University. However, he never lost his love for music, and his bachelor apartment in London houses a grand piano and a clutter of classical record albums.

Horowitz, Vladimir, noted pianist, almost ended his first West Coast concert tour since 1948 before it began. On a preconcert shopping excursion in February, Horowitz found himself wedged in a Seattle supermarket turnstile. "I pushed one way and it would not move," said the 71-year-old musician. "I pushed it the other way. It would not move. I never saw anything like it. I said, 'Good-by, I'm gone forever. Finito.'" After a 15-minute struggle, supermarket employees managed to free Horowitz in time for his sellout concert that night at the Seattle Opera House.

Rock star Elton John shows off his form for the Los Angeles Aztecs professional soccer team. He is one of the owners of the Aztecs.

Korchnoi, Viktor, Russian grand master and second-ranking chess player in the world, lost a game in London on January 17 to 10-year-old Nigel Short of Atherton, England, the youngest of 30 opponents who played Korchnoi in simultaneous matches lasting seven hours. Korchnoi took his loss in the 40-move game gracefully and afterward inscribed a book to the boy, "In honor of your victory." Nigel, who is London champion among youngsters under 14, was unawed by the grand master. "I wasn't scared of him," the boy said. "He tried to wear me down, but I caught him in the endgame."

Lackey, E. Dent, 75, former mayor of Niagara Falls, N.Y., married Ruth Hillis, his late wife's sister, on April 3, but they decided Niagara Falls was not the place for a honeymoon. Instead, they spent six weeks in New Mexico.

Lennon, John, British rock musician and former member of the influential Beatles group, won formal permission to stay in the United States on July 27, after a three-year court battle. His request for resident status was denied in 1973 because of a 1968 conviction in England for possessing marijuana. Lennon claimed the marijuana had been planted in his apartment by police. His application for permanent residency was finally approved in a special hearing that was held before immigration Judge Ira Fieldsteel.

McKee, Fran, 49, became the first woman line officer in the United States Navy to be promoted to rear admiral in February. The two previous women admirals were chiefs in the Nurse Corps. McKee, a veteran of 26 years service, commands the naval security force at Fort Meade, Maryland. She holds a chemistry degree from the University of Alabama and a master's degree in international affairs from George Washington University.

Menuhin, Yehudi, became the first musician to receive an honorary doctorate from the Sorbonne in Paris on February 15. In an emotional acceptance speech, the violinist said that the purpose of music was to unite people "around something bigger than our lives." Then, saying that music itself would better explain what he meant, he played a Bach *chaconne* (slow dance movement).

Monnet, Jean, 88, French statesman, was made an honorary citizen of Europe on April 2 for his part in creating the European Community (Common Market) in the 1950s. The heads of the nine Common Market governments joined in citing him for "boldness and breadth of vision" in his plan for European unity. They had hoped to award Monnet the first common European passport, but they could not agree on details for issuing it.

Murchison, Ruby S., 43, of Fayetteville, N.C., was named U.S. Teacher of the Year on March 6. The black educator has spent 22 years in the classroom and teaches seventh grade in a recently integrated school. In accepting the award at a White House ceremony, she outlined her educational philosophy: "I don't teach a subject. I teach children."

Robinson, Walter, 30, an Army sergeant at Fort Bragg, North Carolina, almost succeeded in walking across the Hudson River from New Jersey to Manhattan on January 13. He wore an inflated pontoon on each foot as he made his way over stiff currents and treacherous chunks of ice, but conceded defeat to the sharp ice floes that threatened to puncture his pontoons after nearly reaching the Manhattan shore. Previously, Robinson had crossed the Panama Canal.

Shipp, Otto, 103, of Sylvester, Ga., and his wife, Annie, celebrated 85 years of marriage on June 27. The chapel of Sylvester African Methodist Episcopal Church was packed with well-wishers as they repeated the vows they made in 1891. "Every day I live with her, I like it better and better," Shipp said. His wife added, "There are no secrets. Just do right and treat him as he is — a man."

Sinatra, Frank, singer and actor, took his fourth wife on July 11. The bride, Barbara Marx, a former model and showgirl, was previously married to Zeppo Marx, youngest of the five Marx brothers. The wedding took place behind the heavily guarded gates of Sunnylands, the California estate of Walter H. Annenberg, who is a former ambassador to Great Britain.

Barbara Walters joins the American Broadcasting Company and becomes the first woman to co-anchor a network television news program.

Sousa, John Philip, the March King, was inducted into the Hall of Fame for Great Americans on August 23. Sousa was born in 1854 and wrote more than 130 marches, including a perennial favorite, "The Stars and Stripes Forever." He believed that a march should have "a melody which appeals to the musical and unmusical alike" and should "make a man with a wooden leg step out."

Thomas, Lowell, 84, a veteran of 46 years in network broadcasting, presented his final radio news program on May 14. Thomas made his first broadcast over local station KDKA in Pittsburgh in 1924 and began a network news program in 1930. "Lowell Thomas and the News" had been carried on CBS Radio since 1945. Thomas said, however, that he would not be going into retirement. He would continue his syndicated television series "Lowell Thomas Remembers" and would pursue other business interests. His autobiography, *Good Evening Everybody,* was published during the year.

Thornton, Michael, of London rushed to an old-fashioned defense of the Duchess of Leinster in March. Believing that the 54-year-old duchess had been insulted by three men, including her stepson, Thornton challenged each of them to personal combat. Although Great Britain banned dueling a century ago, Thornton argued, "Dueling is a good way to sort things out. I don't want to kill anyone, I merely want to teach them a lesson."

Uemura, Noami, 35, returned home to Tokyo in May after completing the longest one-man dog-sled trek in history. During an 18-month journey of 7,200 miles (11,600 kilometers) from Greenland to Alaska, he subsisted on caribou, seal, and walrus meat. Uemura had previously climbed Mount Everest and Kilimanjaro and floated 3,600 miles (5,800 kilometers) down the Amazon River. Next he plans to take the dog sled across Antarctica.

Vinson, Doug, hopes to make the name of the 13th President of the United States a household word with his Millard Fillmore Bicentennial bathtub plug. Vinson, a student at the University of Georgia in Athens, is inventor, manufacturer, and promoter of the $2.50 plug. The plug is strictly ornamental and will neither hold back water nor stop leaks. "But," says Vinson, "it makes a good key chain and you can hang it on the end of a light cord so you can find it in the dark. Or you can hang it on the wall."

Zinno, Joseph A., 52, a retired Air Force colonel of Quonset Point, R.I., became the first American to fly a human-powered plane on April 21. Zinno succeeded in raising his plane 1 foot (30 centimeters) above the ground and flew more than 80 feet (24 meters) before coming to a rough landing. The lightweight plane is powered by bicycle pedals that spin a wheel that is connected by a chain to a propeller behind the tiny cockpit.   Kathryn Sederberg

PERU. Economic difficulties continued to plague the military government of President Francisco Morales Bermudez Cerruti in 1976. Throughout the year, the cast of characters around him became increasingly more conservative as he tried to cope with left wing reformists, strikes, and political protests.

Although routine economic statistics are as guarded as military secrets in Peru, Economy and Finance Minister Luís Barua Castañeda, while announcing a series of austerity measures in January, divulged that exports in 1975 had dropped from $1.5 billion to $1.4 billion while imports had climbed from $1.9 billion to $2.5 billion. He said the export stagnation was caused by a drop in copper and other mineral prices; a hiatus in iron-ore exports because an ore-producing subsidiary of U.S.-owned Marcona Mining Company had been nationalized; and a decline in Peru's fish-meal industry because of nationalization and a shortage of anchovies.

Trade Figures for 1976 are still closely held secrets, but outside sources estimate the balance of trade deficit at anywhere from $32 million to $600-million. In addition, it was tacitly acknowledged in international circles that Peru's dreams of becoming a big oil-exporting country would not materialize. Over a four-year period, the government and 18 private companies had lost up to $2 billion exploring without success the jungle around Iquitos near the headwaters of the Amazon.

A stiff 44 per cent devaluation of the peso on June 28 was followed on June 30 with sharp price increases in food, clothing, transportation, and utilities. Meanwhile, the government offered wage increases of only 10 to 15 per cent to offset a six-month inflation rate of 30 per cent. Widespread rioting by financially strapped workers and students that followed forced the government to declare a nationwide state of emergency on July 1.

Cabinet Changes. On July 16, the president removed from his Cabinet all members considered to be leftists. Chief among them was Prime Minister Jorge Fernandez Maldonado, a leader in formulating the ideals of the Peruvian populist revolution. In March, 6 of Lima's 7 nationalized newspapers were purged of leftist editors, and 12 magazines were closed down.

Many restraints that private industry complained about were lifted, and the ambitious scheme of gradually turning 50 per cent of the ownership and management of all companies over to employees was taken under review with an eye to keeping management in professional hands. In September, the government began to study ways of divesting itself of some state industries, a load that has grown since 1968 from 12 to nearly 180.   Everett G. Martin

See also LATIN AMERICA (Facts in Brief Table).

PET. A Lakeland terrier was chosen best-in-show at the 100th Westminster Kennel Club dog show on February 10 in New York City. Ch. Jo-Ni's Red Baron of Crofton, owned by Virginia K. Dickson of La Habra, Calif., topped 3,097 other dogs in the competition. It was the 75th first prize and the 151st blue rosette for the 5-year-old dog, making him the top-winning terrier in American dog-show history.

At the 77th International Kennel Club show in Chicago on March 27 and 28, best-in-show among 3,206 dogs went to a 3-year-old bulldog, Ch. Marinebull's All the Way, owned by Karl and Joyce Dingman of Richfield, Minn.

Pet Population. Efforts continued to control the growing dog and cat populations. In January, the Veterinary Medical Association of New York City voted to provide a low-cost neutering program for pets whose owners cannot afford the standard fees. In February, 150 public officials and other interested persons attending a conference in Denver on dog and cat control heard reports on an experimental birth-control drug that can be mixed into pet food. The drug would add about 5 cents a day to an animal's food cost.

Registration figures for 1975 released by the American Kennel Club in February 1976 showed that poodles were the most popular pure breed in the United States for the 16th consecutive year. Next came German shepherds and Irish setters.

Doberman pinschers advanced from sixth to fourth place. Beagles and dachshunds each dropped a notch to fifth and sixth place, respectively. Cocker spaniels advanced from ninth to seventh place, and miniature schnauzers, Labrador retrievers, and collies completed the list of 10.

In July, four pet shops in the Tampa, Fla., area sold piranhas, a vicious flesh-eating fish barred from sale within the state. The shops believed that the fish were harmless red pacus. Only nine of 23 piranhas that had been accidentally delivered to the shops could be accounted for.

Tom Krause, owner of a pet shop in Elk Grove Village, Ill., reported in September that since the beginning of 1976 he had sold 800 tarantulas as pets, 25 per cent more than in 1975. "Very few people walk into the shop to buy tarantulas," he said, "but when they see them they are intrigued."

Cat Winners. The Cat Fanciers' Association named Gr. Ch. Thaibok Teriyaki, a seal point Siamese male owned by Mr. and Mrs. E. H. Davis of Port Washington, N.Y., as Best Cat of the Year. Best Alter went to a bicolor American shorthair neuter, Gr. Ch. and Gr. Pr. Step-An-Fetch-It, owned by Linda Leigh Buel of Gaithersburg, Md.; and Best Kitten to a red Persian male, Gr. Ch. Jo-Le's Red Buttons, owned by Joseph and Carol Giannuzzi of Syracuse, N.Y.   Theodore M. O'Leary

Ch. Marinebull's All the Way, a bulldog, poses for admirers after taking top honors at the International Kennel Club show in March.

PETROLEUM AND GAS. The world may be heading for a short-term oil shortage as well as a significant increase in prices in 1977, according to a study released in August 1976. The study, by the London office of Walter J. Levy, an influential oil economist, contended that a squeeze in supplies could take place as early as mid-1977 unless Saudi Arabia lifted its production ceiling of 8.8 million barrels a day, because little surplus production capacity is available elsewhere in the Organization of Petroleum Exporting Countries (OPEC) to meet fast-rising short-term demand.

At a December 16 meeting in Qatar, the previously solid stance of OPEC members on oil prices was broken. Eleven members announced a 10 per cent rise in the price of oil on Jan. 1, 1977, but Saudi Arabia and the United Arab Emirates set only a 5 per cent increase for the first six months of 1977. The Saudis also showed their muscle by hinting that they would increase oil production, a move that might undercut the other OPEC producers.

Saudi Arabia is the world's leading oil-exporting nation. It has by far the largest reserves of oil and gas, with proven recoverable reserves of 165 billion barrels compared with 60 billion for Russia and 36-billion for the United States. The Arabian American Oil Company (Aramco) reported the discovery in March of three additional oil fields, equal to more than 20 per cent of the United States total proven reserves.

On January 1, Venezuela assumed full control of its vast, diverse oil industry in the largest single take-over of American property in history. In July, Saudi Arabia announced plans to take over the United States remaining 40 per cent interest in Aramco, the most important oil property in the world, owned by the Standard Oil Company of California; Texaco Incorporated; the Exxon Corporation; and the Mobil Oil Corporation.

Record Russian Exports. Taking advantage of high world prices, Russia shipped a record volume of crude oil to the West, while holding down the growth of both domestic consumption and exports to its East European allies. The flow of Russian crude oil to the West went up 40 per cent to 480,000 barrels a day, while exports to Communist nations rose only 8 per cent to 1.6 million barrels a day.

U.S. Imports rose to record highs in 1976, with domestic output falling. Crude oil imports averaged 5.6 million barrels a day, up from the 1975 average of 4.78 million barrels a day. Federal Energy Administration figures showed consumption up 3.7 per cent, with gasoline use advancing 6.7 per cent. However, gasoline production stood at a record 7.24 million barrels a day in a typical summer week. With the nation's refineries operating at an average 92.4 per cent of capacity, an average of 13.67 million barrels of crude oil were processed daily. Trends indicated that the Arab nations and

Nigeria were increasing their shares of the U.S. market, while the nation's traditional suppliers, Venezuela and Canada, were contributing less. On June 11, Canada announced it would cut its oil exports to the United States 60,000 barrels a day to a new daily level of 450,000 barrels.

Oil Pricing. The lapse of government heating-oil controls on June 30 opened the way for price rises. The American Petroleum Institute (API) forecast at the end of September that, with the approach of winter, costs in the New York City area would rise to about 41 cents per gallon (11 cents per liter) compared with 38 cents per gallon (10 cents per liter) in 1975. The nation entered the heating season with 214.9 million barrels of heating oil, some 3.5 million barrels more than in 1975.

Sea Drilling. Despite the opposition of coastal states to drilling for oil along their shores, exploratory drilling in U.S. Atlantic coastal waters began in 1976. The United States Department of the Interior leased 93 federal tracts in the area for a total of $1.13 billion on August 17. The leasing followed the refusal of the Supreme Court of the United States to set aside its 1975 ruling that the federal government has the exclusive rights to all of the oil or gas resources that lie along the Atlantic outer continental shelf.

Alaska Pipeline. In June, the Interior Department and the Department of Transportation's State Pipeline Safety Program ordered an independent investigation of weld X rays and repair records for 30,800 mainline pipe welds completed in 1975 on the $7.7-billion Alaska oil pipeline project. The audit, which cost $4.5 million, identified more than 3,000 welds with "deficiencies, irregularities, or discontinuities," including 28 cracks. With more than 10 per cent of the welds requiring repair at a cost that could go as high as $55 million, government officials expressed concern that possible repairs could delay the planned opening of the 798-mile (1,284-kilometer) pipeline, scheduled for mid-1977, until November 1977. The Alyeska Pipeline Service Company, which is building the pipeline and conducted the audit, blamed lax federal supervision for the serious breakdown.

Contractors and some 4,000 workers coped with bad weather and difficult construction conditions to prepare a safe base for the $1-billion oil-storage and shipping complex at the pipeline's Valdez terminus on the southern coast of Alaska. The danger of a possible earthquake, such as the one that leveled Valdez in 1964, made it crucial to dig foundations down to bedrock. The 1,000-acre (405-hectare) terminal site is the largest construction site in the pipeline project.

Natural Gas. The Federal Power Commission (FPC) on July 27 approved a natural gas price increase that almost tripled the amount producers may charge for interstate natural gas. This could

Massive storage and transport facilities near completion at the southern end of the 798-mile (1,284-kilometer) trans-Alaska pipeline at Valdez.

have cost consumers up to $1.5 billion a year. The American Gas Association, an industry group, said the increase would add 6 per cent to the bill of the average residential customer, who paid $205 for natural gas in 1975. In October 1976, acknowledging an error in cost estimates, the FPC cut the price rise by 25 per cent.

Canadian Minister of Energy, Mines, and Resources Alastair W. Gillespie in June announced a 21 per cent, two-stage increase in the price of natural gas shipped to the United States. Federal Energy Administrator Frank G. Zarb said that the increase would cost consumers in the United States $322 million more per year. The first increase went into effect in September, and another, of 14 per cent, was scheduled for Jan. 1, 1977. Zarb said that the impact of the increase would be felt mainly by consumers in New York, Vermont, and the Far Western states.

Tenneco Chemicals, Incorporated, of Houston signed a contract in October to buy 262 billion cubic yards (200 billion cubic meters) of liquefied natural gas from Sonatrach, the Algerian national oil and gas company. The liquefied gas will be processed in Canada at Saint John, N.B., and sent by pipeline to the United States for sale on the East Coast. Deliveries are scheduled to begin in 1981 and will continue for 20 years.   Mary E. Jessup

See also ENERGY.

PHILADELPHIA, the nation's birthplace, celebrated the American Revolution Bicentennial on July 4, 1976, with a re-enactment of the signing of the Declaration of Independence, an address by President Gerald R. Ford in front of Independence Hall, the ringing of the Liberty Bell, and one of the largest parades ever organized. At least 1 million persons participated in the festivities.

The Liberty Bell, which had been moved from Independence Hall to a nearby steel-and-glass structure, was struck with a rubber mallet at 2 P.M., giving the signal for bells to be rung throughout Philadelphia and the nation. Meanwhile, 30,000 persons held their own events to protest the official observances.

Queen Elizabeth II of Great Britain visited Philadelphia on July 6 and presented a 6.5-short-ton (5.9-metric-ton) bell, Great Britain's Bicentennial gift to the United States.

Recall Attempt. The Pennsylvania Supreme Court ruled on September 30 that a move to recall Philadelphia Mayor Frank L. Rizzo from office was unconstitutional. The recall move started on April 17, with its leaders accusing Rizzo of abuse of power and fiscal irresponsibility. Rizzo had announced in January that the city faced at least an $80-million budget deficit and needed to raise taxes on wages, businesses, and real estate. His opponents charged that he had concealed the financial problems during his 1975 re-election campaign. Rizzo's popularity was further damaged when he announced plans to close Philadelphia General Hospital, a municipally supported facility that served many of the city's poor. He also made political enemies by divorcing himself from the local regular Democratic Party early in the year and by suing a Philadelphia newspaper for libel.

The recall movement gathered about 211,000 signatures on petitions, far more than the 145,448 signatures required. But the city's Board of Commissioners rejected the petitions on August 24, ruling that only about 86,500 signatures were valid. The board's action was then overruled in September by Common Pleas Court Judge David N. Savitt, who ordered the recall question placed on the November 2 election ballot. But the matter was ended by the state high court's ruling that the city's recall procedure was unconstitutional.

Legionnaires' Disease. Twenty-nine persons died and 151 others were hospitalized by a mysterious disease that struck persons who had some connection with a July American Legion convention or the Roman Catholic International Eucharistic Congress held in Philadelphia's Bellevue Stratford Hotel. Investigators failed to find anything at the hotel that may have caused the illness. Nevertheless, the hotel suffered a loss of business and had to close in November.   James M. Banovetz

PHILIPPINES. Earthquakes and typhoons rocked the Philippines in 1976. The worst of a series of earthquakes occurred under the Celebes Sea on August 17. Its shock damaged the island of Mindanao and the Sulu Archipelago and generated tidal waves from 15 to 20 feet (4 to 6 meters) high that flooded coastal areas. At least 6,000 persons were killed. Half the bodies were washed out to sea by the receding waves and never recovered. The worst typhoon was Olga in late May, which killed 215 persons and left more than 60,000 homeless because of flooding on the island of Luzon.

The Political Scene. On October 16, the fourth popular referendum since President Ferdinand E. Marcos established martial law in 1972 overwhelmingly approved the continuance of martial law and the establishment of a parliament. Marcos said he planned to hold elections in 1977 for about 120 members of the parliament. A step toward this was the convening of a new Legislative Advisory Council on September 21. Composed of 28 Cabinet members, 91 community assembly leaders, and 13 regional delegates, it lacked any direct power. The council in effect replaced an interim national assembly provided under the 1973 Constitution until parliamentary government could be set up. Marcos had refused to convene the assembly because it would have included in its membership some of his political opponents.

Criticism of the regime continued. A rally in Manila on October 10 against the referendum turned into the first riot in four years, and 34 persons were injured. Diosdado Macapagal, Marcos' predecessor as president, accused him of "blatant dictatorship." Amnesty International and a Roman Catholic organization of some 12,000 priests and nuns accused the government of torturing prisoners. Marcos denied some charges, but after Amnesty International said political prisoners were tortured "freely and with extreme cruelty," the government announced on September 28 that a military court would investigate charges of torture by the armed forces.

The national capital was changed on May 31 from Quezon City to Manila. Most government offices had always been near downtown Manila rather than in Quezon City, a suburb.

Foreign Affairs. The Philippines finished realigning its foreign policy to end isolation from Communist countries by establishing diplomatic relations with Russia on June 2, while Marcos was in Moscow, and with Vietnam on July 12.

The New People's Army of Maoist-style revolutionaries increased its activities despite the capture of some leaders. Marcos said a Muslim separatist movement in the southern islands had killed some 4,000 persons in recent years, and there were still 1,000 fighting.   Henry S. Bradsher

See also ASIA (Facts in Brief Table).

PHOTOGRAPHY. Technical changes using electronics made cameras more compact and automated in 1976. Most talked about was the Canon AE-1, a small 35-millimeter (mm), single-lens-reflex (SLR) model that incorporates more electronic circuits than any previous camera. Its makers claim the circuits eliminate 300, or 20 per cent, of the mechanical parts otherwise needed.

The new design makes the camera smaller and lighter. It also allows the use of a unique automatic flash unit that electronically resets the shutter and diaphragm to the proper settings. Automated assembly has kept the Canon AE-1's price quite low compared with similar advanced cameras. The camera is expected to have a great influence on future designs from other camera makers.

Other Camera Advances. The Rolleiflex SL 2000, another advanced 35-mm SLR camera, was shown as a working model at the 1976 *photokina*—world's fair of photography—in Cologne, West Germany, in September. The camera was not yet available for sale at year's end. It offers a choice of presetting either the shutter speed or the aperture. When the photographer sets one, the camera automatically provides the other setting.

Two of the smallest 35-mm SLR cameras yet developed were shown by the Asahi camera company. The Pentax ME is completely automatic, and the Pentax MX is manually controlled. Each cam-

A photographer shows the picture he took with the Eastman Kodak Company's self-developing camera, which went on the market in 1976.

Fuji Photo Film Company of Japan introduced a color-negative film with a 400 ASA speed rating. The film went on sale in Japan in October, and in the United States at the end of the year. It is the fastest color film available. Eastman has a similar film under development.

Photo Collecting. While photography continued to grow as a medium for science and industry and for active photo hobbyists, it also grew as an art form among collectors of old photographs. Print auctions in such cities as New York and London featured the work of famous photographers of the 1800s and early 1900s. Prices set new highs. For example, a complete set of *Camera Work,* edited by the American photographer Alfred Stieglitz, brought $60,000.

Business Developments. Photographic industry sales were about 9 per cent above the 1975 level, representing a slowing of the 11 per cent average yearly growth rate the industry enjoyed between 1967 and 1975. Color photography continued to dominate. Interest in photography among high school and college students continued high, though future professional prospects were limited.

Several men and women who influenced international photography died during the year. Among them were Americans Paul Strand, Imogen Cunningham, Man Ray, and Minor White, and Czechoslovak photographer Josef Sudek.   Kenneth Poli

era is about 5 inches (12.7 centimeters) across and weighs just over 16 ounces (455 grams).

Eastman Kodak Company finally entered the self-developing photographic market during the summer after seven years of developmental work. Polaroid Corporation, which has monopolized the field since 1948, immediately filed suit in Canada, Great Britain, and the United States, charging patent infringement. The cases are expected to take up to 10 years to settle. Meanwhile, Polaroid in January introduced a new, lower-priced version of its SX-70 camera.

New Lenses. Zoom lenses with variable focal lengths became more common in shorter ranges, such as 28 to 85 mm and 35 to 70 mm. *Catadioptric* (combined lens-and-mirror optical systems) and mirror lenses in focal lengths of 500, 600, and 800 mm were shown in shorter and lighter mounts.

Several manufacturers showed prototype movie cameras featuring autofocus lenses. They automatically focus on a subject without manual help.

Photo Hobbyists. More hobbyists started darkrooms to process and print their own color-negative and slide films. Manufacturers of darkroom materials continued to increase the variety of plastic-coated, quickly processed enlarging papers. Interest increased in positive-to-positive (slide-to-print) materials that eliminated the need for an intermediate negative.

PHYSICS. Significant experiments in 1976 dealt with both the strongest and weakest forces in nature. These are the strong force, which holds protons and neutrons together in the atomic nucleus, and gravity, a force so weak that bodies of astronomical size are needed for experiments.

Naked Charm. Protons, neutrons, pions, and other subnuclear particles that experience the strong force are thought to be made up of tinier constituents called *quarks* even though individual quarks have yet to be observed directly. Many physicists originally liked the quark theory because it is simple. Only three types of quarks and three corresponding antiparticles called *antiquarks* accounted for all the dozens of particles that experience the strong force.

Gradually, however, new information persuaded some physicists that nature was not quite so simple. In 1964, theoreticians James Bjorken of the Stanford Linear Accelerator Center (SLAC) in Palo Alto, Calif., and Sheldon L. Glashow, now at Harvard University, suggested that a fourth type of quark might exist. It differed from the other three quarks because it had a special property arbitrarily called *charm.*

The charmed-quark theory gained support late in 1974 when experimenters at SLAC and Brookhaven National Laboratory in Upton, N.Y., independently discovered a new particle called the psi. It appeared to be a charmed quark and its antiparticle bound together. Subsequently, researchers found a whole family of psi particles that fit the charmed-quark theory. But physicists were hard-pressed to explain why no one had found a particle with net, or *naked,* charm. Such a particle has a charmed quark whose charm is not canceled out by a second anti-charmed quark.

Enter the D Particle. Finally, in August 1976, physicists from SLAC and the University of California, Berkeley, reported the discovery of a genuinely charmed particle. Large numbers of them appeared in experiments at SLAC. The new particle is called the D particle. It is electrically neutral, is about twice as heavy as the proton, and is believed to be composed of a charmed quark and an ordinary antiquark. In September, the same California experimenters reported observing a charged version of the D particle. Although unconfirmed, still more charmed particles appear to be lurking in their data. In October, researchers at the Fermi National Accelerator Laboratory in Batavia, Ill., reported evidence of even heavier charmed particles.

All these new particles satisfy predictions by Glashow and his Harvard colleagues in 1975. The stunning success of the theory reveals a new dimension in elementary particles with possible implications going far beyond the study of the strong force.

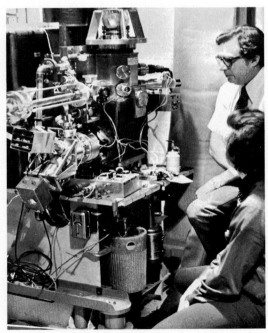

University of Chicago physicists examine the powerful electron microscope they used to make the first "motion pictures" of atoms in action.

Lunar Laser Ranging. In March, two groups of American scientists published independent analyses of data accumulated over nearly six years on the orbital motion of the moon. The data included round-trip flight times for blasts of laser light from the earth that bounced back from a retroreflector array placed on the moon by *Apollo* astronauts. Scientists calculated the earth-moon distance with the incredibly small uncertainty of about 16 inches (41 centimeters). Such ultraprecise measurements of the moon's motion enabled them to check predictions of various modern theories of gravity. The findings support Albert Einstein's general theory of relativity.

New Heavy Nuclei? Many physicists have believed for years that stable atomic nuclei might exist containing many more protons than the 106 in the heaviest element known before 1976. In June, scientists from the University of California, Davis; the Oak Ridge National Laboratory in Tennessee; and Florida State University in Tallahassee reported evidence for an element with 126 protons in its nucleus. They based their claim on X rays emitted when a tiny beam of protons bombarded specially selected particles of monazite. Other experimenters were unable to confirm the report.

In September, a team of Russian nuclear scientists reported the synthesis of element 107. See CHEMISTRY. Thomas O. White

PITTSBURGH teachers on Jan. 26, 1976, ended a strike that had closed Pittsburgh schools for eight weeks. The teachers agreed to a new contract calling for salary increases of 11.3 per cent in 1976, 8.3 per cent in 1977, and 5.1 per cent in 1978.

Common Pleas Court Judge Donald E. Ziegler had ordered the striking teachers to return to their jobs on January 3. The teachers refused, and the Pittsburgh Board of Public Education called for contempt citations. The judge instead ordered both sides to resume negotiations and established a citizens' fact-finding panel to study the dispute.

Fines Levied. The strike continued, and the judge found 18 union leaders guilty of contempt of court on January 8. Four days later, he fined the union $25,000 plus an additional $10,000 per day for each additional day of the strike. He also levied a $100 per day fine against each teacher for each day he or she stayed off work. On January 14, the judge ordered the union's offices padlocked and its assets frozen in an attempt to collect the fines. The January 26 settlement ended the threat of jail sentences for union leaders, but the court refused to cancel $105,000 in contempt fines.

The strike issues included distribution of the funds, class sizes, discipline, and job security. The strike affected 62,300 pupils, 3,800 teachers, and 800 paraprofessionals.

Mayor Peter Flaherty announced on May 6 that

he would not be a candidate for re-election to a third term in 1977. But he refused to rule out the possibility that he might run for the Pennsylvania governorship.

Economic Indicators. Department store sales in the Pittsburgh area increased by 12.1 per cent, but construction activity fell 3.1 per cent over a one-year period ending in August. Factory workers' wages increased an average of 10.7 per cent during the year to $13,536. The cost of living increased 4.2 per cent between July 1975 and July 1976. The U.S. Department of Labor estimated a family of four would need $10,000 a year to sustain a minimum standard of living in the area. Unemployment in the region stood at 7.7 per cent at midyear, but the total number of persons employed fell 1.1 per cent. Food costs, however, fell 0.4 per cent between July 1975 and July 1976.

The United States Steel Corporation and federal, state, and local environmental agencies announced on October 11 that they had reached a $600-million antipollution agreement for cleaning up emissions from the company's suburban Clairton Coke Works. Under it, the company must complete installation of antipollution equipment by 1983.

Federal Bureau of Investigation figures showed that serious crime in the area fell 2.8 per cent between 1970 and 1975. The national rate in major cities rose 38 per cent.   James M. Banovetz

POETRY. In a year of bountiful new works from veteran poets, John Ashbery's *Self-Portrait in a Convex Mirror* was the most widely praised book in the United States in 1976. This elegant, complex, philosophical verse positioned Ashbery as one of America's leading contemporary poetic figures. *The New Oxford Book of American Verse,* edited by critic Richard Ellmann, replaced F. O. Matthiessen's classic 1950 anthology, establishing a revised point of critical departure for American poetry.

Significant Works. Memorable career achievements were embodied in *Selected Poems* by Robert Lowell, twice winner of the Pulitzer Prize; *New and Collected Poems* by Archibald MacLeish; *Selected Poems* by Robert Creeley; and *Collected Poems* from both George Oppen and Robert Francis.

New books from proven talents included James Dickey's *The Zodiac,* a narrative that explored man's tenuous links to the universe. Another book-length poem, John Hollander's *Reflections on Espionage,* told an intriguing spy story in verse form. *The Mind-Reader* by Richard Wilbur exhibited a witty, urbane style. Louis Simpson's *Searching for the Ox* celebrated everyday things that "give the world color, shape, form, and reason."

From Trinidad, the rich, provocative songs of Derek Walcott's *Sea Grapes* were noteworthy. *Viper Jazz* offered cryptic, adventuresome poems by James Tate. Michael Benedikt's *Night Cries* proved

the finest collection of prose poems this year. Other significant volumes were *Jack Straw's Castle* by Thom Gunn, Philip Levine's *The Names of the Lost,* Stephen Berg's *Grief, The Heisenberg Variations* by John Bricuth, *A Swim Off the Rocks* by Howard Moss, and *Another Look,* verse with a classical twist from Horace Gregory.

Younger Poets emerged with exceptional collections. Notable were Dave Smith's splendid *Cumberland Station,* Albert Goldbarth's *Comings Back,* and *Train Windows* by David Evans. The Yale Younger Poets Prize went to Carolyn Forche for *Gathering the Tribes.* Other promising new poets were Michael Hogan, David St. John, Tess Gallagher, James Bertolino, David Cloutier, and Thomas Johnson.

Robert Fitzgerald's new edition of the *Iliad* and Richard Howard's version of E. M. Cioran's *A Short History of Decay* were outstanding translations. Important criticism came from Derek Traversi in *T. S. Eliot: The Longer Poems;* Donald Davis's *Ezra Pound;* and Judith Kroll's study of Sylvia Plath, *Chapters in Mythology.*

Major posthumous collections included the works of British-born W. H. Auden; Austin Clarke, the Irish master; and Italy's Cesare Pavese. Poets Charles Resnikoff, L. E. Sissman, and Walter Lowenfels died during the year.   G. E. Murray

Robert Fitzgerald accepts the first Harold Morton Landon Translation Award in February for his version of Homer's epic the *Iliad.*

POLAND. Political and economic strain put the Communist Party leadership on the defensive in 1976. The *Sejm* (legislature) adopted amendments to Poland's 1952 Constitution on February 10. Pressure from Roman Catholic leaders and intellectuals forced the government to moderate its proposed amendments. For example, Russia was not singled out for a special relationship nor were civil rights tied to compliance with state duties as the government had wanted.

Stefan Cardinal Wyszynski, the Catholic primate of Poland, publicly denounced the government's proposals on January 25. Stanislaw Stomma, leader of the five-member Catholic faction in the Sejm, was the only legislator to abstain from voting. He was not slated for re-election on March 21. Konstanty Lubienski assumed leadership of the faction and was made a member of the Council of State.

Workers Riot. Council of Ministers Chairman Piotr Jaroszewicz announced on June 24 that prices of basic foods, unchanged since 1971, would rise dramatically on June 26 — meat by 69 per cent, butter 50 per cent, sugar 100 per cent, and poultry 30 per cent. He also said the government would pay farmers more for their produce. Workers in a tractor factory in a Warsaw suburb protested by going on strike on June 25, and rioting workers tore up part of the main railway track from Warsaw to western Europe. In Radom, an industrial town south of Warsaw, crowds set fire to the Communist Party Headquarters, looted food stores, and battled police. The government canceled the price hikes on June 25, but said it planned to raise some prices later in the year. In September, however, the whole project was put off until well into 1978. The government reported that 78 persons were arrested and tried for their part in the June food riots.

Supply Problems continued to afflict Poland. To stop hoarding, sugar rationing began in August, and coal rationing came in November, despite the fact that Poland sold less coal to the West than was planned in the first nine months of the year.

Communist Party First Secretary Edward Gierek led a delegation to Moscow on November 9 and 10 that discussed Russian aid to Poland. He obtained promises of help with grain and other commodities. French President Valéry Giscard d'Estaing had talks with Gierek during a hunting trip in Poland in mid-November. Gierek told the Central Committee on December 1 that economic investments would have to be cut through 1980 because of the need to import $1.5 billion worth of grain and meat.

West Germany and Poland finally settled claims for individual Polish contributions to the German pension fund during the German occupation of Poland in World War II.   Chris Cviic

See also EUROPE (Facts in Brief Table); WEST GERMANY.

POLLUTION. See ENVIRONMENT.

POPULATION, WORLD. As of Dec. 31, 1976, world population totaled about 4.3 billion, a gain of nearly 90 million during the year. The world birth rate was 35 births per 1,000 population per year; the death rate was 14 per 1,000. At the existing growth rate of about 2.2 per cent a year, the world's total population would double in about 31 years.

In terms of birth and death rates, the developed section — Europe, Russia, North America, temperate South America, Australia-New Zealand, and Japan — with a population of 1.2 billion, had a birth rate of about 16.5 per 1,000 and a death rate of about 9 per 1,000. The developing section — about 3-billion persons in Asia, Africa, and tropical Latin America — had a birth rate of 37 and a death rate of 13.5 per thousand.

Kuwait had the fastest-growing population at a rate of 6.1 per cent annually, almost three times the world rate. The second fastest was Libya at 4.1 per cent. The United States rate was 1.3 per cent. Austria, Barbados, Great Britain, and Malta have achieved zero population growth. Niger, Rhodesia, and Swaziland tied for the highest birth rate, 52 a year for every 1,000 population. The U.S. rate was 14.7. East and West Germany had the lowest, 10.

Food Outlook. As human numbers increased, annual world grain production declined. The available grain in 1976 was down to 604 pounds (274

THE MILWAUKEE JOURNAL

kilograms) per capita from 686 pounds (311 kilograms) in 1973.

Population control – the effort to bring birth rates into balance with modern low death rates – remained a major concern of most demographers. In 1976, more than 60 of the developing countries had population policies or family-planning programs of one kind or another. In the Philippines, the government's commission on population issued a decree establishing family-planning offices in every municipality. In India, the government adopted a broad new birth-control policy that included raising the minimum marriage age and paying more money to people who voluntarily submitted to sterilization. Several Indian states sponsored legislation to compel people who have two or three children to be sterilized.

In the United States, Congress enacted legislation prohibiting the use of federal Medicaid funds for abortions, except under certain conditions. President Gerald R. Ford vetoed the bill on September 29, but Congress overrode the veto on September 30. On October 22, a United States District Court in New York City ruled the bill unconstitutional. Then, on November 8, the Supreme Court of the United States denied a request to block enforcement of the District Court's ruling. This meant that the bill would not go into effect for a period of some months, if ever. Robert C. Cook

PORTUGAL. Prime Minister Mario Alberto Nobre Lopez Soares announced austerity measures on Sept. 9, 1976, to combat Portugal's desperate economic situation. The package included wage and price controls, an increase on imports surcharges from 20 to 30 per cent, and credit policies to cut consumption and stimulate production and exports. Soares told the nation that its future depended on the people's will to work. He attacked the "cancer of absenteeism," working hours wasted in political meetings, and counterproductive strikes.

A report by economists at the Massachusetts Institute of Technology commissioned by the Bank of Portugal prompted the measures. The report said the government must cut wages by 30 per cent or face galloping inflation, which ran as high as 50 per cent. Unemployment was 16 per cent, and the balance-of-payments deficit increased by $4 million per day.

Election Violence. Soares decided to form a minority government after his Socialist Party received 35 per cent of the votes in National Assembly elections on April 25. A total of 24 per cent went to the liberal Popular Democrats and 16 per cent to the conservative Center Democrats. Communists took 15 per cent. Nine smaller parties split the remaining votes. Violence marred the assembly election campaign and continued into the presidential campaign that followed.

New President. On June 27, General Antonio Dos Santos Ramalho Eanes, the army chief of staff, became Portugal's first democratically elected president in 50 years. A heart attack on June 23 felled candidate José Pinheiro de Azevedo, the prime minister. With Socialist support, Ramalho Eanes got 61.5 per cent of the votes, and Azevedo 14.4 per cent. Radical left wing candidate Otelo Saraiva de Carvalho had 16.5 per cent, and Communist Octavio Pato got 7.6 per cent. Ramalho Eanes was sworn in on July 14 and appointed Soares as prime minister. Ramalho Eanes said the first objective would be to maintain the rule of law and stamp out "insurrectionist activities." Soares promised only "hard work and austerity." See RAMALHO EANES, ANTONIO DOS SANTOS.

Nurses, shop assistants, and cabdrivers went on strike during the pre-election months. Thousands of teachers demonstrated on October 12 to protest government changes in education. The prolonged drought brought electric power cuts; in July, elevators and air conditioners were ordered turned off.

In a step toward European Community (Common Market) membership, Portugal became the 19th member of the Council of Europe on September 22. The council is a political and environmental forum. Kenneth Brown

See also EUROPE (Facts in Brief Table).

After taking oath of office July 14, Portugal's President Antonio Ramalho Eanes, left, greets Mario Soares, who soon was named premier.

POSTAL SERVICE, UNITED STATES. Unhappy over the costs and delays of delivering the mail, Congress voted in 1976 to take a hard look at the U.S. Postal Service and see if it needs a major overhaul. Final approval came on September 10, creating a commission to investigate mounting complaints by mail users and to make recommendations for changes in rate-making procedures and service to the public.

The commission was to report its findings by March 15, 1977. The report was expected to begin a major congressional review of postal operations. The commission's main assignment was to propose ways for the Postal Service to become financially sound.

Growing Subsidies. Congress established the study panel in a bill that provided an extra $1-billion subsidy to keep the postal system operating through September 1977. The lawmakers also approved a ban on cutbacks in service or increases in rates through March 15, 1977. Because of the long delays involved in approving rate increases, this action effectively froze postal charges for all of 1977.

Despite sharp hikes in rates, the Postal Service has required more than $3 billion in federal subsidies since it was created as a semi-independent business in 1971. The total deficit was expected to reach $4.9 billion by the end of September 1977.

Postmaster General Benjamin F. Bailar said the latest $1-billion subsidy was an essential investment in modern mail-handling facilities. Congress was far more critical of the Postal Service. Showing its displeasure, the House voted to resume control over the $50-billion annual postal budget. The Senate refused to go along, and the proposal died.

The creation of a commission to study postal operations was a compromise. President Gerald R. Ford, leaders of Congress, large postal users, and the postal unions all supported the move.

Other Developments. Congress also insisted on a greater flow of information from the Postal Service in the future. The subsidy legislation requires the postal budget to be sent to Congress and postal officials to testify at Senate and House hearings in the first two months of each year. Another provision forbids the closing of any post office without 60 days public notice. Postal patrons were granted the right to appeal a shut-down decision to the Postal Rate Commission, an independent agency.

A United Parcel Service strike, which disrupted postal service for 12 weeks by swelling mail volume in 15 eastern states, ended on December 9 when Teamster members approved a new contract.

A New Rate Schedule went into effect on July 18. It increased rates for second-class mail, special delivery, money orders, and registered mail, and lowered rates for third-class commercial mail. The 13-cent rate for first-class letters remained unchanged.   William J. Eaton

POVEDA BURBANO, ALFREDO (1926-   ), became the presiding member of a three-man military junta that seized control of Ecuador in a peaceful coup d'état on Jan. 11, 1976 (see ECUADOR). Poveda, an admiral in the Ecuadorean Navy, was joined by the chiefs of the army and air force in the junta that ousted President Guillermo A. Rodriguez Lara. The coup was the latest of more than 50 that have marked Ecuador's 146-year history. Poveda and his associates are considered to be conservative and pro-American.

Poveda was born in Ambato, the capital of Tungurahua province on Jan. 24, 1926. He was educated at Ecuador's Naval Academy and received further naval training at schools in Argentina, Brazil, Great Britain, and the United States. He rose steadily through the ranks, becoming a captain in 1958, rear admiral in 1972, and vice-admiral in 1975.

Poveda served in a variety of posts. He was head of naval logistics in 1959 and became chief of naval intelligence in the following year. In 1963, he joined the office of the naval chief of staff and served in several staff positions during the next 10 years. Poveda joined the Cabinet in 1973 as minister of government and police. He was named fleet commander in 1975 and in the same year became chief of Ecuador's Joint Armed Forces Command, a position he held until the January coup.

He is married to Alicia Pizzimbono. Edward G. Nash

POWELL, ANTHONY (1905-   ), British novelist, published *Hearing Secret Harmonies* in April 1976, the 12th and last novel of his sequence *A Dance to the Music of Time*.

Powell is considered one of the best novelists now writing British fiction. He has written many novels, some highly praised for their wit and satire, and an important biography of John Aubrey, the famous English chronicler of the 1600s. Powell also worked briefly as a motion-picture script writer both in England and in Hollywood, and wrote a review column for the *London Daily Telegraph*.

In *A Dance to the Music of Time,* Powell describes the changing nature of the upper classes in England after 1914. The novels are told in the first person by one of the characters, Nicholas Jenkins. Powell insists he had no elaborately worked-out scheme when he started writing the series in the 1940s. The first volume, *A Question of Upbringing,* was published in 1951, and the series includes *The Acceptance of The World* (1953) and *The Military Philosophers* (1969). "The thing just grew," Powell says. "The more I did it, the less I understood. If the thing's working properly, what happens to the characters is inevitable."

Born in London, the son of a British Army officer, Powell attended Eton and Oxford University. He is married to Lady Violet Pakenham, daughter of the fifth Earl of Longford. Foster Stockwell

PRESIDENT OF THE UNITED STATES. Gerald R. Ford lost his bid for election as President on Nov. 2, 1976. Ford had been appointed Vice-President by former President Richard M. Nixon in 1973. He assumed the presidency on Aug. 9, 1974, when Nixon resigned in the wake of the Watergate scandal. After a brief vacation in Palm Springs, Calif., following the November 2 election, President Ford returned to Washington, D.C., to finish out his term, which was to end on Jan. 20, 1977, and to cooperate with President-elect James Earl (Jimmy) Carter, Jr., in the transition period.

Relations with Congress. In his State of the Union message delivered to a joint session of the 94th Congress on Jan. 19, 1976, President Ford asked Congress to act in the spirit of a "new realism." This was in keeping with his consistent efforts to limit government spending and to pursue a conservative economic policy. However, Ford's philosophy led to repeated clashes with the Democrat-controlled Congress.

In its second session, Congress continued to approve new social welfare programs despite the President's threats of vetoes. During his entire term in office, President Ford vetoed 66 bills, most of them for programs he regarded as inflationary, wasteful, or unnecessary. In 1976, he vetoed 22 bills. According to Ford, his vetoes saved the government about $9 billion during his presidential career.

President Ford regarded the vetoes as basic to the U.S. constitutional system of checks and balances. He declared that he vetoed unwise legislation in order to "protect the American people from unrealistic responses to their very real needs." Among the bills he vetoed in 1976 were appropriations for public works and job programs, regulation of strip mining, development of a nonpolluting automobile engine, and an on-site picketing bill.

Five of the President's vetoes — including a bill he vetoed in 1975 — were overridden by the second session of the 94th Congress. Among these were appropriations for health, education, and welfare and public-service jobs programs. See CONGRESS OF THE UNITED STATES.

Ford's Budget. On January 21, the President presented a budget of $394.2 billion for fiscal 1977 (Oct. 1, 1976, to Sept. 30, 1977). The budget provided for increases in defense expenditures and cuts or savings in other federal programs. President Ford estimated that the fiscal 1977 deficit would be about $43 billion. Congress in September set a budget ceiling of $413.1 billion for fiscal 1977.

In June, the Office of Management and Budget (OMB) revealed that the federal deficit for fiscal 1976 (July 1, 1975, to June 30, 1976) was $65.6-billion — $10.4 billion less than anticipated. In October, the OMB announced that the federal government had spent about $11.4 billion less than Congress had appropriated.

President Ford presides over the opening of the Lyndon B. Johnson Memorial in Washington, D.C., as Lady Bird Johnson, seated, listens.

Domestic Issues. Throughout the year, President Ford tried to steer a conservative, prudent course to hold the lid on inflation, even though unemployment remained high.

On October 9, the President signed a proclamation restricting beef imports to help U.S. cattlemen. He raised price-support loans for livestock-grain farmers on October 13, an action that the Department of Agriculture had not recommended. Democratic critics charged that the President was acting with his eye on the election, but Ford denied that these actions to help U.S. farmers were politically motivated.

President Ford criticized court-ordered busing to achieve desegregation in the nation's schools. He questioned its propriety and its effectiveness. White House press secretary Ronald H. Nessen revealed on May 18 that the President had asked Attorney General Edward H. Levi to look for a test case to take to the Supreme Court of the United States so that the court could re-evaluate the use of busing to force school integration. The President on June 24 sent Congress proposed legislation for curbing court-ordered busing. He said his proposals were intended to make busing a tool of last resort for achieving school integration. However, Congress did not act on his suggested legislation, and the Supreme Court several times declined to review cases challenging busing programs. This, in effect, let stand the lower-court rulings on which the busing programs were based.

Foreign Policy. The President and Congress had fewer disagreements over foreign policy in 1976 than in previous years. But despite the President's opposition, Congress in January cut off covert U.S. aid to pro-Western factions in the Angolan civil war. Many members of Congress feared the Ford Administration might involve the United States in a Vietnam-like situation in Angola. In June, Congress passed a military-aid bill that included a ban on aid to Angola and also to Chile. But for the most part, Congress did not intervene in the Ford Administration's foreign policy in 1976.

President Ford signed a treaty with Russia on May 28 in Washington, D.C. The pact limited the size of underground nuclear explosions for peaceful purposes and provided for on-site inspection for nuclear tests under some circumstances. Russian Communist leader Leonid I. Brezhnev signed the treaty in Moscow. This marked the first time that Russia had agreed to any form of on-site inspection. The treaty complemented the 1974 agreement limiting underground nuclear weapons tests. Eventually, both treaties must be ratified by the Senate.

North Koreans killed two U.S. military officers and wounded four enlisted men in Korea's demilitarized zone on August 18. The Americans, part of a United Nations peacekeeping force, were trimming a tree that was blocking the view from an observation post. President Ford warned that North Korea was responsible for the incident. Acting at once to strengthen the U.S. military presence in Korea, he ordered jet fighters and Navy ships into the area. On August 21, North Korean President Kim Il-song conceded that the incident was "regretful." The U.S. military alert ended on September 7. See ARMED FORCES; KOREA, NORTH.

The General Accounting Office (GAO) reported on October 5 that its study of the *Mayaguez* affair – in which Cambodians seized a U.S. merchant ship – indicated that the President had not exhausted all diplomatic procedures before ordering the U.S. attack on Cambodia in May 1975. In the attack, which was staged to free the *Mayaguez* and its 39 crewmen, 38 Americans were killed, 3 were missing, and 53 were wounded. President Ford criticized the GAO report for both its substance and the fact that it was released just before the November 2 election.

The President sent Secretary of State Henry A. Kissinger to Africa in April and again in September to try to mediate the southern African racial crisis, particularly the dispute between Rhodesia's black nationalists and the white-minority government. Kissinger succeeded in getting Rhodesian Prime Minister Ian D. Smith to agree to black-majority rule in two years. However, the black nationalists insisted on a faster turnover of government. See AFRICA; RHODESIA.

Spy Agency Reform. Investigations by congressional committees in 1976 stimulated reform of the nation's intelligence-gathering agencies. At a televised news conference on February 17, President Ford announced that George H. W. Bush, director of the Central Intelligence Agency, would chair a new committee to supervise intelligence operations. A three-member independent supervisory board made up of private citizens was also established. The National Security Council retained responsibility for the overall direction of intelligence policy.

On February 18, the President issued an executive order limiting the surveillance of, and collection of information about, U.S. citizens by federal agencies. The order also prohibited federal agents from engaging in assassination plots in other countries. At the same time, President Ford sent legislation to Congress making it a serious crime for a federal employee to divulge information about the methods used by the federal government to collect and evaluate intelligence information.

On March 10, President Ford revealed plans to enlarge the Foreign Intelligence Advisory Board from 10 to 17 members. The new members included former Defense Secretary Melvin R. Laird and former Treasury Secretary John B. Connally, Jr.

The President suggested on July 19 that Congress establish a permanent prosecutor's office to investigate charges of wrongdoing by federal officials.

Swine Flu. When medical specialists warned in March that an influenza epidemic might sweep the country in the winter of 1976-1977, Ford asked for and Congress granted $135 million to produce a vaccine against the so-called swine flu. The President actively promoted a national immunization program, with the vaccine provided free. After the program began in October, Ford was inoculated in the presence of reporters and photographers to encourage all Americans to receive the protection. However, the program was surrounded by controversy, and it was halted in December when several persons became paralyzed after receiving the flu shot. See PUBLIC HEALTH (Close-Up).

Political Problems. As President, Ford was also titular head of the Republican Party. However, his leadership was sharply contested in 1976 by former California Governor Ronald Reagan, a conservative, who challenged Ford for the presidential nomination. In response, the President actively campaigned in the 1976 primary elections. He reacted to conservative Republican charges that he was selling out U.S. interests by downplaying his policy of détente with Russia. He won the Republican nomination on August 19 on the first ballot at the Republican National Convention in Kansas City, Mo. Ford named Senator Robert J. Dole of Kansas, former Republican National Committee Chairman, as his running mate. See REPUBLICAN PARTY.

In his acceptance speech, President Ford challenged Carter, the Democratic presidential candidate, to televised debates. Carter readily accepted, and the debates were conducted under the auspices of the League of Women Voters. President Ford debated Carter three times – on September 23 in Philadelphia, October 6 in San Francisco, and October 22 in Williamsburg, Va. The first debate covered domestic issues; the second, foreign policy; and the third was open to any issue. During the second debate, Ford made a statement that was widely regarded as a serious political blunder; he claimed Eastern Europe was free of Russian domination. See ELECTIONS; TELEVISION.

Cabinet Problems. On January 14, John T. Dunlop resigned as secretary of labor, after President Ford vetoed a construction-picketing bill that would have expanded picketing rights for workers at construction sites. Dunlop had supported the bill and Ford had earlier assured him it would receive presidential approval. Dunlop resigned to preserve his high standing with labor. President Ford appointed Willie J. Usery, Jr., as secretary of labor on January 22 (see USERY, WILLIE JULIAN, JR.).

President Ford faced a serious political problem in October that was precipitated by Secretary of Agriculture Earl L. Butz, who had made a "highly offensive" racial slur about black Americans. Because Butz was popular with farmers, Ford was reportedly reluctant to ask for his resignation. So he

King Juan Carlos I of Spain gives Betty Ford's hand a courtly kiss as he and Queen Sophia, right, arrive for an official White House visit.

reprimanded Butz on October 1. However, Butz was forced to resign on October 4 because of the storm of public criticism. Butz also apologized for his "gross indiscretion." President Ford accepted the resignation with regret, calling Butz "this good and decent man." On November 4, the President named Acting Secretary of Agriculture John A. Knebel to succeed Butz.

On February 25, the President named former Pennsylvania Governor William W. Scranton chief U.S. delegate to the United Nations, replacing Daniel P. Moynihan (see SCRANTON, WILLIAM WARREN). On March 19, the President named Thomas S. Gates, Jr., to head the U.S. liaison mission to the People's Republic of China.

The President did not travel outside U.S. territory during 1976. He left the mainland only once, for a two-day conference in Puerto Rico in June. He hosted an economic summit conference of the leaders of industrialized nations at Dorado Beach. While in Puerto Rico, he warned Cuba not to interfere in U.S.-Puerto Rican relations.

Although President Ford did not travel abroad, he traveled extensively in the United States during the year – first to secure the Republican Party's presidential nomination, then to campaign against Democratic candidate Carter.   Carol L. Thompson

See also CABINET; ELECTIONS; FORD, GERALD R.; UNITED STATES, GOVERNMENT OF THE.

PRINCE EDWARD ISLAND, Canada's smallest province, worried over shortages and high energy prices in 1976. Totally dependent on oil-fired generators for electricity, the island experienced the highest power costs in Canada. Premier Alexander B. Campbell's Liberal government emphasized conservation and research into alternative sources of supply.

By-elections on November 8 sent three Progressive Conservatives and one Liberal to the provincial legislature. Among them was the newly chosen Conservative leader, J. Angus MacLean, formerly a member of the federal Parliament and a Cabinet minister in the John Diefenbaker government. The Liberals still held a comfortable 24 to 8 edge over the Conservatives in the legislature.

The legislature opened on March 5, and the budget was presented later in the month. After budget increases that averaged 25 per cent for each of the previous three years, a 9.5 per cent ceiling was imposed on spending growth for 1976-1977.

Minister of Veterans Affairs Daniel J. MacDonald, Prince Edward Island's representative in the Trudeau Cabinet, announced on October 28 that almost the entire federal Department of Veterans Affairs would be moved from Ottawa, Ont., to Charlottetown, P.E.I., within five years. About 650 jobs would be transferred as part of a plan to decentralize the public service.   David M. L. Farr

Prisoners reduced part of the British Columbia penitentiary in New Westminster to rubble in September during uprising over security measures.

PRISON. The plight of political prisoners and allegations of torture in many prisons throughout the world received increased attention during 1976. Amnesty International, a London-based human-rights group, issued a report in September that accused 112 countries – virtually every major government in the world – of incarcerating "prisoners of conscience" and stated that torture is practiced "as essentially a state activity" in nearly half of these countries.

Other reports listed Cuba, India, Indonesia, Iran, and Russia among nations that detained from 10,000 to 100,000 political prisoners each. Allegations of torture ranged from police brutality and prison-guard violence in the United States to systematic, sophisticated physical and psychological tortures that are reportedly institutionalized in about 40 countries.

U.S. Prisons. Disillusioned with the rehabilitative potential of prisons, the United States continued to de-emphasize indeterminate sentences, a post-World War II reform that allowed early release for prisoners making satisfactory progress. Several states, including Connecticut, Massachusetts, and Missouri, passed laws mandating minimum jail terms upon conviction for certain crimes, and Maine became the first state to abolish its parole board in favor of short, set jail terms. Continually rising crime figures and statistics show that

career criminal repeaters are responsible for a disproportionate share of offenses. With this in mind, Attorney General Edward H. Levi urged in June that the practice of leaving sentencing to the discretion of federal judges be sharply curtailed and that the U.S. Parole Commission be abolished.

The nation's state and federal prison population continued to grow, reaching a record 250,000 during 1976. A survey by *Corrections* magazine found 24,134 prisoners in federal institutions and 225,582 inmates in state prisons on January 1, a 10.5 per cent increase over the preceding year.

Research Ending. Norman A. Carlson, director of the U.S. Bureau of Prisons, announced on March 1 that the last medical-research program in federal prisons, a drug study at a Lexington, Ky., addiction center, would be phased out by Jan. 1, 1977. Despite the new ban on federal participation, at least 18 state prison systems still allow research using prisoners.

The year's bloodiest prison disturbances occurred at Nevada State Prison in Carson City. Racially inspired fighting on September 27 injured 36 inmates. In a resumption of hostilities on October 10, two prisoners were stabbed to death and 11 others injured.   David C. Beckwith

PRIZES. See AWARDS AND PRIZES; CANADIAN LIBRARY ASSOCIATION; CANADIAN LITERATURE; FASHION; NOBEL PRIZES.

PROTESTANTISM

PROTESTANTISM. Much Protestant attention throughout the world focused on the role that piety played in the 1976 United States presidential campaign. Both President Gerald R. Ford and Democrat James Earl (Jimmy) Carter, Jr., were active members of Protestant churches and identified themselves with evangelical or conservative interests. President Ford, an Episcopalian, made no secret of the fact that he regularly participated in congressional prayer breakfasts organized by evangelical congressmen and that his son Michael was an evangelical seminary student.

Carter, a Baptist, was even more visibly connected with the evangelical wing of Protestantism. He made references to the fact that he had been "born again" and acknowledged a personal decision for and an acceptance of Jesus Christ as his savior.

Such an overt profession of faith in public life matched the spiritual style of many Americans in the 1970s, because large numbers of citizens had come to speak openly about their religious feelings. At the same time, it was disconcerting to those whose experiences differed vastly from Carter's Baptist expressions that were so at home in the American South.

Both Ford and Carter were accused of exploiting religious issues, but both also protested that the mass media insisted on bringing them up. Carter in particular was involved in some old-fashioned debates over separation of church and state when he was criticized by anti-abortion groups. While both Carter and Ford opposed most abortions as private citizens, neither seemed to feel that support of a constitutional change to prohibit abortions was in order. Ford's rejection of constitutional measures was less emphatic than Carter's, and the Democrat was frequently pressed to defend himself on a subject that he and much of the public regarded as a minor issue in the campaign.

The focus on the piety and spirituality of the candidates was not matched by any sustained discussion of the part religion would play in policy issues. A number of church leaders organized Religion and the Presidency (RAP) in Washington, D.C., in January. It was to have been a forum in which the moral and religious side of national controversies would be aired. But few church leaders and even fewer important primary candidates paid attention to the calls for theological discussion of the issues that came from RAP.

Churches and the Bicentennial. Protestant piety showed up in another public arena during 1976. The American Revolution Bicentennial celebration called forth from the churches many memorial services to the religious liberty won by them or deeded to them about 200 years earlier. Many congregations recalled the part that Protestant leadership played in helping form the 200-year-old republic. Fears by some Protestant leaders that the commem-

oration might result in an orgy of state worship, of idolizing the American nation, and of ritual flag-waving were generally not realized. Countless congregations and church-related college campuses used the occasion to examine connections between religion and American history or the civil order.

Protestant themes often come to focus in the conventions of the various denominations. For example, the liveliest debates at several conventions had to do with homosexuality. Should the churches recognize homosexual love on a par with heterosexual love? Should they ordain homosexuals to the holy ministry? While "gay activists" were among the more vocal groups at these conventions, and while their following grew, they tended to meet setbacks when denominations voted. The United Methodist Church, some 10 million strong, held its general convention in Portland, Ore., in May. Despite much urging, delegates overwhelmingly refused to endorse recognition of homosexuality, though the leaders and delegates, like those in other large churches, encouraged ministry to homosexual Christians. The United Presbyterian Church in the United States of America followed a similar line.

Ordination of Women. The other issue having to do with the sex of Christian ministers, the ordination of women, was not as urgent as it had been in many churches in recent years. Perhaps this was

F. Donald Coggan, archbishop of Canterbury, addresses Episcopal Church Convention, which approved ordination of women in September.

because its advocates had already won many victories. There was one dramatic exception. The Episcopal Church, meeting in Minneapolis, Minn., in September, could no longer postpone action on this issue that had troubled the body for some years.

While the majority of the delegates seemed in advance to favor such ordination, the minority was strong and vocal. Some of its leaders threatened to leave the Episcopal Church as it was presently constituted, or to remain as vigorously protesting dissidents, if women were ordained as priests. They cited the length of the church's tradition against such ordination and the complications such an act would raise for Episcopal relations with Roman Catholic and Eastern Orthodox Christians. Yet, by slight majorities, both the House of Bishops and the House of Delegates at Minneapolis voted to ordain women. See ROMAN CATHOLIC CHURCH.

Another controversial Episcopal issue was the choice of a service book for worship. Episcopalians have long cherished the *Book of Common Prayer,* first published in 1549. For 12 years, the American Episcopalians had studied revisions of the prayer book. After much experiment and dissension, they decided to vote on adopting a revised edition at Minneapolis. Again, traditionalists argued against tampering with what was time-honored and pointed to the grand cadences and phrases of the old book. Yet the convention voted for the revision.

Lutheran Strife. Also on the denominational front, the strife-torn Lutheran Church–Missouri Synod moved beyond the point of reconciliation between the conservative and moderate parties. By year's end, not a single proposal for concord remained on the books as the conservatives completed their efforts to control the church. President Jacob A. O. Preus in April ousted four district presidents who continued to authorize the ordination of graduates of the moderate Concordia Seminary in Exile (Seminex) after the Synod outlawed Seminex. These presidents, along with four others who sympathized with them, formed the center of a new church movement. In some cases, their congregations began to move away from the Missouri Synod.

The English District, one of the four whose president was removed, voted in June to become an independent English Synod, which it had been before 1911. It linked with other moderate congregations and jurisdictions in December to form the Association of Evangelical Lutheran Churches.

In Dublin, Ireland, the 13th World Methodist Congress issued a call for continued talks with the Roman Catholic Church on world church unity and for similar discussions with the Lutheran and Eastern Orthodox churches. The congress also urged respect for human rights in countries where racism, discrimination, and economic oppression deprive people of freedom. More than 2,000 delegates attended the six-day congress.

The Membership Decline in the largest U.S. Protestant churches generally slowed or was arrested, according to statistical evidence, but many of them still cut their staffs in an economy move. Growth was centered in the more conservative evangelical churches. But the evangelicals also experienced increasing internal tensions in 1976. For example, *Christianity Today* editor Harold Lindsell, in his book *The Battle for the Bible,* drew a dividing line between those who accepted the idea that the Bible was literally free from error in matters of science and geography and those who had other grounds for accepting its full authority. He named individuals and evangelical institutions he believed did not meet his standards in the matter of strict belief in the Bible's inerrancy. Some of those he named, especially the prestigious Fuller Theological Seminary in Pasadena, Calif., vigorously defended themselves against Lindsell's charges.

Reaction to Lindsell's book suggested that he may have misjudged the strength of opposition to his position among the evangelicals. In any case, he revealed some of the varieties present in today's evangelical movement. The movement was also divided over the issue of ordaining women, over the degrees and styles of social action churches should engage in, and over many points of theology and living styles.   Martin E. Marty

See also RELIGION.

PSYCHOLOGY. The work of a British psychologist long regarded as a leading authority on the relationship of heredity to intelligence was declared suspect and without scientific value in 1976. Cyril L. Burt's research had been unquestioned and was highly influential before his death in 1971.

Burt held that intelligence is predetermined at birth and largely unchangeable. His view helped to shape a rigid, three-tiered British school system based on IQ tests given to children at the age of 11. The scientific articles written by Burt that are now being questioned were based on studies of the IQ's of identical twins reared in separate homes. They had been considered landmarks in psychology because they appeared to be models of scientific rigor.

Leon J. Kamin, a Princeton University psychologist, led the criticism of Burt's work. He cited instances of questionable scientific thought, including biased language, virtually impossible statistical correlations, fabrication of data, and favorable reviews of his own books by Burt under pseudonyms. It is also now believed that two collaborators cited by Burt in his published articles never existed.

The discrediting of Burt's work is particularly significant, because his writings have been a major buttress of the view that blacks inherit inferior intelligence, a position taken by such scientists as Arthur R. Jensen of the University of California and William B. Shockley of Stanford University.

Schizophrenia. Workers at two laboratories in 1976 studied the effects of morphinelike peptides on the behavior of rats. Their results suggest that schizophrenia, the most common form of psychosis, may be based on an imbalance in the supply of these naturally occurring peptides in the brain.

Floyd Bloom, David Segal, Nicholas Ling, and Roger Guillemin of the Salk Institute for Biological Studies and the University of California, San Diego, injected the peptides into the large fluid-filled cavities in rats' brains. Within minutes, the peptides blocked the rats' responses to painful stimuli. Moreover, one of the peptides induced rigidity in their muscles. See BIOCHEMISTRY.

Yasuko F. Jacquet and Neville Marks, working at the New York State Research Institute for Neurochemistry, injected the same peptides into the periaqueductal gray area of the brain stem and found effects quite similar to those obtained in the California studies, despite the small area of brain tissue stimulated. Jacquet and Marks pointed to the similarity between the effects they obtained and the effects of a wide variety of neuroleptic drugs now used to treat certain types of schizophrenia. They also concluded that the disease probably results from a peptide imbalance in the brain. This conclusion may lead to new ways of treating schizophrenic patients.   Robert W. Goy

See also MENTAL HEALTH.

PUBLIC HEALTH. The World Health Organization (WHO) came closer in 1976 to its goal of eliminating smallpox. The only cases reported were in Ethiopia and Somalia. If no new cases occur within the next two years, WHO will declare the disease, which killed millions of people in past centuries, officially eradicated. WHO began its smallpox eradication drive in 1967, a year in which 2 million persons died of the disease.

In the United States, smallpox vaccinations have become almost as extinct as the disease they were designed to prevent. The 26 states that required smallpox vaccinations for children entering school had dropped those requirements by 1976. A massive swine flu campaign ran into complications in 1976, however. See Close-Up.

The Nation's Health. In a report sent to Congress and President Gerald R. Ford in January, the U.S. Department of Health, Education, and Welfare pronounced the American people healthier than ever. Infant death rates were lower and life expectancy longer, according to the report. It also showed that the death rate for heart disease among Americans 55 to 64 years old dropped almost 15 per cent during the preceding six years. Deaths from cancer rose 4 per cent in the same age group. The major causes of death among young people were accidents and homicides.

Deaths from heart attack and heart disease fell below 1 million for the first time since 1967, according to the National Heart and Lung Institute. Better ways of diagnosing and treating heart problems were credited with the drop, which represents a decline of more than 30 per cent since 1950. Heart attack is still the nation's number-one killer, however, even though the heart attack death rate is 7 per cent below what it was in 1970.

Smoking Studies showed that Americans were smoking fewer and milder cigarettes. The Center for Disease Control in Atlanta, Ga., released a study showing that the number of adults who smoked dropped from more than half of all adults in 1964, the year smoking was linked to cancer by the surgeon general, to fewer than 40 per cent in 1975.

Adults who smoke seem to be turning to cigarettes that contain less tar and nicotine. The American Cancer Society reported in September 1976 that such cigarettes cause markedly fewer deaths from lung cancer and heart disease than do the high-tar, high-nicotine brands.

Bubonic Plague posted one of the worst years in recent times. The United States reported 25 cases, the highest total in 50 years. All of the cases reported were in Western states. Health officials explained that the plague is cyclical, and the high incidence seems to be part of an upswing.   Dianne Rafalik

See also HEALTH AND DISEASE; MEDICINE.

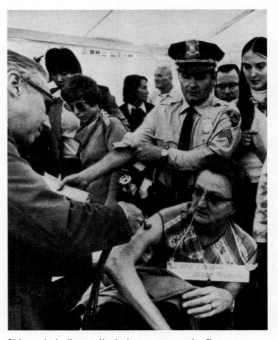

Citizens in Indianapolis, Ind., are among the first to get swine flu inoculations as the national immunization program opens in October 1976.

Flap over The Flu Campaign

The United States mounted its largest public health effort in history in 1976 to immunize all Americans against swine flu, a virus similar to the Spanish influenza that killed more than 20 million people throughout the world in 1918 and 1919. The new viral strain was discovered at Fort Dix, N.J., where it killed a young Army recruit on Feb. 5, 1976, and infected several others. The Center for Disease Control in Atlanta, Ga., determined on February 14 that the new virus was similar to the one that caused the 1918 flu pandemic.

Acting on the advice of some of the nation's top health experts, President Gerald R. Ford announced a national immunization program on March 24 and asked Congress for $135 million to "inoculate every man, woman, and child in the country." Congress quickly approved the funds.

The World Health Organization, noting that no other country had reported any incidence of swine flu, reacted to the President's announcement with surprise. In the United States, critics of the program questioned whether the likelihood of a swine flu epidemic had been overstated, whether the new virus was as deadly as Spanish flu, and whether the sudden decision to inoculate the entire population was simply an election-year ploy.

Supporters argued that the dangers of the virus, to which most Americans had no immunity, were too great not to take action. New flu strains, which generally appear about every 10 years, usually take a high toll. The last new strain, the Hong Kong flu, afflicted some 51-million Americans and killed at least 20,000 of them in 1968 and 1969.

Researchers began developing the new vaccine in April from swine flu viruses injected into fertilized hen eggs and cultivated for several days. After tests involving some 5,000 persons of all ages, production of the vaccine began in June. Almost immediately, the program suffered serious setbacks.

Parke Davis and Company, one of the four pharmaceutical companies manufacturing the vaccine, produced about 2 million doses using the wrong strain of virus. Then the insurance companies that traditionally provide liability coverage for vaccine manufacturers refused to cover this vaccine for fear of damage suits over adverse reactions. Under Administration pressure, Congress on August 10 passed legislation providing manufacturers of swine flu vaccine with a federal shield against damage suits.

Because of these delays, the vaccination drive did not begin until October 1, several months behind schedule. The first flu shots were given to the highest-risk groups – the aged and the chronically ill. Then the program ground to a halt in nine states on October 12 after the deaths of several elderly persons who had received flu shots. No connection between the shots and the deaths was proved, however, and the inoculations resumed.

Then, on December 16, federal officials again suspended the immunization program because of concern that the shots were possibly linked to a series of cases of paralysis. Of 94 reported cases of paralysis, 51, including four deaths, involved persons who had received swine flu shots between one and three weeks before the onset of the paralysis.

Federal epidemiologists reported that they could neither prove nor disprove the possible connection between the swine flu shots and the paralysis. But, to be on the safe side, the officials ordered that the program be discontinued. In all, only some 35 million adults, more than 100 million fewer than the government's goal, had been inoculated.

The swine flu program may forever trigger one question: Was it necessary? President Ford's advisers were convinced they could not wait for further developments before making a decision. There was only one confirmed outbreak of the new flu virus, but no one could foretell if it would become the next pandemic strain. To develop a vaccine that could combat the virus, work had to start immediately. So the advisers urged national immunization because it was better to gamble with money than with lives.

Dianne Rafalik

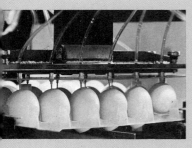

Swine flu vaccine incubates in eggs.

PUBLISHING. The first major revision of the 67-year-old United States Copyright Law was signed by President Gerald R. Ford on Oct. 20, 1976. As a result, the United States became eligible for membership in the Bern Union, the most important international copyright agreement. Under the new law, a copyright will expire 50 years after the death of the author, composer, or creator of the work. Formerly, copyrights expired after a maximum of 56 years from the time they were taken out.

The law established new rules for royalty-free photocopying of any copyrighted materials. In general, a school or library may make limited copies without liability, but wholesale reproduction to avoid paying a subscription price is prohibited. The measure provides that a book or magazine published outside the United States may be eligible for copyright protection starting in 1982.

Business Developments. Doubleday & Company, the largest U.S. hard-cover book publisher, acquired Dell Publishing Company, one of the top five paperback publishers, in April for a reported $35 million.

Simon & Schuster founded Hampshire Press as a wholly owned but independent hard-cover publishing subsidiary in October. James H. Silberman left his post as editor in chief of the adult division at Random House to head Hampshire Press.

Meanwhile, university presses were having a tough struggle with rising costs and reduced subsidies from their schools. To meet the economic crisis, many cut back their staffs, scaled down publishing activities, and joined together in programs. Several began investigating the possibility of publishing more commercially marketable books, such as cookbooks or even fiction.

Paperback Boom. Members of the American Book Sellers Association were cheered at their annual meeting in Chicago in June to learn of an upsurge in paperback book sales. Major booksellers reported that the dollar volume of paperback sales in many cases were equaling or exceeding that of hard-covers. They gave partial credit to television, citing several instances where a TV documentary has stimulated enough interest in a subject that viewers buy a book about it.

Simon & Schuster, hard-cover publisher of *The Final Days,* a book about President Richard M. Nixon's last days in office, sold the paperback rights to Avon Books in April for $1,550,000, a record for a nonfiction book. The paperback version was to be published on May 3, 1977, or one week after it was taken off *The New York Times* best-seller list, whichever came first. Another paperback sale saw the rights to the late Dame Agatha Christie's mystery novel *Sleeping Murder* go to Bantam Books for $1.1 million. Gerald B. Healey

See CANADIAN LITERATURE; LITERATURE; MAGAZINE; NEWSPAPER; POETRY; RECORDINGS.

PUERTO RICO. San Juan's Mayor Carlos Romero Barcelo scored a stunning upset in the gubernatorial election held on Nov. 2, 1976, defeating incumbent Governor Rafael Hernández Colón. Although Romero Barcelo won by only 2 per cent, his New Progressive Party swept to control of both houses of the legislature.

Romero Barcelo, an advocate of statehood for Puerto Rico, indicated that his first task would be to rebuild the sagging economy. About 20 per cent of the work force was unemployed, and half the island's population received food stamps. The island's gross national product had declined 2.4 per cent. Wages were generally low, averaging about $2.59 an hour for industrial workers.

Leaders of seven industrialized nations attended a conference hosted by President Gerald R. Ford at Dorado Beach in June. They agreed to adopt a mutual go-slow policy of economic growth they hoped would solve common problems.

On December 31, Ford said he would recommend statehood for Puerto Rico when the 95th Congress convened in January 1977. President-elect James Earl (Jimmy) Carter, Jr., said on Jan. 1, 1977, that Congress should do nothing "until the Puerto Rican people themselves expressed a preference for statehood." Paul C. Tullier

See also LATIN AMERICA (Facts in Brief Table).

PULITZER PRIZES. See AWARDS AND PRIZES.

QUEBEC. The dramatic provincial election on Nov. 15, 1976, startled most Canadians. A party committed to the separation and independence of Quebec decisively defeated the federal Liberal government of Premier J. Robert Bourassa. Bourassa lost his seat, while his party, which went into the election with 96 seats in a 110-member National Assembly, emerged with only 26.

The separatist Parti Québécois increased its standing from 6 seats to 71 and its share of the popular vote from 30 to 41 per cent. René Lévesque, its founding leader and the new premier of Quebec, played down separation in the campaign, emphasizing charges of corruption and ineptitude in the Bourassa government. He also skillfully exploited voter discontent with such Liberal policies as the official language law and a reduction in milk quotas for dairy farmers. Lévesque promised to hold a referendum before pressing for separation. His first tasks, he said, were to reform the provincial administration and grapple with financial problems. See LÉVESQUE, RENÉ.

The Liberals also lost support to a rejuvenated Union National Party under a new leader, Rodrigue Biron. The party increased its standing from one seat to 11. Two representatives of minor parties were elected. David M. L. Farr

See also CANADA and articles on the other provinces.

RADIO. There were more than twice as many radios as television sets throughout the world in 1976. The United Nations Educational, Scientific, and Cultural Organization reported in August a global total of 881 million radios and 365 million TV sets. There were about 24,270 radio stations. In the United States, which has more radios than any other country, radio advertising sales were expected to be 20 per cent higher than in 1975, making 1976 another record sales year.

The National Broadcasting Company (NBC) celebrated its 50th year as America's first full-fledged radio network. Starting on October 10, it featured five specials on NBC history. The network's inaugural broadcast was aired from New York City on Nov. 15, 1926, over 25 stations in 21 cities ranging as far west as Kansas City.

Programming. An outstanding example of quality radio drama was the National Public Radio network's prestigious series "Earplay." It launched its 1976-1977 season on October 10 with *Listening,* an 80-minute drama written especially for radio by playwright Edward Albee.

A *Broadcasting* magazine survey of the top 50 radio markets showed that the most popular station formats were, in order, contemporary music (best-selling records), beautiful music (soft, melodic, romantic music), middle-of-the-road music, and country music, followed by news and talk shows. The surprisingly strong showing of beautiful music formats reflected a growing trend for stations to switch from rock to a softer musical sound.

NBC announced in November that it would cease operating its all-news radio service by mid-1977. The News and Information Service had lost millions of dollars since it was founded in June 1975 to provide around-the-clock news to local stations.

Government Regulation. The Federal Communications Commission (FCC) declared in July that it was unconstitutional for government to regulate station program formats and said that entertainment decisions should be left to the discretion of the stations. The controversial declaration was in direct conflict with several court decisions. The Supreme Court of the United States was expected to ultimately decide the issue.

In May, the FCC announced a six-month freeze on applications for AM and FM station licenses, starting on June 30, so it could catch up on a backlog of 800 applications.

The American Broadcasting Company bought WMAL-AM and FM in Washington, D.C., from Washington Star Communications for $16 million, subject to FCC approval. The FCC had sought to force Washington Star Communications to give up the station on the ground that one company should not own broadcasting and newspaper properties in the same market. The company publishes the *Washington Star.*   June Bundy Csida

Veteran commentator Lowell Thomas tapes his final news program in New York City in May, ending a 46-year radio network career.

RAILROAD operations in the United States improved substantially in 1976, and major legislation offered federal financial aid to the industry. Consolidated Rail Corporation (Conrail), a federally sponsored successor to Penn Central Transportation Company and some smaller bankrupt Northeastern lines, started up in April.

As the economy strengthened, U.S. railroads registered profits of $253.1 million through September, a turnaround from a deficit of $128.5 million in the similar 1975 period, the Association of American Railroads (AAR) said. But the AAR blamed rising wages and other cost increases for a 32 per cent drop in third-quarter profits.

Operating revenues reached $13.8 billion in the first nine months, 15.7 per cent ahead of the same period in 1975. The Interstate Commerce Commission (ICC) allowed railroads to raise freight rates by up to 4 per cent on October 7, after permitting increases averaging 4.7 per cent earlier in the year. A December 22 decision allowed an additional 4 per cent hike, effective Jan. 7, 1977.

Conrail began operations on April 1 with $2.1-billion in federal money and a slimmed-down rail network. Shippers said early Conrail service improved, but some other railroads complained about government-subsidized competition. Government plans for substantial rail competition in the Northeast were dealt a blow on March 23 when labor negotiations collapsed, preventing the Chessie System, Incorporated, and the Southern Railway from taking over some of the lines involved in the restructuring. Conrail absorbed the lines instead.

The new railroad said it incurred a net loss of $66.4 million in its first six months, through September 30. Meanwhile, a major court battle began over how much former creditors of the Penn Central Railroad and other bankrupt railroads should be paid for selling their assets to Conrail.

Federal Aid. Congress enacted on January 28 the Railroad Revitalization and Regulatory Reform Act of 1976, which gave Conrail its final shape and funding. President Gerald R. Ford signed the bill on February 5, but implementation of the law was slow during the year. The law authorized major loans and other federal financing for railroads in general, sought to impel rail mergers, relaxed some ICC rate and other regulations, and offered $1.8-billion to improve the Boston-to-Washington, D.C., passenger-train corridor. The National Railroad Passenger Corporation (Amtrak) agreed on August 29 to purchase the corridor from Conrail.

Amtrak said its ridership rose 6.7 per cent through September. Improved track enabled Amtrak to speed up a number of runs on October 1 for the first time in years. The corporation's fiscal 1977 operating deficit was estimated at $483 million, up from $357 million in fiscal 1976.   Albert R. Karr

RAMALHO EANES, ANTONIO DOS SANTOS

(1935-   ), became Portugal's president on July 14, 1976. The stern army general won 61.5 per cent of the votes as a law-and-order candidate on June 27 in Portugal's first free presidential election in 50 years (see PORTUGAL). The rigid, austere Ramalho Eanes vowed to respect Portugal's new democratic institutions and defend democratic rights.

Ramalho Eanes was born on Jan. 25, 1935, in the village of Alcains in east-central Portugal. He attended nearby Castelo Branco Lyceum before beginning his military career. He attended a military academy, the Army Officers Training Center, and the Institute for Higher Military Studies, then served in most of Portugal's colonial wars. He was in Angola when Prime Minister Marcello Caetano's government was overthrown on April 25, 1974.

Following the coup, Ramalho Eanes returned to Portugal to direct the government television station, but was forced out by Communists for "incomprehensible neutrality." He helped to quell a leftist military rebellion on Nov. 25, 1975, and was named chief of staff of the army. His decisive leadership during the uprising earned him a reputation as the only man who could control the army and won the support of Portugal's three major parties.

Ramalho Eanes's wife, María Manuela Neto Portugal, has a law degree and works in the Ministry of Education.   Robert K. Johnson

REAGAN, RONALD (1911-   ), a staunch conservative and former governor of California, almost won the Republican presidential nomination in 1976. Reagan won many primary victories over incumbent President Gerald R. Ford, and when the Republican National Convention convened on August 16 in Kansas City, Mo., Reagan's candidacy had prevented Ford from lining up enough delegates to ensure a first-ballot nomination.

As part of his campaign strategy, Reagan charged that the Ford Administration was selling out United States power in the Western Hemisphere to the Russians. He also demanded continued U.S. sovereignty over the Panama Canal.

In a political surprise, Reagan named Pennsylvania Senator Richard S. Schweiker, a liberal, as his vice-presidential running mate on July 26. This move was designed partly to attract liberal Republicans. Instead, Reagan lost conservative support.

After a 44-minute ovation when his name was placed in nomination at the convention, Reagan lost to Ford by 117 votes on the first ballot – 1,070 to 1,187. But at Ford's invitation, he addressed the convention on August 19 and urged party unity.

On September 1, he said he was returning to radio broadcasting and would campaign for Ford. But in his campaign addresses, he seldom spoke of Ford by name.   Carol L. Thompson

See also FORD, GERALD R.; REPUBLICAN PARTY.

RECORDINGS. After 15 years of debate, the U.S. Congress cleared a new copyrights bill on Oct. 1, 1976, a major event for the recording industry, composers, lyricists, and music publishers. President Gerald R. Ford signed the bill on October 20. The new measure, first major revision in the law since 1909, extends the life of a copyright of any composition from 56 years after the copyright is obtained to 50 years after the composer's death. Other provisions raise the rates that songwriters, publishers, and artists receive from record companies for their compositions. Royalties on records increase from 2 cents to 2.75 cents per composition or half a cent per minute of playing time, whichever is higher. For the first time, jukebox owners will have to pay a licensing fee to copyright-collection societies.

The growing popularity of disco music resulted in a new record, a 12-inch (30.5-centimeter)-diameter single. Available at both 45 and 33⅓ revolutions per minute, the records play for about six minutes. Because grooves are spaced farther apart, the new, large singles have improved sound fidelity. Some of them were sold to the public for $3; others were distributed free of charge to disk jockeys in discothèques.

Pop, rock, and jazz records accounted for the vast majority of record sales in 1975. Figures released in 1976 showed 1975 album sales of $1.5-billion, and singles totaled $183 million. Prerecord-

Country singer C. W. McCall recorded "Convoy,"
a song about truckers who use citizens band
(CB) radios, and it became a big best seller.

ed tapes of all types accounted for another $692-million in sales.

Clive J. Davis, former president of CBS Records, pleaded guilty in a New York City federal court in September to one count of income tax evasion and was fined $10,000. After leaving CBS Records, Davis launched a new company, Arista Records, and this label played a major role in establishing such artists as Barry Manilow and the Bay City Rollers (see MUSIC, POPULAR).

United States recording companies celebrated the American Revolution Bicentennial by releasing a few timely albums and singles, but none became major hits. In a program commemorating the event, a chain of U.S. radio stations exchanged radio personalities with an Australian station.

Classical and Semiclassical. The vogue for ragtime composer Scott Joplin's music continued, principally through the original cast recording by Gunther Schuller and the Houston Grand Opera of Joplin's 1911 opera *Treemonisha*. Other notable albums were George Gershwin's 1935 opera *Porgy and Bess* by the Cleveland Orchestra and Chorus; a suite for flute and jazz piano performed by Jean-Pierre Rampal and Claude Bolling; Beverly Sills's album of Victor Herbert music; and Beethoven's *Symphony No. 5* by the Vienna Philharmonic Orchestra.   Leonard Feather

RED CROSS. See COMMUNITY ORGANIZATIONS.

RELIGION seemed increasingly to be an element that intensified conflict between nations and the peoples within them in 1976. The Arab-Israeli struggle, long preoccupied with issues of land and honor, even took on the dimensions of a holy war, though leaders on both sides tried to keep explicitly religious motives and issues from becoming central to the clashes. In early autumn, however, specific acts of vandalism at sacred sites were charged against the other party by both Arabs and Israelis. See JEWS AND JUDAISM.

The civil war in Lebanon made headlines throughout the year, and the names "Christian" and "Muslim" were always associated with the warring parties. People who shared these faiths beyond Lebanese borders seemed at a loss to know what, if anything, to do to help their fellow believers. The battles were increasingly described as hopeless, and religious peacemakers found little hearing during the months of nearly indiscriminate killing in Lebanon. See LEBANON.

Southern Africa also demanded world attention during the year. Issues of regime and revolution there involved religious forces. In South Africa, the ruling powers continued to try to justify their policies of *apartheid* (racial separation) and white supremacy on religious grounds, and the official church generally supported these efforts. But this approach was challenged in August when a racially mixed delegation of the Reformed Ecumenical Synod confronted Prime Minister Balthazar Johannes Vorster in Cape Town. The two sides made little progress toward understanding, but the delegation was promised future meetings with Vorster. The Lutheran World Federation, meanwhile, was more aggressive in accusing the Vorster government of promoting "institutional violence."

Civil war continued in Rhodesia, where a white minority government controlled all the political machinery. Religious groups on both sides were heard more frequently. The black leadership included the exiled Bishop Abel Muzorewa, an internationally recognized United Methodist Church spokesman, who talked in despairing terms of efforts at peaceful settlement. More extreme was Ndabaningi Sithole, a United Church of Christ minister, who gave support to guerrilla warfare to overthrow the white minority government.

In Ethiopia, National Democratic Revolution Program leaders tried to establish a socialist Peoples Democratic Republic of Ethiopia after the death of Emperor Haile Selassie I. They listed Christian missionaries as the chief subversive force against their regime and arrested the deposed head of the Ethiopian Orthodox Church, Patriarch Abuna Tewoflos, and several of his bishops in February.

In Malawi, Jehovah's Witnesses continued to be persecuted and jailed despite international protests. The sect was banned in Malawi in 1967.

U.S. Church Membership Reported for Bodies with 150,000 or More Members*

African Methodist Episcopal Church	1,166,301
African Methodist Episcopal Zion Church	1,024,974
American Baptist Association	1,071,000
American Baptist Churches in the U.S.A.	1,603,033
The American Lutheran Church	2,415,687
Armenian Church of America, Diocese of the (including Diocese of California)	372,000
Assemblies of God	1,239,197
Baptist Missionary Association of America	215,788
Christian Church (Disciples of Christ)	1,302,164
Christian Churches and Churches of Christ	1,049,816
Christian Methodist Episcopal Church	466,718
Christian Reformed Church	287,503
Church of God (Anderson, Ind.)	166,259
Church of God (Cleveland, Tenn.)	343,249
The Church of God in Christ	425,000
The Church of God in Christ, International	501,000
The Church of Jesus Christ of Latter-day Saints	2,336,715
Church of the Brethren	179,336
Church of the Nazarene	441,093
Churches of Christ	2,400,000
Conservative Baptist Association of America	300,000
The Episcopal Church	2,857,513
Free Will Baptists	227,434
General Association of Regular Baptist Churches	250,000
Greek Orthodox Archdiocese of North and South America	1,950,000
International General Assembly of Spiritualists	164,072
Jehovah's Witnesses	560,897
Jewish Congregations	6,115,000
Lutheran Church in America	2,986,078
The Lutheran Church-Missouri Synod	2,763,545
National Baptist Convention of America	2,668,799
National Baptist Convention, U.S.A., Inc.	5,500,000
National Primitive Baptist Convention, Inc.	250,000
Orthodox Church in America	1,000,000
Polish National Catholic Church of America	282,411
Presbyterian Church in the U.S.	878,126
Progressive National Baptist Convention, Inc.	521,692
Reformed Church in America	355,052
Reorganized Church of Jesus Christ of Latter Day Saints	157,762
The Roman Catholic Church	48,881,872
The Salvation Army	384,817
Seventh-day Adventists	495,699
Southern Baptist Convention	12,733,124
Unitarian-Universalist Association	184,552
United Church of Christ	1,818,762
The United Methodist Church	9,957,710
United Pentecostal Church, International	300,000
The United Presbyterian Church in the U.S.A.	2,657,699
Wisconsin Evangelical Lutheran Synod	395,440

*Majority of figures are for the years 1975 and 1976.

Source: National Council of Churches, *Yearbook of American and Canadian Churches* for 1977.

Religion in Russia remained a point of abrasion. Of greatest concern was the continuing Russian inhibition of Jews who wished to emigrate, especially to Israel. But Christians also complained that religious freedom in Russia was still restricted. Baptist leaders in particular urged the Soviet government to permit their members to worship in freedom and to propagate their faith without persecution.

In the United States, Sun Myung Moon of the Unification Church ended his four-year ministry to America with a mass rally in Washington, D.C., on September 19. Moon's highly publicized and criticized movement faced, among other problems, an impending congressional investigation of its finances and its evangelizing methods. Some critics charged that the sect was linked to the South Korean government and was a massive religious lobbying effort on behalf of that government's policies.

The Nation of Islam, better known as the Black Muslims, changed its name in October to the World Community of Islam in the West in part to fight its image as a black separatist group. "We are not Black Muslims and never have been," their chief minister, Wallace D. Muhammad, explained. "We're not black separatists. We're a world community — a community that encompasses everybody." Martin E. Marty

See also EASTERN ORTHODOX CHURCHES; PROTESTANTISM; ROMAN CATHOLIC CHURCH.

REPUBLICAN PARTY. After eight years of ruling the executive branch of the federal government, the Republicans in November 1976 lost control of the White House to Democratic challenger James Earl (Jimmy) Carter, Jr. Gerald R. Ford, the nation's only nonelected President, became the first incumbent to be defeated since 1932.

After trailing by about 30 per cent in polls taken in July, Ford made a remarkable comeback in the final weeks of the campaign. Ford received 48.02 per cent of the popular vote to Carter's 50.08 per cent. Less than 2 per cent went to Eugene J. McCarthy and other candidates. In the Electoral College, Ford lost by a vote of 297 to 240. Although Ford carried the state of Washington, one elector gave his vote to Republican Ronald Reagan. To win, a candidate needs 270 electoral votes.

Ford did best in the Western, Rocky Mountain, and Great Plains states, where Republicans are traditionally strong. But he also carried Connecticut, Illinois, New Jersey, Virginia, and Michigan.

Election Setbacks. The Republicans failed to increase their low numbers in Congress despite the close presidential race. Only 143 Republicans were elected to the House of Representatives in November, while the Democrats won 292 seats. In the Senate, the Republicans gained only one seat. The count for the new Senate stood at 61 Democrats to 38 Republicans and 1 Independent.

President Ford, running mate Robert Dole, and their wives raise their
arms in jubilation at the Republican National Convention in Kansas City.

Republicans also suffered a setback in gubernatorial elections. The number of Republican governors dropped from 13 to 12. See ELECTIONS; STATE GOVERNMENT.

Ford's Campaign appealed to voters to keep him in office on the basis of his record. He argued that he had done a good job considering the enormous problems of recession and inflation and the lack of trust in government he inherited when he replaced Richard M. Nixon in 1974.

As the underdog in the race, Ford challenged Carter to a series of three televised debates, each viewed by an estimated 85 million Americans. In the second debate, on foreign policy and defense, Ford blundered by saying that Eastern Europe was not under the domination of Russia. Observers regarded this as a costly mistake that halted his momentum when he was just short of pulling even with Carter.

The Primary Fight. Before facing Carter, Ford had a tough primary challenge from Reagan, a former California governor and a champion of conservative Republicans. The President won early primary election tests in New Hampshire, Florida, and Illinois. However, Reagan gained a victory in North Carolina on March 23 that turned the tide. Reagan then swept the Texas, Indiana, Georgia, Alabama, Nebraska, Arkansas, Idaho, and Nevada primaries.

Fighting back, Ford won in Kentucky, Tennessee, Oregon, Michigan, Maryland, Ohio, and New Jersey, while Reagan gathered up 167 delegates in the winner-take-all primary in California, his home state.

Because of his contest with Reagan, Ford took several actions to appease conservatives. For example, to blunt criticism that he had made too many concessions to Russia, Ford banned the word *détente* from his Administration's vocabulary. In January, he vetoed a bill that would have expanded the picketing rights of construction unions, even though he had earlier promised to sign it.

Battle for the Uncommitted. When the Republican Party completed its delegate-selection process on July 17, *The New York Times* estimated that Ford had 1,102 delegates and Reagan 1,063, with 94 not committed to either candidate. Ford took the extraordinary step of arriving in Kansas City, Mo., before the Republican National Convention convened so that he could court votes from uncommitted delegates and shore up his support.

Reagan announced before the convention that he would select liberal Senator Richard S. Schweiker of Pennsylvania as his vice-presidential running mate if he won the nomination. The move was regarded as an effort to win over some uncommitted delegates from Pennsylvania and other states in the Northeast. But it startled many of Reagan's hard-

Conservative hopeful Ronald Reagan, left,
and running mate Richard S. Schweiker confer
before the Republican National Convention.

line conservative followers, and some observers believe that Reagan lost as many delegates as he gained by the surprise maneuver.

The President's six-month campaign against Reagan for the Republican nomination ended in success. On August 19, he won a first-ballot victory, polling 1,187 votes to 1,070 for Reagan. One delegate voted for Secretary of Commerce Elliot L. Richardson, and one abstained. Since 1,130 votes were required to win the nomination, the President had a paper-thin margin of 57 votes.

Ford then selected Senator Robert J. Dole of Kansas as his running mate. This disappointed moderates, who predicted that Dole would not help – and might even hinder – the ticket.

Conservatives' Convention. Sharp clashes within the rules and platform committees at the convention dramatized the Ford-Reagan division within the party. Raucous floor demonstrations and frequent booing provided further evidence.

Such ultraconservatives as Senator Jesse A. Helms of North Carolina, a leading Reagan backer, influenced the Republican platform, giving it a strong conservative flavor. The party platform supported constitutional amendments to ban abortion and school busing. It approved allowing nonsectarian prayers in public schools and opposed national health insurance and federal registration of firearms. The platform also called for an end to federal

deficit spending and endorsed tax cuts for the oil industry, business, investors, and parents of college students.

Reagan forces prevailed on a foreign-policy platform plank that was widely viewed as criticism of President Ford and Secretary of State Henry A. Kissinger. It criticized the 1975 Helsinki agreement with Russia that recognized Soviet influence in Eastern Europe, and it praised the controversial Russian novelist Alexander I. Solzhenitsyn, whom Ford did not invite to the White House during Solzhenitsyn's 1975 visit to Washington, D.C. Nevertheless, Ford's supporters decided not to contest adoption of the plank.

In one of their few platform victories, Ford's backers narrowly prevailed over Reaganites to reaffirm Republican support for ratification of the Equal Rights Amendment that would establish legal equality for women.

Test Vote. The Ford forces chose to fight it out with the Reaganites on the convention floor over one issue, however. Reagan backers proposed that Ford be required to name his running mate – as Reagan had done – before the balloting on the presidential nomination. This was viewed by both sides as a test of Reagan's delegate strength.

The vote on the running-mate proposal turned out to be almost identical to the later vote on the nomination; 1,180 delegates voted against, and 1,069 for, the Reagan plan; 10 abstained. This was an unmistakable sign of Ford's narrow but firm control of the convention.

Plea for Harmony. After winning the nomination, Ford made an unusual gesture. He invited his defeated opponent to appear on the podium and address the convention delegates. Reagan accepted and asked for harmony within the Republican Party so that Ford could win election.

After the convention, Reagan campaigned for Ford. He sent several of his top staff assistants to work for the Ford campaign. Despite rumblings of discontent, few conservatives defected from Ford in November. Nevertheless, the Republicans could not hold on to the White House.

Former President Nixon's name was never mentioned during the convention proceedings, nor in any of the resolutions adopted by the delegates. However, his picture and a brief article about him appeared in the official convention program.

After the election, Republican National Chairwoman Mary Louise Smith announced that she would resign early in 1977. And in December, President Ford met with Reagan, Vice-President Nelson A. Rockefeller, and former Treasury Secretary John B. Connally, Jr., to discuss the future of the party.   William J. Eaton

See also DOLE, ROBERT J.; FORD, GERALD R.; NIXON, RICHARD M.; PRESIDENT OF THE UNITED STATES; REAGAN, RONALD.

RETAILING. Consumer spending in the United States set a brisk pace in the first quarter of 1976 and then softened to a flat third quarter. A colder than usual October in much of the United States quickened the retail-sales tempo, which abated again in November. Retailers enjoyed modest gains over the strong 1975 Christmas season, ending 1976 with an overall gain of from 8 to 10 per cent in nonfood operations. Considerable consumer purchasing power was siphoned into automobile sales, which topped 1975 sales by more than 20 per cent.

However, profits did not keep pace with sales increases because of persistent inflationary pressures on operating costs. More U.S. stores than ever opened on Sundays and on holidays.

Shopping Centers. About 75 per cent of the volume of retail firms with annual sales of more than $1 million is now produced by branch stores, most of them in shopping centers, according to the National Retail Merchants Association. A 1976 census made by *Chain Store Age,* a trade magazine, indicates that 57 per cent of all general merchandise sales are made in shopping-center stores. Annual shopping-center sales in 1976 rose to more than $200 million, against $153 million in 1974.

New store openings slowed in 1976. Retailers found that productivity per square foot or meter of sales area continued to decline after adjustments for inflated prices. Catalog showrooms eased their expansion. Because of the 1975 bankruptcy of the giant W. T. Grant Company chain, however, many store locations became available for quick occupancy. The most desirable were rapidly leased by chains and department stores. Because of its aggressive store-opening program, the S. S. Kresge Company (K-Mart) edged the J. C. Penney Company as the retailer with sales second only to Sears Roebuck and Company.

Pilferage Continued to plague stores. Shortages were about 2 per cent in department stores and almost 2.5 per cent in specialty stores, despite added security precautions.

Stores along the U.S.-Mexico border suffered substantial sales losses after the sharp August drop in value of the Mexican peso.

A major concern was the strike of United Parcel Service employees that lasted from mid-September to December 9. United Parcel handles about 55 per cent of all parcels in the United States, and the added load on the U.S. Postal Service caused delays in mail deliveries. Smaller retailers, heavily dependent on fast handling of small shipments, were particularly victimized by the strike.

In merchandising, retailers felt no strong fashion direction to stimulate sales of women's apparel. Video games had strong demand, as did shower-massagers and citizens band radios. See COMMUNICATIONS (Close-Up). Joseph R. Rowen

RHODE ISLAND. See STATE GOVERNMENT.

RHODESIA. Blacks and whites edged closer in 1976 to a negotiated settlement of their long conflict over who should rule Rhodesia. Although the black population of about 6.4 million greatly outnumbered the 270,000 whites, a white-minority government declared Rhodesia independent of Great Britain in November 1965. In 1966, the United Nations (UN) imposed economic sanctions against Rhodesia. This attempt to force the white-minority government, under Prime Minister Ian D. Smith, to accept a transition to black-majority rule was not successful. So Rhodesian black nationalists began a guerrilla war in December 1972.

A Breakthrough appeared to occur on Sept. 24, 1976, when Smith's government agreed to a United States-British plan for black rule within two years. During the transition, Rhodesia would be ruled by a biracial interim government.

Smith's government was under strong pressure from several fronts. An increased number of guerrillas were infiltrating from Mozambique. As of late October, an estimated 3,000 insurgents were operating within Rhodesia. Mozambique, which until 1975 had been under Portuguese colonial rule, joined in the UN economic sanctions on March 3 and closed its border with Rhodesia. As a result, much of Rhodesia's export-import trade had to be diverted to longer, more expensive shipping routes.

The white Rhodesians probably could not fight a sustained civil war without substantial help from South Africa. But South Africa seemed unwilling to provide such support. South African Prime Minister Balthazar Johannes Vorster reportedly told Smith in a meeting on September 19 that he should not expect continued military aid. U.S. Secretary of State Henry A. Kissinger, at the same meeting, then presented the U.S.-British plan.

Britain called Rhodesian black and white leaders to a conference in Geneva, Switzerland, on October 28. Four main leaders represented black nationalists: Bishop Abel Muzorewa, head of the African National Council; Ndabaningi Sithole, president of the Zimbabwe African National Union; Joshua Nkomo, president of the rival Zimbabwe African People's Union; and Robert Mugape of the Zimbabwe People's Army, the main guerrilla force.

Nkomo and Mugape demanded black rule within a year. Smith insisted on two years. The conference deadlocked until November 29, when participants agreed to shelve the independence-date issue and discuss the interim government.

Another deadlock ensued. Smith insisted on the U.S.-British plan for an equal black-white interim government. He also wanted the police and military left under white control during the transition. The black nationalists termed this unacceptable. Nkomo and Mugape demanded a predominantly black interim government. John D. Esseks

See also AFRICA (Facts in Brief Table).

RICHARDSON, ELLIOT LEE (1920-   ), was sworn in as U.S. secretary of commerce on Feb. 2, 1976, replacing Rogers C. B. Morton. It was Richardson's fourth Cabinet post in the Administrations of Presidents Richard M. Nixon and Gerald R. Ford. See CABINET, UNITED STATES.

Richardson had earlier served as secretary of health, education, and welfare (HEW); secretary of defense; and U.S. attorney general. He became a national celebrity in October 1973 when he resigned as attorney general rather than obey Nixon's order to fire the Watergate special prosecutor, Archibald Cox.

Richardson was born in Boston on July 20, 1920. He served in the Army during World War II, then earned his law degree from Harvard University in 1947. He worked as a law clerk for a U.S. appeals court judge in 1947 and 1948 and for Supreme Court Justice Felix Frankfurter in 1948 and 1949, then entered private law practice.

President Dwight D. Eisenhower named Richardson assistant secretary of HEW in 1957, and he was elected attorney general of Massachusetts in 1966. He entered the Nixon Administration as an undersecretary of state in 1969.

Richardson married Anne Francis Hazard in 1952. They have three children.   Darlene R. Stille

ROADS AND HIGHWAYS. See TRANSPORTATION.

ROCKEFELLER, NELSON ALDRICH (1908-   ), Vice-President of the United States, played a minor part in domestic politics during 1976. He had withdrawn in November 1975 from consideration for the 1976 Republican vice-presidential nomination. Nevertheless, he traveled extensively in his official capacity, representing the United States.

Bicentennial Activities. In March and April, the Vice-President and his wife Margarette (Happy) Rockefeller toured six nations — Australia, New Zealand, Malaysia, Iran, Tunisia, and France — in honor of the American Revolution Bicentennial celebration. In Australia, Rockefeller was the target of an anti-American demonstration. Rockefeller returned to the United States on April 4.

On July 2, the Vice-President appeared with President Gerald R. Ford at the National Archives in Washington, D.C., for a Bicentennial celebration opening the archives to the public for 72 hours to display the Declaration of Independence. Two days later, Rockefeller viewed "Operation Sail" in New York Harbor. The spectacle featured a flotilla of tall-masted sailing vessels that gathered in New York Harbor for the Bicentennial celebration. The Vice-President was the official reviewer, stationed on the cruiser U.S.S. *Wainwright*.

Waning Political Life. In the course of the election campaign, Vice-President Rockefeller supported Ford's candidacy against the challenge from the Republican far right spearheaded by former California Governor Ronald Reagan. Reagan's many primary victories prevented Ford from arriving at the Republican National Convention with a first-ballot victory ensured. See REAGAN, RONALD; REPUBLICAN PARTY.

As a top party official, Rockefeller naturally shared the spotlight at the Republican National Convention in Kansas City, Mo., in August. He testified on August 9 to the Republican platform subcommittee on foreign policy, substituting for Secretary of State Henry A. Kissinger. On August 16, he addressed the convention's opening session, praising the Ford Administration and attacking the "pussyfooting prose" of Democratic presidential candidate James Earl (Jimmy) Carter, Jr. On August 19, Rockefeller placed the name of Kansas Senator Robert J. Dole in nomination for the vice-presidency, and the convention approved the choice. See DOLE, ROBERT J.

At a closed meeting of Georgia Republicans on April 15, the Vice-President suggested that two aides on the staff of Senator Henry M. Jackson (D., Wash.) had Communist connections. After his remarks were published by the *Atlanta Journal* on April 21, Rockefeller formally apologized in the Senate for engaging "in unsubstantiated speculation."   Carol L. Thompson

See also FORD, GERALD RUDOLPH.

ROMAN CATHOLIC CHURCH. No major crises or reverses were experienced by the Roman Catholic Church in 1976. However, several Catholic leaders in Latin America were victims of the terror tactics used by authoritarian governments to counter alleged "leftist" leanings of Catholics who promoted basic human rights. A continuing governmental campaign of repression in Argentina led to the murders of eight clergymen noted for their work with the poor. Pope Paul VI called attention to these atrocities on September 27 and said that the church in Argentina wanted only to serve the people in a climate of "serenity and safety for all."

After Orlando Letelier, an exile and former Chilean ambassador to the United States, was assassinated by a bomb blast in Washington, D.C., on September 21, protesters marched to Saint Matthew's Cathedral in Washington on September 26, condemning the Chilean military junta. Bishop James Rausch, general secretary of the National Conference of Catholic Bishops, eulogized Letelier at the cathedral for his commitment to human rights. See CHILE.

Carmelite Bishop Daniel Lamont of Umtali, Rhodesia, was sentenced to 10 years at hard labor on September 22 for failing to report the presence of alleged terrorists at Catholic missions and for advising missionaries not to inform on these blacks. Bishop Lamont said that he had informed the

A special Mass for the handicapped is celebrated during Roman Catholic International Eucharistic Congress, held in Philadelphia in August 1976.

blacks of their human rights and had provided them with medical supplies at mission stations.

In the United States, Archbishop Joseph L. Bernardin, president of the National Conference of Catholic Bishops, sounded an optimistic note in a magazine interview in May. He said that the trials of the church in the United States during the previous 10 years had a purifying effect on the beliefs and practices of American Catholics.

Abortion continued as an important subject for Americans. The Administrative Board of the U.S. Catholic Conference issued a policy statement on February 15 supporting a constitutional amendment to ban abortion, but denying that the church was seeking to form a voting bloc or was endorsing a particular political candidate.

The Executive Committee of the U.S. Catholic Conference conferred with presidential candidates James Earl (Jimmy) Carter, Jr., (on August 31) and Gerald R. Ford (on September 10). The statements they issued after these meetings led some members of the public to conclude that the bishops had endorsed President Ford. But Archbishop Bernardin denied that the bishops had endorsed the President.

The discussion of the right-to-life issue involved in the abortion controversy had a parallel in the continuing debate over "the right to a peaceful death." The New Jersey Supreme Court ruled on March 31 that life-support systems used to keep Karen Quinlan alive could be terminated by a joint decision of her father and physicians, in consultation with an ethics committee or similar body of the institution in which the comatose girl had been hospitalized. The girl's Catholic parents, as well as her parish priest, favored a "peaceful death" for Karen. The life-support systems were terminated on May 22, but she was still living at year's end.

On June 21, the Supreme Court of the United States upheld a Maryland law that provides for state aid to private colleges, including church-related institutions. But the court also held that the aid must have a "secular" purpose, that the primary effect must not be to advance religion, and that there must not be any excessive entanglement of the state in church affairs.

The Vatican's Congregation for the Doctrine of the Faith issued a declaration on sexual ethics that was released in the United States on January 15. It rejected sexual union before marriage, homosexual acts, and masturbation. Some American Catholic theologians viewed the declaration as out of line with contemporary understanding of behavior.

Ordaining Women. Support for the ordination of women to the priesthood continued to increase in 1976. The General Convention of the Episcopal Church in the United States voted in September to approve the ordination of women, a decision that encouraged Catholic advocates of such a move. But some Catholic ecumenists believed that the Episcopal Church decision might impair its relations with the Roman Catholic and Orthodox churches, which are officially opposed to such ordinations. See PROTESTANTISM.

Call to Action Conference. More than 1,300 delegates, representing the most diversified deliberative group in U.S. Catholic history, met in Detroit in October. They met to formulate a "call to action" in eight areas of concern — church, family, neighborhood, work, race and ethnicity, personhood, nationhood, and humankind. In preliminary work, the preparatory committees analyzed 800,000 responses to a nationwide questionnaire. The most divisive issues at these early meetings were the Catholic teaching on birth control, especially in relation to rights of conscience, and the question of the ordination of women. Conference recommendations, which included proposals for changes in church views toward divorced and remarried Catholics, are to be reviewed by the American bishops in 1977, with final decisions to be made by the Holy See in Rome.

The conference was the result of an unparalleled effort by the nation's bishops to create dialogue on the concerns of church members. According to several leaders and delegates, the assembly exceeded most expectations, raising justice priorities and providing an extraordinary model for conducting national consultation. There was speculation during and after the conference that such an assembly might become a regular feature of church life. Such a move would represent a fundamental change in the way the church conducts its national affairs.

Eucharistic Congress. The 41st International Eucharistic Congress began on August 1 in Philadelphia and closed on August 8 with 100,000 persons, including President Ford, crowding into Kennedy Stadium. Among the noted speakers dealing with the congress theme, "The Hungers of the Human Family," were social activist Dorothy Day; Bishop Fulton J. Sheen; Mother Teresa of Calcutta, India; and Archbishop Helder Cámara of Brazil. One of the participants was William W. Cardinal Baum of Washington, D.C., who had received the cardinal's hat from Pope Paul VI on May 24 in Saint Peter's Church in Rome.

The purpose of Eucharistic congresses, since the first was convened in 1881 in Lille, France, is to emphasize the central place of Christ's love as portrayed in the sacrifice on the cross and celebrated in the liturgy of the Mass. The only other Eucharistic Congress in America was held in 1926 in Chicago.

Bishop Marcel Lefebvre, retired archbishop of Dakar, Senegal, stirred up a hornet's nest by demanding the right to offer Mass in Latin in the Tridentine rite, contrary to the present liturgical laws. Bishop Lefebvre was suspended by Pope Paul on July 24, after illegally ordaining 13 priests in Switzerland.

John Ogilvie, a Scottish Jesuit who was hanged in 1615 for refusing to recognize King James's religious superiority over the pope, was canonized in Saint Peter's on October 17 by Pope Paul.

Ecumenical Affairs. Catholic-Jewish relations attained an unprecedented degree of amity in the United States, due at least in part to the felicitous greetings to the Jewish people expressed by the American Bishops in their 1975 statement on Catholic-Jewish relations. See JEWS AND JUDAISM.

Muslim and Catholic scholars met in Tripoli, Libya, in February, but the results were disappointing. Grave misunderstandings arose, partially because of language difficulties, and the Vatican finally rejected parts of the joint report, especially that condemning Zionism as racism.

Catholic Membership. The Official Catholic Directory reported that there were 80,035 converts to Catholicism in 1976, compared with 75,123 in 1975. The total Catholic population in the United States increased about 180,000 to 48,881,872. The number of priests dropped by 62 to 58,847. There were 130,995 nuns in 1976, compared with 135,225 in 1975. High school enrollment in Catholic schools was 895,825 in 1976, down about 15,000, and elementary school enrollment was down some 22,000 to 2,576,856.   John B. Sheerin

ROMANIA improved its relations with Russia and other Warsaw Pact nations in 1976 while trying to forge stronger links with the West and developing nations. President Nicolae Ceausescu paid a state visit to Russia in August and met with Communist Party General Secretary Leonid I. Brezhnev. Ceausescu emphasized that Romania had no claims on its former province of Bessarabia, now the Moldavian Soviet Socialist Republic. He also attended the East Berlin conference of 29 European Communist parties in June.

Romania signed a number of economic pacts with Russia in September. Russia agreed to give Romania technical and financial aid in steel, petrochemical, and other heavy industries. Brezhnev visited Romania for talks with Ceausescu in November. Later, the Warsaw Pact Consultative Committee met in Bucharest for the first time in 10 years.

Western Ties. In November, Romania signed a 10-year trade agreement with the United States and a textile agreement with the European Community (Common Market), the first member of East Europe's Council for Mutual Economic Assistance to do so. Romania gained membership in the Group of 77 of the United Nations Conference on Trade and Development in Manila, the Philippines, in February. But its bid to become a full member of the nonaligned nations movement at the fifth conference in Colombo, Sri Lanka, failed in

August. Romania instead became a permanent observer-member.

Romania played an active part in the first conference on Balkan economic cooperation, held in Athens, Greece, from January 29 to February 5. Ceausescu visited Kuwait in March and Turkey in May. He also met with Bulgaria's State Council Chairman Todor Zhivkov in June following the signing of various trade agreements.

Relations with West Germany deteriorated slightly after a disagreement over the emigration of German-speaking Romanian citizens. Reunification of families and permission for mixed marriages were at issue in relations with France and Sweden.

Ceausescu shuffled the Council of Ministers on June 15. The most interesting change was the appointment of General Ion Ionita, minister of defense since 1966, as deputy prime minister. General Ion Coman took over as defense minister.

Agriculture remained Romania's top domestic priority. Farm output fell between 25 and 50 per cent below plans for 1975, and the 1976 harvest was not good.   Chris Cviic

See also EUROPE (Facts in Brief Table).

ROTARY INTERNATIONAL. See COMMUNITY ORGANIZATIONS.

ROWING. See SPORTS.

RUBBER. See MANUFACTURING.

RUSSIA. Political relations with the West marked time in 1976 against the background of growing Western skepticism about détente. But financial indebtedness to the West increased as trade rose. Russia had problems not only with the Communist parties of Western Europe, but also with the countries of Eastern Europe.

The 25th Communist Party Congress met in Moscow from February 24 to March 5 and reaffirmed the foreign and domestic policies of General Secretary Leonid I. Brezhnev. The congress reelected Brezhnev for another five-year term despite reports of his ill health.

The congress dismissed only one member of the Politburo, the party's top body. He was Dmitri S. Polyansky, who was replaced by Valentin K. Mesyats as minister of agriculture on March 16. Polyansky retained his seat on the Central Committee and later became ambassador to Japan. The Politburo gained two new members—Grigory V. Romanov, party secretary from Leningrad, and Dmitri F. Ustinov, who on April 29 succeeded Marshal Andrei A. Grechko as minister of defense. Grechko died on April 26.

The most senior military post within Russia's military alliance—chief of staff of the Warsaw Pact—became vacant on April 23 when General Sergei Shtemenko died. The post was filled in Octo-

General Secretary Leonid I. Brezhnev delivers the keynote address to the 25th Communist Party Congress, held in Moscow, February 24 to March 5.

ber by General Anatoly Gribkov. Council of Ministers Chairman Aleksey Nikolayevich Kosygin reportedly suffered a heart attack while swimming in August, but Russian officials did not confirm the story. Kosygin appeared in public in October, but rumors of his poor health and impending dismissal continued. Nikolai A. Tikhonov became first deputy prime minister on September 2, reportedly to look after the defense industries that had been Ustinov's responsibility before his promotion.

Communist Rift. Leaders of the Spanish and French Communist parties did not attend the February party congress, during which a rift developed between the pro-Russian "loyalist" delegations and the "Eurocommunists" — delegates from West Europe who insisted on each party's right to hold domestic political interests above the Kremlin's.

A two-day conference of 29 European Communist parties began on June 29 in East Berlin. Only Iceland and Albania did not send representatives. Russia had been trying to organize the conference for two years as a prelude to a world Communist conference that would excommunicate China. However, it ended without mentioning China or adopting any "common tasks" or ideological platforms. On the contrary, the conference affirmed each party's right to pursue its own independent "road to socialism."

Attempts to better relations with Romania and Yugoslavia met with some success. Brezhnev visited Romania from November 22 to 24 (see ROMANIA). He met President Josip Broz Tito of Yugoslavia in East Berlin on May 28 and paid a three-day visit to Belgrade in November (see YUGOSLAVIA).

Chinese-Russian Tensions. Efforts to improve relations with China after Chairman Mao Tsetung's death in September met with rebuffs. China's European ally, Albania, openly rejected Russia's overtures at the Albanian party congress in November. However, Russia and China resumed talks about their disputed border in December.

Foreign Minister and Politburo member Andrei A. Gromyko visited Japan in January, but he failed to break the deadlock over a peace treaty. Russia refused to hand over four small islands north of the Japanese island of Hokkaido that it has occupied since 1945. Relations with Japan suffered a further setback when a Russian pilot landed his MIG-25 jet fighter at an air base in Hakodate, Hokkaido Island, on September 6 and asked for political asylum in the United States. The Japanese angered the Russians by refusing to extradite the pilot and by delaying return of the plane until Japanese and American specialists could examine it. The disassembled jet was returned to Russia in November. See ARMED FORCES.

Russia claimed a 200-nautical-mile fishing zone in December, following similar action by Canada, the United States, and other countries. The move

Dissident historian Andrei Amalrik clutches his cat in Amsterdam, the Netherlands, in July after emigrating from Russia with his wife, Gyusel.

further hampered the already difficult peace-treaty negotiations with Japan.

Strained U.S. Relations. Russia's relations with the United States continued to be strained in the wake of the successful Russian backing of Cuba's intervention in Angola in late 1975 and early 1976 (see ANGOLA). U.S. Secretary of State Henry A. Kissinger visited Moscow in January in an unsuccessful effort to break the deadlock in the second phase of Strategic Arms Limitation Talks.

On May 28, President Gerald R. Ford in Washington, D.C., and Brezhnev in Moscow signed a treaty to limit underground nuclear explosions for peaceful purposes. The pact provided for U.S. on-site inspection of Russian tests. Further U.S.-Russian negotiations were postponed until after James Earl (Jimmy) Carter, Jr., took office as President in January 1977.

African Policy. Russia tried to block Kissinger's efforts to bring about a peaceful settlement in southern Africa. A Marxist movement delegation from Namibia (South West Africa), led by Sam Nujoma, visited Russia in August and received promises of support for its armed struggle against South Africa. Angola's President Agostinho Neto visited Russia in May and again in October. On October 8, he signed a friendship treaty with Russia.

Relations with Egypt reached a new low on March 14 when President Anwar al-Sadat canceled the 1971 treaty of friendship with Russia and expelled Soviet warships. Talks between Foreign Minister Gromyko and the Egyptian foreign minister in November failed to improve relations.

Dissent and Emigration. Russia continued to crack down on all forms of dissent but showed some regard for world opinion. The government announced plans to relax travel restrictions on Western correspondents in Russia after March 31. Plans were also made to increase by 18 the number of Western newspapers sold in Russia as a token of a Soviet desire to fulfill provisions of the 1975 Helsinki Conference on European Security and Cooperation. But in November 1976, Russia and other Soviet-bloc states refused visas to a special commission of the United States Congress set up to check fulfillment of the Helsinki agreements.

Harassment of political dissidents in Russia increased. Andrei D. Sakharov, a physicist and human rights activist, and his wife, Yelena, scuffled with police and were detained briefly at the slander trial of Tartar dissident Mustafa Dzhemilev in the provincial town of Omsk in Siberia in April. Mathematician Leonid Plyushch was released from a psychiatric prison hospital after more than two years detention in January and allowed to travel to France. Historian Andrei Amalrik was allowed to emigrate to the Netherlands in July. Jewish emigration from Russia continued on the same scale as in 1975. Emigration procedures, however, were slightly relaxed in January.

The Economy. The Supreme Soviet of the U.S.S.R. (parliament) approved a new five-year plan on October 29. Its main weight was to be put into agriculture and modernizing existing industries. National income was to rise 26 per cent, industrial output 36 per cent, real per capita income 23 per cent, and overall agricultural output 16 per cent. Industrial output in the first nine months of 1976 rose 4.8 per cent, compared with the first nine months of 1975. But only five of the 19 ministries concerned with consumer goods reached their targets in the five-year plan completed in 1975.

Brezhnev reported to the Central Committee on October 25 that the 1976 grain harvest would meet or exceed the 1973 record of 245.3 million short tons (222.5 million metric tons). Nevertheless, Russia was not expected to be self-sufficient in food for at least five years, and the government continued to buy Western grain. Russia's trade with the West jumped from $10.1 billion in the first half of 1975 to $13.3 billion in the first half of 1976 — 31 per cent of all Soviet foreign trade. The trade deficit with capitalist countries was about $3 billion in the first half of 1976 and was expected to reach $5 billion by the end of the year.   Chris Cviic

See also Europe (Facts in Brief Table); Norway; Space Exploration.

RWANDA. See Africa.

SAFETY. The House of Commons in Great Britain approved a controversial measure on March 1, 1976, making it compulsory to wear automobile safety belts. The measure made drivers and front-seat passengers liable to a maximum fine of $100 for not wearing safety belts. The bill passed by a vote of 249 to 139, despite the complaints of critics who argued that the bill eroded individual liberty and who questioned the government's right to impose legal penalties on an individual's decision to endanger his own life.

In the United States, Secretary of Transportation William T. Coleman, Jr., put off a final decision on December 6 on whether to require automobile makers to install the controversial safety airbag in all new automobiles. Instead, he urged the nation's automakers to take part in a limited program to demonstrate the effectiveness of airbags. Coleman said he hoped to work out a plan whereby "at least two companies" would agree to make and sell a combined total of 500,000 1977 and 1978 model cars equipped with airbags.

Accidental Deaths and Death Rates

	1975		1976†	
	Number	**Rate††**	**Number**	**Rate†**
Motor Vehicle	47,000	22.1	46,320	21.6
Work	12,600	5.9	12,200	5.7
Home	25,500	12.0	24,500	11.4
Public	22,500	10.6	21,500	10.6
Total*	102,500	48.3	101,000	47.2

†For 12-month period up to Aug. 30, 1976.

††Deaths per 100,000 population.

*The total does not equal the sum of the four classes because *Motor Vehicle* includes some deaths also included in *Work* and *Home.*

Source: National Safety Council estimates.

Traffic Accidents. Public opposition to the mandatory 55-mile (89-kilometer)-per-hour speed limit continued on a wide front in the United States in 1976. One organization of police chiefs cited the limit as unpopular and a "burden on law officers." Safety officials continued to support the law, however. They said a steady reduction in traffic fatalities had been maintained since the 55-mile-per-hour speed limit was imposed in 1974 in response to the Arab oil embargo.

Safety officials reported that about 27,000 lives had been saved over the three-year period. They credited the lower speeds and the changes lower speeds brought in the driving habits of U.S. motorists for the lower traffic toll.

However, traffic accidents increased slightly in the first eight months of 1976, with 30,420 persons killed compared with 30,000 during the same period in 1975, according to the National Safety Council (NSC). The reason for this increase, the NSC said, was that people were traveling more in 1976. NSC officials said deaths increased at almost the same rate as mileage on the highway.

Accidental Deaths. Accidents continued to be the fourth leading cause of death in the United States and were the leading cause among all persons from 1 to 38 years of age. Accidents claimed more lives among young people from 15 to 24 than all other causes combined, about four times more than the next leading cause, homicide.

According to the NSC, accidental deaths in the United States were exceeded only by heart disease, cancer, and stroke. Of all the accident fatalities recorded annually, 45 per cent result from motor-vehicle accidents; 15 per cent are from falls; 8 per cent are the result of drowning; and 6 per cent are caused by fires, burns, and other injuries associated with fires.

Accidents in 1975, last year for which U.S. figures were available in 1976, cost $47.1 billion. About $15.4 billion was in lost wages, and $7 billion was in indirect costs of work accidents—such as time lost by others. Other costs included $6.2 billion in medical expenses; $6.3 billion in insurance administration and claim-adjustment costs; $8 billion in motor-vehicle property-damage costs; and about $4.2 billion in fire losses.   Vincent L. Tofany

SAILING. See BOATING.

SAINT LOUIS ranked as one of the less expensive major U.S. cities in which to live in 1976. According to the Department of Labor, a family of four needed $14,961 in annual income to live in modest comfort in the city. Living costs in the St. Louis area rose 5.4 per cent between June 1975 and June 1976, while food costs increased by 3.3 per cent.

The city staged major Bicentennial festivities downtown during the July 4 weekend. A 20-block area was set aside for free concerts, theatrical performances, and fireworks.

On April 14, a statue of Thomas Jefferson was unveiled at the Gateway Arch visitors' center. The statue was designed to serve as the symbolic centerpiece of the city's Jefferson National Expansion Memorial.

New Airport. William T. Coleman, Jr., U.S. secretary of transportation, announced plans on September 1 to develop a new airport to serve the St. Louis metropolitan area in the 1990s and beyond. The new facility was scheduled to be built on 18,650 acres (7,547 hectares) near the Illinois communities of Columbia and Waterloo, about 19 miles (31 kilometers) southeast of downtown St. Louis. Coleman had hoped that the decision to build a new airport, which would take over most commercial operations from the Lambert-St. Louis Airport, would end the controversy over where the area's major airfield should be located.

Coleman indicated that Lambert-St. Louis Airport would be unsuitable for the needs of the 1990s, but Missouri Governor Christopher S. Bond argued that existing technology could be used to modernize it. Furthermore, the Missouri-St. Louis Metropolitan Airport Authority, along with several Missouri counties, immediately filed suit in federal court to block Coleman's plan to build in Illinois.

Public Scandal continued to plague East St. Louis, Ill. The East St. Louis police chief, a lieutenant, and an assistant to the mayor were convicted on November 10 of accepting bribes to protect illegal gambling.

A federal report released on March 2 noted that the rate of violent crimes in St. Louis had continued to increase since 1972 despite $140 million in federal aid for law enforcement. The study blamed the failure on political pressure to plan and implement anticrime programs hastily.

The Economy. Chrysler Corporation announced plans in June for the $20-million expansion of an automobile plant in the St. Louis area. The new facility will add an estimated 1,000 new jobs in the area. A strike of beer-truck drivers kept most major brands of beer out of St. Louis taverns from early April until June 28, when workers accepted a three-year contract.   James M. Banovetz

SALVATION ARMY. See COMMUNITY ORGANIZATIONS.

SAN FRANCISCO-OAKLAND. A labor confrontation with national ramifications took place in San Francisco on March 31, 1976. More than 1,700 city workers went on strike to protest the city's plan to lower their wages. The strikers were testing whether municipal unions could impose wage demands upon a city in the face of determined opposition by both the elected leadership and the voters.

Employee wage rates were high, with street sweepers earning $17,000 a year, while carpenters and electricians made more than $21,000. In a 1975 referendum, voters by a 2-to-1 margin favored ending the city's system of tying pay raises for craft-union city workers to those won by unions in private industry. The 1976 strike began when the city moved to implement what it considered the referendum's objectives by cutting the annual salaries of craft workers by up to $3,000.

Long Strike. Although 2,000 bus and streetcar employees respected the craft-workers' picket lines and stopped public transit in the city, 14,000 other municipal workers reported to their jobs. Minor violence broke out on April 14 when strikers attempted to prevent people from entering City Hall.

Labor leaders discarded a plan for a general strike when longshoremen and teamsters failed to support the strikers. The craft workers also did not succeed in winning support from Democratic political leaders. The unions rejected a city offer to sub-

In the absence of sanitation workers, volunteer citizens shovel garbage off the streets of San Francisco during a city workers' strike.

SARKIS, ELIAS (1924-   ), was inaugurated as president of war-torn Lebanon on Sept. 23, 1976. He had been elected by the Lebanese parliament on May 8, as the country entered its second year of bloody civil war. He succeeded Sleiman Frangie, who defeated him for the presidency in 1970. Sarkis won the 1976 election with the backing of Syria and conservative Maronite Christians. As the Arab peacekeeping force, largely Syrian, enforced a cease-fire in November, Sarkis began the difficult task of rebuilding Lebanon. See LEBANON.

Sarkis was born into a shopkeeping family on July 20, 1924, in Shibaniyah, a mountain village east of Beirut. He was educated in Beirut and earned a law degree in 1948 from St. Joseph University. He soon entered the Lebanese civil service and gained a reputation for hard work and meticulous attention to administrative detail. He has maintained a nonpolitical posture in Lebanon's highly charged political world. Sarkis was head of the presidential office under President Fouad Chehab from 1958 to 1964. He later served as governor of Lebanon's central bank.

Sarkis is a Maronite Christian, as all of Lebanon's presidents have been by custom. He rarely displays emotion and is known in Lebanon as the "Quiet Man" and the "Sphinx."

A bachelor, Elias Sarkis has few close friends. He hunts occasionally.   Edward G. Nash

SASKATCHEWAN. The Canadian province's 10 potash mines, which produce about 40 per cent of the world's supply and sell most of it to the United States, became the center of controversy in 1976. Premier Allan Blakeney's New Democratic Party government in late 1975 had introduced a bill that would allow the province to purchase and operate the mines. Liberal opposition delayed the bill's passage until Jan. 28, 1976.

The government charged that the potash companies had refused to expand production when called upon and had challenged provincial taxation. The opposition responded that the move was unfair to private companies and would hurt Saskatchewan's ability to attract investment capital.

The Blakeney government bought its first mine from U.S. owners on August 12, paying $128.5 million, almost all in cash, for the property. The purchase gave the government-owned Potash Corporation of Saskatchewan about 15 per cent of the province's capacity. The government hoped eventually to acquire 50 per cent of capacity.

The 1976 budget proposed spending $1.3 billion, up 16.4 per cent from 1975. It imposed additional taxes, including a surtax on higher incomes. The New Democratic Party held 39 seats in the 61-seat legislature, the Liberals had 15, and the Conservatives held 7.   David M. L. Farr

See also CANADA.

mit the issue to a referendum. The Board of Supervisors claimed that mail they received ran 95 per cent in favor of a hard line against the unions.

Seventy-five workers returned to their jobs at city housing facilities on April 21. The remaining strikers returned to their jobs on May 3, at their existing wage rates, after the city promised there would be no retribution against the strikers. The city also agreed to remove two antilabor issues from the June election ballot. Both sides agreed to submit the pay dispute to an 11-member panel composed of labor and city representatives. Although the five union representatives disagreed, the panel recommended pay cuts, which took effect July 1.

Crime. Four black men were convicted on March 13 and sentenced to life imprisonment for the so-called Zebra murders of whites in 1973 and 1974.

Joseph Freitas, San Francisco's new district attorney, announced that he would not prosecute prostitution cases. Instead, he indicated that his office would devote its resources to fighting violent crimes and enforcing laws protecting consumers.

The U.S. Department of Transportation on July 21 awarded $16.7 million to finance new and expanded public transit facilities.   James M. Banovetz

SAN MARINO. See EUROPE.

SÃO TOMÉ AND PRÍNCIPE. See AFRICA; Section Five, SÃO TOMÉ AND PRÍNCIPE and SÃO TOMÉ.

SAUDI ARABIA

SAUDI ARABIA established diplomatic relations with the Marxist government of Yemen (Aden) on March 10, 1976. The move was an effort to build an Arabian Peninsula-Persian Gulf regional front against outside influences and reconcile differences, notably between Oman and Yemen (Aden).

Saudi Arabia turned increasingly to the United States for military hardware and know-how, spending more than $3 billion in 1976. Despite these heavy expenditures, the government announced on June 27 a 1976-1977 budget balanced at $31.4 billion. Defense accounted for 29 per cent of the total. Anticipated oil revenues showed a 14.4 per cent increase. At a December meeting of the Organization of Petroleum Exporting Countries (OPEC), Saudi Arabia, along with the United Arab Emirates, refused to raise oil prices more than 5 per cent, thus creating the first break in the previously solid OPEC front. See PETROLEUM AND GAS.

Vast oil revenues and monetary reserves of $24.6-billion enabled Saudi Arabia to continue aid to other nations. It granted $100 million to Yemen (Aden), $36 million to Sudan, and $20 million to Zaire. William Spencer

See also MIDDLE EAST (Facts in Brief Table).

SCHOOL. See CIVIL RIGHTS; EDUCATION; Section One, FOCUS ON EDUCATION; Section Three, THE LOSING WAR AGAINST ILLITERACY.

SCIENCE AND RESEARCH. On July 20, 1976, seven years to the day after a man first walked on the moon, a spacecraft landed successfully on Mars. Within an hour, *Viking 1* transmitted the first picture of the planet's surface to Earth, revealing a barren, rocky, brick-red plain under a pink sky.

Buoyed by their success in guiding a spacecraft to a relatively safe landing site in the Chryse Basin on Mars, scientists at the Jet Propulsion Laboratory in Pasadena, Calif., chose a somewhat bumpier location for *Viking 2*. But it was one that promised to have more moisture and thus a greater chance for harboring life. The second lander touched down in the Plain of Utopia on September 3.

The search for life, however, produced ambiguous results. Scientists had hypothesized several large forms of life that might inhabit Mars. These were given fanciful scientific names, including *petrophages* (rock eaters), but no life appeared in the photographs. Instruments that can detect the products of photosynthesis and metabolism from microscopic organisms yielded results that indicate Mars may harbor life, but scientists suspect that the instruments were merely detecting a chemical reaction in the soil samples. See SPACE EXPLORATION; Section One, FOCUS ON SCIENCE.

Loch Ness Monster. The existence of at least one earthbound animal remained as controversial

President Gerald R. Ford signs a bill establishing Office of Science and Technology Policy before an approving Vice-President and congressmen.

as that of life on Mars. From June through August 1976, a scientific expedition led by Boston lawyer and educator Robert Rines searched in Scotland's murky Loch Ness for a sea monster long reported living there. In December 1975, the respected scientific journal *Nature* had published photographs of a blurry object claimed to be the Loch Ness monster. The pictures and accompanying sonar records were made the previous summer by Rines. He described the monster as from 45 to 60 feet (14 to 18 meters) long with a 9- to 12-foot (3- to 4-meter) neck and diamond-shaped flippers. The monster was tentatively classified as *Nessiteras rhombopteryx* to bring it under the protection of British conservation laws. But despite a systematic search in 1976, financed by the Academy of Applied Science in Boston and *The New York Times,* the monster was not found.

Spray-Can Aerosols damage the environment and will eventually have to be regulated, a committee of the National Academy of Sciences (NAS) concluded in September. The chemical reaction between fluorocarbons from spray cans and ozone in the atmosphere remains so uncertain, however, that the NAS recommended against any immediate action. The danger is that enough of the ozone layer in the stratosphere may be destroyed to admit large quantities of ultraviolet light, increasing the risk of skin cancer and endangering plant and animal life.

Science Adviser. Legislation creating two new presidential science advisory groups was finally passed in May, about three years after President Richard M. Nixon abolished the White House office on science. H. Guyford Stever, director of the National Science Foundation, became the first director of the Office of Science and Technology Policy, the President's science adviser.

Simon Ramo, a founder of TRW, Incorporated, an aerospace and electronics concern, was appointed to head the other new office, the President's Committee on Science and Technology. This committee will conduct a major survey of the current state of scientific research and development in the United States.

Genetic Engineering. Safeguards to prevent the escape of dangerous new microorganisms that may be created through genetic manipulation were formally established by the National Institutes of Health (NIH), Bethesda, Md. The controls are along the lines set forth at the historic Asilomar Conference held in February 1976 in Pacific Grove, Calif. They specify precautions for laboratories conducting such research with NIH funds, and other government agencies are expected to impose similar regulations on such grants.

In genetic-engineering research, molecular pieces of genes made of deoxyribonucleic acid (DNA) are transferred from one organism to another, creating a mutant genetic material with tailor-made

Russian Roulette

properties. Possible benefits of such research include new types of crops that could be designed to thrive in harsh environments. But dangers also lurk, because new strains of bacteria might accidentally be created that would cause diseases for which there are no known cures.

Geneticists also passed two landmarks in the creation of artificial genes. Harvard biologist Argiris Efstratiadis and his colleagues announced in January that they had completely synthesized a mammalian gene for the first time. The gene is one that controls hemoglobin production in rabbits. Har Gobind Khorana, co-winner of the 1968 Nobel Prize for Physiology or Medicine, and his co-workers at the Massachusetts Institute of Technology announced in August the first successfully created gene that actually worked in a living cell. They introduced the man-made gene for protein synthesis into a bacterium.

New Particles. Elementary-particle physicists became more convinced than ever that subatomic particles possess a distinguishing property whimsically called *charm.* The first particle that seemed to openly display this quality was reported by Stanford University physicists in June. Later discoveries indicated that whole new families of charmed particles may exist, opening the way for breakthroughs in elementary-particle theory.   John H. Douglas

See also the various science articles.

SCRANTON, WILLIAM WARREN (1917-   ),

a millionaire businessman and former Pennsylvania governor, was sworn in on March 15, 1976, as United States permanent representative to the United Nations. He succeeded Daniel P. Moynihan, who resigned on February 29. Scranton brought a relaxed style to the U.S. mission and avoided confrontations during touchy debates. He gave partial support to a May 26 Security Council measure that deplored Israeli settlements in occupied Arab lands, which raised questions about continued strong U.S. support of Israel. See UNITED NATIONS (UN).

Born in Madison, Conn., his family's summer home, he was educated at Yale University. After service as an Army pilot during World War II, he received a Yale law degree in 1946. He served as a congressman from 1961 to 1963 and as governor from 1963 to 1967.

Scranton unsuccessfully challenged Senator Barry Goldwater of Arizona for the Republican presidential nomination in 1964. Later he served on various government commissions and as director of such giant corporations as IBM World Trade Corporation and the Sun Oil Company.

Scranton married Mary Lowe Chamberlin in 1942. They have four children and make their home in Dalton, Pa.   Robert K. Johnson

SCULPTURE. See VISUAL ARTS.

SEATTLE became a major professional sports center in 1976, gaining major-league football and baseball franchises. The football club, the Seattle Seahawks, is a National Football League (NFL) expansion team in the National Conference's Western Division. See FOOTBALL.

Major-league baseball returned to Seattle after a seven-year absence. On February 7, the American League and a six-man group headed by Seattle businessman Lester Smith and entertainer Danny Kaye agreed to place an expansion team in the city in 1977. The owners agreed to pay about $5.3 million for the franchise and signed a 20-year lease for the Seattle Mariners to play in the King County domed stadium, the Kingdome. See BASEBALL.

The Kingdome, a 65,000-seat arena, was dedicated in March. In addition to the baseball team, the Seahawks, the Sounders soccer team, and the Supersonics basketball team play there.

Area Violence. Bombs exploded at an electrical company substation and at the offices of a supermarket chain on January 1. The Seattle Police Department blamed an underground revolutionary group. The bombing caused an estimated $100,000 damage to the electrical company's substation.

A state Fisheries Department patrol officer shot and wounded a man aboard a commercial fishing boat that was allegedly trying to ram the patrol

The first fleet of articulated—or "bendable"—buses in the United States is to be delivered to the metropolitan Seattle transit authority in 1977.

boat in Puget Sound in October. Fisheries officials saw the incident as one of a series involving commercial fishermen opposed to the closing of salmon-fishing areas to all but American Indians.

Environment and Energy. Seattle erected a structure to support a park over a short stretch of Interstate Route 5 in the downtown area. The 6-acre (2.43-hectare) park, complete with trees, grass, and even a waterfall, cost $14 million. Officials claimed it would have cost more to purchase a comparable amount of land in the same general area.

The Environmental Protection Agency (EPA) reported on April 30 that it had found evidence of asbestos fibers in Seattle's drinking water. But the EPA indicated that the tests were inconclusive and that further testing would be conducted. Scientists believe that asbestos fibers may be linked to cancer.

The Seattle Trust and Savings Bank announced in July that it would offer loans at reduced interest rates for homes, cars, and boats that were specially designed to conserve energy. The interest-rate reductions ranged from 0.5 to 0.75 per cent.

Living Costs increased only 3.4 per cent between August 1975 and May 1976. Food prices rose 2.2 per cent from June 1975 to June 1976. The Department of Labor reported that a family of four would need an annual income of $15,787 to live moderately in the area. James M. Banovetz

SENEGAL. See AFRICA.

SEYCHELLES became an independent republic within the British Commonwealth on June 28, 1976. The 92-island chain, which lies in the Indian Ocean just off the northeast African coast, thus ended 162 years of British colonial rule. A coalition government was formed under President James Richard Mancham and Prime Minister France Albert Rene. Mancham had been chief minister under the colonial administration, and Rene was leader of the United Party.

Agreement on independence was reached in January after four days of talks in London. A key issue involved three islands – Aldabra, Farquhar, and Des Roches – which had been leased for a long time from Great Britain by the United States. Under the agreement reached on January 22, the lease was terminated and the three islands were turned over to the Seychelles government by the United States on independence day. Victoria, on Mahé Island, remained the capital. President Mancham said the government hoped to expand tourism and fishing, the two main industries.

The government was also investigating the possibility of developing offshore banking and financial facilities that would enable Seychelles to become the "Switzerland of the Indian Ocean" by providing a tax haven for foreign funds. Paul C. Tullier

See also AFRICA (Facts in Brief Table); Section Five, SEYCHELLES and VICTORIA.

SHAW, TIM (1957-), a record-setting American swimmer, was awarded the James E. Sullivan Memorial Trophy in February 1976. The award is made annually by the Amateur Athletic Union (AAU) to the outstanding amateur athlete in the United States for athletic achievement the previous year and for exemplifying the amateur creed.

Shaw, a student at California State College in Long Beach, set world records in 1975 in the 400-, 800-, and 1,500-meter free-style swimming events. He swam on the Long Beach Swim Club 800-meter free-style relay team that set a world record at the 1975 AAU outdoor championships. He also won three individual gold medals in the World Aquatic Championships in Cali, Colombia, in July 1975. Because of his performance, Shaw was named Male Swimmer of the Year by *Swimming World* magazine and won the Prize Eminence Award of the International Amateur Swimming Federation.

Illness and injury – anemia, a staph infection, and a sore shoulder – held Shaw back in 1976. But he recovered sufficiently to make the U.S. Olympic team and win a silver medal for his second-place finish in the 400-meter free-style at the 1976 Summer Olympic Games in Montreal, Canada, in July.

The son of Mr. and Mrs. Burt Shaw, he was born on Nov. 8, 1957. Shaw is the 17th California resident to win the Sullivan award. Joseph P. Spohn

See also OLYMPIC GAMES; SWIMMING.

SHIP AND SHIPPING. Commercial ship demand declined worldwide in 1976 as orders for crude-oil tankers slumped further. Lloyd's Register of Shipping said there were 2,164 merchant vessels being built on June 30, 5 per cent fewer than in June 1975. Shipbuilding orders, including ships under construction, fell to 4,195 from 4,798. Tonnage of vessels on order plunged 34 per cent to 67.1 million gross tons, as large-tanker orders were canceled.

United States shipbuilders held orders totaling $17 billion. The Maritime Administration (Marad) reported commercial-vessel orders valued at $4.6-billion on November 1, up from $4.3 billion in 1975. Some 77 vessels were scheduled for completion by 1980, down from 80 a year earlier.

U.S. Navy contracts maintained a healthy pace. The order book for Navy work in December was about $12.8 billion, against an estimated $11.4 billion in 1975. New orders included an additional *Trident* nuclear-powered submarine, a destroyer tender, and two auxiliary oil tenders (see ARMED FORCES). Several shipbuilders claimed the Navy owed them a total of $1.9 billion, and some threatened to halt production on the disputed projects.

Supertanker Demand improved somewhat, but overcapacity was still high. The total tanker capacity laid up throughout the world in November was down about 30 per cent from March. Some tankers re-entered the oil-charter market as shipping rates

Tugboats move the tanker *Batillus,* called the world's largest in 1976, between docks in March to complete construction in St. Nazaire, France.

between the Persian Gulf and Europe increased, partly reflecting increased oil buying in advance of an expected price boost.

In the United States, more tankers were laid up because of difficulties in getting grain shipments to Russian ports. Marad and Soviet officials could not agree on a grain-shipping rate to take effect when the rate of $16 per metric ton expired on Dec. 31, 1976. Government and industry officials complained in general that Russian rates deeply undercut international shipping charges. Russia agreed on July 16 to raise its rates to match those of other lines, and U.S. Federal Maritime Commission Chairman Karl E. Bakke said the move would improve "stability in ocean trade." In October, Russia sought to join two North Atlantic shipping conferences, a move expected to pave the way for more cooperation between Russia and other ship lines.

R. J. Reynolds Industries, Incorporated, disclosed on September 10 that its Sea-Land Service subsidiary had paid $19 million in "possibly illegal" rebates to shippers — one of several illegal shipping-concern rebates reported in 1976.   Albert R. Karr

See also TRANSPORTATION.

SHOOTING. See HUNTING; SPORTS.

SIERRA LEONE. See AFRICA.

SIKKIM. See ASIA.

SINGAPORE. See ASIA.

SKATING. See HOCKEY; ICE SKATING.

SKIING. From 1967, when World Cup skiing began, to 1976, only one woman competed every year. She was Rosi Mittermaier of West Germany, and in 1976, at age 25, she became the world's most successful skier.

Mittermaier won gold medals in the women's downhill and the special slalom and finished second to Kathy Kreiner of Canada in the giant slalom in the Winter Olympic Games at Innsbruck, Austria, in February. But she considered the World Cup more important, and she won the women's title easily. Ingemar Stenmark of Sweden became men's champion.

The World Cup races ran from December 1975 to March 1976 in six European nations, Colorado, and Quebec. There were 27 slalom, giant slalom, downhill, and combined events in 14 meets for men, 26 events in 14 meets for women.

Mittermaier totaled 281 points against 214 for second-place Lise-Marie Morerod of Switzerland. The leading American women were Cindy Nelson of Lutsen, Minn., who finished in eighth place, and Lindy Cochran of Richmond, Vt., who tied for 20th place.

The 20-year-old Stenmark scored 249 points, followed by Piero Gros of Italy with 205 and Gustavo Thoeni of Italy with 190. Thoeni had won the title four times in the five previous years. Jim Hunter of Calgary, Canada, finished 13th. Phil Mahre of

White Pass, Wash., who tied for 14th place, was the ranking American.

Mittermaier, a small, bubbling woman, had been hampered in other years by various injuries and lack of concentration. After the season, she retired. See MITTERMAIER, ROSI.

In professional skiing, Henri Duvillard of France easily won the 1976 tour championship. From December 1975 to April 1976, there were 11 meets in the United States, Ontario, and Quebec involving 21 head-to-head slalom and giant slalom competitions. The 28-year-old Duvillard, a short, grim man, won 15 of the 21 races and $66,900.

Nordic Skiing. The brightest performance in the history of American Nordic skiing came in the Winter Olympics when 20-year-old Bill Koch of Guilford, Vt., unexpectedly won the silver medal in the 30-kilometer cross-country race. Koch finished sixth in the 15-kilometer race.

The dangerous sport of ski flying—ski jumping for distance—had an impressive year. Hans-Georg Aschenbach of East Germany, an Olympic champion, set a North American record of 505 feet (154 meters) February 29 at Ironwood, Mich. Five days later, 17-year-old Toni Innauer, who won an Olympic silver medal, and Falko Weisspflog of East Germany set a world record of 570 feet (174 meters) at Oberstdorf, West Germany.   Frank Litsky

See also OLYMPIC GAMES.

SOCCER, the leading spectator sport in most other nations, continued to grow in the United States in 1976. The North American Soccer League (NASL), the major professional circuit, and the American Soccer League (ASL), older but smaller and less affluent, reported record attendance and public interest.

The NASL played from April to August with 20 teams—18 of them in the United States and 2 (Toronto and Vancouver) in Canada. Attendance averaged 10,300 per game for 240 games and totaled almost 2.5 million.

The ASL, with most of its players Americans, played the same season, and for the first time it went coast to coast. Its five new teams—Los Angeles, Tacoma, Utah, Oakland, and Sacramento—formed the Western Division. Attendance for the 11 teams totaled 287,752 for 118 games.

The NASL realigned into two conferences and four divisions. The division winners were the Tampa Bay Rowdies (the 1975 league champions), Chicago Sting, Minnesota Kicks, and San Diego Earthquakes. The Toronto Metros won the championship by defeating Minnesota, 3-0, in the playoff final on August 28 in Seattle. The Los Angeles Skyhawks won the ASL title the day before by beating the New York Apollos, 2-1, in Los Angeles.

The players voted Pelé of the New York Cosmos the NASL's Most Valuable Player, with George

Best of the Los Angeles Aztecs second, and Giorgio Chinaglia of the Cosmos, the scoring champion, third. Pelé, a 35-year-old Brazilian and the most celebrated player in soccer history, finished third in scoring with 13 goals and a record 18 assists.

The U.S. professional season was interrupted in May for a round-robin competition for the American Bicentennial Soccer Cup. Brazil won the series from Italy, England, and the United States.

Other Winners. Among the most successful European teams were Anderlecht of Belgium, Liverpool of England, and the Glasgow Rangers of Scotland. Anderlecht won the European Cup Winners Cup, and Bayern Munich won the European Champions Cup for the third straight year. Anderlecht then defeated Bayern Munich, 5-3, in a two-game total-goal series for the European Supercup. Liverpool won the English League first-division title for a record ninth time and its second European Federation Cup (formerly the EUFA Cup) in three years. The Glasgow Rangers swept the Scottish League first-division title, Scottish League Cup, and Scottish Association Cup.

Qualifying matches started among 95 nations for the 1978 World Cup competition in Argentina. Fourteen teams would qualify and join the two automatic qualifiers—defending champion West Germany and host Argentina.   Frank Litsky

British star George Best, left, came out of retirement to play soccer with the Los Angeles Aztecs in the U.S. and Fulham in England.

SOCIAL SECURITY

SOCIAL SECURITY taxes rose for more than 19-million workers in the United States at the end of 1976. James B. Cardwell, commissioner of the U.S. Social Security Administration, announced on October 6 that the wage base on which the taxes are levied was being increased from $15,300 to $16,500 on Jan. 1, 1977. At the same time, the maximum amount that a beneficiary can earn and still get all his or her social security checks was increased to $3,000, up from $2,760.

The new base of $16,500 will result in additional taxes of $2.3 billion on 1977 earnings without increasing the taxes paid by workers who earn $15,-300 or less in a year. The tax rates of 5.85 per cent of taxable earnings for both employees and employers and 7.9 per cent for self-employed people were not changed. The tax increase for those who earn more than $15,300 will range up to a maximum of $70.20 a year each for a wage earner and his employer, and $94.80 for a self-employed person.

Medicare Rates Increase. The Social Security Administration in September ordered a 19 per cent increase in the amount of money the nation's 25-million Medicare recipients must pay for hospital or nursing-home costs. Effective Jan. 1, 1977, the recipient must pay the first $124 of a hospital bill for any stay of fewer than 60 days, up from the 1976 figure of $104.

The new ruling also means a recipient must pay 19 per cent more for hospitalization of more than 60 days and for post-hospital admittances in skilled nursing homes. The record 19 per cent hike followed a 13 per cent increase that went into effect less than a year earlier.

Commissioner Cardwell said the increase was necessary to keep pace with hospital costs that have been rising twice as fast as the cost of living. See HOSPITAL.

Loophole Closed. President Gerald R. Ford signed a bill into law on October 19 that would protect the social security benefits of thousands of workers employed by charitable organizations.

The new law protects those employees of charitable organizations who have had social security benefits withheld from their pay even though proper forms have not been filed. The charitable organizations involved had unwittingly failed to follow proper procedures.

The Supreme Court of the United States on December 13 upheld the social security policy of denying benefits to a divorced woman under age 62 with a dependent child, while paying benefits to a married woman in the same situation.

Social security regulations were changed to make them conform to a 1975 decision by the Supreme Court of the United States granting benefits to widowed fathers for the care of their children. An estimated 15,000 widowed fathers were made eligible for benefits by the decision.   Joseph P. Anderson

SOCIAL WELFARE. The trend of the poor nations getting poorer and the rich richer continued in 1976. United Nations Secretary-General Kurt Waldheim told delegates to the United Nations (UN) Conference on Human Settlements in Vancouver, Canada, on May 31 that a century of misdirected technological progress had left the world with more impoverished people than ever before. He said that the crucial accumulation of problems among human settlements was not due primarily to the explosive growth of world population, but to a lack of national and international planning that called for "urgent remedial action" and "better forms of social organization."

The poor countries of the world have taken resolute action to cope with their problems, according to a report issued in September by the World Bank. Thanks partly to funds received from governmental institutions and private lenders, all but the poorest of the developing countries have been able to maintain relatively high rates of growth, the bank said.

Among the poorest countries, most of which are in Asia and Africa and contain more than a billion people, the annual growth rate was only 2.8 per cent. This growth rate was nearly offset by population increases, so they had little real growth in per-capita terms.

The Organization of Petroleum Exporting Countries (OPEC) in January reduced their pledged aid to poor nations from $1 billion to $800-million after Ecuador and Indonesia withdrew from the commitment because of domestic financial woes. An OPEC spokesman said that the aid fund, which will provide "interest-free, long-term loans to developing countries," would go into operation as soon as the member nations ratified the agreement. The credits, which are to be used for balance-of-payments support or special development projects, will be allotted without geographic, racial, or political considerations.

In the United States, social welfare came in for much critical discussion in 1976. The former director of the U.S. Office of Management and Budget, Roy L. Ash, predicted that the cost of federal income-maintenance programs would reach 33 per cent of the gross national product by the year 2000. But Senator Edmund S. Muskie (D., Me.) cited a study by the Senate Committee on the Budget contradicting these figures. Muskie said the sharp rise in some programs was caused by trends that will not continue at the same fast rate of growth.

The nation's governors, meeting in Hershey, Pa., in July, called upon the Administration and Congress to establish one centrally administered welfare program by the end of 1977, with a national minimum-payment level adjusted regionally for variations in the cost of living. They said that state and local governments would save millions of dollars if welfare payments were made under one program instead of the eight now in operation. The governors' plan also called on the federal government to assume a larger proportion of the cost of welfare payments and administration of the system.

Both the Republican and Democratic party 1976 election platforms criticized the complicated welfare system and called for its overhaul. The Democrats went beyond that to propose an income-maintenance program, most of which would be financed by the federal government. The Republicans opposed such moves toward more federalization.

Social Services Bill. Congress on September 30 overrode President Gerald R. Ford's veto of a measure that appropriated $56.6 million for social services. The measure provided federal funds for such social programs as those devoted to education, employment, health, and welfare.

President Ford based his veto "purely and simply on the issue of fiscal responsibility," pointing out that the bill contained $4 billion more than he had asked for. Members of Congress who voted to override said that the bill was a way of getting billions of dollars to the people who need them most, and that the bill made a commitment to improving the quality of life for many Americans.

The Number of Poor people in the United States increased by 2.5 million in 1975, the largest single rise since the government began keeping poverty statistics in 1959. The largest proportional increases occurred among those who did not ordinarily dominate the poverty statistics – whites, families with a male head, and those who are not elderly. The government defined the poverty level in 1976 as $5,500 for a nonfarm family of four.

One factor in the increased number of poor people was inflation. The purchasing power of the American family declined in 1975 for the second consecutive year as it had in four of the previous six.

Another factor was the recession that created long-term unemployment for many people. The Bureau of the Census said 4.3 million individuals – more than twice the 1974 total – were unemployed so long in 1975 that they exhausted their unemployment benefits.

Possibly the most striking aspect of the 10.7 per cent increase in people living in poverty was the identity of the groups most heavily affected. There was a 12.9 per cent increase in the number of whites and a 6.1 per cent increase in the number of blacks. However, blacks still constituted 31 per cent of the poor, though they make up less than 12 per cent of the total population.

Similarly, the number of poor individuals living in families headed by a man increased 15.3 per cent, while the number living in families headed by a woman went up 4.5 per cent. But a disproportionate number of the poor are still found in families headed by women.   Joseph P. Anderson

SOMALIA. See AFRICA.

SOUTH AFRICA experienced some of the worst racial disorders in its history in 1976. The trouble began in the black township of Soweto near Johannesburg on June 16, when more than 10,000 black high school students marched in protest against a government regulation that some of their classes be taught in Afrikaans, the language of the dominant white minority of Dutch descent. Rioting broke out, and police shot and killed several students.

The disorders spread to 10 surrounding townships and to three black universities. On June 25, the government estimated that 174 blacks and two whites were killed.

The government canceled the language order in July. But blacks harbored many other grievances spawned by the white regime, such as housing and job discrimination and inadequate public services. For example, blacks working in cities live in townships outside the cities, under South Africa's *apartheid* system of racial separation.

Mass arrests followed the June disturbances in Soweto, and about 20,000 students attempted to march on Johannesburg in August in protest against the detentions. Police fired on the marchers, who then began trying to prevent Soweto's black workers from going to their jobs in Johannesburg.

Serious violence began in black townships near Cape Town and Port Elizabeth in August and broke out in Johannesburg itself on September 23. From June to December, about 400 persons were killed in the civil disorders.

Emerging Black Power. The protests helped unite rural and urban black leaders. South Africa's white government had tried to win the cooperation of rural tribal chiefs with such policies as setting aside tribal homelands that would supposedly become sovereign states. The first of these, the Transkei, became independent on October 26 (see TRANSKEI). However, on August 21, leaders of seven other homelands issued a statement sympathizing with the plight of urban blacks and rejecting the so-called independence for their lands. They met in October with black trade unionists and urban leaders to unite against apartheid.

The protests elicited sympathy from important white groups in South Africa. On August 19, the influential Transvaal Chamber of Commerce called for black self-government in the townships, better housing, and an end to job and wage discrimination. White church groups and opposition political parties in Parliament also advocated reforms.

Minor Concessions. The white government responded with minor concessions. It announced on August 20 that blacks living in townships could purchase homes without a time limit on how long they could live in them. Previously, blacks had been restricted to 30-year land leases. On September 23, the government granted permission for sports teams of different races to compete against each other.

South Africa's Balthazar Johannes Vorster, right, greets Rhodesia's Ian Smith, who visited Pretoria for talks on his country's racial strife.

The black homeland leaders warned in their August 21 statement that blacks would not be content with "mere window dressing" concessions. Nothing short of a complete restructuring of the government to allow black participation would do. But on October 18, Prime Minister Balthazar Johannes Vorster made it clear that he would not allow blacks to participate in government.

On November 9, the United Nations General Assembly passed 10 resolutions supporting the efforts of the black majority to gain power, calling for an economic boycott and arms embargo against South Africa, and banning South Africa from all international sports competition. The South African government responded that it would never yield to international pressure.

In regional affairs, South Africa cooperated with the United States in persuading the white-minority government of Rhodesia to accept a transition to black-majority rule within two years (see RHODESIA). South Africa also agreed to independence for Namibia (South West Africa) by Dec. 31, 1978 (see NAMIBIA).   John D. Esseks

See also AFRICA (Facts in Brief Table); OLYMPIC GAMES.

SOUTH AMERICA. See LATIN AMERICA and articles on Latin American countries.

SOUTH CAROLINA. See STATE GOVERNMENT.

SOUTH DAKOTA. See STATE GOVERNMENT.

SPACE EXPLORATION. Two United States *Viking* spacecraft made the first landings on Mars in 1976 and sent back spectacular pictures of the Martian surface. *Viking 1* touched down on July 20 and sent pictures back to Earth showing a reddish desert strewn with rocks of all sizes. The *Viking 2* spacecraft landed on September 3 on a Martian plain called Utopia, 4,600 miles (7,400 kilometers) northeast of the *Viking 1* site. Photographs again showed a reddish, sandy, rock-littered surface and a horizon broken by eroded crater rims and flat mesas.

Search for Life was a prime goal of the *Viking* missions. A 10-foot (3-meter) arm with a scoop picked up soil samples and delivered them to three special chambers in the spacecraft for chemical analysis. Scientists had found no positive proof of life as we know it on Earth by the end of the year. However, puzzling chemical reactions led some scientists to say that *Viking* discovered either a new form of life or a new form of chemistry. See ASTRONOMY; Section One, FOCUS ON SCIENCE.

Russian Space Feats. While *Viking 1* radioed back the first photographs from the surface of Mars, Russian cosmonauts Boris V. Volynov and Vitaly Zholobov orbited the Earth aboard the space laboratory *Salyut 5*. The space lab went into orbit on June 22, and the cosmonauts followed it aloft in the *Soyuz 21* spacecraft on July 6. After 49 days in space, Soviet officials brought the cosmonauts back to Earth because they suffered from "a state of sensory deprivation, a sort of sensory hunger." The two landed in Kazakhstan on August 24.

Cosmonauts flew again in September and October, but they did not reoccupy the *Salyut 5* space lab. *Soyuz 23* developed a failure in its automatic control systems, and Vyacheslav Zudov and Valery Rozhdestvensky made a perilous emergency landing at midnight on a stormswept lake in Kazakhstan 48 hours after launch. The landing, on October 16, was the first by cosmonauts on water.

Space-Shuttle Progress. The National Aeronautics and Space Administration (NASA) issued a call in July for 30 astronauts to serve as pilots and crew on space-shuttle flights. The first shuttle orbiter – scheduled to rocket into orbit like a spacecraft and land on Earth like an airplane in 1979 – was unveiled in September by Rockwell International Corporation.

Although no U.S. astronauts flew in space in 1976, they kept busy preparing for space-shuttle flights. Crews were named for the first two test flights, which involve flying training craft to a landing from an altitude of 35,000 feet (10,700 meters). The shuttle orbiter can carry a *Spacelab* in its cargo bay in which astronauts will live and work. In February, one astronaut and two space scientists conducted a seven-day simulated mission aboard a

mock-up *Spacelab* at the Johnson Space Center near Houston. *Spacelab* is being built by the European Space Agency, a group formed by West European countries.

Venus Probed. Scientists used a new radar system to get the first detailed pictures of a large portion of cloud-shrouded Venus. Installed at Arecibo Ionospheric Observatory in Puerto Rico, the radar system revealed what planetologists believe is a lava flow as big as Oklahoma. The feature consists of large lava-filled basins, resembling the maria on the Moon, and ridges that may have been thrown up by geologic processes similar to those that created mountains on Earth.

Sun Studied. The second *Helios* space probe, launched by West Germany in January, obtained new information about the Sun. It passed 27 million miles (43 million kilometers) from the Sun's surface on April 16, a record close approach.

Other Satellites. NASA launched the world's most powerful communications satellite in January 1976. Jointly developed by the United States and Canada, the Communications Technology Satellite boasts 200 watts of power to transmit written messages, television pictures, and voice communications. *Marisat* satellites were positioned over the Atlantic, Pacific, and Indian oceans to facilitate maritime communications.
William J. Cromie

A rock-strewn desert was part of the first panoramic view of the surface of Mars that was sent to Earth on July 20 by the unmanned *Viking 1*.

SPAIN moved slowly and painfully toward democracy in 1976. On March 2, King Juan Carlos I challenged the regime that put him on the throne. He told members of the right wing Council of Ministers that they must help bring about "the profound reforms the country needs." If not, he indicated, he would by-pass them or call a national referendum to strengthen his powers.

Prime Minister Adolfo Suarez Gonzalez announced on September 10 a government reform bill calling for elections in 1977. Both houses of a proposed parliament to replace the present *Cortes* (parliament) will be elected by universal suffrage, he said. Suarez said the aim was simple – to move from an authoritarian to a democratic system. The Cortes accepted the reforms on November 18, and voters approved them on December 15.

New Political Freedom. The government lifted a ban on political parties other than the official Nationalist Movement on June 9. Spain's opposition groups held a "summit meeting," the first in 40 years, on September 5 and called for a peaceful formation of a new democratic constitution. The government also moved to legalize independent trade unions on October 8. The reform measure was linked to wage controls and price freezes until Sept. 30, 1977, an attack on the 20 per cent annual rate of inflation.

Prime Minister Carlos Arias Navarro resigned on July 1, and Juan Carlos appointed Suarez, then of the National Movement, as a surprise successor. See SUAREZ GONZALEZ, ADOLFO.

Unrest and Protest. Soldiers broke up a strike of Madrid subway workers on January 6. Protests over inflation and wage controls mounted, and the government averted a national rail strike on January 19 by drafting into the army all 62,000 employees. Weeklong strikes for higher wages disrupted Spain's postal system in July and September. Riot police and demonstrators clashed repeatedly, and bomb explosions in eight cities injured at least 12 persons on July 17 and 18. Juan Carlos signed a royal decree on July 30 granting amnesty for all political prisoners and exiles except those sentenced for terrorist acts.

The Basques continued their agitation for separation. An adviser to the king, Juan Maria de Araluce Villar, and four members of his escort were killed in an ambush in San Sebastian on October 4. Separatists kidnaped another adviser on December 11 and demanded the release of political prisoners.

Spain devalued the peseta 11 per cent on February 9 to reduce a mounting trade deficit. Spain said it will apply for membership in the European Community (Common Market).   Kenneth Brown

See also EUROPE (Facts in Brief Table).

King Juan Carlos I, center, watches quietly as Adolfo Suarez Gonzalez, left, is sworn in as prime minister of Spain on July 5.

SPORTS. Players in the four major professional team sports – baseball, football, basketball, and hockey – gained new freedom in 1976. The most dramatic results came in baseball when 24 major-league players from 13 clubs went on the auction block in November. They played the 1976 season without signed contracts and became free agents.

The players were offered in a special draft in what *The New York Times* columnist Red Smith called "mankind's first auction of freed slaves." Each could be chosen by as many as 12 clubs plus his 1976 club, and he could sign with any of those clubs by February 1977. If unsigned by then, he could sign with any club.

Eight of the players – including Reggie Jackson, Bert Campaneris, Joe Rudi, and Gene Tenace – came from the Oakland A's. The 24 players were among the best in baseball, and many signed million-dollar contracts. Jackson got $2.9 million over five years from the New York Yankees.

Two days after the draft, Bill Campbell, a relief pitcher for the Minnesota Twins, became the first free agent to sign. Eight months earlier, he would have signed with the Twins for $30,000. After the draft, he signed with the Boston Red Sox for $1-million over four years. See BASEBALL.

The National Football League Players Association continued sporadic negotiations with the club owners. The players seemed in no rush to reach agreement because federal courts again ruled in their favor in antitrust suits against the league.

A United States District Court on September 8 declared the player draft illegal, and a Court of Appeals on October 18 reaffirmed the ruling that the so-called Rozelle rule was illegal. The Rozelle rule stated that when a player whose contract and option year had expired signed with a new club, his new team had to compensate his old club.

The courts suggested that the players and club owners resolve their differences in a new contract. The courts indicated that a draft and compensation agreement would be acceptable even if it somewhat limited free movement of players. See FOOTBALL.

The National Hockey League and its players association signed such an agreement in May. A month later, 81 players became free agents, but a player's new club had to compensate his old club.

The National Basketball Association and its players in April settled a 1970 class action suit brought by Oscar Robertson, once a leading player. They agreed that after the 1975-1976 season the owners would abolish the option clause, the contract provision that gave the club an option on a player's services for another year. See BASKETBALL.

Among the Winners in 1976 were:

Curling. The United States won the world championship in March in Duluth, Minn., by defeating Scotland, 6-5, in the final. The United States rink, from Hibbing, Minn., consisted of Bruce Roberts, a 33-year-old grade-school teacher, and three relatives.

London mountain climbers can practice on walls like this one in the city's Sobell Sports Centre. It stands about 30 feet (9 meters) high.

Fencing. Russia, which won three of the eight titles in the 1975 world championships, took three of the eight in the 1976 Olympic Games. Peter Westbrook of New York City surprisingly won the saber competition in the Martini & Rossi international tournament in New York, then finished second to Thomas Loconczy of New York City in the national championships.

Handball. Fred Lewis of Miami, Fla., again dominated the professional tour, winning six of the eight tournaments and $8,800 of the $50,000 in prize money. Vern Roberts, Jr., of Lake Forest, Ill., became the U.S. Handball Association four-wall champion, and his brothers Jack and Chris won national titles for youngsters.

Rowing. East Germany, which had dominated international rowing for almost a decade, won most of the Olympic gold medals. Harvard, the outstanding American college eight, passed up the Intercollegiate Rowing Association regatta. California borrowed the Harvard shell and won the varsity title.

Shooting. Margaret Murdock of Topeka, Kans., a 33-year-old Army captain, became the first woman shooter on a U.S. Olympic team and the first woman to win an Olympic shooting medal. She finished second to Lanny Bassham of Bedford, Tex., in small-bore rifle, three positions. Lones Wigger of Carter, Mont., shut out of an Olympic berth, defeated Bassham in winning a ninth U.S. championship in August.

Weight Lifting. Vassili Alexeev of Russia, 34 years old and 344 pounds (156 kilograms), kept his Olympic super-heavyweight title and set a world record of 561 pounds (254 kilograms) for the clean and jerk. The only American medal was a silver to middle heavyweight Lee James of Manchester, Pa. Three lifters, including an American, Phil Grippaldi of Belleville, N.J., were disqualified when tests showed the presence in their bodies of anabolic steroids, banned muscle-building drugs.

Wrestling. Russia won 12 of the 20 gold medals in the Olympics and 5 of the 10 weight divisions in the World Cup in Toledo, Ohio. Middleweight John Peterson of Comstock, Wis., who won a silver medal in 1972, won the only American gold. His brother, Ben, took a silver.

Other Champions. *Archery,* world field champions: men, Tommy Presson, Sweden; women, Anne Marie Lehmann, West Germany. U.S. target champions: men, Darrell Pace, Reading, Ohio; women, Luann Ryon, Riverside, Calif. *Badminton,* U.S. open champions: men, Paul Whetnall, England; women, Gillian Gilks, England. All-England champions: men, Rudy Hartono, Indonesia; women, Gillian Gilks. *Biathlon,* world champion: Heikki Ikola, Finland. U.S. champion: Peter Dascoulias, Tilton, N.H. *Billiards,* world pocket champion: Larry Lisciotti, Manchester, Conn. U.S. pocket champions: men, Tom Jennings, Edison, N.J.; women, Jean Balukas, Brooklyn, N.Y. *Canoeing,* U.S. 500-meter champions: canoe, Andy Weigand, Arlington, Va.; men's kayak, Steve Kelly, Bronx, N.Y.; women's kayak, Ann Turner, St. Charles, Ill. *Casting,* U.S. all-around champion: Steve Rajeff, San Francisco. *Court tennis,* world champion: Howard Angus, England; U.S. champion, Gene Scott, New York City. *Cross-country,* U.S. champions: AAU, Rick Rojas, Boulder, Colo.; NCAA, Henry Rono, Washington State. *Cycling,* world champions: pro road, Freddy Maertens, Belgium; amateur road, Walter Baumgartner, Switzerland; women's sprint, Sheila Young, Detroit. *Field hockey,* women's World Cup: West Germany. *Gymnastics,* American Cup all-around champions: men, Bart Conner, Morton Grove, Ill.; women, Nadia Comaneci, Romania. *Hang gliding,* world champion: Brian Porter, Merced, Calif. *Judo,* U.S. grand champion: Pat Burris, Anaheim, Calif. *Karate,* AAU women's champion: Mary Gaeta, Bloomfield, N.J. *Lacrosse,* U.S. champions: NCAA, Cornell; club, Mount Washington Lacrosse Club, Baltimore. *Modern pentathlon,* U.S. champion: Robert Neiman, Hinsdale, Ill. *Motorcycling,* U.S. grand national champion: Jim Springsteen, Flint, Mich. *Parachuting,* world overall champion: Greg Surabko, Russia. *Polo,* U.S. open champion: Willow Bend, Dallas. *Racquetball,* U.S. champions: men, Charles Brumfield, San Diego; women, Peggy Steding, Odessa, Tex. *Racquets,* U.S. champion: William Surtees, Chicago. *Rodeo,* national high-point scorer: Tom Ferguson, Miami, Okla. *Roller skating,* world champions: men, Thomas Nieder, West Germany; women, Natalie Dunn, East Meadow, N.Y. *Rugby,* Great Britain, Rugby Union: Calcutta Cup, Scotland; county champion, Gloucestershire. Rugby League, Challenge Cup, St. Helens. *Sambo,* U.S. heavyweight champion: Doug Posely, Houston. *Sled-dog racing,* world champion: Dick Moulton, Center Harbor, N.H. *Softball,* U.S. fast-pitch champions: men, Raybestos Cardinals, Stratford, Conn.; women, Raybestos Brakettes, Stratford, Conn. U.S. slow-pitching champion: men, Warren Motors, Jacksonville, Fla.; women, Sorrento's Pizza, Cincinnati. *Squash racquets,* U.S. champions: men, Peter Briggs, New York City; women, Gretchen Spruance, Wilmington, Del. *Squash tennis,* U.S. champion: Pedro Bacallao, New York City. *Surfing,* women's World Cup: Margo Godfrey Oberg, Kauai, Hawaii. *Synchronized swimming,* AAU outdoor champion: Sue Baross, Santa Clara, Calif. *Table tennis,* U.S. open champions: men, Dragutin Surbek, Yugoslavia; women, Kim Soon Ok, South Korea. *Trampoline,* world champions: men, Yevgeni Janes, Russia, and Richard Tison, France (tie); women, Svetlana Levina, Russia. *Volleyball,* AAU champions: men, Honolulu Outriggers; women, Nick's Fish Market, Santa Monica, Calif. International Volleyball Association: San Diego Breakers. *Water polo,* AAU: Concord, Calif. *Water skiing,* U.S. champions: men, Chris Redmond, Canton, Ohio; women, Cindy Todd, Pierson, Fla.   Frank Litsky

See also OLYMPIC GAMES.

SRI LANKA played host in August 1976 to thousands of diplomats at a summit conference of nonaligned nations in Colombo. Under the eye of Prime Minister Sirimavo Bandaranaike, luxury hotels were readied, buildings along the road from the airport to the capital were whitewashed, and thousands of beggars were trucked out of the city to special temporary camps. Although other nations helped with gifts, the conference is believed to have cost Sri Lanka about $30 million.

The country could ill afford such an expenditure. Sri Lanka's per capita income was $120 a year, one of the world's lowest. A severe drought that did not break until October reduced the crop harvest, led to water rationing in Colombo, and caused the flow of the Mahaweli River—the centerpiece of a vast projected irrigation scheme—to drop disastrously.

More than one-third of the rice needed to feed the people had to be imported, most of it from China (in exchange for rubber) and Pakistan. Flour was provided by the United States under the Food for Peace program. General malnutrition was prevented mainly by a rationing system that provided every person with 1 pound (0.45 kilogram) of rice free weekly and another pound at one-third the market price.

Economic Problems, the World Bank noted, were rooted in dependence on two main crops, tea and rubber. Prices of these crops were depressed and fluctuating on the world market. Worse, the country's agricultural production growth barely kept up with its high birth rate. At least one-fifth of the labor force was unemployed, and perhaps thousands more were underemployed. Sri Lanka tried to woo or intimidate foreign investors into bringing funds into the country, but with little success.

Bandaranaike had pledged to hold elections before the spring of 1977. If she were to keep her promise, she would face formidable odds. Although many key posts in the administration were held by her relatives, the government was disunited. The Trotskyites, the former coalition partners with whom she broke in September 1975, stirred up much unrest in 1976.

More Unrest. The economic distress was particularly severe for school graduates unable to find jobs. With the bloody 1971 insurrection of thousands of youths still fresh in people's minds, the government revealed "positive indications" of new insurgent activity in many areas and the discovery of arms caches in the jungle. Even more troublesome was the problem of 2.5 million Hindu Tamils. Restive under the restraints imposed by the mostly Buddhist Sinhalese government, the Tamils in 1976 demanded a separate state, to be called Eelam. Bandaranaike had Tamil leaders arrested. This was an action that could severely affect the fortunes of her Sri Lanka Freedom Party.   Mark Gayn

See also ASIA (Facts in Brief Table).

STAMP COLLECTING. Omnibus stamp issues were used by many nations in 1976 to commemorate such events as the American Revolution Bicentennial, the Olympic Games, and the 100th anniversary of the telephone. Each of the 26 members of the European Postal and Telecommunications Union issued a stamp on the theme of their country's handicrafts.

Of 20 United States commemoratives issued in 1976, 14 were related to the Bicentennial. One of these was a stamp issued in cooperation with Canada. It commemorated Benjamin Franklin who, before U.S. independence, helped to establish postal service in both the American Colonies and Canada. The U.S. and Canadian stamps differed in language and denomination, and slightly in size, but were otherwise identical.

The U.S. Postal Service canceled plans to issue a pane of 32 stamps that, as a unit, reproduced the Declaration of Independence, partly because of a massive protest by collectors. The American Philatelic Society disapproved of the proposed issue, terming it excessive in the context of the numerous other Bicentennial commemoratives. Protests against a 50-state flag issue went unheeded, however, and it attracted wide interest when it appeared on February 23. But collectors complained about sloppy cancellations of the stamps at the respective state-capital post offices. The flag of Tennessee was upside down on that state's stamp, but the Postal Service said the error would not be corrected.

Raymond A. Weil, a New Orleans stamp dealer, paid a record $57,000 for a U.S. one-penny 1851 stamp in New York City on January 31. Weil paid $170,000 at an auction in New York City on June 8 for a block of four of the famous 1918 U.S. airmail inverts. It was the highest price ever paid for a single U.S. stamp item. The seller was Princeton University.

Interphil '76, heralded as the greatest stamp show in United States history, was held in Philadelphia from May 29 to June 6. In connection with this show the Postal Service issued four Bicentennial souvenir sheets of five stamps each that fit together to reproduce famous paintings of Revolutionary events.

Seven Postal Service employees in Tulsa, Okla., were dismissed in August because they found potentially valuable stamps during regular post office sales that they bought at face value of $5 a sheet and then sold to collectors at from $800 to $2,500 a sheet.

The 1975 Christmas stamps showed no denomination, and they were improperly perforated. Experts said the price per sheet might eventually reach $25,000, depending upon the number of sheets in existence. *Theodore M. O'Leary*

STATE GOVERNMENT. The states reduced their general expenditures a total of 10 per cent in fiscal 1976, but they ended the year with a net surplus of only 2.5 per cent of expenditures, or about $2 billion. In a hold-the-line attitude, the states' chief budget officers recommended a cumulative increase in general-fund expenditures during fiscal 1977 of only 7 per cent. They expected general-fund revenues to climb only 10 per cent over fiscal 1976.

Southern and Western states—particularly the so-called sun-belt states of Alabama, Arizona, Arkansas, (southern) California, Florida, Georgia, Louisiana, Mississippi, New Mexico, North Carolina, Oklahoma, South Carolina, Tennessee, Texas, and Virginia—continued to outgrow the Northeastern, Midwestern, and Great Lakes states in population, revenue, and attraction of federal funds. In particular, the sun-belt states netted $13-billion more in federal funds in 1974 than their citizens paid in federal taxes.

Led by New York Governor Hugh L. Carey, the Northeastern industrial states in June 1976 formed a coalition to lobby in Washington, D.C., for a better balance of federal revenues and spending. The so-called frost-belt states, which include 14 industrialized Midwestern and Northeastern states, met in October to review the federal spending imbalance and to formulate strategy.

Meanwhile, several states bailed out their ailing

Canada and the United States observed the American Revolution Bicentennial by jointly issuing stamps featuring Benjamin Franklin.

A steel sculpture by Alexander Calder graces
a reflecting pool of the $2-billion Empire
State Plaza, dedicated July 1 in Albany, N.Y.

cities. Michigan enacted legislation to aid Detroit
to the tune of $27.8 million and authorized the city
to raise garbage-collection taxes. Connecticut authorized $4.5 million for its cities and towns.

Higher Taxes. After a weeklong shut-down of its
schools under a state supreme court order, the New
Jersey legislature enacted the first state income tax
on July 8, aimed at providing an additional $378-
million for schools. Nebraska increased its state income tax rate in August from 15 to 17 per cent of
federal tax liability. Maine increased the state personal income tax by $18.5 million. Rhode Island
raised its sales tax from 5 to 6 per cent for one year.
South Carolina added a 9 per cent surtax to liquor
sales to increase school aid. Gasoline taxes went up
from 10 to 11 cents per gallon (3.8 liters) in Connecticut; from 8.5 to 9.5 cents in Idaho; and from 7
to 8 cents in Kansas.

Several states provided tax breaks. Illinois doubled the state inheritance tax exemption to $40,000.
Kentucky increased its state income tax deduction
to $650 per person. Utah exempted drugs from the
state sales tax and decreased the state income tax.

Six more states provided tax breaks to promote
energy conservation. For example, Michigan eased
property taxes for those buildings that use solar-,
water-, or wind-energy devices. Connecticut, Hawaii, Maryland, and Vermont passed similar laws.
Governor Edmund G. Brown, Jr., of California
signed legislation on July 3 providing $25 million in
loans for homeowners who install solar heating and
cooling systems.

The Elections. Democrats gained one governorship in the 14 contested states on November 2, and
retained a healthy margin of control over the state
legislatures, which had 5,978 seats up for election in
43 states. Voters gave the Democrats control of
both legislative houses in 36 states, while Republicans held complete control in only five states. Other
November ballot issues included referendums to restrict the development of nuclear power, which lost
in six states; to require deposits on beverage containers, which won in two of four states; and to
require the surrender of handguns, which lost in
Massachusetts. See ELECTIONS.

Sunset Laws. Colorado provided the lead for
one of the year's most innovative and controversial
state measures — sunset laws. Colorado's sunset law,
signed in April, provided that about 40 state agencies, boards, commissions, and divisions must undergo legislative scrutiny every six years. They are
to be eliminated if they cannot justify their existence. One-third of the agencies were scheduled for
review in mid-1977. Alabama, Florida, and Louisiana also enacted sunset laws.

First Right-to-Die Law. California in September became the first state to recognize the legality of
living wills, directives authorizing removal of life-
sustaining medical devices. Effective on Jan. 1,

Selected Statistics on State Governments

State	Resident population(a)	Governor	Legislature (b) House (D)	(R)	Senate (D)	(R)	State tax revenue(c)	Tax revenue per capita(d)	Public school enrollment 1975–76(e)	Public school expenditures per pupil in average daily attendance 1975–76(f)
Alabama	3,665	George C. Wallace (D)	105	0	35	0	$ 1,243	$ 339	757	$1,090
Alaska	382	Jay S. Hammond (R)	25	15	12	8	599	1,568	86	2,096
Arizona	2,270	Raul H. Castro (D)	23	37	16	14	1,018	448	483	1,415
Arkansas	2,109	David H. Pryor (D)	96	4	34	1	725	344	451	881
California	21,520	Edmund G. Brown, Jr. (D)	57	23	26	14	10,761	500	4,394	1,320
Colorado	2,583	Richard D. Lamm (D)	30	35	17	18	964	373	563	1,422
Connecticut	3,117	Ella T. Grasso (D)	93	58	22	14	1,264	405	655	1,659
Delaware	582	Pierre du Pont IV (R)	26	15	13	8	359	616	129	1,606
Florida	8,421	Reubin O'D. Askew (D)	92	28	29	10(g)	2,936	349	1,544	1,381
Georgia	4,970	George Busbee (D)	157	23	52	4	1,678	338	1,072	1,114
Hawaii	887	George R. Ariyoshi (D)	39	12	18	7	639	721	175	1,545
Idaho	831	*Cecil D. Andrus (D)	22	48	15	20	329	396	186	1,112
Illinois	11,229	James R. Thompson (R)	92	85	34	25	4,783	426	2,278	1,452
Indiana	5,302	Otis R. Bowen (R)	48	52	28	22	1,916	361	1,177	1,160
Iowa	2,870	Robert D. Ray (R)	60	40	28	22	1,200	418	616	1,455
Kansas	2,310	Robert F. Bennett (R)	64	61	19	21	854	370	446	1,475
Kentucky	3,428	Julian M. Carroll (D)	78	22	30	8	1,404	409	695	986
Louisiana	3,841	Edwin Edwards (D)	101	4	38	1	1,656	431	833	1,082
Maine	1,070	James B. Longley (I)	89	62	12	21	531	496	248	1,197
Maryland	4,144	Marvin Mandel (D)	126	15	39	8	1,960	473	887	1,516
Massachusetts	5,809	Michael S. Dukakis (D)	194	43(h)	33	7	2,728	470	1,200	1,425
Michigan	9,104	William G. Milliken (R)	68	42	24	14	3,769	414	2,121	1,366
Minnesota	3,965	Rudy Perpich (D)	104	30	49	18	2,219	560	884	1,516
Mississippi	2,354	Cliff Finch (D)	119	3	50	2	874	371	509	997
Missouri	4,778	Joseph P. Teasdale (D)	115	48	24	10	1,444	302	994	1,186
Montana	753	Thomas L. Judge (D)	67	33	25	25	278	369	171	1,554
Nebraska	1,553	J. James Exon (D)	49(i) (unicameral)				489	315	316	1,302
Nevada	610	Mike O'Callaghan (D)	35	5	17	3	294	482	136	1,261
New Hampshire	822	Meldrim Thomson, Jr. (R)	179	221	12	12	184	224	171	1,175
New Jersey	7,336	Brendan T. Byrne (D)	49	31	29	10	2,292	312	1,458	1,892
New Mexico	1,168	Jerry Apodaca (D)	48	22	33	9	575	492	280	1,261
New York	18,084	Hugh L. Carey (D)	90	61	25	35	9,780	541	3,411	2,179
North Carolina	5,469	James B. Hunt, Jr. (D)	114	6	46	4	2,060	376	1,169	1,099
North Dakota	643	Arthur A. Link (D)	51	49	18	32	287	447	132	1,207
Ohio	10,690	James A. Rhodes (R)	62	37	21	12	3,309	310	2,314	1,264
Oklahoma	2,766	David L. Boren (D)	79	22	39	9	1,000	362	591	1,130
Oregon	2,329	Robert W. Straub (D)	37	23	24	6	826	355	473	1,501
Pennsylvania	11,862	Milton J. Shapp (D)	118	85	31	19	5,127	432	2,261	1,660
Rhode Island	927	J. Joseph Garrahy (D)	83	17	45	5	389	419	177	1,481
South Carolina	2,848	James B. Edwards (R)	112	12	43	3	1,042	366	622	1,030
South Dakota	686	Richard F. Kneip (D)	22	48	10	25	192	280	153	1,094
Tennessee	4,214	Ray Blanton (D)	66	32	23	9	1,271	302	865	969
Texas	12,487	Dolph Briscoe (D)	123	18	28	3	4,214	337	2,762	1,094
Utah	1,228	Scott M. Matheson (D)	36	39	17	12	474	386	304	1,084
Vermont	476	Richard Snelling (R)	78	72	8	22	475	431	104	1,398
Virginia	5,032	Mills E. Godwin, Jr. (R)	78	17	35	5	1,822	362	1,084	1,197
Washington	3,612	Dixy Lee Ray (D)	62	36	31	18	1,848	512	779	1,443
West Virginia	1,821	John D. Rockefeller IV (D)	91	9	29	5	828	455	401	1,071
Wisconsin	4,609	Patrick J. Lucey (D)	66	33	23	10	2,421	525	968	1,618
Wyoming	390	Ed Herschler (D)	30	31(g)	12	18	193	495	85	1,489
District of Columbia	702								130	1,954

(a) Numbers in thousands, provisional estimates as of July 1, 1976 (Bureau of the Census)
(b) As of Dec. 31, 1976
(c) 1976 preliminary figures in millions (Bureau of the Census)
(d) 1976 preliminary figures in dollars (Bureau of the Census)
(e) Numbers in thousands, fall, 1975 (U.S. Office of Education, *Digest of Education Statistics, 1975*)
(f) Number in dollars, 1975–76 (U.S. Office of Education, *Statistics of Public Elementary and Secondary Day Schools, Fall 1975*)
(g) 1 Independent
(h) 3 Independents
(i) Nonpartisan

*Was to be nominated U.S. secretary of the interior in January 1977

1977, California's Natural Death Act permits a terminally ill patient to direct a physician to withhold or withdraw life-sustaining medical procedures that serve only to postpone death.

A precedent-setting decision ended months of agonizing court pleas on March 31 when the New Jersey Supreme Court ruled that Karen Ann Quinlan's right to privacy included the right for her father, as her guardian, to seek physicians who would agree to disconnect life-sustaining machinery, even if that meant the prospect of death. Quinlan, whose brain had been irreparably damaged in April 1975, did not die when the machinery was removed in May 1976, nor did the debate over the issue of "the right to die with dignity."

More than half the states acted in 1976 to create or modify medical malpractice insurance laws, continuing a trend of recent years. New laws in Alaska, Arizona, Colorado, Delaware, Kentucky, Minnesota, Mississippi, Missouri, New Mexico, Rhode Island, and Virginia authorized joint underwriting associations of insurers to provide medical malpractice coverage.

Ten states — Alaska, Colorado, Connecticut, Florida, Iowa, Kentucky, New Mexico, Pennsylvania, Rhode Island, and Wisconsin — passed laws that enable pharmacists to substitute a generally less expensive generic drug for a prescribed brand-name drug.

Housing Action. California and Illinois passed laws prohibiting banks and mortgage companies from *redlining,* or not providing housing loans to buyers in certain neighborhoods. Arizona provided $35 million in relief for homeowners. Hawaii and Louisiana raised homestead exemptions. In other property-tax breaks, Iowa provided tax relief for the elderly on homes and farms, and Kentucky provided property-tax relief for the blind, elderly, farm owners, and poor.

Toxic Chemical Control. Indiana, Michigan, and Wisconsin passed laws controlling the sale, use, or manufacture of polychlorinated biphenyls (PCB's), industrial chemicals widely used for 40 years in the manufacture of electrical products. PCB's cause cancer in laboratory animals. New York state and the General Electric Company (GE) signed a $7-million pact on September 8 to check the discharge of PCB's and clean up pollution caused by PCB's that GE had been dumping into the Hudson River for 25 years. See CHEMICAL INDUSTRY; ENVIRONMENT.

Death Penalty Ok'd. The July 2 decision of the Supreme Court of the United States upholding capital punishment laws in several states dominated criminal justice in 1976. The decision climaxed years of government action and court rulings. Capital punishment laws in Florida, Georgia, and Texas that gave judges or juries guidelines for meting out the death penalty were upheld. The ruling

voided mandatory death penalty laws that did not contain sentencing guidelines in Louisiana and North Carolina and, later, in Oklahoma. The July ruling placed Utah in the spotlight when convicted murderer Gary Mark Gilmore pleaded for release or swift execution by firing squad. He finally was executed on Jan. 17, 1977. See SUPREME COURT OF THE UNITED STATES.

Within weeks of the Supreme Court decision, Louisiana and Oklahoma acted to bring their capital punishment laws within the ruling. A county circuit court ruled in August that Missouri's death penalty law was unconstitutional, and a state supreme court issued a similar ruling on New York's law in October. The New York decision was appealed to the state's highest court. In a split decision, the Mississippi Supreme Court upheld that state's death penalty law in October.

Other Supreme Court rulings strengthened states' rights. The court struck down on June 24 laws that extend federal minimum-wage and maximum-hour provisions to state and municipal employees. The next day, the court ruled that states have the right to set mandatory retirement ages as long as such regulations serve a legitimate purpose.

Prison Programs. Alabama was one of several states taking action to correct overcrowded prisons. Florida authorized a two-year pilot program for contracts between prisoners and the state on confinement, parole, and release. Colorado enacted a series of prison reform laws, and the legislature appropriated $200,000 for a state master plan for prisons and nearly $1 million for security measures and construction. Kentucky became the first state in the nation to ban commercial bail bonding. Iowa appropriated $1.3 million for a new prison and $4.5 million for community corrections programs.

Victim Compensation and Handguns. Legislatures in Kentucky, Michigan, Ohio, Pennsylvania, and Wisconsin provided for state compensation for crime victims. Colorado and Oklahoma passed new laws requiring criminals to pay their victims for damages. Pennsylvania provided for both state compensation and restitution by criminals.

A dozen states provided new laws regulating the use, sale, or possession of handguns. Kansas and Maine made sentences mandatory for those who use handguns to commit crimes. Mississippi denied parole to criminals who use guns. In Utah, judges may now increase the penalty for criminals who use guns. Florida and Michigan passed laws regulating electronic weapons known as *stun guns.* These weapons shoot darts that electrically stun victims.

New Capital. Alaskan voters chose the site of their new state capital on November 2. Willow, a forested area about 70 miles (113 kilometers) north of Anchorage, won out over two other sites proposed by a selection committee. The capital was to be moved from Juneau by 1980. Ralph Wayne Derickson

STEEL INDUSTRY. United States restrictions on imports of specialty steels, imposed in June 1976, brought sharp reactions from the already troubled European and Japanese steel industries. The import quotas, designed to protect the specialty steel market for U.S. companies, set an import limit of 147,-000 short tons (133,000 metric tons), only slightly less than 1974 and 1975 imports.

The only significant rollback from recent import levels involved shipments from Japan. Nevertheless, European steelmakers began to feel the pinch in the fall, and European Community (Common Market) officials trimmed their production estimates.

For instance, West Germany found itself importing more steel than it exported for the first time in many years. In the last three months of 1976, there were a number of layoffs in the industry.

U.S. Production. The American Iron and Steel Institute (AISI) reported that cumulative steel production through December 4 reached 119.86 million short tons (108.74 million metric tons), 9.2 per cent over the 109.79 million short tons (99.6 million metric tons) of steel poured through Dec. 4, 1975. The AISI noted that much of the increase could be traced to a 50 per cent increase in demand for sheet and strip steel by the automobile industry and by appliance producers, despite much criticized price rises imposed by the leading steelmakers. The latest set of price rises, announced after the November presidential elections, drew strong criticism from President-elect James E. (Jimmy) Carter, Jr., and his staff. The hikes occurred in the face of softening demand for steel — and resulting layoffs — in the final quarter.

Steel from Trash. An innovation in steelmaking was introduced on June 7 when New York City signed a contract with the Ashmont Metal Company, which plans to build a $12-million plant in Brooklyn that will produce steel from metal extracted from burned garbage. The company will build the plant next to a city incinerator. Company officials predict salvaged metal can be turned into some 65 to 70 short tons (59 to 63.5 metric tons) of commercial-grade steel per day.

The Environmental Protection Agency (EPA). Environmental groups and the staff of the Senate Subcommittee on Environmental Pollution questioned the EPA's exemption of eight plants located along a stretch of the Mahoning River in Ohio from regulations limiting the pollutants that can be dumped into lakes and rivers. The plants are owned by the U.S. Steel Corporation, the Republic Steel Corporation, and the Youngstown Sheet and Tube Company. In justifying the exemption, EPA officials agreed with the companies' contention that the old plants were economically marginal and could more cheaply be closed than brought up to EPA standards. When operating at peak level, they provide 24,500 jobs.   Mary E. Jessup

STOCKS AND BONDS. The Dow Jones average of 30 industrial stocks reached a 46-month high of 1,014.79 on Sept. 21, 1976, but then sputtered during the remainder of the year and ended at 1004.64. The 1976 high was 37 points below the all-time peak of 1,051.70 reached on Jan. 11, 1973.

Despite the hesitancy in the last half of the year, prices increased substantially in the first half. Annual lows were recorded the first trading day of 1976 on the New York Stock Exchange, the American Stock Exchange, and the National Association of Securities Dealers over-the-counter market where transactions were registered off the stock exchanges.

Trading volume in 1976 totaled 5.3 billion shares on the New York Stock Exchange, where the greatest number of transactions are made. This was up 13 per cent over the 4.7 billion shares traded in 1975. Volume on the American Stock Exchange amounted to 648 million shares.

Economic Climate. Economic fundamentals and the 1976 election campaign left U.S. investors confused in the last half of the year. Although economic growth validated the business upturn that began in the second quarter of 1975, the rate of real economic growth slowed in the last three quarters of 1976. And the prospect of James Earl (Jimmy) Carter, Jr.'s presidency apparently raised some inves-

Stocks Soar in 1976

Dow Jones industrial averages

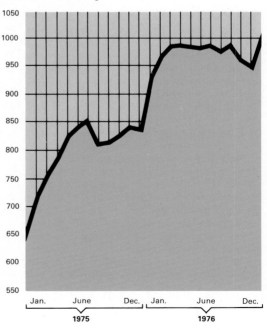

Monthly closings

Heavy trading got 1976 off to a brisk start as evidenced by the piles of paper left on the floor of the New York Stock Exchange in early January.

tors' fears of increased government spending, higher taxes, and renewed inflation.

Despite general concern about inflation, it continued to slow, reflecting slower real growth in the economy and general economic slack. Slower inflation in the United States and most other countries was the major factor in bringing interest rates down. Another factor was the drop in the U.S. federal government deficit compared with a year earlier. The government switched its fiscal year in 1976 to end on September 30, rather than on June 30 as in previous years. This resulted in an apparent reduction in the rate of government spending and eased the burden of financing the federal deficit.

New Stock Issues. Despite more favorable market conditions for borrowers, corporations introduced fewer new stock issues than is usual in an expansionary year. Instead, they rebuilt financial strength by relying on internal earnings. Corporations have relied mainly on bond financing for many years, a preference due to U.S. tax laws that permit interest on bonds to be deducted from income before taxes, whereas stock dividends are paid out of after-tax income. One significant exception was the giant American Telephone and Telegraph Company, which offered a record 12 million new shares of common stock for about $55 a share.

Stock Market Changes. The Securities and Exchange Commission (SEC) continued to push for a competitive and computerized national stock market. In June 1975, the SEC forced major stock exchanges to use a ticker tape that shows transactions both on and off the exchange. It sought rules to allow stock exchange member firms more freedom in executing transactions off the exchanges. Despite its earlier opposition, even the New York Stock Exchange endorsed the principle of a competitive national market, though it contested the SEC's threat to permit members to trade listed stocks off the exchanges. William M. Batten succeeded James J. Needham as New York Stock Exchange chairman on May 19.

Chemical Bank in New York City began offering stock-brokerage services to 19,000 checking-account customers at lower fees than are generally available. Investors paid a $30 annual fee with commissions of only $35 on any transaction up to 500 shares and $55 on transactions up to 1,000 shares.

Dean Witter & Company joined Merrill Lynch, Pierce, Fenner & Smith Incorporated in offering odd-lot brokerage services in 1976. Both brokers dealt in odd lots from their own inventories and did not charge extra fees for such orders.

Strong consumer interest was shown in municipal bond funds, which allowed the small investor to get in on a tax saving formerly available only to large investors. *William G. Dewald*

See also ECONOMICS.

SUAREZ GONZALEZ, ADOLFO (1932-   ), was sworn in as prime minister of Spain on July 5, 1976. The 43-year-old politician was the youngest head of a Spanish government in this century and one of the youngest in Spanish history. He was appointed by King Juan Carlos I, who assumed the throne on the death of General Francisco Franco in 1975. See SPAIN.

Suarez Gonzalez was born in Cebreros, a small Castilian town west of Madrid, on Sept. 25, 1932. After receiving a degree in law from the University of Salamanca, Suarez joined the Madrid Bar Association, where he held various administrative posts. In 1968, he joined the government as governor of Segovia province. Later, he became director-general of the state-run television network; eventually he became deputy secretary-general of a semi-political group, the National Movement. Suarez also maintained close links with Opus Dei, a Roman Catholic lay organization with considerable influence in Spain during the Franco regime.

In mid-1975, Suarez left government service to promote the Union of the Spanish People, a conservative political party that endorsed the cause of King Juan Carlos I. He was appointed prime minister while serving with the party.

Suarez is married and the father of two sons and three daughters. He lives in a quiet residential section in western Madrid. *Paul C. Tullier*

SUDAN. President Gaafar Muhammed Nimeiri on July 2, 1976, survived the third attempt — second in only 10 months — to overthrow him. A mixed force of African mercenaries, Sudanese tribesmen, and army deserters converged on Khartoum for a coup d'état timed to coincide with Nimeiri's return from a three-week visit to the United States, Great Britain, and France. Nimeiri escaped the first attack at Khartoum Airport and rallied government troops to counterattack. Public support for the coup failed to materialize, and the army put down the revolt in fierce fighting that caused some 700 casualties.

The rebel commander, a brigadier general who had been dismissed from service in 1974 for suspected disloyalty, was captured.

The state security court convicted him and 97 other persons of conspiracy with foreign powers to overthrow the regime. All were executed in August.

Nimeiri's Problems. Although Libya was implicated in the conspiracy, the real leaders were members of the National Front, created by a merger of the former opposition Umma Party and the outlawed Muslim Brotherhood. Both groups oppose Nimeiri for suspending parliamentary government and trying to build a one-party state. Death sentences were passed on August 18 at the trial in absentia of former Prime Minister Sadik al-Mahdi and former Finance Minister Sharif Hussein al-Hindi, leaders of the National Front.

Apart from his political difficulties, Nimeiri came under criticism for failure to delegate responsibility, for lack of interest in the problems of non-Arab southern Sudan, and for Sudan's continued economic shortcomings. He reorganized the government on August 26, giving up his posts as prime minister, defense minister, armed forces commander, and secretary-general of the one political party, the Sudan Socialist Union.

Economic Developments included the discovery by oil geologists on August 20 of natural gas deposits in the Red Sea. The Gulf Oil Corporation and Johns-Manville Corporation agreed in February to extract and process asbestos for export from the Angatara and Qala an-Nahl mines. Their joint production was expected to reach 66 million short tons (60 million metric tons) annually.

Other new projects completed were a dry-cell battery plant in Khartoum on February 9, a hemp factory at Abu Naameh on February 12, and the Chinese-built Hasahisa textile mill, which employs 1,700 workers, on June 8.

Outbreaks of a mysterious fever in southern Sudan and neighboring Zaire brought medical teams from the World Health Organization to the remote region in early October. The Sudan disease, similar to Marburg viral disease, killed more than 100 persons.   William Spencer

See also AFRICA (Facts in Brief Table).

SUPREME COURT OF THE UNITED STATES declared capital punishment as a penalty for murder constitutional in a historic ruling on July 2, 1976, setting the stage for the first executions of convicts in the United States since 1967. The moratorium on the death penalty resulted from a 1972 Supreme Court ruling that capital punishment had historically been imposed in a freakish and arbitrary manner and thus violated the Constitution's ban on "cruel and unusual punishment." But on July 2, a 7 to 2 majority in *Gregg v. Georgia* stated that new laws passed by several states since the 1972 ruling had removed that element of chance.

The Controlling Opinion in the death penalty cases was written by Justice Potter Stewart and joined by Justices John Paul Stevens and Lewis F. Powell. It affirmed the death verdict dealt Troy Gregg, convicted of robbing and murdering two men in 1973. The Georgia jury at Gregg's trial found the defendant guilty. In a separate hearing, they determined that one of 10 specific "aggravating circumstances" — he committed the murder for monetary gain — justified the death penalty.

Stewart argued that the requirement for special sentencing provisions in the Georgia law and similar safeguards in Texas and Florida statutes ensure that juries cannot wantonly or arbitrarily impose the death penalty in those states. However, the three justices joined William J. Brennan and Thurgood Marshall, who dissented from the main ruling, in striking down as "unduly harsh and unworkably rigid" new laws in North Carolina and Louisiana that made death mandatory upon conviction for certain crimes. An estimated 300 prisoners convicted under mandatory death statutes in 19 states were spared by the latter ruling.

The court refused to reconsider its July rulings at the start of its new term on October 4. This placed 324 convicts in 16 states with laws similar to Georgia's in immediate danger of death. However, clemency hearings and legal technicalities forestalled executions during 1976. Among the prime candidates for early execution was Gary Gilmore of Utah. His execution date was originally set for November 15, but was stayed three times by legal appeals. The appeals were made by opponents of the death penalty, not by Gilmore, who said he wanted to be executed. He had been convicted of murder and finally was executed on Jan. 17, 1977.

Support for Law Officers. The death penalty decision continued a recent Supreme Court trend toward strengthening the hand of law enforcement officials and prosecutors and trimming protections afforded criminal suspects by the court under the late Chief Justice Earl Warren. The court slashed back sharply on use of the writ of habeas corpus, under which convicts have challenged their state court convictions in federal courts. It also ruled that an individual's Fourth Amendment right to freedom from unreasonable search and seizure does not prevent tax investigators from scrutinizing his accountant and bank records, and it curtailed the use of the exclusionary rule that prevented police from introducing illegally obtained evidence at criminal trials.

Civil Rights. The nation's news media obtained a landmark victory in the ongoing battle known as "free press, fair trial" on June 30 when the court unanimously invalidated a gag order imposed by a judge in a 1975 Nebraska murder trial. Taken together, most observers believed, the opinions in *Nebraska Press Assn. v. Stuart* virtually barred all future gag orders.

The court moved to strengthen previous decisions liberalizing the availability of abortions and cracking down on the spread of allegedly obscene material. In two abortion cases decided on July 1, the court ruled that neither husbands nor parents of minors could legally veto a pregnant woman's decision to have an abortion. Detroit's use of zoning laws to disperse so-called "adult entertainment" establishments, such as bookstores and movie houses, was upheld in a 5 to 4 vote of the court announced on June 24, even though dissenters argued that much of the affected blue material was not legally obscene and should be constitutionally protected.

In two important race-relations cases, the court continued its general expansion of minority rights. The court held 7 to 2 on June 25 that private schools cannot exclude potential students solely on the grounds that they are black. In an 8 to 0 decision on April 20, the court ruled that the U.S. Department of Housing and Urban Development had unconstitutionally followed racial residency patterns in placing new public-housing projects in the Chicago area. This appeared to open the door to such projects in mostly white suburbs.

Other Cases. The court decided on January 30 that the major portions of the 1974 Federal Election Campaign Act were constitutional. The decision allowed public financing of the 1976 federal primary and general elections.

On June 24, by 5 to 4, the court ruled that federal wage and hours laws could not be imposed on state and local governments. The majority suggested that such imposition would destroy the principles of federalism, which apportion powers and responsibilities between federal and state governments.

A 7 to 1 decision on May 24 ruled that a Virginia statute prohibiting price advertising by pharmacists violated antitrust laws. The decision may well foretell similar rulings against advertising bans enforced by other professional groups, including lawyers, doctors, and architects.   David C. Beckwith

SURGERY. See MEDICINE.

SURINAM. See LATIN AMERICA; Section Five, SURINAM and PARAMARIBO.

SWAZILAND. See AFRICA.

SWEDEN. Europe's oldest Socialist government ended after 44 years in power on Sept. 19, 1976, when the Socialist Democratic Party lost a general election. The three opposition parties formed a coalition under Center Party leader Thorbjorn Falldin, a farmer, who took office on October 7. See FALLDIN, THORBJORN.

Falldin's promise to lead the country away from the nuclear age brought down Olof Palme, prime minister since 1969. Palme wanted Sweden to be the world's largest per capita consumer of nuclear power. Falldin told people that more nuclear power was not needed. He called for nuclear power plants already in operation to be dismantled. "The risks of cancer and genetic damage, which could affect generations for thousands of years to come, are too great for us even to consider journeying further into the atomic age," he said. But once in office, Falldin let the nuclear-power program continue.

The September vote gave the non-Socialist parties 180 seats in the single-chamber *Riksdag* (parliament). The Social Democrats and Communists together held 169 seats. The 90.4 per cent voter turnout included 18-year-olds for the first time.

Palme's Difficulties started in April when film director Ingmar Bergman went into temporary exile because, he said, he had been harassed by tax officials and police. Bergman announced on April 22 he would leave Sweden because anyone in his homeland could be attacked by a dictatorial state bureaucracy that "grows like a galloping cancer." He said he had a nervous breakdown after being interrogated on tax-evasion charges that were later dropped. Children's author Astrid Lindgren and actress Bibi Andersson also complained.

Full Employment. Sweden maintained nearly full employment despite deflationary pressure stemming from international recession. In July, the unemployment rate was only 1.3 per cent. The government hoped for economic growth of 6.5 per cent in 1976, led by a nearly 20 per cent increase in exports.

The Riksdag passed a law on June 2 to give employees the right to representation on company boards of directors. Effective on Jan. 1, 1977, the law applies to companies with more than 25 employees. It requires employers to consult unions before making production changes, purchasing new facilities, taking over other companies, or adopting measures that could affect employment.

Monetary Policy. A heavy influx of foreign currency in 1975 led foreign currency reserves to rise $1.3 billion to $3.1 billion at the beginning of 1976. This rise was a major factor in increasing the money supply by 12 per cent, which aided bank liquidity. King Carl XVI Gustaf was married to Silvia Sommerlath, a West German commoner, in Stockholm Cathedral on June 19.   Kenneth Brown

See also EUROPE (Facts in Brief Table).

Silvia Sommerlath, a West German commoner, smiles at her parents during her wedding to King Carl XVI Gustaf of Sweden in Stockholm on June 19.

SWIMMING. American men and East German women were the most impressive swimmers in 1976, winning almost all of the Olympic Games gold medals and breaking almost all of the world records. The individual stars were 20-year-old John Naber of Menlo Park, Calif., and 17-year-old Kornelia Ender of East Germany.

World records were broken often in the East German and the United States Olympic trials. They were broken or tied in 22 of the 26 Olympic events at Montreal, Canada. By year's end, world records had fallen in 13 of the 16 events for men, 14 of the 15 for women.

Of the 13 world records by men, 11 were set by Americans and 2 by foreigners who attended American colleges—Jonty Skinner of South Africa and the University of Alabama and David Wilkie of Scotland and the University of Miami in Florida. Of the 14 records by women, 12 were set by East Germans, 1 by a Russian, and 1 by the United States in the Olympic 400-meter free-style relay.

The American Women had expected to do better. Shirley Babashoff, 19, of Fountain Valley, Calif., had hoped for one or two individual gold medals. Instead, she won four silver, and her only gold came in a relay. She was overshadowed by Ender, who won four gold medals and one silver and broke world records in five events during the year, then retired.

Ender, like most of her teammates, was young and strapping, 5 feet 10 inches (178 centimeters) tall. The American women, perhaps out of frustration, said that they thought the East German women took muscle-building steroid drugs. Rod Strachan of Santa Ana, Calif., winner of the Olympic gold medal in the men's 400-meter individual medley, offered another reason for the success of the East German women: "It's kind of a status symbol for a male to be an athlete in the United States. A girl does not have that kind of respect. In East Germany, you're looked up to whether you're a girl or a boy."

Strachan and Naber helped the University of Southern California win the National Collegiate and Amateur Athletic Union indoor titles. Naber won every Olympic and American backstroke title and broke both the 100- and 200-meter world records. His 200-meter backstroke time of 1 minute 59.19 seconds marked the first breach of the 2-minute barrier.

Other outstanding American men included Brian Goodell, Jim Montgomery, Bruce Furniss, John Hencken, and Mike Bruner, all Olympic champions. The best divers were Phil Boggs of Colorado Springs, Colo., Jennifer Chandler of Lincoln, Ala., and Klaus Dibiasi of Italy, all Olympic champions, and Greg Louganis of El Cajon, Calif.   Frank Litsky

See also OLYMPIC GAMES.

SWITZERLAND held referendums in 1976 on worker participation in management, aid to poor nations, and the workweek. The voters on March 21 rejected both a governmental plan and a union proposal to give workers a greater part in industry-management decisions. On June 13, they vetoed a government proposal to grant an $80-million interest-free loan to the International Development Association, a United Nations agency that helps poor nations. Switzerland spends only 0.14 per cent of its gross national product on foreign aid.

In a third referendum, on December 5, Swiss voters turned down a proposal to shorten the workweek to 40 hours from the standard 44 to 50 hours. They also voted to keep until the end of 1978 the federal price-control office and to extend federal powers to limit the growth of credit.

The Federal Assembly on December 8 elected Minister of Justice Kurt Furgler to become president in 1977. The office is largely ceremonial, and a president can serve only one year at a time.

The government acted in April to stem the inflow of foreign bank notes, especially the Italian lira. The Swiss franc, in rising to new heights, had hurt Switzerland's exports and tourist industry. Incoming cash was limited to $7,900 per person every three months, and in June the central bank interest rate was cut to 2 per cent.   Kenneth Brown

See also EUROPE (Facts in Brief Table).

SYRIA. Massive intervention in the Lebanese civil war by Syrian forces shifted the balance in that struggle in favor of the Lebanese Christians late in 1976. Syria's action produced the most durable of many cease-fires and strengthened prospects for a settlement short of partition.

Although Syrian troops had entered Lebanon as early as April 9, the first major intervention was launched on May 31 when some 4,000 troops and 200 tanks crossed the Lebanese border. The advance met fierce resistance from Muslim leftists and the Palestine Liberation Organization. A cease-fire on June 21 found Syrian forces in effective control of half of Lebanon. The Syrians held their positions throughout the summer, as reinforcements brought their forces to 15,000 troops.

A New Offensive in late September forced the Palestinians from their strategic mountain strongholds and prompted new Arab summit conferences on Lebanon in Riyadh, Saudi Arabia, in late October. Arab leaders agreed there on a new cease-fire to be enforced by an Arab peacekeeping force effectively dominated by Syria's forces, now about 30,000 strong. By mid-November, the Syrian occupation of Lebanon was complete.

President Hafiz al-Asad's Lebanese policy received strong support at home. But the heavy maintenance cost of the intervention – estimated at $2 million per day – dealt a severe blow to the economy. The strain was compounded by the presence of 300,000 Lebanese refugees in Syria.

Economic Prospects. Developments before the Lebanese involvement had indicated a brighter future for Syria. Deposits of uranium estimated at 110-million short tons (100 million metric tons) were discovered on February 6 alongside existing phosphate deposits. A new oil field was discovered at Habari on March 31, and the Alyan oil field, with a capacity of 10,000 barrels per day, went into production on May 23. A record wheat crop produced 2.2 million short tons (2 million metric tons), and cotton and textile exports were expected to bring in $250 million.

The budget announced on April 23 envisaged expenditures at $4.5 billion, 63 per cent covered by locally raised capital and foreign loans. The government even announced the start of a new five-year plan in May, but this was later delayed, and budgetary expenditures were reduced to $3 billion.

Aside from the cost of the Lebanese expedition, there were other negative developments. Iraq cut off oil exports through Syria in a dispute over transit fees; and delays in the delivery of $300 million in aid from Saudi Arabia and Kuwait, who opposed Syria's Lebanon policy, suggested a deficit rivaling 1975's $5 billion.   William Spencer

See also ASAD, HAFIZ AL-; LEBANON; MIDDLE EAST (Facts in Brief Table).

TAIWAN built up both its economy and its military strength in 1976 for the apparently endless confrontation with the Communist regime in the People's Republic of China. A new six-year economic development plan was initiated that emphasized heavy industry and capital-intensive industries – those requiring great outlays of money – instead of the labor-intensive ones that had provided the basis for Taiwan's industrialization. The new emphasis was intended to reduce Taiwan's vulnerability to world economic fluctuations. But dependence on imported oil and other raw materials, and the need to sell exports in order to pay for them, made self-sufficiency impossible.

The plan was intended to increase the gross domestic product – the gross national product minus net payments on foreign investments – 7.5 per cent a year. But figures released on October 1 indicated this target would not be met for 1976.

Defense Plans. Finance Minister Walter H. Fei announced on October 16 that $1.5 billion, 51 per cent of the fiscal 1977 budget, would be spent for defense. Questions arose about Taiwan's efforts to increase its military strength. A controversy over the U.S. training of Taiwanese engineers in inertial-guidance systems at the Massachusetts Institute of Technology resulted in the school's canceling the training program after conceding that it "could have military implications." Taiwan denied

Taiwan's athletes wait in vain in the Detroit airport for permission to compete in Olympic Games in Montreal as the Republic of China.

Olympic participants. Canada later said it would accept the 42 Taiwanese athletes if they did not use a team designation that included the word "China" and did not display the Nationalist Chinese flag. Taiwan, however, refused to accept such a compromise, and its athletes returned home.

The U.S. and China. Premier Chiang Ching-kuo talked more openly than ever before of Taiwan's fears that the Chinese Communists would manage to drive a wedge between his country and the United States. Both the United States and Taiwan, he said, "will benefit from their alliance; each would suffer from a division." The change of administrations in Washington caused some concern in Taiwan. The death in September of Mao Tse-tung, the Communist leader who drove the Nationalists to Taiwan in 1949, did not seem to open any immediate prospects for ending the hostility between Peking and Taipei. See CHINA, PEOPLE'S REPUBLIC OF (Close-Up).

The Kuomintang, the political organization that controls Nationalist China, held its first party congress since 1969 in November. It set basic policy lines, selected a new Central Committee, and made some leadership changes that reflected the advance of a younger generation under Chiang, who was elected head of the party.　　Henry S. Bradsher

See also ASIA (Facts in Brief Table); OLYMPIC GAMES.

reports that it was secretly reprocessing used uranium fuel from its four nuclear power plants in order to obtain material to make atomic bombs.

Olympic Withdrawal. Taiwan withdrew from the 1976 Olympic Games on July 16 because the Canadian government, host for the games, would not permit its team to compete as the Republic of China. Canada, which has full diplomatic relations with the People's Republic of China, said it must compete as Taiwan.

The Canadian action brought protests from many world leaders. President Gerald R. Ford, on July 12, sent a telegram to Philip O. Krumm, head of the U.S. Olympic Committee, saying the Canadian government's stand and the Olympic executive board's move to bar Taiwan was "a bad decision and a bad precedent, if it is upheld." Ford told Krumm that he "deplored the injection of politics into the Olympic athletic competition." International Olympic Committee President Lord Killanin also protested Canada's decision. He said it was "in complete conflict" with the Olympic rules and principles forbidding discrimination on grounds of race, religion, or political affiliation.

The Canadian decision was made under prodding from Peking, according to Allen J. MacEachen, secretary of state for external affairs in Canada. He said the Peking government had formally requested that Canada deny entry to all Taiwanese

TANZANIA. The Chinese-built Tanzam Railroad linking Tanzania and Zambia was formally turned over to the two governments by the People's Republic of China on July 14, 1976. The railroad, financed by the Chinese at a cost of about $400-million, was built under a reciprocal trade and cultural exchange agreement signed in 1969.

Tanzania triggered an international incident on July 9 by being the first African country to announce it would not attend the Olympic Games in Montreal, Canada. Tanzania maintained it was complying with an Organization of African Unity resolution that urged all Africans to boycott the games if New Zealand was represented, because a New Zealand rugby team was playing in South Africa. By July 21, about 30 other nations had joined Tanzania in the boycott. See NEW ZEALAND; OLYMPIC GAMES.

U.S. Secretary of State Henry A. Kissinger visited Tanzania in April to confer with President Julius K. Nyerere. U.S.-Tanzanian relations had deteriorated because of Nyerere's support of the Russian-backed nationalist movement in Angola. A second source of friction was a Tanzanian vote in the United Nations (UN) General Assembly equating Zionism with racism. Earlier, the United States had canceled all development-aid loans to Tanzania because of the UN vote.　　Paul C. Tullier

See also AFRICA (Facts in Brief Table).

TAXATION. President Gerald R. Ford signed the United States first major tax reform legislation since 1969 into law on Oct. 4, 1976. For more than 18 months, congressional committees studied various proposals for reform of the 40,000-page federal tax code before this legislation was made final. Although it was not a comprehensive overhaul of the nation's tax structure, the 1976 legislation filled 1,000 pages and included some major new provisions for corporations and individuals.

The act extended the personal and corporate income tax cuts made in 1975 through fiscal 1977 (Oct. 1, 1976, to Sept. 30, 1977); raised the taxes of upper-income taxpayers by increasing the minimum tax on some so-called preference incomes to 15 per cent; set new limits on tax "shelters"; and revised estate and gift taxes. Allowances for deductible expenses for child care when the child's mother works were also increased.

The full impact that will be made by some of the changes in the 1976 act will not be felt for five years, when the net federal revenue increases will total an estimated $984 million. The act will add an estimated $1.6 billion to federal tax receipts in fiscal 1977. Over a five-year period, the taxes paid by railroads, airlines, shipping firms, insurance companies, and firms with high pollution-control costs will be reduced.

"I have a marvelous machine that takes a simple thing and makes it complicated and unintelligible. I call it Congress."

President Ford hailed the act as "sound, positive, and long overdue," though he did not approve of all its provisions. A tax reform bill had been approved by the House of Representatives in December 1975, but the Senate version of that bill was not approved. Critics said it was a piecemeal travesty of tax reform that catered to special interests and would have cost the federal government an estimated $300 million a year in lost revenue.

Congress extended the temporary cuts on tax withholding rates twice during 1976 — in June and September — before the tax reform bill of 1976 was finally approved.

Federal Tax Collections brought in a total of $302.5 billion in fiscal 1976. Individual income and employment taxes totaled $233.2 billion; corporation income taxes, $46.8 billion; estate and gift taxes, $5.3 billion; and excise taxes, $17.3 billion.

The Internal Revenue Service (IRS) released a report on 1974 tax payments on May 5. According to the report, 244 Americans with adjusted gross incomes of over $200,000 in 1974 paid no federal income tax in that year. Five of these nontaxpayers had 1974 incomes of more than $1 million. The number and proportion of Americans with high incomes who paid no federal taxes rose in 1974.

IRS Audits. In fiscal 1976, the IRS completed 2.04 million individual tax return audits, compared with 3.2 million in 1975. Since there were a total of 81.3 million individual tax returns filed in 1975, this means that only 4 per cent — or 1 in 25 persons — had a chance of being audited that year. For individuals reporting adjusted gross incomes of $30,000 or more from professional, business, or farm sources, however, the audit figure was 9.3 per cent. And for those individuals who reported having adjusted gross incomes of $50,000 or more, the audit figure was 12.6 per cent.

In the aftermath of the Watergate scandal, American taxpayers were becoming aware of the fact that the audit functions of the IRS could be used illegally to frighten or penalize American taxpayers for political reasons. The Senate Select Committee on Intelligence revealed in April that the IRS, between 1969 and 1973, created intelligence files on more than 11,000 individuals and groups and initiated tax investigations for political reasons. On May 11, IRS Commissioner Donald C. Alexander told the House Subcommittee on Government that in his opinion it was neither necessary nor desirable for the IRS to inform the individuals investigated that their tax returns had been audited because of their political views. At hearings of the Privacy Protection Study Commission on March 11 in Washington, D.C., Alexander revealed that the tax returns of 6,704 individuals had been turned over to the Department of Justice in 1975 for use in criminal, but not tax-related, cases.

Alexander announced in November that taxpayers would find tax form 1040 – the so-called "short form" – more difficult to work with in 1977 because taxpayers will have to compute taxable income and taxes using arithmetical skills.

State and Local Taxes. In fiscal 1976, state tax collections totaled $89.3 billion, up 11.3 per cent over fiscal 1975. During the same period, local taxes totaled about $66.6 billion, 25.4 per cent less than total state tax collections. Local taxes totaled approximately $61.3 billion in fiscal 1975.

Sales and gross-receipts taxes represented the largest source of state tax revenue in fiscal 1976, $47.4 billion, or 53.1 per cent of all state tax revenues. All 50 states collected some form of sales and gross receipts tax. Forty-four states collected a total of $21.5 billion in individual income taxes.

Eight states collected just over half of all state tax revenue in fiscal 1976. California again collected the most tax revenue, $10.8 billion. New York again was second with $9.8 billion, followed in order by Pennsylvania, Illinois, Texas, Michigan, Ohio, and Florida.

The Organization for Economic Cooperation and Development revealed that the Dutch, Swedes, and Norwegians, in that order, are the most highly taxed people in the industrialized countries. These countries take roughly half of the national wealth in taxes.　　　　Carol L. Thompson

TELEVISION gave a spectacular daylong 200th birthday party for the United States on July 4, 1976. The worldwide coverage, most of it live, roamed from Guam to the Grand Canyon in Arizona to London's River Thames to "Operation Sail" and the Tall Ships in New York Harbor. This parade of stately windjammers was the most dazzling sight of all.

Television Series. Campy nostalgia ruled prime-time TV series in 1976. The two most consistently top-rated shows were proletarian hymns of praise to the 1950's – "Happy Days," with new teen idol Henry Winkler as the Fonz, a ducktailed, street-tough motorcyclist; and "Laverne and Shirley," a "Happy Days" spin-off about two bottle cappers in a Milwaukee, Wis., brewery.

Also in the top 10 during the year were two science-fiction series – "The Six-Million-Dollar Man" and its spin-off mate "The Bionic Woman" – and a new fall entry, "Charlie's Angels," featuring three glamorous models as implausible special agents.

"All in the Family," saved perhaps by its blue-collar aura, was the only irreverent comedy still in the top 10 by fall. However, relevancy and daring were still alive and well outside of prime time. "Mary Hartman, Mary Hartman," a syndicated soap opera spoof with Louise Lasser as an Angst-

Challenger Jimmy Carter and President Ford staged three televised debates during the 1976 presidential campaign, the first such meetings since 1960.

ridden housewife, was the most talked-about series of 1976. The National Broadcasting Company's (NBC) "Saturday Night," a live, sometimes savagely tasteless, late-evening satirical revue, was a multi-Emmy winner.

Mini-series, long a mainstay of public television, were the greatest innovations in commercial programming. "Rich Man, Poor Man," a $4.5-million, 12-hour adaptation of Irwin Shaw's novel, started the trend in January. It was in the top 10 every week it ran. "Best Sellers" debuted in the fall with a 10-part version of Taylor Caldwell's *Captains and the Kings.* "Family" and "Executive Suite," other new saga-series, were not limited in episodes but used the continuing-story technique.

Nevertheless, the highest-quality mini-series were still on public television. They included dramatizations of Gustave Flaubert's *Madame Bovary* and W. Somerset Maugham's *Cakes and Ale,* and the $6-million, Emmy-winning "Adams Chronicles," highest-rated series in the history of the Corporation for Public Broadcasting.

Special Programs. The many impressive Public Broadcasting Service (PBS) specials included *Harry S. Truman: Plain Speaking;* Julie Harris in *The Last of Mrs. Lincoln; Six Hundred Millennia: China's History Unearthed;* Sir Alec Guinness in *Caesar and Cleopatra; The Great Apes* and *The Animals*

Nobody Loved, presented by the National Geographic Society; *Dying,* a powerful study of four terminal patients; "Visions," a series featuring works of new playwrights; and the first live telecast of a full-length ballet—the three-hour *Swan Lake* danced by the American Ballet Theater on the "Live from Lincoln Center" series.

Stand-out commercial television specials during the year included *Eleanor and Franklin,* in which Jane Alexander was superb as Eleanor Roosevelt; Susan Clark's Emmy-winning performance as Babe Zaharias in *Babe;* NBC's 4½-hour 50th-anniversary show; *The Lindbergh Kidnapping Case; Judge Horton and the Scottsboro Boys;* and the 1939 film classic *Gone with the Wind.*

The most exciting TV sports events were the Winter and Summer Olympic Games. An estimated 65 million viewers watched the Muhammad Ali-Richard Dunn fight from Munich, West Germany, on May 25.

Presidential Debates. Highlighting TV's blitz coverage of the presidential election campaign were the debates by President Gerald R. Ford and challenger James Earl (Jimmy) Carter, Jr., the first since 1960, and the first debate in history between vice-presidential candidates. Each debate was carried live by the three major networks and via delayed broadcast by PBS.

Kate Jackson, Farrah Fawcett-Majors, and Jaclyn Smith, from left, are "Charlie's Angels." The new series was one of the big TV hits of 1976.

Saga of The Soaps

The soap opera, once considered pablum for the bored housewife, invalid, or slightly simple-minded, has come into its own. More than 20 million persons in the United States—including members of Congress, Ivy League college students, and at least one U.S. Supreme Court justice, Thurgood Marshall—watched television soap operas each week in 1976.

Anthropologists trace the roots of modern soap opera to the 19th-century novel. Charles Dickens, Henry James, Anthony Trollope, and Fyodor Dostoevsky wrote many of their classics in serial form. If sales were slow for the early episodes, the author would alter the plot, just as today's TV soap-opera writers respond to low ratings by changing their story line.

The first motion-picture serial was *The Adventures of Kathlyn* in 1913, followed by *Dolly of the Dailies* and, most famous of all, *The Perils of Pauline,* starring Pearl White. Then, as now, the cliffhanger technique of ending each episode created total involvement between audience and story. White, a former trapeze artist, performed all her own stunts, literally dangling from the edge of a cliff at the end of many episodes.

Purists define the soap opera as a Monday-through-Friday daytime serial, involving many troubled characters in a variety of continuing crises, and usually sponsored by a household-products manufacturer.

There were sporadic attempts at producing soap operas in the 1920s, but the first hit radio serial was "Today's Children," created in 1932 by Irna Phillips, queen of the sudsers. Throughout the 1930s and 1940s, soap operas dominated daytime network radio.

In 1958, radio networks aired 60 hours of soap operas a week. Two years later, the last daytime radio serial went off the air and soap opera became exclusively TV fare. Television's first attempt at soap opera—"A Woman to Remember" in 1947—was a flop, as was "The First Hundred Years" in 1950. Finally, in 1951, two serials—"Search for Tomorrow" and "Love of Life"—made the audience connection.

"Rich Man, Poor Man"

In 1976, the television networks carried 14 daytime soap operas, totaling 45 hours each week. Addicts who miss episodes can catch up on the daily adventures through the monthly *Daytime Serial Newsletter,* which provides plot summaries.

Network soap operas pioneered so-called "adult" themes on television. Long before prime-time shows discovered relevancy, soap operas were venturing to explore venereal disease, abortion, incest, homosexuality, and drugs.

The soap-opera influence has spilled over into other areas of programming. Two new prime-time series in the fall were pure soap opera—"Executive Suite" and "Rich Man, Poor Man II." They followed in the footsteps of such successful mini-sagas as the first "Rich Man, Poor Man," "Upstairs, Downstairs," and "Captains and the Kings," which had a quality-suds flavor.

The most outrageous soap opera was "Mary Hartman, Mary Hartman," Norman Lear's spoof of the genre. The series was syndicated in both daytime and late-night slots on 125 TV stations and drew larger audiences than network competition in some cities.

The New York Times Magazine described "Mary Hartman" as a "cultural signpost." The series was studied at Yale University as "an American house of Atreus." It was also the subject of a University of California extension course.

Some psychiatrists use soap opera as a therapeutic tool because inarticulate patients frequently relate to serial characters with similar problems. Mary Hartman herself, while recuperating from a nervous breakdown in a psychiatric clinic, was encouraged to spend much of her time watching TV soap operas.

Many sociologists believe that soap operas, by being only a slightly exaggerated reflection of American culture, act as a cathartic experience for viewers, thereby establishing what *Time* magazine called "a symbiosis between audience and show." Others simply conclude that everybody loves a good story.   June Bundy Csida

Antiviolence Moves. A *TV Guide* poll showed that at least 80 per cent of the public favored the family-viewing-time rule, whereby network programs aired between 8 P.M. and 9 P.M. in the East (7 P.M. to 8 P.M. in the Central Time Zone) must be suitable for family audiences. Moreover, 47 per cent of those polled advocated less TV violence and sex throughout the entire evening. Violence, opposed by 72 per cent, was deemed even more objectionable than sex. But by the end of the 1975-1976 season, 22 out of 27 family-hour series had been axed, and many program producers considered the family-viewing policy a flop.

Federal District Judge Warren J. Ferguson of Los Angeles ruled the family-hour policy unconstitutional on November 3. The suit had been brought by writers, directors, and actors who felt the policy produced undue restraint on creativity. Ferguson said the policy violated First Amendment guarantees of free speech and had been accepted only under pressure from Federal Communications Commission (FCC) chairman Richard E. Wiley, thus constituting government censorship. However, the judge said the networks could continue the policy on their own.

In addition to the continuing public outcry against TV violence, the American Medical Association and several major advertising agencies and TV sponsors registered protests against video mayhem. On July 29, the National Citizens Committee for Better Broadcasting released a list of the 10 most violent and 10 least violent TV shows, including the names of their sponsors. There was a noticeable reduction of prime-time violence when the new season started in the fall.

Congress Acts. On October 1, Congress passed the first revision of copyright law since 1909. Among other provisions, the bill decrees that cable TV and public television broadcasters must now pay copyright royalties for the first time. It specifically prohibits cable-TV operators from substituting their own commercials on imported broadcast signals.

Congress also passed a $330-million-plus bill funding the Corporation for Public Broadcasting under a matching plan through 1979. In February, underwriting of PBS programs by corporations, endowments, and foundations totaled $19-million, 58 per cent above the previous season.

A study released by the House Oversight and Investigations Subcommittee in early October accused the FCC of favoring the interests of broadcasters over the general public, neglecting its license-renewal responsibilities, and not giving sufficient attention to the development potential of UHF and cable TV.

Network Moves. The Westinghouse Broadcasting Company (Group W) petitioned the FCC in September to undertake a comprehensive re-examination of the networks' relationship with their affiliates. Pending an investigation, Group W demanded an immediate freeze on the expansion of network programs into time occupied by affiliate shows. The move apparently forestalled a yearlong campaign by the networks to expand their 30-minute national news shows to an hour. Westinghouse estimated its stations would lose more than $5-million in sales if the networks went to hourlong news programs.

In a surprise network executive shuffle, Arthur K. Taylor resigned as president of the Columbia Broadcasting System (CBS) on October 13. He was succeeded by John D. Backe, vice-president and head of the CBS Publishing Group. In June, Barbara Walters left NBC's "Today" show to become TV's first network news anchorwoman for the American Broadcasting Company. She started on October 4 at an annual salary of $1 million (see WALTERS, BARBARA).

The Department of Justice on November 18 filed a proposed consent judgment to settle its long-pending civil antitrust case against NBC. The department filed suit against all three networks in April 1972, charging monopoly of TV program production. Under the judgment, NBC agreed to a variety of restrictions on production of entertainment shows for the next 10 years.   June Bundy Csida

TENNESSEE. See STATE GOVERNMENT.

TENNIS. Chris Evert of Fort Lauderdale, Fla.; Bjorn Borg of Sweden; and Jimmy Connors of Belleville, Ill., were the major winners on the $11-million international tennis circuit in 1976. However, their accomplishments were almost overshadowed by international politics and the controversies surrounding Ilie Nastase of Romania and Renee Richards of La Jolla, Calif.

Evert defeated Evonne Goolagong of Australia in the finals of the world's two most important championships—6-4, 4-6, 8-6 in the All-England championships from June 18 to July 3 at Wimbledon and 6-3, 6-0 in the United States Open on September 11 at Forest Hills, N.Y. In late October, at age 21 and a pro for four years, Evert became the first woman athlete to reach $1 million in career earnings. Playing for the Phoenix Racquets, she was voted Woman Rookie of the Year and Most Valuable Player in the World Team Tennis league.

Borg and Connors. The 20-year-old Borg, impassive and methodical, won the Wimbledon title with a 6-4, 6-2, 9-7 triumph over Nastase to become the youngest champion in 45 years. He also won the World Championship Tennis final by beating Guillermo Vilas of Argentina in May, and his third straight United States professional title by besting Harold Solomon of Silver Spring, Md., in Brookline, Mass., in August. Including endorsements, Borg earned a total of about $1 million for the year.

Connors won the United States Open and the $30,000 prize on September 12 by defeating Borg, 6-4, 3-6, 7-6, 6-4, in a superb, thrilling final that lasted 3 hours 10 minutes. During the year, Connors won more than $600,000, the most by any tennis player in one year.

The highest purses in history were $415,000 at Forest Hills and the $315,480 at Wimbledon. At Forest Hills, the winning man and woman received $40,000 each. At Wimbledon, the winning man collected $22,250, the winning woman $17,700. The women players voted to boycott Wimbledon in 1977 and set up a rival tournament unless the prize money they received equals that for the men. But they later agreed to accept purses equal to 80 per cent of the men's total prize money.

Political Problems struck the Federation Cup competition for women and the Davis Cup for men. Russia, Czechoslovakia, and Hungary withdrew from the Federation Cup because South Africa and Rhodesia, despite their racial policies, were allowed to play. The United States beat Australia, 2-1, in the final on August 29 in Philadelphia.

The Davis Cup has become embroiled in international politics, mainly because of South Africa's policy of *apartheid* (racial separation). India's team in 1974 refused to play against South Africa; Colombia and Mexico did the same in 1975. The United States Tennis Association warned in April 1976 that it would withdraw from the Davis Cup competition if South Africa were expelled or defaulting nations were not punished. The United States withdrew on July 1 but returned on July 7.

Russia, which disliked Chile's government, defaulted in the Davis Cup semifinals and was banned from Davis Cup competition. Chile advanced to the finals against Italy, but Italy won its first Davis Cup title on December 18.

Nastase, a Wimbledon finalist and Forest Hills semifinalist, was often outrageous. He harangued and swore at officials and gestured indecently at opponents, officials, and spectators. He was suspended and fined, and he also defaulted, but nothing tempered him.

Renee Richards was Richard Raskind, a New York City ophthalmologist and a ranked player in the men's-35 division, until undergoing a sex-change operation in 1975. After winning a California women's tournament in 1976, Richards entered the $60,000 Tennis Week Open in South Orange, N.J., in August. She advanced to the semifinals after many women players had withdrawn in protest to her presence. When she tried to play in the U.S. Open at Forest Hills, tournament officials quickly introduced a chromosome sex test for all women players. Richards refused to take the test, saying it was unfair.   Frank Litsky

TEXAS. See DALLAS-FORT WORTH; HOUSTON; STATE GOVERNMENT.

THAILAND. The armed forces in Thailand seized power on Oct. 6, 1976. An Administrative Reform Committee of military leaders, headed by Admiral Sangad Chaloryu, ousted the parliamentary government of Prime Minister M. R. Seni Pramot. The committee named a civilian, Thanin Kraiwichian, prime minister to rule under the supervision of the reform committee.

The armed forces had controlled Thailand from the 1930s until 1973, when the last military dictator, Thanom Kittikachorn, resigned after violent student riots in Bangkok. Sanya Dharmasakti then became premier. Parliamentary democracy in 1975 established first Seni and then his brother Khukrit Pramot as prime ministers heading coalition governments. Khukrit resigned on Jan. 12, 1976, after only 10 months in office. He said he could not govern because of left wing pressure to nationalize businesses and banks, legalize the Communist Party, and rush into land reforms.

Violence and Riots. A violent election campaign followed Khukrit's resignation. At least eight leftist leaders were murdered by rightists. Seni's Democratic Party won a strong plurality in April 4 voting, and on April 20 he became prime minister.

Amid the rising tension and polarization between the political right and left in Bangkok, and divisions within the armed forces on whether to try to regain power, Thanom returned from exile on September 19 to enter a Buddhist monastery. Leftist students demonstrated against his presence in Bangkok. This led to a savage attack on demonstrators at Thammasat University on October 6 by right wing groups and heavily armed police. Some 30 students were shot, lynched, or burned to death.

The reform committee then announced its takeover in order to "forestall a Communist plot backed by the Vietnamese." Thanin, a right-wing intellectual with little political experience, was appointed prime minister on October 8. He announced that Thailand would be run for four years by an appointed legislature. Then elections would be phased in gradually, with a fully elected government possible after 16 years.

A New Constitution, decreed on October 22, gave the prime minister the power "to order any action." But his actions required authorization by the reform committee, which became known as the Prime Minister's Advisory Council.

A number of leftists fled from Bangkok to escape arrest. Many joined the Communist-led guerrilla army that had long conducted raids in Thailand with Vietnamese assistance, raising the possibility that the guerrilla force would be greatly expanded.

The last of 48,000 U.S. military men stationed in Thailand left on July 20. About 250 American military advisers remained, and U.S. planes continued to use a Thai air base.   Henry S. Bradsher

See also ASIA (Facts in Brief Table).

THEATER

The musical, an invention of the American theater, held the spotlight in the 1976 Bicentennial observance. A record number of new and old musicals combined song, dance, and story to entertain Broadway audiences. In mid-November, an avid theatergoer could choose from among 17 offerings.

While *A Chorus Line* continued to be the most popular musical, a revival of *Threepenny Opera* by Bertolt Brecht and Kurt Weill, which opened in May 1976, was judged by many as the most artistic.

Using stylized movement and decor, director Richard Foreman of the New York Shakespeare Festival imaginatively conveyed the authors' cynical picture of corruption and exploitation. The play is set in Victorian London but has strong implications for pre-World War II Germany. Raul Julia as Mack the Knife and Ellen Greene as Jenny headed an impressive cast of beggars, criminals, and street-walkers moving like marionettes controlled by a powerful few. The production drew comparisons to

George Gershwin's classic American opera, *Porgy and Bess,* returned to Broadway in a smashing revival staged by the Houston Grand Opera.

another musical, *Chicago,* a popular exposé of corruption in the courts of the 1920s, brilliantly interpreted by director Bob Fosse in terms of Brecht's satirical cabaret theater. The longest-running musical was *Grease,* in its fifth year of re-creating the rock music, dances, and mores of the 1950s.

New Musicals included *Pacific Overtures,* which used features of Japanese Kabuki and Bunraku theaters to tell the story of the Westernization of that country. *Bubbling Brown Sugar* depicted the important contributions of black artists to the development of American musical theater. An all-black version of *Guys and Dolls* demonstrated that the Frank Loesser musical set in Damon Runyon's New York City was a stage classic. Another classic, *My*

Fair Lady, was applauded when its revival appeared just 20 years after its opening in 1956.

George Gershwin's *Porgy and Bess* was revived in an impressive production by the Houston Grand Opera. Its pre-Broadway tour included performances in the Filene Theater at Wolf Trap Farm Park in Vienna, Va., the first U.S. National Park devoted to the performing arts. On a stage of native wood open on three sides to the surrounding park, the talented artists of *Porgy and Bess* impressively portrayed the moving story of the crippled Porgy and the people of Catfish Row in Charleston, S.C. Wolf Trap also presented plays for young audiences at the Children's Theater in the Woods. Virginia folk tales were dramatized on a stage made from a single slab of wood, with a theater shell made of wood bark.

Outdoor Music Dramas were a popular Bicentennial attraction for summer tourists. One of the longest running spectacles is *The Lost Colony,* at Fort Raleigh, near Manteo, N.C. Staged on the spot where Sir Walter Raleigh's colonists landed in 1587, the Paul Green work combines music, dance, and drama to tell of the people of this vanished colony. The show opened in 1937.

New Plays and Playwrights brought vitality to the Broadway scene. *For Colored Girls Who Have Considered Suicide When the Rainbow Is Enuf* is an imaginative saga by Ntozake Shange. Using song, dance, verse, and vignette, seven young black women tell of their experiences, their exploitation, and their achievement of self-realization.

Milan Stitt's first play, *The Runner Stumbles,* arrived on Broadway from the Hartman Theatre in Stamford, Conn. In Austin Pendleton, the play found a skilled director who achieved and sustained tension that was both dramatic and intellectual as the action moved back and forth in time. It explored the conflicts of a priest accused of murdering a nun. David Rabe's final play in his trilogy about the Vietnam War was *Streamers,* a production that originated at the Long Wharf Theatre in New Haven, Conn. The word *streamer* is an Army term for a parachute that fails to open. Using streamers as a metaphor for the chances people take, Rabe focuses on the effects of violence in American society.

The Long Wharf also produced Arthur Miller's new play, *The Archbishop's Ceiling,* which opened in December. The author describes the theme of his new work as "what the soul does under the impact of immense power, how it makes accommodations, and how it transcends the power."

Foreign Stages contributed important works to the theater scene. Harold Pinter's *No Man's Land,* presented by Great Britain's National Theatre, starred Sir John Gielgud and Sir Ralph Richardson in brilliant portrayals of two old men, one rich, one poor. They meet in a pub, go to the rich man's home, and reminisce. Their memories are a "no

Great Britain's massive new National Theatre, which stands near Waterloo Bridge on the River Thames in London, has three theaters.

George Grizzard, Barbara Barrie, and Jack Weston enact the successive visitors in the suite from New York City, Philadelphia, London, and Chicago.

American Classics Revivals included the Phoenix Repertory Theatre's double bill, Tennessee Williams' *27 Wagons Full of Cotton*, and Arthur Miller's *A Memory of Two Mondays*. The first play deals with the rivalry and revenge of rural Southern neighbors, the second with a young boy's impressions of warehouse workers in New York City in the 1930s. Eugene O'Neill's *Long Day's Journey into Night* appeared at the John F. Kennedy Center for the Performing Arts in Washington, D.C., the Brooklyn Academy of Music in New York, and the Goodman Memorial Theatre in Chicago.

Shakespeare's plays were widely performed in 1976. The Royal Shakespeare Company brought a vivid production of *Henry V* to the Brooklyn Academy of Music, with Alan Howard portraying a nonheroic Henry who is deliberately playing the role of hero.

Canada's Stratford Festival began its 23rd season in June with productions of *Hamlet* and William Congreve's *The Way of the World*. Alice Griffin

See also AWARDS AND PRIZES (Arts Awards).

TIMOR. See ASIA; INDONESIA.

TOGO. See AFRICA.

TORNADO. See DISASTERS; WEATHER.

TOYS. See GAMES, MODELS, AND TOYS.

TRACK AND FIELD. The outstanding track and field athletes of 1976 included Olympic decathlon champion Bruce Jenner of San Jose, Calif., and three runners—Alberto Juantorena of Cuba, Lasse Viren of Finland, and Tatiana Kazankina of Russia. All broke world records in the Olympic Games at Montreal, Canada.

The 26-year-old Jenner grew up in Mount Kisco, N.Y., and Sandy Hook, Conn. He lived and trained in San Jose because many of the world's best athletes trained there. "When I train with someone like Al Feuerbach, who is 20 feet better than I am, it makes me do better," he said.

Jenner's System Worked. He had been the world's best decathlon athlete since the 1972 Olympics; he broke the world record for hand timing in August 1975 and June 1976; and he broke the world record for automatic timing in the Olympics. His winning score of 8,618 points for the 10 events bettered the automatic-timed record by 164 points.

It was a fitting finale to track for Jenner, a handsome, vibrant, and demonstrative man. He wanted to be an entertainment star, and the offers started before he left Montreal.

Everyone knew Juantorena was a potential Olympic champion at 400 meters. Few considered him at 800 meters because he had seldom run that distance before the spring of 1976. He ran it so well that he decided to run both races in the Olympics, a

man's land," which "never grows older, but . . . remains forever, icy and silent," like death itself. Two controversial plays from England premièred in Washington, D.C. *Dirty Linen* by Tom Stoppard opened at the West End Theater and was so popular it was transferred to the larger Eisenhower Theater. Set in a committee room of Great Britain's House of Commons, it centers upon an inquiry into the sexual practices of members of Parliament. It possibly refers to the Profumo case of the early 1960s, but viewers noted a relationship to 1976 sex scandals among members of the U.S. Congress. Edward Bond's *The Fool*, offered by the Folger Theatre Group, portrayed the 19th-century English poet John Clare from youthful revolt to final madness.

French writer Marguerite Duras' *Days in the Trees* brought Mildred Dunnock a play worthy of her talents. With great sensitivity, she played a mother who returns to Paris from Vietnam to see her son, with whom she is in conflict. Czechoslovak playwright Pavel Kohout treats the madness of an actor playing the role of Hamlet in *Poor Murderer*. Laurence Luckinbill won praise as the actor who believes he has actually killed Polonius.

Neil Simon again displayed his talent for farce. *California Suite* is a quartet of short plays about couples in a Hollywood hotel suite who are involved in minor crises brought on by divorce, infidelity, incompatibility, and tennis. Tammy Grimes, double never before achieved. With strength that seemed limitless, he won both.

There was no doubt that Viren could win both the Olympic 5,000 and 10,000 meters, because he had done it in the 1972 Olympics. He did it again at Montreal with astounding last-lap speed.

Kazankina, 24 years old and slight, had never won anything of note until she won the 800- and 1,500-meter Olympic gold medals, with a world record in the 800 to go with her month-old world record in the 1,500.

John Walker of New Zealand dominated the men's 1,500-meter run most of the year in the absence of Filbert Bayi of Tanzania. Edwin Moses of Dayton, Ohio, took up the 400-meter hurdles in the spring and won the Olympic gold medal in world-record time. Viktor Saneyev of Russia in the triple jump and Arnie Robinson of San Diego, Calif., in the long jump remained the best in the world. Mac Wilkins of San Jose broke the world discus record four times.

Irena Szewinska of Poland, who was a medalist in the 1964, 1968, and 1972 Olympics, won the gold medal in the women's 400-meter dash at Montreal. She set a world-record time of 49.29 seconds that was truly exceptional. The best American women were Kathy McMillan of Raeford, N.C., in the long jump; Kathy Schmidt of Pacific Palisades,

Calif., in the javelin throw; and Rosalyn Bryant of Chicago in the 400-meter dash.

Pole-Vault Record. There was high drama in the pole vault at the United States Olympic trials in June in Eugene, Ore. Dave Roberts, Earl Bell, and Terry Porter were the only vaulters to clear 18 feet 1/2 inch (5.49 meters), and they won the three berths on the Olympic team. When they continued vaulting, with the bar at a world-record height of 18 feet 8 1/4 inches (5.70 meters), Roberts' pole suddenly snapped in two.

"May I use your pole?" Roberts asked Bell.

"Sure," said Bell, "but wait until I finish."

Bell and Porter missed three times each and were done. Then Roberts, using Bell's pole, cleared 18 feet 8 1/4 inches on his third attempt and took the world record from Bell. It seemed only fair, because Bell's record vault three weeks before had taken the record from Roberts, 25, a student at the University of Florida Medical School.

Dwight Stones of Huntington Beach, Calif., had been a controversial, outspoken, anti-Establishment figure since 1973, when he set a world high-jump record of 7 feet 6 1/2 inches (2.30 meters). His 1976 season included controversy, success, and a glaring defeat. Flopping over the bar backward, he won the National Collegiate indoor and outdoor titles and the Amateur Athletic Union

World Track and Field Records Established in 1976

Event	Holder	Country	Where made	Date	Record
Men					
100 meters	Steve Williams	U.S.A.	Gainesville, Fla.	March 27	:09.90*
	Harvey Glance	U.S.A.	Columbia, S.C.	April 3	:09.90*
	Harvey Glance	U.S.A.	Baton Rouge, La.	May 1	:09.90*
	Steve Williams	U.S.A.	Atlanta, Ga.	May 22	:09.90*
	Don Quarrie	Jamaica	Modesto, Calif.	May 22	:09.90*
800 meters	Alberto Juantorena	Cuba	Montreal	July 25	1:43.50
2,000 meters	John Walker	New Zealand	Oslo, Norway	June 30	4:51.40
400-meter hurdles	Edwin Moses	U.S.A.	Montreal	July 25	:47.64
3,000 steeplechase	Anders Garderud	Sweden	Montreal	July 28	8:08.02
High jump	Dwight Stones	U.S.A.	Philadelphia	August 4	7 ft. 7 1/4 in. (2.32 meters)
Pole vault	Dave Roberts	U.S.A.	Eugene, Ore.	June 22	18 ft. 8 1/4 in. (5.70 meters)
Shot-put	Alexandr Barishnikov	Russia	Paris	July 10	72 ft. 2 1/4 in. (22.00 meters)
Discus throw	Mac Wilkins	U.S.A.	San Jose, Calif.	May 1	232 ft. 6 in. (70.86 meters)
Javelin throw	Miklos Nemeth	Hungary	Montreal	July 26	310 ft. 4 in. (94.58 meters)
Decathlon	Bruce Jenner	U.S.A.	Montreal	July 29-30	8,618 points
Women					
100 meters	Annegret Richter	W. Germany	Montreal	July 25	:11.01
400 meters	Irena Szewinska	Poland	Montreal	July 29	:49.29
800 meters	Tatiana Kazankina	Russia	Montreal	July 26	1:54.94
1,000 meters	Nikolina Shtereva	Bulgaria	Belkemen, Bulgaria	July 4	2:33.80
1,500 meters	Tatiana Kazankina	Russia	Moscow	June 28	3:56.00
3,000 meters	Ludmilla Bragina	Russia	College Park, Md.	August 7	8:27.10
400-meter relay	Oelsner, Stecher, Bodendorf, Bloss	E. Germany	East Berlin	May 29	:42.50
1,600-meter relay	Maletzki, Rohde, Streidt, Brehmer	E. Germany	Montreal	July 31	3:19.23
High jump	Rosemarie Ackermann	E. Germany	Dresden, E. Ger.	May 8	6 ft. 5 1/4 in. (1.96 meters)
Long jump	Sigrun Siegl	E. Germany	Dresden, E. Ger.	May 19	22 ft. 11 1/4 in. (6.99 meters)
Shot-put	Helena Fibingerova	Czechoslovakia	Opava, Czech.	September 26	72 ft. 1 3/4 in. (21.99 meters)
Discus throw	Faina Melnik	Russia	Sochi, Russia	April 24	231 ft. 3 in. (70.50 meters)
Javelin throw	Ruth Fuchs	E. Germany	East Berlin	July 10	226 ft. 9 in. (69.12 meters)

*Equals record

national championship outdoors. He set world indoor records of 7 feet 6¼ inches (2.29 meters) and 7 feet 6½ inches (2.30 meters) on successive nights. Outdoors, after more than 60 unsuccessful attempts in three years at 7 feet 7 inches (2.31 meters), he cleared that height on June 5 at Philadelphia for another world record.

The 22-year-old Stones was a heavy favorite in the Olympics, but he feared that rain and a slippery surface would trouble him more than the others because his run-up was so fast. It rained at Montreal, and he finished third at 7 feet 3 inches (2.21 meters). On a dry surface at Philadelphia four nights later, he raised his world record to 7 feet 7¼ inches (2.32 meters).

It was somewhat of a lost year for Bayi and many other black Africans. Their governments, angry at New Zealand's sports relations with South Africa, refused to allow them in meets in which New Zealanders competed. Injuries and poor performances cost the United States Olympic team such potential medalists as 100-meter recordholder Steve Williams, distance runner Marty Liquori, shot-putter Terry Albritton, and vaulter Dan Ripley. The International Track Association canceled the last half of its professional tour because of unsuccessful recruiting and public apathy.   Frank Litsky

See also OLYMPIC GAMES.

TRANSIT systems in urban areas of the United States in 1976 sustained the gradual rise in ridership that began three years earlier. The American Public Transit Association said that city mass-transit operations carried 5.2 billion passengers through November — 0.7 per cent above the same 1975 period. New York City suffered a 5.7 per cent fall-off in the first 11 months, but ridership rose 18.5 per cent in Cleveland, 4.0 per cent in Chicago, and 4.1 per cent in Miami, Fla. Strikes hampered operations in San Francisco and Los Angeles.

Federal operating subsidies helped to cover growing transit losses and expand services. Officials predicted a nationwide deficit in excess of the $1.7-billion shortfall in 1975. New York City averted a boost in its 50-cent fare by borrowing about $130-million in federal capital-grant funds to cover operating expenses temporarily. Washington, D.C.'s Metro rapid-transit system began operating on March 27, the seventh such system in the United States. But only a 4.6-mile (7-kilometer) downtown stretch of the planned 100-mile (161-kilometer) network was opened in 1976.

Many transit operators introduced new equipment or such promotional services as cut-rate fares to lure passengers. Seattle, Los Angeles, and Washington, D.C., opted for "articulated" buses, which bend in the middle to turn corners more easily (see

The far left lane is reserved for buses and car-pool vehicles during Diamond Lane Express Plan test on Los Angeles' Santa Monica Freeway in March 1976.

SEATTLE). Sault Ste. Marie, Mich., started the first federally funded rural transit bus system, using five small buses to cover three counties in Michigan's Upper Peninsula.

Hedge Handicap Help. How to serve the transit needs of the elderly and the handicapped was a major issue. Some cities began special services for these customers. For example, small buses or vans provided transportation on phone-call demand, many at half fare. But a lawsuit filed in a Philadelphia federal court in June was designed to force the federal government to grant funds only for regular-service transit buses equipped with low floors, hydraulic lifts, or wheelchair ramps for elderly and handicapped riders.

The Urban Mass Transportation Administration (UMTA) discontinued development work on the Transbus, a new bus with a low floor for easier entry. The UMTA ruled on July 27 that transit buses need not have floors 22 inches (56 centimeters) above the ground, but said that future buses must have lower floors than those then in use. Houston and five other cities delayed purchase of advanced buses until a legal dispute between UMTA, bus makers, and buyers – in which Transbus-aid cancellation is a factor – is settled.

Most of the $11.8 billion in transit financing authorized by a 1974 law was committed by the end of 1976 in an election-year spurt of new grants and promises. Major grants or commitments were made to rapid-transit systems being built in Baltimore and Atlanta, Ga., and to three planned commuter-rail projects in New Jersey. Preliminary work was approved for a new system in Honolulu, Hawaii, and pledges of up to $600 million went to Detroit and Miami for major rapid-transit systems or alternative service.

Cost Consciousness. The Department of Transportation (DOT) sought to prevent unbridled expansion of rapid-transit systems. Transportation Secretary William T. Coleman, Jr., said any further escalation of the construction cost of Washington, D.C.'s Metro system beyond the latest official estimate of $4.7 billion would have to come from local funds. DOT encouraged cancellation of urban interstate highway projects and the use of these funds for transit. Both Washington, D.C., and Boston gained approval for carrying out more such highway-to-transit shifts.

UMTA committed up to $269 million on June 10 to fund a *light-rail* project – a modern trolleylike system – in Buffalo, N.Y. This was the first light-rail project approved by UMTA under a new policy of encouraging cities to develop less-costly types of transit lines. The agency said on December 22 that it will pay $220 million for small, automatically controlled "people-mover" systems in Cleveland, Houston, Los Angeles, and St. Paul.   Albert R. Karr

See also TRANSPORTATION.

TRANSKEI was granted formal independence on Oct. 26, 1976, by South Africa. A black homeland set up by the white South African government, it has 1.5 million people; its capital is Umtata.

Chief Kaiser Matanzima became the prime minister at independence. His Transkei National Independence Party won the parliamentary elections held on September 29. However, many leaders of the Democratic Party, which opposed independence, had been arrested before the election.

Almost all the world's governments rejected Transkei's independence. On October 26, the United Nations urged its members not to deal with Transkei. There was broad concern that support for Transkei independence would mean support for South African *apartheid,* or racial separation.

Under apartheid, blacks are supposed to become citizens of one of 10 tribal homelands. Transkei, homeland of the Xhosa, was the first to become independent. However, all 10 homelands comprise only 13 per cent of South Africa's land, while blacks make up about 70 per cent of the population.

Economic opportunities in the homelands are too limited to support the entire black community. The homeland-independence policy is strongly opposed by black nationalists, who seek black-majority rule in a united South Africa.   John D. Esseks

See also AFRICA (Facts in Brief Table); SOUTH AFRICA.

TRANSPORTATION. The improving economy and government moves to help them cheered the United States transportation industries in 1976. Because traffic increased substantially, airlines and railroads reversed previous losses, and truckers enjoyed a sizable rise in profits. Carriers turned to a rapid succession of fare- and rate-increase petitions, and regulatory agencies responded by approving most bids.

Traffic Increases. The total 1976 U.S. transportation tab was about $345 billion, a 9.4 per cent increase over 1975, according to a preliminary estimate by the Transportation Association of America (TAA). The trade group estimated that overall U.S. mainland intercity freight volume rose about 5 per cent, led by a 10 per cent climb in truck traffic. Big-volume pipeline freight was up about 3 per cent, while rail hauling, Great Lakes traffic, and rivers and canals all increased 5 per cent. Air cargo rose about 6 per cent.

The TAA estimated that intercity passenger traffic increased 6.3 per cent, largely because of a 6 per cent boost in automobile travel. It also estimated that rail-passenger traffic rose 5 per cent and air travel 10 per cent; bus traffic fell 2 per cent.

The Federal Highway Administration said auto speeds crept up despite vigorous state enforcement of the federal speed limit of 55 miles (89 kilometers) per hour. The Department of Transportation (DOT) blamed this trend for a 1 per cent rise in highway fatalities through October. Deaths were down sharply in 1974 and 1975 from 1973, when higher speed limits existed. See SAFETY.

Transportation Secretary William T. Coleman, Jr., made major decisions in the waning days of President Gerald R. Ford's Administration. He ruled on February 4 that the British-French supersonic Concorde jetliner be allowed a 16-month trial at New York City and Washington, D.C., airports (see AVIATION). But on December 6, Coleman delayed a final decision on whether to order the controversial airbags installed in all new passenger cars (see AUTOMOBILE).

Coleman recommended to President Ford that part of the airline ticket tax be used to assist airlines in buying new, quieter aircraft. The President called for airline-noise reduction steps, but instead of adopting the recommended plan, he instructed Coleman to hold a public hearing on December 1 on ways to pay for quieter jets. The Federal Railroad Administration worked on regulations for giving financial assistance to railroads as part of a $6.4-billion rail-aid law enacted in February (see RAILROAD).

The Ford Administration pushed for passage of its airline and motor-carrier deregulation bills. But Coleman said in October and November that the measures would be reworked to make them more acceptable to the affected industries (see TRUCK AND TRUCKING). Transport legislation enacted in 1976 included laws setting a 200-nautical-mile U.S. fishing limit; extending until 1980 the airport-aid program, which expired on June 30, 1975; and continuing with little change the highway trust fund through fiscal 1978. The Ford Administration abandoned a 1975 plan to divert most of the federal gasoline tax from the trust fund to the general treasury and the states.

President-elect James Earl (Jimmy) Carter, Jr., announced on December 14 that Representative Brock Adams (D., Wash.) was his choice for transportation secretary. Adams served on the transportation subcommittee of the House Committee on Interstate and Foreign Commerce. He was an author of railroad legislation in 1973 to reorganize bankrupt lines and of the new rail-aid law.

Canada's Transport Commission held hearings on a proposal by Transport Minister Otto E. Lang for a single-service transcontinental passenger-train network, replacing the two existing rail operations. Air service was shut down for nine days in June in Canada by a pilots' strike. The pilots said that a plan to use French in Canadian air-traffic-control communications would be confusing and unsafe. An agreement to leave resolution of the issue to Parliament, after an impartial inquiry, ended the strike on June 28. See CANADA.   Albert R. Karr

See also SHIP AND SHIPPING; TRANSIT.

TRAVEL. World tourism increased about 5 per cent in 1976. There were about 223 million international arrivals throughout the world, and they spent $40 billion. More than 18 million travelers from abroad visited the United States, up 15 per cent. An estimated 23.2 million Americans visited other countries. Of this total, some 12.8 million went to Canada, a 3 per cent decline; 2.8 million visited Mexico, a 3 per cent increase; and 7.5 million traveled overseas, a 7 per cent increase.

About 11.6 million Canadians visited the U.S. in 1976, up 17 per cent, and they spent close to $2-billion. The number of Mexican visitors increased 2 per cent to 2.2 million, and they spent about $1.7-billion. Once again, Japanese tourists constituted the largest group of overseas visitors to the United States. In 1976, some 860,000 Japanese, 1 per cent more than in 1975, came and spent $435 million. British visitors increased by 20 per cent to 525,000, West Germans by 21 per cent to 360,000, and French by 33 per cent to 210,000.

The Devalued Pound drew tourists to Great Britain in droves. They spent $3.5 billion, including $1-billion on shopping. A total of 370,000 tourists from the Middle East, including Iranians, visited London in 1976, nearly 100,000 more than in 1975. British shopkeepers were overjoyed, but some Britons complained of the crowding and inconvenience.

The *Mississippi Queen,* first overnight-cruise paddle-wheel steamboat to be built in 50 years, is commissioned in July at Cincinnati, Ohio.

One or more vacation trips were taken by over 117 million Americans, a 6 per cent increase. Twenty-nine per cent traveled by plane, and 57 per cent by private car. Nearly 100 million Americans toured their own country and spent $85 billion, $10-billion more than in 1975. More than 64 million persons spent nearly $600 million at 35 major U.S. theme parks.

Bicentennial Travel to Boston, New York City, Philadelphia, and Washington, D.C., was a victim of publicity overkill. Frightened off by early predictions of crowded attractions, traffic jams, and "no vacancy" signs, millions of Americans avoided the "colonial corridor." Many who did visit merely darted into town, made a quick run of the free attractions, and then left, assuming that there was no place to stay.

A revival of American travel to Cuba after more than 15 years became a distinct possibility in August. For the first time, the official Cuban tourist agency issued a direct invitation to U.S. tour operators to discuss group trips that could begin as early as the winter of 1977.

Montreal hosted 750,000 visitors between July 17 and August 1 during the Summer Olympic Games. This massive two-week influx of tourists temporarily increased metropolitan Montreal's population by almost 30 per cent.

Scheduled Supersonic Travel across the North Atlantic was inaugurated on May 24 on the London-Washington, D.C., and Paris-Washington, D.C., routes. There was a 20 per cent surcharge on the 1,350-mph (2,172-kph) Concorde flights, with round-trip fares between Washington and Paris costing $1,654 – $352 more than the regular first-class airfare. See AVIATION.

The Civil Aeronautics Board approved Advance Booking Charters (ABC), a new category of charter flights. Effective October 7, passengers no longer needed to be members of an existing group or to purchase hotel or other ground arrangements as part of the air package. They had only to buy their seats at least 45 days in advance for major European destinations and 30 days in advance for others. While the regular summer economy New York-London round-trip fare was $764, an ABC ticket cost $350.

Travel at Sea. Well over 1 million passengers from North America took pleasure cruises aboard luxury vessels based all over the world. Close to 100,000 travelers sailed between New York City and Europe. Four cruise lines – Cunard, Holland America, Carras, and Royal Viking – offered three-day excursions to mainland China, from Hong Kong to Canton and beyond. The *Mississippi Queen,* the first overnight riverboat to be built in the United States in 50 years, began its 18-day maiden voyage from Cincinnati, Ohio, to New Orleans and back on July 27.

This new roller coaster in Eureka, Mo., is billed as the world's longest, fastest, and tallest—with a 92-foot (28-meter) drop.

On the Rails. More than 17 million travelers rode U.S. trains. The USA Railpass, originally devised to attract travelers from abroad, was offered for sale in the United States in 1976. It allowed two weeks of unlimited travel on the Amtrak and Southern Pacific Company routes for $150, three weeks for $200, and 30 days for $250.

On the Road. United States annual highway travel increased by 2 per cent to 1,381 billion vehicle miles (2,223 billion vehicle kilometers). Ridership on intercity buses totaled about 360 million. In August, Greyhound and other bus companies reinstated the 15-day Ameripass, which allowed unlimited travel and stopover privileges for $165. Recreational-vehicle sales in 1976 increased to 523,000, up from 339,000 in 1975.

Room Service. Occupancy rates in the U.S. lodging industry ran about 64 per cent nationally, well below the traditional goal of 75 per cent. The Hyatt Corporation became the fastest-growing U.S. hotel chain, operating more than 40 major hotels. One of the most profitable operations – Club Méditerranée, with 75 resort villages from Tahiti to Senegal – had revenue of more than $200 million. The Middle East experienced a hotel building boom, except in war-torn Lebanon. Five chains opened hotels or had them under contract in seven Middle East countries.   Lynn Beaumont

TRINIDAD AND TOBAGO. See WEST INDIES.

TRUCK AND TRUCKING. The United States trucking industry prospered as the economy moved upward in 1976. Tonnage hauled rose 11 per cent and total motor-carrier revenues increased 15 per cent to $25.3 billion, the American Trucking Associations, Incorporated (ATA), estimated. Net earnings were about $795 million, a 99 per cent climb from the $400-million profit in 1975.

Trucking concerns gained several rounds of freight-rate increase approvals from the Interstate Commerce Commission (ICC). Carriers were granted rate hikes of from 5 to 6 per cent in April and from 2 to 5 per cent in June and July. Rises of about 2 per cent followed in August and September, with a final round of increases in October and November, in the range of from 1 to 5 per cent.

Higher Costs. Motor carriers said they needed rate boosts to cover higher labor costs under a new contract with the International Brotherhood of Teamsters negotiated in early April. The agreement was reached after a short strike that began on April 1. The contract provided wage and fringe-benefit increases of up to 33 per cent over three years. It also obligated employers to provide single hotel or motel rooms for over-the-road drivers and to air-condition truck cabs. The contract applied to about 400,000 Teamsters directly, but could indirectly determine wage rates for many more truck-drivers. See LABOR.

The Teamsters struck United Parcel Service of America, Incorporated, on September 15, and the strike lasted until December 9. Shutdown of the small-package shipments carrier caused a particular pinch in the busy pre-Christmas delivery season.

Deregulation Opposed. The proposal by President Gerald R. Ford's Administration in November 1975 to reduce ICC regulation of motor-carrier rates and market entry ran into tough going. The ATA mounted a vigorous public campaign against the measure, saying the plan would destroy the stability of the trucking industry and cause many small towns to lose truck service. The ICC also opposed the proposal. In Congress, transportation subcommittees held hearings on the proposed motor-carrier legislation, but gave it a cool reception and demanded better justification.

Shortly before the November 2 election, U.S. Secretary of Transportation William T. Coleman, Jr., told an ATA meeting that the Ford Administration recognized some shortcomings in its proposal and would modify it. At the same meeting, Thomas Bertram Lance, who was later picked to be federal budget director by President-elect James Earl (Jimmy) Carter, Jr., said the former Georgia governor understood the truckers' fears of losing protection for their operating certificates if controls were lifted.   Albert R. Karr

See also TRANSPORTATION.

TRUDEAU, PIERRE ELLIOTT (1919-   ), suffered his most severe drop in popularity in 1976 since he became prime minister of Canada eight years earlier. Public opinion polls showed that only about one-third of the Canadians polled approved of Trudeau's leadership, a sharp contrast to his personal standing in previous years.

Trudeau's difficulties arose from two sources. One was economic – the unpopularity, especially among organized labor and business, of his government's wage and price control programs. His drastic change of mind on this issue, after originally opposing controls, hurt his credibility.

The other problem lay in the challenges to Canadian unity. Bilingualism, the principle that brought Trudeau into public life and upon which he had staked his reputation, was under attack both in English-speaking Canada and in French-speaking Quebec. This worked to the advantage of the separatist party in Quebec, which took power in an election on November 15.

Trudeau's most urgent task was to regain a following for his Liberal Party in English-speaking Canada. It was the only way he could avoid the recurring nightmare of Canadian politics in which the electoral support of each of the major parties was confined to one or the other of the two principal language groups.   David M. L. Farr

See also CANADA; QUEBEC.

Unorthodox design of the Hotel du Lac in Tunis, Tunisia, gives it an upside-down appearance, with rooms hanging at the end of each wing.

TUNISIA. The first public criticism of President Habib Bourguiba's one-party regime by anyone other than students surfaced in 1976. Several national leaders, including five former government ministers, appealed publicly to Bourguiba on March 20, the 20th anniversary of Tunisian independence, to allow opposition political parties to form. They blamed his patriarchal leadership for Tunisia's high unemployment and criticized the lack of vocational and technical educational facilities and other national problems.

Tunisia blamed Libyan agents for a March 22 attempt to assassinate Bourguiba and Prime Minister Hedi Nouira. The case generated friction between Tunisia and Libya. The tension was aggravated by the expulsion of Tunisian workers from Libya after the arrest of the agents, but relations improved later.

Tunisia's Economic prospects improved with a record grain harvest of 1.65 million short tons (1.5-million metric tons) and the discovery of new phosphate deposits and an offshore oil field in the Gulf of Gabes. An April 25 agreement with the European Community (Common Market) permits 80 per cent tariff reductions for Tunisian wine, olive oil, and citrus exports to Common Market countries. A new five-year plan announced in March forecast a 7.5 per cent annual growth rate.   William Spencer

See also AFRICA (Facts in Brief Table).

TURKEY. A devastating earthquake, the nation's worst in 40 years, struck the eastern province of Van on Nov. 24, 1976. More than 100 villages were destroyed and more than 4,000 persons were killed. Relief efforts were hampered by a snowstorm and bitter cold in the area.

Tension with Greece over oil exploration rights in the Aegean Sea reached a peak in August, threatening a confrontation similar to the 1974 crisis over Cyprus. The dispute centered around ownership of the Aegean seabed and continental shelf. The 1973 discovery of oil off the Greek island of Thasos raised Turkish hopes of a similar strike. In July and August 1976, the Turkish research ship *MTA Sismik I* searched for oil in waters claimed by the Greeks.

Greece protested to the United Nations Security Council and on August 10 asked the World Court in The Hague, the Netherlands, to issue an injunction against further Turkish exploration. The court rejected the request on September 12, though it deferred judgment on the ownership question. Greco-Turkish talks were stalled at that point.

A successful oil strike would have helped Turkey weather its economic difficulties. But the dispute with Greece helped weld national unity under Prime Minister Suleyman Demirel. Demirel's Justice Party maintained its coalition majority in the Grand National Assembly with no major challenges. There was considerable political violence during the year, but most of it involved conflicts between left wing and right wing students, with the government acting as policeman. Even so, clashes produced 64 deaths and hundreds of injuries.

An Uncertain Economy was the basic factor in the unrest. The unemployment rate reached 20 per cent. Remittances from Turkish workers in Europe, many of them also idled by the economic crunch there, dropped 8 per cent from $500,000 to $399,000. Demirel said on July 10 that exports had increased 82 per cent and would reach $2.5 billion. The five-year plan announced on July 26 would invest $14 billion in 157 industrial projects, including two nuclear power plants. But it was not clear where the financing would come from to pay for this massive industrial investment.

There were some bright spots. On September 17, the Turkish state petroleum organization struck natural gas deposits under the Black Sea with a daily flow of 91.5 million cubic yards (70 million cubic meters). The Kirkuk-Dörtyol pipeline, completed in September, gave Turkey access to Iraqi oil at less than the posted price per barrel.

Agricultural production showed marked improvement in 1976. The wheat harvest of 17.6 million short tons (16.4 million metric tons) was a record for the country.   William Spencer

See also EUROPE (Facts in Brief Table).

UGANDA. Israeli commandos raided Entebbe Airport on the night of July 3, 1976, to rescue 103 hostages held by airline hijackers. The commandos, flown from Israel in three military transport planes, landed without prior permission from the Ugandan government. They met resistance from both the hijackers and Ugandan soldiers. During the fighting, about 20 Ugandans were killed in addition to seven hijackers, three hostages, and one commando.

The Hijacking began on June 27, when pro-Palestinian terrorists seized control of an Air France flight from Tel Aviv to Paris after a stopover in Athens, Greece. The hijackers diverted the plane for refueling in Libya, then ordered it to Entebbe.

There was controversy over Ugandan President Idi Amin Dada's role in the incident. He claimed he made every effort to have the hostages, most of whom were Israeli, released. The hijackers wanted 53 pro-Palestinian prisoners jailed in Europe and Israel released in exchange for the hostages. However, Amin reportedly complicated the negotiations by adding to the list five Ugandans held in Kenya. Moreover, some hostages charged after their release that Ugandan soldiers had cooperated with the hijackers. See ISRAEL; MIDDLE EAST.

On the return flight to Israel, the three Israeli planes refueled in Kenya. Because Kenya's government permitted the refueling, Amin's government allegedly retaliated against Kenyans living in

Uganda. Kenya charged that Amin had murdered hundreds of Kenyans since the raid. Each country accused the other of preparing for a military confrontation. Kenya curtailed the flow of fuel and other goods to landlocked Uganda, claiming Uganda had not paid for $50 million in past shipments. However, on August 7, Kenya and Uganda agreed to normalize relations. See KENYA.

Britain Cuts Ties. Great Britain severed diplomatic relations with Uganda on July 28, the first such action against any member of the British Commonwealth. The disappearance of Dora Bloch, an elderly woman with dual British and Israeli citizenship, was a major cause of the rupture. She had been on the hijacked airliner, but prior to the raid was taken to a Uganda hospital for treatment when she choked on food. After the raid, British authorities could neither visit her in the hospital nor learn of her whereabouts. Underground sources reported she was killed in retaliation for the raid.

On June 10, Amin was reportedly the target of an assassination attempt. Hand grenades thrown during a ceremony he attended reportedly wounded him slightly and killed 10 others. On June 25, Amin was made president for life.   John D. Esseks

See also AFRICA (Facts in Brief Table).

UNEMPLOYMENT. See ECONOMICS; LABOR.

UNION OF SOVIET SOCIALIST REPUBLICS (U.S.S.R.). See RUSSIA.

UNITED ARAB EMIRATES (UAE). Merger of the armed forces of member emirates was postponed again on May 6, 1976, when Dubayy and Ash Shariqah objected to placing their forces under direct presidential command. Dubayy also refused to contribute to the $1.15-billion UAE budget approved by the federal council on May 20. This left Abu Zaby, the richest member, obliged to contribute $1 billion. There was also a dispute between Dubayy and Ash Shariqah over construction of a building on land adjoining their common border.

As a result of these various differences, the council postponed action on a new federal constitution, which was to have gone into effect on July 12, to replace the Provisional Constitution adopted in 1971. Zayid bin Sultan al-Nuhayan of Abu Zaby announced in September that he would not seek re-election to a second term as UAE president because his fellow rulers had failed to support him.

Large oil deposits were found in Ras al Khaymah, one of the poorer emirates, on July 28. The first UAE refinery went into production on April 27. Despite a slowdown in development projects to reduce dependence on oil, the UAE ended 1976 with $890 million in foreign currency reserves. On December 16, the UAE joined Saudi Arabia in announcing it would raise oil prices 5 per cent on Jan. 1, 1977. See PETROLEUM AND GAS.   William Spencer

See also MIDDLE EAST (Facts in Brief Table).

UNITED NATIONS (UN). Arabs, Africans, and their allies fought throughout 1976 for three UN actions — to get Israel out of Arab territories it has occupied since 1967; to set up a Palestinian state there; and to end white rule in South Africa, Namibia (South West Africa), Rhodesia, and the last French colonies in Africa. The Arab-African coalition always prevailed in the General Assembly, which can only recommend that nations do something. However, vetoes by Western countries often stopped them in the Security Council, which alone can order things done.

PLO Participates. The Palestine Liberation Organization (PLO) took part for the first time in the Council's debate on the Palestine question that ended on January 26. The United States vetoed a resolution that called for Israeli withdrawal from Arab territories, establishment of a Palestinian state "in Palestine," return to Israel or compensation of Arab refugees, and guarantees of the sovereignty of all states in the area. The vote was 9 to 1 with Great Britain, Italy, and Sweden abstaining and China and Libya not participating.

In February, Libya and Pakistan initiated a debate on Israel's handling of Arab demonstrations that followed Muslim-Jewish clashes on Old Jerusalem's sacred Temple Mount, and the United States vetoed a resolution on March 25 — on a 14 to

1 vote — that called on Israel to uphold the inviolability of the holy places and to stop changing the "physical, cultural, demographic, and religious character" of Old Jerusalem. Egypt arranged another debate on Israeli actions in occupied territories, and on May 26, the United States alone dissented from a Security Council majority statement that "deplored" Israel's establishment of settlements there. Egypt set up yet another debate on Israel's occupation policies after desecration of Muslim and Jewish religious objects in Abraham's tomb in Hebron. This time, the United States agreed to a Council statement on November 11 that strongly deplored establishment of Israeli settlements in the occupied territories.

Meanwhile, a Palestinian rights committee created by the 1975 General Assembly had sent the Council a report recommending that it fix a timetable for Israel to turn over the occupied territories to the UN by June 1, 1977. The committee also wanted the UN later to give the West Bank of Jordan and the Gaza Strip to the PLO for a "Palestinian national entity." The United States vetoed a resolution on June 29, 1976, upholding Palestinian rights and taking note of the report.

Hostage Issue Raised. On an African complaint, Dahomey (Benin), Libya, and Tanzania proposed that the Council condemn Israel for vio-

In a historic first, Israel and the Palestine Liberation Organization take part in a March 22 Security Council debate on the Middle East.

lating Uganda's sovereignty on July 3 and 4 when airborne Israeli commandos rescued 103 hostages and killed seven pro-Palestinian hijackers and about 20 Ugandan troops at Entebbe Airport. Lacking the votes to win, the Africans withdrew the resolution on July 14.

A British-U.S. resolution to condemn airline hijacking and defend national sovereignty in general got six votes, three short of the nine needed to pass, when two Council members abstained from voting and seven sponsors of the anti-Israeli proposal did not participate in the debate. But the Entebbe rescue prompted West Germany to ask the General Assembly to act against the taking of hostages. The Assembly unanimously adopted a resolution on December 15 that called for establishment of a committee to draft an international treaty against the taking of hostages.

The drive for a Palestinian state ended for the year on November 24 when the General Assembly adopted a resolution sponsored by almost all members of the Palestinian rights committee. The resolution urged the Security Council to reconsider the committee's recommendations and "take necessary measures" to put them into effect. It asked the committee to "exert all efforts" to that end and report back to the Assembly for further debate in 1977. With 30 members abstaining, the tally was 90 to 16 on the resolution. Australia, Canada, Israel, the United States, and some West European and Latin American countries voted "no." That Assembly vote gave Palestinian rights one more "yes" than in two previous debates since PLO leader Yasir Arafat's 1974 UN speech.

"The General Assembly has been hijacked by a group of Arab extremists," Israeli Ambassador Chaim Herzog said.

The Assembly approved a resolution on December 9 asking Secretary-General Kurt Waldheim to resume contacts aimed at reconvening the Geneva conference on the Middle East by March 1, 1977. By a vote of 91 to 11, with 21 abstentions, the Assembly asked for PLO participation in the talks. Israel and the United States voted against both.

South Africa Condemned. The Council unanimously condemned South Africa on June 19 for killing students and other Africans "opposing racial discrimination" in demonstrations that began when the government required that some classes in black schools be taught in the Afrikaans language. The Council condemned South Africa again on July 30 for a July 11 raid on a transit camp for Namibian freedom fighters in Zambia. South Africa denied Zambia's charges. The United States abstained from the 14 to 0 vote. The Council had demanded unanimously on January 30 that South Africa withdraw from Namibia and agree by August 31 to UN-supervised elections there. The deadline passed without such agreement, and the United States,

Britain, and France on October 19 vetoed an arms embargo meant to force South Africa out of Namibia. But the Council was unanimous on March 17 in asking governments to help Mozambique weather the economic shock of joining the UN embargo against Rhodesia, aimed at bringing down the white-minority government there, and in extending that embargo on April 6 to include insurance.

"Africa Session." The 31st Assembly earned its nickname of "Africa session" when it adopted 11 resolutions against South Africa's race-segregating apartheid policy. A resolution approved on October 26 asked governments not to recognize the Transkei, declared independent that day as the first homeland that South Africa has set aside for its black tribes. The other 10 resolutions, passed on November 9, included calls for broad action against apartheid, a 1977 world conference to promote that action, a universal sports boycott of South Africa, aid to apartheid sufferers, and release of South African political prisoners.

One resolution asked UN members to stop economic collaboration with South Africa, implying withdrawal of investments. Another, devised by Sweden as easier to swallow, suggested Security Council action to head off new investments in South Africa. Dovetailing resolutions called for the Council to make its existing anti-apartheid arms embar-

Daniel P. Moynihan, who quit as chief U.S. delegate to the United Nations in February, vetoes anti-Israeli resolution on January 26.

go against South Africa mandatory and for the United States, Britain, and France not to veto a mandatory arms embargo.

Endorses Military Force. The General Assembly approved a resolution on December 20 that, for the first time, endorsed Namibia's "armed struggle" against South Africa. The vote was 107 to 6. Belgium, Britain, France, Luxembourg, the United States, and West Germany voted against the resolution, which also condemned South Africa for its "illegal occupation" of Namibia. Twelve countries abstained.

For the second year, South Africa stayed out of the Assembly to avoid being ordered out, as it was in 1974. But South African Ambassador Roelof F. Botha defended his country in some Council debates, contending that blacks there lived better than blacks elsewhere in Africa.

Angola Joins. On March 31, 1976, the Council condemned "South Africa's aggression against Angola" — meaning aid to the losing side in the civil war there — by a vote of 9 to 0. Britain, France, Italy, Japan, and the United States abstained and China did not participate. The United States and China, backers of the losing side in Angola, complained that Russian arms and Cuban troops had helped the winners. The United States mentioned the Cuban troops on June 23 when it vetoed UN membership for Angola, which needed the Council's recommendation before the Assembly could make it a member. China did not participate in the 13 to 1 vote. The United States abstained when the membership application was revived after the November U.S. elections, and Angola became the 146th member of the UN on December 1.

Nix on Vietnam. Meanwhile, the United States vetoed Vietnam's UN membership application on November 15. William W. Scranton, chief U.S. representative to the UN, said that Vietnam had not given the United States "information available to it" on some 800 Americans missing in action in that country.

On November 26, the Assembly asked the Council to reconsider Vietnam's application "favorably." The tally was 124 to 1 with Israel, Britain, and West Germany abstaining. Scranton cast the negative vote and warned that he would veto it again if the application came up in the Council again. His hard line interrupted a brief post-election U.S. honeymoon with the Arab-African coalition, during which the United States agreed to the November 11 Council criticism of Israel and lifted its veto of Angola. Officials said the American concessions were meant to encourage the Africans not to make trouble for talks in Geneva, Switzerland, on black-majority rule in Rhodesia and to persuade the Arabs to cooperate in Middle East negotiations.

Chief U.S. Delegate Changes. The trend fitted the easygoing image Scranton had won, despite ve-

toes and speeches criticizing the Russians, since he took over as chief U.S. delegate from Daniel P. Moynihan on March 15 (see SCRANTON, WILLIAM W.). Moynihan, whose outspoken manner had provoked Arab and African denunciation and Western disquiet, resigned on February 2. He won election to the U.S. Senate from New York in November. On December 17, President-elect James Earl (Jimmy) Carter, Jr., announced his choice for Scranton's successor as chief delegate — Representative Andrew Young (D., Ga.). Young would be the first black to head the U.S. delegation.

Assembly Business. The General Assembly admitted Seychelles, Indian Ocean islands, as the 145th UN member, soon after opening its three-month 31st session on September 21 and electing Hamilton S. Amerasinghe of Sri Lanka as president. Western Samoa became the 147th UN member on December 15. The Assembly on October 21 elected Canada, India, Mauritius, Venezuela, and West Germany to two-year terms on the Security Council starting in 1977.

Secretary-General Kurt Waldheim was re-elected to a second 5-year term on December 8. The Council had recommended the popular diplomat to the Assembly over Luis Echeverría Alvarez, former president of Mexico, who presented himself as a candidate from the developing nations.

Sessions Abroad. The Economic and Social Council held its own first Africa session in Abidjan, the Ivory Coast, from June 30 to July 9 and issued a set of goals in a "Declaration of Abidjan." The UN Conference on Human Settlement in Vancouver, Canada, from May 31 to June 11, produced recommendations for national and international action to improve cities and towns.

The Fourth UN Conference on Trade and Development, held in Nairobi, Kenya, in May, approved an integrated program to stabilize the prices of 18 commodities, ranging from bananas to iron ore, by issuing buffer stocks financed from a $3-billion common fund.

The General Conference of the UN Educational, Scientific, and Cultural Organization (UNESCO) met for five weeks in Nairobi and readmitted Israel to UNESCO's European regional group on November 22. The U.S. Congress cut off U.S. dues to UNESCO, a fourth of that body's regular income, when Israel's bid to rejoin the group was rejected in Paris in 1974.

The UN Law of the Sea Conference revised its draft for a sea-law treaty in sessions in New York City from March 15 to May 7 and from August 2 to September 17. But it could not agree on the extent to which an international seabed authority should share with private enterprise the mining of ocean-floor nodules that are rich in metals. It scheduled its first 1977 meeting for May 23. See MINES AND MINING; OCEAN.   William N. Oatis

UNITED STATES, GOVERNMENT OF THE

UNITED STATES, GOVERNMENT OF THE. Events in 1976 signaled the stability of the United States and the nation's heartening recovery from the trauma of the Watergate scandal. Those events included the narrow victory in November of Democratic presidential candidate James Earl (Jimmy) Carter, Jr., and the orderly, friendly transition from a Republican to a Democratic Administration in Washington, D.C.

The nation's economy began to recover from the severe recession of 1974-1975, and by the end of the year, the inflation rate was between 5 and 6 per cent, down from the average 9.1 per cent of 1975. However, unemployment remained a problem; the unemployment rate hovered around 8 per cent in December. See ECONOMICS; LABOR.

Intelligence-Gathering Agencies. Both the Central Intelligence Agency (CIA) and the Federal Bureau of Investigation (FBI) came under intense scrutiny in 1976. President Gerald R. Ford announced on February 17 that CIA director George H. W. Bush would chair a new committee to supervise intelligence operations. A three-member board composed of civilians was also established to oversee intelligence gathering. The President issued an executive order on February 18 restricting federal surveillance of U.S. citizens.

On April 28, the Senate Select Committee on Intelligence issued a report charging that the FBI and other U.S. intelligence agencies had illegally spied on U.S. citizens and organizations. FBI documents obtained in a lawsuit brought by the Socialist Workers Party (SWP) showed that the FBI had repeatedly burglarized SWP offices since the late 1950s. Yet the FBI never found evidence to bring a single charge against any member of the SWP. Martin Luther King, Jr., the National Association for the Advancement of Colored People, and former Supreme Court Justice William O. Douglas were among those subjected to illegal surveillance.

Reportedly, Attorney General Edward H. Levi advised the FBI to inform unknowing victims of a 17-year program of FBI harassment, so that the victims could bring lawsuits or order their files destroyed. The Department of Justice also began a probe of FBI abuses.

On August 8, FBI director Clarence M. Kelley declared that he had been "deliberately deceived" about illegal FBI activity. On August 11, he announced that the FBI would be reorganized to prevent further abuses.

The Executive Branch. After campaigning vigorously, President Ford narrowly lost his bid for the presidency in November. He won 48.02 per cent of the popular vote to Carter's 50.08 per cent (see ELECTIONS). Ford prepared to leave the presidency with a government pension of almost $100,000 a year, including a presidential pension of $60,000 a year, plus $96,000 a year for staff and an office.

Major Agencies and Bureaus of the U.S. Government*

Executive Office of the President
President, Gerald R. Ford

Vice-President, Nelson A. Rockefeller
White House Staff Coordinator, Richard B. Cheney
Presidential Press Secretary, Ronald H. Nessen
Central Intelligence Agency—George H. W. Bush, Director
Council of Economic Advisers—Alan Greenspan, Chairman
Council on Environmental Quality—(vacant)
Council on Wage and Price Stability—(vacant)
Domestic Council—James M. Cannon, Executive Director
Economic Policy Board—L. William Seidman, Executive Director
Office of Management and Budget—James T. Lynn, Director
Office of Science and Technology Policy—H. Guyford Stever, Director
Office of Telecommunications Policy—Thomas J. Houser, Director

State Department
Secretary of State, Henry A. Kissinger

Agency for International Development—Daniel Parker, Administrator
U.S. Representative to the United Nations—William W. Scranton

Department of the Treasury
Secretary of the Treasury, William E. Simon

Bureau of Alcohol, Tobacco, and Firearms—Rex D. Davis, Director
Bureau of Engraving and Printing—James A. Conlon, Director
Bureau of the Mint—Mary Brooks, Director
Comptroller of the Currency—(vacant)
Internal Revenue Service—Donald C. Alexander, Commissioner
Treasurer of the United States—Francine Neff
U.S. Customs Service—Vernon D. Acree, Commissioner
U.S. Secret Service—H. Stuart Knight, Director

Department of Defense
Secretary of Defense, Donald H. Rumsfeld

Joint Chiefs of Staff—General George S. Brown, Chairman
Secretary of the Air Force—Thomas C. Reed
Secretary of the Army—Martin R. Hoffmann
Secretary of the Navy—J. William Middendorf II

Department of Justice
Attorney General, Edward H. Levi

Bureau of Prisons—Norman A. Carlson, Director
Drug Enforcement Administration—Peter Bensinger, Administrator
Federal Bureau of Investigation—Clarence M. Kelley, Director
Immigration and Naturalization Service—Leonard F. Chapman, Jr., Commissioner
Law Enforcement Assistance Administration—Richard W. Velde, Administrator
Solicitor General—Robert H. Bork

Department of the Interior
Secretary of the Interior, Thomas S. Kleppe

Bureau of Indian Affairs—Benjamin Reifel, Commissioner
Bureau of Land Management—Curt Berklund, Director
Bureau of Mines—Thomas V. Falkie, Director
Bureau of Outdoor Recreation—John Crutcher, Director
Bureau of Reclamation—Gilbert G. Stamm, Commissioner
Geological Survey—Vincent E. McKelvey, Director
National Park Service—Gary E. Everhardt, Director
Office of Territorial Affairs—Fred Zeder, Director
U.S. Fish and Wildlife Service—Lynn A. Greenwalt, Director

Department of Agriculture
Secretary of Agriculture, John A. Knebel †

Agricultural Economics—Don A. Paarlberg, Director
Agricultural Marketing Service—Donald E. Wilkinson, Administrator

*As of Jan 1, 1977; † nominated but not yet confirmed

Agricultural Stabilization and Conservation Service—Kenneth E. Frick, Administrator
Farmers Home Administration—Frank B. Elliott, Administrator
Federal Crop Insurance Corporation—Melvin R. Peterson, Manager
Forest Service—John R. McGuire, Chief
Rural Electrification Administration—David A. Hamil, Administrator
Soil Conservation Service—Ronello M. Davis, Administrator

Department of Commerce
Secretary of Commerce, Elliot L. Richardson

Bureau of the Census—(vacant)
National Bureau of Standards—Ernest Ambler †, Director
National Oceanic and Atmospheric Administration—Robert M. White, Administrator
Office of Minority Business Enterprise—Alex M. Armendaris, Director
Patent and Trademark Office—C. Marshall Dann, Commissioner

Department of Labor
Secretary of Labor, W. J. Usery, Jr.

Bureau of Labor Statistics—Julius Shiskin, Commissioner
Labor-Management Services Administration—Bernard E. DeLury, Administrator
Occupational Safety and Health Administration—Morton Corn, Administrator

Department of Health, Education, and Welfare
Secretary of Health, Education, and Welfare, F. David Mathews

Administration on Aging—Arthur S. Flemming, Commissioner
Alcohol, Drug Abuse, and Mental Health Administration—James D. Isbister, Administrator
Food and Drug Administration—(vacant)
Health Resources Administration—Kenneth M. Endicott, Administrator
Health Services Administration—Robert van Hoek, Acting Administrator
National Institute of Education—Harold L. Hodgkinson, Director
National Institutes of Health—Donald S. Fredrickson, Director
Office of Consumer Affairs—Virginia H. Knauer, Director
Office of Education—Edward Aguirre, Commissioner
Public Health Service—Theodore Cooper, Administrator
Social and Rehabilitation Service—Robert E. Fulton, Administrator
Social Security Administration—James B. Cardwell, Commissioner

Department of Housing and Urban Development
Secretary of Housing and Urban Development, Carla A. Hills

Community Planning and Development—(vacant)
Federal Disaster Assistance Administration—Thomas P. Dunne, Administrator
Federal Housing Commissioner—(vacant)
Federal Insurance Administration—John Robert Hunter, Acting Administrator
Government National Mortgage Association—David M. deWilde, President
New Communities Administration—James F. Dausch, Administrator

Department of Transportation
Secretary of Transportation, William T. Coleman, Jr.

Federal Aviation Administration—John L. McLucas, Administrator
Federal Highway Administration—Norbert T. Tiemann, Administrator
Federal Railroad Administration—Asaph H. Hall, Administrator
National Highway Traffic Safety Administration—John W. Snow, Administrator
U.S. Coast Guard—Admiral Owen W. Siler, Commandant
Urban Mass Transportation Administration—Robert E. Patricelli, Administrator

Congressional Officials
President of the Senate pro tempore—James O. Eastland

Speaker of the House—Thomas P. O'Neill, Jr.

Architect of the Capitol—George M. White
Comptroller General of the U.S.—Elmer B. Staats
Congressional Budget Office—Alice M. Rivlin, Director
Librarian of Congress—Daniel J. Boorstin
Office of Technology Assessment—Emilio Q. Daddario, Director
Public Printer of the U.S.—Thomas F. McCormick

Independent Agencies
ACTION—Michael P. Balzano, Jr., Director
American Revolution Bicentennial Administration—John W. Warner, Administrator
Civil Aeronautics Board—John E. Robson, Chairman
Civil Service Commission—Robert E. Hampton, Chairman
Commodity Futures Trading Commission—William T. Bagley, Chairman
Community Services Administration—Samuel R. Martinez
Consumer Product Safety Commission—S. John Byington, Chairman
Energy Research and Development Administration—Robert C. Seamans, Jr., Administrator
Environmental Protection Agency—Russell E. Train, Administrator
Equal Employment Opportunity Commission—Ethel Bent Walsh, Acting Chairman
Export-Import Bank—Stephen McKenzie DuBrul, Jr., President
Farm Credit Administration—W. Malcolm Harding, Governor
Federal Communications Commission—Richard E. Wiley, Chairman
Federal Deposit Insurance Corporation—Robert E. Barnett, Chairman
Federal Election Commission—Vernon W. Thomson, Chairman
Federal Energy Administration—Frank G. Zarb, Administrator
Federal Home Loan Bank Board—Garth Marston, Chairman
Federal Maritime Commission—Karl E. Bakke, Chairman
Federal Mediation and Conciliation Service—James F. Scearce, Director
Federal Power Commission—Richard L. Dunham, Chairman
Federal Reserve System—Arthur F. Burns, Board of Governors Chairman
Federal Trade Commission—Calvin J. Collier, Chairman
General Services Administration—Jack M. Eckerd, Administrator
Indian Claims Commission—Jerome K. Kuykendall, Chairman
Interstate Commerce Commission—George M. Stafford, Chairman
National Aeronautics and Space Administration—James C. Fletcher, Administrator
National Credit Union Administration—C. Austin Montgomery, Administrator
National Foundation on the Arts and Humanities—Paul Berman, Director
National Labor Relations Board—Betty Southard Murphy, Chairman
National Mediation Board—David H. Stowe, Chairman
National Science Foundation—Richard C. Atkinson, Acting Director
National Transportation Safety Board—Webster B. Todd, Jr., Chairman
Nuclear Regulatory Commission—Marcus A. Rowden, Chairman
Occupational Safety and Health Review Commission—Frank R. Barnako, Chairman
Overseas Private Investment Corporation—Marshall T. Mays, President
Securities and Exchange Commission—Roderick M. Hills, Chairman
Selective Service System—Byron V. Pepitone, Director
Small Business Administration—Mitchell P. Kobelinski, Administrator
Smithsonian Institution—S. Dillon Ripley, Secretary
Tennessee Valley Authority—Aubrey J. Wagner, Chairman
U.S. Arms Control and Disarmament Agency—Fred C. Ikle, Director
U.S. Commission on Civil Rights—Arthur S. Flemming, Chairman
U.S. Information Agency—(vacant)
U.S. International Trade Commission—Will E. Leonard, Jr., Chairman
U.S. Metric Board—Louis F. Polk †, Chairman
U.S. Postal Service—Benjamin F. Bailar, Postmaster General
Veterans Administration—Richard L. Roudebush, Administrator

Federal Spending and Revenue Receipts

Estimated U.S. Budget for Fiscal 1977*

	Billions of dollars
National defense	101.1
International affairs†	6.8
Science and space research	4.5
Natural resources, environment, energy	13.8
Agriculture	1.7
Commerce and transportation	16.5
Community and regional development	5.5
Education, employment, social services	16.6
Health	34.4
Income security	137.1
Veterans benefits and services	17.2
Law enforcement and justice	3.4
General government	3.4
General revenue sharing	7.4
Interest	41.3
Allowances	2.3
Undistributed funds	−18.8
Total	394.2

*Oct. 1, 1976, to Sept. 30, 1977; all
previous years, July 1 to June 30

†Includes foreign aid

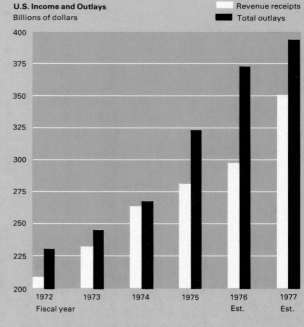

U.S. Income and Outlays
Billions of dollars

☐ Revenue receipts
■ Total outlays

Source: U.S. Office of Management and Budget

There were few differences between the President and Congress in the field of foreign policy in 1976. Most Americans turned their attention away from foreign affairs. Remembering the U.S. failure in Vietnam, they were determined to avoid future foreign entanglements. Responding to this national mood, Congress cut off aid to Angola despite the Administration's urgent request for funds. Nonetheless, President Ford sent Secretary of State Henry A. Kissinger to Africa to act as mediator in the conflict between Rhodesia's white-minority government and its black nationalists. See AFRICA; ANGOLA; RHODESIA.

Changing Administrations. At the end of 1976, public attention focused on Carter's choices to fill Cabinet posts in 1977. But prior to that, there were three changes in President Ford's Cabinet. John T. Dunlop resigned as secretary of labor on January 14, and on January 22 the President named Willie J. Usery, Jr., to that post. On February 2, Elliot L. Richardson, whom Ford had nominated as secretary of commerce in November 1975, succeeded Rogers C. B. Morton in that post. Secretary of Agriculture Earl L. Butz resigned under fire on Oct. 4, 1976, for making a racial slur. Ford named John A. Knebel to replace Butz on November 4.

Major appointments by Ford in 1976 included H. Guyford Stever as director of the Office of Science and Technology Policy and former Pennsylva-

nia Governor William W. Scranton as chief U.S. delegate to the United Nations. See PRESIDENT OF THE UNITED STATES.

In December, Carter announced he would nominate the following persons to Cabinet posts: Cyrus R. Vance as secretary of state; W. Michael Blumenthal as secretary of the treasury; Harold Brown as secretary of defense; Griffin B. Bell as attorney general; Cecil D. Andrus as secretary of the interior; Bob Bergland as secretary of agriculture; Juanita Kreps as secretary of commerce; F. Ray Marshall as secretary of labor; Joseph A. Califano, Jr., as secretary of health, education, and welfare; Patricia Roberts Harris as secretary of housing and urban development; and Brock Adams as secretary of transportation. See CABINET.

The Legislative Branch. Conflict between President Ford and the U.S. Congress produced a stalemate in 1976. The President continued to veto bills he regarded as inflationary or wasteful; Congress continued to press for welfare legislation in an effort to cope with growing unemployment and demands for public works and social services. In his presidential career, Ford vetoed a total of 66 bills passed by the Congress. He vetoed 22 of them in 1976 alone. Congress in 1976 overrode five of Ford's vetoes. Congress on September 16 passed the first major tax-reform legislation since 1969. The President signed it on October 4. See TAXATION.

Social welfare legislation passed by Congress in 1976 provided funds for day-care centers serving low-income families, for public service jobs, for public works projects, and for water-treatment plants. Congress extended Department of Housing and Urban Development housing programs for the elderly and those in low-income groups. It also appropriated funds for higher education and vocational and medical training.

Legislation passed by Congress to protect the environment included the Toxic Substances Control Act, ordering the gradual phase-out of polychlorinated biphenyls; funds for energy research; and expanded funding for national parks.

Consumers benefited when Congress expanded the authority of the Consumer Product Safety Commission. Consumers also stood to gain from passage of a so-called "Sunshine Act," requiring about 50 federal agencies to conduct most of their activities in public. In foreign affairs, Congress cut off aid to factions fighting a civil war in Angola and refused military aid to Chile or any other government systematically torturing political prisoners. See CONGRESS OF THE UNITED STATES; HOUSING; SOCIAL WELFARE; TAXATION.

The Supreme Court of the United States handed down several far-reaching decisions in 1976. The court ruled 6 to 3 on July 1 that a state cannot legally require a woman to have her husband's consent before she can undergo an abortion. It also ruled 5 to 4 that a state cannot require all single women under 18 years of age to secure parental consent before having an abortion.

The court ruled 6 to 3 on March 30 that a Virginia state law prohibiting homosexual acts in private by consenting adults was constitutional. On July 2, the court ruled 7 to 2 that the death penalty for murder is neither cruel nor unusual punishment and is therefore constitutional.

On January 30, the court made several decisions regarding the provisions of the Federal Election Campaign Act of 1974. It held that presidential candidates not receiving federal funds cannot be limited by law in their campaign spending. The same applied to congressional candidates. The court ruled that the Federal Election Commission would have to be restructured, and a reconstituted commission was later approved by Congress.

Other important Supreme Court decisions:
- A judicial gag rule, forbidding press reporting of a crime, is usually unconstitutional.
- Private nonsectarian schools may not exclude applicants because of race.   Carol L. Thompson

See also SUPREME COURT OF THE UNITED STATES; Section One, FOCUS ON THE NATION; Section Five, CARTER, JAMES EARL, JR.

UNITED STATES CONSTITUTION. See CONSTITUTION OF THE UNITED STATES.

UPPER VOLTA. See AFRICA.

URUGUAY. The armed forces ousted President Juan M. Bordaberry Arocena on June 12, 1976, after more than six months of government debate over Uruguay's political future. Vice-President Alberto Demicheli took over as interim president. A National Council of 25 civilians and 21 military officers was formed on June 27 to oversee the country and select a new president. On July 14, the council named its chairman, Aparicio Mendez Manfredini, a 71-year-old conservative lawyer, as president for a five-year term that began officially on September 1.

Bordaberry had been elected to a five-year term in November 1971. He had ruled by decree under a relationship with the military that was never clearly defined since June 1973, after he had dissolved Congress and suspended political parties and labor unions.

The Military, in their communiqué announcing the ouster of Bordaberry, ascribed their differences with him to what they termed his lack of respect for "the deep democratic convictions of our citizenry." Bordaberry, according to the communiqué, wanted to abolish political parties forever and bring the armed forces into the government permanently.

Mendez declared on July 15 that the major political parties, the Blancos and the Colorados, would be allowed to take part in choosing his successor, but only after they were purged of "professional politicians," whose indecisiveness and divisiveness, it was charged, encouraged urban terrorism and near economic collapse. Mendez also said that he planned a "civic purge" to root Marxists out of political institutions and that the country would get a new constitution that disavowed the Marxist concept of "class struggle."

Amnesty International, a London-based organization concerned with the plight of political prisoners, began a worldwide campaign in February to publicize abuses of human rights by the military and police forces in Uruguay. On February 19, it issued a report charging that 22 political prisoners had been tortured to death in Uruguay between May 1972 and November 1975. The organization also asserted that Uruguay had the world's highest proportion of political prisoners—about 6,000 out of a population of 3.1 million.

During the year, dozens of Uruguayans sought political asylum in various foreign embassies in Montevideo, including the Mexican and Colombian embassies. Venezuela suspended diplomatic relations with Uruguay on July 6, a week after alleged Uruguayan security agents abducted a woman who was seeking political asylum on the grounds of the Venezuelan Embassy in Montevideo. In September, the U.S. Congress suspended all aid programs to Uruguay because of human-rights violations there.   Everett G. Martin

See also LATIN AMERICA (Facts in Brief Table).

USERY, WILLIE JULIAN, JR. (1923-   ), was sworn in as U.S. secretary of labor on Feb. 10, 1976. He succeeded John T. Dunlop, who resigned in January after President Gerald R. Ford vetoed a controversial construction-site picketing bill that Dunlop had supported. See LABOR.

Usery was born in Hardwick, Ga., on Dec. 21, 1923. He attended Georgia Military College and went to Mercer University in Macon, Ga., for one year. From 1943 to 1946, he served in the U.S. Navy as a steamfitter. Usery became a welder and joined the International Association of Machinists in 1946. He rose to grand lodge representative and chairman of the union negotiating committee.

Usery was named assistant secretary of labor for labor-management relations in 1969. He became director of the Federal Mediation and Conciliation Service in 1973, and in 1974 he took on the additional duties of special assistant to the President for labor-management negotiations.

As a government mediator, Usery was personally involved in many of the nation's most important labor disputes. He is rated one of the best mediators in labor history and is regarded as a tireless and skillful negotiator by parties on both sides of the bargaining table.   Kathryn Sederberg

UTAH. See STATE GOVERNMENT.

UTILITIES. See COMMUNICATIONS; ENERGY; PETROLEUM AND GAS.

VENEZUELA formally nationalized its oil industry on Jan. 1, 1976. President Carlos Andres Perez, raising the national flag in a ceremony at Lake Maracaibo, declared, "We are not nationalizing because we will earn more money. We are nationalizing because oil is the nation's basic industry . . . and it is neither convenient nor acceptable that it be in foreign hands."

The 21 oil-producing firms – including the U.S.-owned Exxon Corporation, the Shell Oil Company, the Gulf Oil Corporation, and the Mobil Oil Corporation – which had about $5 billion invested in facilities, are to receive $1.1 billion plus $160 million a year for technical assistance.

Political Unrest. On February 14, student rioting erupted in San Felipe, Yaracuy state, after two students were killed during a demonstration for better school facilities. The disorder, which spread quickly to at least 13 other cities, intensified during U.S. Secretary of State Henry A. Kissinger's visit to Caracas from February 16 to 18.

American Kidnaped. On February 27, William Niehous, general manager of the Venezuelan operations of Owens-Illinois, Incorporated, a U.S.-based glassmaking concern, was kidnaped from his Caracas home by left wing subversives. The kidnapers identified themselves in a communiqué to *El Nacional*, a Caracas newspaper, as the Group of Revolutionary Commandos (GCR). They said they

acted to protest government repression and alleged interference in Venezuela's economic policies by the American company.

Police, theorizing that the GCR was an amalgam of small leftist guerrilla groups, arrested and held more than 100 persons in several cities. The death of one suspect stirred widespread protests. The suspect, Jorge Antonio Rodriguez, leader of the tiny Venezuelan Socialist League, was seized on July 20, when police intercepted a ransom payment that an alleged agent of Owens-Illinois was attempting to pay for the release of Niehous. At year's end, Niehous was still in the kidnapers' hands.

Owens-Illinois, ignoring a government admonition to have no dealings with the kidnapers, also paid a $116 bonus to each of its 1,600 employees and financed publication of the guerrillas' manifesto in *The New York Times* and other publications. On April 6, the government angrily declared that the firm had "offended the dignity of the country and promoted the subversion of our constitutional order." In reprisal, it nationalized all of Owens-Illinois' assets.   Everett G. Martin

See also LATIN AMERICA (Facts in Brief Table).

VERMONT. See STATE GOVERNMENT.

VETERANS. See COMMUNITY ORGANIZATIONS.

VICE-PRESIDENT OF THE UNITED STATES. See MONDALE, WALTER F.; ROCKEFELLER, NELSON ALDRICH.

VIETNAM was reunited on July 2, 1976, as the Socialist Republic of Vietnam with Hanoi as its capital. The country had been divided in 1954 into a Communist-ruled northern part and a separate U.S.-backed southern part by the Geneva Agreement that ended French rule in Indochina. Communist efforts to gain control of the entire country succeeded in April 1975, after 18 years of war.

North Vietnamese Army Chief of Staff General Van Tien Dung published in 1976 an account of the final military campaign that said Hanoi was surprised by the speed of the South's collapse and by winning the victory so soon. The victory brought South Vietnam under the regime in Hanoi, which included many southerners in its leadership.

Power in Hanoi emanated from the Vietnam Workers' Party, a Communist organization founded by the late Ho Chi Minh. The South had been run since April 1975 by members of this party and the victorious army.

National Elections were held on April 26 for a National Assembly with 249 seats assigned to the North and 243 to the South. Voters' choices were limited to people approved by the Workers' Party. The new Assembly met in Hanoi from June 24 to July 3. Ton Duc Thang became president of the reunited country, and Pham Van Dong became prime minister. Most of the new leaders had held the same jobs in the North Vietnamese govern-

Float bearing a portrait of Ho Chi Minh leads a Saigon parade on April 26—election day for the joint North and South Vietnam National Assembly.

Communist authorities gradually tightened controls on the South, including setting up special tribunals to deal with economic crimes. Some who had opposed both the defeated Saigon government and the northern victors were reported living under great hardship in prison camps with former members of the Saigon government.

In November, it was announced that Vietnam's war-ravaged railway system was nearly restored. This opened the possibility of traveling from Saigon to Paris in the future.

International Affairs. Hanoi tried to establish normal relations with Southeast Asian countries, succeeding with most. But the military coup in Thailand on October 6 set back progress toward good relations with Bangkok. See THAILAND.

After lengthy sparring by letter, Vietnam and the United States opened talks on normalizing their relations in Paris on November 12. The United States insisted that Hanoi must provide full information on Americans missing in the Vietnam War. Hanoi insisted that the United States had promised in 1973 to provide postwar aid. Washington said North Vietnam's violations of the cease-fire canceled this promise. On November 15, a U.S. veto prevented United Nations membership for Vietnam. Henry S. Bradsher

See also ASIA (Facts in Brief Table).

VIRGINIA. See STATE GOVERNMENT.

ment, and the flag, anthem, and emblem of North Vietnam were also adopted.

The Workers' Party held its fourth congress in mid-December, the first since 1960. The congress in theory is the supreme policy council for the party, and through it for the nation. The new congress was held "to discuss and adopt the socialist revolutionary line in our entire country, the key tasks of the Second [1976 to 1980] Five-Year Plan and the [revised] party statutes, and to elect a new Central Committee." Plans were also made to speed up economic development.

Army Role. The army was given a major economic role, thus keeping it together rather than disbanding it so soldiers could return to civilian work. The Ministry of National Defense became responsible for reconstruction and economic development. In addition to working in everything from industry and transportation to agriculture and fisheries, the army was turned into a "large school for training youths."

A dwindling security role remained for the army, too. Several incidents were reported, including a rebellion by armed dissidents in a Roman Catholic church in Saigon on February 12 in which three persons were killed. The government revealed other armed opposition and sniping at officials, and there were reports of resistance in some rural areas. But, in general, the country seemed peaceful.

VISUAL ARTS. The celebration of the American Revolution Bicentennial was an ongoing focus for the world of art in 1976. Washington, D.C., hosted many exhibitions and became a major culture center. The Smithsonian Institution re-created the 1876 Philadelphia Exposition by reassembling thousands of the objects exhibited there. The Corcoran Gallery of Art presented "America 1976," displaying the works of 45 artists who had been invited by the Department of the Interior to choose subjects in areas under the department's jurisdiction in any of the 50 states.

"The Golden Door," organized by the Hirshhorn Museum and Sculpture Garden, surveyed the ethnic basis of American civilization as seen in the art of 67 foreign-born American artists. Three large retrospective exhibitions of important contemporary Americans were held—the works of Robert Rauschenberg, at the National Collection of Fine Arts; Morris Louis, at the National Gallery of Art; and Hans Hofmann, at the Hirshhorn Museum.

Several major exhibitions also opened their U.S. tours in Washington. One example was "The European Vision of America," organized by the Cleveland Museum of Art and first seen at the National Gallery of Art. "Treasures of Tutankhamon" began a two-year U.S. tour at the National Gallery.

Elsewhere, the Bicentennial was celebrated at the Philadelphia Museum of Art by its "Philadelphia:

300 Years of American Art." At the Pennsylvania Academy of the Fine Arts, "In This Academy" surveyed the importance of that venerable art school with 350 works. In New York City, the Museum of Modern Art assembled "Natural Paradise: Painting in America 1800-1950"; the Whitney Museum of American Art presented "200 Years of American Sculpture"; and the Metropolitan Museum of Art organized an exhibition of the academic sculpture of Daniel Chester French.

Foreign Exchange. Several major exhibitions were seen in the United States and then sent abroad. The Art Gallery of Yale University sent "American Art 1750-1800" to the Victoria and Albert Museum in London. After its display in Cleveland and Washington, "The European Vision of America" went on to Paris.

Among the shows sent to the United States from abroad were 41 Leonardo da Vinci drawings from the Royal Collections at Windsor Castle in England, seen at the Los Angeles County Museum of Art. Eight works of Spain's Francisco Goya were exhibited in New York City and Washington, D.C. It was also hoped that "Sacred Circles: North American Indian Art," organized by the Nelson-Atkins Gallery of Art in Kansas City, Mo., for the Hayward Gallery in London, would be shown in the United States. And, for the first time, the Whitney Museum produced an exhibition to be seen abroad. Its "American Art Since 1950" was organized for the Seibu Art Museum in Tokyo.

Other Important U.S. Exhibitions included "Art Nouveau in Belgium and France 1885-1915," an exhibition of decorative arts organized by the Institute for the Fine Arts at Houston's Rice University and the Art Institute of Chicago. The Art Institute also assembled the unusual "Raiment for the Lord's Service: A Thousand Years of Western Church Vestments." Two other exhibitions focused on early modernist artists. The Museum of Modern Art in New York City presented "The Wild Beasts: Fauvism and Its Affinities," while the Art Institute of Chicago, together with the Guggenheim Museum in New York City, offered the work of the Belgian pre-expressionist James Ensor.

Two of America's favorite artists were also honored with exhibitions. The Metropolitan Museum of Art organized an Andrew Wyeth exhibition, and the Whitney Museum showed Alexander Calder's sculpture. Calder died on November 11, shortly after arriving in New York City for the opening of his show.

The obvious vitality of these many exhibitions did not disguise a continuing sense of uneasiness among practicing artists about the present meaning of creating art. Traditional painting and sculpture

Artist Christo's *Running Fence* of shimmering nylon stretched along the California coast for 24½ miles (40 kilometers) for two weeks in September.

Restorer carefully cleans drawings, believed to be by Michelangelo, that line the walls of a room under the Medici Chapel in Florence, Italy.

Major Acquisitions of artwork included *Lavender Mist* by the pioneer American abstract-expressionist painter, Jackson Pollock. One of the last of his works in private hands, *Lavender Mist* was bought by the National Gallery of Art for $2-million. The Cleveland Museum of Art bought a major work by one of the greatest Italian painters, Michelangelo Merisi da Caravaggio. The whereabouts of *The Martyrdom of Saint Andrew* had been unknown until it reappeared in Spain in 1973. It is now one of only five works by Caravaggio in the United States. The Brooklyn Museum exchanged 11 paintings and $200,000 for the large romantic-realist painting *Storm in the Rocky Mountains* by the mid-19th century artist Albert Bierstadt. The Museum of Modern Art in New York City purchased *The Swimming Pool,* a long cutout by Henri Matisse. Meant as a model for ceramic wall sculpture, the important work will replace Picasso's *Guernica* in the museum's collection. According to Picasso's will, *Guernica* must be returned to Spain when democracy is restored there.

Art at Auction. Prices for art continued to show both the increasing rarity of older works and the continuing value accorded to any great work of art. *Still Life with Japanese Print,* a painting by Paul Gauguin, was sold for $1.4 million, the second highest recorded price for postimpressionist art. A record price for an American painting in Great Britain was reached with the $320,000 paid for the early 19th-century *Washington and his Generals at Yorktown* by James Peale. A landscape by the British romantic Joseph M. W. Turner was sold for $684,000. One of the year's sensational prices was the $260,000 paid for a small Chinese porcelain vase from the Ming dynasty that had been sold for $150 in 1940. The $190,000 paid for a Mark Rothko established an auction record for works of the American abstract-expressionist school.

Financial Problems continued to plague many American museums. Among attempted solutions were drastic service cuts and wider use of mandatory entrance fees. The most dramatic proposal was that of the Museum of Modern Art in New York City to build a 40-story condominium apartment building over the museum to ensure future income. Museums also continued to seek greater federal and corporate support.

Building Activity included the completion of the new East Wing of the Art Institute of Chicago. In addition to providing more gallery space, the wing will house the Louis Sullivan Room, a reconstruction of the trading room of the now-demolished Chicago Stock Exchange designed by the great architect. In New York City, the Cooper-Hewitt Museum of Decorative Arts and Design reopened in the former Andrew Carnegie mansion. Joshua B. Kind

VITAL STATISTICS. See CENSUS, UNITED STATES; POPULATION, WORLD.

materials were still used; for instance, the style known as photo-realism — mimicking photography — has achieved recent popularity. Also eclectic production — combining several modernist idioms, such as constructivist geometry and expressionist artistic freedom — has begun to appear more frequently. Nonetheless, many artists feel that work created in these ways is becoming less valuable. This may account for the continuing interest in nontraditional materials and attitudes that started in the late 1960s. They include minimal, process, conceptual, and performance art, as well as the use of craft, film, and video materials.

Picasso and Others. In Paris, the heirs to the enormous estate of Pablo Picasso — some 1,500 paintings, 3,000 drawings, and 500 sculptures — announced that about 20 per cent of these works would be turned over to the French government to establish a Picasso Museum. The museum will be near the controversial, newly opened, $200-million culture complex, *Centre Beaubourg,* in Paris.

A large exhibition in Paris celebrated the centenary of the death of Jean François Millet, best known for *The Angelus.* Three hundred paintings seen at the Tate Gallery in London honored the 200th anniversary of the birth of John Constable. Several large drawings thought to be by Michelangelo were discovered in a room under the Medici Chapel in Florence, Italy.

WALTERS, BARBARA (1931-   ), became the first woman to co-anchor a television network evening newscast in the United States on Oct. 4, 1976, when she joined Harry Reasoner on the American Broadcasting Company (ABC) evening news program. A five-year contract for a reported $1 million a year lured her away from the National Broadcasting Company (NBC) "Today" show after 15 years and made her the highest-paid TV news personality.

Born Sept. 25, 1931, in Boston, Walters grew up there, in New York City, and in Miami Beach, Fla., moving as fortunes changed for her father, a nightclub impresario. She graduated from Sarah Lawrence College in Bronxville, N.Y., in 1953 with a B.A. degree in English and a desire to teach. Instead, she joined a New York City television station where she learned to research, write, film, and edit. She joined the "Today" show as a writer in 1961.

One of the best interviewers in television, Walters took over another NBC talk program, "Not for Women Only," in 1971. At ABC, she moderated the third televised debate between President Gerald R. Ford and James Earl (Jimmy) Carter, Jr. on October 22.

She married Lee Guber in 1963, but they were divorced in 1976. They have a daughter, Jacqueline Dena.   Robert K. Johnson

WASHINGTON. See SEATTLE; STATE GOV'T.

WASHINGTON, D.C. President Gerald R. Ford and a number of high-ranking government officials gathered at the National Archives in Washington, D.C., on July 2, 1976, to pay tribute to the Declaration of Independence as part of the American Revolution Bicentennial celebration. Virtually all the city's museums and galleries featured Bicentennial shows, and the Smithsonian Institution opened its new National Air and Space Museum on July 1.

Local Government. A proposed amendment to the U.S. Constitution, which eventually would have given residents of the District of Columbia a voting member in the House of Representatives, failed to gain approval of the House on March 23. The measure fell 45 votes short of the two-thirds majority required to approve a constitutional amendment.

A U.S. Senate report released on June 19 concluded that the District of Columbia government was losing millions of revenue dollars annually because of inadequate bookkeeping. The report recommended an overhaul of the district's money-management system, but noted that it would take two years and about $20 million just to get the books in shape for auditing.

The initial 4.6-mile (7.4-kilometer) segment of Washington's planned 98-mile (158-kilometer) rapid-transit system opened in March. Daily ridership was two to three times the expected 8,500 pas-

President Ford and his wife, Betty, attend the ceremony at which Dean Francis B. Sayre dedicates the nave of Washington Cathedral on July 8.

sengers. The federal government gave Washington a \$15.7-million mass-transit grant on July 21 to help finance new and expanded facilities.

Police Affairs. Washington newspapers reported in January that the Central Intelligence Agency (CIA) had provided Washington, D.C., police with equipment and training for electronic surveillance and burglary. The CIA claimed its action was legal and indicated that the CIA assisted the police because of "tangible threats of terrorist groups within their jurisdiction."

The Supreme Court of the United States on June 7 upheld the validity of tests given to applicants for the Washington police force by a 7 to 2 vote. A federal appellate court had previously ruled the tests had a "racially disproportionate impact" and were therefore unfair to minority applicants.

A former Chilean Cabinet member and ambassador to the United States, Orlando Letelier, was killed on September 21, when a bomb exploded under his car. Prominent U.S. congressmen accused agents of Chile's military government of carrying out the assassination.

Unemployment Declines. A U.S. Department of Labor report on May 5 showed that unemployment in Washington had fallen below 6 per cent. Living costs rose 4 per cent between August 1975 and May 1976. Food costs rose 3.8 per cent between June 1975 and June 1976.   James M. Banovetz

WEATHER. Western Europe suffered its worst drought in memory in 1976. Crops in Belgium, Italy, and West Germany wilted under a relentless summer sun. French and Swiss farmers, unable to find pasture for their cattle, had to slaughter thousands of the animals. A rainwear factory in Scotland closed its doors. And at the Wimbledon tennis championships in England in June and July, more than 500 spectators fainted in the heat in a day. The governments of Great Britain and Belgium took drastic action in August, imposing stiff fines for wasting water.

In the United States, the weather was erratic. The North-Central States experienced one of the worst droughts ever recorded, with crops in the Dakotas, Iowa, Minnesota, Nebraska, and Wisconsin suffering the most. Southern California's drought was broken by heavy rains during the second week of September. The lettuce crop was severely damaged by this rain, raising prices and reducing the quality of lettuce that reached the market. The early fall was considerably colder than normal over the southeastern two-thirds of the country, with record snows in the Texas Panhandle during the last week of October.

Pollution Study. In early April, the U.S. Air Force performed a series of research flights in the stratosphere for the National Center for Atmospheric Research and the National Oceanic and Atmospheric Administration (NOAA) to determine the cause of ozone depletion. Ozone in the upper atmosphere shields the earth from harmful ultraviolet radiation.

Samples of air were taken from the stratosphere to be analyzed for nitrogen oxides, acidic vapors, fluorocarbons, and chlorine compounds. In theory, one chlorine atom can destroy thousands of ozone molecules by a cyclic process if the chlorine is not removed in the process. The presence of sufficient quantities of hydrogen chloride could remove the chlorines and thus reduce the ozone destruction. The data collected on the research flights were being studied.

Many areas suffer from ozone pollution near the earth's surface. Until 1976, scientists assumed that ozone near the ground dissipates at night and is manufactured anew by automobile and other exhaust products during the following day. However, they found in 1976 that each day's pollution rises at night only to descend again the next day.

In another NOAA study, a manned balloon was used to determine the rate at which pollutants are dispersed at various levels in the atmosphere. The study, called Project Da Vinci, was made in June over St. Louis. The balloon was equipped with more than 1 short ton (0.9 metric ton) of instruments. Many small balloons were released from the parent craft, and they stayed at heights of 1,000 to 3,000 feet (300 to 900 meters), where most of the earth's pollutants are mixed with the atmosphere. Researchers studied particle size, shape, and composition and analyzed the possible effects of pollution on weather.

Climatic Change. Scientists performing research for the National Science Foundation have discovered a warming trend in Antarctica and other parts of the extreme Southern Hemisphere. The warming trend appears to be greater in magnitude than the recent cooling trend observed in the Northern Hemisphere. Its most likely cause is an increase of carbon dioxide in the atmosphere. But the researchers believe that the cause will not be fully known without more study of the upper air weather and the factors that affect the earth's *albedo,* the amount of solar energy reflected.

A three-day conference on solar physics and related fields was held in Boulder, Colo., in April to discuss the relationship of solar output to changes in the earth's climate. Much of the discussion concerned the periodicity (intervals) of sunspots and whether this has an effect on weather and climate. It was pointed out that the "Little Ice Age" in the 1600s occurred during a 40-year period when no sun spots were observed. Many of the scientists believe that a relationship exists, but that further research is needed for proof.   Edward W. Pearl

See also DISASTERS.

WEIGHT LIFTING. See OLYMPIC GAMES; SPORTS.

WEST INDIES. The number of small nations emerging in the Caribbean continued to grow in 1976. Anguilla was constitutionally established as a self-governing British territory on February 10 (see ANGUILLA). In self-governing Antigua, an associated state within the Commonwealth of Nations, Labor Party leader Vere Bird was elected prime minister on February 18.

On August 1, Trinidad and Tobago dissolved its ties to the British Crown by adopting a new charter to replace its 1962 Constitution. Under the new document, Trinidad and Tobago became a republic with a president elected head of the government by the two houses of Parliament. In the general elections held on September 13, the ruling People's National Movement Party captured 24 of the 36 seats at stake in the House of Representatives. Prime Minister Eric E. Williams was named to his fifth consecutive five-year term.

The Democratic Action Congress, a major opposition party, captured only two seats. However, the Labor Front, another opposition party, won 10 seats in the Senate and promised to act as a counterweight to Williams' centrist policies.

Barbados Results. J. M. G. Adams, leader of the Barbados Labor Party, was sworn in as prime minister on September 3 after an election that gave his party 17 of the 24 seats in the House of Assembly against 7 for the Democratic Labor Party headed by Errol W. Barrow, who had served as prime minister for 15 years. Adams pledged a free national health service and the elimination of corporate and trade taxes, as well as a 5 per cent sales tax, a charter for women, and a program to fight unemployment.

Terrorist Activities continued to plague Jamaica. On January 6, violence erupted in Kingston. Tenement housing and other buildings were destroyed by fire bombings, and terrorist groups exchanged gunfire with police and army forces. Despite an immediate declaration of martial law, the disturbances continued sporadically. On June 19, the government declared a state of emergency. During the preceding 5½ months, about 100 persons had been killed. The government claimed the violence was part of a "destabilization campaign" by conservative forces against Prime Minister Michael N. Manley's Democratic Socialist government. On November 2, an attempt was made to assassinate Edward Seaga, leader of the Jamaican Labor Party. Manley was re-elected and his party increased its strength in Parliament in a landslide election victory on December 15.   Paul C. Tullier

See also LATIN AMERICA (Facts in Brief Table).

WEST VIRGINIA. See STATE GOVERNMENT.
WILDLIFE. See CONSERVATION.
WISCONSIN. See STATE GOVERNMENT.
WRESTLING. See OLYMPIC GAMES; SPORTS.
WYOMING. See STATE GOVERNMENT.

YEMEN (ADEN) established diplomatic relations with Saudi Arabia on March 10, 1976, marking an unspectacular but dramatic shift in policy. The agreement did not merely solidify relations between basically antagonistic regimes – Saudi Arabia is a conservative monarchy, while Aden is a one-party Marxist-Leninist state. It also brought Aden an immediate $100 million in aid for its struggling economy. The Aden regime also agreed to a cease-fire with Oman along their common border, though it continued to give moral support to rebels fighting in the southern Omani province of Dhofar.

On November 25, Aden forces shot down an Iranian fighter plane from Oman that had violated Yemeni airspace near the eastern border. Officials called it the latest of repeated violations by military and spy planes. Oman said the plane was on a training flight and had not crossed the border when it was fired on.

Amnesty International reported on May 17 that from 2,000 to 10,000 political prisoners were in jail in Aden but that many of their sentences had been reduced to a 15-year maximum. The report also concluded that no organized opposition existed to the ruling National Front (NF), but the NF's internal divisions were underscored by the attempted assassination in Cairo, Egypt, on August 6 of former Prime Minister Muhammad Ali Haitham. Aden's consul in Cairo, Saif Muhsen, was arrested for complicity in the attempt.

Red Dependence. Despite the move to normalize relations with its neighbors, Yemen was still heavily dependent on Communist aid for economic development. The largest share of foreign aid came from mainland China, and three Chinese-built, Chinese-financed projects went into operation on June 19. They were an expanded saltworks in Aden, a wire and farm-tools plant near Khormaksar, and a fish cannery and fish-meal processing plant in Aden. The latter has an annual export capacity of 500 short tons (453 metric tons). Other Communist aid included an agreement with North Korea for a soap factory.

Yemen also received loans from Abu Zaby for $9-million for fishing equipment and $450,000 from Libya for a health clinic on remote Socotra Island. The International Development Association (IDA) gave credits of $7 million on February 19 for a project to improve agricultural production for 5,000 farm families in the Hadhramaut Valley. A second IDA credit of $3.2 million, along with $13-million from the Arab Fund for Economic and Social Development, would finance expansion of Aden harbor, used little since the Suez Canal reopened in 1975. Instead of the 500 per cent increase in shipping into Aden projected when the canal was restored to service, the 1976 increase was about 50 per cent.   William Spencer

See also MIDDLE EAST (Facts in Brief Table).

YEMEN (SANA), despite its meager resources and limited economic prospects, continued to attract external support in 1976. Aid came from a number of sources. Saudi Arabia, its main backer, agreed on April 13 to pay the salaries of 754 Egyptian teachers employed in Yemen and to provide additional teachers. The Saudi Development Fund also contributed $48 million for roads, rural health clinics, and water-supply projects, all desperately needed in this land where annual per capita income is $90.

Saudi support in particular enabled Command Council Chairman Ibrahim Mohamed al-Hamdi to embark on a cautious policy of Western contacts. On April 28, the Ford Administration notified Congress of plans to sell Yemen $139 million in military equipment, to be paid for by Saudi Arabia.

The budget issued on July 15 estimated revenues of $180 million and expenditures of $260 million, the $80-million deficit up sharply from 1975's $58-million. Nevertheless, the government went ahead on October 1 with its first Five-Year Plan. The Inter-Parliamentary Union, meeting in Mexico City, expelled Yemen on April 19 because Hamdi dissolved Yemen's Parliament in 1975. William Spencer

See also MIDDLE EAST (Facts in Brief Table).

YOUNG MEN'S CHRISTIAN ASSOCIATION (YMCA). See COMMUNITY ORGANIZATIONS.
YOUNG WOMEN'S CHRISTIAN ASSOCIATION (YWCA). See COMMUNITY ORGANIZATIONS.

YOUTH ORGANIZATIONS continued their efforts to serve people in 1976 with programs designed to develop skills, improve opportunities, and relieve social and personal problems that affect the young.

Boy Scouts of America (BSA) will expand the role of women in adult BSA posts, BSA President Arch Monson announced on February 25 in Washington, D.C. The changes include the removal of all sex qualifications for leaders of Cub Scout packs. With the exception of scoutmaster and assistant scoutmaster, all positions in the Scout program will now be open to women. In addition, the BSA intends to drop all sex requirements for attendance at Wood Badge Programs, the highest leadership training programs in the Scout movement. Monson said the action was "recognition of the extremely valuable contribution of women to the Boy Scouts of America in its 66 years of service to youth."

"Exploring," the coeducational program for young adults 15 through 20 years old, was also expanded. Nationwide BSA programs emphasized conservation, the American Revolution Bicentennial, physical fitness, and religious principles. During the summer, nearly 800 Eagle Scouts assisted visitors and demonstrated crafts in Washington, D.C.

The President's Council on Physical Fitness and Sports honored the BSA for its outstanding contribution to physical fitness.

BSA membership stood at 5.3 million at the beginning of 1976. Harvey L. Price was named acting chief scout executive, and Monson, a San Francisco business executive and civic leader, was reelected to a second term as president of BSA.

Boys' Clubs of America. "Project Team," a three-year alcohol-abuse-prevention program, received a second-year grant renewal from the National Institute on Alcohol Abuse and Alcoholism of the Department of Health, Education, and Welfare. New programs emphasizing health services, alternatives to the juvenile justice system, clarification of personal values, and the responsibilities of future leadership were being developed.

More than 1,000 Boys' Club workers representing nearly 1,100 Boys' Clubs in 700 communities in the United States attended the annual conference in New Orleans in May. National Boy of the Year for 1976, Robert Lee Fisher of the Boys' Club of Pasadena, Calif., was presented with a plaque by President Gerald R. Ford proclaiming him the boy who best "typifies juvenile decency in action."

Camp Fire Girls had more than 350 councils in 30,000 communities in the United States developing programs to meet community needs. These include day-care programs, coed activities, career-development seminars, storefront recreational programs, and activities for young people with special needs and interests.

Camp Fire continued its emphasis on the development of the individual in small groups such as "Blue Birds," "Adventurers," "Discovery," and "Horizon Club."

4-H Clubs. About 5½ million 4-H'ers between the ages of 9 and 19 worked under the guidance of 550,000 adult and teen volunteer leaders in 1976. Their theme for the year was "4-H '76 – Spirit of Tomorrow."

Of the total 4-H membership, 23 per cent live on farms, 40 per cent in towns with fewer than 10,000 persons, and 17 per cent in towns and cities of from 10,000 to 50,000. Nearly 20 per cent live in metropolitan areas of more than 50,000 persons.

Thirty young farmers from the United States and Russia participated in the first international 4-H exchange program between the two nations. Twenty-three young men and women with strong backgrounds in agriculture and 4-H exchanged places with counterparts from Poland for a work-study experience.

Future Farmers of America (FFA) achieved great success in the first full year of its "Food for America" program. The program telling the story of agriculture was presented to about 500,000 elementary school students.

FFA hosted a world conference on agricultural education at its November national convention in Kansas City, Mo. The 200 representatives from 24 countries discussed methods of improving agriculture and increasing the world food supply. At the convention, awards were presented to the Star Farmer of America and the Star Agribusinessman of America. See AGRICULTURE.

FFA membership continued to grow at the rate of about 15,000 a year. There are now 500,385 members in 8,072 chapters in the United States.

Girl Scouts of the United States of America lit candles – symbolic "flames of freedom" – across the continent on March 12, 1976, as part of their three-year American Revolution Bicentennial project. Many of these ceremonies took place at state capitals. First lady Betty Ford, honorary Girl Scout president, lit the first candle on Oct. 26, 1975, in Washington, D.C.

The Reader's Digest Foundation again awarded grants to Cadette and Senior Girl Scouts for special community projects in 1976. Twenty-seven grants totaling more than $8,500 went to Girl Scout groups in 18 states for such projects as developing safe bicycle routes, restoring historic landmarks, and creating miniparks for senior citizens.

The National Board of Directors appointed Frances R. Hesselbein of Johnstown, Pa., as national executive director of Girl Scouts of the U.S.A.

Girls Clubs of America (GCA) adopted the following goals at its 31st annual conference: To take a leading role as an advocate for the rights of girls of all backgrounds and abilities; to give girls opportunities to recognize their worth as human beings and to develop their full potential; to help girls become knowledgeable, creative, and active participants in a representative society; to develop and maintain quality programs and high standards of evaluation in girls' clubs; and to expand the capabilities and strengths of Girls Clubs of America.

Two hundred and fifty local Girls Clubs were implementing these goals in their daily work with 205,000 girls from 6 to 18 in all parts of the United States. Some 67 per cent of these girls were from low-income families.

Junior Achievement (JA) launched Project Business, a program for ninth-grade students, in 1976 after four years of experimentation. Designed to teach the basic tenets of the free-enterprise economic system and to increase young people's knowledge of how business operates, Project Business brings a local business person to a social studies or economics class once a week to work with the students. This specially trained volunteer leads class discussions, conducts visits to offices and industrial sites, and talks about business career opportunities.

In the second semester of the 1975-1976 school year, 6,000 students in 33 cities were enrolled in 213 Project Business classes. Thanks in part to a $755,-910 grant from the W. K. Kellogg Foundation of Battle Creek, Mich., business consultants in 3,500 classrooms will conduct Project Business for 98,000 students in 175 cities by 1979.   Joseph P. Anderson

YUGOSLAVIA improved its relations with Russia in 1976 and at the same time strengthened its economic and political ties with both the West and the developing countries. At home, the government crackdown against dissidents continued.

President Josip Broz Tito attended the East Berlin conference of 29 European Communist parties in June and met with Russian Communist Party General Secretary Leonid I. Brezhnev. The two leaders met again in Belgrade for three days in November, at which time Brezhnev reaffirmed Russia's respect for Yugoslavia's independence.

Relations with Bulgaria improved after talks in Sofia, Bulgaria, in September. But relations with Austria deteriorated sharply following Austria's decision in July to hold a language census in November to see how many Slovenes and Croats live in Austria, especially in the province of Carinthia. Yugoslavia condemned the census and Austrian policy in general as "statistical genocide" (see AUSTRIA). Albanian Communist Party leader Enver Hoxha criticized Yugoslavia for allowing Russian ships into Yugoslav ports.

Dissident Crackdown. General Franjo Herljevic, secretary for internal affairs, told the Federal Assembly in July that Yugoslav security forces had uncovered 13 "subversive" groups since 1974 and arrested 237 of their members. For example, 11 Croatian nationalists were convicted in Zagreb in June on charges of planning sabotage and assassinations. Five were sentenced to death, but their sentences were commuted. About 30 pro-Moscow hardliners, mainly Serbs, were tried and sentenced.

A Belgrade court sentenced Vladimir Dapcevic to death on July 5 for crimes against the state. Dapcevic denied charges that he was the leader of anti-Tito dissidents in Russia and Western Europe. He accused Yugoslav authorities of having kidnaped him from Bucharest, Romania, in 1975 while on a visit from Belgium. His sentence was commuted to 20 years in prison.

Jet Hijack. Four Croatian-born men and an American woman hijacked a New York-to-Chicago Trans World Airlines jet on September 10. They gave themselves up in Paris on September 12 after having propaganda leaflets advocating Croatia's separation from Yugoslavia dropped on major cities. They were returned to the United States and charged with air piracy and the murder of a New York City policeman, who died trying to dismantle a bomb that the hijackers allegedly left behind.

The European Community (Common Market) announced in November it would offer Yugoslavia substantial financial aid. Yugoslavia's 1976 grain harvest was good. Imports dropped 9 per cent in the first nine months, while exports rose 22 per cent. Nevertheless, food prices increased as much as 30 per cent.   Chris Cviic

See also EUROPE (Facts in Brief Table).

YUKON TERRITORY. The Canadian federal government answered Indian land claims in the territory in 1976 by proposing to give the Indians 1,200 square miles (3,100 square kilometers) of land for their exclusive use, as well as a cash award of $50-million. Yukon Indians criticized the proposal, claiming that it did not match the 1974 Quebec offer to the Indians of James Bay. Although it was not possible to reach a settlement during the year, the Council of Yukon Indians carried out a program of community education in preparation for further negotiations with Ottawa. Northern Affairs Minister Warren Allmand told the Yukon Legislative Council that the territory would not become a province until arrangements were made to allow its Indians to have a greater part in the government.

A strike beginning on March 8 at the Anvil zinc-lead mine in the southern Yukon, the most important mine in the territory, threatened the $228-million mining industry, the main industry of the Yukon. A mediator succeeded in ending the long dispute on November 19. Better news came with the start of open-cut mining on a promising barite deposit at Macmillan Pass, north of Ross River. Barite is used in oil drilling.

Arthur Pearson, a 38-year-old biologist, succeeded James Smith as commissioner of the Yukon Territory on July 1.   David M. L. Farr

See also CANADA.

ZAIRE experienced serious economic difficulties in 1976. In March, the government of President Mobutu Sese Seko devalued Zaire's currency by 42 per cent in terms of United States dollars. Imports had far outstripped exports. One reason for this was a steep slide during 1975 in world market prices for copper, Zaire's most important export. Another problem was the country's large foreign debt. It was having difficulty meeting the heavy payments. In June, foreign governments that had lent Zaire money agreed to reschedule payments.

Donald H. Rumsfeld, the U.S. secretary of defense, arrived in Zaire on June 17 to discuss Zaire's defense needs, particularly after the victory of the Russian-backed faction in neighboring Angola's civil war. Thousands of Cuban troops were also present in Angola (see ANGOLA). During Rumsfeld's visit, Zaire reportedly received assurances that U.S. military assistance would be increased to $28 million from about $19 million.

Zaire had backed the losing faction in the Angolan civil war. Nevertheless, on February 28, Mobutu's government extended diplomatic recognition to the government of the Popular Movement for the Liberation of Angola (MPLA). Zaire also pledged that anti-MPLA forces would not be allowed to use its territory.   John D. Esseks

See also AFRICA (Facts in Brief Table).

ZAMBIA. See AFRICA.

ZOOLOGY. Zoologists at Duke University in Durham, N.C., discovered in 1976 that sea gulls dangle their feet to get rid of excess body heat that builds up when they fly. The scientists found that gulls disperse fully 80 per cent of the heat produced during flight through their feet. The flow of blood to the feet increases greatly, and heat is dispersed by the superficial capillaries.

Birds have no sweat glands to cool their bodies. Experts believe that many birds get rid of excess heat through the lining of their mouths and breathing passages. Sea gulls drink salt water and have to spend energy to pump out the excess salt through salt glands in their skulls to keep their body fluids from becoming too salty. If they were to use evaporation from the respiratory tract as other birds do, their body fluids would become too salty and perhaps damage their biological systems.

Sensitive Sharks. Zoologists in Leningrad, Russia, studied the special types of sense organs found in sharks and skates that are receptive to weak electric currents. The receptors, called the ampullae of Lorenzini, consist of pores in the head region that lead through ducts to tiny sacs that are surrounded by sensory cells. Sharks and skates use these receptors to sense tiny electric pulses produced by body parts of their prey, such as the heart, even when the prey hides in the sand on the ocean bottom.

The Russians have discovered that the ampullae of Lorenzini are also responsive to tiny changes in the earth's magnetic field. Some of the receptors are responsive when the fish is moving in one direction, and others respond when it moves in another direction. They form a kind of built-in compass.

Amorous Hogs. When a *boar* (male hog) breathes on a *sow* (female), she stands immobilized, and courtship can proceed easily. Zoologists in Munich, West Germany, found in 1976 that the immobilized sow is responding to a chemical substance in the breath of the amorous boar. The chemical is a pheromone called 16-unsaturated c-19 steroid. The German scientists have also found this chemical in the sweat of humans, and in greater quantities in males than in females. They speculate that the substance exuded by perspiring men might affect the sexual responsiveness of women, but undoubtedly not in the drastic fashion in which female hogs are immobilized. Human beings are not as acutely attuned to the sense of smell. However, odor is probably more important to us than we realize, at least on a subconscious level.

Steven Boyd, a researcher at the Woods Hole Oceanographic Institution in Massachusetts reported in May that tadpoles practice a unique form of birth control that affects fish. The tadpoles apparently release a chemical substance that blocks the reproduction of small fish in the same pond. The mechanism assures tadpoles their share of the limited resources of the pond.   Barbara N. Benson

ZOOS AND AQUARIUMS continued to improve their exhibits in 1976. Among the largest opened were "Big Cat Country" at the St. Louis Zoological Park and the William Mann lion and tiger grottoes at the National Zoological Park in Washington, D.C. Other new feline exhibits included a cheetah run at the Columbus (Ohio) Zoo and a puma exhibit at the Brookfield Zoo near Chicago.

Lincoln Park Zoo in Chicago transferred its collection of great apes to a new building featuring high climbable structures. An outdoor gorilla exhibit opened at the San Antonio Zoo, and others were under construction at the Cincinnati, Columbus, and Denver zoos.

A flamingo lagoon was completed at the Los Angeles Zoo, and a modern wing was added to the aviary at the Detroit Zoo. The new Seattle Aquarium was scheduled to open in 1977, and construction was underway on the Minnesota State Zoo in Mankato and on the Dade County Zoo outside Miami.

Promoting Breeding. Most of the new exhibits were designed to promote breeding of animals. Even in older exhibits, better diets and more knowledgeable care brought substantial achievements in propagating rare and endangered species.

The National Zoo, for example, has recorded 50 pygmy hippopotamus births. The Dallas Zoo has reached the third generation in its herd of Suni antelope, and the St. Louis Zoo bred a mottled owl for the first time in captivity. Sea catfish, a marine species that incubates its eggs in the male fish's mouth, were successfully hatched at Chicago's Shedd Aquarium, while the Belle Isle Aquarium in Detroit bred freshwater sting rays.

Several zoos had to start birth-control programs for their large cats because of limited space and the difficulty in finding a place for them in the wild. Some of the Atlanta Zoo's crocodiles, however, were shipped to the wilds of Mexico for release there.

Conservation. In keeping with the Convention on International Trade in Endangered Species, the U.S. Congress added 159 species to the list of endangered animals. The list includes such zoo favorites as the Indian elephant, Bactrian camel, chimpanzee, black rhino, and mountain zebra. See Section Two, LAST CHANCE FOR THE SEA TURTLE.

The taking of killer whales became a highly publicized and controversial matter when a team from Sea World of San Diego attempted to make a federally permitted capture of such a whale in Puget Sound, Wash., in early 1976. Legislation was later introduced to ban capture of the species, but more than 100,000 letters were sent to congressional representatives protesting such an extreme measure. The species is already covered by the Marine Mammal Protection Act.

George B. Rabb

Siberian tiger in a realistic exhibit at Brookfield Zoo near Chicago gets its food by triggering a mechanism inside an artificial deer's ribcage.

Section Five

World Book Supplement

In its function of keeping WORLD BOOK owners up to date, THE WORLD BOOK YEAR BOOK herewith presents significant new articles from the 1977 edition of THE WORLD BOOK ENCYCLOPEDIA.

JAMES E. CARTER, JR.

James E Carter Jr [signature]

NIXON
37th President
1969—1974

FORD
38th President
1974—1977

CARTER, JAMES EARL, JR. (1924-   ), was elected President of the United States in 1976, climaxing a remarkable rise to national fame. Carter had been governor of Georgia from 1971 to 1975 and was little known elsewhere at the beginning of 1976. But then he won 18 primary elections and became the Democratic candidate for President. Carter, known by the nickname Jimmy, defeated President Gerald R. Ford in the 1976 election.

Before Carter won election as governor, he served in the Georgia Senate. He had managed his family warehouse business and farm before entering politics. Carter also had been an officer in the United States Navy. He was the first graduate of the U.S. Naval Academy to become chief executive.

When Carter took office as President, the nation was challenged mainly by economic problems. The economy was gradually recovering from a severe recession that had struck in 1974, but the unemployment rate remained high. Carter pledged during his campaign to reduce unemployment and to encourage steady growth in the economy.

Carter also promised government concern for needy Americans. He once said: "We should make our major investments in people, not in buildings and weapons. The poor, the weak, the aged, the afflicted must be treated with respect and compassion and with love. . . . The test of any government is not how popular it is with the powerful, but how honestly and fairly it deals with the many who must depend on it."

In appearance and manner, Carter was calm, reserved, and soft-spoken. His friends knew him as a man of great personal warmth and charm. In politics, Carter was an able, energetic campaigner with an iron will and a determination to win every fight. According to his political aides, he demanded hard work and set high standards but pushed himself the hardest.

Early Life

Boyhood. James Earl Carter, Jr., was born on Oct. 1, 1924, in Plains, Ga. He had two sisters, Gloria (1926-   ) and Ruth (1929-   ), and a brother, William Alton III (1937-   ).

Carter's father, a farmer and small businessman, was born in Georgia. He ran a farm products store on the family farm in the rural community of Archery, a few miles west of Plains. Carter's mother, Lillian

Jack J. Spalding, the contributor of this article, is Editor of the Atlanta Journal.

Gordy Carter, also had been born in Georgia. She met her future husband in Plains. They became engaged in 1921, while she was training as a registered nurse, and were married two years later.

The Carters lived in Plains when Jimmy was born. Four years later, they moved to the farm in Archery. Jimmy grew up there and helped with the farm chores during his boyhood. He also developed an early interest in business. When the sandy-haired boy was about 5 years old, he began to sell boiled peanuts on the streets of Plains. He earned about $1 a day on weekdays and about $5 on Saturdays. At the age of 9, Jimmy bought five huge bales of cotton for 5 cents a pound. He stored the cotton and sold it a few years later, when the price had more than tripled.

Education. Jimmy went to public school in Plains. He shared his mother's love of reading and received good grades. A schoolmate later remembered that Jimmy "was always the smartest in the class." The boy's favorite subjects included history, literature, and music. As a teen-ager, he played on the high school basketball team.

In 1941, following graduation from high school, Carter entered Georgia Southwestern College in nearby Americus. In 1942, a boyhood dream came true when he received an appointment to the United States Naval Academy in Annapolis, Md. "Even as a grammar school child, I read books about the Navy and Annapolis," Carter recalled. However, he lacked the mathematics courses required for admission to the academy and enrolled at Georgia Institute of Technology to fulfill this requirement. Carter entered the academy in 1943. He did especially well in electronics, gunnery, and naval tactics and graduated in 1946, ranking 59th in a class of 820.

Carter's Family. In 1945, Carter had started to date Rosalynn Smith (Aug. 18, 1927-   ) of Plains. She was the best friend of his sister Ruth. Rosalynn's father, a garage mechanic, died when she was 13 years old. She took a part-time job as cleaning girl in a beauty shop to help pay the family's expenses.

Jimmy and Rosalynn were married on July 7, 1946, about a month after he graduated from the Naval Academy. They had four children—John William (1947-   ), James Earl III (1950-   ), Donnel Jeffrey (1952-   ), and Amy Lynn (1967-   ).

Naval Career. Carter spent his first two years in the Navy chiefly as an electronics instructor. He served first on the U.S.S. *Wyoming* and later on the U.S.S. *Mississippi*. These battleships were being used to test new equipment. Near the end of his period on the *Mississippi*,

Charles M. Rafshoon

The United States flag had 50 stars when James E. Carter, Jr., became President.

Carter volunteered for submarine duty. He graduated from submarine-training school in December 1948, ranking third in a class of 52. Carter was then assigned to the submarine U.S.S. *Pomfret* and, in 1950, to the U.S.S. *K-1*, a submarine designed for antisubmarine warfare.

In 1952, Carter joined a select group of officers who were developing the world's first nuclear-powered submarines. He became engineering officer of the nuclear submarine *Sea Wolf*. Carter served under Captain Hyman G. Rickover, who pioneered the nuclear project. Carter later wrote that Rickover "had a profound effect on my life—perhaps more than anyone except my own parents. . . . He expected the maximum from us, but he always contributed more."

A turning point in Carter's life occurred in 1953, when his father died of cancer. Carter felt he was needed in Plains to manage the family businesses. But Rosalynn

----

IMPORTANT DATES IN CARTER'S LIFE

1924 (Oct. 1) Born in Plains, Ga.
1946 Graduated from the United States Naval Academy.
1946 (July 7) Married Rosalynn Smith.
1946-1953 Served in the United States Navy.
1962 Elected to the Georgia Senate.
1964 Reelected to the Georgia Senate.
1970 Elected governor of Georgia.
1976 Elected President of the United States.

----

had no desire to return to Plains, and she argued against his leaving the Navy. Carter later called their disagreement "the first really serious argument in our marriage." He resigned from the Navy that year with the rank of lieutenant senior grade.

Return to Plains

Businessman and Civic Leader. Soon after Carter returned to Plains, he took over the family farm and a peanut warehouse that his father had established in the town. He studied modern farming techniques at the Agricultural Experiment Station in Tifton, Ga. During the late 1950's and the 1960's, Carter expanded the warehouse and bought new machinery for the farm. The family businesses thrived under his management.

Carter devoted much time to civic affairs. He served on the Sumter County Board of Education from 1955 to 1962, the last two years as chairman. Carter also became a deacon and Sunday-school teacher of the Plains Baptist Church and a member of the local hospital and library boards.

Carter was widely respected in Plains. But his views on racial issues often differed from those of most of his neighbors. He disapproved of the segregation laws that separated blacks and whites in schools and other public facilities throughout the South. During the 1950's, these laws came under increasing attack by federal courts and civil rights workers. Many Southerners formed local chapters of the White Citizens' Council, an organization designed to help preserve segregation.

543

Young Jimmy, shown at the age of 2, lived in the small town of Plains, Ga., for the first four years of his life.

Carter's Boyhood Home was this wooden clapboard house on a farm in Archery, Ga., just west of Plains. His family lived in the house from 1928 to 1949. Jimmy worked on the farm and sold peanuts in Plains. He also attended school in Plains.

A chapter was established in Plains in 1955, and Carter was asked to join. He refused to do so and declared that he would rather move from Plains.

In 1965, Carter's church considered a proposal to ban blacks from Sunday services. At that time, black civil rights workers were trying to integrate various Southern churches. Carter urged his congregation to defeat the measure, but only his family and one other church member voted against it.

State Senator. In 1962, Carter ran for the Georgia Senate. He received a stormy introduction to state politics. On the day of the Georgia primary election, Carter saw voters marking their ballots openly in front of the election supervisor in the town of Georgetown. He charged that this action violated Georgia voting laws.

But the supervisor, who was the political boss of the area and a supporter of Carter's opponent, ignored the protest.

The results of the primary election showed that Carter had lost by only a few votes. He angrily challenged the results in court. Just three days before the general election, he was declared to be the Democratic nominee. Carter beat his Republican opponent by about 1,000 votes. He was reelected to the Senate in 1964. As a state senator, Carter worked hard for reforms in education.

Steps to the Governorship. In 1966, Carter became a candidate for the Democratic nomination for governor of Georgia. He was defeated in the primary election. But Carter, determined to win the governorship, de-

At the Age of 13, the sandy-haired Carter attended a camp near Covington, Ga.

Carter's Parents, Lillian and James E. Carter, Sr., were born in Georgia. She was a registered nurse, and he was a farmer and businessman.

cided later that year to run for the office again in 1970. From 1966 to 1970, he worked to increase his understanding of Georgia's problems and made about 1,800 speeches throughout the state.

In 1970, political experts gave Carter little chance of winning the Democratic nomination for governor. The heavily favored candidate was Carl E. Sanders, a liberal who had served as governor from 1963 to 1967. During the campaign, Carter opposed the busing of students to achieve racial balance in schools. He also took other stands that were important to Georgia's rural, conservative voters. Carter's critics charged he was appealing for the support of segregationists. Carter won the nomination. In the general election, he defeated his Republican opponent, Hal Suit, an Atlanta television newscaster, by about 200,000 votes.

Governor of Georgia

Carter began his term as governor in January 1971 and quickly made clear that he would work to aid all needy Georgians. In his inaugural address, he declared: "I say to you quite frankly that the time for racial discrimination is over. No poor, rural, weak, or black person should ever have to bear the additional burden of being deprived of the opportunity of an education, a job, or simple justice." This speech brought Carter his first nationwide attention.

Political Reformer. During Carter's campaign for the governorship, he had promised to make the state government more efficient. Soon after he took office, he set up task forces of leaders from education, industry, and state government to study every state agency. One task force member later recalled that the new governor "was right there with us, working just as hard, digging just as deep into every little problem. It was his program and he worked on it as hard as anybody, and the final prod-

uct was distinctly his." As a result of this detailed study, Carter merged about 300 state agencies and boards into about 30 agencies.

Carter also pushed a series of reforms through the legislature. One of the most important ones was a law to provide equal state aid to schools in the wealthy and poor areas of Georgia. Other reforms set up community centers for retarded children and increased educational programs for convicts. At Carter's urging, the legislature passed laws to protect the environment, preserve historic sites, and decrease secrecy in government. Carter took pride in a program he introduced for the appointment of judges and state government officials. Under this program, all such appointments were based on merit, rather than political influence.

Concern for Blacks. Carter opened many job opportunities for blacks in the Georgia state government. During his administration, the number of black appointees on major state boards and agencies increased from 3 to 53. The number of black state employees rose by about 40 per cent.

Carter also established a project to honor notable black Georgians. In 1973, he appointed a committee to nominate blacks for the portrait galleries in the State Capitol. Pictures of many prominent Georgia men and women hung there, but none were of blacks. The committee's first choice was Martin Luther King, Jr. A portrait of the famous civil rights leader was hung in the Capitol in 1974.

Plans for the Presidency. While serving as governor, Carter became increasingly active in national activities of the Democratic Party. He headed the 1972 Democratic Governors' Campaign Committee, which worked to help elect the party's candidates for governor. He

Carter Family Album from Charles M. Rafshoon

As a Submarine Officer in the United States Navy, Carter, *second from left,* served aboard the U.S.S. *K-1,* a submarine designed for antisubmarine warfare. He later joined a group of officers who were developing the world's first nuclear-powered submarines.

Charles M. Rafshoon

In Private Life, Carter managed his family's business holdings, which included a peanut warehouse in Plains and nearby farmland. He is shown driving a load of peanuts to the warehouse.

also served as chairman of the Democratic National Campaign Committee in 1974.

At about the middle of his term as governor, Carter began to consider running for President in 1976. Georgia law prohibited a governor from serving two consecutive terms. But Carter also saw no heavy favorite for the Democratic presidential nomination. In addition, he believed that voters would support a leader from outside Washington, D.C., who offered bold, new solutions to the nation's problems.

Carter's mother later recalled that she learned in September 1973 of his plan to seek the presidency. She asked him what he intended to do after leaving the governorship, and Carter replied, "I'm going to run

for President." She asked, "President of what?", and he answered: "Momma, I'm going to run for President of the United States, and I'm going to win."

In December 1974, a month before his term as governor expired, Carter announced his candidacy for the 1976 Democratic presidential nomination. He was still little known outside Georgia.

Presidential Candidate

Rise to Prominence. Carter began to work full time for the nomination soon after leaving office as governor in January 1975. He campaigned outside Georgia for about 250 days that year but attracted little attention. In October 1975, a public opinion poll that ranked possible contenders for the Democratic presidential nomination did not even mention him.

In January 1976, Carter began a whirlwind rise to national prominence. That month, he received the most votes in an Iowa caucus, the first contest to elect delegates to the 1976 Democratic National Convention. In February, Carter won the year's first presidential primary election, in New Hampshire. By then, 10 other Democrats were seeking the nomination. Carter's chief opponents were Senator Henry M. Jackson of Washington, Representative Morris K. Udall of Arizona, and Governor George C. Wallace of Alabama. In March, Carter beat Wallace in the Florida primary. Soon afterward, a public opinion poll showed that Carter was the top choice of Democrats for the nomination.

Many voters liked Carter largely because he had not served in Washington, D.C. He became a symbol of their desire for a leader without ties to various interest groups in the nation's capital. Carter also attracted much support with his vow to restore moral leadership to the presidency. Public confidence in government had been shaken by the Watergate scandal, which led to the resignation of President Richard M. Nixon (see WATERGATE). Vice-President Gerald R. Ford succeeded Nixon as President. But Ford's popularity fell sharply after he pardoned Nixon for any federal crimes Nixon may have committed as President.

Carter's popularity continued to grow during the spring. In April, he won important primary victories over Udall in Wisconsin and Jackson in Pennsylvania.

Johnson Publishing Co.

As Governor of Georgia, Carter began a project to honor noted black Georgians by hanging their portraits in the State Capitol. In 1974, a portrait of Martin Luther King, Jr., became the first to be hung. Carter and Mrs. King attended the ceremony, *left.*

The *table* in the article on ELECTORAL COLLEGE gives the electoral vote by states for both Carter, the winner, and Ford.

Carter entered nearly all of the nation's 31 presidential primaries and won 18 of them. As a result, Democratic leaders throughout the country endorsed his candidacy.

Carter easily won the nomination for President on the first ballot at the Democratic National Convention in New York City. At his request, Senator Walter F. Mondale of Minnesota was nominated for Vice-President. The Republicans nominated Ford and his vice-presidential choice, Senator Robert J. Dole of Kansas.

The 1976 Election. Many political observers believed that Carter's nomination would unite the Democratic Party. Since 1964, millions of conservative Democrats in the South had supported Republican presidential candidates. But in 1976, most of these men and women were expected to vote for Carter.

In the presidential campaign, Carter charged that Ford had failed to deal effectively with high unemployment. During the summer and autumn of 1976, about 8 per cent of the nation's workers had no jobs. Carter promised to help create more jobs by increasing federal spending and encouraging business expansion. Ford argued that Carter's plans would lead to rapid inflation.

The campaign included the second series of nationally televised debates between rival presidential candidates. The first series took place in 1960, between John F. Kennedy, the Democratic candidate, and Richard M. Nixon, the Republican nominee. In the 1976 presidential election, Carter and Mondale defeated Ford and Dole. JACK J. SPALDING

Related Articles in WORLD BOOK include:

Democratic Party
Ford, Gerald R.
Mondale, Walter F.
President of the United States

Charles M. Rafshoon

Carter's Family. Standing are, *left to right,* son James, daughter-in-law Caron, grandson Jason, son John, and daughter-in-law Judy. Seated are Mrs. Carter, the President, daughter-in-law Annette, son Jeffrey, and, *foreground,* daughter Amy.

Outline

I. **Early Life**
   A. Boyhood
   B. Education
   C. Carter's Family
   D. Naval Career

II. **Return to Plains**
   A. Businessman and Civic Leader
   B. State Senator
   C. Steps to the Governorship

III. **Governor of Georgia**
   A. Political Reformer
   B. Concern for Blacks
   C. Plans for the Presidency

IV. **Presidential Candidate**
   A. Rise to Prominence
   B. The 1976 Election

Questions

What boyhood dream came true for Carter in 1942?

How did Carter receive a stormy introduction to statewide politics in Georgia?

In what special project did Carter work as a naval officer?

What conditions influenced Carter's decision to seek the presidency?

How did Carter help honor notable black Georgians while he was governor of Georgia?

How did Carter first gain nationwide attention?

Which of Carter's views often differed with those of most of his neighbors in Plains?

Why was Carter's nomination for President expected to unite the Democratic Party in the 1976 election?

What were some ways Carter earned money as a boy?

Why did Carter resign from the Navy in 1953?

Keystone

Nomination in 1976 brought this happy response from Carter and his running mate, Senator Walter F. Mondale of Minnesota.

Cary S. Wolinsky, Stock, Boston — Chester Peterson, Jr., *Farm Journal*

The Food Supply in Poor and Rich Countries differs greatly, in many cases because of differences in farm output. At the left, farmers in Nepal receive a ration of rice seed, which will produce barely enough food for their needs. At the right, a U.S. farmer harvests a huge crop of soybeans.

FOOD SUPPLY

FOOD SUPPLY is the total amount of food available to all the people in the world. No one can live without food, and so the supply of food has always been one of the human race's chief concerns. The food supply depends mainly on the world's farmers. They raise the crops and livestock that provide most of our food. The world's food supply varies from year to year because the production of crops and livestock varies. Some years, terrible losses result from droughts, floods, or other natural disasters. Yet the world's population grows every year, and so the worldwide demand for food also constantly increases. Food shortages and famines occur when the food supply falls short of the amount needed.

The food supply varies not only from year to year but also from country to country. Most of the poor, *developing* nations of Africa, Asia, and Latin America seldom have enough food for most of their people. Millions of people in these countries go hungry. During years of famine, millions may die of starvation. In almost all *developed* nations, on the other hand, the majority of people have an adequate diet. But in few countries is the food supply equally distributed. In nearly every nation, some people have more than enough to eat while others live in constant hunger.

Most people in the developed countries have an adequate diet for several reasons. Almost all the developed nations lie in the world's *temperate* regions—that is, be-

Lester R. Brown, the contributor of this article, is President of Worldwatch Institute, a private, nonprofit organization that researches problems of worldwide concern, including food supply problems. He is also the author of By Bread Alone *and other books on the food supply.*

tween the tropics and the polar areas. The soil and climate in temperate regions are generally well suited for farming. In addition, the developed nations have money for agricultural research and so have been able to solve various problems associated with agriculture in temperate regions. Most farmers in the developed countries can afford the fertilizers and other materials needed to produce large amounts of food. Finally, the developed countries have enough food because their population grows more slowly than their food supply.

Unlike the developed countries, most developing nations lie in or near the tropics. The soil and climate in these regions are generally not so well suited to large-scale food production as they are in temperate regions. Nor do the developing nations have much money for agricultural research. As a result, they have made relatively little progress in solving the problems of tropical agriculture. In addition, many farmers in the developing countries cannot afford to buy the fertilizers and other materials they need to produce more food. All these conditions limit food production. But the developing nations have too little food chiefly because their population grows nearly as fast as—or faster than—their food supply.

The world's population passed 4 billion in the mid-1970's and is increasing about 2 per cent a year. At this rate of growth, the number of people in the world will double in 35 years. Food production must also double during this time to feed the added people.

Many experts believe that food production will be unable to keep up with population growth unless the birth rate falls sharply. This theory was first developed in detail by the British economist Thomas Robert Malthus in the late 1700's (see MALTHUS, THOMAS ROBERT). In the past, population growth was controlled mainly by a high death rate. But during the 1900's, improved

548

living standards and medical advances have reduced the death rate in the majority of countries. Today, most people who agree with Malthus consider family planning to be the only practical method of reducing population growth. This article discusses these and other food supply problems. It also discusses human food needs, food sources, and food supply programs.

Basic Human Food Needs

Experts usually determine the adequacy of a person's diet by the amount of *calories* and *protein* it provides. Protein is one of the chief *nutrients* (nourishing substances) found in food. It is needed to build and maintain body cells. Other nutrients are *carbohydrates* (starches and sugars), fats, minerals, and vitamins. Calories are units of energy supplied by food. Carbohydrates and fats normally provide most of the calories in the human diet. Protein supplies the rest. People who lack sufficient calories in their diet are said to be *undernourished*. A person whose diet seriously lacks any nutrient is said to be *malnourished*. Protein malnutrition is by far the most common type of malnutrition.

The majority of people who do not get enough protein in their diet also lack sufficient calories. To make up for a continuing lack of calories, the human body changes more and more protein into energy. As a result, less protein is available to build and maintain body cells. Most malnutrition is therefore protein-calorie malnutrition—an inadequate supply of both protein and calories in the diet. As many as 500 million persons throughout the world—about an eighth of the world's

population—suffer from protein-calorie malnutrition. The great majority of these people live in developing countries, and most are young children. Many victims die before they are 5 years old. Many others grow up with severe mental and physical handicaps. See NUTRITION (Protein-Calorie Malnutrition).

Calories. The amount of calories a person needs each day depends on the person's sex, age, body build, and degree of physical activity. A husky house painter, for example, requires far more calories than does a slightly built office worker. The United Nations (UN) estimates that a moderately active man of average weight—that is, 143 pounds (65 kilograms)—needs at least 3,000 calories a day. A moderately active woman of average weight—that is, 121 pounds (55 kilograms)—needs about 2,200. Children and young people up to 19 years of age require an average of 820 to 3,070 calories, depending on sex, weight, and age.

Daily calorie *consumption* (intake) by all people in the poorest developing countries averages under 2,000—far less than most people require. In many developed countries, daily calorie consumption averages over 3,200—far more than most people require.

Protein in the human diet consists of *animal protein* and *plant protein*. Dairy products, eggs, fish, and meat are the chief sources of animal protein. The best sources of plant protein are members of the pea family. These plants, which are called *legumes* or *pulses*, include beans, peas, and peanuts. *Cereal grains* also supply plant pro-

Per Capita Distribution of the World's Calorie Supply

This graph shows the number of food calories that would be available daily *per capita* (for each person) in the world's major regions if the calories were divided equally among all the people in the region. The dotted red line indicates the daily calorie requirement for a moderately active woman of average weight—that is, 121 pounds (55 kilograms). The dotted blue line shows the requirement for a moderately active man of average weight—that is, 143 pounds (65 kilograms).

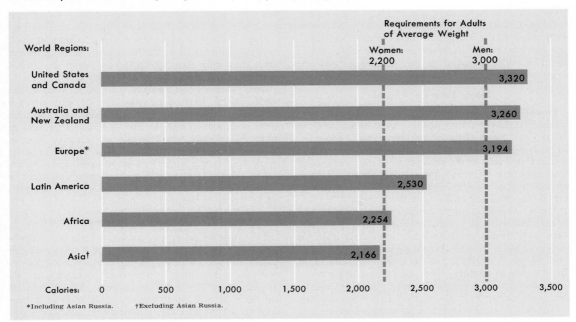

Sources: *Population, Food Supply, and Agricultural Development,* FAO, 1975. *Handbook on Human Nutritional Requirements,* FAO, 1974. Supply figures are 1969-1971 averages.

FOOD SUPPLY

tein. The main cereal grains are barley, corn, millet, oats, rice, rye, sorghum, and wheat.

Protein is made up of molecules called *amino acids*. The human body must have certain amino acids to build and maintain body cells. Most sources of animal protein provide all the essential amino acids—and in the proportions the body requires. These food sources can thus supply all of a person's daily protein needs. On the other hand, many sources of plant protein do not supply the complete combination of amino acids. One or more of the essential amino acids are missing or insufficient. For example, cereal grains by themselves do not provide a full combination of amino acids. But if grain is eaten together with certain legumes, especially protein-rich soybeans, it can meet a person's protein needs. See PROTEIN.

People differ in their protein requirements, just as they do in their calorie requirements. But a person's protein needs also depend on the quality of the protein consumed. People require less protein if their diet includes some animal protein than if it includes only plant protein. The UN estimates that a man of average weight needs at least 37 grams of protein daily, if the protein is entirely animal protein. A woman of average weight needs about 29 grams. Children and young people up to 19 years of age require an average of 14 to 38 grams. In every case, a person's requirement increases if the protein is mainly plant protein.

Daily protein consumption by all people in the poorest developing countries averages about 40 grams. But most of the protein is plant protein. Average protein consumption in these countries therefore falls short of the minimum requirement. In addition, most people in these countries have too few calories in their diet. As a result, much of the protein they consume is used to meet their energy needs rather than to build and maintain body cells. Protein consumption by all people in many developed countries averages as high as 80 to 100 grams daily. Most of the protein is animal protein and therefore far exceeds the minimum need. The extra protein provides added calories. If the calories exceed the amount required, the body stores the excess as fat.

Major Sources of Food

Cereal Grains are the world's most important food source. Worldwide, they supply more than half the calories and much of the protein that people consume. Grain is also a chief ingredient in most livestock feed and so is involved in the production of meat, eggs, and dairy products. Cereal grains are of such great importance that food experts often use the size of the grain supply as a measure of the total food supply.

Almost all the grain grown in developing countries is *food grain*—that is, people consume it directly as food. They may simply cook the grain as a main dish. Or they may use it to make bread, noodles, or some other food. People in developed countries also consume grain directly. But in addition, they use much of the grain as *feed grain*, which is fed to livestock. People consume this grain indirectly in the form of livestock products.

Grains used chiefly as feed in some countries are used chiefly as food in other countries. For example, most of the corn grown in the United States is used for livestock

Per Capita Protein Supply in the United States and India

In the United States, a developed country, the daily per capita protein supply is twice as large as in India, a developing country. In addition, the supply of high-quality, animal protein in the United States is five times as large as in India.

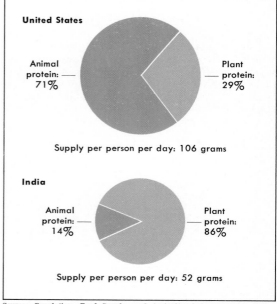

United States

Animal protein: 71%

Plant protein: 29%

Supply per person per day: 106 grams

India

Animal protein: 14%

Plant protein: 86%

Supply per person per day: 52 grams

Source: *Population, Food Supply, and Agricultural Development*, FAO, 1975. Figures are 1969-1971 averages.

feed. But in some African and Latin-American countries, corn is an important food grain.

Livestock and Fish are the main sources of animal protein. On a worldwide basis, meat, eggs, and dairy products supply about 85 to 90 per cent of the animal protein in the human diet. Fish provide a large percentage of the animal protein in certain countries, such as Japan, Norway, and the Philippines. But worldwide, fish supply only about 10 to 15 per cent of the animal protein people consume.

Other Major Food Sources. In certain areas of the world, people depend heavily on food sources other than grain, livestock, or fish. Soybeans and other legumes rank second only to rice as a source of food in many Asian countries. Potatoes are a major food in parts of Europe and South America. People in some tropical areas rely largely on such native foods as bananas, *cassava* (a starchy root), and sweet potatoes or yams. Of all these foods, only legumes provide an adequate supply of essential amino acids.

Conditions That Affect the Food Supply

The world's food supply consists mainly of food produced during the current year. But it also includes *reserves*, or *stocks*, left over from previous years. Food reserves are necessary to help prevent shortages after bad farming years. To build up reserves, the countries of the world overall must produce more food in a year than they consume. But few countries produce a surplus. The United States produces by far the largest surplus. Argentina, Australia, Canada, and New Zealand also regularly produce a food surplus, though far less than that produced by the United States.

Most countries produce either just enough food to meet their needs or not enough. If a country fails to produce enough food for all its people, it must import additional supplies or face a shortage. Most developed countries that do not produce sufficient food can afford to import the extra supplies they need. Great Britain and Japan are examples of such countries. But most developing countries cannot afford to import all the additional food their people require. Since the early 1950's, world food production has doubled, but so has the worldwide demand. As a result, many countries rely on food imports, chiefly from the United States.

The amount of food a country produces depends partly on its agricultural resources, such as land and water. No country has an unlimited supply of these resources. The worldwide food supply is thus affected by (1) limited agricultural resources and (2) the ever-increasing demand for food. The food supply within countries is also affected by problems of distribution.

Limited Agricultural Resources. Farming requires various resources—especially land, water, energy, and fertilizer. Land is the chief agricultural resource. Land used for growing crops must be fairly level and fertile. But most of the world's good cropland is already in use,

The Relation Between Food Production and Population

This graph shows the percentage contributions to world food production and world population of each of the major world regions. Asia, Africa, and Latin America have 75 per cent of the world's people but produce less than 45 per cent of its food.

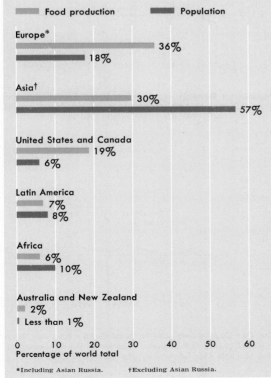

Food production   Population

Europe*
36%
18%

Asia†
30%
57%

United States and Canada
19%
6%

Latin America
7%
8%

Africa
6%
10%

Australia and New Zealand
2%
Less than 1%

0   10   20   30   40   50   60
Percentage of world total

*Including Asian Russia.   †Excluding Asian Russia.

Source: FAO. Figures are for 1975.

and most of the unused land lies in remote areas, far from markets and transportation.

All crops require water to grow, but rainfall is distributed unevenly over the earth's surface. Some farmers can depend on rainfall for all the water they need. Other farmers must use irrigation water—if it is available—because the rainfall is too light or uncertain. But the supply of irrigation water is limited, and farmers in some countries use nearly all the available supply.

Many farmers depend heavily on energy resources—particularly petroleum fuels—to operate tractors, irrigation pumps, and other farm equipment. They use fertilizers—especially nitrogen fertilizers—to enrich the soil. At present, most nitrogen fertilizers are made from natural gas. But the world's supplies of petroleum and natural gas are strictly limited. In fact, the supplies may become extremely short or nearly exhausted by the early 2000's. Farmers will therefore need other sources for energy and nitrogen fertilizers.

Meanwhile, the cost of petroleum fuels and fertilizer has soared. Most farmers in developed countries can afford the higher costs. But many farmers in developing countries cannot and so are unable to increase their food production. In every country, higher prices for energy and fertilizer add to the cost of food.

Increased use of agricultural resources can help farmers produce more food. But it can also cause environmental problems. For example, increased use of nitrogen fertilizers sometimes creates a build-up of nitrogen compounds in the soil. Rain water eventually washes these compounds into rivers and streams, where they contribute to water pollution.

Increased Demand for Food chiefly reflects the growth in the population of the world. To a lesser extent, it also reflects higher living standards, which allow people to eat both bigger and better meals.

The Effect of Population Growth. Experts measure a country's food supply by the amount that would be available *per capita* (for each person) if the food were distributed equally among all the people. The food supply thus depends not only on the total amount of food but also on the number of people who must be fed.

The developed and developing countries both increased food production more than 25 per cent during the 1960's. During this period, the population of the developed nations grew about 10 per cent. The amount of food available per capita in these countries therefore increased greatly. But the population of the developing countries grew nearly 25 per cent during the 1960's. The population growth therefore almost equaled the gain in food production, and so little food was left over to help improve people's diets. In some developing nations, the population increases faster than food production. The per capita food supply in these countries thus continually declines.

In an attempt to avoid disastrous food shortages in the future, many developing countries have promoted birth control programs (see BIRTH CONTROL). But lack of education and various other social and economic obstacles have prevented the programs from reaching or influencing most of the people.

The Effect of Higher Living Standards. As people improve their living standards, especially through in-

FOOD SUPPLY

creased personal income, they usually eat more food. In time, they also generally begin to eat more expensive foods, particularly more meat. Greater meat consumption calls for an increase in the amount of grain used for livestock feed. For this reason, many countries with a high standard of living also have a high per capita consumption of grain.

The people of the United States directly consume an average of about 150 pounds (68 kilograms) of grain per person annually. But about 1,500 pounds (680 kilograms) of grain per person is fed to U.S. livestock each year. Americans consume this grain indirectly in the form of meat, eggs, and dairy products. Total per capita grain consumption in the United States thus averages about 1,650 pounds (748 kilograms) annually.

Total per capita grain consumption in the developing countries averages about 400 pounds (180 kilograms) a year. Almost all this grain is consumed directly. On the average, people in the United States therefore consume more than four times as much grain as do people in the developing countries.

Distribution Problems. In many developing countries, the majority of people are too poor to buy all the food they need. Much of the available supply therefore goes to the small minority of people who can afford it. The developing countries also lack modern facilities for the transportation and storage of food. In many cases, supplies cannot be delivered immediately to every area where they are needed, and they cannot be safely stored to await shipment. As a result, large quantities of food spoil or are eaten by mice, rats, and insects.

Methods to Increase the Food Supply

Most increases in the food supply result from greater farm output. Farm output can be increased in two main ways: (1) by developing new farmland and (2) by making existing farmland more productive. Two other methods to increase the food supply involve (1) reducing the demand for feed grain and (2) developing new sources of food.

Developing New Farmland is difficult and costly. The largest areas of land that could be developed for farming lie in Africa south of the Sahara and in the Amazon River Basin of South America. Much of this land is covered with dense forests, and the tropical soil and climate are not ideal for farming. As a result, the countries that control the two regions often have difficulty getting farmers to settle and develop the land.

Making Farmland More Productive. Farmers have two main methods of making their land more productive. (1) They may increase their use of irrigation, energy, and fertilizer. (2) They may use improved varieties of grains and livestock, which produce higher crop yields and larger amounts of livestock products. Farmers in developed countries have used both methods during much of the 1900's. In the 1950's and 1960's, farmers in some developing countries also adopted both methods to increase their production of wheat and rice. Their effort proved so successful that it has been called the *Green Revolution.*

The development of high-yield varieties of rice and wheat made the Green Revolution possible. But the revolution also required greater use of irrigation water,

The Growth in Food Production and Population

The developing countries have difficulty improving their food supply because their population grows nearly as fast as—or faster than—their food production. The reverse is true of most developed countries. The three graphs below illustrate this difference.

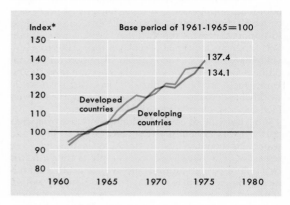

The Growth of Food Production in the developing countries equaled that in the developed countries from 1961 through 1975.

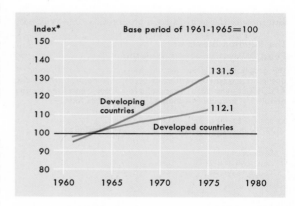

Population Growth was much less in the developed nations from 1961 through 1975 than it was in the developing nations.

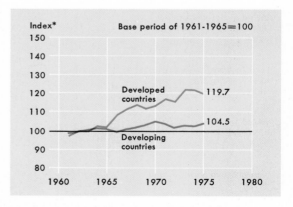

The Per Capita Increase in Food Production was therefore much greater in the developed countries. The developing nations had little food left over to help improve people's diets.

*Shows changes in relation to the base period of 1961-1965.
Source: FAO.

energy, and fertilizer. Many farmers got the water from wells and installed electric or diesel-powered pumps to bring the water to the surface. To get the highest yields, farmers had to enrich their soil with fertilizers. During the 1960's, these methods helped such countries as India and Mexico double their wheat production.

The Green Revolution can continue to make farmland more productive. For example, if farmers in the tropics have enough water, fertilizer, and other essential resources, they can grow two or three crops a year on the same land, instead of one crop. But the Green Revolution's ability to increase the food supply is limited. As we have seen, many farmers in developing countries cannot afford the additional resources that the Green Revolution requires. But in any case, greater use of these resources makes land more productive only up to a point. Most farmers in the United States, for example, use 7 to 10 times as much fertilizer on each unit of land as do most farmers in developing countries. But U.S. grain yields are only about twice as large as those in developing countries.

Although farmland can be made more productive, the ever-rising costs of energy and fertilizer drive food prices higher and higher. And millions of people throughout the world cannot afford to buy all the food they need even at lower prices. Ways must therefore be found to expand food production at a cost that most people can afford.

The best hope for making farmland more productive lies with agricultural research. For example, research scientists are working to develop varieties of grain that not only produce higher yields but also have other improved characteristics. Such a grain might supply a more complete combination of amino acids, make more efficient use of water and fertilizer, and provide better resistance to insects and disease. But it is extremely difficult to develop a plant variety that has so many different characteristics. The necessary research therefore takes much time and money.

Marc & Evelyne Bernheim, Woodfin Camp, Inc.

Research in Tropical Agriculture seeks to increase food production in developing countries, most of which lie in the tropics. This researcher in India is studying tropical plant diseases.

Reducing the Demand for Feed Grain would increase the amount of calories and protein available for human consumption. This increase would occur because livestock consume more calories and protein than they produce. Beef cattle are especially inefficient in this respect. For every 8 to 10 pounds (3.6 to 4.5 kilograms) of grain that beef cattle consume, they produce only 1 pound (0.45 kilogram) of meat. But 8 pounds of grain supplies about 10 times as many calories and more than 4 times as much protein as a pound of beef supplies.

In the past, almost all beef cattle grazed on grass and other *forage* up to the time they were slaughtered. But since the mid-1900's, many cattle-fattening establishments called *feed lots* have opened in the United States, Canada, and certain other developed countries. A feed lot fattens cattle on grain. Today, most U.S. beef cattle are fattened on feed lots and so consume enormous quantities of grain. The demand for feed grain would lessen greatly if the cattle industry returned to its earlier practice of raising cattle chiefly on forage. Some cattle raisers have already made the change. As a result, the percentage of cattle fattened on U.S. feed lots declined in the mid-1970's.

The demand for feed grain would also decline if people in the developed countries ate less meat. Most people in the United States, for example, could probably reduce their meat consumption as much as 30 per cent without ill effects.

Developing New Sources of Food. Such oilseed crops as coconuts, cottonseed, peanuts, and soybeans are all valuable sources of protein. Soybeans have an especially high protein content and have long been an important food in Asia, where they originated. But with this exception, none of these oilseed crops is a major source of food anywhere in the world. Instead, the crops are grown mainly for their oil, which is used to make such products as margarine and salad dressing. The protein, however, remains in the meal, the part of the seed that is left after the oil has been removed. Most of the meal is used for livestock feed.

Since the mid-1900's, food processors have been working to make the protein in oilseed meal available for human consumption. They have developed a variety of inexpensive, specially flavored foods from soybean meal. Some of these products, especially those in beverage form, have been successfully marketed in developing countries in various parts of the world. Food processors are now working to convert coconut, cottonseed, and peanut meal into foods that will have a broad appeal. All three crops are widely grown in the tropics and so could provide millions of people in developing countries with inexpensive protein.

Scientists and food processors have also developed methods of enriching food. For example, scientists have produced artificial amino acids, which can be added to bread and other grain products to improve the quality of their protein.

Food Supply Programs

Various organizations sponsor programs to increase and improve the world's food supply. The chief international organizations include two United Nations

FOOD SUPPLY

(UN) agencies—the Food and Agriculture Organization (FAO) and the World Bank. Another major agency, the Organization for Economic Cooperation and Development (OECD), is made up of developed non-Communist countries. The World Food Council, a group of food experts appointed by the UN, helps coordinate the work of the various international organizations. Many developed nations have set up their own agencies to help increase the world's food supply.

A number of important food supply programs are sponsored by religious and other private groups. For example, the Rockefeller Foundation, an organization founded in the United States by the Rockefeller family, has long been one of the biggest contributors to agricultural research in developing countries.

Technical and Financial Programs work to expand farm output in developing countries. The FAO sponsors the chief technical assistance programs. These programs are designed mainly to train farmers in modern agricultural methods. The United Nations Development Program also sponsors technical aid programs (see UNITED NATIONS [Economic and Technical Aid]). Most financial help for agriculture in the developing countries is in the form of low-interest loans. The OECD, the World Bank, and various regional banks associated with the World Bank provide most of the loans. In 1976, the UN established the International Fund for Agricultural Development to obtain additional loan funds from prosperous UN members. The United States offers technical aid and loans chiefly through its Agency for International Development.

Food Aid Programs provide shipments of food to countries that need emergency aid. Members of the OECD contribute most of this aid. The United States is the largest contributor. Most U.S. assistance is administered through the federal government's Food for Peace program. The World Food Program, sponsored by the UN and the FAO, channels donations from individual countries to nations in need of aid. Many private charitable organizations also supply food aid.

Research Programs. Various scientific research programs seek to increase both the quality and the quantity of the food supply. For example, a variety of corn with an improved amino acid content was developed in the 1960's. But the new variety gives relatively low yields. Scientists are now working to develop a high-yield variety with the improved amino acid content.

Research scientists are also seeking ways to conserve agricultural resources. As we have seen, some of this research is aimed at developing varieties of grain that make more efficient use of water and fertilizer. Animal scientists are conducting similar experiments to develop varieties of cattle that produce more meat from the same amount of feed.

Many research projects are carried out at about 10 agricultural research institutes jointly sponsored by the FAO, the World Bank, the Ford and Rockefeller foundations, and several other organizations. The institutes have been established in developing countries, and each specializes in a particular type of research. In Mexico, for example, the International Center for the Improvement of Maize and Wheat is trying to produce improved varieties of corn, wheat, and certain other grains.

Alain Nogues, Sygma

Emergency Food Supplies are provided for thousands of disaster victims annually. These Red Cross workers are distributing emergency rations to victims of a flood in Bangladesh.

Some of the institutes, such as the International Rice Research Institute in the Philippines, are working to develop varieties of plants and livestock that are specially suited to tropical climates. For more information on agricultural research, see AGRICULTURAL RESEARCH SERVICE; RESEARCH (Agriculture).

A World Food Reserve. In 1974, representatives from 130 countries attended a UN-sponsored World Food Conference in Rome. The representatives adopted a plan to set up a unified world food reserve. The world's reserves now consist of the individual reserves of the major exporting countries. Each country administers its own reserve. Under the new plan, each country will continue to hold its own reserve, but it will work with participating countries in the use of the reserve. Reserve supplies can thus be directed to parts of the world where they are needed most.   LESTER R. BROWN

Related Articles. See AGRICULTURE, FOOD, and NUTRITION with their lists of *Related Articles*. See also the following articles:

Agency for International Development	Food for Peace
Birth Control	Foreign Aid
Famine	Green Revolution
Fishing Industry	Population
Food and Agriculture Organization	Standard of Living
	Technical Assistance
	World Bank

FAMINE is a prolonged food shortage that causes widespread hunger and death. Throughout history, famine has struck at least one area of the world every few years. Most of the developing nations of Africa, Asia, and Latin America have barely enough food for their people. Millions in these countries go hungry. When food production or imports drop for any reason, famine may strike and thousands or millions of people may die.

Causes of Famine

Many famines have more than one cause. For example, the great Bengal famine of 1943 in eastern India was caused by both natural and historical events. World War II created a general food shortage and led to the cutoff of rice imports from Burma, which had been occupied by the Japanese. Then a cyclone destroyed much farmland. Famine struck, and more than $1\frac{1}{2}$ million persons died.

Nearly all famines result from crop failures. The chief causes of crop failure include (1) *drought* (prolonged lack of rain), (2) too much rainfall and flooding, and (3) plant diseases and pests. Many other factors may also help create a famine.

Drought ranks as the chief cause of famine. Certain regions of China, India, and Russia have always been those hardest hit by famine. All three have large areas, near deserts, where the rainfall is light and variable. In a dry year, crops in those areas fail and famine may strike. In the 1870's, for example, dry weather in the Deccan plateau of southern India caused a famine that took about 5 million lives. During the same period, a famine in China killed more than 9 million persons.

In the late 1960's and early 1970's, lack of rain produced widespread famine in a region of Africa called the Sahel. The estimated number of deaths was about a million. The Sahel lies just south of the Sahara. It includes parts of Chad, Mali, Mauritania, Niger, Senegal, the Sudan, Upper Volta, and other nations.

Too Much Rainfall may also bring famine. Rivers swollen by heavy rains overflow their banks and destroy farmland. Other crops rot in the field because of the excess water. In the 1300's, several years of heavy rains created widespread famine in western Europe. The Hwang Ho River in northern China is called *China's Sorrow* because it often floods, ruining crops and bringing famine. In 1929 and 1930, flooding along this river caused a famine that killed about 2 million persons.

Plant Diseases and Pests sometimes produce famine. During the 1840's, a plant disease destroyed most of Ireland's potato crop. Between 1841 and 1851, Ireland's population dropped by about $2\frac{1}{2}$ million persons through starvation, disease, and emigration.

Other Causes of famine include both natural and human ones. Such natural disasters as cyclones, earthquakes, early frosts, and tidal waves may affect a large area, destroying enough crops to create a famine. War may result in a famine if many farmers leave their fields and join the armed forces. In some cases, an army has deliberately created a famine to starve an enemy into surrender. The army destroys stored food and growing crops and sets up a blockade to cut off the enemy's food supply. Blockades prevented shipments of food from reaching the region of Biafra during the Nigerian Civil War (1967-1970). A famine resulted, and more than a million Biafrans probably starved.

Poor transportation may also contribute to a famine because of the difficulty of shipping food where it is needed. Many of the famines in China, India, and Russia resulted largely from primitive transportation. For example, a famine in what is now the state of Uttar Pradesh in northern India killed about 800,000 persons in 1837 and 1838. Lack of transportation prevented the shipment of grain from other areas of India.

Effects of Famine

The chief effects of famine include (1) death and disease, (2) destruction of livestock and seed, (3) crime and other social disorders, and (4) migration.

Death and Disease are the main and most immediate effects of famine. People who lack sufficient food lose weight and grow extremely weak. Many famine victims become so feeble that they die from diarrhea or some other simple ailment. The weakened condition of a starvation victim is called *marasmus*. Old people and young children are the first to die.

Children who have some food but do not receive enough protein develop a condition called *kwashiorkor*. One of its symptoms is *edema* (puffy swelling of the face, forearms, and ankles). Changes in the color and texture of the hair and skin also may occur. Young famine victims who do not die from kwashiorkor or starvation may grow up with severe mental and physical handicaps.

Famines also increase the possibility of epidemics. Cholera, typhus, and other diseases take many lives because people weakened by hunger do not recover easily from disease. Large numbers of the victims have fled from their homes and live in crowded refugee camps where disease spreads quickly. People frequently must drink impure water, which can carry disease.

David Austen, Stock, Boston

Famine Victims receive food and other emergency aid from their government and such international agencies as the Red Cross and United Nations (UN). The people shown above are waiting for food at a famine relief center in Dacca, Bangladesh.

FAMINE

Destruction of Livestock and Seed during a famine prolongs the disaster. Many farm animals die or are killed for food. Farmers, to avoid starvation, may have to eat all their seed before the planting season begins. Such damaging losses hinder them from returning to a normal life and may lower production levels.

Crime and Other Social Disorders increase during a famine. Such crimes as looting, prostitution, and theft multiply. Desperate people steal food and other items they could not obtain otherwise. They may sell stolen goods to buy something to eat. There may be scattered outbreaks of violence, particularly near food distribution centers. However, large riots rarely occur.

Migration. Large numbers of famine victims leave their homes and flock to cities or other areas where food may be available. In the confusion, parents and children may be separated, leading to panic. Youths may band together to obtain food by looting or theft.

Prolonged famine may result in emigration. The potato famine in Ireland caused about a million persons to settle in other countries, chiefly the United States.

Fighting Famine

The United Nations (UN) and several other international organizations provide emergency help for famine victims. Various agencies also work to increase the world's food supply and thus prevent future famines. Many nations hope to prevent famine by increasing their food production. If a nation can build up a large enough reserve of food, regional crop failures will not cause disastrous shortages. For additional information about world food programs and methods of producing more food, see the WORLD BOOK articles on UNITED NATIONS (Fighting Hunger) and FOOD SUPPLY (Methods to Increase the Food Supply; Food Supply Programs).

If a nation's population grows as fast as its food production, little food will be left over to build up a reserve. For this reason, many nations have promoted birth control programs to limit their population growth (see BIRTH CONTROL [In Other Countries]). However, such programs have had little effect in areas where large numbers of people remain poor. Many poor people want large families so the children can help with the work and, later, care for the parents.   JEAN MAYER

ANGOLA is an independent nation on the southwest coast of Africa. Its official name is the People's Republic of Angola. Angola covers 481,354 square miles (1,246,700 square kilometers) and has a population of about 6,340,000. Cabinda, in the northwest, is a district of Angola, though the Congo River and Zaire separate it from the rest of the country.

Most of Angola's people live in rural areas and work on farms. The nation produces a variety of crops and ranks as a world leader in coffee production. Angola also has many natural resources, including diamonds, iron ore, and petroleum. Luanda, the capital and largest city, is a major African seaport.

Angola became independent in November 1975. Parts of it had been ruled by Portugal for most of the period since the 1500's. Shortly before Angola gained independence, a civil war broke out between rival groups that wanted to rule the country. The war lasted until early 1976 and greatly influenced the nation's life.

George Peabody & Associates

Angolan Children help draw the family water supply at a well in a rural village, *above*. Most of the people of Angola live in rural areas and work as farmers and herders.

Government of Angola is controlled by the nation's only political party, called the Popular Movement for the Liberation of Angola (MPLA). The party bases its policies on the philosophy of Karl Marx, one of the chief founders of Communism. The party leader serves as president, head of state, and commander in chief of the armed forces. The party's Central Committee, headed by a premier, is the chief policymaking body.

People. Almost all the people of Angola are black Africans. The blacks belong to several ethnic groups. Before the nation became independent, more than 400,000 Europeans and *mestizos* (persons of mixed black African and white ancestry) lived in Angola. Most of them fled during the civil war.

More than 80 per cent of Angola's people live in rural areas. The rural people work as farmers and herders and many raise just enough food for their own use. Most of the Europeans and mestizos who did not

---
———————— FACTS IN BRIEF ————————

Capital: Luanda.

Official Language: Portuguese.

Area: 481,354 sq. mi. (1,246,700 km²). *Greatest Distances*— north-south, 850 mi. (1,368 km); east-west, 800 mi. (1,287 km). *Coastline*—928 mi. (1,493 km).

Elevation: *Highest*—Môco, 8,595 ft. (2,620 m). *Lowest*— sea level.

Population: *Estimated 1977 Population*—6,340,000; distribution, 18 per cent urban, 82 per cent rural; density, 13 persons per sq. mi. (5 per km²). *1970 Census*— 5,673,046; *Estimated 1982 Population*—6,863,000.

Chief Products: *Agriculture*—coffee, corn, sugar cane, tobacco; *Manufacturing*—food processing, cement, chemicals, textiles; *Mining*—diamonds, petroleum.

Flag: The flag has two horizontal stripes. The red stripe represents Angola's struggle for independence, and the black stripe symbolizes Africa. The yellow emblem in the center has a five-pointed star that stands for socialism, a half cogwheel for industry, and a machete for agriculture. Adopted in 1975. See FLAG (picture: Flags of Africa).

Money: *Basic Unit*—escudo. See ESCUDO; MONEY (table).

leave the country live in cities. They own small businesses or hold other jobs that require technical and management skills. Europeans and mestizos once held most of these jobs, but blacks have replaced many of them.

Most black Angolans speak a language that belongs to the Bantu language group (see BANTU). Europeans, mestizos, and educated blacks speak Portuguese, Angola's official language. About half the people, including most of the city dwellers, are Christians. Other Angolans practice religions based on the worship of ancestors and spirits. Only about 30 per cent of the people can read and write.

Land and Climate. Angola forms part of the large inland plateau of southern Africa. The country consists chiefly of hilly grasslands, but a rocky desert covers the south. The land gradually rises from the interior to the west, where it drops sharply to a narrow coastal plain. Most of the coastal plain has little natural vegetation. Tropical forests grow in the north.

Angola has many rivers and more than 900 miles (1,400 kilometers) of coastline. Some of the rivers flow north into the Congo River, and others flow west into the Atlantic Ocean. A few, including the Cunene and the Cuanza, serve as waterways to the interior.

Temperatures in the coastal plain region average about 70° F. (21° C) in January and about 60° F. (16° C) in June. Most of the inland region has slightly higher temperatures. From 40 to 60 inches (100 to 150

Angola

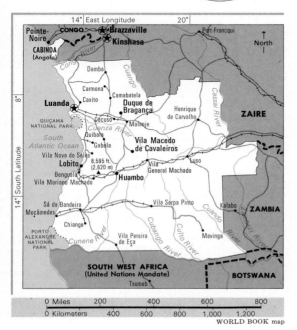

Capital	⊛
Other City or Town	●
Road	——
Rail Line	⟷
MOUNTAIN	▲
River	⌒

WORLD BOOK map

centimeters) of rain falls annually on the northern coast and in most of the interior. Only about 2 inches (5 centimeters) of rain falls yearly in the desert.

Economy of Angola is based largely on agriculture. However, mining and manufacturing have become increasingly important to the nation. The main food crops include bananas, cassava, corn, and sugar cane. Angola also produces several crops for export, including coffee and tobacco.

Angola has vast deposits of copper, diamonds, iron ore, and petroleum. Cabinda provides most of the petroleum, the nation's leading export. Angolan industries produce cement, chemicals, processed foods, and textiles.

The nation has about 27,300 miles (44,000 kilometers) of roads. An extensive railroad system serves many Angolan cities and provides neighboring Zambia and Zaire with an important link to the sea. Angola has 35 radio stations and two daily newspapers.

History. Prehistoric peoples lived in what is now Angola as early as 50,000 B.C. Bantu-speaking peoples settled there about 2,000 years ago. The Portuguese established bases in Angola during the 1500's. By the early 1600's, Angola had become a major source of slave labor for Portugal's colony in Brazil. In 1641, the Dutch forced the Portuguese out of Angola and took over the slave trade. Portugal regained control in 1648. During the 1800's, after the decline of the slave trade, Portuguese planters began to grow corn, sugar cane, and tobacco in Angola.

Portugal began to improve Angola's economy after the Portuguese dictator Antonio de Oliveira Salazar came to power in the late 1920's. Thousands of Portuguese moved to Angola and established businesses there.

During the 1950's, many Angolans began to demand freedom from Portuguese rule. In 1956, they organized the Popular Movement for the Liberation of Angola (MPLA). Many members of the MPLA revolted in Luanda in 1961. The rioting quickly spread throughout the country and soon developed into a bloody guerrilla war. A Portuguese army that included a large number of Angolans put down the uprising. The MPLA rebels then set up guerrilla bases in neighboring countries.

Cultural and political differences began to divide the Angolan rebels after the 1961 revolt. In 1962, a group of northern rebels formed the Front for the Liberation of Angola (FNLA). Four years later, southern rebels organized the National Union for the Total Independence of Angola (UNITA).

In 1974, Portuguese military officers overthrew the government of Portugal. In January 1975, they decided to grant independence to Angola. At first, the Angolans agreed to set up a government consisting of representatives of all three rebel groups. But each group wanted to head the government, and a civil war broke out over which would rule.

Angola gained independence from Portugal on Nov. 11, 1975. But the civil war continued between the MPLA and the FNLA and UNITA, whose forces had united. The MPLA received considerable aid from two Communist nations, Russia and Cuba. Russia supplied military equipment and Cuba sent troops. The Russians and Cubans supported the MPLA because it followed

ANGOLA

J. P. Laffont, Sygma

Luanda, the capital and largest city of Angola, has many modern buildings and broad, tree-lined streets. A deep natural harbor helps make it one of the leading African seaports.

the socialist philosophy of Karl Marx, one of the chief founders of Communism. Russia and Cuba hoped Angola would become a Communist nation if the MPLA won the war. The MPLA defeated its enemies in April 1976 and formed a Marxist government. But its president, Agostinho Neto, denied that the government was a Communist dictatorship.

Neto's government faced many problems. For example, the departure of most of the Europeans who had lived in Angola resulted in a serious shortage of technicians and executives. Some important positions were filled by blacks and by specialists from Russia and Cuba. But many businesses could not be managed properly, and industrial production declined rapidly.

The government began several programs to overcome the effects of the civil war. It took control of many businesses and started to train teachers and technicians. Russia, Cuba, and other Communist countries provided financial and technical aid. But the government also encouraged non-Communist nations to invest in Angolan businesses.   LEWIS HENRY GANN

LUANDA, *loo AHN duh* (pop. 600,000), is the capital and largest city of Angola, and the country's chief industrial center and port. It lies on the west coast of Africa, along the Atlantic Ocean (see ANGOLA [map]).

Industrial facilities in Luanda include foundries; sawmills; textile mills; and cement, printing, and food processing plants. An airport and a railroad serve the city.

The Portuguese ruled Angola as a colony for about 400 years until the country gained independence in 1975. They founded Luanda in 1576, and the city became the main center of Portuguese settlement in Angola. The Portuguese built many impressive European-style structures in Luanda, including a fortress; churches; libraries; houses; and business, government, and university buildings. Run-down areas called *shantytowns* lie outside the city.

Civil war broke out after Angola became independent, and almost all the Portuguese left. Today, most of Luanda's people are black Africans.   LEWIS HENRY GANN

CAPE VERDE is an African country that consists of 10 main islands and 5 tiny islands. It lies in the Atlantic Ocean, about 400 miles (640 kilometers) west of Dakar, Senegal, on the African mainland.

Cape Verde has a population of about 305,000 and a total land area of 1,557 square miles (4,033 square kilometers). São Tiago, the largest island, covers 383 square miles (992 square kilometers). Santo Antão is the second largest island, followed by Boa Vista, Fogo, São Nicolau, Maio, São Vicente, Sal, Brava, and Santa Luzia. Santa Luzia and the five islets are uninhabited.

Praia, the capital of Cape Verde, is on São Tiago (see PRAIA). Mindelo, on São Vicente, is the country's largest city and chief port. Portugal ruled the islands from the 1460's until 1975, when Cape Verde gained independence.

Government. Cape Verde is a republic. The people elect a 56-member legislature called the People's Assembly, which selects a president and a premier. The Assembly also appoints a Cabinet of eight members, headed by the premier. The president serves as the chief of state.

Cape Verde has only one political party, the African Party for the Independence of Guinea and Cape Verde. It is usually called the PAIGC, the initials of the party's name in Portuguese. The PAIGC is also the only political party in Guinea-Bissau, an African mainland nation southeast of Cape Verde.

People. About 70 per cent of the people of Cape Verde have mixed black African and Portuguese ancestry. Black Africans make up most of the rest of the population.

Cape Verde has an extremely low standard of living because many of its people cannot find work. The country's chief industries, farming and fishing, provide workers with only a bare income. Famines have occurred frequently through the years, and many of the people are undernourished. Since the mid-1900's, hundreds of thousands of Cape Verdians have emigrated to Brazil, Portugal, the United States, and other countries.

Most Cape Verdians speak a local Creole dialect based on ancient Portuguese and various African languages. The majority of the people are Roman Catholics, but many also practice *animism,* the belief that everything in nature has a soul.

Cape Verde has about 500 elementary schools and several high schools and technical schools. About 75 per cent of the people can read and write.

─────── **FACTS IN BRIEF** ───────

Capital: Praia.

Form of Government: Republic.

Total Land Area: 1,557 sq. mi. (4,033 km²). *Coastline*—600 mi. (966 km).

Elevation: *Highest*—Pico, 9,281 ft. (2,829 m). *Lowest*—sea level.

Population: *Estimated 1977 Population*—305,000; distribution, 90 per cent rural, 10 per cent urban; density, 197 persons per sq. mi. (76 per km²). *1970 Census*—272,071. *Estimated 1982 Population*—333,000.

Chief Products: Bananas, salt, sugar cane.

Flag: A black star framed by two curved ears of corn lies on a red vertical stripe at the left. A yellow horizontal stripe appears over a green one at the right. See FLAG (picture: Flags of Africa).

Money: *Basic Unit*—escudo.

* National capital
* Settlement
+ Elevation above sea level
Road

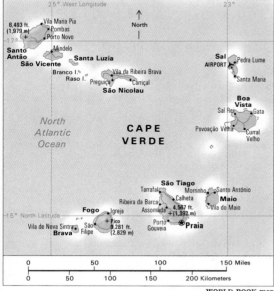

25° West Longitude — 23°

North

6,493 ft.
(1,979 m) Vila Maria Pia
Pombas
Porto Novo
Santo
Antão Mindelo
São Vicente Santa Luzia
Branco I.
Raso I. Preguiça Carriçal
São Nicolau
Sal
AIRPORT
Pedra Lume
Santa Maria

North
Atlantic
Ocean

CAPE
VERDE

Boa
Vista
Sal Rei Gata
Povoação Velha Curral
Velho

São Tiago
Tarrafal Morrinho Santo António
Ribeira da Barca Calheta Maio
Fogo Assomada 4,567 ft. Vila do Maio
Igreja +(1,392 m)
Vila de Nova Sintra Pico Porto
São 9,281 ft. Gouveia Praia
Brava Filipe (2,829 m)

0 50 100 150 Miles
0 50 100 150 200 Kilometers

WORLD BOOK map

Duncan Carse

Cape Verde's Rugged, Mountainous Land lies barren after years of drought. Few plants can grow in the volcanic ash that covers São Vicente, *above*, and most of the country's other islands.

Land and Climate. The islands of Cape Verde were formed by volcanic eruptions that occurred from $2\frac{1}{2}$ to 65 million years ago. The only remaining active volcano is on Fogo Island. Most of the islands have rugged, mountainous land, with tall cliffs ranging along the coastlines.

Cape Verde has a warm, dry climate, with average annual temperatures that range from 68° F. (20° C) to 77° F. (25° C). A continual shortage of rain makes most of the land too dry to support plant life. The country becomes even drier during January and February, when sandstorms blow in from the Sahara.

Economy of Cape Verde is underdeveloped. Agriculture is the country's major industry, but most of the land cannot be farmed because of its dryness. A drought that began in 1968 and continued into the 1970's caused about a 90 per cent drop in agricultural production. Most of the country's livestock died during the drought. Cape Verde's chief crops include coffee beans; sugar cane; bananas and other fruits; and such vegetables as beans, corn, and tomatoes.

During the mid-1900's, Cape Verde worked to develop its fishing industry. Lobsters and tuna are the main catches. The country's mining industry produces salt and *pozzuolana*, a volcanic rock used by the cement industry. Both these products are exported.

Before Cape Verde became independent in 1975, it relied almost entirely on Portugal for economic support. Since then, it has received food aid from the United Nations and financial aid from various other countries.

Cape Verde has three radio stations and two newspapers. The islands have a total of only about 920 miles (1,480 kilometers) of roads. There is no railroad service, and boats operate among the islands only infrequently. Sal Island has an airport, and several of the other islands have small landing strips.

History. Portuguese explorers discovered the islands of Cape Verde about 1460. The islands were uninhabited at the time, and the Portuguese began to settle there about two years later. They planted cotton, fruit trees, and sugar cane and brought slaves from the African mainland to work the land.

Slave trading became Cape Verde's most important commercial activity during the 1500's and 1600's, and the islands prospered. Slaves learned how to work on plantations there before being shipped to the Americas and elsewhere. The slave trade declined in the late 1600's, and the prosperity ended. Economic conditions improved slightly in the mid-1800's, when Mindelo became an important refueling port for ships crossing the Atlantic.

Portugal ruled Cape Verde and what is now Guinea-Bissau under one government until 1879, when each became a separate Portuguese colony. Cape Verde became a Portuguese overseas province in 1951, and its people assumed a greater role in the government. The PAIGC fought to overthrow Portuguese rule from the mid-1950's until 1975, when Cape Verde became an independent country. Guinea-Bissau had won independence in 1974, and the two nations have worked to unite under a single government.

KRISTIN W. HENRY and CLEMENT HENRY MOORE

PRAIA

PRAIA, *PRĪ ah* (pop. 21,494), is the capital of Cape Verde, an island country west of the African mainland. Most of the nation's government activity takes place in Praia, and the city is also a seaport and a trading center. Praia lies on the southeastern coast of São Tiago, the largest island of Cape Verde. For location, see CAPE VERDE (map).

Historians do not know when Praia was founded, but the city had been established by 1572. The Portuguese ruled Cape Verde from the 1460's until 1975, when it became an independent country. They made Praia the capital in 1770. KRISTIN W. HENRY and CLEMENT HENRY MOORE

COMOROS, *KAHM oh rohz,* is a small African country made up of several islands. It lies in the Indian Ocean between the mainland of Africa and the island country of Madagascar. The Comoros island group consists of four main islands—Anjouan, Grande Comore, Mayotte, and Moheli—and several smaller ones.

All the islands belonged to France until 1975. Three of the four largest islands declared their independence that year, but Mayotte chose to remain a French possession. The Comorian government considers Mayotte part of the country, but the people of Mayotte have voted to stay under French rule.

The country's official name is the *Republic of the Comoros.* The islands, including Mayotte, have a total area of 838 square miles (2,171 square kilometers) and a population of about 320,000. Most Comorians live in rural villages. Moroni, on Grande Comore, is the capital and largest city. About 18,000 people live there.

Government. A 13-member National Executive Council governs Comoros and appoints a president who serves as head of state. The president's responsibilities include land reform and national defense. He names a Cabinet and a prime minister to assist him.

People. Most of the people of Comoros have mixed ancestry. They are descendants of Arabs, black Africans, and other groups. Almost all Comorians are farmers, but few of them raise enough crops to feed even themselves. They must import large supplies of rice, their chief food. The people also eat such foods as bananas, coconuts, and yams.

Major problems in the islands include disease, hunger, and lack of education. Illness and malnutrition occur frequently, and the nation has a shortage of physicians and hospitals. Only about a third of the children complete elementary school, and few go on to high school.

Most Comorians are Muslims and speak Arabic or Swahili. French, the official language of the country, is widely understood, though most Comorians do not speak or write it.

FACTS IN BRIEF

Capital: Moroni.

Official Language: French.

Form of Government: Republic.

Total Land Area: 838 square miles (2,171 km²). *Coastline*—243 mi. (391 km).

Elevation: *Highest*—Mont Kartala, 7,746 ft. (2,361 m). *Lowest*—sea level.

Population: *Estimated 1977 Population*—320,000; distribution, 96 per cent rural, 4 per cent urban; density, 381 persons per sq. mi. (147 per km²). *1966 Census*—243,948. *Estimated 1982 Population*—360,000.

Chief Products: bananas, cloves, coconuts, corn, perfume plants, rice, spices, vanilla, yams.

Flag: A red field covers two-thirds of the flag. A green field lies beneath. A crescent moon and four five-pointed stars are in the upper left-hand corner. Adopted in 1975. See FLAG (picture: Flags of Africa).

Money: Basic Unit—Franc.

Land and Climate. Most of the Comoro Islands were formed by volcanoes. Mont Kartala, a volcano on Grande Comore, is still active. Plateaus and valleys created by flowing lava lie beneath the volcanic peaks of the islands. Swamps form the shorelines of almost all the islands.

Comoros has a cool, dry climate. A hot, rainy season lasts from November through April. The heavy rains during this period provide the islands with their only natural source of drinking water. The people store the water for year-round use.

Thase Daniel, Bruce Coleman Inc.

The Comoro Islands have many open-air markets, including the one in Moroni, the nation's capital and largest city. Merchants spread their wares on the ground to attract strolling shoppers.

Comoros

✳	National capital
•	Settlement
+	Elevation above sea level
——	Road

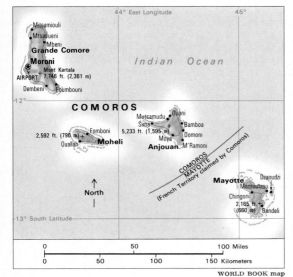

WORLD BOOK map

In 1975, Anjouan, Grande Comore, and Moheli voted for complete independence, but Mayotte voted to remain under French protection. France recognized the independence of the three islands but continued to rule Mayotte as a possession. In 1976, the people of Mayotte again voted for French rule.

Several Comorian governments have held power for short periods since independence was declared. In 1976, the National Executive Council appointed a president. The Comorian government also planned to name a governor for each of the islands, and a commissioner to deal with the question of independence for Mayotte.   LEWIS HENRY GANN

MORONI (pop. 18,000) is the capital and largest city of Comoros, an island country southeast of the African mainland. The city lies on the west coast of Grande Comore, the largest island of Comoros. For location, see COMOROS (map).

Moroni is the nation's center of government, trade, and tourism. Muslims from many countries visit the city's beautiful *mosque* (Muslim house of worship). The chief *lycée* (secondary school) of Comoros is located in Moroni.   LEWIS HENRY GANN

MOZAMBIQUE, *MOH zuhm BEEK*, is a country on the southeast coast of Africa. It covers 302,330 square miles (783,030 square kilometers) and has a population of about 10 million. Mozambique is slightly larger than Texas and has about three-fourths as many people as that state.

About 90 per cent of the people of Mozambique live in rural areas. Most of the urban centers lie near the coast. Maputo is the capital, largest city, and chief port. Mozambique is noted for its many fine harbors, and its excellent port facilities are used by some neighboring countries. Mozambique was governed by Portugal from the early 1500's until 1975. The country became independent that year after a 10-year struggle against Portuguese rule.

Government of Mozambique is controlled by the nation's only political party, the Front for the Liberation of Mozambique. The party, known as Frelimo,

Economy. Comoros is one of the world's poorest nations. It has no major industry, and no valuable minerals have been found there. Comorians have an average annual income of only about $100.

The economy of Comoros depends almost entirely on agriculture. The people raise such crops as bananas, coconuts, rice, and yams for food. They export cloves, perfume plants, spices, and vanilla. Comoros must import about three times as much as it exports. The country trades chiefly with France, Madagascar, the United States, and West Germany.

Until 1975, France gave the Comoro Islands about $18 million in annual aid. France cut off this aid after three of the main islands declared their independence. The loss has caused serious damage to the economy of Comoros.

Grande Comore has an airport and a radio station. Only the larger towns of the islands have electricity, and the country has a total of only about 150 miles (241 kilometers) of paved roads.

History. The first people who lived in the Comoro Islands came from mainland Africa, Madagascar, and Malaysia. Historians know little about them or when they came to the islands.

During the 1400's, Arabs landed on the Comoros and took over the islands. For the next 400 years, Arab sultans ruled each island as a separate kingdom.

France seized Mayotte in 1843 and by 1886 had gained control of the rest of the islands. The French granted the islands self-rule in 1961.

───────── **FACTS IN BRIEF** ─────────

Official Name: *República Popular de Moçambique* (People's Republic of Mozambique).

Capital: Maputo.

Official Language: Portuguese.

Area: 302,330 sq. mi. (783,030 km²). *Coastline*—1,556 mi. (2,504 km). *Greatest Distances*—north-south, 1,100 mi. (1,770 km); east-west, 680 mi. (1,094 km).

Elevation: *Highest*—Mt. Binga, 7,992 ft. (2,436 m). *Lowest*—sea level.

Population: *Estimated 1977 Population*—9,810,000; distribution, 92 per cent rural, 8 per cent urban; density, 34 persons per sq. mi. (13 per km²). *1970 Census*—8,233,834. *Estimated 1982 Population*—11,210,000.

Chief Products: Cashews, coconuts, cotton, sugar.

Flag: The flag has four wedge-shaped diagonal stripes of green, red, black, and yellow, which are separated by white bands. In the upper left corner, a white cog wheel encloses a book, which has a gun and a hoe crossed over it. See FLAG (picture: Flags of Africa).

Money: *Basic Unit*—Escudo. See MONEY (table: Values).

MOZAMBIQUE

bases its policies on the philosophy of Karl Marx and V. I. Lenin, two founders of Communism. The president of Frelimo is also the nation's president. The highest governmental power lies with the party's Central Committee, which is made up of 15 members appointed by Frelimo. The party also appoints the 210 members of the People's Assembly, Mozambique's legislative body. This group meets twice a year. Its Permanent Committee handles legislative matters between sessions.

People. Almost all Mozambicans are black Africans. Other groups, including Arabs, Europeans, and Pakistanis, make up less than 2 per cent of the population. Most of the blacks belong to groups that speak a Bantu language. Differences among the various languages limit communication among the groups. Few blacks can speak Portuguese, the country's official language. Some Mozambicans speak English when conducting business activities.

Most Mozambicans are farmers, but their techniques are extremely primitive. Some farmers use the *slash and burn* method, which involves cutting and burning forest trees to clear an area for planting. Farmers in some areas of the country use more modern techniques.

About 75 per cent of the people practice traditional African religions. Many of this group are *animists*, who believe that everything in nature has a soul. Others worship the spirits of their ancestors. Most of the remaining 25 per cent are either Roman Catholics or Muslims.

Only about 15 per cent of Mozambique's population can read and write, but the government has begun programs to improve education. A university was established in Maputo in 1962.

Land and Climate. Almost half of Mozambique is covered by a flat plain that extends inland from the coast. The land rises steadily beyond the plain, and high plateaus and mountains run along much of the western border. Sand dunes and swamps line the coast. Grasslands, treeless plains, and tropical forests cover much of the country.

Many sizable rivers flow east through Mozambique into the Indian Ocean, and their basins have extremely fertile soil. Cashew trees and coconut palms grow throughout the country. Animal life in Mozambique includes crocodiles, lions, rhinoceroses, and zebras.

Mozambique has a basically tropical climate, but temperatures and rainfall vary considerably in different areas. Temperatures average 68° F. (20° C) in July and 80° F. (27° C) in January. About 80 per cent of the annual rainfall occurs from November to March. The rainfall ranges from about 16 to 48 inches (41 to 122 centimeters).

Economy of Mozambique is not well developed. The government, which owns all the farmland and the major industries, is working to increase agricultural production and industrial development.

Mozambique

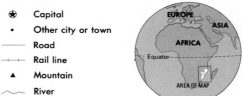

- ✹ Capital
- • Other city or town
- —— Road
- ⊢⊣⊢ Rail line
- ▲ Mountain
- ⌇ River

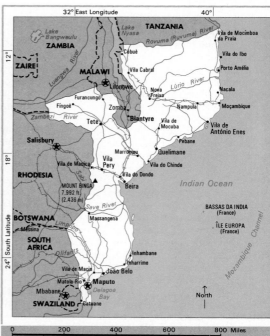

WORLD BOOK map

Jerry Frank, DPI

Maputo, the capital of Mozambique, is a leading African port. Ships from many countries carry cargo to and from the city. Maputo lies on Delagoa Bay, an inlet of the Indian Ocean.

Editorial Photocolor Archives

Outdoor Markets, where people buy food and other goods, serve as shopping centers in many parts of Mozambique. The market shown above is near Maputo.

Editorial Photocolor Archives

A Rural Village near Tete in northwestern Mozambique, consists of a cluster of huts with thatched roofs. The people of the village farm the land and graze livestock nearby.

Agriculture is Mozambique's major industry, but only about 5 per cent of the farmland is cultivated. The nation is a leading producer of cashews. Other important crops include coconuts, cotton, and sugar.

Mozambique's economy depends partly on payments by South Africa and Malawi for the use of railroads and port facilities. In addition, many Mozambicans work in South African mines.

Mozambique produces more than 300,000 short tons (270,000 metric tons) of coal yearly. Industrial development has been slow and has occurred mainly in the food-processing and oil-refining industries.

Mozambique has about 23,900 miles (38,460 kilometers) of roads and several railroads. An airport operates in Maputo. One television station, three radio stations, and four daily newspapers serve the nation.

History. People have lived in the area that is now Mozambique since the 4000's B.C. Bantu-speaking people settled there before A.D. 100, and Arabs lived in the area by the 800's. Portuguese explorers first visited Mozambique in 1497. They established a trading post there in 1505, and the country became a slave-trading center. However, most of Mozambique remained undeveloped until the late 1800's.

Through the years, Portuguese control of Mozambique was threatened by Arabs, Africans, and some European nations. In 1885, Africa was divided among various European powers, and Mozambique was recognized as a Portuguese colony. Borders similar to those of present-day Mozambique were established in 1891.

Towns and railroads were built in Mozambique during the late 1800's and early 1900's, and the Portuguese population rose. In the 1950's, many blacks became increasingly discontented with white Portuguese rule. Frelimo was established in 1961 as a guerrilla movement. It began military attacks against the

Portuguese in 1964 and gained control of part of northern Mozambique. Fighting between Frelimo and Portuguese forces continued for 10 years.

Portugal agreed in 1974 to grant independence to its colonies, and Mozambique became an independent nation on June 25, 1975. Frelimo established a government that took control of all education, health and legal services, land, housing, and major industries. Most of the Portuguese left Mozambique at that time.

In March 1976, Mozambique closed its border with Rhodesia to protest that country's white minority government. This action has cost Mozambique about $100 million in annual income from Rhodesian use of its railroads and ports. In addition, the government has limited the number of Mozambican workers in South Africa, which also has a white minority government.

Border fighting broke out between Mozambican and Rhodesian troops. Many black Rhodesians fled to Mozambique to use bases there in their fight against the Rhodesian government.   LEWIS HENRY GANN

See also MAPUTO.

MAPUTO (pop. 354,684; met. area pop. 750,000) is the capital and largest city of Mozambique. It has an excellent harbor and is the chief port of Mozambique and several nearby countries. It lies on Delagoa Bay in southern Mozambique (see MOZAMBIQUE [map]).

The Portuguese founded the city about 1780 and named it Lourenço Marques. The city became the major white settlement in Mozambique, but most of the whites left in 1975 after Mozambique gained independence from Portugal. In 1976, the city's name was changed to Maputo.

The main sections of Maputo have wide, tree-lined streets and large beaches. The fortress of Nossa Senhora da Conceição, built in 1871, is a famous landmark. The city's major industries include cement-making, food processing, and tourism.   LEWIS HENRY GANN

563

PAPUA NEW GUINEA

PAPUA NEW GUINEA, *PAP oo uh noo GIHN ee,* is an independent nation in the Pacific Ocean, northeast of Australia. It consists of part of New Guinea plus a chain of tropical islands that extend more than 1,000 miles (1,600 kilometers).

Papua New Guinea has a total land area of 178,260 square miles (461,691 square kilometers) and a population of about 2,667,000. The eastern half of the island of New Guinea makes up most of the country. The rest of Papua New Guinea consists of the islands of the Bismarck Archipelago; Bougainville and Buka in the Solomon Islands; the D'Entrecasteaux Islands; the Louisiade Archipelago; the Trobriand Islands; and Woodlark Island. Port Moresby, on New Guinea, is the capital and largest city.

European explorers first visited various islands of Papua New Guinea during the early 1500's. The islands came under Australian rule in the early 1900's and gained independence in 1975.

Government. Papua New Guinea is a constitutional monarchy and a member of the Commonwealth of Nations. The British monarch serves as head of state and is represented on the islands by a governor general. The people elect a national legislature, which selects a prime minister to head the government.

People. About 98 per cent of the population of Papua New Guinea are Melanesians, a dark-skinned people with black, woolly hair. Other groups on the islands include Australians and Chinese. Most of the people live in small villages. They farm the land and raise just enough food for their own needs.

The people of Papua New Guinea speak more than 700 languages. As a result, many individuals have difficulty communicating with one another. About half the population are Christians. The other half practice primitive religions based on ancestor worship. Only about 25 per cent of the children attend elementary school, and less than 3 per cent go on to high school.

Land and Climate. The islands of Papua New Guinea form part of a series of underwater mountains, many of which are active or inactive volcanoes. Thick tropical forests cover about 80 per cent of the land. Eastern New Guinea has several mountain ranges. Rivers flow down the mountain valleys and form wide deltas near the shore. Large swamps cover much of the coastal land. The other islands have similar land formations.

Papua New Guinea has a hot, humid climate. The temperature averages from 75° to 82° F. (24° to 28° C) in the lowlands and about 68° F. (20° C) in the highlands. An average of about 80 inches (203 centimeters) of rain falls annually.

Economy of Papua New Guinea is based largely on agriculture. Almost all the people work on farms. The chief farm products include cocoa, coconuts, coffee, rubber, sweet potatoes, tea, and yams. Copper, which is mined on the island of Bougainville, ranks as the most valuable resource. It accounts for more than 60 per cent of the value of Papua New Guinea's exports.

The country has about 10,000 miles (16,000 kilometers) of roads, most of them unpaved. A national airline provides transportation among the islands. Papua New Guinea has 29 radio stations and 2 newspapers.

History. People lived in what is now Papua New Guinea as early as 50,000 years ago. In the early 1500's, Spanish and Portuguese explorers landed on the islands. The Dutch and English visited several of the islands during the next 300 years. In 1884, Germany seized northeastern New Guinea and the islands off its shore. Later that same year, Great Britain took over

---

FACTS IN BRIEF

Capital: Port Moresby.

Form of Government: Constitutional monarchy.

Total Land Area: 178,260 sq. mi. (461,691 km²). *Greatest Distances Between Islands*—north-south, 730 mi. (1,174 km); east-west, 1,040 mi. (1,674 km).

Elevation: *Highest*—Mount Wilhelm, 14,793 ft. (4,509 m) above sea level. *Lowest*—sea level.

Population: *Estimated 1977 Population*—2,667,000; distribution, 99 per cent rural, 1 per cent urban; density, 16 persons per sq. mi. (6 per km²). *1971 Census*—2,489,936; *Estimated 1982 Population*—2,803,000.

Chief Products: *Agriculture*—cocoa, coconuts, coffee, rubber, tea, timber. *Mining*—copper, gold, silver.

Flag: The rectangular flag is divided diagonally from upper left to lower right. A golden bird of paradise is in the upper section, which is red. Five stars representing the Southern Cross appear in the lower section, which is black. See FLAG (picture: Flags of Asia and the Pacific).

Money: *Basic Unit*—kina.

Mary S. McCarthy, Tom Stack & Associates

Port Moresby, Papua New Guinea's capital and largest city, lies on the hot, humid coast of southeastern New Guinea. Many houses in the city, such as those shown in this photograph, are built on stilts to keep them cooler and protect them from moisture.

Papua New Guinea

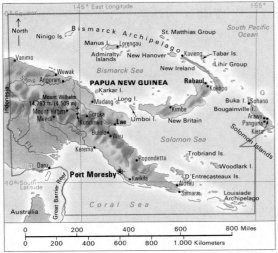

✳	National capital
•	City or settlement
+	Elevation above sea level
—	Road

WORLD BOOK map

southeastern New Guinea and the nearby islands. In 1905, Britain gave these possessions to Australia, which named the islands the Territory of Papua. In late 1914, just after the beginning of World War I, Australian troops seized the islands held by Germany. These islands came under official Australian rule in 1921.

Japanese forces invaded the islands in 1942, during World War II. They held much of New Guinea and several of the other islands until 1944, when Allied troops retook them. After the war ended in 1945, the northern islands came under the control of Australia. Australia united the northern and southern islands in 1949.

Papua New Guinea became independent on Sept. 16, 1975. The government made plans to modernize the country, but political unrest on some of the islands held back this program. For example, Bougainville declared itself independent in late 1975. It rejoined Papua New Guinea early in 1976.   DAVID A. M. LEA

See also NEW GUINEA; PORT MORESBY.

PORT MORESBY (pop. 66,244) is the capital and largest city of Papua New Guinea, a country in the South Pacific Ocean. It lies on a deep harbor on the southeastern coast of the island of New Guinea. For location, see PAPUA NEW GUINEA (map).

Port Moresby has been an important trade center since it became the capital of British New Guinea in 1885. During World War II (1939-1945), it served as an Allied military base and was bombed by Japanese forces.

The city became the capital of Papua New Guinea in 1975, when the nation gained independence. Since

SÃO TOMÉ AND PRÍNCIPE

then, it has attracted several industries, including paint manufacturing and boat building. The city was named for the British explorer Captain John Moresby, who sailed into its harbor in 1873.   DAVID A. M. LEA

See also NEW GUINEA (picture); PAPUA NEW GUINEA (picture).

SÃO TOMÉ AND PRÍNCIPE, *SOWN taw MEH, PREEN see puh,* is an African country that consists of two main islands and several tiny islands. The two main islands—São Tomé Island and Príncipe Island—give the country its name. The islands lie in the Gulf of Guinea, about 180 miles (290 kilometers) west of Libreville, Gabon, on the African mainland.

São Tomé and Príncipe has a total land area of 372 square miles (964 square kilometers). It is less than a third as large as Rhode Island, the smallest state of the United States. São Tomé Island is much larger than Príncipe Island. It accounts for almost 90 per cent of the country's area and has about 90 per cent of its people. Most of the 84,000 people of São Tomé and Príncipe live in rural areas and work on farms. The city of São Tomé, on São Tomé Island, is the nation's capital and largest city.

São Tomé and príncipe became an independent nation in 1975. It previously had been ruled by Portugal for most of the period since the late 1400's. During the 1500's, São Tomé Island became a center of the African slave trade.

Government. São Tomé and Príncipe is a republic. The people elect a national assembly, and the assembly chooses a president. The president appoints a prime minister and a Cabinet to help him run the government.

People. About 70 per cent of the people of São Tomé and Príncipe are *Creoles* (persons of mixed black African and European ancestry). Africans from mainland countries form the second largest population group. Europeans account for a small percentage of the population.

Many of the Creoles own small farms or businesses, or work as fishermen or laborers. Some of the Europeans own farms, and others have jobs that require technical or management skills. Most of the Africans from the mainland are laborers who work at low-paying jobs.

FACTS IN BRIEF ─────

Capital: São Tomé (city).

Form of Government: Republic.

Total Land Area: 372 sq. mi. (964 km²). *Coastline*—98 mi. (158 km).

Elevation: *Highest*—Pico de São Tomé, 6,640 ft. (2,024 m). *Lowest*—sea level.

Population: *Estimated 1977 Population*—84,000; distribution, 85 per cent rural, 15 per cent urban; density, 225 persons per sq. mi. (87 per km²). *1970 Census*—73,811. *Estimated 1982 Population*—93,000.

Chief Products: Cocoa, coconuts, coffee, copra, livestock.

Flag: The flag has green horizontal stripes at the top and bottom, a yellow horizontal stripe in the center, and a red triangle near the staff. Two black stars symbolizing the country's two main islands appear on the yellow stripe. Adopted in 1975. See FLAG (picture: Flags of Africa).

Money: *Basic Unit*—escudo.

SÃO TOMÉ AND PRÍNCIPE

Portuguese is the most widely used language in São Tomé and Príncipe. Many Creoles and Europeans speak a dialect based on Portuguese as it was spoken hundreds of years ago. Roman Catholicism is the main religion among the Creoles and Europeans. The mainland Africans use the language and practice the religion of the country of their origin. By law, children in São Tomé and Príncipe are required to complete elementary school, but many do not do so. Relatively few children go on to high school.

Land and Climate. The islands of São Tomé and Príncipe are part of a series of extinct volcanoes. The western part of São Tomé Island rises sharply from the sea, and forests grow near the shore. Inland, formations of basalt rock rise steeply toward the center of the island. The land gradually slopes downward from the center to the east coast. There, volcanic ash has formed deep deposits of fertile soil. Príncipe Island has a similar land pattern.

São Tomé and Príncipe islands lie a little north of the equator. The country has hot, humid weather from September through May; and hot, dry weather from June through August. The average annual temperature varies from 77° F. (25° C) in the lowlands to about 65° F. (18° C) in the highlands. The annual rainfall averages 16 inches (41 centimeters).

Economy of São Tomé and Príncipe is based on agriculture, but fishing is also important. The country has little manufacturing or mining.

About 90 per cent of the nation's cultivated land belongs to agricultural companies that operate large commercial farms. The other 10 per cent is divided among about 11,000 small farm owners. The chief products of São Tomé and Príncipe are cocoa, coconuts, coffee, copra, and livestock.

São Tomé and Príncipe has about 180 miles (290 kilometers) of roads. An airport lies near the city of São Tomé.

History. Portuguese explorers discovered the islands of São Tomé and Príncipe in 1470, during the great age of Portuguese discovery. The islands were uninhabited at the time.

About 1485, Portugal began to send convicts, exiles, and settlers to the islands. These people tried to raise sugar, which was in great demand in Europe. But, because of the great physical labor required, there were not enough of them to produce large sugar crops. The Portuguese then started to bring slaves from the African mainland to work on the sugar plantations. The islands soon ranked among the world's leading sugar producers.

In the mid-1500's, many slaves on São Tomé Island revolted against the plantation owners. A number of owners abandoned their plantations, and sugar production declined. By that time, many nations were involved in the African slave trade. São Tomé Island became a major center of it. Slaves from the mainland of Africa were sent to São Tomé and then shipped to the Americas and elsewhere.

The Dutch and the French ruled São Tomé Island during periods of the 1600's and 1700's, but the Portuguese regained control. In the 1800's, Portuguese planters began to grow coffee and cocoa in São Tomé and

São Tomé and Príncipe

⊛	National capital
•	Settlement
+	Elevation above sea level
——	Road
——	Railroad

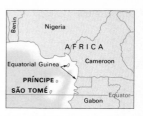

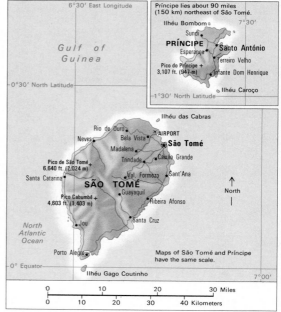

WORLD BOOK map

Príncipe. They used slave labor to help raise these crops.

Portugal and most other nations ended slavery in the 1800's. But the Portuguese continued to bring mainland Africans to São Tomé and Príncipe as contract laborers. These workers were treated harshly, and they revolted unsuccessfully from time to time during the 1800's and 1900's.

In the mid-1900's, many people in São Tomé and Príncipe began demanding an end to Portuguese rule. The islands gained independence on July 12, 1975. The new country's leaders announced plans to distribute the farmland among more people. They also called for investment by foreign industries.   JAMES W. FERNANDEZ

See also São Tomé.

SÃO TOMÉ, *SOWN taw MEH* (pop. 17,380), is the capital and largest city of São Tomé and Príncipe, an island country west of the African mainland. The city lies on the northeast coast of São Tomé Island. For location, see São Tomé and Príncipe (map).

The city of São Tomé serves as a trading and shipping center for farm products of São Tomé and Príncipe. The country's only airport is near the capital. The Portuguese discovered São Tomé Island in 1470 and founded the city about 1500.   JAMES W. FERNANDEZ

SEYCHELLES, *say SHEHL* or *say SHEHLZ,* is an African country that consists of about 90 islands in the Indian Ocean. The islands are scattered over 400,000 square miles (1,035,995 square kilometers), about 1,000 miles (1,600 kilometers) east of the African mainland.

Seychelles has a total land area of 145 square miles (376 square kilometers) and a population of 62,000. It is about one-ninth as large as Rhode Island, the smallest state of the United States. The largest island, Mahé, covers about 55 square miles (142 square kilometers). Approximately 85 per cent of the population lives on Mahé. Most of the rest of the people live on the next largest islands, Praslin and La Digue. Many of the smaller islands are uninhabited. Victoria, on Mahé, is the nation's capital, chief port, and only town. Seychelles was ruled by Great Britain from 1814 until 1976, when it became independent.

Government. Seychelles is a republic. The people elect a president and a 25-member Legislative Assembly. The president selects 10 members of the Assembly to serve in his Cabinet.

Seychelles has two major political parties, the Seychelles Democratic Party (SDP) and the Seychelles Peoples United Party (SPUP). The SDP favors maintaining close ties with Great Britain, but the SPUP wants a strong alliance with other African nations.

People. About 90 per cent of the people of Seychelles have mixed African and European ancestry. The others are Chinese, Europeans of British or French origin, and people from India.

About 35 per cent of the nation's workers are employed by the government. Another 25 per cent work in the construction industry, and about 15 per cent are farmers.

English is the country's official language, but most of the people speak Creole, a dialect of French. Almost all Seychellois children attend elementary school, but only about a third go on to high school. Approximately 60 per cent of the people can read and write. Most Seychellois are Roman Catholics.

Seychelles has a severe overpopulation problem. The government has tried to hold down the population growth by encouraging birth control and emigration.

Many Seychellois men and women live together without being married, and about half the children are born to unmarried couples. In many cases, the woman provides clothing for herself and the children, and the man buys his own clothes and food for the family.

Land and Climate. Seychelles consists of granite islands and coral islands. The granite islands have streams, mountains, and white, sandy beaches. The soil is fertile. But the land has many rocks, making farming difficult. The coral group is made up of *atolls* (ring-shaped coral islands) and low islands with reefs that rise a few feet above sea level. These islands cannot support much plant life, and many of them are uninhabited.

Cinnamon grows wild on much of Mahé, and coconut palms flourish on many of the islands. The *coco de mer,* a double coconut that weighs as much as 50 pounds (23 kilograms), grows only in Seychelles. The country has many unusual species of plants and birds, and giant tortoises also live there.

Seychelles has a hot, moist climate. Annual temperatures average from 75° F. (24° C) to 86° F. (30° C). The average annual rainfall ranges from 52 inches (132 centimeters) on some of the coral islands to 92 inches (234 centimeters) on Mahé.

Economy of Seychelles is based on tourism. The country's remote location and beautiful beaches attract many vacationers. The tourist trade increased the need for hotels and restaurants, which led to the development of a construction industry during the 1970's.

A shortage of suitable farmland limits agricultural production in Seychelles. Cinnamon, coconuts, and

Seychelles

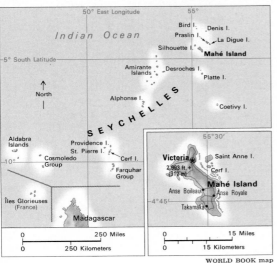

WORLD BOOK map

FACTS IN BRIEF

Capital: Victoria.

Official Language: English.

Form of Government: Republic.

Total Land Area: 145 sq. mi. (376 km²). *Coastline*—305 mi. (491 km).

Elevation: *Highest*—Morne Seychellois, 2,993 ft. (912 m), on Mahé Island. *Lowest*—sea level.

Population: *Estimated 1977 Population*—62,000; distribution, 69 per cent rural, 31 per cent urban; density, 427 persons per sq. mi. (165 per km²). *1971 Census*—52,650. *Estimated 1982 Population*—71,000.

Chief Products: Cinnamon, coconuts, copra.

Flag: The flag has a white diagonal cross with red triangular side panels and royal blue triangular panels at top and bottom. Adopted June 29, 1976. See FLAG (picture: Flags of Africa).

Money: *Basic Unit*—rupee.

Victoria, on the island of Mahé, is the capital and chief port of Seychelles. The harbor was rebuilt in 1975 to accommodate ocean-going vessels up to 700 feet (210 meters) long.

copra (dried coconut meat) are the country's chief products. A growing fishing industry contributes to the economy.

Seychelles has about 125 miles (201 kilometers) of roads. An airport operates on Mahé, and a ferry travels daily among the three largest islands. The country has one radio station and two daily newspapers.

History. Portuguese sailors discovered Seychelles in the early 1500's. The islands were uninhabited at the time, and for the next 250 years they served chiefly as a hiding place for pirates. In 1742, an expedition from Île de France (now Mauritius) explored Mahé. France claimed the islands in 1756.

About 1770, a group of white planters and African slaves came from Île de France and settled on Mahé. For many years, Seychelles served as a supply station for French ships sailing to India and the East Indies.

During the 1790's, war broke out between France and several European nations, including Great Britain. A treaty signed in 1814 gave Seychelles to Britain. Conditions in Seychelles declined under British rule. Britain did not establish schools there until 1944, and political parties were not organized until the 1960's. During the early 1970's, many Seychellois began to demand an end to British rule. Seychelles became independent in June 1976.   BURTON BENEDICT

See also VICTORIA.

VICTORIA (pop. 13,736) is the capital, chief port, and only town of Seychelles, an island country east of the African mainland. The town lies on the east coast of Mahé, the largest island of Seychelles. For location, see SEYCHELLES (map).

Almost all the government activity and commercial business of Seychelles takes place in Victoria. The town has a modern port that was built in 1975. Landmarks include a small replica of a clock tower in London; Government House, a two-story mansion built in 1911; a Roman Catholic cathedral; and a botanic garden.

The French founded the town in 1788 and named it Port Royal. The British took control of Seychelles in 1814. They renamed the town in 1841 in honor of Queen Victoria of Great Britain.   BURTON BENEDICT

SURINAM, *soo rih NAHM,* is a country on the northeast coast of South America. Mountainous rain forests cover about 80 per cent of Surinam, and most of the people live in the flat coastal area. Surinam has an area of 63,037 square miles (163,265 square kilometers) and a population of about 444,000. The country is slightly larger than Georgia but has less than a tenth as many people as that state. About a third of the people live in Paramaribo, the capital, largest city, and chief port. The Netherlands ruled the country during most of the period from 1667 until 1975, when Surinam gained independence. Before it became independent, Surinam was also known as *Dutch Guiana.*

Government. Surinam is a parliamentary democracy. The people elect a Parliament of 39 members. The political party with the majority of representatives in Parliament selects a prime minister and a 13-member Council of Ministers, the prime minister's cabinet.

Surinam's Extensive River System is the nation's chief means of transportation. The people use dugout canoes, such as the one shown above, on waterways in the thick rain forests that cover most of the country.

Capital: Paramaribo.

Official Language: Dutch.

Form of Government: Parliamentary Democracy.

Area: 63,037 sq. mi. (163,265 km²). *Coastline*—226 mi. (364 km). *Greatest Distances*—north-south, 285 mi. (459 km); east-west, 280 mi. (451 km).

Elevation: *Highest*—Mt. Julianatop, 4,218 ft. (1,286 m). *Lowest*—sea level.

Population: *Estimated 1977 Population*—444,000; distribution, 60 per cent rural, 40 per cent urban; density, 8 persons per sq. mi. (3 per km²). *1971 Census*—384,903. *Estimated 1982 Population*—505,000.

Chief Products: Aluminum, bananas, bauxite, rice.

National Anthem: "Opo Kondre Men Oen Opo" ("Get Up People, Get Up").

Flag: The flag has five horizontal stripes of green, red, white, red, and green. A yellow five-pointed star lies in the center. See FLAG (picture: Flags of South America).

Money: *Basic Unit*—guilder.

Surinam's political parties are based on ethnic background. The country has two major parties. The National Combination Party consists primarily of *Creoles*, who are people with mixed European and black African ancestry. The United Reform Party represents the *Hindustanis*, who are the descendants of people from India.

People of many ethnic backgrounds live in Surinam. Hindustanis make up more than a third of the population, and another third are Creoles. The rest of the people are, in order of number, Indonesians, black Africans, American Indians, Chinese, and Europeans.

Each ethnic group in Surinam has preserved its own culture, religion, and language. Dutch is the nation's official language, but the various groups use a Creole dialect as a common language.

Some Hindustanis in Surinam own and operate small farms, and others are skilled industrial workers. Most of the Creoles work in government or for business companies. Many Indonesians are tenant farmers, who rent their land.

Black Africans in Surinam are called *Bush Negroes*. They are the descendants of a group of blacks who escaped from slavery in the 1600's. Most Bush Negroes live in the rain forests and follow African tribal customs.

About 70 per cent of Surinam's people can read and write. The law requires children from 7 to 12 years old to attend elementary school, and some go on to high school. Surinam has one university, in Paramaribo.

Land and Climate. Surinam has a narrow coastal area of flat swampland that has been drained for farming. This area extends inland 10 to 50 miles (16 to 80 kilometers) to a sandy plain that rises about 150 feet (46 meters) high. Mountainous rain forests with about 2,000 kinds of trees lie farther inland, and a high grassy *savanna* (treeless plain) runs along the southwest border. Rivers flow north through Surinam to the Atlantic.

The climate of Surinam is warm and moist, with an average annual temperature of 81° F. (27° C). The annual rainfall averages 76 inches (193 centimeters) in western Surinam and 95 inches (241 centimeters) in Paramaribo.

Economy of Surinam is based on mining and metal processing. The country is a leading producer of baux-

ite, an ore from which aluminum is made. Raw bauxite and aluminum account for about 90 per cent of Surinam's exports.

Agriculture also has an important part in Surinam's economy. Rice, a major export crop, is grown on about three-fourths of the farmland. Other crops include bananas, coconuts, and sugar. The forests yield a large supply of hardwoods from which Surinam's lumber industry produces logs and plywood.

The country's chief means of transportation is an extensive system of rivers. Surinam has only about 800 miles (1,300 kilometers) of main roads, and railroad service is limited. An international airport operates near Paramaribo. Surinam has three major newspapers, a television station, and five radio stations.

History. Christopher Columbus sighted what is now Surinam in 1498, and Spaniards and Portuguese explored the area during the 1500's. In 1651, British explorers built the first permanent settlement there. They established cotton and sugar cane plantations and brought slaves from Africa to work the land. The settlement prospered rapidly. In 1667, the Dutch took control of it and in exchange gave the British what became the state of New York.

Surinam

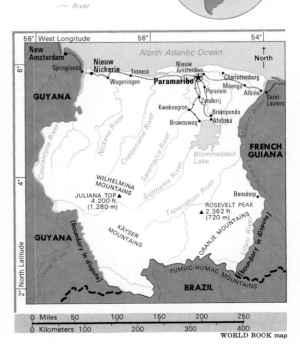

★ Capital
● Other City or Town
—— Road
+—+ Rail Line
▲ MOUNTAIN
〜 River

WORLD BOOK map

569

Paramaribo is Surinam's capital, largest city, and chief port. Low wooden buildings, *above,* line the streets of the city, a center of business, cultural, and government activity. About a third of Surinam's people live in Paramaribo.

Leon V. Kofod

Surinam suffered economic setbacks during the 1700's as a result of slave uprisings and Dutch neglect. In the early 1800's, ownership of the colony shifted several times between Great Britain and The Netherlands. In 1815, Britain gave up its claim to Surinam, and the Dutch regained control. The Dutch abolished slavery in 1863 and brought laborers from India and Indonesia to work on the plantations. However, plantation farming declined during the early 1900's, and many people moved to urban areas.

Surinam became a self-governing Dutch territory in 1954. During the 1970's, the Creoles led a movement for full independence, which was supported by the Dutch government. But the Hindustanis opposed independence, and racial conflicts occurred in Surinam for the first time. Shortly before Surinam gained independence in November 1975, thousands of its people emigrated to The Netherlands. This emigration caused a shortage of skilled labor and greatly restricted economic development in Surinam. GARY BRANA-SHUTE

PARAMARIBO, *PAR uh MAR uh BOH* (pop. 150,-000), is the capital, largest city, and chief port of Surinam, a country in northeastern South America. About half of the people in Surinam live in and around Paramaribo. The city lies on the Surinam River, 12 miles (20 kilometers) inland from the Atlantic Ocean. For location, see SURINAM (map). Industrial firms in Paramaribo manufacture aluminum, plywood, and various other products. The city is the home of the University of Surinam and the Surinam Museum.

Paramaribo grew up around a British fort built in the mid-1600's. After the abolition of slavery in 1863, many former slaves moved to Paramaribo. The city's population grew rapidly, and industrial development began in the early 1900's. Most of the buildings in Paramaribo are made of wood, and over the years, fires have caused much damage to the city. GARY BRANA-SHUTE

CHINESE LITERATURE is one of the oldest and greatest of the world's literatures. Chinese writers have produced important works for almost 3,000 years.

During most of China's history, the Chinese did not consider literature a separate art form. They expected all cultured people to write in a graceful, elegant style, regardless of the topic. Many masterpieces of Chinese literature deal with subjects that some Western writers regard as nonliterary. These topics include history, philosophy, politics, religion, and science.

Until the 1900's, government service was the occupation of greatest prestige in China. For more than 1,000 years, people gained a government position primarily by passing an examination that tested their ability to compose both poetry and prose. Almost all of China's greatest writers before the 1900's were government officials. Most of them received their appointments because of their skill with words.

Many works of Chinese literature teach a moral lesson or express a political philosophy. These themes appear especially in the writings of Confucians. Confucianism is a philosophy founded by Confucius, who lived from about 551 to 479 B.C. It was the dominant Chinese philosophy until the 1900's. Many other writers were Buddhists or Taoists, rather than Confucians. Buddhism was a major Chinese religion, and Taoism was both an important religion and a philosophy. The Buddhists and Taoists were less interested than the Confucians in morality and politics. But they used literature to express their religious and philosophical ideas.

During the 1900's, Chinese literature has made a sharp break with the past. This break resulted partly from the influence of Western culture on Chinese writers. But the rise of the Communist Party to power in China made an even greater impact. Ever since the Chinese Communists took control in 1949, they have required Chinese writers to stress Communist ideals.

Early Chinese Literature

Beginnings. The first significant work of Chinese literature was a collection of 300 poems called the *Classic of Songs.* The earliest of these poems probably date back to the 1100's B.C. Some of the poems may have originated as songs about farming, love, and the hardships of war. Others were used in such ceremonies as weddings and religious sacrifices.

The earliest prose in Chinese literature was a collection of historical writings called the *Classic of Documents.* It consists largely of speeches supposedly made by the earliest Chinese rulers. However, the speeches were probably fiction written during the Chou dynasty (about 1027 to 256 B.C.).

The *Classic of Songs* and the *Classic of Documents,* along with several other books, formed the basis of Confucianism. The Confucians considered these books to be models of literary excellence. They also honored them as works of moral wisdom because the books emphasized Confucian ideals of duty, moderation, proper conduct, and public service.

Taoism probably began during the 300's B.C., partly as a reaction against Confucianism. Unlike the Confucians, the Taoists believed people should avoid social

Leisure Enough to Spare (1360), an ink painting on paper by Yao T'ing-mei; the Cleveland Museum of Art, John L. Severance Fund

Traditional Chinese Poetry was closely associated with painting. A poet painted this scroll and wrote the poem at the left. The poem describes the beauties of nature and the pleasures of solitude.

obligations and live simply and close to nature. Taoist ideas strongly influenced poets who wrote about the beauties of nature. Taoism produced two literary masterpieces. The first, *The Classic of the Way and the Virtue*, was probably written by Lao Tzu, the founder of Taoism. Most of the other work, the *Chuang Tzu*, is credited to Chuang Tzu, a philosopher.

An important collection of poems called the *Elegies of Ch'u* appeared during the 300's B.C. Most of them were probably written by a poet named Ch'ü Yüan. Many of the poems describe flights to imaginary regions inhabited by mythical creatures, gods, and spirits.

Poetry. Perhaps the four greatest Chinese poets lived during the T'ang dynasty (A.D. 618-907). They were, in the order of their birth, Wang Wei, Li Po, Tu Fu, and Po Chü-i.

Wang Wei wrote four-line poems that delicately describes scenes from nature. His works, with their emphasis on quiet and contemplation, show the influence of Buddhism.

Li Po wrote imaginative poems about his dreams and fantasies and his love of wine. Unlike most other poets of his time, he wrote in the style of old Chinese ballads.

Tu Fu is considered China's greatest poet by many critics. He surpassed all other T'ang poets in range of style and subject matter. In some of his early poems, Tu Fu expressed disappointment at failing an examination for government service. A bloody rebellion from 755 to 757 inspired him to write poems condemning the absurdity he saw in war. In his late poems, Tu Fu emphasized clever use of language, developing a style that influenced Chinese poets for centuries.

Po Chü-i wrote satiric poems in ballad style. The poems protested against various government policies and programs of his day.

Drama and Fiction developed as important forms of Chinese literature during the 1200's. Chinese plays resemble European opera, combining singing and dancing with dialogue. The two most famous Chinese plays are *The Western Chamber*, written by Wang Shih-fu, and *Injustice to Tou O*, written by Kuan Han-Ch'ing. Both plays were written in the 1200's. T'ang Hsien-tsu ranks as the greatest Chinese playwright. His most notable play was *Peony Pavilion* (about 1600).

Lo Kuan-chung, who died about 1400, rewrote traditional historical tales into long, complicated stories that resemble novels by Western authors. Lo wrote *Romance of the Three Kingdoms*, which describes the struggle for power among three rival states during the A.D. 100's and 200's. Lo and a writer named Shih Nai-en wrote *Water Margin*, also known as *All Men Are Brothers*. It tells about an outlaw gang that may actually have existed in the A.D. 1100's.

Wu Ch'eng-en, an author of the 1500's, wrote a comic masterpiece called *Monkey*. He based this novel on a pilgrimage of a Buddhist monk to India in the A.D. 600's. An unknown writer of the 1500's wrote *Golden Lotus*, a famous novel about moral corruption. *Dream of the Red Chamber*, perhaps the greatest Chinese novel, was written by Ts'ao Hsüeh-ch'in in the 1700's. It describes the decline of a prominent aristocratic family.

Modern Chinese Literature

Until the 1800's, China was almost isolated from the West. Many European missionaries and traders traveled to China during the 1800's, and the Chinese were gradually exposed to Western culture. By the early 1900's, the works of most Chinese authors showed some influence of Western literature. The most important Chinese author of the early 1900's was Lu Hsün, who wrote satiric short stories of social criticism.

The Chinese Communists, led by Mao Tse-tung, came to power in 1949 after a long civil war. The Communists demanded that all literature serve the new state. They ordered writers to create works that could be easily understood by the peasants, soldiers, and workers. The heroes of literary works had to represent the working class. Some older writers attacked the new literature, which they considered dull. The government prohibited these writers from publishing their works.

Today, the most widely read writings in China are the poems and sayings of Mao Tse-tung. But writers who live outside China produce the most significant Chinese literature. Their works are published in Taiwan and Hong Kong. Many of these writers live in the United States, and their works reflect knowledge of both traditional Chinese literature and Western literature. The chief authors of this group include Yang Mu, Pai Hsien-yung, and Yü Kuang-chung.   DAVID R. KNECHTGES

Swimming is an exciting sport and a popular form of recreation. The swimmers at the left dive into a pool at the start of a championship race. The women in the center perform a graceful movement in a sport called *synchronized swimming*. At the right, an instructor teaches children how to swim.

SWIMMING

SWIMMING is the act of moving through water by using the arms and legs. Swimming is a popular form of recreation, an important international sport, and a healthful exercise.

People of all ages—from the very young to the elderly—swim for fun. Throughout the world, millions of people enjoy swimming in lakes, oceans, and rivers. Others swim in indoor or outdoor pools. Many schools, recreation centers, motels, apartment buildings, and private clubs have an indoor or outdoor pool. Thousands of communities provide pools for local residents. Many families even have a pool in their backyard.

During the 1900's, swimming has become a major competitive sport. Thousands of swimmers compete in meets held by schools, colleges, and swimming clubs. The best international swimmers take part in annual meets in many parts of the world. Swimming races have always been a highlight of the Summer Olympic Games, which take place every four years. Many long-distance swimmers attempt such feats as swimming across the English Channel or from the southern California coast to Santa Catalina Island.

Good swimmers can also enjoy a variety of other

Don Van Rossen, the contributor of this article, is Aquatics Director and Head Swim Coach at the University of Oregon.

water sports. Such sports include springboard and platform diving, surfing, water skiing, water polo, and scuba diving and other kinds of skin diving. In addition, the ability to swim well makes such sports as fishing and boating safer and more enjoyable. Above all, the ability to swim may save a person's life in an emergency in the water.

Swimming is one of the best exercises for keeping physically fit. Swimming improves heart action, aids blood circulation, and helps develop firm muscles.

Water Safety

Swimming, boating, fishing, and other water sports are among the most popular forms of recreation. Yet many people lack knowledge of water safety rules or take dangerous chances. Every year, almost 9,000 persons drown in the United States and about 1,000 persons in Canada. Most of these drownings would not occur if everyone knew how to swim and observed basic water safety rules. The following discussion deals with basic rules and techniques that could save your life or help you save another person's life.

First of all, know how to swim. Many schools provide swimming lessons as part of their physical education program. Adults can learn to swim at public and private pools and at recreation centers.

Never swim alone. Always swim with a companion and know where that person is at all times. Swim only in areas protected by lifeguards. If such an area is not available, be sure that the bottom has no snags, trash,

WORLD BOOK photo

ica, the Boy Scouts, the Girl Scouts, the YMCA, the YWCA, and various other organizations offer water safety programs. Many of these organizations also teach lifesaving skills to experienced swimmers.

Swimming Kicks and Strokes

Swimmers move their legs, feet, arms, and hands in certain ways to propel themselves through the water easily and quickly. The movements of the legs and feet are called *kicks*. These movements combined with movements of the arms and hands are called *strokes*.

The Basic Kicks. Swimmers use four types of kicks: (1) the flutter kick, (2) the breaststroke kick, (3) the dolphin kick, and (4) the scissors kick. Each of these kicks is used in doing one or more of the strokes described later in this section.

The Flutter Kick is the most popular kick and the easiest for most swimmers to learn. To do the flutter kick, you rapidly whip your legs up and down from the hips, alternating one leg with the other. The legs should be fairly straight, close together, and relaxed. The power to do the flutter kick should come from the thigh muscles.

The Breaststroke Kick begins with your legs fully extended and the toes pointed to the rear. You then bring your heels toward the hips just under the surface of the water. As your feet near the hips, bend your knees and extend them outward. Turn your ankles so the toes also point outward. Then, without pause, push your feet backward and squeeze your legs together until the toes again point to the rear.

The Dolphin Kick resembles the flutter kick. But in the dolphin kick, you move both of your legs up and down at the same time.

The Scissors Kick begins with your body turned to either side. Your legs are together and the toes pointed back. Draw your knees up and then spread your legs wide apart like the open blades of a scissors, moving your top leg forward from the hip. Then snap both legs together to their original position in a scissorslike action.

The Basic Strokes are (1) the front crawl, (2) the backstroke, (3) the breaststroke, (4) the butterfly, and (5) the sidestroke.

The Front Crawl is the fastest and most popular stroke. You move your arms in a steady, circular motion in combination with the flutter kick. One hand reaches forward above the water while the other pulls beneath the water. You breathe by turning your head to one side just as the hand on that side passes your leg. You inhale through the mouth. You exhale through the mouth or nose, but you keep your face in the water while exhaling.

The Backstroke, or *back crawl*, is performed as you lie on your back. It is a restful stroke because your face is always out of the water and breathing is easy. As in the front crawl, each arm alternately moves in a steady, circular motion in and out of the water while your legs do the flutter kick.

The Breaststroke is another restful stroke. It is done in combination with the breaststroke kick. You begin with your face in the water, arms and legs fully extended, and the palms facing outward. You then sweep out your arms as your hands push downward

or weeds. If you swim in the ocean or a river, you should know about tides and currents.

Water for diving should be deep and clear. Never dive into unfamiliar waters, and always look carefully for other swimmers before you dive. When swimming, stay away from diving boards and diving platforms.

Whether you are a beginning or experienced swimmer, a knowledge of *survival bobbing* can help you survive an accident or other difficulty in the water. Survival bobbing enables you to float a long time on your stomach while using very little energy. You fill your lungs with air and relax your body. Your arms and legs hang down limply, and your chin flops down to the chest. The air in your lungs holds your back above the water's surface. When you need a breath, you quickly exhale through the nose, lift your face out of the water, and inhale through your mouth. You then return to the restful, floating position. You can raise your mouth higher out of the water for a breath by pressing your hands down or squeezing your legs gently together.

Only a trained lifeguard should attempt a swimming rescue. But even if you are a nonswimmer, you can help a swimmer in trouble. If the person is close by, you can extend a board, pole, shirt, towel, or similar object and pull the swimmer to safety. But be sure to lie down or keep your body low to avoid being pulled into the water. If the swimmer is too far away to reach an object, you can throw a life preserver, a board, or any other object that will float and support the swimmer.

The American Red Cross, the Boys' Clubs of Amer-

SWIMMING

Basic Swimming Strokes

The Front Crawl

The Backstroke

The Breaststroke

The Butterfly

and outward. The hands continue to circle and come together under the chin. As the hands begin to push down, you lift your head for a breath. Finally, you again extend your arms and legs and glide forward. You then repeat the sequence. You make a breast-stroke kick at the end of the stroke as your arms extend for the glide.

The Butterfly is a difficult stroke to learn, but it is smooth and graceful if performed correctly. In this stroke, you swing both arms forward above the water and then pull them down and back to your legs. As your arms start to move toward your legs, you lift your head forward and take a breath. Then you dip your head into the water and exhale as your arms move forward again. You make two dolphin kicks during each complete stroke, one as your hands enter the water and the other as your arms pass under your body.

The Sidestroke is done on your side, whichever side is more comfortable. Your head rests on your lower arm, which is extended ahead with the palm turned downward. The top arm is at your side. The palm of the lower hand presses down in the water until it is beneath the shoulder. At the same time, the top hand slides up to meet the lower hand. The legs do a scissors kick while the lower arm returns to an extended position and the palm of the upper hand pushes toward the feet. You then glide forward before repeating the sequence.

Other Strokes. Swimmers use a number of other strokes besides the basic five. The most important include the *dog paddle* and the *elementary backstroke*. To perform the dog paddle, cup your hands and rotate them in a circular motion underwater, with one hand forward when the other one is back. You do a flutter kick with the dog paddle. Your head remains out of the water throughout the stroke. The elementary backstroke, like the regular

backstroke, is performed on your back. You bring your hands up along the sides of your body to your shoulders. Next you turn out the hands and stretch the fingers outward. Then you push your hands down and glide. Swimmers do the breaststroke kick or scissors kick with this stroke.

Swimming as a Sport

The Federation Internationale de Natation Amateur (FINA) governs international swimming and other water sports at the amateur level. The FINA consists of national associations from about 100 countries. These associations include the Amateur Athletic Union (AAU) of the United States, the Canadian Federation of Amateur Aquatics, the Amateur Swimming Union of Australia, and the Amateur Swimming Association of Great Britain.

The Pool. Swim meets are held in both *long-course* pools, which measure 50 meters (164 feet) long, and *short-course* pools, which measure 22.885 meters (75 feet) long. Long-course pools are divided into 6, 8, or 10 lanes, each of which is 2.4 meters (8 feet) wide. Short-course pools have 6 or 8 lanes. Each lane measures 2.1 or 2.4 meters (7 or 8 feet) wide. In U.S. championship meets, 8 lanes must be used in both long- and short-course pools. The FINA recognizes world records set only in long-course pools.

Water in a regulation pool must be at least 4 feet (1.2 meters) deep and have a temperature of about 78° F. (26° C). Floats called *lane dividers* run the length of the pool. They mark lane boundaries and help keep the surface of the water calm.

Kinds of Races. Swimmers participate in five kinds of races—freestyle, breaststroke, backstroke, butterfly, and individual medley. In a freestyle race, a swimmer

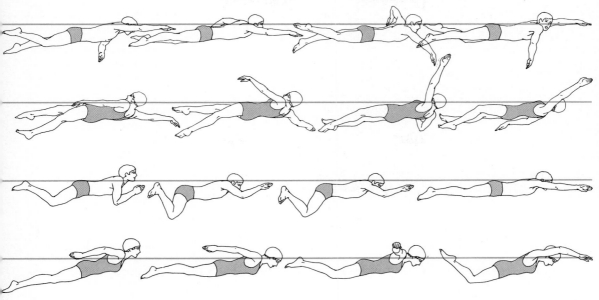

WORLD BOOK illustrations by Robert Keys

A Regulation Swimming Pool   Swimming pools are divided into lanes for races, one lane for each swimmer in a race. Wall targets, lane lines, and a midpool line guide each swimmer. Near each end of the pool, a flag line is hung over the water to warn swimmers in backstroke races that they are approaching the end of the lane.

WORLD BOOK diagram by Arthur Grebetz

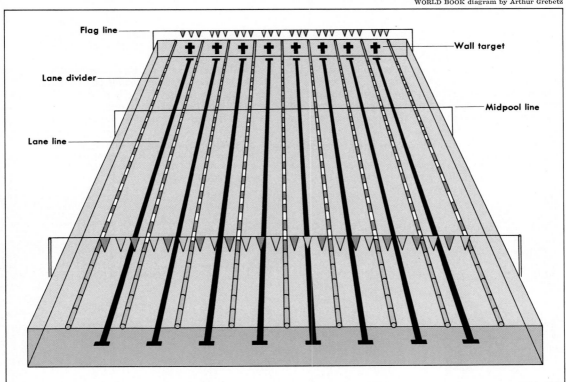

Flag line —
Wall target
Lane divider —
Midpool line
Lane line —

Team stunt performed by the Santa Clara (Calif.) Aquamaids;
Lee Pillsbury, *Swimming World*

Synchronized Swimming is a women's water sport in which swimmers *synchronize* (match) graceful, acrobatic movements to music. Competition is divided into solo, duet, and team events.

may choose any stroke. But swimmers always use the front crawl because it is the fastest stroke. In the individual medley, athletes swim an equal distance of each of the four strokes.

In national and international meets, individual freestyle races are held at distances of 100, 200, 400, 800, and 1,500 meters. Breaststroke, backstroke, and butterfly events are 100 and 200 meters long. The individual medley covers 200 and 400 meters.

Team *relays* are among the most exciting swimming races. A team consists of four swimmers, each of whom swims an equal distance. Men's and women's teams participate in a 400-meter freestyle relay, a 400-meter medley relay, and an 800-meter freestyle relay. In the medley relay, each member of the team swims a different stroke for 100 meters.

Swim Meets are held at various levels of competition, from local to international. So many swimmers participate in competitive swimming that qualifying times are

established for large meets. Swimmers must at least equal the qualifying times for the races they hope to enter to be eligible for those events.

Large meets have several officials. The chief official is the referee. The referee supervises the other officials and makes sure that the swimmers follow regulations.

Each swimmer in a race is assigned a lane. The swimmers with the fastest qualifying times get the center lanes, and the slowest swimmers receive the outside lanes. The race begins at the sound of the starter's gun or horn. During the race, lane judges watch each swimmer's strokes and the turns at the end of the pool. An illegal stroke or turn disqualifies a swimmer.

In many meets, an electronic timing and judging system determines the order of finish and each swimmer's time to $\frac{1}{1,000}$ of a second. The system begins automatically at the starter's signal. It records the time for each swimmer as the swimmer's hand touches a plate attached to the end of the pool.

Starts and Turns. A swimmer's performance in a race partly depends on the skill used in starting the race and in turning at the end of each lap. At the start of a freestyle, breaststroke, or butterfly race, a swimmer gains time by diving as far as possible through the air before hitting the water. In these races, swimmers dive off a raised starting platform. In backstroke events, they begin in the water with their back to the lane. They hold a starting block attached to the end of the pool. At the starting signal, with their back slightly arched, the swimmers use both feet to push off from the pool's end as forcibly as possible.

Fast turns also save a swimmer time. Freestyle and backstroke swimmers use the *flip*, or *somersault*, turn. In this turn, they make an underwater somersault to reverse their direction after touching the end of the pool. Breaststroke and butterfly swimmers use an *open* turn, in which they keep their head above the water while reversing their direction.

Training. Most young people interested in competitive swimming begin by racing against swimmers in their own age group. In the United States, the AAU has established an age-group program for young swimmers. This program divides swimmers into four groups:

Starting a Swimming Race   A skillful start plays an important part in a swimmer's performance in a race. The swimmer first wraps his toes around the edge of the starting block and looks straight ahead, *left.* He swings his arms back, elbows straight, and begins to dive, *center.* Over the water, *right,* he arches his back slightly, lowers his head, and raises his arms. He should hit the water at a slight angle.

Chicago Park District (WORLD BOOK photos)

(1) age 10 and under; (2) ages 11 and 12; (3) ages 13 and 14; and (4) ages 15 to 18.

Most swimmers in age-group programs work out once or twice a day for five or six days each week. And they follow this schedule for 11 months every year. Their training includes land and water exercises to increase endurance, speed, and strength. They also practice kicks and strokes. To keep up their energy and to help avoid illnesses, all swimmers are advised to eat a well-balanced diet and to get plenty of rest.

Synchronized Swimming is a water sport for women that combines grace, rhythm, and acrobatic skills. In

this sport, swimmers perform certain movements to music that they have selected. They *synchronize* (match) these movements with the rhythm and mood of the music.

Synchronized swimming was once called *water ballet.* It began as a form of exhibition swimming at water shows and remains a popular feature of such shows. In 1952, the first international rules were established for synchronized swimming as a sport.

Competition is divided into solo, duet, and team

WORLD SWIMMING RECORDS*†

Event	Time	Holder	Country	Made At	Date
Men's Events					
100-meter freestyle	50.59 s.	James Montgomery	United States	Kansas City, Kans.	Aug. 23, 1975
200-meter freestyle	1 m. 50.32 s.	Bruce Furniss	United States	Kansas City, Kans.	Aug. 21, 1975
400-meter freestyle	3 m. 53.31 s.	Tim Shaw	United States	Kansas City, Kans.	Aug. 20, 1975
800-meter freestyle	8 m. 09.60 s.	Tim Shaw	United States	Mission Viejo, Calif.	July 12, 1975
1,500-meter freestyle	15 m. 20.91 s.	Tim Shaw	United States	Long Beach, Calif.	June 21, 1975
100-meter breaststroke	1 m. 03.88 s.	John Hencken	United States	Concord, Calif.	Aug. 31, 1974
200-meter breaststroke	2 m. 18.21 s.	John Hencken	United States	Concord, Calif.	Sept. 1, 1974
100-meter butterfly	54.27 s.	Mark Spitz	United States	Munich	Aug. 31, 1972
200-meter butterfly	2 m. 00.70 s.	Mark Spitz	United States	Munich	Aug. 28, 1972
100-meter backstroke	56.30 s.	Roland Matthes	East Germany	Munich	Sept. 4, 1972
200-meter backstroke	2 m. 01.87 s.	Roland Matthes	East Germany	Belgrade	Sept. 6, 1973
200-meter individual medley	2 m. 06.08 s.	Bruce Furniss	United States	Kansas City, Kans.	Aug. 23, 1975
400-meter individual medley	4 m. 28.89 s.	Andras Hargitay	Hungary	Vienna	Aug. 20, 1974
400-meter freestyle relay	3 m. 24.85 s.	National Team (B. Furniss, J. Montgomery, A. Coan, J. Murphy)	United States	Cali, Colombia	July 23, 1975
800-meter freestyle relay	7 m. 30.54 s.	Long Beach Swim Club (R. Favero, T. Shaw, S. Furniss, B. Furniss)	United States	Kansas City, Kans.	Aug. 22, 1975
400-meter medley race	3 m. 48.16 s.	National Team (M. Stamm, T. Bruce, M. Spitz, J. Heidenreich)	United States	Munich	Sept. 4, 1972
Women's Events					
100-meter freestyle	56.22 s.	Kornelia Ender	East Germany	Cali, Colombia	July 26, 1975
200-meter freestyle	2 m. 02.27 s.	Kornelia Ender	East Germany	Dresden, East Germany	March 15, 1975
400-meter freestyle	4 m. 14.76 s.	Shirley Babashoff	United States	Long Beach, Calif.	June 20, 1975
800-meter freestyle	8 m. 43.48 s.	Jennifer Turrall	Australia	London	March 31, 1975
1,500-meter freestyle	16 m. 33.94 s.	Jennifer Turrall	Australia	Concord, Calif.	Aug. 25, 1974
100-meter breaststroke	1 m. 12.28 s.	Renate Vogel	East Germany	Concord, Calif.	Sept. 1, 1974
200-meter breaststroke	2 m. 34.99 s.	Karla Linke	East Germany	Vienna	Aug. 19, 1974
100-meter butterfly	1 m. 01.24 s.	Kornelia Ender	East Germany	Cali, Colombia	July 24, 1975
200-meter butterfly	2 m. 13.76 s.	Rosemarie Kother	East Germany	Belgrade	Sept. 8, 1973
100-meter backstroke	1 m. 02.98 s.	Ulrike Richter	East Germany	Vienna	Aug. 18, 1974
200-meter backstroke	2 m. 15.46 s.	Birgit Treiber	East Germany	Cali, Colombia	July 25, 1975
200-meter individual medley	2 m. 18.83 s.	Ulrike Tauber	East Germany	Wittenberg, East Germany	June 10, 1975
400-meter individual medley	4 m. 52.20 s.	Ulrike Tauber	East Germany	Wittenberg, East Germany	June 7, 1975
400-meter freestyle relay	3 m. 49.37 s.	National Team (K. Ender, B. Krause, C. Hempel, U. Bruckner)	East Germany	Cali, Colombia	July 26, 1975
400-meter medley relay	4 m. 13.78 s.	National Team (U. Richter, R. Vogel, R. Kother, K. Ender)	East Germany	Vienna	Aug. 24, 1974

*Includes only records set in 50-meter pools.
†Officially recognized as of Jan. 1, 1976.

Source: *Amateur Athlete Yearbook* © 1976, Amateur Athletic Union of the United States.

SWIMMING

events. A team may have four to eight members. Each solo, duet, or team event has two sections—*stunts* and *routines*. Stunts are acrobatic movements. Routines combine stunts with swimming strokes to create various patterns. Routines in international competition have a time limit of five minutes.

More than 30 stunts may be used in international competition. They are divided into two series. The second series is more difficult than the first. Swimmers must perform three stunts from the first series and two from the second.

The *dolphin* is an example of a commonly performed stunt. It is also used in many routines. A swimmer begins the dolphin by floating on her back. She then pulls herself under the water head first, makes a complete circle, and returns to the floating position. In the *dolphin bent knee* stunt, a swimmer bends one knee while performing the circular movement underwater.

Judges award points for each stunt and routine. After each stunt, the judges grade a swimmer according to the difficulty of the stunt and how well she performed it. The judges give each routine two scores, one for *execution* and one for *style*. The execution score reflects the skill a swimmer showed in performing the stunts and strokes. The style score includes how well a swimmer synchronized her movements with the music.

In water shows and swimming exhibitions, swimmers often base their synchronized-swimming routines on a story or a theme. For example, they might act out such a tale as *Alice in Wonderland* with the aid of a narrator. Or the swimmers might choose such a theme as the seasons of the year and expressively interpret each season's mood.   DON VAN ROSSEN

Related Articles in WORLD BOOK include:

Outline

I. Water Safety

II. Swimming Kicks and Strokes
  A. The Basic Kicks
  B. The Basic Strokes

III. Swimming as a Sport
  A. The Pool
  B. Kinds of Races
  C. Swim Meets
  D. Starts and Turns
  E. Training
  F. Synchronized Swimming

Questions

How can a nonswimmer help a swimmer in trouble?
What are the five basic swimming strokes?
How do swimmers start in a backstroke race?
What part does music play in synchronized swimming?
What are some basic water safety rules?
Why is swimming a good exercise for keeping physically fit?
How often do most swimmers in age-group programs work out?
What is a freestyle race?
What is survival bobbing?
How does a swimmer do the flutter kick?

SWIMMING POOL. Millions of people in the United States and other countries enjoy the fun and recreation provided by swimming pools. Some pools are used for swimming competition. This article discusses backyard pools. For information on pools used in swim meets, see the WORLD BOOK article on SWIMMING.

Manufacturers produce a wide variety of backyard pools. Both the expense and the type of swimming activities planned should be considered when selecting a pool. There are two main kinds of backyard swimming pools, *in-ground pools* and *above-ground pools*.

In-ground pools are pools in which the water is below the surface of the ground. Most of these pools cost at least as much as a new automobile, but they last almost indefinitely. Many in-ground pools are made of concrete or fiberglass. Others consist of a vinyl liner in a shell of steel, aluminum, or special wood. Many in-ground pools have diving boards.

Above-ground pools are pools in which the water is in a metal or plastic frame above the surface of the ground. Such pools are less expensive than in-ground pools. However, they do not last as long. Some above-ground pools are small and shallow, and so they provide only limited opportunities for swimming.

Any backyard pool should have basic equipment. Ladders are necessary for getting into and out of the pool. A filtration system for removing impurities from the water is essential. The pool should also have an automatic *skimmer*, a device that keeps the water surface free of trash.

Critically reviewed by the NATIONAL SWIMMING POOL INSTITUTE

Coleco

A Backyard Swimming Pool provides fun and exercise for the entire family. The motor and cylindrical tank at the lower left are part of a filtration system. This system keeps the water clean by continuously circulating it through a filter.

A Diver soars into the air after leaping from a 3-meter springboard. This board is one of the two kinds used in diving meets. The other is the 1-meter springboard, shown at the bottom of the picture. Divers also compete from a 10-meter platform, shown at the top. The 7.5-meter platform, *center*, is used for practice.

Albert Schoenfield, *Swimming World*

DIVING is a popular water sport. A diver leaps from a springboard or a platform and performs daring acrobatics in the air before plunging into the water. Skillful divers combine strength and grace with great courage while spinning and twisting toward the water as fast as 30 miles (48 kilometers) per hour. Some athletes dive from platforms as high as a three-story building.

Unlike swimming, diving emphasizes technique rather than endurance or speed. Champion divers require many years to perfect their skills. Therefore, most of them are older than champion swimmers. Many teen-age swimmers win national or international championships, but most divers do not reach their peak until their early 20's.

Some divers perform comic or trick dives at water shows, and others plunge into the ocean from towering cliffs. Such divers have great skill and daring, but they perform for entertainment, not in athletic competition. This article discusses diving as a sport. For information on other forms of diving, see the WORLD BOOK articles on DIVING, UNDERWATER; SKIN DIVING; and SPEARFISHING.

Types of Diving

National and international diving meets consist of two types of competition, *springboard diving* and *platform diving*. In springboard diving, the diver uses the spring

Micki King, the contributor of this article, is a United States Air Force officer who won the gold medal in springboard diving at the 1972 Summer Olympic Games.

from a bouncing board to gain the height necessary to perform a dive. In platform diving, the diver jumps from a high, stationary surface. The great height of the platform gives him or her enough time to perform a dive.

Springboard Diving is more popular than platform diving because more pools have springboards than platforms. Most school, community, and hotel and motel pools have at least one diving board.

Diving boards used in meets measure 16 feet (5 meters) long and 20 inches (51 centimeters) wide. They extend about 6 feet (1.8 meters) beyond the edge of the pool. Springboard diving competitions are held on 1-meter and 3-meter boards, which are 1 meter (3 feet) or 3 meters (10 feet) above the water. In the Olympic Games, springboard diving is held only on the 3-meter board. The United States national championship, and some other diving meets have separate events on each board.

During the 1960's, the development of aluminum diving boards revolutionized springboard diving and greatly increased its popularity as a spectator sport. Aluminum springboards are narrower and much more flexible than the earlier thick wooden ones. The aluminum boards provide greater spring, enabling divers to gain more height. This increased height allows athletes to perform difficult dives that previously had been possible only from a platform.

Platform Diving. Diving platforms for meets must be at least 20 feet (6 meters) long and 6½ feet (2 meters) wide. They are covered with matting to prevent ath-

DIVING

letes from slipping. Diving platforms are 10 meters (33 feet) above the water. Some platforms have levels that are 5 meters (16 feet) or 7.5 meters (25 feet) high, but divers use them only for practice, not for competition.

Diving Techniques

Diving is safe for properly trained athletes, but good diving requires proper coaching and equipment. Beginners risk serious injury if they do not learn proper techniques. Difficult dives performed in meets should never be attempted from a backyard or motel pool diving board.

The most important movement for a successful dive consists of the *approach* and the *hurdle*. The approach consists of the first steps taken by the diver on the board or platform. The hurdle is the last step—actually a short jump—which takes him or her to the edge. Some dives that are performed from the platform do not require an approach or hurdle because the diver starts at the edge.

Many elements contribute to a proper approach and hurdle. For example, the approach steps should be natural and even in length. Steps that are too long or too short may result in shifts in weight that can cause imbalance. Expert divers watch the end of the board throughout the approach. They must then watch their feet as they land on the board in their hurdle. They do this by dropping their eyes but keeping the head straight. In springboard diving, the arms swing down in time with the downward push of the board. They swing up as the board rebounds. In platform diving, the arms are kept extended overhead as the diver lands on the end of the platform.

Correct technique is particularly important in springboard diving. The diver must time the hurdle and take-off to exactly match the rebound of the board. If the athlete's timing is off by even a split second, the dive may be spoiled.

All dives involve certain actions that divers must follow precisely while in the air. Ideally, a diver enters the water vertically, with the body straight and the toes pointed. If the diver hits the water head first, his or her arms should be extended in front of the head in line with the body. If the dive requires the athlete to enter feet first, the arms should be straight and close to the body.

Kinds of Dives

There are five basic kinds of dives. These dives, in the order in which they are performed in the Olympic Games, are (1) forward, (2) back, (3) reverse, (4) inward, and (5) forward with a half twist.

Each of the five dives represents a group of dives. Each group consists of the basic dives and a number of variations of them. All the variations in the first four groups include at least one somersault. Most twist dives combine somersaults with twists. To do a twist, a diver turns his or her body one complete revolution in the air.

Divers perform forward, back, reverse, and inward dives in one of three positions: (1) layout or straight, (2) pike, and (3) tuck. In the layout position, the diver keeps the body straight. In the pike position, the athlete bends at the hips and keeps the knees straight. In the tuck position, he or she draws the knees up toward the chest and grasps the lower legs with the hands. A fourth position, called the *free* position, is used only in certain twist dives. This is the general name for any position used in dives that involve twisting and somersaulting.

The illustrations on page 202 show examples of the five kinds of dives and the three diving positions.

Diving Meets

The United States, Canada, and many other countries hold national championship diving meets annually. In addition, international competitions are held throughout the year.

Diving meets are held both indoors and outdoors. Men and women compete separately, but they perform the same dives and use the same boards and platforms. Every meet consists of required and optional dives. The judging and scoring procedures are also the same for men's and women's diving.

Beginning a Springboard Dive A diver must perform a series of movements to begin a dive properly. The most important movements for most dives are the *approach* and the *hurdle*. (1) The approach consists of the diver's first steps on the springboard. (2) The hurdle is a short jump that takes the athlete to the edge of the board. (3) The diver's arms swing down as the board goes down. (4) They swing up as the board rebounds. (5) The take-off lifts the diver high into the air.

WORLD BOOK illustrations by Robert Keys

Kinds of Dives Five kinds of dives are performed in a meet. These dives, in the order in which they are performed, are (1) forward, (2) back, (3) reverse, (4) inward, and (5) forward with a half twist. Divers perform the first four dives in one of three positions: layout or straight, pike, and tuck. In a number of twist dives, divers use the *free* position, which may include a layout, a pike, or a tuck.

WORLD BOOK illustrations by Robert Keys

Forward dive
(layout position)

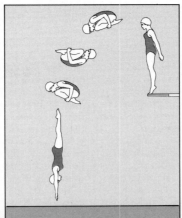

Forward 1½-somersault dive
(tuck position)

Back dive
(layout position)

Reverse dive
(layout position)

Inward dive
(pike position)

Half-twist dive
(free position)

The top national and international diving meets are conducted under regulations established by the Federation Internationale de Natation Amateur (FINA). This organization is the international governing body for swimming and diving.

Required and Optional Dives. In most meets, the athletes must perform 11 dives—5 required dives and 6 optional ones. The required dives must be performed by all the competitors, but the divers may select their optional dives from an approved list.

The required part of the program consists of one dive from each of the five groups—forward, back, reverse, inward, and twist. One optional dive must also be performed from each group. The diver may choose his or her sixth optional dive from any of the groups.

Judging and Scoring. Each dive in a meet is scored by three to seven judges. The judges evaluate every diver's approach, technique, grace and execution in the air, and entry into the water.

The FINA assigns each required and optional dive a *degree of difficulty*. Difficulty is based on the number of twists and somersaults, and whether the dive is performed from a springboard or platform.

The judges award points and half points on a scale of 0 to 10. A score of 5 to 6 points is considered satisfactory, 6½ to 8 points good, and 8½ to 10 points very good.

After the judges evaluate a dive, their scores are added up and then multiplied by the degree of difficulty. The result is the athlete's score for that dive. The scores for all 11 dives are totaled to figure the diver's score for the meet. MICKI KING

See also SWIMMING; OLYMPIC GAMES (table: Swimming and Diving).

GENETIC ENGINEERING

GENETIC ENGINEERING, in its broadest sense, refers to any artificial process that alters the genetic makeup of an organism or its offspring. Such alteration can be caused by chemicals, X rays, and even selective breeding. However, most scientists use the term *genetic engineering* to describe the process whereby specific genes can be added to or removed from an organism.

Genes are the hereditary material of cells, and they control many characteristics of an organism. By changing the genes of an organism, scientists can provide it with different traits. The offspring of the modified organism will also have these characteristics because genes are passed from generation to generation.

Genetic engineering research increased greatly during the mid-1970's. Most of this work has involved transplanting genes from animals and plants into bacteria. By allowing the altered bacteria to reproduce, researchers can obtain many identical copies of the transferred animal or plant genes. Studies of these genes have helped increase scientists' knowledge of the structure and function of hereditary material.

In the future, genetic engineering may be used in medicine, agriculture, and industry. Scientists may learn to transfer into bacteria the human genes for producing such body chemicals as hormones and antibodies. The altered bacteria and their offspring could then produce these valuable substances, which physicians use to treat various diseases. If scientists learn to repair or replace defective genes, genetic engineering could help cure victims of certain genetic diseases. In addition, genetic engineering might lead to the development of high-yield crops and livestock, thus expanding the world's food supply. Industry may help protect the environment by using genetically engineered bacteria to "eat up" pollutants.

Many scientists have expressed concern over the possible dangers of genetic engineering research. For example, they fear this research could unintentionally develop bacteria and viruses that are better able to cause disease or resist drugs. In 1975, scientists from the United States, Russia, and about 15 other countries drew up research guidelines to guard against such dangers. ANN H. FERRELL

STRESS is a body condition that may occur when a person faces a threatening or unfamiliar situation. Such situations include illness, the loss of a job, and even a promotion or being elected class president. Stress causes a person's energy and strength to increase temporarily. The body also increases its defenses against diseases. All these bodily changes may help an individual overcome challenges and dangers.

If stress continues for weeks or months, it may damage or exhaust certain organs and lead to various illnesses. Physicians believe that people can help themselves stay in good health by avoiding lengthy stress.

Causes of Stress are called *stressors*. They may include any unusual demand on a person's body or mind.

Illness causes stress because it forces the body to activate its defenses against disease. Stress also results when the body must heal an injury or adapt to such environmental hazards as noise or extreme cold.

In addition, stress may occur when a person must adapt to an unfamiliar situation—whether the change seems favorable or unfavorable. For example, most people experience stress when they welcome a new baby to their family or mourn the death of a close relative. A change in a person's income, marital status, place of residence, or even diet may also trigger stress.

An event that causes great stress for one person may present only a minor difficulty for another. A person's physical condition affects his or her ability to handle stressors. An individual's response also depends on whether he or she feels in control of the situation. A difficulty may cause little stress if a person can predict, overcome, or at least understand it.

How Stress Affects the Body. Stress alters the functioning of most parts of the body, including the brain, the muscles, and the internal organs. These changes increase a person's ability to meet a variety of stressors. In fact, the changes caused by stress may prepare an individual for dangers that are not present. For example, stress heightens certain bodily defenses against germs.

Stress begins with certain bodily changes that last from a few minutes to a few hours. Their effects include keener senses and increased energy and strength. Other changes develop gradually and may continue for weeks or months if a stressor persists. They heighten the body's ability to check inflammation and to destroy germs and poisons. Stress also causes the body to build up its stores of sugar, which supplies energy.

A part of the brain called the *hypothalamus* regulates the body's responses to stressors. Nerve or chemical signals alert the hypothalamus when a stressor occurs. The hypothalamus then releases chemical messengers called *hormones* from various glands into the blood.

The short-term changes of stress result chiefly from the hormone *epinephrine*, also called *adrenalin*. This hormone is secreted by the inner part of each adrenal gland. Most long-term changes are set off by *cortisol* and other hormones from the outer part of each adrenal. Hormones from such glands as the pancreas, the pituitary, and the thyroid also play a role in stress.

Stress-Related Illnesses. Prolonged stress may temporarily exhaust the adrenal glands or other organs that help the body maintain enough energy and resist disease. As a result, a person may feel extremely fatigued and have little ability to fight illness. Lengthy stress also weakens the skin and internal membranes. Rashes, ulcers, or other disorders of the skin, stomach, or intestines may result. Other conditions associated with stress include high blood pressure and long-term malfunction of such glands as the adrenals, pancreas, pituitary, and thyroid.

Extremely prolonged and severe stress can lead to potentially fatal conditions. Such conditions include *cardiac arrest* (heart failure) and *shock* (a general weakening of the vital processes).

Physicians recommend three main ways to help prevent stress-related illnesses. (1) Avoid continual stress. A person facing a long series of stressors should plan periods of relaxation. (2) Learn to handle troublesome situations with a minimum of stress. The WORLD BOOK article on HEALTH (Keeping Your Mind Healthy) includes suggestions that may help reduce stress. (3) Pay special attention to your health when stress does occur. A healthful way of life and appropriate medical care can prevent a stress-related illness from developing or becoming serious. HANS SELYE

Dictionary Supplement

This section lists important words from the 1977 edition of
THE WORLD BOOK DICTIONARY. This dictionary, first published
by Field Enterprises Educational Corporation in 1963, keeps abreast
of our living language with a program of continuous editorial revision.
The following supplement has been prepared under the direction
of the editors of THE WORLD BOOK ENCYCLOPEDIA and
Clarence L. Barnhart, editor in chief of THE WORLD BOOK DICTIONARY.
It is presented as a service to owners of the dictionary and as an
informative feature to subscribers of THE WORLD BOOK YEAR BOOK.

A a

altered state of consciousness, any deviation from the normal activity of the mind or brain: *Drug experience can be understood only if it is viewed as an altered state of consciousness rather than as a pharmacological event* (Andrew Weil). *Telepathy, clairvoyance, mystical transports, and other altered states of consciousness may be latent in most, if not all, of us* (New Yorker). *Abbr:* ASC (no periods).

a|pa|min (ā′pə min), *n.* a substance, derived from bee venom, that is poisonous to nervous tissue, used experimentally in neurology and medicine: *Apamin is the smallest neurotoxic polypeptide known, and it is the only one whose interaction with the spinal cord is well established* (Science). [< Latin *ap*(is) bee + English *amin*(o acid)]

au|to|trans|fu|sion (ô′tō trans fyü′zhən), *n.* a method of returning a patient's blood to his system upon recapturing and processing it after internal bleeding in surgery or because of trauma: *to perform autotransfusion ... the blood lost is collected, filtered, and processed, and then introduced back into the patient's circulatory system* (Byron T. Scott).

B b

B cell, or **B-cell** (bē′sel′), *n.* a type of lymphocyte that produces antibodies, characterized by many fingerlike protrusions on its surface: *Both the B-cells and T-cells reside primarily in the body's lymphoid tissues.... From these tissues, the cells recirculate through the body and continually monitor for the presence of potential attackers* (Time). [< *B*(ursa of Fabricius, an organ in chickens where the cell was first found to originate) + *cell*]

beef|a|lo (bē′fə lō), *n., pl.* **-loes** or **-los**. *U.S.* any one of a breed of beef cattle developed by interbreeding Herefords and Charolaises with buffaloes. [blend of *beef* and *buffalo*]

big dress, a loose-fitting dress made in the style of the Big Look; droop.

Big Look, a fashion in women's clothes characterized by loose, broad, voluminous designs: *The Big Look differed from the midi in that it brought the fabric flowing in immense yardages about the body* (Kathryn Z. Livingston).

bi|o|gas (bī′ō gas′), *n.* a mixture of methane and carbon dioxide produced by bacterial action on organic waste matter and used as a cheap form of fuel: *Biogas burns in a slightly modified methane burner with a sufficiently hot flame for cooking* (Gerald Leach).

bi|o|haz|ard (bī′ō haz′ərd), *n.* any danger or peril resulting from biological research: *The control of biohazards is a new kind of problem in cancer research. Only recently it has become apparent that viruses, which had been thought to be species-specific, can cross from one species to another and thus spread disease* (New Scientist).

blax|ploi|ta|tion (blaks′ploi tā′shən), *n. U.S.* the production of films and plays with black actors for black audiences: *For every blaxploitation movie, 10 white-exploitation movies of cheap thrills of violence ... are made and exhibited in, I venture, far more theaters and drive-ins than black films* (Psychology Today). [blend of *black* and *exploitation*, patterned on *sexploitation*]

bow shock, or **bow|shock** (bou′-shok′), *n.* the shock wave caused by the impact of a planet's magnetic field on solar wind: *About 20 minutes before the spacecraft reached its closest distance to Mercury (about 466 miles), there were very clear signs of a bow shock* (Science News).

burn bag, a bag used to burn completely discarded documents: *Most of the bureau's less savory assignments had been recorded in special "pink memorandums" or "Do Not File" reports destined for the burn bag* (Newsweek).

C c

cardiopulmonary resuscitation, = CPR.

CCD (no periods), charge-coupled device.

cel|lu|lite (sel′yə līt, -ə lēt), *n.* fatty deposits beneath the skin, forming undesirable dimpling: *American women didn't share their French sisters' concern about cellulite—their word for those orange-peel-like lumps on limbs and posteriors that are so embarrassingly evident at bathing-suit time* (New York Times Book Review). [< French *cellulite* < *cellule* cell]

charge-cou|pled device (chärj′kup′-əld), a semiconductor silicon chip with a dense array of tiny cells in which mobile electric charges can be stored and transferred from cell to cell by the external manipulation of voltages: *Charge-coupled devices can be used in small, sensitive cameras that replace bulky television equipment, or as digital information storage units* (Science News).

code (kōd), *n., v.,* **cod|ed, cod|ing.** *— n.* **5** a lines and numbers printed on a product for identification by an optical scanner: *the code on the cover of a paperback.* **b** = Universal Product Code.

cod war, a prolonged conflict between nations over fishing rights in territorial waters: *For the third time since World War II, Iceland and Britain are near blows in what citizens of both nations call the cod war* (Time).

co|ev|o|lu|tion (kō ev′ə lü′shən), *n. Biology.* evolution of two or more forms or organisms together or in response to one another: *Ultraviolet pigments ... have probably played an important part in the coevolution of flowers with ultraviolet-sensitive insects* (New Scientist).

D d

dilatancy theory, a theory that the measurable change in volume of rocks under pressure can be used to predict earthquake: *The dilatancy theory arose after seismologists noticed that in the months before several earthquakes, compressional waves in the vicinity of the quake site slowed down, then speeded up again* (Science News).

dis|par|lure (dis′pär lur′), *n.* a synthetic form of the sex attractant of the female gypsy moth, more potent than gyplure: *Availability of the synthetic pheromone disparlure has ... greatly increased the efficiency of the trapping program, and led to the possibility of direct control of the moth* (Mortin Beroza). [< (Porthetria) *dispar,* species name of the gypsy moth + English *lure*]

droop (drūp), *v., n. — v.i.* **2** Also, **Droop.** a wide, loose, flowing dress similar to the tent dress: *On Fifth Avenue, the droops were out in droves, completely concealing even the shapeliest women's protrusions* (New York Times). [< Scandinavian (compare Old Icelandic *drūpa*). See related etym. at **drop**.]

E e

earth shoe, a thick-soled, low-heeled shoe designed to raise the sole of the foot for more natural wear and greater comfort: *She got rid of the demure blue patent pumps she had been wearing and substituted earth shoes, supremely comfortable but odd-looking* (Maclean's).

element 106, an artificial, radioactive chemical element, the 14th of the transuranium elements and the third of the transactinides, produced by bombarding californium with oxygen ions or by bombarding lead nuclei with chromium and molybdenum ions.

e|lint or **ELINT** (i lint′), *n.* **1** a ship or aircraft equipped with electronic monitoring apparatus for gathering secret intelligence; spy ship or spyplane: *"How would we feel if a Russian 'elint' suddenly showed up four miles off our Polaris base at Charleston, S.C., in company with three Soviet destroyers?" one official asked* (New York Times). **2** information obtained by this means: *U.S. intelligence learned of the mishap through ELINT* (Time). [< *el*(ectronic) *int*(elligence)]

ERA (no periods) or **E.R.A.**, **3** Equal Rights Amendment (a proposed constitutional amendment stating that "equality of rights under the law shall not be denied or abridged by the United States or any state on account of sex"): *Proponents of ERA redoubled efforts to obtain the required total of 38 approving states needed by 1979 to make it law* (Caroline Bird).

eth|no|cide (eth′nə sīd), *n.* the systematic destruction of an ethnic culture: *Those missionaries who, by the verdict of Bishop Alejo Ovelar, "are implicated in the grave crime of ethnocide"... would see nothing wrong in the destruction of the racial identity of Indians* (Sunday Times Magazine). [< *ethno-* + *-cide²*]

F f

fac|toid (fak′toid), *n.* a contrived fact; something having no existence except as an item reported in the news media: *Juggling facts, guesses, and factoids as suits his fancy, ... he loses authority as both biographer and novelist* (George P. Elliott). [American English (coined by Norman Mailer) < *fact* + *-oid*]

First World, the developed or industrialized countries of the world: *He tries to prick the conscience of the First World for its complicity in the Third World's troubles* (Time).

G g

GIGO (no periods), garbage in, garbage out: *New technology and curriculum changes, he says, can be beneficial, but "it's a matter of GIGO ... You put garbage into a computer, you get garbage out."* Simply investing money into new ideas isn't *enough* (Science News).

glitz|y (glit′sē), *adj.,* **glitz|i|er, glitz|i| est.** *Informal.* gaudy; garish; tawdry: *glitzy costumes. For him, decadence is glitzy camp* (Pauline Kael). [< German *glitz*(ern) to glitter + English -*y*¹] — **glitz′i|ness,** *n.*

glu|on (glü′on), *n.* a hypothetical neutral component of elementary particles that holds together subnucleons such as partons and quarks: *The mass of the gluon can be estimated ... as 10 billion or possibly tens of billions of electron volts* (Science News). [< glue + -*on*]

gorp (gôrp), *n. U.S.* a mixture of nuts, sweets, and the like, eaten as a snack: *I took a ration of gorp— soybeans, sunflower seeds, oats, pretzels, Wheat Chex, raisins, and kelp— and poured another ration into Carol's hands* (John McPhee). [perhaps < earlier *U.S. Slang gorp,* verb, to eat greedily]

gra|no|la (grə nō′lə), *n.* a mixture of natural cereals, often sold as a health food: *Rows of unfamiliar foodstuffs are appearing in middle-class cupboards: brown rice by the bucketful, as well as packages of adsuki, granola, gomasio, ginseng and miso* (Time). [American English, probably < Italian *grano* grain + augmentative suffix -*ola*]

H h

Heim|lich maneuver (hīm′lik), a procedure to prevent choking on something lodged in the windpipe by grasping the victim from behind and locking one's hands in a fist so the thumb is against the victim's abdomen, slightly above the navel and below the ribcage, and with a quick squeeze forcing the fist up under the diaphragm to expel air through the windpipe: *The Heimlich maneuver has been credited with saving more than 160 lives in the first nine months since it was described* (Irwin J. Polk). [< Henry J. *Heimlich,* an American surgeon who devised it] .

Hus|tle (hus′əl), *n., v.,* **-tled, -tling.** — *n.* **1** a lively, syncopated ballroom dance with various steps, figures, and patterns performed by couples in close contact: *The Hustle is a dance of posture, rigor, and coordination ... that demands little floor space* (New York Times). **2** music for this dance. — *v.i.* to dance the Hustle: *Hustling is done to specially written dance music* (The New York Sunday News). [< *hustle*]

hy|per|al|i|men|ta|tion (hī′pər al′ə-men tā′shən), *n.* the use of intravenous feeding to provide all the calories, vitamins, minerals, and other nutrients required by individual patients: *Surgeons in hospitals around the world now use hyperalimentation in the treatment of various types of intestinal ulcers, cancers and blockages* (Science News).

I i

in|flump (in flump′), *n.* = slumpflation. [blend of *inflation* and *slump*]

i|tai-i|tai (ē′tī ē tī), *n.* a bone and kidney disease caused by the ingestion of cadmium from contaminated fish and shellfish: *Another painful new disease called itai-itai (literally, ouch-ouch) derived from cadmium flowing ... from a mining and smelting factory* (Time). [< Japanese *itai-itai,* reduplication of *itai,* a cry of pain]

J j

jay² (jā), *n. U.S. Slang.* a marijuana cigarette. [< pronunciation of *j* for *joint* (def. 9)]

J particle, = psi particle. [< the letter *J,* because of its resemblance to the Chinese character for (Samuel) *Ting,* a physicist at the Brookhaven National Laboratory who discovered the particle]

K k

kid|vid (kid′vid), *n. U.S.* children's television programs as an industry: *In that special region of television land known as kidvid, ... says one broadcaster, "We don't think of them as little people, but as little customers"* (New York Times Magazine). [< *kid*¹ (def. 5) + *vid*(eo)]

L l

layered look, a fashion in women's clothes in which a variety of garments are worn one over the other: *It was my first overexposure to the so-called "layered look" from Paris—a turtleneck with a blouse, with a sweater, with a vest, with a raincoat, with a cape* (Eli N. Evans).

leisure suit, a man's suit consisting of a light, shirt-styled jacket and matching trousers, designed especially for leisure-time wear.

M m

M-1 or **M₁** (em′wun′), *n. Economics.* currency and demand deposits.

M-2 or **M₂** (em′tü′), *n. Economics.* M-1 plus time deposits and certificates of deposit.

MARV (märv), *n., v.* — *n.* **1** a long-range missile with nuclear warheads that can be maneuvered after reentry into the earth's atmosphere to evade interception by defensive missiles. **2** any one of the warheads on this missile. — *v.t.* to equip with a MARV: *The U.S. has already MIRVed a good number of its missiles and hopes eventually to MARV others* (Time). [< *MA*(neuverable) *R*(eentry) *V*(ehicle)]

MCP (no periods), **Informal.** male chauvinist pig: *A Doll's House, one of the genuine Ibsen masterpieces, was ... rescued by Claire Bloom and Anthony Hopkins as Nora and her MCP husband Torvald* (National Review).

Mi|ran|da card (mi ran′də), *U.S.* a card carried by police on which is printed the constitutional rights read to an accused person, usually upon arrest: *Police used a Miranda card to read a Mexican immigrant his rights before arresting him in connection*

with the barroom slaying (New York Post). [< Ernesto *Miranda,* 1942-1976, the defendant in a case (1966) in which the U.S. Supreme Court ruled a defendant must be informed of his rights prior to questioning]

mood stone, an artificial gem that is supposed to change color to reflect the mood of the wearer, made of quartz incorporating liquid crystals.

Moon|ie (mü′nē), *n.* a follower of Sun Myung Moon, born 1921, a Korean evangelist preaching a blend of fundamentalist Christianity and Eastern mysticism: *Young Moonies, who also are encouraged to donate their personal possessions and bank accounts to the movement, receive no pay* (New York Sunday News).

N n

neutral current, *Nuclear Physics.* a hypothetical flow of particles involving the weak interaction in which no electric charge is transferred; a stream of neutral W particles: *Evidence supporting the existence of neutral currents was obtained in experiments using a neutrino beam and a 12-ft. bubble chamber filled with liquid hydrogen* (Lawrence W. Jones).

nine (nīn), *n., adj.* — *n.* **b** *Especially British.* the countries comprising the European Economic Community since 1973; the nine nations of the Common Market: *The Nine are due to agree then on a new round of farm price increases* (Manchester Guardian Weekly). [Old English *nigon*]

no-fault (nō′fôlt′), *adj. U.S.* **2** having to do with any legal action in which fault is eliminated as a ground for finding against either party: *I take note of the rising pressures for no-fault divorce ... and what I would call no-fault medical malpractice* (Shana Alexander).

O o

O.A., Overeaters Anonymous.

open marriage, a marriage based on the complete equality and freedom of both partners: *"Open marriage" covenants ... permit each party to form a variety of relationships—by no means just physical—with members of the opposite sex* (Newsweek).

P p

point-of-sale (point′əv sāl′), *adj.* of or having to do with a computerized system of recording sales information when a sale is made: *The records are maintained inside the computer and are continuously updated by the point-of-sale information* (John R. Rice).

primal therapy or **primal scream therapy,** a form of group psychotherapy which encourages members to re-enact experiences of early child-

---

Pronunciation Key: hat, āge, cãre, fär; let, ēqual, tèrm; it, īce; hot, ōpen, ôrder; oil, out; cup, pùt, rüle; child; long; thin; ᴛʜen; zh, measure; ə represents **a** in about, **e** in taken, **i** in pencil, **o** in lemon, **u** in circus.

hood to release their repressed anger or pain: *The main technique that primal therapy uses is to persuade the patient to become a baby* (New Scientist).

psi particle, an electrically neutral elementary particle with a very large mass and long lifetime, produced by the collision of an electron and a positron; J particle: *A new fundamental particle, the psi particle, ... was thought possibly to consist of two new quarks* (John Newell).

Q q

Quaa|lude (kwä′lüd), *n. Trademark.* a nonbarbiturate sedative, widely used as a narcotic and considered addictive: *Most popular among the downs are ... newer soporifics such as Quaaludes* (New York Times).

quad|ra|disc (kwod′rə disk′), *n.* a quadraphonic record.

R r

restriction enzyme or **endonuclease**, an enzyme that cleaves the DNA strands of a species at a specific site which matches the DNA fragment of another species cut by the same enzyme, enabling segments of DNA from different sources to be joined in new combinations: *A recently discovered class of enzymes called "restriction enzymes" has made gene insertions possible, but ... has also created potential biohazards* (Science News).

right-to-lif|er (rīt′to lī′fər), *n.* a person who opposes legalized abortion.

ripple effect, a spreading effect, result, or influence: *Supplies of automobiles were stacking up ... and the ripple effect of the auto-industry slowdown had not even been felt yet* (New Yorker).

rock opera, an opera with rock'n'roll music: *There are pitfalls aplenty ... in his screen translation of the bally-hooed Broadway rock opera* (Newsweek).

RPV (no periods), remotely piloted vehicle (an unmanned aircraft controlled from the ground for use in aerial reconnaissance, target practice, bomb delivery, and the like): *The USAF has set up a new organization to manage RPV programmes, and is considering the use of RPVs fitted with warheads as "kamikaze" planes* (New Scientist).

S s

sea-floor spreading (sē′flôr′, -flōr′), the process by which the sea floor is being continuously formed and spread by upwellings from the earth's mantle along the mid-ocean ridges when crustal plates move apart, and continuously destroyed by the sinking of the sea floor into the mantle when plates push against each other: *In the study of sea-floor spreading and plate tectonics, continental margins assume special significance, for it is there that plate interactions or early stages of spreading occur* (Science News).

sig|ni|fy|ing (sig′nə fī ing, -in), *n. U.S.* a verbal game or contest among black youths, in which a series of insults are exchanged to test the par-

ticipants' restraint and ability with words: *Girls are also the objects of much signifyin' by male students. The signifyin' may relate to a girl's looks or ... her boyfriend* (Today's Education).

slump|fla|tion (slump flā′shən), *n. Economics.* inflation accompanied by a steady decline in business and employment; inflump: *The $16 billion in rebates and tax credits might be too weak to jolt the economy out of its alarming slumpflation* (Time). *Stagflation changed into the still more unspeakable slumpflation* (Manchester Guardian Weekly). [blend of *slump* and *inflation*]

sta|ple|punc|ture (stā′pəl pungk′-chər), *n.* the insertion of tiny wire staples into the external ear as a form of acupuncture supposed to reduce the appetite or eliminate drug-withdrawal symptoms: *Staplepuncture ... is based on the theory—so far unconfirmed—that there are "obesity nerve endings" in the ear* (Time). [< *staple*[1] + (acu)*puncture*]

stroke[2] (strōk), *v.,* **stroked, strok|ing,** *n. — v.t.* **2** *Figurative.* **a** to manipulate by cajoling; persuade by soothing words or flattery: *The White House counsel received a "happy Easter" phone call from the President, but he recognized it ... as a 'stroking' call* (Newsweek). **b** to boost the ego of: *It's Show Biz, man—a bunch a' egomaniacal people using a captive audience to stroke themselves* (Atlantic). *— n.* **2** an act or means of stroking someone: *(Figurative.) It is the function of the Parent to enforce an Injunction ... along with reinforcing "strokes"* (New York Times Magazine). [Middle English *stroken,* Old English *strācian.* See related etym. at **strike.**]

swine flu, a virulent form of influenza caused by a filterable virus originally isolated in swine: *The very possibility that the swine flu virus had once again become infectious to humans was enough to trigger a series of triphammer decisions* (New York Sunday News).

T t

Ta|ser (tā′zer), *n., v. — n. Trademark.* a handheld weapon somewhat like a flashlight that fires a dart attached to long wires which transmit electric shock that immobilizes a person temporarily: *The Taser ... paralyzes you until the barbs are removed or the current is switched off* (New Scientist). *— v.t.* to attack or disable with a Taser. [< *T*(ele-) *A*(ctive) *S*(hock) *E*(lectronic) *R*(epulsion)]

T cell, or **T-cell** (tē′sel′), *n.* a type of lymphocyte that attacks foreign bodies directly, destroying them chemically, derived from the thymus gland and distinguished from a B cell by its relatively smooth surface: *Since T cells do not secrete antibodies and B cells do, it seems plausible that T cells might cause B cells to produce antibodies* (Science News). [< *T*(hymuse derived) *cell*]

TM (no periods), Transcendental Meditation: *Readers were most interested in the Eastern religions and practices—TM, Yoga, and Zen* (National Review).

tu|bu|lin (tü′byə lin, tyü′-), *n.* globular protein that is the basic structural unit of microtubules: *Microtubules from any kind of eukaryotic flagella and cilia are composed of related proteins called tubulin* (Scientific American).

TVP (no periods), *Trademark.* textured vegetable protein (an engineered food made from processed soybeans): *TVP and ground meat will soon be sold in most markets as "soy patties" or "fortified burgers"* (Harriet Van Horne).

U u

Universal Product Code, *U.S.* code on the labels of supermarket products in a computerized system of checkout and inventory: *The Universal Product Code ... is the coded symbol of lines and spaces now on the labels of about 60 per cent of the products in markets* (New York Post). *Abbr:* UPC (no periods).

up-front (up′frunt′), *adj. U.S. Informal.* not concealed; direct; forthright: *an up-front attitude toward racism. The up-front public business he had to do ... was done for him by his surrogates* (Newsweek).

V v

vi|ro|gene (vī′rō jēn′), *n.* a virus-producing gene: *The virogene can code for transforming protein, internal and external viral antigens, polymerases, and other enzymes that go into the making of a complete virus* (Science).

W w

white market, the lawful buying and selling of any item in short supply or of ration coupons to prevent a black market from springing up: *To minimize racketeering, any rationing ought to be coupled with what has been called the "white market"—a kind of legal black market* (Time).

X x

X-o|gen (eks′ō jen), *n. Astronomy.* an unidentified molecule detected through radio emission in the region of various constellations, including Orion and Sagittarius: *X-ogen's close correspondence with hydrogen cyanide leads to the conclusion that its structure has similarities with that of hydrogen cyanide* (Science News).

Y y

yecch (yuk, yuᴴ), *interj. U.S. Informal.* an exclamation of disgust: *"You ask a guy today how the economy will be in three weeks and he'll say 'Yecch!'"* (Newsweek).

Z z

Zim|bab|we|an (zim bäb′wē ən), *n., adj. — n.* a native or inhabitant of Zimbabwe, the African nationalist name of Rhodesia: *To demonstrate on the Rhodesia question, the young Zimbabweans ... raised hand-drawn posters in the gallery* (London Times). *— adj.* of or having to do with Zimbabwe or Zimbabweans.

Index

How to Use the Index

This index covers the contents of the 1975, 1976, and 1977 editions of THE WORLD BOOK YEAR BOOK.

Each index entry is followed by the edition year (in *italics*) and the page number, as:
ADVERTISING, *77-172, 76-166, 75-184*

This means that information about Advertising begins on the pages indicated for each of the editions.

An index entry that is the title of an article appearing in THE YEAR BOOK is printed in capital letters, as: **AUTOMOBILE.** An entry that is not an article title, but a subject discussed in an article of some other title, is printed: **Pollution.**

The various "See" and "See also" cross references in the index list are to other entries within the index. Clue words or phrases are used when two or more references to the same subject appear in the same edition of THE YEAR BOOK. These make it easy to locate the material on the page, since they refer to an article title or article subsection in which the reference appears, as:
Emission standards: automobile, *77-206, 76-198, 75-214;* environment, *77-318*

The indication *"il."* means that the reference is to an illustration only. An index entry in capital letters followed by *"WBE"* refers to a new or revised WORLD BOOK ENCYCLOPEDIA article that is printed in the supplement section, as:
CHINESE LITERATURE, *WBE, 77-570*

A

INDEX

Acknowledgments

The publishers acknowledge the following sources for illustrations. Credits read from left to right, top to bottom, on their respective pages. An asterisk (*) denotes illustrations created exclusively for THE YEAR BOOK. All maps, charts, and diagrams were prepared by THE YEAR BOOK staff unless otherwise noted.

3	Jet Propulsion Laboratory
8	Wide World
9	United Press Int.; Wide World; Keystone
10	Wide World; Joe Bulaitis, Camera Press, London; Wide World
11	United Press Int.; Wide World; Wide World; Wide World
12	Wide World
13	Bob West, Photo Trends; Wide World; Jet Propulsion Laboratory
14	Wide World; Henri Bureau, Sygma; Wide World
15	Pictorial Parade; Wide World; Wide World
16	Wide World
18	Wide World; United Press Int.; Joe Bulaitis, Camera Press, London; Wide World; Salhani, Sygma; United Press Int.; Keystone; Keystone; *Newsweek*
20	Camerapix from Keystone
21	Denis Cameron, Sygma
22-23	Wide World
24	Wide World; Wide World; Wide World; Wide World; Photo Trends; Keystone; Keystone; Keystone; Wide World
26	Wide World
27	NBC
28	Keystone
30	General Motors; Keystone; Tim Janicke; Wide World; Wide World; Wide World; Wide World; Arthur Grace, NYT Pictures; Wide World
32	Wide World
33	Amana Refrigeration, Inc.
34	Institute for Biomedical Engineering, University of Utah
36	Jet Propulsion Laboratory; Wide World; Wide World; Oceaneering International, Inc.; Wide World; Wide World; Wide World; Jet Propulsion Laboratory
38-40	Jet Propulsion Laboratory
41	Massachusetts Institute of Technology
42	WORLD BOOK photo*; Wide World; American Library Association; Wm. Franklin McMahon*; Wide World; WORLD BOOK photo*; WORLD BOOK photo*; Wide World; Wide World
44	WORLD BOOK photo*
45	Bernard Gotfryd, *Newsweek*
46	Wide World
47	Fred C. Eckhardt, Jr.*
48	*Ladies' Home Journal* from Wide World; WFLD-32, Chicago; NYT Pictures; Keystone; Sandy Solmon; NYT Pictures; Wide World; CBS
50	Friedman-Abeles
51	Guthrie Theater
53	WORLD BOOK photo*
54	Wide World; A. Dejean, Sygma; Wide World; Wide World; Wide World; Wide World; Wide World; United Press Int.; Chicago Black Hawks
55	Joseph A. Erhardt*
56-58	Wide World
60	Joseph A. Erhardt*
62	Bill Mauldin*
63	Mauldin, © 1960 *St. Louis Post-Dispatch*; Joseph A. Erhardt*; Joseph A. Erhardt*
64-65	Joseph A. Erhardt*
66	Thomas Nast, *Harpers Weekly,* 1871; Museum of Fine Arts, Boston; Reprinted by Permission of Curtis Brown, Ltd. Copyright © 1946 by David Low
68	Bill Mauldin*
69	Joseph A. Erhardt*
70	Copyright 1949, 1951 by Bill Mauldin from *Bill Mauldin's Army;* Mauldin, © 1967 *Chicago Sun-Times;* © 1971 Mauldin, *Chicago Sun-Times*
71	© 1971 Mauldin, *Chicago Sun-Times;* Mauldin, © 1975 *Chicago Sun-Times;* Mauldin, © 1976 *Chicago Sun-Times;* © 1965 Mauldin, *Chicago Sun-Times*
72	Oliphant, Los Angeles Times Syndicate © 1976 *Washington Star;* MacNelly, *The Richmond News Leader* © 1976 by Chicago Tribune; Conrad, © *The Los Angeles Times,* 1976; Copyright 1976 by Herblock in *The Washington Post*
73-75	Joseph A. Erhardt*
76	Joseph A. Erhardt*; Bill Mauldin, National Park Service
78	WORLD BOOK photo by Baldev*; Joseph A. Erhardt*
79	Joseph A. Erhardt*
81	Joseph A. Erhardt*; Joseph A. Erhardt*
83	Joseph A. Erhardt*; John Launois, Black Star; Joseph A. Erhardt*
86	Marc & Evelyne Bernheim, Woodfin Camp, Inc.
88	United Nations; John Launois, Black Star; United Nations
90	WORLD BOOK photo*; Wm. Franklin McMahon*
92	Steven Scher, Black Star
94	Ted Rozumalski, Black Star; Floyd M. Herdrick, DPI; Doug Wilson, Black Star; Fred Ward, Black Star
95	Floyd M. Herdrick, DPI; Gene Daniels, Black Star
96	Gabe Palmer, The Image Bank
97	Susan Gallagher, Black Star; Dan McCoy, Black Star; Martin Levick, Black Star
98	Doug Wilson, Black Star; Martin Levick, Black Star; Dennis Brack, Black Star
99	Doug Wilson, Black Star; Bob Weinreb, Black Star
100	Mark Klamkin, Black Star; Gerald Holly, Black Star; Tom Ebenhoh, Black Star
101	Bob Jones, Jr., Black Star; Lee Lockwood, Black Star; Warren Uzzle, Black Star
102	John Gordon, Black Star; Harry Schaefer, Black Star
103	Fred Ward, Black Star; Mark Klamkin, Black Star
104	John Rees, Black Star; Zalesky-Clemmer, Black Star; Doug Wilson, Black Star
105	Bill Grimes, Black Star; Frank Aleksandrowicz, Black Star
106	Doug Wilson, Black Star; Bob Jones, Jr., Black Star; Dan McCoy, Black Star
107	Bob Jones, Jr., Black Star
108-120	John Faulkner*
122-123	George Suyeoka*
125	Robert Frerck; Raymond V. Schoder, S.J.
126	George Suyeoka*
128	Smithsonian Institution; Smithsonian Institution; George Suyeoka*
130	The Newberry Library, Chicago, Edward E. Ayer Collection
132	Lin Caufield Photographers, Inc.*
133	Parks Canada
134	British Library Board (Rare Book Division, New York Public Library, Astor, Lenox and Tilden Foundations)
136	Peter C. H. Pritchard
139	Harry McNaught*
142	Nicholas DeVore, Bruce Coleman Inc.
143	Peter C. H. Pritchard; Ron Church, Tom Stack & Assoc.
144	David Hughes, Bruce Coleman Inc.; Peter C. H. Pritchard
146	Archie Carr; Keith Gillett, Tom Stack & Assoc.; Jack Egan, Tom Stack & Assoc.; Keith Gillett, Tom Stack & Assoc.
147	Robert L. Dunne, Bruce Coleman Inc.; Keith Gillett, Tom Stack & Assoc.
148	Jack Egan, Island Resources Foundation; Jack Egan, Island Resources Foundation; Jack Egan, Tom Stack & Assoc.
150-151	Peter C. H. Pritchard
154	Bettmann Archive; Bettmann Archive; The Newberry Library, Chicago; Brown Brothers
157	The Newberry Library, Chicago
158	Culver Pictures
160-162	Brown Brothers
163	Historical Pictures Service; *The Centennial Exposition*
165	The Newberry Library, Chicago
167	Bettmann Archive
169	Historical Pictures Service
172	Wide World
173	*Advertising Age*
174-175	Wide World
178	Berges, Sygma
179	Camerapix from Keystone
180	Dann Perszyk
182-183	Tim Janicke
184	Eupra
185-186	American Library Association
187	Henri Bureau, Sygma
188	Wide World
190	John A. Graham, © National Geographic Society
191	American Institute of Architects
192	United Press Int.
193-194	Wide World
196-197	Keystone

A Preview of 1977

January

S	M	T	W	T	F	S
						1
2	3	4	5	6	7	8
9	10	11	12	13	14	15
16	17	18	19	20	21	22
23	24	25	26	27	28	29
30	31					

1 **New Year's Day.**

4 **95th Congress** convenes for first session.

6 **Epiphany,** 12th day of Christmas, celebrates visit of the Three Wise Men.
Holiday of the Three Hierarchs, Eastern Orthodox holy day, commemorating Saints Basil, Gregory, and John Chrysostom.

31 **Australia Day,** commemorates Captain Arthur Phillips' landing in 1788 at site where Sydney now stands.

February

S	M	T	W	T	F	S
		1	2	3	4	5
6	7	8	9	10	11	12
13	14	15	16	17	18	19
20	21	22	23	24	25	26
27	28					

1 **Boy Scouts of America Anniversary Celebration** through February 28.

2 **Ground-Hog Day.** Legend says six weeks of winter weather will follow if ground hog sees its shadow.

12 **Abraham Lincoln's Birthday,** observed in 26 states.

14 **Saint Valentine's Day,** festival of romance and affection.

15 **Susan B. Anthony Day,** commemorates the birth of the suffragist leader.

18 **Chinese New Year,** begins year 4675 of the ancient Chinese calendar, the Year of the Serpent.

21 **George Washington's Birthday,** according to law, is now legally celebrated by federal employees, the District of Columbia, and 42 states on the third Monday in February, not on the actual anniversary, the 22nd.

22 **Mardi Gras,** last celebration before Lent, observed in New Orleans and in many Roman Catholic countries.

23 **Ash Wednesday,** first day of Lent, the penitential period that precedes Easter.

March

S	M	T	W	T	F	S
		1	2	3	4	5
6	7	8	9	10	11	12
13	14	15	16	17	18	19
20	21	22	23	24	25	26
27	28	29	30	31		

1 **Easter Seal Campaign** through April 10.
Red Cross Month through March 31.

4 **Purim,** commemorates the saving of Jews through the death of the ancient Persian despot Haman.

6 **Girl Scout Week,** through March 12, marks the organization's 65th birthday.

13 **Camp Fire Girls Birthday Week,** to March 19, marks 67th birthday of the organization.

17 **St. Patrick's Day,** honoring the patron saint of Ireland.

20 **First Day of Spring,** 12:43 P.M., E.S.T.

27 **National Boys' Club Week** through April 2.

April

S	M	T	W	T	F	S
					1	2
3	4	5	6	7	8	9
10	11	12	13	14	15	16
17	18	19	20	21	22	23
24	25	26	27	28	29	30

1 **April Fools' Day.**
Cancer Control Month through April 30.

3 **Palm Sunday,** marks Jesus' final entry into Jerusalem along streets festively covered with palm branches.
Holy Week, through April 9, commemorates the Crucifixion and Resurrection of Jesus Christ.
Passover, or Pesah, first day, starting the 15th day of the Hebrew month of Nisan. The eight-day festival celebrates the deliverance of the ancient Jews from bondage in Egypt.

7 **Maundy Thursday,** celebrates Christ's injunction to love each other.

8 **Good Friday,** marks the death of Jesus on the cross. It is observed as a public holiday in 17 states.

10 **Easter Sunday,** commemorating the Resurrection of Jesus Christ.
Eastern Orthodox Easter Sunday.

17 **National Library Week** through April 23.

30 **Walpurgis Night,** according to legend, the night of the witches' Sabbath gathering in Germany's Harz Mountains.

May

S	M	T	W	T	F	S
1	2	3	4	5	6	7
8	9	10	11	12	13	14
15	16	17	18	19	20	21
22	23	24	25	26	27	28
29	30	31				

1 **May Day,** observed as a festival of spring in many countries.
Law Day, U.S.A.
National Music Week through May 8.

7 **Kentucky Derby** at Churchill Downs, Louisville, Ky.

8 **Mother's Day.**

9 **Salvation Army Week** through May 15.

19 **Ascension Day,** 40 days after Easter Sunday, commemorating the ascent of Jesus into heaven.

23 **Shabuot,** Jewish Feast of Weeks, marks the revealing of the Ten Commandments to Moses on Mount Sinai.

29 **Whitsunday,** or Pentecost, the seventh Sunday after Easter, commemorating the descent of the Holy Spirit upon Jesus' 12 apostles.

30 **Memorial Day,** according to law, is the last Monday in May.

June

S	M	T	W	T	F	S
			1	2	3	4
5	6	7	8	9	10	11
12	13	14	15	16	17	18
19	20	21	22	23	24	25
26	27	28	29	30		

6 **Stratford Festival,** drama and music, Ontario, Canada, through October 15.
D-Day, commemorates the day the Allies landed to assault the German-held continent of Europe in 1944.

11 **Queen's Official Birthday,** marked by trooping of the colors in London.

12 **National Flag Week** through June 18.

19 **Father's Day.**

21 **First Day of Summer,** 7:14 A.M., E.S.T.

27 **Freedom Week** through July 4.

July

S	M	T	W	T	F	S
					1	2
3	4	5	6	7	8	9
10	11	12	13	14	15	16
17	18	19	20	21	22	23
24	25	26	27	28	29	30
31						

1 **Dominion Day** (Canada), celebrates the confederation of the provinces in 1867.

4 **Independence Day,** marks Continental Congress's adoption of Declaration of Independence in 1776.

14 **Bastille Day** (France), commemorates popular uprising against Louis XVI in 1789 and seizure of the Bastille, the infamous French prison.

15 **Saint Swithin's Day.** According to legend, if it rains on this day, it will rain for 40 days.

17 **Captive Nations Week** through July 23.

20 **Moon Day,** the anniversary of man's first landing on the Moon in 1969.

24 **Tishah B'ab,** Jewish fast day, on ninth day of Hebrew month of Ab, marking Babylonians' destruction of the First Temple in Jerusalem in 587 B.C.; Roman destruction of the Second Temple in A.D. 70; and Roman suppression of Jewish revolt in A.D. 135.

25 **Salzburg International Music and Drama Festival,** Salzburg, Austria, through August 27.

August

S	M	T	W	T	F	S
	1	2	3	4	5	6
7	8	9	10	11	12	13
14	15	16	17	18	19	20
21	22	23	24	25	26	27
28	29	30	31			

14 **V-J Day** (original) marks Allied victory over Japan in 1945.

15 **Feast of the Assumption,** Roman Catholic and Eastern Orthodox holy day, celebrates the ascent of the Virgin Mary into heaven.

17 **Ramadan,** the ninth month of the Muslim calendar begins, observed by fasting.

19 **National Aviation Day.**

21 **Edinburgh International Festival,** music, drama, and film, through September 10.

26 **Women's Equality Day,** commemorating the ratification of the 19th Amendment, giving women the vote.

September

S	M	T	W	T	F	S
				1	2	3
4	5	6	7	8	9	10
11	12	13	14	15	16	17
18	19	20	21	22	23	24
25	26	27	28	29	30	

5 **Labor Day** in the United States and Canada.

13 **Rosh Hashanah,** or Jewish New Year, the year 5738 beginning at sunset. It falls on the first day of the Hebrew month of Tishri and lasts for two days.

22 **Yom Kippur,** or Day of Atonement, most solemn day in the Jewish calendar, marking the end of the period of penitence.
First Day of Autumn, 10:30 P.M., E.S.T.

23 **American Indian Day,** honoring native Americans.

27 **Sukkot,** or Feast of Tabernacles, begins the nine-day Jewish observance, which originally celebrated the end of harvest season.
Harvest Moon, the full moon nearest the autumnal equinox of the sun, shines with special brilliance for several days and helps farmers in the Northern Hemisphere to get more field work done after sunset.

October

S	M	T	W	T	F	S
						1
2	3	4	5	6	7	8
9	10	11	12	13	14	15
16	17	18	19	20	21	22
23	24	25	26	27	28	29
30	31					

1 **Anniversary of the 1949 Chinese Communist Revolution,** China's national holiday.

2 **National Employ the Physically Handicapped Week** through October 8.
National 4-H Week through October 8.
Fire Prevention Week through October 8.

9 **Leif Ericson Day,** honoring early Norse explorer of North America.
National Y-Teen Week through October 15.

10 **Thanksgiving Day,** Canada.
Columbus Day, commemorates Columbus' discovery of America in 1492. Previously celebrated on October 12.

23 **National Cleaner Air Week** through October 29.

24 **Veterans Day,** observed on the fourth Monday in October.

31 **Halloween,** or All Hallows' Eve.
Reformation Day, celebrated by Protestants, marks the day in 1517 when Martin Luther nailed his Ninety-Five Theses of protest to the door of a church in Wittenberg, Germany.
United Nations Children's Fund (UNICEF) Day.

November

S	M	T	W	T	F	S
		1	2	3	4	5
6	7	8	9	10	11	12
13	14	15	16	17	18	19
20	21	22	23	24	25	26
27	28	29	30			

1 **All Saints' Day,** observed by the Roman Catholic Church.
Christmas Seal Campaign through December 31.

5 **Guy Fawkes Day** (Great Britain), marks the failure of a plot to blow up King James I and Parliament in 1605 with ceremonial burning of Guy Fawkes in effigy.

7 **National Children's Book Week** through November 13.

8 **Election Day,** United States.

13 **American Education Week** through November 19.

24 **Thanksgiving Day,** United States.

27 **Advent,** first of the four Sundays in the season preceding Christmas.

December

S	M	T	W	T	F	S
				1	2	3
4	5	6	7	8	9	10
11	12	13	14	15	16	17
18	19	20	21	22	23	24
25	26	27	28	29	30	31

2 **Pan American Health Day.**

5 **Hanukkah,** or Feast of Lights, eight-day Jewish holiday beginning on the 25th day of the Hebrew month of Kislev that celebrates the Jewish defeat of the Syrian tyrant Antiochus IV in 165 B.C. and the rededication of The Temple in Jerusalem.

6 **Saint Nicholas Day,** when children in parts of Europe receive gifts.

10 **Nobel Prize Ceremony,** in Stockholm, Sweden, and Oslo, Norway.

15 **Bill of Rights Day,** marks the ratification of that document in 1791.

21 **First Day of Winter,** 6:24 P.M., E.S.T.

25 **Christmas.**

31 **New Year's Eve.**